A TOPICAL APPROACH TO LIFE-SPAN DEVELOPMENT

FIFTH EDITION

John W. Santrock

University of Texas at Dallas

McGraw Hill

Connect
Learn
Succeed™

Published by McGraw-Hill, an imprint of The McGraw-Hill Companies, Inc., 1221 Avenue of the Americas, New York, NY 10020. Copyright © 2010, 2008, 2007, 2005, 2002. All rights reserved. No part of this publication may be reproduced or distributed in any form or by any means, or stored in a database or retrieval system, without the prior written consent of The McGraw-Hill Companies, Inc., including, but not limited to, in any network or other electronic storage or transmission, or broadcast for distance learning.

This book is printed on acid-free paper.

2 3 4 5 6 7 8 9 0 DOW/DOW 0

ISBN: 978-0-07-337093-4
MHID: 0-07-337093-2

Vice President, Editorial: *Michael Ryan*
Director, Editorial: *Beth Mejia*
Publisher: *Michael J. Sugarman*
Executive Editor: *Krista Bettino*
Executive Marketing Manager: *James R. Headley*
Marketing Manager: *Yasuko Okada*
Director of Development: *Nancy Crochiere*
Developmental Editor: *Barbara A. Conover*
Editorial Coordinator: *Megan Stotts*
Production Managers: *Karol Jurado/Marilyn Rothenberger*
Manuscript Editor: *Beatrice Sussman*
Permissions Editor: *Marty Moga*
Cover Designer: *Laurie Entringer*
Cover Image: *Geoff Turner/Taxi/Getty Images*
Text Designer: *Pam Verros*
Photo Research: *LouAnn Wilson*
Senior Production Supervisor: *Tandra Jorgensen*
Composition: *9.5/12 Meridien by Aptara®, Inc.*
Printing: *45# New Era Thin Plus by RR Donnelley & Sons*

Credits: The credits section for this book begins on page 759 and is considered an extension of the copyright page.

Library of Congress Cataloging-in-Publication Data

Santrock, John W.
    A topical approach to life-span development / John W. Santrock.—5th ed.
        p. cm.
    Rev. ed. of: Life span development. 4th ed. c2008.
    ISBN-13: 978-0-07-337093-4 (hardcover : alk. paper)
    ISBN-10: 0-07-337093-2 (hardcover : alk. paper) 1. Developmental psychology—Textbooks.
I. Santrock, John W. Life span development. II. Title.
    BF713.S257 2010
    305.2—dc22

                                                                        2009036321

The Internet addresses listed in the text were accurate at the time of publication. The inclusion of a Web site does not indicate an endorsement by the authors or McGraw-Hill, and McGraw-Hill does not guarantee the accuracy of the information presented at these sites.

www.mhhe.com

With special appreciation to my wife, Mary Jo

About the Author

John W. Santrock

Received his Ph.D. from the University of Minnesota in 1973. He taught at the University of Charleston and the University of Georgia before joining the psychology department at the University of Texas at Dallas. He has been a member of the editorial boards of *Developmental Psychology* and *Child Development*. His research on father custody is widely cited and used in expert witness testimony to promote flexibility and alternative considerations in custody disputes. John has also authored these exceptional McGraw-Hill texts: *Child Development*, twelfth edition; *Children*, eleventh edition; *Adolescence*, thirteenth edition; *Life-Span Development*, twelfth edition; *Essentials of Life-Span Development*, first edition; *Human Adjustment*, first edition; and *Educational Psychology*, fourth edition.

For many years, John was involved in tennis as a player, teaching professional, and coach of professional tennis players. He has been married for more than 40 years to his wife, Mary Jo, who is a Realtor. He has two daughters—Tracy, who is a Realtor, and Jennifer, who is a medical sales specialist. He has one granddaughter, Jordan, age 18 and two grandsons, Alex age 5, and Luke, age 3. Tracy recently completed the New York Marathon, and Jennifer was in the top 100 ranked players on the Women's Professional Tennis Tour. In the last decade, John also has spent time painting expressionist art.

John Santrock, teaching an undergraduate class

Brief Contents

Contents

SECTION 1 THE LIFE-SPAN PERSPECTIVE 2

SECTION 2 BIOLOGICAL PROCESSES, PHYSICAL DEVELOPMENT, AND HEALTH 50

SECTION 3 COGNITIVE PROCESSES AND DEVELOPMENT 204

S E C T I O N 4 **SOCIOEMOTIONAL PROCESSES AND
DEVELOPMENT 340**

SECTION 6 ENDINGS 640

Expert Consultants

Life-span development has become an enormous, complex field, and no single author, or even several authors, can possibly keep up with all of the rapidly changing content in the many different areas of life-span development. To solve this problem, author John Santrock sought the input of leading experts about content in a number of areas of life-span development. The experts provided detailed evaluations and recommendations in their area(s) of expertise. The biographies and photographs of the experts, who literally represent a who's who in the field of life-span development, follow.

Charles Nelson

Dr. Nelson is one of the world's leading experts on the development of the brain. He currently is a professor of pediatrics at Harvard Medical School, and holds the Richard David Scott Chair in Pediatric Developmental Medicine Research at Children's Hospital, Boston (where he also serves as director of Research in Developmental Medicine). Dr. Nelson received his Ph.D. from McGill University and formerly was a professor at Purdue University and the Institute of Child Development, University of Minnesota. He has a long-standing theoretical interest in the effects of early experience on brain and behavioral development. One of Dr. Nelson's main research interests is the ontogeny of memory and face recognition. He studies both typically developing children and children at risk for neurodevelopmental disorders, and he uses behavioral, electrophysiological (ERP), and metabolic (MRI) methods in his research. He served on the National Academy of Sciences panel that wrote *From Neurons to Neighborhoods,* and from 1997–2005, directed the John D. and Catherine T. MacArthur Foundation Research Network on *Early Experience and Brain Development.*

> *. . . I thought the chapters (Chapter 1, "Introduction," Chapter 2, "Biological Beginnings" and Chapter 3, "Physical Development and Biological Aging") were terrific: well written and well researched.*
>
> **—CHARLES NELSON**

Rachel Keen

Dr. Keen is one of the world's leading experts on perceptual-motor development. Formerly Rachel Keen Clifton, she currently is a professor of psychology at the University of Virginia and previously held that position at the University of Massachuetts–Amherst. She obtained her Ph.D. from the Institute of Child Development at the University of Minnesota. Dr. Keen is a former president of the International Society on Infant Studies and recently received the Distinguished Scientist Award from the Society for Research in Child Development. Dr. Keen has been awarded research grants from the National Institutes of Health, the National Science Foundation, and the March of Dimes. She held a Research Scientist Award from the National Institute of Mental Health for 20 years. Dr. Keen has served on the editorial boards of *Developmental Psychology, Child Development, Infant Behavior and Development,* and the *Journal of Experimental Child Psychology.* She also is a former editor of the *Monographs of the Society for Research in Child Development.*

> *First, I am delighted that John Santrock's chapter (5, "Motor, Sensory, and Perceptual Development") continues to improve with each edition, and this current edition is the best yet. . . . Once again, he has done his homework so that the text is up-to-date, and the references cited are always appropriate. I think his scholarship for a text of this sort is outstanding.*
>
> **—RACHEL KEEN**

Ross Parke

Dr. Parke is one of the world's leading experts on socioemotional development and family processes. He currently is Professor Emeritus at the University of California–Riverside, where he formerly was Distinguished Professor of Psychology and director of the Center for Family Studies. Dr. Parke obtained his Ph.D. from the University of Waterloo, Ontario, Canada. He is a past president of Division 7, the Developmental Psychology Division, of the American Psychological Association, and has received the G. Stanley Hall Award from this APA division. Dr. Parke also is a Fellow of the American Association for the Advancement of Science. He currently is the editor of the *Journal of Family Psychology* and has served as editor of *Developmental Psychology* and as associate editor of *Child Development.* Dr. Parke has authored and edited a number of books, including *Child Psychology* (with Mavis Hetherington and Mary Gauvain), *Throwaway Dads* (with Armin Brott), *Family-Peer Relationships* (with Gary Ladd), *Children in Time and Place* (with Glen Elder and John Modell), and *Exploring Family Relationships with Other Social Contexts* (with Sheppard Kellam). His research has focused on early social relationships in infancy and childhood. Dr. Parke is well known for his early work on the effects of punishment,

aggression, and child abuse, as well as his research on the father's role in infancy and early childhood. His current research focuses on links between family and peer social systems, and on the impact of economic stress on families of diverse ethnic backgrounds.

This chapter (14, "Families, Lifestyles, and Parenting") covers the main issues very well and includes an impressive list of recent references.

—**Ross Parke**

Robert J. Sternberg

Dr. Sternberg, widely recognized as one of the world's leading experts on the cognitive aspects of children's development, currently is Dean of the School of Arts and Sciences and a professor of psychology at Tufts University. He is also an honorary professor of psychology in the Department of Psychology at the University of Heidelberg (Germany). Prior to Tufts, Dr. Sternberg was IBM Professor of Psychology and Education in the Department of Psychology, a professor of management in the School of Management, and director of the Center for the Psychology of Abilities, Competencies, and Expertise at Yale. This center, now relocated to Tufts, seeks to have an impact on science, education, and society. He is a former president of the American Psychological Association and is president-elect of the International Association for Cognitive Education and Psychology. Dr. Sternberg received his Ph.D. from Stanford University in 1975 and his B.A. summa cum laude, *Phi Beta Kappa,* with honors with exceptional distinction in psychology, from Yale University in 1972. He also holds honorary doctorates from numerous universities including the

University of Heidelberg (Germany), Complutense University of Madrid (Spain), University of Leuven (Belgium), University of Cyprus, University of Paris V (France), and St. Petersburg State University (Russia). Dr. Sternberg is the author of more than 1,200 journal articles, book chapters, and books, and has received over $20 million in government and other grants and contracts for his research. The central focus of his research is on intelligence, creativity, and wisdom, and he also has studied love and close relationships as well as hate. This research has been conducted on five different continents. Among his many awards are the Sir Francis Galton Award from the International Association of Empirical Aesthetics, the Arthur W. Staats Award from the American Psychological Foundation and the Society for General Psychology, and the E. L. Thorndike Award for Career Achievement in Educational Psychology Award from the Society for Educational Psychology of the American Psychological Association (APA). He has been listed in the *APA Monitor on Psychology* as one of the top 100 psychologists of the twentieth century, and is listed by the ISI as one of its most highly cited authors (top .05 percent) in psychology and psychiatry.

Gigliana Melzi

Dr. Melzi is a leading expert on language development. She currently is a professor in the Department of Applied Psychology at New York University's Steinhardt School of Culture, Education, and Human Development, where she also is director of undergraduate studies. Dr. Melzi obtained her doctoral degree from Boston University. She has published articles and chapters focusing on the early literacy and language development of Spanish-speaking Latino children living in the United States and in their countries of origin. In one line of research, Dr. Melzi has investigated the daily literacy activities of immigrant parents and their impact on children's school performance. She also has conducted research on various discourse

and linguistic features of Spanish-speaking mother–child dyads from nonimmigrant and immigrant Latin American families across various socioeconomic groups. Currently, Dr. Melzi is funded by the National Institutes of Health and the Administration for Children and Families (ACF) in the U.S. Department of Health and Human Services for her work on educational involvement of Latino Head Start families.

Thanks for the opportunity to read the chapter (9, "Language Development"). I enjoyed it very much. . . . It does present language development in a very accessible manner. I commend the author for doing so.

—**Gigliana Melzi**

Susanne Denham

Dr. Denham is a leading expert on children's emotional development. She currently is a professor of psychology and director of the Applied Developmental Psychology program at George Mason University. Dr. Denham obtained her Ph.D. from the University of Maryland–Baltimore County. Apart from using her experience as a mother of three children to initiate and explore research on children's emotional development, she also has used her 11-year hands-on experience as a school psychologist to inform her research. Dr. Denham has authored numerous articles and two books on varying topics, from emotional and social competence in preschoolers and older children to developmental psychopathology. These projects have been supported by the National Institute of Mental Health, the National Science Foundation, and the W. T. Grant Foundation. Dr. Denham has also studied the development of forgiveness in children with the support of "A Campaign for Forgiveness Research" of the John Templeton Foundation.

> I think the chapter (10, "Emotional Development") is comprehensive, thoughtful, and generally very complete, as well as topical in that it will be of interest to students.
>
> —SUSANNE DENHAM

Crystal Park

Dr. Park is a leading expert on coping with stress and the psychological aspects of religion. She currently is a professor in clinical psychology at the University of Connecticut–Storrs and also is affiliated with the University of Connecticut Center for Health, Intervention, and Prevention. Dr. Park obtained her Ph.D. from the University of Delaware and completed a postdoctoral fellowship at the University of California–San Francisco. Her research focuses on multiple aspects of coping with stressful events, including the roles of religious beliefs and religious coping, the phenomenon of stress-related growth, and the making of meaning from highly stressful life events. In recent years, Dr. Park has been examining these issues in the context of traumatic events and life-threatening illnesses, especially cancer and congestive heart failure. She is currently principal investigator of research on mediators of the effects of spirituality on well-being in congestive heart failure patients; a meaning-making writing intervention in people with post-traumatic stress disorder; and the quality of life in younger cancer survivors. She is co-editor of *The Handbook of the Psychology of Religion and Spirituality* and the recently published *Medical Illness and Positive Life Change: Can Crisis Lead to Personal Transformation?*

> I very much like the way that the sections of the book I read (Chapter 4, "Health"; Chapter 13, "Moral Development, Values, and Religion"; and Chapter 17, "Death, Dying, and Grieving") are written. The interweaving of current research and simple, solid frames are great, and should really allow students to understand and remember. The writing is clear and easy to read. You make this easy, and I know it isn't.
>
> —CRYSTAL PARK

Seth Kalichman

Dr. Kalichman is one of the world's leading experts on sexuality. He currently is a professor in the Department of Psychology at the University of Connecticut and director of the Southeast HIV and AIDS Research and Evaluation (SHARE) Project. Dr. Kalichman obtained his Ph.D. in clinical-community psychology from the University of South Carolina. His research focuses on social and behavioral aspects of AIDS, especially sexual risk behavior intervention research in the United States and South Africa, research that is supported by the National Institutes of Health and the National Institute on Alcohol Abuse and Alcoholism. Dr. Kalichman was the recipient of the Distinguished Scientific Award for Early Career Contribution to Psychology in Health awarded by the American Psychological Association and Distinguished Scientist Award from the Society for Behavioral Medicine. He currently is the editor of the journal *AIDS and Behavior* and the author of *Denying AIDS: Conspiracy Theories, Pseudoscience, and Human Tragedy*, with all royalties from the sale of *Denying AIDS* donated to purchase HIV treatments in Africa.

> This sexual development chapter (12, "Gender and Sexuality") has numerous updated references and reads as very contemporary narrative. . . . I think that the perspective taken in this chapter does reflect the current thinking in the field. The chapter is well balanced between biological and social aspects of sexual development. The integration of relevant areas that is achieved is also certainly in keeping with the field.
>
> —SETH KALICHMAN

Preface

Most textbooks on life-span development are chronologically organized. Why present life-span development topically? In a topical approach, students can see the processes involved in a particular aspect of development in a single chapter and often in a particular part of a chapter. In contrast, in a chronologically organized textbook, a topic such as the development of the brain appears in a number of chapters—typically early in the book in an infancy chapter, later in a childhood chapter, and then again toward the end of the book in an aging chapter. Examining life-span development topically allows developmental changes through the life-span to be described in close proximity to one another and helps students make better connections between them.

The positive comments of instructors who adopted the four editions of this book, students who have studied it, and leading experts in the field confirm the increasing interest in teaching life-span development with a topical approach. *A Topical Approach to Life-Span Development*, fifth edition, is not just an age-stage text with a chronological-within-topical-organization. When key chronological, sequential changes take place, they are emphasized. The focus, though, is mainly on the processes of development, how these processes function, and how they change developmentally throughout the life span.

The three main themes of the book are research, applications, and contexts. It is very important for students to have a firm grasp of the research foundation of the field. They also want to know how this information can be applied in the real world and how contextual variations—especially those that involve culture, ethnicity, and gender—affect development. These themes are woven throughout the book and featured in interludes that examine in depth a specific aspect of research, applications, and contexts. These three themes—research, applications, and contexts—continue as important themes in the fifth edition of *A Topical Approach to Life-Span Development*.

For this edition of *A Topical Approach to Life-Span Development*, I have also expanded coverage in a number of key areas, incorporated the latest research and applications, and fine-tuned the features of the book that make learning easier and more engaging.

First I describe the thrust of these changes in general terms. Then I provide a detailed description of the chapter-by-chapter changes.

RESEARCH AND CONTENT

Above all, a topical life-span development text must have a solid research foundation. This edition has a more extensive research orientation than the previous editions and includes the latest, most contemporary research.

Research Citations

A Topical Approach to Life-Span Development, fifth edition, is truly a twenty-first-century presentation of the field of life-span development with more than 1,600 citations from 2006 to 2010 alone, as well as classic references from the twentieth century.

Content

Many new content areas have been added and many others updated and expanded. Significant content changes are detailed on a chapter-by-chapter basis later in the Preface.

Research in Life-Span Development Interludes

A *Research in Life-Span Development* interlude appears in each chapter. These interludes provide an in-depth look at research on a topic covered in the chapter. New *Research* interludes include "Memory in the A.M. and P.M. and Memory for Something Meaningful" (Chapter 1); updated coverage of Tiffany Field's massage therapy research (Field & Diego, 2008), including a new figure on massage therapy and preterm infants' stress behaviors (Hernandez-Reif, Diego, & Field, 2007) (Chapter 2); and "Fast Track" (Thomas & the Conduct Problems Prevention Research Group, 2009; Dodge & others, 2008; Slough, McMahon, & the Conduct Problems Prevention Research Group, 2008) (Chapter 13).

Expert Research Consultants

Life-span development has become an enormous, complex field, and no single author can possibly be an expert in all areas of life-span development. To be certain of presenting definitive and current research accurately, I have sought the input of leading experts in many different areas of life-span development. These consultants graciously provided detailed evaluations and recommendations in their areas of expertise. The expert research consultants for *A Topical Approach to Life-Span Development*, fifth edition, are:

Charles Nelson, *Harvard University and Children's Hospital, Boston*	Physical development and the development of the brain
Rachel Keen, *University of Virginia*	Motor, sensory, and perceptual development
Ross Parke, *University of California at Riverside*	Families, lifestyles, and parenting
Robert J. Sternberg, *Tufts University*	Intelligence
Gigliana Melzi, *New York University*	Language development
Susanne Denham, *George Mason University*	Emotional development
Crystal Park, *University of Connecticut*	Health and aging, values and religion, and death, dying, and grieving
Seth Kalichman, *University of Connecticut*	Gender and sexuality

APPLICATIONS AND CONTEXTS

It is important not only to present the scientific foundations of life-span development to students, but also to describe real-world applications and the contexts of development.

Applications

There is increasing interest in the real-world applications of research. In this text, I have made every effort to provide applied examples of concepts and to give students a sense that the field of life-span development has personal meaning for them. Applications are woven throughout the book and also are emphasized in an *Applications in Life-Span Development* interlude that appears in each chapter. New *Applications* interludes include "Improving Family Policy" (McLoyd & others, 2009) (Chapter 1) and "Cognitive Training with Older Adults" (Chapter 7).

In addition to the applications discussed in each chapter, a Careers in Life-Span Development Appendix follows Chapter 1. It describes a number of careers in education/research, clinical/counseling, medical/nursing/physical development, and families/relationships categories. In addition, new to this edition are a number of *Careers in Life-Span Development* profiles. In every chapter, a *Careers* profile describes a person's work—and, in most cases, a photograph shows the individual at work.

Contexts

Contextual variations in development are discussed throughout the text and in *Contexts of Life-Span Development* interludes, which highlight cultural and ethnic aspects of development. New and updated *Contexts of Life-Span Development* interludes include "Women's Struggle for Equality: An International Journey" (UNICEF, 2009, 2010) (Chapter 1), updated coverage of family leave policies around the world (Tolani & Brooks-Gunn, 2008) (Chapter 10), "Improving Resources for Families in Impoverished

Areas" (Duncan, Huston, & Weisner, 2007; Huston & others, 2006) (Chapter 15), and "Work and Retirement Around the World" (HSBC Insurance, 2007) (Chapter 16). Other new *Contexts of Life-Span Development* interludes are described later, in the section on the chapter-by-chapter changes.

ACCESSIBILITY AND INTEREST

Many students today juggle numerous responsibilities in addition to their coursework. To help them make the most of their study time, I have made this book as accessible as possible without watering down the content. The writing, organization, and learning system of *A Topical Approach to Life-Span Development* will engage students and provide a clear overview of life-span development.

Writing

Across five editions of this text, I have honed the writing to improve accessibility for students. In particular, I have sought to clearly define concepts and provide relevant examples of the concepts to promote understanding.

The Learning System

I strongly believe that students not only should be challenged to study hard and think more deeply and productively about life-span development, but also should be provided with effective learning tools. Feedback from instructors and students has confirmed that the learning system in this book increases understanding and retention of the content.

Students struggle to find the main ideas in their courses, especially in life-span development, which includes so much material. The learning system centers on learning goals that, together with the main text headings, keep the key ideas in front of the reader from the beginning to the end of the chapter. Each chapter has no more than five main headings and corresponding learning goals, which are presented side-by-side in the chapter-opening spread. At the end of each main section of a chapter, the learning goal is repeated in a feature called Review and Reflect, which prompts students to review the key topics in the section and poses a question to encourage them to think critically about what they have read. At the end of the chapter, under the heading Reach Your Learning Goals, the learning goals guide students through the bulleted chapter review.

In addition to the verbal tools just described, visual organizers, or maps, that link up with the learning goals are presented at the beginning of each major section in the chapter. At the end of each chapter, the section maps are assembled into a complete map of the chapter to provide a visual review guide. The complete learning system, including many additional features not mentioned here, is illustrated in the Visual Tour for Students.

CHAPTER-BY-CHAPTER CHANGES

Numerous changes were made in each of the 17 chapters in *A Topical Approach to Life-Span Development*, fifth edition. Here are the major ones.

CHAPTER 1
INTRODUCTION

- Significant updating of research and citations
- Revised definition of gender based on expert consultant Diane Halpern's (2006) input
- Expanded discussion of poverty and children, including updated statistics on the percentage of U.S. children living in poverty (Federal Interagency Forum on Child and Family Statistics, 2008)
- New *Contexts of Life-Span Development* interlude, "Women's Struggle for Equality: An International Journey" (UNICEF 2009, 2010), including a new figure
- New description of the life of 17-year-old Doly Akter and her efforts to improve the lives of females in the slum where she lives in Dhaka, Bangladesh
- New *Applications in Life-Span Development* interlude: "Improving Family Policy" (Minnesota Family Investment Program, 2009)
- Description of recent research revealing the cumulative effects of poverty on physiological indices of stress in children (Evans & Kim, 2007)
- New *Research in Life-Span Development* interlude: "Memory in the A.M. and P.M. and Memory for Something Meaningful"
- New section, Connecting Biological, Cognitive, and Socioemotional Processes (Diamond, 2009; Diamond, Casey, & Munakata, 2010)
- New description of the rapidly emerging fields of developmental cognitive neuroscience and developmental social neuroscience to illustrate the interface of biological, cognitive, and socioemotional processes (Diamond, Casey, & Munakata, 2010; Johnson, 2009)
- Extensively updated and expanded coverage of the link between age and happiness, including recent research that indicates happiness increases with age (Yang, 2008)
- Deleted section, A Historical Perspective

CHAPTER 2
BIOLOGICAL BEGINNINGS

- Considerable rewriting and editing of content for improved clarification and student learning
- Extensive research and citation updating
- Expanded criticisms of evolutionary psychology
- Updated coverage of brain development in the prenatal period (Moulson & Nelson, 2008; Nelson, 2009)
- Updated material on the approximate number of genes that humans possess (20,500) (Ensemble Human, 2008)
- Description of recent research on the characteristics of boys with Klinefelter syndrome (Ross & others, 2008)
- Updated and expanded coverage of fragile X syndrome, including a new photograph of a boy with fragile X syndrome (Ono, Farzin, & Hagerman, 2008)

- Inclusion of recent research on cognitive deficits in boys with fragile X syndrome (Hooper & others, 2008)
- New coverage of the underutilization of the only drug (hydroxyurea) approved to treat sickle-cell anemia in adolescents and adults, and current research that is underway to determine if the drug is effective in treating babies
- Description of a recent research review on how genetic counseling clients interpret risk (Sivell & others, 2008)
- New material on the concept of gene-gene interaction (Chen & others, 2009; Jylhava & others, 2009)
- Updated and expanded discussion of heredity-environment interaction (Barry, Kochanska, & Philibert, 2008; Shen, 2009)
- New section and coverage of the concept of G × E, which involves the interaction of a specific measured variation in the DNA sequence and a specific measured aspect of the environment (Cheok & others, 2009; Diamond, 2009)
- Discussion of a recent G × E interaction study on the gene *5-HTTLPR* and how the long version of the gene likely serves a protective function in children's parental loss (Caspers & others, 2009)
- New description of recent research on secure attachment in infancy serving as a protective factor in the development of self-regulation in early childhood for children at risk because they have the short version of the *5-HTTLPR* gene (Kochanska, Philibert, & Barry, 2009)
- New coverage of the field of pharmacogenetics and how it reflects G × E (Berlin, Paul, & Vesell, 2009; Lima & others, 2009)
- New final paragraph on the interaction of heredity and environment interaction that emphasizes development as a co-construction of biology, culture, and the individual
- New section on the extensive recent research on the potential for using noninvasive prenatal diagnosis (NIPD) as an alternative to chorionic villus sampling and amniocentesis (Avent & others, 2008; Finning & Chitty, 2008)
- New figure showing a fetal MRI
- Description of a recent research study indicating that exercise in pregnancy is linked to a reduced risk of preterm birth (Hegaard & others, 2008)
- New description of what the field of behavioral teratology involves (DiPietro, 2008)
- New commentary that male fetuses are far more likely to be affected by teratogens than female fetuses (DiPietro, 2008)
- Inclusion of information from a recent research review of aspirin and reproductive outcomes (James, Bancazio, & Price, 2008)
- Coverage of a recent study on caffeine intake during pregnancy and risk for miscarrage (Weng, Odouli, & Li, 2008)
- Change of label from FAS to FASD (fetal alcohol spectrum disorders) in keeping with recently developed terminology and expanded coverage of FASD (Olson, King, & Jirikowic, 2008)
- Description of recent research on maternal smoking and inttention/hyperactivity in children (Knopik, 2009; Pinkhardt & others, 2009)

- Coverage of recent research on the harmful effects of cocaine use during pregnancy on growth, language development, and attention (Accornero & others, 2007; Lewis & others, 2007; Richardson, Goldschmidt, & Larkby, 2008)

- Description of a recent study linking prenatal cocaine exposure to an increased likelihood of being in special education and receiving support services (Levine & others, 2008)

- Inclusion of information about a recent study that revealed negative neonatal outcomes following exposure to methamphetamine in the prenatal period (Smith & others, 2008)

- Description of a recent study on prenatal marijuana exposure and lower intelligence in childhood (Goldschmidt & others, 2008)

- Coverage of recent analysis proposing that fetal programming from an overweight pregnant woman is likely linked to the offspring's being overweight in childhood and adolescence (McMillen & others, 2008)

- Updated and expanded material on the offspring of diabetic mothers (Gluck & others, 2009; Eriksson, 2009)

- Coverage of a recent study that revealed a substantial reduction in preterm birth when women took folic acid for one year prior to conceiving (Bukowski & others, 2008)

- Updated research on fetal mercury exposure and developmental outcomes (Triche & Hossain, 2007)

- Description of a recent research review on maternal stress during pregnancy and negative developmental outcomes in offspring (Talge & others, 2007)

- Coverage of recent studies showing that declines in stress during pregnancy linked to a lower incidence of preterm birth (Glynn & others, 2008) and positive prenatal and birth outcomes (Diego & others, 2009; Field & others, 2009)

- Description of a recent study indicating positive benefits in CenteringPregnancy groups (Klima & others, 2009)

- Coverage of a successful home nurse visiting program, the Nurse Family Partnership, conducted by David Olds and his colleagues (2007), which has produced positive outcomes for mothers and their children

- Discussion of recent research on a home visitation program that reduced the incidence of low birth weight infants (Lee & others, 2009)

- Updated coverage of trends in cesarean delivery (National Center for Health Statistics, 2007)

- Description of a recent national study comparing neonatal death rates of cesarean delivery with no labor complications to neonatal death rates involving planned vaginal delivery (MacDorman & others, 2008)

- Description of a recent study linking preterm birth with dropping out of school, including a new figure (Geeta & others, 2008)

- Description of a recent MRI study of brain deficiencies in children born very preterm (Swamy, Ostbye, & Skjaerven, 2008)

- Updated research about the use of progestin in reducing the risk of preterm birth (Fonseca & others, 2007; Lamant & Jaggat, 2007)

- Discussion of recent research indicating that low birth weight children have more difficulties in socializing and have different lifestyles as emerging adults and adults than their normal birth weight counterparts (Kajantie & others, 2008; Moster, Lie, & Markestad, 2008; Schmidt & others, 2008)

- Description of two recent experimental studies revealing the benefits of kangaroo care (Gathwala, Singh, & Balhara, 2008; Suman, Udani, & Nanavati, 2008)

- Updated coverage of the *Research in Life-Span Development* interlude on Tiffany Field's massage therapy research, including recent research on the effects of massage therapy on preterm infants' stress behaviors, with a new figure illustrating the results (Field & Diego, 2008; Field, Diego, & Hernandez-Reif, 2008; Hernandez-Reif, Diego, & Field, 2007)

CHAPTER 3
PHYSICAL DEVELOPMENT AND BIOLOGICAL AGING

- Extensive revising, editing, and updating of the discussion of puberty

- New discussion of precocious puberty (Blakemore, Berenbaum, & Liben, 2009).

- Inclusion of recent information on a longitudinal study of the sequence of pubertal events in boys and girls (Susman & others, 2009)

- Inclusion of recent information that early-maturing girls are less likely to graduate from high school and more likely to cohabit and marry earlier (Cavanagh, 2009)

- Description of a recent study of increased height in Chinese adolescents, especially during puberty, from the 1950s through 2005 (Ji & Chen, 2008)

- New figure of the major endocrine glands and their roles in pubertal development

- Inclusion of information about a recent study on early-maturing girls and trying cigarettes and alcohol without their parents' knowledge (Westling & others, 2008)

- Description of a recent study of menopausal transition on women's quality of life in Taiwan (Cheng & others, 2008)

- New material on Mark Johnson and his colleagues' (2009) view of the powerful neural leadership and organizational role of the prefrontal cortex during development

- New material on which individuals are most often the perpetrators of shaken baby syndrome (National Center for Shaken Baby Syndrome, 2008)

- Inclusion of new material on the increasing focal activation of the brain in middle and late childhood (Durston & others, 2006)

- Description of recent research that revealed a link between the volume of the amygdala in young adolescents and their aggressive behavior when interacting with parents (Whittle & others, 2008)

- Coverage of recent research on changes in the brain in adolescence and resistance to peer pressure (Paus & others, 2008)

- New material on the current consensus that under normal conditions it is unlikely that adults lose brain cells per se (Nelson, 2008)

- Description of recent research indicating links between aerobic fitness, greater volume in the hippocampus, and better memory (Erickson & others, 2009)

- Coverage of recent information that new brain cells survive longer when rats are cognitively challenged to learn something (Shors, 2009)

- New material on individual differences in brain lateralization and aging, including a new figure showing an fMRI scan of 81-year-old T. Boone Pickens' brain (Helman, 2008)

- Updated and expanded material on sleep patterns in infancy (Sadeh, 2008)

- Expanded discussion of REM sleep in infancy and question raised about whether we can know for sure whether infants dream

- Coverage of a recent study indicating that infants who sleep in bedrooms with a fan have a lower risk of SIDS (Coleman-Phox, Odouli, & Li, 2008)

- Expanded and updated description of young children's sleep patterns and adjustment (National Sleep Foundation, 2009)

- Inclusion of recent research on a link between inadequate sleep and injuries that require attention in preschool children (Koulouglioti, Cole, & Kitzman, 2008)

- Description of a recent longitudinal study on characteristics linked to young children's having bad dreams (Simard & others, 2008)

- Inclusion of recent research on bedtime sleep resistance and problem behaviors in children (Carvalho Bos & others, 2009)

- Description of recent research on short sleep duration and being overweight in childhood (Nixon & others, 2008; Patel & Hu, 2008)

- Discussion of a recent study linking sleep problems from 3 to 8 years of age with the early onset of drug use and depression in adolescence (Wong, Brower, & Zucker, 2009)

- Coverage of a recent national study of adolescent sleep patterns, including developmental changes from the ninth through the twelfth grade as well as a new figure illustrating the changes (Eaton & others, 2008).

- New photograph of an adolescent girl's sleep being monitored in Mary Carskadon's sleep laboratory at Brown University

- Updated description of life expectancy based on recent statistics (Heron & others, 2008; National Center for Health Statistics, 2008)

- New coverage of a surprising gender difference in centenarians' physical and cognitive functioning that favors men (Perls, 2007; Terry & others, 2008)

- New coverage of susceptibility and longevity genes (Concannon & others, 2009; Hinks & others, 2009)

- Updated and expanded discussion of the role that telomerase inhibition might play in reducing cancerous cells (Effros, 2009; Wu & others, 2009)

- Coverage of a recent study linking vitamin C and E use in women with telomere length (Xu & others, 2009)

- Coverage of a recent study linking smoking with higher concentrations of free radicals (Reddy Thavanti & others, 2008)

 **CHAPTER 4
HEALTH**

- New *Diversity in Life-Span Development* interlude, "Culture and Health," describing the Ni-Hon-San Study that explores links between culture and health

- Description of a recent study indicating that taking a high level of supplemental vitamin C was linked to a lower incidence of hip fractures in older women (Sahni & others, 2009)

- Inclusion of recent research on the *apo4* gene and onset of Alzheimer disease (Sando & others, 2008)

- Updated description of the number of U.S. adults with Alzheimer disease in 2009 (Alzheimer's Association, 2009)

- Updated description of the percentage of individuals estimated to develop Alzheimer disease in the next 10 years at age 65, 75, and 85 for women and men, including a new figure (Alzheimer's Association, 2009)

- Expanded coverage of MCI, including the use of fMRI scans with individuals who have MCI to predict which of these individuals are likely to develop Alzheimer disease

- Description of recent research on cortical thickness and MCI (Wang & others, 2009)

- Coverage of recent research on the use of deep brain stimulation in treating Parkinson disease (Troster, 2009; Zahodne & others, 2009)

- Discussion of recent research indicating that certain types of dancing improve the movement skills of individuals with Parkinson disease (Hackney & Earhart, 2009)

- New figure on the decline in the percentage of older adults who are living in nursing homes

- Inclusion of material from a recent research review by the American Academy of Pediatrics indicating no link between breast feeding and children's allergies (Greer & others, 2008)

- Extensive updating, revision, and expansion of material on breast feeding based on a recent large-scale research review (Agency for Healthcare Quality and Research, 2007)

- Description of recent research linking breast feeding with a lower incidence of metabolic syndrome in midlife women (Ram & others, 2008)

- Discussion of an important issue related to the correlational nature of breast versus bottle feeding studies (Agency for Healthcare Quality and Research, 2007)

- Inclusion of information from a recent national survey of 4- to 18-year-olds' consumption of fat in their diet (Kranz, Lin, & Wagstaff, 2007)

- New discussion of the role of caregiver feeding behavior and styles in young children's eating behavior (Black & Hurley, 2007; Black & Lozoff, 2008)

- Recent information about changes in the WIC program for 2009 (Food & Nutrition Service, 2009)

- Inclusion of recent research on the changes and effectiveness of various aspects of the WIC program (Black & others, 2009; Heinig & others, 2009; Olson & others, 2009a, b)

- Coverage of a recent large-scale U.S. study on the percentage of children 2 to 19 years of age who have weight problems and the recent leveling off in overweight categories (Ogden, Carroll, & Flegal, 2008)

- Updated material on the increase in overweight children in many countries around the world (Chan, 2008; Li & others, 2008).

- Inclusion of a recent study that found children's weight at 5 years of age was significantly related to their weight at 9 years of age (Gardner & others, 2009)

- Discussion of a recent study on developmental changes in the percentage of overweight children from 4 to 11 years of age, depending on whether they have lean or obese parents (Semmler & others, 2009)

- Coverage of a recent large-scale U.S. study indicating a higher percentage of being overweight or obese for African American and Latino children than for non-Latino White children (Benson, Baer, & Kaelber, 2009)

- Description of recent studies linking high levels of watching TV with being overweight in childhood (Wells & others, 2008)

- Coverage of a study of adolescents that found a relation between excess body fat and watching TV and playing video games more on weekends (Vicente-Rodriguez & others, 2008)

- Expanded and updated coverage of the developmental outcomes of children who are overweight

- Coverage of a recent study indicating a link between body mass index and waist circumference in childhood and metabolic syndrome in adulthood (Sun & others, 2008)

- Description of a recent study on how peers perceived obese children (Zeller, Reiter-Purtill, & Ramey, 2008)

- Description of a recent study indicating the percent of overweight male and female adolescents who become obese adults (Wang & others, 2008)

- Inclusion of recent research on the positive role that keeping a food diary has on losing weight (Hollis & others, 2008)

- Updated coverage of overweight and obesity, including projections of the percentage of Americans who will be overweight in 2030 (Beydoun & Wang, 2009)

- Inclusion of recent research on the link between overweight and depression (Ball, Burton, & Brown, 2009)

- Updated discussion of dieting, including a recent research review of diet-plus-exercise programs in weight loss (Wu & others, 2009)

- Coverage of a recent study of calorie restriction and verbal memory in older adults (Witte & others, 2009)

- Discussion of a recent study focused on whether underweight women and men live longer (Wandell, Carlsson, & Theobald, 2009)

- Description of recent large-scale studies of men indicating that taking vitamin C and vitamin E did not prevent cardiovascular disease (Gaziano & others, 2009; Sesso & others, 2008)

- Coverage of a recent study finding no links between diet supplementation with antioxidant vitamins and cancer incidence/death (Lin & others, 2009)

- Coverage of the increased concern about the sedentary lifestyles of children in a number of countries around the world (Dowda & others, 2009; Liu & others, 2008)

- Inclusion of information about three recent studies focused on increasing young children's physical activity (Beets & Foley, 2008; Brown & others, 2009; Trost, Fees, & Dzewaltowski, 2008)

- Description of recent research on the benefits of an intensive resistance training program on reducing children's body fat and increasing their muscle strength (Benson, Torode, & Fiatarone Singh, 2008)

- Inclusion of recent research indicating the amount of daily physical activity that is associated with lower odds of childhood obesity (Wittmeier, Mollard, & Kriellaars, 2008)

- Description of a recent study linking aerobic exercise to an increase in planning skills in overweight children (Davis & others, 2007)

- Updating of the trends in the percentage of U.S. adolescents who ate fruits and vegetables on a regular basis (Eaton & others, 2008)

- Inclusion of a recent research review on family factors linked to whether or not adolescents eat fruits and vegetables (Pearson, Biddle, & Gorely, 2008)

- New description of a recent national study of U.S. 9- to 15-year-old boys' and girls' exercise patterns showing a significant decline in physical activity from 9 to 15 years of age, including a new figure (Nader & others, 2008)

- Coverage of a recent study that revealed a positive role of aerobic exercise fitness on 9-year-old girls' performance on a cognitive control task that required them to inhibit irrelevant responses to obtain correct solutions (Hillman & others, 2009)

- Updated coverage of ethnicity by gender rates of exercise for U.S. adolescents (Eaton & others, 2008)

- Coverage of a recent national study showing that 13 years of age is when a decline in exercise occurs in many adolescents and factors that increase the likelihood that adolescents will engage in regular exercise (Kahn & others, 2008)

- Inclusion of recent research on links between watching TV and using computers and exercise rates of adolescents (Chen, Liou, & Wu, 2008)

- Inclusion of recent research on exercise and reduction of colon and rectal cancer risk (Howard & others, 2008)

- New material on the positive role of exercise in older adults' cellular functioning, including a recent study on exercise and white blood cells in the tips of chromosomes (Cherkas & others, 2008)

- Coverage of a recent national study revealing that older adults have only slightly increased their level of exercise in recent years, including a new figure (Centers for Disease Control and Prevention, 2008)

- Description of recent research on adolescents who eat dinner with their families and lower incidences of drug abuse (CASA, 2007)

- Updated results from the Monitoring the Future Study regarding adolescent substance use and abuse (Johnston & others, 2008)

- Inclusion of a recent study on a link between systolic blood pressure during exercise and increased long-term survival (Hedberg & others, 2009)

- New material on the role of exercise in improving immune system functioning in older adult women (Sakamoto & others, 2009)

- Description of a recent longitudinal study on physical fitness, weight, and longevity across a 12-year period (Sui & others, 2007)

- Coverage of a longitudinal study of regular exercise at 72 years of age and its link to still being alive at 90 years of age (Yates & others, 2008)

- New commentary about the increasing demand for home-care workers because of the increase in the population of older adults and their preference to stay out of nursing homes (Moos, 2007)

- Updated results from the Monitoring the Future Study regarding adolescent substance use and abuse (Johnston & others, 2009)

- Description of recent research on how early educational success provides important protection against developing drug problems in adolescence (Bachman & others, 2008)

- Coverage of a recent study of the percentage of college students who abstain from drinking alcohol (Huang & others, 2009)

- Coverage of two recent research studies that found a protective effect of moderate drinking in the health and longevity of older adults (Rozzini, Ranhoff, & Trabucchi, 2007; Strandberg & others, 2007)

- New discussion of the role that resveratrol plays in increasing longevity through moderate drinking and description of its link to a key enzyme, SIRT1 (Mukerjee & others, 2009)

- Inclusion of recent research indicating that red wine, but not white wine, killed several lines of cancer cells (Wallenborg & others, 2009)

CHAPTER 5

MOTOR, SENSORY, AND PERCEPTUAL DEVELOPMENT

- Description of recent research on infants' walking patterns and their occasional large steps (Badaly & Adolph, 2008)

- Updated coverage of cultural variation in infant motor development (Adolph, Karasik, & Tamis-LeMonda, 2010)

- Description of a recent study linking children's physical fitness and the mastery of motor skills (Haga, 2008)

- Coverage of a recent experimental study of physical activity in older adults at risk for mobility disability (Rejeski & others, 2008)

- Inclusion of a recent study on mobility restrictions in older adults predicted by a lower level of physical activity and a higher level of adiposity (Koster & others, 2008)

- Coverage of recent research on obesity and mobility restrictions in older adults (Houston & others, 2009)

- Updated information about the development of visual acuity in young infants (Aslin & Lathrop, 2008)

- New section on the perception of occluded objects

- New material on the age at which infants develop the ability to perceive that occluded objects are complete

- Discussion of Scott Johnson's (2009a, b, c) view on why infants are able to develop the ability to perceive occluded objects as complete

- New description of a recent study by Bennett Bertenthal and his colleagues (2007) on infants' predictive tracking of briefly occluded moving objects

- New discussion of the success in speaking and understanding speech in congenitally deaf children when they undergo cochlear implant surgery early in their development (Peters & others, 2007)

- Description of a recent study of adolescents' use of MP3 players and their perception of low personal vulnerability for hearing problems (Vogel & others, 2008)

- Expanded coverage of hearing problems in older adults (Fowler & Leigh-Paffenroth, 2007)

- New material on the use of stem cells as an alternative to cochlear implants in neurosensory hearing loss (Pauley & others, 2008)

- Description of a recent study indicating a decline in the detection of smells in older adults but an increase in perceived pleasantness of a smell (Markovic & others, 2007)

- New main section, Nature, Nurture, and Perceptual Development, examining nativist and empiricist views of perception (Arterberry, 2008; Slater & others, 2009)

- Updated and expanded coverage of perceptual-motor coupling, including how infants develop new perceptual-motor couplings.

CHAPTER 6
COGNITIVE DEVELOPMENTAL APPROACHES

- Revised, improved figure on Piaget's three mountains task, providing students with a better understanding of the concept of egocentrism

- Expanded analysis of object permanence, including Andrew Meltzoff's (2008; Meltzoff & Moore, 1998) criticisms of the violation of expectations method as an accurate measure of object permanence

- New section on the nature-nurture issue in infant cognitive development

- New discussion of Elizbeth Spelke's (2000; Spelke & Kinzler, 2007, 2009) core knowledge approach

- New coverage of the intriguing question of whether young infants have a sense of number

- Description of a recent study on the area of the brain activated when 3-month-old infants were observing changes in the number of objects compared with changes in the type of objects (Izard, Dehaene-Lambertz, & Dehaene, 2008)

- Inclusion of criticism of Spelke's core knowledge approach by Mark Johnson (2008)

- Expanded and updated conclusion to what are the focus and most difficult task infant researchers face in determining the influence of nature and nurture (Aslin, 2009)

- Expanded description of criticisms of Vygotsky (Gauvain, 2008)

CHAPTER 7
INFORMATION PROCESSING

- Reduction of introductory overview of information processing to allow for inclusion of recent research and increasing interest in developmental changes in attention, memory, thinking, and metacognition

- Expanded and updated coverage of attention, including developmental changes in orienting/investigative and sustained attention (Courage & Richards, 2008)

- Expanded and updated discussion of habituation and its importance in infant development (Slater, Field, & Hernandez-Reif, 2007)

- New coverage of advances in executive attention and sustained attention in early childhood (Rothbart & Gartstein, 2008)

- Discussion of a recent study that linked children's attention problems at 54 months of age with a lower level of social skills in peer relations in the first and third grades (NICHD Early Child Care Research Network, 2009)

- New description of exercises used in some European kindergartens to improve young children's attention (Mills & Mills, 2000; Posner & Rothbart, 2007)

- New discussion of multitasking and its distracting effects on adolescents' allocation of attention, especially when engaging in a challenging task (Bauerlein, 2008; Begley & Interlandi, 2008)

- Inclusion of results from a study of episodic memory in 18- to 94-year-olds (Siedlecki, 2007)

- Expanded discusion of working memory and aging, including explanation of deficits in working memory in older adults because of their less efficient inhibition in preventing irrelevant information from entering working memory and their increased distractibility (Lustig & Hasher, 2009)

- New coverage of the reminiscence bump in autobiographical memory, including recent research on the role of perceived control and influence on later development in such memories (Gluck & Bluck, 2007)

- Description of recent research on cohort effects on cognitive aging (Zelinski & Kennison, 2007)

- Expanded and updated coverage of concept formation and categorization in infancy (Quinn, 2009a, b)

- Description of recent research on the early development of intense interests in particular categories, including strong gender differences, including a new figure (DeLoache, Simcock, & Macari, 2007)

- Expanded discussion of concept formation and categorization in infancy and a new final summary statement about the infant's remarkable degree of learning power (Diamond, Casey, & Munakata, 2010; Mandler, 2004, 2009)

- Description of recent research on more than 107,000 students in 41 countries linking family, economic, and cultural influences to science achievement (Chiu, 2007)

- Description of a decision-making study on how graduated driver licensing (GDL) reduces adolescent crashes and fatalities (Keating, 2007)

- Inclusion of new material about the importance of social contexts, especially peers and how their presence activates the brain's reward pathways, in adolescent decision making (Steinberg, 2008)

- Description of a recent study on aging and decision making (Isella & others, 2008)

- Expanded and updated coverage of cognitive neuroscience and aging, including activity increases in older adults' frontal and parietal regions while they are engaging in tasks that require cognitive control processes, such as attention (Grady, 2008; Gutchess & others, 2005)

- New coverage of Denise Park and Patricia Reuter-Lorenz' (2009) scaffolding view of the aging, adaptive brain and cognition

- Coverage of recent research involving data from the Victoria Longitudinal Study that supports the "use it or lose it" concept (Bielak & others, 2007)

- Inclusion of research in men in their seventies, indicating that reading daily reduced their mortality (Jacobs & others, 2008)

- New photo and description of the Young@Heart chorus to illustrate the "use it" side of "use it or lose it"

- Coverage of a recent study linking years of education and cognitive ability in 79-year-olds (Gow & others, 2008)

- Description of age-related cognitive decline in adults with mood disorders, such as depression (Gualtieri & Johnson, 2008)
- New *Applications in Life-Span Development* interlude: "Cognitive Training with Older Adults"
- Much expanded and updated coverage of the young child's theory of mind with considerable input from leading expert Candice Mills
- Description of a recent study linking children's theory of mind to cognitive processes (Wellman & others, 2008)
- Coverage of a recent study linking young children's theory of mind competence with later metamemory skills (Lockl & Schneider, 2007)
- New discussion of reasons to question false-belief understanding as a pivotal point in the development of a theory of mind
- New figures that show stimuli used in theory of mind research

CHAPTER 8
INTELLIGENCE

- Considerable editing and updating of the discussion of intelligence based on feedback from expert consultant Robert J. Sternberg
- Expansion of discussion on what intelligence is, including variations of what Sternberg and Vygotsky might include in their views of what intelligence involves
- New material on the most recent revision of the Stanford Binet test, the Stanford-Binet 5, which now provides scores on five subtests and an overall composite score
- Deletion of some of the historical work on the role of heredity in intelligence
- Deletion of section on group intelligence tests
- New material on the increased interest in emotional intelligence, as well as criticism of the concept (Cox & Nelson, 2008)
- New description of the Bayley-IIII, including its two new scales—socio-emotional and adaptive—that are assessed by questionnaires given to the infant's primary caregiver (Lennon & others, 2008)
- New discussion of Sternberg's recent application of his triarchic theory of intelligence to the concept of wisdom, including an emphasis on teaching wisdom in schools (Sternberg, 2009d, e; Sternberg, Jarvin, & Grigorenko, 2009; Sternberg, Jarvin, & Reznitskaya, 2010)
- New section, The Neuroscience of Intelligence
- Discussion of the link between overall brain size and intelligence
- Coverage of recent research on a distributed neural network that involves the frontal and parietal lobes and the neural network's link to intelligence (Colom, Jung, & Haier, 2007; Colom & others, 2009; Jung & Hair, 2007)
- Description of the link between a higher level of intelligence and a higher volume of gray matter in the brain (Colom, Jung, & Haier, 2007; Luders & others, 2009)

- New material on the role of neurological speed in intelligence
- New conclusion to the section on heredity/environment and intelligence, tying the conclusion to the nature-nurture issue first discussed in Chapter 1
- New mention of an IQ of 130 as the low threshold for giftedness as being arbitrary
- New commentary about the reason that gifted children don't always become gifted adults
- New discussion of John Colombo and his colleagues' (2004, 2009) research on attempting to predict from infancy which infants will have high cognitive ability as children
- New material on developmental changes in giftedness in childhood and adolescence, with increased emphasis on domain-specific giftedness (Horowitz, 2009; Keating, 2009; Matthews, 2009)

CHAPTER 9
LANGUAGE DEVELOPMENT

- Revised, updated, and expanded coverage of early language development based on leading expert Beverly Goldfield's recommendations
- Movement of recognizing speech sounds before babbling in the section on early development of language in infancy
- New section on gestures to indicate their importance in early language development and expansion of this topic
- Expanded discussion of infants' understanding of words before speaking first word
- New material on cross-linguistic differences in the early acquisition of verbs in English, Mandarin Chinese, Korean, and Japanese
- Expanded discussion of early word learning to include individual variations in the use of whole phrases and the referential/expressive distinction
- New material on explanations for young children's rapid word learning, including fast mapping and other processes (Pan & Uccelli, 2009)
- Updated description of 3-year-olds' phonological advances (Menn & Stoel-Gammon, 2009)
- Expanded and updated coverage of young children's improvements in pragmatics (Aktar & Herold, 2008)
- Coverage of a recent study linking maternal sensitivity and negative intrusiveness to young children's language development (Pungello & others, 2009)
- Expanded discussion of emergent literacy skills in young children, including a recent study linking maternal education with emergent literacy skills (Korat, 2009)
- Coverage of a recent study of key factors in young children's early literacy experiences in low-income families (Rodriguez & others, 2009)

- Heightened emphasis on the importance of teachers in the development of students' writing skills based on the observations made by Michael Pressley and his colleagues (2007)

- Updated and expanded coverage of writing skills (Graham, 2009; Harris & others, 2008)

- Discussion of a recent meta-analysis of the most effective intervention factors in improving the writing quality of fourth- through twelfth-grade students (Graham & Perin, 2007)

- Coverage of a recent research review on which cognitive processes used in one language transfer more easily to learning a second language (Bialystok, 2007)

- Expanded and updated discussion of research indicating more complex conclusions about whether there are sensitive periods in learning a second language (Thomas & Johnson, 2008)

 CHAPTER 10
EMOTIONAL DEVELOPMENT

- Updated and expanded description of separation protest in infants (Kagan, 2008)

- Expanded and updated coverage of infant smiling, including new figure showing the characteristics of an intense smile by a 6-month-old (Messinger, 2008)

- New discussion of anticipatory smiling in infancy and its link to social competence in early childhood (Parlade & others, 2009)

- Expanded and updated discussion of advances in young children's understanding of emotions (Cole & others, 2009)

- Reorganization of the discussion of emotional development in early childhood into these categories based on expert Susan Denham's recommendation: expressing emotions, understanding emotions, and regulating emotions

- Updated and expanded coverage of children's outcomes following a disaster (Kar, 2009)

- Description of recent studies indicating that older adults are more inclined to use passive emotion regulation strategies (such as distracting themselves from the problem and suppressing feelings) and less inclined to express anger in solving interpersonal problems than younger adults are (Blanchard-Fields & Coats, 2007; Coats & Blanchard-Fields, 2008)

- Description of a recent study on older adults' social networks (Cornwell, Laumann, & Schumm, 2008)

- New discussion of developmental changes in temperament characteristics (Rothbart & Gartstein, 2008)

- New coverage of the importance of considering the multiple temperament dimensions of children rather than classifying them on a single dimension (Bates, 2008)

- Discussion of a recent study of effortful control and children's adjustment problems in China and the United States (Zhou, Lengua, & Wang, 2009)

- Description of a recent study indicating an interaction between temperament style and the type of child care young children experience (Pluess & Belsky, 2009)

- New discussion of the normative development of temperament and the emergence of individual differences in temperament, including connection of the emergence of effortful control to development of the brain's frontal lobes (Bates, 2008)

- Description of recent research on factors that benefited children with a difficult temperament (Bradley & Corwyn, 2008)

- Expanded coverage of the role of locomotion in social orientation and motivation (Thompson, 2008)

- Coverage of a recent meta-analysis of studies using the still-face paradigm and links between affect and secure attachment (Mesman, van IJzendoorn, & Bakersman-Kranenburg, 2009)

- New summary section: Infants' Social Sophistication and Insight (Thompson, 2009a, b)

- New commentary about how recent findings regarding infants' earlier social understanding may be linked to understanding goals and intentions in Bowlby's phase 3 of attachment rather than in phase 4 (Thompson, 2008)

- Discussion of a recent study of maternal sensitivity in parenting and infant attachment security (Finger & others, 2009)

- Coverage of a recent longitudinal study on infant attachment and cognitive development in the elementary school years (O'Connor & McCartney, 2007)

- New commentary about the most consistent link between early attachment and subsequent development occurring for insecure disorganized babies (Bates, 2008)

- Description of recent research indicating a gene × environment interaction between disorganized attachment, the short version of the serontonin transporter gene—*5-HTTLPR*—and a low level of maternal responsiveness (Spangler & others, 2009)

- Important new section, Developmental Social Neuoroscience and Attachment, including recent theory and views on the role of the brain neuroanatomy, neurotransmitters, and hormones in the development of mother-infant attachment (Bales & Carter, 2009; de Haan & Gunnar, 2009; Gonzales, Atkinson, & Fleming, 2009)

- New figure that shows likely key brain structures in infant-mother attachment

- New figure on the dramatic increase in the percentage of U.S. fathers who stay at home full-time with their children and the results of a recent study of stay-at-home fathers (Rochlen & others, 2005)

- New figure on the primary care arrangements for children under 5 years of age with employed mothers (Clarke-Stewart & Miner, 2008)

- Updated and expanded coverage of family leave policies around the world related to childbirth in the *Contexts of Life-Span Development* interlude (Tolani & Brooks-Gunn, 2008)

- Inclusion of recent research on the positive outcomes that develop when low-income parents select higher-quality child care (McCartney & others, 2007)

- Expanded and updated material on the important role of sensitive parenting in child outcomes for children in child care (Friedman, Melhuish, & Hill, 2009; Thompson, 2009c)

- Description of recent research on quality of child care and children's vocabulary development (Belsky & others, 2007)

- Coverage of recent research on emotion-dismissing parents and children's poor emotion regulation (Lunkenheimer, Shields, & Cortina, 2007)

- Updated discussion of Joseph Allen's (2007, 2008; Allen & others, 2004, 2007) research on attachment and its link to competent adolescent development

- Description of a recent study of adolescent attachment styles and peer relations (Dykas, Ziv, & Cassidy, 2008)

- Updated coverage of dating and romantic relationships in adolescence (Connolly & McIsaac, 2009)

- Discussion of two recent studies of adolescent girls' romantic involvement and its link to co-rumination, depressive symptoms, and emotionally unavailable parents (Starr & Davila, 2008; Steinberg & Davila, 2008)

- New coverage of three stages in the development of romantic relationships in adolescence (Connolly & McIsaac, 2009)

- New material on the percentage of adolescents who are early and late bloomers in developing romantic relationships (Connolly & McIsaac, 2009)

- Coverage of a recent study of adolescents' romantic experience and links to various aspects of adjustment (Furman, Low, & Ho, 2009)

- Description of a recent study of how a dating partner influences an adolescent's adjustment (Simons, Aiken, & Prinstein, 2008)

- Extensively updated and expanded material on adult attachment (Feeney & Monin, 2008; Mikulincer & Shaver 2008; Shaver & Mikulincer, 2010)

- Description of a recent study on adult attachment patterns in women and female orgasm (Cohen & Belsky, 2008)

- New material showing a link between the serotonin transporter gene (*5-HTTLPR*) and unresolved adult attachment (Caspers & others, 2009)

- New discussion of Internet matchmaking, including a comparison with online matchmaking and in-person initiation of relationships (Holmes, Little, & Welsh, 2009; Masters, 2008)

 CHAPTER 11
THE SELF, IDENTITY, AND PERSONALITY

- Expanded explanation of why young children have unrealistically positive self-descriptions (Thompson, 2008)

- Inclusion of information about a recent study linking low self-esteem in childhood with depression in adolescence and early adulthood (Orth & others, 2008)

- Coverage of a recent study on a link between relationship authenticity and an increase in self-esteem during adolescence (Impett & others, 2008)

- New material on narcissism, including recent research on self-esteem, narcissism, shame, and aggression in adolescents (Thomaes & others, 2008)

- Discussion of the controversy about whether recent generations of adolescents and emerging adults are more narcissistic than earlier generations and recent research on this topic (Trzesniewski, Donnellan, & Robins, 2008a, b; Twenge & others, 2008a, b)

- Expanded discussion of self-esteem and possible selves in middle-aged and older adults (Smith, 2009)

- New section, Some Contemporary Thoughts on Identity (Azmitia, Syed, & Radmacher, 2008; Phinney, 2008)

- New discussion of William Damon's (2008) book, *The Path to Purpose*, and his views on why too many of today's youth are struggling to find a path to a positive identity

- Expanded and updated description of why college often stimulates a greater integration of identity at a higher level (Phinney, 2008)

- Inclusion of recent research on ethnic identity in Navajo adolescents (Jones & Galliher, 2007)

- Description of a recent longitudinal study of ethnic identity resolution and proactive coping with discrimination (Umana-Taylor & others, 2008)

- Coverage of a recent study indicating the importance of exploration in ethnic identity development (Whitehead & others, 2009)

- Discussion of a recent study of Latino youth indicating a link between growth in identity exploration and an increase in self-esteem (Umana-Taylor, Gonzales-Backen, & Guimond, 2009)

- New discussion of the key role that conscientiousness plays in adolescent adjustment and competence, including description of a number of recent research studies (Anderson & others, 2007; Noftee & Robins, 2007; Roberts & others, 2009)

- Coverage of recent research on developmental changes across the life span in the Big Five factors of personality (Allemand, Zimprich, & Hendriks, 2008; Donnellan & Lucas, 2008)

- Coverage of a recent study of the components of conscientiousness that increased in the transition to late adulthood (Jackson & others, 2009)

- Inclusion of a study on conscientiousness as a predictor of mortality risk from childhood through late adulthood (Martin, Friedman, & Schwarz, 2007)

- Substantial updating and expansion of conclusions about stability and change in personality development based on a recent review by Brent Roberts and Daniel Mroczek (2008)

 CHAPTER 12
GENDER AND SEXUALITY

- New major opening section, What Is Gender?

- Updated and expanded discussion of gender identity (Blakemore, Berenbaum, & Liben, 2009; Egan & Perry, 2001)

- Inclusion of a recent study on developmental changes in sex-typed behavior (Golombok & others, 2008)

- New discussion of a recent longitudinal study of the acquisition of gender labels in infancy and their link to sex-typed play (Zosuls & others, 2009)

- Coverage of a recent longitudinal study on a decline in male- and female-typed activities from 7 to 19 years of age (McHale & others, 2009)

- Coverage of a recent study linking higher prenatal testosterone levels to increased male-typical play in 6- to 10-year-old boys and girls (Auyeung & others, 2009)

- Expanded and updated discussion of gender differences in mothers' and fathers' parenting interactions with their children and adolescents (Galambos, Berenbaum, & McHale, 2009)

- New commentary about boys having more rigid gender stereotypes than girls (Blakemore, Berenbaum, & Liben, 2009)

- Coverage of a recent study of 3- to 10-year-old boys' and girls' gender stereotyping (Miller & others, 2009)

- New material on no gender differences in overall intelligence but differences in some cognitive areas (Blakemore, Berenbaum, & Liben, 2009; Galambos, Berenbaum, & McHale, 2009)

- Description of a recent research review on gender and visuo-spatial skills (Halpern & others, 2007)

- Updated coverage of gender similarities and differences in the brain (Blakemore, Berenbaum, & Liben, 2009)

- Discussion of a recent large-scale national study of 7 million U.S. students showing no major gender differences in math (Hyde & others, 2008)

- Description of how there is still gender disparity in math, science, and technology careers despite girls' school achievement gains in math and science (Watt, 2008; Watt & Eccles, 2008)

- Coverage of recent national assessments indicating that U.S. girls have much stronger literacy skills (reading, writing) than U.S. boys, who are only slightly better than U.S. girls in math and science (National Assessment of Educational Progress, 2007)

- At the request of reviewers and adopters, deleted section on androgyny and gender-role classification

- Coverage of recent research comparing same-sex couples with opposite-sex dating, engaged, and married dyads (Roisman & others, 2008)

- Inclusion of recent research on the percentage of lesbians and gay males who have encountered various forms of harassment and discrimination (Herek, 2009)

- Discussion of a recent research review on adolescents, sex, and the media (Brown & Strasburger, 2007)

- Updated description of HIV and AIDS in the United States (National Center for Health Statistics, 2009)

- Updated discussion of HIV and AIDS around the world and especially in sub-Saharan African (Campbell, 2009; UNAIDS, 2008)

- Discussion of recent research on a link between men's sexual narcissism and their sexual aggression (Widman & McNulty, 2009)

- Description of a recent national study on the percentage of U.S. high school students who were currently sexually active (Eaton & others, 2008)

- Inclusion of recent data on ethnic variations in first sexual intercourse

- Coverage of recent research on a link between various risk factors and early sexual intercourse (Hyde & Price, 2007)

- Description of a recent research review on factors linked to having sexual intercourse earlier in adolescence (Zimmer-Gembeck & Helfand, 2008)

- Discussion of a large-scale U.S. study on the increase in the use of a contraceptive during the last time high school students had sexual intercourse (Centers for Disease Control and Prevention, 2008)

- Inclusion of information about a recent longitudinal study linking attention problems and disruptive aggressive behavior at school entry to a constellation of problems in middle school, which in turn were related to early initiation of sexual activity (Schofield & others, 2008)

- Coverage of a recent study that revealed a link between maternal communication about sex and a reduction in risky sexual behavior by Latino adolescents (Trejos-Castillo & Vazonyi, 2009)

- Coverage of a recent study of middle school students indicating that better academic achievement was a protective factor in keeping boys and girls from engaging in early initiation of sexual intercourse (Laflin, Wang, & Barry, 2008)

- Description of recent national data on the U.S. adolescent birth rate, indicating an increase in 2006, including a new figure of trends (Child Trends, 2008)

- Description of a national study documenting the high percentage of daughters of teenage mothers who become pregnant themselves, and other risk factors in the daughters' lives for becoming pregnant (Meade, Kershaw, & Ickovics, 2008)

- New coverage of information comparing ethnic groups on the likelihood of having a second child in adolescence (Rosengard, 2009)

- Coverage of a recent research review indicating that abstinence-only education is not effective in delaying sexual intercourse in adolescence and is not effective in reducing HIV-risk behaviors (Underhill, Montgomery, & Operario, 2007)

- Description of a recent study that revealed that adolescents who experienced comprehensive sex education reported fewer pregnancies than adolescents who were given abstinence-only or no sex education (Kohler, Manhart, & Lafferty, 2008)

- Inclusion of information about recent studies indicating that sexual assault and rape are more likely to occur when alcohol and marijuana are being used (Messman-Moore & others, 2008; Young & others, 2008)

- Inclusion of data from a recent national study on the percentage of U.S. ninth- to twelfth-grade students who have been forced to have sexual intercourse (Eaton & others, 2008)

- Discussion of a recent study on the percentage of U.S. 12- to 18-year-old girls who experience various types of sexual harassment (Leaper & Brown 2008)

- Coverage of a recent study on factors that increase menopausal symptoms (Sabia & others, 2008)

- Coverage of recent research studies in a number of countries indicating that coinciding with the decrease in HRT in recent years has been a related decline in breast cancer (Dobson, 2009; Parkin, 2009; Vankrunkelsven & others, 2009)

- Discussion of two recent research reviews that conclude HRT does not maintain or improve cognitive functioning in post-menopausal women (Hogervorst & others, 2009; Lethaby & others, 2009)

- New material on a large-scale longitudinal study on the sexual functioning of women as they made the transition through menopause (Avis & others, 2009)

- Updated description of recent studies documenting the effectiveness and sexual satisfaction of men with erectile dysfunction after taking Viagra (Abdo & others, 2008; McCullough & others, 2008)

- New material on the percentage of men with erectile dysfunction who report that it has impaired their self-esteem and harmed their relationship with their partner (Mirone & others, 2009)

- Description of a recent study indicating that Viagra improves the self-esteem, confidence, and relationships of men with erectile dysfunction (Glina & others, 2009)

- New material on a link between a low level of testosterone and the presence of metabolic syndrome and a high level of triglycerides (Corona & others, 2009)

- Discussion of a recent experimental study showing that lifestyle changes in exercise and diet can reduce erectile dysfunction (Esposito & others, 2009)

- Expanded and updated coverage of health and sexual activity in late adulthood, including further information from a large-scale study of older adults (Lindau & others, 2007)

- New material on a recent large-scale study of the main sexual problems reported by 40- to 80-year-old U.S. men and women (Laumann & others, 2009)

CHAPTER 13
MORAL DEVELOPMENT, VALUES, AND RELIGION

- New information about how most young adolescents around the world use moral judgment of mutuality (stage 3) that makes intimate friendships possible (Gibbs, 2009)

- Coverage of a recent research review of cross-cultural studies of Kohlberg's moral judgment stages, including the role of perspective taking (Gibbs & others, 2007)

- Updated conclusions about whether gender differences in moral orientation are as strong as Gilligan suggests (Blakemore, Berenbaum, & Liben, 2009)

- New section on young children's development of a conscience (Kochanska & Aksan, 2007)

- Coverage of a recent study linking an early mutually responsive orientation between parents and their infant, a decrease in power assertive discipline in early childhood, and an increase in the young child's internalization and self-regulation (Kochanska & others, 2008)

- Inclusion of recent information that 40 of 50 states now have mandates regarding character education (Carr, 2008)

- Coverage of the recent acceptance of using a care perspective as part of character education (Noddings, 2008; Sherblom, 2008)

- Description of a recent study on service learning and academic adjustment (Schmidt, Shumow, & Kackar, 2007)

- Inclusion of a recent study of gender differences in service learning (Webster & Worrell, 2008)

- New section on cheating, including recent research and information about why students cheat and strategies for preventing cheating (Anderman & Murdock, 2007; Stephens, 2008)

- Description of a recent large-scale study of 50- to 79-year-olds in 21 countries revealing that volunteering was common (HSBC Insurance, 2007)

- Coverage of a recent study indicating a steady increase in volunteering from 57 to 85 years of age (Cornwell, Laumann, & Schumm, 2008)

- Description of recent research on maternal monitoring and a lower incidence of delinquency in Latino girls (Loukas, Suizzo, & Prelow, 2007)

- Coverage of a recent study linking early child abuse with delinquency (Lansford & others, 2007)

- Discussion of a recent study implicating harsh discipline at 8 to 10 years of age was a predictor of which adolescent delinquents would persist in criminal activity after age 21 (Farrington, Ttofi, & Coid, 2009)

- Coverage of a recent longitudinal experimental study involving parenting intervention with divorced mothers and sons and a subsequent lower level of delinquency (Forgatch & others, 2009)

- Coverage of a recent study linking parents' lack of knowledge of their young adolescents' whereabouts and the adolescents' engagement in delinquency later in adolescence (Lahey & others, 2008)

- Inclusion of recent research studies on the role of peer rejection and deviant peers in predicting delinquency (Bowman, Prelow, & Weaver, 2007; Vitaro, Pedersen, & Brendgen, 2007)

- New material on the importance of self-control and intelligence in whether adolescents will become delinquents

- Updated coverage of college students' values, including a recent increase in developing a meaningful philosophy of life (Pryor & others, 2008)

- New discussion of William Damon's (2008) *The Path to Purpose* and its link to youths' development of values

- New description and photograph of Nina Vasan, founder of ACS Teens, a nationwide group of adolescent volunteers, one of the individuals Damon (2008) highlighted as exemplifying a youth who is developing a clear path to purpose

- Updated and expanded coverage of links between cognitive changes and adolescents' religious and spiritual development (Good & Willoughby, 2008)

- Inclusion of recent research on a link between regular religious attendance and a lower risk of mortality (Gillum & others, 2008)

- Description of recent research comparing aspects of religion in African American, Caribbean Black, and non-Latino White older adults (Taylor, Chatters, & Jackson, 2007)

- New *Research in Life-Span Development* interlude, "Fast Track," providing very recent information about an extensive intervention with high-risk kindergarten children and outcomes of the intervention in adolescence (Conduct Problems Prevention Research Group, 2007; Dodge & the Conduct Problems Prevention Research Group, 2007; Thomas & the Conduct Problems Prevention Research Group, 2009)

- Description of recent research on the percentage of U.S. parents with children at home who pray with the children and send their children to religious education programs (Pew Research Center, 2008)

- Discussion of a recent study of changes in religiousness (Koenig, McGue, & Iacono, 2008) and attending religious services from 14 to 25 years of age, including a new figure

- Coverage of a recent study of Indonesian Muslim 13-year-olds' religious involvement and social competence (French & others, 2008)

- Description of a recent national survey of U.S. adults' religious beliefs and behavior (Pew Research Center, 2008)

- Inclusion of information about a large-scale study in Mexico linking a lower likelihood of cigarette smoking with religious factors (Benjamins & Buck, 2008)

- Coverage of a recent study indicating that certain aspects of religion are related to lower levels of worry, anxiety, and depressive symptoms (Rosmarin, Krumrei, & Andersson, 2009)

- Discussion of a recent study that compared different religious coping styles and adjustment (Ross & others, 2009)

- Description of a recent study of older adults linking religious attendance with a lower risk of depression (Aranda, 2008)

 CHAPTER 14
FAMILIES, LIFESTYLES, AND PARENTING

- New discussion of the extensive increase in Latino and Asian families in the United States in recent years and examination of how immigrant families differ from longtime residents (Liu & others, 2009; Tewari & Alvarez, 2009)

- Updated figures on the percentage of single adults in the United States (U.S. Census Bureau, 2008)

- Updated coverage of the dramatic increase in the number of people who cohabit in the United States, including an updated figure (Popenoe, 2009)

- Description of a recent study on the percentage of women who cohabited before the age of 24 (Schoen, Landale, & Daniels, 2007)

- Coverage of a recent study indicating that cohabiting women experience an elevated risk of partner violence (Brownridge, 2008)

- Discussion of recent research that found a link between cohabitation prior to becoming engaged and negative marital outcomes (Rhoades, Stanley, & Markham, 2009)

- Updated statistics on the age of first marriage in the United States (U.S. Census Bureau, 2008)

- Description of the recent trend in the increase in number of divorces from 2005 to 2007 after a long downward trend since 1980 (Popenoe, 2009)

- New description of characteristics of the partner that are likely to lead to a divorce (Hoelter, 2009)

- Inclusion of recent research comparing stressful recent experiences in single, married, and divorced adults (American Psychological Association, 2007)

- Updated information on the percentage of married persons 18 and older with "very happy" marriages, including an updated figure (Popenoe, 2009)

- Updated coverage of the age of first marriage in countries around the world (Waite, 2009)

- Coverage of a recent study focused on marital satisfaction in middle-aged and older adults (Henry & others, 2007)

- Expanded discussion of divorce in late adulthood, including cohort effects and gender differences (Peek, 2009)

- New material on the characteristics and timing of adults who get remarried (Waite, 2009)

- Updated and expanded discussion of the benefits and problems that characterize remarriage (Waite, 2009)

- Description of recent research on relationship quality across ten years in gay male, lesbian, and heterosexual couples (Kurdek, 2008)

- New comparison of the percentage of 40- to 44-year-old U.S. women who remained childless in 1976 and 2006 (U.S. Census Bureau, 2008)

- Expanded and updated discussion of parental monitoring to include factors related to adolescents' willingness to disclose information to parents (Smetana & others, 2009)

- New section, Further Thoughts on Parenting Styles, including the interest in "unpacking" components of parenting styles, plus material on caution in interpreting studies of parenting styles and children's development, especially because they are correlational in nature

- Discussion of the increasing number of recent research studies that have found negative developmental outcomes for children who have been physically punished by their parents (Mulvaney & Mebert, 2007)

- Description of a recent study on coparenting and young children's effortful control (Karreman & others, 2008)

- New coverage of data indicating that child neglect occurs up to three times as often as child abuse (Benoit, Coolbear, & Crawford, 2008)

- New material on links between neighborhoods and child maltreatment (Coulton & others, 2007; Kimbrough-Melton & Campbell, 2008)

- New discussion of a recent multigenerational study on outcomes for mothers with a history of sexual abuse during childhood and the mothers' offspring (Noll & others, 2009)

- New information about abnormal stress hormone levels in children who have been maltreated (Gunnar & Fisher, 2006), including new figure

- New material on adolescent outcomes of child abuse and neglect (Wekerle & others, 2009)

- Description of recent research linking attachment in adolescence with patterns of intimacy in emerging adulthood (Mayseless & Scharf, 2007)

- Discussion of a recent longitudinal study of secure attachment in adolescence and outcomes in emerging adulthood (Allen & others, 2009)

- Inclusion of information about greater protection and monitoring of daughters than sons in Latino families compared with non-Latino White families (Allen & others, 2008)

- Description of a recent study of parent-adolescent conflict in Latino families (Crean, 2008)

- Updated coverage of birth order based on a recent review (Paulhus, 2008)

- New description of a link between working mothers and a reduction in children's (especially girls') gender stereotyping (Goldberg & Lucas-Thompson, 2008)

- Inclusion of information about a recent study on increased depression in the adolescent daughters in divorced families (Oldehinkel & others, 2008)

- Added commentary that the problems children from divorced families experience often stem from active marital conflict in the predivorce period (Thompson, 2008)

- New main section, Adoptive Parents and Adopted Children

- Description of a recent research review on the self-esteem of adopted and nonadopted children, and transracial and same-race adoptees (Juffer & van IJzendoorn, 2007)

- Description of recent research on secure attachment in adolescence and capacity for romantic intimacy in emerging adulthood (Mayseless & Scharf, 2007)

- Description of developmental changes in sibling relationships from childhood to adolescence (East, 2009)

- Description of a recent study on support between adult siblings (Voorpostel & Blieszner, 2008)

- Inclusion of recent research on why the grandparent role is important in middle and late adulthood (Thiele & Whelan, 2008)

- New discussion of how trends in longevity and childbearing delay are influencing grandparenting availability (Szinovacz, 2009)

- Expanded and updated coverage of grandparents as full-time caregivers for grandchildren (Silverstein, 2009)

- Description of a recent study of grandparenting and adolescent adjustment in single-parent, stepparent, and two-parent biological families (Attar-Schwartz & others, 2009)

- Inclusion of a recent study on relationships between aging parents and their children (Fingerman & others, 2007)

- Expanded and updated description of the closeness of women's relationships across generations (Merrill, 2009)

- Inclusion of information about two recent studies that document how various characteristics influence the degree to which individuals have intergenerational contact (Bucx, Knijn, & Hagendoorn, 2008; Sarkisian & Gerstel, 2008)

- Description of a recent large-scale study in 21 countries on intergenerational ties and family responsibility (HSBC Insurance, 2007)

- Coverage of a recent study documenting the stronger role of mothers in intergenerational connections than of fathers (Monserud, 2008)

- Coverage of a recent intergenerational study of divorce and secure attachment (Crowell, Treboux, & Brockmeyer, 2009)

 ## CHAPTER 15
PEERS AND THE SOCIOCULTURAL WORLD

- New discussion of the early development of friendships during the preschool years (Howes, 2009)

- Updated and expanded discussion of the connected worlds of parent-child and peer relations (Hartup, 2008; Ross & Howe, 2009)

- Expanded and updated description of links between parent and peer relations (McDowell & Parke, 2009)

- New section on contextual influences on peer relations (Brown & Deitz, 2009; Brown & others, 2008; Prinstein & Dodge, 2008)

- New section on individual difference factors in peer relations (Brown & Deitz, 2009; Brown & others, 2008)

- Description of a recent study linking the personality trait of negative emotionality to adolescents' negative interactions with a friend or romantic partner (Hatton & others, 2008)

- Expanded and updated material on which adolescents are most likely to conform to their peers (Prinstein, 2007; Prinstein & Dodge, 2008; Prinstein & others, 2009)

- Discussion of recent research on age differences in resistance to peer influence (Steinberg & Monahan, 2007)

- Description of a recent study of developmental outcomes for young adolescents who are unpopular with their peers (McElhaney, Antonishak, & Allen, 2008)

- Updated and expanded discussion of bullying, including the roles of social contexts and the larger peer group (Salmivalli & Peets, 2009)

- New coverage of the adaptive and maladaptive changes associated with being popular with peers (Allen & others, 2005)

- Expanded and updated description of developmentally advantageous and disadvantageous friendships (Hartup, 2009; Snyder & others, 2008)

- Description of recent research on girls and friendships with older boys (Poulin & Pedersen, 2007)

- Inclusion of material on the positive aspect of girls' friendships with achievement-oriented best friends and discussion of how this is linked to taking math courses in high school (Crosnoe & others, 2008)

- Coverage of recent research indicating the importance of friends' grade-point average in adolescent development (Cook, Deng, & Morgano, 2007)

- New discussion of the talk-featured, gossip aspect of friendship in adolescence (Buhrmester & Chong, 2009)

- Discussion of recent research on friendship co-rumination, and depression in adolescence (Rose, Carlson, & Waller, 2007)

- Expanded material on friendship in older adults, including comparison of the friendships of young adults and older adults (Zettel-Watson & Rook, 2009)

- Coverage of a recent study on the importance for unmarried older adults of being embedded in a friendship network (Fiori, Smith, & Antonucci, 2007)

- New description of three factors most often associated with living the "good life" as an older adult in most cultures (Fry, 2007)

- Updated coverage of the importance of social support and social integration in late adulthood, including cultural variations in social support (Antonucci, Akiyama, & Sherman, 2007; Loucks & others, 2006; Rooks & others, 2007)

- Description of a recent study on older adults' social networks (Cornwell, Laumann, & Schumm, 2008)

- Inclusion of a recent study on the happiness, self-efficacy, and optimism of centenarians (Jopp & Rott, 2006)

- Expanded and updated material on social play as the main context for most young children's interactions with peers (Coplan & Arbeau, 2009)

- Description of how the increased use of electronic media has resulted in less time for play in childhood (Linn, 2008)

- Updated coverage of social play (Sumaroka & Bernstein, 2008)

- Expanded coverage of pretend play, including Catherine Garvey's and Angeline Lillard's views

- Description of a recent study on adolescents' participation in structured activities and initiative (Watts & Caldwell; 2008)

- Inclusion of a recent national study of older adults' participation in leisure activities (Hughes, McDowell, & Brody, 2008)

- New discussion of a recent cross-cultural comparison of U.S. and Chinese seventh- and eighth-graders' academic and motivational behavior (Wang & Pomerantz, 2009)

- New coverage of a recent analysis by Carolyn Tamis-LeMonda and her colleagues (2008), describing the importance of cultural values in parenting practices and how in many families children and adolescents are reared in a context of individualistic and collectivistic values

- New introductory discussion on technology, the media, and culture focused on positive and negative aspects of how the technology revolution is affecting children and youth (Bauerlein, 2008; Egbert, 2009)

- New material on the dramatic increase in media multitasking by children and youth and how, if this is factored into media use figures, children and adolescents now use electronic media an average of eight hours per day (Roberts, Henriksen, & Foehr, 2009; Roberts & Foehr, 2008)

- New coverage of recent research on the high risk of texting while driving a truck that included videotaping of more than 6 million miles of driving by the truckers (Blanco & others, 2009; Hanowski & others, 2009)

- New description of the link between a high level of TV viewing and obesity in children and youth (Escobar-Chaves & Anderson, 2008)

- Updated discussion of media violence and conclusions about how it influences adolescents based on two recent research reviews (Escobar-Chaves & Anderson, 2008; Wilson, 2008)

- New information about one positive aspect of video game use—improvement in visuospatial skills (Schmidt & Vandewater, 2008)

- Expanded and updated coverage of links between time spent watching TV and whether it is linked to ADHD (Schmidt & Vandewater, 2008)

- Coverage of three recent studies by Douglas Gentile and his colleagues (2009) that illustrate a link between playing prosocial video games and an increase in prosocial behavior

- Description of a recent survey of the significant threat minors encounter with both online and offline bullying (Palfrey & others, 2009)

- Discussion of recent research on adolescent self-disclosure on the Internet and which gender benefits more from self-disclosing with friends on the Internet (Schouten, Valkenburg, & Peter, 2007; Valkenburg & Peter, 2009)

- Description of a recent study of the sequence of using various electronic communication technologies by college females and males (Yang & Brown, 2009)

- Coverage of a recent study of pubertal timing and what adolescent boys do online (Skoog, Stattin, & Kerr, 2009)

- Updated coverage of older adults' use of technology (Hickman, Rogers, & Fisk, 2007)

- Inclusion of information about a recent study linking neighborhood disadvantage, parenting behavior, and child outcomes (Kohen & others, 2008)

- Updated U.S. poverty statistics for U.S. children (Federal Interagency Forum on Child and Family Statistics, 2008)

- Inclusion of recent data on the much higher percentage of children and adolescents living in poverty in female-headed households compared with married families (Federal Interagency Forum on Child and Family Statistics, 2008)

- Updated statistics on the percent of children and adolescents in African American, Latino, and non-Latino white families living in poverty (Federal Interagency Forum on Child and Family Statistics, 2008)

- New *Contexts of Life-Span Development* interlude, "Improving Resources for Families in Impoverished Areas: The New Hope Program" including recent research by Aletha Huston and her colleagues (Duncan, Huston, & Weisner, 2007; Huston & others, 2006) on intervening in impoverished families

- New discussion of how adolescents in poverty likely are more aware of their social disadvantage and its associated stigma than are children (McLoyd & others, 2009)

- Updated data on the percentage of older adults living in poverty (U.S. Census Bureau, 2008)

- New description of the link between poverty and increased health outcomes in older adults (Gerst & Mutchler, 2009; Wight & others, 2008)

- Coverage of a recent study indicating that low SES increases the risk of death in older adults (Krueger & Chang, 2008)

CHAPTER 16
SCHOOLS, ACHIEVEMENT, AND WORK

- New figure describing the recently updated recommendations for developmentally appropriate education of the National Association for the Education of Young Children (NAEYC, 2009)

- Updated material on Project Head Start, including information about its being the largest federally funded program for U.S. children (Hagen & Lamb-Parker, 2008)

- Considerable editing of material on children with disabilities based on expert consultant Karen Harris' recommendations

- Updated description of the percentage of students with disabilities who receive special services (National Center for Education Statistics, 2008b)

- Revised definition of learning disabilities to more closely approximate the U.S. government's definition

- Coverage of trends in the percentage of students with learning disabilities who receive special services (National Center for Education Statistics, 2008b)

- New description of the variation that occur across states and school systems in how learning disabilities are defined and diagnosed (Bender, 2008)

- Added description of how an ADHD diagnosis requires that the characteristics appear early in childhood and be debilitating for the child

- New material on how school teams are not supposed to diagnose ADHD and why (Bender, 2008)

- New material documenting a three-year delay in the thickening of the cerebral cortex in children with ADHD, including a new figure

- New coverage about neurotransmitters, such as serotonin, and ADHD (Hercigonja Novkovic & others, 2009; Levy, 2009; Rader, McCauley, & Callen, 2009)

- Description of a recent meta-analysis indicating that behavior management treatments are effective in reducing the effects of ADHD (Fabiano & others, 2009)

- Discussion of a recent experimental study that found atomoxetine combined with a psychoeducational treatment was effective in reducing children's ADHD symptoms (Svanborg & others, 2009)

- New section, Autism Spectrum Disorders, including very recent views on these disorders (Anderson & others, 2009; Gong & others, 2009).

- New information about the recent increase in the estimate of the number of children with autism spectrum disorders

- Inclusion of recent research linking autism spectrum disorders to genetic mutations on chromosome 16 in approximately 1 out of 100 cases of these disorders (Weiss & others, 2008)

- New discussion of gender and autism, including Baron-Cohen's (2008) argument that autism reflects an extreme male brain

- New figure showing the percentage of U.S. students with disabilities who spent time in the regular classroom in a recent school year (National Center for Education Statistics, 2007)

- Description of a recent study linking chronic poverty to adverse cognitive development outcomes in children (Najman & others, 2009)

- Inclusion of information about a recent study illustrating the importance of mastery goals in students' effort in mathematics (Chouinard, Karsenti, & Roy, 2007)

- New description of how the U.S. government's No Child Left Behind legislation promotes a performance rather than a mastery orientation (Schunk, Pintrich, & Meece, 2008)

- New section, Conclusions about Intrinsic and Extrinsic Motivation (Cameron & Pierce, 2008; Eccles & Roeser, 2009)

- New coverage that emphasizes how mastery and performance goals aren't always mutually exclusive—and that for many children combining mastery and performance orientations benefits them (Anderman & Anderman, 2010; Schunk, Pintrich, & Meece, 2008)

- Description of a recent observational study of teachers in 12 classrooms to determine the learning factors that are linked to teachers with high, average, and low expectations for students' success (Rubie-Davies, 2007)

- Discussion of a recent study on teachers' and mothers' expectations and their link with children's achievement outcomes (Benner & Mistry, 2007)

- Coverage of a recent study indicating that teachers' positive expectations help to protect students from the influence of parents' negative expectations (Wood, Kaplan, & McLoyd, 2007)

- New main section, Purpose, focusing on the importance of purpose in achievement and the low percentage of parents who engage youth in discussions about purpose (Damon, 2008)

- New description of the lack of resources to support learning in the homes of students from low-income families (Schunk, Pintrich, & Meece, 2008)

- Description of a recent study comparing discipline problems in sixth-graders in middle school versus sixth-graders in elementary school (Cook & others, 2008)

- Updated statistics on school dropouts, including the substantial decrease in Latino dropouts since 2000 (National Center for Education Statistics, 2008a)

- Coverage of a recent study indicating the importance of parents in reducing the likelihood adolescents will drop out of school (Englund, Egeland, & Collins, 2008)

- Expanded and updated description of the positive outcomes of the "I Have a Dream" Foundation (2009), including a recent evaluation of the Houston program

- Description of the recent initiative by the Bill and Melinda Gates Foundation (2006, 2008) to reduce the dropout rate in schools with high dropout rates by keeping high-risk students with the same teachers across the high school years

- New discussion of the recent results from the large-scale international assessment of fourth-grade students' math and science scores with a focus on how U.S. students compare to students in other countries (TIMMS, 2008)

- New discussion of Phyllis Moen's (2009a) view of the career mystique and how it has changed in recent years

- Expanded and updated coverage of work during adolescence, including a new figure on the percentage of employed students in the United States and the number of hours they work each week (Staff, Messersmith, & Schulenberg, 2009)

- Updated coverage of the percentage of full-time U.S. college students who are employed (National Center for Education Statistics, 2008c)

- Description of a projected increase in women's share of the U.S. labor force through 2016 (*Occupational Outlook Handbook*, 2008–2009)

- New discussion of Damon's (2008) views on a path to purpose and career development

- Description of how many adults today have changing expectations for work, yet too often employers aren't meeting those expectations (Grywacz, 2009; Moen, 2009a, b)

- Coverage of a recent national survey on stress in the workplace (American Psychological Association, 2007)

- Expanded discussion of issues involved in dual-earner couples based on Phyllis Moen's (2009a, b) recent views

- New discussion of the percentage of older adults in the workforce, including a new figure (U.S. Bureau of Labor Statistics, 2008)

- New material on the significant increase in full-time employment and substantial downturn in part-time employment of older adults in the United States, including a new figure (U.S. Bureau of Labor Statistics, 2008)

- Coverage of the increasing trend for midlife couples to have to plan for two retirements, his and hers (Moen & Altobelli, 2007; Moen, Kelly, & Magennis, 2008)

- Updated and expanded coverage of the complexity of life paths older adults follow when they reach retirement age, as well as the varied reasons some older adults continue to work when they reach retirement age, based on expert consultant Phyllis Moen's (2007) ideas

- Description of baby boomers' delayed retirement plans (Frey, 2007)

- New *Contexts of Life-Span Development* interlude, "Work and Retirement Around the World," describing a recent large-scale study of 21,000 40- to 79-year-old adults in 21 countries, including a new figure (HSBC Insurance, 2007)

- Coverage of a 2007 U.S. retirement survey indicating how workers have some misconceptions about retirement and the income and long-term care they will receive (Helman, VanDerhei, & Copeland, 2007)

- Description of how important planning is for adjustment in retirement, especially for women, who are more likely to live longer than men and more likely to be alone (Moen, 2007)

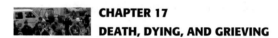

CHAPTER 17
DEATH, DYING, AND GRIEVING

- Extensive research and citation updating

- Discussion of a recent study of contradictions in individuals' end-of-life decisions about themselves and relatives (Sviri & others, 2009)

- Coverage of a recent study of the percentage of patients who had a living will and had discussed health-care wishes with their family (Clements, 2009)

- Added commentary in the coverage of what constitutes a good death (Carr, 2009)

- Description of a recent study on the lack of information doctors tend to provide to dying individuals about how long they are likely to live (Harrington & Smith, 2008)

- Updated information about the legality of assisted suicide—in 2008, assisted suicide became legal in Montana and in 2009 it became legal in Washington State

- Update on the countries allowing euthanasia (Pasman & others, 2009; Watson, 2009)

- Coverage of a recent study of terminally ill cancer patients' views on physician-assisted suicide (Wilson & others, 2007)

- Updated description of suicide rates in adolescence and new information about the increase in suicide in emerging adulthood (Minino, Heron, & Smith, 2006; Parks & others, 2006)

- New figure illustrating trends in the percentage of U.S. adolescents who seriously considered committing suicide

- Updated rates of suicide in countries around the world (World Health Organization, 2009)

- New discussion of the cultural contexts of suicide attempts, including a new figure on ethnic variations in suicide attempts by U.S. adolescents (Goldston & others, 2007)
- Coverage of a recent study on the influence of suicide attempts by members of an adolescent's social groups on the adolescent's probability of attempting suicide (de Leo & Heller, 2008)
- Inclusion of recent research linking thwarted belongingness and perception of being a burden to others with suicidal thoughts (Van Orden & others, 2008)
- Description of a recent study on preteen alcohol use and suicide attempts in adolescence (Swahn, Bossarte, & Sullivent, 2008)
- Coverage of a recent study indicating that as individuals move closer to death, they become more spiritual (Park, 2008)
- Description of recent research indicating that yearning and acceptance are more common responses than depression following the death of a loved one (Maciejewski & others, 2007)
- New coverage of the increasingly used term of "prolonged grief" by Holly Prigerson and others (Maciejewski & others, 2007)
- Added commentary about how difficult the coping process is for parents following the death of a child (De Lisle-Porter & Podruchneg, 2009; Reder & Sorwint, 2009)
- Discussion of a recent study on the benefits of volunteering for widows following the death of a spouse (Li, 2007)
- Inclusion of a recent study of a decrease in the life satisfaction over time in 80-plus-year-old individuals whose spouse died (Berg & others, 2009)
- Description of a recent study on meaning in life and anger in bereaved spouses (Kim, 2009)
- Description of a recent study indicating that when older adults engaged in helping behavior following a spouse's death, they experienced an accelerated decline in depressive symptoms (Brown & others, 2008)
- Updated information about the significant increase in the percentage of Americans who are cremated (Cremation Association of North America, 2008)
- Discussion of trends in death, mourning, and funerals (Callahan, 2009)

ACKNOWLEDGMENTS

I very much appreciate the support and guidance provided to me by many people at McGraw-Hill. Beth Mejia, Editorial Director, has done a marvelous job of directing and monitoring the development and publication of this text. Mike Sugarman, Publisher, has brought a wealth of publishing knowledge and vision to bear on improving my texts. Krista Bettino, Executive Editor, deserves special mention for the superb work she has done as the new editor for this book. The Developmental Editor,

Barbara Conover, has done an excellent job of editing the manuscript and handling the page-by-page changes to this new edition. Nancy Crochiere, Director of Development, has done a superb job of organizing and monitoring the many tasks necessary to move this book through the editorial process. Megan Stotts, Sarah DeHaas, and AJ Lafererra, Editorial Coordinators, have done a competent job of obtaining reviewers and handling many editorial chores. James Headley, Marketing Manager, has contributed in numerous positive ways to this book. Beatrice Sussman did a superb job as the book's copy editor. Marilyn Rothenberger did a terrific job in coordinating the book's production. LouAnn Wilson, Photo Researcher, did excellent work in tracking down elusive photographs for the book.

I also want to thank my wife, Mary Jo, our children, Tracy and Jennifer, and our grandchildren, Jordan, Alex, and Luke, for their wonderful contributions to my life and for helping me to better understand the marvels and mysteries of life-span development.

REVIEWERS

I owe a special gratitude to the reviewers who provided detailed feedback about the book.

Expert Consultants

I already listed the expert consultants earlier in the Preface. Their photographs and biographies appear on pages xiv–xvi. Life-span development has become an enormous, complex field, and no single author can possibly be an expert in all areas of the field. To solve this problem, in the fourth edition and in this fifth edition, I have sought the input of leading experts in many different areas of life-span development. The experts have provided me with detailed recommendations of new research to include. The panel of experts is literally a who's who in the field of life-span development.

Charles Nelson, *Harvard University and Children's Hospital, Boston*	Physical development and the development of the brain
Rachel Keen, *University of Virginia*	Motor, sensory, and perceptual development
Ross Parke, *University of California at Riverside*	Families, lifestyles, and parenting
Robert J. Sternberg, *Tufts University*	Intelligence
Gigliana Melzi, *New York University*	Language development
Susanne Denham, *George Mason University*	Emotional development
Crystal Park, *University of Connecticut*	Health and aging, values and religion, and death, dying, and grieving
Seth Kalichman, *University of Connecticut*	Gender and sexuality

General Text Reviewers

I also owe a great deal of thanks to the instructors teaching the life-span course who have provided feedback about the book. Many of the changes in *A Topical Approach to Life-Span Development*, fifth edition, are based on their input. For their suggestions, I thank these individuals:

Prerevision Reviewers

Sunshine Corwan, *University of Central Oklahoma*
Troianne Grayson, *Florida Community College at Jacksonville, South Campus*
La Tishia Horrell, *Ivy Tech Community College*
Gary Leka, *University of Texas–Pan American*
Madeline Rex-Lear, *University of Texas at Arlington*

Reviewers for the Fifth Edition

Terra Bartee, *Cisco Junior College*
Janet Boseovski, *University of North Carolina at Greensboro*
Rick Chandler, *Itawamba Community College*
Dawn Young, *Boissier Parish Community College*
Carolyn Fallahi, *Central Connecticut State University*
Alisha Janowsky, *University of Central Florida*
Gabriela Martorell, *Portland State University*
Lois Oestreich, *Salt Lake Community College*
Pam Terry, *Gordon College*

Reviewers for Previous Editions

Anora Ackerson, *Kalamazoo Community College*
Randy Allen, *Barton Community College*
Denise M. Arehart, *University of Colorado–Denver*
Harriet Bachner, *Northeastern State University*
Catherine E. Barnard, *Kalamazoo Valley Community College*
Andrea Backschneider, *University of Houston*
Sheri Bauman, *University of Arizona*
Jay Belsky, *Birkbeck College, University of London*
James E. Birren, *University of California, Los Angeles*
Tracie L. Blumentritt, *University of Wisconsin–La Crosse*
John Bonvillian, *University of Virginia*
Brenda Butterfield, *University of Minnesota–Duluth*
Ann Calhoun-Sauls, *Belmont Abbey College*
Silvia Canetto, *Colorado State University*
Richard S. Chandler, *Itawamba Community College*
Andrea D. Clements, *East Tennessee State University*
Gregory Cutler, *Bay de Noc Community College*
Scott Delys, *North Central Texas College*
Kimberly DuVall, *James Madison University*
Marion A. Eppler, *East Carolina University*
Dan P. Fawaz, *Georgia Perimeter College*
E. Richard Ferraro, *University of North Dakota*
Fan Flovell, *Eastern Kentucky University*
James Forbes, *Angelo State University*
Tom Frangicetto, *Northampton Community College*
James Garbarino, *Cornell University*
Janet Gebelt, *University of Portland*

Gilbert Gottlieb, *University of North Carolina, Chapel Hill*
Elena Grigorenko, *Yale University*
James Guinee, *University of Central Arkansas*
Yvette Harris, *Miami (Ohio) University*
Carol H. Hoare, *George Washington University*
Scott Hofer, *Pennsylvania State University*
William Hoyer, *Syracuse University*
Fergus Hughes, *University of Wisconsin*
Mary P. Hughes Stone, *San Francisco State University*
Janet Shibley Hyde, *University of Wisconsin–Madison*
Emily J. Johnson, *University of Wisconsin at LaCrosse*
Robert Kastenbaum, *Emeritus, Arizona State University*
Kevin Keating, *Broward Community College*
Sue Kelley, *Lycoming College*
Rachel Keen, *University of Massachusetts–Amherst*
Melanie Killian, *University of Maryland*
Suzanne G. Krinsky, *University of Southern Colorado*
Kathleen Lawler, *University of Tennessee*
Richard P. Lanthier, *George Washington University*
Gloria Lopez, *Sacramento City College*
James Marcia, *Simon Fraser University*
Linda Mayes, *Yale University*
Katrina McDaniel, *Barton College*
Sharon McNeely, *Northeastern Illinois University*
Salvador Macias III, *University of South Carolina*
Carole Martin, *Colorado College*
Gabriela A. Martorell, *Portland State University*
Lara Mayeux, *University of Oklahoma–Norman*
Patricia A. Mills, *Miami University*
Daniel K. Mroczek, *Fordham University*
Winnie Mucherah, *Ball State University*
Bridget Murphy-Kelsey, *University of Oklahoma*
Margaret M. Norwood, *Thomas Nelson Community College*
Pamela Balls Organista, *University of San Francisco*
Scott Peterson, *Cameron University*
Rob Palkovitz, *University of Delaware*
Denise Park, *University of Illinois, Urbana–Champaign*
Warren Phillips, *Iowa State University*
Janet Polivy, *University of Toronto*
James S. Previte, *Victor Valley College*
Janet Reis, *University of Illinois–Urbana*
Elizabeth Rodriguez, *Salt Lake City Community College*
Theresa Sawyer, *Carroll Community College*
Kim Schrenk, *Montana State University*
Pamela Schuetze, *Buffalo State College*
Matthew Scullin, *West Virginia University*
Rebecca Shiner, *Colgate University*
Thomas D. Spencer, *San Francisco State University*
Robert B. Stewart, Jr., *Oakland University*
Ross Thompson, *University of California–Davis*
Jonathan Tudge, *University of North Carolina–Greensboro*
Robin Valeri, *St. Bonaventure University*
Kay Walsh, *James Madison University*
Allan Wigfield, *University of Maryland*
Clarissa Willis, *Arkansas Technical University*
Linda M. Woolf, *Webster University*

SUPPLEMENTS

The supplements listed here may accompany *A Topical Approach to Life-Span Development,* fifth edition. Please contact your McGraw-Hill representative for details concerning policies, prices, and availability.

For the Instructor

The instructor side of the Online Learning Center at http://www.mhhe.com/santrockldt5e contains the Instructor's Manual, Test Bank files, PowerPoint slides, Image Gallery, CPS Questions, and other valuable material to help you design and enhance your course. Ask your local McGraw-Hill representative for your password.

Instructor's Manual *by Troianne Grayson, Florida Community College at Jacksonville* Each chapter of the *Instructor's Manual* is introduced by a Total Teaching Package Outline. This fully integrated tool helps instructors more easily locate and choose among the many resources available for the course by linking each element of the Instructor's Manual to a particular teaching topic within the chapter. These elements include chapter outlines, lecture suggestions, classroom activities, discussion board prompts, suggested journal entries, personal applications, research projects, film and video lists, Web site suggestions, and handouts.

Test Bank and Computerized Test Bank *by Veronica Rowland* This comprehensive Test Bank includes more than 2,000 factual, conceptual, and applied multiple-choice, as well as approximately 25 essay questions per chapter. Every question indicates the correct answer, is identified by type of question (conceptual, applied, or factual), refers to the chapter topic it addresses, and indicates the page number in the text where the corresponding material can be found. All test questions are compatible with EZ Test, McGraw-Hill's Computerized Test Bank program.

Powerpoint Slides *by L. Ann Butzin, Owens Community College* These presentations cover the key points of each chapter and include charts and graphs from the text. They can be used as is, or you may modify them to meet your specific needs.

CPS Questions *by Alisha Janowky, University of Central Florida* These questions, formatted for use with the interactive Classroom Performance System, are organized by chapter and designed to test factual, applied, and conceptual understanding. These test questions are also compatible with EZTest, McGraw-Hill's Computerized Test Bank program.

McGraw-Hill's Visual Asset Database for Life–Span Development ("VAD") McGraw-Hill's Visual Assets Database for Life-span Development (VAD 2.0) (www.mhhe.com/vad) is an online database of videos for use in the developmental psychology classroom, created specifically for instructors. You can customize classroom presentations by downloading the videos to your computer and showing the videos on their own or insert them into your course cartridge or PowerPoint presentations. All of the videos are available with or without captions. Ask your McGraw-Hill representative for access information.

McGraw-Hill Contemporary Learning Series/Annual Editions: Human Development This reader is a collection of articles on topics related to the latest research and thinking in human development. Annual Editions are updated regularly and include useful features such as a topic guide, an annotated table of contents, unit overviews, and a topical index.

For the Student

For the Student Online Learning Center (OLC) This companion Web site, at www.mhhe.com/santrockldt5e offers a wide variety of student resources. **Multiple Choice, True/False,** and **Matching Tests** for each chapter reinforce key principles, terms, and ideas, and cover all the major concepts discussed throughout the text. Entirely different from the test items in the Test Bank, the questions have been written to quiz students but also to help them learn. Key terms from the text are reproduced in a **Glossary of Key Terms** where they can be accessed in alphabetical order for easy reference and review. **Decision-Making Scenarios** present students with the opportunity to apply the information in the chapter to realistic situations, and see what effects their decisions have. Streamable online **Videos** reinforce chapter content.

Visual Tour for Students

This book provides you with important study tools to help you more effectively learn about life-span development. Especially important is the learning goals system that is integrated throughout each chapter. In the visual walk-through of features, pay special attention to how the learning goals system works.

THE LEARNING GOALS SYSTEM

Using the learning goals system will help you to learn the material more easily. Key aspects of the learning goals system are the learning goals, chapter maps, Review and Reflect, and Reach Your Learning Goals sections, which are all linked together.

At the beginning of each chapter, you will see a page that includes both a chapter outline and three to six learning goals that preview the chapter's main themes and underscore the most important ideas in the chapter. Then, at the beginning of each major section of a chapter, you will see a mini–chapter map that provides you with a visual organization of the key topics you are about to read in the section. At the end of each section is Review and Reflect, in which the learning goal for the section is restated, a series of review questions related to the mini–chapter map are asked, and a question that encourages you to think critically about a topic related to the section appears. At the end of the chapter, you will come to a section titled Reach Your Learning Goals. This includes an overall chapter map that visually organizes all of the main headings, a restatement of the chapter's learning goals, and a summary of the chapter's content that is directly linked to the chapter outline at the beginning of the chapter and the questions asked in the Review part of Review and Reflect within the chapter. The Reach Your Learning Goals summary essentially answers the questions asked in the within-chapter Review sections.

CHAPTER OPENING OUTLINE AND LEARNING GOALS

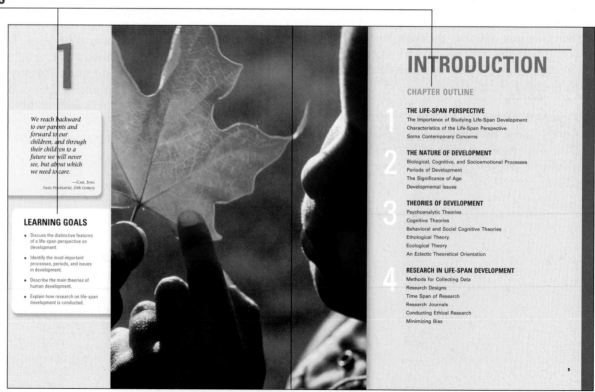

1

We reach backward to our parents and forward to our children, and through their children to a future we will never see, but about which we need to care.

—CARL JUNG
Swiss Psychiatrist, 20th Century

LEARNING GOALS

- Discuss the distinctive features of a life-span perspective on development.
- Identify the most important processes, periods, and issues in development.
- Describe the main theories of human development.
- Explain how research on life-span development is conducted.

INTRODUCTION

CHAPTER OUTLINE

1 THE LIFE-SPAN PERSPECTIVE
The Importance of Studying Life-Span Development
Characteristics of the Life-Span Perspective
Some Contemporary Concerns

2 THE NATURE OF DEVELOPMENT
Biological, Cognitive, and Socioemotional Processes
Periods of Development
The Significance of Age
Developmental Issues

3 THEORIES OF DEVELOPMENT
Psychoanalytic Theories
Cognitive Theories
Behavioral and Social Cognitive Theories
Ethological Theory
Ecological Theory
An Eclectic Theoretical Orientation

4 RESEARCH IN LIFE-SPAN DEVELOPMENT
Methods for Collecting Data
Research Designs
Time Span of Research
Research Journals
Conducting Ethical Research
Minimizing Bias

5

MINI–CHAPTER MAP

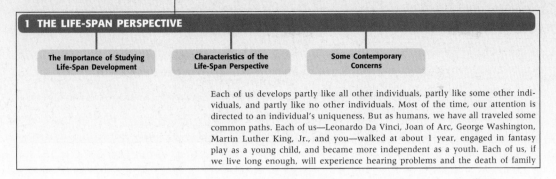

1 THE LIFE-SPAN PERSPECTIVE

| The Importance of Studying Life-Span Development | Characteristics of the Life-Span Perspective | Some Contemporary Concerns |

Each of us develops partly like all other individuals, partly like some other individuals, and partly like no other individuals. Most of the time, our attention is directed to an individual's uniqueness. But as humans, we have all traveled some common paths. Each of us—Leonardo Da Vinci, Joan of Arc, George Washington, Martin Luther King, Jr., and you—walked at about 1 year, engaged in fantasy play as a young child, and became more independent as a youth. Each of us, if we live long enough, will experience hearing problems and the death of family

REVIEW AND REFLECT

Review and Reflect: Learning Goal 1

 Discuss the distinctive features of a life-span perspective on development

REVIEW
- What is meant by the concept of development? Why is the study of life-span development important?
- What are eight main characteristics of the life-span perspective? What are three sources of contextual influences?
- What are some contemporary concerns in life-span development?

REFLECT
- Imagine what your development would have been like in a culture that offered fewer or distinctly different choices. How might your development have been different if your family had been significantly richer or poorer?

REACH YOUR LEARNING GOALS

Reach Your Learning Goals

Introduction

1 THE LIFE-SPAN PERSPECTIVE: DISCUSS THE DISTINCTIVE FEATURES OF A LIFE-SPAN PERSPECTIVE ON DEVELOPMENT

| The Importance of Studying Life-Span Development |

- Development is the pattern of change that begins at conception and continues through the human life span. It includes both growth and decline. Studying life-span development helps prepare us to take responsibility for children, gives us insight about our own lives, and gives us knowledge about what our lives will be like as we age.

| Characteristics of the Life-Span Perspective |

- The life-span perspective includes these basic conceptions: Development is lifelong, multidimensional, multidirectional, and plastic; its study is multidisciplinary; it is embedded in contexts; it involves growth, maintenance, and regulation of loss; and it is a co-construction of biological, cultural, and individual factors. Three important sources of contextual influences are (1) normative age-graded influences, (2) normative history-graded influences, and (3) nonnormative life events.

OTHER LEARNING SYSTEM FEATURES

RESEARCH IN LIFE-SPAN DEVELOPMENT INTERLUDE

One *Research in Life-Span* interlude appears in every chapter. The *Research* interludes describe a life-span research study or program and are designed to acquaint you with how research in life-span development is conducted.

Research in Life-Span Development

MEMORY IN THE A.M. AND P.M. AND MEMORY FOR SOMETHING MEANINGFUL

Laura Helmuth (2003) described how researchers are finding that certain testing conditions have exaggerated age-related declines in performance in older adults. Optimum testing conditions are not the same for young adults as they are for older adults. Most researchers conduct their studies in the afternoon, a convenient time for researchers and undergraduate participants. Traditional-aged college students

Applications in Life-Span Development

IMPROVING FAMILY POLICY

In the United States, the national government, state governments, and city governments all play a role in influencing the well-being of children (Children's Defense Fund, 2008, 2009). When families fail or seriously endanger a child's well-being, governments often step in to help. At the national and state levels, policy makers have debated for decades whether helping poor parents ends up helping their children as well. Researchers are providing some answers by examining the effects of specific policies (Huston & Bentley, 2010).

For example, the Minnesota Family Investment Program (MFIP) was designed in the 1990s primarily to influence the behavior of adults—specifically, to move adults off the welfare rolls and into paid employment. A key element of the program was that it guaranteed that adults participating in the program would receive more income if they worked than if they did not. When the adults' income rose, how did that affect their children? A study of the effects of MFIP found that increases in the incomes of working poor parents were linked with benefits for their children (Gennetian & Miller, 2002). The children's achievement in school improved, and their behavior problems decreased. A current MFIP study is examining the influence of specific services on low-income families at risk for child maltreatment and other negative outcomes for children (Minnesota Family Investment Program, 2009).

Developmental psychologists and other researchers have examined the effects of many other government policies. They are seeking ways to help families living in poverty improve their well-being, and they have offered many suggestions for improving government policies (Johnson, Tarrant, & Brooks-Gunn, 2008; McLoyd & others, 2009).

These children live in a slum area of a small Vermont town where the unemployment rate is very high because of a decline in industrial jobs. *What should be the government's role in improving the lives of these children?*

APPLICATIONS IN LIFE-SPAN DEVELOPMENT INTERLUDE

Every chapter has one *Applications in Life-Span Development* interlude, which provides applied information about parenting, education, or health and well-being related to a topic in the chapter.

CONTEXTS OF LIFE-SPAN DEVELOPMENT INTERLUDE

Once each chapter a *Contexts of Life-Span Development* interlude appears to provide information about social contexts related to a chapter topic. Diversity and culture are especially emphasized in the *Contexts* interludes.

Contexts of Life-Span Development

WOMEN'S STRUGGLE FOR EQUALITY: AN INTERNATIONAL JOURNEY

The educational and psychological conditions of women around the world are a serious concern (UNICEF, 2009, 2010). Inadequate educational opportunities, violence, and mental health issues are just some of the problems faced by many women.

One analysis found that a higher percentage of girls than boys around the world have never had any education (UNICEF, 2004) (see Figure 1.3). The countries with the fewest females being educated are in Africa, where in some areas, girls and women are receiving no education at all. Canada, the United States, and Russia have the highest percentages of educated women. In developing countries, 67 percent of women over the age of 25 (compared with 50 percent of men) have never been to school. At the beginning of the twenty-first century, 80 million more boys than girls were in primary and secondary educational settings around the world (United Nations, 2002).

Women in every country experience violence, often from someone close to them (Humphreys, 2007). Abuse by partners occurs in one of every six households in the United States, with the vast majority of the abuse being directed at women by men (White & Frabutt, 2006). Although most countries around the world now have battered women's shelters, beating women continues to be accepted and expected behavior in some countries (UNICEF, 2009, 2010).

FIGURE 1.3 Percentage of Children 7 to 18 Years of Age Around the World Who Have Never Been to School of Any Kind. When UNICEF (2004) surveyed the education that children around the world are receiving, it found that far more girls than boys receive no formal schooling at all.

(Graph: y-axis "Percentage of children 7 to 18 years of age" from 0 to 20; legend: Girls, Boys; x-axis categories: Nonpoor, Poor)

KEY TERMS AND GLOSSARY

Key terms appear in boldface. Their definitions appear in the margin near where they are introduced.

> **development** The pattern of change that begins at conception and continues through the life span. Most development involves growth, although it also includes decline brought on by aging and dying.

history—as an infant, a child, an adolescent, or an adult. Perhaps you want to know more about what your life will be like as you move through the adult years—as a middle-aged adult, or as an adult in old age, for example. Or perhaps you have just stumbled onto this course, thinking that it sounded intriguing and that the study of the human life span might raise some provocative issues. Whatever your reasons, you will discover that the study of life-span development is

Key terms also are listed and page-referenced at the end of each chapter.

KEY TERMS

development 6	gender 10	Erikson's theory 22	naturalistic observation 31
life-span perspective 7	social policy 11	Piaget's theory 23	standardized test 31
normative age-graded influences 8	biological processes 14	Vygotsky's theory 24	case study 31
	cognitive processes 14	information-processing theory 24	descriptive research 32
normative history-graded influences 8	socioemotional processes 14	social cognitive theory 25	correlational research 32
	nature-nurture issue 19		correlation coefficient 32
nonnormative life events 8	stability-change issue 19	ethology 26	experiment 33

Key terms are alphabetically listed, defined, and page-referenced in a Glossary at the end of the book.

GLOSSARY

A

A-not-B error Also called AB̄ error; this occurs when infants make the mistake of selecting the familiar hiding place (A) rather than the new hiding place (B̄) as they progress into substage 4 in Piaget's sensorimotor stage. 213

Alzheimer disease A progressive, irreversible brain disorder characterized by a gradual deterioration of memory, reasoning, language, and, eventually, physical function. 142

amygdala A part of the brain's limbic system that is the seat of emotions such as anger. 116

androgens A class of sex hormones—an impor-

and controls on children's actions; extensive verbal give-and-take is allowed, and parents are warm and nurturant toward the child. 525

autism spectrum disorders (ASDs) Also called pervasive developmental disorders, these range from the severe disorder labeled autistic disorder to the milder disorder called Asperger syndrome. Chil-

QUOTATIONS

These appear at the beginning of a section, beginning of the chapter, and in the margins of the chapter to further stimulate thought about a topic.

> *One's children's children's children. Look back to us as we look to you; we are related by our imaginations. If we are able to touch, it is because we have imagined each other's existence, our dreams running back and forth along a cable from age to age.*
>
> —ROGER ROSENBLATT
> *American Writer, 20th Century*

Middle and late childhood is the developmental period from about 6 to 11 years of age, approximately corresponding to the elementary school years. During this period, the fundamental skills of reading, writing, and arithmetic are mastered. The child is formally exposed to the larger world and its culture. Achievement becomes a more central theme of the child's world, and self-control increases.

Adolescence is the developmental period of transition from childhood to early adulthood, entered at approximately 10 to 12 years of age and ending at 18 to 21 years of age. Adolescence begins with rapid physical changes—dramatic gains in height and weight, changes in body contour, and the development of sexual characteristics such as enlargement of the breasts, growth of pubic and facial hair, and deepening of the voice. At this point in development, the pursuit of independence and an identity are prominent. Thought is more logical, abstract, and idealistic. More time is spent outside the family.

Early adulthood is the developmental period that begins in the late teens or early twenties and lasts through the thirties. It is a time of establishing personal and economic independence, career development, and, for many, selecting a mate, learning to live with someone in an intimate way, starting a family, and rearing children.

Middle adulthood is the developmental period from approximately 40 years of age to about 60. It is a time of expanding personal and social involvement and

CRITICAL-THINKING AND CONTENT QUESTIONS IN PHOTOGRAPH CAPTIONS

Most photographs have a caption that ends with a critical-thinking or knowledge question in italics to stimulate further thought about a topic.

Vygotsky's Sociocultural Cognitive Theory Like Piaget, the Russian developmentalist Lev Vygotsky (1896–1934) maintained that children actively construct their knowledge. However, Vygotsky (1962) gave social interaction and culture far more important roles in cognitive development than Piaget did. **Vygotsky's theory** is a sociocultural cognitive theory that emphasizes how culture and social interaction guide cognitive development.

Vygotsky portrayed the child's development as inseparable from social and cultural activities (Gredler, 2008; Holzman, 2009). He argued that cognitive development involves learning to use the inventions of society, such as language, mathematical systems, and memory strategies. Thus, in one culture, children might learn to count with the help of a computer; in another, they might learn by using beads. According to Vygotsky, children's social interaction with more-skilled adults and peers is indispensable to their cognitive development (Gauvain, 2008). Through this interaction, they learn to use the tools that will help them adapt and be successful in their culture. In Chapter 6, "Schools," we examine ideas about learning and teaching that are based on Vygotsky's theory.

There is considerable interest today in Lev Vygotsky's sociocultural cognitive theory of child development. *What were Vygotsky's basic claims about children's development?*

The Information-Processing Theory Information-processing **theory** emphasizes that individuals manipulate information, monitor it,

CAREERS IN LIFE-SPAN DEVELOPMENT APPENDIX

A Careers in Life-Span Development Appendix that describes a number of careers appears following Chapter 1.

Appendix

Careers in Life-Span Development

The field of life-span development offers an amazing breadth of careers that can provide extremely satisfying work. College and university professors teach courses in many areas of life-span development. Teachers impart knowledge, understanding, and skills to children and adolescents. Counselors, clinical psychologists, nurses, and physicians help people of different ages to cope more effectively with their lives and improve their well-being.

These and many other careers related to life-span development offer numerous rewards. By working in the field of life-span development, you can help people to improve their lives, understand yourself and others better, possibly advance the

medical/nursing/physical development; and families/relationships. These are not the only career options in life-span development, but the profiles should give you an idea of the range of opportunities available. The profile for each career will describe the work and address the amount of education required and the nature of the training. The Web site for this book gives more detailed information about these careers in life-span development.

EDUCATION/RESEARCH

Numerous careers in life-span development involve education or research. The opportunities range from college professor to

CAREERS IN LIFE-SPAN DEVELOPMENT PROFILES

Throughout the book, *Careers in Life-Span Development* profiles feature a person working in a life-span field related to the chapter's content.

Careers in Life-Span Development

Pam Reid, Educational and Development Psychologist

When she was a child, Pam Reid liked to play with chemistry sets. Reid majored in chemistry during college and wanted to become a doctor. However, when some of her friends signed up for a psychology class as an elective she also decided to take the course. She was intrigued by learning about how people think, behave, and develop—so much so that she changed her major to psychology. Reid went on to obtain her Ph.D. in psychology (American Psychological Association 2003, p. 16).

For a number of years, Reid was professor of education and psychology at the University of Michigan, where she also was a research scientist at the Institute for Research on Women and Gender. Her main focus has been on how children and adolescents develop social skills with a special interest in the development of African American girls (Reid & Zalk 2001). In 2004, Reid become Provost and Executive Vice-President at Roosevelt University in Chicago, and in 2007 became president of Saint Joseph College in Hartford, Connecticut.

Pam Reid (*back row, center*) with graduate students she mentored at the University of Michigan.

KEY PEOPLE

The most important theorists and researchers are listed and page-referenced at the end of each chapter.

KEY PEOPLE

Paul Baltes 7	Sigmund Freud 21	Lev Vygotsky 24	Albert Bandura 25
Marian Wright Edelman 11	Erik Erikson 22	Robert Siegler 25	Konrad Lorenz 26
Bernice Neugarten 18	Jean Piaget 23	B. F. Skinner 25	Urie Bronfenbrenner 27

E-LEARNING TOOLS

This feature appears at the end of each chapter and consists of four parts: *Taking It to the Net* Internet problem-solving exercises, *Self-Assessment*, which consists of one or more self-evaluations, *Health and Well-Being, Parenting, and Education* exercises, which provide an opportunity to practice decision-making skills related to real-world applications, and *Video Clips*, which are available online. By going to the Online Learning Center for this book, where you can complete these valuable and enjoyable exercises, you will find many learning activities to improve your knowledge and understanding of the chapter.

E-LEARNING TOOLS

Connect to **www.mhhe.com/santrockldt5e** to research the answers and complete these exercises. In addition, you'll find a number of other resources and valuable study tools for Chapter 1, "Introduction," on this Web site.

Taking It to the Net

1. You have been asked to prepare a document on the current structure of early childhood care in your state. Are the needs of the children in your state being met? What are the strengths and weaknesses of the current structure in your state?

2. Deanna wants to enroll her 7-year-old son, Victor, in clinical trials for attention deficit hyperactivity disorder treatment research. Victor's father is overseas on business for two months. Is it necessary that Victor's father consent to allow Victor to participate? Does the research group need Victor's approval before accepting him as a subject?

3. Carmen is completing her Ph.D. in clinical psychology. She is interested in geropsychology. What are some of the specialty areas in this field?

Self-Assessment

To evaluate yourself on topics related to this chapter, complete these self-assessments:

- *Evaluating My Interest in a Career in Life-Span Development*
- *Models and Mentors in My Life*

Health and Well-Being, Parenting, and Education

Build your decision-making skills by trying your hand at the health and well-being, parenting, and education exercises.

Video Clips

The Online Learning Center includes the following videos for this chapter:

- *Careers in Developmental Psychology*
- *Research Methods for Studying Infants*
- *Continuity and Change*

A TOPICAL APPROACH TO LIFE-SPAN DEVELOPMENT

THE LIFE-SPAN PERSPECTIVE

All the world's a stage.
And all the men and
women merely players.
They have their exits and
their entrances, and one
man in his time plays
many parts.

—WILLIAM SHAKESPEARE
English Playwright, 17th Century

This book is about human development—its universal features,

its individual variations, its nature. Every life is distinct, a new

biography in the world. Examining the shape of life-span

development allows us to understand it better. *A Topical*

Approach to Life-Span Development is about the rhythm

and meaning of people's lives, about turning mystery into

understanding, and about weaving a portrait of who each of us

was, is, and will be. In Section 1, you will read "Introduction"

(Chapter 1).

1

> *We reach backward*
> *to our parents and*
> *forward to our*
> *children, and through*
> *their children to a*
> *future we will never*
> *see, but about which*
> *we need to care.*
>
> —CARL JUNG
> *Swiss Psychiatrist, 20th Century*

LEARNING GOALS

◆ Discuss the distinctive features
  of a life-span perspective on
  development.

◆ Identify the most important
  processes, periods, and issues
  in development.

◆ Describe the main theories of
  human development.

◆ Explain how research on life-span
  development is conducted.

INTRODUCTION

CHAPTER OUTLINE

PREVIEW

This book is a window into the journey of human development—your own and that of every other member of the human species. Every life is distinct, a new biography in the world. Examining the shape of life-span development helps us to understand it better. In this first chapter, we explore what it means to take a life-span perspective on development, examine the nature of development, discuss theories of development, and outline how science helps us to understand it.

1 THE LIFE-SPAN PERSPECTIVE

The Importance of Studying Life-Span Development	Characteristics of the Life-Span Perspective	Some Contemporary Concerns

Each of us develops partly like all other individuals, partly like some other individuals, and partly like no other individuals. Most of the time, our attention is directed to an individual's uniqueness. But as humans, we have all traveled some common paths. Each of us—Leonardo Da Vinci, Joan of Arc, George Washington, Martin Luther King, Jr., and you—walked at about 1 year, engaged in fantasy play as a young child, and became more independent as a youth. Each of us, if we live long enough, will experience hearing problems and the death of family members and friends. This is the general course of our **development,** the pattern of movement or change that begins at conception and continues through the human life span.

In this section, we explore what is meant by the concept of development and why the study of life-span development is important. We outline the main characteristics of the life-span perspective and discuss various sources of contextual influences. In addition, we examine some contemporary concerns in life-span development.

The Importance of Studying Life-Span Development

How might people benefit from examining life-span development? Perhaps you are, or will be, a parent or a teacher. If so, responsibility for children is, or will be, a part of your everyday life. The more you learn about them, the better you can deal with them. Perhaps you hope to gain some insight about your own history—as an infant, a child, an adolescent, or an adult. Perhaps you want to know more about what your life will be like as you move through the adult years—as a middle-aged adult, or as an adult in old age, for example. Or perhaps you have just stumbled onto this course, thinking that it sounded intriguing and that the study of the human life span might raise some provocative issues. Whatever your reasons, you will discover that the study of life-span development is filled with intriguing information about who we are, how we came to be this way, and where our future will take us.

Most development involves growth, but it also includes decline and dying. In exploring development, we examine the life span from the point of conception until the time when life—at least, life as we know it—ends. You will see yourself as an infant, as a child, and as an adolescent, and be stimulated to think about how those years influenced the kind of individual you are today. And you will see yourself as a young adult, as a middle-aged adult, and as an adult in old age, and be motivated

development The pattern of change that begins at conception and continues through the life span. Most development involves growth, although it also includes decline brought on by aging and dying.

life-span perspective The perspective that development is lifelong, multidimensional, multidirectional, plastic, multidisciplinary, and contextual; involves growth, maintenance, and regulation of loss; and is constructed through biological, sociocultural, and individual factors working together.

to think about how your experiences today will influence your development through the remainder of your adult years.

Characteristics of the Life-Span Perspective

Although growth and development are dramatic during the first two decades of life, development is not something that happens only to children and adolescents. The *traditional approach* to the study of development emphasizes extensive change from birth to adolescence (especially during infancy), little or no change in adulthood, and decline in old age. But a great deal of change does occur in the five or six decades after adolescence. The *life-span approach* emphasizes developmental change throughout adulthood as well as childhood (Blazer & Steffens, 2009; Charles & Carstensen, 2010; Hoyer & Roodin, 2009).

The recent increase in human life expectancy has contributed to the popularity of the life-span approach to development. The upper boundary of the *human life span* (based on the oldest age documented) is 122 years, as indicated in Figure 1.1; this maximum life span of humans has not changed since the beginning of recorded history. What has changed is *life expectancy:* the average number of years that a person born in a particular year can expect to live. In the twentieth century alone, life expectancy in the United States increased by 30 years, thanks to improvements in sanitation, nutrition, and medicine (see Figure 1.2). As we end the first decade of the twenty-first century, the life expectancy in the United States is 78 years of age (Centers for Disease Control and Prevention, 2008). Today, for most individuals in developed countries, childhood and adolescence represent only about one-fourth of their lives.

The belief that development occurs throughout life is central to the life-span perspective on human development, but this perspective has other characteristics as well. According to life-span development expert Paul Baltes (1939–2006), the **life-span perspective** views development as lifelong, multidimensional, multidirectional, plastic, multidisciplinary, and contextual, and as a process that involves growth, maintenance, and regulation of loss (Baltes, 1987, 2003; Baltes, Lindenberger, & Staudinger, 2006). In Baltes' view, it is important to understand that development is constructed through biological, sociocultural, and individual factors working together. Let's look at each of these characteristics.

Development Is Lifelong   In the life-span perspective, early adulthood is not the endpoint of development; rather, no age period dominates development. Researchers increasingly study the experiences and psychological orientations of adults at different points in their lives. Later in this chapter, we consider the age periods of development and their characteristics.

Development Is Multidimensional   At every age, your body, your mind, your emotions, and your relationships change and affect each other. Development consists of biological, cognitive, and socioemotional dimensions. Even within one of these dimensions, there are many components—for example, attention, memory, abstract thinking, speed of processing information, and social intelligence are just a few of the components of the cognitive dimension.

Development Is Multidirectional   Throughout life, some dimensions or components of a dimension expand and others shrink. For example, when one language (such as English) is acquired early in development, the capacity for acquiring second and third languages (such as Spanish and Chinese) decreases later in development, especially after early childhood (Levelt, 1989). During adolescence, as individuals establish romantic relationships, their time spent with friends may decrease. During late adulthood, older adults might become wiser by being able to call on

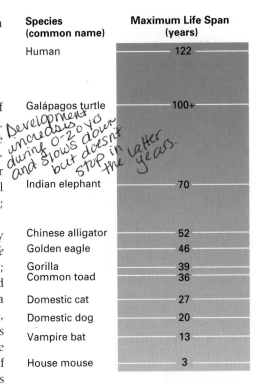

Species (common name)	Maximum Life Span (years)
Human	122
Galápagos turtle	100+
Indian elephant	70
Chinese alligator	52
Golden eagle	46
Gorilla	39
Common toad	36
Domestic cat	27
Domestic dog	20
Vampire bat	13
House mouse	3

FIGURE 1.1 Maximam Recorded Life Span for Different Species. Our only competitor for the maximum recorded life span is the Galápagos turtle.

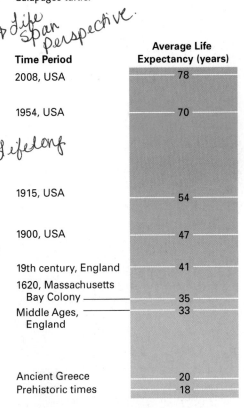

Time Period	Average Life Expectancy (years)
2008, USA	78
1954, USA	70
1915, USA	54
1900, USA	47
19th century, England	41
1620, Massachusetts Bay Colony	35
Middle Ages, England	33
Ancient Greece	20
Prehistoric times	18

FIGURE 1.2 Human Life Expectancy at Birth from Prehistoric to Contemporary Times. It took 5,000 years to extend human life expectancy from 18 to 41 years of age.

Paul Baltes, a leading architect of the life-span perspective of development, conversing with one of the long-time research participants (now 96 years of age) in the Berlin Aging Study, which he directed. She joined the study in the early 1990s and has participated six times in extensive physical, medical, psychological, and social assessments. In her professional life, she was a practicing medical doctor.

normative age-graded influences Influences that are similar for individuals in a particular age group.

normative history-graded influences Influences that are common to people of a particular generation because of historical circumstances.

nonnormative life events Unusual occurrences that have a major impact on an individual's life.

Nonnormative life events, such as Hurricane Katrina in August 2005, are unusual circumstances that have a major impact on a person's life. Here a woman and her children are shown in a Houston shelter for those left homeless by the devastating hurricane.

experience to guide their intellectual decision making, but they perform more poorly on tasks that require speed in processing information (Baltes & Kuntzman, 2007).

Development Is Plastic   Developmentalists debate how much plasticity people have in various dimensions at different points in their development. *Plasticity* means the capacity for change. For example, can you still improve your intellectual skills when you are in your seventies or eighties? Or might these intellectual skills be fixed by the time you are in your thirties, so that further improvement is impossible? Researchers have found that the cognitive skills of older adults can be improved through training and developing better strategies (Boron, Willis, & Schaie, 2007). However, possibly we possess less capacity for change when we become old (Baltes, Reuter-Lorenz, & Rösler, 2006). The search for plasticity and its constraints is a key element on the contemporary agenda for developmental research (Kochanska, Philibert, & Barry, 2009; Siegler & others, 2009).

Developmental Science Is Multidisciplinary   Psychologists, sociologists, anthropologists, neuroscientists, and medical researchers all share an interest in unlocking the mysteries of development through the life span. How do your heredity and health limit your intelligence? Do intelligence and social relationships change with age in the same way around the world? How do families and schools influence intellectual development? These are examples of research questions that cut across disciplines.

Development Is Contextual   All development occurs within a context, or setting. Contexts include families, neighborhoods, schools, peer groups, churches, university laboratories, cities, countries, and so on. Each of these settings is influenced by historical, economic, social, and cultural factors (Shiraev & Levy, 2010).

Contexts, like individuals, change. Thus, individuals are changing beings in a changing world. As a result of these changes, contexts exert three types of influences (Baltes, 2003): (1) normative age-graded influences, (2) normative history-graded influences, and (3) nonnormative or highly individualized life events. Each of these types can have a biological or an environmental impact on development. **Normative age-graded influences** are similar for individuals in a particular age group. These influences include biological processes such as puberty and menopause. They also include sociocultural, environmental processes such as beginning formal education (usually at about age 6 in most cultures) and retirement (which takes place in the fifties and sixties in most cultures).

Normative history-graded influences are common to people of a particular generation because of historical circumstances. For example, in their youth American baby boomers shared the experience of the Cuban missile crisis, the assassination of John F. Kennedy, and the Beatles invasion. Other examples of normative history-graded influences include economic, political, and social upheavals such as the Great Depression in the 1930s, World War II in the 1940s, the civil rights and women's rights movements of the 1960s and 1970s, the terrorist attacks of 9/11/2001, as well as the integration of computers, cell phones, and Ipods into everyday life in recent decades (Schaie, 2008a, b; 2009). Long-term changes in the genetic and cultural makeup of a population (due to immigration or changes in fertility rates) are also part of normative historical change.

Nonnormative life events are unusual occurrences that have a major impact on the individual's life. These events do not happen to all people, and when they do occur they can influence people in different ways. Examples include the death of a parent when a child is young, pregnancy in early adolescence, a fire that destroys a home, winning the lottery, or getting an unexpected career opportunity.

Development Involves Growth, Maintenance, and Regulation of Loss

Baltes and his colleagues (2006) assert that the mastery of life often involves conflicts and competition among three goals of human development: growth, maintenance, and regulation of loss. As individuals age into middle and late adulthood, the maintenance and regulation of loss in their capacities take center stage away from growth. Thus, a 75-year-old man might aim not to improve his memory or his golf swing but to maintain his independence and merely to play golf.

Development Is a Co-Construction of Biology, Culture, and the Individual

Development is a co-construction of biological, cultural, and individual factors working together (Baltes, Reuter-Lorenz, & Rösler, 2006). For example, the brain shapes culture, but it is also shaped by culture and the experiences that individuals have or pursue. In terms of individual factors, we can go beyond what our genetic inheritance and environment give us. We can author a unique developmental path by actively choosing from the environment the things that optimize our lives (Rathunde & Csikszentmihalyi, 2006).

Some Contemporary Concerns

Pick up a newspaper or magazine and you might see headlines like these: "Political Leanings May Be Written in the Genes," "Mother Accused of Tossing Children into Bay," "Gender Gap Widens," "FDA Warns About ADHD Drug," "Heart Attack Deaths Higher in Black Patients," "Test May Predict Alzheimer Disease." Researchers using the life-span perspective are examining these and many other topics of contemporary concern. The roles that health and well-being, parenting, education, and sociocultural contexts play in life-span development, as well as how social policy is related to these issues, are a particular focus of this textbook.

Health and Well-Being   Health professionals today recognize the power of lifestyles and psychological states in health and well-being (Insel & Roth, 2009; Hahn, Payne, & Lucas, 2009; Worthington, 2010). In every chapter of this book, issues of health and well-being are integrated into our discussion.

Parenting and Education   Can two gay men raise a healthy family? Are children harmed if both parents work outside the home? Are U.S. schools failing to teach children how to read and write and calculate adequately? We hear many questions like these related to pressures on the contemporary family and the problems of U.S. schools (Ballentine & Hammock, 2009; McCoy & Keen, 2009; Patterson, 2009). In later chapters, we analyze child care, the effects of divorce, parenting styles, intergenerational relationships, early childhood education, relationships between childhood poverty and education, bilingual education, new educational efforts to improve lifelong learning, and many other issues related to parenting and education.

Sociocultural Contexts and Diversity   Health, parenting, and education—like development itself—are all shaped by their sociocultural context (Tamis-LeMonda & McFadden, 2010; Taylor & Whittaker, 2009). To analyze this context, four concepts are especially useful: culture, ethnicity, socioeconomic status, and gender.

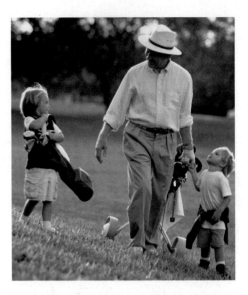

How might growth versus maintenance and regulation be reflected in the development of this grandfather and his two grandchildren?

Children learn to love when they are loved

Culture encompasses the behavior patterns, beliefs, and all other products of a particular group of people that are passed on from generation to generation. Culture results from the interaction of people over many years. A cultural group can be as large as the United States or as small as an isolated Appalachian town. Whatever its size, the group's culture influences the behavior of its members (Shiraev & Levy, 2010). **Cross-cultural studies** compare aspects of two or more cultures. The comparison provides information about the degree to which development is similar, or universal, across cultures, or instead is culture-specific (Hayashino & Chopra, 2009).

Ethnicity (the word *ethnic* comes from the Greek word for "nation") is rooted in cultural heritage, nationality, race, religion, and language. African Americans, Latinos, Asian Americans, Native Americans, European Americans, and Arab Americans are examples of broad ethnic groups in the United States. Diversity exists within each ethnic group (Florence, 2010; Hernandez, Denton, & Macartney, 2010).

Socioeconomic status (SES) refers to a person's position within society based on occupational, educational, and economic characteristics. Socioeconomic status implies certain inequalities. Differences in the ability to control resources and to participate in society's rewards produce unequal opportunities (Coltrane & others, 2008; Healey, 2009; Huston & Bentley, 2010).

Gender refers to the characteristics of people as males and females. Few aspects of our development are more central to our identity and social relationships than gender (Best, 2010; Blakemore, Berenbaum, & Liben, 2009).

The sociocultural context of the United States has become increasingly diverse in recent years. Its population includes a greater variety of cultures and ethnic groups than ever before. This changing demographic tapestry promises not only the richness that diversity produces but also difficult challenges in extending the American dream to all individuals (Grigorenko & Takanishi, 2010; Spring, 2010; Tewari & Alvarez, 2008). We discuss sociocultural contexts and diversity in each chapter. In addition, a *Contexts of Life-Span Development* interlude appears in every chapter. The first one, about women's international struggle for equality, appears here.

culture The behavior patterns, beliefs, and all other products of a group that are passed on from generation to generation.

cross-cultural studies Comparison of one culture with one or more other cultures. These provide information about the degree to which development is similar, or universal, across cultures, and the degree to which it is culture-specific.

ethnicity A characteristic based on cultural heritage, nationality characteristics, race, religion, and language.

socioeconomic status (SES) Refers to a person's position in society based on occupational, educational, and economic characteristics.

gender The characteristics of people as males or females.

Contexts of Life-Span Development

WOMEN'S STRUGGLE FOR EQUALITY: AN INTERNATIONAL JOURNEY

The educational and psychological conditions of women around the world are a serious concern (UNICEF, 2009, 2010). Inadequate educational opportunities, violence, and mental health issues are just some of the problems faced by many women.

One analysis found that a higher percentage of girls than boys around the world have never had any education (UNICEF, 2004) (see Figure 1.3). The countries with the fewest females being educated are in Africa, where in some areas, girls and women are receiving no education at all. Canada, the United States, and Russia have the highest percentages of educated women. In developing countries, 67 percent of women over the age of 25 (compared with 50 percent of men) have never been to school. At the beginning of the twenty-first century, 80 million more boys than girls were in primary and secondary educational settings around the world (United Nations, 2002).

Women in every country experience violence, often from someone close to them (Humphreys, 2007). Abuse by partners occurs in one of every six households in the United States, with the vast majority of the abuse being directed at women by men (White & Frabutt, 2006). Although most countries around the world now have battered women's shelters, beating women continues to be accepted and expected behavior in some countries (UNICEF, 2009, 2010).

FIGURE 1.3 Percentage of Children 7 to 18 Years of Age Around the World Who Have Never Been to School of Any Kind. When UNICEF (2004) surveyed the education that children around the world are receiving, it found that far more girls than boys receive no formal schooling at all.

Doly Akter, age 17, lives in a slum in Dhaka, Bangladesh, where sewers overflow, garbage rots in the streets, and children are undernourished. Nearly two-thirds of young women in Bangladesh get married before they are 18. Doly recently organized a club supported by UNICEF in which girls go door-to-door to monitor the hygiene habits of households in their neighborhood. The monitoring had led to improved hygiene and health in the families. Also, her group has managed to stop several child marriages by meeting with parents and convincing them that it is not in their daughter's best interests. When talking with parents in their neighborhoods, the girls in the club emphasize the importance of staying in school and how this will improve their daughters' future. Doly says that the girls in her UNICEF group are far more aware of their rights than their mothers ever were. (UNICEF, 2007).

Gender also influences mental health (Blakemore, Berenbaum, & Liben, 2009). A study of depression in high-income countries found women were twice as likely as men to be diagnosed as depressed (Nolen-Hoeksema, 1990). In the United States, from adolescence through adulthood, females are more likely than males to be depressed (Davison & Neale, 2010). Why? Some experts suggest that more women are diagnosed with depression than actually have depression (Nolen-Hoeksema, 2010). Some argue that inequities such as low pay and unequal employment opportunities have contributed to the greater incidence of depression in females than males (Whiffen, 2001). In the view of some researchers, problems like these are likely to be addressed only when women share equal power with men (UNICEF, 2009).

Social Policy   **Social policy** is a government's course of action designed to promote the welfare of its citizens. Values, economics, and politics all shape a nation's social policy. Out of concern that policy makers are doing too little to protect the well-being of children and older adults, life-span researchers are increasingly undertaking studies that they hope will lead to effective social policy (Balsano, Theokas, & Bobek, 2009; Gupta, Thornton, & Huston, 2008).

Statistics such as infant mortality rates, mortality among children under 5, and the percentage of children who are malnourished or living in poverty provide benchmarks for evaluating how well children are doing in a particular society. For many years, Marian Wright Edelman, a tireless advocate of children's rights, has pointed out that indicators like these place the United States at or near the lowest rank for industrialized nations in the treatment of children.

Children who grow up in poverty represent a special concern (Huston & Bentley, 2010; McLoyd & others, 2009). In 2006, approximately 17.4 percent of U.S. children were living in families below the poverty line (Federal Interagency Forum on Child and Family Statistics, 2008). This is an increase from 2001 (16.2 percent) but down from a peak of 22.7 percent in 1993. As indicated in Figure 1.4, one study found that a higher percentage of U.S. children in poor families than in middle-income families were exposed to family turmoil, separation from a parent, violence, crowding, excessive noise, and poor housing (Evans & English, 2002). A recent study also revealed that the more years children spent living in poverty, the more their physiological indices of stress were elevated (Evans & Kim, 2007).

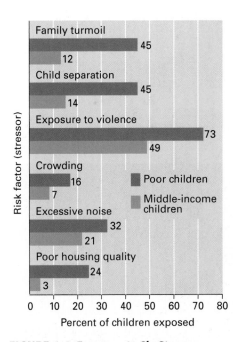

FIGURE 1.4 Exposure to Six Stressors Among Poor and Middle-Income Children. One recent study analyzed the exposure to six stressors among poor children and middle-income children (Evans & English, 2002). Poor children were much more likely to face each of these stressors.

social policy A government's course of action designed to promote the welfare of its citizens.

Marian Wright Edelman, president of the Children's Defense Fund (shown here interacting with young children), has been a tireless advocate of children's rights and has been instrumental in calling attention to the needs of children. *What are some of these needs?*

The U.S. figure of 17.4 percent of children living in poverty is much higher than those from other industrialized nations. For example, Canada has a child poverty rate of 9 percent and Sweden has a rate of 2 percent.

Edelman says that parenting and nurturing the next generation of children are our society's most important functions and that we need to take them more seriously than we have in the past. To read about efforts to improve the lives of children through social policies, see the *Applications in Life-Span Development* interlude that follows.

Applications in Life-Span Development

IMPROVING FAMILY POLICY

In the United States, the national government, state governments, and city governments all play a role in influencing the well-being of children (Children's Defense Fund, 2008, 2009). When families fail or seriously endanger a child's well-being, governments often step in to help. At the national and state levels, policy makers have debated for decades whether helping poor parents ends up helping their children as well. Researchers are providing some answers by examining the effects of specific policies (Huston & Bentley, 2010).

For example, the Minnesota Family Investment Program (MFIP) was designed in the 1990s primarily to influence the behavior of adults—specifically, to move adults off the welfare rolls and into paid employment. A key element of the program was that it guaranteed that adults participating in the program would receive more income if they worked than if they did not. When the adults' income rose, how did that affect their children? A study of the effects of MFIP found that increases in the incomes of working poor parents were linked with benefits for their children (Gennetian & Miller, 2002). The children's achievement in school improved, and their behavior problems decreased. A current MFIP study is examining the influence of specific services on low-income families at risk for child maltreatment and other negative outcomes for children (Minnesota Family Investment Program, 2009).

Developmental psychologists and other researchers have examined the effects of many other government policies. They are seeking ways to help families living in poverty improve their well-being, and they have offered many suggestions for improving government policies (Johnson, Tarrant, & Brooks-Gunn, 2008; McLoyd & others, 2009).

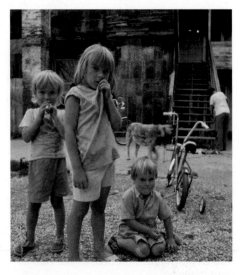

These children live in a slum area of a small Vermont town where the unemployment rate is very high because of a decline in industrial jobs. *What should be the government's role in improving the lives of these children?*

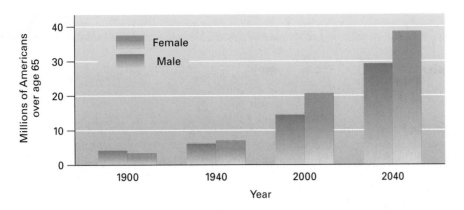

FIGURE 1.5 The Aging of America. The number of Americans over 65 has grown dramatically since 1900 and is projected to increase further from the present to the year 2040. A significant increase will also occur in the number of individuals in the 85-and-over group. Centenarians—persons 100 years of age or older—are the fastest-growing age group in the United States, and their numbers are expected to swell in the coming decades (Perls, 2007).

At the other end of the life span, the well-being of older adults also creates policy issues (Blazer & Steffens, 2009; Moody, 2009). Key concerns are escalating health-care costs and the access of older adults to adequate health care (Ferrini & Ferrini, 2008). One study found that the health-care system fails older adults in many areas (Wenger & others, 2003). For example, older adults received the recommended care for general medical conditions such as heart disease only 52 percent of the time; they received appropriate care for undernutrition and Alzheimer disease only 31 percent of the time.

These concerns about the well-being of older adults are heightened by two facts. First, the number of older adults in the United States is growing dramatically, as Figure 1.5 shows. Second, many of these older Americans are likely to need society's help. Compared with earlier decades, U.S. adults today are less likely to be married, more likely to be childless, and more likely to be living alone. As the older population continues to expand in the twenty-first century, an increasing number of older adults will be without either a spouse or children— traditionally the main sources of support for older adults (Connides, 2009). These individuals will need social relationships, networks, and supports (Fiori, Antonucci, & Akiyama, 2009).

Review and Reflect: Learning Goal 1

 Discuss the distinctive features of a life-span perspective on development

REVIEW

- What is meant by the concept of development? Why is the study of life-span development important?
- What are eight main characteristics of the life-span perspective? What are three sources of contextual influences?
- What are some contemporary concerns in life-span development?

REFLECT

- Imagine what your development would have been like in a culture that offered fewer or distinctly different choices. How might your development have been different if your family had been significantly richer or poorer?

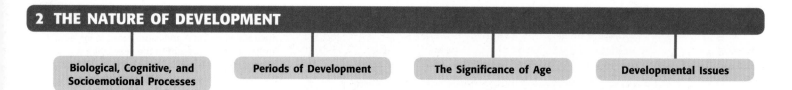

2 THE NATURE OF DEVELOPMENT

Biological, Cognitive, and Socioemotional Processes	Periods of Development	The Significance of Age	Developmental Issues

In this section, we explore what is meant by developmental processes and periods, as well as variations in the way age is conceptualized. We examine key developmental issues, how they describe development, and strategies we can use to evaluate them.

A chronicle of the events in any person's life can quickly become a confusing and tedious array of details. Two concepts help provide a framework for describing and understanding an individual's development: developmental processes and periods of development.

Biological, Cognitive, and Socioemotional Processes

At the beginning of this chapter, we defined *development* as the pattern of change that begins at conception and continues through the life span. The pattern is complex because it is the product of biological, cognitive, and socioemotional processes (see Figure 1.6).

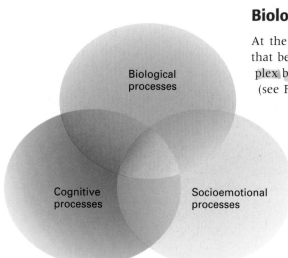

FIGURE 1.6 Processes Involved in Development. Development involves the interaction of biological, cognitive, and socioemotional processes.

Biological Processes **Biological processes** produce changes in an individual's physical nature. Genes inherited from parents, the development of the brain, height and weight gains, changes in motor skills, nutrition, exercise, the hormonal changes of puberty, and cardiovascular decline are all examples of biological processes that affect development.

Cognitive processes **Cognitive processes** refer to changes in the individual's thought, intelligence, and language. Watching a colorful mobile swinging above the crib, putting together a two-word sentence, memorizing a poem, imagining what it would be like to be a movie star, and solving a crossword puzzle all involve cognitive processes.

Socioemotional Processes **Socioemotional processes** involve changes in the individual's relationships with other people, changes in emotions, and changes in personality. An infant's smile in response to a parent's touch, a toddler's aggressive attack on a playmate, a school-age child's development of assertiveness, an adolescent's joy at the senior prom, and the affection of an elderly couple all reflect the role of socioemotional processes in development.

Connecting Biological, Cognitive, and Socioemotional Processes Biological, cognitive, and socioemotional processes are inextricably intertwined (Diamond, 2009; Diamond, Casey, & Munakata, 2010). Consider a baby smiling in response to a parent's touch. This response depends on biological processes (the physical nature of touch and responsiveness to it), cognitive processes (the ability to understand intentional acts), and socioemotional processes (the act of smiling often reflects a positive emotional feeling, and smiling helps to connect us in positive ways with other human beings). Nowhere is the connection across biological, cognitive, and socioemotional processes more obvious than in two rapidly emerging fields:

- *Developmental cognitive neuroscience,* which explores links between development, cognitive processes, and the brain (Diamond, Casey, & Munakata, 2010)
- *Developmental social neuroscience,* which examines connections between socioemotional processes, development, and the brain (de Haan & Gunnar, 2009; Johnson & others, 2009)

biological processes Processes that produce changes in an individual's physical nature.

cognitive processes Processes that involve changes in an individual's thought, intelligence, and language.

socioemotional processes Processes that involve changes in an individual's relationships with other people, emotions, and personality.

In many instances, biological, cognitive, and socioemotional processes are bidirectional. For example, biological processes can influence cognitive processes and vice versa. Thus, although usually we study the different processes of development (biological, cognitive, and socioemotional) in separate locations, keep in mind that we are talking about the development of an integrated individual with a mind and body that are interdependent.

Periods of Development

The interplay of biological, cognitive, and socioemotional processes produces the periods of the human life span (see Figure 1.7). A *developmental period* refers to a time frame in a person's life that is characterized by certain features. For the purposes of organization and understanding, we commonly describe development in terms of these periods. The most widely used classification of developmental periods involves the eight-period sequence shown in Figure 1.7. Approximate age ranges are listed for the periods to provide a general idea of when a period begins and ends.

The *prenatal period* is the time from conception to birth. It involves tremendous growth—from a single cell to an organism complete with brain and behavioral capabilities—and takes place in approximately a nine-month period.

Infancy is the developmental period from birth to 18 or 24 months. Infancy is a time of extreme dependence upon adults. During this period, many psychological activities—language, symbolic thought, sensorimotor coordination, and social learning, for example—are just beginning.

Early childhood is the developmental period from the end of infancy to age 5 or 6. This period is sometimes called the "preschool years." During this time, young children learn to become more self-sufficient and to care for themselves, develop school readiness skills (following instructions, identifying letters), and spend many hours in play with peers. First grade typically marks the end of early childhood.

FIGURE 1.7 Processes and Periods of Development. The unfolding of life's periods of development is influenced by the interaction of biological, cognitive, and socioemotional processes.

Periods of Development

| Prenatal period (conception to birth) | Infancy (birth to 18–24 months) | Early childhood (2–5 years) | Middle and late childhood (6–11 years) | Adolescence (10–12 to 18 years) | Early adulthood (20s to 30s) | Middle adulthood (40s to 60s) | Late adulthood (60s–70s to death) |

Biological processes

Cognitive processes

Socioemotional processes

Processes of Development

*O*ne's children's children's children. Look back to us as we look to you; we are related by our imaginations. If we are able to touch, it is because we have imagined each other's existence, our dreams running back and forth along a cable from age to age.

—ROGER ROSENBLATT
American Writer, 20th Century

Middle and late childhood is the developmental period from about 6 to 11 years of age, approximately corresponding to the elementary school years. During this period, the fundamental skills of reading, writing, and arithmetic are mastered. The child is formally exposed to the larger world and its culture. Achievement becomes a more central theme of the child's world, and self-control increases.

Adolescence is the developmental period of transition from childhood to early adulthood, entered at approximately 10 to 12 years of age and ending at 18 to 21 years of age. Adolescence begins with rapid physical changes—dramatic gains in height and weight, changes in body contour, and the development of sexual characteristics such as enlargement of the breasts, growth of pubic and facial hair, and deepening of the voice. At this point in development, the pursuit of independence and an identity are prominent. Thought is more logical, abstract, and idealistic. More time is spent outside the family.

Early adulthood is the developmental period that begins in the late teens or early twenties and lasts through the thirties. It is a time of establishing personal and economic independence, career development, and, for many, selecting a mate, learning to live with someone in an intimate way, starting a family, and rearing children.

Middle adulthood is the developmental period from approximately 40 years of age to about 60. It is a time of expanding personal and social involvement and responsibility; of assisting the next generation in becoming competent, mature individuals; and of reaching and maintaining satisfaction in a career.

Late adulthood is the developmental period that begins in the sixties or seventies and lasts until death. It is a time of life review, retirement, and adjustment to new social roles involving decreasing strength and health.

Late adulthood has the longest span of any period of development, and—as noted earlier—the number of people in this age group has been increasing dramatically. As a result, life-span developmentalists have been paying more attention to differences within late adulthood (Scheibe, Freund, & Baltes, 2007). Paul Baltes and Jacqui Smith (2003) argue that a major change takes place in older adults' lives as they become the "oldest old," on average at about 85 years of age. For example, the "young old" (classified as 65 through 84 in this analysis) have substantial potential for physical and cognitive fitness, retain much of their cognitive capacity, and can develop strategies to cope with the gains and losses of aging. In contrast, the oldest old (85 and older) show considerable loss in cognitive skills, experience an increase in chronic stress, and are more frail (Baltes & Smith, 2003). Nonetheless, as we see in later chapters, considerable variation exists in how much the oldest old retain their capabilities.

Thus, Baltes and Smith concluded that considerable plasticity and adaptability characterize adults from their sixties until their mid-eighties but that the oldest old have reached the limits of their functional capacity, which makes interventions to improve their lives difficult. Nonetheless, as described in later chapters, considerable variation exists in how much the oldest old retain their capabilities (Perls, 2007). As you will see in the *Research in Life-Span Development* interlude, contexts play an important role in how well older adults perform.

Research in Life-Span Development

MEMORY IN THE A.M. AND P.M. AND MEMORY FOR SOMETHING MEANINGFUL

Laura Helmuth (2003) described how researchers are finding that certain testing conditions have exaggerated age-related declines in performance in older adults. Optimum testing conditions are not the same for young adults as they are for older adults. Most researchers conduct their studies in the afternoon, a convenient time for researchers and undergraduate participants. Traditional-aged college students in their late teens and early twenties are often more alert and function more optimally in the afternoon, but about 75 percent of older adults are "morning people," performing at their best early in the day (Helmuth, 2003).

Lynn Hasher and her colleagues (2001) tested the memory of college students 18 to 32 years of age and community volunteers 58 to 78 years of age in the late afternoon (about 4 to 5 p.m.) and in the morning (about 8 to 9 a.m.). Regardless of the time of day, the younger college students performed better than the older adults on the memory tests, which involved recognizing sentences from a story and memorizing a list of words. However, when the participants took the memory tests in the morning rather than in the late afternoon, the age difference in performance decreased considerably (see Figure 1.8).

The relevance of information also affects memory. Thomas Hess and his colleagues (2003) asked younger adults (18 to 30 years of age) and older adults (62 to 84 years of age) to listen to a drawn-out description that was identified as either someone's experiences on a first job or their experiences while searching for a retirement home. The younger adults remembered the details of both circumstances. However, the older adults showed a keen memory for the retirement-home search but not for the first-job experience.

In short, researchers have found that age differences in memory are robust when researchers ask for information that doesn't matter much, but when older adults are asked about information that is relevant to their lives, differences in the memory of younger and older adults often decline considerably (Hasher, 2003). Thus, the type of information selected by researchers may produce an exaggerated view of declines in memory with age.

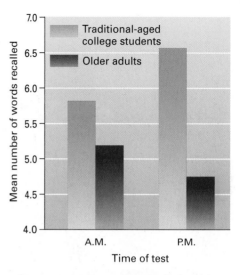

FIGURE 1.8 Memory, Age, and Time of Day Tested (a.m. or p.m.). In one study, traditional-aged college students performed better than older adults in both the a.m. and the p.m. Note, however, that the memory of the older adults was better when they were tested in the morning than in the afternoon, whereas the memory of the traditional-aged college students was not as good in the morning as it was in the afternoon (Hasher & others, 2001).

Life-span developmentalists who focus on adult development and aging increasingly describe life-span development in terms of four "ages" (Baltes, 2006; Willis & Schaie, 2006):

First age: Childhood and adolescence

Second age: Prime adulthood, twenties through fifties

Third age: Approximately 60 to 79 years of age

Fourth age: Approximately 80 years and older

The major emphasis in this conceptualization is on the third and fourth ages, especially the increasing evidence that individuals in the third age are healthier and can lead more active, productive lives than their predecessors in earlier generations. However, when older adults reach their eighties, especially 85 and over (fourth age), health and well-being decline for many individuals.

The Significance of Age

In the earlier description of developmental periods, an approximate age range was linked with each period. But there are also variations in the capabilities of individuals of the same age, and we have seen how changes with age can be exaggerated. How important is age when we try to understand an individual?

Age and Happiness   Is one age in life better than another? When researchers have studied this question, consistent answers have not been forthcoming. Some studies of adults have indicated that happiness increases with age (Rodgers, 1982); others reveal no differences in happiness for adults of different ages (Ingelhart, 1990); and yet others have found a U-shaped result with the lowest happiness occurring at 30 to 40 years of age (Mroczek & Kolarz, 1998). However, an increasing number of studies indicate that at least in the United States adults are happier as they age (Charles, Reynolds, & Gatz, 2001; Erlich & Isaacowitz, 2002).

(Top) Dawn Russel, competing in the broad jump in a recent Senior Olympics competition in Oregon; *(bottom)* a sedentary, overweight middle-aged man. *Even if Dawn Russel's chronological age is older, might her biological age be younger than the middle-aged man's?*

Consider a recent large-scale U.S. study of approximately 28,000 individuals from 18 to 88 that revealed happiness increased with age (Yang, 2008). For example, about 33 percent were very happy at 88 years of age compared with only about 24 percent in their late teens and early twenties. Why might older people report as much or more happiness and life satisfaction as younger people? Despite the increase in physical problems and losses older adults experience, they are more content with what they have in their lives, have better relationships with the people who matter to them, are less pressured to achieve, have more time for leisurely pursuits, and have many years of experience that may help them adapt better to their circumstances with wisdom than younger adults do (Cornwell, Schumm, & Laumann, 2008; Ram & others, 2008). Also in the study, baby boomers (those born from 1946 to 1964) reported being less happy than individuals born earlier—possibly because they are not lowering their aspirations and idealistic hopes as they age as did earlier generations. Because growing older is a certain outcome of living, it is good to know that we are likely to be just as happy or happier as older adults than when we were younger.

Conceptions of Age   According to some life-span experts, chronological age is not very relevant to understanding a person's psychological development (Botwinick, 1978). Chronological age is the number of years that have elapsed since birth. But time is a crude index of experience, and it does not cause anything. Chronological age, moreover, is not the only way of measuring age. Just as there are different domains of development, there are different ways of thinking about age.

Age has been conceptualized not just as chronological age but also as biological age, psychological age, and social age (Hoyer & Roodin, 2009). *Biological age* is a person's age in terms of biological health. Determining biological age involves knowing the functional capacities of a person's vital organs. One person's vital capacities may be better or worse than those of others of comparable age. The younger the person's biological age, the longer the person is expected to live, regardless of chronological age.

Psychological age is an individual's adaptive capacities compared with those of other individuals of the same chronological age. Thus, older adults who continue to learn, are flexible, are motivated, control their emotions think clearly, and are engaging in more adaptive behaviors than their chronological age-mates who do not continue to learn, are rigid, are unmotivated, do not control their emotions, and do not think clearly (Park & Reuter-Lorenz, 2009). Reflecting the importance of psychological age, a longitudinal study of more than 1,200 individuals across seven decades revealed that the personality trait of conscientiousness (being organized, careful, and disciplined, for example) predicted lower mortality (frequency of death) risk from childhood through late adulthood (Martin, Friedman, & Schwartz, 2007).

Social age refers to social roles and expectations related to a person's age. Consider the role of "mother" and the behaviors that accompany the role (Hoyer & Roodin, 2009). In predicting an adult woman's behavior, it may be more important to know that she is the mother of a 3-year-old child than to know whether she is 20 or 30 years old.

Life-span expert Bernice Neugarten (1988) argues that in U.S. society chronological age is becoming irrelevant. The 28-year-old mayor, the 35-year-old grandmother, the 65-year-old father of a preschooler, the 55-year-old widow who starts a business, and the 70-year-old student illustrate that old assumptions about the proper timing of life events no longer govern our lives. We still have some expectations for when certain life events—such as getting married, having children, and retiring—should occur. However, chronological age has become a less accurate predictor of these life events in our society. Moreover, issues such as how to deal with intimacy and how to cope with success and failure appear and reappear throughout the life span.

From a life-span perspective, an overall age profile of an individual involves not just chronological age but also biological age, psychological age, and social age. For example, a 70-year-old man (chronological age) might be in good physical health

PEANUTS: © United Feature Syndicate, Inc.

(biological age), be experiencing memory problems and not be coping well with the demands placed on him by his wife's recent hospitalization (psychological age), and have a number of friends with whom he regularly golfs (social age).

Developmental Issues

Is your own journey through life marked out ahead of time, or can your experiences change your path? Are the experiences you have early in your journey more important than later ones? Is your journey more like taking an elevator up a skyscraper with distinct stops along the way or more like a cruise down a river with smoother ebbs and flows? These questions point to three issues about the nature of development: the roles played by nature and nurture, by stability and change, and by continuity and discontinuity.

Nature and Nurture   The **nature-nurture issue** involves the extent to which development is influenced by nature and by nurture. Nature refers to an organism's biological inheritance, nurture to its environmental experiences.

According to those who emphasize the role of nature, just as a sunflower grows in an orderly way—unless flattened by an unfriendly environment—so too the human grows in an orderly way. An evolutionary and genetic foundation produces commonalities in growth and development (Buss, 2008; Hyde, 2009). We walk before we talk, speak one word before two words, grow rapidly in infancy and less so in early childhood, experience a rush of sex hormones in puberty, reach the peak of our physical strength in late adolescence and early adulthood, and then physically decline. Proponents of the importance of nature acknowledge that extreme environments—those that are psychologically barren or hostile—can depress development. However, they believe that basic growth tendencies are genetically programmed into humans (Brooker, 2009).

By contrast, others emphasize the importance of nurture, or environmental experiences, in development (Thompson, 2009a). Experiences run the gamut from the individual's biological environment (nutrition, medical care, drugs, and physical accidents) to the social environment (family, peers, schools, community, media, and culture).

Stability and Change   Is the shy child who hides behind the sofa when visitors arrive destined to become a wallflower at college dances, or might the child become a sociable, talkative individual? Is the fun-loving, carefree adolescent bound to have difficulty holding down a 9-to-5 job as an adult? These questions reflect the **stability-change issue,** which involves the degree to which early traits and characteristics persist through life or change.

Many developmentalists who emphasize stability in development argue that stability is the result of heredity and possibly early experiences in life. Developmentalists who emphasize change take the more optimistic view that later experiences can produce change. Recall that in the life-span perspective, plasticity, the potential for change, exists throughout the life span. Experts such as Paul Baltes (2003) argue

nature-nurture issue Debate about whether development is primarily influenced by nature or nurture. Nature refers to an organism's biological inheritance, nurture to its environmental experiences. The "nature proponents" claim biological inheritance is the more important influence on development; the "nurture proponents" claim that environmental experiences are more important.

stability-change issue Debate as to whether and to what degree we become older renditions of our early experience (stability) or whether we develop into someone different from who we were at an earlier point in development (change).

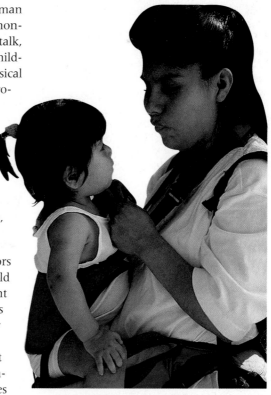

What is the nature of the early- and later-experience issue in development?

that with increasing age and on average older adults often show less capacity for change in the sense of learning new things than younger adults. However, many older adults continue to be good at practicing what they have learned in earlier times.

The roles of early and later experience are an aspect of the stability-change issue that has long been hotly debated (Kagan, 2010; Park & Reuter-Lorenz, 2009). Some argue that unless infants experience warm, nurturant caregiving in the first year or so of life, their development will never be optimal (Berlin, Cassidy, & Appleyard, 2008). The later-experience advocates see children as malleable throughout development and later sensitive caregiving as equally important to earlier sensitive caregiving (Siegler & others, 2009).

Continuity and Discontinuity   When developmental change occurs, is it gradual or abrupt? Think about your own development for a moment. Did you gradually become the person you are? Or did you experience sudden, distinct changes in your growth? For the most part, developmentalists who emphasize nurture describe development as a gradual, continuous process. Those who emphasize nature often describe development as a series of distinct stages.

The **continuity-discontinuity issue** focuses on the degree to which development involves either gradual, cumulative change (continuity) or distinct stages (discontinuity). In terms of continuity, as the oak grows from seedling to giant oak, it becomes more and more an oak—its development is continuous (see Figure 1.9). Similarly, a child's first word, though seemingly an abrupt, discontinuous event, is actually the result of weeks and months of growth and practice. Puberty might seem abrupt, but it is a gradual process that occurs over several years.

In terms of discontinuity, as an insect grows from a caterpillar to a chrysalis to a butterfly, it passes through a sequence of stages in which change is qualitatively rather than quantitatively different. Similarly, at some point a child moves from not being able to think abstractly about the world to being able to do so. This is a qualitative, discontinuous change in development rather than a quantitative, continuous change.

Evaluating the Developmental Issues   Most life-span developmentalists acknowledge that development is not all nature or all nurture, not all stability or all change, and not all continuity or all discontinuity (D'Onofrio, 2008). Nature and nurture, stability and change, continuity and discontinuity characterize development throughout the human life span.

Although most developmentalists do not take extreme positions on these three important issues, there is spirited debate regarding how strongly development is influenced by each of them (Blakemore, Berenhaum, & Liben, 2009; Schaie, 2009).

Continuity

Discontinuity

FIGURE 1.9 Continuity and Discontinuity in Development. *Is our development like that of a seedling gradually growing into a giant oak? Or is it more like that of a caterpillar suddenly becoming a butterfly?*

continuity-discontinuity issue Debate that focuses on the extent to which development involves gradual, cumulative change (continuity) or distinct stages (discontinuity).

Review and Reflect: Learning Goal 2

2   Identify the most important processes, periods, and issues in development

REVIEW
- What are three key developmental processes?
- What are eight main developmental periods?
- How is age related to development?
- What are three main developmental issues?

REFLECT
- Do you think there is a best age to be? If so, what is it? Why?

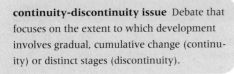

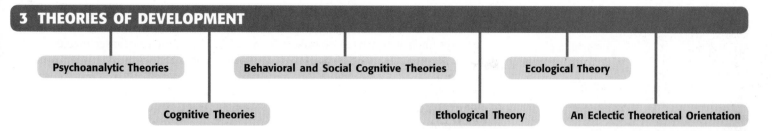

3 THEORIES OF DEVELOPMENT

- **Psychoanalytic Theories**
  - **Cognitive Theories**
- **Behavioral and Social Cognitive Theories**
  - **Ethological Theory**
- **Ecological Theory**
  - **An Eclectic Theoretical Orientation**

How can we answer questions about the roles of nature and nurture, stability and change, and continuity and discontinuity in development? How can we determine, for example, whether special care can repair the harm inflicted by child neglect or whether memory declines in older adults can be prevented? The scientific method is the best tool we have to answer such questions.

The *scientific method* is essentially a four-step process: (1) conceptualize a process or problem to be studied, (2) collect research information (data), (3) analyze data, and (4) draw conclusions.

In step 1, when researchers are formulating a problem to study, they often draw on theories and develop hypotheses. A **theory** is an interrelated, coherent set of ideas that helps to explain phenomena and make predictions. It may suggest **hypotheses,** which are specific assertions and predictions that can be tested. For example, a theory on mentoring might state that sustained support and guidance from an adult make a difference in the lives of children from impoverished backgrounds because the mentor gives the children opportunities to observe and imitate the behavior and strategies of the mentor.

This section outlines key aspects of five theoretical orientations to development: psychoanalytic, cognitive, behavioral and social cognitive, ethological, and ecological. Each contributes an important piece to the life-span development puzzle. Although the theories disagree about certain aspects of development, many of their ideas are complementary rather than contradictory. Together they let us see the total landscape of life-span development in all its richness.

Psychoanalytic Theories

Psychoanalytic theories describe development as primarily unconscious (beyond awareness) and heavily colored by emotion. Psychoanalytic theorists emphasize that behavior is merely a surface characteristic and that a true understanding of development requires analyzing the symbolic meanings of behavior and the deep inner workings of the mind. Psychoanalytic theorists also stress that early experiences with parents extensively shape development. These characteristics are highlighted in the main psychoanalytic theory, that of Sigmund Freud (1856–1939).

Freud's Theory As Freud listened to, probed, and analyzed his patients, he became convinced that their problems were the result of experiences early in life. He thought that as children grow up, their focus of pleasure and sexual impulses shifts from the mouth to the anus and eventually to the genitals. As a result, we go through five stages of psychosexual development: oral, anal, phallic, latency, and genital (see Figure 1.10).

theory An interrelated, coherent set of ideas that helps to explain phenomena and make predictions.

hypotheses Specific assumptions and predictions that can be tested to determine their accuracy.

psychoanalytic theories Theories that describe development as primarily unconscious and heavily colored by emotion. Behavior is merely a surface characteristic, and the symbolic workings of the mind have to be analyzed to understand behavior. Early experiences with parents are emphasized.

Sigmund Freud, the pioneering architect of psychoanalytic theory. *How did Freud portray development?*

FIGURE 1.10 Freudian Stages. According to Freud, people develop through five psychosexual stages in which the focus of pleasure changes.

Oral Stage	**Anal Stage**	**Phallic Stage**	**Latency Stage**	**Genital Stage**
Infant's pleasure centers on the mouth.	Child's pleasure focuses on the anus.	Child's pleasure focuses on the genitals.	Child represses sexual interest and develops social and intellectual skills.	A time of sexual reawakening; source of sexual pleasure becomes someone outside the family.
Birth to 1½ Years	*1½ to 3 Years*	*3 to 6 Years*	*Years to Puberty*	*Puberty Onward*

Erikson's Stages	Developmental Period
Integrity versus despair	Late adulthood (60s onward)
Generativity versus stagnation	Middle adulthood (40s, 50s)
Intimacy versus isolation	Early adulthood (20s, 30s)
Identity versus identity confusion	Adolescence (10 to 20 years)
Industry versus inferiority	Middle and late childhood (elementary school years, 6 years to puberty)
Initiative versus guilt	Early childhood (preschool years, 3 to 5 years)
Autonomy versus shame and doubt	Infancy (1 to 3 years)
Trust versus mistrust	Infancy (first year)

FIGURE 1.11 Erikson's Eight Life-Span Stages. Like Freud, Erikson proposed that individuals go through distinct, universal stages of development. Thus, in terms of the continuity-discontinuity issue both favor the discontinuity side of the debate. Notice that the timing of Erikson's first four stages is similar to that of Freud's stages. *What are implications of saying that people go through stages of development?*

Our adult personality, Freud (1917) claimed, is determined by the way we resolve conflicts between sources of pleasure at each stage and the demands of reality.

Freud's theory has been significantly revised by a number of psychoanalytic theorists. Many of today's psychoanalytic theorists argue that Freud overemphasized sexual instincts; they place more emphasis on cultural experiences as determinants of an individual's development. Unconscious thought remains a central theme, but thought plays a greater role than Freud envisioned. Next, we consider the ideas of an important revisionist of Freud's ideas—Erik Erikson.

Erikson's Psychosocial Theory Erik Erikson recognized Freud's contributions but stressed that Freud misjudged some important dimensions of human development. For one thing, Erikson (1950, 1968) said we develop in psychosocial stages, rather than in psychosexual stages, as Freud maintained. According to Freud, the primary motivation for human behavior is sexual in nature; according to Erikson, it is social and reflects a desire to affiliate with other people. According to Freud, our basic personality is shaped in the first five years of life; according to Erikson, developmental change occurs throughout the life span. Thus, in terms of the early-versus-later-experience issue described earlier in the chapter, Freud viewed early experiences as far more important than later experiences, whereas Erikson emphasized the importance of both early and later experiences.

In **Erikson's theory,** eight stages of development unfold as we go through life (see Figure 1.11). At each stage, a unique developmental task confronts individuals with a crisis that must be resolved. According to Erikson, this crisis is not a catastrophe but a turning point marked by both increased vulnerability and enhanced potential. The more successfully individuals resolve the crises, the healthier their development will be.

Trust versus mistrust is Erikson's first psychosocial stage, which is experienced in the first year of life. Trust in infancy sets the stage for a lifelong expectation that the world will be a good and pleasant place to live.

Autonomy versus shame and doubt is Erikson's second stage. This stage occurs in late infancy and toddlerhood (1 to 3 years). After gaining trust in their caregivers, infants begin to discover that their behavior is their own. They start to assert their sense of independence or autonomy. They realize their *will.* If infants and toddlers are restrained too much or punished too harshly, they are likely to develop a sense of shame and doubt.

Initiative versus guilt, Erikson's third stage of development, occurs during the preschool years. As preschool children encounter a widening social world, they face new challenges that require active, purposeful, responsible behavior. Feelings of guilt may arise, though, if the child is irresponsible and is made to feel too anxious.

Industry versus inferiority is Erikson's fourth developmental stage, occurring approximately in the elementary school years. Children now need to direct their energy toward mastering knowledge and intellectual skills. The negative outcome is that the child may develop a sense of inferiority—feeling incompetent and unproductive.

During the adolescent years individuals face finding

Erik Erikson with his wife, Joan, an artist. Erikson generated one of the most important developmental theories of the twentieth century. *Which stage of Erikson's theory are you in? Does Erikson's description of this stage characterize you?*

out who they are, what they are all about, and where they are going in life. This is Erikson's fifth developmental stage, (*identity versus identity confusion*) If adolescents explore roles in a healthy manner and arrive at a positive path to follow in life, they achieve a positive identity; if they do not, identity confusion reigns.

(*Intimacy versus isolation*) is Erikson's sixth developmental stage, which individuals experience during the early adulthood years. At this time, individuals face the developmental task of forming intimate relationships. If young adults form healthy friendships and an intimate relationship with another, intimacy will be achieved; if not, isolation will result.

(*Generativity versus stagnation*), Erikson's seventh developmental stage, occurs during middle adulthood. By *generativity* Erikson means primarily a concern for helping the younger generation to develop and lead useful lives. The feeling of having done nothing to help the next generation is stagnation.

(*Integrity versus despair*) is Erikson's eighth and final stage of development, which individuals experience in late adulthood. During this stage, a person reflects on the past. If the person's life review reveals a life well spent, integrity will be achieved; if not, the retrospective glances likely will yield doubt or gloom—the despair Erikson described.

Evaluating Psychoanalytic Theories   Contributions of psychoanalytic theories include an emphasis on a developmental framework, family relationships, and unconscious aspects of the mind. Criticisms include a lack of scientific support, too much emphasis on sexual underpinnings, and an image of people that is too negative.

Cognitive Theories

Whereas psychoanalytic theories stress the importance of the unconscious, cognitive theories emphasize conscious thoughts. Three important cognitive theories are Piaget's cognitive developmental theory, Vygotsky's sociocultural cognitive theory, and information-processing theory.

Piaget's Cognitive Developmental Theory   Piaget's theory states that children go through four stages of cognitive development as they actively construct their understanding of the world. Two processes underlie this cognitive construction of the world: organization and adaptation. To make sense of our world, we organize our experiences. For example, we separate important ideas from less important ideas, and we connect one idea to another. In addition to organizing our observations and experiences, we adapt, adjusting to new environmental demands (Byrnes, 2008; Carpendale, Muller, & Bibok, 2008).

Piaget (1954) also proposed that we go through four stages in understanding the world (see Figure 1.12). Each age-related stage consists of a distinct way of thinking,

Erikson's theory Theory that proposes eight stages of human development. Each stage consists of a unique developmental task that confronts individuals with a crisis that must be resolved.

Piaget's theory Theory stating that children actively construct their understanding of the world and go through four stages of cognitive development.

FIGURE 1.12 Piaget's Four Stages of Cognitive Development. According to Piaget, distinct ways of thinking characterize children of different ages.

Sensorimotor Stage	Preoperational Stage	Concrete Operational Stage	Formal Operational Stage
The infant constructs an understanding of the world by coordinating sensory experiences with physical actions. An infant progresses from reflexive, instinctual action at birth to the beginning of symbolic thought toward the end of the stage.	The child begins to represent the world with words and images. These words and images reflect increased symbolic thinking and go beyond the connection of sensory information and physical action.	The child can now reason logically about concrete events and classify objects into different sets.	The adolescent reasons in more abstract, idealistic, and logical ways.
Birth to 2 Years of Age	*2 to 7 Years of Age*	*7 to 11 Years of Age*	*11 Years of Age Through Adulthood*

Jean Piaget, the famous Swiss developmental psychologist, changed the way we think about the development of children's minds. *What are some key ideas in Piaget's theory?*

a *different* way of understanding the world. Thus, according to Piaget, the child's cognition is *qualitatively* different in one stage compared with another. What are Piaget's four stages of cognitive development?

The *sensorimotor stage,* which lasts from birth to about 2 years of age, is the first Piagetian stage. In this stage, infants construct an understanding of the world by coordinating sensory experiences (such as seeing and hearing) with physical, motoric actions—hence the term *sensorimotor.*

The *preoperational stage,* which lasts from approximately 2 to 7 years of age, is Piaget's second stage. In this stage, children begin to go beyond simply connecting sensory information with physical action and represent the world with words, images, and drawings. However, according to Piaget, preschool children still lack the ability to perform what he calls *operations,* which are internalized mental actions that allow children to do mentally what they previously could only do physically. For example, if you imagine putting two sticks together to see whether they would be as long as another stick, without actually moving the sticks, you are performing a concrete operation.

The *concrete operational stage,* which lasts from approximately 7 to 11 years of age, is the third Piagetian stage. In this stage, children can perform operations that involve objects, and they can reason logically when the reasoning can be applied to specific or concrete examples. For instance, concrete operational thinkers cannot imagine the steps necessary to complete an algebraic equation, which is too abstract for thinking at this stage of development.

The *formal operational stage,* which appears between the ages of 11 and 15 and continues through adulthood, is Piaget's fourth and final stage. In this stage, individuals move beyond concrete experiences and think in abstract and more logical terms. As part of thinking more abstractly, adolescents develop images of ideal circumstances. They might think about what an ideal parent is like and compare their parents to this ideal standard. They begin to entertain possibilities for the future and are fascinated with what they can be. In solving problems, they become more systematic, developing hypotheses about why something is happening the way it is and then testing these hypotheses. We will examine Piaget's cognitive developmental theory further in Chapters 5, "Motor, Sensory, and Perceptual Development," 7, "Information Processing," 9, "Language Development," and 11, "The Self, Identity, and Personality."

There is considerable interest today in Lev Vygotsky's sociocultural cognitive theory of child development. *What were Vygotsky's basic claims about children's development?*

Vygotsky's Sociocultural Cognitive Theory Like Piaget, the Russian developmentalist Lev Vygotsky (1896–1934) maintained that children actively construct their knowledge. However, Vygotsky (1962) gave social interaction and culture far more important roles in cognitive development than Piaget did. **Vygotsky's theory** is a sociocultural cognitive theory that emphasizes how culture and social interaction guide cognitive development.

Vygotsky portrayed the child's development as inseparable from social and cultural activities (Gredler, 2008; Holzman, 2009). He argued that cognitive development involves learning to use the inventions of society, such as language, mathematical systems, and memory strategies. Thus, in one culture, children might learn to count with the help of a computer; in another, they might learn by using beads. According to Vygotsky, children's social interaction with more-skilled adults and peers is indispensable to their cognitive development (Gauvain & Parke, 2010). Through this interaction, they learn to use the tools that will help them adapt and be successful in their culture. In Chapter 6, "Schools," we examine ideas about learning and teaching that are based on Vygotsky's theory.

The Information-Processing Theory Information-processing **theory** emphasizes that individuals manipulate information, monitor it, and strategize about it. Unlike Piaget's theory, but like Vygotsky's theory, information-processing theory does not describe development as stage-like. Instead, according to this theory, individuals develop a gradually increasing capacity for processing information, which allows them to acquire increasingly complex knowledge and skills (Halford, 2008).

Robert Siegler (2007), a leading expert on children's information processing, states that thinking is information processing. In other words, when individuals perceive, encode, represent, store, and retrieve information, they are thinking. Siegler emphasizes that an important aspect of development is learning good strategies for processing information. For example, becoming a better reader might involve learning to monitor the key themes of the material being read.

Evaluating Cognitive Theories   Contributions of cognitive theories include a positive view of development and an emphasis on the active construction of understanding. Criticisms include skepticism about the pureness of Piaget's stages and too little attention to individual variations.

Behavioral and Social Cognitive Theories

Behaviorism essentially holds that we can study scientifically only what we can directly observe and measure. Out of the behavioral tradition grew the belief that development is observable behavior that we can learn through experience with the environment (Klein, 2009). In terms of the continuity-discontinuity issue discussed earlier in this chapter, the behavioral and social cognitive theories emphasize continuity in development and argue that development does not occur in stage-like fashion. Let's explore two versions of behaviorism: Skinner's operant conditioning and Bandura's social cognitive theory.

Skinner's Operant Conditioning   According to B. F. Skinner (1904–1990), through *operant conditioning* the consequences of a behavior produce changes in the probability of the behavior's occurrence. A behavior followed by a rewarding stimulus is more likely to recur, whereas a behavior followed by a punishing stimulus is less likely to recur. For example, when an adult smiles at a child after the child has done something, the child is more likely to engage in that behavior again than if the adult gives the child a disapproving look.

In Skinner's (1938) view, such rewards and punishments shape development. For Skinner the key aspect of development is behavior, not thoughts and feelings. He emphasized that development consists of the pattern of behavioral changes that are brought about by rewards and punishments. For example, Skinner would say that shy people learned to be shy as a result of experiences they had while growing up. It follows that modifications in an environment can help a shy person become more socially oriented.

Bandura's Social Cognitive Theory   Some psychologists agree with the behaviorists' notion that development is learned and is influenced strongly by environmental interactions. However, unlike Skinner, they also see cognition as important in understanding development. **Social cognitive theory** holds that behavior, environment, and cognition are the key factors in development.

American psychologist Albert Bandura (1925–) is the leading architect of social cognitive theory. Bandura (Bandura, 2001, 2007, 2008, 2009, 2010a,b) emphasizes that cognitive processes have important links with the environment and behavior. His early research program focused heavily on *observational learning* (also called *imitation*,

B. F. Skinner was a tinkerer who liked to make new gadgets. The younger of his two daughters, Deborah, was raised in Skinner's enclosed Air-Crib, which he invented because he wanted to control her environment completely. The Air-Crib was sound-proofed and temperature controlled. Debbie, shown here as a child with her parents, is currently a successful artist, is married, and lives in London. *What do you think about Skinner's Air-Crib?*

Vygotsky's theory Sociocultural cognitive theory that emphasizes how culture and social interaction guide cognitive development.

information-processing theory Theory emphasizing that individuals manipulate information, monitor it, and strategize about it. Central to this theory are the processes of memory and thinking.

social cognitive theory Theoretical view which holds that behavior, environment, and cognition are the key factors in development.

Albert Bandura has been one of the leading architects of social cognitive theory. *What is the nature of his theory?*

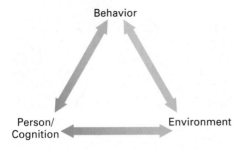

FIGURE 1.13 Bandura's Social Cognitive Model. The arrows illustrate how relations between behavior, person/cognition, and environment are reciprocal rather than unidirectional.

or *modeling*), which is learning that occurs through observing what others do. For example, a young boy might observe his father yelling in anger and treating other people with hostility; with his peers, the young boy later acts very aggressively, showing the same characteristics as his father's behavior. Social cognitive theorists stress that people acquire a wide range of behaviors, thoughts, and feelings through observing others' behavior and that these observations form an important part of life-span development.

What is *cognitive* about observational learning in Bandura's view? He proposes that people cognitively represent the behavior of others and then sometimes adopt this behavior themselves.

Bandura's (2001, 2007, 2008, 2009, 2010a,b) model of learning and development includes three elements: behavior, the person/cognition, and the environment. An individual's confidence that he or she can control his or her success is an example of a person factor; strategies are an example of a cognitive factor. As shown in Figure 1.13, behavior, person/cognition, and environmental factors operate interactively.

Evaluating Behavioral and Social Cognitive Theories   Contributions of the behavioral and social cognitive theories include an emphasis on scientific research and environmental determinants of behavior. Criticisms include too little emphasis on cognition in Skinner's view and giving inadequate attention to developmental changes.

Ethological Theory

Ethology stresses that behavior is strongly influenced by biology, is tied to evolution, and is characterized by critical or sensitive periods. These are specific time frames during which, according to ethologists, the presence or absence of certain experiences has a long-lasting influence on individuals.

European zoologist Konrad Lorenz (1903–1989) helped bring ethology to prominence. In his best-known research, Lorenz (1965) studied the behavior of greylag geese, which will follow their mothers as soon as they hatch. Lorenz separated the eggs laid by one goose into two groups. One group he returned to the goose to be hatched by her. The other group was hatched in an incubator. The goslings in the first group performed as predicted. They followed their mother as soon as they hatched. However, those in the second group, which saw Lorenz when they first hatched, followed him everywhere, as though he were their mother. Lorenz marked

Konrad Lorenz, a pioneering student of animal behavior, is followed through the water by three imprinted greylag geese. Describe Lorenz's experiment with the geese. *Do you think his experiment would have the same results with human babies? Explain.*

the goslings and then placed both groups under a box. Mother goose and "mother" Lorenz stood aside as the box lifted. Each group of goslings went directly to its "mother." Lorenz called this process *imprinting,* the rapid, innate learning that involves attachment to the first moving object that is seen.

John Bowlby (1969, 1989) illustrated an important application of ethological theory to human development. Bowlby stressed that attachment to a caregiver over the first year of life has important consequences throughout the life span. In his view, if this attachment is positive and secure, the individual will likely develop positively in childhood and adulthood. If the attachment is negative and insecure, life-span development will likely not be optimal. In Chapter 10, "Emotional Development," we explore the concept of infant attachment in much greater detail.

In Lorenz's view, imprinting needs to take place at a certain, very early time in the life of the animal, or else it will not take place. This point in time is called a *critical period*. A related concept is that of a *sensitive period*, and an example of this is the time during infancy when, according to Bowlby, attachment should occur in order to promote optimal development of social relationships.

Another theory that emphasizes biological foundations of development— evolutionary psychology—is presented in Chapter 2, "Biological Beginnings," along with views on the role of heredity in development. In addition, we examine a number of biological theories of aging in Chapter 3, "Physical Development and Biological Aging."

Evaluating Ethological Theory   Contributions of ethological theory include a focus on the biological and evolutionary basis of development, and the use of careful observations in naturalistic settings. Criticisms include too much emphasis on biological foundations and a belief that the critical and sensitive period concepts might be too rigid.

Ecological Theory

While ethological theory stresses biological factors, ecological theory emphasizes environmental factors. One ecological theory that has important implications for understanding life-span development was created by Urie Bronfenbrenner (1917–2005).

Bronfenbrenner's ecological theory (1986, 2004; Bronfenbrenner & Morris, 1998, 2006) holds that development reflects the influence of several environmental systems. The theory identifies five environmental systems: microsystem, mesosystem, exosystem, macrosystem, and chronosystem (see Figure 1.14).

The *microsystem* is the setting in which the individual lives. Contexts within it include the person's family, peers, school, and neighborhood. It is in the microsystem that the most direct interactions with social agents take place—with parents, friends, and teachers, for example. The individual is not a passive recipient of experiences in these settings, but someone who helps to construct the settings.

The *mesosystem* involves relations between microsystems or connections between contexts. Examples are the relation of family experiences to school experiences, school experiences to church experiences, and family experiences to peer experiences. For example, children whose parents have rejected them may have difficulty developing positive relations with teachers.

The *exosystem* consists of links between a social setting in which the individual does not have an active role and the individual's immediate context. For example, a husband's or child's experience at home may be influenced by a mother's experiences at work. The mother might receive a promotion that requires more travel,

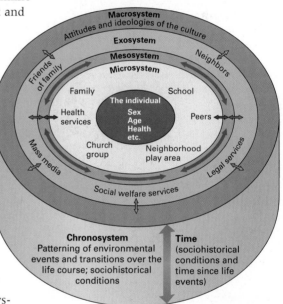

FIGURE 1.14 Bronfenbrenner's Ecological Theory of Development. Bronfenbrenner's ecological theory consists of five environmental systems: microsystem, mesosystem, exosystem, macrosystem, and chronosystem.

ethology Theory stressing that behavior is strongly influenced by biology, is tied to evolution, and is characterized by critical or sensitive periods.

Bronfenbrenner's ecological theory Bronfenbrenner's environmental systems theory that focuses on five environmental systems: microsystem, mesosystem, exosystem, macrosystem, and chronosystem.

which might increase conflict with the husband and change patterns of interaction with the child.

The *macrosystem* involves the culture in which individuals live. Remember from earlier in the chapter that culture refers to the behavior patterns, beliefs, and all other products of a group of people that are passed on from generation to generation. Remember also that cross-cultural studies—the comparison of one culture with one or more other cultures—provide information about the generality of development.

The *chronosystem* consists of the patterning of environmental events and transitions over the life course, as well as sociohistorical circumstances. For example, divorce is one transition. Researchers have found that the negative effects of divorce on children often peak in the first year after the divorce (Hetherington, 1993, 2006). By two years after the divorce, family interaction is more stable. As an example of sociohistorical circumstances, consider how the opportunities for women to pursue a career have increased since the 1960s.

Bronfenbrenner (2004; Bronfenbrenner & Morris, 2006) subsequently added biological influences to his theory, describing it as a *bioecological* theory. Nonetheless, it is still dominated by ecological, environmental contexts (Ceci, 2000).

What can make children resilient when they face adverse contexts? Ann Masten (2001, 2004, 2007, 2009a,b) analyzed the research literature on resilience and concluded that resilient children have a number of different kinds of positive characteristics and support in their lives including positive individual traits (such as good intellectual functioning), family ties (close relationships in a caring family), and extrafamilial supports (connections with competent, caring adults outside the family). Figure 1.15 summarizes the sources of resilience that may come from individual, family, and extrafamilial contexts.

Evaluating Ecological Theory   Contributions of the theory include a systematic examination of macro- and microdimensions of environmental systems, and attention to connections between environmental systems. Criticisms include giving inadequate attention to biological factors, as well as placing too little emphasis on cognitive factors.

An Eclectic Theoretical Orientation

No single theory described in this chapter can explain entirely the rich complexity of life-span development, but each has contributed to our understanding of development. Psychoanalytic theory best explains the unconscious mind. Erikson's theory best describes the changes that occur in adult development. Piaget's, Vygotsky's, and the information-processing views provide the most complete description of cognitive development. The behavioral and social cognitive and ecological theories have been the most adept at examining the environmental determinants of development. The ethological theories have highlighted biology's role and the importance of sensitive periods in development.

In short, although theories are helpful guides, relying on a single theory to explain development is probably a mistake. This book instead takes an **eclectic theoretical orientation,** which does not follow any one theoretical approach but rather selects from each theory whatever is considered its best features. In this way, you can view the study of development as it actually exists—with different theorists

Urie Bronfenbrenner developed ecological theory, a perspective that is receiving increased attention. *What is the nature of ecological theory?*

Source	Characteristic
Individual	Good intellectual functioning
	Appealing, sociable, easygoing disposition
	Self-confidence, high self-esteem
	Talents
	Faith
Family	Close relationship to caring parent figure
	Authoritative parenting: warmth, structure, high expectations
	Socioeconomic advantages
	Connections to extended supportive family networks
Extrafamilial context	Bonds to caring adults outside the family
	Connections to positive organizations
	Attending effective schools

FIGURE 1.15 Characteristics of Resilient Children.

eclectic theoretical orientation An orientation that does not follow any one theoretical approach, but rather selects from each theory whatever is considered the best in it.

THEORY	ISSUES	
	Continuity/discontinuity, early versus later experiences	**Biological and environmental factors**
Psychoanalytic	Discontinuity between stages—continuity between early experiences and later development; early experiences very important; later changes in development emphasized in Erikson's theory	Freud's biological determination interacting with early family experiences; Erikson's more balanced biological-cultural interaction perspective
Cognitive	Discontinuity between stages in Piaget's theory; continuity between early experiences and later development in Piaget's and Vygotsky's theories; no stages in Vygotsky's theory or information-processing theory	Piaget's emphasis on interaction and adaptation; environment provides the setting for cognitive structures to develop; information-processing view has not addressed this issue extensively but mainly emphasizes biological-environmental interaction
Behavioral and social cognitive	Continuity (no stages); experience at all points of development important	Environment viewed as the cause of behavior in both views
Ethological	Discontinuity but no stages; critical or sensitive periods emphasized; early experiences very important	Strong biological view
Ecological	Little attention to continuity/discontinuity; change emphasized more than stability	Strong environmental view

FIGURE 1.16 A Comparison of Theories and Issues in Life-Span Development.

making different assumptions, stressing different empirical problems, and using different strategies to discover information. Figure 1.16 compares the main theoretical perspectives in terms of how they view important developmental issues in children's development.

Review and Reflect: Learning Goal 3

3 **Describe the main theories of human development**

REVIEW

- How can theory and hypotheses be defined? What are the four steps of the scientific method? What are two main psychoanalytic theories? What are some contributions and criticisms of the psychoanalytic theories?
- What are three main cognitive theories? What are some contributions and criticisms of the cognitive theories?
- What are two main behavioral and social cognitive theories? What are some contributions and criticisms of the behavioral and social cognitive theories?
- What is the nature of ethological theory? What are some contributions and criticisms of the theory?
- What characterizes ecological theory? What are some contributions and criticisms of the theory?
- What is an eclectic theoretical orientation?

REFLECT

- Which of the life-span theories do you think best explains your own development? Why?

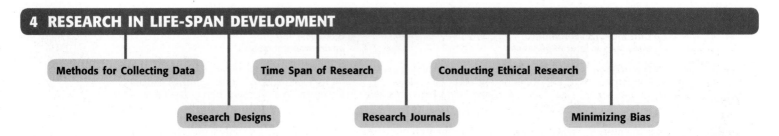

4 RESEARCH IN LIFE-SPAN DEVELOPMENT

Methods for Collecting Data

Research Designs

Time Span of Research

Research Journals

Conducting Ethical Research

Minimizing Bias

> *Science refines everyday thinking.*
>
> —ALBERT EINSTEIN
> *German-born American Physicist, 20th Century*

If they follow an eclectic orientation, how do scholars and researchers determine that one feature of a theory is somehow better than another? The scientific method discussed earlier in this chapter provides the guide. Through scientific research, they can test and refine the features of theories.

Generally, research in life-span development is designed to test hypotheses, which in some cases are derived from the theories just described. Through research, theories are modified to reflect new data, and occasionally new theories arise. How are data about life-span development collected? What types of research designs are used to study life-span development? And what are some ethical considerations in conducting research on life-span development?

Methods for Collecting Data

Whether we are interested in studying attachment in infants, the cognitive skills of children, or social relationships in older adults, we can choose from several ways of collecting data. Here we consider the measures most often used, beginning with observation.

A researcher observes teacher-child interaction through a one-way mirror in a child-care program.

Observation   Scientific observation requires an important set of skills (Jackson, 2008). For observations to be effective, they have to be systematic. We have to have some idea of what we are looking for. We have to know whom we are observing, when and where we will observe, how we will make our observations, and how we will record them.

Where should we make our observations? We have two choices: the laboratory and the everyday world.

When we observe scientifically, we often need to control certain factors that determine behavior but are not the focus of our inquiry (McBurney & White, 2010). For this reason, some research in life-span development is conducted in a **laboratory,** a controlled setting where many of the complex factors of the "real world" are absent. For example, suppose you want to observe how children react when they see other people act aggressively. If you observe children in their homes or schools, you have no control over how much aggression the children observe, what kind of aggression they see, which people they see acting aggressively, or how other people treat the children. In contrast, if you observe the children in a laboratory, you can control these and other factors and therefore have more confidence about how to interpret your observations.

Laboratory research does have some drawbacks, however, including the following:

- It is almost impossible to conduct research without the participants knowing they are being studied.

- The laboratory setting is unnatural and therefore can cause the participants to behave unnaturally.

- People who are willing to come to a university laboratory may not fairly represent groups from diverse cultural backgrounds.

- People who are unfamiliar with university settings, and with the idea of "helping science," may be intimidated by the laboratory setting.

laboratory A controlled setting in which many of the complex factors of the "real world" are removed.

naturalistic observation Observing behavior in real-world settings.

standardized test A test with uniform procedures for administration and scoring. Many standardized tests allow a person's performance to be compared with the performance of other individuals.

case study An in-depth look at a single individual.

Naturalistic observation provides insights that we sometimes cannot achieve in the laboratory (Graziano & Raulin, 2010). **Naturalistic observation** means observing behavior in real-world settings, making no effort to manipulate or control the situation. Life-span researchers conduct naturalistic observations at sporting events, child-care centers, schools, work settings, malls, and other places people live in and frequent.

Naturalistic observation was used in one study that focused on conversations in a children's science museum (Crowley & others, 2001). When visiting exhibits at the science museum, parents were three times as likely to engage boys than girls in explanatory talk. This finding suggests a gender bias that encourages boys more than girls to be interested in science (see Figure 1.17).

Survey and Interview   Sometimes the best and quickest way to get information about people is to ask them for it. One technique is to *interview* them directly. A related method is the *survey*—sometimes referred to as a *questionnaire*—which is especially useful when information from many people is needed (Gay, Mills, & Airasian, 2009). A standard set of questions is used to obtain peoples' self-reported attitudes or beliefs about a particular topic. In a good survey, the questions are clear and unbiased, allowing respondents to answer unambiguously.

Surveys and interviews can be used to study a wide range of topics from religious beliefs to sexual habits to attitudes about gun control to beliefs about how to improve schools. Surveys and interviews may be conducted in person, over the telephone, and over the Internet.

One problem with surveys and interviews is the tendency of participants to answer questions in a way that they think is socially acceptable or desirable rather than to say what they truly think or feel (Creswell, 2008). For example, on a survey or in an interview some individuals might say that they do not take drugs even though they do.

Standardized Test   A **standardized test** has uniform procedures for administration and scoring. Many standardized tests allow a person's performance to be compared with that of other individuals; thus they provide information about individual differences among people (Kingston, 2008). One example is the Stanford-Binet intelligence test, which is described in Chapter 8, "Intelligence." Your score on the Stanford-Binet test tells you how your performance compares with that of thousands of other people who have taken the test (Bart & Peterson, 2008).

One criticism of standardized tests is that they assume a person's behavior is consistent and stable, yet personality and intelligence— two primary targets of standardized testing—can vary with the situation. For example, a person may perform poorly on a standardized intelligence test in an office setting but score much higher at home, where he or she is less anxious.

Case Study   A **case study** is an in-depth look at a single individual. Case studies are performed mainly by mental health professionals when, for either practical or ethical reasons, the unique aspects of an individual's life cannot be duplicated and tested in other individuals. A case study provides information about one person's experiences; it may focus on nearly any aspect of the subject's life that helps the researcher understand the person's mind, behavior, or other attributes. In later chapters, we discuss vivid case studies, such as that of Michael Rehbein, who had much of the left side of his brain removed at 7 years of age to end severe epileptic seizures.

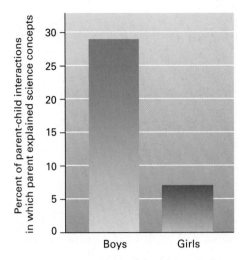

FIGURE 1.17 Parents' Explanations of Science to Sons and Daughters at a Science Museum. In a naturalistic observation study at a children's science museum, parents were more than three times more likely to explain science to boys than to girls (Crowley & others, 2001). The gender difference occurred regardless of whether the father, the mother, or both parents were with the child, although the gender difference was greatest for father's science explanations to sons and daughters.

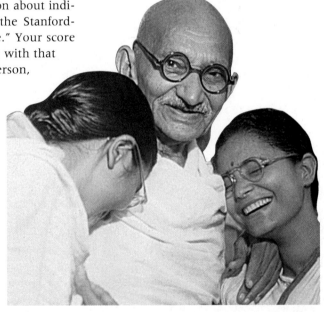

Mahatma Gandhi was the spiritual leader of India in the middle of the twentieth century. Erik Erikson conducted an extensive case study of Gandhi's life to determine what contributed to his identity development. *What are some limitations of the case study approach?*

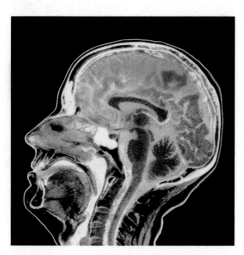

This fMRI scan of a 51-year-old male shows atrophy in the cerebral cortex of the brain, which occurs in various disorders including stroke and Alzheimer disease. The area of the upper cerebral cortex (where higher-level brain functioning such as thinking and planning occur) is colored dark red. Neuroimaging techniques such as the fMRI are helping researchers to learn more about how the brain functions as people develop and age, as well as what happens to the brain when aging diseases such as stroke and Alzheimer disease are present.

A case study can provide a dramatic, in-depth portrayal of an individual's life, but we must be cautious when generalizing from this information. The subject of a case study is unique, with a genetic makeup and personal history that no one else shares. In addition, case studies involve judgments of unknown reliability. Researchers who conduct case studies rarely check to see if other professionals agree with their observations or findings.

Physiological Measures Researchers are increasingly using physiological measures when they study development at different points in the life span (Hofheimer & Lester, 2008; Nelson, 2009). For example, as puberty unfolds, the blood levels of certain hormones increase. To determine the nature of these hormonal changes, researchers analyze blood samples from adolescent volunteers (Susman & Dorn, 2009).

Another physiological measure that is increasingly being used is neuroimaging, especially *functional magnetic resonance imaging (fMRI)*, in which electromagnetic waves are used to construct images of a person's brain tissue and biochemical activity (Park & Reuter-Lorenz, 2009). We will have much more to say about neuroimaging and other physiological measures in later chapters.

Research Designs

In conducting research on life-span development, in addition to a method for collecting data, you also need a research design. There are three main types of research design: descriptive, correlational, and experimental.

Descriptive Research All of the data-collection methods that we have discussed can be used in **descriptive research,** which aims to observe and record behavior. For example, a researcher might observe the extent to which people are altruistic or aggressive toward each other. By itself, descriptive research cannot prove what causes some phenomenon, but it can reveal important information about people's behavior (Leedy & Ormrod, 2010; McMillan & Schumacher, 2010).

Correlational Research In contrast to descriptive research, correlational research goes beyond describing phenomena; it provides information that will help us to predict how people will behave. In **correlational research,** the goal is to describe the strength of the relationship between two or more events or characteristics. The more strongly the two events are correlated (or related or associated), the more effectively we can predict one event from the other (Howell, 2010).

For example, to study if children of permissive parents have less self-control than other children, you would need to carefully record observations of parents' permissiveness and their children's self-control. You might observe that the higher a parent was in permissiveness, the lower the child was in self-control. You would then analyze these data statistically to yield a numerical measure, called a **correlation coefficient,** a number based on a statistical analysis that is used to describe the degree of association between two variables. The correlation coefficient ranges from +1.00 to −1.00. A negative number means an inverse (reversed) relation. In the example just given, you might find an inverse correlation between permissive parenting and children's self-control with a coefficient of, say, −.30. By contrast, you might find a positive correlation of +.30 between parental monitoring of children and children's self-control.

The higher the correlation coefficient (whether positive or negative), the stronger the association between the two variables. A correlation of 0 means that there is no association between the variables. A correlation of −.40 is stronger than a correlation of +.20 because we disregard whether the correlation is positive or negative in determining the strength of the correlation.

descriptive research A type of research that aims to observe and record behavior.

correlational research A type of research that strives to describe the strength of the relationship between two or more events or characterists.

correlation coefficient A number based on a statistical analysis that is used to describe the degree of association between two variables.

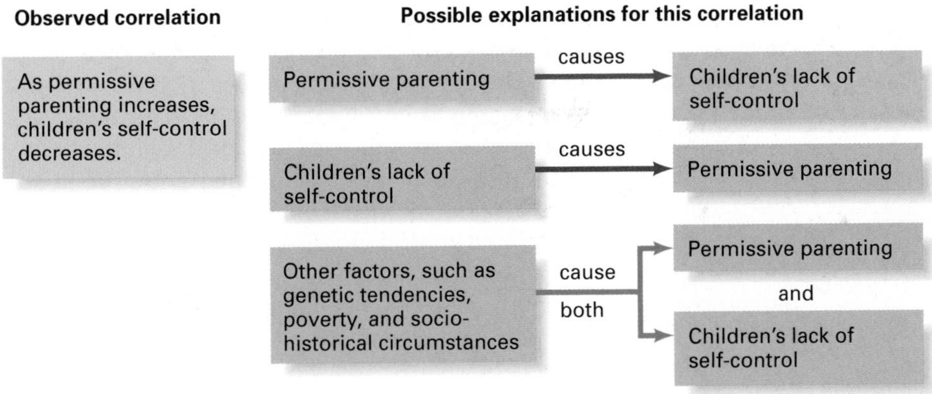

Observed correlation

| As permissive parenting increases, children's self-control decreases. |

Possible explanations for this correlation

Permissive parenting — causes → Children's lack of self-control

Children's lack of self-control — causes → Permissive parenting

Other factors, such as genetic tendencies, poverty, and socio-historical circumstances — cause both → Permissive parenting and Children's lack of self-control

FIGURE 1.18 Possible Explanations for Correlational Data. An observed correlation between two events cannot be used to conclude that one event caused the other. Some possibilities are that the second event caused the first event or that a third, unknown event caused the correlation between the first two events.

A caution is in order, however. Correlation does not equal causation (Wiersman & Jurs, 2009). The correlational finding just mentioned does not mean that permissive parenting necessarily causes low self-control in children. It could mean that, but it also could mean that a child's lack of self-control caused the parents to throw up their arms in despair and give up trying to control the child. It also could mean that other factors, such as heredity or poverty, caused the correlation between permissive parenting and low self-control in children. Figure 1.18 illustrates these possible interpretations of correlational data.

Experimental Research To study causality, researchers turn to experimental research. An **experiment** is a carefully regulated procedure in which one or more factors believed to influence the behavior being studied are manipulated while all other factors are held constant. If the behavior under study changes when a factor is manipulated, the manipulated factor has caused the behavior to change. In other words, the experiment has demonstrated cause and effect. The cause is the factor that was manipulated. The effect is the behavior that changed because of the manipulation. Nonexperimental research methods (descriptive and correlational research) cannot establish cause and effect because they do not involve manipulating factors in a controlled way (Mitchell & Jolley, 2010).

Independent and Dependent Variables Experiments include two types of changeable factors, or variables: independent and dependent. An *independent variable* is a manipulated, influential, experimental factor. It is a potential cause. The label "independent" is used because this variable can be manipulated independently of other factors to determine its effect. An experiment may include one independent variable or several of them.

A *dependent variable* is a factor that can change in an experiment, in response to changes in the independent variable. As researchers manipulate the independent variable, they measure the dependent variable for any resulting effect.

For example, suppose that you are conducting a study to determine whether pregnant women could change the breathing and sleeping patterns of their newborn babies by meditating during pregnancy. You might require one group of pregnant women to engage in a certain amount and type of meditation each day while another group would not meditate; the meditation is thus the independent variable. When the infants are born, you would observe and measure their breathing and sleeping patterns. These patterns are the dependent variable, the factor that changes as the result of your manipulation.

Experimental and Control Groups Experiments can involve one or more experimental groups and one or more control groups. An *experimental group* is a group whose experience is manipulated. A *control group* is a comparison group that is as

experiment Carefully regulated procedure in which one or more factors believed to influence the behavior being studied are manipulated while all other factors are held constant.

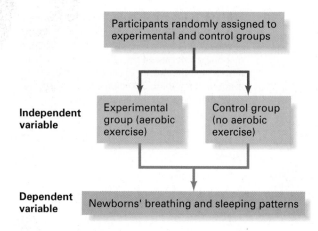

Participants randomly assigned to experimental and control groups

Independent variable

Experimental group (aerobic exercise)   Control group (no aerobic exercise)

Dependent variable   Newborns' breathing and sleeping patterns

FIGURE 1.19 Principles of Experimental Research.

much like the experimental group as possible and that is treated in every way like the experimental group except for the manipulated factor (independent variable). The control group serves as a baseline against which the effects of the manipulated condition can be compared.

Random assignment is an important principle for deciding whether each participant will be placed in the experimental group or in the control group. Random assignment means that researchers assign participants to experimental and control groups by chance. It reduces the likelihood that the experiment's results will be due to any preexisting differences between groups (Graziano & Raulin, 2010). In the example of the effects of meditation by pregnant women on the breathing and sleeping patterns of their newborns, you would randomly assign half of the pregnant women to engage in meditation over a period of weeks (the experimental group) and the other half not to meditate over the same number of weeks (the control group). Figure 1.19 illustrates the nature of experimental research.

Time Span of Research

Researchers in life-span development have a special concern with studies that focus on the relation of age to some other variable. They have several options: Researchers can study different individuals of different ages and compare them or they can study the same individuals as they age over time.

Cross-Sectional Approach   The **cross-sectional approach** is a research strategy that simultaneously compares individuals of different ages. A typical cross-sectional study might include three groups of children: 5-year-olds, 8-year-olds, and 11-year-olds. Another study might include a group of 15-year-olds, 25-year-olds, and 45-year-olds. The groups can be compared with respect to a variety of dependent variables: IQ, memory, peer relations, attachment to parents, hormonal changes, and so on. All of these comparisons can be accomplished in a short time. In some studies, data are collected in a single day. Even in large-scale cross-sectional studies with hundreds of subjects, data collection does not usually take longer than several months to complete.

The main advantage of the cross-sectional study is that the researcher does not have to wait for the individuals to grow up or become older. Despite its efficiency, though, the cross-sectional approach has its drawbacks. It gives no information about how individuals change or about the stability of their characteristics. It can obscure the increases and decreases of development—the hills and valleys of growth and development. For example, a cross-sectional study of life satisfaction might reveal average increases and decreases, but it would not show how the life satisfaction of individual adults waxed and waned over the years. It also would not tell us whether the same adults who had positive or negative perceptions of life satisfaction in early adulthood maintained their relative degree of life satisfaction as they became middle-aged or older adults.

Longitudinal Approach   The **longitudinal approach** is a research strategy in which the same individuals are studied over a period of time, usually several years or more. For example, in a longitudinal study of life satisfaction, the same adults might be assessed periodically over a 70-year time span—at the ages of 20, 35, 45, 65, and 90, for example.

Longitudinal studies provide a wealth of information about vital issues such as stability and change in development and the importance of early experience for later development, but they do have drawbacks (Gibbons, Hedeker, & DuToit, 2009). They are expensive and time consuming. The longer the study lasts, the more participants drop out—they move, get sick, lose interest, and so forth. The participants who remain may be dissimilar to those who drop out, biasing the outcome of the

cross-sectional approach A research strategy in which individuals of different ages are compared at one time.

longitudinal approach A research strategy in which the same individuals are studied over a period of time, usually several years or more.

cohort effects Effects due to a person's time of birth, era, or generation but not to actual age.

study. Those individuals who remain in a longitudinal study over a number of years may be more responsible and conformity-oriented, for example, or they might have more stable lives.

Cohort Effects A *cohort* is a group of people who are born at a similar point in history and share similar experiences as a result, such as living through the Vietnam War or growing up in the same city around the same time. These shared experiences may produce a range of differences among cohorts. For example, people who were teenagers during World War II are likely to differ from people who were teenagers during the booming 1990s in their educational opportunities and economic status, in how they were raised, and in their attitudes toward sex and religion. In life-span development research, **cohort effects** are due to a person's time of birth, era, or generation but not to actual age.

Cohort effects are important because they can powerfully affect the dependent measures in a study ostensibly concerned with age (Schaie, 2008a, b; 2009). Researchers have shown it is especially important to be aware of cohort effects when assessing adult intelligence (Schaie, 1996). Individuals born at different points in time—such as 1930, 1960, and 1990—have had varying opportunities for education. Individuals born in earlier years had less access to education, and this fact may have a significant effect on how this cohort performs on intelligence tests.

Cross-sectional studies can show how different cohorts respond, but they can confuse age changes and cohort effects. Longitudinal studies are effective in studying age changes but only within one cohort.

Research Journals

Regardless of whether you pursue a career in life-span development, psychology, or some related scientific field, you can benefit by learning about the journal process. As a student, you might be required to look up original research in journals. As a parent, teacher, or nurse you might want to consult journals to obtain information that will help you understand and work more effectively with people. And, as an inquiring person, you might look up information in journals after you have heard or read something that piqued your curiosity.

A journal publishes scholarly and academic information, usually in a specific domain—like physics, math, sociology, or, our current interest, life-span development. Scholars in these fields publish most of their research in journals, which are the source of core information in virtually every academic discipline.

An increasing number of journals publish information about life-span development. Among the leading journals in life-span development are *Developmental Psychology, Child Development, Pediatrics, Pediatric Nursing, The Journals of Gerontology, Infant Behavior and Development, Journal of Research on Adolescence, Journal of Adult Development, Journal of Gerontological Nursing, Psychology and Aging, Human Development,* and many others. Also, a number of journals that do not focus solely on development publish articles on various aspects of human development. These journals include *Journal of Educational Psychology, Sex Roles, Journal of Cross-Cultural Research, Journal of Marriage and the Family,* and *Journal of Consulting and Clinical Psychology.*

Every journal has a board of experts who evaluate articles submitted for publication. Each submitted paper is accepted or rejected on the basis of such factors as its contribution to the field, methodological excellence, and clarity of writing. Some of the most prestigious journals reject as many as 80 to 90 percent of the articles submitted.

Journal articles are usually written by professionals for other professionals in the specialized field of the journal's focus; therefore, they often contain technical language and terms specific to the discipline that are difficult for nonprofessionals

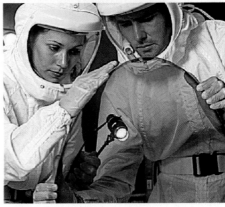

Cohort effects are due to a person's time of birth or generation but not actually to age. Think for a moment about growing up in (a) the Great Depression and (b) today. *How might your development be different depending on which of these time frames has dominated your life? your parents' lives? your grandparents' lives?*

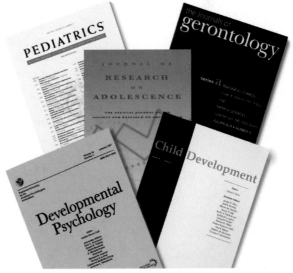

Research journals are the core of information in virtually every academic discipline. Those shown here are among the increasing number of research journals that publish information about life-span development. *What are the main parts of a research article that present findings from original research?*

to understand. Their organization often takes this course: abstract, introduction, method, results, discussion, and references.

The *abstract* is a brief summary that appears at the beginning of the article. The abstract lets readers quickly determine whether the article is relevant to their interests. The *introduction* introduces the problem or issue that is being studied. It includes a concise review of research relevant to the topic, theoretical ties, and one or more hypotheses to be tested. The *method* section consists of a clear description of the subjects evaluated in the study, the measures used, and the procedures that were followed. The method section should be sufficiently clear and detailed so that by reading it another researcher could repeat or replicate the study. The *results* section reports the analysis of the data collected. In most cases, the results section includes statistical analyses that are difficult for nonprofessionals to understand. The *discussion* section describes the author's conclusions, inferences, and interpretation of what was found. Statements are usually made about whether the hypotheses presented in the introduction were supported, limitations of the study, and suggestions for future research. The last part of the journal article, called *references,* includes bibliographic information for each source cited in the article. The references section is often a good source for finding other articles relevant to the topic that interests you.

Where do you find journals such as those described above? Your college or university library likely has some of them, and some public libraries also carry journals. Online resources such as PsycINFO and PubMed, which can facilitate the search for journal articles, are available to students on many campuses.

Conducting Ethical Research

Ethics in research may affect you personally if you ever serve as a participant in a study. In that event, you need to know your rights as a participant and the responsibilities of researchers to assure that these rights are safeguarded.

If you ever become a researcher in life-span development yourself, you will need an even deeper understanding of ethics. Even if you only carry out experimental projects in psychology courses, you must consider the rights of the participants in those projects. A student might think, "I volunteer in a home for the mentally retarded several hours per week. I can use the residents of the home in my study to see if a particular treatment helps improve their memory for everyday tasks." But without proper permissions, the most well-meaning and considerate studies still violate the rights of the participants.

Today, proposed research at colleges and universities must pass the scrutiny of a research ethics committee before the research can begin (Kimmel, 2007). In addition, the American Psychological Association (APA) has developed ethics guidelines for its members. The code of ethics instructs psychologists to protect their participants from mental and physical harm. The participants' best interests need to be kept foremost in the researcher's mind (Wiersman & Jurs, 2009). APA's guidelines address four important issues:

1. *Informed consent.* All participants must know what their research participation will involve and what risks might develop. Even after informed consent is given, participants must retain the right to withdraw from the study at any time and for any reason.
2. *Confidentiality.* Researchers are responsible for keeping all of the data they gather on individuals completely confidential and, when possible, completely anonymous.
3. *Debriefing.* After the study has been completed, participants should be informed of its purpose and the methods that were used. In most cases, the experimenter also can inform participants in a general manner beforehand about the purpose of the research without leading participants to behave in a way they think the experimenter is expecting.

4. *Deception.* In some circumstances, telling the participants beforehand what the research study is about substantially alters the participants' behavior and invalidates the researcher's data. Thus, researchers may deceive the participants about the details of the study. In all cases of deception, however, the psychologist must ensure that the deception will not harm the participants and that the participants will be *debriefed* (told the complete nature of the study) as soon as possible after the study is completed.

Minimizing Bias

Studies of life-span development are most useful when they are conducted without bias or prejudice toward any group of people (Banks, 2010). Of special concern is bias based on gender and bias based on culture or ethnicity.

Gender Bias   For most of its existence, our society has had a strong gender bias, a preconceived notion about the abilities of women and men that prevented individuals from pursuing their own interests and achieving their potential (Etaugh & Bridges, 2010; UNICEF, 2009, 2010). Gender bias also has had a less obvious effect within the field of life-span development. For example, it is not unusual for conclusions to be drawn about females' attitudes and behaviors from research conducted with males as the only participants (Matlin, 2008).

Furthermore, when researchers find gender differences, their reports sometimes magnify those differences (Denmark & others, 1988). For example, a researcher might report that 74 percent of the men in a study had high achievement expectations versus only 67 percent of the women and go on to talk about the differences in some detail. In reality, this might be a rather small difference. It also might disappear if the study were repeated or the study might have methodological problems that don't allow such strong interpretations.

Pam Reid is a leading researcher who studies gender and ethnic bias in development. To read about Pam's interests, see the *Careers in Life-Span Development* profile.

Careers in Life-Span Development

Pam Reid, Educational and Development Psychologist

When she was a child, Pam Reid liked to play with chemistry sets. Reid majored in chemistry during college and wanted to become a doctor. However, when some of her friends signed up for a psychology class as an elective she also decided to take the course. She was intrigued by learning about how people think, behave, and develop—so much so that she changed her major to psychology. Reid went on to obtain her Ph.D. in psychology (American Psychological Association 2003, p. 16).

For a number of years, Reid was professor of education and psychology at the University of Michigan, where she also was a research scientist at the Institute for Research on Women and Gender. Her main focus has been on how children and adolescents develop social skills with a special interest in the development of African American girls (Reid & Zalk 2001). In 2004, Reid become Provost and Executive Vice-President at Roosevelt University in Chicago, and in 2007 became president of Saint Joseph College in Hartford, Connecticut.

Pam Reid (*back row, center*) with graduate students she mentored at the University of Michigan.

Look at these two photographs, one of them mainly White males, the other of a diverse group of females and males from different ethnic groups, including some White individuals. Consider a topic in life-span development, such as parenting, love or cultural values. *If you were conducting research on this topic, might the results of the study be different depending on whether the participants in your study were the individuals in the photograph on the top or those on the bottom?*

ethnic gloss Use of an ethnic label such as African American or Latino in a superficial way that portrays an ethnic group as being more homogeneous than it really is.

Cultural and Ethnic Bias   The realization that research on life-span development needs to include more people from diverse ethnic groups has also been building (Graham, 2006; Kim & others, 2009). Historically, people from ethnic minority groups (African American, Latino, Asian American, and Native American) were excluded from most research in the United States and simply thought of as variations from the norm or average. If minority individuals were included in samples and their scores didn't fit the norm, they were viewed as confounds or "noise" in data and discounted. Given the fact that individuals from diverse ethnic groups were excluded from research on life-span development for so long, we might reasonably conclude that people's real lives are perhaps more varied than research data have indicated in the past.

Researchers also have tended to overgeneralize about ethnic groups (Banks, 2010; Liu & others, 2009). **Ethnic gloss** is using an ethnic label such as African American or Latino in a superficial way that portrays an ethnic group as being more homogeneous than it really is (Trimble, 1988). For example, a researcher might describe a research sample like this: "The participants were 60 Latinos." A more complete description of the Latino group might be something like this: "The 60 Latino participants were Mexican Americans from low-income neighborhoods in the southwestern area of Los Angeles. Thirty-six were from homes in which Spanish is the dominant spoken language, 24 from homes in which English is the main spoken language. Thirty were born in the United States, 30 in Mexico. Twenty-eight described themselves as Mexican American, 14 as Mexican, 9 as American, 6 as Chicano, and 3 as Latino." Ethnic gloss can cause researchers to obtain samples of ethnic groups that are not representative of the group's diversity, which can lead to overgeneralization and stereotyping.

The continued growth of minority families in the United States in approaching decades will mainly be due to the immigration of Latino and Asian families. Researchers need "to take into account their acculturation level and generational status of parents and children," and how they influence family processes and child outcomes (Parke & Buriel, 2006, p. 487). More attention also needs to be given to biculturalism because the complexity of diversity means that some children of color identify with two or more ethnic groups. And language development research needs to focus more on second-language acquisition (usually English) and bilingualism and how they are linked to school achievement.

Review and Reflect: Learning Goal 4

4 **Explain how research on life-span development is conducted**

REVIEW

- What methods do researchers use to collect data on life-span development?
- What research designs are used to study human development?
- How is research conducted on the time span of people's lives?
- What characterizes research journals?
- What are researchers' ethical responsibilities to the people they study?
- How can gender, cultural, and ethnic bias affect the outcome of a research study?

REFLECT

- Imagine that you are conducting a research study on the sexual attitudes and behaviors of adolescents. What ethical safeguards should you use in conducting the study?

Reach Your Learning Goals

Introduction

1 THE LIFE-SPAN PERSPECTIVE: DISCUSS THE DISTINCTIVE FEATURES OF A LIFE-SPAN PERSPECTIVE ON DEVELOPMENT

The Importance of Studying Life-Span Development

Characteristics of the Life-Span Perspective

Some Contemporary Concerns

- Development is the pattern of change that begins at conception and continues through the human life span. It includes both growth and decline. Studying life-span development helps prepare us to take responsibility for children, gives us insight about our own lives, and gives us knowledge about what our lives will be like as we age.

- The life-span perspective includes these basic conceptions: Development is lifelong, multidimensional, multidirectional, and plastic; its study is multidisciplinary; it is embedded in contexts; it involves growth, maintenance, and regulation of loss; and it is a co-construction of biological, cultural, and individual factors. Three important sources of contextual influences are (1) normative age-graded influences, (2) normative history-graded influences, and (3) nonnormative life events.

- Health and well-being, parenting, education, sociocultural contexts and diversity, and social policy are all areas of contemporary concern that are closely tied to life-span development. Important dimensions of the sociocultural context include culture, ethnicity, socioeconomic status, and gender. There is increasing interest in social policy issues related to children and to older adults.

2 THE NATURE OF DEVELOPMENT: IDENTIFY THE MOST IMPORTANT PROCESSES, PERIODS, AND ISSUES IN DEVELOPMENT

Biological, Cognitive, and Socioemotional Processes

Periods of Development

The Significance of Age

Developmental Issues

- Three key developmental processes are biological, cognitive, and socioemotional. Development is influenced by an interplay of these processes.

- The life-span is commonly divided into these periods of development: prenatal, infancy, early childhood, middle and late childhood, adolescence, early adulthood, middle adulthood, and late adulthood. Increasingly, life-span developmentalists have described the human life span in terms of four ages with a special focus on the third age (about 60 to 79 years of age) and fourth age (about 80 years and older).

- According to some experts on life-span development, too much emphasis is placed on chronological age. An increasing number of studies have found that as adults get older they are happier. We often think of age only in terms of chronological age, but a full evaluation of age requires consideration of chronological, biological, psychological, and social age. Neugarten emphasizes that we are moving toward a society in which chronological age is only a weak predictor of development in adulthood.

- The nature-nurture issue focuses on the extent to which development is mainly influenced by nature (biological inheritance) or nurture (environmental experiences). The stability-change issue focuses on the degree to which we become older renditions of our early experience or develop into someone different from who we were earlier in development. A special aspect of the stability-change issue is the extent to which development is determined by early versus later experiences. Developmentalists describe development as continuous (gradual, a cumulative change) or as discontinuous (abrupt, a sequence of stages). Most developmentalists recognize that extreme positions on the nature-nurture, stability-change, and continuity-discontinuity issues are unwise. Despite this consensus, there is still spirited debate on these issues.

3   THEORIES OF DEVELOPMENT: DESCRIBE THE MAIN THEORIES OF HUMAN DEVELOPMENT

Psychoanalytic Theories

- A theory is an interrelated, coherent set of ideas that helps to explain phenomena and to make predictions. Hypotheses are specific assertions and predictions, often derived from theory, that can be tested. The scientific method involves four main steps: (1) conceptualize a problem, (2) collect data, (3) analyze data, and (4) draw conclusions. Theory is often involved in conceptualizing a problem. According to psychoanalytic theories, development primarily depends on the unconscious mind and is heavily couched in emotion. Freud also argued that individuals go through five psychosexual stages. Erikson's theory emphasizes eight psychosocial stages of development: trust versus mistrust, autonomy versus shame and doubt, initiative versus guilt, industry versus inferiority, identity versus identity confusion, intimacy versus isolation, generativity versus stagnation, and integrity versus despair. Contributions of psychoanalytic theories include an emphasis on a developmental framework, family relationships, and unconscious aspects of the mind. Criticisms include a lack of scientific support, too much emphasis on sexual underpinnings, and an image of people that is too negative.

Cognitive Theories

- Three main cognitive theories are Piaget's, Vygotsky's, and information-processing theory. Cognitive theories emphasize thinking, reasoning, language, and other cognitive processes. Piaget proposed a cognitive developmental theory in which children use their cognition to adapt to their world. In Piaget's theory, children go through four cognitive stages: sensorimotor, preoperational, concrete operational, and formal operational. Vygotsky's sociocultural cognitive theory emphasizes how culture and social interaction guide cognitive development. The information-processing approach emphasizes that individuals manipulate information, monitor it, and strategize about it. Contributions of cognitive theories include an emphasis on the active construction of understanding and a positive view of development. Criticisms include giving too little attention to individual variations and skepticism about the pureness of Piagetian stages.

Behavioral and Social Cognitive Theories

- Two main behavioral and social cognitive theories are Skinner's operant conditioning and Bandura's social cognitive theory. In Skinner's operant conditioning, the consequences of a behavior produce changes in the probability of the behavior's occurrence. In social cognitive theory, behavior, environment, and cognition are key factors in development. Bandura emphasizes reciprocal interactions among person/cognition, behavior, and environment. Contributions of the behavioral and social cognitive theories include an emphasis on scientific research and a focus on environmental determinants of behavior. Criticisms include inadequate attention to developmental changes and too little emphasis on cognition in Skinner's view.

Ethological Theory

- Ethology stresses that behavior is strongly influenced by biology, is tied to evolution, and is characterized by critical or sensitive periods. Contributions of ethological theory include a focus on the biological and evolutionary basis of development. Criticisms include a belief that the concepts of critical and sensitive periods may be too rigid.

Ecological Theory

- Ecological theory emphasizes environmental contexts. Bronfenbrenner's environmental systems view of development proposes five environmental systems: microsystem, mesosystem, exosystem, macrosystem, and chronosystem. Contributions of the theory include a systematic examination of macro- and microdimensions of environmental systems and attention to connections between environmental systems. Criticisms include giving inadequate attention to biological factors, as well as a lack of emphasis on cognitive factors.

An Eclectic Theoretical Orientation

- An eclectic orientation does not follow any one theoretical approach but rather selects from each theory whatever is considered the best in it.

4   RESEARCH IN LIFE-SPAN DEVELOPMENT: EXPLAIN HOW RESEARCH ON LIFE-SPAN DEVELOPMENT IS CONDUCTED

Methods for Collecting Data

- Methods for collecting data about life-span development include observation (in a laboratory or a naturalistic setting), survey (questionnaire) or interview, standardized test, case study, and physiological measures.

Research Designs

- Three main research designs are descriptive, correlational, and experimental. Descriptive research aims to observe and record behavior. The goal of correlational research is to describe the strength of the relationship between two or more events or characteristics. Experimental research involves conducting an experiment, which can determine cause and effect. An independent variable is the manipulated, influential, experimental factor. A dependent variable is a factor that can change in an experiment, in response to changes in the independent variable. Experiments can involve one or more experimental groups and control groups. In random assignment, researchers assign participants to experimental and control groups by chance.

Time Span of Research

- When researchers decide about the time span of their research, they can conduct cross-sectional or longitudinal studies. Life-span researchers are especially concerned about cohort effects.

Research Journals

- Research journals publish scholarly and academic information, usually in a specific domain, such as infancy, adolescence, or aging. An expanding number of research journals provide information about a wide range of topics on life-span development.

Conducting Ethical Research

- Researchers' ethical responsibilities include seeking participants' informed consent, ensuring their confidentiality, debriefing them about the purpose and potential personal consequences of participating, and avoiding unnecessary deception of participants.

Minimizing Bias

- Researchers need to guard against gender, cultural, and ethnic bias in research. Every effort should be made to make research equitable for both females and males. Individuals from varied ethnic backgrounds need to be included as participants in life-span research, and overgeneralization about diverse members within a group must be avoided.

KEY TERMS

development 6
life-span perspective 7
normative age-graded
    influences 8
normative history-graded
    influences 8
nonnormative life events 8
culture 10
cross-cultural studies 10
ethnicity 10
socioeconomic status
    (SES) 10

gender 10
social policy 11
biological processes 14
cognitive processes 14
socioemotional processes 14
nature-nurture issue 19
stability-change issue 19
continuity-discontinuity
    issue 20
theory 21
hypotheses 21
psychoanalytic theories 21

Erikson's theory 22
Piaget's theory 23
Vygotsky's theory 24
information-processing
    theory 24
social cognitive theory 25
ethology 26
Bronfenbrenner's ecological
    theory 27
eclectic theoretical
    orientation 28
laboratory 30

naturalistic observation 31
standardized test 31
case study 31
descriptive research 32
correlational research 32
correlation coefficient 32
experiment 33
cross-sectional approach 34
longitudinal approach 34
cohort effects 35
ethnic gloss 38

KEY PEOPLE

Paul Baltes 7
Marian Wright Edelman 11
Bernice Neugarten 18

Sigmund Freud 21
Erik Erikson 22
Jean Piaget 23

Lev Vygotsky 24
Robert Siegler 25
B. F. Skinner 25

Albert Bandura 25
Konrad Lorenz 26
Urie Bronfenbrenner 27

E-LEARNING TOOLS

Connect to **www.mhhe.com/santrockldt5e** to research the answers and complete these exercises. In addition, you'll find a number of other resources and valuable study tools for Chapter 1, "Introduction," on this Web site.

Taking It to the Net

1. You have been asked to prepare a document on the current structure of early childhood care in your state. Are the needs of the children in your state being met? What are the strengths and weaknesses of the current structure in your state?

2. Deanna wants to enroll her 7-year-old son, Victor, in clinical trials for attention deficit hyperactivity disorder treatment research. Victor's father is overseas on business for two months. Is it necessary that Victor's father consent to allow Victor to participate? Does the research group need Victor's approval before accepting him as a subject?

3. Carmen is completing her Ph.D. in clinical psychology. She is interested in geropsychology. What are some of the specialty areas in this field?

Self-Assessment

To evaluate yourself on topics related to this chapter, complete these self-assessments:

- *Evaluating My Interest in a Career in Life-Span Development*
- *Models and Mentors in My Life*

Health and Well-Being, Parenting, and Education

Build your decision-making skills by trying your hand at the health and well-being, parenting, and education exercises.

Video Clips

The Online Learning Center includes the following videos for this chapter:

- *Careers in Developmental Psychology*
- *Research Methods for Studying Infants*
- *Continuity and Change*

Appendix

Careers in Life-Span Development

The field of life-span development offers an amazing breadth of careers that can provide extremely satisfying work. College and university professors teach courses in many areas of life-span development. Teachers impart knowledge, understanding, and skills to children and adolescents. Counselors, clinical psychologists, nurses, and physicians help people of different ages to cope more effectively with their lives and improve their well-being.

These and many other careers related to life-span development offer numerous rewards. By working in the field of life-span development, you can help people to improve their lives, understand yourself and others better, possibly advance the state of knowledge in the field, and have an enjoyable time while you are doing these things. Many careers in life-span development pay reasonably well. For example, psychologists earn well above the median salary in the United States.

If you are considering a career in life-span development, would you prefer to work with infants? Children? Adolescents? Older adults? As you go through this term, try to spend some time with people of different ages. Observe their behavior. Talk with them about their lives. Think about whether you would like to work with people of this age in your life's work.

In addition, to find out about careers in life-span development, you might talk with people who work in various jobs. For example, if you have some interest in becoming a school counselor, call a school, ask to speak with a counselor, and set up an appointment to discuss the counselor's career and work. If you have an interest in becoming a nurse, call the nursing department at a hospital and set up an appointment to speak with the nursing coordinator about a nursing career.

Another way of exploring careers in life-span development is to work in a related job while you are in college. Many colleges and universities offer internships or other work experiences for students who major in specific fields. Course credit or pay is given for some of these jobs. Take advantage of these opportunities. They can help you decide if this is the right career for you, and they can help you get into graduate school, if you decide you want to go.

An advanced degree is not absolutely necessary for some careers in life-span development, but usually you can considerably expand your opportunities (and income) by obtaining a graduate degree. If you think you might want to go to graduate school, talk with one or more professors about your interests, keep a high grade-point average, take appropriate courses, and realize that you likely will need to take the Graduate Record Examination at some point.

Upcoming sections of the text will profile a number of careers in four areas: education/research; clinical/counseling; medical/nursing/physical development; and families/relationships. These are not the only career options in life-span development, but the profiles should give you an idea of the range of opportunities available. The profile for each career will describe the work and address the amount of education required and the nature of the training. The Web site for this book gives more detailed information about these careers in life-span development.

EDUCATION/RESEARCH

Numerous careers in life-span development involve education or research. The opportunities range from college professor to child-care director to school psychologist.

College/University Professor

Professors teach courses in life-span development at many types of institutions, including research universities with master's or Ph.D. programs in life-span development, four-year colleges with no graduate programs, and community colleges. The courses in life-span development are offered in many different programs and schools, including psychology, education, nursing, child and family studies, social work, and medicine. In addition to teaching at the undergraduate or graduate level (or both), professors may conduct research, advise students or direct their research, and serve on college or university committees. Research is part of a professor's job description at most universities with master's and Ph.D. programs, but some college professors do not conduct research and focus instead on teaching.

Teaching life-span development at a college or university almost always requires a Ph.D. or master's degree. Obtaining a Ph.D. usually takes four to six years of graduate work; a master's degree requires approximately two years. The training involves taking graduate courses, learning to conduct research, and attending and presenting papers at professional meetings. Many graduate students work as teaching or research assistants for professors in an apprenticeship relationship that helps them to become competent teachers and researchers.

Researcher

Some individuals in the field of life-span development work in research positions. They might work for a university, a government agency such as the National Institute of Mental Health, or private industry. They generate research ideas, plan studies, carry out the research, and usually attempt to publish the research in a scientific journal. A researcher often works

Careers in Life-Span Development

Valerie Pang, Professor of Teacher Education

Valerie Pang is a professor of teacher education of San Diego State University and formerly was an elementary school teacher. Like Dr. Pang, many professors of teacher education have a doctorate and have experience in teaching at the elementary or secondary school level.

Pang earned a doctorate at the University of Washington. She has received a Multicultural Educator Award from the National Association of Multicultural Education for her work on culture and equity; She also was given the Distinguished Scholar Award from the American Educational Research Association's Committee on the Role and Status of Minorities in Education.

Pang (2005) believes that competent teachers need to:

- Recognize the power and complexity of cultural influences on students.
- Be sensitive to whether their expectations for students are culturally biased.
- Evaluate whether they are doing a good job of seeing life from the perspective of students who come from different cultures.

Valerie Pang is a professor in the School of Education of San Diego State University and formerly an elementary school teacher. Valerie believes it is important for teachers to create a caring classroom that affirms all students.

in collaboration with other researchers. One researcher might spend much of his or her time in a laboratory; another researcher might work out in the field, such as in schools, hospitals, and so on. Most researchers in life-span development have either a master's degree or Ph.D.

Elementary or Secondary School Teacher

Elementary and secondary school teachers teach one or more subject areas, preparing the curriculum, giving tests, assigning grades, monitoring students' progress, conducting parent-teacher conferences, and attending workshops. Becoming an elementary or secondary school teacher requires a minimum of an undergraduate degree. The training involves taking a wide range of courses with a major or concentration in education as well as completing supervised practice teaching.

Exceptional Children (Special Education) Teacher

Teachers of exceptional children spend concentrated time with children who have a disability such as attention deficit hyperactivity disorder (ADHD), mental retardation, or cerebral palsy, or with children who are gifted. Usually some of their work occurs outside the students' regular classroom, and some of it inside the students' regular classroom. The exceptional children teacher works closely with the student's regular classroom teacher and parents to create the best educational

program for the student. Teachers of exceptional children often continue their education after obtaining their undergraduate degree and attain a master's degree.

Early Education Educator

Early childhood educators work on college faculties and usually teach in community colleges that award an associate degree in early childhood education. They have a minimum of a master's degree in their field. In graduate school, they take courses in early child education and receive supervisory training in child-care or early childhood programs.

Preschool/Kindergarten Teacher

Preschool teachers teach mainly 4-year-old children, and kindergarten teachers primarily teach 5-year-old children. They usually have an undergraduate degree in education, specializing in early childhood education. State certification to become a preschool or kindergarten teacher usually is required.

Family and Consumer Science Educator

Family and consumer science educators may specialize in early childhood education or instruct middle and high school students about such matters as nutrition, interpersonal relationships, human sexuality, parenting, and human development.

Hundreds of colleges and universities throughout the United States offer two- and four-year degree programs in family and consumer science. These programs usually require an internship. Additional education courses may be needed to obtain a teaching certificate. Some family and consumer educators go on to graduate school for further training, which provides a background for possible jobs in college teaching or research.

Educational Psychologist

Educational psychologists most often teach in a college or university and conduct research in such areas of educational psychology as learning, motivation, classroom management, and assessment. They help train students for positions in educational psychology, school psychology, and teaching. Most educational psychologists have a doctorate in education, which takes four to six years of graduate work.

School Psychologist

School psychologists focus on improving the psychological and intellectual well-being of elementary, middle/junior, and high school students. They give psychological tests, interview students and their parents, consult with teachers, and may provide counseling to students and their families. They may work in a centralized office in a school district or in one or more schools.

School psychologists usually have a master's or doctoral degree in school psychology. In graduate school, they take courses in counseling, assessment, learning, and other areas of education and psychology.

Gerontologist

Gerontologists usually work in research in some branch of the federal or state government. They specialize in the study of aging with a particular focus on government programs for older adults, social policy, and delivery of services to older adults. In their research, gerontologists define problems to be studied, collect data, interpret the results, and make recommendations for social policy. Most gerontologists have a master's or doctoral degree and have taken a concentration of coursework in adult development and aging.

CLINICAL/COUNSELING

A wide variety of clinical and counseling jobs are linked with life-span development. These range from child clinical psychologist to adolescent drug counselor to geriatric psychiatrist.

Clinical Psychologist

Clinical psychologists seek to help people with psychological problems. They work in a variety of settings, including colleges and universities, clinics, medical schools, and private practice.

Some clinical psychologists only conduct psychotherapy; others do psychological assessment and psychotherapy; some also do research. Clinical psychologists may specialize in a particular age group, such as children (child clinical psychologist) or older adults (often referred to as a geropsychologist).

Clinical psychologists have either a Ph.D. (which involves clinical and research training) or a Psy.D. degree (which only involves clinical training). This graduate training usually takes five to seven years and includes courses in clinical psychology and a one-year supervised internship in an accredited setting toward the end of the training. Many geropsychologists pursue a year or two of postdoctoral training. Most states require clinical psychologists to pass a test in order to become licensed in the state and to call themselves clinical psychologists.

Psychiatrist

Psychiatrists obtain a medical degree and then do a residency in psychiatry. Medical school takes approximately four years and the psychiatry residency another three to four years. Unlike most psychologists (who do not go to medical school), psychiatrists can administer drugs to clients. (Recently, several states have given clinical psychologists the right to prescribe drugs.)

Like clinical psychologists, psychiatrists might specialize in working with children (child psychiatry) or with older adults (geriatric psychiatry). Psychiatrists might work in medical schools in teaching and research roles, in medical clinics or hospitals, or in private practice. In addition to administering drugs to help improve the lives of people with psychological problems, psychiatrists also may conduct psychotherapy.

Counseling Psychologist

Counseling psychologists work in the same settings as clinical psychologists and may do psychotherapy, teach, or conduct research. Many counseling psychologists do not do therapy with individuals who have severe mental disorders, such as schizophrenia.

Counseling psychologists go through much the same training as clinical psychologists, although in a graduate program in counseling rather than clinical psychology. Counseling psychologists have either a master's degree or a doctoral degree. They also must go through a licensing procedure. One type of master's degree in counseling leads to the designation of licensed professional counselor.

School Counselor

School counselors help students to cope with adjustment problems, identify their abilities and interests, develop academic plans, and explore career options. The focus of the job depends on the age of the children. High school counselors advise students about vocational and technical training and admissions requirements for college, as well as about taking entrance exams, applying for financial aid, and choosing a major. Elementary school counselors mainly counsel students about social and personal problems. They may observe children in the classroom and at play as part of their work.

School counselors may work with students individually, in small groups, or even in a classroom. They often consult with parents, teachers, and school administrators when trying to help students. School counselors usually have a master's degree in counseling.

Career Counselor

Career counselors help individuals to identify their best career options and guide them in applying for jobs. They may work in private industry or at a college or university. They usually interview individuals and give them vocational and/or psychological tests to identify appropriate careers that fit their interests and abilities. Sometimes they help individuals to create resumes or conduct mock interviews to help them feel comfortable in a job interview. They might arrange and promote job fairs or other recruiting events to help individuals obtain jobs.

Rehabilitation Counselor

Rehabilitation counselors work with individuals to identify career options, develop adjustment and coping skills to maximize independence, and resolve problems created by a disability. A master's degree in rehabilitation counseling or guidance or counseling psychology is generally considered the minimum education requirement.

Social Worker

Many social workers are involved in helping people with social or economic problems. They may investigate, evaluate, and attempt to rectify reported cases of abuse, neglect, endangerment, or domestic disputes. They may intervene in families and provide counseling and referral services to individuals and families. Some social workers specialize in a certain area. For example, a medical social worker might coordinate support services to people with a long-term disability; family-care social workers often work with families with children or an older adult who needs support services. Social workers often work for publicly funded agencies at the city, state, or national level, although increasingly they work in the private sector in areas such as drug rehabilitation and family counseling.

Social workers have a minimum of an undergraduate degree from a school of social work that includes coursework in sociology and psychology. Some social workers also have a master's or doctoral degree. For example, medical social workers have a master's degree in social work (M.S.W.) and complete graduate coursework and supervised clinical experiences in medical settings.

Drug Counselor

Drug counselors provide counseling to individuals with drug-abuse problems. Some drug counselors specialize in working with adolescents or older adults. They may work on an individual basis with a substance abuser or conduct group therapy. They may work in private practice, with a state or federal government agency, with a company, or in a hospital.

At a minimum, drug counselors complete an associate's or certificate program. Many have an undergraduate degree in substance-abuse counseling, and some have master's and doctoral degrees. Most states provide a certification procedure for obtaining a license to practice drug counseling.

MEDICAL/NURSING/PHYSICAL DEVELOPMENT

This third main area of careers in life-span development includes a wide range of careers in the medical and nursing areas, as well as jobs pertaining to improving some aspect of a person's physical development.

Obstetrician/Gynecologist

An obstetrician/gynecologist prescribes prenatal and postnatal care, performs deliveries in maternity cases, and treats diseases and injuries of the female reproductive system. Becoming an obstetrician/gynecologist requires a medical degree plus three to five years of residency in obstetrics/gynecology. Obstetricians may work in private practice, a medical clinic, a hospital, or a medical school.

Pediatrician

A pediatrician monitors infants' and children's health, works to prevent disease or injury, helps children attain optimal health, and treats children with health problems. Pediatricians have earned a medical degree and completed a three- to five-year residency in pediatrics.

Pediatricians may work in private practice, a medical clinic, a hospital, or a medical school. Many pediatricians on the faculty of medical schools also teach and conduct research on children's health and diseases.

Geriatric Physician

Geriatric physicians diagnose medical problems of older adults, evaluate treatment options, and make recommendations for nursing care or other arrangements. They have a medical degree and specialized in geriatric medicine by doing a three- to five-year residency. Like other doctors, geriatric physicians may work in private practice, a medical clinic, a hospital, or a medical school. Those in medical school settings may not only treat older adults but also teach future physicians and conduct research.

Careers in Life-Span Development

Katherine Duchen Smith, Nurse and Child-Care Health Consultant

Katherine Duchen Smith has a master's degree in nursing and works as a child-care health consultant. She lives in Ft. Collins, Colorado, and in 2004 was appointed as the public relations chair of the National Association of Pediatric Nurse Practitioners (NAP-NAP), which has more than 6,000 members.

Smith provides health consultation and educational services to child-care centers, private schools, and hospitals. She also teaches in the Regis University Family Nurse Practitioner Program. Smith developed an interest in outreach and public-relations activities during her five-year term as a board member for the Fort Collins Poudre Valley Hospital System. Later, she became the organization's outreach consultant.

As child-care health consultants, nurses might provide telephone consultation and link children, families, or staff with primary care providers. In underserved areas, they might also be asked to administer immunizations, help chronically ill children access specialty care, or develop a comprehensive health promotion or injury prevention program for caregivers and families.

Katherine Duchen Smith (*left*), nurse and child-care health consultant, at a child-care center where she is a consultant.

Neonatal Nurse

Neonatal nurses deliver care to newborn infants. They may work with infants born under normal circumstances or premature and critically ill neonates. A minimum of an undergraduate degree in nursing with a specialization in the newborn is required. This training involves coursework in nursing and the biological sciences, as well as supervised clinical experiences.

Nurse-Midwife

A nurse-midwife formulates and provides comprehensive care to expectant mothers as they prepare to give birth, guides them through the birth process, and cares for them after the birth. The nurse-midwife also may provide care to the newborn, counsel parents on the infant's development and parenting, and provide guidance about health practices. Becoming a nurse-midwife generally requires an undergraduate degree from a school of nursing. A nurse-midwife most often works in a hospital setting.

Pediatric Nurse

Pediatric nurses monitor infants' and children's health, work to prevent disease or injury, and help children attain optimal health. They may work in hospitals, in schools of nursing, or with pediatricians in private practice or at a medical clinic.

Pediatric nurses have a degree in nursing that takes two to five years to complete. They take courses in biological sciences, nursing care, and pediatrics, usually in a school of nursing. They also undergo supervised clinical experiences in medical settings. Some pediatric nurses go on to earn a master's or doctoral degree in pediatric nursing.

Geriatric Nurse

Geriatric nurses seek to prevent or intervene in the chronic or acute health problems of older adults. They may work in hospitals, nursing homes, schools of nursing, or with geriatric medical specialists or psychiatrists in a medical clinic or in private practice.

Like pediatric nurses, geriatric nurses take courses in a school of nursing and obtain a degree in nursing, which takes from two to five years. They complete courses in biological sciences, nursing care, and mental health as well as supervised clinical training in geriatric settings. They also may obtain a master's or doctoral degree in their specialty.

Physical Therapist

Physical therapists work with individuals who have a physical problem due to disease or injury to help them function as competently as possible. They may consult with other professionals and coordinate services for the individual. Many physical therapists work with people of all ages, although some specialize in working with a specific age group, such as children or older adults.

Physical therapists usually have an undergraduate degree in physical therapy and are licensed by a state. They take courses and experience supervised training in physical therapy.

Occupational Therapist

Occupational therapists initiate the evaluation of clients with various impairments and manage their treatment. They help people regain, develop, and build skills that are important for independent functioning, health, well-being, security, and happiness.

An occupational therapist (OTR) may have an associate, bachelor's, master's, and/or doctoral degree with education ranging from two to six years. Training includes occupational therapy courses in a specialized program. National certification is required and licensing/registration is required in some states.

Therapeutic/Recreation Therapist

Therapeutic/recreation therapists maintain or improve the quality of life for people with special needs through intervention, leisure education, and recreation. They work in hospitals, rehabilitation centers, local government agencies, and at-risk youth programs, as well as other settings. Becoming a therapeutic/recreation therapist requires an undergraduate degree with coursework in leisure studies and a concentration in therapeutic recreation. National certification is usually required. Coursework in anatomy, special education, and psychology is beneficial.

Audiologist

Audiologists assess and identify the presence and severity of hearing loss, as well as problems in balance. They may work in a medical clinic, with a physician in private practice, in a hospital, or in a medical school.

An audiologist completes coursework and supervised training to earn a minimum of an undergraduate degree in hearing science. Some audiologists also go on to obtain a master's or doctoral degree.

Speech Therapist

Speech therapists identify, assess, and treat speech and language problems. They may work with physicians, psychologists, social workers, and other health-care professionals in a team approach to help individuals with physical or psychological problems that involve speech and language. Some speech therapists specialize in working with individuals of a particular age or people with a particular type of speech disorder.

Speech therapists have a minimum of an undergraduate degree in speech and hearing science or in a type of communi-

cations disorder. They may work in private practice, hospitals and medical schools, and government agencies.

Genetic Counselor

Genetic counselors identify and counsel families at risk for genetic disorders. They work as members of a health-care team, providing information and support to families who have members who have genetic defects or disorders or are at risk for a variety of inherited conditions. They also serve as educators and resource people for other health-care professionals and the public. Almost one-half work in university medical centers; one-fourth work in private hospital settings.

Genetic counselors have specialized graduate degrees and experience in medical genetics and counseling. Most enter the field after majoring in undergraduate school in such disciplines as biology, genetics, psychology, nursing, public health, or social work.

FAMILIES/RELATIONSHIPS

A number of careers and jobs related to life-span development focus on working with families and relationship problems. These range from home health aide to marriage and family therapist.

Home Health Aide

A home health aide provides services to older adults in the older adults' homes, helping them with basic self-care tasks. No higher education is required for this position. There is brief training by an agency.

Child Welfare Worker

Child protective services in each state employ child welfare workers. They protect children's rights, evaluate any maltreatment, and may have children removed from their homes if necessary. A child social worker has a minimum of an undergraduate degree in social work.

Child Life Specialist

Child life specialists work with children and their families when the child needs to be hospitalized. They monitor the child's activities, seek to reduce the child's stress, and help the child to cope and to enjoy the hospital experience as much as possible. Child life specialists may provide parent education and develop individualized treatment plans based on an assessment of the child's development, temperament, medical plan, and available social supports. Child life specialists have an undergraduate degree. They have taken courses in child development and education and usually completed additional courses in a child life program.

Marriage and Family Therapist

Marriage and family therapists work on the principle that many individuals who have psychological problems benefit when psychotherapy is provided in the context of a marital or family relationship. Marriage and family therapists may provide marital therapy, couple therapy to individuals in a relationship who are not married, and family therapy to two or more members of a family.

Marriage and family therapists have a master's or a doctoral degree. They complete a training program in graduate school similar to a clinical psychologist's but with the focus on marital and family relationships. In most states, it is necessary to go through a licensing procedure to practice marital and family therapy.

BIOLOGICAL PROCESSES, PHYSICAL DEVELOPMENT, AND HEALTH

*Babies are such a nice
way to start people.*

—Don Herold
American Writer, 20th Century

The rhythm and meaning of life involve biological foundations.

How, from so simple a beginning, can endless forms develop

and grow and mature? What was this organism, what is it and

what will it be? In Section 2, you will read and study four

chapters: "Biological Beginnings" (Chapter 2), "Physical

Development and Biological Aging" (Chapter 3), "Health"

(Chapter 4), and "Motor, Sensory, and Perceptual Development"

(Chapter 5).

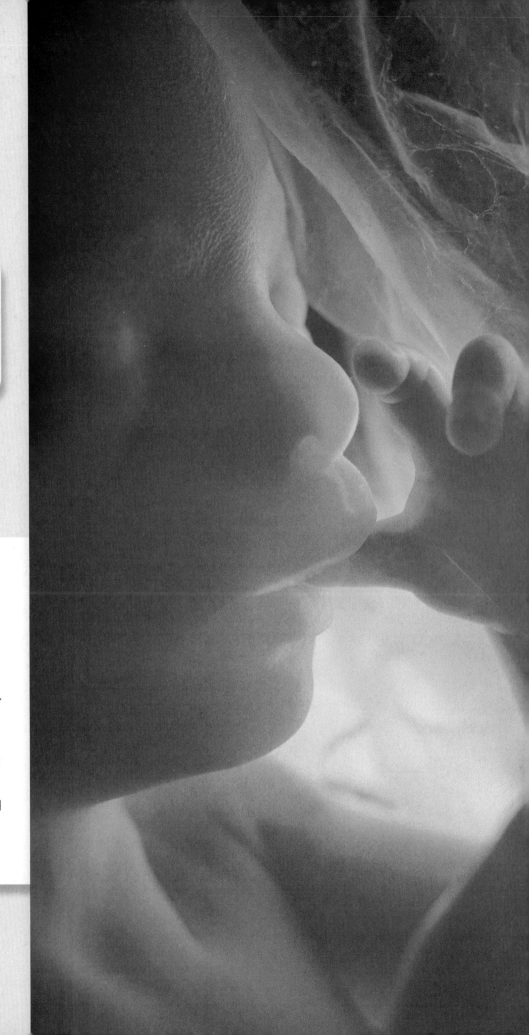

2

*There was a star
danced, and under
that I was born.*

—WILLIAM SHAKESPEARE
English Playwright, 17th Century

LEARNING GOALS

◆ Discuss the evolutionary
perspective on life-span
development.

◆ Describe what genes are and how
they influence human development.

◆ Explain some of the ways that
heredity and environment interact
to produce individual differences in
development.

◆ Characterize the course of prenatal
development and its hazards.

◆ Summarize how birth takes place.

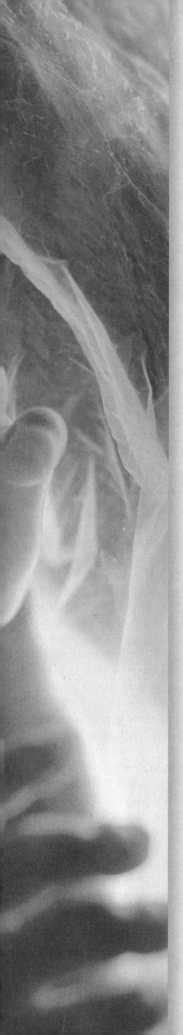

BIOLOGICAL BEGINNINGS

CHAPTER OUTLINE

1 THE EVOLUTIONARY PERSPECTIVE

Natural Selection and Adaptive Behavior

Evolutionary Psychology

2 GENETIC FOUNDATIONS OF DEVELOPMENT

The Collaborative Gene

Genes and Chromosomes

Genetic Principles

Chromosomal and Gene-Linked Abnormalities

3 HEREDITY AND ENVIRONMENT INTERACTION: THE NATURE-NURTURE DEBATE

Behavior Genetics

Heredity-Environment Correlations

Shared and Nonshared Environmental Influences

The Epigenetic View and Gene $\times$ Environment (G $\times$ E) Interaction

Conclusions About Heredity-Environment Interaction

4 PRENATAL DEVELOPMENT

The Course of Prenatal Development

Prenatal Diagnostic Tests

Hazards to Prenatal Development

Prenatal Care

5 BIRTH

The Birth Process

Assessing the Newborn

Low Birth Weight and Preterm Infants

Bonding

PREVIEW

Organisms are not like billiard balls, moved by simple external forces to predictable positions on life's table. Environmental experiences and biological foundations work together to make us who we are. In this chapter, we explore life's biological beginnings and experiences, charting growth from conception through the prenatal period and examining the birth process itself. We will begin our exploration of biological foundations by exploring possible evolutionary influences.

1 THE EVOLUTIONARY PERSPECTIVE

Natural Selection and Adaptive Behavior

Evolutionary Psychology

In evolutionary time, humans are relative newcomers to earth. As our earliest ancestors left the forest to feed on the savannahs, and then to form hunting societies on the open plains, their minds and behaviors changed, and they eventually established humans as the dominant species on earth. How did this evolution come about?

Natural Selection and Adaptive Behavior

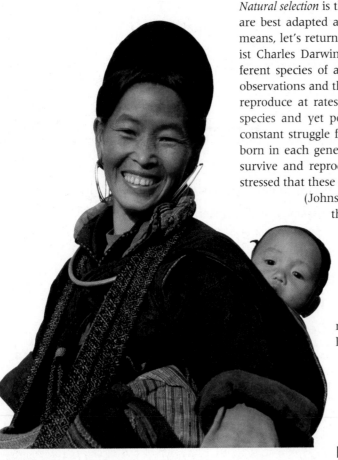

Natural selection is the evolutionary process by which those individuals of a species that are best adapted are the ones that survive and reproduce. To understand what this means, let's return to the middle of the nineteenth century, when the British naturalist Charles Darwin (1809–1892) was sailing around the world, observing many different species of animals in their natural surroundings. Darwin, who published his observations and thoughts in *On the Origin of Species* (1859), noted that most organisms reproduce at rates that would cause enormous increases in the population of most species and yet populations remain nearly constant. He reasoned that an intense, constant struggle for food, water, and resources must occur among the many young born in each generation, because many of the young do not survive. Those that do survive and reproduce pass on their characteristics to the next generation. Darwin stressed that these survivors are better *adapted* to their world than are the nonsurvivors (Johnson & Losos, 2010). The best-adapted individuals survive to leave the most offspring. Over the course of many generations, organisms with the characteristics needed for survival make up an increased percentage of the population. Over many, many generations, this could produce a gradual modification of the whole population.

If environmental conditions change, however, other characteristics might become favored by natural selection, moving the species in a different direction (Mader, 2010). All organisms must adapt to particular places, climates, food sources, and ways of life. An eagle's claws are a physical adaptation that facilitates predation. *Adaptive behavior* is behavior that promotes an organism's survival in the natural habitat (Enger, Ross, & Bailey, 2009). For example, attachment between a caregiver and a baby ensures the infant's closeness to a caregiver for feeding and protection from danger, thus increasing the infant's chances of survival.

Evolutionary Psychology

Although Darwin introduced the theory of evolution by natural selection in 1859, his ideas only recently have become a popular framework for

How does the attachment of this Vietnamese baby to its mother reflect the evolutionary process of adaptive behavior?

explaining behavior. Psychology's newest approach, **evolutionary psychology,** emphasizes the importance of adaptation, reproduction, and "survival of the fittest" in shaping behavior. "Fit" in this sense refers to the ability to bear offspring that survive long enough to bear offspring of their own. In this view, natural selection favors behaviors that increase reproductive success, the ability to pass your genes to the next generation (Bjorklund, 2007).

David Buss (1995, 2004, 2008) has been especially influential in stimulating new interest in how evolution can explain human behavior. He notes that just as evolution shapes our physical features, such as body shape and height, it also pervasively influences how we make decisions, how aggressive we are, what are our fears, and our mating patterns. For example, assume that our ancestors were hunters and gatherers on the plains and that men did most of the hunting and women stayed close to home gathering seeds and plants for food. If you have to travel some distance from your home in an effort to find and slay a fleeing animal, you need not only certain physical traits but also the ability for certain types of spatial thinking. Men born with these traits would be more likely than men without them to survive, to bring home lots of food, and to be considered attractive mates—and thus to reproduce and pass on these characteristics to their children. In other words, these traits would provide a reproductive advantage for males and, over many generations, men with good spatial thinking skills might become more numerous in the population. Critics point out that this scenario might or might not have actually happened.

Evolutionary Developmental Psychology   Recently, interest has grown in using the concepts of evolutionary psychology to understand human development (Greve & Bjorklund, 2009). Following are some ideas proposed by evolutionary developmental psychologists (Bjorklund & Pellegrini, 2002).

An extended childhood period evolved because humans require time to develop a large brain and learn the complexity of human societies. Humans take longer to become reproductively mature than any other mammal (see Figure 2.1). During this extended childhood period, they develop a large brain and the experiences needed to become competent adults in a complex society.

Many evolved psychological mechanisms are domain-specific. That is, the mechanisms apply only to a specific aspect of a person's makeup. According to evolutionary psychology, information processing is one example. In this view, the mind is not a general-purpose device that can be applied equally to a vast array of problems. Instead, as our ancestors dealt with certain recurring problems such as hunting for food and finding shelter, specialized modules evolved that process information related to those problems—for example, a module for physical knowledge for tracking animals, a module for mathematical knowledge for trading, and a module for language.

Evolved mechanisms are not always adaptive in contemporary society. Some behaviors that were adaptive for our prehistoric ancestors may not serve us well today. For example, the food-scarce environment of our ancestors likely led to humans' propensity to gorge when food is available and to crave high-calorie foods, a trait that might lead to an epidemic of obesity when food is plentiful. Critics of evolutionary psychology argue that the concept of evolved mechanisms cannot be tested scientifically.

Evolution and Life-Span Development   In evolutionary theory, what matters is that individuals live long enough to reproduce and pass on their characteristics (Brooker, 2009). So why do humans live so long after reproduction? Perhaps evolution favored longevity because having older people around improves the survival rates of babies. Possibly having grandparents alive to care for the young while parents were out hunting and gathering food created an evolutionary advantage.

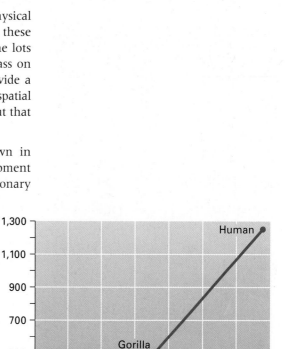

FIGURE 2.1 The Brain Sizes of Various Primates and Humans in Relation to the Length of the Childhood Period. Compared with other primates, humans have both a larger brain and a longer childhood period. *What conclusions can you draw from this graph?*

evolutionary psychology Emphasizes the importance of adaptation, reproduction, and "survival of the fittest" in shaping behavior.

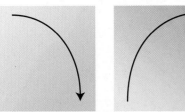

Evolutionary selection benefits decrease with age

Need for culture increases with age

Life span

Life span

FIGURE 2.2 Baltes' View of Evolution and Culture Across the Life Span.

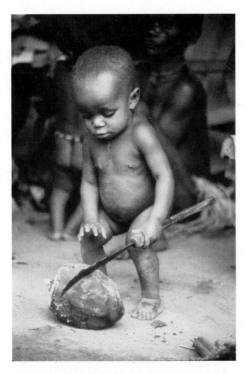

Children in all cultures are interested in the tools that adults in their cultures use. For example, this 11-month-old boy from the Efe culture in the Democratic Republic of the Congo in Africa is trying to cut a papaya with an *apopau* (a smaller version of a machete). *Might the infant's behavior be evolutionary-based or be due to both biological and environmental conditions?*

chromosomes Threadlike structures made up of deoxyribonucleic acid, or DNA.

DNA A complex molecule that contains genetic information and has a double helix shape.

genes Units of hereditary information composed of DNA. Genes direct cells to reproduce themselves and assemble proteins that direct body processes.

According to life-span developmentalist Paul Baltes (2003), the benefits conferred by evolutionary selection decrease with age. Natural selection has not weeded out many harmful conditions and nonadaptive characteristics that appear among older adults. Why? Natural selection operates primarily on characteristics that are tied to reproductive fitness, which extends through the earlier part of adulthood. Thus, says Baltes, selection primarily operates during the first half of life.

As an example, consider Alzheimer disease, an irreversible brain disorder characterized by gradual deterioration. This disease typically does not appear until age 70 or later. If it were a disease that struck 20-year-olds, perhaps natural selection would have eliminated it eons ago.

Thus, unaided by evolutionary pressures against nonadaptive conditions, we suffer the aches, pains, and infirmities of aging. And, as the benefits of evolutionary selection decrease with age, argues Baltes, the need for culture increases (see Figure 2.2). That is, as older adults weaken biologically, they need culture-based resources such as cognitive skills, literacy, medical technology, and social support. For example, older adults may need help and training from other people to maintain their cognitive skills (Park & Reuter-Lorenz, 2009).

Evaluating Evolutionary Psychology Although the popular press gives a lot of attention to the ideas of evolutionary psychology, it remains just one theoretical approach. Like the theories described in Chapter 1, "Introduction," it has limitations, weaknesses, and critics. Common criticisms are that much of evolutionary psychology cannot be tested scientifically and that it relies mainly on post-hoc (after the fact) explanations.

Another criticism was offered by Albert Bandura (1998), whose social cognitive theory was described in Chapter 1, "Introduction." He acknowledges the influence of evolution on human adaptation but rejects what he calls "one-sided evolutionism," which views social behavior as the product of evolved biology. An alternative is a *bidirectional* view, in which environmental and biological conditions influence each other. In this view, evolutionary pressures created changes in biological structures that allowed the use of tools, which enabled our ancestors to manipulate the environment, constructing new environmental conditions. In turn, environmental innovations produced new selection pressures that led to the evolution of specialized biological systems for consciousness, thought, and language.

In other words, evolution has given us body structures and biological potentialities but it does not dictate behavior. People have used their biological capacities to produce diverse cultures—aggressive and pacific, egalitarian, and autocratic.

Review and Reflect: Learning Goal 1

 Discuss the evolutionary perspective on life-span development

REVIEW

- How can natural selection and adaptive behavior be defined?
- What is evolutionary psychology? What basic ideas about human development are proposed by evolutionary psychologists? How might evolutionary influences have different effects at different points in the life span? How can evolutionary psychology be evaluated?

REFLECT

- Which is more persuasive to you: the views of evolutionary psychologists or their critics? Why?

2 GENETIC FOUNDATIONS OF DEVELOPMENT

- **The Collaborative Gene**
- **Genetic Principles**
- **Genes and Chromosomes**
- **Chromosomal and Gene-Linked Abnormalities**

How are characteristics that suit a species for survival transmitted from one generation to the next? Darwin did not know because genes and the principles of genetics had not yet been discovered. Each of us carries a "genetic code" that we inherited from our parents. Because a fertilized egg carries this human code, a fertilized human egg cannot grow into an egret, eagle, or elephant.

The Collaborative Gene

Each of us began life as a single cell weighing about one twenty-millionth of an ounce! This tiny piece of matter housed our entire genetic code—instructions that orchestrated growth from that single cell to a person made of trillions of cells, each containing a replica of the original code. That code is carried by our genes (Hyde, 2009). What are genes and what do they do? For the answer, we need to look into our cells.

The nucleus of each human cell contains **chromosomes**, which are threadlike structures made up of deoxyribonucleic acid, or DNA. **DNA** is a complex molecule that has a double helix shape, like a spiral staircase, and it contains genetic information. **Genes,** the units of hereditary information, are short segments of DNA, as you can see in Figure 2.3. They direct cells to reproduce themselves and to assemble proteins. Proteins, in turn, are the building blocks of cells as well as the regulators that direct the body's processes (Akey, 2009; Hoefnagels, 2009).

Each gene has its own location, its own designated place on a particular chromosome. Today, there is a great deal of enthusiasm about efforts to discover the specific locations of genes that are linked to certain functions and to certain diseases (Brooker, 2009; Hyde, 2009). An important step in this direction was accomplished when the Human Genome Project and the Celera Corporation completed a preliminary map of the human *genome*—the complete set of developmental instructions for creating proteins that initiate the making of a human organism (Antonarkis, 2009).

One of the big surprises of the Human Genome Project was a report indicating that humans have only about 30,000 genes (U.S. Department of Energy, 2001). More recently, the number of human genes has been revised further downward to approximately 20,500 (Ensemble Human, 2008). Scientists had thought that humans had as many as 100,000 or more genes. They had also maintained that each gene programmed just one protein. In fact, because humans appear to have far more proteins than they have genes, there cannot be a one-to-one correspondence between genes and proteins (Commoner, 2002). Each gene is not translated, in automaton-like fashion, into one and only one protein. A gene does not act independently, as developmental psychologist David Moore (2001) emphasized by titling his book *The Dependent Gene.*

A positive result from the Human Genome Project. Shortly after Andrew Gobea was born, his cells were genetically altered to prevent his immune system from failing.

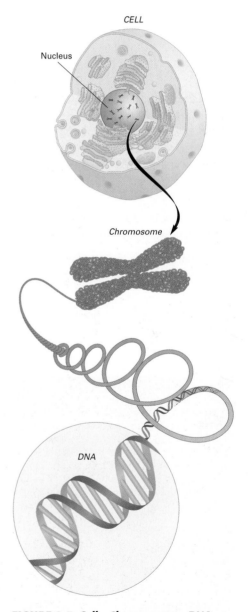

FIGURE 2.3 Cells, Chromosomes, DNA, and Genes. (*Top*) The body contains trillions of cells. Each cell contains a central structure, the nucleus. (*Middle*) Chromosomes are threadlike structures located in the nucleus of the cell. Chromosomes are composed of DNA. (*Bottom*) DNA has the structure of a spiral staircase. A gene is a segment of DNA.

Rather than being a group of independent genes, the human genome consists of many genes that collaborate both with each other and with nongenetic factors inside and outside the body. The collaboration operates at many points. For example, the cellular machinery mixes, matches, and links small pieces of DNA to reproduce the genes, and that machinery is influenced by what is going on around it.

Whether a gene is turned "on," working to assemble proteins, is also a matter of collaboration. The activity of genes (*genetic expression*) is affected by their environment (Gottlieb, 2007). For example, hormones that circulate in the blood make their way into the cell where they can turn genes "on" and "off." And the flow of hormones can be affected by environmental conditions, such as light, day length, nutrition, and behavior. Numerous studies have shown that external events outside of the original cell and the person, as well as events inside the cell, can excite or inhibit gene expression (Gottlieb, 2007). For example, one recent study revealed that an increase in the concentration of stress hormones such as cortisol produced a fivefold increase in DNA damage (Flint & others, 2007).

In short, a single gene is rarely the source of a protein's genetic information, much less of an inherited trait (Gottlieb, Wahlsten, & Lickliter, 2006). Rather than being a group of independent genes, the human genome consists of many genes that collaborate both with each other and with nongenetic factors inside and outside the body.

Genes and Chromosomes

Genes are not only collaborative, they are enduring. How do genes manage to get passed from generation to generation and end up in all of the trillion cells in the body? Three processes explain the heart of the story: mitosis, meiosis, and fertilization.

Mitosis, Meiosis, and Fertilization   All cells in your body, except the sperm and egg, have 46 chromosomes arranged in 23 pairs. These cells reproduce by a process called **mitosis.** During mitosis, the cell's nucleus—including the chromosomes—duplicates itself and the cell divides. Two new cells are formed, each containing the same DNA as the original cell, arranged in the same 23 pairs of chromosomes.

However, a different type of cell division—**meiosis**—forms eggs and sperm (or *gametes*). During meiosis, a cell of the testes (in men) or ovaries (in women) duplicates its chromosomes but then divides *twice*, thus forming four cells, each of which has only half of the genetic material of the parent cell (Mader, 2010). By the end of meiosis, each egg or sperm has 23 *unpaired* chromosomes.

During **fertilization,** an egg and a sperm fuse to create a single cell, called a **zygote** (see Figure 2.4). In the zygote, the 23 unpaired chromosomes from the egg and the 23 unpaired chromosomes from the sperm combine to form one set of 23 paired chromosomes—one chromosome of each pair from the mother's egg and the other from the father's sperm. In this manner, each parent contributes half of the offspring's genetic material.

Figure 2.5 shows 23 paired chromosomes of a male and a female. The members of each pair of chromosomes are both similar and different: Each chromosome in the pair contains varying forms of the same genes, at the same location on the chromosome. A gene for hair color, for example, is located on both members of one pair of chromosomes, in the same location on each. However, one of those chromosomes might carry the gene for blond hair; the other chromosome in the pair might carry the gene for brown hair.

Do you notice any obvious differences between the chromosomes of the male and the chromosomes of the female in Figure 2.5? The

mitosis Cellular reproduction in which the cell's nucleus duplicates itself; two new cells are formed, each containing the same DNA as the original cell, arranged in the same 23 pairs of chromosomes.

meiosis A specialized form of cell division that occurs to form eggs and sperm (or gametes).

fertilization A stage in reproduction whereby an egg and a sperm fuse to create a single cell, called a zygote.

zygote A single cell formed through fertilization.

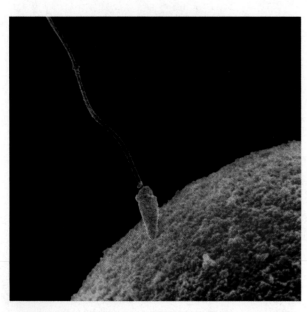

FIGURE 2.4 A Single Sperm Penetrating an Egg at the Point of Fertilization.

difference lies in the 23rd pair. Ordinarily, in females this pair consists of two chromosomes called *X chromosomes*; in males the 23rd pair consists of an X and a *Y chromosome*. The presence of a Y chromosome is what makes an individual male.

Sources of Variability Combining the genes of two parents in offspring increases genetic variability in the population, which is valuable for a species because it provides more characteristics for natural selection to operate on (Hyde, 2009; Mader, 2010). In fact, the human genetic process creates several important sources of variability.

First, the chromosomes in the zygote are not exact copies of those in the mother's ovaries and the father's testes. During the formation of the sperm and egg in meiosis, the members of each pair of chromosomes are separated, but which chromosome in the pair goes to the gamete is a matter of chance. In addition, before the pairs separate, pieces of the two chromosomes in each pair are exchanged, creating a new combination of genes on each chromosome. Thus, when chromosomes from the mother's egg and the father's sperm are brought together in the zygote, the result is a truly unique combination of genes (Starr, Evers, & Starr 2010).

If each zygote is unique, how do identical twins exist? *Identical twins* (also called monozygotic twins) develop from a single zygote that splits into two genetically identical replicas, each of which becomes a person. *Fraternal twins* (called dizygotic twins) develop from separate eggs and separate sperm, making them genetically no more similar than ordinary siblings.

Another source of variability comes from DNA (Cummings, 2009). Chance, a mistake by cellular machinery, or damage from an environmental agent such as radiation may produce a *mutated gene,* which is a permanently altered segment of DNA (Enger, Ross, & Bailey, 2009).

Even when their genes are identical, however, people vary. The difference between genotypes and phenotypes helps us to understand this source of variability. All of a person's genetic material makes up his or her **genotype.** However, not all of the genetic material is apparent in our observed and measurable characteristics. A **phenotype** consists of observable characteristics. Phenotypes include physical characteristics (such as height, weight, and hair color) and psychological characteristics (such as personality and intelligence).

For each genotype, a range of phenotypes can be expressed, providing another source of variability (Gottlieb, 2007). An individual can inherit the genetic potential to grow very large, for example, but good nutrition, among other things, will be essential to achieving that potential.

Genetic Principles

What determines how a genotype is expressed to create a particular phenotype? Much is unknown about the answer to this question (Hartwell, 2008; Talaro, 2008).

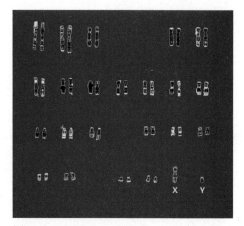

(a)

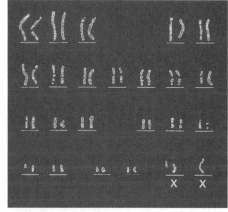

(b)

FIGURE 2.5 The Genetic Difference Between Males and Females. Set (*a*) shows the chromosome structure of a male, and set (*b*) shows the chromosome structure of a female. The last pair of 23 pairs of chromosomes is in the bottom right box of each set. Notice that the Y chromosome of the male is smaller than the X chromosome of the female. To obtain this kind of chromosomal picture, a cell is removed from a person's body, usually from the inside of the mouth. The chromosomes are stained by chemical treatment, magnified extensively, and then photographed.

Calvin and Hobbes   by Bill Watterson

genotype All of a person's actual genetic material.

phenotype Observable and measurable characteristics such as height, hair color, and intelligence.

However, a number of genetic principles have been discovered, among them those of dominant-recessive genes, sex-linked genes, genetic imprinting, and polygenically determined characteristics.

Dominant-Recessive Genes Principle   In some cases, one gene of a pair always exerts its effects; it is *dominant*, overriding the potential influence of the other gene, called the *recessive* gene. This is the *dominant-recessive genes principle*. A recessive gene exerts its influence only if the two genes of a pair are both recessive. If you inherit a recessive gene for a trait from each of your parents, you will show the trait. If you inherit a recessive gene from only one parent, you may never know you carry the gene. Brown hair, farsightedness, and dimples rule over blond hair, nearsightedness, and freckles in the world of dominant-recessive genes.

Can two brown-haired parents have a blond-haired child? Yes, they can. Suppose that each parent has a dominant gene for brown hair and a recessive gene for blond hair. Since dominant genes override recessive genes, the parents have brown hair, but both are carriers of blondness and pass on their recessive genes for blond hair. With no dominant gene to override them, the recessive genes can make the child's hair blond.

Sex-Linked Genes   Most mutated genes are recessive. When a mutated gene is carried on the X chromosome, the result is called *X-linked inheritance*. It may have very different implications for males than for females (Peterson, Wang, & Willems, 2008). Remember that males have only one X chromosome. Thus, if there is an altered, disease-creating gene on the X chromosome, males have no "backup" copy to counter the harmful gene and therefore may carry an X-linked disease. However, females have a second X chromosome, which is likely to be unchanged. As a result, they are not likely to have the X-linked disease. Thus, most individuals who have X-linked diseases are males. Females who have one changed copy of the X gene are known as "carriers," and they usually do not show any signs of the X-linked disease. Hemophilia and fragile X syndrome, which we discuss later in the chapter, are examples of X-linked inheritance diseases (Pierce & other, 2007).

Genetic Imprinting   *Genetic imprinting* occurs when the expression of a gene has different effects depending on whether the mother or the father passed on the gene (Horsthemke & Buiting, 2008). A chemical process "silences" one member of the gene pair. For example, as a result of imprinting, only the maternally derived copy of the expressed gene might be active, while the paternally derived copy of the same expressed gene is silenced—or vice versa. Only a small percentage of human genes appear to undergo imprinting, but it is a normal and important aspect of development (Hampton, 2008). When imprinting goes awry, development is disturbed, as in the case of Beckwith-Wiedemann syndrome, a growth disorder, and Wilms tumor, a type of cancer (Gropman & Adams, 2007).

Polygenic Inheritance   Genetic transmission is usually more complex than the simple example we have examined thus far (Hartwell, 2008). Few characteristics reflect the influence of only a single gene or pair of genes. Most are determined by the interaction of many different genes; they are said to be *polygenically determined*. Even a simple characteristic such as height, for example, reflects the interaction of many genes, as well as the influence of the environment.

The term *gene-gene interaction* is increasingly used to describe studies that focus on the interdependence of two or more genes in influencing characteristics, behavior, diseases, and development (Li & others, 2008). For example, recent studies have documented gene-gene interaction in cancer (Chen & others, 2009) and cardiovascular disease (Jylhava & others, 2009).

Chromosomal and Gene-Linked Abnormalities

Sometimes, abnormalities characterize the genetic process. Some of these abnormalities involve whole chromosomes that do not separate properly during meiosis. Other abnormalities are produced by harmful genes.

Chromosomal Abnormalities Sometimes, when a gamete is formed, the sperm or ovum does not have its normal set of 23 chromosomes. The most notable examples involve Down syndrome and abnormalities of the sex chromosomes (see Figure 2.6).

Down Syndrome An individual with **Down syndrome** has a round face, a flattened skull, an extra fold of skin over the eyelids, a protruding tongue, short limbs, and retardation of motor and mental abilities (Fidler, 2008). The syndrome is caused by the presence of an extra copy of chromosome 21 (Visootsak & Sherman, 2007). It is not known why the extra chromosome is present, but the health of the male sperm or female ovum may be involved (Hodapp & Dykens, 2006).

Down syndrome appears approximately once in every 700 live births. Women between the ages of 16 and 34 are less likely to give birth to a child with Down syndrome than are younger or older women. African American children are rarely born with Down syndrome.

Sex-Linked Chromosomal Abnormalities Recall that a newborn normally has either an X and a Y chromosome, or two X chromosomes. Human embryos must possess at least one X chromosome to be viable. The most common sex-linked chromosomal abnormalities involve the presence of an extra chromosome (either an X or Y) or the absence of one X chromosome in females.

Klinefelter syndrome is a chromosomal disorder in which males have an extra X chromosome, making them XXY instead of XY. Males with this disorder have undeveloped testes, and they usually have enlarged breasts and become tall (Bojesen & Gravholt, 2007). A recent study revealed significant impairment in language, academic, attentional, and motor abilities in boys with the syndrome (Ross & others, 2008). Klinefelter syndrome occurs approximately once in every 800 live male births.

Fragile X syndrome is a chromosomal disorder that results from an abnormality in the X chromosome, which becomes constricted and often breaks. Mental

These athletes, many of whom have Down syndrome, are participating in a Special Olympics competition. Notice the distinctive facial features of the individuals with Down syndrome, such as a round face and a flattened skull. *What causes Down syndrome?*

Down syndrome A chromosomally transmitted form of mental retardation, caused by the presence of an extra copy of chromosome 21.

Klinefelter syndrome A chromosomal disorder in which males have an extra X chromosome, making them XXY instead of XY.

fragile X syndrome A chromosomal disorder involving an abnormality in the X chromosome, which becomes constricted and often breaks.

Name	Description	Treatment	Incidence
Down syndrome	An extra chromosome causes mild to severe retardation and physical abnormalities.	Surgery, early intervention, infant stimulation, and special learning programs	1 in 1,900 births at age 20 1 in 300 births at age 35 1 in 30 births at age 45
Klinefelter syndrome	An extra X chromosome causes physical abnormalities.	Hormone therapy can be effective	1 in 800 males
Fragile X syndrome	An abnormality in the X chromosome can cause mental retardation, learning disabilities, or short attention span.	Special education, speech and language therapy	More common in males than in females
Turner syndrome	A missing X chromosome in females can cause mental retardation and sexual underdevelopment.	Hormone therapy in childhood and puberty	1 in 2,500 female births
XYY syndrome	An extra Y chromosome can cause above-average height.	No special treatment required	1 in 1,000 male births

FIGURE 2.6 Some Chromosomal Abnormalities. *Note:* Treatment does not necessarily erase the problem but may improve the individual's adaptive behavior and quality of life.

A boy with fragile X syndrome.

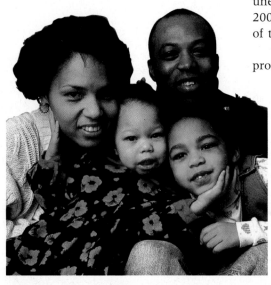

During a physical examination for a college football tryout, Jerry Hubbard, 32, learned that he carried the gene for sickle-cell anemia. Daughter Sara is healthy, but daughter Avery (in the print dress) has sickle-cell anemia. *If you were a genetic counselor, would you recommend that this family have more children? Explain.*

Turner syndrome A chromosomal disorder in females in which either an X chromosome is missing, making the person XO instead of XX, or part of one X chromosome is deleted.

XYY syndrome A chromosomal disorder in which males have an extra Y chromosome.

deficiency frequently is an outcome, but it may take the form of mental retardation, a learning disability, or a short attention span. A recent study revealed that boys with fragile X syndrome were characterized by cognitive deficits in inhibition, memory, and planning (Hooper & others, 2008). This disorder occurs more frequently in males than in females, possibly because the second X chromosome in females negates the effects of the other abnormal X chromosome (Ono, Farzin, & Hagerman, 2008).

Turner syndrome is a chromosomal disorder in females in which either an X chromosome is missing, making the person XO instead of XX, or part of one X chromosome is deleted. Females with Turner syndrome are short in stature and have a webbed neck. They might be infertile and have difficulty in mathematics, but their verbal ability is often quite good (Murphy & Mazzocco, 2008) Turner syndrome occurs in approximately 1 of every 2,500 live female births.

The **XYY syndrome** is a chromosomal disorder in which the male has an extra Y chromosome (Isen & Baker, 2008). Early interest in this syndrome focused on the belief that the extra Y chromosome found in some males contributed to aggression and violence. However, researchers subsequently found that XYY males are no more likely to commit crimes than are XY males (Witkin & others, 1976).

Gene-Linked Abnormalities Abnormalities can be produced not only by an uneven number of chromosomes, but also by harmful genes (Presson & Jenner, 2008). More than 7,000 such genetic disorders have been identified, although most of them are rare.

Phenylketonuria (PKU) is a genetic disorder in which the individual cannot properly metabolize phenylalanine, an amino acid. It results from a recessive gene and occurs about once in every 10,000 to 20,000 live births. Today, phenylketonuria is easily detected, and it is treated by a diet that prevents an excess accumulation of phenylalanine. If phenylketonuria is left untreated, however, excess phenylalanine builds up in the child, producing mental retardation and hyperactivity. Phenylketonuria accounts for approximately 1 percent of institutionalized individuals who are mentally retarded, and it occurs primarily in non-Latino Whites.

The story of phenylketonuria has important implications for the nature-nurture issue. Although phenylketonuria is a genetic disorder (nature), how or whether a gene's influence in phenylketonuria is played out depend on environmental influences since the disorder can be treated (nurture) (Ney & others, 2008). That is, the presence of a genetic defect *does not* inevitably lead to the development of the disorder *if* the individual develops in the right environment (one free of phenylalanine).

Sickle-cell anemia, which occurs most often in African Americans, is a genetic disorder that impairs the body's red blood cells. Red blood cells carry oxygen to the body's cells and are usually shaped like a disk. In sickle-cell anemia, a recessive gene causes the red blood cell to become a hook-shaped "sickle" that cannot carry oxygen properly and dies quickly. As a result, the body's cells do not receive adequate oxygen, causing anemia and often early death (King, DeBraun, & White, 2008). About 1 in 400 African American babies is affected by sickle-cell anemia. One in 10 African Americans is a carrier, as is 1 in 20 Latin Americans. A National Institutes of Health (2008) panel recently concluded that the only FDA-approved drug to treat sickle-cell anemia in adolescents and adults—hydroxyurea—has been underutilized. Research is currently being conducted in a study named Baby HUG to determine if the drug works with babies.

Other diseases that result from genetic abnormalities include cystic fibrosis, diabetes, hemophilia, Huntington disease, spina bifida, and Tay-Sachs disease (Dunn & others, 2008). Figure 2.7 provides further information about these diseases. Someday,

Name	Description	Treatment	Incidence
Cystic fibrosis	Glandular dysfunction that interferes with mucus production; breathing and digestion are hampered, resulting in a shortened life span.	Physical and oxygen therapy, synthetic enzymes, and antibiotics; most individuals live to middle age.	1 in 2,000 births
Diabetes	Body does not produce enough insulin, which causes abnormal metabolism of sugar.	Early onset can be fatal unless treated with insulin.	1 in 2,500 births
Hemophilia	Delayed blood clotting causes internal and external bleeding.	Blood transfusions/injections can reduce or prevent damage due to internal bleeding.	1 in 10,000 males
Huntington disease	Central nervous system deteriorates, producing problems in muscle coordination and mental deterioration.	Doesn't usually appear until age 35 or older; death likely 10 to 20 years after symptoms appear.	1 in 20,000 births
Phenylketonuria (PKU)	Metabolic disorder that, left untreated, causes mental retardation.	Special diet can result in average intelligence and normal life span.	1 in 14,000 births
Sickle-cell anemia	Blood disorder that limits the body's oxygen supply; it can cause joint swelling, as well as heart and kidney failure.	Penicillin, medication for pain, antibiotics, and blood transfusions.	1 in 400 African American children (lower among other groups)
Spina bifida	Neural tube disorder that causes brain and spine abnormalities.	Corrective surgery at birth, orthopedic devices, and physical/medical therapy.	2 in 1,000 births
Tay-Sachs disease	Deceleration of mental and physical development caused by an accumulation of lipids in the nervous system.	Medication and special diet are used, but death is likely by 5 years of age.	One in 30 American Jews is a carrier.

FIGURE 2.7 Some Gene-Linked Abnormalities.

scientists may identify why these and other genetic abnormalities occur and discover how to cure them.

Dealing with Genetic Abnormalities   Every individual carries DNA variations that might predispose the person to serious physical disease or mental disorder. But not all individuals who carry a genetic disorder display the disorder. Other genes or developmental events sometimes compensate for genetic abnormalities (Gottlieb, 2007). For example, recall the earlier example of phenylketonuria—even though individuals might carry the genetic disorder of phenylketonuria, it is not expressed when phenylalanine is replaced by other nutrients in their diet.

Thus, genes are not destiny, but genes that are missing, nonfunctional, or mutated can be associated with disorders (Gaff, Williams, & McInerney, 2008). Identifying such genetic flaws could enable doctors to predict an individual's risks, recommend healthy practices, and prescribe the safest and most effective drugs (Blaine & others, 2008).

However, this knowledge might bring important costs as well as benefits. Who would have access to a person's genetic profile? An individual's ability to land and hold jobs or obtain insurance might be threatened if it is known that a person is considered at risk for some disease. For example, should an airline pilot or a neurosurgeon who is predisposed to develop a disorder that makes one's hands shake be required to leave that job early?

Genetic counselors, usually physicians or biologists who are well versed in the field of medical genetics, understand the kinds of problems just described, the odds of encountering them, and helpful strategies for offseting some of their effects (Sivell & others, 2008). To read about the career and work of a genetic counselor, see the *Careers in Life-Span Development* profile.

phenylketonuria (PKU) A genetic disorder in which an individual cannot properly metabolize phenylalanine, an amino acid; PKU is now easily detected—but, if left untreated, results in mental retardation and hyperactivity.

sickle-cell anemia A genetic disorder that affects the red blood cells and occurs most often in African Americans.

Careers in Life-Span Development

Holly Ishmael, Genetic Counselor

Holly Ishmael is a genetic counselor at Children's Mercy Hospital in
Kansas City. She obtained an undergraduate degree in psychology
from Sarah Lawrence College and then a master's degree in genetic
counseling from the same college. She uses many of the principles
discussed in this chapter in her genetic counseling work.

Ishmael says, "Genetic counseling is a perfect combination
for people who want to do something science-oriented, but need
human contact and don't want to spend all of their time in a lab or
have their nose in a book" (Rizzo, 1999, p. 3).

There are approximately thirty graduate genetic counseling
programs in the United States. If you are interested in this profession, you can obtain further information from the National Society
of Genetic Counselors at www.nsgc.org.

Holly Ishmael (*left*) in a genetic counseling session.

Review and Reflect: Learning Goal 2

2 **Describe what genes are and how they influence human development**

REVIEW
- What are genes?
- How are genes passed on?
- What basic principles describe how genes interact?
- What are some chromosomal and gene-linked abnormalities?

REFLECT
- What possible ethical issues regarding genetics and development might arise in the future?

---

3 HEREDITY AND ENVIRONMENT INTERACTION: THE NATURE-NURTURE DEBATE

Behavior Genetics

Shared and Nonshared Environmental Influences

Conclusions About Heredity-Environment Interaction

Heredity-Environment Correlations

The Epigenetic View and Gene × Environment (G × E) Interaction

Is it possible to untangle the influence of heredity from that of environment and
discover the role of each in producing individual differences in development? When
heredity and environment interact, how does heredity influence the environment,
and vice versa?

Behavior Genetics

Behavior genetics is the field that seeks to discover the influence of heredity and environment on individual differences in human traits and development (Kandler, Rieman, & Kampfe, 2009). Note that behavior geneticists do not determine the extent to which genetics or the environment affects an individual's traits. Instead, they try to figure out what is responsible for the differences among people—that is, to what extent do people differ because of differences in genes, environment, or a combination of these? To study the influence of heredity on behavior, behavior geneticists often use either twins or adoption situations (Goldsmith, 2008; Mustelin & others, 2009).

In the most common **twin study,** the behavioral similarity of identical twins (who are genetically identical) is compared with the behavioral similarity of fraternal twins. Recall that although fraternal twins share the same womb, they are no more genetically alike than brothers or sisters. Thus, by comparing groups of identical and fraternal twins, behavior geneticists capitalize on the basic knowledge that identical twins are more similar genetically than are fraternal twins (Isen & others, 2009; Wood & others, 2008). For example, one study found that conduct problems were more prevalent in identical twins than in fraternal twins; the researchers concluded that the study demonstrated an important role for heredity in conduct problems (Scourfield & others, 2004).

However, several issues complicate interpretation of twin studies. For example, perhaps the environments of identical twins are more similar than the environments of fraternal twins. Adults might stress the similarities of identical twins more than those of fraternal twins, and identical twins might perceive themselves as a "set" and play together more than fraternal twins do. If so, the influence of the environment on the observed similarities between identical and fraternal twins might be very significant.

In an **adoption study,** investigators seek to discover whether the behavior and psychological characteristics of adopted children are more like those of their adoptive parents, who have provided a home environment, or more like those of their biological parents, who have contributed their heredity (Loehlin, Horn, & Ernst, 2007). Another form of the adoption study compares adoptive and biological siblings.

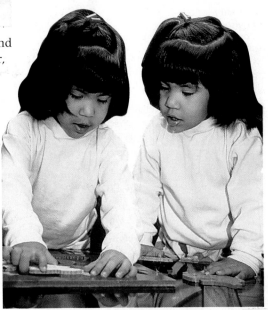

Twin studies compare identical twins with fraternal twins. Identical twins develop from a single fertilized egg that splits into two genetically identical organisms. Fraternal twins develop from separate eggs, making them genetically no more similar than nontwin siblings. *What is the nature of the twin study method?*

Monozygotic - one egg

Dizygotic -

Heredity-Environment Correlations   Backdoor

The difficulties that researchers encounter when they interpret the results of twin studies and adoption studies reflect the complexities of heredity-environment interaction. Some of these interactions are *heredity-environment correlations*—that is, individuals' genes may influence the types of environments to which they are exposed. In a sense, individuals "inherit" environments that may be related or linked to genetic "propensities" (Plomin, DeFries, & Fulker, 2007). Behavior geneticist Sandra Scarr (1993) described three ways that heredity and environment are correlated (see Figure 2.8):   Backdoor

- **Passive genotype-environment correlations** occur because biological parents, who are genetically related to the child, provide a rearing environment for the child. For example, the parents might have a genetic predisposition to be intelligent and read skillfully. Because they read well and enjoy reading, they provide their children with books to read. The likely outcome is that their children, given their own inherited predispositions from their parents and their book-filled environment, will become skilled readers.

- **Evocative genotype-environment correlations** occur because a child's characteristics elicit certain types of environments. For example, active, smiling children receive more social stimulation than passive, quiet children do. Cooperative, attentive children evoke more pleasant and instructional responses from the adults around them than uncooperative, distractible children do.

behavior genetics The field that seeks to discover the influence of heredity and environment on individual differences in human traits and development.

twin study A study in which the behavioral similarity of identical twins is compared with the behavioral similarity of fraternal twins.

adoption study A study in which investigators seek to discover whether, in behavior and psychological characteristics, adopted children are more like their adoptive parents, who provided a home environment, or more like their biological parents, who contributed their heredity. Another form of the adoption study is to compare adoptive and biological siblings.

passive genotype-environment correlations Correlations that exist when the biological parents, who are genetically related to the child, provide a rearing environment for the child.

evocative genotype-environment correlations Correlations that exist when the child's characteristics elicit certain types of environments.

Heredity-Environment Correlation	Description	Examples
Passive	Children inherit genetic tendencies from their parents and parents also provide an environment that matches their own genetic tendencies.	Musically inclined parents usually have musically inclined children and they are likely to provide an environment rich in music for their children.
Evocative	The child's genetic tendencies elicit stimulation from the environment that supports a particular trait. Thus genes evoke environmental support.	A happy, outgoing child elicits smiles and friendly responses from others.
Active (niche-picking)	Children actively seek out "niches" in their environment that reflect their own interests and talents and are thus in accord with their genotype.	Libraries, sports fields, and a store with musical instruments are examples of environmental niches children might seek out if they have intellectual interests in books, talent in sports, or musical talents, respectively.

FIGURE 2.8 Exploring Heredity-Environment Correlations.

- **Active (niche-picking) genotype-environment correlations** occur when children seek out environments that they find compatible and stimulating. *Niche-picking* refers to finding a setting that is suited to one's abilities. Children select from their surrounding environment some aspects that they respond to, learn about, or ignore. Their active selections of environments are related to their particular genotype. For example, outgoing children tend to seek out social contexts in which to interact with people, whereas shy children don't. Children who are musically inclined are likely to select musical environments in which they can successfully perform their skills. How these "tendencies" come about is discussed shortly under the topic of the epigenetic view.

Scarr notes that the relative importance of the three genotype-environment correlations changes as children develop from infancy through adolescence. In infancy, much of the environment that children experience is provided by adults. Thus, passive genotype-environment correlations are more common in the lives of infants and young children than they are for older children and adolescents who can extend their experiences beyond the family's influence and create their environments to a greater degree.

Notice that this analysis gives the preeminent role in development to heredity: The analysis describes how heredity may influence the types of environments that children experience. Critics argue that the concept of heredity-environment correlation gives heredity too much of a one-sided influence in determining development because it does not consider the role of prior environmental influences in shaping the correlation itself (Gottlieb, 2007). Before considering this criticism and a different view of the heredity-environment linkage, let's take a closer look at how behavior geneticists analyze the environments involved in heredity-environment interaction.

Shared and Nonshared Environmental Influences

Behavior geneticists have argued that to understand the environment's role in differences between people, we should distinguish between shared and nonshared environments (Kirkpatrick, McGue, & Iacono, 2009). That is, we should consider experiences that children share in common with other children living in the same home, and experiences that are not shared (Ozaki & Ando, 2009; Wardle & others, 2008).

Shared environmental experiences are siblings' common experiences, such as their parents' personalities or intellectual orientation, the family's socioeconomic status, and the neighborhood in which they live. By contrast, **nonshared environmental experiences** are a child's unique experiences, both within the family and outside the family, that are not shared with a sibling. For example, siblings often have different peer groups, different friends, and different teachers at school.

Behavior geneticist Robert Plomin (2004) has found that shared environment accounts for little of the variation in children's personality or interests. In other words, even though two children live under the same roof with the same parents,

active (niche-picking) genotype-environment correlations Correlations that exist when children seek out environments they find compatible and stimulating.

shared environmental experiences Siblings' common experiences, such as their parents' personalities or intellectual orientation, the family's socioeconomic status, and the neighborhood in which they live.

nonshared environmental experiences The child's own unique experiences, both within the family and outside the family, that are not shared by another sibling; thus, experiences occurring within the family can be part of the "nonshared environment."

their personalities are often very different. Further, Plomin argues that heredity influences the nonshared environments of siblings through the heredity-environment correlations we described earlier. For example, a child who has inherited a genetic tendency to be athletic is likely to spend more time in environments related to sports, whereas a child who has inherited a tendency to be musically inclined is more likely to spend time in environments related to music.

The Epigenetic View and Gene × Environment (G × E) Interaction

Critics argue that the concept of heredity-environment correlation gives heredity too much of a one-sided influence in determining development because it does not consider the role of prior environmental influences in shaping the correlation itself (Gottlieb, 2007). However, earlier in the chapter we discussed how genes are collaborative, not determining an individual's traits in an independent manner, but rather in an interactive manner with the environment.

The Epigenetic View   In line with the concept of a collaborative gene, Gilbert Gottlieb (2007) emphasizes the **epigenetic view,** which states that development is the result of an ongoing, bidirectional interchange between heredity and the environment. Figure 2.9 compares the heredity-environment correlation and epigenetic views of development.

Let's look at an example that reflects the epigenetic view. A baby inherits genes from both parents at conception. During prenatal development, toxins, nutrition, and stress can influence some genes to stop functioning, while others become stronger or weaker. During infancy, the same environmental experiences such as toxins, nutrition, stress, learning, and encouragement continue to modify genetic activity and the activity of the nervous system that directly underlies behavior. Heredity and environment operate together—or collaborate—to produce a person's intelligence, temperament, height, weight, ability to pitch a baseball, ability to read, and so on (Gottlieb, 2007).

Gene × Environment (G × E) Interaction   An increasing number of studies are exploring how the interaction of heredity and environment influence development, including interactions that involve specific DNA sequences (Barry, Kochanska, & Philibert, 2008; Diamond, 2009; Nilsson & others, 2009; Pauli-Pott & others, 2009; Shen, 2009). One research study found that individuals who have a short version of a genotype labeled *5-HTTLPR* (a gene involving the neurotransmitter serotonin) have an elevated risk of developing depression only if they also have stressful lives (Caspi & others, 2003). Thus, the specific gene did not link directly to the development of depression, but rather interacted with environmental exposure to stress to predict whether individuals would develop depression. In a recent study, adults who experienced parental loss as young children were more likely to have unresolved attachment as adults only when they had the short version of the *5-HTTLPR* gene (Caspers & others, 2009). The long version of the serotonin transporter gene apparently provided some protection and ability to cope better with parental loss. And another recent study revealed that a secure attachment relationship in infancy was a protective factor for the development of self-regulation in early childhood for children at risk because they have the short version of the *5-HTTLPR* gene (Kochanska, Philibert, & Barry, 2009).

The type of research just described is referred to as **gene × environment (G × E) interaction**—the interaction of a specific measured variation in DNA and a specific measured aspect of the environment (Diamond, 2009; Moffitt, Caspi, & Rutter, 2006). The field of *pharmacogenetics* is the study of gene-environment interaction involving the individual's genotype and drug treatment (the environment factor) (Cheok & others, 2009). The goal of many pharmacogenetic studies is to discover if certain drugs are safer or more dangerous to use if the individual's genotype is known (Berlin, Paul, & Vesell, 2009; Lima & others, 2009).

Tennis stars Venus and Serena Williams. *What might be some shared and nonshared environmental experiences they had while they were growing up that contributed to their tennis stardom?*

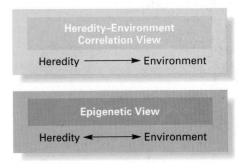

FIGURE 2.9 Comparison of the Heredity-Environment Correlation and Epigenetic Views of Development.

epigenetic view   Perspective that emphasizes that development is the result of an ongoing, bidirectional interchange between heredity and environment.

gene × environment (G × E) interaction   The interaction of a specific measured variation in the DNA and a specific measured aspect of the environment.

Conclusions About Heredity-Environment Interaction

*T*he interaction of heredity and environment is so extensive that to ask which is more important, nature or nurture, is like asking which is more important to a rectangle, height or width.

—WILLIAM GREENOUGH
Contemporary Developmental Psychologist, University of Illinois at Urbana

If an attractive, popular, intelligent girl is elected president of her senior class in high school, is her success due to heredity or to environment? Of course, the answer is both.

The relative contributions of heredity and environment are not additive. That is, we can't say that such-and-such a percentage of nature and such-and-such a percentage of experience make us who we are. Nor is it accurate to say that full genetic expression happens once, around conception or birth, after which we carry our genetic legacy into the world to see how far it takes us. Genes produce proteins throughout the life span, in many different environments. Or they don't produce these proteins, depending in part on how harsh or nourishing those environments are.

The emerging view is that complex behaviors have some *genetic loading* that gives people a propensity for a particular developmental trajectory (Guo & Tillman, 2009; Petrill & others, 2009; Plomin & others, 2009). However, the actual development requires more: an environment. And that environment is complex, as is the mixture of genes we inherit (Thompson, 2009a). Environmental influences range from the things we lump together under "nurture" (such as parenting, family dynamics, schooling, and neighborhood quality) to biological encounters (such as viruses, birth complications, and even biological events in cells).

If heredity and environment interact to determine the course of development, is that all there is to answering the question of what causes development? Are children completely at the mercy of their genes and environment as they develop? Their genetic heritage and environmental experiences are pervasive influences on their development. But in thinking about what causes development, it is important to think about development as the co-construction of biology, culture, *and* the individual child. Children not only are the outcomes of their heredity and the environment they experience, but they also can author a unique developmental path by changing the environment. As one psychologist recently concluded:

> In reality, we are both the creatures and creators of our worlds. We are . . . the products of our genes and environments. Nevertheless, . . . the stream of causation that shapes the future runs through our present choices. . . . Mind matters. . . . Our hopes, goals, and expectations influence our future. (Myers, 2010, p. 168)

Review and Reflect: Learning Goal 3

 Explain some of the ways that heredity and environment interact to produce individual differences in development

REVIEW

- What is behavior genetics?
- What are three types of heredity-environment correlations?
- What is meant by the concepts of shared and nonshared environmental experiences?
- What is the epigenetic view of development?
- What conclusions can be reached about heredity-environment interaction?

REFLECT

- Someone tells you that she has analyzed her genetic background and environmental experiences and reached the conclusion that environment definitely has had little influence on her intelligence. What would you say to this person about her ability to make this self-diagnosis?

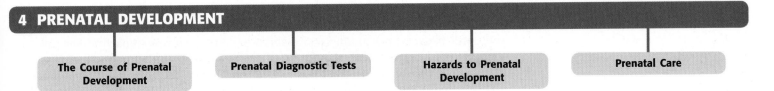

4 PRENATAL DEVELOPMENT

- The Course of Prenatal Development
- Prenatal Diagnostic Tests
- Hazards to Prenatal Development
- Prenatal Care

Conception occurs when a single sperm cell from the male unites with an ovum (egg) in the female's fallopian tube in a process called fertilization. Over the next few months, the genetic code discussed earlier directs a series of changes in the fertilized egg, but many events and hazards will influence how that egg develops and becomes a person.

The Course of Prenatal Development

Prenatal development lasts approximately 266 days, beginning with fertilization and ending with birth. It can be divided into three periods: germinal, embryonic, and fetal. An especially important and fascinating aspect of the prenatal period is the development of the brain.

The Germinal Period The **germinal period** is the period of prenatal development that takes place in the first two weeks after conception. It includes the creation of the fertilized egg, called a zygote, cell division, and the attachment of the zygote to the uterine wall.

Rapid cell division by the zygote begins the germinal period (recall from earlier in the chapter that this cell division occurs through a process called *mitosis*). By approximately one week after conception, the differentiation of these cells—their specialization for different tasks—has already begun. At this stage, the group of cells, now called the *blastocyst*, consists of an inner mass of cells that will eventually develop into the embryo and the *trophoblast*, an outer layer of cells that later provides nutrition and support for the embryo. *Implantation*, the attachment of the zygote to the uterine wall, takes place about 10 to 14 days after conception.

The Embryonic Period The **embryonic period** is the period of prenatal development that occurs from two to eight weeks after conception. During the embryonic period, the rate of cell differentiation intensifies, support systems for cells form, and organs begin to appear.

This period begins as the blastocyst attaches to the uterine wall. The mass of cells is now called an *embryo*, and three layers of cells form. The embryo's *endoderm* is the inner layer of cells, which will develop into the digestive and respiratory systems. The *ectoderm* is the outermost layer, which will become the nervous system, sensory receptors (ears, nose, and eyes, for example), and skin parts (hair and nails, for example). The *mesoderm* is the middle layer, which will become the circulatory system, bones, muscles, excretory system, and reproductive system. Every body part eventually develops from these three layers. The endoderm primarily produces internal body parts, the mesoderm primarily produces parts that surround the internal areas, and the ectoderm primarily produces surface parts.

As the embryo's three layers form, life-support systems for the embryo develop rapidly. These life-support systems include the amnion, the umbilical cord (both of which develop from the fertilized egg, not the mother's body), and the placenta. The amnion is like a bag or an envelope and contains a clear fluid in which the developing embryo floats. The amniotic fluid provides an environment that is temperature and humidity controlled, as well as shockproof. The *umbilical cord* contains two arteries and one vein, and it connects the baby to the placenta. The *placenta* consists of a disk-shaped group of tissues in which small blood vessels from the mother and the offspring intertwine but do not join.

> *The history of man for nine months preceding his birth would, probably, be far more interesting, and contain events of greater moment than all three score and ten years that follow it.*
>
> —SAMUEL TAYLOR COLERIDGE
> *English Poet, Essayist, 19th Century*

germinal period The period of prenatal development that takes place in the first two weeks after conception; it includes the creation of the zygote, continued cell division, and the attachment of the zygote to the wall of the uterus.

embryonic period The period of prenatal development that occurs from two to eight weeks after conception. During the embryonic period, the rate of cell differentiation intensifies, support systems for the cells form, and organs appear.

Very small molecules—oxygen, water, salt, food from the mother's blood, as well as carbon dioxide and digestive wastes from the offspring's blood—pass back and forth between the mother and embryo or fetus. Large molecules cannot pass through the placental wall; these include red blood cells and harmful substances, such as most bacteria, maternal wastes, and hormones. The complex mechanisms that govern the transfer of substances across the placental barrier are still not entirely understood (Cetin & Alvino, 2009).

By the time most women know they are pregnant, the major organs have begun to form. **Organogenesis** is the name given to the process of organ formation during the first two months of prenatal development. While they are being formed, the organs are especially vulnerable to environmental changes (Mullis & Tonella, 2008).

The Fetal Period The **fetal period** is the prenatal period of development that begins two months after conception and lasts for seven months, on the average. Growth and development continue their dramatic course during this time.

Three months after conception, the fetus is about 3 inches long and weighs about 3 ounces. It has become active, moving its arms and legs, opening and closing its mouth, and moving its head. The face, forehead, eyelids, nose, and chin are distinguishable, as are the upper arms, lower arms, hands, and lower limbs. The genitals can be identified as male or female. By the end of the fourth month, the fetus has grown to 6 inches in length and weighs 4 to 7 ounces. For the first time, the mother can feel arm and leg movements.

By the end of the fifth month, the fetus is about 12 inches long and weighs close to a pound. Structures of the skin have formed—toenails and fingernails, for example. By the end of the sixth month, the eyes and eyelids are completely formed, and a fine layer of hair covers the head. A grasping reflex is present and irregular breathing movements occur.

As early as six months of pregnancy (about 24 to 25 weeks after conception), the fetus for the first time has a chance of surviving outside the womb—that is, it is *viable*. Infants born earlier than about 32 weeks of pregnancy usually need help breathing because their lungs are not yet fully mature. By the end of the seventh month, the fetus is about 16 inches long and now weighs about 3 pounds.

During the last two months of prenatal development, fatty tissues develop, and the functioning of various organ systems—heart and kidneys, for example—steps up. During the eighth and ninth months, the fetus grows longer and gains substantial weight—about another 4 pounds. At birth, the average American baby weighs 7½ pounds and is about 20 inches long.

An overview of some of the main developments we have discussed and some more specific changes in prenatal development are presented in Figure 2.10. In addition to describing prenatal development in terms of germinal, embryonic, and fetal periods, it also can be divided into equal periods of three months, called *trimesters*. Remember that the three trimesters are not the same as the three prenatal periods we have discussed. The germinal and embryonic periods occur in the first trimester. The fetal period begins toward the end of the first trimester and continues through the second and third trimesters. Viability (the chances of surviving outside the womb) occurs at the beginning of the third trimester.

The Brain One of the most remarkable aspects of the prenatal period is the development of the brain (Fair & Schlaggar, 2008; Nelson, 2009). By the time babies are born, they have approximately 100 billion **neurons,** or nerve cells, which handle information processing at the cellular level. During prenatal development, neurons spend time moving to the right locations and are starting to become connected. The basic architecture of the human brain is assembled during the first two trimesters of prenatal development. The third trimester of prenatal development and the first two years of postnatal life are characterized by connectivity and functioning of neurons (Moulson & Nelson, 2008).

organogenesis Process of organ formation that takes place during the first two months of prenatal development.

fetal period The prenatal period of development that begins two months after conception and lasts for seven months, on average.

neurons Nerve cells that handle information processing at the cellular level.

	First trimester (first 3 months)		
Prenatal growth	**Conception to 4 weeks** • Is less than 1/10 inch long • Beginning development of spinal cord, nervous system, gastrointestinal system, heart, and lungs • Amniotic sac envelopes the preliminary tissues of entire body • Is called a "zygote"	**8 weeks** • Slightly more than 1 inch long • Face is forming with rudimentary eyes, ears, mouth, and tooth buds • Arms and legs are moving • Brain is forming • Fetal heartbeat is detectable with ultrasound • Is called an "embryo"	**12 weeks** • Is about 3 inches long and weighs about 1 ounce • Can move arms, legs, fingers, and toes • Fingerprints are present • Can smile, frown, suck, and swallow • Sex is distinguishable • Can urinate • Is called a "fetus"	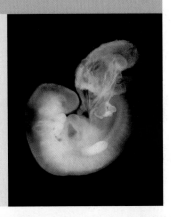

	Second trimester (middle 3 months)		
Prenatal growth	**16 weeks** • Is about 5½ inches long and weighs about 4 ounces • Heartbeat is strong • Skin is thin, transparent • Downy hair (lanugo) covers body • Fingernails and toenails are forming • Has coordinated movements; is able to roll over in amniotic fluid	**20 weeks** • Is 10 to 12 inches long and weighs ½ to 1 pound • Heartbeat is audible with ordinary stethoscope • Sucks thumb • Hiccups • Hair, eyelashes, eyebrows are present	**24 weeks** • Is 11 to 14 inches long and weighs 1 to 1½ pounds • Skin is wrinkled and covered with protective coating (vernix caseosa) • Eyes are open • Waste matter is collected in bowel • Has strong grip	

	Third trimester (last 3 months)		
Prenatal growth	**28 weeks** • Is 14 to 17 inches long and weighs 2½ to 3 pounds • Is adding body fat • Is very active • Rudimentary breathing movements are present	**32 weeks** • Is 16½ to 18 inches long and weighs 4 to 5 pounds • Has periods of sleep and wakefulness • Responds to sounds • May assume the birth position • Bones of head are soft and flexible • Iron is being stored in liver	**36 to 38 weeks** • Is 19 inches long and weighs 6 pounds • Skin is less wrinkled • Vernix caseosa is thick • Lanugo is mostly gone • Is less active • Is gaining immunities from mother	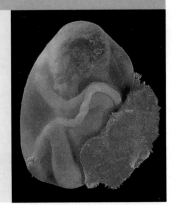

FIGURE 2.10 The Three Trimesters of Prenatal Development.

As the human embryo develops inside its mother's womb, the nervous system begins forming as a long, hollow tube located on the embryo's back. This pear-shaped *neural tube*, which forms at about 18 to 24 days after conception, develops out of the ectoderm. The tube closes at the top and bottom ends at about 24 days after conception. Figure 2.11 shows that the nervous system still has a tubular appearance six weeks after conception.

Two birth defects related to a failure of the neural tube to close are anencephaly and spina bifida. The highest regions of the brain fail to develop when fetuses have anencephaly, and they die in the womb, during childbirth, or shortly after birth

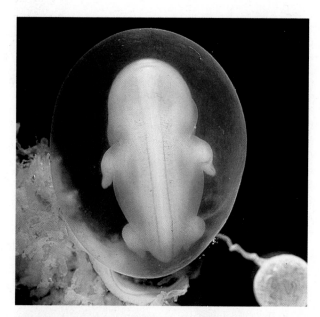

FIGURE 2.11 Early Formation of the Nervous System.
The photograph shows the primitive, tubular appearance of the nervous system at six weeks in the human embryo.

These individuals are members of the Spina Bifida Association of Greater New Orleans. The association is made up of parents, family members, children, and adults with spina bifida, and health professionals who provide care for individuals born with spina bifida and their families.

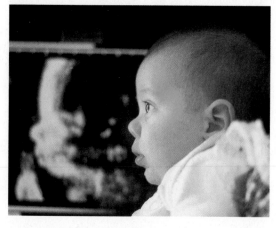

A 6-month-old infant poses with the ultrasound sonography record taken four months into the baby's prenatal development. *What is ultrasound sonography?*

(Levene & Chervenak, 2009). Spina bifida results in varying degrees of paralysis of the lower limbs. Individuals with spina bifida usually need assistive devices such as crutches, braces, or wheelchairs. A strategy that can help to prevent neural tube defects is that women take adequate amounts of the B vitamin folic acid, a topic we discuss later in the chapter (Bell & Oakley, 2009; Johnston, 2008).

In a normal pregnancy, once the neural tube has closed, a massive proliferation of new immature neurons begins to takes place about the fifth prenatal week and continues throughout the remainder of the prenatal period. The generation of new neurons is called *neurogenesis*. At the peak of neurogenesis, it is estimated that as many as 200,000 neurons are being generated every minute (Brown, Keynes, & Lumsden, 2001).

At approximately 6 to 24 weeks after conception, *neuronal migration* occurs (Moulson & Nelson, 2008). During this stage, cells move outward from their point of origin to their appropriate locations and create the different levels, structures, and regions of the brain (Kuriyama & Mayor, 2009). Once a cell has migrated to its target destination, it must mature and develop a more complex structure.

About the 23rd prenatal week, connections between neurons begin to occur, a process that continues postnatally (Nelson, 2009). Chapter 3, "Physical Development and Biological Aging," presents details about the complex structure of neurons, their connectivity, and the development of the brain from infancy through late adulthood.

Prenatal Diagnostic Tests

One choice open to prospective parents is whether or not to have prenatal testing done. A number of tests can indicate whether a fetus is developing normally, including ultrasound sonography, fetal MRI, chorionic villus sampling, amniocentesis, maternal blood screening, and noninvasive prenatal diagnosis (NIPD).

An ultrasound test is often conducted seven weeks into a pregnancy and at various times later in pregnancy. *Ultrasound sonography* is a prenatal medical procedure in which high-frequency sound waves are directed into the pregnant woman's abdomen. The echo from the sounds is transformed into a visual representation of the fetus' inner structures. This technique can detect many structural abnormalities in the fetus, including microencephaly, a form of mental retardation involving an abnormally small brain; it can also determine the number of fetuses and give clues to the baby's sex (Gerards & others, 2008).

The development of brain-imaging techniques has led to increasing use of *fetal MRI* to diagnose fetal malformations (Garel, 2008; Obenauer & Maestre, 2008) (see Figure 2.12). MRI, or magnetic resonance imaging, uses a powerful magnet and radio images to generate detailed images of the body's organs and structures. Currently, ultrasound is still the first choice in fetal screening, but fetal MRI can provide more detailed images than ultrasound. In many instances, ultrasound will indicate a possible abnormality and then fetal MRI will be used to obtain a clearer, more detailed image (Muhler & others, 2007). Among the fetal malformations that fetal MRI may be able to detect better than ultrasound sonography are certain central nervous system, chest, gastrointestinal, genital/urinary, and placental abnormalities (Fratelli & others, 2007).

At some point between 9.5 and 12.5 weeks of pregnancy, chorionic villus sampling may be used to detect genetic defects and chromosome abnormalities

(Csaba, Bush, & Saphier, 2006). *Chorionic villus sampling* is a prenatal medical procedure in which a small sample of the placenta (the vascular organ that links the fetus to the mother's uterus) is removed. Diagnosis takes about 10 days.

Between the 15th and 18th weeks of pregnancy, amniocentesis may be performed. *Amniocentesis* is a prenatal medical procedure in which a sample of amniotic fluid is withdrawn by syringe and tested for chromosomal or metabolic disorders. The later that amniocentesis is performed, the better is its diagnostic potential. The earlier that it is performed, the more useful it is in deciding how to handle a pregnancy (Li & others, 2006). It may take two weeks for enough cells to grow and for amniocentesis test results to be obtained.

During the 16th to 18th weeks of pregnancy, maternal blood screening may be performed. *Maternal blood screening* identifies pregnancies that have an elevated risk for birth defects such as spina bifida and Down syndrome. The current blood test is called the *triple screen* because it measures three substances in the mother's blood. After an abnormal triple screen result, the next step is usually an ultrasound examination. If an ultrasound does not explain the abnormal triple screen results, amniocentesis is typically used.

Noninvasive prenatal diagnosis (NIPD) is increasingly being used as an alternative to such procedures as chorionic villus sampling and amniocentesis (Avent & others, 2008). At this point, NIPD has mainly focused on the isolation and examination of fetal cells circulating in the mother's blood and the analysis of cell-free fetal DNA in maternal plasma (Finning & Chitty, 2008; Norbury & Norbury, 2008). Researchers are exploring the potential for using NIPD to confirm a baby's sex as early as five weeks after conception and to diagnose Down syndrome (Avent & others, 2008; Hahn, Zhong, & Holzgreve, 2008). Being able to detect an offspring's sex and various diseases and defects so early raises ethical concerns about couples' motivation to terminate a pregnancy (Newsom, 2008; van den Heuvel & Marteau, 2008).

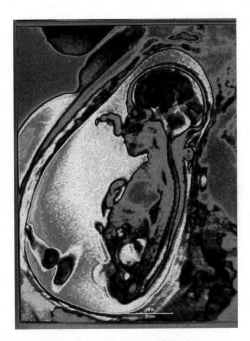

FIGURE 2.12 A Fetal MRI, Which Is Increasingly Being Used in Prenatal Diagnosis of Fetal Malformations.

Hazards to Prenatal Development

The mother's womb protects most babies as they develop. Despite this protection, the environment can affect the embryo or fetus in many well-documented ways.

General Principles   A **teratogen** is any agent that can potentially cause a birth defect or negatively alter cognitive and behavioral outcomes. The field of study that investigates the causes of birth defects is called *teratology*. Some exposures to teratogens do not cause physical birth defects but can alter the developing brain and influence cognitive and behavioral functioning, in which case the field of study is called *behavioral teratology* (DiPietro, 2008).

Teratogens include drugs, incompatible blood types, environmental pollutants, infectious diseases, nutritional deficiencies, maternal stress, and advanced maternal and paternal age. In fact, thousands of babies are born deformed or mentally retarded every year as a result of events that occurred in the mother's life as early as one or two months *before* conception. As we further discuss teratogens, you will see that factors related to the father also can influence prenatal development.

So many teratogens exist that practically every fetus is exposed to at least some teratogens. For this reason, it is difficult to determine which teratogen causes which problem. In addition, it may take a long time for the effects of a teratogen to show up. Only about half of all potential effects appear at birth.

The dose, the genetic susceptibility, and the time of exposure to a particular teratogen influence both the severity of the damage to an embryo or fetus and the type of defect:

- *Dose.* The dose effect is obvious—the greater the dose of an agent, such as a drug, the greater the effect.
- *Genetic susceptibility.* The type or severity of abnormalities caused by a teratogen is linked to the genotype of the pregnant woman and the genotype of

teratogen Any agent that can potentially cause a birth defect or negatively alter cognitive and behavioral outcomes.

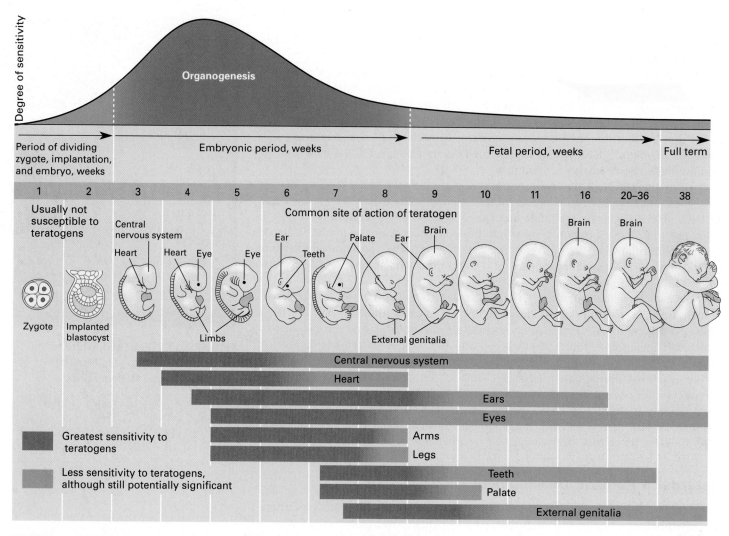

FIGURE 2.13 Teratogens and the Timing of Their Effects on Prenatal Development. The danger of structural defects caused by teratogens is greatest early in embryonic development, during the period of organogenesis (red color). Later assaults by teratogens (blue-green color) are more likely to stunt growth or cause problems of organ function instead of causing structural damage.

the embryo or fetus. For example, how a mother metabolizes a particular drug can influence the degree to which the drug effects are transmitted to the embryo or fetus. Differences in placental membranes and placental transport also affect exposure. The extent to which an embryo or fetus is vulnerable to a teratogen may also depend on its genotype (Marinucci & others, 2009). Also, for unknown reasons, male fetuses are far more likely to be affected by teratogens than female fetuses (DiPietro, 2008).

- *Time of exposure.* Teratogens do more damage when they occur at some points in development rather than at others. Damage during the germinal period may even prevent implantation. In general, the embryonic period is more vulnerable than the fetal period.

Figure 2.13 summarizes additional information about the effects of time of exposure to a teratogen. The probability of a structural defect is greatest early in the embryonic period, when organs are being formed (Lu & Lu, 2008). Each body structure has its own critical period of formation. Recall from Chapter 1, "Introduction," that a *critical period* is a fixed time period very early in development during which certain experiences or events can have a long-lasting effect on development. The critical period for the nervous system (week 3) is earlier than that for arms and legs (weeks 4 and 5).

After organogenesis is complete, teratogens are less likely to cause anatomical defects. Instead, exposure during the fetal period is more likely instead to stunt growth or to create problems in the way organs function. To examine some key teratogens and their effects, let's begin with drugs.

Prescription and Nonprescription Drugs Many U.S. women are given prescriptions for drugs while they are pregnant—especially antibiotics, analgesics, and asthma medications. Prescription as well as nonprescription drugs, however, may have negative effects on the embryo or fetus (Weiner & Buhischi, 2009).

Prescription drugs that can function as teratogens include antibiotics, such as streptomycin and tetracycline; some antidepressants; certain hormones, such as progestin and synthetic estrogen; and Accutane (which often is prescribed for acne) (Garcia-Bournissen & others, 2008). Nonprescription drugs that can be harmful include diet pills and aspirin (Norgard & others, 2006). A recent research review indicated that low doses of aspirin pose no harm for the fetus but that high doses can contribute to maternal and fetal bleeding (James, Brancazio, & Price, 2008).

Psychoactive Drugs Psychoactive drugs are drugs that act on the nervous system to alter states of consciousness, modify perceptions, and change moods. Examples include caffeine, alcohol, and nicotine, as well as illegal drugs such as cocaine, marijuana, and heroin.

Caffeine People often consume caffeine by drinking coffee, tea, or colas, or by eating chocolate. A recent study revealed that pregnant women who consumed 200 or more milligrams of caffeine a day (equal to about two or more 8-ounce containers of coffee or five or more 12-ounce cans of cola) had an increased risk of miscarriage (Weng, Odouli, & Li, 2008). Taking into account such results, the U.S. Food and Drug Administration recommends that pregnant women either not consume caffeine or consume it only sparingly.

Alcohol Heavy drinking by pregnant women can be devastating to offspring (Borwoski & Niebyl, 2008). **Fetal alcohol spectrum disorders (FASD)** are a cluster of abnormalities and problems that appear in the offspring of mothers who drink alcohol heavily during pregnancy (Olson, King, & Jirikowic, 2008). The abnormalities include facial deformities and defective limbs, face, and heart. Most children with FASD have learning problems, and many are below average in intelligence; some are mentally retarded (Caley & others, 2008; Cuzon & others, 2008). A recent study revealed that children with FASD have impaired memory development (Pei & others, 2008). Although many mothers of FASD infants are heavy drinkers, many mothers who are heavy drinkers do not have children with FASD or have one child with FASD and other children who do not have it.

Drinking alcohol during pregnancy, however, can have serious effects on offspring even when they are not afflicted with FASD. Serious malformations such as those produced by FASD are not found in infants born to mothers who are moderate drinkers, but even moderate drinking can have a negative effect on the offspring (Howell & others, 2006).

What are some guidelines for alcohol use during pregnancy? The U.S. Surgeon General recommends that *no* alcohol be consumed during pregnancy. And research suggests that it may not be wise to consume alcohol at the time of conception. One study revealed that when both men and women drank alcohol during the week in which they conceived a baby, the risk of early pregnancy loss increased (Henriksen & others, 2004). And a recent study revealed that although both non-Latino White women and African American women lowered their alcohol intake when they became pregnant, non-Latino White women lowered their alcohol intake more than

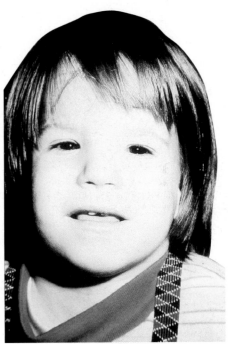

Fetal alcohol spectrum disorders (FASD) are characterized by a number of physical abnormalities and learning problems. Notice the wide-set eyes, flat cheekbones, and thin upper lip in this child with FASD.

fetal alcohol spectrum disorders (FASD)
A cluster of abnormalities that appears in the offspring of mothers who drink alcohol heavily during pregnancy.

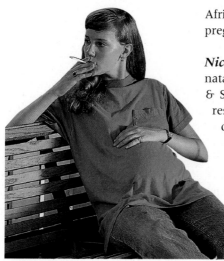

What are some links between expectant mothers' cigarette smoking and outcomes for their offspring?

African American women (Morris & others, 2008). In sum, it is recommended that pregnant women avoid drinking alcohol entirely.

Nicotine   Cigarette smoking by pregnant women can also adversely influence prenatal development, birth, and postnatal development (Cooper & Moley, 2008; Shea & Steiner, 2008). Preterm births and low birth weights, fetal and neonatal deaths, respiratory problems, and sudden infant death syndrome (SIDS, also known as crib death) are all more common among the offspring of mothers who smoked during pregnancy (Henderson, 2008; Landau, 2008). Maternal smoking during pregnancy also has been identified as a risk factor for the development of attention deficit hyperactivity disorder in offspring (Knopik, 2009; Pinkhardt & others, 2009). For example, a recent study revealed that children whose mothers smoked during pregnancy were more likely to have a higher level of inattention and hyperactivity than children whose mothers did not smoke in pregnancy (Obel & others, 2009). A recent research review also indicated that environmental tobacco smoke was linked to increased risk of low birth weight in offspring (Leonardi-Bee & others, 2008).

Intervention programs designed to help pregnant women stop smoking can reduce some of smoking's negative effects, especially by raising birth weights (Barron & others, 2007). A recent study revealed that women who quit smoking during pregnancy had offspring with higher birth weight than their counterparts who continued smoking (Jaddoe & others, 2008).

Cocaine   Does cocaine use during pregnancy harm the developing embryo and fetus? The most consistent finding is that cocaine exposure during prenatal development is associated with reduced birth weight, length, and head circumference (Smith & others, 2001). Also, in other studies, prenatal cocaine exposure has been linked to lower arousal, less effective self-regulation, higher excitability, and lower quality of reflexes at 1 month of age (Lester & others, 2002); to impaired motor development in the second year of life and a slower growth rate through 10 years of age (Richardson, Goldschmidt, & Willford, 2008); to impaired language development and information processing (Beeghly & others, 2006; Lewis & others, 2007), including attention deficits in preschool and elementary school children (Accornero & others, 2007; Noland & others, 2005); and to increased likelihood of being in a special education program that involves support services (Levine & others, 2008).

Some researchers argue that these findings should be interpreted cautiously. Why? Because other factors in the lives of pregnant women who use cocaine (such as poverty, malnutrition, and other substance abuse) often cannot be ruled out as possible contributors to the problems found in their children (Hurt & others, 2005). For example, cocaine users are more likely than nonusers to smoke cigarettes, use marijuana, drink alcohol, and take amphetamines.

Despite these cautions, the weight of research evidence indicates that children born to mothers who use cocaine are likely to have neurological and cognitive deficits (Field, 2007; Mayer & Zhang, 2009; Richardson, Goldschmidt, & Larkby, 2008). Cocaine use by pregnant women is strongly discouraged.

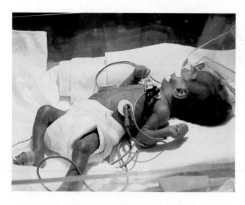

This baby was exposed to cocaine prenatally. *What are some of the possible effects on development of being exposed to cocaine prenatally?*

Methamphetamine   Methamphetamine, like cocaine, is a stimulant, speeding up an individual's nervous system. Babies born to mothers who use methamphetamine, or "meth," during pregnancy are at risk for a number of problems, including high infant mortality, low birth weight, and developmental and behavioral problems (Forrester & Merz, 2007). A recent study revealed that meth exposure during prenatal development was linked to decreased arousal, increased stress, and poor movement quality in newborns (Smith & others, 2008).

Marijuana   An increasing number of studies find that marijuana use by pregnant women has negative outcomes for offspring (Williams & Ross, 2007). A recent study found that prenatal marijuana exposure was related to lower intelligence in children (Goldschmidt & others, 2008). Another study revealed that prenatal marijuana exposure was linked with depressive symptoms at 10 years of age (Gray & others, 2005). An additional study indicated that prenatal exposure to marijuana was related to marijuana use at 14 years of age (Day, Goldschmidt, & Thomas, 2006). In sum, marijuana use is not recommended for pregnant women.

Heroin   It is well documented that infants whose mothers are addicted to heroin show several behavioral difficulties (Steinhausen, Blattman, & Pfund, 2007). The difficulties include withdrawal symptoms, such as tremors, irritability, abnormal crying, disturbed sleep, and impaired motor control. Many still show behavioral problems at their first birthday, and attention deficits may appear later in development. The most common treatment for heroin addiction, methadone, is associated with very severe withdrawal symptoms in newborns (Binder & Vavrinkova, 2008).

Incompatible Blood Types   Incompatibility between the mother's and father's blood type poses another risk to prenatal development. Blood types are created by differences in the surface structure of red blood cells. One type of difference in the surface of red blood cells creates the familiar blood groups—A, B, O, and AB. A second difference creates what is called Rh-positive and Rh-negative blood. If a surface marker, called the *Rh factor*, is present in an individual's red blood cells, the person is said to be Rh-positive; if the Rh-marker is not present, the person is said to be Rh-negative. If a pregnant woman is Rh-negative and her partner is Rh-positive, the fetus may be Rh-positive. If the fetus' blood is Rh-positive and the mother's is Rh-negative, the mother's immune system may produce antibodies that will attack the fetus. The result can be any number of problems, including miscarriage or stillbirth, anemia, jaundice, heart defects, brain damage, or death soon after birth (Moise, 2005).

Generally, the first Rh-positive baby of an Rh-negative mother is not at risk, but with each subsequent pregnancy the risk increases. A vaccine (RhoGAM) may be given to the mother within three days of the child's birth to prevent her body from making antibodies that will attack future Rh-positive fetuses. Also, babies affected by Rh incompatibility can be given blood transfusions before or right after birth.

Maternal Diseases   Maternal diseases and infections can produce defects in offspring by crossing the placental barrier, or they can cause damage during birth. Rubella (German measles) is one disease that can cause prenatal defects. Women who plan to have children should have a blood test before they become pregnant to determine if they are immune to the disease (Dontigny & others, 2008).

Syphilis (a sexually transmitted infection) is more damaging later in prenatal development—four months or more after conception. When syphilis is present at birth, problems can develop in the central nervous system and gastrointestinal tract (Johnson, Erbelding, & Ghanem, 2007). Most states require that pregnant women be given a blood test to detect the presence of syphilis.

Another infection that has received widespread attention recently is genital herpes. Newborns contract this virus when they are delivered through the birth canal of a mother with genital herpes (Hollier & Wendel, 2008). If an active case of genital herpes is detected in a pregnant woman close to her delivery date, a cesarean section (in which the infant is delivered through an incision in the mother's abdomen) can be performed to keep the virus from infecting the newborn (Sellner & others, 2009).

Acquired immune deficiency syndrome (AIDS) is a sexually transmitted syndrome that is caused by the human immunodeficiency virus (HIV), which destroys the body's immune system. A mother can infect her offspring with HIV in three ways: (1) during gestation across the placenta, (2) during delivery through contact with maternal blood or fluids, and (3) postpartum (after birth) through breast feeding. The transmission of HIV through breast feeding is especially a problem in many developing countries (UNICEF, 2009). Babies born to HIV-infected mothers can be

Because the fetus depends entirely on its mother for nutrition, it is important for the pregnant woman to have good nutritional habits. In Kenya, this government clinic provides pregnant women with information about how their diet can influence the health of their fetus and offspring. *What might the information about diet be like?*

(1) infected and symptomatic (show AIDS symptoms), (2) infected but asymptomatic (not show AIDS symptoms), or (3) not infected at all. An infant who is infected and asymptomatic may still develop HIV symptoms up until 15 months of age.

The increasingly widespread disease of diabetes, characterized by high levels of sugar in the blood, also affects offspring (Most & others, 2009; Oostdam & others, 2009). A recent large-scale study revealed that from 1999 to 2005 twice as many women and five times as many adolescents giving birth had diabetes (Lawrence & others, 2008). The increase in diabetes likely was fueled by the dramatic increase in being overweight or obese.

A research review indicated that when newborns have physical defects they are more likely to have diabetic mothers (Eriksson, 2009). Women who have gestational diabetes also may deliver very large infants (weighing 10 pounds or more), and the infants themselves are at risk for diabetes (Gluck & others, 2009).

Maternal Diet and Nutrition A developing embryo or fetus depends completely on its mother for nutrition, which comes from the mother's blood. The nutritional status of the embryo or fetus is determined by the mother's total caloric intake, including her intake of proteins, vitamins, and minerals. Children born to malnourished mothers are more likely than other children to be malformed.

Being overweight before and during pregnancy can also put the embryo or fetus at risk, and an increasing number of pregnant women in the United States are overweight (Chu & others, 2009; Reece, 2008). Recent studies indicated that prepregnancy maternal obesity increased the risk of stillbirth and neonatal death, and was linked with defects in the central nervous system of offspring (Anderson & others, 2005; Guelinckx & others, 2008). Further, a recent analysis proposed that overnutrition in fetal life (due to overeating on the part of the pregnant woman) results in a series of neuroendocrine changes in the fetus that in turn program the development of fat cells and of the appetite regulation system (McMillen & others, 2008). In this analysis, it was predicted that such early fetal programming is likely linked to being overweight in childhood and adolescence.

One aspect of maternal nutrition that is important for normal prenatal development is folic acid, a B-complex vitamin (Goh & Koren, 2008). A recent study of more than 34,000 women taking folic acid either alone or as part of a multivitamin for at least one year prior to conceiving was linked with a 70 percent lower risk of delivering from 20 to 28 weeks and a 50 percent lower risk of delivering between 28 to 32 weeks (Bukowski & others, 2008). As we discussed earlier in the chapter, a lack of folic acid is linked with neural tube defects in offspring, such as spina bifida (Ryan-Harshman & Aldoori, 2008). The U.S. Department of Health and Human Services (2009) recommends that pregnant women consume a minimum of 400 micrograms of folic acid per day (about twice the amount the average woman gets in one day). Orange juice and spinach are examples of foods rich in folic acid.

Eating fish is often recommended as part of a healthy diet, but pollution has made many fish a risky choice for pregnant women. Some fish contain high levels of mercury, which is released into the air both naturally and by industrial pollution (Oken & Bellinger, 2008). When mercury falls into the water, it can become toxic and accumulate in large fish, such as shark, swordfish, king mackerel, and some species of large tuna. Mercury is easily transferred across the placenta, and the embryo's developing brain and nervous system are highly sensitive to the metal (Gliori & others, 2006). Researchers have found that prenatal mercury exposure is linked to adverse outcomes, including miscarriage, preterm birth, and lower intelligence (Triche & Hossain, 2007).

The U.S. Food and Drug Administration (2004) has provided the following recommendations for women of childbearing age and young children: Do not eat shark, swordfish, king mackerel, or tilefish; eat up to 12 ounces (two average meals) a week of fish and shellfish that are low in mercury, such as shrimp, canned light tuna, salmon, pollock, and catfish.

PCBs (polychlorinated biphenyls) are chemicals that were used in manufacturing until they were banned in the 1970s in the United States, but they are still present in landfills, sediments, and wildlife. One concern focuses on pregnant women eating PCB-polluted fish (Hertz-Picciotto & others, 2008). A recent research review concluded that PCB-polluted fish pose a potential risk to prenatal neurodevelopment (Korrick & Sagiv, 2008).

Emotional States and Stress   When a pregnant woman experiences intense fears, anxieties, and other emotions, physiological changes occur that may affect her fetus (Entringer & others, 2009). For example, producing adrenaline in response to fear restricts blood flow to the uterine area and can deprive the fetus of adequate oxygen. Also, maternal stress may increase the level of corticotropin-releasing hormone (CRH), a precursor of the stress hormone cortisol, early in pregnancy (Latendresse, 2009). Elevated levels of CRH and cortisol in the fetus have been linked to premature delivery in infants (Field, 2007). A recent study also revealed that a decline in stress during pregnancy was linked to a lower incidence of preterm birth (Glynn & others, 2008).

A recent research review concluded that pregnant women with high levels of stress are at increased risk for having a child with emotional or cognitive problems, attention deficit hyperactivity disorder (ADHD), and language delay (Talge & others, 2007). The review indicated that still unknown is the type of stress that is most detrimental, but research suggests that stress in the woman's relationship with a partner is one candidate.

Might maternal depression also have an adverse effect on prenatal development and birth? A recent study revealed maternal depression was linked to preterm birth and slower prenatal growth rates (Diego & others, 2009). In this study, mothers who were depressed had elevated cortisol levels, which likely contributed to the negative outcomes for the fetus and newborn. Another recent study found that depressed African American pregnant women had elevated levels of anxiety, anger, daily hassles, sleep disturbance, and cortisol (Field & others, 2009). This combination of negative maternal factors may contribute to the higher rate of preterm and low birth weight African American newborns.

Maternal Age   When possible harmful effects on the fetus and infant are considered, two maternal ages are of special interest: adolescence and 35 and older (Malizia, Hacker, & Penzias, 2009). The mortality rate of infants born to adolescent mothers is double that of infants born to mothers in their twenties. Although this high rate probably reflects the immaturity of the mother's reproductive system, poor nutrition, lack of prenatal care, and low socioeconomic status may also play a role (Smithbattle, 2007).

Maternal age is also linked to the risk that a child will have Down syndrome, a form of mental retardation that was discussed earlier in the chapter (Allen & others, 2009). A baby with Down syndrome rarely is born to a mother 16 to 34 years of age. However, when the mother reaches 40 years of age, the probability is slightly over 1 in 100 that a baby born to her will have Down syndrome, and by age 50 it is almost 1 in 10.

When mothers are 35 years and older, risks also increase for low birth weight, preterm delivery, and fetal death (Fretts, Zera, & Heffner, 2008; Mbugua Gitau & others, 2009). One study found that low birth weight delivery increased 11 percent and preterm delivery increased 14 percent in women 35 years and older (Tough & others, 2002).

We still have much to learn about the role of the mother's age in pregnancy and childbirth (Montan, 2007). As women remain active, exercise regularly, and are careful about their nutrition, their reproductive systems may remain healthier at older ages than was thought possible in the past. For example, in one study, two-thirds of the pregnancies of women 45 years and older in Australia were free of complications (Callaway, Lust, & McIntrye, 2005).

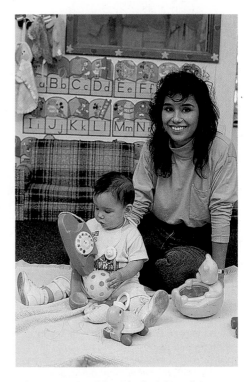

What are some of the risks for infants born to adolescent mothers?

In one study, in China, the longer fathers smoked the greater the risk that their children would develop cancer (Ji & others, 1997). *What are some other paternal factors that can influence the development of the fetus and the child?*

Paternal Factors So far, we have discussed how characteristics of the mother—such as drug use, disease, nutrition and diet, emotional states, and age—can influence prenatal development and the development of the child. Might there also be some paternal risk factors? Men's exposure to lead, radiation, certain pesticides, and petrochemicals may cause abnormalities in sperm that lead to miscarriage or diseases, such as childhood cancer (Cordier, 2008). It has been speculated that, when fathers take cocaine, it may attach itself to sperm and cause birth defects, but the evidence for this effect is not yet strong. In one study, long-term use of cocaine by men was related to low sperm count, low motility, and a higher number of abnormally formed sperm (Bracken & others, 1990). Cocaine-related infertility appears to be reversible if users stop taking the drug for at least one year.

The father's smoking during the mother's pregnancy also can cause problems for the offspring. In one study, heavy paternal smoking was associated with the risk of early pregnancy loss (Venners & others, 2005).

The father's age also makes a difference (Fear & others, 2007). About 5 percent of children with Down syndrome have older fathers. The offspring of older fathers also face increased risk for other birth defects, including dwarfism and Marfan syndrome, which involves head and limb deformities.

Environmental Hazards Many aspects of our modern industrial world can endanger the embryo or fetus (O'Connor & Roy, 2008). Some specific hazards to the embryo or fetus include radiation, toxic wastes, and other chemical pollutants (Orecchia, Lucignani, & Tosi, 2008; Raabe & Müller, 2008).

Women and their physicians should weigh the risk of an X-ray when an actual or potential pregnancy is involved (Menias & others, 2007). However, a routine diagnostic X-ray of a body area other than the abdomen, with the woman's abdomen protected by a lead apron, is generally considered safe (Brent, 2009).

Environmental pollutants and toxic wastes are also sources of danger to unborn children. Among the dangerous pollutants are carbon monoxide, mercury, and lead, as well as certain fertilizers and pesticides (Hu & others, 2007).

Despite these many potential hazards during prenatal development, it is important to keep in mind that most of the time prenatal development does not go awry and development proceeds along the positive path that was described at the beginning of the chapter. The *Applications in Life-Span Development* interlude that follows outlines some of the steps that prospective parents can take to increase the chances for healthy prenatal development.

An explosion at the Chernobyl nuclear power plant in the Ukraine produced radioactive contamination that spread to surrounding areas. Thousands of infants were born with health problems and deformities as a result of the nuclear contamination, including this boy whose arm did not form. *Other than radioactive contamination, what are some other types of environmental hazards to prenatal development?*

Applications in Life-Span Development

A HEALTHY PREGNANCY

A helpful initial strategy for women is to begin preparing for pregnancy before becoming pregnant. Women should consult with their physician about discontinuing any medications that might harm the offspring, including acne medications and tranquilizers. If they smoke or drink alcohol, they need to break these habits before becoming pregnant. It also is wise to reduce caffeine intake and begin taking a multiple vitamin with iron, making sure it has at least 0.4 mg of folic acid. Avoiding fish with high levels of mercury is another good strategy.

In addition to healthy eating, moderate regular exercise is linked with fewer discomforts in pregnancy and an improved sense of well-being (Rafla, Nair, & Kumar,

2008). For example, one study revealed that regular exercise during the second half of pregnancy reduced the low back pain of expectant mothers (Garshasbi & Faghih Zadeh, 2005). And a recent study found that, compared with sedentary pregnant women, women who engaged in light leisure time physical activity had a 24 percent reduced likelihood of preterm delivery, and those who participated in moderate to heavy leisure time physical activity had a 66 percent reduced risk of preterm delivery (Hegaard & others, 2008). However, it is important for expectant mothers not to exercise too strenuously, which can increase the probability of bleeding or preterm labor. Walking, swimming, and stretching are among recommended exercises for expectant mothers.

Another important aspect of having a healthy pregnancy is to talk with a physician about the use of prenatal tests to assess the health of the developing fetus, a topic that we discussed earlier in this chapter. Another important step in a healthy pregnancy is to obtain early prenatal care, which we discuss next.

How might a woman's exercise in pregnancy benefit her and her offspring?

Prenatal Care

Information about teratogens and other prenatal hazards is one of the many benefits that expectant mothers gain from prenatal care. Although prenatal care varies enormously, it usually involves a defined schedule of visits for medical care, which typically include screening for manageable conditions and treatable diseases that can affect the baby or the mother (Mennuti, 2008). In addition to medical care, prenatal programs often include comprehensive educational, social, and nutritional services.

Research contrasting the experiences of mothers who had prenatal care and those who did not supports the significance of prenatal care (McFarlin, 2009). Researchers have found that low birth weight and preterm deliveries are common among U.S. mothers who receive no prenatal care. And, in one study, the absence of prenatal care increased the risk for preterm birth by almost threefold in both non-Latino White and African American women (Stringer & others, 2005).

Inadequate prenatal care may help explain a disturbing fact: Rates of infant mortality and low birth weight indicate that many other nations have healthier babies than does the United States (Flynn, Budd, & Modelski, 2008; Hueston, Geesey, & Diaz, 2008). In many countries that have a lower percentage of low birth weight infants than the United States, mothers receive either free or very low cost prenatal and postnatal care, and they can receive paid maternity leave from work that ranges from 9 to 40 weeks. In Norway and the Netherlands, prenatal care is coordinated with a general practitioner, an obstetrician, and a midwife.

An innovative program that is rapidly expanding in the United States is Centering-Pregnancy (Massey, Rising, & Ickovics, 2006; Steming, 2008). This relationship-centered program provides complete prenatal care in a group setting. CenteringPregnancy replaces traditional 15-minute physician visits with 90-minute peer group support settings and self-examination led by a physician or certified nurse-midwife. Groups of up to ten women (and often their partners) meet regularly, beginning at 12 to 16 weeks of pregnancy. The sessions emphasize empowering women to play an active role in experiencing a positive pregnancy. A recent study revealed that CenteringPregnancy groups made more prenatal visits, had higher breast feeding rates, and were more satisfied with their prenatal care than women in individual care (Klima & others, 2009).

Some prenatal programs for parents focus on home visitation (Lee & others, 2009). Research evaluations indicate that the Nurse Family Partnership created by David Olds and his colleagues (2004, 2007) is successful. The Nurse Family Partnership involves home visits by trained nurses beginning in the second or third trimester of

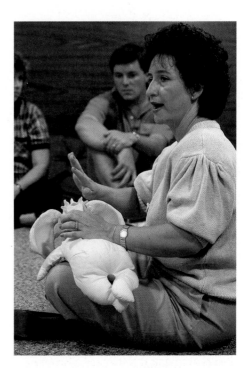

Early prenatal education classes focus on such topics as changes in the development of the fetus. Later classes focus on preparation for the birth and care of the newborn. *To what extent should fathers, as well as mothers, participate in these classes?*

A CenteringPregnancy program. This rapidly increasing program alters routine prenatal care by bringing women out of exam rooms and into relationship-oriented groups.

prenatal development. The extensive program consists of approximately 50 home visits from the prenatal period through 2 years of age. The home visits focus on the mother's health, access to health care, parenting, and improvement of the mother's life by providing her guidance in education, work, and relationships. Research revealed that the Nurse Family Partnership has numerous positive outcomes including fewer pregnancies, better work circumstances, and stability in relationship partners for the mother, and improved academic success and social development for the child (Olds & others, 2004, 2007). In another home visitation program, high-risk pregnant women and adolescents, many living in poverty conditions, were provided biweekly home visitation services that encouraged healthy prenatal behavior, social support, and links to medical and other community services (Lee & others, 2009). Compared with a control group of pregnant women and adolescents who did not receive the home visits, the home visitation group gave birth to fewer low birth weight infants.

Many cultures and ethnic groups have differing views of pregnancy. In the *Contexts of Life-Span Development* interlude that follows, we explore these beliefs.

Contexts of Life-Span Development

CULTURAL BELIEFS ABOUT PREGNANCY

All cultures have beliefs and practices that surround life's major events, and one such event is pregnancy. When a woman who has immigrated to the United States becomes pregnant, the beliefs and practices of her native culture may be as important as, or more so than, those of the mainstream U.S. culture that now surrounds her. The conflict between cultural tradition and Western medicine may pose a risk for the pregnancy and a challenge for the health-care professional who wishes to give proper care while respecting the woman's values.

The American Public Health Association (2006) has identified a variety of cultural beliefs and practices that are observed among various immigrant groups, such as:

- *Food cravings*. Latin American, Asian, and some African cultures believe that it is important for a pregnant woman's food cravings to be satisfied because they are thought to be the cravings of the baby. If cravings are left unsatisfied, the baby might take on certain unpleasant personality and/or physical traits, perhaps characteristic of the food (Taylor, Ko, & Pan, 1999). As an example, in African cultures women often eat soil, chalk, or clay during pregnancy; this is believed to satisfy the baby's hunger as well as affirming soil as a symbol of female fertility (American Public Health Association, 2006).

- *"Hot-cold" theory of illness*. Many cultures in Latin America, Asia, and Africa characterize foods, medications, and illnesses as "hot" or "cold"; this terminology has to do not with temperature or spiciness, but with traditional definitions and categories. Most of these cultures view pregnancy as a "hot" condition, although the Chinese view it as "cold" (Taylor, Ko, & Pan, 1999). As a result, a woman may resist taking a prescribed medication because of concern that it could create too much "heat" and cause a miscarriage; in Indian culture, iron-rich foods are also considered unacceptably "hot" for pregnant women (DeSantis, 1998).

- *Extended family*. In many immigrant cultures, the extended family is a vital support system, and health-care decisions are made based on the needs of the family over those of the individual. Western health-care providers need to be sensitive to this dynamic, which runs counter to today's practices of protecting patient confidentiality and autonomy.

- *Stoicism.* In many Asian cultures, stoicism is valued, as suffering is seen as part of life (Uba, 1992). Physicians are also viewed with great respect. As a result, a pregnant Asian woman may behave submissively and avoid voicing complaints to her health-care provider, but she may privately fail to follow the provider's advice (Assanand & others, 1990).

Some cultures treat pregnancy simply as a natural occurrence; others see it as a medical condition (Walsh, 2006). How expectant mothers behave during pregnancy may depend in part on the prevalence of traditional home-care remedies and folk beliefs, the importance of indigenous healers, and the influence of health-care professionals in their culture. In various cultures, women may consult herbalists and/or faith healers during pregnancy (Mbonye, Neema, & Magnussen, 2006).

Health-care workers should assess whether a woman's beliefs or practices pose a threat to her or the fetus. If they do, health-care professionals should consider a culturally sensitive way to handle the problem (Kenner, Sugrue, & Finkelman, 2007).

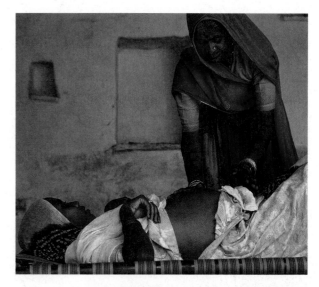

In India, a midwife checks on the size, position, and heartbeat of a fetus. Midwives deliver babies in many cultures around the world. *What are some cultural variations in prenatal care?*

Review and Reflect: Learning Goal 4

 4 **Characterize the course of prenatal development and its hazards**

REVIEW

- What is the course of prenatal development? How does the brain develop in the prenatal period?
- What are some prenatal diagnostic tests?
- What are some of the main hazards to prenatal development?
- What do prenatal care programs provide?

REFLECT

- What can be done to convince women who are pregnant not to smoke or drink? Consider the role of health-care providers, the role of insurance companies, and specific programs targeted at women who are pregnant.

5 BIRTH

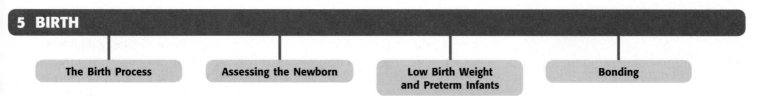

| The Birth Process | Assessing the Newborn | Low Birth Weight and Preterm Infants | Bonding |

Many importance circumstances are involved in the birth of a baby. Let's explore the birth process, examining variations in how it occurs and in its outcomes.

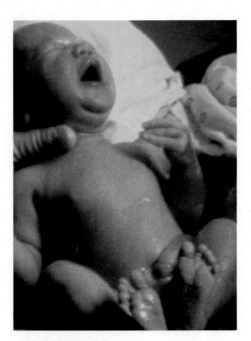

After the long journey of prenatal development, birth takes place. During birth the baby is on a threshold between two worlds. *What is the fetus/newborn transition like?*

The Birth Process

Nature writes the basic script for how birth occurs, but parents make important choices about conditions surrounding birth. We look first at the sequence of physical steps when a child is born.

Stages of Birth   Childbirth—or labor—occurs in three stages. In the first stage, uterine contractions are 15 to 20 minutes apart at the beginning and last up to a minute. These contractions cause the woman's cervix (the opening into the birth canal) to stretch and open. As the first stage progresses, the contractions come closer together, appearing every two to five minutes. Their intensity increases too. By the end of the first birth stage, contractions dilate the cervix to an opening of about 4 inches, so that the baby can move from the uterus to the birth canal. For a woman having her first child, the first stage lasts an average of 6 to 12 hours; it is the longest of the three stages.

The second birth stage begins when the baby's head starts to move through the cervix and the birth canal. It terminates when the baby completely emerges from the mother's body. For a first birth, this stage lasts approximately 1½ hours, and for later births the second stage averages 45 minutes in length. With each contraction, the mother bears down hard to push the baby out of her body. By the time the baby's head is out of the mother's body, the contractions come almost every minute and last for about a minute.

Afterbirth is the third stage, at which time the placenta, umbilical cord, and other membranes are detached and expelled. This final stage is the shortest of the three birth stages, lasting only minutes.

Childbirth Setting and Attendants   In the United States, most births take place in hospitals. Some women with good medical histories and low risk for problems may choose a delivery at home or in a freestanding birth center, which is usually staffed by nurse-midwives. Births at home are far more common in many other countries—for example, in Holland, 35 percent of the babies are born at home. Some critics worry that the U.S. tendency to view birth through a medical lens may lead to unnecessary medical procedures (Hausman, 2005).

The person who helps a mother during birth varies across cultures. In U.S. hospitals, it has become the norm for fathers or birth coaches to be with the mother throughout labor and delivery. In the East African Nigoni culture, men are completely excluded from the childbirth process. When a woman is ready to give birth, female relatives move into the woman's hut and the husband leaves, taking his belongings (clothes, tools, weapons, and so on) with him. He is not permitted to return until after the baby is born. In some cultures, childbirth is an open, community affair. For example, in the Pukapukan culture in the Pacific Islands, women give birth in a shelter that is open for villagers to observe.

Midwifery is the norm throughout most of the world (Tiran, 2008; Wickham, 2009). In Holland, more than 40 percent of babies are delivered by midwives rather than by doctors (Treffers & others, 1990). But in 2003, 91 percent of U.S. births were attended by physicians, and only 8 percent of women who delivered a baby in the United States were attended by a midwife (Martin & others, 2005). In the United States, most midwives are nurses who have been specially trained in delivering babies. Compared with physicians, certified nurse-midwives generally spend more time with patients during prenatal visits, place more emphasis on patient counseling and education, provide more emotional support, and are more likely to be with the patient one-on-one during the entire labor and delivery process, aspects that may explain the more positive outcomes for babies delivered by certified nurse-midwives (Davis, 2005).

In many countries, a doula attends a childbearing woman. *Doula* is a Greek word that means "a woman who helps." A *doula* is a caregiver who provides continuous

A woman in the African !Kung culture giving birth in a sitting position. Notice the help and support being given by another woman. *What are some cultural variations in childbirth?*

physical, emotional, and educational support for the mother before, during, and after childbirth. Doulas remain with the mother throughout labor, assessing and responding to her needs. Researchers have found positive effects when a doula is present at the birth of a child (Campbell & others, 2006).

Methods of Childbirth   U.S. hospitals often allow the mother and her obstetrician a range of options regarding their method of delivery. Key choices involve whether or not to use medication, whether to use any of a number of nonmedicated techniques to reduce pain, and when to resort to a cesarean delivery.

Medication   Three basic kinds of drugs that are used for labor are analgesia, anesthesia, and oxytocics. *Analgesia* is used to relieve pain. Analgesics include tranquilizers, barbiturates, and narcotics (such as Demerol). *Anesthesia* is used in late first-stage labor and during expulsion of the baby to block sensation in an area of the body or to block consciousness. In normal births, there is a trend toward not using general anesthesia, which blocks consciousness, because general anesthesia can be transmitted through the placenta to the fetus (Lieberman & others, 2005). *Oxytocin* is a synthetic hormone that is used to stimulate contractions; pitocin is the most widely used oxytocin (Ratcliffe, 2008). The benefits and risks of oxytocin as a part of childbirth continue to be debated (Vasdev, 2008).

Predicting how a drug will affect an individual woman and her fetus is difficult (Smith, 2009). A particular drug might have only a minimal effect on one fetus yet have a much stronger effect on another. The drug's dosage also is a factor.

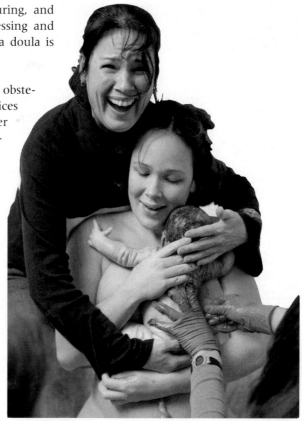

A doula assisting a birth. *What types of support do doulas provide?*

Natural and Prepared Childbirth   Today, at least some medication is used in the typical childbirth, but elements of natural childbirth and prepared childbirth remain popular (Davidson, London, & Ladewig, 2008). **Natural childbirth** is the method that aims to reduce the mother's pain by decreasing her fear through education about childbirth and by teaching her to use breathing methods and relaxation techniques during delivery. French obstetrician Ferdinand Lamaze developed a method similar to natural childbirth that is known as **prepared childbirth,** or the Lamaze method. It includes a special breathing technique to control pushing in the final stages of labor, as well as detailed education about anatomy. The Lamaze method has become very popular in the United States. The pregnant woman's partner usually serves as a coach, who attends childbirth classes with her and helps her with her breathing and relaxation during delivery.

Proponents of current prepared childbirth methods emphasize that when information and support are provided, women *know* how to give birth. To read about one nurse whose research focuses on fatigue during childbearing and breathing exercises during labor, see the *Careers in Life-Span Development* profile.

Other Nonmedicated Techniques to Reduce Pain   The effort to reduce stress and control pain during labor has recently led to an increase in the use of some old and some new nonmedicated techniques (Field, 2007; Moleti, 2009; Simkin & Bolding, 2004). These include waterbirth, massage, acupuncture, hypnosis, and music therapy.

Waterbirth involves giving birth in a tub of warm water. Some women go through labor in the water and get out for delivery; others remain in the water for delivery. The rationale for waterbirth is that the baby has been in an amniotic sac for many months and that delivery in a similar environment is likely to be less stressful for the baby and the mother. Mothers get into the warm water when contractions become close together and intense. Getting into the water too soon can

natural childbirth Method attempting to reduce the mother's pain by decreasing her fear through education about childbirth and relaxation techniques during delivery.

prepared childbirth Developed by French obstetrician Ferdinand Lamaze, a childbirth strategy similar to natural childbirth but one that includes a special breathing technique to control pushing in the final stages of labor and details about anatomy and physiology.

Careers in Life-Span Development

Linda Pugh, Perinatal Nurse

Perinatal nurses work with childbearing women to support health and growth during the childbearing experience. Linda Pugh (Ph.D., R.N.C.) is a perinatal nurse on the faculty at the Johns Hopkins University School of Nursing. She is certified as an inpatient obstetric nurse and specializes in the care of women during labor and delivery. Pugh teaches nursing to both undergraduate and graduate students. In addition to educating professional nurses and conducting research, Pugh consults with hospitals and organizations about women's health issues.

Pugh's research interests include nursing interventions with low-income breast feeding women, discovering ways to prevent and ameliorate fatigue during childbearing, and using effective breathing exercises during labor.

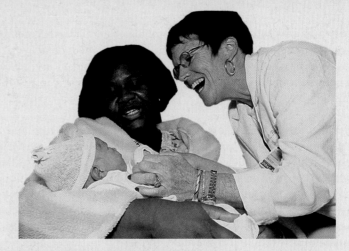

Linda Pugh (*right*) with a mother and her newborn.

What characterizes the use of waterbirth in delivering a baby?

cause labor to slow or stop. Researchers have found positive results for mothers and offspring when waterbirth is used appropriately (Thoni & Moroder, 2004).

Massage is increasingly used as a procedure prior to and during delivery (Field, 2007; Kimber & others, 2008). Researchers have found that massage can reduce pain and anxiety during labor (Chang, Chen, & Huang, 2006).

Acupuncture, the insertion of very fine needles into specific locations in the body, is considered a standard procedure to reduce the pain of childbirth in China, although it only recently has begun to be used in the United States for this purpose (Moleti, 2009). One research review indicated that only a limited number of studies had been conducted on the use of acupuncture in childbirth but that it appears to be safe and may have positive effects (Smith & Crowther, 2004).

Hypnosis, the induction of a psychological state of altered attention and awareness in which the individual is unusually responsively to suggestions, is also increasingly being used during childbirth (Mottershead, 2006). Some studies have indicated positive effects of hypnosis for reducing pain during childbirth (Barabasz & Perez, 2007).

Music therapy during childbirth, which involves the use of music to reduce stress and manage pain, is increasingly being used (Cepeda & others, 2006). Few research studies have been conducted to determine its effectiveness.

Cesarean Delivery Normally, the baby's head comes through the vagina first. But if the baby is in a *breech position*, the baby's buttocks are the first part to emerge. In 1 of every 25 deliveries, the baby's head is still in the uterus when the rest of the body is out. Breech births can cause respiratory problems and mental defects because of oxygen loss. As a result, if the baby is in a breech position, a cesarean section or a cesarean delivery is usually performed. In a *cesarean delivery*, the baby is removed from the mother's uterus through an incision made in her abdomen (Tita & others, 2009).

Cesarean deliveries are safer than breech deliveries. Cesarean deliveries also are performed if the baby is lying crosswise in the uterus, if the baby's head is too large to pass through the mother's pelvis, if the baby develops complications, or if the mother is bleeding vaginally. Cesarean deliveries can be life-saving, but they do bring risks. Compared with vaginal deliveries, they involve a higher infection rate, longer hospital stays, and the greater expense and stress that accompany any surgery. A recent national study of all U.S. live births and infant deaths from 1999 to 2002 revealed that cesarean deliveries with no labor complications resulted in a neonatal death rate that was 2.4 times that of planned vaginal deliveries (MacDorman & others, 2008).

The benefits and risks of cesarean sections continue to be debated (Declercq & others, 2008; Greene, 2009). Some critics note that too many babies are delivered by cesarean section in the United States (Chaillet & Dumont, 2007). More cesarean sections are performed in the United States than in any other country in the world. The cesarean delivery rate jumped 5 percent from 2002 to 2006 in the United States to 31 percent of all births, the highest level since these data began to be reported on birth certificates in 1989 (National Center for Health Statistics, 2007). Higher cesarean delivery rates may be due to a better ability to identify infants in distress during birth and the increase in overweight and obese pregnant women. Also, some doctors may be overly cautious and recommend a cesarean delivery to defend against a potential lawsuit.

The Transition from Fetus to Newborn   Much of our discussion of birth so far has focused on the mother. Being born also involves considerable stress for the baby. During each contraction, when the placenta and umbilical cord are compressed as the uterine muscles draw together, the supply of oxygen to the fetus is decreased. If the delivery takes too long, the baby can develop *anoxia*, a condition in which the fetus or newborn has an insufficient supply of oxygen. Anoxia can cause brain damage (Smith, 2008).

The baby has considerable capacity to withstand the stress of birth. Large quantities of adrenaline and noradrenaline, hormones that protect the fetus in the event of oxygen deficiency, are secreted in stressful circumstances. These hormones increase the heart's pumping activity, speed up heart rate, channel blood flow to the brain, and raise the blood-sugar level. Never again in life will such large amounts of these hormones be secreted. This circumstance underscores how stressful it is to be born and also how well prepared and adapted the fetus is for birth (Van Beveren, 2008).

At the time of birth, the baby is covered with what is called *vernix caseosa*, a protective skin grease. This vernix consists of fatty secretions and dead cells, thought to help protect the baby's skin against heat loss before and during birth.

Immediately after birth, the umbilical cord is cut. Before birth, oxygen came from the mother via the umbilical cord, but now the baby is self-sufficient and can breathe on its own. Now 25 million little air sacs in the lungs must be filled with air. These first breaths may be the hardest ones an individual takes.

Assessing the Newborn

Almost immediately after birth, after the baby and mother have become acquainted, a newborn is taken to be weighed, cleaned up, and tested for signs of developmental problems that might require urgent attention (Als & Butler, 2008). The **Apgar Scale** is widely used to assess the health of newborns at one and five minutes after birth. The Apgar Scale evaluates infants' heart rate, respiratory effort, muscle tone, body color, and reflex irritability. An obstetrician or a nurse does the evaluation and gives the newborn a score, or reading, of 0, 1, or 2 on each of these five health signs (see Figure 2.14). A total score of 7 to 10 indicates that the newborn's condition is good. A score of 5 indicates there may be developmental difficulties. A score of 3 or below signals an emergency and indicates that the baby might not survive.

Apgar Scale A widely used method to assess the health of newborns at one and five minutes after birth; it evaluates infants' heart rate, respiratory effort, muscle tone, body color, and reflex irritability.

Score	0	1	2
Heart rate	Absent	Slow—less than 100 beats per minute	Fast—100–140 beats per minute
Respiratory effort	No breathing for more than one minute	Irregular and slow	Good breathing with normal crying
Muscle tone	Limp and flaccid	Weak, inactive, but some flexion of extremities	Strong, active motion
Body color	Blue and pale	Body pink, but extremities blue	Entire body pink
Reflex irritability	No response	Grimace	Coughing, sneezing and crying

FIGURE 2.14 The Apgar Scale.

Brazelton Neonatal Behavioral Assessment Scale (NBAS) A test given within 24 to 36 hours after birth to assess newborns' neurological development, reflexes, and reactions to people.

Neonatal Intensive Care Unit Network Neurobehavioral Scale (NNNS) An "offspring" of the NBAS, a test that provides a more comprehensive analysis of the newborn's behavior, neurological and stress responses, and regulatory capacities.

low birth weight infants Infants that weigh less than 5½ pounds at birth.

The Apgar Scale is especially good at assessing the newborn's ability to respond to the stress of delivery and the new environment (Oberlander & others, 2008). It also identifies high-risk infants who need resuscitation.

For a more thorough assessment of the newborn, the Brazelton Neonatal Behavioral Assessment Scale or the Neonatal Intensive Care Unit Network Neurobehavioral Scale may be used. The **Brazelton Neonatal Behavioral Assessment Scale (NBAS)** is performed within 24 to 36 hours after birth. It is also used as a sensitive index of neurological competence in the weeks or months after birth and as a measure in many studies of infant development (Mamtani, Patel, & Kulkarni, 2008). The NBAS assesses the newborn's neurological development, reflexes, and reactions to people. A very low NBAS score can indicate brain damage, or stress to the brain that may heal in time.

An "offspring" of the NBAS, the **Neonatal Intensive Care Unit Network Neurobehavioral Scale (NNNS)** provides a more comprehensive analysis of the newborn's behavior, neurological and stress responses, and regulatory capacities (Lester, Tronick, & Brazelton, 2004). Whereas the NBAS was developed to assess normal, healthy, term infants, T. Berry Brazelton, along with Barry Lester and Edward Tronick, developed the NNNS to assess the at-risk infant. It is especially useful for evaluating preterm infants (although it may not be appropriate for those less than 30 weeks' gestational age) and substance-exposed infants (Boukydis & Lester, 2008; Smith & others, 2008).

Low Birth Weight and Preterm Infants

Three related conditions pose threats to many newborns: having a low birth weight, being preterm, and being small for date. **Low birth weight infants** weigh less than 5½ pounds at birth. *Very low birth weight* newborns weigh under 3 pounds, and *extremely low birth weight newborns* under 2 pounds. **Preterm infants** are those born three weeks or more before the pregnancy has reached its full term—in other words, 35 or fewer weeks after conception. **Small for date infants** (also called *small for gestational age infants*) are those whose birth weight is below normal when the length of the pregnancy is considered. They weigh less than 90 percent of all babies of the same gestational age. Small for date infants may be preterm or full-term.

In 2006, 12.8 percent of U.S. infants were born preterm—a 36 percent increase since the 1980s (National Center for Health Statistics, 2009). The increase in preterm birth is likely due to such factors as the increasing number of births to women 35 years and older, increasing rates of multiple births, increased management of maternal and fetal conditions (for example, inducing labor preterm if medical technology indicates it will increase the likelihood of survival), increased substance abuse (tobacco, alcohol), and increased stress (Goldenberg & Culhane, 2007).

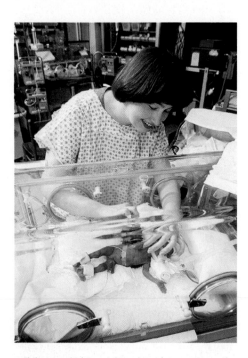

A "kilogram kid," weighing less than 2.3 pounds at birth. *What are some long-term outcomes for weighing so little at birth?*

Incidences and Causes of Low Birth Weight Most, but not all, preterm babies are also low birth weight babies. The incidence of low birth weight varies considerably from country to country. In some developing countries, such as India and Sudan, where poverty is rampant and the health and nutrition of mothers are poor, the percentage of low birth weight babies reaches as high as 31 percent (UNICEF, 2005) (see Figure 2.15). In the United States, there has been an increase in low birth weight infants in the last two decades, and the U.S. low birth weight rate of 8.1 percent in 2004 is considerably higher than that of many other developed countries (Hoyert & others, 2006). For example, only 4 percent of the infants born in Sweden, Finland, the Netherlands, and Norway are low birth weight.

The causes of low birth weight also vary. In the developing world, low birth weight stems mainly from the mother's poor health and nutrition (Vorster & Kruger, 2007). Diseases such as diarrhea and malaria, which are common in developing countries, can impair fetal growth if the mother becomes infected while she is pregnant. In developed countries, cigarette smoking during pregnancy is the leading cause of low birth weight (Nabet & others, 2007).

Recently, there has been considerable interest generated in the role that progestin might play in reducing preterm births (Basaran, 2007; Thorton, 2007). In one study, weekly injections of the hormone progesterone, which is naturally produced by the ovaries, lowered the rate of preterm births by one-third (Meis & Peaceman, 2003). Other recent studies provide further support for the use of progestin in the second trimester of pregnancy in reducing the risk of preterm delivery (Fonseca & others, 2007; Lamont & Jaggat, 2007).

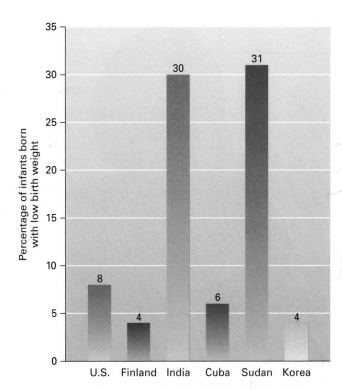

FIGURE 2.15 Percentage of Infants Born with Low Birth Weight in Selected Countries.

Consequences of Low Birth Weight Although most preterm and low birth weight infants are healthy, as a group they have more health and developmental problems than normal birth weight infants (Minde & Zelkowitz, 2008; Santo, Portuguez, & Nunes, 2009). Approximately 50 percent of all low birth weight children are enrolled in special education programs.

For preterm birth, the terms *extremely preterm* and *very preterm* are increasingly used (Smith, 2008). *Extremely preterm infants* are those born less than 28 weeks preterm, and *very preterm infants* are those born less than 33 weeks of gestational age. Figure 2.16 shows the results of a recent Norwegian study indicating that the earlier preterm infants are born the more likely they will drop out of school (Swamy, Ostbye, & Skjaerven, 2008). A recent research review also revealed that very preterm infants had lower IQ scores, had less effective information-processing skills, and were more at risk for behavioral problems than full-term infants (Johnson, 2007).

The number and severity of these problems increase when infants are born very early and as their birth weight decreases (Allen, 2008; Casey, 2008). Survival rates for infants who are born very early and very small have risen, but with this improved survival rate have come increases in rates of severe brain damage. The earlier the birth and the lower the birth weight, the greater is the likelihood of brain injury. A recent MRI study revealed that adolescents who had experienced very preterm birth were more likely to show reduced prefrontal lobe and corpus callosum functioning than were full-term adolescents (Narberhaus & others, 2008).

An increasing number of studies also indicate that low birth weight infants have more difficulty in socializing and have different lifestyles as emerging adults and adults (Kajantie & others, 2008; Moster, Lie, & Markestad, 2008). For example, in one study, as adults, extremely low birth weight infants were more likely to report that they were more inhibited and had a lower level of emotional well-being than normal birth weight infants were likely to report as adults (Schmidt & others, 2008).

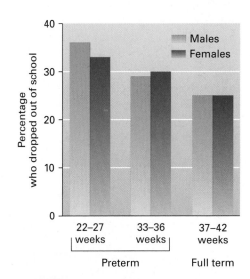

FIGURE 2.16 Percentage of Preterm and Full-Term Birth Infants Who Dropped Out of School.

preterm infants Infants born three weeks or more before the pregnancy has reached its full term.

small for date infants Infants whose birth weights are below normal when the length of pregnancy is considered; also called small for gestational age infants. Small for date infants may be preterm or full-term.

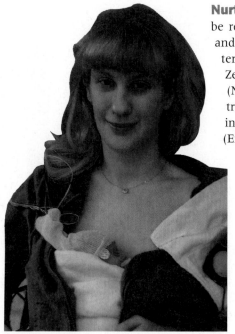

A new mother practicing kangaroo care. *What is kangaroo care?*

kangaroo care A way of holding a preterm infant so that there is skin-to-skin contact.

Nurturing Preterm Infants   Some effects of being born low in birth weight can be reduced or even reversed. Intensive enrichment programs that provide medical and educational services for both the parents and the children can improve short-term outcomes for low birth weight children (Lee & others, 2009; Minde & Zelkowitz, 2008). Currently, the two most popular neonatal intensive care unit (NICU) interventions that involve parents are breast feeding and **kangaroo care,** treatment for preterm infants that involves skin-to-skin contact. Recent surveys indicated that kangaroo care is used from 82 to 97 percent by nurses in NICUs (Engler & others, 2002; Field & others, 2006). Also in one of these surveys, massage therapy was used in 37 percent of the NICUs (Field & others, 2006).

In kangaroo care, the baby, wearing only a diaper, is held upright against the parent's bare chest, much as a baby kangaroo is carried by its mother. Kangaroo care is typically practiced for two to three hours per day, over an extended time in early infancy (Johnson, 2007).

Why use kangaroo care with preterm infants? Preterm infants often have difficulty coordinating their breathing and heart rate, and the close physical contact with the parent provided by kangaroo care can help to stabilize the preterm infant's heartbeat, temperature, and breathing (Walters & others, 2007). Further, preterm infants who experience kangaroo care have longer periods of sleep, gain more weight, decrease their crying, have longer periods of alertness, and have earlier hospital discharge (Ludington-Hoe & others, 2006). Two recent experimental studies revealed that low birth weight infants randomly assigned to kangaroo mother care compared with traditional mother care gained more weight, were less likely to experience hypothermia and hypoglycemia, and were more strongly attached to their mother (Gathwala, Singh, & Balhara, 2008; Suman, Udani, & Nanavati, 2008). A recent study also revealed that kangaroo care decreased pain responses in preterm infants (Johnston & others, 2009). Kangaroo care increasingly is being recommended for full-term infants as well (Ferber & Makhoul, 2008; Walters & others, 2008).

Many preterm infants experience less touch than full-term infants because they are isolated in temperature-controlled incubators (Chia, Sellick, & Gan, 2006). The research of Tiffany Field has led to a surge of interest in the role that massage might play in improving the developmental outcomes for preterm infants. To read about her research, see the following *Research in Life-Span Development* interlude.

Research in Life-Span Development

TIFFANY FIELD'S RESEARCH ON MASSAGE THERAPY

Throughout history and in many cultures, caregivers have massaged infants. In Africa and Asia, infants are routinely massaged by parents or other family members for several months after birth. In the United States, interest in using touch and massage to improve the growth, health, and well-being of infants has been stimulated by the research of Tiffany Field (2001, 2003, 2007; Field & Diego, 2008; Field, Diego, & Hernandez-Reif, 2007, 2008; Field & others, 2006; Hernandez-Reif, Diego, & Field, 2007), director of the Touch Research Institute at the University of Miami School of Medicine.

In a recent study, preterm infants in a neonatal intensive care unit (NICU) were randomly assigned to a massage therapy group or a control group. For five consecutive days, the preterm infants in the massage group were given three 15-minute moderate-pressure massages (Hernandez-Reif, Diego, & Field, 2007). Behavioral observations of the following stress behaviors were made on the first and last days of the study: crying, grimacing, yawning, sneezing, jerky arm and leg movements, startles, and finger flaring. The various stress behaviors were summarized in a composite stress behavior index. As indicated in Figure 2.17, massage had a stress-reducing effect on the preterm infants,

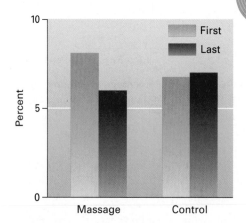

FIGURE 2.17 Preterm Infants Show Reduced Stress Behaviors and Activity After Five Days of Massage Therapy (Hernandez-Reif, Diego, & Field, 2007). Infant Behavior and Development, 30.

which is especially important because they encounter numerous stressors while they are hospitalized.

In another study, Field and her colleagues (2004) tested a more cost-effective massage strategy. They taught mothers how to massage their full-term infants rather than having health-care professionals do the massage. Beginning from day one of the newborn's life to the end of the first month, once a day before bedtime the mothers massaged the babies using either light or moderate pressure. Infants who were massaged with moderate pressure gained more weight, performed better on the orientation scale of the Brazelton, were less excitable and less depressed, and were less agitated during sleep.

Field has demonstrated the benefits of massage therapy for infants who face a variety of problems. For example, preterm infants exposed to cocaine as a fetus who received massage therapy gained weight and improved their scores on developmental tests (Wheeden & others, 1993). Another study investigated 1- to 3-month-old infants born to depressed adolescent mothers (Field & others, 1996). The infants of depressed mothers who received massage therapy had lower stress—as well as improved emotionality, sociability, and soothability—compared with the nonmassaged infants of depressed mothers.

In a research review of massage therapy with preterm infants, Field and her colleagues (2004) concluded that the most consistent findings involve two positive results: (1) increased weight gain and (2) discharge from the hospital from three to six days earlier than infants not receiving massage therapy.

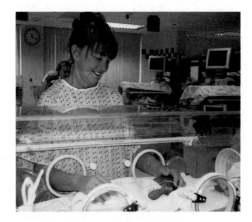

Shown here is Tiffany Field massaging a newborn infant. *What types of infants has massage therapy been shown to help?*

Bonding

A special component of the parent-infant relationship is **bonding,** the formation of a connection, especially a physical bond between parents and the newborn in the period shortly after birth. Sometimes hospitals seem determined to deter bonding. Drugs given to the mother to make her delivery less painful can make the mother drowsy, interfering with her ability to respond to and stimulate the newborn. Mothers and newborns are often separated shortly after delivery, and preterm infants are isolated from their mothers even more than are full-term infants.

Do these practices do any harm? Some physicians stress that during the period shortly after birth, the parents and newborn need to form an emotional attachment as a foundation for optimal development in years to come (Kennell, 2006; Kennell & McGrath, 1999). Is there evidence that close contact between mothers in the first several days after birth is critical for optimal development later in life? Although some research supports this bonding hypothesis (Klaus & Kennell, 1976), a body of research challenges the significance of the first few days of life as a critical period (Bakeman & Brown, 1980; Rode & others, 1981). Indeed, the extreme form of the bonding hypothesis—that the newborn must have close contact with the mother in the first few days of life to develop optimally—simply is not true.

Nonetheless, the weakness of the bonding hypothesis should not be used as an excuse to keep motivated mothers from interacting with their newborns. Such contact brings pleasure to many mothers. In some mother-infant pairs—including preterm infants, adolescent mothers, and mothers from disadvantaged circumstances—early close contact may establish a climate for improved interaction after the mother and infant leave the hospital.

Many hospitals now offer a *rooming-in* arrangement, in which the baby remains in the mother's room most of the time during its hospital stay. However, if parents choose not to use this rooming-in arrangement, the weight of the research suggests that this decision will not harm the infant emotionally (Lamb, 1994).

bonding The formation of a close connection, especially a physical bond between parents and their newborn in the period shortly after birth.

Review and Reflect: Learning Goal 5

5 **Summarize how birth takes place**

REVIEW

- What are the three main stages of birth? What are some different birth strategies? What is the transition from fetus to newborn like for the infant?
- What are three measures of neonatal health and responsiveness?
- What are the outcomes for children if they are born preterm or with a low birth weight?
- What is bonding? How is it linked to child outcomes?

REFLECT

- If you are a female, which birth strategy do you prefer? Why? If you are a male, how involved would you want to be in helping your partner through pregnancy and the birth of your baby?

Biological Beginnings

1 THE EVOLUTIONARY PERSPECTIVE: DISCUSS THE EVOLUTIONARY PERSPECTIVE ON LIFE-SPAN DEVELOPMENT

Natural Selection and Adaptive Behavior

- Natural selection is the process by which those individuals of a species that are best adapted survive and reproduce. Darwin proposed that natural selection fuels evolution. In evolutionary theory, adaptive behavior is behavior that promotes the organism's survival in a natural habitat.

Evolutionary Psychology

- Evolutionary psychology holds that adaptation, reproduction, and "survival of the fittest" are important in shaping behavior. Ideas proposed by evolutionary developmental psychology include the view that an extended childhood period is needed to develop a large brain and learn the complexity of human social communities. According to Baltes, the benefits resulting from evolutionary selection decrease with age mainly because of a decline in reproductive fitness. At the same time, cultural needs increase. Like other theoretical approaches to development, evolutionary psychology has limitations. Bandura rejects "one-sided evolutionism" and argues for a bidirectional link between biology and environment. Biology allows for a broad range of cultural possibilities. Evolution has given us bodily structures and biological potential, but it does not dictate our behavior.

2 GENETIC FOUNDATIONS OF DEVELOPMENT: DESCRIBE WHAT GENES ARE AND HOW THEY INFLUENCE HUMAN DEVELOPMENT

The Collaborative Gene

- Short segments of DNA constitute genes, the units of hereditary information that direct cells to reproduce and manufacture proteins. Genes act collaboratively, not independently.

Genes and Chromosomes

- Genes are passed on to new cells when chromosomes are duplicated during the process of mitosis and meiosis, which are two ways in which new cells are formed. When an egg and a sperm unite in the fertilization process, the resulting zygote contains the genes from the chromosomes in the father's sperm and the mother's egg. Despite this transmission of genes from generation to generation, variability is created in several ways, including the exchange of chromosomal segments during meiosis, mutations, and the distinction between a genotype and a phenotype.

Genetic Principles

- Genetic principles include those involving dominant-recessive genes, sex-linked genes, genetic imprinting, and polygenic inheritance.

Chromosomal and Gene-Linked Abnormalities

- Chromosomal abnormalities produce Down syndrome, which is caused by the presence of an extra copy of chromosome 21, as well as sex-linked chromosomal abnormalities such as Klinefelter syndrome, fragile X syndrome, Turner syndrome, and XYY syndrome. Gene-linked abnormalities involve harmful genes. Gene-linked disorders include phenylketonuria (PKU) and sickle-cell anemia. Genetic counseling offers couples information about their risk of having a child with inherited abnormalities.

3 HEREDITY AND ENVIRONMENT INTERACTION: THE NATURE-NURTURE DEBATE: EXPLAIN SOME OF THE WAYS THAT HEREDITY AND ENVIRONMENT INTERACT TO PRODUCE INDIVIDUAL DIFFERENCES IN DEVELOPMENT

Behavior Genetics

- Behavior genetics is the field that seeks to discover the influence of heredity and environment on individual differences in human traits and development. Methods used by behavior geneticists include twin studies and adoption studies.

Heredity-Environment Correlations

- In Scarr's heredity-environment correlations view, heredity may influence the types of environments that children experience. She describes three genotype-environment correlations: passive, evocative, and active (niche-picking). Scarr notes that the relative importance of these three genotype-environment correlations changes as children develop.

Shared and Nonshared Environmental Influences

- Shared environmental experiences refer to siblings' common experiences, such as their parents' personalities or intellectual orientation, the family's socioeconomic status, and the neighborhood in which they live. Nonshared environmental experiences involve the child's unique experiences, both within a family and outside a family, that are not shared with a sibling. Many behavior geneticists argue that differences in the development of siblings are due to nonshared environmental experiences (and heredity) rather than shared environmental experiences.

The Epigenetic View and Gene × Environment (G × E) Interaction

- The epigenetic view emphasizes that development is the result of an ongoing, bidirectional interchange between heredity and environment. The interaction of a specific measured variation in DNA and a specific measured aspect of the environment is referred to as gene × environment (G × E) interaction.

Conclusions About Heredity-Environment Interaction

- Complex behaviors have some genetic loading that gives people a propensity for a particular developmental trajectory. However, actual development also requires an environment, and that environment is complex. The interaction of heredity and environment is extensive. Much remains to be discovered about the specific ways that heredity and environment interact to influence development.

4 PRENATAL DEVELOPMENT: CHARACTERIZE THE COURSE OF PRENATAL DEVELOPMENT AND ITS HAZARDS

The Course of Prenatal Development

- Prenatal development is divided into three periods: germinal (first two weeks after conception), which ends when the zygote (a fertilized egg) attaches to the uterine wall; embryonic (two to eight weeks after conception), during which the embryo differentiates into three layers, life-support systems develop, and organ systems begin to form (organogenesis); and fetal (two months after conception until about nine months, or when the infant is born), a time when organ systems have matured to the point at which life can be sustained outside of the womb. The growth of the brain during prenatal development is nothing short of remarkable. By the time babies are born they have approximately 100 billion neurons, or nerve cells. The term neurogenesis means the formation of new neurons. The nervous system begins with the formation of a neural tube at 18 to 24 days after conception. Proliferation and migration are two processes that characterize brain development in the prenatal period. The basic architecture of the brain is formed in the first two trimesters of prenatal development.

Prenatal Diagnostic Tests

- Amniocentesis, ultrasound sonography, fetal MRI, chorionic villus sampling, maternal blood screening, and noninvasive prenatal diagnosis (NIPD) are used to determine whether a fetus is developing normally. There has been a dramatic increase in research on less invasive diagnosis, such as fetal MRI and NIPD.

Hazards to Prenatal Development

- A teratogen is any agent that can potentially cause a birth defect or negatively alter cognitive and behavioral outcomes. The dose, time of exposure, and genetic susceptibility influence the severity of the damage to an unborn child and the type of defect that occurs. Prescription drugs that can be harmful include antibiotics, some antidepressants, and certain hormones; nonprescription drugs that can be harmful include diet pills and aspirin. The psychoactive drugs caffeine, alcohol, nicotine, cocaine, methamphetamine, marijuana, and heroin are potentially harmful to offspring. For example, fetal alcohol spectrum disorders (FASD) are a cluster of abnormalities that appear in offspring of mothers who drink heavily during pregnancy. Even when pregnant women drink moderately (one to two drinks a day), negative effects on their offspring have been found. Cigarette smoking by pregnant women also has serious adverse effects on prenatal and child development (such as low birth weight). Incompatibility of the mother's and the father's blood types can be harmful to the fetus. Problems may also result if a pregnant woman has rubella (German measles), syphilis, genital herpes, or AIDS. A developing fetus depends entirely on its mother for nutrition, and it may be harmed if the mother is malnourished, is overweight, has a diet deficient in folic acid, or consumes significant amounts of fish polluted by mercury or PCBs. High anxiety and stress in the mother are linked with less than optimal prenatal and birth outcomes. Maternal age can negatively affect the offspring's development if the mother is an adolescent or 35 and older. Paternal factors that can adversely affect prenatal development include exposure to lead, radiation, certain pesticides, and petrochemicals. Potential environmental hazards include radiation, environmental pollutants, and toxic wastes.

Prenatal Care

- Prenatal care programs provide information about teratogens and other prenatal hazards. In addition, various medical conditions are screened for, and medical care is given in a defined schedule of visits. Prenatal classes often provide nutritional, social, and educational services.

5 BIRTH: SUMMARIZE HOW BIRTH TAKES PLACE

The Birth Process

- Childbirth occurs in three stages. The first stage, which lasts about 6 to 12 hours for a woman having her first child, is the longest stage. The cervix dilates to about 4 inches at the end of the first stage. The second stage begins when the baby's head moves through the cervix and ends with the baby's complete emergence. The third stage is afterbirth. Childbirth strategies involve the childbirth setting and attendants. In many countries, a doula attends a childbearing woman. Methods of delivery include medicated, natural and prepared, and cesarean. An increasing number of nonmedicated techniques, such as waterbirth, are being used to reduce childbirth pain. Being born involves considerable stress for the baby, but the baby is well prepared and adapted to handle the stress. Anoxia—insufficient oxygen supply to the fetus/newborn—is a potential hazard.

Assessing the Newborn

- For many years, the Apgar Scale has been used to assess the newborn's health. The Brazelton Neonatal Behavioral Assessment Scale (NBAS) examines the newborn's neurological development, reflexes, and reactions to people. The Neonatal Intensive Care Unit Network Neurobehavioral Scale (NNNS) was created to assess the at-risk infant.

Low Birth Weight and Preterm Infants

- Low birth weight infants weigh less than 5½ pounds, and they may be preterm (born three weeks or more before the pregnancy has reached its full term) or small for date (infants whose birth weight is below normal when the length of pregnancy is considered; also called small for gestational age). Small for date infants may be preterm or full-term. Although most low birth weight infants are normal and healthy, as a group they have more health and developmental problems than normal birth weight infants. Kangaroo care and massage therapy have been shown to have benefits for preterm infants.

| Bonding |

- Bonding is the formation of a close connection, especially a physical bond between parents and the newborn shortly after birth. Early bonding has not been found to be critical in the development of a competent infant.

KEY TERMS

evolutionary
 psychology 55
chromosomes 57
DNA 57
genes 57
mitosis 58
meiosis 58
fertilization 58
zygote 58
genotype 59
phenotype 59
Down syndrome 61
Klinefelter syndrome 61
fragile X syndrome 61
Turner syndrome 62

XYY syndrome 62
phenylketonuria (PKU) 62
sickle-cell anemia 62
behavior genetics 65
twin study 65
adoption study 65
passive genotype-
 environment
 correlations 65
evocative genotype-
 environment
 correlations 65
active (niche-picking)
 genotype-environment
 correlations 66

shared environmental
 experiences 66
nonshared environmental
 experiences 66
epigenetic view 67
gene × environment (G × E)
 interaction 67
germinal period 69
embryonic period 69
organogensis 70
fetal period 70
neurons 70
teratogen 73
fetal alcohol spectrum
 disorders (FASD) 75

natural childbirth 85
prepared childbirth 85
Apgar Scale 87
Brazelton Neonatal
 Behavioral Assessment
 Scale (NBAS) 88
Neonatal Intensive Care
 Unit Network
 Neurobehavioral
 Scale (NNNS) 88
low birth weight infants 88
preterm infants 88
small for date infants 88
kangaroo care 90
bonding 91

KEY PEOPLE

Charles Darwin 54
David Buss 55
Paul Baltes 56
Albert Bandura 56

David Moore 57
Sandra Scarr 65
Robert Plomin 66
Gilbert Gottlieb 67

David Olds 81
Ferdinand
 Lamaze 85
T. Berry Brazelton 88

Barry Lester and Edward
 Tronick 88
Tiffany Field 90

E-LEARNING TOOLS

Connect to **www.mhhe.com/santrockldt5e** to research the answers and complete these exercises. In addition, you'll find a number of other resources and valuable study tools for Chapter 2, "Biological Beginnings," on this Web site.

Taking It to the Net

1. Ahmahl, a biochemistry major, is writing a psychology paper on the potential dilemmas that society and scientists may face as a result of the decoding of the human genome. What are some of the main issues or concerns that Ahmahl should address in his paper?

2. Brandon and Katie are thrilled to learn that they are expecting their first child. They are curious about the genetic makeup of their unborn child and want to know (a) what disorders might be identified through prenatal genetic testing; and (b) which tests, if any, Katie should undergo to help determine the health of their child.

3. Jaime's doctor has told her that he has some concerns regarding her newborn son's low score on the Brazelton Neonatal Behavioral Assessment Scale (NBAS). Jaime would like to know more about the NBAS, including what it measures and what kind of assessment activities are involved.

Self-Assessment

To evaluate your genetic history and prenatal issues, complete these self-assessments:

- *Prenatal Genetic Screening Questionnaire*
- *My Family Health Tree*

Health and Well-Being, Parenting, and Education

Build your decision-making skills by trying your hand at the health and well-being, parenting, and education exercises.

Video Clips

The Online Learning Center includes the following video for this chapter:

- *Midwifery*

3

To be seventy years young is sometimes far more cheerful and hopeful than to be forty years old.

—Oliver Wendell Holmes, Sr.
American Physician & Poet, 19th Century

LEARNING GOALS

◆ Discuss major changes in the body through the life span.

◆ Describe how the brain changes through the life span.

◆ Summarize how sleep patterns change as people develop.

◆ Explain longevity and the biological aspects of aging.

PHYSICAL DEVELOPMENT AND BIOLOGICAL AGING

CHAPTER OUTLINE

PREVIEW

Think about how much you have changed physically and will continue to change as you age. We come into this life as small beings. But we grow very rapidly in infancy, more slowly in childhood, and once again more rapidly during puberty, and then experience another slowdown. Eventually we decline, but many older adults are still physically robust. In this chapter, we explore changes in body growth, the brain, and sleep across the life span. We also examine longevity and evaluate some fascinating ideas about why we age.

1 BODY GROWTH AND CHANGE

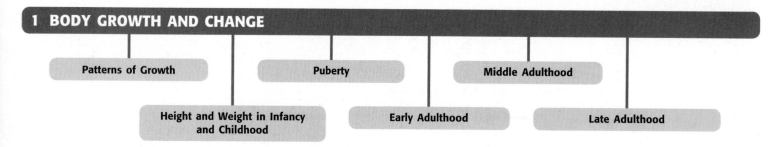

In life's long journey, we go through many bodily changes. We grow up, we grow out, we shrink. The very visible changes in height and weight are accompanied by less visible ones in bones, lungs, and every other organ of the body. These changes will help shape how we think about ourselves, how other people think about us, and what we are capable of thinking, doing, and feeling. Are there strict timelines for these changes? Are they set in our genes? Let's begin by studying some basic patterns of growth and then turn to bodily changes from the time we are infants through the time we are older adults.

Patterns of Growth

The **cephalocaudal pattern** is the sequence in which the fastest growth in the human body occurs at the top, with the head. Physical growth in size, weight, and feature differentiation gradually works its way down from the top to the bottom (for example, neck, shoulders, middle trunk, and so on). This same pattern occurs in the head area, because the top parts of the head—the eyes and brain—grow faster than the lower parts, such as the jaw. During prenatal development and early infancy, the head constitutes an extraordinarily large proportion of the total body (see Figure 3.1).

In most cases, sensory and motor development proceeds according to the cephalocaudal principle. For example, infants see objects before they can control their

FIGURE 3.1 Changes in Proportions of the Human Body During Growth. As individuals develop from infancy through adulthood, one of the most noticeable physical changes is that the head becomes smaller in relation to the rest of the body. The fractions listed refer to head size as a proportion of total body length at different ages.

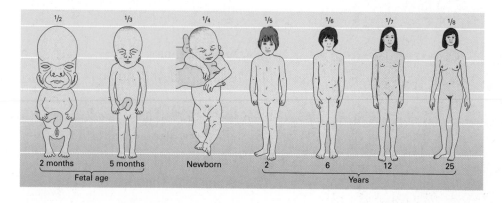

torso, and they can use their hands long before they can crawl or walk. However, one study contradicted the cephalocaudal principle because infants reached for toys with their feet before using their hands (Galloway & Thelen, 2004). In this study, infants on average first contacted the toy with their feet when they were 12 weeks old and with their hands when they were 16 weeks old. Thus, contrary to long-standing beliefs, early leg movements can be precisely controlled, some aspects of development that involve reaching do not involve lengthy practice, and early motor behaviors don't always develop in a strict cephalocaudal pattern.

The **proximodistal pattern** is the growth sequence that starts at the center of the body and moves toward the extremities. An example is the early maturation of muscular control of the trunk and arms, compared with that of the hands and fingers. Further, infants use the whole hand as a unit before they can control several fingers.

Height and Weight in Infancy and Childhood

Height and weight increase rapidly in infancy (Lampl, 2008). Then, they take a slower course during the childhood years.

Infancy The average North American newborn is 20 inches long and weighs 7½ pounds. Ninety-five percent of full-term newborns are 18 to 22 inches long and weigh between 5½ and 10 pounds.

In the first several days of life, most newborns lose 5 to 7 percent of their body weight. Once infants adjust to sucking, swallowing, and digesting, they grow rapidly, gaining an average of 5 to 6 ounces per week during the first month. They have doubled their birth weight by the age of 4 months and have nearly tripled it by their first birthday. Infants grow about 1 inch per month during the first year, reaching approximately 1½ times their birth length by their first birthday.

Infants' rate of growth slows considerably in the second year of life (Wolraich & others, 2008). By 2 years of age, infants weigh approximately 26 to 32 pounds, having gained a quarter to half a pound per month during the second year; now they have reached about one-fifth of their adult weight. The average 2-year-old is 32 to 35 inches tall, which is nearly one-half of adult height.

Early Childhood As the preschool child grows older, the percentage of increase in height and weight decreases with each additional year (Cooper & others, 2008). Girls are only slightly smaller and lighter than boys during these years. Both boys and girls slim down as the trunks of their bodies lengthen. Although their heads are still somewhat large for their bodies, by the end of the preschool years most children have lost their top-heavy look. Body fat also shows a slow, steady decline during the preschool years. Girls have more fatty tissue than boys; boys have more muscle tissue.

Growth patterns vary individually (Burns & others, 2009). Think back to your preschool years. This was probably the first time you noticed that some children were taller than you, some shorter; some were fatter, some thinner; some were stronger, some weaker. Much of the variation is due to heredity, but environmental experiences are also involved. A review of the height and weight of children around the world concluded that two important contributors to height differences are ethnic origin and nutrition (Meredith, 1978). Also, urban, middle-socioeconomic-status, and firstborn children were taller than rural, lower-socioeconomic-status, and later-born children. The children whose mothers smoked during pregnancy were half an inch shorter than

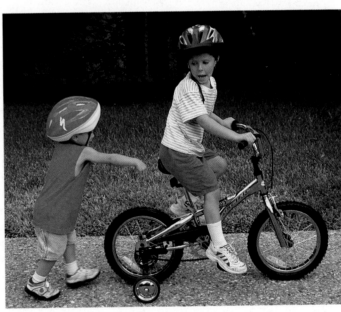

The bodies of 5-year-olds and 2-year-olds are different from one another. The 5-year-old not only is taller and heavier, but also has a longer trunk and legs than the 2-year-old. *What might be some other physical differences between 2- and 5-year-olds?*

cephalocaudal pattern The sequence in which the fastest growth occurs at the top—the head—with physical growth in size, weight, and feature differentiation gradually working from top to bottom.

proximodistal pattern The sequence in which growth starts at the center of the body and moves toward the extremities.

the children whose mothers did not smoke during pregnancy. In the United States, African American children are taller than non-Latino White children.

Why are some children unusually short? The culprits are congenital factors (genetic or prenatal problems), growth hormone deficiency, a physical problem that develops in childhood, maternal smoking during pregnancy, or an emotional difficulty. One research review found that although children with short stature on average score lower than children of normal or tall stature on tests of motor skills, intelligence, and achievement, few short children score outside the normal range for these skills (Wheeler & others, 2004).

Growth hormone deficiency is the absence or deficiency of growth hormone produced by the pituitary gland to stimulate the body to grow. Growth hormone deficiency may occur during infancy or later in childhood (Oswiecimska & others, 2008). It is estimated that as many as 10,000 to 15,000 U.S. children have growth hormone deficiency (Stanford University Medical Center, 2008). Without treatment, most children with growth hormone deficiency will not reach a height of 5 feet. Treatment for this hormone deficiency involves regular injections of growth hormone and usually lasts several years (Rosenfeld & Bakker, 2008). Some children receive daily injections, others several times a week.

Children who are chronically sick are shorter than their counterparts who are rarely sick. Children who have been physically abused or neglected may secrete too little growth hormone, which can restrict their physical growth.

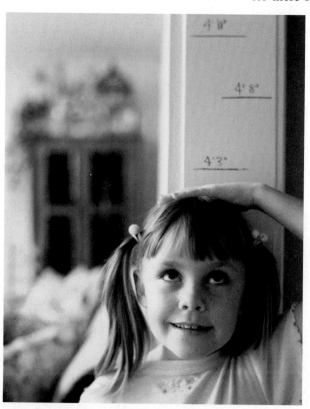

What characterizes physical growth during middle and late childhood?

Middle and Late Childhood
The period of middle and late childhood involves slow, consistent growth. This is a period of calm before the rapid growth spurt of adolescence.

During the elementary school years, children grow an average of 2 to 3 inches a year. At the age of 8, the average girl and the average boy are 4 feet 2 inches tall. During the middle and late childhood years, children gain about 5 to 7 pounds a year. The average 8-year-old girl and the average 8-year-old boy weigh 56 pounds. The weight increase is due mainly to increases in the size of the skeletal and muscular systems, as well as the size of some body organs. Muscle mass and strength gradually increase as "baby fat" decreases in middle and late childhood (Hockenberry & Wilson, 2009).

The loose movements and knock-knees of early childhood give way to improved muscle tone in middle and late childhood. The increase in muscular strength is due to heredity and to exercise. Children also double their strength capabilities during these years. Because of their greater number of muscle cells, boys tend to be stronger than girls.

Changes in proportions are among the most pronounced physical changes in middle and late childhood. Head circumference, waist circumference, and leg length decrease in relation to body height. A less noticeable physical change is that bones continue to harden during middle and late childhood but yield to pressure and pull more than mature bones.

Puberty

Puberty is a period of rapid physical maturation involving hormonal and bodily changes that take places in early adolescence. We begin our exploration of puberty by focusing on sexual maturation, height, and weight; we then explore hormonal changes, discuss timing and variations in puberty, and conclude by describing puberty's psychological accompaniments.

Sexual Maturation, Height, and Weight
Think back to the onset of your puberty. Of the striking changes that were taking place in your body, what was the

growth hormone deficiency The absence or deficiency of growth hormone produced by the pituitary gland to stimulate body growth.

puberty A period of rapid physical maturation involving hormonal and bodily changes during early adolescence.

first to occur? Researchers have found that male pubertal characteristics typically develop in this order: increase in penis and testicle size, appearance of straight pubic hair, minor voice change, first ejaculation (which usually occurs through masturbation or a wet dream), appearance of curly pubic hair, onset of maximum growth in height and weight, growth of hair in armpits, more detectable voice changes, and, finally, growth of facial hair.

What is the order of appearance of physical changes in females? First, either the breasts enlarge or pubic hair appears. A recent longitudinal study revealed that on average, girls' breast development preceded their pubic hair development by about two months (Susman & others, 2009). Later, hair appears in the armpits. As these changes occur, the female grows in height and her hips become wider than her shoulders. **Menarche**—a girl's first menstruation—comes rather late in the pubertal cycle. Initially, her menstrual cycles may be highly irregular. For the first several years, she may not ovulate every menstrual cycle; some girls do not ovulate at all until a year or two after menstruation begins. No voice changes comparable to those in pubertal males occur in pubertal females. By the end of puberty, the female's breasts have become more fully rounded.

Marked weight gains coincide with the onset of puberty. During early adolescence, girls tend to outweigh boys, but by about age 14 boys begin to surpass girls. Similarly, at the beginning of the adolescent period, girls tend to be as tall as or taller than boys of their age, but by the end of the middle school years most boys have caught up or, in many cases, surpassed girls in height. A recent study examined 7- to 18-year-old Chinese children and adolescents' height from the 1950s through 2005 (Ji & Chen, 2008). In general, there were significant increases in height across this time frame with the greatest increase occurring during puberty. The researchers concluded that improved nutrition, health, and socioeconomic conditions were likely responsible for the increases in adolescents' height.

As indicated in Figure 3.2, the growth spurt occurs approximately two years earlier for girls than for boys. The mean age at the beginning of the growth spurt in girls is 9; for boys, it is 11. The peak rate of pubertal change occurs at 11½ years for girls and 13½ years for boys. During their growth spurt, girls increase in height about 3½ inches per year, boys about 4 inches. Boys and girls who are shorter or taller than their peers before adolescence are likely to remain so during adolescence; however, as much as 30 percent of an individual's height in late adolescence is unexplained by his or her height in the elementary school years.

Hormonal Changes

Behind the first whisker in boys and the widening of hips in girls is a flood of **hormones,** powerful chemical substances secreted by the endocrine glands and carried through the body by the bloodstream. The endocrine system's role in puberty involves the interaction of the hypothalamus, the pituitary gland, and the gonads (see Figure 3.3). The **hypothalamus,** a structure in the brain, is involved with eating and sexual behavior. The **pituitary gland,** an important endocrine gland, controls growth and regulates other glands; among these, the **gonads**—the testes in males, the ovaries in females—are particularly important in giving rise to pubertal changes in the body.

How do the gonads, or sex glands, work? The pituitary sends a signal via **gonadotropins** (hormones that stimulate the testes or ovaries) to the appropriate gland to manufacture hormones. These hormones give rise to such changes as the production of sperm in males and menstruation and the release of eggs from the ovaries in females. The pituitary gland, through interaction with the hypothalamus, detects when the optimal level of hormones is reached and responds and maintains it with additional gonadotropin secretion (Susman & Dorn, 2009).

Not only does the pituitary gland release gonadotropins that stimulate the testes and ovaries, but through interaction with the hypothalamus the pituitary gland also secretes hormones that either directly lead to growth and skeletal maturation or

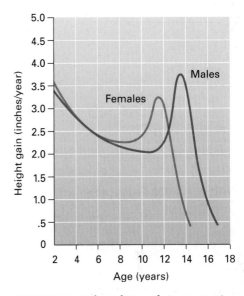

FIGURE 3.2 Pubertal Growth Spurt. On the average, the peak of the growth spurt that characterizes pubertal change occurs two years earlier for girls (11½) than for boys (13½).

menarche A girl's first menstrual period.

hormones Powerful chemical substances secreted by the endocrine glands and carried through the body by the bloodstream.

hypothalamus A structure in the brain that is involved with eating and sexual behavior.

pituitary gland An important endocrine gland that controls growth and regulates other glands.

gonads The sex glands—the testes in males, the ovaries in females.

gonadotropins Hormones that stimulate the testes or ovaries.

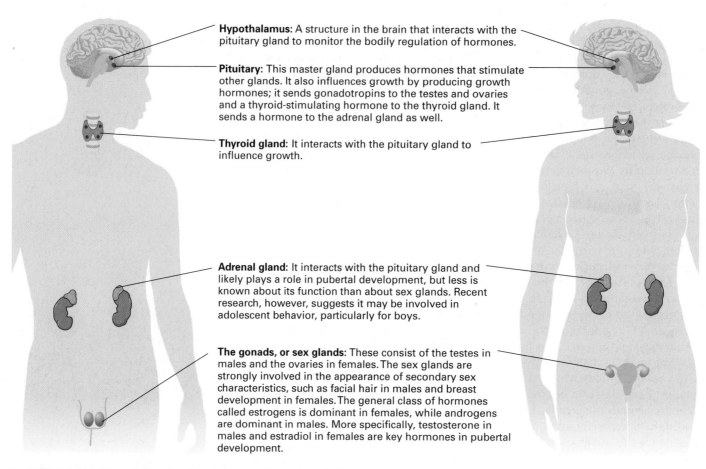

Hypothalamus: A structure in the brain that interacts with the pituitary gland to monitor the bodily regulation of hormones.

Pituitary: This master gland produces hormones that stimulate other glands. It also influences growth by producing growth hormones; it sends gonadotropins to the testes and ovaries and a thyroid-stimulating hormone to the thyroid gland. It sends a hormone to the adrenal gland as well.

Thyroid gland: It interacts with the pituitary gland to influence growth.

Adrenal gland: It interacts with the pituitary gland and likely plays a role in pubertal development, but less is known about its function than about sex glands. Recent research, however, suggests it may be involved in adolescent behavior, particularly for boys.

The gonads, or sex glands: These consist of the testes in males and the ovaries in females. The sex glands are strongly involved in the appearance of secondary sex characteristics, such as facial hair in males and breast development in females. The general class of hormones called estrogens is dominant in females, while androgens are dominant in males. More specifically, testosterone in males and estradiol in females are key hormones in pubertal development.

FIGURE 3.3 The Major Endocrine Glands Involved in Pubertal Change.

produce growth effects through interaction with the thyroid gland, located at the base of the throat.

The concentrations of certain hormones increase dramatically during adolescence (Susman & Dorn, 2009). **Testosterone** is a hormone associated in boys with the development of genitals, an increase in height, and a change in voice. **Estradiol** is a type of estrogen associated in girls with breast, uterine, and skeletal development. In one study, testosterone levels increased eighteenfold in boys but only twofold in girls during puberty; estradiol increased eightfold in girls but only twofold in boys (Nottelmann & others, 1987). Thus, both testosterone and estradiol are present in the hormonal makeup of both boys and girls, but testosterone dominates in male pubertal development, estradiol in female pubertal development (Richmond & Rogol, 2007).

The same influx of hormones that grows hair on a male's chest and increases the fatty tissue in a female's breasts may also contribute to psychological development in adolescence. In one study of boys and girls ranging in age from 9 to 14, a higher concentration of testosterone was present in boys who rated themselves as more socially competent (Nottelmann & others, 1987). However, hormonal effects by themselves do not account for adolescent development (Graber, 2008; Dorn & others, 2006). For example, in one study, social factors were much better predictors of young adolescent girls' depression and anger than hormonal factors (Brooks-Gunn & Warren, 1989). Behavior and moods also can affect hormones. Stress, eating patterns, exercise, sexual activity, tension, and depression can activate or suppress various aspects of the hormonal system. In sum, the hormone-behavior link is complex (Susman & Dorn, 2009).

testosterone A hormone associated in boys with the development of genitals, an increase in height, and a change in voice.

estradiol A hormone associated in girls with breast, uterine, and skeletal development.

Timing and Variations in Puberty   In the United States—where children mature up to a year earlier than children in European countries—the average age of menarche has declined significantly since the mid-nineteenth century (see Figure 3.4). Fortunately, however, we are unlikely to see pubescent toddlers, since what has happened in the past century is likely the result of improved nutrition and health.

Why do the changes of puberty occur when they do, and how can variations in their timing be explained? The basic genetic program for puberty is wired into the species (McAnarney, 2008). However, nutrition, health, and other environmental factors also affect puberty's timing and makeup (Hermann-Giddens, 2007).

For most boys, the pubertal sequence may begin as early as age 10 or as late as 13½, and may end as early as age 13 or as late as 17. Thus the normal range is wide enough that, given two boys of the same chronological age, one might complete the pubertal sequence before the other one has begun it. For girls, menarche is considered within the normal range if it appears between the ages of 9 and 15.

Precocious puberty is the term used to describe the very early onset and rapid progression of puberty. Judith Blakemore and her colleagues (2009, p. 58) recently described the following characteristics of precocious puberty. Precocious puberty is usually diagnosed when pubertal onset occurs before 8 years of age in girls and before 9 years of age in boys. Precocious puberty occurs approximately 10 times more often in girls than in boys. When precocious puberty occurs, it usually is treated by medically suppressing gonadotropic secretions, which temporarily stops pubertal change. The reasons for this treatment is that children who experience precocious puberty are ultimately likely to have short stature, early sexual capability, and the potential for engaging in age-inappropriate behavior (Blakemore, Berenbaum, & Liben, 2009).

Psychological Accompaniments of Puberty   What are some links between puberty and psychological characteristics? How do early and late maturation influence adolescents' psychological development?

Body Image   One psychological aspect of puberty is certain for both boys and girls: Adolescents are preoccupied with their bodies (Jones, Bain, & King, 2008; Mueller, 2009). Perhaps you looked in the mirror on a daily, and sometimes even hourly, basis to see if you could detect anything different about your changing body. Preoccupation with one's body image is strong throughout adolescence, but it is especially acute during puberty, a time when adolescents are more dissatisfied with their bodies than in late adolescence.

Gender differences characterize adolescents' perceptions of their bodies. In general, throughout puberty girls are less happy with their bodies and have more negative body images than boys (Bearman & others, 2006). As pubertal change proceeds, girls often become more dissatisfied with their bodies, probably because their body fat increases. In contrast, boys become more satisfied as they move through puberty, probably because their muscle mass increases (Bearman & others, 2006).

Early and Late Maturation   Did you enter puberty early, late, or on time? When adolescents mature earlier or later than their peers, they often perceive themselves differently (Susman & Dorn, 2009). In the Berkeley Longitudinal Study conducted some years ago, early-maturing boys perceived themselves more positively and had more successful peer relations than did late-maturing boys (Jones, 1965). The findings for early-maturing girls were similar but not as strong as for boys. When the late-maturing boys were in their thirties, however, they had developed a more positive identity than the early-maturing boys had (Peskin, 1967). Perhaps the late-maturing boys had had more time to explore life's options, or perhaps the early-maturing boys continued to focus on their physical status instead of paying attention to career development and achievement.

Adolescents show a strong preoccupation with their changing bodies and develop images of what their bodies are like. *Why might adolescent males have more positive body images than adolescent females?*

precocious puberty The term used to describe the very early onset and rapid progression of puberty.

What are some outcomes of early and late maturation in adolescence?

An increasing number of researchers have found that early maturation increases girls' vulnerability to a number of problems (Mendle, Turkheimer, & Emery, 2007; Westling & others, 2008). Early-maturing girls are more likely to smoke, drink, be depressed, have an eating disorder, struggle for earlier independence from their parents, and have older friends; and their bodies are likely to elicit responses from males that lead to earlier dating and earlier sexual experiences (Wiesner & Ittel, 2002). For example, a recent study revealed that early-maturing girls were more likely to try cigarettes and alcohol without their parents' knowledge (Westling & others, 2008). And early-maturing girls are less likely to graduate from high school and also cohabit and marrier earlier (Cavanagh, 2009). Apparently as a result of their social and cognitive immaturity, combined with early physical development, early-maturing girls are easily lured into problem behaviors, not recognizing the possible long-term effects of these on their development.

Early Adulthood

After the dramatic physical changes of puberty, the years of early adulthood seem an uneventful time in the body's history. Physical changes during these years may be subtle, but they do continue.

Height remains rather constant during the early adulthood years. Peak functioning of the body's joints also usually occurs in the twenties. Many individuals also reach a peak of muscle tone and strength in their late teens and twenties (Candow & Chilibeck, 2005). However, these may begin to decline in the thirties. Sagging chins and protruding abdomens may also appear for the first time. Muscles start to have less elasticity, and aches may begin to show in places not felt before.

Middle Adulthood

Like the changes of early adulthood, midlife physical changes are usually gradual. Although everyone experiences some physical change due to aging in the middle adulthood years, the rates of aging vary considerably from one individual to another. Genetic makeup and lifestyle factors play important roles in whether and when chronic diseases will appear. (In Chapter 4, "Health," we explore these diseases.)

Physical Appearance Individuals lose height in middle age, and many gain weight. On average, from 30 to 50 years of age, men lost about ½ inch in height, then may lose another ¾ inch from 50 to 70 years of age (Hoyer & Roodin, 2009). The height loss for women can be as much as 2 inches from 25 to 75 years of age. Note that there are large variations in the extent to which individuals become shorter with aging. The decrease in height is due to bone loss in the vertebrae. On average, body fat accounts for about 10 percent of body weight in adolescence; it makes up 20 percent or more in middle age.

Noticeable signs of aging usually are apparent by the forties or fifties. The skin begins to wrinkle and sag because of a loss of fat and collagen in underlying tissues (Farage & others, 2009). Small, localized areas of pigmentation in the skin produce aging spots, especially in areas that are exposed to sunlight, such as the hands and face. The hair thins and grays because of a lower replacement rate and a decline in melanin production. Fingernails and toenails develop ridges and become thicker and more brittle.

Since a youthful appearance is stressed in many cultures, many Americans whose hair is graying, whose skin is wrinkling, whose bodies are sagging, and whose teeth are yellowing strive to make themselves look younger. Undergoing cosmetic surgery, dyeing hair, purchasing wigs, enrolling in weight reduction programs, participating in exercise regimens, and taking heavy doses of vitamins are common in middle age. Baby boomers have shown a strong interest in plastic surgery and Botox,

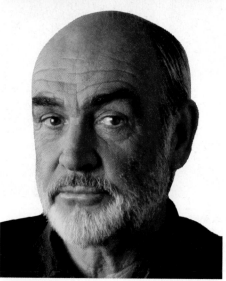

Famous actor Sean Connery as a young adult in his twenties (*top*) and as a middle-aged adult in his fifties (*bottom*). *What are some of the most outwardly noticeable signs of aging in the middle adulthood years?*

which may reflect their desire to take control of the aging process (Niamtu, 2009).

Strength, Joints, and Bones   The term *sarcopenia* is given to age-related loss of muscle mass and strength. The rate of muscle loss with age occurs at a rate of approximately 1 to 2 percent per year past the age of 50. A loss of strength especially occurs in the back and legs. Exercise can reduce the decline involved in sarcopenia (Johnson, De Lisio, & Parise, 2008).

Maximum bone density occurs by the mid to late thirties. From this point on, there is a progressive loss of bone. The rate of bone loss begins slowly but accelerates in the fifties (Burke & others, 2003). Women experience about twice the rate of bone loss as men. By the end of midlife, bones break more easily and heal more slowly (Wehren & others, 2005).

Cardiovascular System   The level of cholesterol in the blood increases through the adult years (Betensky, Contrada, & Leventhal, 2009). Cholesterol comes in two forms: LDL (low-density lipoprotein) and HDL (high-density lipoprotein). LDL is often referred to as "bad" cholesterol because when the level of LDL is too high, it sticks to the lining of blood vessels, a condition that can lead to atherosclerosis (hardening of the arteries). HDL is often referred to as "good" cholesterol because when it is high and LDL is low, the risk of cardiovascular disease is lessened (Gao & others, 2009). Scientists are not sure why HDL is protective but theorize that it may scour the walls of blood vessels and help to remove LDL from them. In middle age, cholesterol begins to accumulate on the artery walls, which are thickening. The result is an increased risk of cardiovascular disease. Cholesterol levels are influenced by heredity, but LDL can be reduced and HDL increased by eating food that is low in saturated fat and cholesterol and by exercising regularly (Masley & others, 2008).

Blood pressure, too, usually rises in the forties and fifties, and high blood pressure (hypertension) is linked with an increased rate of mortality (Krakoff, 2008). At menopause, a woman's blood pressure rises sharply and usually remains above that of a man through life's later years (S. Taler, 2009).

An increasing problem in middle and late adulthood that involves the cardiovascular system is the *metabolic syndrome*, a condition characterized by hypertension, obesity, and insulin resistance (Shin, Yun, & Park, 2009). Metabolic syndrome often leads to the development of diabetes and cardiovascular disease (Knuiman & others, 2009). In a longitudinal study, metabolic syndrome was a significant predictor of experiencing a heart attack or death over the course of seven years in elderly Mexican Americans (Otiniano & others, 2005). Weight loss and exercise are strongly recommended in the treatment of metabolic syndrome (Dupuy & others, 2007).

Lungs   There is little change in lung capacity through most of middle adulthood. However, at about the age of 55, the proteins in lung tissue become less elastic. This change, combined with a gradual stiffening of the chest wall, decreases the lungs' capacity to shuttle oxygen from the air people breathe to the blood in their veins (Simpson & others, 2005).

For smokers, however, the picture is different and bleaker. As shown in Figure 3.4, the lung capacity of individuals who are smokers drops precipitously in middle age. However, if the individuals quit smoking their lung capacity improves, although not to the level of individuals who have never smoked (Williams, 1995).

Sexuality   **Climacteric** is a term that is used to describe the midlife transition in which fertility declines. **Menopause** is the time in middle age, usually in the late forties or early fifties, when a woman's menstrual periods cease. The average age

Members of the Maasai tribe in Kenya, Africa, can stay on a treadmill for a long time because of their active lives. Heart disease is extremely low in the Masai tribe, which also can be attributed to their energetic lifestyle.

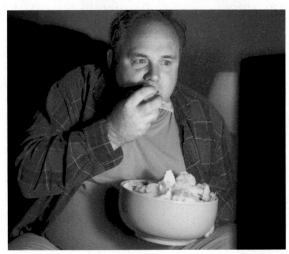

What characterizes metabolic syndrome?

climacteric The midlife transition in which fertility declines.

menopause The time in middle age, usually in the late forties or early fifties, when a woman's menstrual periods cease.

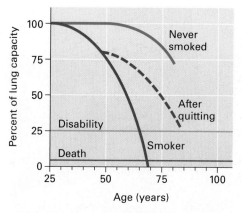

FIGURE 3.4 The Relation of Lung Capacity to Age and Cigarette Smoking. Lung capacity shows little change through middle age for individuals who have not smoked. However, smoking is linked with reduced lung capacity in middle-aged and older adults. When individuals stop smoking, their lung capacity becomes greater than those who continue to smoke, but not as great as the lung capacity of individuals who have never smoked.

Researchers have found that almost 50 percent of Canadian and American women have occasional hot flashes, but only one in seven Japanese women do (Lock, 1998). *What factors might account for these variations?*

at which women have their last period is 52. A small percentage of women—10 percent—go through menopause before 40. Just as puberty has been coming earlier, however, menopause has been coming later (Birren, 2002). Specific causes of the later incidence of menopause have not been documented, but improved nutrition and lower incidence of infectious diseases may be the reasons.

Menopause involves a dramatic decline in the production of estrogen by the ovaries. This decline may produce "hot flashes," nausea, fatigue, and rapid heartbeat, for example. Cross-cultural studies reveal wide variations in the menopause experience. For example, hot flashes are uncommon in Mayan women (Beyene, 1986). Asian women report fewer hot flashes than women in Western societies (Payer, 1991). It is difficult to determine whether these cross-cultural variations are due to genetic, dietary, reproductive, or cultural factors.

Menopause is not the negative experience for most women that it was once thought to be (Dillaway, 2005). A recent study in Taiwan found no significant effect of menopausal transition on women's quality of life (Cheng & others, 2007). However, the loss of fertility is an important marker for women (Wise, 2006).

Do men go through anything like the menopause that women experience? That is, is there a male menopause? During middle adulthood, most men do not lose their capacity to father children, although there usually is a modest decline in their sexual hormone level and activity (Baum & Crespi, 2008; Kohler & others, 2008). Testosterone production begins to decline about 1 percent a year during middle adulthood, and this decline can reduce sexual drive. Sperm count usually shows a slow decline, but men do not lose their fertility.

We have more to say about the climacteric and the sexual attitudes and behaviors of middle-aged women and men in Chapter 12, "Gender and Sexuality."

Late Adulthood

Late adulthood brings an increased risk of physical disability, but there is considerable variability in rates of decline in functioning (Terry & others, 2008). What factors are involved in the successful maintenance of functional abilities? One analysis involved the MacArthur Research Network on Successful Aging Study, a three-site longitudinal study of successful aging in women and men aged 70 to 79 years of age. In this study, physical performance (such as walking efficiency, maintaining balance, and repeatedly standing up and sitting down) did decline with age, but there was considerable individual variation (Seeman & others, 1995). The physical performance of older adults in poor health from low-income backgrounds was inferior to that of their higher-income, healthy counterparts. A majority of the older adults maintained their physical performance over a three-year period in their seventies, and some even improved their performance during this time.

Physical Appearance The changes in physical appearance that take place in middle adulthood become more pronounced in late adulthood. Most noticeable are facial wrinkles and age spots.

Our weight usually drops after we reach 60 years of age, likely because we lose muscle, which also gives our bodies a more "sagging" look (Harridge & Saltin, 2007). The good news is that exercise and weight lifting can help slow the decrease in muscle mass and improve the older adult's body appearance.

Circulatory System Significant changes also take place in the circulatory system of older adults (Betensky, Contrada, & Leventhal, 2009). In one analysis, 57 percent of 80-year-old men and 60 percent of 81-year-old women had hypertension, and 32 percent of the men and 31 percent of the women had experienced a stroke (Aronow, 2007).

In the past, a 65-year-old with a blood pressure reading of 160/90 would have been told, "For your age, that is normal." Now a healthier diet, exercise, and/or medication might be prescribed to lower blood pressure. Today, most experts on aging even recommend that consistent blood pressures above 120/80 should be treated to reduce the risk of heart attack, stroke, or kidney disease (Frankin, 2006). A rise in blood pressure with age can be linked with illness, obesity, stress, stiffening of blood vessels, or lack of exercise (McEniery & others, 2008). The longer any of these factors persist, the worse the individual's blood pressure gets (Miura & others, 2009; Yamasue & others, 2008). Various drugs, a healthy diet, and exercise can reduce the risk of cardiovascular disease in older adults (Hedberg & others, 2009).

Geriatric nurses can be especially helpful to older adults who experience acute or chronic illness. To read about the work of one geriatric nurse, see the *Careers in Life-Span Development* profile.

Careers in Life-Span Development

Sarah Kagan, Geriatric Nurse

Sarah Kagan is a professor of nursing at the University of Pennsylvania School of Nursing. She provides nursing consultation to patients, their families, nurses, and physicians on the complex needs of older adults related to their hospitalization. She also consults on research and the management of patients who have head and neck cancers. Kagon also teaches in the undergraduate nursing program where she directs the course, Nursing Care in the Older Adult. In 2003, she was awarded a MacArthur Fellowship for her work in the field of nursing.

In Kagan's own words:

I'm lucky to be doing what I love—caring for older adults and families—and learning from them so that I can share this knowledge and develop or investigate better ways of caring. My special interests in the care of older adults who have cancer allow me the intimate privilege of being with patients at the best and worst times of their lives. That intimacy acts as a beacon—it reminds me of the value I and nursing as a profession contribute to society and the rewards offered in return (Kagan, 2008, p. 1).

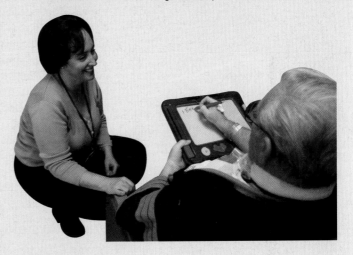

Sarah Kagan with a patient

Review and Reflect: Learning Goal 1

1 Discuss major changes in the body through the life span

REVIEW

- What are cephalocaudal and proximodistal patterns?
- How do height and weight change in infancy and childhood?
- What changes characterize puberty?
- What physical changes occur in early adulthood?
- How do people develop physically during middle adulthood?
- What is the nature of physical changes in late adulthood?

REFLECT

- How old were you when you started puberty? How do you think this timing affected your social relationships and development?

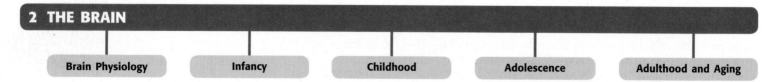

2 THE BRAIN

| Brain Physiology | Infancy | Childhood | Adolescence | Adulthood and Aging |

Until recently, little was known for certain about how the brain changes as we grow and age. Today, dramatic progress is being made in understanding these changes (Nelson, 2009). The study of age-related changes in the brain is one of the most exciting frontiers in science. As we saw in Chapter 2, "Biological Beginnings," remarkable changes already have occurred in the brain during prenatal development. Here we consider the changes in the brain from infancy through late adulthood.

In every change of the body we have described so far, the brain is involved in some way. Structures of the brain help to regulate not only behavior but also metabolism, blood pressure, the release of hormones, and other aspects of the body's physiology. As the rest of the body is changing, what is happening in the brain?

Not long ago, scientists thought that our genes determined how our brains were "wired" and that, unlike most cells, the cells in the brain responsible for processing information stopped dividing at some point early in childhood. Whatever brain your heredity dealt you, you were essentially stuck with it. This view, however, turned out to be wrong. Instead, principles of the life-span perspective discussed in Chapter 1, "Introduction," apply to the brain. For example, it changes throughout life, in both positive and negative ways. It has "plasticity," and its development depends on context (Nelson, 2009; Reeb & others, 2008). What you do and how you live can change the development of your brain.

The old view of the brain in part reflected the fact that scientists did not have the technology that could detect and map sensitive changes in the brain as it develops. The creation of sophisticated brain-scanning techniques has allowed better detection of these changes. Before exploring these changes, let's examine some key structures of the brain and how they function.

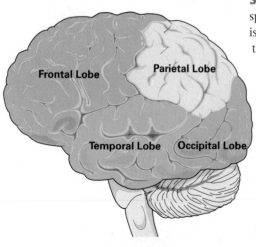

FIGURE 3.5 The Human Brain's Hemispheres. The two hemispheres of the human brain are clearly seen in this photograph.

FIGURE 3.6 The Brain's Four Lobes. Shown here are the locations of the brain's four lobes: frontal, occipital, temporal, and parietal.

Brain Physiology

The brain includes a number of major structures. As we discussed in Chapter 2, "Biological Beginnings," the key components of these structures are *neurons*, nerve cells that handle information processing.

Structure and Function   Looked at from above, the brain has two halves, or hemispheres (see Figure 3.5). The top portion of the brain, farthest from the spinal cord, is known as the *forebrain*. Its outer layer of cells, the cerebral cortex, covers it like a thin cap. The *cerebral cortex* is responsible for about 80 percent of the brain's volume and is critical in perception, thinking, language, and other important functions.

Each hemisphere of the cortex has four major areas, called *lobes*. Although the lobes usually work together, each has a somewhat different primary function (see Figure 3.6):

- *Frontal lobes* are involved in voluntary movement, thinking, personality, and intentionality or purpose.
- *Occipital lobes* function in vision.
- *Temporal lobes* have an active role in hearing, language processing, and memory.
- *Parietal lobes* play important roles in registering spatial location, attention, and motor control.

Deeper in the brain, beneath the cortex, lie other key structures. These include the hypothalamus and the pituitary gland as well as the *amygdala*, which plays an

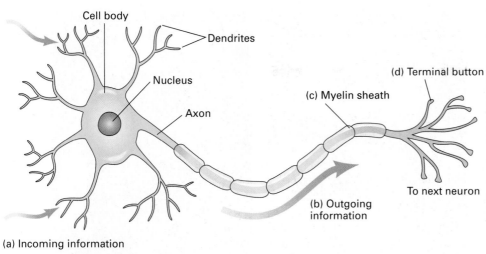

Cell body
Dendrites
(d) Terminal button
(c) Myelin sheath
Nucleus
Axon
To next neuron
(b) Outgoing information
(a) Incoming information

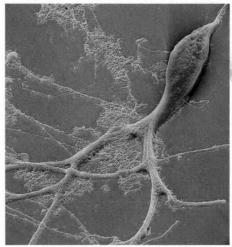

Neuron - cell

FIGURE 3.7 The Neuron. (*a*) The dendrites of the cell body receive information from other neurons, muscles, or glands through the axon. (*b*) Axons transmit information away from the cell body. (*c*) A myelin sheath covers most axons and speeds information transmission. (*d*) As the axon ends, it branches out into terminal buttons. At the right is an actual photograph of a neuron.

important role in emotions, and the *hippocampus*, which is especially important in memory and emotion.

Neurons How do these structures work? As we discussed earlier, the neurons process information. Figure 3.7 shows some important parts of the neuron, including the axon and dendrites. Basically, an axon sends electrical signals away from the central part of the neuron. At tiny gaps called synapses, the axon communicates with the dendrites of other neurons, which then pass the signals on. The communication in the synapse occurs through the release of chemical substances known as neurotransmitters.

As Figure 3.7 shows, most axons are covered by a myelin sheath, which is a layer of fat cells. The sheath helps impulses travel faster along the axon, increasing the speed and efficiency with which information travels from neuron to neuron in a process called **myelination** (Fair & Schlaggar, 2008). Myelination also may be involved in providing energy to neurons.

Which neurons get which information? Clusters of neurons known as *neural circuits* work together to handle particular types of information. The brain is organized in many neural circuits. For example, one neural circuit is important in attention and working memory. This type of memory holds information for a brief time and is like a "mental workbench" as we perform a task (Baddeley, 2007). This neural circuit, which lies in the prefrontal cortex area of the frontal lobes, uses the neurotransmitter dopamine.

To some extent, the type of information handled by neurons depends on whether they are in the left or the right hemisphere of the cortex (Bortfeld, Favaj, & Boas, 2009; Spironelli & Angrilli, 2008). Speech and grammar, for example, depend on activity in the left hemisphere in most people; humor and the use of metaphors depend on activity in the right hemisphere (Imada & others, 2007). This specialization of function in one hemisphere of the cerebral cortex or the other is called **lateralization.** However, most neuroscientists agree that complex functions such as reading or performing music involve both hemispheres (Stroobant, Buijs, & Vingerhoets, 2009). Labeling people as "left-brained" because they are logical thinkers and "right-brained" because they are creative thinkers does not correspond to the way the brain's hemispheres work. For the most part, complex thinking is the outcome of communication between both hemispheres of the brain (Ligeois & others, 2008).

myelination The process of encasing axons with a myelin sheath, which helps increase the speed and efficiency of information processing.

lateralization Specialization of function in one hemisphere or the other of the cerebral cortex.

FIGURE 3.8 Early Deprivation and Brain Activity. These two photographs are PET (positron-emission tomography) scans (which use radioactive tracers to image and analyze blood flow and metabolic activity in the body's organs) of the brains of (*a*) a normal child and (*b*) an institutionalized Romanian orphan who experienced substantial deprivation since birth. In PET scans, the highest to lowest brain activity is reflected in the colors of red, yellow, green, blue, and black, respectively. As can be seen, red and yellow show up to a much greater degree in the PET scan of the normal child than that of the deprived Romanian orphan.

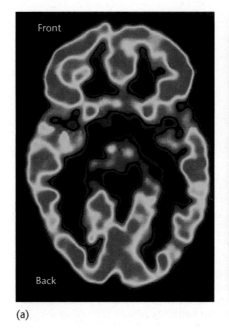

(a)

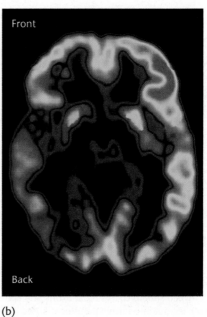

(b)

(a)

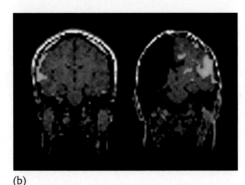

(b)

FIGURE 3.9 Plasticity in the Brain's Hemispheres. (*a*) Michael Rehbein at 14 years of age. (*b*) Michael's right hemisphere (*right*) has reorganized to take over the language functions normally carried out by corresponding areas in the left hemisphere of an intact brain (*left*). However, the right hemisphere is not as efficient as the left, and more areas of the brain are recruited to process speech.

The degree of lateralization may change as people develop through the human life span. Let's now explore a number of age-related changes in the brain.

Infancy

As we saw in Chapter 2, "Biological Beginnings," brain development occurs extensively during the prenatal period. The brain's development is also substantial during infancy and later (Johnson, Grossman, Farroni, 2009; Nelson, 2009).

Because the brain develops so extensively, an infant's head should always be protected from falls or other injuries, and a baby should never be shaken. *Shaken baby syndrome,* which includes brain swelling and hemorrhaging, affects hundreds of babies in the United States each year (Altimer, 2008; Mraz, 2009). A recent analysis found that fathers most often were the perpetrators of shaken baby syndrome, followed by child-care providers, and a boyfriend of the victim's mother (National Center on Shaken Baby Syndrome, 2008).

As an infant walks, talks, runs, shakes a rattle, smiles, and frowns, changes in its brain are occurring. Consider the description in Chapter 2, "Biological Beginnings," of how the infant begins life as a single cell and nine months later is born with a brain and nervous system that contain approximately 100 billion nerve cells, or neurons. What determines how those neurons are connected to communicate with each other?

Early Experience and the Brain Children who grow up in a deprived environment may have depressed brain activity (Reeb & others, 2008). As shown in Figure 3.8, a child who grew up in the unresponsive and unstimulating environment of a Romanian orphanage showed considerably depressed brain activity compared with a normal child.

Are the effects of deprived environments reversible? There is reason to think that at least for some individuals the answer is yes (Guzzetta & others, 2008). The brain demonstrates both flexibility and resilience. Consider 14-year-old Michael Rehbein. At age 7, he began to experience uncontrollable seizures—as many as 400 a day. Doctors said the only solution was to remove the left hemisphere of his brain where the seizures were occurring. Recovery was slow, but his right hemisphere began to reorganize and take over functions that normally occur in the brain's left hemisphere, including speech (see Figure 3.9).

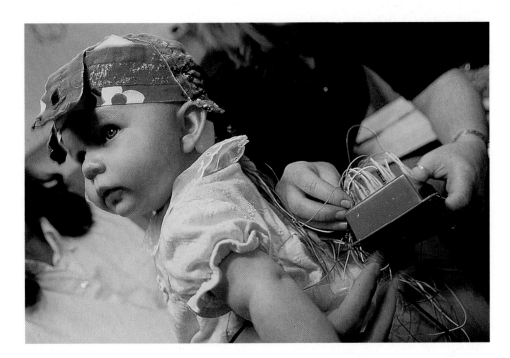

FIGURE 3.10 Measuring the Activity in an Infant's Brain. By attaching up to 128 electrodes to a baby's scalp, Charles Nelson and his colleagues have studied the brain's activity in the infant's ability to recognize faces and remember.

Neuroscientists note that what wires the brain—or rewires it, in the case of Michael Rehbein—is repeated experience (Nash, 1997). Each time a baby tries to touch an attractive object or gazes intently at a face, tiny bursts of electricity shoot through the brain, knitting together neurons into circuits. The results are some of the behavioral milestones we discuss in this and other chapters.

In sum, the infant's brain is waiting for experiences to determine how connections are made. Before birth, it appears that genes mainly direct basic wiring patterns. Neurons grow and travel to distant places awaiting further instructions (Sheridan & Nelson, 2008). After birth, the inflowing stream of sights, sounds, smells, touches, language, and eye contact help shape the brain's neural connections.

Studying the brain's development in infancy is not as easy as it might seem. Even the latest brain-imaging technologies (described in Chapter 1, "Introduction,") cannot make out fine details in adult brains and cannot be used with babies (de Haan & Martinos, 2008). Positron-emission tomography (PET) scans pose a radiation risk to babies, and infants wriggle too much to capture accurate images using magnetic resonance imaging (MRI) (Marcus, Mulrine, & Wong, 1999). However, among the researchers who are making strides in finding out more about the brain's development in infancy are Charles Nelson and his colleagues (Nelson, 2007, 2009; Moulson & Nelson, 2008; Sheridan & Nelson, 2008) (see Figure 3.10).

Changing Neurons   At birth, the newborn's brain is about 25 percent of its adult weight. By the second birthday, the brain is about 75 percent of its adult weight. Two key developments during these first two years involve the myelin sheath (the layer of fat cells that speeds up the electrical impulse along the axon) and connections between dendrites.

Myelination, the process of encasing axons with a myelin sheath, begins prenatally and continues after birth (see Figure 3.11). Myelination for visual pathways occurs rapidly after birth, being completed in the first six months. Auditory myelination is not completed until 4 or 5 years of age. Some aspects of myelination continue even into adolescence. Indeed, the most extensive changes in myelination in the frontal lobes occur during adolescence (Steinberg, 2008).

Dramatic increases in dendrites and synapses (the tiny gaps between neurons across which neurotransmitters carry information) also characterize the development

Myelin Sheath   Axon

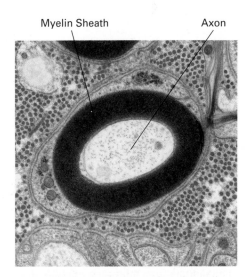

FIGURE 3.11 A Myelinated Nerve Fiber. The myelin sheath, shown in brown, encases the axon (white). This image was produced by an electron microscope that magnified the nerve fiber 12,000 times. *What role does myelination play in the brain's development?*

FIGURE 3.12 Dendritic Spreading. Note the increase in connections among neurons over the course of the first two years of life. Reprinted by permission of the publisher from *The Postnatal Development of the Human Cerebral Cortex*, Vols. 1-VIII, by Jesse LeRoy Conel, Cambridge, Mass.: Harvard University Press, Copyright © 1939, 1975 by the President and Fellows of Harvard College.

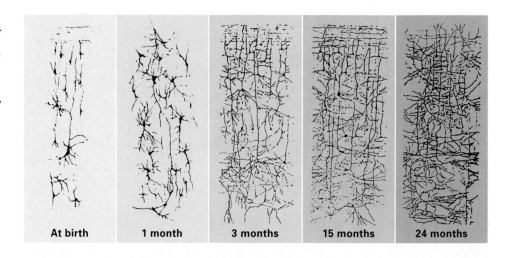

At birth · 1 month · 3 months · 15 months · 24 months

of the brain in the first two years of life (see Figure 3.12). Nearly twice as many of these connections are made as will ever be used (Huttenlocher & Dabholkar, 1997; Huttenlocher & others, 1991). The connections that are used become strengthened and survive, while the unused ones are replaced by other pathways or disappear (Giedd, 2008). That is, connections are "pruned." Figure 3.14 vividly illustrates the growth and later pruning of synapses in the visual, auditory, and prefrontal cortex areas of the brain (Huttenlocher & Dabholkar, 1997).

As shown in Figure 3.13, "blooming and pruning" vary considerably by brain region in humans (Thompson & Nelson, 2001). For example, the peak synaptic overproduction in the area concerned with vision occurs about the fourth postnatal month, followed by a gradual pruning until the middle to end of the preschool years (Huttenlocher & Dabholkar, 1997). In areas of the brain involved in hearing and language, a similar, though somewhat later, course is detected. However, in the *prefrontal cortex* (the area of the brain where higher-level thinking and self-regulation occur), the peak of overproduction occurs at just after 3 years of age. Both heredity and environment are thought to influence synaptic overproduction and subsequent pruning.

Changing Structures At birth, the hemispheres already have started to specialize: Newborns show greater electrical activity in the left hemisphere than in the right hemisphere when they are listening to speech sounds (Hahn, 1987).

FIGURE 3.13 Synaptic Density in the Human Brain from Infancy to Adulthood. The graph shows the dramatic increase in synaptic density, and then pruning, in three regions of the brain: visual cortex, auditory cortex, and prefrontal cortex. Synaptic density is believed to be an important indication of the extent of connectivity between neurons.

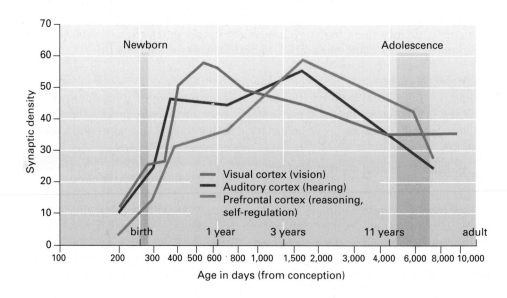

The areas of the brain do not mature uniformly (Fischer, 2008; Nelson, 2009). The frontal lobe is immature in the newborn. As neurons in the frontal lobe become myelinated and interconnected during the first year of life, infants develop an ability to regulate their physiological states (such as sleep) and gain more control over their reflexes. Cognitive skills that require deliberate thinking do not emerge until later (Bell & Fox, 1992).

At about 2 months of age, the motor control centers of the brain develop to the point at which infants can suddenly reach out and grab a nearby object. At about 4 months, the neural connections necessary for depth perception begin to form. And at about 12 months, the brain's speech centers are poised to produce one of infancy's magical moments: when the infant utters its first word.

Childhood

The brain and other parts of the nervous system continue developing through childhood (Diamond, Casey, & Munakata, 2010). These changes enable children to plan their actions, to attend to stimuli more effectively, and to make considerable strides in language development.

During early childhood, the brain and head grow more rapidly than any other part of the body. Figure 3.14 shows how the growth curve for the head and brain advances more rapidly than the growth curve for height and weight. Some of the brain's increase in size is due to myelination and some is due to an increase in the number and size of dendrites. Some developmentalists conclude that myelination is important in the maturation of a number of children's abilities (Fair & Schlaggar, 2008). For example, myelination in the areas of the brain related to hand-eye coordination is not complete until about 4 years of age. A functional magnetic resonance imaging (fMRI) study of children (mean age, 4 years) found that those who were characterized by developmental delay of motor and cognitive milestones had significantly reduced levels of myelination (Pujol & others, 2004). Myelination in the areas of the brain related to focusing attention is not complete until the end of the middle or late childhood.

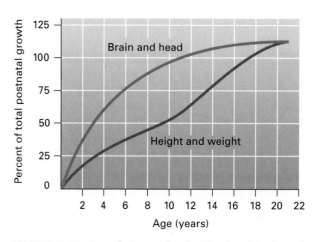

FIGURE 3.14 Growth Curves for the Head and Brain and for Height and Weight. The more rapid growth of the brain and head can easily be seen. Height and weight advance more gradually over the first two decades of life.

Still, the brain in early childhood is not growing as rapidly as in infancy. However, the anatomical changes in the child's brain between the ages of 3 and 15 are dramatic. By repeatedly obtaining brain scans of the same children for up to four years, scientists have found that children's brains experience rapid, distinct bursts of growth (Thompson & others, 2000). The amount of brain material in some areas can nearly double in as little as one year, followed by a drastic loss of tissue as unneeded cells are purged and the brain continues to reorganize itself. The overall size of the brain does not increase dramatically from 3 to 15. What does dramatically change are local patterns within the brain (Thompson & others, 2000). From 3 to 6 years of age, the most rapid growth occurs in the frontal lobe areas involved in planning and organizing new actions and in maintaining attention to tasks. From ages 6 through puberty, the most dramatic growth takes place in the temporal and parietal lobes, especially in areas that play major roles in language and spatial relations.

Total brain volume stabilizes by the end of middle and late childhood, but significant changes in various structures and regions of the brain continue to occur during middle and late childhood. In particular, the brain pathways and circuitry involving the prefrontal cortex, the highest level in the brain, continue to increase in middle and late childhood (Diamond, Casey, & Munakata, 2010). In a recent study, researchers found less diffusion and more focal activation in the prefrontal cortex from 7 to 30 years of age (Durston & others, 2006). The activation change was accompanied by increased efficiency in cognitive performance, especially in *cognitive control*, which involves flexible and effective control in a number of areas.

These areas concern controlling attention, reducing interfering thoughts, inhibiting motor actions, and being cognitively flexible in switching between competing choices (Diamond, Casey, & Munakata, 2010).

Developmental neuroscientist Mark Johnson and his colleagues (2009) recently proposed that the prefrontal cortex likely orchestrates the functions of many other brain regions during development. As part of this neural leadership and organizational role, the prefrontal cortex may provide an advantage to neural connections and networks that include the prefrontal cortex. In their view, the prefrontal cortex likely coordinates the best neural connections for solving a problem.

Adolescence

Until recently, little research has been conducted on developmental changes in the brain during adolescence. Although research in this area is still in its infancy, an increasing number of studies are under way (Casey, Jones, & Hare, 2008; Whittle & others, 2008). Scientists now note that the adolescent's brain is different from the child's brain, and that in adolescence the brain is still growing (McAnarney, 2008; Paus, 2009).

Earlier we indicated that connections between neurons become "pruned" as children and adolescents development. What results from this pruning is that by the end of adolescence individuals have "fewer, more selective, more effective neuronal connections than they did as children" (Kuhn, 2009, p. 153). And this pruning indicates that the activities adolescents choose to engage in and not to engage in influence which neural connections will be strengthened and which will disappear.

Among the most important structural changes in the brain during adolescence are those involving the corpus callosum, the prefrontal cortex, and the amygdala. The **corpus callosum,** a large bundle of axon fibers that connects the brain's left and right hemispheres, thickens in adolescence, and this improves adolescents' ability to process information (Giedd, 2008; Giedd & others, 2009). Advances in the development of the **prefrontal cortex**—the highest level of the frontal lobes that is involved in reasoning, decision making, and self-control— continue through the emerging adult years, approximately 18 to 25 years of age, or later (Powell, 2006). However, the **amygdala**— a part of the brain's limbic system that is the seat of emotions such as anger—matures much earlier than the prefrontal cortex. Figure 3.15 shows the locations of the corpus callosum, prefrontal cortex, and amygdala. A recent study of 137 early adolescents revealed a positive link between the volume of the amygdala and the duration of adolescents' aggressive behavior during interactions with parents (Whittle & others, 2008).

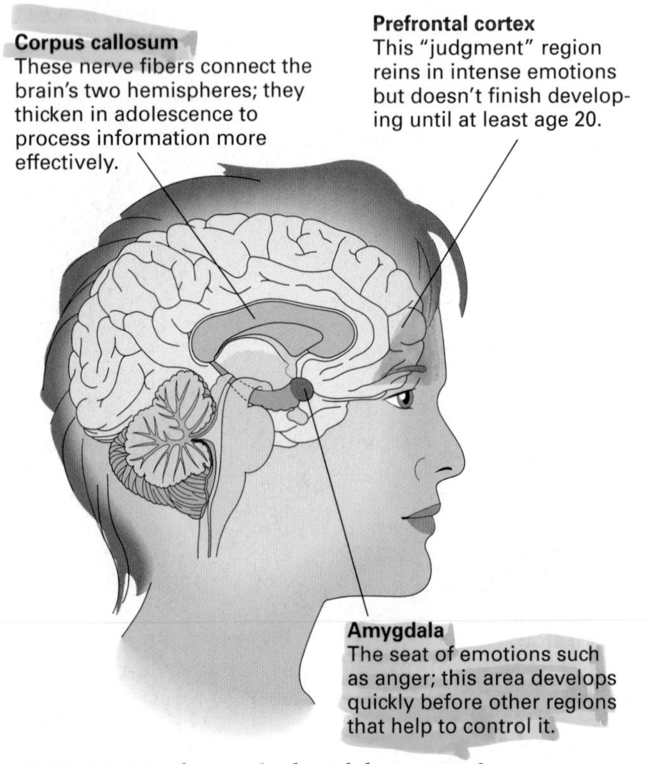

Leading researcher Charles Nelson (2003) points out that although adolescents are capable of very strong emotions, their prefrontal cortex hasn't adequately developed to the point at which they can control these passions. It is as if the prefrontal cortex doesn't yet have the brakes to slow down the amygdala's emotional intensity. Or consider this interpretation of the development of emotion and cognition in adolescents: "early activation of strong 'turbo-charged' feelings with a relatively un-skilled set of 'driving skills' or cognitive abilities to modulate strong emotions and motivations" (Dahl, 2004, p. 18).

Of course, a major issue is which comes first, biological changes in the brain or experiences that stimulate these changes? (Lerner, Boyd, & Du, 2009). Consider a recent study in which the prefrontal cortex thickened and more brain connections formed when adolescents resisted peer pressure (Paus & others, 2008). Scientists have yet to determine whether the brain changes come first or

corpus callosum A large bundle of axon fibers that connects the brain's left and right hemispheres.

prefrontal cortex The highest level of the frontal lobes that is involved in reasoning, decision making, and self-control.

amygdala A part of the brain's limbic system that is the seat of emotions such as anger.

Corpus callosum
These nerve fibers connect the brain's two hemispheres; they thicken in adolescence to process information more effectively.

Prefrontal cortex
This "judgment" region reins in intense emotions but doesn't finish developing until at least age 20.

Amygdala
The seat of emotions such as anger; this area develops quickly before other regions that help to control it.

FIGURE 3.15 Changes in the Adolescent Brain.

whether the brain changes are the result of experiences with parents, peers, and others. Once again, we encounter the nature-nurture issue that is so prominent in examining development through the life span.

Are there implications of what we now know about changes in the adolescent's brain for taking drugs and the legal system? According to leading expert Jay Giedd (2007, pp. 1–2D), "Biology doesn't make teens rebellious or have purple hair or take drugs. It does not mean you are going to do drugs, but it gives you more of a chance to do that."

Let's further consider the developmental disjunction between the early development of the amygdala and the later development of the prefrontal cortex. This disjunction may account for an increase in risk taking and other problems in adolescence. To read further about risk-taking behavior in adolescence, see the *Applications in Life-Span Development* interlude.

Applications in Life-Span Development

STRATEGIES FOR HELPING ADOLESCENTS REDUCE THEIR RISK-TAKING BEHAVIOR

Novelty - New

Beginning in early adolescence, individuals seek experiences that create high-intensity feelings. . . . Adolescents like intensity, excitement, and arousal. They are drawn to music videos that shock and bombard the senses. Teenagers flock to horror and slasher movies. They dominate queues waiting to ride high-adrenaline rides at amusement parks. Adolescence is a time when sex, drugs, very loud music, and other high-stimulation experiences take on great appeal. It is a developmental period when an appetite for adventure, a predilection for risks, and desire for novelty and thrills seem to reach naturally high levels. While these patterns of emotional changes are evidence to some degree in most adolescents, it is important to recognize the wide range of individual differences during this period of development. (Dahl, 2004, p. 6)

The self-regulatory skills necessary to inhibit risk taking often don't develop until later in adolescence or emerging adulthood (Casey, Jones, & Hare, 2008). And, as we just saw, this gap between the increase in risk-taking behavior and the delay in self-regulation is linked to brain development in the limbic system (involved in pleasure seeking and emotion) taking place earlier than development of the frontal lobes (involved in self-regulation) (Giedd & others, 2009; Paus, 2009; Steinberg, 2009).

What can be done to help adolescents satisfy their motivation for risk taking without compromising their health? As Laurence Steinberg (2004, p. 58) argues, one strategy is to limit

How might developmental changes in the brain be involved in adolescent risk taking? What are some strategies for reducing adolescent risk taking?

opportunities for immature judgment to have harmful consequences. . . . Thus, strategies such as raising the price of cigarettes, more vigilantly enforcing laws governing the sale of alcohol, expanding access to mental health and contraceptive services, and raising the driving age would likely be more effective than strategies aimed at making adolescents wiser, less impulsive, and less short-sighted.

It is also important for parents, teachers, mentors, and other responsible adults to effectively monitor adolescents' behavior (Dahl, 2007). In many cases, adults decrease their monitoring of adolescents too early, leaving them to cope with tempting situations alone or with friends and peers. When adolescents are in tempting and dangerous situations with minimal adult supervision, their inclination to engage in risk-taking behavior combined with their lack of self-regulatory skills can make them vulnerable to a host of negative outcomes.

Adulthood and Aging

Changes in the brain continue during adulthood. Most of the research on the brains of adults, however, has focused on the aging brain of older adults. What are some of the general findings about the aging brain? How much plasticity and adaptiveness does it retain?

The Shrinking, Slowing Brain   On average, the brain loses 5 to 10 percent of its weight between the ages of 20 and 90. Brain volume also decreases (Bondare, 2007). One study found that the volume of the brain was 15 percent less in older adults than younger adults (Shan & others, 2005). Scientists are not sure why these changes occur but note they might result from a decrease in dendrites and damage to the myelin sheath that covers axons. The current consensus is that under normal conditions adults are unlikely to lose brain cells per se (Nelson, 2008).

Some areas shrink more than others. The prefrontal cortex is one area that shrinks with aging, and recent research has linked this shrinkage with a decrease in working memory and other cognitive activities in older adults (Isella & others, 2008).

A general slowing of function in the brain and spinal cord begins in middle adulthood and accelerates in late adulthood (Birren, 2002). Both physical coordination and intellectual performance are affected. For example, after age 70, many adults no longer show a knee jerk and by age 90 most reflexes are much slower (Spence, 1989). The slowing of the brain can impair the performance of older adults on intelligence tests and various cognitive tasks, especially those that are timed (Birren, 2002). For example, one recent neuroimaging study revealed that older adults were more likely to be characterized by slower processing in the prefrontal cortex during retrieval of information on a cognitive task than were younger adults (Rypma, Eldreth, & Rebbechi, 2007).

Aging has also been linked to a reduction in the production of some neurotransmitters, including acetylcholine, dopamine, and gamma-aminobutyric acid (GABA) (Jagust & D'Esposito, 2009). Some researchers conclude that reductions in acetylcholine may be responsible for small declines in memory functioning and even with the severe memory loss associated with Alzheimer disease, which we will discuss in Chapter 4, "Health" (Holzgrabe & others, 2007). Normal age-related reductions in dopamine may cause problems in planning and carrying out motor activities (Erixon-Lindroth & others, 2005). Severe reductions in the production of dopamine have been linked with age-related diseases characterized by a loss of motor control, such as Parkinson disease (Hauser & Zesiewicz, 2007). GABA helps to control the preciseness of the signal sent from one neuron to another, decreasing "noise," but its production decreases with aging (Yuan, 2008).

The Adapting Brain   If the brain were a computer, this description of the aging brain might lead you to think that it could not do much of anything. However, unlike a computer, the brain has remarkable repair capability (Jessberger & Gage, 2008; Park & Reuter-Coronz, 2009). Even in late adulthood, the brain loses only a portion of its ability to function, and the activities older adults engage in can influence the brain's development (Erickson & others, 2007). For example, in a recent fMRI study, higher levels of aerobic fitness were linked with greater volume in the hippocampus, which translates into better memory (Erickson & others, 2009).

Can adults, even aging adults, generate new neurons? Researchers have found that **neurogenesis,** the generation of new neurons, does occur in lower mammalian species, such as mice (Zhu & others, 2009). Also, research indicates that exercise and an enriched, complex environment can generate new brain cells in mice and that stress reduces their survival rate (Segovia, Arco, & Mora, 2009; Vander Borght & others, 2009) (see Figure 3.16). Researchers recently have discovered that if rats are cognitively challenged to learn something, new brain cells survive longer (Shors, 2009).

neurogenesis The generation of new neurons.

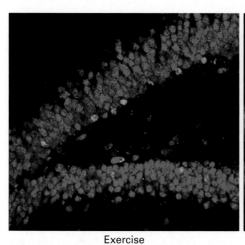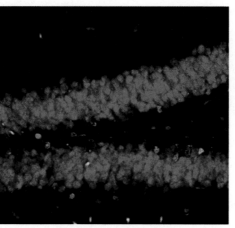

Exercise   Enriched Environment

FIGURE 3.16 Generating New Nerve Cells in Adult Mice. Researchers have found that exercise (running) and an enriched environment (a larger cage and many toys) can cause brain cells to divide and form new brain cells (Kempermann, van Praag, & Gage, 2000). Cells were labeled with a chemical marker that becomes integrated into the DNA of dividing cells (red). Four weeks later, they were also labeled to mark neurons (nerve cells). As shown here, both the running mice and the mice in an enriched environment had many cells that were still dividing (red) and others that had differentiated into new nerve cells (orange).

It also is now accepted that neurogenesis can occur in humans (Aimone, Wiles, & Gage, 2009; Hagg, 2009; Libert, Cohen, & Guarente, 2008). However, researchers have documented neurogenesis only in two brain regions, the hippocampus, which is involved in memory, and the olfactory bulb, which is involved in smell (Gould, 2007; Leasure & Decker, 2009). It also is not known what functions these new brain cells perform, and at this point researchers have documented that they last for only several weeks (Nelson, 2006). Researchers currently are studying factors that might inhibit and promote neurogenesis, including various drugs, stress, and exercise (van Praag, 2008, 2009). They also are examining how the grafting of neural stem cells to various regions of the brain, such as the hippocampus, might increase neurogenesis (Duan & others, 2008; Farin & others, 2009).

Dendritic growth can occur in human adults, possibly even in older adults (Eliasieh, Liets, & Chalupa, 2007). One study compared the brains of adults at various ages (Coleman, 1986). From the forties through the seventies, the growth of dendrites increased. However, in people in their nineties, dendritic growth no longer occurred. This dendritic growth might compensate for the possible loss of neurons through the seventies but not in the nineties. Lack of dendritic growth in older adults could be due to a lack of environmental stimulation and activity.

Stanley Rapaport (1994), chief of the neurosciences laboratory at the National Institute on Aging, demonstrated another way in which the aging brain can adapt. He compared the brains of younger and older people engaged in the same tasks. The older brains had rewired themselves to compensate for losses. If one neuron was not up to the job, neighboring neurons helped to pick up the slack. Rapaport concluded that as brains age, they can shift responsibilities for a given task from one region to another.

Changes in lateralization may provide one type of adaptation in aging adults (Angel & others, 2009; Cabeza, 2002; Cabeza, Nyberg, & Park, 2009). Recall that lateralization is the specialization of function in one hemisphere of the brain or the other. Using neuroimaging techniques, researchers recently found that brain activity in the prefrontal cortex is lateralized less in older adults than in younger adults when they are engaging in cognitive tasks (Cabeza, 2002; Rossi & others, 2005). For example, Figure 3.17 shows that when younger adults are given the task of recognizing words they have previously seen, they process the information primarily in the right hemisphere; older adults are more likely to use both hemispheres (Madden & others, 1999).

The decrease in lateralization in older adults might play a compensatory role in the aging brain. That is, using both hemispheres may improve the cognitive functioning of older adults. Support for this view comes from another study in which

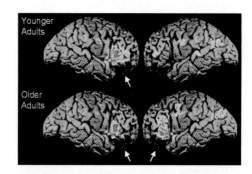

FIGURE 3.17 The Decrease in Brain Lateralization in Older Adults. Younger adults primarily used the right prefrontal region of the brain (*top left photo*) during a recall memory task, whereas older adults used both the left and right prefrontal regions (*bottom two photos*).

Left Hemisphere   **Right Hemisphere**

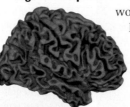

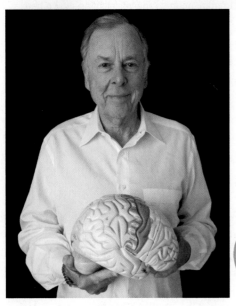

FIGURE 3.18 Individual Differences in Hemispheric Specialization in Older Adults. On tough questions—such as "Are 'zombie' and 'unicorn' living or nonliving?"—the red patches indicate that 81-year-old T. Boone Pickens was relying mainly on the left hemisphere of his brain to make a decision. Most older adults show a stronger bilateral activation, using both hemispheres more equally than Pickens, whose lateralization was more characteristic of younger adults.

older adults who used both brain hemispheres were faster at completing a working memory task than their counterparts who primarily used only one hemisphere (Reuter-Lorenz & others, 2000). However, the decrease in lateralization may be a mere by-product of aging; it may reflect an age-related decline in the brain's ability to specialize functions. In this view, during childhood the brain becomes increasingly differentiated in terms of its functions; as adults become older, this process may reverse. Support for the dedifferentiation view is found in the higher intercorrelations of performance on cognitive tasks in older adults than in younger adults (Baltes & Lindenberger, 1997). Of course, there are individual differences in how the brain changes in older adults. Consider highly successful businessman 81-year-old T. Boone Pickens, who continues to lead a highly active lifestyle, regularly exercising and engaging in cognitively complex work. Undergoing a recent fMRI in cognitive neuroscientist Denise Park's laboratory, when Pickens was presented various cognitive tasks, instead of both hemispheres being active, Pickens' left hemisphere was still dominant just as the case with most younger adults (Helman, 2008). Indeed, as the cognitive tasks became more complex, the more Pickens used the left hemisphere of his brain (see Figure 3.18). To read further about aging and the brain, see the *Research in Life-Span Development* interlude.

Research in Life-Span Development

THE NUN STUDY

The Nun Study, directed by David Snowdon, is an intriguing, ongoing investigation of aging in 678 nuns, many of whom are from a convent in Mankato, Minnesota (Snowdon, 1997, 2002, 2003; Tyas & others, 2007). Each of the 678 nuns agreed to participate in annual assessments of their cognitive and physical functioning. They also agreed to donate their brains for scientific research when they die, and they are the largest group of brain

Two participants in the Mankato Nun Study. *Left*: Sister Marcella Zachman (*left*) finally stopped teaching at age 97. At 99, she helped ailing nuns exercise their brains by quizzing them on vocabulary or playing a card game called Skip-Bo, at which she would deliberately lose. Sister Mary Esther Boor (*right*), also pictured at 99 years of age, was a former teacher who stayed alert by doing puzzles and volunteering to work the front desk. She died at the age of 107 and taught for more than 80 years. *Right*: A technician holds the brain of a deceased Mankato nun. The nuns donate their brains for research that explores the effects of stimulation on brain growth.

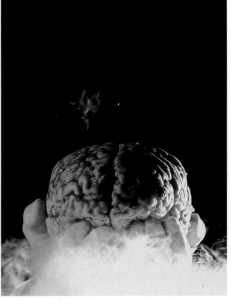

donors in the world. Examination of the nuns' donated brains, as well as others, has led neuroscientists to believe that the brain has a remarkable capacity to change and grow, even in old age. The Sisters of Notre Dame in Mankato lead an intellectually challenging life, and brain researchers believe this contributes to their quality of life as older adults and possibly to their longevity.

Findings from the Nun Study so far include:

- Idea density, a measure of linguistic ability assessed early in the adult years (age 22), was linked with higher brain weight, fewer incidences of mild cognitive impairment, and fewer characteristics of Alzheimer disease in 75- to 95-year-old nuns (Riley & others, 2005).

- Positive emotions early in adulthood were linked to longevity (Danner, Snowdon, & Friesen, 2001). Handwritten autobiographies from 180 nuns, composed when they were 22 years of age, were scored for emotional content. The nuns whose early writings had higher scores for positive emotional content were more likely to still be alive at 75 to 95 years of age than their counterparts whose early writings were characterized by negative emotional content.

- Sisters who had taught for most of their lives showed more moderate declines in intellectual skills than those who had spent most of their lives in service-based tasks, a finding supporting the notion that stimulating the brain with intellectual activity keeps neurons healthy and alive (Snowdon, 2002).

- Sisters with high levels of folic acid showed little evidence of Alzheimer-like damage to their brain after death (Snowdon & others, 2000). Possibly the substantial folic acid in the blood means less chance of having a stroke and possibly helps to protect the brain from decline.

This and other research provides hope that scientists will discover ways to tap into the brain's capacity to adapt in order to prevent and treat brain diseases (Jagust & others, 2008). For example, scientists might learn more effective ways to help older adults recover from strokes (Ijzerman, Renzenbrink, & Geurts, 2009). Even when areas of the brain are permanently damaged by stroke, new message routes can be created to get around the blockage or to resume the function of that area (de la Torre, 2008).

Review and Reflect: Learning Goal 2

 2 Describe how the brain changes through the life span

REVIEW

- What are the major areas of the brain, and how does it process information?
- How does the brain change in infancy?
- What characterizes the development of the brain in childhood?
- How can the changes in the brain during adolescence be summarized?
- What is the aging brain like?

REFLECT

- If you could interview the Mankato nuns, what would you want to ask them?

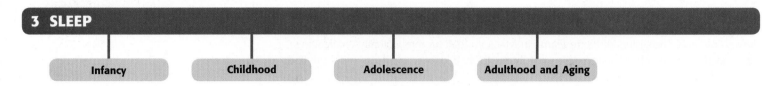

3 SLEEP

| Infancy | Childhood | Adolescence | Adulthood and Aging |

Sleep restores, replenishes, and rebuilds our brains and bodies. Some neuroscientists maintain that sleep gives neurons that are active while we are awake a chance to shut down and repair themselves (National Institute of Neurological Disorders and Stroke, 2009). How do our sleeping patterns change across the life span?

Infancy

How much do infants sleep? Can any special problems develop regarding infants' sleep?

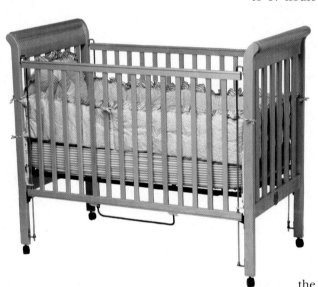

The Sleep/Wake Cycle   When we were infants, sleep consumed more of our time than it does now (Sadeh, 2008; Taveras & others, 2008). Newborns sleep 16 to 17 hours a day, although some sleep more and others less—the range is from a low of about 10 hours to a high of about 21 hours. Their longest period of sleep is not always between 11 p.m. and 7 a.m. Although total sleep remains somewhat consistent for young infants, their sleep during the day does not always follow a rhythmic pattern. An infant might change from sleeping several long bouts of 7 or 8 hours to three or four shorter sessions only several hours in duration. By about 1 month of age, most infants have begun to sleep longer at night. By 6 months of age, they usually have moved closer to adult-like sleep patterns, spending their longest span of sleep at night and their longest span of waking during the day (Sadeh, 2008).

The most common infant sleep-related problem reported by parents is night waking. Surveys indicate that 20 to 30 percent of infants have difficulty going to sleep at night and night waking (Sadeh, 2008). What factors are involved in infant night waking? Infant night-waking problems have consistently been linked to excessive parental involvement in sleep-related interactions with their infant (Sadeh, 2008).

Cultural variations characterize infant sleeping patterns. For example, in the Kipsigis culture in the African country of Kenya, infants sleep with their mothers at night and are permitted to nurse on demand (Super & Harkness, 1997). During the day, they are strapped to their mothers' backs, accompanying them on their daily rounds of chores and social activities. As a result, Kipsigis infants do not sleep through the night until much later than American infants. During their first eight months, Kipsigis infants rarely sleep longer than three hours at a stretch, even at night. This pattern contrasts with that of many American infants, who generally begin to sleep up to eight hours a night by 8 months of age.

REM Sleep   In REM sleep, the eyes flutter beneath closed lids; in non-REM sleep, this type of eye movement does not occur and sleep is quieter. Figure 3.19 shows developmental changes in the average number of total hours spent in REM and non-REM sleep. By the time they reach adulthood, individuals spend about one-fifth of their night in REM sleep, and REM sleep usually appears about one hour after non-REM sleep. However, about half of an infant's sleep is REM sleep, and infants often begin their sleep cycle with REM sleep rather than non-REM sleep (Sadeh, 2008). A much greater amount of time is taken up by REM sleep in infancy than at any other point in the life span. By the time infants reach 3 months of age, the percentage of time they spend in REM sleep falls to about 40 percent, and REM sleep no longer begins their sleep cycle.

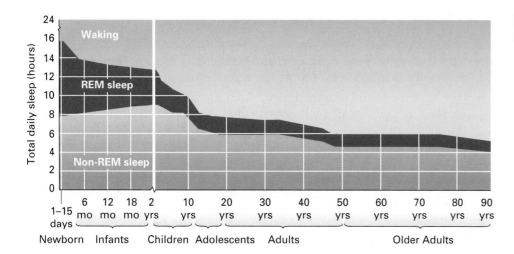

FIGURE 3.19 Sleep Across the Human Life Span.

Why do infants spend so much time in REM sleep? Researchers are not certain. The large amount of REM sleep may provide infants with added self-stimulation, since they spend less time awake than do older children. REM sleep also might promote the brain's development in infancy (Graven, 2006).

When adults are awakened during REM sleep, they frequently report that they have been dreaming, but when they are awakened during non-REM sleep they are much less likely to report they have been dreaming (Cartwright & others, 2006). Since infants spend more time than adults in REM sleep, can we conclude that they dream a lot? We don't know whether infants dream or not, because they don't have any way of reporting dreams.

Shared Sleeping   Some child experts stress that there are benefits to shared sleeping (as when an infant sleeps in the same bed with its mother). They state that it can promote breast feeding, lets the mother respond more quickly to the baby's cries, and allows her to detect breathing pauses in the baby that might be dangerous (Nelson & others, 2005). Sharing a bed with a mother is common practice in many countries, such as Guatemala and China, whereas in others, such as the United States and Great Britain, most newborns sleep in a crib, either in the same room as the parents or in a separate room.

Shared sleeping remains a controversial issue, with some experts recommending it, others arguing against it (Mitchell, 2007; Sadeh, 2008). The American Academy of Pediatrics Task Force on Infant Positioning and SIDS (AAPTFIPS) (2000) recommends against shared sleeping. They argue that in some instances bed sharing might lead to sudden infant death syndrome (SIDS), as could be the case if a sleeping mother rolls over on her baby. Recent studies have found that bed sharing is linked with a greater incidence of SIDS, especially when parents smoke (Alm, Lagercrantz, & Wennergren, 2006; Bajanowsk & others, 2008).

SIDS   **Sudden infant death syndrome (SIDS)** is a condition that occurs when infants stop breathing, usually during the night, and die suddenly without an apparent cause. SIDS remains the highest cause of infant death in the United States with nearly 3,000 infant deaths attributed to it annually. Risk of SIDS is highest at 2 to 4 months of age (Centers for Disease Control and Prevention, 2008).

Since 1992, The American Academy of Pediatrics (AAP) has recommended that infants be placed to sleep on their backs to reduce the risk of SIDS, and the frequency of prone sleeping among U.S. infants has dropped dramatically (AAPTFIPS, 2000). Researchers have found that SIDS does indeed decrease when infants sleep on their backs rather than their stomachs or sides (Dwyer & Ponsonby, 2009; McMullen, Lipke, & LeMura, 2009). Among the reasons given for prone sleeping being a high-risk factor for SIDS are that it impairs the infant's arousal from sleep and restricts the infant's ability to swallow effectively (Mitchell, 2009).

sudden infant death syndrome (SIDS)
Condition that occurs when an infant stops breathing, usually during the night, and suddenly dies without an apparent cause.

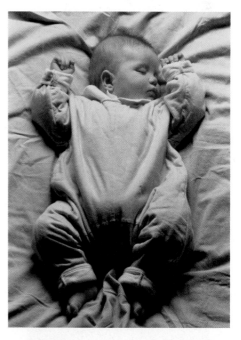

Is this a good sleep position for this 3-month-old infant? Why or why not?

In addition to sleeping in a prone position, researchers have found that the following are risk factors for SIDS:

- SIDS is more likely to occur in infants who do not use a pacifier when they go to sleep than in those who do use a pacifier (Li & others, 2006).
- Low birth weight infants are 5 to 10 times more likely to die of SIDS than are their normal-weight counterparts (Horne & others, 2002).
- Infants whose siblings have died of SIDS are two to four times as likely to die of it (Lenoir, Mallet, & Calenda, 2000).
- Six percent of infants with *sleep apnea,* a temporary cessation of breathing in which the airway is completely blocked, usually for 10 seconds or longer, die of SIDS (McNamara & Sullivan, 2000).
- African American and Eskimo infants are four to six times as likely as all others to die of SIDS (Ige & Shelton, 2004).
- SIDS is more common in lower socioeconomic groups (Mitchell & others, 2000).
- SIDS is more common in infants who are passively exposed to cigarette smoke (Shea & Steiner, 2008).
- SIDS is more common if infants sleep in soft bedding (McGarvey & others, 2006).
- SIDS is less common when infants sleep in a bedroom with a fan. A recent study revealed that sleeping in a bedroom with a fan lowers the risk of SIDS by 70 percent (Coleman-Phox, Odouli, & Li, 2008).
- SIDS occurs more often in infants with abnormal brain stem functioning involving the neurotransmitter serotonin (Kinney & others, 2009; Machaalani & Waters, 2008).

Childhood

Experts recommend that young children get 11 to 13 hours of a sleep each night (National Sleep Foundation, 2009). Most young children sleep through the night and have one daytime nap (Davis, Parker, & Montgomery, 2004).

Following is a sampling of recent research on factors linked to children's sleep problems. A national survey indicated that children who do not get adequate sleep are more likely to show depressive symptoms, have problems at school, have a father in poor health, live in a family characterized by frequent disagreements and heated arguments, and live in an unsafe neighborhood than are children who get adequate sleep (Smaldone, Honig, & Byrne, 2007). One study also revealed that marital conflict was linked to disruptions in children's sleep (El-Sheikh & others, 2006). Another study revealed that preschool children who did not get adequate sleep were more likely to experience injuries that required medical attention (Koulouglioti, Cole, & Kitzman, 2008). Yet another recent study revealed that children who had sleep problems from 3 to 8 years of age were more likely to develop adolescent problems, such as early onset of drug use and depression (Wong, Brower, & Zucker, 2009). And recent research indicates that short sleep duration in children is linked with being overweight (Nixon & others, 2008; Patel & Hu, 2008).

Not only is the amount of sleep children get important, but so is uninterrupted sleep. One study revealed that disruption in 4- to 5-year-old children's sleep (variability in amount of sleep, variability in bedtime, and lateness in going to bed) was linked to less optimal adjustment in preschool (Bates & others, 2002). And a recent study found that bedtime resistance was associated with conduct problems or hyperactivity in children (Carvalho Bos & others, 2009).

Helping the child to slow down before bedtime often contributes to less resistance in going to bed. Reading the child a story, playing quietly with the child in the bath, and letting the child sit on the caregiver's lap while listening to music are quieting activities.

What are some links between children's sleep patterns and other aspects of development?

Children can experience a number of sleep problems (Nevsimalova, 2009; Sadeh, 2008). One estimate indicates that more than 40 percent of children experience a sleep problem at some point in their development (Boyle & Cropley, 2004).

Among the sleep problems that children can develop are nightmares and night terrors. *Nightmares* are frightening dreams that awaken the sleeper, more often toward the morning than just after the child has gone to bed at night. Almost every child has an occasional nightmare, but persistent nightmares might indicate that the child is feeling too much stress during waking hours. A recent study revealed that preschool children who tended to have bad dreams were characterized by a difficult temperament at 5 months of age and anxiousness at 17 months of age (Simard & others, 2008).

Night terrors are characterized by sudden arousal from sleep and an intense fear, usually accompanied by a number of physiological reactions, such as rapid heart rate and breathing, loud screams, heavy perspiration, and physical movement (Bruni & others, 2008). In most instances, the child has little or no memory of what happened during the night terror. Night terrors are less common than nightmares and occur more often in deep sleep than do nightmares. Many children who experience night terrors return to sleep rather quickly. These sleep disruptions are not believed to reflect any emotional problems in children.

Adolescence

Might changing sleep patterns in adolescence contribute to adolescents' health-compromising behaviors? Recently there has been a surge of interest in adolescent sleep patterns (Moseley & Gradisar, 2009; Noland & others, 2009).

In a recent national survey of youth, only 31 percent of U.S. adolescents got eight or more hours of sleep on an average school night (Eaton & others, 2008). In this study, the percentage of adolescents getting this much sleep on an average school night decreased as they got older (see Figure 3.20). One study revealed that adolescents who got inadequate sleep (eight hours or less) on school nights were more likely to feel more tired or sleepy, more cranky and irritable, fall asleep in school, be in a depressed mood, and drink caffeinated beverages than their counterparts who got optimal sleep (nine or more hours). And in another study of adolescents, getting less sleep at night was linked to higher levels of anxiety, depression, and fatigue the next day (Fuligni & Hardway, 2006).

Mary Carskadon (2002, 2004, 2005, 2006) has conducted a number of research studies on adolescent sleep patterns. She has found that adolescents sleep an average of 9 hours and 25 minutes when given the opportunity to sleep as long as they like. Most adolescents get considerably less sleep than this, especially during the week. This creates a sleep debt, which adolescents often try to make up on the weekend. Carskadon also has found that older adolescents are often more sleepy during the day than are younger adolescents. She concludes that this was not because of factors such as academic work and social pressures. Rather, her research suggests that adolescents' biological clocks undergo a hormonal phase shift as they get older. This pushes the time of wakefulness to an hour later than when they were young adolescents. Carskadon has found that the shift was caused by a delay in the nightly presence of the hormone *melatonin,* which is produced by the brain's pineal gland in preparation for the body to sleep. Melatonin is secreted at about 9:30 p.m. in younger adolescents but is produced approximately an hour later in older adolescents, which delays the onset of sleep.

Carskadon determined that early school starting times can result in grogginess and lack of attention in class and poor performance on tests. Based on this research, schools in Edina, Minnesota, made the decision to start classes at 8:30 a.m. instead of 7:25 a.m. Discipline problems and the number of students who report an illness or depression have dropped. Test scores in Edina have improved for high school students, but not for middle school students—results that support Carskadon's idea that older adolescents are more affected by earlier school start times than younger adolescents are.

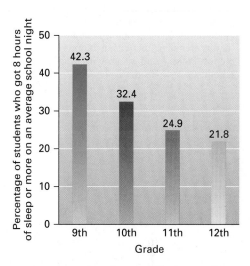

FIGURE 3.20 Developmental Changes in U.S. Adolescents' Sleep Patterns on an Average School Night.

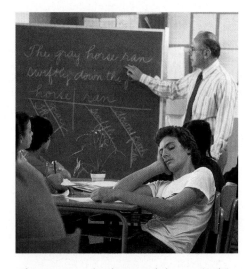

What are some developmental changes in sleep patterns during adolescence? How might these influence alertness at school?

In Mary Carskadon's sleep laboratory at Brown University, an adolescent girl's brain activity is being monitored. Carskadon (2005) says that in the morning, sleep-deprived adolescents' "brains are telling them its night time . . . and the rest of the world is saying it's time to go to school" (p. 19).

A longitudinal study further documented the negative outcomes of sleep loss during early adolescence (Fredrikson & others, 2004). The researchers examined the sleep patterns of 2,259 students from the sixth through the eighth grade. Over the course of the study, students who engaged in less sleep were more depressed and had lower self-esteem. Another study found that inadequate sleep during adolescence was linked to ineffective stress management, a low level of exercise, and having an unhealthy diet (Chen, Wang, & Jeng, 2006).

Adulthood and Aging

It is not only many adolescents who are getting inadequate sleep. Many adults don't get enough either. The average American adult gets just under seven hours of sleep a night. How much sleep do adults need to function optimally the next day? An increasing number of experts note that eight hours of sleep or more per night are necessary to be at your best the next day. These experts argue that many adults have become sleep deprived (Banks & Dinges, 2008). Work pressures, school pressures, family obligations, and social obligations often lead to long hours of wakefulness and irregular sleep/wake schedules (Dorrian & others, 2008).

Some aspects of sleep become more problematic in middle age (Alessi, 2007; McCrae & Dubyak, 2009). The total number of hours slept usually remains the same as in early adulthood, but beginning in the forties, wakeful periods are more frequent and there is less of the deepest type of sleep. The amount of time spent lying awake in bed at night begins to increase in middle age, which can produce a feeling of being less rested in the mornings (Abbott, 2003). Sleep problems in middle-aged adults are more common in individuals who take a higher number of prescription drugs, are obese, have cardiovascular disease, or are depressed (Miller & Cappuccio, 2007).

Beginning in middle adulthood and continuing through late adulthood, the timing of sleep also changes (Abbott, 2003). Many older adults go to bed earlier at night and wake up earlier in the morning (Liu & Liu, 2005). Many older adults also take a nap in the afternoon.

Insomnia increases in late adulthood, with almost half of older adults reporting that they experience some degree of insomnia (Hofman & Swaab, 2006). Many of the sleep problems of older adults are associated with health problems (National Sleep Foundation, 2003). Here are some strategies to help older adults sleep better at night: Avoid caffeine, avoid over-the-counter sleep remedies, stay physically active during the day, stay mentally active, and limit naps.

Review and Reflect: Learning Goal 3

3 **Summarize how sleep patterns change as people develop**

REVIEW

- How can sleep be characterized in infancy?
- What changes occur in sleep during childhood?
- How does adolescence affect sleep?
- What changes in sleep take place during adulthood and aging?

REFLECT

- How much sleep do you get on the average each night? Do you get enough sleep to function optimally the next day? Explain.

4 LONGEVITY

| Life Expectancy and Life Span | Centenarians | Biological Theories of Aging |

What do we really know about longevity? How long do most people live, and what distinguishes people who live a very long time? What is life likely to be like for those who live to a very ripe old age, and why do we age in the first place?

Life Expectancy and Life Span

We are no longer a youthful society. As more individuals live to older ages, the proportion of individuals at different ages has become increasingly similar. Indeed, the concept of a period called "late adulthood" is a recent one—until the twentieth century, most individuals died before they reached 65.

Recall from Chapter 1, "Introduction," that a much greater percentage of persons live to an older age. However, the life span has remained virtually unchanged since the beginning of recorded history. **Life span** is the upper boundary of life, the maximum number of years an individual can live. The maximum life span of humans is approximately 120 to 125 years of age. *Life expectancy* is the number of years that will probably be lived by the average person born in a specific year. Improvements in medicine, nutrition, exercise, and lifestyle have increased our life expectancy an average of 31 additional years since 1900. Sixty-five-year-olds in the United States today can expect to live an average of 18 more years (20 for females, 16 for males) (National Center for Health Statistics, 2006). The average life expectancy of individuals born today in the United States is 78.1 years (National Center for Health Statistics, 2008).

How does the United States fare in life expectancy, compared with other countries around the world? We do considerably better than some, a little worse than some others (Powell, 2009). Japan has the highest life expectancy at birth today (82 years) (Guillot, 2009). Differences in life expectancies across countries are due to such factors as health conditions and medical care throughout the life span.

Life expectancy also differs for various ethnic groups within the United States and for men and women (Guillot, 2009). For example, the life expectancy of African Americans (73) in the United States is five years lower than the life expectancy for non-Latino Whites (78) (National Center for Health Statistics, 2008). Non-Latino White women have a life expectancy of 81, followed by African American women (77), non-Latino White men (76 years), and African American men (70 years) (Heron & others, 2008).

Today, the overall life expectancy for females is 80.7 years of age, for males 75.4 years of age (Heron & others, 2008). Beginning in the mid-thirties, females outnumber males; this gap widens during the remainder of the adult years. By the time adults are 75 years of age, more than 61 percent of the population is female; for those 85 and over, the figure is almost 70 percent female. Why can women expect to live longer than men? Social factors such as health attitudes, habits, lifestyles, and occupation are probably important (Saint Onge, 2009). For example, men are more likely than women to die from the leading causes of death in the United States, such as cancer of the respiratory system, motor vehicle accidents, cirrhosis of the liver, emphysema, and coronary heart disease (Yoshida & others, 2006). These causes of death are associated with lifestyle. For example, the sex difference in deaths due to lung cancer and emphysema occurs because men are heavier smokers than women.

The sex difference in longevity is also influenced by biological factors. In virtually all species, females outlive males. Women have more resistance to infections

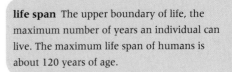

life span The upper boundary of life, the maximum number of years an individual can live. The maximum life span of humans is about 120 years of age.

Frenchwoman Jeanne Louise Calment recently died at age 122. It has been claimed that some people have lived longer, but scientists say the maximum human life span is about 120 to 125 years.

and degenerative diseases. For example, the female's estrogen production helps to protect her from arteriosclerosis (hardening of the arteries) (Vina & others, 2005). And the additional X chromosome that women carry in comparison to men may be associated with the production of more antibodies to fight off disease.

Centenarians

In industrialized countries, the number of centenarians (individuals 100 years and older) is increasing at a rate of approximately 7 percent each year (Perls, 2007). In the United States, there were only 15,000 centenarians in 1980, a number that had risen to 77,000 in 2000, and it is projected that this number will reach more than 800,000 by 2050. The United States has the most centenarians followed by Japan, China, and England/Wales (Hall, 2008). It is estimated that there are 75 to 100 supercentenarians (individuals 110 years or older) in the United States and about 300 to 450 worldwide (Perls, 2007).

A disproportionate number of centenarians are women. However, although women are more likely to attain exceptional longevity than men, among centenarians men are more likely to be healthier than women (Perls, 2007). Though far fewer in number, male centenarians have better physical and cognitive functioning than their female counterparts (Terry & others, 2008a). One explanation for this gender difference in centenarians' health is that to reach exceptional old age men may need to be in excellent health (Perls, 2007). By contrast, women may be more adaptive in living with illnesses when they are older and thus can reach an exceptional old age in spite of having a chronic disability.

What chance do you have of living to be 100? Genes play an important role in surviving to an extreme old age (Bostock, Soiza, & Whalley, 2009). There is increasing interest in studying *susceptibility genes*—those that make the individual more vulnerable to specific diseases or acceleration of aging, and *longevity genes*—those that make the individual less vulnerable to certain diseases and more likely to live to an older age (Concannon & others, 2009; Hinks & others, 2009). But as indicated in Figure 3.21, there are also other factors at work such as family history, health (weight, diet, smoking, and exercise), education, personality, and lifestyle (Barbieri & others, 2009). To further examine the factors that are involved in living to a very old age, read the following *Contexts of Life-Span Development* interlude.

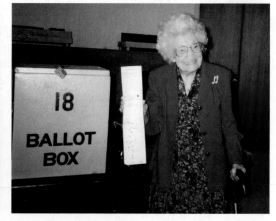

Three participants in the New England Centenarian Study: (*left*) Adelaide Kruger, age 101, watering her flowers; (*middle*) Waldo McBurney, age 104, is an active beekeeper, gardener, and runner who has earned five gold medals and set international records in track and field events in his age group; (*right*) Daphne Brann, age 110, voting in an election.

This survey gives you a rough guide for predicting your longevity. The basic life expectancy for males is age 75, and for females is 80. Write down your basic life expectancy. If you are in your fifties or sixties, you should add ten years to the basic figure because you have already proved yourself to be a durable individual. If you are over age 60 and active, you can even add another two years.

Life Expectancy

Decide how each item applies to you and add or subtract the appropriate number of years from your basic life expectancy.

1. Family history
___ Add five years if two or more of your grandparents lived to 80 or beyond.
___ Subtract four years if any parent, grandparent, sister, or brother died of a heart attack or stroke before 50.
___ Subtract two years if anyone died from these diseases before 60.
___ Subtract three years for each case of diabetes, thyroid disorder, breast cancer, cancer of the digestive system, asthma, or chronic bronchitis among parents or grandparents.

2. Marital status
___ If you are married, add four years.
___ If you are over twenty-five and not married, subtract one year for every unmarried decade.

3. Economic status
___ Add two years if your family income is over $60,000 per year.
___ Subtract three years if you have been poor for the greater part of your life.

4. Physique
___ Subtract one year for every ten pounds you are overweight.
___ For each inch your girth measurement exceeds your chest measurement deduct two years.
___ Add three years if you are over forty and not overweight.

5. Exercise
___ Add three years if you exercise regularly and moderately (jogging three times a week).
___ Add five years if you exercise regularly and vigorously (long-distance running three times a week).
___ Subtract three years if your job is sedentary.
___ Add three years if your job is active.

6. Alcohol
___ Add two years if you are a light drinker (one to three drinks a day).
___ Subtract five to ten years if you are a heavy drinker (more than four drinks per day).
___ Subtract one year if you are a teetaler.

7. Smoking
___ Subtract eight years if you smoke two or more packs of cigarettes per day.
___ Subtract two years if you smoke one to two packs per day.
___ Subtract two years if you smoke less than one pack.
___ Subtract two years if your regularly smoke a pipe or cigars.

8. Disposition
___ Add two years if you are a reasoned, practical person.
___ Subtract two years if you are aggressive, intense, and competitive.
___ Add one to five years if you are basically happy and content with life.
___ Subtract one to five years if you are often unhappy, worried, and often feel guilty.

9. Education
___ Subtract two years if you have less than a high school education.
___ Add one year if you attended four years of school beyond high school.
___ Add three years if you attended five or more years beyond high school.

10. Environment
___ Add four years if you have lived most of your life in a rural environment.
___ Subtract two years if you have lived most of your life in an urban environment.

11. Sleep
___ Subtract five years if you sleep more than nine hours a day.

12. Temperature
___ Add two years if your home's thermostat is set at no more than 68° F.

13. Health care
___ Add three years if you have regular medical checkups and regular dental care.
___ Subtract two years if you are frequently ill.

___ **Your Life Expectancy Total**

FIGURE 3.21 Can You Live to Be 100?

Contexts of Life-Span Development

LIVING LONGER IN OKINAWA

Individuals live longer on the Japanese island of Okinawa in the East China Sea than anywhere else in the world. In Okinawa, there are 34.7 centenarians for every 100,000 inhabitants, the highest ratio in the world. In comparison, the United States

(continued on next page)

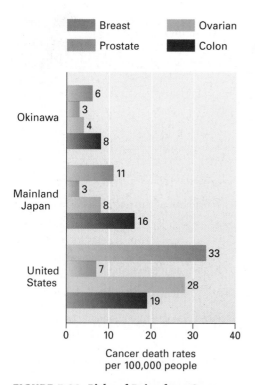

FIGURE 3.22 Risks of Dying from Cancer in Okinawa, Japan, and the United States. The risk of dying from different forms of cancer is lower in Okinawa than in the United States and mainland Japan (Willcox, Willcox, & Suzuki, 2002). Okinawans eat lots of tofu and soy products, which are rich in flavonoids (believed to lower the risk of breast and prostate cancer). They also consume large amounts of fish, especially tuna, mackerel, and salmon, which reduce the risk of breast cancer.

has about 10 centenarians for every 100,000 residents. The life expectancy in Okinawa is one of the highest in the world—81.2 years of age (86 for women, 78 for men). And Okinawa has the highest prevalence of centenarians in the world (Wilcox & others, 2008).

What is responsible for such longevity in Okinawa? Some possible explanations include the following (Willcox, Willcox, & Suzuki, 2002; Willcox & others, 2007, 2008):

- *Diet.* Okinawans eat very healthy food—heavy on grains, fish, and vegetables; light on meat, eggs, and dairy products. The risk of dying of cancer is far lower among Okinawans than among Japanese mainland and Americans (see Figure 3.22). About 100,000 Okinawans moved to Brazil and quickly adopted the eating regimen of their new home, one heavy on red meat. The result: The life expectancy of the Brazilian Okinawans is now 17 years lower than Japanese Okinawan's 81 years!

- *Low-stress lifestyle.* The easygoing lifestyle in Okinawa more closely resembles that of a laid-back South Sea island than that of the high-stress world on the Japanese mainland.

- *Caring community.* Okinawans look out for each other and do not isolate or ignore their older adults. If older adults need help, they don't hesitate to ask a neighbor. Such support and caring are likely responsible for Okinawa having the lowest suicide rate among older women in East Asia, an area noted for its high suicide rate among older women.

- *Activity.* Many older adults in Okinawa are active, engaging in such activities as taking walks and working in their gardens. Many older Okinawans also continue working at their jobs.

- *Spirituality.* Many older adults in Okinawa find a sense of purpose in spiritual matters. Prayer is commonplace and believed to ease the mind of stress and problems.

Toshiko Taira, 80, weaves cloth from the fibers of banana trees on a loom in Okinawa. She, like many Okinawans, believes that such sense of purpose helps people to live longer.

Biological Theories of Aging

Even if we stay remarkably healthy, we begin to age at some point. In fact, life-span experts argue that biological aging begins at birth (Schaie, 2000). What are the biological explanations of aging? Intriguing explanations of why we age are provided by four biological theories: cellular clock theory, free-radical theory, mitochondrial theory, and hormonal stress theory.

Cellular Clock Theory

Cellular clock theory is Leonard Hayflick's (1977) theory that cells can divide a maximum of about 75 to 80 times and that, as we age, our cells become less capable of dividing. Hayflick found that cells extracted from adults in their fifties to seventies divided fewer than 75 to 80 times. Based on the ways cells divide, Hayflick places the upper limit of the human life-span potential at about 120 to 125 years of age.

cellular clock theory Leonard Hayflick's theory that the maximum number of times human cells can divide is about 75 to 80. As we age, our cells have less capability to divide.

free-radical theory A microbiological theory of aging that states that people age because when their cells metabolize energy, they generate waste that includes unstable oxygen molecules, known as free radicals, that damage DNA and other cellular structures.

In the last decade, scientists have tried to fill in a gap in cellular clock theory (Liew & Norbury, 2009; Zou & others, 2009). Hayflick did not know why cells die. The answer may lie at the tips of chromosomes, at *telomeres*, which are DNA sequences that cap chromosomes (Shay & Wright, 2007).

Each time a cell divides, the telomeres become shorter and shorter (see Figure 3.23). After about 70 or 80 replications, the telomeres are dramatically reduced and the cell no longer can reproduce. A recent study revealed that healthy centenarians had longer telomeres than unhealthy centenarians (Terry & others, 2008b). Another recent study found that women with higher intakes of vitamins C and E had longer telomeres than women with lower intakes of these vitamins (Xu & others, 2009).

Injecting the enzyme *telomerase* into human cells grown in the laboratory can substantially extend the life of the cells beyond the approximately 70 to 80 normal cell divisions (Aubert & Lansdorp, 2008). However, telomerase is present in approximately 85 percent of cancerous cells and thus may not produce healthy life extension of cells (Fakhoury, Nimmo, & Autexier, 2007). To capitalize on the high presence of telomerase in cancerous cells, researchers currently are investigating gene therapies that inhibit telomerase and lead to the death of cancerous cells while keeping healthy cells alive (Effros, 2009; Wu & others, 2009).

Free-Radical Theory   A second microbiological theory of aging is **free-radical theory,** which states that people age because when cells metabolize energy, the by-products include unstable oxygen molecules known as free radicals (Chebab & others, 2008). The free radicals ricochet around the cells, damaging DNA and other cellular structures (Afanas'ev, 2009). The damage can lead to a range of disorders, including cancer and arthritis (Farooqui & Farooqui, 2009). Overeating is linked with an increase in free radicals, and researchers recently have found that calorie restriction—a diet restricted in calories although adequate in proteins, vitamins, and minerals—reduces the oxidative damage created by free radicals (Keijer & van Schothorst, 2008). And a recent study revealed a greater concentration of free radicals in 20- to 80-year-old smokers than nonsmokers (Reddy Thavanati & others, 2008).

Mitochondrial Theory   There is increasing interest in the role that *mitochondria*—tiny bodies within cells that supply energy for function, growth, and repair—might play in aging (Boveris & Navarro, 2008) (see Figure 3.24). **Mitochondrial theory** states that aging is due to the decay of mitochondria. It appears that this decay is primarily due to oxidative damage and loss of critical micronutrients supplied by the cell (Druzhyna, Wilson, & LeDoux, 2008; Figueiredo & others, 2009).

How do this damage and the loss of nutrients occur? Among the by-products of mitochondrial energy production are the free radicals just described. According to the mitochondrial theory, the damage caused by free radicals initiates a self-perpetuating cycle in which oxidative damage causes impairment of mitochondrial function, which results in the generation of even greater amounts of free radicals. The result is that over time, the affected mitochondria become so inefficient that they cannot generate enough energy to meet cellular needs (Kadenbagh, Ramzan, & Voght, 2009; Reddy Thavanati & others, 2008). One recent study revealed that exercise in older adults increased mitochondrial activity in their cells (Menshikova & others, 2006).

Defects in mitochondria are linked with cardiovascular disease, neurodegenerative diseases such as dementia, and decline in liver functioning (Kim, Wei, & Sowers, 2008). However, it is not known whether the defects in mitochondria cause aging or are merely accompaniments of the aging process (Van Remmen & Jones, 2009).

Hormonal Stress Theory   The three theories of aging that we have discussed so far-cellular clock, free radical, and mitochondrial-attempt to explain again at the

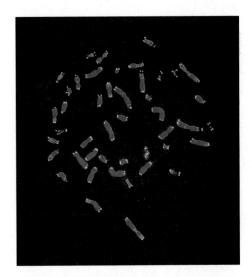

FIGURE 3.23 Telomeres and Aging. The above photograph shows telomeres lighting up the tips of chromosomes.

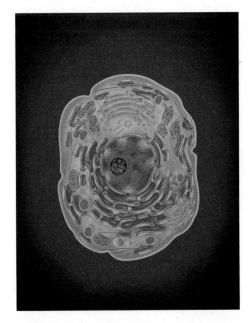

FIGURE 3.24 Mitochondria. This color-coded illustration of a typical cell shows mitochondria in green. The illustration also includes the nucleus (pink) with its DNA (brown). *What that changes in mitochondria might be involved in aging?*

mitochondrial theory The theory that aging is caused by the decay of mitochondria, tiny cellular bodies that supply energy for function, growth, and repair.

cellular level. In contrast, **hormonal stress theory** argues that aging in the body's hormonal system can lower resistance to stress and increase the likelihood of disease.

Normally, when people experience stressors, the body responds by releasing certain hormones. As people age, the hormones stimulated by stress remain at elevated levels longer than when they were younger (Brown-Borg, 2008; Simm & others, 2008). These prolonged, elevated levels of stress-related hormones are associated with increased risks for many diseases, including cardiovascular disease, cancer, diabetes, and hypertension (Epel, 2009).

A variation of hormonal stress theory has emphasized the contribution of a decline in immune system functioning with aging (Swain & Nikolich-Zugich, 2009; Walston & others, 2009). Aging contributes to immune system deficits that give rise to infectious diseases in older adults (Bauer, Jeckel, & Luz, 2009; Suvas, 2008). The extended duration of stress and diminished restorative processes in older adults may accelerate the effects of aging on immunity.

Which of these biological theories best explains aging? That question has not yet been answered. It might turn out that all of these biological processes contribute to aging (Miller, 2009).

Review and Reflect: Learning Goal 4

 4 **Explain longevity and the biological aspects of aging**

REVIEW

- What is the difference between life span and life expectancy? What sex differences exist in longevity?
- What characterizes centenarians?
- What are the four main biological theories of aging?

REFLECT

- If we could lengthen the maximum human life span, would this increase be beneficial? If so, to whom?

---

hormonal stress theory The theory that aging in the body's hormonal system can lower resistance to stress and increase the likelihood of disease.

Reach Your Learning Goals

Physical Development and Biological Aging

---

1 BODY GROWTH AND CHANGE: DISCUSS MAJOR CHANGES IN THE BODY THROUGH THE LIFE SPAN

Patterns of Growth

- Human growth follows cephalocaudal (fastest growth occurs at the top with the head) and proximodistal patterns (growth starts at the center of the body and moves toward the extremities).

Height and Weight in Infancy and Childhood

- Height and weight increase rapidly in infancy and then take a slower course during childhood. Growth patterns vary individually. Physically abused or neglected children may experience growth hormone deficiency, restricting their growth. Head circumference, waist circumference, and leg length decrease relative to body height in middle and late childhood.

Puberty

- Puberty is a rapid physical maturation involving hormonal and bodily changes that takes place in early adolescence. A number of changes occur in sexual maturation. The growth spurt involves height and weight and occurs about two years earlier for girls than boys. Extensive hormonal changes characterize puberty. Puberty began occurring much earlier in the twentieth century mainly because of improved health and nutrition. The basic genetic program for puberty is wired into the nature of the species, but nutrition, health, and other environmental factors affect puberty's timing and makeup. Adolescents show heightened interest in their bodies and body images. Younger adolescents are more preoccupied with these images than older adolescents. Adolescent girls often have a more negative body image than do adolescent boys. Early maturation often favors boys, at least during early adolescence, but as adults, late-maturing boys have a more positive identity than do early-maturing boys. Early-maturing girls are at risk for a number of developmental problems.

Early Adulthood

- In early adulthood, height remains rather constant. Many individuals reach their peak of muscle tone and strength in their late teens and twenties; however, these can decline in the thirties.

Middle Adulthood

- In middle adulthood, changes usually are gradual. Visible signs of aging, such as the wrinkling of skin, usually appear in the forties and fifties. Middle-aged individuals also tend to lose height and gain weight. Strength, joints, and bones show declines in middle age. The cardiovascular system declines in functioning, and at about 55 years of age lung capacity begins to decline, more so in smokers than nonsmokers. The climacteric is a term used to describe the midlife transition in which fertility declines. Menopause is the time in middle age, usually in the later forties or early fifties, when a woman's menstrual periods cease. Men do not experience an inability to father children in middle age, although their testosterone level declines.

Late Adulthood

- In late adulthood, outwardly noticeable physical changes become more prominent, individuals get shorter, and weight often decreases because of muscle loss. The circulatory system declines further.

---

2 THE BRAIN: DESCRIBE HOW THE BRAIN CHANGES THROUGH THE LIFE SPAN

Brain Physiology

- The brain has two hemispheres, each of which has four lobes (frontal, occipital, temporal, and parietal). Throughout the brain, nerve cells called neurons process information. Communication among neurons involves the axon, dendrites, synapses, neurotransmitters, and the myelin sheath. Clusters of neurons, known as neural circuits, work together to handle specific types of information. Specialization of functioning does occur in the brain's hemispheres, as in language, but for the most part both hemispheres are at work in most complex functions.

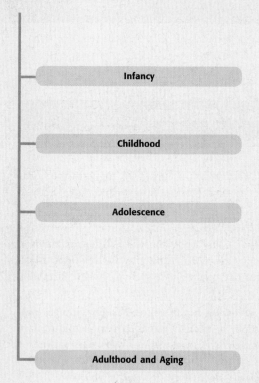

Infancy

- Researchers have found that early experience influences the brain's development. Myelination begins prenatally and continues after birth. In infancy, one of the most impressive changes in the brain is the enormous increase in dendrites and synapses. These connections between neurons are overproduced and pruned.

Childhood

- During early childhood, the brain and head grow more rapidly than any other part of the body. Researchers have found that dramatic anatomical changes in brain patterns occur from 3 to 15 years of age, often involving spurts of brain activity and growth. In middle and late childhood, focal brain activation increases.

Adolescence

- The corpus callosum, a large bundle of axon fibers that connects the brain's left and right hemispheres, thickens in adolescence, and this thickening improves the adolescent's ability to process information. The prefrontal cortex, the highest level of the frontal lobes that are involved in reasoning, decision making, and self-control, continues to mature through emerging adulthood or later. The amygdala, the part of the limbic system that is the seat of emotions such as anger, matures earlier than the prefrontal cortex. The later development of the prefrontal cortex combined with the earlier maturity of the amygdala may explain the difficulty adolescents have in putting the brakes on their emotional intensity.

Adulthood and Aging

- On average, the brain loses 5 to 10 percent of its weight between the ages of 20 and 90. Brain volume also decreases with aging. Shrinking occurs in some areas of the brain, such as the prefrontal cortex, more than in other areas. A general slowing of function characterizes the central nervous system beginning in middle adulthood and increasing in late adulthood. A decline in the production of some neurotransmitters is related to aging. Neurogenesis has been demonstrated in lower mammals and can occur in humans. It appears that dendritic growth can occur in adults. The brain has the capacity to virtually rewire itself to compensate for loss in older adults. Another change is a decrease in brain lateralization in older adults.

---

3   SLEEP: SUMMARIZE HOW SLEEP PATTERNS CHANGE AS PEOPLE DEVELOP

Infancy

- Newborns sleep about 16 to 17 hours a day. By about 6 months of age, most infants have sleep patterns similar to those of adults. REM sleep occurs more in infancy than in childhood and adulthood. Sleeping arrangements vary across cultures. A special concern is sudden infant death syndrome.

Childhood

- Most young children sleep through the night and have one daytime nap. However, some children develop sleep problems, such as persistent nightmares and night terrors.

Adolescence

- Many adolescents stay up later and sleep longer in the morning than when they were children. Recent interest focuses on biological explanations of these developmental changes in sleep during adolescence and their link to school success.

Adulthood and Aging

- An increasing concern is that adults do not get enough sleep. In middle age, wakeful periods may interrupt nightly sleep more often. Many older adults go to bed earlier and wake up earlier the next morning. Almost half of older adults report having some insomnia.

---

4   LONGEVITY: EXPLAIN LONGEVITY AND THE BIOLOGICAL ASPECTS OF AGING

Life Expectancy and Life Span

- Life expectancy is the number of years an individual is expected to live when he or she is born. Life span is the maximum number of years any member of a species has been known to live. On the average, females live about five years longer than males

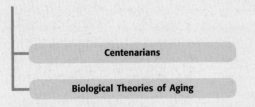

Centenarians

Biological Theories of Aging

do. The sex difference is likely due to biological and social factors. An increasing number of individuals live to be 100 or older.

- Heredity, family history, health, education, personality, and lifestyle are important factors in living to be a centenarian. The ability to cope with stress also is important.

- Four biological theories are cellular clock theory, free-radical theory, mitochondrial theory, and hormonal stress theory. Hayflick proposed the cellular clock theory, which states that cells can divide a maximum of about 75 to 80 times and that, as we age, our cells become less capable of dividing. Telomeres are likely involved in explaining why cells lose their capacity to divide. According to free-radical theory, people age because unstable oxygen molecules called free radicals are produced in the cells. According to mitochondrial theory, aging is due to the decay of mitochondria, tiny cellular bodies that supply energy for function, growth, and repair. According to hormonal stress theory, aging in the body's hormonal system can lower resistance to stress and increase the likelihood of disease.

KEY TERMS

cephalocaudal pattern 100
proximodistal pattern 101
growth hormone
   deficiency 102
puberty 102
menarche 103
hormones 103
hypothalamus 103

pituitary gland 103
gonads 103
gonadotropins 103
testosterone 104
estradiol 104
precocious puberty 105
climacteric 107
menopause 107

myelination 111
lateralization 111
corpus callosum 116
prefrontal cortex 116
amygdala 116
neurogenesis 118
sudden infant death
   syndrome (SIDS) 123

life span 127
cellular clock theory 130
free-radical theory 131
mitochondrial theory 131
hormonal stress theory 132

KEY PEOPLE

Judith Blakemore 105
Charles Nelson 113

Mark Johnson 116
Laurence Steinberg 117

Stanley Rapaport 119

Leonard Hayflick 130

E-LEARNING TOOLS

Connect to **www.mhhe.com/santrockldt5e** to research the answers and complete these exercises. In addition, you'll find a number of other resources and valuable study tools for Chapter 3, "Physical Development and Biological Aging," on this Web site.

Taking It to the Net

1. June's only child, 12-year-old Suzanne, is starting to show all the physical signs of puberty. What behavioral changes in Suzanne should June expect as a result of puberty?

2. Unfortunately, Kathryn's family does not have a history of longevity. Kathryn feels doomed by heredity. She has heard about the Okinawa Centenarian Study, and she is curious to learn more about the life habits of the participants. Is there anything Kathryn can do to increase her chances of living to an old age?

Self-Assessment

To evaluate yourself in regard to your sleep, complete this self-assessment:

- *Do You Get Enough Sleep?*

Health and Well-Being, Parenting, and Education

Build your decision-making skills by trying your hand at the health and well-being, parenting, and education exercises.

Video Clips

The Online Learning Center includes the following videos for this chapter:

- *Have I Changed Since Age 20?*
- *Physical Changes at Age 72*

4

Nothing can be changed until it is faced.

—JAMES BALDWIN
American Novelist, 20th Century

LEARNING GOALS

◆ Describe developmental changes in health.

◆ Characterize developmental changes in nutrition and eating behavior.

◆ Summarize the roles of exercise in child and adult health.

◆ Evaluate substance use in adolescence and adulthood.

HEALTH

CHAPTER OUTLINE

PREVIEW

Life is more than just living. It is important to live healthily. As we grow and develop through the life span, we have many opportunities to engage in health-enhancing or health-compromising behaviors, either by our choosing or because of the contexts provided by our caregivers. In this chapter, we explore many aspects of health, including illness and disease, nutrition and eating behavior, exercise, and substance use.

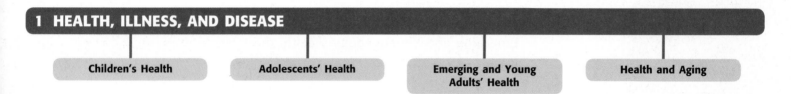

1 HEALTH, ILLNESS, AND DISEASE

| Children's Health | Adolescents' Health | Emerging and Young Adults' Health | Health and Aging |

Changing patterns of illness have fueled an interest in searching not just for biological causes of health, illness, and disease, but for psychological and sociocultural causes as well. With these multiple causes in mind, let's now examine changes in health through the human life span.

Children's Health

There are many causes for children's health. In this chapter, we focus on two of the most important influences: prevention and poverty. Among the topics we consider that further impact the health of children are immunization, accidents, and access to health care.

Prevention Although the dangers of many diseases for children have greatly diminished, it is still important for parents to keep their children on a timely immunization schedule (Russ, Regaldo, & Halfon, 2008). The recommended ages for various immunizations are shown in Figure 4.1.

In addition to immunization, another important aspect of preventing health problems in children is to avoid accidents, which are the leading cause of death in children (Wolraich & others, 2008). Infants need close monitoring as they gain locomotor and manipulative skills, along with a strong curiosity to explore the environment (Betz & Sowden, 2008). Aspiration of foreign objects, suffocation, falls, poisoning, burns, and motor vehicle accidents are among the most common accidents in infancy (Burns & others, 2009).

The status of children's motor, cognitive, and socioemotional development makes their health-care needs unique. For example, think about how the infant's and young child's motor skills are inadequate to ensure their personal safety while riding in an automobile. Adults must take preventive measures to restrain infants and young children in car seats. Young children also lack the cognitive skills, including reading ability, to discriminate between safe and unsafe household substances. And they may lack the impulse control to keep from running out into a busy street while chasing a ball or toy.

Caregivers play an important role in children's health (Herrmann, King, & Weitzman, 2008; Worthman, 2010). For example, children exposed to tobacco smoke in the home are more likely to develop wheezing symptoms and asthma than children in nonsmoking homes (Carlsen & Carlsen, 2008; Dong & others, 2008). By driving

Age	Immunization
Birth	Hepatitis B
2 months	Diphtheria Polio Influenza
4 months	Diphtheria Polio Influenza
6 months	Diphtheria Influenza
1 year	TB test
15 months	Measles Mumps Rubella Influenza
18 months	Diphtheria Polio
4 to 6 years	Diphtheria Polio
11 to 12 years	Measles Mumps Rubella
14 to 16 years	Tetanus-diphtheria

FIGURE 4.1 Recommended Immunization Schedule for Infants and Children.

at safe speeds, decreasing or eliminating drinking—especially before driving—and not smoking around children, caregivers enhance their children's health (Bolte & others, 2009; Chang, 2009).

Poverty   Of special concern in the United States is the poor health of many young children from low-income families. An estimated 7 percent of U.S. children have no usual source of health care. Approximately 11 million preschool children in the United States are malnourished. Their malnutrition places their health at risk. Many have poor resistance to diseases—including minor ones, such as colds, and major ones, such as influenza.

What is the best way to improve the health of children who live in poverty? Some experts argue that offering medical care is not enough. If you give an antibiotic to a child with a sore throat who then returns to a home where she will be cold and hungry, have you provided good health care? One approach to children's health aims to treat not only medical problems of the individual child but the conditions of the entire family. In fact, some programs seek to identify children who are at risk for problems and then try to alter the risk factors in an effort to prevent illness and disease (Worthman, 2010).

Why is adolescence often a key juncture in health?

Adolescents' Health

How important is adolescence in the development of health habits? How do parents and peers influence the health of adolescents?

Adolescence is a critical juncture in the adoption of behaviors relevant to health (Ozer & Irwin, 2009). Many of the factors linked to poor health habits and early death in the adult years begin during adolescence (Nyaronga & Wickrama, 2009).

Social contexts, including families, peers, and schools, influence adolescent health. Parents and older siblings can be important models of health-enhancing behaviors. In the National Longitudinal Study of Health, based on data collected from more than 12,000 seventh- through twelfth-graders, youth who did not eat dinner with a parent five or more days a week had dramatically higher rates of smoking cigarettes, using marijuana, getting into fights, and initiating sexual activity (Council of Economic Advisors, 2000). Parental caring and monitoring often combine to produce less risk taking in youth.

Peers also can influence adolescents' health (Youngblade, Storch, & Nackashi, 2007). Adolescents who have a limited capacity to resist dares often engage in risk taking at the urging of their peers. Peer pressure can instigate such health-compromising behaviors as cigarette smoking, substance abuse, early sexual activity, and violence (Loeber, Burke, & Pardini, 2009).

Because adolescents spend so much time in school, it is not surprising that what goes on there can influence their health behavior. Teachers, like parents, can serve as important health role models.

Health experts increasingly recognize that whether adolescents will develop a health problem or be healthy depends primarily on their own behavior (Robbins, Powers, & Burgess, 2008). Improving adolescent health involves (1) reducing adolescents' health-compromising behaviors, such as drug abuse, violence, unprotected sexual intercourse, and dangerous driving; and (2) increasing health-enhancing behaviors, such as eating nutritiously, exercising, and wearing seat belts.

Identifying adolescents' unmet needs and setting goals for health promotion are important steps to take in maximizing adolescent development.

—SUSAN MILLSTEIN
Contemporary Psychologist, University of California–San Francisco

Emerging and Young Adults' Health

Emerging adults have more than twice the mortality rate of adolescents (Park & others, 2006) (see Figure 4.2). As indicated in Figure 4.2, males are mainly responsible for the higher mortality rate of emerging adults.

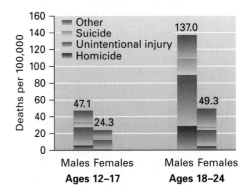

FIGURE 4.2 Mortality Rates of U.S. Adolescents and Emerging Adults.

Although emerging adults have a higher death rate than adolescents, emerging adults have few chronic health problems, and they have fewer colds and respiratory problems than when they were children (Rimsza & Kirk, 2005). Most college students know what it takes to prevent illness and promote health, but many don't fare very well when it comes to applying this information to themselves (Lenz, 2004).

In emerging and early adulthood, few individuals stop to think about how their personal lifestyles will affect their health later in their adult lives (Sakamaki & others, 2005). As young adults, many of us develop a pattern of not eating breakfast, not eating regular meals and relying on snacks as our main food source during the day, eating excessively to the point where we exceed the normal weight for our age, smoking moderately or excessively, drinking moderately or excessively, failing to exercise, and getting by with only a few hours of sleep at night (Cousineau, Goldstein, & Franco, 2005). These lifestyles are associated with poor health, which in turn impacts life satisfaction (Robbins, Power, & Burgess, 2008). In the Berkeley Longitudinal Study—in which individuals were evaluated over a period of 40 years—physical health at age 30 predicted life satisfaction at age 70, more so for men than for women (Mussen, Honzik, & Eichorn, 1982).

There are some hidden dangers in the peaks of performance and health in emerging and early adulthood. Young adults can draw on physical resources for a great deal of pleasure, often bouncing back easily from physical stress and abuse. However, this practice can lead them to push their bodies too far. The negative effects of abusing one's body might not show up in emerging adulthood or the first part of early adulthood, but they probably will surface later in early adulthood or in middle adulthood (Lenz, 2004).

Health and Aging

Aging can bring on new health problems, such as Alzheimer disease. Keep in mind, though, that many older adults are healthy. For example, only 17 percent of U.S. adults from 65 to 74 years of age have a disability. As shown in Figure 4.3, the percentage of Americans without a disability continues above 50 percent until they reach 85 years and older.

Chronic Disorders   **Chronic disorders** are characterized by a slow onset and long duration. Chronic disorders are rare in early adulthood, increase in middle adulthood, and become common in late adulthood (Kane, 2007).

The most common chronic disorders in middle age differ for females and males. The most common chronic disorders in middle adulthood for U.S. women, in order, are arthritis, hypertension, and sinus problems; the most common ones for U.S. men are hypertension, arthritis, hearing impairments, and heart disease. Men have a higher incidence of fatal chronic conditions (such as coronary heart disease, cancer, and stroke); women have a higher incidence of nonfatal ones (such as sinus problems, varicose veins, and bursitis). Older women have higher incidences of arthritis and hypertension, and are more likely to have visual problems, but are less likely to have hearing problems than older men are.

Cancer recently replaced cardiovascular disease as the leading cause of death in U.S. middle-aged adults. The same realignment of causes of death has also occurred in 65- to 74-year-olds with cancer now the leading cause of death in this age group (National Center for Health Statistics, 2008a, b, c). The decline in cardiovascular disease in middle-aged and older adults is due to improved drugs, a decrease in smoking, better diet, and an increase in exercise.

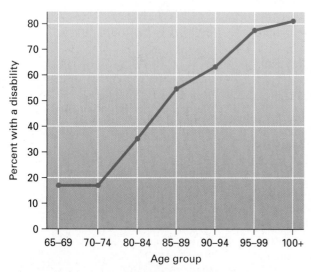

Note: Data for the 75 to 79 age group were unavailable.

FIGURE 4.3 Percentage of U.S. Older Adults of Different Ages Who Have a Disability.

chronic disorders Disorders characterized by slow onset and long duration.

However, in the 75 to 84 and 85-and-over age groups, cardiovascular disease still is the leading cause of death (National Center for Health Statistics, 2008a, b, c). As individuals age through the late adult years, the older they are the more likely they will die of cardiovascular disease than cancer (National Center for Health Statistics, 2008a, b, c).

Even when adults over the age of 65 have a physical impairment, many of them can still carry on their everyday activities or work. Chronic conditions associated with the greatest limitation on work are heart conditions (52 percent), diabetes (34 percent), asthma (27 percent), and arthritis (27 percent).

Low income is also strongly related to health problems in late adulthood (Aldwin, Spiro, & Park, 2006). Approximately three times as many poor as non-poor older adults report that their activities are limited by chronic disorders.

Normal aging involves some loss of bone tissue from the skeleton. However, in some instances loss of bone tissue can become severe. **Osteoporosis** involves an extensive loss of bone tissue. Osteoporosis is the main reason many older adults walk with a marked stoop (Ishikawa & others, 2009). Women are especially vulnerable to osteoporosis, the leading cause of broken bones in women (Bessette & others, 2009). Approximately 80 percent of osteoporosis cases in the United States occur in females, 20 percent in males. Almost two-thirds of all women over the age of 60 are affected by osteoporosis. This aging disorder is most common in non-Latina White, thin, and small-framed women.

Osteoporosis is related to deficiencies in calcium, vitamin D, estrogen, and lack of exercise (Bonjour & others, 2009). To prevent osteoporosis, young and middle-aged women should eat foods rich in calcium, get more exercise, and avoid smoking (Duque, Demontiero, & Troen, 2009). Calcium-rich foods include dairy products (low-fat milk and low-fat yogurt, for example) and certain vegetables (such as broccoli, turnip greens, and kale) (Lanham-New, 2008). A recent study revealed that taking a high supplement level of vitamin C was linked to fewer hip fractures in older women (Sahni & others, 2009). Aging women should also get bone density checks (Hourigan & others, 2008). Drugs such as alendronate (Fosamax) can be used to reduce the risk of osteoporosis (Suzuki & others, 2008). A program of regular exercise has the potential to reduce osteoporosis (Iwamoto & others, 2009; Yokoya & others, 2009).

Health problems that accompany aging not only can involve bones, muscles, and the cardiovascular system. Culture is an important influence on health. To read about the role of culture in coronary disease, see the *Diversity in Life-Span Development* interlude.

What characterizes osteoporosis? What are some strategies for reducing osteoporosis?

Diversity in Life-Span Development

CULTURE AND HEALTH

Culture plays an important role in coronary disease. Cross-cultural psychologists maintain that studies of immigrants shed light on the role culture plays in health. When people migrate to another culture, their health practices are likely to change, whereas their genetic predispositions to certain disorders remain constant (Jorgensen, Borch-Johnsen, & Bjerregaard, 2006).

Consider the Ni-Hon-San Study (Nippon–Honolulu–San Francisco), an ongoing study of approximately 12,000 Japanese men in Hiroshima and Nagasaki (Japan), Honolulu, and San Francisco. In the study, the Japanese men living in Japan have had the lowest rate of coronary heart disease, those living in Honolulu have had an intermediate rate, and those living in San Francisco have had the highest rate. The Japanese

(continued on next page)

osteoporosis A disorder that involves an extensive loss of bone tissue and is the main reason many older adults walk with a marked stoop. Women are especially vulnerable to osteoporosis.

In the Ni-Hon-San Study, what health variations were found for Japanese men living in Japan (left), Honolulu (middle), and San Francisco (right)?

men's cholesterol level, glucose level, and weight all increased as they migrated. Why? As the Japanese men migrated farther away from Japan, they acculturated, and their health practices, such as diet, changed. The Japanese men in California, for example, ate 40 percent more fat than the men in Japan.

Conversely, Japanese men in California have much lower rates of cerebrovascular disease (stroke) than Japanese men living in Japan. Businessmen in Japan tend to consume vast quantities of alcohol and to chain-smoke, both of which are high-risk factors for stroke. Stroke was the leading cause of death in Japan until it was surpassed by cancer in 1981. However, death rates from stroke for Japanese American men are at the same level as those of non-Latino White American men. Researchers suspect that this level is related to a change in behavior. That is, Japanese American men consume less alcohol and smoke less than their counterparts in Japan.

Health problems that accompany aging also can involve neurological disorders. Next, we examine a neurological disorder in aging that has dramatically increased in recent decades—Alzheimer disease.

Alzheimer Disease   **Dementia** is a global term for any neurological disorder in which the primary symptom is deterioration of mental functioning. Individuals with dementia often lose the ability to care for themselves and can lose the ability to recognize familiar surroundings and people (including family members) (Mast & Healy, 2009). It is estimated that 23 percent of women and 17 percent of men 85 years of age and over have dementia (Alzheimer's Association, 2009). Dementia is a broad category, and it is important that every effort is made to determine a specific cause of the deteriorating mental functioning in an older adult (Whitehouse, 2007).

One form of dementia is **Alzheimer disease**—a progressive, irreversible brain disorder that is characterized by a gradual deterioration of memory, reasoning, language, and eventually, physical function. In 2009, an estimated 5.3 million adults in the United States had Alzheimer disease, and it is projected that 10 million baby boomers (individuals born from 1946 to 1964) will develop Alzheimer disease in their lifetime (Alzheimer's Association, 2009). Figure 4.4 shows the estimated risks for developing Alzheimer disease at different ages for women and men (Alzheimer's Association, 2009). Women are likely to develop Alzheimer disease because they live longer than men, and their longer life expectancy increases the

dementia A global term for any neurological disorder in which the primary symptom is deterioration of mental functioning.

Alzheimer disease A progressive, irreversible brain disorder characterized by a gradual deterioration of memory, reasoning, language, and, eventually, physical function.

number of years during which they can develop Alheimer disease. It is estimated that Alzheimer disease triples the health-care costs of Americans 65 years of age and older (Alzheimer's Association, 2009). Because of the increasing prevalence of Alzheimer disease, researchers have stepped up their efforts to discover the causes of the disease and find more effective ways to treat it (Chiba & others, 2009; O'Bryant & others, 2009).

Because of differences in onset, Alzheimer also is now described as *early onset* (initially occurring in individuals younger than 65 years of age) or *late onset* (which has its initial onset in individuals 65 years of age and older). Early-onset Alzheimer disease is rare (about 10 percent of all cases) and generally affects people 30 to 60 years of age.

Alzheimer disease involves a deficiency in the important brain messenger chemical acetylcholine, which plays an important role in memory (Pepeu & Giovannini, 2009). Also, as Alzheimer disease progresses, the brain shrinks and deteriorates (see Figure 4.5). The deterioration of the brain in Alzheimer disease is characterized by the formation of *amyloid plaques* (dense deposits of protein that accumulate in the blood vessels) and *neurofibrillary tangles* (twisted fibers that build up in neurons) (Tabira, 2009). Researchers are focusing their efforts on ways to interrupt the progress of amyloid plaques and neurofibrillary tangles in Alzheimer patients (Nathalie & Jean-Noel, 2008; Norberg, 2008).

Although scientists are not certain what causes Alzheimer disease, age is an important risk factor and genes also likely play an important role (Williamson, Goldman, & Marder, 2009). The number of individuals with Alzheimer disease doubles every five years after the age of 65. A protein called *apolipoprotein E (apoE)*, which is linked to increasing presence of plaques and tangles in the brain, could play a role in as many as one-third of the cases of Alzheimer disease (Golanska & others, 2009; Lane & He, 2009). A recent study of almost 12,000 pairs of twins in Sweden found that identical twins were both more likely to develop Alzheimer disease than fraternal twins, suggesting a genetic influence on the disease (Gatz & others, 2006). And another recent study revealed that the presence of the *apoE* gene lowers the age of onset of Alzheimer disease (Sando & others, 2008).

Although individuals with a family history of Alzheimer disease are at greater risk, the disease is complex and likely caused by a number of factors, including lifestyles (Avramopoulos, 2009). For many years, scientists have known that a healthy diet plus exercise and weight control can lower the risk of cardiovascular disease. Now, they are finding that these healthy lifestyle factors may also lower the risk of Alzheimer disease. Researchers have revealed that older adults with Alzheimer disease are more likely to also have cardiovascular disease than individuals who do not have Alzheimer disease (Helzner & others, 2009). Autopsies show that brains with the telltale signs of tangles and plaques of Alzheimer patients are three times more common in individuals with cardiovascular disease (Sparks & others, 1990). Recently, more cardiac risk factors have been implicated in Alzheimer disease—obesity, smoking, atherosclerosis, and high cholesterol (Abellan & others, 2009; Sonnen & others, 2009; Sottero & others, 2009).

As with many problems associated with aging, exercise may also reduce the risk of Alzheimer disease (Middleton & others, 2007). One study of more than 2,000 men 71 to 93 years of age revealed that those who walked less than one-fourth of a mile a day were almost twice as likely to develop Alzheimer disease than their male counterparts who walked more than two miles a day (Abbott & others, 2004).

Early Detection and Alzheimer Disease   *Mild cognitive impairment (MCI)* represents a transitional state between the cognitive changes of normal aging and very early Alzheimer disease and other dementias (Peterson & Negash, 2008). Estimates indicate that as many as 10 to 20 percent of individuals 65 years of age and older have

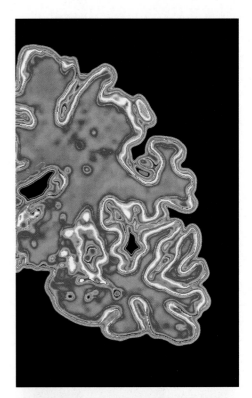
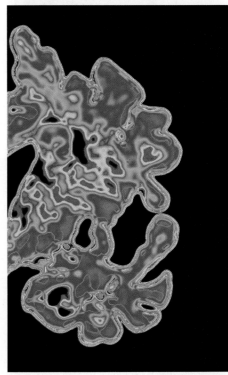

FIGURE 4.4 Two Brains: Normal Aging and Alzheimer Disease. The top computer graphic shows a slice of a normal aging brain, the bottom photograph a slice of a brain ravaged by Alzheimer disease. Notice the deterioration and shrinking in the Alzheimer disease brain.

MCI (Alzheimer's Association, 2009). Some individuals with MCI do not go on to develop Alzheimer disease, but MCI is a risk factor for Alzheimer disease.

Distinguishing between individuals who merely have age-associated declines in memory and those with MCI is difficult, as is predicting which individuals with MCI will subsequently develop Alzheimer disease. One effort in this regard is to have individuals with MCI undergo an fMRI (functional magnetic resonance imaging) brain scan (Pihlajamaki, Jauhiainen, & Soininen, 2009). If the scan shows that certain brain regions involved in memory are smaller than those of individuals without memory impairments, the individual is more likely to progress to Alzheimer disease (Alzheimer's Association, 2009). Also, recent research indicates that individuals without MCI have a higher degree of cortical thickness than individuals with MCI (Wang & others, 2009). Also, fMRI scans can detect changes in the brain that are fairly typical of early Alzheimer disease even before symptoms develop (Matsuda, 2007).

Longitudinal studies have indicated that certain aspects of memory may provide indicators of subsequent dementia and Alzheimer disease (Johnson & others, 2009). In one study, performance on a short verbal recall memory task in individuals with no indication of the presence of Alzheimer disease was linked to whether Alzheimer disease was present in the individuals 10 years later (Tierney & others, 2005). In another study, older adults whose episodic memory was impaired in an initial assessment were more than twice as likely to develop Alzheimer disease over a 10-year period as those with impairments in other cognitive domains such as semantic memory, working memory, and visuospatial ability (Aggarwal & others, 2005).

Drug Treatment of Alzheimer Disease Several drugs called cholinerase inhibitors have been approved by the U.S. Food and Drug Administration to treat Alzheimer disease. They are designed to improve memory and other cognitive functions by increasing levels of acetylcholine in the brain (Orhan & others, 2009; Pepeu & Giovannini, 2009). Keep in mind, though, that the drugs used to treat Alzheimer disease only slow the downward progression of the disease; they do not treat its cause (Rafii & Aisen, 2009). These drugs slow the worsening of Alzheimer symptoms for approximately 6 to 12 months for about 50 percent of the individuals who take them (Alzheimer's Association, 2009). Also, no drugs have yet been approved by the U.S. Food and Drug Administration for the treatment of MCI (Alzheimer's Association, 2009).

Caring for Individuals with Alzheimer Disease A special and growing concern is caring for Alzheimer patients (Cooper & others, 2008). Health-care professionals note that the family can be an important support system for the Alzheimer patient, but this support can have severe costs for the family, who can become emotionally and physically drained by the extensive care required for a person with Alzheimer disease (Vellone & others, 2008). For example, depression has been reported in 50 percent of family caregivers for Alzheimer patients (Redinbaugh, MacCallum, & Kiecolt-Glaser, 1995). A meta-analysis found that female caregivers reported providing more caregiving hours and higher levels of burden and depression, as well as lower levels of well-being and physical health, than male caregivers (Pinquart & Sorensen, 2006).

Respite care (services that provide temporary relief for those who are caring for individuals with disabilities, illnesses, or the elderly) has been developed to help people who have to meet the day-to-day needs of Alzheimer patients. This type of care provides an important break away from the burden of providing chronic care (Tompkins & Bell, 2009). To read further about individuals who care for Alzheimer patients, see the *Research in Life-Span Development* interlude.

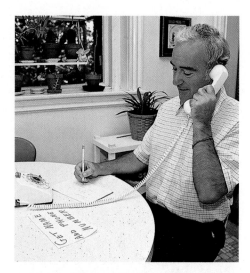

Memory loss is a common characteristic of Alzheimer disease. Written reminders, like those shown here, can help individuals with Alzheimer remember daily tasks.

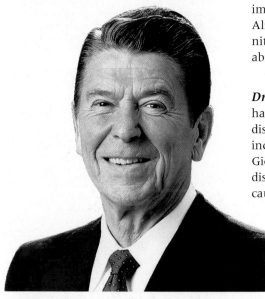

Former president Ronald Reagan was diagnosed with Alzheimer disease at age 83.

A wife comforting her husband who has Alzheimer disease. *What are some concerns about the family caregivers of individuals with Alzheimer disease?*

Research in Life-Span Development

THE STRESS OF CARING FOR AN ALZHEIMER PATIENT AT HOME

Researchers have recently found that the stress of caring for an Alzheimer patient at home can prematurely age the immune system, putting caregivers at risk for developing age-related diseases (Glaser & Kiecolt-Glaser, 2005; Graham, Christian, & Kiecolt-Glaser, 2006; Mausbach & others, 2007). In one study, 119 older adults who were caring for a spouse with Alzheimer disease or another form of dementia (which can require up to 100 hours a week of time) were compared with 106 older adults who did not have to care for a chronically ill spouse (Kiecolt-Glazer & others, 2003). The age of the older adults upon entry into the study ranged from 55 to 89 with an average age of 70.

Periodically during the six-year study, blood samples were taken and the levels of a naturally produced immune chemical called interleukin-6, or IL-6, were measured. IL-6 increases with age and can place people at risk for a number of illnesses, including cardiovascular disease, type 2 diabetes, frailty, and certain cancers. The researchers found that the levels of IL-6 increased much faster in the Alzheimer caregivers than in the older adults who did not have to care for a critically ill spouse (see Figure 4.5).

Each time IL-6 was assessed by drawing blood, the participants also completed a 10-item perceived stress scale to assess the extent they perceived their daily life during the prior week as "unpredictable, uncontrollable, and overloading" (Kiecolt-Glazer & others, 2003, p. 9091). Participants rated each item from 0 (never) to 4 (very often). Alzheimer caregivers reported greater stress than the noncaregiver controls across each of the six annual assessments.

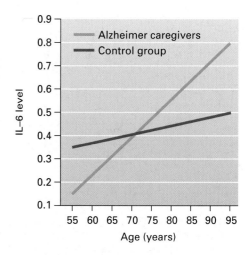

FIGURE 4.5 Comparison of IL-6 Levels in Alzheimer Caregivers and a Control Group of Noncaregivers. Notice that IL-6 (an immune chemical that places individuals at risk for a number of diseases) increased for both the Alzheimer caregivers and the control group of noncaregivers. However, also note that IL-6 increased significantly more in the Alzheimer caregivers. A higher score for IL-6 reflects a higher level of the immune chemical.

Parkinson disease A chronic, progressive disease characterized by muscle tremors, slowing of movement, and partial facial paralysis.

Parkinson Disease Another type of dementia is **Parkinson disease,** a chronic, progressive disease characterized by muscle tremors, slowing of movement, and partial facial paralysis. Parkinson disease is triggered by degeneration of dopamine-producing neurons in the brain (Swanson, Sesso, & Emborg, 2009). The neurotransmitter dopamine is necessary for normal brain functioning. Why these neurons degenerate is not known. The main treatment for Parkinson disease involves administering drugs that enhance the effect of dopamine (dopamine agonists) in the disease's earlier stages and later administering the drug L-dopa, which is converted by the brain into dopamine (LeWitt, 2009). However, it is difficult to determine the correct level of dosage of L-dopa, and it loses its efficacy over time (Nomoto & others, 2009).

Another treatment for advanced Parkinson disease is deep brain stimulation (DBS), which involves implantation of electrodes within the brain. The electrodes are then stimulated by a pacemaker-like device. Recent studies indicated that deep brain stimulation may provide benefits for individuals with Parkinson disease (Troster, 2009; Zahodne & others, 2009). Other recent studies indicate that certain types of dance, such as the tango, can improve the movement skills of individuals with Parkinson disease (Hackney & Earhart, 2009). Stem cell transplantation and gene therapy offer hope for the future in treating Parkinson disease (Isacson & Kordower, 2009; Trimmer & Bennett, 2009).

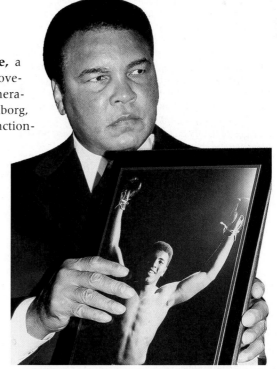

Muhammad Ali, one of the world's leading sports figures, has Parkinson disease.

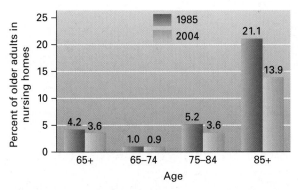

FIGURE 4.6 Percent of U.S. Older Adults Living in Nursing Homes: 1985 to 2004. *Note:* The Lewin Group calculations are based on the 1985 and 2004 National Nursing Home Survey (NNHS), National Center for Health Statistics.

Mathilde Spett (*right*), who is 91 years old, injured herself in a fall but recently graduated from a walker to a cane and learned how to stay on a better diet with the help of home-care aide Marilyn Ferguson (*left*). The demand for home-care aides is predicted to increase dramatically in the next several decades because of the likely doubling of the 65-year-and-older population and older adults' preference for remaining out of nursing homes (Moos, 2007). Not only is it important to significantly increase the number of health-care professionals to treat older adults, it is also very important that they not harbor negative stereotypes of older adults and that they show very positive attitudes toward them.

FIGURE 4.7 Perceived Control and Mortality. In the study by Rodin and Langer (1977), nursing home residents who were encouraged to feel more in control of their lives were more likely to be alive 18 months later than those who were treated to feel more dependent on the nursing home staff.

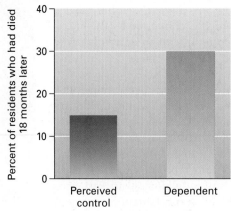

Health Treatment for Older Adults The development of alternative home and community-based care has decreased the percentage of older adults who are living in nursing homes (Katz & others, 2009; Russell & Rice, 2009). Still, as older adults age, their probability of being in a nursing home increases (see Figure 4.6). What is the quality of nursing homes and extended-care facilities for older adults? What is the relationship between older adults and health-care providers?

The quality of nursing homes and other extended-care facilities for older adults varies enormously and is a source of continuing national concern (Eskildsen & Price, 2009). More than one-third are seriously deficient. They fail federally mandated inspections because they do not meet the minimum standards for physicians, pharmacists, and various rehabilitation specialists (occupational and physical therapists). Further concerns focus on the patient's right to privacy, access to medical information, safety, and lifestyle freedom within the individual's range of mental and physical capabilities.

Because of the inadequate quality of many nursing homes and the escalating costs for nursing home care, many specialists in the health problems of the aged stress that home health care, elder-care centers, and preventive medicine clinics are good alternatives (Katz & others, 2009). They are potentially less expensive than hospitals and nursing homes. They also are less likely to engender the feelings of depersonalization and dependency that occur so often in residents of institutions. Currently, there is an increased demand for but shortage of home-care workers because of the increase in population of older adults and their preference to stay out of nursing homes (Moos, 2007).

In a classic study focused on the way older adults are cared for in nursing homes, Judith Rodin and Ellen Langer (1977) found that an important factor related to health, and even survival, in a nursing home is the patient's feelings of control and self-determination. A group of elderly nursing home residents were encouraged to make more day-to-day choices and thus feel they had more responsibility for control over their lives. They began to decide such matters as what they ate, when their visitors could come, what movies they saw, and who could come to their rooms. A similar group in the same nursing home was told by the administrator how caring the nursing home was and how much the staff wanted to help, but these elderly nursing home residents were given no opportunities to take more control over their lives. Eighteen months later, the residents given responsibility and control were more alert and active, and said they were happier, than the residents who were encouraged only to feel that the staff would try to satisfy their needs. And the "responsible" or "self-control" group had significantly better improvement in their health than did the "dependent" group. Even more important was the finding that after 18 months only half as many nursing home residents in the "responsibility" group had died as in the "dependent" group (see Figure 4.7). Perceived control over one's environment, then, can literally be a matter of life or death.

Review and Reflect: Learning Goal 1

1 **Describe developmental changes in health**

REVIEW

- How can children's health be characterized?
- What is the nature of adolescents' health?
- What characterizes the health of emerging and young adults?
- How extensively does health decline in old age?

REFLECT

- What changes in your lifestyle right now might help you to age more successfully when you get older?

2 NUTRITION AND EATING BEHAVIOR

| Infancy | Childhood | Adolescence | Adult Development and Aging |

Nutritional needs, eating behavior, and related issues vary to some extent across the life span. Let's begin by exploring what takes place with infants.

Infancy

For infants, the importance of receiving adequate energy and nutrients in a loving and supportive environment cannot be overstated (Black & others, 2009). From birth to 1 year of age, human infants triple their weight and increase their length by 50 percent. Because infants vary in their nutrient reserves, body composition, growth rates, and activity patterns, their nutrient needs vary as well. However, because parents need guidelines, nutritionists recommend that infants consume approximately 50 calories per day for each pound they weigh—more than twice an adult's requirement per pound.

Breast Versus Bottle Feeding   For the first four to six months of life, human milk or an alternative formula is the baby's source of nutrients and energy. For years, debate has focused on whether breast feeding is better for the infant than bottle feeding. The growing consensus is that breast feeding is better for the baby's health (Lawrence, 2008; Thorley, 2009). Since the 1970s, breast feeding by U.S. mothers has soared (see Figure 4.8). In 2004, more than two-thirds of U.S. mothers breast fed their newborns, and more than a third breast fed their 6-month-olds. The American Academy of Pediatrics (AAP) and the American Dietetic Association strongly endorse breast feeding throughout the infant's first year (AAP Work Group on Breastfeeding, 1997; James & Dobson, 2005).

What are some of the benefits of breast feeding? The following conclusions have been reached based on the current state of research:

Evaluation of Benefits for the Child

- *Gastrointestinal infections.* Breast fed infants have fewer gastrointestinal infections (Newburg & Walker, 2007).

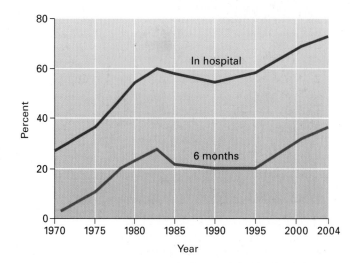

FIGURE 4.8 Trends in Breast Feeding in the United States: 1970 to 2004.

- *Lower respiratory tract infections.* Breast fed infants have fewer lower respiratory tract infections (Ip & others, 2007).

- *Allergies.* A recent research review by the American Academy of Pediatrics indicated that there is no evidence that breast feeding reduces the risk of allergies in children (Greer & others, 2008). The research review also concluded that modest evidence exists for feeding hyperallergenic formulas to susceptible babies if they are not solely breast fed.

- *Asthma.* The recent research review by the American Academy of Pediatrics concluded that exclusive breast feeding for three months protects against wheezing in babies, but whether it prevents asthma in older children is unclear (Greer & others, 2008).

- *Otitis media.* Breast fed infants are less likely to develop this middle ear infection (Rovers, de Kok, & Schilder, 2006).

- *Atopic dermatitis.* Breast fed babies are less likely to have this chronic inflammation of the skin (Snijders & others, 2007). The recent research review by the American Academy of Pediatrics also concluded that for infants with a family history of allergies, breast feeding exclusively for at least four months is linked to a lower risk of skin rashes (Greer & others, 2008).

- *Overweight and obesity.* Consistent evidence indicates that breast fed infants are less likely to become overweight or obese in childhood, adolescence, and adulthood (Moschonis, Grammatikaki, & Manios, 2007).

- *Diabetes.* Breast fed infants are less likely to develop type 1 diabetes in childhood (Ping & Hagopian, 2006) and type 2 diabetes in adulthood (Villegas & others, 2008).

- *SIDS.* Breast fed infants are less likely to experience SIDS (Ip & others, 2007).

In a large-scale research review, no conclusive evidence for the benefits of breast feeding was found for children's cognitive development and cardiovascular system (Agency for Healthcare Research and Quality, 2007).

Evaluation of Benefits for the Mother

- *Breast cancer.* Consistent evidence indicates a lower incidence of breast cancer in women who breast feed their infants (Shema & others, 2007).

- *Ovarian cancer.* Evidence also reveals a reduction in ovarian cancer in women who breast feed their infants (Jordan & others, 2008).

- *Type 2 diabetes.* Some evidence suggests a small reduction in type 2 diabetes in women who breast feed their infants (Ip & others, 2007).

In a large-scale research review, no conclusive evidence could be found for the maternal benefits of breast feeding on return to prepregnancy weight, osteoporosis, and postpartum depression (Agency for Healthcare Research and Quality, 2007). However, a recent study revealed that women who breast fed their infants had a lower incidence of metabolic syndrome (a disorder characterized by obesity, hypertension, and insulin resistance) in midlife (Ram & others, 2008).

The AAP Work Group on Breastfeeding (1997) strongly endorses breast feeding throughout the first year of life. Are there circumstances when mothers should not breast feed? Yes, a mother should not breast feed (1) if the mother is infected with HIV or some other infectious disease that can be transmitted through her milk, (2) if she has active tuberculosis, or (3) if she is taking any drug that may not be safe for the infant (Berlin, Paul, & Vesell, 2009; Buhimschi & Weiner, 2009; Fadnes & others, 2009).

Some women cannot breast feed their infants because of physical difficulties; others feel guilty if they terminate breast feeding early. Mothers may also worry that they are depriving their infants of important emotional and psychological benefits if they bottle feed rather than breast feed. Some researchers have found, however,

Human milk, or an alternative formula, is a baby's source of nutrients for the first four to six months. The growing consensus is that breast feeding is better for the baby's health, although controversy still swirls about the issue of breast feeding versus bottle feeding. *Why is breast feeding strongly recommended by pediatricians?*

that there are no psychological differences between breast fed and bottle fed infants (Ferguson, Harwood, & Shannon, 1987; Young, 1990).

A further issue in interpreting the benefits of breast feeding was underscored in a recent large-scale research review (Agency for Healthcare Quality and Research, 2007). While highlighting a number of breast feeding benefits for children and mothers, the report issued a caution about breast feeding research: None of the findings implies causality. Breast versus bottle feeding studies are correlational, not experimental, and women who breast feed are wealthier, older, more educated, and likely more health-conscious than their bottle feeding counterparts, characteristics that could explain why breast fed children are healthier.

Malnutrition in Infancy   When they are severely malnourished, infants fail to grow adequately and they are listless. Very severe malnutrition usually takes the form of marasmus or kwashiorkor. **Marasmus** is severe malnutrition due to insufficient caloric intake. Infants with marasmus have a shrunken, wasted, elderly appearance. **Kwashiorkor** is severe malnutrition caused by a deficiency in protein. The child's abdomen and feet swell with fluids. Otherwise, children with kwashiorkor may look well fed. In fact, their vital organs are collecting whatever nutrients are present, depriving other parts of the body. The disease usually appears between 1 to 3 years of age. Marasmus and kwashiorkor are serious problems in developing countries, with as many as 50 percent of deaths under the age of 5 in these countries due to such severe protein-energy malnutrition (UNICEF, 2003). The incidence of marasmus and kwashiorkor in the United States is rare, although there still is concern about energy and nutrient intakes in infants from low-income families.

Nutritional supplements for infants can also improve their cognitive development. In a longitudinal investigation conducted over two decades in rural Guatemala, Ernesto Pollitt and his colleagues (1993) found that giving malnourished infants or children protein supplements and increased calories had long-term effects on cognitive development. Both the socioeconomic status of the children and the period during which the nutritional supplements were given influenced the effects of the supplements. For example, the children in the lowest socioeconomic groups benefited more than the children in the higher socioeconomic groups. Also, when supplements were given only after the children were 2 years old, they still had a positive influence, but the effect on cognitive development was less powerful.

Pediatric nurses can play an important role in improving the lives of malnourished children and advising parents on feeding practices. To read about the work of one pediatric nurse, see the *Careers in Life-Span Development* profile.

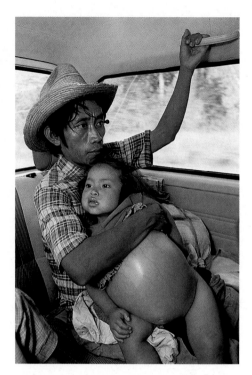

This Honduran child has kwashiorkor. Notice the telltale sign of kwashiorkor: a greatly expanded abdomen without the appearance of such expansion in other body areas, such as arms and legs. *What are some other characteristics of kwashiorkor?*

Childhood

Malnutrition continues to be a major threat to millions during the childhood years (Schiff, 2009). Malnutrition and starvation are a daily fact of life for children in many developing countries (UNICEF, 2009).

Poor nutrition is a special concern in the lives of infants from low-income families. To address this problem in the United States, the WIC (Women, Infants, and Children) program provides federal grants to states for healthy supplemental foods, health-care referrals, and nutrition education for women from low-income families beginning in pregnancy, and to infants and young children up to 5 years of age who are at nutritional risk (Food & Nutrition Service, 2009; WIC New York, 2009). WIC serves approximately 7,500,000 participants in the United States. In 2009, WIC made changes in the program to promote breast feeding and provide more nutritious food (Food & Nutrition Service, 2009; WIC New York, 2009):

- *Increase breast feeding.* WIC staff are being trained in lactation counseling and in most programs, peer counseling services are available to pregnant women and new mothers.

marasmus Severe malnutrition due to insufficient caloric intake.

kwashiorkor Severe malnutrition caused by a deficiency in protein in which the child's legs and abdomen swell with fluids.

Careers in Life-Span Development

Barbara Deloin, Pediatric Nurse

Barbara Deloin is a pediatric nurse in Denver, Colorado. She practices nursing in the Pediatric Oral Feeding Clinic and is involved in research as part of an irritable infant study for the Children's Hospital in Denver. She also is on the faculty of nursing at the Colorado Health Sciences Center. Deloin previously worked in San Diego, where she was coordinator of the Child Health Program for the County of San Diego.

Her research interests focus on children with special health-care needs, especially high-risk infants and children, and promoting positive parent-child experiences. She is a former president of the National Association of Pediatric Nurse Associates and Practitioners.

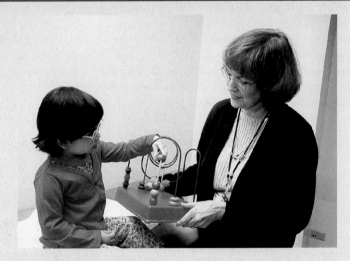

Barbara Deloin, working with a child with special health-care needs.

- *Provide food lower in fat content.* Only 1 percent or skim milk is available for children 2 years of age and older and women; low-fat cheese and tofu are options.
- *Distribute food higher in fiber, and include more vegetables and fruits.* Vouchers provlded to low-income families encourage the consumption of whole-grain cereals and breads, as well as more vegetables and fruits.
- *Have food available that is more culturally appropriate.* For example, brown rice or whole-grain tortillas can be substituted for whole-grain breads; calcium-set tofu or calcium-fortified soy milk can be substituted for cow's milk.

An increasing research initiative is exploring ways to improve the WIC program and assess its influence on mothers, infants, and young children's nutrition and health (Black & others, 2009; Hannan & others, 2009; Heinig & others, 2009; Olson & others, 2009a). A recent study revealed that a WIC program that introduced peer counseling services for pregnant women increased breast feeding initiation by 27 percent (Olson & others, 2009b). Another recent study found that entry in the first trimester of pregnancy to the WIC program in Rhode Island reduced maternal cigarette smoking (Brodsky, Viner-Brown, & Handler, 2009).

Eating Behavior and Parental Feeding Styles   For most children in the United States, insufficient food is not the key problem. Instead, receiving poor nutrition as a result of unhealthy eating habits and being overweight threaten their present and future health (Bolling & Daniel, 2008). A national assessment found that most children's diets need improvement (Federal Interagency Forum on Child and Family Statistics, 2002). In this assessment, only 27 percent of 2- to 5-year-old children were categorized as having good diets. Their diets worsened as they became older—only 13 percent of 6- to 9-year-old children had healthy diets. Although some health-conscious parents may be providing too little fat in their infants' and children's diets, other parents are raising their children on diets in which the percentage of fat is far too high (Schiff, 2009). And in a recent national survey, 4- to 18-year-olds often consumed the high-fat varieties of milk, yogurt, cheese, ice cream, and dairy-based toppings (Kranz, Lin, Wagstaff, 2007).

Parental Feeding Styles   Children's eating behavior is strongly influenced by their caregivers' behavior (Black & Hurley, 2007). Children's eating behavior improves when caregivers eat with children on a predictable schedule, model eating healthy food, make mealtimes pleasant occasions, and engage in certain feeding styles. Distractions from television, family arguments, and competing activities should be minimized so that children can focus on eating. A sensitive/responsive caregiver feeding style, in which the caregiver is nurturant, provides clear information about what is expected, and appropriately responds to children's cues, is recommended (Black & Hurley, 2007). Forceful and restrictive caregiver behaviors are not recommended. For example, a restrictive feeding style is linked to children being overweight (Black & Lozoff, 2008).

Overweight Children   Being overweight has become a serious problem in childhood (Frisco, 2009; Li & others, 2009). The Centers for Disease Control and Prevention (2009) has a category of obesity for adults but does not have an obesity category for children and adolescents because of the stigma the label may bring. Rather they have categories for being overweight or at-risk for being overweight in childhood and adolescence. These categories are determined by body mass index (BMI), which is computed by a formula that takes into account height and weight. Only children and adolescents at or above the 95th percentile of BMI are included in the overweight category, and those at or above the 85th percentile are included in the at-risk category for being overweight category.

What are some concerns about overweight children?

The percentages of young children who are overweight or at risk for being overweight in the United States has increased dramatically in recent decades, and the percentages are likely to grow unless changes occur in children's lifestyles (Benson, Baer, & Kaelber, 2009). A recent study revealed that in 2003 to 2006, 11 percent of U.S. 2- to 19-year-olds were obese, 16 percent were overweight, and 38 percent were at risk for being overweight (Ogden, Carroll, & Flegal, 2008). The good news from this large-scale study is that the percentages in these categories have started to level off rather than increase, as they had been doing in the last several decades.

Still, the levels of child obesity, overweight, and risk for being overweight are still far too high (Frisco, 2009). Note that girls are more likely than boys to be overweight, and this gender difference occurs in many countries (Sweeting, 2008). In a recent large-scale U.S. study, African American and Latino children were more likely to be overweight or obese than non-Latino White children (Benson, Baer, & Kaelber, 2009).

It is not just in the United States that children are becoming more overweight. Recent surveys and policy prescriptions in Australia, mainland China, Hong Kong, and other countries indicate that children in many countries around the world are becoming more overweight (Chan, 2008; Li & others, 2008).

The risk for overweight young children of continuing to be overweight when they become older was documented in one study. In that study, 80 percent of the children who were at risk for being overweight at 3 years of age were also at risk for being overweight or were overweight at 12 years of age (Nader & others, 2006). Another study found that children's weight at 5 years of age was significantly linked to their weight at 9 years of age (Gardner & others, 2009). And another study revealed that the prevalence of being overweight remained stable from 4 to 11 years of age for children with lean parents but more than doubled across this time frame for children with obese parents (17 percent to 45 percent) (Semmler & others, 2009).

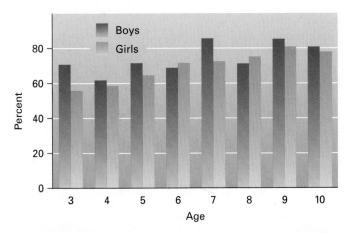

FIGURE 4.9 **Relation to Being Overweight in Childhood with Being Overweight in Adulthood.** *Note:* Data show the chance that children who are in the 95th percentile among their peers in terms of weight are likely to be overweight when they are 35.

Being overweight in childhood also is linked to being overweight in adulthood. In one study, a high percentage of children who were in the 95th percentile among their peers in terms of weight are still likely to be overweight when they are in their thirties (Guo & others, 2002) (see Figure 4.9). Another study revealed that girls who were overweight in childhood were 11 to 30 times more likely to be obese in adulthood than girls who were not overweight in childhood (Thompson & others, 2007). And a recent study found that children with high body mass index and waist circumference are at risk for metabolic syndrome (a constellation of factors including obesity, high blood pressure, and type 2 diabetes that place individuals at risk for developing cardiovascular disease) in adulthood (Sun & others, 2008).

Many parents do not recognize that their children are overweight. One recent study of parents with 2- to 17-year-old children revealed that few parents of overweight children perceived their children to be too heavy and were not worried about the children's weight (Eckstein & others, 2006).

Heredity and Environment Both heredity and environment influence whether children will become overweight (Li & others, 2009). Recent genetic analysis indicates that heredity is an important factor in children becoming overweight (Wardle & others, 2008). Overweight parents tend to have overweight children, even if they are not living in the same household (Wardlaw & Hempl, 2007). One study found that the greatest risk factor for being overweight at 9 years of age was a parent being overweight (Agras & others, 2004).

Environmental factors that influence whether children become overweight or not include the greater availability of food (especially food high in fat content), energy-saving devices, declining physical activity, parental monitoring of children's eating habits, the context in which a child eats, and heavy TV watching (Byrd-Williams & others, 2008; Shoup & others, 2008). The American culture provides ample encouragement of overeating in children. Food is everywhere children go and easily accessed—in vending machines, fast-food restaurants, and so on (Rosenheck, 2008). Also, the portion size that children eat in meals in the United States has grown. A recent study revealed a link between high levels of watching TV with being overweight in childhood (Wells & others, 2008). Another study found that an excess of body fat in adolescents was related to watching TV and playing video games more on weekends (Vicente-Rodriguez & others, 2008).

Consequences of Obesity The increase in overweight children in recent decades is cause for great concern because being overweight raises the risk for many medical and psychological problems (Oude & others, 2009; Pott & others, 2009). Overweight children are at risk for developing pulmonary problems, such as sleep apnea (which involves upper-airway obstruction), and having hip problems (Tauman & Gozal, 2006). Diabetes, hypertension (high blood pressure), and elevated blood cholesterol levels also are common in children who are overweight (Viikari & others, 2009). Once considered rare, hypertension in children has become increasingly common in overweight children (Jafar, 2009). Overweight children with cardiovascular problems are more likely to come from low-socioeconomic-status families than from higher-status ones (Longo-Mbenza, Lukoki, & M'buyambia-Kabangu, 2007). Social and psychological consequences of being overweight in childhood include low self-esteem, depression, and some exclusion of obese children from peer groups (Datar & Sturm, 2004; Gibson & others, 2008). A recent study revealed that obese children were perceived as less attractive, more tired, and more socially withdrawn than nonobese peers (Zeller, Reiter-Purtill, & Ramey, 2008).

Treatment of Obesity   Many experts recommend a program that includes a combination of diet, exercise, and behavior modification to help children lose weight (Wittmeier, Mollard, & Kriellaars, 2008). Exercise is an especially important component of a successful weight-loss program for overweight children (Benson, Torode, & Fiatrone Singh, 2008).

Obesity-intervention programs with children are usually conducted through schools and often focus on teaching children and parents about developing a healthy diet, exercising more, and reducing TV viewing time (Shaya & others, 2008). In the intervention program Planet Health, parents and children are encouraged to work together to change their home environment, such as reducing TV time (Gortmaker & others, 1999). Other programs combine activities at school with materials that are sent home to parents.

Adolescence

Nutrition and being overweight are also key problems among adolescents. A comparison of adolescents in 28 countries found that U.S. adolescents ate more junk food than teenagers in most other countries (World Health Organization, 2000). The National Youth Risk Survey found that U.S. high school students decreased their intake of fruits and vegetables from 1999 through 2007 (Eaton & others, 2008) (see Figure 4.10). A recent research review found that these two family factors were linked to increased fruit and vegetable consumption by adolescents: availability of fruits and vegetables in the home and consumption of fruits and vegetables by parents (Pearson, Biddle, & Gorely, 2009). Thus, parents play an important role in adolescents' nutrition through the food choices they make available to adolescents and serving as models for healthy or unhealthy nutrition.

Not surprisingly, the percentage of overweight adolescents has been increasing. Being overweight increased from 11 to 17 percent for U.S. 12- to 19-year-olds from the early 1990s through 2004 (National Center for Health Statistics, 2006). A recent study found 62 percent of the male and 73 percent of the female adolescents in the 85th to 94th percentile of body mass index (BMI) became obese adults (Wang & others, 2008). In this study, of those who were at the 95th percentile and higher for BMI, 80 percent of the male and 92 percent of the female adolescents became obese adults.

Are there ethnic variations in being overweight during adolescence? A survey by the National Center for Health Statistics (2002) found that African American girls and Latino boys have especially high risks of being overweight during adolescence (see Figure 4.11). Another study revealed that the higher obesity rate for African American girls is linked with a diet higher in calories and fat, as well as with sedentary behavior (Sanchez-Johnsen & others, 2004).

What types of interventions have been successful in reducing overweight in adolescents? One review indicated that clinical approaches focusing on the individual adolescent and including a combination of calorie restriction, exercise (walking or biking to school, participating in a regular exercise program), reduction of sedentary activity (watching TV, playing video games), and behavioral therapy (such as keeping weight-loss diaries and rewards for meeting goals) have been moderately effective in helping overweight adolescents lose weight (Fowler-Brown & Kahwati, 2004).

Anorexia Nervosa   **Anorexia nervosa** is an eating disorder that involves the relentless pursuit of thinness through starvation. Anorexia nervosa is a serious disorder that can lead to death. Three main characteristics of anorexia nervosa are as follows:

- Weighing less than 85 percent of what is considered normal for a person's age and height.

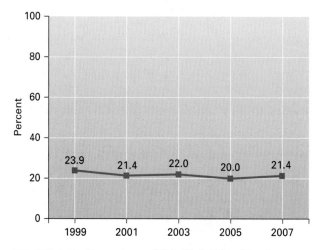

FIGURE 4.10 Percentage of U.S. High School Students Who Ate Fruits and Vegetables Five or More Times a Day, 1999 to 2007. *Note:* This shows the percentage of high school students over time who had eaten fruits and vegetables (100% fruit juice, fruit, green salad, potatoes—excluding french fries, fried potatoes, or potato chips—carrots, or other vegetables) five or more times a day during the preceding seven days (Eatson & others, 2008).

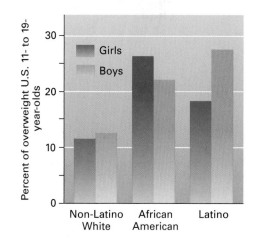

FIGURE 4.11 Percentage of Overweight U.S. Adolescent Boys and Girls in Different Ethnic Groups.

anorexia nervosa An eating disorder that involves the relentless pursuit of thinness through starvation.

These overweight adolescent girls are attending a weight-management camp. *In the research review by Fowler-Brown and Kahwati (2004), what clinical approaches have been moderately successful helping in adolescents lose weight?*

Anorexia nervosa has become an increasing problem for adolescent girls and emerging adult women. *What are some possible causes of anorexia nervosa?*

bulimia nervosa An eating disorder in which the individual consistently follows a binge-and-purge eating pattern.

- Having an intense fear of gaining weight. The fear does not decrease with weight loss.
- Having a distorted image of their body shape (Rigaud & others, 2007). Even when the individuals are extremely thin, they see themselves as too fat. They never think they are thin enough, especially in the abdomen, buttocks, and thighs. They usually weigh themselves frequently, often take their body measurements, and gaze critically at themselves in mirrors (Seidenfeld, Sosin, & Rickert, 2004).

Anorexia nervosa typically begins in the early to middle teenage years, often following an episode of dieting and some type of life stress (Lee & others, 2005). It is about ten times more likely to characterize females than males. Although most U.S. adolescent girls have been on a diet at some point, slightly less than 1 percent ever develop anorexia nervosa (Walters & Kendler, 1994). When anorexia nervosa does occur in males, the symptoms and other characteristics (such as a distorted body image and family conflict) are usually similar to those reported by females with the disorder (Araceli & others, 2005).

Most anorexics are non-Latino White adolescent or young adult females from well-educated, middle- and upper-income families that are competitive and high-achieving (Schmidt, 2003). They set high standards, become stressed about not being able to reach the standards, and are intensely concerned about how others perceive them (Striegel-Moore, Silberstein, & Rodin, 1993). Unable to meet these high expectations, they turn to something they can control: their weight. The dieting behaviors of anorexics were once largely hidden. Today, however, social-networking Web sites, such as MySpace and Facebook, connect thousands of anorexics who are able to share pro-ana (pro-anorexic) information on how to deprive their bodies and become unhealthily thin. Problems in family functioning are increasingly being found to be linked to the appearance of anorexia nervosa in adolescent girls (Benninghoven & others, 2007), and a recent research review indicated that family therapy is often the most effective treatment of adolescent girls with anorexia nervosa (Bulik & others, 2007).

The fashion image in the American culture which emphasizes that "thin is beautiful" contributes to the incidence of anorexia nervosa (Polivy & others, 2003). This image is reflected in the saying, "You never can be too rich or too thin." The media portrays thin as beautiful in their choice of fashion models, which many adolescent girls want to emulate. And many adolescent girls who strive to be thin hang out together. A recent study of adolescent girls revealed that friends often share similar body image and eating problems (Hutchinson & Rapee, 2007). In this study, an individual girl's dieting and extreme weight-loss behavior could be predicted from her friends' dieting and extreme weight-loss behavior.

Bulimia Nervosa Although anorexics control their eating by restricting it, most bulimics cannot. **Bulimia nervosa** is an eating disorder in which the individual consistently follows a binge-and-purge eating pattern. The bulimic goes on an eating binge and then purges by self-inducing vomiting or using a laxative. Although many people binge and purge occasionally and some experiment with it, a person is considered to have a serious bulimic disorder only if the episodes occur at least twice a week for three months (Napierski-Prancl, 2009).

As with anorexics, most bulimics are preoccupied with food, have a strong fear of becoming overweight, and are depressed or anxious (Speranza & others,

2005). A recent study revealed that bulimics overvalued their body weight and shape, and this overvaluation was linked to higher depression and lower self-esteem (Hrabosky & others, 2007). Unlike anorexics, people who binge and purge typically fall within a normal weight range, which makes bulimia more difficult to detect.

Bulimia nervosa typically begins in late adolescence or early adulthood. About 90 percent of bulimics are women. Approximately 1 to 2 percent of women are estimated to develop bulimia nervosa. Many women who develop bulimia nervosa were somewhat overweight before the onset of the disorder, and the binge eating often began during an episode of dieting. One study of adolescent girls found that increased dieting, pressure to be thin, exaggerated importance of appearance, body dissatisfaction, depression symptoms, low self-esteem, and low social support predicted binge eating two years later (Stice, Presnell, & Spangler, 2002).

Adult Development and Aging

Nutrition and eating behavior continue to play important roles in adult physical development and health. Among the topics we discuss in this section are obesity, exercising and dieting to lose weight, and links between aging, weight, and nutrition.

Obesity   Obesity is not only a problem for many children, it is also a serious and pervasive problem for many adults (Wardlaw & Smith, 2009). The prevalence of obesity in U.S. adults increased from 23 percent in the early 1990s to 32 percent in 2004 (National Center for Health Statistics, 2006). More than 60 percent of U.S. adults are overweight or obese (National Center for Health Statistics, 2006). The National Health and Nutrition Examination Survey (NHANES) recently projected that 86 percent of Americans will be overweight or obese by 2030 if current weight trends continue (Beydoun & Wang, 2009). And a study of more than 168,000 adults in 63 countries revealed that worldwide 40 percent of the men and 30 percent of the women were overweight, and 24 percent of the men and 27 percent of the women were obese (Balkau & others, 2007).

Overweight and obesity are linked to increased risk of hypertension, diabetes, and cardiovascular disease (Gurevich-Panigrahi & others, 2009; Schiff, 2009). For individuals who are 30 percent overweight, the probability of dying in middle adulthood increases by about 40 percent. Overweight and obesity also are associated with mental health problems. For example, a recent study revealed that overweight women were more likely to be depressed than women who were not overweight (Ball, Burton, & Brown, 2009).

What causes obesity? Some individuals do inherit a tendency to be overweight (Li & others, 2007). Only 10 percent of children who do not have obese parents become obese themselves, whereas 40 percent of children who become obese have one obese parent. Further, 70 percent of children who become obese have two obese parents. Researchers also have documented that animals can be inbred to have a propensity for obesity (Allan, Eisen, & Pomp, 2005). And identical human twins have similar weights, even when they are reared apart.

Evolutionary psychology offers some insight into our problems with obesity. The human gustatory system and taste preferences developed at a time when reliable food sources were scarce. Our earliest ancestors probably developed a preference for sweets, because ripe fruit, which is a concentrated source of sugar (and calories), was so accessible. Today many people still have a "sweet tooth," but unlike our ancestors' ripe fruit that contained sugar plus vitamins and minerals, the soft drinks and candy bars we snack on today often fill us with empty calories.

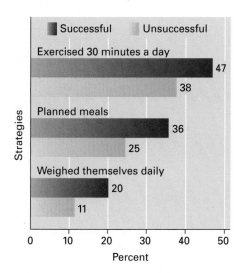

FIGURE 4.12 Comparison of Strategies in Successful and Unsuccessful Dieters.

Strong evidence of the environment's influence on weight is the doubling of the rate of obesity in the United States since 1900. This dramatic increase in obesity likely is due to greater availability of food (especially food high in fat), energy-saving devices, and declining physical activity (Li & others, 2007). Further evidence of the environment's influence on weight comes from a study on obesity in immigrants who had been in the United States for a varied number of years (Goel & others, 2004). Obesity was present in 8 percent of the immigrants who had been in the United States for one year or less but 19 percent of the immigrants who had lived in the United States for 15 years or more.

Exercising and Dieting The most effective programs for losing weight include exercise (Wardlaw & Smith, 2009). A recent research review concluded that adults who engaged in diet-plus-exercise programs lost more weight than diet-only programs (Wu & others, 2009). Exercise not only burns up calories, but continues to elevate the person's metabolic rate for several hours *after* exercising. A recent study of approximately 2,000 U.S. adults found that exercising 30 minutes a day, planning meals, and weighing themselves daily were the main strategies used by successful dieters compared with unsuccessful dieters (Kruger, Blanck, & Gillespse, 2006) (see Figure 4.12). A recent study also revealed that obese adults in a diet program who kept a food diary for six or seven days a week had double the weight loss compared with obese adults who did not keep a food diary (Hollis & others, 2008).

Even when diets do produce weight loss, they can place the dieter at risk for other health problems (Cunningham & Hyson, 2006). One main concern focuses on weight cycling—yo-yo dieting—in which the person is in a recurring cycle of weight loss and weight gain (Janacek & others, 2005). Also, liquid diets and other very-low-calorie strategies are linked with gallbladder damage.

With these problems in mind, when overweight people diet and maintain their weight loss, they do become less depressed and reduce their risk for a number of health-impairing disorders (Mensah & Brown, 2007).

Calorie Restriction and Longevity Scientists have accumulated considerable evidence that calorie restriction in laboratory animals (in most cases rats) can increase the animals' life span (Wei & others, 2008). Animals fed diets restricted in calories, although adequate in protein, vitamins, and minerals, live as much as 40 percent longer than animals given unlimited access to food (Jolly, 2005). And chronic problems such as cardiovascular, kidney, and liver disease appear at a later age (Fontana, 2009). Calorie restriction also delays biochemical alterations such as the age-related rise in cholesterol and triglycerides observed in both humans and animals (Fontana, 2008, 2009). And recent research indicates that calorie restriction may provide neuroprotection for an aging central nervous system (Contestabile, 2009; Newton & others, 2008) (see Figure 4.13). For example, a recent study revealed that following calorie restriction for three months, the verbal memory of older adults improved (Witte & others, 2009).

No one knows for certain how calorie restriction works to increase the life span of animals (Anderson & Weindruch, 2007). Some scientists note that it might lower the level of free radicals and reduce oxidative stress in cells (Hunt & others, 2006). For example, one study found that calorie restriction slowed the age-related increase in oxidative stress (Ward & others, 2005). Others argue that calorie restriction might trigger a state of emergency called "survival mode" in which the body eliminates all unnecessary functions to focus only on staying alive. This survival mode likely is the result of evolution in which calorie restriction allowed animals to survive periods of famine, and thus the genes remain in the genomes of animal and human species today (Chen & Guarente, 2007).

Whether similar very-low-calorie diets can stretch the human life span is not known (Shanley & Kirkwood, 2006). In some instances, the animals in these studies ate 40 percent less than normal. In humans, a typical level of calorie restriction involves a 30 percent decrease, which translates into about 1,120 calories a day for the average woman and 1,540 for the average man.

Do underweight women and men live longer lives? A recent study revealed that women who were 20 pounds or more underweight lived longer even after controlling for smoking, hypertension, alcohol intake, and other factors (Wandell, Carlsso, & Theobald, 2009). In this study, underweight men did not live longer when various factors were controlled.

The Growing Controversy Over Vitamins and Aging   For years, most experts on aging and health argued that a balanced diet was all that was needed for successful aging; vitamin supplements were not recommended. However, recent research suggests the possibility that some vitamin supplements—mainly a group called "antioxidants," which includes vitamin C, vitamin E, and beta-carotene—help to slow the aging process and improve the health of older adults.

The theory is that antioxidants counteract the cell damage caused by free radicals, which are produced both by the body's own metabolism and by environmental factors such as smoking, pollution, and bad chemicals in the diet (Flora, 2007). When free radicals cause damage (oxidation) in one cell, a chain reaction of damage follows. Antioxidants act much like a fire extinguisher, helping to neutralize free-radical activity.

Some research studies find links between the antioxidant vitamins and health (Marko & others, 2007). One study linked low blood vitamin C concentration in older adults with an earlier incidence of death (Fletcher, Breeze, & Shetty, 2003). However, recent large-scale studies of men revealed that taking vitamin C and vitamin E did not prevent cardiovascular disease (Gaziano & others, 2009; Sesso & others, 2008). And another recent study indicated that diet supplementation with vitamins C, E, and beta-carotene had no effect on cancer incidence or cancer death (Lin & others, 2009).

There is no evidence that antioxidants can increase the human life span, but some aging and health experts argue that vitamin C and beta-carotene can reduce a person's risk of becoming frail and sick in the later adult years (Korantzopoulos & others, 2007). However, there are still a lot of blanks and uncertainties in what we know. That is, we don't know which vitamins should be taken, how large a dose should be taken, what the restraints are, and so on. Critics also argue that the key experimental studies documenting the effectiveness of the vitamins in slowing the aging process have not been conducted. The studies in this area thus far have been so-called *population studies* that are correlational rather than experimental in nature. Other factors—such as exercise, better health practices, and good nutritional habits—might be responsible for the positive findings about vitamins and aging rather than vitamins themselves. Also, the free-radical theory is a theory and not a fact, and is only one of a number of theories about why we age.

With these uncertainties in mind, some aging experts still recommend vitamin supplements in the following range: 250 to 1,000 milligrams of vitamin C and 15 to 30 milligrams of beta-carotene.

Possible links between vitamins and cognitive performance in older adults also have been the focus of increased research attention. For example, a recent study revealed that individuals 65 years of age and older who took higher levels of antioxidant vitamins had less cognitive decline than their counterparts who took lower levels (Wengreen & others, 2007). Some studies have found that taking B vitamins, especially folate, B_6, and B_{12}, is positively related to cognitive performance in older adults (Feng & others, 2006). However, other studies indicate that taking B vitamins and other supplemental vitamins has no effect on the cognitive functioning of older adults (McNeill & others, 2007).

FIGURE 4.13 Calorie Restriction in Monkeys. Shown here are two monkeys at the Wisconsin Primate Research Center. Both are 24 years old. The monkey in the top photograph was raised on a calorie-restricted diet, while the monkey in the bottom photograph was raised on a normal diet. Notice that the monkey on the calorie-restricted diet looks younger; he also has lower glucose and insulin levels. The monkey raised on a normal diet has higher triglycerides and more oxidative damage to his cells.

> **Review and Reflect: Learning Goal 2**
>
> **2** **Characterize developmental changes in nutrition and eating behavior**
>
> **REVIEW**
>
> - What are some important aspects of nutrition and eating behavior in infancy?
> - What are some key nutritional problems in American children?
> - How can eating behavior and disorders in adolescence be characterized?
> - What are some controversies and issues in nutrition and eating behavior in the adult years?
>
> **REFLECT**
>
> - How good are you at eating nutritiously and healthily? Have your lifestyle and behavior in this area affected your health? Might they affect your health in the future?

3 EXERCISE

Childhood and Adolescence	Adulthood	Aging and Longevity

We have just seen the important role exercise plays in losing weight. Exercise is linked with many aspects of being physically and mentally healthy. Let's explore exercise throughout the life span.

Childhood and Adolescence

American children and adolescents are not getting enough exercise (Fahey, Insel, & Roth, 2009; Slawta & Deneui, 2009). Educators and policy makers in the United States and numerous countries around the world, including China, Finland, and Great Britain, have become very concerned about the sedentary lifestyles of many children and adolescents in their countries (Dowda & others, 2009; Liu & others, 2008).

Childhood   Because of their activity level and the development of large muscles, especially in the arms and legs, children need daily exercise (Rink, 2009). Television watching is linked with low activity and obesity in children (Gable, Chang, & Krull, 2007). A related concern is the dramatic increase in computer use by children. Reviews of research have concluded that the total time that children spend in front of a television or computer screen places them at risk for reduced activity and possible weight gain (Rey-Lopez & others, 2008). For example, a recent study revealed that the more adolescents watched television and used computers, the less likely they were to engage in regular exercise (Chen, Liou, & Wu, 2008). One study revealed that children who watched two or more hours of TV a day were less likely to participate in organized physical activities and less likely to have two or more servings of fruit a day than their counterparts who watched less than two hours of TV a day (Salmon, Campbell, & Crawford, 2006). A longitudinal study found that a higher incidence of watching TV in childhood and adolescence was linked with being overweight, being less physically fit, and having higher cholesterol levels at 26 years of age (Hancox, Milne, & Poulton, 2004).

The following three recent studies address aspects of families and schools that influence young children's physical activity levels:

- Observations of 3- to 5-year-old children during outdoor play at preschools revealed that the preschool children were mainly sedentary even when participating in outdoor play (Brown & others, 2009). In this study, throughout the day the preschoolers were sedentary 89 percent of the time, engaged in light activity 8 percent of the time, and participated in moderate to vigorous physical activity only 3 percent of the time.

- Preschool children's physical activity was enhanced by family members engaging in sports together and by parents' perception that it was safe for their children to play outside (Beets & Foley, 2008).

- Incorporation of a "move and learn" physical activity curriculum increased the activity level of 3- to 5-year-old children in a half-day preschool program (Trost, Fees, & Dzewaltowski, 2008).

What are some good strategies for increasing children's exercise?

Researchers and educators are increasingly exploring strategies that will increase children's exercise participation (McGuigan & others, 2009; Rink, 2009). Following are three recent studies that address ways to increase children's exercise:

- A high-intensity resistance training program decreased children's body fat and increased their muscle strength (Benson, Torode, & Fiatarone Singh, 2008).

- Forty-five minutes of moderate physical activity and 15 minutes of vigorous physical activity daily were related to decreased odds of children being overweight (Wittmeier, Mollard, & Kriellaars, 2008).

- Aerobic exercise was linked to increases in an important cognitive activity—planning—in overweight 9-year-old children (Davis & others, 2007).

In another recent study, 9-year-old girls who were more physically fit (as measured on a field test of aerobic capacity) showed better cognitive performance on a cognitive control task that involved inhibiting task-irrelevant information to obtain correct solutions than 9-year-old girls who were less physically fit (Hillman & others, 2009).

Adolescence Researchers have found that individuals become less active as they reach and progress through adolescence (Butcher & others, 2008; Hills, King, & Armstrong, 2007). A recent national study of U.S. 9- to 15-year-olds revealed that almost all 9- and 11-year-olds met the federal government's moderate to vigorous exercise recommendations per day (a minimum of 60 minutes daily), but only 31 percent of 15-year-olds met the recommendations on weekdays, and on weekends only 17 percent met the recommendations (Nader & others, 2008). The recent national study also found that adolescent boys were more likely to engage in moderate to vigorous exercise than girls. Figure 4.14 shows the average amount of exercise of the U.S. boys and girls from 9 to 15 years of age on weekdays and weekends. Another recent national study of U.S. adolescents revealed that physical activity increased until 13 years of age in boys and girls but then declined through 18 years of age (Kahn & others, 2008). In this study, adolescents were more likely to engage in regular exercise when they perceived it was important to present a positive body image to their friends and when exercise was important to their parents.

Ethnic differences in exercise participation rates of U.S. adolescents also occur, and these rates vary by gender. As indicated in Figure 4.15, in the National Youth Risk Survey, non-Latino White boys exercised the most, African American girls the least (Eaton & others, 2008).

FIGURE 4.14 Average Amount of Moderate to Vigorous Exercise Engaged in by U.S. 9- to 15-years-olds on Weekdays and Weekends. *Note:* The federal government recommends 60 minutes of moderate to vigorous physical activity per day.

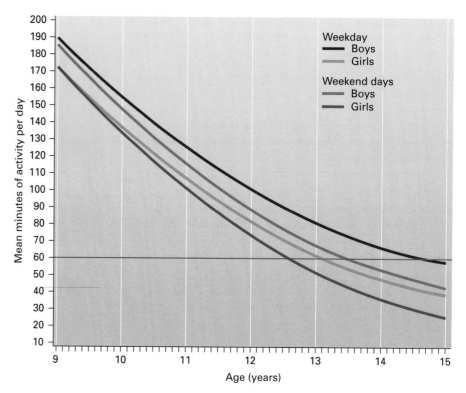

FIGURE 4.15 Exercise Rates of U.S. High School Students: Gender and Ethnicity. *Note:* Data are for high school students who were physically active doing any kind of physical activity that increased their heart rate and made them breathe hard some of the time for a total of at least 60 minutes a day on five or more of the seven days preceding the survey.

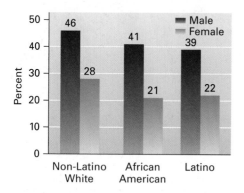

In 2007, Texas became the first state to test student's physical fitness. The student shown here is performing the trunk lift. Other assessments include aerobic exercise, muscle strength, and body fat. Assessments will be done annually.

aerobic exercise Sustained activity that stimulates heart and lung functioning.

Low levels of exercise by adolescents not only appear in general exercise data but also in participation in P.E. classes (Floriani & Kennedy, 2008; Rink, 2009). Participation in P.E. classes was especially low for African American and Latino adolescents. Adolescents are less likely to take a P.E. class in high school than in middle school (MMWR, 2006). The percentage of high school students who take a daily physical education class decreased from 42 percent in 1991 to 33 percent in 2005 (MMWR, 2006).

Some ways to get children and adolescents to exercise more follow:

- Improve physical fitness classes in schools.
- Offer more physical activity programs run by volunteers at school facilities.
- Have children plan community and school exercise activities that really interest them.
- Encourage families to focus on physical activity and challenge parents to exercise more.

Adulthood

The benefits of exercise continue in adulthood. Both moderate and intense exercise produce important physical and psychological gains (Robbins, Powers, & Burgess, 2008). The enjoyment and pleasure we derive from exercise added to its physical benefits make exercise one of life's most important activities.

One of the primary health benefits of exercise is prevention of heart disease (Anspaugh, Hamrick, & Rosato, 2009). Some people get the benefits of vigorous exercise on the job. For example, longshoremen who are on their feet all day, and lift, push, and carry heavy cargo, have about half the risk of fatal heart attacks as co-workers like crane drivers and clerks, who have physically less demanding jobs. Even getting hogs to jog has documented the cardiovascular benefits of exercise (see Figure 4.16). A recent study also revealed that exercise was linked with reduced risk of developing colon and rectal cancer (Howard & others, 2008).

Although exercise designed to strengthen muscles and bones or to improve flexibility is important to fitness, many health experts stress aerobic exercise. **Aerobic exercise** is sustained activity—jogging, swimming, or cycling, for example—that stimulates heart and lung functioning. Elaborate studies of 17,000 male alumni of Harvard University found that those who exercised strenuously on a regular basis had a lower risk of heart disease and were more likely to be alive in their middle adulthood years than their more sedentary counterparts (Lee, Hsieh, & Paffenbarger, 1995; Paffenbarger & others, 1993).

Some health experts conclude that, regardless of other risk factors (smoking, high blood pressure, overweight, heredity), if you exercise enough to burn more than 2,000 calories a week, you can cut your risk of heart attack by an impressive two-thirds (Sherwood, Light, & Blumenthal, 1989). But burning up 2,000 calories a week through exercise requires a lot of effort, far more than most of us are willing to expend. To burn 300 calories a day through exercise, you would have to do one of the following: swim or run for about 25 minutes, walk for 45 minutes at about 4 miles an hour, or participate in aerobic dancing for 30 minutes.

As a more realistic goal, many health experts recommend that adults engage in 45 minutes or more of moderate physical activity on most, preferably all, days of the week. Most recommend that you should try to raise your heart rate to at least 60 percent of your maximum heart rate. However, only about one-fifth of adults are active at these recommended levels of physical activity.

Researchers have found that exercise benefits not only physical health but mental health as well. In particular, exercise improves self-esteem and reduces anxiety and depression (Brenes & others, 2007). Meta-analyses have shown that exercise can be as effective in reducing depression as psychotherapy (Richardson & others, 2005). One study of more than 600 adults found that exercise was associated with positive mental health and obesity with poor mental health (Rohrer, Pierce, & Blackburn, 2005). To read about ways to incorporate regular exercise into your life, see the *Applications in Life-Span Development* interlude.

FIGURE 4.16 The Jogging Hog Experiment. Jogging hogs reveal the dramatic effects of exercise on health. In one investigation, a group of hogs was trained to run approximately 100 miles per week (Bloor & White, 1983). Then, the researchers narrowed the arteries that supplied blood to the hogs' hearts. The hearts of the jogging hogs developed extensive alternate pathways for blood supply, and 42 percent of the threatened heart tissue was salvaged compared with only 17 percent in a control group of nonjogging hogs.

Applications in Life-Span Development

EXERCISE

Here are some helpful strategies for building exercise into your life:

- *Reduce TV time.* Heavy TV viewing by college students is linked to poor health (Shields, 2006). Replace some of your TV time with exercise.
- *Chart your progress.* Systematically recording your exercise workouts will help you to chart your progress. This strategy is especially helpful over the long term.
- *Get rid of excuses.* People make up all kinds of excuses for not exercising. A typical excuse is, "I don't have enough time." You likely do have enough time.
- *Imagine the alternative.* Ask yourself whether you are too busy to take care of your own health. What will your life be like if you lose your health?
- *Learn more about exercise.* The more you know about exercise, the more you are likely to start an exercise program and continue it.

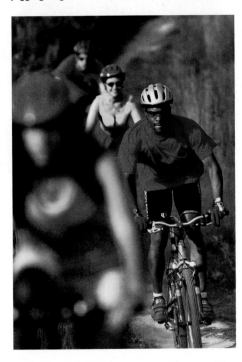

What exercise goals have you set for yourself?

Aging and Longevity

Although we may be in the evening of our lives in late adulthood, we are not meant to live out our remaining years passively. Everything we know about older adults

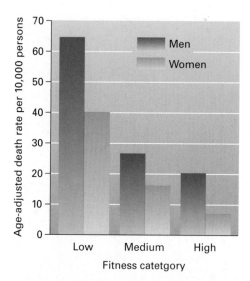

FIGURE 4.17 Physical Fitness and Mortality. In this study of middle-aged and older adults, being moderately fit or highly fit meant that individuals were less likely to die over a period of eight years than their low-fitness (sedentary) counterparts (Blair & others, 1989).

suggests they are healthier and happier the more active they are. Can regular exercise lead to a healthier late adulthood and increase longevity? Let's examine several research studies on exercise and aging.

In one study, exercise literally meant a difference in life or death for middle-aged and older adults (Blair, 1990). More than 10,000 men and women were divided into categories of low fitness, medium fitness, and high fitness (Blair & others, 1989). Then they were studied over a period of eight years. As shown in Figure 4.17, sedentary participants (low fitness) were more than twice as likely to die during the eight-year time span of the study than those who were moderately fit and more than three times as likely to die as those who were highly fit. The positive effects of being physically fit occurred for both men and women in this study. Further, a recent study revealed that 60-year-old and older adults who were in the lowest fifth in terms of physical fitness as determined by a treadmill test were four times more likely to die over a 12-year period than their counterparts who were in the top fifth of physical fitness (Sui & others, 2007). Also, in this study, older adults who were physically fit but overweight had a lower mortality risk over the 12 years than their normal-weight counterparts who were low in fitness. And a longitudinal study found that men who exercised regularly at 72 years of age had a 30 percent higher probability of still being alive at 90 years of age than their sedentary counterparts (Yates & others, 2008).

Gerontologists increasingly recommend strength training in addition to aerobic activity and stretching for older adults (Suetta & others, 2008). The average person's lean body mass declines with age—about 6.6 pounds of lean muscle are lost each decade during the adult years. The rate of loss accelerates after age 45. Weight lifting can preserve and possibly increase muscle mass in older adults (Johnson, De Lisio, & Parise, 2008).

Exercise is an excellent way to maintain health (Deeny & others, 2008; Temple & others, 2008). The current recommended level of aerobic activity for adults 60 years of age and older is 30 minutes of moderately intense activity, such as brisk walking or riding a stationary bicycle, five or more days a week, and strength training on two or more days a week (Der Ananian & Prohaska, 2007). Flexibility and balance exercises also are recommended.

Researchers continue to document the positive effects of exercise in older adults (Rizvi, 2007). Exercise helps people to live independent lives with dignity in late adulthood. At 80, 90, and even 100 years of age, exercise can help prevent older adults from falling down or even being institutionalized. Being physically fit means being able to do the things you want to do, whether you are young or old.

Researchers who study exercise and aging have discovered the following:

• *Exercise is linked to increased longevity.* In a longitudinal study of Chinese women, those who exercised regularly were less likely to die over approximately a six-year time period (Matthews & others, 2007). A recent study also revealed that systolic blood pressure during exercise was linked to an increase in long-term survival of 75-year-olds (Hedberg & others, 2009). In one analysis, energy expenditure by older adults during exercise that burns up at least 1,000 calories a week was estimated to increase life expectancy by about 30 percent, and burning up 2,000 calories a week in exercise was estimated to increase life expectancy by about 50 percent (Lee & Skerrett, 2001).

• *Exercise is related to prevention of common chronic diseases.* Exercise can reduce the risk of developing cardiovascular disease, type 2 diabetes, osteoporosis, stroke, and breast cancer (Yassine & others, 2009).

• *Exercise is associated with improvement in the treatment of many diseases.* When exercise is used as part of the treatment, individuals with these diseases show improvement in symptoms: arthritis, pulmonary disease, congestive heart failure, coronary artery disease, hypertension, type 2 diabetes, obesity, and Alzheimer disease (Coker & others, 2009; Rimmer & others, 2009).

- *Exercise improves older adults' cellular functioning.* Researchers increasingly are finding that exercise improves cellular functioning in older adults (Boveris & Navarro, 2008). For example, a recent study revealed that the tips of chromosomes contained more white blood cells when older adults had a higher level of physical activity during leisure time (Cherkas & others, 2008).

- *Exercise improves immune system functioning in older adults.* A recent study revealed that following exercise, a number of components of immune system functioning in older adult women improved (Sakamoto & others, 2009).

- *Exercise can optimize body composition and reduce the decline in motor skills as aging occurs.* Exercise can increase muscle mass and bone mass, as well as decrease bone fragility (Gu & others, 2009). A recent study found that participation in exercise activities was linked to a delay in the onset and progression of frailty (Peterson & others, 2009).

- *Exercise reduces the likelihood that older adults will develop mental health problems and can be effective in the treatment of mental health problems.* For example, exercise reduces the likelihood that older adults will develop depression and can be effective in treating depression in older adults (Brenes & others, 2007).

- *Exercise is linked to improved brain and cognitive functioning in older adults.* Exercise increases brain volume in older adults (Erickson & others, 2009). Also, older adults who exercise process information more effectively than older adults who don't exercise (Williamson & others, 2009).

Despite the extensive documentation of exercise's power to improve older adults' health and quality of life, a recent national survey revealed that older adults have increased their exercise levels only slightly in recent years (Centers for Disease Control and Prevention, 2008) (see Figure 4.18). Possible explanations of older adults' failure to substantially increase their exercise focus on such factors as chronic illnesses, life crises (such as a spouse's death) that disrupt exercise schedules, embarrassment of being around others who are in better shape (especially if they haven't exercised much earlier in life), and the "why bother?" factor (not believing that exercise will improve their lives much) (Painter, 2008). And, as we have seen, it is never too later to start exercising, and older adults can significantly benefit from regular exercise.

What are some of the benefits of exercise for older adults?

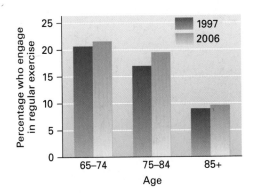

FIGURE 4.18 Regular Exercise by U.S. Older Adults: 1997 to 2006.

Review and Reflect: Learning Goal 3

 Summarize the roles of exercise in child and adult health

REVIEW
- How extensively do U.S. children and adolescents exercise?
- What roles does exercise play in adult health?
- How does exercise influence development in aging adults?

REFLECT
- Suppose a middle-aged person asked this question: "What would give me the greatest advantage: exercising more or eating less?" What would your answer be?

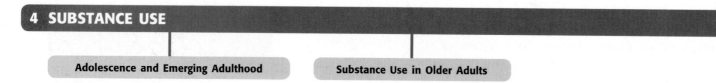

4 SUBSTANCE USE

Adolescence and Emerging Adulthood Substance Use in Older Adults

Besides exercising, another important healthy practice is to avoid using substances such as alcohol, cigarettes, and other psychoactive drugs (Kinney, 2009). For example, in one longitudinal study, individuals who did not abuse alcohol at age 50 were more likely to still be alive and healthy at 75 to 80 years of age than their counterparts who abused alcohol at age 50 (Vaillant, 2002).

In Chapter 2, "Biological Beginnings," we described the negative effects on the fetus and developing child that can result from substance use by the pregnant mother. Here we examine substance use by adolescents, emerging adults, and older adults.

Adolescence and Emerging Adulthood

Cigarette smoking begins primarily in childhood and adolescence, and many alcoholics established their drinking habits during secondary school or college (Wood, Vinson, & Sher, 2001). In fact, most adolescents and emerging adults use drugs at some point, whether limited to alcohol, caffeine, and cigarettes or extended to marijuana, cocaine, and other so-called "hard" drugs. However, drug use poses a special hazard to development when adolescents and emerging adults use drugs as a way of coping with stress. This practice can interfere with the development of coping skills and responsible decision making. Drug use in early adolescence has more detrimental long-term effects on the development of responsible, competent behavior than drug use in late adolescence (Newcomb & Bentler, 1989).

Trends in Adolescent Drug Use Each year since 1975, Lloyd Johnston and his colleagues at the Institute of Social Research at the University of Michigan have monitored the drug use of America's high school seniors in a wide range of public and private high schools. Since 1991, they also have surveyed drug use by eighth- and tenth-graders. In 2008, the University of Michigan study, called the Monitoring the Future Study, surveyed more than 46,000 students in nearly 400 secondary schools.

According to this study, the proportions of eighth-, tenth-, and twelfth-grade U.S. students who used any illicit drug declined in the late 1990s and first years of the twenty-first century (Johnston & others, 2009) (see Figure 4.19). Nonetheless, even with the recent decline in use, the United States still has one of the highest rates of adolescent drug use of any industrialized nation. For example, one study revealed that a higher percentage of U.S. adolescents have used an illicit drug than adolescents in most European countries (Hibell & others, 2004).

How extensive is alcohol use by U.S. adolescents? Sizeable declines in adolescent alcohol use have occurred in recent years (Johnston & others, 2009). The percentage of U.S. eighth-graders saying that they had had any alcohol to drink in the past 30 days fell from a 1996 high of 26 percent to 16 percent in 2008. The 30-day prevalence fell among tenth-graders from 39 percent in 2001 to 29 percent in 2008 and among high school seniors from 72 percent in 1980 to 43 percent in 2008. Binge drinking (defined in the University of Michigan surveys as having five or more drinks in a row in the last two weeks) by high school seniors

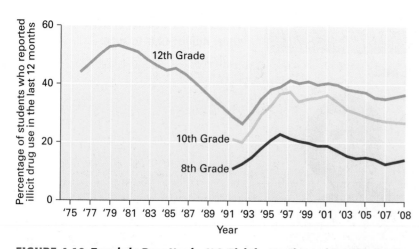

FIGURE 4.19 Trends in Drug Use by U.S. Eighth-, Tenth-, and Twelfth-Grade Students. This graph shows the percentage of U.S. eighth-, tenth-, and twelfth-grade students who reported having taken an illicit drug in the last 12 months from 1991 to 2008, for eighth- and tenth-graders, and from 1975 to 2008, for twelfth-graders (Johnston & others, 2009).

declined from 41 percent in 1980 to 28 percent in 2008. Binge drinking by eighth- and tenth-graders also has dropped in recent years. A consistent sex difference occurs in binge drinking, with males engaging in this more than females.

Cigarette smoking among U.S. adolescents peaked in 1996 and 1997 and has gradually declined since then (Johnston & others, 2009). Following peak use in 1996, smoking rates for U.S. eighth-graders have fallen by 50 percent. In 2008, the percentages of adolescents who said they had smoked cigarettes in the last 30 days were 20 percent (twelfth grade), 12 percent (tenth grade), and 7 percent (eighth grade).

Cigarette smoking (in which the active drug is nicotine) is one of the most serious yet preventable health problems. Smoking is likely to begin in grades 7 through 9, although sizable portions of youth are still establishing regular smoking habits during high school and college. Risk factors for becoming a regular smoker in adolescence include having a friend who smokes, a weak academic orientation, and low parental support (Tucker, Ellickson, & Klein, 2003).

An alarming recent trend is the use of prescription painkillers by adolescents (Forrester, 2007). A 2004 survey revealed that 18 percent of U.S. adolescents had used Vicodin (acetaminophen and hydrocodone) at some point in their lifetime, and 10 percent had used OxyContin (oxycodone) (Partnership for a Drug-Free America, 2005). These drugs fall into the general class of drugs called narcotics, and they are highly addictive. In this recent national survey, 9 percent of adolescents said they had abused cough medications to intentionally get high. Adolescents cite the medicine cabinets of their parents or of friends' parents as the main source for their prescription painkillers (Johnston & others, 2008).

Eighteen-year-old Paul Michaud (*above*) began taking OxyContin in high school. Michaud says, "I was hooked," Now he is in drug treatment.

The Roles of Development, Parents, Peers, and Educational Success A special concern involves adolescents who begin to use drugs early in adolescence or even in childhood (Patrick, Abar, & Maggs, 2009). A recent study revealed that individuals who began drinking alcohol before 14 years of age were more likely to become alcohol dependent than their counterparts who began drinking alcohol at 21 years of age or older (Hingson, Heeren, & Winter, 2006). A longitudinal study of individuals from 8 to 42 years of age also found that early onset of drinking was linked to increased risk of heavy drinking in middle age (Pitkanen, Lyra, & Pulkkinen, 2005).

Parents, peers, and social support can play important roles in preventing adolescent drug abuse. Positive relationships with parents and others can reduce adolescents' drug use (Chassin, Hussong, & Beltran, 2009; Hoffman, 2009). In one study, parental control and monitoring were linked with a lower incidence of problem behavior by adolescents, including substance abuse (Fletcher, Steinberg, & Williams-Wheeler, 2004). A recent study also revealed that adolescents who averaged having less than two family dinners a week were more likely to drink alcohol, smoke cigarettes, and abuse prescription drugs than their adolescent counterparts who averaged five or more family dinners a week (CASA, 2007). Another recent study of more than 5,000 middle school students revealed that having friends in their school's social network and having fewer friends who use substances were related to a lower level of substance use (Ennett & others, 2006).

Educational success is also a strong buffer for the emergence of drug problems in adolescence. A recent analysis by Jerald Bachman and his colleagues (2008) revealed that early educational achievement considerably reduced the likelihood that adolescents would develop drug problems, including those involving alcohol abuse, smoking, and abuse of various illicit drugs.

What roles do parents play in adolescents' drug use?

What kinds of problems are associated with binge drinking in college?

Emerging Adults' Drug Use The transition from high school to college may be a critical transition in alcohol abuse (Schulenberg & others, 2001). The large majority of emerging adults recognize that drinking is common among individuals their age and is largely acceptable, even expected by their peers. They also perceive that they get some social and coping benefits from alcohol use and even occasional heavy drinking. A recent study revealed that only 20 percent of college students reported that they abstain from drinking alcohol (Huang & others, 2009).

In 2005, approximately 40 percent of U.S. college students reported that they drink heavily, a rate that was unchanged since 1993 (Johnston & others, 2006). The effects of heavy drinking take a toll. In a national survey of drinking patterns on 140 campuses, almost half of the binge drinkers reported problems that included missing classes, physical injuries, troubles with police, and having unprotected sex (Wechsler & others, 1994). This survey also found that binge-drinking college students were eleven times more likely to drive after drinking, and twice as likely to have unprotected sex, than college students who did not binge drink.

A special concern is the increase in binge drinking by females during emerging adulthood (Young & others, 2005). One study found a 125 percent increase in binge drinking at all-women colleges from 1993 through 2001 (Wechsler & others, 2002).

Fortunately, by the time individuals reach their mid-twenties, many have reduced their use of alcohol and drugs. That is the conclusion reached by Gerald Bachman and his colleagues (2002) in a longitudinal analysis of more than 38,000 individuals (see Figure 4.20). They were evaluated from the time they were high school seniors through their twenties.

Do individuals smoke cigarettes more in emerging adulthood than adolescence? According to a U.S. survey, 18- to 25-year-olds reported a smoking rate than was substantially higher than the rate of 12- to 17-year-olds and higher than the rate of individuals who were 26 years and older (Substance Abuse and Mental Health Services Administration, 2005). Thus, cigarette smoking peaks in emerging adulthood (Park & others, 2006).

Substance Use in Older Adults

As indicated earlier, alcohol and substance abuse peak in emerging adulthood and then decline somewhat by the mid-twenties. Of course, alcohol and substance abuse continue to raise serious health concerns for many adults in early and middle adulthood (Ksir, Chart, & Ray, 2008).

There also is concern about alcohol and substance abuse in older adults, although a national survey found that binge drinking declines through the late adulthood

FIGURE 4.20 Binge Drinking in the Adolescence–Early Adulthood Transition. Note that the percentage of individuals engaging in binge drinking peaked at 21 to 22 years of age and then began to gradually decline through the remainder of the twenties. Binge drinking was defined as having five or more alcoholic drinks in a row in the past two weeks.

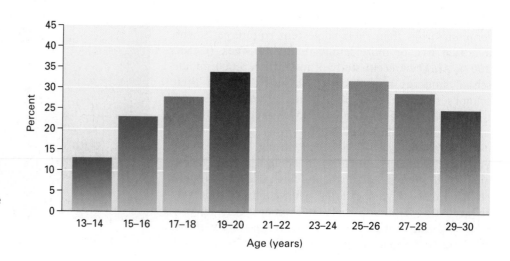

years (National Center for Health Statistics, 2002) (see Figure 4.21). Indeed, a majority (58 percent) of U.S. adults 65 years and older completely abstain from alcohol, an increase from 38 percent of 45- to 64-year-olds. The reasons for these declines are usually attributed to an increase in illness and disease.

Despite these declines in alcohol use, the Substance Abuse and Mental Health Services Administration (2005) has identified substance abuse among older adults as the "invisible epidemic" in the United States. The belief is that substance abuse often goes undetected in older adults, and there is concern about older adults who abuse not only illicit drugs but prescription drugs as well (Segal, 2007). The consequences of abuse—such as depression, inadequate nutrition, congestive heart failure, and frequent falls—may erroneously be attributed to other medical or psychological conditions (Hoyer & Roodin, 2009). As the number of older adults rises, substance abuse is likely to characterize an increasing number of older adults (Atkinson, Ryan, & Turner, 2001). For older adults who are taking multiple medications, the dangers of substance abuse rise. For example, when combined with tranquilizers or sedatives, alcohol use can impair breathing, produce excessive sedation, and even be fatal.

Despite the concerns about substance abuse in adulthood, researchers have revealed a protective effect of moderate alcohol use in older adults (Strandberg & others, 2007). One study revealed better physical and mental health, and increased longevity, in older adults who drank moderately compared with those who drank heavily or did not drink at all (Rozzini, Ranhoff, & Trabucchi, 2007). The explanation of moderate drinking's benefits involve better physical and mental performance, being more open to social contacts, and being able to assert mastery over one's life.

Researchers have especially found that moderate drinking of red wine is linked to better health and increased longevity (Kaur & others, 2007). Explanation of the benefits of red wine center on its connection to lowering stress and reduced risk of coronary heart disease. A chemical in the skin of red wine grapes—resveratrol—has been hypothesized to play a key role in red wine's health benefits, although solid evidence for this link has yet to be found (Goswami & Das, 2009; Issuree & others, 2009; Park & others, 2009; Shakibaei, Harikumar, & Aggarwal, 2009). A recent study did find that red wine, but not white, killed several lines of cancer cells (Wallenborg & others, 2009). Scientists are exploring how resveratrol might activate SIRT1, an enzyme that is involved in DNA repair and aging (Mukerjee & others, 2009).

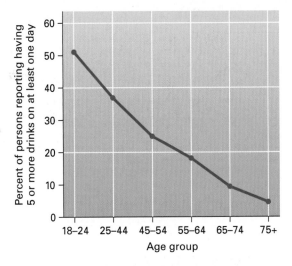

FIGURE 4.21 Age and the Consumption of Five or More Drinks on at Least One Day in the United States. The graph shows the considerable decline in having five or more drinks on at least one day as people get older (National Center for Health Statistics, 2002).

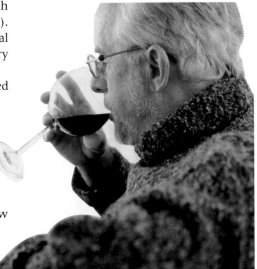

What might explain the finding that drinking red wine in moderation is linked to better health and increased longevity?

Review and Reflect: Learning Goal 4

4 **Evaluate substance use in adolescence and adulthood**

REVIEW

- How extensively do adolescents take drugs? What factors are linked with drug abuse by adolescents? What is the nature of substance use in college students and young adults?
- How can substance use in older adults be described?

REFLECT

- Do you know someone who has a drug problem? If so, describe the nature of the problem. Is the person willing to admit to having a problem?

Reach Your Learning Goals

Health

---

1   HEALTH, ILLNESS, AND DISEASE: DESCRIBE DEVELOPMENTAL CHANGES IN HEALTH.

Children's Health

- Prevention and poverty are important factors in children's health. Children need timely immunizations. Accident prevention is a key aspect of children's health. Of special concern are children living in poverty, who often are malnourished.

Adolescents' Health

- Adolescence is a critical juncture in health because many health habits—good or bad—still are being formed. Social contexts, including family, peers, and schools, influence the health of adolescents.

Emerging and Young Adults' Health

- Few emerging and young adults have chronic health problems. Many emerging and young adults don't stop to think about how their personal lifestyles will affect their health later in their lives. Emerging adults have double the mortality rate of adolescents.

Health and Aging

- Chronic disorders increase in middle-aged adults and are common in older adults. Osteoporosis is a concern, especially among older women. Dementias, especially Alzheimer disease, are a major health problem. Another type of dementia is Parkinson disease. A special concern is the quality of nursing homes for older adults and the treatment of older adults in nursing homes.

---

2   NUTRITION AND EATING BEHAVIOR: CHARACTERIZE DEVELOPMENTAL CHANGES IN NUTRITION AND EATING BEHAVIOR

Infancy

- The importance of adequate energy intake consumed in a loving and supportive environment in infancy cannot be overstated. The growing consensus is that breast feeding is better for the baby's health than bottle feeding. Marasmus and kwashiorkor are diseases caused by severe malnutrition. Nutritional supplements can improve infants' cognitive development.

Childhood

- Poor nutrition in children from low-income families is a special concern. Other concerns about children's nutrition focus on fat content in their diet and obesity. Thirty-eight percent of U.S. 2- to 19-year-olds are at risk for being overweight. Obesity increases a child's risk of developing many medical and psychological problems. Hypertension, diabetes, and elevated cholesterol levels are common in overweight children.

Adolescence

- Nutrition and being overweight are also key problems among adolescents. Anorexia nervosa and bulimia nervosa can develop in adolescence; most anorexics and bulimics are women.

Adult Development and Aging

- Obesity is a major concern in adulthood, and dieting is pervasive. Calorie restriction is associated with longevity, but a balanced diet along with exercise is usually recommended for older adults. Controversy surrounds whether antioxidant vitamins can reduce the risk for disease.

---

3   EXERCISE: SUMMARIZE THE ROLES OF EXERCISE IN CHILD AND ADULT HEALTH

Childhood and Adolescence

- Most children and adolescents are not getting nearly enough exercise. Too much TV and computer time can result in reduced activity and weight gain. Individuals become less active as they progress through adolescence.

Adulthood

- Both moderate and intense exercise produce physical and psychological advantages, such as lowered risk of heart disease, reduced anxiety, and increased self-esteem.

Aging and Longevity

- Regular exercise can lead to a healthier life as a middle-aged and older adult and increase longevity.

4 SUBSTANCE USE: EVALUATE SUBSTANCE USE IN ADOLESCENCE AND ADULTHOOD

Adolescence and Emerging Adulthood

- The United States has one of the highest adolescent drug use rates of any industrialized country. Alcohol, cigarette smoking, and prescription painkillers are special concerns. Development, parents, peers, and educational success play important roles in preventing drug abuse in adolescents. About forty percent of U.S. college students say they drink heavily. Substance use peaks in emerging adulthood and then often decreases by the mid-twenties.

Substance Use in Older Adults

- Alcohol use declines in older adults, although abuse is more difficult to detect in older adults than in younger adults. There is concern about older adults who abuse prescription drugs and illicit drugs.

KEY TERMS

chronic disorders 140	Alzheimer disease 142	kwashiorkor 149	aerobic exercise 161
osteoporosis 141	Parkinson disease 145	anorexia nervosa 153	
dementia 142	marasmus 149	bulimia nervosa 154	

KEY PEOPLE

Judith Rodin and Ellen Langer 146

Ernesto Pollitt 149

Lloyd Johnston 164

E-LEARNING TOOLS

Connect to **www.mhhe.com/santrock1dt5e** to research the answers and complete these exercises. In addition, you'll find a number of other resources and valuable study tools for Chapter 4, "Health," on this Web site.

Taking It to the Net

1. Eric's 72-year-old mother, Jane, has been diagnosed with Alzheimer disease. Eric plans to move Jane from her apartment to his home, where he will take care of her as long as he can. What things should he do to make his home safe for Jane?

2. Darren and Angie are concerned that Heather, their 17-year-old daughter, may have an eating disorder. Heather denies that she has a problem and insists that she looks fat despite her extremely low body weight. What should Darren and Angie do to help Heather? Are there doctors who specialize in the treatment of eating disorders?

3. Donald started smoking as an adolescent, and he has been smoking a pack of cigarettes a day for at least 20 years. He wants to quit but has decided he needs some form of nicotine replacement for a while. What are the pros and cons of the nicotine patch versus nicotine gum?

Self-Assessment

To evaluate yourself on topics related to your health, complete these self-assessments:

- *Is Your Lifestyle Good for Your Health?*
- *My Health Habits*
- *Do I Abuse Drugs?*

Health and Well-Being, Parenting, and Education

Build your decision-making skills by trying your hand at the health and well-being, parenting, and education exercises.

Video Clips

The Online Learning Center includes the following videos for this chapter:

- *Bulimia*
- *Children and Nutrition*
- *Eating Disorders*
- *Have I Changed Since Age 20?*
- *Obesity*

5

The setting sun, and
music at close,
As the last taste of
sweets, is sweetest last,
Writ in remembrance
more than things
long past.

—WILLIAM SHAKESPEARE
English Playwright, 17th Century

LEARNING GOALS

◆ Describe how motor skills develop.

◆ Outline the course of sensory and
perceptual development.

◆ Discuss the connection between
perception and action.

MOTOR, SENSORY, AND PERCEPTUAL DEVELOPMENT

CHAPTER OUTLINE

PREVIEW

Think about what is required for us to find our way around our environment, to play sports, or to create art. These activities require both active perception and precisely timed motor actions. Neither innate, automatic movements nor simple sensations are enough to let us do the things we take for granted every day. How do we develop perceptual and motor abilities, and what happens to them as we age? In this chapter, we focus first on the development of motor skills, then on sensory and perceptual development, and finally on the coupling of perceptual-motor skills.

1 MOTOR DEVELOPMENT

| The Dynamic Systems View | Reflexes | Gross Motor Skills | Fine Motor Skills |

dynamic systems theory A theory proposed by Esther Thelen that seeks to explain how infants assemble motor skills for perceiving and acting.

reflexes Built-in reactions to stimuli that govern the newborn's movements, which are automatic and beyond the newborn's control.

rooting reflex A newborn's built-in reaction that occurs when the infant's cheek is stroked or the side of the mouth is touched. In response, the infant turns its head toward the side that was touched, in an apparent effort to find something to suck.

Most adults are capable of coordinated, purposive actions of considerable skill, including driving a car, playing golf, and typing effectively on a computer keyboard. Some adults have extraordinary motor skills, such as those involved in winning an Olympic pole vault competition, painting a masterpiece, or performing heart surgery. Look all you want at a newborn infant, and you will observe nothing even remotely approaching these skilled actions. How, then, do the motor behaviors of adults come about?

The Dynamic Systems View

Developmentalist Arnold Gesell (1934) thought his painstaking observations had revealed how people develop their motor skills. He had discovered that infants and children develop rolling, sitting, standing, and other motor skills in a fixed order and within specific time frames. These observations, said Gesell, show that motor development comes about through the unfolding of a genetic plan, or *maturation.*

Later studies, however, demonstrated that the sequence of developmental milestones is not as fixed as Gesell indicated and not due as much to heredity as Gesell argued (Adolph & Joh, 2009; Adolph, Karasik, & Tamis-LeMonda, 2010). In the last two decades, the study of motor development experienced a renaissance as psychologists developed new insights about *how* motor skills develop (Spencer, 2009; Thelen & Smith, 1998, 2006). One increasingly influential theory is dynamic systems theory, proposed by Esther Thelen.

According to **dynamic systems theory,** infants assemble motor skills for perceiving and acting. Notice that perception and action are coupled according to this theory (Thelen & Smith, 2006). To develop motor skills, infants must perceive something in the environment that motivates them to act and use their perceptions to fine-tune their movements. Motor skills represent solutions to the infant's goals (Clearfield & others, 2009).

How is a motor skill developed according to this theory? When infants are motivated to do something, they might create a new motor behavior. The new behavior is the result of many converging factors: the development of the nervous system, the body's physical properties and its possibilities for movement, the goal the child is motivated to reach, and the environmental support for the skill (von Hofsten, 2008). For example, babies learn to walk only when maturation of the nervous

Esther Thelen is shown conducting an experiment to discover how infants learn to control their arms to reach and grasp for objects. A computer device is used to monitor the infant's arm movements and to track muscle patterns. Thelen's research is conducted from a dynamic systems perspective. *What is the nature of this perspective?*

system allows them to control certain leg muscles, when their legs have grown enough to support their weight, and when they want to move.

Mastering a motor skill requires the infant's active efforts to coordinate several components of the skill. Infants explore and select possible solutions to the demands of a new task; they assemble adaptive patterns by modifying their current movement patterns. The first step occurs when the infant is motivated by a new challenge—such as the desire to cross a room—and gets into the "ballpark" of the task demands by taking a couple of stumbling steps. Then, the infant "tunes" these movements to make them smoother and more effective. The tuning is achieved through repeated cycles of action and perception of the consequences of that action. According to the dynamic systems view, even universal milestones, such as crawling, reaching, and walking, are learned through this process of adaptation: Infants modulate their movement patterns to fit a new task by exploring and selecting possible configurations (Adolph, Karasik, & Tamis-LeMonda, 2010; Spencer & others, 2009; Thelen & Smith, 2006).

To see how dynamic systems theory explains motor behavior, imagine that you offer a new toy to a baby named Gabriel (Thelen & others, 1993). There is no exact program that can tell Gabriel ahead of time how to move his arm and hand and fingers to grasp the toy. Gabriel must adapt to his goal—grasping the toy—and the context. From his sitting position, he must make split-second adjustments to extend his arm, holding his body steady so that his arm and torso don't plow into the toy. Muscles in his arm and shoulder contract and stretch in a host of combinations, exerting a variety of forces. He improvises a way to reach out with one arm and wrap his fingers around the toy.

Thus, according to dynamic systems theory, motor development is not a passive process in which genes dictate the unfolding of a sequence of skills over time (Spencer, 2009). Rather, the infant actively puts together a skill to achieve a goal within the constraints set by the infant's body and environment. Nature and nurture, the infant and the environment, are all working together as part of an ever-changing system.

As we examine the course of motor development, we will see how dynamic systems theory applies to some specific skills. First, though, let's examine how the story of motor development begins with reflexes.

Reflexes

The newborn is not completely helpless. Among other things, it has some basic reflexes (Pedroso, 2008). For example, the newborn automatically holds its breath and contracts its throat to keep water out. **Reflexes** are built-in reactions to stimuli; they govern the newborn's movements, which are automatic and beyond the newborn's control. Reflexes are genetically carried survival mechanisms. They allow infants to respond adaptively to their environment before they have had the opportunity to learn.

The rooting and sucking reflexes are important examples. Both have survival value for newborn mammals, who must find a mother's breast to obtain nourishment. The **rooting reflex** occurs when the infant's cheek is stroked or the side of the mouth is touched. In response, the infant turns its head toward the side that was touched in an apparent effort to find something to suck. The **sucking reflex** occurs when newborns automatically suck an object placed in their mouth. This reflex enables newborns to get nourishment before they have associated a nipple with food; it also serves as a self-soothing or self-regulating mechanism.

Another example is the **Moro reflex,** which occurs in response to a sudden, intense noise or movement (see Figure 5.1). When startled, the newborn arches its back, throws back its head, and flings out its arms and legs. Then the newborn rapidly closes its arms and legs. The Moro reflex is believed to be a way of grabbing for support while falling; it would have had survival value for our primate ancestors.

The experiences of the first three years of life are almost entirely lost to us, and when we attempt to enter into a small child's world, we come as foreigners who have forgotten the landscape and no longer speak the native tongue.

—**SELMA FRAIBERG**
Developmentalist and Child Advocate, 20th Century

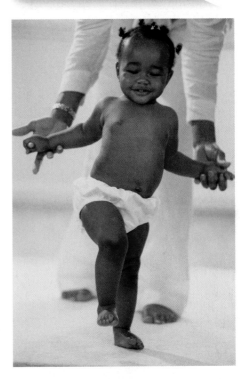

How might dynamic systems theory explain the development of learning to walk?

sucking reflex A newborn's built-in reaction of automatically sucking an object placed in its mouth. The sucking reflex enables the infant to get nourishment before it has associated a nipple with food.

Moro reflex A startle response that occurs in reaction to a sudden, intense noise or movement. When startled, the newborn arches its back, throws its head back, and flings out its arms and legs. Then the newborn rapidly closes its arms and legs to the center of the body.

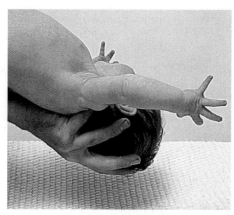

Moro reflex

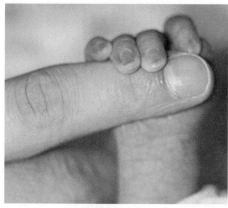

Grasping reflex

FIGURE 5.1 The Moro Reflex and the Grasping Reflex.

What are some developmental changes in posture during infancy?

Some reflexes—coughing, sneezing, blinking, shivering, and yawning, for example—persist throughout life. They are as important for the adult as they are for the infant. Other reflexes, though, disappear several months following birth, as the infant's brain matures, and voluntary control over many behaviors develops. The rooting and Moro reflexes, for example, tend to disappear when the infant is 3 to 4 months old.

The movements of some reflexes eventually become incorporated into more complex, voluntary actions. One important example is the **grasping reflex,** which occurs when something touches the infant's palms (see Figure 5.1). The infant responds by grasping tightly. By the end of the third month, the grasping reflex diminishes, and the infant shows a more voluntary grasp. As its motor development becomes smoother, the infant will grasp objects, carefully manipulate them, and explore their qualities.

Although reflexes are automatic and inborn, differences in reflexive behavior are soon apparent. For example, the sucking capabilities of newborns vary considerably. Some newborns are efficient at forceful sucking and obtaining milk; others are not as adept and get tired before they are full. Most infants take several weeks to establish a sucking style that is coordinated with the way the mother is holding the infant, the way milk is coming out of the bottle or breast, and the infant's temperament (Blass, 2008).

Pediatrician T. Berry Brazelton (1956) observed how infants' sucking changed as they grew older. Over 85 percent of the infants engaged in considerable sucking behavior unrelated to feeding. They sucked their finger, their fists, and pacifiers. By the age of 1 year, most had stopped the sucking behavior, but as many as 40 percent of children continue to suck their thumbs after they have started school (Kessen Haith, & Salapatek, 1970). Most developmentalists do not attach a great deal of significance to this behavior.

Gross Motor Skills

Ask any parents about their baby, and sooner or later you are likely to hear about one or more motor milestone, such as "Cassandra just learned to crawl," "Jesse is finally sitting alone," or "Angela took her first step last week." Parents proudly announce such milestones as their children transform themselves from babies unable to lift their heads to toddlers who grab things off the grocery store shelf, chase a cat, and participate actively in the family's social life (Thelen, 2000). These milestones are examples of **gross motor skills,** skills that involve large-muscle activities, such as moving one's arms and walking.

The Development of Posture

How do gross motor skills develop? As a foundation, these skills require postural control (Adolph & Joh, 2009). For example, to track moving objects, you must be able to control your head in order to stabilize your gaze; before you can walk, you must be able to balance on one leg.

Posture is more than just holding still and straight. Posture is a dynamic process that is linked with sensory information in the skin, joints, and muscles, which tell us where we are in space; in vestibular organs in the inner ear that regulate balance and equilibrium; and in vision and hearing (Thelen & Smith, 2006).

Newborn infants cannot voluntarily control their posture. Within a few weeks, though, they can hold their heads erect, and soon they can lift their heads while prone. By 2 months of age, babies can sit while supported on a lap or an infant seat, but they cannot sit independently until they are 6 or 7 months of age. Standing also develops gradually during the first year of life. By about 8 to 9 months of age, infants usually learn to pull themselves up and hold onto a chair, and they often can stand alone by about 10 to 12 months of age.

Learning to Walk   Locomotion and postural control are closely linked, especially in walking upright (Adolph & Joh, 2009; Adolph, Karasik, & Tamis-LeMonda, 2010). To walk upright, the baby must be able both to balance on one leg as the other is swung forward and to shift the weight from one leg to the other.

Even young infants can make the alternating leg movements that are needed for walking. The neural pathways that control leg alternation are in place from a very early age, possibly even at birth or before. A recent study found that 3-day-old infants adapted their stepping pattern to visual input (Barbu-Roth & others, 2009). In this study, the very young infants took more steps when they saw a visual treadmill moving beneath their feet than their counterparts who saw a stationary image or an image that rotated. This study also illustrates the key concept of the coupling of perception and action in dynamic systems theory. Infants also engage in frequent alternating kicking movements throughout the first six months of life when they are lying on their backs. Also when 1- to 2-month-olds are given support with their feet in contact with a motorized treadmill, they show well-coordinated, alternating steps.

If infants can produce forward stepping movements so early, why does it take them so long to learn to walk? The key skills in learning to walk appear to be stabilizing balance on one leg long enough to swing the other forward and shifting the weight without falling. This is a difficult biomechanical problem to solve, and it takes infants about a year to do it.

When infants learn to walk, they typically take small steps because of their limited balance control and strength. However, a recent study revealed that infants occasionally take a few large steps that even exceed their leg length, and these large steps indicate increased balance and strength (Badaly & Adolph, 2008).

In learning to locomote, infants learn what kinds of places and surfaces are safe for locomotion (Adolph & Joh, 2009; Gil, Adolph, & Vreijken, 2009). Karen Adolph (1997) investigated how experienced and inexperienced crawling infants and walking infants go down steep slopes (see Figure 5.2). Newly crawling infants, who averaged about 8½ months in age, rather indiscriminately went down the steep slopes, often falling in the process (with their mothers next to the slope to catch them). After weeks of practice, the crawling babies became more adept at judging which slopes were too steep to crawl down and which ones they could navigate safely. New walkers also could not judge the safety of the slopes, but experienced walkers accurately matched their skills with the steepness of the slopes. They rarely fell downhill, either refusing to go down the steep slopes or going down backward in a cautious manner. Experienced walkers perceptually assessed the situation—looking, swaying, touching, and thinking before they moved down the slope. With experience, both the crawlers and the walkers learned to avoid the risky slopes where they would fall, integrating perceptual information with the development of a new motor behavior. In this research, we again see the importance of perceptual-motor coupling in the development of motor skills. Thus, practice is very important in the development of new motor skills (Adolph & Joh, 2009; Adolph & others, 2008).

The First Year: Motor Development Milestones and Variations   Figure 5.3 summarizes important accomplishments in gross motor skills during the first year, culminating in the ability to walk easily. The timing of these milestones, especially the later ones, may vary by as much as two to four months, and experiences can modify the onset of these accomplishments. For example, since 1992, when pediatricians began recommending that parents place their babies on their backs when they sleep, fewer babies crawled and those who did crawled later (Davis & others, 1998). Also, some infants do not follow the standard sequence of motor accomplishments (Eaton, 2008). For example, many American infants never crawl on their belly or on their hands and knees. They may discover an idiosyncratic form of

Newly crawling infant

Experienced walker

FIGURE 5.2 The Role of Experience in Crawling and Walking Infants' Judgments of Whether to Go Down a Slope. Karen Adolph (1997) found that locomotor experience rather than age was the primary predictor of adaptive responding on slopes of varying steepness. Newly crawling and walking infants could not judge the safety of the various slopes. With experience, they learned to avoid slopes where they would fall. When expert crawlers began to walk, they again made mistakes and fell, even though they had judged the same slope accurately when crawling. Adolph referred to this as the *specificity of learning* because it does not transfer across crawling and walking.

grasping reflex A reflex that occurs when something touches an infant's palms. The infant responds by grasping tightly.

gross motor skills Motor skills that involve large-muscle activities, such as walking.

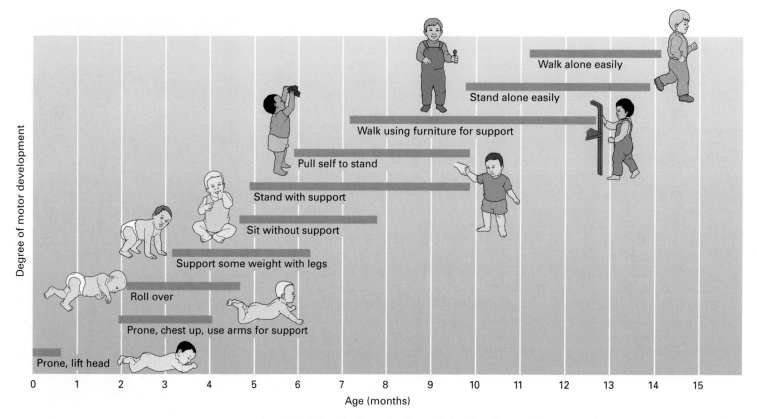

FIGURE 5.3 Milestones in Gross Motor Development.

locomotion before walking, such as rolling, or they might never locomote until they get upright (Adolph & Joh, 2009). In the African Mali tribe, most infants do not crawl (Bril, 1999).

According to Karen Adolph and Sarah Berger (2005), "the old-fashioned view that growth and motor development reflect merely the age-related output of maturation is, at best, incomplete. Rather, infants acquire new skills with the help of their caregivers in a real-world environment of objects, surfaces, and planes."

Development in the Second Year   The motor accomplishments of the first year bring increasing independence, allowing infants to explore their environment more extensively and to initiate interaction with others more readily. In the second year of life, toddlers become more motorically skilled and mobile. Motor activity during the second year is vital to the child's competent development and few restrictions, except for safety, should be placed on their adventures.

By 13 to 18 months, toddlers can pull a toy attached to a string and use their hands and legs to climb up a number of steps. By 18 to 24 months, toddlers can walk quickly or run stiffly for a short distance, balance on their feet in a squat position while playing with objects on the floor, walk backward without losing their balance, stand and kick a ball without falling, stand and throw a ball, and jump in place.

Can parents give their babies a head start on becoming physically fit and physically talented through structured exercise classes? Most infancy experts recommend against structured exercise classes for babies. But there are other ways of guiding infants' motor development. Caregivers in some cultures do handle babies vigorously, and such treatment might advance motor development, as we discuss in the *Contexts of Life-Span Development* interlude.

Contexts of Life-Span Development

CULTURAL VARIATIONS IN GUIDING INFANTS' MOTOR DEVELOPMENT

Mothers in developing countries tend to stimulate their infants' motor skills more than mothers in more developed countries (Hopkins, 1991). In many African, Indian, and Caribbean cultures, mothers massage and stretch their infants during daily baths (Adolph, Karasik, & Tamis-LeMonda, 2010). Mothers in the Gusii culture of Kenya also encourage vigorous movement in their babies (Hopkins & Westra, 1988).

Do these cultural variations make a difference in the infant's motor development? When caregivers provide babies with physical guidance by physically handling them in special ways (such as stroking, massaging, or stretching) or by giving them opportunities for exercise, the infants often reach motor milestones earlier than infants whose caregivers have not provided these activities (Adolph, Karasik, & Tamis-LeMonda, 2010). For example, Jamaican mothers expect their infants to sit and walk alone two to three months earlier than English mothers do (Hopkins & Westra, 1990).

Nonetheless, even when infants' motor activity is restricted, many infants still reach the milestones of motor development at a normal age. For example, Algonquin infants in Quebec, Canada, spend much of their first year strapped to a cradle board. Despite their inactivity, these infants still sit up, crawl, and walk within an age range similar to that of infants in cultures who have had much greater opportunity for activity.

(*Top*) In the Algonquin culture in Quebec, Canada, babies are strapped to a cradle board for much of their infancy. (*Bottom*) In Jamaica, mothers massage and stretch their infants' arms and legs. *To what extent do cultural variations in the activity infants engage in influence the time at which they reach motor milestones?*

Childhood   The preschool child no longer has to make an effort to stay upright and to move around. As children move their legs with more confidence and carry themselves more purposefully, moving around in the environment becomes more automatic.

At 3 years of age, children enjoy simple movements, such as hopping, jumping, and running back and forth, just for the sheer delight of performing these activities. They take considerable pride in showing how they can run across a room and jump all of 6 inches. The run-and-jump will win no Olympic gold medals, but for the 3-year-old the activity is a source of considerable pride and accomplishment.

At 4 years of age, children are still enjoying the same kind of activities, but they have become more adventurous. They scramble over low jungle gyms as they display their athletic prowess. Although they have been able to climb stairs with one foot on each step for some time, they are just beginning to be able to come down the same way.

At 5 years of age, children are even more adventuresome than they were at 4. It is not unusual for self-assured 5-year-olds to perform hair-raising stunts on practically any climbing object. They run hard and enjoy races with each other and their parents.

During middle and late childhood, children's motor development becomes much smoother and more coordinated than it was in early childhood. For example, only one child in a thousand can hit a tennis ball over the net at the age of 3, yet by the age of 10 or 11 most children can learn to play the sport. Running, climbing, skipping rope, swimming, bicycle riding, and skating are just a few of the many physical skills elementary school children can master. And, when mastered, these physical skills are a source of great pleasure and accomplishment. A recent study of 9-year-olds revealed that those who were more physically fit had

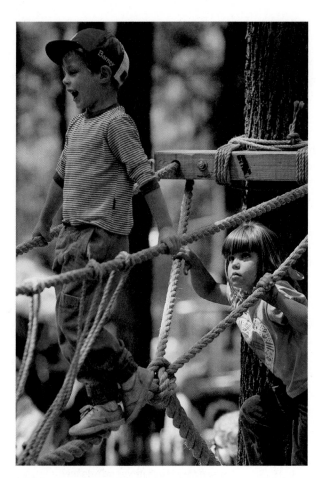

What are some developmental changes in children's motor development in early childhood and middle and late childhood?

a better mastery of motor skills (Haga, 2008). In gross motor skills involving large-muscle activity, boys usually outperform girls.

As children move through the elementary school years, they gain greater control over their bodies and can sit and pay attention for longer periods of time. However, elementary school children are far from being physically mature, and they need to be active. Elementary school children become more fatigued by long periods of sitting than by running, jumping, or bicycling (Rink, 2009). Physical action is essential for these children to refine their developing skills, such as batting a ball, skipping rope, or balancing on a beam. Children benefit from exercise breaks periodically during the school day on the order of 15 minutes every two hours (Keen, 2005). In sum, elementary school children should be engaged in active, rather than passive, activities.

Organized sports are one way of encouraging children to be active and to develop their motor skills. Schools and community agencies offer programs for children that involve baseball, soccer, football, basketball, swimming, gymnastics, and other sports. For children who participate in them, these programs may play a central role in their lives.

Participation in sports can have both positive and negative consequences for children (Coatsworth, & Conway, 2009; Gaudreau, Amiot, & Vallerand, 2009). Participation can provide exercise, opportunities to learn how to compete, self-esteem, persistence, and a setting for developing peer relations and friendships (Theokas, 2009). Further, participating in sports reduces the likelihood that children will become obese (Sturm, 2005). For example, in one recent study, Mexican youth who did not participate in sports were more likely to be overweight or obese than those who participated (Salazar-Martinez & others, 2006). One study also revealed that participation in sports for three hours per week or more beyond regular physical education classes was related to increased physical fitness and lower fat mass in 9-year-old boys (Ara & others, 2004). However, sports also can bring pressure to achieve and win, physical injuries, a distraction from academic work, and unrealistic expectations for success as an athlete (Lawrence, Shaha, & Lillis, 2008; Siow, Cameron, & Ganley, 2008).

Few people challenge the value of sports for children when conducted as part of a school's physical education or intramural program. However, some critics question the appropriateness of highly competitive, win-oriented sports teams, especially when they involve championship play and media publicity. Such activities not only put undue stress on children but also may teach them a win-at-all-costs philosophy. Overly ambitious parents, coaches, and community boosters can unintentionally create a highly stressful atmosphere in children's sports. When parental, organizational, or community prestige becomes the central focus of the child's participation in sports, the danger of exploitation clearly is present. Programs oriented toward such purposes often require long and arduous training sessions over many months and years, frequently leading to specialization at too early an age. In such circumstances, adults often transmit to the child the distorted view that the sport is the most important aspect of the child's existence.

In thinking about the influence of sports on children's development, it is important to keep in mind that just participating in sports does not necessarily lead to benefits for children (Theokas, 2009). It is the quality of the participation experience that confers benefits. Also, in many research studies, the influence of sports is considered in a general way, yet different sports have different characteristics, demands, and patterns of interaction with coaches, parents, and the community. The *Applications in Life-Span Development* interlude examines the roles of parents and coaches in children's sports.

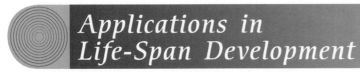

Applications in Life-Span Development

PARENTS AND CHILDREN'S SPORTS

Most sports psychologists stress that it is important for parents to show an interest in their children's sports participation. Most children want their parents to watch them perform in sports. Many children whose parents do not come to watch them play in sporting events feel that their parents do not adequately support them. However, some children become extremely nervous when their parents watch them perform, or they get embarrassed when their parents cheer too loudly or make a fuss. If children request that their parents not watch them perform, parents should respect their children's wishes (Schreiber, 1990).

Parents should compliment their children for their sports performance. In the course of a game, there are dozens of circumstances when the child has done something positive—parents should stress a child's good performance, even if the child has limited abilities. Parents can tell their children how much the children hustled in the game and how enthusiastically they played. Even if the child strikes out in a baseball game, a parent can say, "That was a nice swing."

If parents do not become overinvolved, they can help their children build their physical skills and help them emotionally—discussing with them how to deal with a difficult coach, how to cope with a tough loss, and how to put in perspective a poorly played game. Parents need to carefully monitor their children as they participate in sports for signs of developing stress. If the problems appear to be beyond the intuitive skills of a volunteer coach or parent, a consultation with a counselor or clinician may be needed. Also, the parent needs to be sensitive to whether the sport in which the child is participating is the best one for the child and whether the child can handle its competitive pressures.

Some guidelines provided by the Women's Sports Foundation (2001) in its booklet *Parents' Guide to Girls' Sports* can benefit both parents and coaches of all children in sports:

The Dos

- Make sports fun; the more children enjoy sports, the more they will want to play.
- Remember that it is okay for children to make mistakes; it means they are trying.
- Allow children to ask questions about the sport and discuss the sport in a calm, supportive manner.
- Show respect for the child's sports participation.
- Be positive and convince the child that he or she is making a good effort.
- Be a positive role model for the child in sports.

The Don'ts

- Yell or scream at the child.
- Condemn the child for poor play or continue to bring up failures long after they happen.
- Point out the child's errors in front of others.
- Expect the child to learn something immediately.
- Expect the child to become a pro.
- Ridicule or make fun of the child.
- Compare the child to siblings or to more talented children.
- Make sports all work and no fun.

What are some of the possible positive and negative aspects of children's participation in sports?

Adolescence and Adulthood Gross motor skills typically improve during adolescence. Most of us reach our peak physical performance before the age of 30, often between the ages of 19 and 26. This peak occurs both for the average young adult and for outstanding athletes. Even though athletes keep getting better than their predecessors—running faster, jumping higher, and lifting more weight—the age at which they reach their peak performance has remained virtually the same (Schultz & Curnow, 1988). Most swimmers and gymnasts reach their peak in their late teens. Many athletes, including track performers in sprint races (100-, 200-yard dashes), peak in their early to mid-twenties. Golfers and marathon runners tend to peak in their late twenties or even early thirties.

After an individual reaches the age of 30, most biological functions begin to decline, although the decline of specific organs can vary considerably (McCarter, 2006). The decrement in general biological functioning that begins at about age 30 occurs at a rate of about 0.75 to 1 percent a year. Decrements often occur in cardiovascular functioning, muscle strength, bone tissue (especially for females), neural function, balance, and flexibility.

People slow down in late adulthood. Older adults move slower than young adults (Rossit & Harvey, 2008). This difference occurs across a wide range of movement difficulty (see Figure 5.4). General slowing of movement in older adults has been found in everyday tasks such as moving from one place to another and continuous movement (Mollenkopf, 2007; Woollacott, 2007).

Adequate mobility is an important aspect of maintaining an independent and active lifestyle in late adulthood (Baezner & others, 2008; Callisaya & others, 2008). One recent study of the functional ability of noninstitutionalized 70-plus-year-olds revealed that over an eight-year period, the most deterioration occurred in their mobility (Holstein & others, 2007). A recent study revealed that obesity was linked to mobility limitation in older adults (Houston & others, 2009). The good news is that regular walking decreases the onset of physical disability in older adults (Newman & others, 2006). Also, exercise and appropriate weight lifting can help to reduce the decrease in muscle mass and improve the older person's body appearance (Peterson & others, 2009).

No matter how well individuals take care of themselves, aging eventually produces declines in biological functions (Veranazza-Martin & others, 2008). But, as we discussed in Chapter 1, "Introduction," chronological age (an individual's age since birth) does differ from biological age (an individual's biological health).

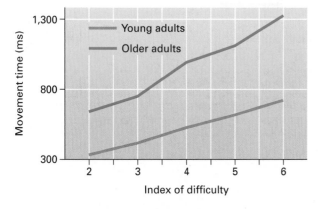

FIGURE 5.4 Movement and Aging. Older adults take longer to move than young adults, and this occurs across a range of movement difficulty (Ketcham & Stelmach, 2001).

Motor skills decline less in older adults who are active and biologically healthy. *What is the difference between chronological age and biological age?*

Aging individuals who are active and biologically healthy perform motor skills at a higher level than their less active, less healthy aging counterparts. As we saw in Chapter 4, "Health," physical activity can have positive effects on motor skills in older adults. For example, one study found that exercise and an active lifestyle that included extensive walking protected against mobility loss in 70- to 79-year-old adults (Visser & others, 2005). Also, in a recent study, 70- to 89-year-olds at risk for mobility disability were randomly assigned to 12 months of either physical activity or a successful aging educational intervention (Rejeski & others, 2008). Older adults who engaged in physical activity showed more mobility gains than those in the educational intervention. And a recent study revealed that a higher level of physical activity and a lower level of adiposity (fatness) were linked to lower mobility restrictions in older adults (Koster & others, 2008).

Fine Motor Skills

Whereas gross motor skills involve large-muscle activity, **fine motor skills** involve finely tuned movements. Buttoning a shirt, typing, or anything that requires finger dexterity demonstrates fine motor skills.

Infancy   Infants have hardly any control over fine motor skills at birth, but newborns do have many components of what will become finely coordinated arm, hand, and finger movements.

The onset of reaching and grasping marks a significant achievement in infants' ability to interact with their surroundings (van Hof, van der Kamp, & Savelsbergh, 2008). During the first two years of life, infants refine how they reach and grasp (Barrett & Needham, 2008; Needham, 2009). Initially, infants reach by moving their shoulders and elbows crudely, swinging toward an object. Later, when infants reach for an object they move their wrists, rotate their hands, and coordinate their thumb and forefinger. Infants do not have to see their own hands in order to reach for an object (Clifton & others, 1993). Cues from muscles, tendons, and joints, not sight of the limb, guide reaching by 4-month-old infants.

Infants refine their ability to grasp objects by developing two types of grasps. Initially, infants grip with the whole hand, which is called the *palmer grasp.* Later, toward the end of the first year, infants also grasp small objects with their thumb and forefinger, which is called the *pincer grip.* Their grasping system is very flexible. They vary their grip on an object depending on its size, shape, and texture, as well as the size of their own hands relative to the object's size. Infants grip small objects with their thumb and forefinger (and sometimes their middle finger too), whereas they grip large objects with all of the fingers of one hand or both hands.

Perceptual-motor coupling is necessary for the infant to coordinate grasping (Keen, 2005). Which perceptual system the infant is most likely to use in coordinating grasping varies with age. Four-month-old infants rely greatly on touch to determine how they will grip an object; eight-month-olds are more likely to use vision as a guide (Newell & others, 1989). This developmental change is efficient because vision lets infants preshape their hands as they reach for an object.

Experience plays a role in reaching and grasping. In one study, 3-month old infants participated in play sessions wearing "sticky mittens"—"mittens with palms that stuck to the edges of toys and allowed the infants to pick up the toys" (Needham, Barrett, & Peterman, 2002, p. 279) (see Figure 5.5). Infants who participated in sessions with the mittens grasped and manipulated objects earlier in their development than a control group of infants who did not receive the "mitten" experience. The experienced infants looked at the objects longer, swatted at them more during visual contact, and were more likely to mouth the objects.

A young girl using a pincer grip to pick up puzzle pieces.

fine motor skills Motor skills that involve finely tuned movements, such as any activity that requires finger dexterity.

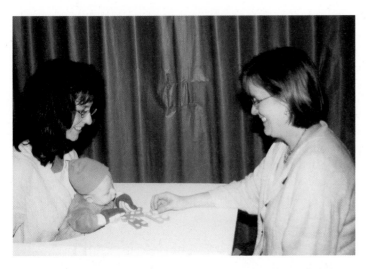

FIGURE 5.5 Infants' Use of "Sticky Mittens" to Explore Objects.
Amy Needham and her colleagues (2002) found that "sticky mittens" enhanced young infants' object exploration skills.

Just as infants need to exercise their gross motor skills, they also need to exercise their fine motor skills (Barrett, Davis, & Needham, 2007; Needham, 2009). Especially when they can manage a pincer grip, infants delight in picking up small objects. Many develop the pincer grip and begin to crawl at about the same time, and infants at this time pick up virtually everything in sight, especially on the floor, and put the objects in their mouth. Thus, parents need to be vigilant in regularly monitoring what objects are within the infant's reach (Keen, 2005).

Childhood and Adolescence As children get older, their fine motor skills improve (Sveistrup & others, 2008). At 3 years of age, children have had the ability to pick up the tiniest objects between their thumb and forefinger for some time, but they are still somewhat clumsy at it. Three-year-olds can build surprisingly high block towers, each block placed with intense concentration but often not in a completely straight line. When 3-year-olds play with a form board or a simple puzzle, they are rather rough in placing the pieces. Even when they recognize the hole that a piece fits into, they are not very precise in positioning the piece. They often try to force the piece in the hole or pat it vigorously.

By 4 years of age, children's fine motor coordination has become much more precise. Sometimes 4-year-old children have trouble building high towers with blocks because, in their desire to place each of the blocks perfectly, they may upset those already stacked. By age 5, children's fine motor coordination has improved further. Hand, arm, and fingers all move together under better command of the eye. Mere towers no longer interest the 5-year-old, who now wants to build a house or a church, complete with steeple, though adults may still need to be told what each finished project is meant to be.

Increased myelination of the central nervous system is reflected in the improvement of fine motor skills during middle and late childhood. (Recall from Chapter 3, "Physical Development and Biological Aging," that *myelination* involves the covering of the axon with a myelin sheath, a process that increases the speed with which information travels from neuron to neuron.) Children use their hands more adroitly as tools. Six-year-olds can hammer, paste, tie shoes, and fasten clothes. By 7 years of age, children's hands have become steadier. At this age, children prefer a pencil to a crayon for printing, and reversal of letters is less common. Printing becomes smaller. At 8 to 10 years of age, children can use their hands independently with more ease and precision; children can now write rather than print words. Letter size becomes smaller and more even. At 10 to 12 years of age, children begin to show manipulative skills similar to the abilities of adults. The complex, intricate, and rapid movements needed to produce fine-quality crafts or to play a difficult piece on a musical instrument can be mastered. Girls usually outperform boys in fine motor skills.

Adult Development Fine motor skills may undergo some decline in middle and late adulthood as dexterity decreases, although for most healthy individuals, fine motor skills, such as reaching and grasping, continue to be performed in functional ways. However, pathological conditions may result in weakness or paralysis of an individual's hands, in which case performance of fine motor skills may be impossible.

Slowed movement is one way in which fine motor skills may decline (Newell, Vaillancourt, & Sosnoff, 2006). For example, older adults are slower in their handwriting than younger adults are, although many older adults continue to perform handwriting competently (Dixon, Kurzman, & Friesen, 1993). Two explanations of the slower motor behavior of older adults are (1) neural noise and (2) strategy (Ketcham & Stelmach, 2001).

Neural noise refers to an increase in irregular neural activity in the central nervous system, which could affect a wide range of sensorimotor activities (Welford, 1984). Older adults are thought to have higher neural noise than younger adults (Walker, Philbin, & Fisk, 1997). An increase in neural noise disturbs the processing of incoming signals, delaying their interpretation and implementation. The consequences are slower and more variable movement performance by older adults.

Aging adults also may engage in *strategies* to compensate for declines in their gross and fine motor skills (Ketcham & Stelmach, 2001). Many older adults are strongly motivated to perform a task as accurately as possible (Salthouse, 1988). When they try to perform motor activities (such as handwriting or typing on a computer) too fast, older adults are prone to make more errors than younger adults, so they may slow their movements to execute a task more accurately.

Older adults are capable of learning new motor tasks just as younger adults are, although older adults typically do this at a slower rate of improvement (Ketcham & Stelmach, 2001). Thus, practice and training programs may minimize declines in motor function.

What are some changes in fine motor skills in aging adults? How can aging adults compensate for declines in motor skills?

Review and Reflect: Learning Goal 1

1 **Describe how motor skills develop**

REVIEW

- What is the dynamic systems view of motor development?
- What are reflexes? What are some reflexes of infants?
- What are gross motor skills, and how do they develop?
- What are fine motor skills? How do fine motor skills develop?

REFLECT

- How would you evaluate the benefits and drawbacks of allowing an 8-year-old to play Little League baseball?

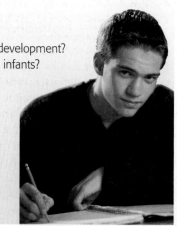

2 SENSORY AND PERCEPTUAL DEVELOPMENT

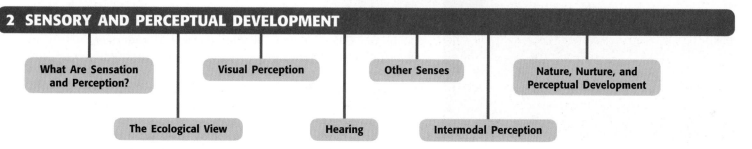

What Are Sensation and Perception?   The Ecological View   Visual Perception   Hearing   Other Senses   Intermodal Perception   Nature, Nurture, and Perceptual Development

Right now, I am looking at my computer screen to make sure the words are being printed accurately as I am typing them. My perceptual and motor skills are working together. Recall that even control of posture uses information from the senses. And, when people grasp an object, they use perceptual information about the object to adjust their motions.

How do these sensations and perceptions develop? Can a newborn see? If so, what can it perceive? What about the other senses—hearing, smell, taste, touch, and pain? What are they like in the newborn, and how do they develop? How do sensation and perception change when adults become older? These are among the intriguing questions that we explore in this section.

What Are Sensation and Perception?

How does a newborn know that her mother's skin is soft rather than rough? How does a 5-year-old know what color his hair is? How does a 10-year-old know that a firecracker is louder than a cat's meow? Infants and children "know" these things because of information that comes through the senses. Without vision, hearing, touch, taste, smell, and other senses, we would be isolated from the world; we would live in dark silence, a tasteless, colorless, feelingless void.

Sensation occurs when information interacts with sensory *receptors*—the eyes, ears, tongue, nostrils, and skin. The sensation of hearing occurs when waves of pulsating air are collected by the outer ear and conducted through the bones of the inner ear and the *cochlea*, where mechanical vibrations are converted into electrical impulses. Then the electrical impulses move to the *auditory nerve*, which transmits them to the brain. The sensation of vision occurs as rays of light contact the eyes and become focused on the *retina*, where light is converted into electrical impulses. Then the electrical impulses are transmitted by the *optic nerve* to the visual centers of the brain.

Perception is the interpretation of what is sensed. The air waves that contact the ears might be interpreted as noise or as musical sounds, for example. The physical energy transmitted to the retina of the eye might be interpreted as a particular color, pattern, or shape, depending on how it is perceived.

The Ecological View

For the past several decades, much of the research on perceptual development in infancy has been guided by the ecological view of Eleanor and James J. Gibson (E. Gibson, 1969, 1989, 2001; J. Gibson, 1966, 1979). They argue that we do not have to take bits and pieces of data from sensations and build up representations of the world in our minds. Instead, our perceptual system can select from the rich information that the environment itself provides.

According to the Gibsons' **ecological view,** we directly perceive information that exists in the world around us. Perception brings us into contact with the environment in order to interact with and adapt to it. Perception is designed for action. Perception gives people such information as when to duck, when to turn their bodies through a narrow passageway, and when to put up their hands to catch something.

In the Gibsons' view, all objects have **affordances,** which are opportunities for interaction offered by objects that fit within our capabilities to perform activities. A pot may afford you something to cook with, and it may afford a toddler something to bang. Adults immediately know when a chair is appropriate for sitting, when a surface is safe for walking, or when an object is within reach. We directly and accurately perceive these affordances by sensing information from the environment—the light or sound reflecting from the surfaces of the world—and from our own bodies through muscle receptors, joint receptors, and skin receptors.

sensation Reaction that occurs when information interacts with sensory receptors—the eyes, ears, tongue, nostrils, and skin.

perception The interpretation of sensation.

ecological view The view proposed by the Gibsons that people directly perceive information in the world around them. Perception brings people in contact with the environment in order to interact with it and adapt to it.

affordances Opportunities for interaction offered by objects that fit within our capabilities to perform activities.

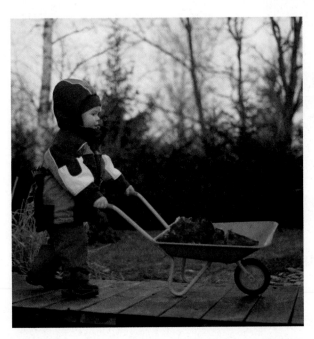

How would you use the Gibsons' ecological theory of perception and the concept of affordance to explain the role that perception is playing in this toddler's activity?

An important developmental question is, What affordances can infants or children detect and use? In one study, for example, when babies who could walk were faced with a squishy waterbed, they stopped and explored it, then chose to crawl rather than walk across it (Gibson & others, 1987). They combined perception and action to adapt to the demands of the task.

Similarly, as we discussed earlier in the section on motor development, infants who were just learning to crawl or just learning to walk were less cautious when confronted with a steep slope than experienced crawlers or walkers were (Adolph, 1997; Adolph & Joh, 2009). The more experienced crawlers and walkers perceived that a slope *affords* the possibility not only for faster locomotion but also for falling. Again, infants coupled perception and action to make a decision about what do in their environment. Through perceptual development, children become more efficient at discovering and using affordances.

Studying the infant's perception has not been an easy task. The *Research in Life-Span Development* interlude describes some of the ingenious ways researchers study the infant's perception.

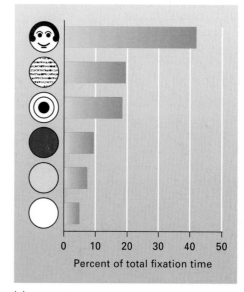

(a)

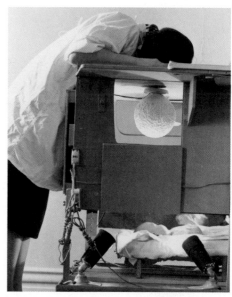

(b)

FIGURE 5.6 Fantz' Experiment on Infants' Visual Perception. (*a*) Infants 2 to 3 weeks old preferred to look at some stimuli more than others. In Fantz' experiment, infants preferred to look at patterns rather than at color or brightness. For example, they looked longer at a face, a piece of printed matter, or a bull's-eye than at red, yellow, or white discs. (*b*) Fantz used a "looking chamber" to study infants' perception of stimuli.

Research in Life-Span Development

STUDYING THE NEWBORN'S PERCEPTION

The creature has poor motor coordination and can move itself only with great difficulty. Although it cries when uncomfortable, it uses few other vocalizations. In fact, it sleeps most of the time, about 16 to 17 hours a day. You are curious about this creature and want to know more about what it can do. You think to yourself, "I wonder if it can see. How could I find out?"

You obviously have a communication problem with the creature. You must devise a way that will allow the creature to "tell" you that it can see. While examining the creature one day, you make an interesting discovery. When you move an object horizontally in front of the creature, its eyes follow the object's movement.

The creature's head movement suggests that it has at least some vision. In case you haven't already guessed, the creature you have been reading about is the human infant, and the role you played is that of a researcher interested in devising techniques to learn about the infant's visual perception. After years of work, scientists have developed research methods and tools sophisticated enough to examine the subtle abilities of infants and to interpret their complex actions (Bendersky & Sullivan, 2007).

Visual Preference Method

Robert Fantz (1963) was a pioneer in this effort. Fantz made an important discovery that advanced the ability of researchers to investigate infants' visual perception: Infants look at different things for different lengths of time. Fantz placed infants in a "looking chamber," which had two visual displays on the ceiling above the infant's head. An experimenter viewed the infant's eyes by looking through a peephole. If the infant was fixating on one of the displays, the experimenter could see the display's reflection in the infant's eyes. This arrangement allowed the experimenter to determine how long the infant looked at each display. Fantz (1963) found that infants only 2 days old look longer at patterned stimuli, such as faces and concentric circles, than at red, white, or yellow discs. Infants 2 to 3 weeks old preferred to look at patterns—a face, a piece of printed matter, or a bull's-eye—longer than at red, yellow, or white discs (see Figure 5.6). Fantz's research method—studying whether infants can distinguish one stimulus from another by measuring the length of time they attend to different stimuli—is referred to as the **visual preference method.**

visual preference method A method developed by Fantz to determine whether infants can distinguish one stimulus from another by measuring the length of time they attend to different stimuli.

(continued on next page)

Habituation and Dishabituation

Another way that researchers have studied infant perception is to present a stimulus (such as a sight or a sound) a number of times. If the infant decreases its response to the stimulus after several presentations, this change indicates that the infant is no longer interested in looking at the stimulus. If the researcher now presents a new stimulus, the infant's response will recover—an indication that the infant could discriminate between the old and new stimulus (Snyder & Torrence, 2008).

Habituation is the name given to decreased responsiveness to a stimulus after repeated presentations of the stimulus. **Dishabituation** is the recovery of a habituated response after a change in stimulation. Newborn infants can habituate to repeated sights, sounds, smells, or touches (Rovee-Collier, 2004). Among the measures researchers use in habituation studies are sucking behavior (sucking stops when the young infant attends to a novel object), heart and respiration rates, and the length of time the infant looks at an object. Figure 5.7 shows the results of one study of habituation and dishabituation with newborns (Slater, Morison, & Somers, 1988).

High-Amplitude Sucking

To assess an infant's attention to sound, researchers often use a method called *high-amplitude sucking*. In this method, infants are given a nonnutritive nipple to suck, and the nipple is connected to

> a sound generating system. Each suck causes a noise to be generated and the infant learns quickly that sucking brings about this noise. At first, babies suck frequently, so the noise occurs often. Then, gradually, they lose interest in hearing repetitions of the same noise and begin to suck less frequently. At this point, the experimenter changes the sound that is being generated. If the babies renew vigorous sucking, we infer that they have discriminated the sound change and are sucking more because they want to hear the interesting new sound. (Menn & Stoel-Gammon, 2009, p. 67)

Other Methods

A technique that can be used to determine if an infant can see or hear is the *orienting response,* which involves turning one's head toward a sight or sound. Another technique,

habituation Decreased responsiveness to a stimulus after repeated presentations of the stimulus.

dishabituation The recovery of a habituated response after a change in stimulation.

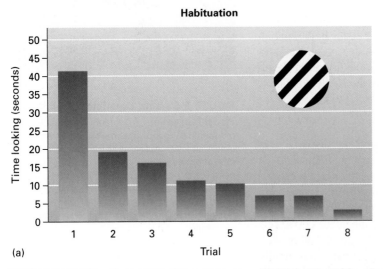

(a)

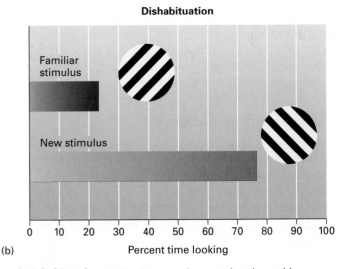

(b)

FIGURE 5.7 Habituation and Dishabituation. In the first part of one study, 7-hour-old newborns were shown the stimulus in (*a*). As indicated, the newborns looked at it an average of 41 seconds when it was first presented to them (Slater, Morison, & Somers, 1988). Over seven more presentations of the stimulus, they looked at it less and less. In the second part of the study, infants were presented with both the familiar stimulus to which they had just become habituated (*a*) and a new stimulus (shown in *b*, which was rotated 90 degrees). The newborns looked at the new stimulus three times as much as the familiar stimulus.

tracking, measures eye movements that follow (*track*) a moving object; it can be used to evaluate an infant's early visual ability. A *startle response* can be used to determine an infant's reaction to a noise (Bendersky & Sullivan, 2007).

Equipment

Technology can facilitate the use of most methods for investigating the infant's perceptual abilities. Videotape equipment allows researchers to investigate elusive behaviors. High-speed computers make it possible to perform complex data analysis in minutes. Other equipment records respiration, heart rate, body movement, visual fixation, and sucking behavior, which provide clues to what the infant is perceiving. For example, some researchers use equipment that detects if a change in infants' respiration follows a change in the pitch of a sound. If so, it suggests that the infants have heard the pitch change. Thus, scientists have become ingenious at assessing the development of infants, discovering ways to "interview" them even though they cannot yet talk.

Visual Perception

Some important changes in visual perception as we age can be traced to differences in how the eye itself functions over time. These changes in the eye's functioning influence, for example, how clearly we can see an object, whether we can differentiate its colors, at what distances, and in what light. But the differences between what the newborn sees and what a toddler or an adult sees go far beyond those that can be explained by changes in the eye's functioning, as we discuss in this section.

Infancy   Psychologist William James (1890/1950) called the newborn's perceptual world a "blooming, buzzing confusion." More than a century later, we can safely say that he was wrong (Slater, Field, & Hernandez-Reif, 2007). Even the newborn perceives a world with some order. That world, however, is far different from the one perceived by the toddler or the adult.

Visual Acuity   Just how well can infants see? At birth, the nerves and muscles and lens of the eye are still developing. As a result, newborns cannot see small things that are far away. The newborn's vision is estimated to be 20/240 on the well-known Snellen chart used for eye examinations, which means that a newborn can see at 20 feet what a normal adult can see at 240 feet (Aslin & Lathrop, 2008). In other words, an object 20 feet away is only as clear to the newborn as it would be if it were 240 feet away from an adult with normal vision (20/20). By 6 months of age, though, on *average* vision is 20/40 (Aslin & Lathrop, 2008).

Infants show an interest in human faces soon after birth (Quinn & others, 2009). Figure 5.8 shows a computer estimation of what a picture of a face looks like to an infant at different ages from a distance of about 6 inches. Infants spend more time looking at their mother's face than a stranger's face as early as 12 hours after being born (Bushnell, 2003). By 3 months of age, infants match voices to faces, distinguish between male and female faces, and discriminate between faces of their own ethnic group and those of other ethnic groups (Kelly & others, 2007, 2009; Pascalis & Kelly, 2008).

Even very young infants soon change the way they gather information from the visual world, including human faces (Aslin & Lathrop, 2008). By using a special mirror arrangement, researchers projected an image of human faces in front of infants' eyes so that the infants' eye movements could be photographed (Maurer &

 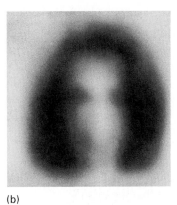  

(a) (b) (c) (d)

FIGURE 5.8 Visual Acuity During the First Months of Life. The four photographs represent a computer estimation of what a picture of a face looks like to a 1-month-old (*a*), 2-month-old (*b*), 3-month-old (*c*), and 1-year-old (*d*, which approximates the visual acuity of an adult).

Salapatek, 1976). As Figure 5.9 shows, the 2-month-old scans much more of the face than the 1-month-old, and the 2-month-old spends more time examining the internal details of the face. Thus, the 2-month-old gains more information about the world than does the 1-month-old.

Also, as we discussed in the *Research in Life-Span Development* interlude, young infants can perceive certain patterns. With the help of his "looking chamber," Robert Fantz (1963) revealed that even 2- to 3-week-old infants prefer to look at patterned displays rather than nonpatterned displays. For example, they prefer to look at a normal human face rather than one with scrambled features, and prefer to look at a bull's-eye target or black and white stripes rather than a plain circle.

Color Vision   The infant's color vision also improves (Aslin & Lathrop, 2008). By 8 weeks, and possibly by even 4 weeks, infants can discriminate some colors (Kelly, Borchert, & Teller, 1997). By 4 months of age, they have color preferences that mirror adults in some cases, preferring saturated colors such as royal blue over pale blue, for example (Bornstein, 1975). In part, these changes in vision reflect maturation. Experience, however, is also necessary for color vision to develop normally (Sugita, 2004).

Perceptual Constancy   Some perceptual accomplishments are especially intriguing because they indicate that the infant's perception goes beyond the information provided by the senses (Arterberry, 2008; Slater, Field, & Hernandez-Reif, 2007). This is the case in *perceptual constancy*, in which sensory stimulation is changing but perception of the physical world remains constant. If infants did not develop perceptual constancy, each time they saw an object at a different distance or in a different orientation, they would perceive it as a different object. Thus, the development of perceptual constancy allows infants to perceive their world as stable. Two types of perceptual constancy are size constancy and shape constancy.

Size constancy is the recognition that an object remains the same even though the retinal image of the object changes as you move toward or away from the object. The farther away from us an object is, the smaller its image is on our eyes. Thus, the size of an object on the retina is not sufficient to tell us its actual size. For example, you perceive a bicycle standing right in front of you as smaller than the car parked across the street, even though the bicycle casts a large image on your eyes than the car does. When you move away from the bicycle, you do

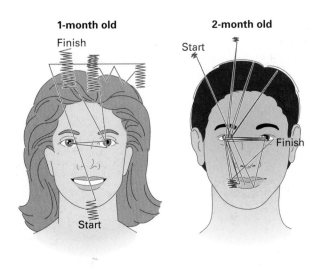

1-month old
Finish

2-month old
Start

Finish

Start

FIGURE 5.9 How 1- and 2-Month-Old Infants Scan the Human Face.

size constancy Recognition that an object remains the same even though the retinal image of the object changes as you move toward or away from the object.

not perceive it to be shrinking even though its image on your retinas shrinks; you perceive its size as constant.

But what about babies? Do they have size constancy? Researchers have found that babies as young as 3 months of age show size constancy (Bower, 1966; Day & McKenzie, 1973). However, at 3 months of age, a baby's ability is not full-blown. It continues to develop until 10 or 11 years of age (Kellman & Banks, 1998).

Shape constancy is the recognition that an object remains the same shape even though its orientation to us changes. Look around the room you are in right now. You likely see objects of varying shapes, such as tables and chairs. If you get up and walk around the room, you will see these objects from different sides and angles. Even though your retinal image of the objects changes as you walk and look, you will still perceive the objects as the same shape.

Do babies have shape constancy? As with size constancy, researchers have found that babies as young as 3 months of age have shape constancy (Bower, 1966; Day & McKenzie, 1973). Three-month-old infants, however, do not have shape constancy for irregularly-shaped objects, such as tilted planes (Cook & Birch, 1984).

Perception of Occluded Objects   Look around the context where you are now. You likely see that some objects are partly occluded by other objects that are in front of them—possibly a desk behind a chair, some books behind a computer, or a car parked behind a tree. Do infants perceive an object as complete when it is occluded by an object in front of it?

In the first two months of postnatal development, infants don't perceive occluded objects as complete, instead perceiving only what is visible (Johnson, 2009a). Beginning at about 2 months of age, infants develop the ability to perceive that occluded objects are whole (Slater, Field, & Hernandez-Reif, 2007). How does perceptual completion develop? In Scott Johnson's (2004, 2009a, b, c; Johnson & others, 2000) research, learning, experience, and self-directed exploration via eye movements play key roles in the development of perceptual completion in young infants.

Many of the objects in the world that are occluded appear and disappear behind closer objects, as when you are walking down the street and see cars appear and disappear behind buildings as they move or you move. Can infants predictively track briefly occluded moving objects? They develop the ability to track briefly occluded moving objects at about 3 to 5 months of age (Bertenthal, 2008). A recent study explored 5- to 9-month-old infants' ability to track moving objects that disappeared gradually behind an occluded partition, disappeared abruptly, or imploded (shrank quickly in size) (Bertenthal, Longo, & Kenny, 2007). In this study, the infants were more likely to accurately predict the moving object when it disappeared gradually rather than abruptly or imploding.

Depth Perception   Might infants even perceive depth? To investigate this question, Eleanor Gibson and Richard Walk (1960) constructed a miniature cliff with a drop-off covered by glass in their laboratory. They placed infants on the edge of this visual cliff and had their mothers coax them to crawl onto the glass (see Figure 5.10). Most infants would not crawl out on the glass, choosing instead to remain on the shallow side, an indication that they could perceive depth.

The 6- to 12-month-old infants in the visual cliff experiment had extensive visual experience. Do younger infants without this experience still perceive depth? Since younger infants do not crawl, this question

shape constancy Recognition that an object remains the same even though its orientation to us changes.

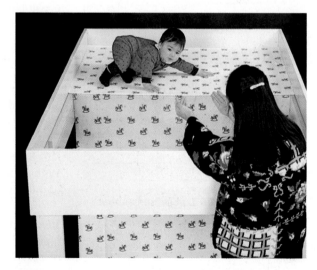

FIGURE 5.10 Examining Infants' Depth Perception on the Visual Cliff. Eleanor Gibson and Richard Walk (1960) found that most infants would not walk out on the glass over the drop-off, which indicated that they had depth perception.

is difficult to answer. Two- to four-month-old infants show differences in heart rate when they are placed directly on the deep side of the visual cliff instead of on the shallow side (Campos, Langer, & Krowitz, 1970). However, these differences might mean that young infants respond to differences in some visual characteristics of the deep and shallow cliffs, with no actual knowledge of depth. Although researchers do not know exactly how early in life infants can perceive depth, we do know that infants develop the ability to use binocular cues to depth by about 3 to 4 months of age.

Nature, Nurture, and the Development of Infants' Visual Perception   There has been a longstanding interest in how strongly infants' visual perception is influenced by nature or nurture (Arterberry, 2008). A recent analysis concluded that much of vision develops from innate (nature) foundations and that the basic foundation of many visual abilities can be detected at birth, while others unfold maturationally (Kellman & Arterberry, 2006). Environmental experiences (nurture) likely refine or calibrate many visual functions, and they may be the driving force behind some functions.

Childhood   Children become increasingly efficient at detecting the boundaries between colors (such as red and orange) at 3 to 4 years of age (Gibson, 1969). When they are about 4 or 5 years old, most children's eye muscles are adequately developed so that they can move their eyes efficiently across a series of letters. Many preschool children are farsighted, unable to see close up as well as they can see far away. By the time they enter the first grade, though, most children can focus their eyes and sustain their attention effectively on close-up objects.

What are the signs of vision problems in children? They include rubbing the eyes, blinking or squinting excessively, appearing irritable when playing games that require good distance vision, shutting or covering one eye, and tilting the head or thrusting it forward when looking at something. A child who shows any of these behaviors should be examined by an ophthalmologist.

After infancy, children's visual expectations about the physical world continue to develop. In one study, 2- to 4½-year-old children were given a task in which the goal was to find a toy ball that had been dropped through an opaque tube (Hood, 1995). As shown in Figure 5.11, if the ball is dropped into the tube at the top right, it will land in the box at the bottom left. However, in this task, most of the 2-year-olds, and even some of the 4-year-olds, persisted in searching in the box immediately beneath the dropping point. For them, gravity ruled and they had failed to perceive the end location of the curved tube.

How do children learn to deal with situations like that in Figure 5.11, and how do they come to understand other laws of the physical world? These questions are addressed by studies of cognitive development, which we discuss in Chapters 6, "Cognitive Developmental Approaches," and 7, "Information Processing."

Adulthood   Vision changes little after childhood until the effects of aging emerge. With aging, declines in visual acuity, color vision, and depth perception occur. Several diseases of the eye also may emerge in aging adults (Cimaroli, 2009).

Visual Acuity   Accommodation of the eye—the eye's ability to focus and maintain an image on the retina—declines most sharply between 40 and 59 years of age. This loss of accommodation is what is commonly known as *presbyopia*. In particular, middle-aged individuals begin to have difficulty viewing close objects. The eye's blood supply also diminishes, although usually not until the fifties or sixties. The reduced blood supply may decrease the visual field's size and account for an increase in the eye's *blind spot,* the location where the retina does not register any light. And there is some evidence that the retina becomes less sensitive

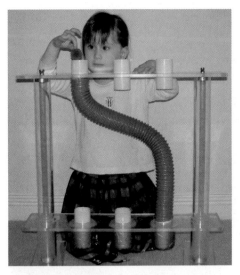

FIGURE 5.11 Visual Expectations About the Physical World. When young children see the ball dropped into the tube, many of them will search for it immediately below the dropping point.

accommodation of the eye   The eye's ability to focus and maintain an image on the retina.

to low levels of illumination (Hughes, 1978). As a result, middle-aged adults begin to have difficulty reading or working in dim light. Presbyopia is correctable with bifocals, reading glasses, laser surgery, or implantation of intraocular lenses (Glasser, 2008; Tewari & Sha, 2008).

In late adulthood, the decline in vision that began for most adults in early or middle adulthood becomes more pronounced (Lindenberger & Ghisletta, 2009; Sharts-Hopko, 2009). Night driving is especially difficult, to some extent because tolerance for glare diminishes (Babizhayev, Minasyan, & Richer, 2009). *Dark adaptation* is slower—that is, older individuals take longer to recover their vision when going from a well-lighted room to semidarkness. The area of the visual field becomes smaller, an indication that the intensity of a stimulus in the peripheral area of the visual field needs to be increased if the stimulus is to be seen. Events taking place away from the center of the visual field might not be detected (Fozard & Gordon-Salant, 2001).

This visual decline often can be traced to a reduction in the quality or intensity of light reaching the retina. At 60 years of age, the retina receives only about one-third as much light as it did at 20 years of age (Scialfa & Kline, 2007). In extreme old age, these changes might be accompanied by degenerative changes in the retina, causing severe difficulty in seeing. Large-print books and magnifiers might be needed in such cases.

One extensive study of visual changes in adults found that the age of older adults was a significant factor in how extensively their visual functioning differed from that of younger adults (Brabyn & others, 2001). Beyond 75, and more so beyond age 85, older adults showed significantly worse performance on a number of visual tasks when compared with young adults and older adults in their sixties and early seventies. The greatest decline in visual perception beyond 75, and especially beyond 85, involved glare. The older adults, especially those 85 and older, fared much worse in being able to see clearly when glare was present, and they took much longer to recover from glare than did younger adults (see Figure 5.12). For example, whereas young adults recover vision following glare in less than 10 seconds, 50 percent of 90-year-olds have not recovered vision after 1.5 minutes.

Older adults also show a decline in motion sensitivity (Schieber, 2006). In terms of practical applications of this decline, researchers have found that compared with younger drivers, older drivers underestimate the time needed for an approaching vehicle to reach their location (Staplin, Lococo, & Sim, 1993). This decline in the accuracy of effortless perceptual guidance means that older adult drivers need to expend cognitive effort when driving, especially when approaching intersections.

Color Vision   Color vision also may decline with age in older adults as a result of the yellowing of the lens of the eye (Scialfa & Kline, 2007). This decline is most likely to occur in the green-blue-violet part of the color spectrum. As a result, older adults may have trouble accurately matching closely related colors such as navy socks and black socks.

Depth Perception   As with many areas of perception, depth perception changes little after infancy until adults become older. Depth perception typically declines in late adulthood; thus, it can be difficult for the older adult to determine how close or far away or how high or low something is (Bian & Andersen, 2009). A decline in depth perception can make steps or street curbs difficult to manage.

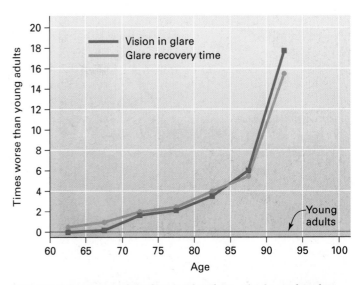

FIGURE 5.12 Rates of Decline in Visual Functioning Related to Glare in Adults of Different Ages. Older adults, especially those 85 and older, fare much worse than younger adults in being able to see clearly when glare is present, and their recovery from glare is much slower. These data were collected from a random sample of community-dwelling older adults living in Marin County, California. For each age, the factor by which the group's median performance was worse than normative values for young adults is shown.

What are some concerns about older adults' driving based on changes in visual perception?

FIGURE 5.13 Macular Degeneration. This simulation of the effect of macular degeneration shows how individuals with this eye disease can see their peripheral field of vision but can't clearly see what is in their central visual field.

A decrease in contrast sensitivity is one factor that diminishes the older adult's ability to perceive depth. Light-dark contrast is produced by the amount of light reflected by surfaces (a light object is brighter than a dark object). The difference in contrast makes objects that contrast with the background easier to see. Compared with younger adults, older adults need sharper contrasts and sharper edges around an object to differentiate it from its background.

Diseases of the Eye   Three diseases that can impair the vision of older adults are cataracts, glaucoma, and macular degeneration:

- **Cataracts** involve a thickening of the lens of the eye that causes vision to become cloudy, opaque, and distorted (Sugimoto, Kuze, & Uji, 2008). By age 70, approximately 30 percent of individuals experience a partial loss of vision due to cataracts. Initially, cataracts can be treated by glasses; if they worsen, a simple surgical procedure can remove them (Chung & others, 2009).

- **Glaucoma** involves damage to the optic nerve because of the pressure created by a buildup of fluid in the eye (Lacey, Cate, & Broadway, 2009). Approximately 1 percent of individuals in their seventies and 10 percent of those in their nineties have glaucoma, which can be treated with eyedrops. If left untreated, glaucoma can ultimately destroy a person's vision (Musch & others, 2009).

- **Macular degeneration** is a disease that involves deterioration of the *macula* of the retina, which corresponds to the focal center of the visual field (see Figure 5.13). Individuals with macular degeneration may have relatively normal peripheral vision but be unable to see clearly what is right in front of them (Redmond & White, 2008; Rovner & others, 2009). It affects 1 in 25 individuals from 66 to 74 years of age and 1 in 6 of those 75 years old and older. One recent study found that cigarette smoking is a contributing factor in macular degeneration (Schmidt & others, 2006). If the disease is detected early, it can be treated with laser surgery (Cook, Patel, & Tufail, 2008). However, macular degeneration is difficult to treat and thus a leading cause of blindness in older adults (Wang & others, 2009).

Hearing

Can the fetus hear? What kind of changes in hearing take place in infancy? When does hearing begin to decline in adulthood?

The Fetus, Infant, and Child   During the last two months of pregnancy, as the fetus nestles in its mother's womb, it can hear sounds such as the mother's voice, music, and so on (Kisilevsky & others, 2009; Morokuma & others, 2008). Two psychologists wanted to find out if a fetus that heard Dr. Seuss' classic story *The Cat in the Hat* while still in the mother's womb would prefer hearing the story after birth (DeCasper & Spence, 1986). During the last months of pregnancy, sixteen women read *The Cat in the Hat* to their fetuses. Then, shortly after they were born, the mothers read either *The Cat in the Hat* or a story with a different rhyme and pace, *The King, the Mice and the Cheese* (which was not read to them during prenatal development). The infants sucked on a nipple in a different way when the mothers read the two stories, suggesting that the infants recognized the pattern and tone of *The Cat in the Hat* (see Figure 5.14). This study illustrates not only that a fetus can hear but also that it has a remarkable ability to learn even before birth.

cataracts A thickening of the lens of the eye that causes vision to become cloudy, opaque, and distorted.

glaucoma Damage to the optic nerve because of the pressure created by a buildup of fluid in the eye.

macular degeneration A vision problem in the elderly that involves deterioration of the macula of the retina.

The fetus can also recognize the mother's voice, as a recent study demonstrated (Kisilevsky & others, 2003). Sixty term fetuses (mean gestational age, 38.4 weeks) were exposed to a tape recording either of their mother or of a female stranger reading a passage. The sounds of the tape were delivered through a loudspeaker held just above the mother's abdomen. Fetal heart rate increased in response to the mother's voice but decreased in response to the stranger's voice.

What kind of changes in hearing take place during infancy? They involve perception of a sound's loudness, pitch, and localization:

- *Loudness.* Immediately after birth, infants cannot hear soft sounds quite as well as adults can; a stimulus must be louder to be heard by a newborn than by an adult (Trehub & others, 1991). For example, an adult can hear a whisper from about 4 to 5 feet away, but a newborn requires that sounds be closer to a normal conversational level to be heard at that distance.

- *Pitch.* Infants are also less sensitive to the pitch of a sound than adults are. *Pitch* is the perception of the frequency of a sound. A soprano voice sounds high pitched, a bass voice low pitched. Infants are less sensitive to low-pitched sounds and are more likely to hear high-pitched sounds (Aslin, Jusczyk, & Pisoni, 1998). By 2 years of age, infants have considerably improved their ability to distinguish sounds with different pitches.

- *Localization.* Even newborns can determine the general location from where a sound is coming, but by 6 months of age they are more proficient at *localizing* sounds or detecting their origins. Their ability to localize sounds continues to improve in the second year (Saffran, Werker, & Werner, 2006).

Most children's hearing is adequate, but early hearing screening in infancy needs to be conducted (Durieux-Smith, Fitzpatrick, & Whittingham, 2008; Korres & others, 2008). About 1 in 1,000 newborns is deaf and 6 in 1,000 have some degree of hearing loss. Hearing aids or surgery can improve hearing for many of them (O'Gorman, Hamid, & Fox, 2005).

Cochlear implants—small, electronic devices that directly stimulate the auditory nerve—are now done routinely for congenitally deaf children, even as early as 12 months of age. Many of the hearing-impaired children who have early cochlear implant surgery show good progress with their speech and understanding others' speech, which allows them to function effectively in a hearing world (Peters & others, 2007).

Otitis media is a middle-ear infection that can impair hearing temporarily. If it continues too long, it can interfere with language development and socialization (Maruthy & Mannarukrishnaiah, 2008). As many as one-third of all U.S. children from birth to 3 years of age have three or more episodes. In some cases, the infection can develop into a more chronic condition in which the middle ear becomes filled with fluid, and this can seriously impair hearing. Treatments for otitis media include antibiotics and placement of a tube in the inner ear to drain fluid (Park & others, 2008; Zhou & others, 2008).

Adolescence   Most adolescents' hearing is excellent. However, anyone who listens to loud sounds for sustained periods of time runs the risk of developing hearing problems. H.E.A.R. (Hearing Education and Awareness for Rockers) was founded by rock musicians whose hearing has been damaged by their exposure to high-volume rock music. Increasingly, rock musicians, such as the group Metallica, wear earplugs when they are playing their music. Listening to music at high levels on iPods and MP3 players also may contribute to hearing problems in youth (Vogel & others, 2008a). In a recent study, adolescents reported that they typically play their MP3 players at maximum volume and were generally aware of the risks of loud music exposure (Vogel & others, 2008b). However, most adolescents expressed low personal vulnerability to loud music exposure. We further

(a)

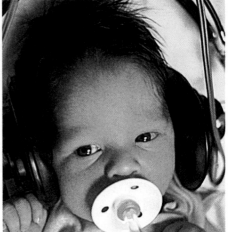
(b)

FIGURE 5.14 Hearing in the Womb.
(*a*) Pregnant mothers read *The Cat in the Hat* to their fetuses during the last few months of pregnancy. (*b*) When they were born, the babies preferred listening to a recording of their mothers reading *The Cat in the Hat*, as evidenced by their sucking on a nipple, rather than another story, *The King, the Mice and the Cheese.*

What are some concerns about adolescents who listen to loud music?

explore adolescents' sense of low personal vulnerability in Chapter 6, "Cognitive Development Approaches."

Adulthood and Aging   Few changes in hearing are believed to take place during the adult years until middle adulthood (Feeny & Sanford, 2004). Hearing can start to decline by the age of 40. Sensitivity to high pitches usually declines first. The ability to hear low-pitched sounds does not seem to decline much in middle adulthood, though. Men usually lose their sensitivity to high-pitched sounds sooner than women do, but this sex difference might be due to men's greater exposure to noise in occupations such as mining and automobile work.

Hearing impairment usually does not become much of an impediment until late adulthood (Fozard, 2000). Only 19 percent of individuals from 45 to 54 years of age experience some type of hearing problem, but for those 75 to 79, the figure reaches 75 percent (Harris, 1975). It has been estimated that 15 percent of the population over the age of 65 is legally deaf, usually due to degeneration of the *cochlea,* the primary neural receptor for hearing in the inner ear (Adams, 2009).

Two devices can be used to minimize the problems linked to hearing loss: (1) hearing aids that amplify sound to reduce middle ear based conductive hearing loss, and (2) cochlear implants that restore some hearing following neurosensory hearing loss (Pauley & others, 2008). Currently, researchers are exploring the use of stem cells as an alternative to the use of cochlear implants (Pauley & others, 2008).

Earlier, in the discussion of vision, we considered research on the importance of the age of older adults in determining the degree of their visual decline. Age also is a factor in the degree of hearing decline in older adults (Lavoie, Mehta, & Thornton, 2008). As indicated in Figure 5.15, the declines in vision and hearing are much greater in individuals 75 years and older than in individuals 65 to 74 years of age (Charness & Bosman, 1992).

A longitudinal study examined changes in hearing over a 10-year period, beginning at 80 years of age (Hietanen & others, 2004). A significant deterioration in hearing sensitivity occurred across the eighties. Although there was a substantial decline in measured hearing ability, self-perceptions of hearing difficulties changed very little across the 10 years. Hearing aids were not used by more than 75 percent of the older adults, an indication that the use of hearing aids in older adults deserves closer scrutiny.

Older adults often don't recognize that they have a hearing problem, deny that they have one, or accept it as a part of growing old (Fowler & Leigh-Paffenroth, 2007). Older women are more likely to seek treatment for their hearing problem than are older adult men (Fowler & Leigh-Paffenroth, 2007).

AGE

Perceptual System	65 to 74 years	75 years and older
Vision	There is a loss of acuity even with corrective lenses. Less transmission of light occurs through the retina (half as much as in young adults).	There is a significant loss of visual acuity and a decrease in the size of the perceived visual field. The ability to see effectively when glare is present decreases as does the recovery of vision after experiencing glare. Visual dysfunction from cataracts and glaucoma increases.
Hearing	There is a significant loss of hearing at high frequencies and some loss at middle frequencies. These losses can be helped by a hearing aid.	There is a significant loss at high and middle frequencies. A hearing aid is more likely to be needed than in young-old age.

FIGURE 5.15 Vision and Hearing Decline in Old Age and Late Old Age.

Vision impairment and hearing loss among older adults can significantly influence their health and functioning (Berry, Kelley-Bock, & Rei, 2008). One study found that 20 percent of individuals 70 years and older had both visual and hearing impairment, and the dual impairment was associated with greater difficulty in performing daily activities, such as preparing meals, shopping, and using a telephone (Brennan, Horowitz, & Su, 2005). Another study revealed that individuals 70 years and older with only hearing loss reported that they were less healthy, engaged in fewer activities, and participated less in social roles than their counterparts without sensory loss (Crews & Campbell, 2004). In this study, older adults with only vision loss showed even more impairment in health and functioning than those with only hearing loss, and those with both vision and hearing loss had the most decline in health and functioning. Hearing loss in older adults is also linked to increased depression (Levy, Slade, & Gill, 2006).

Other Senses

As we develop, we not only obtain information about the world from our eyes and our ears. We also gather information about the world through sensory receptors in our skin, nose, and tongue.

Touch and Pain   Do newborns respond to touch (called *tactile stimulation*)? Can they feel pain? How does the perception of touch and pain change with age?

Infancy   Do newborns respond to touch? Can they feel pain?

Newborns do respond to touch. A touch to the cheek produces a turning of the head; a touch to the lips produces sucking movements.

Newborns can also feel pain (Field & Hernandez-Reif, 2008; Gunnar & Quevado, 2007). If and when you have a son and consider whether he should be circumcised, the issue of an infant's pain perception probably will become important to you. Circumcision usually is performed on young boys about the third day after birth. Will your young son experience pain if he is circumcised when he is 3 days old? An investigation by Megan Gunnar and her colleagues (1987) found that newborn infant males cried intensely during circumcision. The circumcised infants also display amazing resiliency. Within several minutes after the surgery, they can nurse and interact in a normal manner with their mothers. And, if allowed to, the newly circumcised newborns drift into a deep sleep, which seems to serve as a coping mechanism.

For many years, doctors performed operations on newborns without anesthesia. This practice was accepted because of the dangers of anesthesia and because of the supposition that newborns do not feel pain. As researchers demonstrated that newborns can feel pain, the practice of operating on newborns without anesthesia is being challenged. Anesthesia now is used in some circumcisions (Taddio, 2008).

Adulthood   There has been little research on developmental changes in touch and pain after infancy until the middle and late adulthood years. Changes in touch are associated with aging (Harkins & Scott, 2007). One study found that older adults could detect touch much less in the lower extremities (ankles, knees, and so on) than in the upper extremities (wrists, shoulders, and so on) (Corso, 1997). Also, in one study, older adults were much less sensitive to touch on their forefinger and foot than were younger adults (Stevens & others, 2003). For most older adults, though, a decline in touch sensitivity is not problematic (Hoyer & Roodin, 2009). And a recent study revealed that older adults who are blind retain a high level of touch sensitivity, which likely is linked to their use of active touch in their daily lives (Legge & others, 2008).

Older adults are less sensitive to pain and suffer from it less than younger adults do (Gagliese, 2009). Although decreased sensitivity to pain can help older adults

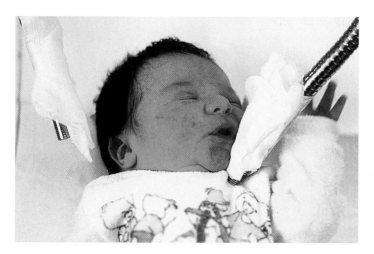

FIGURE 5.16 Newborns' Preference for the Smell of Their Mother's Breast Pad. In the experiment by MacFarlane (1975), 6-day-old infants preferred to smell their mother's breast pad rather than a clean one that had never been used, but 2-day-old infants did not show the preference, indicating that this odor preference requires several days of experience to develop.

cope with disease and injury, it can be harmful if it masks injury or illness that needs to be treated.

Smell Newborns can differentiate odors (Doty & Shah, 2008). The expressions on their faces seem to indicate that they like the way vanilla and strawberry smell but do not like the way rotten eggs and fish smell (Steiner, 1979). In one investigation, 6-day-old infants who were breast fed showed a clear preference for smelling their mother's breast pad rather than a clean breast pad (MacFarlane, 1975) (see Figure 5.16). However, when they were 2 days old, they did not show this preference, an indication that they require several days of experience to recognize this odor.

A decline in sensitivity to odors may occur as early as the twenties and continues to decline through each subsequent decade of life through the nineties (Margran & Boulton, 2005). Beginning in the sixties, the decrease in sensitivity to smells becomes more noticeable to most people (Hawkes, 2006). A majority of individuals 80 years of age and older experience a significant reduction in smell (Lafreiere & Mann, 2009). An fMRI study found that older adults had less activity in the olfactory pathways of the brain than younger adults did, and this lower brain activity was related to a lower sensitivity to the smells of lavender and spearmint (Wang & others, 2005). Also, a decline in the sense of smell can reduce the ability to detect smoke from a fire.

The decline in the olfactory system can reduce older adults' enjoyment of food and their life satisfaction. If elderly individuals need to be encouraged to eat more, compounds that stimulate the olfactory nerve are sometimes added to food. Further, a recent study of 19 to 39, 40 to 59, and 60 and older adults revealed that although adults' ability to detect a smell declined as they got older, the perceived pleasantness of a smell increased in the older group (Markovic & others, 2007).

Taste Sensitivity to taste might be present even before birth (Doty & Shah, 2008). When saccharin was added to the amniotic fluid of a near-term fetus, swallowing increased (Windle, 1940). In one study, even at only 2 hours of age, babies made different facial expressions when they tasted sweet, sour, and bitter solutions (Rosenstein & Oster, 1988) (see Figure 5.17). At about 4 months of age, infants

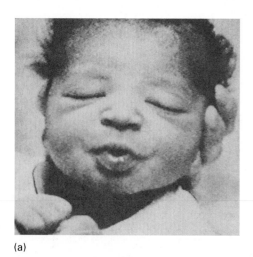
(a)
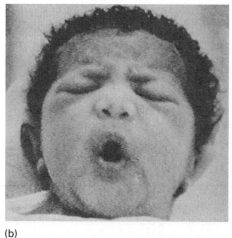
(b)
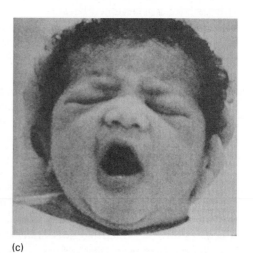
(c)

FIGURE 5.17 Newborns' Facial Responses to Basic Tastes. Facial expressions elicited by (a) a sweet solution, (b) a sour solution, and (c) a bitter solution.

begin to prefer salty tastes, which as newborns they had found to be aversive (Doty & Shah, 2008).

One study found a significant reduction in the ability of older adults to recognize sweet, salty, sour, and bitter tastes (Fukunaga, Uematsu, & Sugimoto, 2005). As with smell, there is less decline in taste in healthy older adults than in unhealthy older adults. However, when even relatively healthy older adults take medications, their taste sensitivity declines (Roberts & Rosenberg, 2006). Many older adults prefer highly seasoned foods (sweeter, spicier, saltier) to compensate for their diminished taste and smell (Hoyer & Roodin, 2009). This preference can lead to increased eating of nonnutritious, highly seasoned "junk food."

Researchers have found that older adults show a greater decline in their sense of smell than in their taste (Schiffman, 2007). Smell, too, declines less in healthy older adults than in their less healthy counterparts.

Intermodal Perception

Imagine that you are playing basketball or tennis. You are experiencing many visual inputs—the ball is coming and going, other players are moving around, and so on. However, you are experiencing many auditory inputs as well: the sound of the ball bouncing or being hit, the grunts and groans, and so on. There is good correspondence between much of the visual and auditory information: When you see the ball bounce, you hear a bouncing sound; when a player stretches to hit a ball, you hear a groan. When you look at and listen to what is going on, you do not experience just the sounds or just the sights; you put all these things together. You experience a unitary episode. This is **intermodal perception,** which involves integrating information from two or more sensory modalities, such as vision and hearing.

How is intermodal perception involved in this context in which a boy is listening to headphones while working on a computer?

Early, exploratory forms of intermodal perception exist even in newborns (Bahrick & Hollich, 2008). For example, newborns turn their eyes and their head toward the sound of a voice or rattle when the sound is maintained for several seconds (Clifton & others, 1981), but the newborn can localize a sound and look at an object only in a crude way (Bechtold, Bushnell, & Salapatek, 1979). These early forms of intermodal perception become sharpened with experience in the first year of life (Hollich, Newman, & Jusczyk, 2005). In one study, infants as young as 3½ months old looked more at their mother when they also heard her voice and longer at their father when they also heard his voice (Spelke & Owsley, 1979). Thus even young infants can coordinate visual-auditory information involving people.

Can young infants put vision and sound together as precisely as adults do? In the first six months, infants have difficulty connecting sensory input from different modes, but in the second half of the first year they show an increased ability to make this connection mentally.

Thus, babies are born into the world with some innate abilities to perceive relations among sensory modalities, but their intermodal abilities improve considerably through experience (Banks, 2005). As with all aspects of development, in perceptual development, nature and nurture interact and cooperate (Banks, 2005).

Nature, Nurture, and Perceptual Development

Now that we have discussed many aspects of perceptual development, let's explore one of developmental psychology's key issues as it relates to perceptual development: the nature-nurture issue. There has been a long-standing interest in how strongly infants' perception is influenced by nature or nurture (Aslin, 2009; Johnson, 2009a, b, c; Slater & others, 2009). In the field of perceptual development, nature proponents are referred to as *nativists* and those who emphasize learning and experience are called *empiricists*.

intermodal perception The ability to integrate information about two or more sensory modalities, such as vision and hearing.

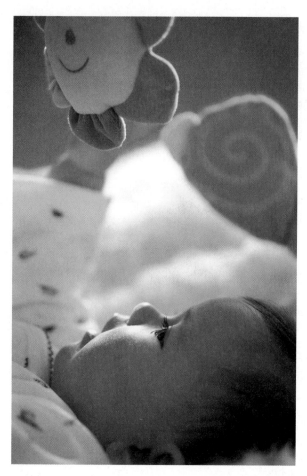

What roles do nature and nurture play in the infant's perceptual development?

In the nativist view, the ability to perceive the world in a competent, organized way is inborn or innate. At the beginning of our discussion of perceptual development, we examined the ecological view of the Gibsons' because it has played such a pivotal role in guiding research in perceptual development. The Gibsons' ecological view leans toward a nativist explanation of perceptual development because it holds that perception is direct and evolved over time to allow the detection of size and shape constancy, a three-dimensional world, intermodal perception, and so on early in infancy. However, the Gibsons' view is not entirely nativist because they emphasized that perceptual development involves distinctive features that are detected at different ages (Slater & others, 2009).

The Gibsons' ecological view is quite different than Piaget's constructivist view, (discussed in Chapter 1, "Introduction,") which reflects an empiricist approach to explaining perceptual development. According to Piaget, much of perceptual development in infancy must await the development of a sequence of cognitive stages for infants to construct more complex perceptual tasks. Thus, in Piaget's view, the ability to perceive size and shape constancy, a three-dimensional world, intermodal perception, and so on develops later in infancy than the Gibsons envision.

Today, it is clear that an extreme empiricist position on perceptual development is unwarranted. Much of early perception develops from innate (nature) foundations, and the basic foundation of many perceptual abilities can be detected in newborns, whereas others unfold maturationally (Arterberry, 2008; Kellman & Arterberry, 2006). However, as infants develop, environmental experiences (nurture) refine or calibrate many perceptual functions, and they may be the driving force behind some functions. The accumulation of experience with and knowledge about their perceptual world contributes to infants' ability to perceive coherent perceptions of people and things (Slater & others, 2009). Thus, a full portrait of perceptual development includes the influence of nature, nuture, and a developing sensitivity to information (Arterberry, 2008).

Review and Reflect: Learning Goal 2

2 **Outline the course of sensory and perceptual development**

REVIEW

- What are sensation and perception?
- What is the ecological view of perception? What are some research methods used to study infant perception?
- How does vision develop?
- How does hearing develop?
- How do touch and pain develop? How does smell develop? How does taste develop?
- What is intermodal perception, and how does it develop?
- What roles do nature and nurture play in perceptual development?

REFLECT

- What would you do to stimulate the hearing of a 1-year-old infant?

3 PERCEPTUAL-MOTOR COUPLING

As we come to the end of this chapter, we return to the important theme of perceptual-motor coupling. The distinction between perceiving and doing has been a time-honored tradition in psychology. However, a number of experts on perceptual and motor development question whether this distinction makes sense (Adolph & Joh, 2009; Bertenthal, 2008; Thelen & Smith, 2006). The main thrust of research in Esther Thelen's dynamic systems approach is to explore how people assemble motor behaviors for perceiving and acting. The main theme of the ecological approach of Eleanor and James J. Gibson is to discover how perception guides action. Action can guide perception, and perception can guide action. Only by moving one's eyes, head, hands, and arms and by moving from one location to another can an individual fully experience his or her environment and learn how to adapt to it. Perception and action are coupled (Corbetta & Snapp-Childs, 2009).

Babies, for example, continually coordinate their movements with perceptual information to learn how to maintain balance, reach for objects in space, and move across various surfaces and terrains (Adolph, Karasik, & Tamis-LeMonda, 2010; Thelen & Smith, 2006). They are motivated to move by what they perceive. Consider the sight of an attractive toy across the room. In this situation, infants must perceive the current state of their bodies and learn how to use their limbs to reach the toy. Although their movements at first are awkward and uncoordinated, babies soon learn to select patterns that are appropriate for reaching their goals.

Equally important is the other part of the perception-action coupling. That is, action educates perception (Adolph, Karasik, & Tamis-LeMonda, 2010). For example, watching an object while exploring it manually helps infants to discriminate its texture, size, and hardness. Locomoting in the environment teaches babies about how objects and people look from different perspectives, or whether surfaces will support their weight. Individuals perceive in order to move and move in order to perceive. Perceptual and motor development do not occur in isolation from each other but instead are coupled.

Perception and action are coupled throughout the human life span.

How do infants develop new perceptual-motor couplings? Recall from our discussion earlier in this chapter that in the traditional view of Gesell, infants' perceptual-motor development is prescribed by a genetic plan to follow a fixed and sequential progression of stages in development. The genetic determination view has been replaced by the dynamic systems view that infants learn new perceptual-motor couplings by assembling skills for perceiving and acting. New perceptual-motor coupling is not passively accomplished; rather, the infant actively develops a skill to achieve a goal within the constraints set by the infant's body and the environment.

Driving a car illustrates the coupling of perceptual and motor skills. The decline in perceptual-motor skills in late adulthood makes driving a car difficult for many older adults (Okonkwo & others, 2008). Drivers over the age of 65 are involved in more accidents than middle-aged adults because of such mistakes as improper turns, not yielding the right of way, and not obeying traffic signs; their younger counterparts are more likely to have accidents because they are speeding (Sterns, Barrett, & Alexander, 1985). Older adults can compensate for declines in perceptual-motor skills by driving shorter distances, choosing less congested routes, and driving only in daylight.

Review and Reflect: Learning Goal 3

 Discuss the connection between perception and action

REVIEW

- How are perception and motor actions coupled in development?

REFLECT

- Describe two examples not given in the text in which perception guides action. Then describe two examples not given in the text in which action guides perception.

Reach Your Learning Goals

Motor, Sensory, and Perceptual Development

1   MOTOR DEVELOPMENT: DESCRIBE HOW MOTOR SKILLS DEVELOP

The Dynamic Systems View

- Thelen's dynamic systems theory seeks to explain how motor behaviors are assembled by infants for perceiving and acting. Perception and action are coupled. According to this theory, motor skills are the result of many converging factors, such as the development of the nervous system, the body's physical properties and its movement possibilities, the goal the child is motivated to reach, and environmental support for the skill. In the dynamic systems view, motor development is far more complex than the result of a genetic blueprint.

Reflexes

- Reflexes—built-in reactions to stimuli—govern the newborn's movements. They include the sucking, rooting, and Moro reflexes. Some reflexes such as sneezing and yawning persist through life; other reflexes disappear several months following birth.

Gross Motor Skills

- Gross motor skills involve large-muscle activities. Key skills developed during infancy include control of posture and walking. Gross motor skills improve dramatically in the childhood years. The peak of physical performance often occurs from 19 to 26 years of age. In general, older adults show a slowing of movement, but motor skills decline less in those who engage in a higher level of physical activity.

Fine Motor Skills

- Fine motor skills involve finely tuned motor actions. The onset of reaching and grasping marks a significant accomplishment. Fine motor skills continue to develop through the childhood years and then experience some decline with aging. Neural noise and strategy have been proposed as possible explanations for the slowing of motor behavior in older adults. Practice and training programs can help minimize decline in aging adults' motor function.

2   SENSORY AND PERCEPTUAL DEVELOPMENT: OUTLINE THE COURSE OF SENSORY AND PERCEPTUAL DEVELOPMENT

What Are Sensation and Perception?

- Sensation occurs when information interacts with sensory receptors. Perception is the interpretation of sensation.

The Ecological View

- Created by the Gibsons, the ecological view states that people directly perceive information that exists in the world. Perception brings people in contact with the environment in order to interact with and adapt to it. Affordances provide opportunities for interaction offered by objects that fit within our capabilities to perform activities. Researchers have developed a number of methods to assess the infant's perception, including the visual preference method (which Fantz used to determine young infants' interest in looking at patterned over nonpatterned displays), habituation and dishabituation, and tracking.

Visual Perception

- The infant's visual acuity increases dramatically in the first year of life. Infants can distinguish some colors by 8 weeks of age, and possibly by as early as 4 weeks. Young infants systematically scan human faces. By 3 months of age, infants show size and shape constancy. At approximately 2 months of age, infants develop the ability to perceive that occluded objects are complete. In Gibson and Walk's classic study, infants as young as 6 months of age had depth perception. Much of vision develops from biological foundations, but environmental experiences can contribute to the development of visual perception. During the preschool years, children become better

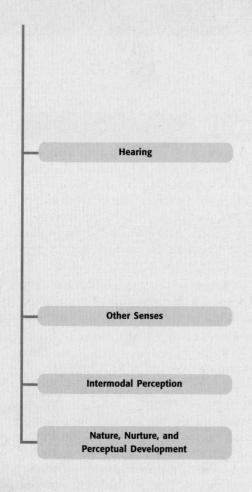

Hearing

Other Senses

Intermodal Perception

Nature, Nurture, and Perceptual Development

at differentiating colors and scanning the visual world. After the early adult years, visual acuity declines. Eye accommodation decreases the most from 40 to 59 years of age. In older adults, the yellowing of the eye's lens reduces color differentiation, and the ability to see the periphery of a visual field declines. Significant declines in visual functioning related to glare characterize adults 75 years and older and even more so those 85 years and older. Three diseases that can impair the vision of older adults are cataracts, glaucoma, and macular degeneration.

• The fetus can hear sounds such as the mother's voice and music during the last two months of pregnancy. Immediately after birth newborns can hear, but their sensory threshold is higher than that of adults. Developmental changes in the perception of loudness, pitch, and localization of sound occur during infancy. Most children's hearing is adequate, but one special concern is otitis media. A concern in adolescence is listening to loud music for prolonged periods of time, which can damage hearing. Hearing can start to decline by the age of 40, especially sensitivity to high-pitched sounds. However, hearing impairment usually doesn't become much of an impediment until late adulthood. About 15 percent of the over-65 population is estimated to be legally deaf. Hearing aids can diminish hearing problems for many older adults.

• Newborns can respond to touch and feel pain. Sensitivity to pain decreases in late adulthood. Newborns can differentiate odors, and sensitivity to taste may be present before birth. Smell and taste may decline in late adulthood, although in healthy individuals the decline is minimal.

• Crude, exploratory forms of intermodal perception—the ability to relate and integrate information from two or more sensory modalities—are present in newborns and become sharpened over the first year of life.

• In perception, nature advocates are referred to as nativists and nurture proponents are called empiricists. The Gibsons' ecological view that has guided much of perceptual development research leans toward a nativist approach but still allows for developmental changes in distinctive features. Piaget's constructivist view leans toward an empiricist approach, emphasizing that many perceptual accomplishments must await the development of cognitive stages in infancy. A strong empiricist approach is unwarranted. A full account of perceptual development includes the roles of nature, nurture, and the developing sensitivity to information.

3   PERCEPTUAL-MOTOR COUPLING: DISCUSS THE CONNECTION BETWEEN PERCEPTION AND ACTION

• Perception and action often are not isolated but rather are coupled. Action can guide perception and perception can guide action. Individuals perceive in order to move and move in order to perceive.

KEY TERMS

dynamic systems theory 172	gross motor skills 174	visual preference method 185	accommodation of the eye 190
reflexes 173	fine motor skills 181	habituation 186	cataracts 192
rooting reflex 173	sensation 184	dishabituation 186	glaucoma 192
sucking reflex 173	perception 184	size constancy 188	macular degeneration 192
Moro reflex 173	ecological view 184	shape constancy 189	intermodal perception 197
grasping reflex 174	affordances 184		

KEY PEOPLE

Esther Thelen 172
T. Berry Brazelton 174
Karen Adolph 175

Eleanor and James
J. Gibson 185
Robert Fantz 185

William James 187
Scott Johnson 189
Richard Walk 189

Megan Gunnar 195

E-LEARNING TOOLS

Connect to **www.mhhe.com/santrockldt5e** to research the answers to complete these exercises. In addition, you'll find a number of other resources and valuable study tools for Chapter 5, "Motor, Sensory, and Perceptual Development," on this Web site.

Taking It to the Net

1. Ten-year-old Kristin is a new member of her soccer league's select team. Kristin's parents are reluctant to allow Kristin to participate in a program that has a reputation for being intensely competitive. If they allow her to participate, what can they do to make it a healthy experience for themselves and for Kristin?

2. Patty's 85-year-old mother, who lives with her and her family, has begun eating less and less. She tells Patty, "Eating is no fun anymore. I can't taste anything." What can Patty do to make meals more appealing for her mother?

Self-Assessment

To think further about how you believe parents should interact with their babies to effectively promote their physical development, complete this self-assessment:

- *My Beliefs About Nurturing a Baby's Physical Development*

Health and Well-Being, Parenting, and Education

Build your decision-making skills by trying your hand at the health and well-being, parenting, and education exercises.

Video Clips

The Online Learning Center includes the following videos for this chapter:

- *Infant Perception*
- *Pattern Perception at 4 Months*

COGNITIVE PROCESSES AND DEVELOPMENT

*Learning is an ornament
in prosperity, a refuge in
adversity.*

—ARISTOTLE
Greek Philosopher, 4th Century B.C.

Children thirst to know and understand. They construct their

own ideas about the world around them and are remarkable for

their curiosity, intelligence, and language. And it is always in

season for the old to learn. In Section 3, you will read four

chapters: "Cognitive Developmental Approaches" (Chapter 6),

"Information Processing" (Chapter 7), "Intelligence" (Chapter 8),

and "Language Development" (Chapter 9).

6

The mind is an enchanting thing.

—MARIANNE MOORE
American Poet, 20th Century

LEARNING GOALS

- ◆ Discuss the key processes and four stages in Piaget's theory.

- ◆ Apply Piaget's theory to education, and evaluate Piaget's theory.

- ◆ Identify the main concepts in Vygotsky's theory, and compare it with Piaget's theory.

- ◆ Describe cognitive changes in adulthood.

COGNITIVE DEVELOPMENTAL APPROACHES

CHAPTER OUTLINE

PREVIEW

Cognitive developmental approaches place a special emphasis on how individuals actively construct their thinking. They also focus heavily on how thinking changes from one point in development to another. In this chapter, we focus on the cognitive developmental approaches of Jean Piaget and Lev Vygotsky. We also explore the possibility that adults think in a qualitatively more advanced way than adolescents do.

1 PIAGET'S THEORY OF COGNITIVE DEVELOPMENT

Processes of Development	Sensorimotor Stage	Preoperational Stage	Concrete Operational Stage	Formal Operational Stage

Piaget is shown here with his family. Piaget's careful observations of his three children—Lucienne, Laurent, and Jacqueline—contributed to the development of his cognitive theory.

Poet Nora Perry asks, "Who knows the thoughts of a child?" As much as anyone, Piaget knew. Through careful observations of his own three children—Laurent, Lucienne, and Jacqueline—and observations of and interviews with other children, Piaget changed perceptions of the way children think about the world.

Piaget's theory is a general, unifying story of how biology and experience sculpt cognitive development. Piaget thought that, just as our physical bodies have structures that enable us to adapt to the world, we build mental structures that help us to adapt to the world. *Adaptation* involves adjusting to new environmental demands. Piaget stressed that children actively construct their own cognitive worlds; information is not just poured into their minds from the environment. He sought to discover how children at different points in their development think about the world and how systematic changes in their thinking occur.

Processes of Development

What processes do children use as they construct their knowledge of the world? Piaget developed several concepts to answer this question; especially important are schemes, assimilation, accommodation, organization, equilibrium, and equilibration.

Schemes   As the infant or child seeks to construct an understanding of the world, said Piaget (1954), the developing brain creates schemes. These are actions or mental representations that organize knowledge. In Piaget's theory, behavioral schemes (physical activities) characterize infancy and mental schemes (cognitive activities) develop in childhood (Lamb, Bornstein, & Teti, 2002). A baby's schemes are structured by simple actions that can be performed on objects such as sucking, looking, and grasping. Older children have schemes that include strategies and plans for solving problems. By the time we have reached adulthood, we have constructed an enormous number of diverse schemes, ranging from how to drive a car to balancing a budget to the concept of fairness.

Assimilation and Accommodation   To explain how children use and adapt their schemes, Piaget offered two concepts: assimilation and accommodation. **Assimilation** occurs when children use their existing schemes to deal with new information or experiences. Think about a toddler who has learned the word *car* to identify the family's car. The toddler might call all moving vehicles on roads "cars," including

schemes In Piaget's theory, actions or mental representations that organize knowledge.

assimilation Piagetian concept in which children use existing schemes to incorporate new information.

motorcycles and trucks; the child has assimilated these objects to his or her existing scheme. **Accommodation** occurs when children adjust their schemes to take new information and experiences into account. The child soon learns that motorcycles and trucks are not cars and fine-tunes the category to exclude motorcycles and trucks, accommodating the scheme.

Assimilation and accommodation operate even in very young infants. New-borns reflexively suck everything that touches their lips; they assimilate all sorts of objects into their sucking scheme. By sucking different objects, they learn about their taste, texture, shape, and so on. After several months of experience, though, they construct their understanding of the world differently. Some objects, such as fingers and the mother's breast, can be sucked, and others, such as fuzzy blankets, should not be sucked. In other words, they accommodate their sucking scheme.

Organization   To make sense out of their world, said Piaget, children cognitively organize their experiences. **Organization** in Piaget's theory is the grouping of isolated behaviors and thoughts into a higher-order system. Continual refinement of this organization is an inherent part of development. A child who has only a vague idea about how to use a hammer may also have a vague idea about how to use other tools. After learning how to use each one, the child relates these uses, organizing his knowledge.

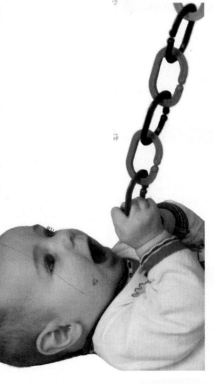

In Piaget's view, what is a scheme? What schemes might this young infant be displaying?

Equilibration and Stages of Development   Assimilation and accommodation always take the child to a higher ground, according to Piaget. In trying to understand the world, the child inevitably experiences cognitive conflict, or *disequilibrium*. That is, the child is constantly faced with counterexamples to his or her existing schemes and with inconsistencies. For example, if a child believes that pouring water from a short and wide container into a tall and narrow container changes the amount of water, then the child might be puzzled by where the "extra" water came from and whether there is actually more water to drink. The puzzle creates disequilibrium; for Piaget, an internal search for equilibrium creates motivation for change. The child assimilates and accommodates, adjusting old schemes, developing new schemes, and organizing and reorganizing the old and new schemes. Eventually, the organization is fundamentally different from the old organization; it is a new way of thinking.

In short, according to Piaget, children constantly assimilate and accommodate as they seek equilibrium. There is considerable movement between states of cognitive equilibrium and disequilibrium as assimilation and accommodation work in concert to produce cognitive change. **Equilibration** is the name Piaget gave to this mechanism by which children shift from one stage of thought to the next.

The result of these processes, according to Piaget, is that individuals go through four stages of development. A different way of understanding the world makes one stage more advanced than another. Cognition is *qualitatively* different in one stage compared with another. In other words, the way children reason at one stage is different from the way they reason at another stage. Figure 6.1 provides a brief description of the four Piagetian stages.

Sensorimotor Stage

The **sensorimotor stage** lasts from birth to about 2 years of age. In this stage, infants construct an understanding of the world by coordinating sensory experiences (such as seeing and hearing) with physical, motoric actions—hence the term "sensorimotor." At the beginning of this stage, newborns have little more than reflexes with which to work. At the end of the sensorimotor stage, 2-year-olds can produce

accommodation Piagetian concept of adjusting schemes to fit new information and experiences.

organization Piagetian concept of grouping isolated behaviors and thoughts into a higher-order, more smoothly functioning cognitive system.

equilibration A mechanism that Piaget proposed to explain how children shift from one stage of thought to the next.

sensorimotor stage The first of Piaget's stages, which lasts from birth to about 2 years of age; infants construct an understanding of the world by coordinating sensory experiences (such as seeing and hearing) with physical, motoric actions.

Sensorimotor Stage	**0–2 Years**
Infants gain knowledge of the world from the physical actions they perform on it. Infants coordinate sensory experiences with these physical actions. An infant progresses from reflexive, instinctual action at birth to the beginning of symbolic thought toward the end of the stage.	

Preoperational Stage	**2–7 Years**
The child begins to use mental representations to understand the world. Symbolic thinking, reflected in the use of words and images, is used in this mental representation, which goes beyond the connection of sensory information with physical action. However, there are some constraints on the child's thinking at this stage, such as egocentrism and centration.	

Concrete Operational Stage	**7–11 Years**
The child can now reason logically about concrete events, understands the concept of conservation, organizes objects into hierarchical classes (classification), and places objects in ordered series (seriation).	

Formal Operational Stage	**11–15 Years**
The adolescent reasons in more abstract, idealistic, and logical (hypothetical-deductive) ways.	

FIGURE 6.1 Piaget's Four Stages of Cognitive Development.

I wish I could travel by the road that crosses the baby's mind, and out beyond all bounds; where messengers run errands for no cause between the kingdoms of kings of no history; where reason makes kites of her laws and flies them, and truth sets facts free from its fetters.

—Rabindranath Tagore
Bengali Poet and Essayist, 20th Century

complex sensorimotor patterns and use primitive symbols. We first discuss Piaget's descriptions of how infants develop. Later we consider criticisms of his view.

Substages Piaget divided the sensorimotor stage into six substages: (1) simple reflexes; (2) first habits and primary circular reactions; (3) secondary circular reactions; (4) coordination of secondary circular reactions; (5) tertiary circular reactions, novelty, and curiosity; and (6) internalization of schemes (see Figure 6.2).

Simple reflexes, the first sensorimotor substage, corresponds to the first month after birth. In this substage, sensation and action are coordinated primarily through reflexive behaviors, such as rooting and sucking. Soon the infant produces behaviors that resemble reflexes in the absence of the usual stimulus for the reflex. For example, a newborn will suck a nipple or bottle only when it is placed directly in the baby's mouth or touched to the lips. But soon the infant might suck when a bottle or nipple is only nearby. Even in the first month of life, the infant is initiating action and actively structuring experiences.

First habits and primary circular reactions is the second sensorimotor substage, which develops between 1 and 4 months of age. In this substage, the infant coordinates sensation and two types of schemes: habits and primary circular reactions. A *habit* is a scheme based on a reflex that has become completely separated from its eliciting stimulus. For example, infants in substage 1 suck when bottles are put to their lips or when they see a bottle. Infants in substage 2 might suck even when no bottle is present. A *circular reaction* is a repetitive action.

A *primary circular reaction* is a scheme based on the attempt to reproduce an event that initially occurred by chance. For example, suppose an infant accidentally sucks his fingers when they are placed near his mouth. Later, he searches for his fingers to suck them again, but the fingers do not cooperate because the infant cannot coordinate visual and manual actions.

Habits and circular reactions are stereotyped—that is, the infant repeats them the same way each time. During this substage, the infant's own body remains the infant's center of attention. There is no outward pull by environmental events.

Secondary circular reactions is the third sensorimotor substage, which develops between 4 and 8 months of age. In this substage, the infant becomes more object oriented, moving beyond preoccupation with the self. The infant's schemes are not intentional or goal-directed, but they are repeated because of their consequences. By chance, an infant might shake a rattle. The infant repeats this action for the sake of its fascination. This is a *secondary circular reaction:* an action repeated because of its consequences. The infant also imitates some simple actions, such as the baby talk or burbling of adults, and some physical gestures. However, the baby imitates only actions that she is already able to produce.

Coordination of secondary circular reactions is Piaget's fourth sensorimotor substage, which develops between 8 and 12 months of age. To progress into this substage, the infant must coordinate vision and touch, hand and eye. Actions become more outwardly directed. Significant changes during this substage involve the coordination of schemes and intentionality. Infants readily combine and recombine previously learned schemes in a coordinated way. They might look at an object and grasp it simultaneously, or they might visually inspect a toy, such as a rattle, and finger it simultaneously, exploring it tactilely. Actions are even more outwardly directed than before. Related to this coordination is the second achievement—the presence of intentionality. For example, infants might manipulate a stick in order to bring a desired toy within reach, or they might knock over one block to reach and play with another one.

Substage	Age	Description	Example
1 Simple reflexes	Birth to 1 month	Coordination of sensation and action through reflexive behaviors.	Rooting, sucking, and grasping reflexes; newborns suck reflexively when their lips are touched.
2 First habits and primary circular reactions	1 to 4 months	Coordination of sensation and two types of schemes: habits (reflex) and primary circular reactions (reproduction of an event that initially occurred by chance). Main focus is still on the infant's body.	Repeating a body sensation first experienced by chance (sucking thumb, for example); then infants might accommodate actions by sucking their thumb differently than they suck on a nipple.
3 Secondary circular reactions	4 to 8 months	Infants become more object-oriented, moving beyond self-preoccupation; repeat actions that bring interesting or pleasurable results.	An infant coos to make a person stay near; as the person starts to leave, the infant coos again.
4 Coordination of secondary circular reactions	8 to 12 months	Coordination of vision and touch—hand-eye coordination; coordination of schemes and intentionality.	Infant manipulates a stick in order to bring an attractive toy within reach.
5 Tertiary circular reactions, novelty, and curiosity	12 to 18 months	Infants become intrigued by the many properties of objects and by the many things they can make happen to objects; they experiment with new behavior.	A block can be made to fall, spin, hit another object, and slide across the ground.
6 Internalization of schemes	18 to 24 months	Infants develop the ability to use primitive symbols and form enduring mental representations.	An infant who has never thrown a temper tantrum before sees a playmate throw a tantrum; the infant retains a memory of the event, then throws one himself the next day.

FIGURE 6.2 Piaget's Six Substages of Sensorimotor Development.

Tertiary circular reactions, novelty, and curiosity is Piaget's fifth sensorimotor substage, which develops between 12 and 18 months of age. In this substage, infants become intrigued by the many properties of objects and by the many things that they can make happen to objects. A block can be made to fall, spin, hit another object, and slide across the ground. *Tertiary circular reactions* are schemes in which the infant purposely explores new possibilities with objects, continually doing new things to them and exploring the results. Piaget says that this stage marks the starting point for human curiosity and interest in novelty.

Internalization of schemes is Piaget's sixth and final sensorimotor substage, which develops between 18 and 24 months of age. In this substage, the infant develops the ability to use primitive symbols. For Piaget, a *symbol* is an internalized sensory image or word that represents an event. Primitive symbols permit the infant to think about concrete events without directly acting them out or perceiving them. Moreover, symbols allow the infant to manipulate and transform the represented events in simple ways. In a favorite Piagetian example, Piaget's young daughter saw a matchbox being opened and closed. Later, she mimicked the event by opening and closing her mouth. This was an obvious expression of her image of the event.

Object Permanence Imagine how chaotic and unpredictable your life would be if you could not distinguish between yourself and your world. This is what the life of a newborn must be like, according to Piaget. There is no differentiation between the self and world; objects have no separate, permanent existence.

This 17-month-old is in Piaget's stage of tertiary circular reactions. *What might the infant do to suggest that she is in this stage?*

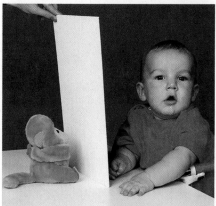

FIGURE 6.3 Object Permanence. Piaget argued that object permanence is one of infancy's landmark cognitive accomplishments. For this 5-month-old boy, "out of sight" is literally out of mind. The infant looks at the toy monkey (*top*), but when his view of the toy is blocked (*bottom*), he does not search for it. Several months later, he will search for the hidden toy monkey, reflecting the presence of object permanence.

By the end of the sensorimotor period, objects are both separate from the self and permanent. **Object permanence** is the understanding that objects continue to exist even when they cannot be seen, heard, or touched. Acquiring the sense of object permanence is one of the infant's most important accomplishments, according to Piaget.

How can anyone know whether an infant has a sense of object permanence or not? The principal way that object permanence is studied is by watching an infant's reaction when an interesting object disappears (see Figure 6.3). If infants search for the object, it is assumed that they believe it continues to exist.

Object permanence is just one of the basic concepts about the physical world developed by babies. To Piaget, children, even infants, are much like little scientists, examining the world to see how it works. The *Research in Life-Span Development* interlude describes some of the ways in which adult scientists try to discover what these "baby scientists" are finding out about the world.

Research in Life-Span Development

OBJECT PERMANENCE AND CAUSALITY

Two accomplishments of infants that Piaget examined were the development of object permanence and the child's understanding of causality. Let's examine two research studies that address these topics.

In both studies, Renée Baillargeon and her colleagues used a research method that involves *violation of expectations*. In this method, infants see an event happen as it normally would. Then, the event is changed, often in a way that creates a physically impossible event. If infants look longer at the changed event, their reaction indicates they are surprised by it. In other words, it is interpreted to indicate that the infant had certain expectations about the world that were violated.

In one study focused on object permanence, researchers showed infants a toy car that moved down an inclined track, disappeared behind a screen, and then reemerged at the other end, still on the track (Baillargeon & DeVos, 1991) (see Figure 6.4a). After this sequence was repeated several times, something different occurred: A toy mouse was placed *behind* the tracks but was hidden by the screen while the car rolled by (see Figure 6.4b). This was the "possible" event. Then, the researchers created an "impossible event": The toy mouse was placed *on* the tracks but was secretly removed after the screen was lowered so that the car seemed to go through the mouse (see Figure 6.4c). In this study, infants as young as 3½ months of age looked longer at the

FIGURE 6.4 Using the Violation of Expectations Method to Study Object Permanence In Infants. If infants looked longer at (c) than at (b), researchers reasoned that the impossible event in (c) violated the infants' expectations and that they remembered that the toy mouse existed.

object permanence The Piagetian term for one of an infant's most important accomplishments: understanding that objects continue to exist even when they cannot directly be seen, heard, or touched.

(a) Practice (No toy mouse)

(b) Possible event (Toy mouse behind the track)

(c) Impossible event (Toy mouse on the track)

impossible event than at the possible event, an indication that they were surprised by it. Their surprise suggested that they remembered not only that the toy mouse still existed (object permanence) but where it was located.

Another study focused on the infant's understanding of causality (Kotovsky & Baillargeon, 1994). In this research, a cylinder rolls down a ramp and hits a toy bug at the bottom of the ramp. By 5½ and 6½ months of age, after infants have seen how far the bug will be pushed by a medium-sized cylinder, their reactions indicate that they understand that the bug will roll farther if it is hit by a large cylinder than if it is hit by a small cylinder. Thus, by the middle of the first year of life, these infants understood that the size of a moving object determines how far it will move a stationary object that it collides with.

In Baillargeon's (2008; Baillargeon & others, 2009) view, infants have a preadapted, innate bias called the *principle of persistence* that explains their assumption that objects don't change their properties—including how solid they are, their location, their color, and their form—unless some external factor (a person moves the object, for example) obviously intervenes. Shortly, we revisit the extent to which nature and nurture are at work in the changes that take place in the infant's cognitive development.

The research findings discussed in this interlude and other research indicate that infants develop object permanence earlier than Piaget proposed (Baillargeon & others, 2009; Luo, Kaufman, & Baillargeon, 2009). Indeed, as you will see in the next section, a major theme of infant cognitive development today is that infants are more cognitively competent than Piaget envisioned.

Evaluating Piaget's Sensorimotor Stage   Piaget opened up a new way of looking at infants with his view that their main task is to coordinate their sensory impressions with their motor activity. However, the infant's cognitive world is not as neatly packaged as Piaget portrayed it, and some of Piaget's explanations for the cause of change are debated. In the past several decades, sophisticated experimental techniques have been devised to study infants, and there have been a large number of research studies on infant development. Much of the new research suggests that Piaget's view of sensorimotor development needs to be modified (Baillargeon & others, 2009; Johnson, 2009a, b, c; Spelke & Kinzler, 2009; Quinn & Bhatt, 2009; Woodward & Needham, 2009).

The A-not-B Error   One modification concerns Piaget's claim that certain processes are crucial in transitions from one stage to the next. The data do not always support his explanations. For example, in Piaget's theory, an important feature in the progression into substage 4, *coordination of secondary circular reactions*, is an infant's inclination to search for a hidden object in a familiar location rather than to look for the object in a new location. For example, if a toy is hidden twice, initially at location A and subsequently at location B, 8- to 12-month-old infants search initially and correctly at location A. But, when the toy is subsequently hidden at location B, they make the mistake of continuing to search for it at location A. **A-not-B error** (also called AB̄ error) is the term used to describe this common mistake. Older infants are less likely to make the A-not-B error because their concept of object permanence is more complete.

Researchers have found, however, that the A-not-B error does not show up consistently (Sophian, 1985). The evidence indicates that A-not-B errors are sensitive to the delay between hiding the object at B and the infant's attempt to find it (Diamond, 1985). Thus, the A-not-B error might be due to a failure in memory. Another explanation is that infants tend to repeat a previous motor behavior (Clearfield & others, 2006; Smith, 1999).

Perceptual Development and Expectations   A number of theorists, such as Eleanor Gibson (2001) and Elizabeth Spelke (1991; Spelke & Kinzler, 2007, 2009), argue

A-not-B error Also called AB̄ error; this occurs when infants make the mistake of selecting the familiar hiding place (A) rather than the new hiding place (B̄) as they progress into substage 4 in Piaget's sensorimotor stage.

that infants' perceptual abilities are highly developed very early in development. Spelke argues that young infants interpret the world as having predictable occurrences. For example, in Chapter 5, "Motor, Sensory, and Perceptual Development," we discussed research that demonstrated the presence of intermodal perception—the ability to coordinate information from two or more sensory modalities, such as vision and hearing—by 3½ months of age, much earlier than Piaget would have predicted (Spelke & Owsley, 1979).

Research also suggests that infants develop the ability to understand how the world works at a very early age (Baillargeon & others, 2009). For example, by the time they are 3 months of age, infants develop expectations about future events. Marshall Haith and his colleagues (Canfield & Haith, 1991; Haith, Hazen, & Goodman, 1988) presented pictures to infants in either a regular alternating sequence (such as left, right, left, right) or an unpredictable sequence (such as right, right, left, right). When the sequence was predictable, the 3-month-old infants began to anticipate the location of the picture, looking at the side on which it was expected to appear. However, younger infants did not develop expectations about where a picture would be presented.

What revisions in Piaget's theory of sensorimotor development do contemporary researchers conclude need to be made?

What kinds of expectations do infants form? Are we born expecting the world to obey basic physical laws, such as gravity, or when do we learn about how the world works? Experiments by Elizabeth Spelke (1991, 2000; Spelke & Hespos, 2001) have addressed these questions. She placed babies before a puppet stage and showed them a series of actions that are unexpected if you know how the physical world works—for example, one ball seemed to roll through a solid barrier, another seemed to leap between two platforms, and a third appeared to hang in midair (Spelke, 1979). Spelke measured and compared the babies' looking times for unexpected and expected actions. She concluded that, by 4 months of age, even though infants do not yet have the ability to talk about objects, move around objects, manipulate objects, or even see objects with high resolution, they expect objects to be solid and continuous. However, at 4 months of age, infants do not expect an object to obey gravitational constraints (Spelke & others, 1992). Similarly, research by Renée Baillargeon (1995, 2004) documents that infants as young as 3 to 4 months expect objects to be *substantial* (in the sense that other objects cannot move through them) and *permanent* (in the sense that objects continue to exist when they are hidden).

In sum, researchers such as Baillargeon and Spelke conclude that infants see objects as bounded, unitary, solid, and separate from their background, possibly at birth or shortly thereafter, but definitely by 3 to 4 months of age—much earlier than Piaget envisioned. Young infants still have much to learn about objects, but the world appears both stable and orderly to them.

However, some critics, such as Andrew Meltzoff (2008; Meltzoff & Moore, 1998), argue that Spelke's and Baillargeon's research relies on how long infants look at unexpected events and thus assess infants' *perceptual expectations* about where and when objects will reappear rather than tapping their *knowledge* about where the objects are when they are out of sight. Meltzoff points out that whether infants act on their perception is an important aspect of assessing object permanence and states that it does not appear that young infants can act on the information. Thus, Meltzoff (2008) concludes that whether longer looking time is a valid measure of object permanence and how early infants develop object permanence remain controversial.

The Nature-Nurture Issue   In considering the big issue of whether nature or nature plays the more important role in infant development, Elizabeth Spelke (Spelke, 2000; Spelke & Kinzler, 2007, 2009) comes down clearly on the side of nature. Spelke endorses a **core knowledge approach,** which states that infants are born

*I*nfants know that objects are substantial and permanent at an earlier age than Piaget envisioned.

—Renée Baillargeon
Contemporary Psychologist, University of Illinois

core knowledge approach States that infants are born with domain-specific innate knowledge systems. Among these domain-specific knowledge systems are those involving space, number sense, object permanence, and language.

with domain-specific innate knowledge systems. Among these domain-specific knowledge systems are those involving space, number sense, object permanence, and language. Strongly influenced by evolution, the core knowledge domains are theorized to be prewired to allow infants to make sense of their world. After all, Spelke concludes, how could infants possibly grasp the complex world in which they live if they didn't come into the world equipped with core sets of knowledge. In this approach, the innate core knowledge domains form a foundation around which more mature cognitive functioning and learning develop. The core knowledge approach argues that Piaget greatly underestimated the cognitive abilities of infants, especially young infants.

An intriguing domain of core knowledge that has been investigated in young infants is whether they have a sense of number. Spelke concludes that they do. Using the violation of expectations method discussed in the *Research in Life-Span Development* interlude, Karen Wynn (1992) conducted an early experiment on infants' sense of number. Five-month-old infants were shown one or two Mickey Mouse dolls on a puppet stage. Then the experimenter hid the doll(s) behind a screen and visibly removed or added one. Next, when the screen was lifted, the infants looked longer when they saw the incorrect number of dolls. Spelke and her colleagues (Hyde & Spelke, 2009; Lipton & Spelke, 2004; Spelke & Kinzler, 2007; Xu, Spelke, & Goddard, 2005) have found that infants can distinguish between different numbers of objects, actions, and sounds. Efforts to find further support for infants' sense of number are extending to assessments of brain activity. For example, a recent study of 3-month-olds observing changes either in the identity of objects or the number of objects revealed that changes in the type of objects activated a region of the brain's temporal lobe, whereas changes in the number of objects activated an additional region of the parietal lobe (Izard, Dehaene-Lambertz, & Dehaene, 2008). In older children and adults, number sense activates the same region of the parietal lobe activated in the 3-month-old infants in this study.

Not everyone agrees with Spelke's conclusions about young infants' math skills (Cohen, 2002). One criticism is that infants in the number experiments are merely responding to changes in the display that violated their expectations.

In criticizing the core knowledge approach, British developmental psychologist Mark Johnson (2008) says that the infants Spelke assesses in her research already have accumulated hundreds, and in some cases even thousands, of hours of experience in grasping what the world is about, which gives considerable room for the environment's role in the development of infant cognition (Highfield, 2008). According to Johnson (2008), infants likely come into the world with "soft biases to perceive and attend to different aspects of the environment, and to learn about the world in particular ways." Although debate about the cause and course of infant cognitive development continues, most developmentalists today agree that Piaget underestimated the early cognitive accomplishments of infants and that both nature and nurture are involved in infants' cognitive development.

Conclusions   In sum, many researchers conclude that Piaget wasn't specific enough about how infants learn about their world and that infants, especially young infants, are more competent than Piaget thought (Baillargeon & others, 2009; Diamond, Casey, & Munakata, 2010; Spelke & Kinzler, 2009). As they have examined the specific ways that infants learn, the field of infant cognition has become very specialized. There are many researchers working on different questions, with no general theory emerging that can connect all of the different findings (Nelson, 1999). Their theories often are local theories, focused on specific research questions, rather than grand theories like Piaget's (Kuhn, 1998). If there is a unifying theme, it is that investigators in infant development seek to understand more precisely how developmental changes in cognition take place and the big issue of nature and nurture (Aslin, 2009; Woodward & Needham, 2009). As they seek to answer more precisely the contributions of nature and nurture to infant development, researchers face the

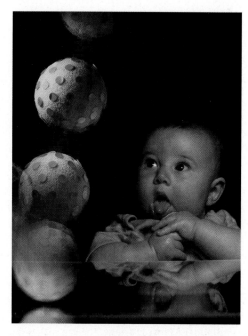

A 4-month-old in Elizabeth Spelke's infant perception laboratory is tested to determine if she knows that an object in motion will not stop in midair. Spelke concluded that at 4 months babies don't expect objects like these balls to obey gravitational constraints, but that they do expect objects to be solid and continuous. Research by Spelke, Renée Baillargeon, and others suggest that infants develop an ability to understand how the world works earlier than Piaget envisioned. However, critics such as Andrew Meltzoff fault their research and conclude there is still controversy about how early some infant cognitive accomplishments occur.

difficult task of determining whether the course of acquiring information, which is very rapid in some domains, is best accounted for by an innate set of biases (that is, core knowledge), or by the extensive input of environmental experiences to which the infant is exposed (Aslin, 2009).

Preoperational Stage

The cognitive world of the preschool child is creative, free, and fanciful. The imagination of preschool children works overtime, and their mental grasp of the world improves. Piaget described the preschool child's cognition as preoperational. What did he mean?

The **preoperational stage,** which lasts from approximately 2 to 7 years of age, is the second Piagetian stage. In this stage, children begin to represent the world with words, images, and drawings. They form stable concepts and begin to reason. At the same time, the young child's cognitive world is dominated by egocentrism and magical beliefs.

Because Piaget called this stage "preoperational," it might sound like an unimportant waiting period. Not so. However, the label *preoperational* emphasizes that the child does not yet perform **operations,** which are reversible mental actions that allow children to do mentally what before they could do only physically. Mentally adding and subtracting numbers are examples of operations. *Preoperational thought* is the beginning of the ability to reconstruct in thought what has been established in behavior. It can be divided into two substages: the symbolic function substage and the intuitive thought substage.

The Symbolic Function Substage The **symbolic function substage** is the first substage of preoperational thought, occurring roughly between the ages of 2 and 4. In this substage, the young child gains the ability to mentally represent an object that is not present. This ability vastly expands the child's mental world (Carlson & Zelazo, 2008). Young children use scribble designs to represent people, houses, cars, clouds, and so on; they begin to use language and engage in pretend play. However, although young children make distinct progress during this substage, their thought still has important limitations, two of which are egocentrism and animism.

Egocentrism is the inability to distinguish between one's own perspective and someone else's perspective. Piaget and Barbel Inhelder (1969) initially studied young children's egocentrism by devising the three mountains task (see Figure 6.5). The child walks around the model of the mountains and becomes familiar with what the mountains look like from different perspectives and can see that there are different objects on the mountains. The child is then seated on one side of the table on which the mountains are placed. The experimenter moves a doll to different locations around the table, at each location asking the child to select from a series of photos the one photo that most accurately reflects the view that the doll is seeing. Children in the preoperational stage often pick their own view rather than the

preoperational stage The second Piagetian developmental stage, which lasts from about 2 to 7 years of age; children begin to represent the world with words, images, and drawings.

operations Reversible mental actions that allow children to do mentally what before they had done only physically.

symbolic function substage The first substage of preoperational thought, occurring roughly between the ages of 2 and 4. In this substage, the young child gains the ability to represent mentally an object that is not present.

egocentrism The inability to distinguish between one's own and someone else's perspective; an important feature of preoperational thought.

FIGURE 6.5 The Three Mountains Task.
The mountain model on the far left shows the child's perspective from view A, where he or she is sitting. The four squares represent photos showing the mountains from four different viewpoints of the model—A, B, C, and D. The experimenter asks the child to identify the photo in which the mountains look as they would from position B. To identify the photo correctly, the child has to take the perspective of a person sitting at spot B. Invariably, a child who thinks in a preoperational way cannot perform this task. When asked what a view of the mountains looks like from position B, the child selects Photo 1, taken from location A (the child's own view at the time) instead of Photo 2, the correct view.

Model of Mountains

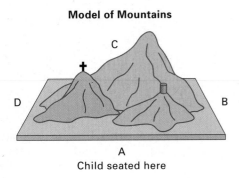

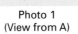

| Photo 1 | Photo 2 | Photo 3 | Photo 4 |
| (View from A) | (View from B) | (View from C) | (View from D) |

doll's view. Preschool children frequently show the ability to take another's perspective on some tasks but not others.

Animism, another limitation of preoperational thought, is the belief that inanimate objects have lifelike qualities and are capable of action (Gelman & Opfer, 2004). A young child might show animism by saying, "That tree pushed the leaf off, and it fell down" or "The sidewalk made me mad; it made me fall down." A young child who uses animism fails to distinguish the appropriate occasions for using human and nonhuman perspectives.

Possibly because young children are not very concerned about reality, their drawings are fanciful and inventive. Suns are blue, skies are yellow, and cars float on clouds in their symbolic, imaginative world. One 3½-year-old looked at a scribble he had just drawn and described it as a pelican kissing a seal (see Figure 6.6a). The symbolism is simple but strong, like abstractions found in some modern art. Twentieth-century Spanish artist Pablo Picasso commented, "I used to draw like Raphael but it has taken me a lifetime to draw like young children." In the elementary school years, a child's drawings become more realistic, neat, and precise (see Figure 6.6b). Suns are yellow, skies are blue, and cars travel on roads (Winner, 1986).

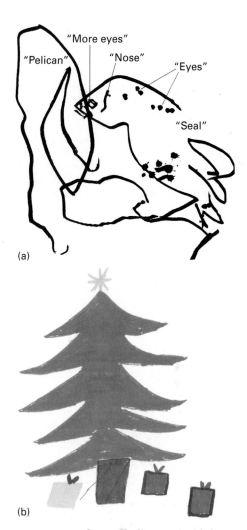

(a)

(b)

FIGURE 6.6 The Symbolic Drawings of Young Children. (*a*) A 3½-year-old's symbolic drawing. Halfway into this drawing, the 3½-year-old artist said it was "a pelican kissing a seal." (*b*) This 11-year-old's drawing is neater and more realistic but also less inventive.

The Intuitive Thought Substage

The **intuitive thought substage** is the second substage of preoperational thought, occurring between approximately 4 and 7 years of age. In this substage, children begin to use primitive reasoning and want to know the answers to all sorts of questions. Consider 4-year-old Tommy, who is at the beginning of the intuitive thought substage. Although he is starting to develop his own ideas about the world he lives in, his ideas are still simple, and he is not very good at thinking things out. He has difficulty understanding events that he knows are taking place but that he cannot see. His fantasized thoughts bear little resemblance to reality. He cannot yet answer the question "What if?" in any reliable way. For example, he has only a vague idea of what would happen if a car were to hit him. He also has difficulty negotiating traffic because he cannot do the mental calculations necessary to estimate whether an approaching car will hit him when he crosses the road.

By the age of 5, children have just about exhausted the adults around them with "why" questions. The child's questions signal the emergence of interest in reasoning and in figuring out why things are the way they are. Following are some samples of the questions children ask during the questioning period of 4 to 6 years of age (Elkind, 1976):

What makes you grow up?

Who was the mother when everybody was a baby?

Why do leaves fall?

Why does the sun shine?

Piaget called this substage *intuitive* because young children seem so sure about their knowledge and understanding yet are unaware of how they know what they know. That is, they know something but know it without the use of rational thinking.

"I still don't have all the answers, but I'm beginning to ask the right questions."

animism A facet of preoperational thought— the belief that inanimate objects have lifelike qualities and are capable of action.

intuitive thought substage The second substage of preoperational thought, occurring between approximately 4 and 7 years of age. Children begin to use primitive reasoning and want to know the answers to all sorts of questions.

FIGURE 6.7 Piaget's Conservation Task. The beaker test is a well-known Piagetian test to determine whether a child can think operationally—that is, can mentally reverse actions and show conservation of the substance. (*a*) Two identical beakers are presented to the child. Then, the experimenter pours the liquid from B into C, which is taller and thinner than A or B. (*b*) The child is asked if these beakers (A and C) have the same amount of liquid. The preoperational child says "no." When asked to point to the beaker that has more liquid, the preoperational child points to the tall, thin beaker.

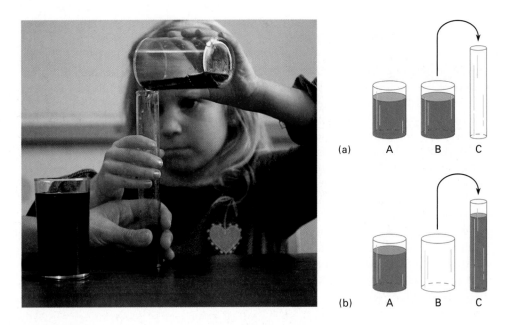

Centration and the Limits of Preoperational Thought One limitation of preoperational thought is **centration,** a centering of attention on one characteristic to the exclusion of all others. Centration is most clearly evidenced in young children's lack of **conservation,** the awareness that altering an object's or a substance's appearance does not change its basic properties. For example, to adults, it is obvious that a certain amount of liquid stays the same, regardless of a container's shape. But this is not at all obvious to young children. Instead, they are struck by the height of the liquid in the container; they focus on that characteristic to the exclusion of others.

The situation that Piaget devised to study conservation is his most famous task. In the conservation task, children are presented with two identical beakers, each filled to the same level with liquid (see Figure 6.7). They are asked if these beakers have the same amount of liquid, and they usually say yes. Then the liquid from one beaker is poured into a third beaker, which is taller and thinner than the first two. The children are then asked if the amount of liquid in the tall, thin beaker is equal to that which remains in one of the original beakers. Children who are less than 7 or 8 years old usually say no and justify their answers in terms of the differing height or width of the beakers. Older children usually answer yes and justify their answers appropriately ("If you poured the water back, the amount would still be the same").

In Piaget's theory, failing the conservation-of-liquid task is a sign that children are at the preoperational stage of cognitive development. The failure demonstrates not only centration but also an inability to mentally reverse actions. To understand this concept, see the conservation-of-matter example shown in Figure 6.8. In the column on "matter" you'll see that preoperational children say the longer shape has more clay because they assume that "longer is more." Preoperational children cannot mentally reverse the clay-rolling process to see that the amount of clay is the same in both the shorter ball shape and the longer stick shape.

In Figure 6.8 we see that, in addition to failing the conservation-of-liquid task, preoperational children also fail to conserve number, matter, and length. However, children often vary in their performance on different conservation tasks. Thus, a child might be able to conserve volume but not number.

Some developmentalists do not believe Piaget was entirely correct in his estimate of when children's conservation skills emerge. For example, Rochel Gelman (1969) showed that when the child's attention to relevant aspects of the conservation task is improved, the child is more likely to conserve. Gelman has also demonstrated that attentional training on one dimension, such as number, improves the preschool child's performance on another dimension, such as mass. Thus, Gelman

centration The focusing of attention on one characteristic to the exclusion of all others.

conservation The awareness that altering the appearance of an object or a substance does not change its basic properties.

Type of conservation	Initial presentation	Manipulation	Preoperational child's answer
Number	Two identical rows of objects are shown to the child, who agrees they have the same number.	One row is lengthened and the child is asked whether one row now has more objects.	Yes, the longer row.
Matter	Two identical balls of clay are shown to the child. The child agrees that they are equal.	The experimenter changes the shape of one of the balls and asks the child whether they still contain equal amounts of clay.	No, the longer one has more.
Length	Two sticks are aligned in front of the child. The child agrees that they are the same length.	The experimenter moves one stick to the right, then asks the child if they are equal in length.	No, the one on the top is longer.

FIGURE 6.8 Some Dimensions of Conservation: Number, Matter, and Length. *What characteristics of preoperational thought do children demonstrate when they fail these conservation tasks?*

noted that conservation appears earlier than Piaget thought and that attention is especially important in explaining conservation.

Concrete Operational Stage

Piaget proposed that the **concrete operational stage** lasts from approximately 7 to 11 years of age. In this stage, children can perform concrete operations, and they can reason logically as long as reasoning can be applied to specific or concrete examples. Remember that *operations* are mental actions that are reversible, and *concrete operations* are operations that are applied to real, concrete objects. When a child adds two apples together with four apples and concludes that there are now six apples, she is performing a concrete operation.

The conservation tasks described earlier indicate whether children are capable of concrete operations. Concrete operations allow the child to consider several characteristics rather than to focus on a single property of an object. In the clay example, the preoperational child is likely to focus on height *or* width. The concrete operational child coordinates information about both dimensions.

Are there cultural variations in the development of conservation skills? To read about this topic, see the *Contexts of Life-Span Development* interlude.

Contexts of Life-Span Development

CONSERVATION SKILLS AROUND THE WORLD

Psychologist Patricia Greenfield (1966) conducted a series of studies among Wolof children in the West African nation of Senegal to see if Piaget's theory of concrete operational thought is universal. Using Piaget's beaker tasks, she found that only 50 percent of the 10- to 13-year-olds understood the principle of conservation. Comparable studies among cultures in central Australia, New Guinea (an island north of Australia), the Amazon jungle region of Brazil, and rural Sardinia (an island off the coast of Italy) yielded strongly similar results (Dasen, 1977). These findings suggested that adults in some cultures do not reach the stage of concrete operational thought. However, if this were so, such adults

(continued on next page)

concrete operational stage The third Piagetian stage, which lasts from approximately 7 to 11 years of age; children can perform concrete operations, and logical reasoning replaces intuitive reasoning as long as the reasoning can be applied to specific or concrete examples.

The age at which children acquire conservation skills is related to the extent to which the culture provides practice relevant to the concept of conservation. The children shown here live in Nepal, and they have extensive experience as potters. They gain an understanding of the concept of conservation of quantity earlier than children the same age who do not have experience manipulating a material like clay.

seriation The concrete operation that involves ordering stimuli along a quantitative dimension (such as length).

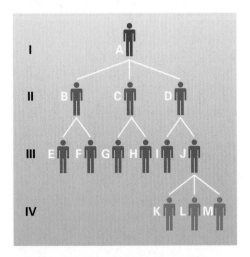

FIGURE 6.9 Classification: An Important Ability in Concrete Operational Thought. A family tree of four generations (*I to VI*): The pre-operational child has trouble classifying the members of the four generations; the concrete operational child can classify the members vertically, horizontally, and obliquely (up and down and across). For example, the concrete operational child understands that a family member can be a son, a brother, and a father, all at the same time.

would be severely handicapped in everyday life. Like preschool children, they would be unable to think through the implications of their actions and would be unable to coordinate various kinds of information about objects. They also would be incapable of going beyond an egocentric perspective to understand another person's point of view.

Some researchers maintain that the failure to find concrete operational thought in various cultures is due to inadequate communication between the experimenter and the children. For example, one study involved two cultural groups from Cape Breton, Nova Scotia—one English-speaking European, the other Micmac First Nation peoples. No difference in conservation abilities appeared between the groups of 10- to 11-year-olds when they were interviewed in their native languages (Nyiti, 1982). The Micmac children all spoke their ancestral tongue at home but had also spoken English since the first grade. When the Micmac children were interviewed in English, they understood the concept of conservation only half as well as the English-speaking children of European descent did. This study illustrates the importance of communication between the experimenter and the research participants in cross-cultural studies.

Researchers have also investigated whether a child's ability to use the concept of conservation can improve if the child comes from a culture in which conservation is not widely practiced (Greenfield & Suzuki, 1998). In one study, rural aboriginal Australian children performed some exercises similar to Piaget's beaker task (Dasen, Ngini, & Lavalée, 1979). This "training" improved their performance on the beaker task. Even so, their grasp of the conservation concept lagged behind that of children from the Australian city of Canberra by approximately three years. These findings suggest that the aboriginal culture does not provide practice that is relevant to the conservation concept.

In sum, the age at which individuals acquire conservation skills is associated with the degree to which their culture provides relevant practice. However, such cross-cultural differences tend to disappear when the studies are conducted by experimenters who are familiar with the language of the people being studied or when the participants receive special training (Cole, 2006).

What other abilities are characteristic of children who have reached the concrete operational stage? One important skill is the ability to classify or divide things into different sets or subsets and to consider their interrelationships. Consider the family tree of four generations that is shown in Figure 6.9 (Furth & Wachs, 1975). This family tree suggests that the grandfather (A) has three children (B, C, and D), each of whom has two children (E through J), and that one of these children (J) has three children (K, L, and M). A child who comprehends the classification system can move up and down a level, across a level, and up and down and across within the system. The concrete operational child understands that person J can at the same time be father, brother, and grandson, for example.

Children who have reached the concrete operational stage are also capable of **seriation,** which is the ability to order stimuli along a quantitative dimension (such as length). To see if students can serialize, a teacher might haphazardly place eight sticks of different lengths on a table. The teacher then asks the students to order the sticks by length. Many young children end up with two or three small groups of "big" sticks or "little" sticks, rather than a correct ordering of all eight sticks. Another mistaken strategy they use is to evenly line up the tops of the sticks but ignore the bottoms. The concrete operational thinker who is capable of seriation simultaneously understands that each stick must be longer than the one that precedes it and shorter than the one that follows it.

Another aspect of reasoning about the relations between classes is **transitivity,** which is the ability to logically combine relations to understand certain conclusions. In this case, consider three sticks (A, B, and C) of differing lengths. A is the longest, B is intermediate in length, and C is the shortest. Does the child understand that, if A is longer than B and B is longer than C, then A is longer than C? In Piaget's theory, concrete operational thinkers who are capable of transitivity do; preoperational thinkers do not.

Formal Operational Stage

Last stage

So far we have studied the first three of Piaget's stages of cognitive development: sensorimotor, preoperational, and concrete operational. What are the characteristics of the fourth and final stage?

The **formal operational stage,** which appears between 11 and 15 years of age, is the fourth and final Piagetian stage. In this stage, individuals move beyond concrete experiences and think in abstract and more logical ways. As part of thinking more abstractly, adolescents develop images of ideal circumstances. They might think about what an ideal parent is like and compare their parents to their ideal standards. They begin to entertain possibilities for the future and are fascinated with what they can be. In solving problems, formal operational thinkers are more systematic and use logical reasoning.

Abstract, Idealistic, and Logical Thinking   The abstract quality of the adolescent's thought at the formal operational level is evident in the adolescent's verbal problem-solving ability. Whereas the concrete operational thinker needs to see the concrete elements A, B, and C to be able to make the logical inference that if A = B and B = C, then A = C, the formal operational thinker can solve this problem merely through verbal presentation.

Another indication of the abstract quality of adolescents' thought is their increased tendency to think about thought itself. One adolescent commented, "I began thinking about why I was thinking about what I was. Then I began thinking about why I was thinking about what I was thinking about what I was." If this sounds abstract, it is, and it characterizes the adolescent's enhanced focus on thought and its abstract qualities.

Accompanying the abstract nature of formal operational thought in adolescence is thought full of idealism and possibilities. Although children frequently think in concrete ways, or in terms of what is real and limited, adolescents begin to engage in extended speculation about ideal characteristics—qualities they desire in themselves and in others. Such thoughts often lead adolescents to compare themselves with others in regard to such ideal standards. And the thoughts of adolescents are often fantasy flights into future possibilities. It is not unusual for the adolescent to become impatient with these newfound ideal standards and to become perplexed over which of many ideal standards to adopt.

As adolescents are learning to think more abstractly and idealistically, they are also learning to think more logically. Children are more likely to solve problems in a trial-and-error fashion. Adolescents begin to think more as a scientist thinks, devising plans to solve problems and

transitivity The ability to logically combine relations to understand certain conclusions. Piaget argued that an understanding of transitivity is characteristic of concrete operational thought.

formal operational stage The fourth and final Piagetian stage, which appears between the ages of 11 and 15; individuals move beyond concrete experiences and think in more abstract and logical ways.

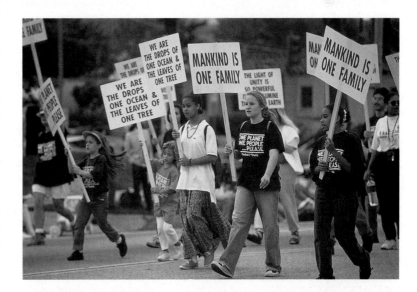

Might adolescents' ability to reason hypothetically and to evaluate what is ideal versus what is real lead them to engage in demonstrations, such as this protest related to better ethnic relations? What other causes might be attractive to adolescents' newfound cognitive abilities of hypothetical-deductive reasoning and idealistic thinking?

Many adolescent girls spend long hours in front of the mirror, depleting cans of hairspray, tubes of lipstick, and jars of cosmetics. *How might this behavior be related to changes in adolescent cognitive and physical development?*

I check my look in the mirror. I wanna change my clothes, my hair, my face.

—BRUCE SPRINGSTEEN
Contemporary American Rock Star

hypothetical-deductive reasoning Piaget's formal operational concept that adolescents have the cognitive ability to develop hypotheses about ways to solve problems and can systematically deduce which is the best path to follow in solving the problem.

adolescent egocentrism The heightened self-consciousness of adolescents, which is reflected in adolescents' beliefs that others are as interested in them as they are in themselves, and in adolescents' sense of personal uniqueness and invincibility.

systematically testing solutions. They use **hypothetical-deductive reasoning**—that is, they develop hypotheses, or best guesses, and systematically deduce, or conclude, which is the best path to follow in solving the problem.

One example of hypothetical-deductive reasoning involves a modification of the familiar game Twenty Questions. Individuals are shown a set of 42 color pictures, displayed in a rectangular array (six rows of seven pictures each), and are asked to determine which picture the experimenter has in mind (that is, which is "correct"). The individuals are allowed to ask only questions to which the experimenter can answer yes or no. The object of the game is to select the correct picture by asking as few questions as possible. Adolescents who are deductive hypothesis testers formulate a plan and test a series of hypotheses, which considerably narrows the field of choices. The most effective plan is a "halving" strategy (*Q*: Is the picture in the right half of the array?).

Assimilation (incorporating new information into existing knowledge) dominates the initial development of formal operational thought, and these thinkers perceive the world subjectively and idealistically. Later in adolescence, as intellectual balance is restored, these individuals accommodate to the cognitive upheaval that has occurred (they adjust to the new information).

Some of Piaget's ideas on formal operational thought are being challenged, however (Keating, 2004; Kuhn, 2008, 2009). There is much more individual variation in formal operational thought than Piaget envisioned (Kuhn, 2008, 2009). Only about one in three young adolescents is a formal operational thinker. Many American adults never become formal operational thinkers, and neither do many adults in other cultures.

Adolescent Egocentrism   In addition to thinking more logically, abstractly, and idealistically—characteristics of Piaget's formal operational thought stage—in what other ways do adolescents change cognitively? David Elkind (1978) described how adolescent egocentrism governs the way that adolescents think about social matters. **Adolescent egocentrism** is the heightened self-consciousness of adolescents, which is reflected in their belief that others are as interested in them as they are themselves, and in their sense of personal uniqueness and invincibility. Elkind argued that adolescent egocentrism can be dissected into two types of social thinking—imaginary audience and personal fable.

The **imaginary audience** refers to the aspect of adolescent egocentrism that involves feeling one is the center of everyone's attention and sensing that one is on stage. An adolescent boy might think that others are as aware of a few hairs that are out of place as he is. An adolescent girl walks into her classroom and thinks that all eyes are riveted on her complexion. Adolescents especially sense that they are "on stage" in early adolescence, believing they are the main actors and all others are the audience.

According to Elkind, the **personal fable** is the part of adolescent egocentrism that involves an adolescent's sense of personal uniqueness and invincibility. Adolescents' sense of personal uniqueness makes them feel that no one can understand how they really feel. For example, an adolescent girl thinks that her mother cannot possibly sense the hurt she feels because her boyfriend has broken up with her. As part of their effort to retain a sense of personal uniqueness, adolescents might craft stories about themselves that are filled with fantasy, immersing themselves in a world that is far removed from reality. Personal fables frequently show up in adolescent diaries.

Adolescents also often show a sense of invincibility—feeling that although others might be vulnerable to tragedies, such as a terrible car wreck, these things won't happen to them. As a result, some adolescents engage in risky behaviors such as drag racing, drug use, and having sexual intercourse without using contraceptives or barriers against sexually transmitted infections (STIs) (Alberts, Elkind, & Ginsberg, 2007). For example, one study found that eleventh- and twelfth-grade females who were high in adolescent egocentrism were more likely to say they would not get pregnant from engaging in sex without contraception than were their counterparts who were low in adolescent egocentrism (Arnett, 1990). And a recent study of sixth- through twelfth-graders revealed that a sense of invincibility was linked to engaging in risky behaviors, such as smoking cigarettes, drinking alcohol, and delinquency, whereas a sense of personal uniqueness was related to depression and suicidal thoughts (Aalsma, Lapsley, & Flannery, 2006).

Reason to question the accuracy of the invulnerability aspect of the personal fable is provided by research that reveals many adolescents don't consider themselves invulnerable (Bruine de Bruin, Parker, & Fischoff, 2007). Indeed, some research studies suggest that, rather than perceiving themselves to be invulnerable, most adolescents tend to portray themselves as vulnerable to experiencing a premature death (Jamieson & Romer, 2008; Reyna & Rivers, 2008).

Review and Reflect: Learning Goal 1

 1 **Discuss the key processes and four stages in Piaget's theory**

REVIEW

- What are the key processes in Piaget's theory of cognitive development? What are Piaget's four stages of cognitive development?
- What are the main characteristics of the sensorimotor stage?
- What are the main characteristics of the preoperational stage?
- What are the main characteristics of the concrete operational stage?
- What are the main characteristics of the formal operational stage?

REFLECT

- Do you consider yourself to be a formal operational thinker? Do you still sometimes feel like a concrete operational thinker? Give examples.

2 APPLYING AND EVALUATING PIAGET'S THEORY

Piaget and Education   **Evaluating Piaget's Theory**

What are some applications of Piaget's theory to education? What are the main contributions and criticisms of Piaget's theory?

Piaget and Education

Piaget was not an educator, but he provided a sound conceptual framework for viewing learning and education. Here are some ideas in Piaget's theory that can be applied to teaching children (Elkind, 1976; Heuwinkel, 1996):

1. *Take a constructivist approach.* Piaget emphasized that children learn best when they are active and seek solutions for themselves. Piaget opposed teaching methods that treat children as passive receptacles. The educational implication of Piaget's view is that, in all subjects, students learn best by making discoveries, reflecting on them, and discussing them, rather than by blindly imitating the teacher or doing things by rote.

imaginary audience That aspect of adolescent egocentrism that involves feeling one is the center of attention and sensing that one is on stage.

personal fable The part of adolescent egocentrism that involves an adolescent's sense of personal uniqueness and invincibility.

What are some educational strategies that can be derived from Piaget's theory?

2. *Facilitate rather than direct learning.* Effective teachers design situations that allow students to learn by doing. These situations promote students' thinking and discovery. Teachers listen, watch, and question students, to help them gain better understanding. Don't just examine what students think and what is the product of their learning. Rather, carefully observe them and find out how they think. Ask relevant questions to stimulate their thinking, and ask them to explain their answers.

3. *Consider the child's knowledge and level of thinking.* Students do not come to class with empty minds. They have many ideas about the physical and natural world. They have concepts of space, time, quantity, and causality. These ideas differ from the ideas of adults. Teachers need to interpret what a student is saying and respond in a way that is not too far from the student's level. Also, Piaget suggested that it is important to examine children's mistakes in thinking, not just what they get correct, to help guide them to a higher level of understanding.

4. *Use ongoing assessment.* Individually constructed meanings cannot be measured by standardized tests. Math and language portfolios (which contain work in progress as well as finished products), individual conferences in which students discuss their thinking strategies, and students' written and verbal explanations of their reasoning can be used to evaluate progress.

5. *Promote the student's intellectual health.* When Piaget came to lecture in the United States, he was asked, "What can I do to get my child to a higher cognitive stage sooner?" He was asked this question so often here compared with other countries that he called it the American question. For Piaget, children's learning should occur naturally. Children should not be pushed and pressured into achieving too much too early in their development, before they are maturationally ready. Some parents spend long hours every day holding up large flash cards with words on them to improve their baby's vocabulary. In the Piagetian view, this is not the best way for infants to learn. It places too much emphasis on speeding up intellectual development, involves passive learning, and will not work.

6. *Turn the classroom into a setting of exploration and discovery.* What do actual classrooms look like when the teachers adopt Piaget's views? Several first- and second-grade math classrooms provide some good examples (Kamii, 1985, 1989). The teachers emphasize students' own exploration and discovery. The classrooms are less structured than what we think of as a typical classroom. Workbooks and predetermined assignments are not used. Rather, the teachers observe the students' interests and natural participation in activities to determine what the course of learning will be. For example, a math lesson might be constructed around counting the day's lunch money or dividing supplies among students. Often, games are prominently used in the classroom to stimulate mathematical thinking. For example, a version of dominoes teaches children about even-numbered combinations. A variation on tic-tac-toe involves replacing Xs and Os with numbers. Teachers encourage peer interaction during the lessons and games because students' different viewpoints can contribute to advances in thinking.

Evaluating Piaget's Theory

What were Piaget's main contributions? Has his theory withstood the test of time?

Contributions   Piaget, the founder of the present field of children's cognitive development, was a giant in the field of developmental psychology. Psychologists owe him a long list of masterful concepts of enduring power and fascination: assimilation, accommodation, object permanence, egocentrism, conservation, and others. Psychologists also owe him the current vision of children as active, constructive thinkers (Carpendale, Muller, & Bibok, 2008). And they have a debt to him for creating a theory that has generated a huge volume of research on children's cognitive development.

Piaget also was a genius when it came to observing children. His careful observations showed us inventive ways to discover how children act on and adapt to their world. Piaget showed us some important things to look for in cognitive development, such as the shift from preoperational to concrete operational thinking. He also showed us how children need to make their experiences fit their schemes (cognitive frameworks) yet simultaneously adapt their schemes to experience. Piaget revealed how cognitive change is likely to occur if the context is structured to allow gradual movement to the next higher level. Concepts do not emerge suddenly, full-blown, but instead develop through a series of partial accomplishments that lead to increasingly comprehensive understanding (Haith & Benson, 1998).

Criticisms Piaget's theory has not gone unchallenged. Questions are raised about estimates of children's competence at different developmental levels, stages, the training of children to reason at higher levels, and culture and education.

Estimates of Children's Competence Some cognitive abilities emerge earlier than Piaget thought (Carpendale, Muller, & Bibok, 2008; Halford, 2008). For example, as previously noted, some aspects of object permanence emerge earlier than he believed. Even 2-year-olds are nonegocentric in some contexts. When they realize that another person will not see an object, they investigate whether the person is blindfolded or looking in a different direction. Some understanding of the conservation of number has been demonstrated as early as age 3, although Piaget did not think it emerged until 7. Young children are not as uniformly "pre" this and "pre" that (precausal, preoperational) as Piaget thought.

Other cognitive abilities also can emerge later than Piaget thought (Byrnes, 2008; Kuhn, 2008). Many adolescents still think in concrete operational ways or are just beginning to master formal operations. Even many adults are not formal operational thinkers. In sum, recent theoretical revisions highlight more cognitive competencies of infants and young children and more cognitive shortcomings of adolescents and adults (Byrnes, 2008; Scholnick, 2008).

Stages In terms of timing and stages, some cognitive abilities have been found to emerge earlier than Piaget had thought, others later (Bauer, 2009; Kuhn, 2008). Recent reviews conclude that the evidence does not support Piaget's view that prior to age 11 children don't engage in abstract thinking and that from 11 years on they do (Kuhn, 2008; Wigfield, Brynes, & Eccles, 2006). Thus, adolescents' cognitive development is not as stage-like as Piaget thought.

Effects of Training Some children who are at one cognitive stage (such as preoperational) can be trained to reason at a higher cognitive stage (such as concrete operational). This discovery poses a problem for Piaget's theory. He argued that such training is only superficial and ineffective, unless the child is at a maturational transition point between the stages (Gelman & Williams, 1998).

Culture and Education Culture and education exert stronger influences on children's development than Piaget maintained (Gauvain, 2008; Holzman, 2009; Maynard, 2008). For example, the age at which children acquire conservation skills is related to how much practice their culture provides in these skills. An outstanding teacher and education in the logic of math and science can promote concrete and formal operational thought.

An Alternative View **Neo-Piagetians** argue that Piaget got some things right but that his theory needs considerable revision. They give more emphasis to how children

An outstanding teacher and education in the logic of science and mathematics are important cultural experiences that promote the development of operational thought. Schooling and education likely play more important roles in the development of operational thought than Piaget envisioned. *What are some other criticisms of Piaget's theory?*

neo-Piagetians Developmentalists who have elaborated on Piaget's theory, emphasizing attention to children's strategies; information-processing speed; the task involved; and division of the problem into more precise, smaller steps.

use attention, memory, and strategies to process information (Case, 1987, 1999). They especially stress that a more accurate portrayal of children's thinking requires attention to children's strategies; the speed at which children process information; the specific task involved; and the division of problems into smaller, more precise steps (Morra & others, 2007). In Chapter 7, "Information Processing," we further discuss these aspects of children's thought.

Review and Reflect: Learning Goal 2

 Apply Piaget's theory to education, and evaluate Piaget's theory

REVIEW

- How can Piaget's theory be applied to educating children?
- What are some key contributions and criticisms of Piaget's theory?

REFLECT

- How might thinking in formal operational ways rather than concrete operational ways help students to develop better study skills?

---

3 VYGOTSKY'S THEORY OF COGNITIVE DEVELOPMENT

The Zone of Proximal Development	Scaffolding	Language and Thought	Teaching Strategies	Evaluating Vygotsky's Theory

Piaget's theory is a major developmental theory. Another developmental theory that focuses on children's cognition is Vygotsky's theory. Like Piaget, Lev Vygotsky emphasized that children actively construct their knowledge and understanding. In Piaget's theory, children develop ways of thinking and understanding by their actions and interactions with the physical world. In Vygtosky's theory, children are more often described as social creatures than in Piaget's theory. They develop their ways of thinking and understanding primarily through social interaction (Yasnitsky & Ferrari, 2008). Their cognitive development depends on the tools provided by society, and their minds are shaped by the cultural context in which they live (Gauvain, & Parke, 2010; Holzman, 2009).

We briefly described Vygotsky's theory in Chapter 1. Here we take a closer look at his ideas about how children learn and his view of the role of language in cognitive development.

The Zone of Proximal Development

Vygotsky's belief in the importance of social influences, especially instruction, on children's cognitive development is reflected in his concept of the zone of proximal development. **Zone of proximal development (ZPD)** is Vygotsky's term for the range of tasks that are too difficult for the child to master alone but that can be learned with guidance and assistance from adults or more-skilled children. Thus, the lower limit of the ZPD is the level of skill reached by the child working independently. The upper limit is the level of additional responsibility the child can accept with the assistance of an able instructor (see Figure 6.10). The ZPD captures the child's cognitive skills that are in the process of maturing and can be accomplished only with the

zone of proximal development (ZPD) Vygotsky's term for tasks too difficult for children to master alone but that can be mastered with guidance and assistance from adults or more-skilled children.

assistance of a more-skilled person (Alvarez & del Rio, 2008; Levykh, 2008). Vygotsky (1962) called these the "buds" or "flowers" of development, to distinguish them from the "fruits" of development, which the child already can accomplish independently.

Scaffolding   Closely linked to the idea of the ZPD is the concept of scaffolding. **Scaffolding** means changing the level of support. Over the course of a teaching session, a more-skilled person (a teacher or advanced peer) adjusts the amount of guidance to fit the child's current performance (Daniels, 2007). When the student is learning a new task, the skilled person may use direct instruction. As the student's competence increases, the person gives less guidance.

Dialogue is an important tool of scaffolding in the zone of proximal development. Vygotsky viewed children as having rich but unsystematic, disorganized, and spontaneous concepts. In a dialogue, these concepts meet with the skilled helper's more systematic, logical, and rational concepts. As a result, the child's concepts become more systematic, logical, and rational. For example, a dialogue might take place between a teacher and a child when the teacher uses scaffolding to help a child understand a concept like "transportation."

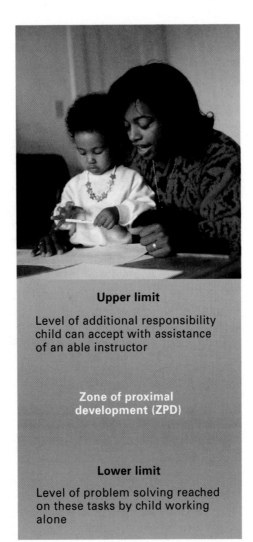

Upper limit

Level of additional responsibility child can accept with assistance of an able instructor

Zone of proximal development (ZPD)

Lower limit

Level of problem solving reached on these tasks by child working alone

FIGURE 6.10 Vygotsky's Zone of Proximal Development. Vygotsky's zone of proximal development has a lower limit and an upper limit. Tasks in the ZPD are too difficult for the child to perform alone. They require assistance from an adult or a more-skilled child. As children experience the verbal instruction or demonstration, they organize the information in their existing mental structures, so they can eventually perform the skill or task alone.

scaffolding In cognitive development, a term Vygotsky used to describe the changing level of support over the course of a teaching session, with the more-skilled person adjusting guidance to fit the child's current performance level.

Language and Thought

The use of dialogue as a tool for scaffolding is only one example of the important role of language in a child's development. According to Vygotsky, children use speech not only for social communication, but also to help them solve tasks. Vygotsky (1962) further believed that young children use language to plan, guide, and monitor their behavior. This use of language for self-regulation is called *private speech*. For Piaget, private speech is egocentric and immature—but for Vygotsky, it is an important tool of thought during the early childhood years (John-Steiner, 2007; Wertsch, 2008).

Vygotsky said that language and thought initially develop independently of each other and then merge. He emphasized that all mental functions have external, or social, origins. Children must use language to communicate with others before they can focus inward on their own thoughts. Children also must communicate externally and use language for a long period of time before they can make the transition from external to internal speech. This transition period occurs between 3 and 7 years of age and involves talking to oneself. After a while, the self-talk becomes second nature to children, and they can act without verbalizing; at this point, children have internalized their egocentric speech in the form of *inner speech*, which becomes their thoughts (Mercer, 2008).

Lev Vygotsky (1896–1934), shown here with his daughter, reasoned that children's cognitive development is advanced through social interaction with more-skilled individuals embedded in a sociocultural backdrop. *How is Vygotsky' theory different from Piaget's?*

Vygotsky held that children who use a lot of private speech are more socially competent than those who don't. He argued that private speech represents an early transition in becoming more socially communicative. For Vygotsky, when young children talk to themselves, they are using language to govern their behavior and guide themselves. For example, a child working on a puzzle might say to herself, "Which pieces should I put together first? I'll try those green ones first. Now I need some blue ones. No, that blue one doesn't fit there. I'll try it over here."

Piaget argued that self-talk is egocentric and reflects immaturity. However, researchers have found support for Vygotsky's view that private speech plays a positive role in children's development (Mercer, 2008; Wertsch, 2008). Researchers have found that children use private speech more when tasks are difficult, when they have made errors, and when they are not sure how to proceed (Berk, 1994). They also have revealed that children who use private speech are more attentive and improve their performance more than children who do not use private speech (Berk & Spuhl, 1995).

Teaching Strategies

Vygotsky's theory has been embraced by many teachers and has been successfully applied to education (Gredler, 2009; Holzman, 2009; Wertsch, 2008). Here are some ways Vygotsky's theory can be incorporated in classrooms:

1. *Assess the child's ZPD.* Like Piaget, Vygotsky did not believe that formal, standardized tests are the best way to assess children's learning. Rather, Vygotsky argued that assessment should focus on determining the child's zone of proximal development. The more-skilled helper presents the child with tasks of varying difficulty to determine the best level at which to begin instruction.
2. *Use the child's ZPD in teaching.* Teaching should begin toward the zone's upper limit, so that the child can reach the goal with help and move to a higher level of skill and knowledge. Offer just enough assistance. You might ask, "What can I do to help you?" Or simply observe the child's intentions and attempts and provide support when needed. When the child hesitates, offer encouragement. And encourage the child to practice the skill. You may watch and appreciate the child's practice or offer support when the child forgets what to do.
3. *Use more-skilled peers as teachers.* Remember that it is not just adults who are important in helping children learn. Children also benefit from the support and guidance of more-skilled children (John-Steiner, 2007).
4. *Monitor and encourage children's use of private speech.* Be aware of the developmental change from externally talking to oneself when solving a problem during the preschool years, to privately talking to oneself in the early elementary school years (Mercer, 2008). In the elementary school years, encourage children to internalize and self-regulate their talk to themselves.
5. *Place instruction in a meaningful context.* Educators today are moving away from abstract presentations of material, instead providing students with opportunities to experience learning in real-world settings. For example, instead of just memorizing math formulas, students work on math problems with real-world implications.
6. *Transform the classroom with Vygotskian ideas.* What does a Vygotskian classroom look like? The Kamehameha Elementary Education Program (KEEP) is based on Vygotsky's theory (Tharp, 1994). The ZPD is the key element of instruction in this program. Children might read a story and then interpret its meaning. Many of the learning activities take place in small groups. All children spend at least 20 minutes each morning in a setting called "Center One." In this context, scaffolding is used to improve children's literary skills. The instructor asks questions, responds to students' queries, and builds on the ideas that students generate. Thousands of children from low-income families have attended KEEP public schools—in Hawaii, on an Arizona Navajo reservation, and in Los Angeles. Compared with a control group of non-KEEP children, the KEEP children

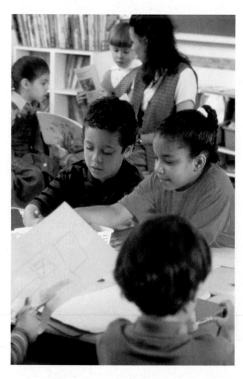

How can Vygotsky's ideas be applied to educating children?

participated more actively in classroom discussion, were more attentive in class, and had higher reading achievement (Tharp & Gallimore, 1988).

To read about the work of a teacher who applies Vygotsky's theory to her teaching, see the *Careers in Life-Span Development* profile about elementary school teacher Donene Polson. The *Applications in Life-Span Development* interlude further explores the implications of Vygotsky's theory for children's education.

Careers in Life-Span Development

Donene Polson, Elementary School Teacher

Donene Polson teaches at Washington Elementary School in Salt Lake City, Utah. Washington is an innovative school that emphasizes the importance of people learning together as a community of learners. Children as well as adults plan learning activities. Throughout the school day, children work in small groups.

Polson says that she loves working in a school in which students, teachers, and parents work together as a community to help children learn. Before the school year begins, she meets with parents at the family's home to prepare for the upcoming year, getting acquainted, and establishing schedules to determine when parents can contribute to classroom instruction. At monthly parent-teacher meetings, Polson and the parents plan the curriculum and discuss how children's learning is progressing. They brainstorm about resources in the community that can be used effectively to promote children's learning.

Applications in Life-Span Development

TOOLS OF THE MIND

Tools of the Mind is an early childhood education curriculum that emphasizes children's development of self-regulation and the cognitive foundations of literacy (Hyson, Copple, & Jones, 2006). The curriculum was created by Elena Bodrova and Deborah Leong (2007) and has been implemented in more than 200 classrooms. Most of the children in the Tools of the Mind programs are at risk because of their living circumstances, which in many instances involve poverty and other difficult conditions such as being homeless and having parents with drug problems.

Tools of the Mind is grounded in Vygotsky's (1962) theory with special attention given to cultural tools and developing self-regulation, the zone of proximal development, scaffolding, private speech, shared activity, and play as important activity. In a Tools of the Mind classroom, dramatic play has a central role. Teachers guide children in creating themes that are based on the children's interests, such as treasure hunt, store, hospital, and restaurant. Teachers also incorporate field trips, visitor presentations, videos, and books in the development of children's play. In addition, they help children develop a play plan, which increases the maturity of their play. Play plans describe what the children expect to do in the play period, including the imaginary context, roles, and props to be used. The play plans increase the quality of their play and self-regulation.

Scaffolding writing is another important theme in the Tools of the Mind classroom. Teachers guide children in planning their own message by drawing a line to stand for each word the child says. Children then repeat the message, pointing to each line as they say the word. Then, a child writes on the lines, trying to represent each word with some letters or symbols. Figure 6.11 shows how the scaffolding writing process improved a 5-year-old child's writing over the course of two months.

(continued on next page)

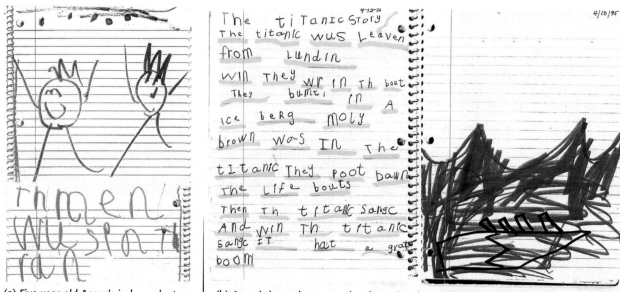

(a) Five-year-old Aaron's independent journal writing prior to using the scaffolded writing technique.

(b) Aaron's journal two months after using the scaffolded writing technique.

FIGURE 6.11 Writing Progress of a 5-Year-Old Boy Over Two Months Using the Scaffolding Writing Process in Tools of the Mind.

Research assessments of children's writing in Tools of the Mind classrooms revealed that they have more advanced writing skills than children in other early childhood programs (Bodrova & Leong, 2007) (see Figure 6.11). For example, they write more complex messages, use more words, spell more accurately, show better letter recognition, and have a better understanding of the concept of a sentence.

Evaluating Vygotsky's Theory

Even though their theories were proposed at about the same time, most of the world learned about Vygotsky's theory later than they learned about Piaget's theory, so Vygotsky's theory has not yet been evaluated as thoroughly. Vygotsky's view of the importance of sociocultural influences on children's development fits with the current belief that it is important to evaluate the contextual factors in learning (Gauvain, & Parke, 2010; Holzman, 2009).

We already have considered several comparisons of Vygotsky's and Piaget's theories, such as Vygotsky's emphasis on the importance of inner speech in development and Piaget's view that such speech is immature. Although both theories are constructivist, Vygotsky's is a **social constructivist approach,** which emphasizes the social contexts of learning and the construction of knowledge through social interaction.

In moving from Piaget to Vygotsky, the conceptual shift is from the individual to collaboration, social interaction, and sociocultural activity (Halford, 2008; Yasnitzky & Ferrari, 2008). The endpoint of cognitive development for Piaget is formal operational thought. For Vygotsky, the endpoint can differ, depending on which skills are considered to be the most important in a particular culture. For Piaget, children construct knowledge by transforming, organizing, and reorganizing previous knowledge. For Vygotsky, children construct knowledge through social interaction (Holzman, 2009). The implication of Piaget's theory for teaching is that children need support to explore their world and discover knowledge. The main implication of Vygotsky's theory for teaching is that students need many opportunities to learn with the teacher and more-skilled peers. In both Piaget's and Vygotsky's theories, teachers serve as facilitators and guides, rather than as directors and molders of learning. Figure 6.12 compares Vygotsky's and Piaget's theories.

social constructivist approach An emphasis on the social contexts of learning and construction of knowledge through social interaction. Vygotsky's theory reflects this approach.

	VYGOTSKY	PIAGET
Sociocultural Context	Strong emphasis	Little emphasis
Constructivism	Social constructivist	Cognitive constructivist
Stages	No general stages of development proposed	Strong emphasis on stages (sensorimotor, preoperational, concrete operational, and formal operational)
Key Processes	Zone of proximal development, language, dialogue, tools of the culture	Schema, assimilation, accommodation, operations, conservation, classification, hypothetical-deductive reasoning
Role of Language	A major role; language plays a powerful role in shaping thought	Language has a minimal role; cognition primarily directs language
View on Education	Education plays a central role, helping children learn the tools of the culture.	Education merely refines the child's cognitive skills that have already emerged.
Teaching Implications	Teacher is a facilitator and guide, not a director; establish many opportunities for children to learn with the teacher and more-skilled peers	Also views teacher as a facilitator and guide, not a director; provide support for children to explore their world and discover knowledge

FIGURE 6.12 Comparison of Vygotsky's and Piaget's theories.

Criticisms of Vygotsky's theory also have surfaced (Karpov, 2006). Some critics point out that Vygotsky was not specific enough about age-related changes (Gauvain, 2008). Another criticism focuses on Vygotsky not adequately describing how changes in socioemotional capabilities contribute to cognitive development (Gauvain, 2008). Yet another criticism is that he overemphasized the role of language in thinking. Also, his emphasis on collaboration and guidance has potential pitfalls. Might facilitators be too helpful in some cases, as when a parent becomes too overbearing and controlling? Further, some children might become lazy and expect help when they might have done something on their own.

Review and Reflect: Learning Goal 3

3 Identify the main concepts in Vygotsky's theory, and compare it with Piaget's theory

REVIEW

- What is the zone of proximal development?
- What is scaffolding?
- How did Vygotsky view language and thought?
- How can Vygotsky's theory be applied to education?
- What are some similarities and differences between Vygotsky's and Piaget's theories?

REFLECT

- Which theory—Piaget's or Vygotsky's—do you like better? Why?

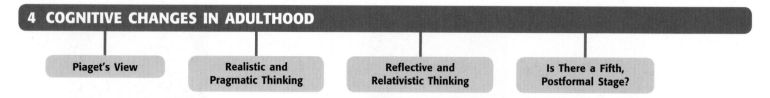

4 COGNITIVE CHANGES IN ADULTHOOD

| Piaget's View | Realistic and Pragmatic Thinking | Reflective and Relativistic Thinking | Is There a Fifth, Postformal Stage? |

We have discussed the theories that Piaget and Vygotsky proposed to account for how the cognitive development of children proceeds. Neither, however, had much to say about cognitive development in adulthood. What do developmentalists know about changes in the way that adults think?

Piaget's View

Recall that, according to Piaget, the formal operational stage of thought begins at 11 to 15 years of age. During this stage, the final one in Piaget's theory, thinking becomes more abstract, idealistic, and logical than the concrete operational thinking of 7- to 11-year-olds. Of course, young adults have more knowledge than adolescents. But, according to Piaget, adults and adolescents use the same type of reasoning. Adolescents and adults think in qualitatively the same way.

Many individuals don't reach the highest level of their formal operational thinking until adulthood. That is, though many individuals begin to plan and hypothesize about intellectual problems as adolescents, they become more systematic and sophisticated at these skills as young adults. Also, many adults do not think in formal operational ways (Keating, 2004).

Realistic and Pragmatic Thinking

Some developmentalists propose that as young adults move into the world of work, their way of thinking does change. One idea is that as they face the constraints of reality that work promotes, their idealism decreases (Labouvie-Vief, 1986).

A related change in thinking was proposed by K. Warner Schaie (1977). He concluded that it is unlikely that adults go beyond the powerful methods of scientific thinking characteristic of the formal operational stage. However, Schaie argued that adults do progress beyond adolescents in their use of intellect. For example, in early adulthood individuals often switch from acquiring knowledge to applying knowledge as they pursue success in their work.

Reflective and Relativistic Thinking

William Perry (1970) also described changes in cognition that take place in early adulthood. He said that adolescents often view the world in terms of polarities—right/wrong, we/they, or good/bad. As youth age into adulthood, they gradually move away from this type of absolutist thinking as they become aware of the diverse opinions and multiple perspectives of others. Thus, in Perry's view, the absolutist, dualistic thinking of adolescence gives way to the reflective, relativistic thinking of adulthood. Other developmentalists also argue that reflective thinking is an important indicator of cognitive change in young adults (Fischer & Bidell, 2006).

Expanding on Perry's view, Gisela Labouvie-Vief (2006) recently proposed that the increasing complexity of cultures in the past century has generated a greater need for more reflective, complex thinking that takes into account the changing nature of knowledge and challenges. She also emphasizes that the key aspects of cognitive development in emerging adulthood include deciding on a specific worldview, recognizing that the worldview is subjective, and understanding that diverse worldviews should be acknowledged. In her perspective, considerable individual variation characterizes the thinking of emerging adults with

What are some possible ways that young adults and adolescents might think differently?

the highest level of thinking attained by only some. She argues that the level of education emerging adults achieve especially influences how likely they will maximize their cognitive potential.

Is There a Fifth, Postformal Stage?

Some theorists have pieced together these descriptions of adult thinking and have proposed that young adults move into a new qualitative stage of cognitive development, postformal thought (Sinnott, 2003). **Postformal thought** is:

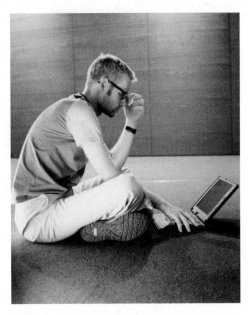

- *Reflective, relativistic, and contextual.* As young adults engage in solving problems, they might think deeply about many aspects of work, politics, relationships, and other areas of life (Labouvie-Vief, 1996). They find that what might be the best solution to a problem at work (with a boss or co-worker) might not be the best solution at home (with a romantic partner). Thus, postformal thought holds that the correct answer to a problem requires reflective thinking and may vary from one situation to another. Some psychologists argue that reflective thinking continues to increase in the forties and fifties (Fischer & Pruyne, 2003).

- *Provisional.* Many young adults also become more skeptical about the truth and seem unwilling to accept an answer as final. Thus, they come to see the search for truth as an ongoing and perhaps never-ending process.

- *Realistic.* Young adults understand that thinking can't always be abstract. In many instances, it must be realistic and pragmatic.

- *Open to emotions and subjective.* Many young adults accept that emotion and subjective factors can influence thinking (Kitchener & King, 1981; Kramer, Kahlbaugh, & Goldston, 1992). For example, as young adults, they understand that a person thinks more clearly in a calm rather than an angry state.

What characterizes a possible fifth stage of cognitive development called postformal thought?

How strong is the evidence for a fifth, postformal stage of cognitive development? Researchers have found that young adults are more likely to engage in postformal thinking than adolescents are (Commons & Richards, 2003; Commons & others, 1989). But critics argue that research has yet to document that postformal thought is a qualitatively more advanced stage than formal operational thought.

There has been little discussion about whether specific cognitive stages might characterize middle and late adulthood. One candidate for a possible stage is "wisdom," which we discuss in Chapter 8, "Intelligence." In addition, researchers have documented many ways in which specific aspects of cognition change during adulthood, and we discuss those in Chapter 7, "Information Processing."

Review and Reflect: Learning Goal 4

4 **Describe cognitive changes in adulthood**

REVIEW

- What is Piaget's view of adult cognitive development?
- Do young adults retain the idealism of the formal operational stage?
- What is Perry's view of cognitive changes from adolescence to adulthood?
- What characteristics have been proposed for a fifth, postformal stage of cognitive development?

REFLECT

- What do you think are the most important cognitive changes that take place in young adults?

postformal thought Thinking that is reflective, relativistic, and contextual; provisional; realistic; and open to emotions and subjective.

Reach Your Learning Goals

Cognitive Developmental Approaches

1 PIAGET'S THEORY OF COGNITIVE DEVELOPMENT: DISCUSS THE KEY PROCESSES AND FOUR STAGES IN PIAGET'S THEORY

Processes of Development

- In Piaget's theory, children construct their own cognitive worlds, building mental structures to adapt to their world. Piaget's key concepts include schemes, assimilation, accomodation, organization, equilibrium, and equilibration. Schemes are actions or mental representations that organize knowledge. Behavioral schemes (physical activities) characterize infancy, whereas mental schemes (cognitive activities) develop in childhood. Adaptation involves assimilation and accommodation. Assimilation occurs when children use existing schemes to deal with new information. Accommodation refers to children's adjusting schemes to take new information and experiences into account. Through organization, children group isolated behaviors into a higher-order, more smoothly functioning cognitive system. Equilibration is a mechanism Piaget proposed to explain how children shift from one cognitive stage to the next. As children experience cognitive conflict in trying to understand the world, they seek equilibrium. The result is equilibration, which brings the child to a new stage of thought. According to Piaget, there are four qualitatively different stages of cognitive development: sensorimotor, preoperational, concrete operational, and formal operational.

Sensorimotor Stage

- In sensorimotor thought, the first of Piaget's four stages, the infant organizes and coordinates sensations with physical movements. The stage lasts from birth to about 2 years of age. Sensorimotor thought has six substages: simple reflexes; first habits and primary circular reactions; secondary circular reactions; coordination of secondary circular reactions; tertiary circular reactions, novelty, and curiosity; and internalization of schemes. One key aspect of this stage is object permanence, the ability of infants to understand that objects continue to exist even though they are no longer observing them. Another aspect involves infants' understanding of cause and effect. In the past several decades, revisions of Piaget's view have been proposed based on research. For example, researchers have found that a stable and differentiated perceptual world is established earlier than Piaget envisioned. The nature-nurture issue is a key aspect of infant cognitive development. Spelke's core knowledge approach is a strong nature view. Most developmentalists conclude that both nature and nurture are important in infant cognitive development.

Preoperational Stage

- Preoperational thought is the beginning of the ability to reconstruct at the level of thought what has been established in behavior. It involves a transition from a primitive to a more sophisticated use of symbols. In preoperational thought, the child does not yet think in an operational way. The symbolic function substage occurs roughly from 2 to 4 years of age and is characterized by symbolic thought, egocentrism, and animism. The intuitive thought substage stretches from about 4 to 7 years of age. It is called intuitive because children seem so sure about their knowledge yet they are unaware of how they know what they know. The preoperational child lacks conservation and asks a barrage of questions.

Concrete Operational Stage

- Concrete operational thought occurs roughly from 7 to 11 years of age. During this stage, children can perform concrete operations, think logically about concrete objects, classify things, and reason about relationships among classes of things. Concrete thought is not as abstract as formal operational thought.

| Formal Operational Stage | • Formal operational thought appears between 11 and 15 years of age. Formal operational thought is more abstract, idealistic, and logical than concrete operational thought. Piaget argues that adolescents become capable of engaging in hypothetical-deductive reasoning. But Piaget did not give adequate attention to individual variation in adolescent thinking. Many young adolescents do not think in hypothetical-deductive ways but rather are consolidating their concrete operational thinking. In addition, adolescents develop a special kind of egocentrism that involves an imaginary audience and a personal fable about being unique and invincible. |

2 APPLYING AND EVALUATING PIAGET'S THEORY: APPLY PIAGET'S THEORY TO EDUCATION, AND EVALUATE PIAGET'S THEORY

| Piaget and Education | • Piaget was not an educator, but his constructivist views have been applied to teaching. These applications include an emphasis on facilitating rather than directing learning, considering the child's level of knowledge, using ongoing assessment, promoting the student's intellectual health, and turning the classroom into a setting of exploration and discovery. |
| Evaluating Piaget's Theory | • We owe to Piaget the field of cognitive development. He was a genius at observing children, and he gave us a number of masterful concepts. Critics, however, question his estimates of competence at different developmental levels, his stage concept, and other ideas. Neo-Piagetians emphasize the importance of information processing. |

3 VYGOTSKY'S THEORY OF COGNITIVE DEVELOPMENT: IDENTIFY THE MAIN CONCEPTS IN VYGOTSKY'S THEORY, AND COMPARE IT WITH PIAGET'S THEORY

The Zone of Proximal Development	• Zone of proximal development (ZPD) is Vygotsky's term for the range of tasks that are too difficult for children to master alone but that can be learned with the guidance and assistance of more-skilled adults and peers.
Scaffolding	• Scaffolding is a teaching technique in which a more-skilled person adjusts the level of guidance to fit the child's current performance level. Dialogue is an important aspect of scaffolding.
Language and Thought	• Vygotsky argued that language plays a key role in cognition. Language and thought initially develop independently, but then children internalize their egocentric speech in the form of inner speech, which becomes their thoughts. This transition to inner speech occurs from 3 to 7 years of age. Vygotsky's view contrasts with Piaget's view that young children's speech is immature and egocentric.
Teaching Strategies	• Applications of Vygotsky's ideas to education include using the child's zone of proximal development and scaffolding, using more-skilled peers as teachers, monitoring and encouraging children's use of private speech, and accurately assessing the zone of proximal development. These practices can transform the classroom and establish a meaningful context for instruction.
Evaluating Vygotsy's Theory	• Like Piaget, Vygotsky emphasized that children actively construct their understanding of the world. Unlike Piaget, he did not propose stages of cognitive development, and he emphasized that children construct knowledge through social interaction. In Vygotsky's theory, children depend on tools provided by the culture, which determines which skills they will develop. Some critics say that Vygotsky overemphasized the role of language in thinking.

4 COGNITIVE CHANGES IN ADULTHOOD: DESCRIBE COGNITIVE CHANGES IN ADULTHOOD

Piaget's View

Realistic and Pragmatic Thinking

Reflective and Relativistic Thinking

Is There a Fifth, Postformal Stage?

- Piaget said that formal operational thought, entered at 11 to 15 years of age, is the final cognitive stage, although adults are more knowledgeable than adolescents.

- Some experts argue that the idealism of Piaget's formal operational stage declines in young adults, being replaced by more realistic, pragmatic thinking.

- Perry said that adolescents often engage in dualistic, absolutist thinking, whereas young adults are more likely to think reflectively and relativistically.

- Postformal thought is reflective, relativistic, and contextual; provisional; realistic; and open to emotions and subjective.

KEY TERMS

schemes 208
assimilation 208
accommodation 209
organization 209
equilibration 209
sensorimotor stage 209
object permanence 212
A-not-B error 213
core knowledge
   approach 214

preoperational stage 216
operations 216
symbolic function
   substage 216
egocentrism 216
animism 217
intuitive thought
   substage 217
centration 218
conservation 218

concrete operational
   stage 219
seriation 220
transitivity 221
formal operational stage 221
hypothetical-deductive
   reasoning 222
adolescent egocentrism 222
imaginary audience 222
personal fable 222

neo-Piagetians 225
zone of proximal
   development (ZPD) 226
scaffolding 227
social constructivist
   approach 230
postformal thought 233

KEY PEOPLE

Jean Piaget 208
Renée Baillargeon 212
Eleanor Gibson 213
Elizabeth Spelke 213
Marshall Haith 214

Andrew Meltzoff 214
Karen Wynn 215
Mark Johnson 215
Barbel Inhelder 216
Rochel Gelman 218

David Elkind 226
Lev Vygotsky 226
Elena Bodrova and Deborah
   Leong 229

K. Warner Schaie 232
William Perry 232
Gisela Labouvie-Vief 232

E-LEARNING TOOLS

Connect to **www.mhhe.com/santrockldt5e** to research the answers and complete these exercises. In addition, you'll find a number of other resources and valuable study tools for Chapter 6, "Cognitive Developmental Approaches," on this Web site.

Taking It to the Net

1. Irene is participating in a debate at the University of Virginia's School of Education regarding the new mandatory testing requirements for all public school children based on state-mandated Standards of Learning (SOL). She will argue that SOL and testing are contrary to Piaget's and Vygotsky's theories about the nature of education and how learning should be assessed. What are some of the arguments she can use?

2. Jack and Marie have not been pleased with the education their children have been receiving. They feel it only emphasizes rote learning. They have found a school that purports to mesh Vygotsky's ideas about constructivism with the use of technology. What kind of classroom activities should they expect? Will their children experience something different from rote learning?

3. Alex is preparing to teach in a community college program designed for adults returning to school to prepare for new careers. How can Alex plan his curriculum to take into account his adult students' cognitive development and learning style?

Self-Assessment

To explore your views on how parents should interact with a baby to effectively promote the baby's cognitive development and to examine how the way you think may change from adolescence to adulthood, complete these self-assessments:

- *My Beliefs About Nurturing a Baby's Mind*
- *Exploring Changes in My Thinking from Adolescence to Adulthood*

Health and Well-Being, Parenting, and Education

Build your decision-making skills by trying your hand at the health and well-being, parenting, and education exercises.

Video Clips

The Online Learning Center includes the following videos for this chapter:

- *Brain Development and Cognition*
- *Lacking Concept of Conservation (Liquid) at Age 3*
- *Lacking Concept of Conservation (Number) at Age 5*
- *Lack of Egocentrism Example at Age 4*
- *Lacking Object Permanence at 4 Months*

7

I think, therefore, I am.

—RENE DESCARTES
Philosopher, 17th Century

LEARNING GOALS

◆ Explain the information-processing approach and its application to development.

◆ Define attention, and outline its developmental changes.

◆ Describe what memory is and how it changes through the life span.

◆ Characterize thinking and its developmental changes.

◆ Define metacognition, and summarize its developmental changes.

INFORMATION PROCESSING

CHAPTER OUTLINE

1 **THE INFORMATION-PROCESSING APPROACH**

2 **ATTENTION**

3 **MEMORY**

4 **THINKING**

5 **METACOGNITION**

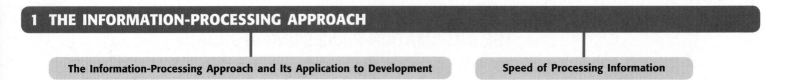

The Information-Processing Approach and Its Application to Development   Speed of Processing Information

What are some of the basic ideas of the information-processing approach? How does processing information change as individuals develop? How important is speed of processing in development?

The Information-Processing Approach and Its Application to Development

As we indicated in Chapter 1, "Introduction," the *information-processing approach* analyzes how individuals manipulate information, monitor it, and create strategies for handling it (Siegler, 2006, 2009). This approach shares some characteristics with the theories of cognitive development that were discussed in Chapter 6, "Cognitive Developmental Approaches." Both those theories and the information-processing approach rejected the behavioral approach that dominated psychology during the first half of the twentieth century. As we discussed in Chapter 1, the behaviorists argued that to explain behavior it is important to examine associations between stimuli and behavior. In contrast, the theories of Piaget and Vygotsky, which were presented in Chapter 6, and the information-processing approach focus on how people think.

Effective information processing involves attention, memory, and thinking (Bauer, 2009; Mayer, 2008). Figure 7.1 is a basic, simplified representation of how information processing works; it omits a great deal and does not indicate the many routes that the flow of information takes. For example, the processes may overlap and not always go in the left-to-right direction indicated in the figure. A number of different processes may be involved in the way memory functions in processing information. The purpose of the model is to get you to begin thinking in a general way about how people process information. In subsequent sections, we consider details about the way people process information and how information processing changes as they develop.

Robert Siegler (2006, 2009) emphasizes that *mechanisms of change* are especially important in the advances children make in cognitive development. According to

FIGURE 7.1 A Basic, Simplified Model of Information Processing.

Siegler, three mechanisms work together to create changes in children's cognitive skills: encoding, automaticity, and strategy construction.

Encoding is the process by which information gets into memory. Changes in children's cognitive skills depend on increased skill at encoding relevant information and ignoring irrelevant information. For example, to a 4-year-old, an *s* in cursive writing is a shape very different from an *s* that is printed. But a 10-year-old has learned to encode the relevant fact that both are the letter *s* and to ignore the irrelevant differences in their shape.

Automaticity refers to the ability to process information with little or no effort. Practice allows children to encode increasing amounts of information automatically. For example, once children have learned to read well, they do not think about each letter in a word as a letter; instead, they encode whole words. Once a task is automatic, it does not require conscious effort. As a result, as information processing becomes more automatic, we can complete tasks more quickly and handle more than one task at a time. If you did not encode words automatically but instead read this page by focusing your attention on each letter in each word, imagine how long it would take you to read it.

Strategy construction is the creation of new procedures for processing information. For example, children's reading benefits when they develop the strategy of stopping periodically to take stock of what they have read so far (Pressley, 2007).

In addition, Siegler (2006, 2009) argues that children's information processing is characterized by *self-modification*. That is, children learn to use what they have learned in previous circumstances to adapt their responses to a new situation. Part of this self-modification draws on **metacognition,** which means "knowing about knowing" (Flavell, 2004). One example of metacognition is what children know about the best ways to remember what they have read. Do they know that they will remember what they have read better if they can relate it to their own lives in some way? Thus, in Siegler's application of information processing to development, children play an active role in their cognitive development.

Speed of Processing Information

A limitation on processing is speed of processing. How fast we process information often influences what we can do with that information. If you are trying to add up in your mind the cost of items you are buying at the grocery store, you need to be able to rapidly compute the sum before you have forgotten the price of the individual items. If someone gives you a phone message, you want to be able to write it down before the person hangs up or before you have forgotten what the person said.

Many everyday tasks are constrained by the time that is available. For example, a child may be told to finish writing a letter in five minutes so that the family can leave. A teacher might give children ten minutes to complete a series of arithmetic problems. In these cases, if the children do not complete the tasks in the time allowed, the cause is uncertain. Perhaps they are simply slow at the physical act of writing, or possibly they are slow in the mental operation of deciding what to say or at spelling words or at doing arithmetic.

Researchers have devised a number of ways to assess processing speed. For example, processing speed can be assessed using a *reaction-time task* in which individuals are asked to push a button as soon as they see a stimulus such as a light. Or individuals might be asked to match letters or match numbers with symbols on a computer screen.

Changes in Speed of Processing There is abundant evidence that the speed with which such tasks are completed improves dramatically across the childhood years (Kail, 2000). Processing speed continues to improve in early adolescence (Kuhn, 2009). For example, in one study, 10-year-olds were approximately 1.8 times slower at processing information than young adults on such tasks as reaction time, letter matching, mental

encoding The process by which information gets into memory.

automaticity The ability to process information with little or no effort.

strategy construction Creation of new procedures for processing information.

metacognition "Knowing about knowing."

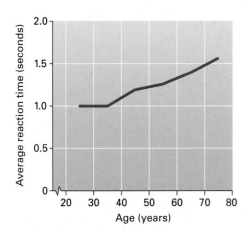

FIGURE 7.2 The Relation of Age to Reaction Time. In one study, the average reaction time began to slow in the forties and this decline accelerated in the sixties and seventies (Salthouse, 1994). The task used to assess reaction time required individuals to match numbers with symbols on a computer screen.

rotation, and abstract matching (Hale, 1990). Twelve-year-olds were approximately 1.5 times slower than young adults, but 15-year-olds processed information on the tasks as fast as the young adults. Also, a recent study of 8- to 13-year-old children revealed that processing speed increased with age, and further that the developmental change in processing speed preceded an increase in working memory capacity (Kail, 2007).

Does processing speed decline in adulthood? In K. Warner Schaie's (1996) Seattle Longitudinal Study, processing speed began declining in middle adulthood. As Figure 7.2 shows, the slowdown in processing speed continues into late adulthood (Salthouse, 2007).

The decline in processing speed in older adults is likely due to a decline in functioning of the brain and central nervous system (Finch, 2009; Salthouse, 2009). Health and exercise may influence how much decline in processing speed occurs (Hillman, Erickson, & Kramer, 2008). One study found that following six months of aerobic exercise older adults showed improvement on reaction-time tasks (Kramer & others, 1999).

Does Processing Speed Matter? How fast children can process information is linked with their competence in thinking (Demetriou & others, 2002). For example, how fast children can articulate a series of words affects how many words they can store and remember.

For some tasks in everyday life, though, speed of processing information may not be important. For example, the strategies that people learn through experience may compensate for any decline in processing speed with age. In general, though, speed is an important aspect of processing information (Hoyer & Roodin, 2009).

Review and Reflect: Learning Goal 1

1 Explain the information-processing approach and its application to development

REVIEW

- What is the information-processing approach, and how can it be applied to development?
- How does processing speed change developmentally?

REFLECT

- The importance of strategies in processing information was discussed in the section you just read. What strategies do you use when you process information?

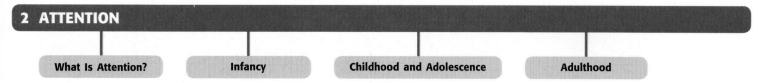

2 ATTENTION

| What Is Attention? | Infancy | Childhood and Adolescence | Adulthood |

The world holds a lot of information to perceive. Right now, you are perceiving the letters and words that make up this sentence. Now look around the setting where you are and pick out something to look at other than this book. After that, curl up the toes on your right foot. In each of these circumstances, you engaged in the process of paying attention. What is attention and what effect does it have? How does it change with age?

What Is Attention?

Attention is the focusing of mental resources. Attention improves cognitive processing for many tasks. At any one time, though, people can pay attention to only a limited amount of information.

Individuals can allocate their attention in different ways. Psychologists have labeled these types of allocation as selective attention, divided attention, sustained attention, and executive attention.

- **Selective attention** is focusing on a specific aspect of experience that is relevant while ignoring others that are irrelevant. Focusing on one voice among many in a crowded room or a noisy restaurant is an example of selective attention. When you switched your attention to the toes on your right foot, you were engaging in selective attention.

- **Divided attention** involves concentrating on more than one activity at the same time. If you are listening to music or the television while you are reading this chapter, you are engaging in divided attention.

- **Sustained attention** is the ability to maintain attention to a selected stimulus for a prolonged period of time. Sustained attention is also called *vigilance*.

- **Executive attention** involves action planning, allocating attention to goals, error detection and compensation, monitoring progress on tasks, and dealing with novel or difficult circumstances.

attention Focusing of mental resources.

selective attention Focusing on a specific aspect of experience that is relevant while ignoring others that are irrelevant.

divided attention Concentration on more than one activity at the same time.

sustained attention The ability to maintain attention to a selected stimulus for a prolonged period of time.

executive attention Cognitive process involving action planning, allocating attention to goals, error detection and compensation, monitoring progress on tasks, and dealing with novel or difficult circumstances.

Infancy

How effectively can infants attend to something? Even newborns can detect a contour and fixate on it. Older infants scan patterns more thoroughly. By 4 months, infants can selectively attend to an object.

Orienting/Investigative Process Attention in the first year of life is dominated by an *orienting/investigative process* (Posner & Rothbart, 2007). This process involves directing attention to potentially important locations in the environment (that is, *where*) and recognizing objects and their features (such as color and form) (that is, *what*) (Courage & Richards, 2008). From 3 to 9 months of age, infants can deploy their attention more flexibly and quickly. Another important type of attention is *sustained attention*, also referred to as *focused attention* (Courage & Richards, 2008). New stimuli typically elicit an orienting response followed by sustained attention. It is sustained attention that allows infants to learn about and remember characteristics of a stimulus as it becomes familiar. Researchers have found that infants as young as 3 months of age engage in 5 to 10

This young infant's attention is riveted on the blue toy frog that has just been placed in front of him. The young infant's attention to the toy frog will be strongly regulated by the processes of habituation and dishabituation. *What characterizes these processes?*

seconds of sustained attention. From this age through the second year, the length of sustained attention increases (Courage & Richards, 2008).

Habituation and Dishabituation Closely linked with attention are the processes of habituation and dishabituation, which we discussed in Chapter 5, "Motor, Sensory, and Perceptual Development" (Kavsek, 2009). If you say the same word or show the same toy to a baby several times in a row, the baby usually pays less attention to it each time. This is *habituation*—decreased responsiveness to a stimulus after repeated presentations of the stimulus. *Dishabituation* is the increase in responsiveness after a change in stimulation. Chapter 5 described some of the measures that researchers use to study whether habituation is occurring, such as sucking behavior (sucking stops when an infant attends to a novel object), heart rates, and the length of time the infant looks at an object.

Infants' attention is strongly governed by novelty and habituation (Courage & Richards, 2008; Snyder & Torrence, 2008). When an object becomes familiar, attention becomes shorter, making infants more vulnerable to distraction (Oakes, Kannass, & Shaddy, 2002). One study found that 10-month-olds were more distractible than 26-month-olds (Ruff & Capozzoli, 2003). Another study revealed that infants who were labeled "short lookers" because of the brief time they focused attention had better memory at 1 year of age than did "long lookers," who had more sustained attention (Courage, Howe, & Squires, 2004).

Researchers study habituation to determine the extent to which infants can see, hear, smell, taste, and experience touch (Slater, Field, & Hernandez-Reif, 2007). Studies of habituation can also indicate whether infants recognize something they have previously experienced. Habituation provides a measure of an infant's maturity and well-being. Infants who have brain damage do not habituate well.

Knowing about habituation and dishabituation can help parents interact effectively with infants. Infants respond to changes in stimulation. Wise parents sense when an infant shows an interest and realize that they may have to repeat something many times for the infant to process information. But if the stimulation is repeated often, the infant stops responding to the parent. In parent-infant interaction, it is important for parents to do novel things and to repeat them often until the infant stops responding. The parent stops or changes behaviors when the infant redirects his or her attention (Rosenblith, 1992).

Joint Attention Another aspect of attention that is an important aspect of infant development is **joint attention,** in which individuals focus on the same object or event. Joint attention requires (1) an ability to track another's behavior, such as following the gaze of someone; (2) one person directing another's attention; and (3) reciprocal interaction. Early in infancy, joint attention usually involves a caregiver pointing or using words to direct an infant's attention. Emerging forms of joint attention occur at about 7 to 8 months of age, but it is not until toward the end of the first year that joint attention skills are frequently observed (Heimann & others, 2006). In a study conducted by Rechele Brooks and Andrew Meltzoff (2005), at 10 to 11 months of age infants first began engaging in "gaze following," looking where another person has just looked (see Figure 7.3). And by their first birthday, infants have begun to direct adults' attention to objects that capture their interest (Heimann & others, 2006).

Joint attention plays important roles in many aspects of infant development and considerably increases infants' ability to learn from other people. Nowhere is this more apparent than in observations of interchanges between caregivers and infants as infants are learning language (Meltzoff & Brooks, 2009; Poulin-Dubois & Graham, 2007). When caregivers and infants frequently engage in joint attention, infants say their first word earlier and develop a larger vocabulary (Flom & Pick, 2003).

joint attention Focus by individuals on the same object or event; requires an ability to track another's behavior, one individual's directing another's attention, and reciprocal interaction.

A mother and her infant daughter engaging in joint attention. *What about this photograph tells you that joint attention is occurring? Why is joint attention an important aspect of infant development?*

(a)   (b)

FIGURE 7.3 Gaze Following in Infancy.
Researcher Rechele Brooks shifts her eyes from the infant to a toy in the foreground (*a*). The infant then follows her eye movement to the toy (*b*). Brooks and colleague Andrew Meltzoff (2005) found that infants begin to engage in this kind of behavior called "gaze following" at 10 to 11 months of age. *Why might gaze following be an important accomplishment for an infant?*

Childhood and Adolescence

The child's ability to pay attention improves significantly during the preschool years (Posner & Rothbart, 2007). Toddlers wander around, shift attention from one activity to another, and seem to spend little time focused on any one object or event. By comparison, the preschool child might be observed watching television for a half hour.

Young children especially make advances in two aspects of attention—executive attention and sustained attention (Courage & Richards, 2008; Rothbart & Gartstein, 2008). Mary Rothbart and Maria Gartstein (2008, p. 332) recently described why advances in executive and sustained attention are so important in early childhood:

> The development of the . . . executive attention system supports the rapid increases in effortful control in the toddler and preschool years. Increases in attention are due, in part, to advances in comprehension and language development. As children are better able to understand their environment, this increased appreciation of their surroundings helps them to sustain attention for longer periods of time.

In at least two ways, however, the preschool child's control of attention is still deficient:

- *Salient versus relevant dimensions.* Preschool children are likely to pay attention to stimuli that stand out, or are *salient,* even when those stimuli are not relevant to solving a problem or performing a task. For example, if a flashy, attractive clown presents the directions for solving a problem, preschool children are likely to pay more attention to the clown than to the directions. After the age of 6 or 7, children attend more efficiently to the dimensions of the task that are relevant, such as the directions for solving a problem. This change reflects a shift to cognitive control of attention, so that children act less impulsively and reflect more.

- *Planfulness.* Although in general young children's planning improves as part of advances in executive attention, when experimenters ask children to judge whether two complex pictures are the same, preschool children tend to use a haphazard comparison strategy, not examining all of the details before making a judgment. By comparison, elementary-school-age children are more likely to systematically compare the details across the pictures, one detail at a time (Vurpillot, 1968) (see Figure 7.4).

In Central European countries, such as Hungary, kindergarten children, participate in exercises designed to improve their attention (Mills & Mills, 2000; Posner & Rothbart, 2007). For example, in one eye-contact exercise, the teacher sits in the center of a circle of children, and each child is required to catch the teacher's eye before being permitted to leave the group. In other exercises created to improve attention, teachers have children participate in stop-go activities during which they

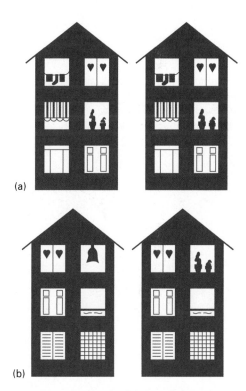

(a)

(b)

FIGURE 7.4 The Planfulness of Attention.
In one study, children were given pairs of houses to examine, like the ones shown here (Vurpillot, 1968). For three pairs of houses, what was in the windows was identical (*a*). For the other three pairs, the windows had different items in them (*b*). By filming the reflection in the children's eyes, it could be determined what they were looking at, how long they looked, and the sequence of their eye movements. Children under 6 examined only a fragmentary portion of each display and made their judgments on the basis of insufficient information. By contrast, older children scanned the windows in more detailed ways and were more accurate in their judgments of which windows were identical.

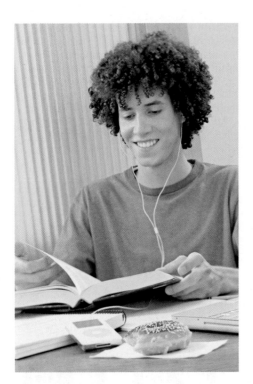

Is multitasking, which involves divided attention, beneficial or distracting?

have to listen for a specific signal, such as a drumbeat or an exact number of rhythmic beats, before stopping the activity.

Preschool children's ability to control and sustain their attention is related to school readiness (Posner & Rothbart, 2007). For example, a study of more than 1,000 children revealed that their ability to sustain their attention at 54 months of age was inked to their school readiness (which included achievement and language skills) (NICHD Early Child Care Research Network, 2005). And in a recent study, children whose parents and teachers rated them higher on a scale of having attention problems at 54 months of age had a lower level of social skills in peer relations in the first and third grades than their counterparts who were rated lower on the attention problems scale at 54 months of age (NICHD Early Child Care Research Network, 2009).

Attention to relevant information increases steadily through the elementary and secondary school years (Davidson, 1996). Processing of irrelevant information decreases in adolescence.

Another important aspect of attention is the ability to shift it from one activity to another as needed. For example, writing a good story requires shifting attention among the competing tasks of forming letters, composing grammar, structuring paragraphs, and conveying the story as a whole. Older children and adolescents are better than younger children at tasks that require shifts of attention.

One trend involving divided attention is adolescents' multitasking, which in some cases involves not just dividing attention between two activities, but even three or more (Bauerlein, 2008). A major influence on the increase in multitasking is the availability of multiple electronic media. Many adolescents have a range of electronic media at their disposal. It is not unusual for adolescents to simultaneously divide their attention to working on homework, while engaging in an instant messaging conversation, surfing the Web, and looking at an iTunes playlist. And a national survey revealed that 50 percent of adolescents made and answered phone calls while driving, and 13 percent (approximately 1.7 million) wrote and/or read text messages while driving (Allstate Foundation, 2005).

Is this multitasking beneficial or distracting? Multitasking expands the information adolescents attend to and forces the brain to share processing resources, which can distract the adolescent's attention from what might be most important at the moment (Begley & Interlandi, 2008).

However, it appears that some high-multitasking adolescents can hold more information in short-term memory and keep it separated into what they need to know and not know (Nash, 2008). But if the key task is at all complex and challenging, such as trying to figure out how to solve a homework problem, multitasking considerably reduces attention to the key task (Myers, 2008).

Adulthood

What happens to attention in adulthood? Attentional skills are often excellent in early adulthood and, of course, the discussion of divided attention and multitasking applies to many adults as well as adolescents. However, in many contexts older adults may not be able to focus on relevant information as effectively as younger adults (Madden, 2007). Consider a study that examined the role that visual attention, involving search, selection, and switching, played in driving risk in older adult drivers (Richardson & Marottoli, 2003). Thirty-five community-dwelling drivers aged 72 and older (mean age, 80) underwent an on-road driving evaluation involving parking lot maneuvers and urban, suburban, and highway driving. They were also given tests of visual attention. The worse their driving, the lower their visual attention score was. Yielding right of way and negotiating safe turns or merges were especially related to visual attention.

Older adults tend to be less adept at selective attention—focusing on a specific aspect of experience while ignoring others—than younger adults are (Rogers & Fisk,

2001). These age differences are minimal if the task involves a simple search (such as determining whether a target item is present on a computer screen) or if individuals have practiced the task (Kramer & Madden, 2008). As the demands on attention increase, however, the performance of older adults declines (Kramer & Madden, 2008). As long as two competing tasks are reasonably easy, age differences among adults are minimal or nonexistent. However, as competing tasks become more difficult, older adults divide attention less effectively than younger adults (Maciokas & Crognale, 2003).

How well do older adults function on tasks that involve vigilance? On tests of simple vigilance, older adults usually perform as well as younger adults—but on complex vigilance tasks, older adults' performance usually drops (Bucur & Madden, 2007).

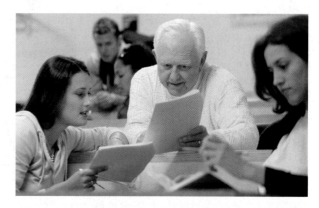

What are some developmental changes in attention in adulthood?

Review and Reflect: Learning Goal 2

 2   **Define attention, and outline its developmental changes**

REVIEW

- What is attention? What are three ways that people allocate their attention?
- How does attention develop in infancy?
- How does attention develop in childhood and adolescence?
- How does attention change during the adult years?

REFLECT

- Imagine that you are an elementary school teacher. Devise some strategies to help children pay attention in class.

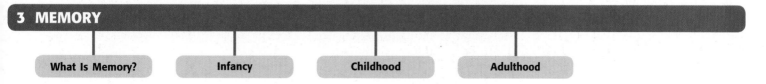

3 MEMORY

| What Is Memory? | Infancy | Childhood | Adulthood |

Twentieth-century American playwright Tennessee Williams once commented that life is all memory except for that one present moment that goes by so quickly that you can hardly catch it going. But just what is memory?

What Is Memory?

Memory is the retention of information over time. Without memory you would not be able to connect what happened to you yesterday with what is going on in your life today. Human memory is truly remarkable when you think of how much information we put into our memories and how much we must retrieve to perform all of life's activities. However, human memory has its imperfections, as we discuss shortly.

Processes of Memory   Researchers study how information is initially placed or encoded into memory, how it is retained or stored after being encoded, and how it

memory Retention of information over time.

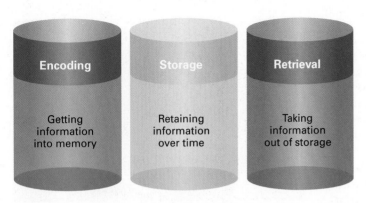

FIGURE 7.5 Processing Information in Memory. As you read about the many aspects of memory in this chapter, think about the organization of memory in terms of these three main activities.

is found or retrieved for a certain purpose later (see Figure 7.5). Encoding, storage, and retrieval are the basic processes required for memory. Failures can occur in any of these processes. Some part of an event might not be encoded, the mental representation of the event might not be stored, or even if the memory exists, you might not be able to retrieve it.

Constructing Memory   Memories may be inaccurate for a number of reasons (Paz-Alonso & others, 2009; Sabbagh, 2009). Memory is not like a tape recorder or a camera or computer memory. People construct and reconstruct their memories. According to **schema theory,** people mold memories to fit information that already exists in their minds. This process is guided by **schemas,** which are mental frameworks that organize concepts and information. Schemas influence the way people encode, make inferences about, and retrieve information. Often when we retrieve information, we fill in the gaps.

We have schemas for all sorts of information. If a teacher tells your class a story about two men and two women who were involved in a train crash in France, students won't remember every detail of the story and will reconstruct the story with their own particular stamp on it. One student might reconstruct the story by saying they died in a plane crash, another might describe three men and three women, another might say the crash was in Germany, and so on. Such reconstruction and distortion are nowhere more apparent than in clashing testimony given by eyewitnesses at trials.

In sum, schema theory accurately predicts that people don't store and retrieve bits of data in computer-like fashion (Baddeley, Eysenck, & Anderson, 2009). We reconstruct the past rather than take an exact photograph of it, and the mind can distort an event as it encodes and stores impressions of it (Bauer, 2009; Kensinger, 2009).

In their study of memory, researchers have not extensively examined the roles that sociocultural factors might play. In the *Contexts of Life-Span Development* interlude, we explore how culture and gender might be linked with memory.

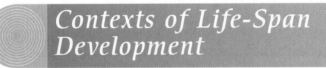

Contexts of Life-Span Development

CULTURE, GENDER, AND MEMORY

A culture sensitizes its members to certain objects, events, and strategies, which in turn can influence the nature of memory (Cole, 2006; Fivush, 2009). In schema theory, a person's background, which is encoded in schemas, is revealed in the way the person reconstructs a story. This effect of cultural background on memory is called the *cultural specificity hypothesis*. It states that cultural experiences determine what is relevant in a person's life and, thus, what the person is likely to remember. For example, imagine that you live on a remote island in the Pacific Ocean and make your livelihood by fishing. Your memory about how weather affects fishing is likely to be highly developed. By contrast, a Pacific Islander might be hard-pressed to encode and recall the details of one hour of MTV. The cultural specificity hypothesis also refers to subgroups within a culture. For example, many basketball fans in the United States can recount an impressive array of National Basketball Association (NBA) statistics. A devout gardener might know the informal and Latin names of all the plants he sees on a garden tour. Our specific interests in our culture and subculture shape the richness of our memory stores and schemas on any given topic.

American children, especially American girls, describe autobiographical narratives "that are longer, more detailed, more specific, and more 'personal' (both in terms of

schema theory Theory stating that people mold memories to fit information that already exists in their minds.

schemas Mental frameworks that organize concepts and information.

mention of self, and mention of internal states), than narratives by children from China and Korea. The pattern is consistent with expectations derived from the finding that in their conversations about past events, American mothers and their children are more elaborative and more focused on autonomous themes . . . and that Korean mothers and their children have less frequent and less detailed conversations about the past . . ." (Bauer, 2006, p. 411).

Gender is another aspect of sociocultural diversity that has been given little attention in memory research until recently (Gertstorf, Herlitz, & Smith, 2006). Researchers have found these gender differences in memory:

- Females are better at episodic memory, which is memory for personal events that include the time and place the event occurred (Halpern, 2001). A longitudinal study examined episodic memory in individuals who initially were 70 to 100 years old over a period of 13 years (Gerstorf, Herlitz, & Smith, 2006). Women had better episodic memory than men at each assessment.

- Females are better than males at emotion-linked memory, such as memory for an emotional film (Cahill & others, 2001). In childhood and adulthood, females' memory narratives include more emotion language and emotional experiences than those of males (Bauer, 2009).

- Males are better than females on tasks that require transformations in visuospatial working memory (Halpern, 2001). These tasks include mental rotation, which involves the imagined motion of stationary objects (such as what a shape would look like if it were rotated in space).

- Females may process information more elaborately and in greater detail, whereas males may be more likely to use schemas or focus on overall information (Guillem & Mograss, 2005).

What are some gender differences in memory?

implicit memory Memory without conscious recollection—memory of skills and routine procedures that are performed automatically.

Infancy

Popular child-rearing expert Penelope Leach (1990) told parents that 6- to 8-month-old babies cannot hold a picture of their mother or father in their mind. And historically psychologists believed that infants cannot store memories until they have language skills. Recently, though, child development researchers have revealed that infants as young as 3 months of age show a limited type of memory.

First Memories   Carolyn Rovee-Collier (1987, 2007) has conducted research that demonstrates infants can remember perceptual-motor information. In a characteristic experiment, she places a baby in a crib underneath an elaborate mobile and ties one end of a ribbon to the baby's ankle and the other end to the mobile. The baby kicks and makes the mobile move (see Figure 7.6). Weeks later, the baby is returned to the crib, but its foot is not tied to the mobile. The baby kicks, apparently trying to make the mobile move. However, if the mobile's makeup is changed even slightly, the baby doesn't kick. If the mobile is then restored to being exactly as it was when the baby's ankle was tied to it, the baby will begin kicking again. According to Rovee-Collier, even by 2½ months the baby's memory is incredibly detailed.

How well can infants remember? Some researchers such as Rovee-Collier (2007, Rovee-Collier & Cuevas, 2009) have concluded that infants as young as 2 to 6 months of age can remember some experiences through when they are 1½ to 2 years of age. However, critics such as Jean Mandler (2000), a leading expert on infant cognition, argue that the infants in Rovee-Collier's experiments are displaying only implicit memory. **Implicit memory** refers to memory without

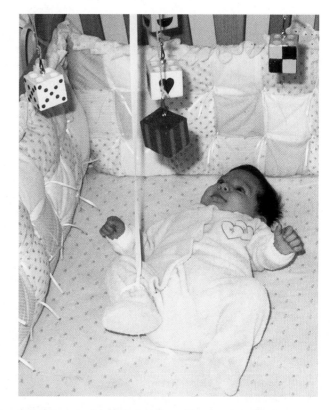

FIGURE 7.6 The Technique Used in Rovee-Collier's Investigation of Infant Memory. In Rovee-Collier's experiment, operant conditioning was used to demonstrate that infants as young as 2½ months of age can retain information from the experience of being conditioned.

Cerebral Cortex
(tan-colored area with wrinkles and folds)

Frontal Lobe

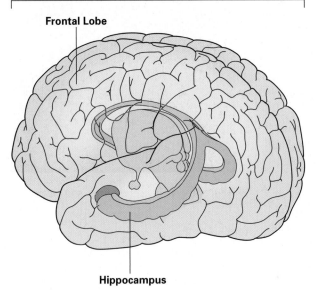

Hippocampus

FIGURE 7.7 Key Brain Structures Involved in Explicit Memory Development in Infancy.

conscious recollection—memories of skills and routine procedures that are performed automatically. In contrast, **explicit memory** refers to the conscious memory of facts and experiences.

When people think about memory, they are usually referring to explicit memory. Most researchers find that babies do not show explicit memory until the second half of the first year (Bauer, 2009). Then, explicit memory improves substantially during the second year of life (Bauer, 2009). In one longitudinal study, infants were assessed several times during their second year (Bauer & others, 2000). Older infants showed more accurate memory and required fewer prompts to demonstrate their memory than younger infants. Researchers have documented that, 6-month-olds can remember information for 24 hours but by 20 months of age infants can remember information they encountered 12 months earlier.

In sum, most of young infants' conscious memories are fragile and short-lived, except for memory of perceptual-motor actions, which can be substantial (Mandler, 2000). Conscious memories improve across the second year of life (Bauer, 2009).

What changes in the brain are linked to infants' memory development? From about 6 to 12 months of age, the maturation of the hippocampus and the surrounding cerebral cortex, especially the frontal lobes, makes the emergence of explicit memory possible (Diamond, Casey, & Munakata, 2010; Nelson, 2009) (see Figure 7.7). Explicit memory continues to improve in the second year, as these brain structures further mature and connections between them increase. Less is known about the areas of the brain involved in implicit memory in infancy.

Infantile Amnesia   Do you remember your third birthday party? Probably not. Most adults can remember little if anything from the first three years of their life (Sabbagh, 2009). This is called *infantile,* or *childhood, amnesia.* The few reported adult memories of life at age 2 or 3 are at best very sketchy (Neisser, 2004). Elementary school children also do not remember much of their early child years. In one study, about three years after leaving preschool, children were much poorer at remembering their former classmates than their teacher was (Lie & Newcombe, 1999). In another study, 10-year-olds were shown pictures of their preschool classmates, and they recognized only about 20 percent of them (Newcombe & Fox, 1994).

What is the cause of infantile amnesia? One reason for the difficulty older children and adults have in recalling events from their infant and early child years is the immaturity of the prefrontal lobes of the brain, which are believed to play an important role in memory for events (Boyer & Diamond, 1992).

Childhood

Children's memory improves considerably after infancy. What are some of the significant strides in memory as children grow older? The progress includes improvements in short-term and long-term memory, as well as the use of strategies.

Short-Term and Working Memory   When people talk about memory, they are usually referring to **long-term memory,** which is relatively permanent and unlimited. When you remember the type of games you enjoyed playing as a child, your first date, or characteristics of the life-span perspective (which we discussed in Chapter 1, "Introduction"), you are drawing on your long-term memory. But when you remember the word you just read, you are using short-term memory. **Short-term**

explicit memory Conscious memory of facts and experiences.

long-term memory A relatively permanent and unlimited type of memory.

short-term memory Retention of information for up to 15 to 30 seconds, without rehearsal of the information. Using rehearsal, individuals can keep the information in short-term memory longer.

working memory A mental "workbench" where individuals manipulate and assemble information when making decisions, solving problems, and comprehending written and spoken language.

memory involves the retention of information for up to 15 to 30 seconds, without rehearsal of the information. Using rehearsal, individuals can keep the information in short-term memory longer (Yen, 2008).

Memory Span Unlike long-term memory, short-term memory has a very limited capacity. One method of assessing that capacity is the memory-span task. You simply hear a short list of stimuli—usually digits—presented at a rapid pace (one per second, for example). Then you are asked to repeat the digits.

Research with the memory-span task suggests that short-term memory increases during childhood. For example, in one investigation, memory span increased from about 2 digits in 2- to 3-year-old children to about 5 digits in 7-year-old children. Between 7 and 13 years of age, memory span increased only by 1½ digits (Dempster, 1981) (see Figure 7.8). Keep in mind, though, that individuals have different memory spans.

Why does memory span change with age? Rehearsal of information is important; older children rehearse the digits more than younger children do. Speed of processing information is important, too, especially the speed with which memory items can be identified. For example, one study tested children on their speed at repeating words presented orally (Case, Kurland, & Goldberg, 1982). Speed of repetition was a powerful predictor of memory span. The children who were able to quickly repeat the presented words were also far more likely to have greater memory spans. Indeed, when the speed of repetition was controlled, the 6-year-olds' memory spans were equal to those of young adults.

Working Memory Short-term memory is like a passive storehouse with shelves to store information until it is moved to long-term memory. Alan Baddeley (1990, 2001, 2007) defines **working memory** as a kind of mental "workbench," where individuals manipulate and assemble information when they make decisions, solve problems, and comprehend written and spoken language (see Figure 7.9). Working memory is described as more active and powerful in modifying information than short-term memory.

Working memory is linked to many aspects of children's development (Baddeley, Eysenck, & Anderson, 2009; Reznick, 2009). For example, children who have better working memory are more advanced in reading comprehension and problem solving than their counterparts with less effective working memory (Bjorklund, 2005).

Children's Long-Term Memory Sometimes the long-term memories of preschoolers seem to be erratic, but young children can remember a great deal of information if they are given appropriate cues and prompts. One area in which children's long-term memory is being examined extensively relates to whether young children should be allowed to testify in court (Pipe & Salmon, 2009; Sabbagh, 2009). Increasingly, young children are being allowed to testify, especially if they are the only witnesses to abuse, a crime, and so forth. Several factors influence the accuracy of a young child's memory (Bruck & Ceci, 1999):

- *There are age differences in children's susceptibility to suggestion.* Preschoolers are the most suggestible age group in comparison with older children and adults (Ceci, Papierno, & Kulkofsky, 2007). For example, preschool children are more susceptible to

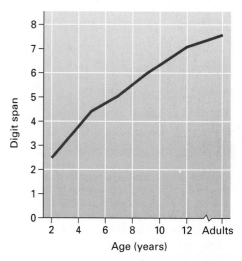

FIGURE 7.8 Developmental Changes in Memory Span. In one study, from 2 years of age to 7 years of age, children's memory span increased about 3 digits to 5 digits (Dempster, 1981). By 12 years of age, memory span had increased on average only another 1½ digits, to 7 digits. *What factors might contribute to the increase in memory span during childhood?*

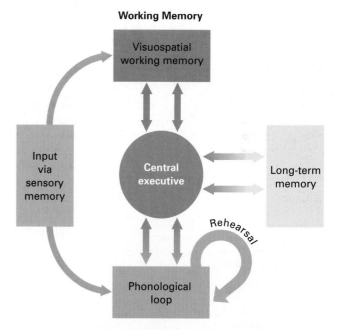

FIGURE 7.9 Working Memory. In Baddeley's working memory model, working memory is like a mental workbench, where a great deal of information processing is carried out. Working memory consists of three main components. The phonological loop and visuospatial working memory serve as assistants, helping the central executive do its work. Input from sensory memory goes to the phonological loop, where information about speech is stored and rehearsal takes place, and visuospatial working memory, where visual and spatial information, including imagery, are stored. Working memory is a limited-capacity system, and information is stored there for only a brief time. Working memory interacts with long-term memory, using information from long-term memory in its work and transmitting information to long-term memory for longer storage.

Four-year-old Jennifer Royal was the only eyewitness to one of her playmates being shot to death. She was allowed to testify in open court, and the clarity of her statements helped to convict the gunman. *What are some issues in whether young children should be allowed to testify in court?*

elaboration Engagement in more extensive processing of information, benefiting memory.

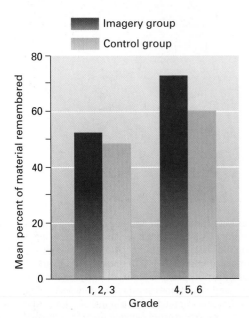

FIGURE 7.10 Imagery and Memory of Verbal Information. Imagery improved older elementary school children's memory for sentences more than younger elementary school children's memory for sentences.

misleading or incorrect post-event information (Ghetti & Alexander, 2004). Despite these age differences, there is still concern about older children when they are subjected to suggestive interviews (Poole & Lindsay, 1996).

- *There are individual differences in susceptibility.* Some preschoolers are highly resistant to interviewers' suggestions, whereas others immediately succumb to the slightest suggestion (Crossman, Scullin, & Melnyk, 2004). A research review concluded that suggestibility is linked to low self-concept, low support from parents, and mothers' insecure attachment in romantic relationships (Bruck & Melnyk, 2004).

- *Interviewing techniques can produce substantial distortions in children's reports about highly salient events.* Children are suggestible not just about peripheral details but also about the central aspects of an event (Bruck, Ceci, & Hembrooke, 1998). Their false claims have been found to persist for at least three months (Ornstein, Gordon, & Larus, 1992). Nonetheless, young children are capable of recalling much that is relevant about an event (Goodman, Batterman-Faunce, & Kenney, 1992). When children do accurately recall an event, the interviewer often has a neutral tone, there is limited use of misleading questions, and there is an absence of any motivation for the child to make a false report (Bruck & Ceci, 1999).

In sum, whether a young child's eyewitness testimony is accurate or not may depend on a number of factors such as the type, number, and intensity of the suggestive techniques the child has experienced (Pipe, 2008; Pipe & Salmon, 2009). It appears that the reliability of young children's reports has as much to do with the skills and motivation of the interviewer as with any natural limitations on young children's memory (Bruck, Ceci, & Principe, 2006).

Children's long-term memory improves even more as they move into the middle and late childhood years. This advance is especially true when they use the strategies that we describe next.

Strategies *Strategies* involve the use of mental activities to improve the processing of information (Bjorklund, Dukes, & Brown, 2009; Siegler, 2009). For memory, rehearsing information and organizing are two typical strategies that older children (and adults) use to remember information more effectively. Rehearsal (repetition) works better for short-term memory. Strategies such as organization, elaborating on the information to be remembered, and making it personally relevant, make long-term memory more effective. Preschool children usually do not use strategies such as rehearsal and organization to remember (Flavell, Miller, & Miller, 2002).

Imagery Creating mental images is another strategy for improving memory (Kellogg, 2007). However, using imagery to remember verbal information works better for older children than for younger children (Schneider & Pressley, 1997). In one study, 20 sentences were presented to first- through sixth-grade children to remember—such as "The angry bird shouted at the white dog" and "The policeman painted the circus tent on a windy day" (Pressley & others, 1987). Children were randomly assigned to an imagery condition (in which they were told to make a picture in their head for each sentence) and a control condition (in which they were told just to try hard). Figure 7.10 shows that the imagery instructions helped older elementary school children (grades 4 through 6) but did not help the younger elementary school children (grades 1 through 3). However, mental imagery can help young schoolchildren to remember pictures (Schneider & Pressley, 1997).

Elaboration One important strategy is **elaboration,** which involves engaging in more extensive processing of information. When individuals engage in elaboration, their memory benefits. Thinking of examples and self-reference are effective ways to elaborate information. Thinking about personal associations with information makes the information more meaningful and helps children to remember it. For example, if the word *win* is on a list of words a child is asked to remember, the child might think of the last time she won a bicycle race.

The use of elaboration changes developmentally (Schneider, 2004). Adolescents are more likely than children to use elaboration spontaneously. Elementary school children can be taught to use elaboration strategies on a learning task, but they will be less likely than adolescents to use the strategies on other learning tasks in the future. Nonetheless, verbal elaboration can be an effective strategy even for young elementary school children.

Fuzzy Trace Theory One theory that emphasizes the reconstructive aspects of memory provides an alternative to strategies in explaining developmental changes in children's memory. Proposed by Charles Brainerd and Valerie Reyna (1993, 2004), **fuzzy trace theory** states that memory is best understood by considering two types of memory representations: (1) verbatim memory trace, and (2) gist. The verbatim memory trace consists of the precise details of the information, whereas *gist* refers to the central idea of the information. When gist is used, fuzzy traces are built up. Although individuals of all ages extract gist, young children tend to store and retrieve verbatim traces. At some point during the early elementary school years, children begin to use gist more and, according to the theory, its use contributes to the improved memory and reasoning of older children because fuzzy traces are more enduring and less likely to be forgotten than verbatim traces (Reyna & Rivers, 2008).

Knowledge An especially important influence on memory is the knowledge that individuals possess about a specific topic or skill (Mayer, 2008; Nippold, 2009). Knowledge influences what people notice and how they organize, represent, and interpret information. This skill, in turn, affects their ability to remember, reason, and solve problems.

One study found that 10- and 11-year-olds who were experienced chess players were able to remember more information about chess pieces than college students who were not chess players (Chi, 1978). In contrast, the college students were able to remember other stimuli better than the children were. Thus, the children's expertise in chess gave them superior memories, but only in chess.

Adulthood

Memory changes during the adult years, but not all memory changes with age in the same way (Hoyer & Roodin, 2009; Kensinger, 2009). Let's look first at working memory and processing speed.

Working Memory and Processing Speed Two important cognitive resources that are linked with aging are working memory and processing speed (Delaloye & others, 2009). Remember that working memory is like a mental "workbench" that allows us to manipulate and assemble information (Baddeley, 2007). One study examined working memory from 6 to 57 years of age (Swanson, 1999). Working memory performance generally increased across childhood, adolescence, and early adulthood, peaked at 45 years of age, and declined at 57 years of age. The increase and decrease in working memory were related to both remembering new information and maintaining the memory of old information. In this study, working memory performance was also linked with reading and math achievement. Researchers have found declines in working memory during the late adulthood years (Delaloye

fuzzy trace theory Theory stating that memory is best understood by considering two types of memory representations: (1) verbatim memory trace, and (2) gist. In this theory, older children's better memory is attributed to the fuzzy traces created by extracting the gist of information.

& others, 2009). Explanation of the decline in working memory in older adults focuses on their less efficient inhibition in preventing irrelevant information from entering working memory and their increased distractibility (Commodari & Guarnera, 2008; Lustig & Hasher, 2009).

Also recall from earlier in the chapter that processing speed declines in middle and late adulthood (Salthouse, 2009). Further, the decline in processing speed is linked with a decline in working memory (Chaytor & Schmitter-Edgecombe, 2004).

Explicit and Implicit Memory   Long-term memory systems include explicit and implicit memory. Recall that *explicit memory* refers to the conscious memory of facts and experiences. Explicit memory is also sometimes called *declarative memory*. Examples of explicit memory include being at a grocery store and remembering that you want to buy something or remembering the events of a movie you have seen.

Explicit memory can be subdivided into episodic memory and semantic memory. **Episodic memory** is the retention of information about the where and when of life's happenings. For example, what was it like when your younger sister or brother was born? What happened to you on your first date? What did you eat for breakfast this morning?

Autobiographical memory is the personal recollection of events and facts. Autobiographical memories are stored as episodic memories. A robust finding in autobiographical memory is called the *reminiscence bump*, in which adults remember more events from the second and third decades of their lives than from other decades (Berntsen & Rubin, 2002). The "bump" is found more for positive than negative life events. A recent study revealed that the "bump" was characterized not only by positive life events but also by high perceived control over the event and high perceived influence of the event on one's later development (Gluck & Bluck, 2007).

Semantic memory is a person's knowledge about the world. It includes a person's fields of expertise (such as knowledge of chess, for a skilled chess player); general academic knowledge of the sort learned in school (such as knowledge of geometry); and "everyday knowledge" about meanings of words, famous individuals, important places, and common things (such as who Nelson Mandela and Mahatma Gandhi are).

Recall that *implicit memory* refers to memory of skills and routine procedures that are performed automatically. (Implicit memory is sometimes referred to as procedural memory.) Examples of implicit memory include unconsciously remembering how to drive a car, swing a golf club, or type on a computer keyboard.

episodic memory Retention of information about the where and when of life's happenings.

semantic memory A person's knowledge about the world, including fields of expertise, general academic knowledge, and "everyday knowledge" about meaning of words, famous individuals, important places, and common things.

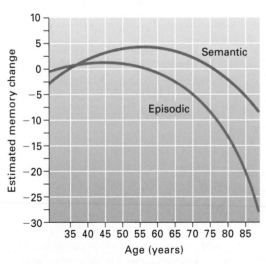

FIGURE 7.11 Changes in Episodic and Semantic Memory in Adulthood.

Aging and Explicit Memory   Younger adults have better episodic memory than older adults have (Cansino, 2009). A recent study of 18- to 94-year-olds revealed that increased age was linked to increased difficulty in retrieving episodic information, facts, and events (Siedlecki, 2007).

Does semantic memory decline with age? Among the tasks that researchers often use to assess semantic memory are vocabulary, general knowledge, and word identification (Baddeley, Eysenck, & Anderson, 2009). Older adults do often take longer to retrieve semantic information, but usually they can ultimately retrieve it. As shown in Figure 7.11, semantic memory continues to increase through the fifties, showing little decline even through the sixties (Rönnlund & others, 2005). Figure 7.11 also shows how the gap between semantic and episodic memory widens during the middle and late adulthood years. In one study, after almost five decades adults picked out their high school classmates with better than 70 percent accuracy (Bahrick, Bahrick, & Wittlinger, 1975). In the *Research in Life-Span Development* interlude, we focus on another study that examined the developmental aspects of semantic memory.

Research in Life-Span Development

HOW WELL DO ADULTS REMEMBER WHAT THEY LEARNED IN HIGH SCHOOL AND COLLEGE SPANISH?

When older adults are assessed for what they learned in high school or college, researchers find neither great durability in memory nor huge deterioration (Salthouse, 1991). In one study, non-Latino adults of various ages in the United States were studied to determine how much Spanish they remembered from classes they had taken in high school or college (Bahrick, 1984). The individuals chosen for the study had used Spanish very little since they initially learned it in high school or college. Not surprisingly, young adults who had taken Spanish classes within the last three years remembered their Spanish best. After that, the deterioration in memory was very gradual (see Figure 7.12). For example, older adults who had studied Spanish 50 years earlier remembered about 80 percent of what young adults did who had studied it in the last three years! The most important factor in the adults' memory of Spanish was not how long ago they studied it but how well they initially learned it—those who got an A in Spanish 50 years earlier remembered more Spanish than adults who got a C when taking Spanish only one year earlier.

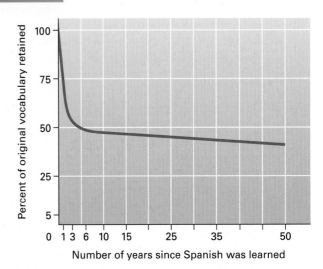

FIGURE 7.12 Memory for Spanish as a Function of Age Since Spanish Was Learned. An initial steep drop occurred over about a three-year period in remembering the vocabulary learned in Spanish classes. However, there was little drop-off in memory for Spanish vocabulary from three years after taking Spanish classes to 50 years after taking them. Even 50 years after taking Spanish classes, individuals still remembered almost 50 percent of the vocabulary.

Although many aspects of semantic memory are reasonably well preserved in late adulthood, a common memory problem for older adults is the *tip-of-the-tongue (TOT) phenomenon,* in which individuals can't quite retrieve familiar information but have the feeling that they should be able to retrieve it (Bucur & Madden, 2007). Researchers have found that older adults are more likely to be experience TOT states than younger adults (Bucur & Madden, 2007).

Aging and Implicit Memory   Implicit memory is less likely to be adversely affected by aging than explicit memory (Yoon, Cole, & Lee, 2009). Thus, older adults are more likely to forget which items they wanted to buy at the grocery store (unless they wrote them down on a list and took it with them) than they are to forget how to drive a car. Their processing speed may be slower when driving the car, but they can remember how to do it.

Source Memory   Source memory is the ability to remember where one learned something. The contexts of source memory might be the physical setting, the emotional context, or the identity of the speaker. Failures of source memory increase with age in the adult years, and they can be embarrassing as when an older adult forgets who told a joke and retells it to the source (Besken & Gulgoz, 2009; Glisky & Kong, 2008). One study examined young and older adults' memory of which of four individuals spoke a word and the gender of the speaker (Simons & others, 2004). Older adults were less likely to remember the identity of the speaker and the speaker's gender than the young adults were. Other studies have also found that source memory declines in older adults (Hernandez & others, 2008; Luber & others, 2004). However, researchers have found that when

source memory The ability to remember where something is learned.

information is more relevant to older adults, age differences in source memory are less robust (Hasher, 2003).

Prospective Memory   **Prospective memory** involves remembering to do something in the future, such as remembering to take your medicine or remembering to do an errand. Some researchers have found a decline in prospective memory with age. However, a number of studies show that determining the cause of the decline is complex and depends on such factors as the nature of the task and what is being assessed (Einstein & McDaniel, 2005; Rendell & others, 2007). For example, age-related deficits occur more often in time-based tasks (such as remembering to call someone next Friday) than in event-based tasks (remembering to tell your friend to read a particular book the next time you see her). Further, declines in prospective memory occur more in laboratory settings than in real-life settings (Bisiacchi, Tarantino, & Ciccola, 2009). Indeed, in some real-life settings, such as keeping appointments, older adults' prospective memory is better than younger adults' (Luo & Craik, 2008).

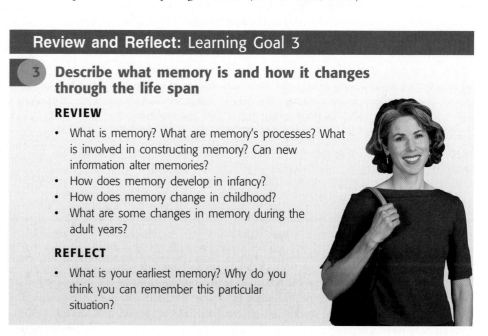

Review and Reflect: Learning Goal 3

3 **Describe what memory is and how it changes through the life span**

REVIEW
- What is memory? What are memory's processes? What is involved in constructing memory? Can new information alter memories?
- How does memory develop in infancy?
- How does memory change in childhood?
- What are some changes in memory during the adult years?

REFLECT
- What is your earliest memory? Why do you think you can remember this particular situation?

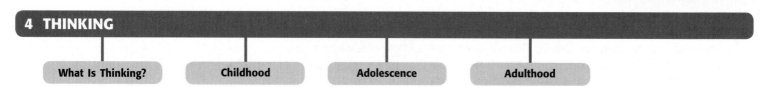

4 THINKING

What Is Thinking?	Childhood	Adolescence	Adulthood

Attention and memory are often steps toward another level of information processing—thinking. What is thinking? How does it change developmentally? What is children's scientific thinking like? Let's explore these questions.

What Is Thinking?

Thinking involves manipulating and transforming information in memory. We think in order to reason, reflect, evaluate ideas, solve problems, and make decisions.

Childhood

To explore thinking in childhood, we examine these questions: To what extent do infants form concepts and engage in categorization? What is critical thinking? How

prospective memory Remembering to do something in the future.

thinking Manipulating and transforming information in memory, in order to reason, reflect, evaluate ideas and solve problems, and make decisions.

can critical thinking be encouraged in schools? What is children's scientific thinking like? How do children solve problems?

Concept Formation and Categorization in Infancy   Along with attention, memory, and imitation, concepts are key aspects of infants' cognitive development (Cohen, 2009; Mandler, 2009). To understand what concepts are, we first have to define *categories*—they group objects, events, and characteristics on the basis of common properties. *Concepts* are ideas about what categories represent, or—said another way—the sort of thing we think category members are. Concepts and categories help us to simplify and summarize information (Oakes, 2008; Rakison & Oakes, 2009). Without concepts, you would see each object and event as unique; you would not be able to make any generalizations.

Do infants have concepts? Yes, they do, although we do not know just how early concept formation begins (Mandler, 2009; Quinn, 2009a, b).

Using habituation experiments like those described earlier in the chapter, some researchers have found that infants as young as 3 months of age can group together objects with similar appearances (Quinn, 2009a, b). This research capitalizes on the knowledge that infants are more likely to look at a novel object than a familiar object.

Jean Mandler (2004, 2009) argues that these early categorizations are best described as *perceptual categorization*. That is, the categorizations are based on similar perceptual features of objects, such as size, color, and movement, as well as parts of objects, such as legs for animals. Mandler (2004) concludes that it is not until about 7 to 9 months of age that infants form *conceptual* categories rather than just making perceptual discriminations between different categories. In one study of 9- to 11-month-olds, infants classified birds as animals and airplanes as vehicles even though the objects were perceptually similar—airplanes and birds with their wings spread (Mandler & McDonough, 1993) (see Figure 7.13).

Further advances in categorization occur in the second year of life (Booth, 2006; Rakison & Oakes, 2009). Many infants' "first concepts are broad and global in nature, such as 'animal' or 'indoor thing.' Gradually, over the first two years these broad concepts become more differentiated into concepts such as 'land animal,' then 'dog,' or to 'furniture,' then 'chair'" (Mandler, 2006, p. 1).

Do some very young children develop an intense, passionate interest in a specific category of objects or activities? A recent study of 11-month-old to 6-year-old children confirmed that they do (DeLoache, Simcock, & Macari, 2007). A striking finding was the large gender difference in categories—with an extreme intense interest in particular categories stronger for boys than girls. Categorization of boys' intense interests focused on vehicles, trains, machines, dinosaurs, and balls; girls' intense interests were more likely to involve dress-ups and books/reading (see Figure 7.14). By the time your author's grandson Alex was 2 years old, he already had developed an intense, passionate interest in the category of vehicles. He categorized vehicles into such subcategories as cars, trucks, earthmoving equipment, and buses. In addition to common classifications of cars into police cars, jeeps, taxis, and such, and trucks into fire trucks, dump trucks, and the like, his categorical knowledge of earthmoving equipment included bulldozers and excavators, and he categorized buses into school buses, London buses, and funky Malta buses (retro buses on the island of Malta). By 2½-years of age, Alex developed an intense, passionate interest in categorizing dinosaurs.

Infants are creating concepts and organizing their world into conceptual domains that will form the backbone of their thought throughout life.

—JEAN MANGLER
*Contemporary Psychologist,
University of California-San Diego*

FIGURE 7.13 Categorization in 9- to 11-Month-Olds. These are the stimuli used in the study that indicated 9- to 11-month-old infants categorized birds as animals and airplanes as vehicles even though the objects were perceptually similar (Mandler & McDonough, 1993).

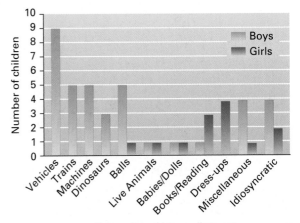

FIGURE 7.14 Categorization of Boys' and Girls' Intense Interests.

The author's grandson Alex at 2 years of age showing his intense, passionate interest in the category of vehicles while playing with a London taxi and a funky Malta bus.

S. GROSS

"For God's sake, think! Why is he being so nice to you?"
© The New Yorker Collection 1998 Sam Gross from cartoonbank.com. All rights reserved. Reprinted with permission.

critical thinking Involves grasping the deeper meaning of ideas, keeping an open mind, and deciding for oneself what to believe or do.

mindfulness Being alert, mentally present, and cognitively flexible while going through life's everyday activities and tasks.

In sum, the infant's advances in processing information—through attention, memory, imitation, and concept formation—is much richer, more gradual, and less stage-like, and occurs earlier than was envisioned by earlier theorists, such as Piaget, (Diamond, Casey, & Munakata, 2010; Johnson, 2009a, b, c; Woodward & Needham, 2009). As leading infant researcher Jean Mandler (2004) concluded, "The human infant shows a remarkable degree of learning power and complexity in what is being learned and in the way it is represented" (p. 304).

Critical Thinking   Regardless of the kind of thinking children and adults engage in, their thinking is fueled by concepts. Currently, both psychologists and educators have considerable interest in critical thinking (Halpern, 2007; Sternberg, 2007).

Critical thinking involves grasping the deeper meaning of ideas, keeping an open mind about different approaches and perspectives, and deciding for oneself what to believe or do. In this book, the second part of the Review and Reflect sections challenges you to think critically about a topic or an issue related to the discussion. Thinking critically includes asking not only what happened, but how and why; examining supposed "facts" to determine whether there is evidence to support them; evaluating what other people say rather than immediately accepting it as the truth; and asking questions and speculating beyond what is known to create new ideas and new information.

According to Ellen Langer (2005), **mindfulness**—being alert, mentally present, and cognitively flexible while going through life's everyday activities and tasks—is an important aspect of thinking critically. Mindful children and adults maintain an active awareness of the circumstances in their life and are motivated to find the best solutions to tasks. Mindful individuals create new ideas, are open to new information, and operate from a single perspective. By contrast, mindless individuals are entrapped in old ideas, engage in automatic behavior, and operate from a single perspective.

In the view of critics such as Jacqueline and Martin Brooks (1993, 2001), few schools teach students to think critically. Schools spend too much time on getting students to give a single correct answer rather than encouraging students to come up with new ideas and rethink conclusions. Too often teachers ask students to recite, define, describe, state, and list rather than to analyze, infer, connect, synthesize, criticize, create, evaluate, think, and rethink. As a result, many schools graduate students who think superficially, staying on the surface of problems rather than becoming deeply engaged in meaningful thinking.

To read about one developmental psychologist who used her training in cognitive development to pursue a career in an applied area, see the *Careers in Life-Span Development* profile.

Scientific Thinking   Some aspects of thinking are specific to a particular domain, such as mathematics, science, or reading. We explore reading in Chapter 9, "Language Development." Here we examine scientific thinking by children.

Like scientists, children ask fundamental questions about reality and seek answers to problems that seem utterly trivial or unanswerable to other people (such as "Why is the sky blue?"). Do children generate hypotheses, perform experiments, and reach conclusions about their data in ways resembling those of scientists?

Scientific reasoning often is aimed at identifying causal relations. Like scientists, children place a great deal of emphasis on causal mechanisms. Their understanding of how events are caused weighs more heavily in their causal inferences than even such strong influences as whether the cause happened immediately before the effect.

There also are important differences between the reasoning of children and the reasoning of scientists (Gallagher, 2007). Children are more influenced by happenstance events than by an overall pattern (Kuhn, 2006). Often, children maintain their old theories regardless of the evidence (Kuhn, Schauble, & Garcia-Mila, 1992).

Careers in Life-Span Development

Helen Schwe, Developmental Psychologist and Toy Designer

Helen Schwe obtained a Ph.D. from Stanford University in developmental psychology but she now spends her days talking with computer engineers and designing "smart" toys for children. Smart toys are designed to improve children's problem-solving and symbolic thinking skills.

When she was a graduate student, Schwe worked part-time for Hasbro toys, testing its children's software on preschoolers. Her first job after graduate school was with Zowie entertainment, which was subsequently bought by LEGO. According to Schwe, "Even in a toy's most primitive stage of development, you see children's creativity in responding to challenges, their satisfaction when a problem is solved or simply their delight when they are having fun" (p. 50). In addition to conducting experiments and focus groups at different stages of a toy's development, Helen also assesses the age-appropriateness of a toy. Most of her current work focuses on 3- to 5-year-old children.

(Source: Schlegel, 2000, pp. 50–51)

Helen Schwe, a developmental psychologist, with some of the "smart" toys she designed.

Children might go through mental gymnastics trying to reconcile seemingly contradictory new information with their existing beliefs. For example, after learning about the solar system, children sometimes conclude that there are two earths, the seemingly flat world in which they live and the round ball floating in space that their teacher described.

Children also have difficulty designing experiments that can distinguish among alternative causes. Instead, they tend to bias the experiments in favor of whatever hypothesis they began with. Sometimes they see the results as supporting their original hypothesis even when the results directly contradict it. Thus, although there are important similarities between children and scientists, in their basic curiosity and in the kinds of questions they ask, there are also important differences in the degree to which they can separate theory and evidence and in their ability to design conclusive experiments (Lehrer & Schauble, 2006).

Too often, the skills scientists use, such as careful observation, graphing, self-regulatory thinking, and knowing when and how to apply one's knowledge to solve problems, are not routinely taught in schools (Bybee, Powell, & Trowbridge, 2008). Children have many concepts that are incompatible with science and reality. Good teachers perceive and understand a child's underlying scientific concepts, then use the concepts as a scaffold for learning (Magnusson & Palinscar, 2005). Effective science teaching helps children distinguish between fruitful errors and misconceptions, and detect plainly wrong ideas that need to be replaced by more accurate conceptions (Bass, Contant, & Carin, 2009).

It is important for teachers to at a minimum initially scaffold students' science learning, extensively monitor their progress, and ensure that they are learning science content (Chiapetta & Koballa, 2010). Thus,

Elementary school science teacher, Luis Recalde, holds up a seaweed specimen in one of the hands-on, high-interest learning contexts he creates for students. Recalde, a fourth- and fifth-grade science teacher at Vincent E. Mauro Elementary School, in New Haven, Connecticut, uses every opportunity to make science fascinating and motivating for students to learn. Recalde infuses hands-on science experiences with energy and enthusiasm. To help students get a better sense of what it is like to be a scientist, he brings lab coats to the classroom for students to wear. He holds science fair workshops for teachers and often gives up his vacation time to help students with science projects.

in pursuing science investigations, students need to "learn inquiry skills *and* science content" (Lehrer & Schauble, 2006).

How might family, economic, and cultural experiences be linked to children's science achievement? A recent study of more than 107,000 students in 41 countries examined this question (Chiu, 2007). Students had higher science achievement scores when they lived in two-parent families, experienced more family involvement, lived with fewer siblings, their schools had more resources, they lived in wealthier countries, or they lived in countries with more equal distribution of household income.

Solving Problems   Children face many problems that they must solve in order to adapt effectively, both in school and out of school. *Problem solving* involves finding an appropriate way to attain a goal. What are some ways that children solve problems?

Using Strategies to Solve Problems   In Michael Pressley's view (Pressley, 2003, 2007), the key to education is helping students learn a rich repertoire of strategies for solving problems. Good thinkers routinely use strategies and effective planning to solve problems. Pressley argues that when children are given instruction about effective strategies, they often can apply strategies that they had not used on their own. Pressley emphasizes that children benefit when the teacher models the appropriate strategy, verbalizes the steps in the strategy, and then guides the children to practice the strategy. Their practice is supported by the teacher's feedback until the children can effectively execute the strategy autonomously.

When instructing children about employing the strategy, the teacher also should explain how using the strategy will benefit them. Children need to be motivated to learn and to use the strategies. Just having children learn a new strategy is usually not enough for them to continue to use it and to transfer the strategy to new situations. For effective maintenance and transfer, children should be encouraged to monitor the effectiveness of the new strategy by comparing their performance on tests and other assessments.

Learning to use strategies effectively often takes time. Initially, it takes time to execute the strategies and to practice them. "Practice" means that children use the effective strategy over and over again until they perform it automatically. To execute the strategies effectively, they need to have the strategies in long-term memory, and extensive practice makes this possible.

Do children use one strategy or multiple strategies in memory and problem solving? They often use more than one strategy (Siegler, 2006, 2009). Most children benefit from generating a variety of alternative strategies and experimenting with different approaches to a problem, discovering what works well, when, and where. This approach is especially true for children from the middle elementary school grades on, although some cognitive psychologists believe that even young children should be encouraged to practice varying strategies (Siegler, 2006, 2009).

Pressley and his colleagues (Pressley, 2007; Pressley & others, 2001, 2003, 2004) have spent considerable time in recent years observing the use of strategy instruction by teachers and strategy use by students in elementary and secondary school classrooms. They conclude that teachers' use of strategy instruction is far less complete and intense than what is needed for students to learn how to use strategies effectively. They argue that education needs to be restructured so that students are provided with more opportunities to become competent strategic learners.

A final point about strategies is that many strategies depend on prior knowledge (Pressley, 2007). For example, students can't apply organizational strategies to a list of items unless they know the correct categories into which the items fall.

Using Analogies to Solve Problems   An *analogy* involves correspondence in some respects between things that are dissimilar. The development of *analogical problem* *solving* resembles that of scientific reasoning. Even very young children can draw reasonable analogies under some circumstances and use them to solve problems (Freeman & Gehl, 1995). Under other circumstances, however, even college students fail to draw seemingly obvious analogies. This resemblance is not coincidental, because scientific reasoning often depends on drawing useful analogies.

Ann Brown and her collaborators (Brown, 1990; Brown, Kane, & Echols, 1986) have demonstrated some of the types of analogical reasoning that occur even as early as 1 and 2 years of age. When 1- and 2-year-olds are shown that a curved stick can be used as a tool to pull in a toy that is too far away to be reached unaided, they draw the correct analogy in choosing which stick to use the next time. They do not choose sticks on the basis of their being the same color as the stick they used before. They also do not just choose objects that look exactly like the tool they saw that demonstrated to be effective (such as a curved cane); instead they identify the essential property and will choose whichever objects have it (they will choose a straight rake as well as the curved cane). The 2-year-olds were more likely than the 1-year-olds to learn the initial task without any help, but once they learned the task, both 1- and 2-year-olds drew the right analogy to new problems.

Successful analogical problem solving often involves tools more abstract than curved sticks for hauling in objects that are beyond one's reach. Maps and verbal descriptions of routes, for example, often help us to figure out how to get where we want to go (DeLoache, Miller, & Pierroutsakos, 1998). Recent studies of toddlers' abilities to use scale models to guide their problem-solving activities show that dramatic developments occur in such tool use quite early in development (DeLoache, 2004).

Judy DeLoache (1989) created a situation in which 2½- and 3-year-olds were shown a small toy hidden within a scale model of a room. The child was then asked to find the toy in a real room that was a bigger version of the scale model. If the toy was hidden under the armchair in the scale model, it was also hidden under the armchair in the real room. Considerable development occurred between 2½ and 3 years of age on this task. Thirty-month-old children rarely could solve the problem; by 36 months they generally could.

What was the source of the 2½-year-olds' difficulty on the task? It was not inability to understand how any type of symbol could represent another situation. Shown line drawings or photographs of the larger room, 2½-year-olds had no difficulty finding the object. Instead, the difficulty seemed to come from the toddlers' simultaneously viewing the scale model as a symbol of the larger room and as an object in itself. Surprising consequences followed from this insight. Allowing children to play with the scale model before using it as a symbol worsened their performance, presumably because playing with it made them think of it more as an object in itself. Conversely, putting the scale model in a glass case, where the children could not handle it at all, resulted in the children more often being able to use it successfully to find the object hidden in the larger room. The general lesson is that young children can use a variety of tools to draw analogies, but they easily can forget that an object is being used as a symbol of something else and instead take it as being of interest as an object in its own right.

Judy DeLoache (*left*) has conducted research that focuses on young children's developing cognitive abilities. She has demonstrated that children's symbolic representation between 2½ and 3 years of age enables them to find a toy in a real room that is a much bigger version of the scale model.

Adolescence

How does critical thinking change in adolescence? How do adolescents make decisions?

Critical Thinking   If a solid basis of fundamental skills (such as literacy and math skills) is not developed during childhood, critical-thinking skills are unlikely to mature in adolescence. For the subset of adolescents who lack fundamental skills, potential gains in adolescent thinking are not likely. For other adolescents, this time is an important transitional period in the development of critical thinking (Keating,

1990, 2004). Some of the cognitive changes that allow improved critical thinking in adolescence are these:

- Increased speed, automaticity, and capacity of information processing, which free cognitive resources for other purposes
- More knowledge in a variety of domains
- An increased ability to construct new combinations of knowledge
- A greater range and more spontaneous use of strategies or procedures such as planning, considering alternatives, and cognitive monitoring

In one study of fifth-, eighth-, and eleventh-graders, critical thinking increased with age but still only occurred in 43 percent of even the eleventh-graders. Many adolescents showed self-serving biases in their reasoning (Klaczynski & Narasimham, 1998).

Decision Making   Adolescence is a time of increased decision making—which friends to choose; which person to date; whether to have sex, buy a car, go to college, and so on (Kuhn, 2008, 2009; Reyna & Rivers, 2008). How competent are adolescents at making decisions? In some reviews, older adolescents are described as more competent than younger adolescents, who in turn are more competent than children (Keating, 2004). Compared with children, young adolescents are more likely to generate different options, examine a situation from a variety of perspectives, anticipate the consequences of decisions, and consider the credibility of sources. And older adolescents are better at decision making than younger adolescents.

However, older adolescents' decision-making skills are far from perfect and being able to make competent decisions does not guarantee that one will make them in everyday life, where breadth of experience often comes into play (Gerrard & others, 2008; Sunstein, 2008). As an example, driver-training courses improve adolescents' cognitive and motor skills to levels equal to, or sometimes superior to, those of adults. However, driver training has not been effective in reducing adolescents' high rate of traffic accidents, although recently researchers have found that implementing a graduated driver licensing (GDL) program can reduce crash and fatality rates for adolescent drivers (Keating, 2007). GDL components include a learner's holding period, practice-driving certification, night-driving restriction, and passenger restriction.

Most people make better decisions when they are calm rather than emotionally aroused. This circumstance may especially be true for adolescents (Rivers, Reyna, & Mills, 2008; Steinberg & others, 2009). Recall from our discussion of brain development in Chapter 3, "Physical Development and Biological Aging," that adolescents have a tendency to be emotionally intense. Thus, the same adolescent who makes a wise decision when calm may make an unwise

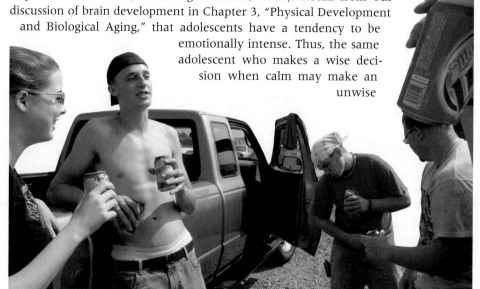

How do emotions and social contexts influence adolescents' decision making?

decision when emotionally aroused (Casey, Getz, & Galvan, 2008). In the heat of the moment, then, adolescents' emotions may especially overwhelm their decision-making ability.

The social context plays a key role in adolescent decision making. For example, adolescents' willingness to make risky decisions is more likely to occur in contexts where substances and other temptations are readily available (Gerrard & others, 2008; Reyna & Rivers, 2008). Recent research reveals that the presence of peers in risk-taking situations increases the likelihood that adolescents will make risky decisions (Steinberg, 2008). In one study of risk taking involving a simulated driving task, the presence of peers increased an adolescent's decision to engage in risky driving by 50 percent but had no effect on adults (Gardner & Steinberg, 2005). One view is that the presence of peers activates the brain's reward system, especially dopamine pathways (Steinberg, 2008).

One proposal to explain adolescent decision making is the **dual-process model,** which states that decision making is influenced by two cognitive systems—one analytical and one experiential, which compete with each other (Klacyznski, 2001; Reyna & Farley, 2006). The dual-process model emphasizes that it is the experiential system—monitoring and managing actual experiences—that benefits adolescents' decision making, not the analytical system. In this view, adolescents don't benefit from engaging in reflective, detailed, higher-level cognitive analysis about a decision, especially in high-risk, real-world contexts. In such contexts, adolescents just need to know that there are some circumstances that are so dangerous that they need to be avoided at all costs (Mills, Reyna, & Estrada, 2008). However, some experts on adolescent cognition argue that in many cases adolescents benefit from both analytical and experiential systems (Kuhn, 2009).

Adulthood

Earlier in the chapter, we examined the changes that take place in speed of processing information, attention, and memory during adulthood. Here we focus on some gains in thinking during the middle adulthood years and the challenges that older adults face.

Practical Problem Solving and Expertise
Nancy Denney (1986, 1990) observed circumstances such as how young and middle-aged adults handled a landlord who would not fix their stove and what they did if a bank failed to deposit a check. She found that the ability to solve such practical problems improved through the forties and fifties as individuals accumulated practical experience. However, since Denney's research, other studies on everyday problem-solving and decision-making effectiveness across the adult years have been conducted; a recent meta-analysis of these studies indicated both remained stable in early and middle adulthood, then declined in late adulthood (Thorton & Dumke, 2005). However, in late adulthood, older adults' everyday problem-solving and decision-making effectiveness benefited when individuals were highly educated and the content of the problems involved interpersonal matters. Further, a recent study revealed that older adults are better at solving emotionally laden and interpersonal problems than younger adults (Blanchard-Fields, 2007). However, a recent study revealed that older adults showed less effective decision making on a complex laboratory task that required sustained attention than did younger adults (Isella & others, 2008).

Experience as well as years of learning and effort may bring the rewards of **expertise,** or extensive, highly organized knowledge and understanding of a particular domain. Because it takes so long to attain, expertise often shows up more among middle-aged or older adults than among younger adults (Clancy & Hoyer, 1994; Kim & Hasher, 2005). Individuals may be experts in areas as diverse as physics, art, or knowledge of wine.

Stephen J. Hawking is a world-renowned expert in physics. Hawking authored the best-selling book, *A Brief History of Time*. Hawking has a neurological disorder that prevents him from being able to walk or talk. He communicates with the aid of a voice-equipped computer. *What distinguishes experts from novices?*

dual-process model States that decision making is influenced by two systems—one analytical and one experiential, which compete with each other; in this model, it is the experiential system—monitoring and managing actual experiences—that benefits adolescent decision making.

expertise Having extensive, highly organized knowledge and understanding of a particular domain.

How are education, work, and health linked to cognitive functioning in older adults?

Whatever their area of expertise, within that domain experts tend to process information differently from the way novices do (Bransford & others, 2006). Here are some of the characteristics that distinguish experts from novices:

- Experts are more likely to rely on their accumulated experience to solve problems.
- Experts often process information automatically and analyze it more efficiently when solving a problem in their domain than novices do.
- Experts have better strategies and shortcuts to solving problems in their domain than novices do.
- Experts are more creative and flexible in solving problems in their domain than novices are (Csikszentmihalyi, 1997).

Decision Making Despite declines in many aspects of memory, such as working memory and long-term memory, many older adults preserve decision-making skills reasonably well (Healey & Hasher, 2009). In some cases, though, age-related decreases in memory will impair decision making. However, older adults especially perform well when decision making is not constrained by time pressures and when the decision is meaningful for them (Yoon, Cole, & Lee, 2009).

Education, Work, and Health Education, work, and health are three important influences on the cognitive functioning of older adults. They are also three of the most important factors involved in understanding why cohort effects need to be taken into account in studying the cognitive functioning of older adults. Indeed, cohort effects are very important to consider in the study of cognitive aging. For example, a recent study of two cohorts tested 16 years apart revealed that at age 74, the average performance on a wide range of cognitive tasks for older adults from the more recent cohort was equal to those of the older adults from the earlier cohort when they were 15 years younger (Zelinski & Kennison, 2007).

Education Successive generations in America's twentieth century were better educated, and this trend continues in the twenty-first century (Manheimer, 2007). Not only were today's older adults more likely to go to college when they were young adults than were their parents or grandparents, but more older adults are returning to college today to further their education than in past generations. Educational experiences are positively correlated with scores on intelligence tests and information-processing tasks, such as memory (Tucker-Drob, Johnson, & Jones, 2009; Wilson & others, 2009). A recent study revealed that more years of education were linked to higher cognitive ability in 79-year-olds (Gow & others, 2008).

Work Successive generations have also had work experiences that include a stronger emphasis on cognitively oriented labor (Elias & Wagster, 2007). Our great-grandfathers and grandfathers were more likely to be manual laborers than were our fathers, who are more likely to be involved in cognitively oriented occupations. As the industrial society continues to be replaced by the information society, younger generations will have more experience in jobs that require considerable cognitive investment. The increased emphasis on complex information processing in jobs likely enhances an individual's intellectual abilities (Schooler, 2007).

In one study, substantive complex work was linked with higher intellectual functioning in older adults (Schooler, Mulatu, & Oates, 1999). This research is consistent with findings in a wide range of disciplines, including animal-based neurobiology studies, which strongly suggest that exposure to complex environments increases intellectual functioning throughout the life course (Kemperman, Gast, & Gage, 2002).

Health Successive generations have also been healthier in late adulthood as better treatments for a variety of illnesses (such as hypertension) have been developed. Many of these illnesses have a negative impact on cognitive functioning (Dahle, Jacobs, & Raz, 2009). Hypertension has been linked to lower cognitive performance in a number of studies, not only in older adults but also in young and middle-aged adults (Newman & others, 2009). Thus, some of the decline in intellectual performance found for older adults is likely due to health-related factors rather than to age per se (Dahle, Jacobs, & Raz, 2009).

K. Warner Schaie (1994) concluded that although some diseases—such as hypertension and diabetes—are linked to cognitive drop-offs, they do not directly cause mental decline. Rather, the lifestyles of the individuals with the diseases might be the culprits. For example, overeating, inactivity, and stress are related to both physical and mental decline (Lee & others, 2007). And researchers have found age-related cognitive decline in adults with mood disorders, such as depression (Gualtieri & Johnson, 2008).

As we saw in Chapter 4, "Health," a number of research studies have found that exercise is linked to improved cognitive functioning (Erickson & others, 2009; Hillman, Erickson, & Kramer, 2008). Walking or any other aerobic exercise appears to get blood and oxygen pumping to the brain, which can help people think more clearly (Studenski & others, 2006).

The mental health of older adults can also influence their cognitive functioning. For example, a recent study revealed that depressive symptoms predicted cognitive decline in older adults (Chodosh & others, 2007).

Cognitive Neuroscience and Aging In Chapter 3, "Physical Development and Biological Aging," we indicated that certain regions of the brain are involved in links between aging and cognitive functioning. In this section, we further explore the substantial increase in interest in the brain's role in aging and cognitive functioning. As we saw in Chapter 1, "Introduction," the field of *developmental cognitive neuroscience* has emerged as the major discipline that studies links between development, the brain, and cognitive functioning (Diamond, Casey, & Munakata, 2010). This field especially relies on brain-imaging techniques, such as functional magnetic resonance imaging (fMRI) and positron-emission tomography (PET), to reveal the areas of the brain that are activated when individuals are engaging in certain cognitive activities (Kennedy & Raz, 2009; Meeks & Jeste, 2009; Schiavone & others, 2009). For example, as an older adult is asked to encode and then retrieve verbal materials or images of scenes, the older adult's brain activity will be monitored by an fMRI brain scan.

Changes in the brain can influence cognitive functioning, and changes in cognitive functioning can influence the brain (Grady, 2008). For example, aging of the brain's prefrontal cortex may produce a decline in working memory. And when older adults do not regularly use their working memory, neural connections in the prefrontal lobe may atrophy. Further, cognitive interventions that activate older adults' working memory may increase these neural connections.

Although in its infancy as a field, the cognitive neuroscience of aging is beginning to uncover some important links between aging, the brain, and cognitive functioning. These include the following:

- Neural circuits in specific regions of the brain's prefrontal cortex decline, and this decline is linked to poorer performance by older adults on complex reasoning tasks, working memory, and episodic memory tasks (Hedden & Gabrielli, 2004) (see Figure 7.15).

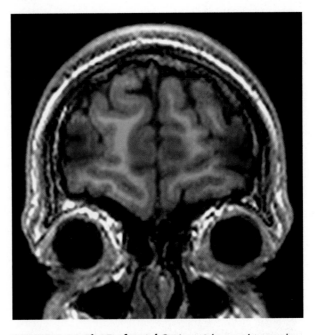

FIGURE 7.15 The Prefrontal Cortex. Advances in neuroimaging are allowing researchers to make significant advances in connecting changes in the brain with cognitive development. Shown here is an fMRI of the brain's prefrontal cortex. *What links have been found between the prefrontal cortex, aging, and cognitive development?*

- Recall from Chapter 3, "Physical Development and Biological Aging," that older adults are more likely than younger adults to use both hemispheres of the brain to compensate for aging declines in attention, memory, and language (Dennis & Cabeza, 2008; Grady, 2008).

- Functioning of the hippocampus declines less than the functioning of the frontal lobes in older adults. However, further indication of possible compensation for memory decline in aging was found in a study of increased activation of the frontal lobes. Possibly this increased activation compensates for declining activation of the hippocampus (Gutchess & others, 2005).

- Patterns of neural differences with age are larger for retrieval than for encoding (Park & Gutchess, 2005).

- Compared with younger adults, older adults show greater activity in the frontal and parietal regions while they are engaging in tasks that require cognitive control processes such as attention (Grady, 2008).

- An increasing number of cognitive and fitness training studies include brain-imaging techniques such as fMRI to assess the results of such training on brain function (Erickson & others, 2009; Hillman, Erickson, & Kramer, 2008; Williamson & others, 2009). In one study, older adults who walked one hour a day three days a week for six months showed increased volume in the frontal and temporal lobes of the brain (Colcombe & others, 2006).

Denise Park and Patricia Reuter-Lorenz (2009) recently proposed a neurocognitive scaffolding view of connections between the aging brain and cognition. In this view, increased activation in the prefrontal cortex with aging reflects an adaptive brain that is compensating for the challenges of declining neural structures and function, and declines in various aspects of cognition, including working memory and long-term memory. Scaffolding involves the use of complementary neural circuits to protect cognitive functioning in an aging brain. Among the factors that can strengthen brain scaffolding are cognitive engagement and exercise.

Use It or Lose It   Changes in cognitive activity patterns might result in disuse and consequent atrophy of cognitive skills. This concept is captured in the concept of "use it or lose it." The mental activities that likely benefit the maintenance of cognitive skills in older adults are activities such as reading books, doing crossword puzzles, and going to lectures and concerts. "Use it or lose it" also is a significant component of the engagement model of cognitive optimization that emphasizes how intellectual and social engagement can buffer age-related declines in intellectual development (Park & Reuter-Lorenz, 2009). These studies support the "use or lose it" concept and the engagement model of cognitive optimization:

The Young@Heart chorus—whose average age is 80—performing. Young@Heart became a hit documentary in 2008. The documentary displays the singing talents, energy, and optimism of a remarkable group of older adults, who clearly are on the "use it" side of "use it or lose it."

- In the Victoria Longitudinal Study, when middle-aged and older adults participated in intellectually engaging activities it served to buffer them against cognitive decline (Hultsch & others, 1999). Recent analyses of the participants in this study revealed that engagement in cognitively complex activities was linked to faster and more consistent processing speed (Bielak & others, 2007).

- In a 4½-year longitudinal study of 801 Catholic priests 65 years and older, those who regularly read books, did crossword puzzles, or otherwise exercised their minds were 47 percent less likely to develop Alzheimer disease than the priests who rarely engaged in these activities (Wilson & others, 2002).

- A recent study revealed that reading daily was linked to reduced mortality in men in their seventies (Jacobs & others, 2008).

Cognitive Training If an older adult is losing cognitive skills, can those skills be retrained? Two key conclusions can be derived from research: (1) training can improve the cognitive skills of many older adults, but (2) there is some loss in plasticity in late adulthood (Hoyer & Roodin, 2009). To read further about cognitive training studies with older adults, see the *Applications in Life-Span Development* interlude.

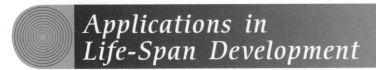

Applications in Life-Span Development

COGNITIVE TRAINING WITH OLDER ADULTS

What activities are part of successful cognitive training? A seven-year longitudinal study by Sherry Willis and Carolyn Nesselroade (1990) used cognitive training to help adults maintain fluid intelligence (the ability to reason abstractly) with advancing age. The older adults were taught strategies for identifying the rule or pattern required to solve problems. The trainer modeled correct strategies for solving problems. Individuals practiced on training items, received feedback about the correct solutions to practice problems, and participated in group discussion. After this cognitive training, adults in their seventies and eighties performed at a higher level than they had in their late sixties.

A recent study had older adults participate in a 20-week activity called Senior Odyssey, a team-based program involving creative problem solving that is derived from the Odyssey of the Mind program for children and emerging adults (Stine-Morrow & others, 2007). In a field experiment, compared with a control group who did not experience Senior Odyssey, the Senior Odyssey participants showed improved processing speed, somewhat improved creative thinking, and increased mindfulness. As described earlier in the chapter, *mindfulness* involves generating new ideas, being open to new information, and being aware of multiple perspectives (Langer, 2007).

Sherry Willis (*right*) assessing the cognitive skills of aging adults. Willis has shown that older adults can be trained to improve their reasoning ability. She especially notes that it is important for adults to use their cognitive abilities and believes that maintaining an active mental life is important.

Another recent study trained older adults to increase their processing speed (Ball, Edwards, & Ross, 2007). As a result of the training, older adults increased their processing speed, and the gain was maintained for two years. The benefits of the processing speed training translated into improvements in everyday activities, such as safer driving performance.

Researchers are also finding that improving the physical fitness of older adults can improve their cognitive functioning (Boron, Willis, & Schaie, 2007; Kramer & Morrow, 2009). A review of studies revealed that aerobic fitness training improved the planning, scheduling, working memory, resistance to distraction, and processing involving multiple tasks in older adults (Colcombe & Kramer, 2003).

In sum, the cognitive vitality of older adults can be improved through cognitive and fitness training (Erickson & others, 2009; Kramer & Morrow, 2009). However, benefits have not been observed in all studies (Salthouse, 2007). Further research is needed to determine more precisely which cognitive improvements occur in older adults (Margrett & Deshpande-Kamat, 2009; Park & Reuter-Lorenz, 2009).

Review and Reflect: Learning Goal 4

4 **Characterize thinking and its developmental changes**

REVIEW

• What is thinking?
• What characterizes concept formation and categorization in infancy? What is critical thinking? Do children and scientists think in the same ways? What are two important aspects of problem solving?
• What are some changes in thinking during adolescence?
• What are some changes in thinking in adulthood?

REFLECT

• Choose an area in which you consider yourself at least somewhat of an expert. Compare your ability to learn in this field with the ability of a novice.

5   METACOGNITION

What Is Metacognition?   **Theory of Mind**   **Metamemory in Children**   **Metacognition in Adolescence and Adulthood**

As you read at the beginning of this chapter, *metacognition* is "knowing about knowing" (Flavell, 2004). In this section, we examine the role of metacognition in performing cognitive tasks, children's memory abilities, and metacognition in adolescents and adults.

What Is Metacognition?

Metacognition can take many forms. It includes knowledge about when and where to use particular strategies for learning or for solving problems. **Metamemory,** individuals' knowledge about memory, is an especially important form of metacognition. Metamemory includes general knowledge about memory, such as knowing that recognition tests (for example, multiple-choice questions) are easier than recall tests (for example, essay questions). It also encompasses knowledge about one's own memory, such as knowing whether you have studied enough for an upcoming test.

Metacognition helps people to perform many cognitive tasks more effectively (Flavell, 2004; Pressley, 2007). In one study, students were taught metacognitive skills to help them solve math problems (Cardelle-Elawar, 1992). In each of 30 daily lessons involving math story problems, a teacher guided low-achieving students to recognize when they did not know the meaning of a word, did not have all of the information necessary to solve a problem, did not know how to subdivide the problem into specific steps, or did not know how to carry out a computation. After the 30 daily lessons, the students who were given this metacognitive training had better math achievement and attitudes toward math.

Theory of Mind

Even young children are curious about the nature of the human mind. They have a **theory of mind,** which refers to awareness of one's own mental processes and the mental processes of others. Studies of theory of mind view the child as "a thinker who is trying to explain, predict, and understand people's thoughts, feelings, and utterances" (Harris, 2006, p. 847). Researchers are increasingly discovering that children's theory of mind is linked to cognitive processes (Wellman & others, 2008). For example, a recent study found that theory of mind competence at age 3 is related to a higher level of metamemory at age 5 (Lockl & Schneider, 2007).

Developmental Changes   Children's theory of mind changes as they develop through childhood (Astington & Dack, 2008; Doherty, 2008; Gelman, 2009). Some changes occur quite early in development, as we see next.

From 18 months to 3 years of age, children begin to understand three mental states:

- *Perceptions.* By 2 years of age, children recognize that another person will see what's in front of her own eyes instead of what's in front of the child's eyes (Lempers, Flavell, & Flavell, 1977), and by 3 years of age, they realize that looking leads to knowing what's inside a container (Pratt & Bryant, 1990).

- *Emotions.* The child can distinguish between positive (for example, happy) and negative (sad, for example) emotions. A child might say, "Tommy feels bad."

- *Desires.* All humans have some sort of desires. But when do children begin to recognize that someone else's desires may different than from their own? Toddlers recognize that if people want something, they will try to get it. For instance, a child might say, "I want my mommy."

Two- to three-year-olds understand the way that desires are related to actions and to simple emotions. For example, they understand that people will search for what they want and that if they obtain it, they are likely to feel happy, but if they don't they will keep searching for it and are likely to feel sad or angry (Wellman & Woolley, 1990). Children also refer to desires earlier and more frequently than they refer to cognitive states such as thinking and knowing (Bartsch & Wellman, 1995).

One of the landmark developments in understanding others' desires is recognizing that someone else may have different desires from one's own (Astington & Dack, 2008). Eighteen-month-olds understand that their own food preferences may not match the preferences of others—they will give an adult the food to which she says "Yummy!" even if the food is something that the infants detest (Repacholi & Gopnik, 1997). As they get older, they can verbalize that they themselves do not like something but an adult might (Flavell & others, 1992).

Between the ages of 3 to 5, children come to understand that the mind can represent objects and events accurately or inaccurately. The realization that people can have *false beliefs*—beliefs that are not true—develops in a majority of children by the time they are 5 years old (Wellman, Cross, & Watson, 2001) (see Figure 7.16). This point is often described as a pivotal one in understanding the mind—recognizing that beliefs are not just mapped directly into the mind from the surrounding world, but also that different people can have different, and sometimes incorrect, beliefs (Liu & others, 2008). In a classic false-belief task, young children were shown a Band-Aids box and asked what was inside (Jenkins & Astington, 1996). To the children's surprise, the box actually contained pencils. When asked what a child who had never seen the box would think was inside, 3-year-olds typically responded, "Pencils." However, the 4- and 5-year-olds, grinning at the

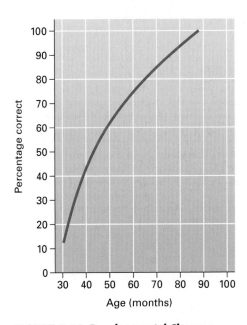

FIGURE 7.16 Developmental Changes in False-Belief Performance. False-belief performance—the child's understanding that a person has a false belief which contradicts reality—dramatically increases from 2½ years of age through the middle of the elementary school years. In a summary of the results of many studies, 2½-year-olds gave incorrect responses about 80 percent of the time (Wellman, Cross, & Watson, 2001). At 3 years 8 months, they were correct about 50 percent of the time and after that gave increasingly correct responses.

metamemory   Knowledge about memory.

theory of mind   Awareness of one's own mental processes and the mental processes of others.

Sally   Anne

FIGURE 7.17 The Sally and Anne False-Belief Task. In the false-belief task, the skit above in which Sally has a basket and Anne has a box is shown to children. Sally places a toy in her basket and then leaves. While Sally is gone and can't watch, Anne removes the toy from Sally's basket and places it in her box. Sally then comes back and the children are asked where they think Sally will look for her toy. Children are said to "pass" the false-belief task if they understand that Sally looks in her basket first before realizing the toy isn't there.

anticipation of the false beliefs of other children who had not seen what was inside the box, were more likely to say "Band-Aids."

In a similar task, children are told a story about Sally and Anne: Sally places a toy in a basket and then leaves the room (see Figure 7.17). In her absence, Anne takes the toy from the basket and places it in a box. Children are asked where Sally will look for the toy when she returns. The major finding is that 3-year-olds tend to fail false-belief tasks, saying that Sally will look in the box (even though Sally could not know that the toy has moved to this new location). Four-year-olds and older children tend to pass the task, correctly saying that Sally will have a "false belief"—she will think the object is in the basket, even though that belief is now false. The conclusion from these studies is that children younger than 4 years old do not understand that it is possible to have a false belief.

However, there are reasons to question the focus on this one supposedly pivotal moment in the development of a theory of mind. For example, the false-belief task is a complicated one that involves a number of factors such as the characters in the story and all of their individual actions (Bloom & German, 2000). Children also have to disregard their own knowledge in making predictions about what others would think, which is difficult for young children (Birch & Bloom, 2003). Another important issue is that there is more to understanding the minds of others than this false-belief task would indicate.

One example of a limitation in 3- to 5-year-olds' understanding the mind is how they think about thinking. Preschoolers often underestimate when mental activity is likely occurring. For example, they sometimes think that a person who is sitting quietly or reading is not actually thinking very much (Flavell, Green, & Flavell, 1995). Their understanding of their own thinking is also limited. One study revealed that even 5-year-olds have difficulty reporting their thoughts (Flavell, Green, & Flavell, 1995). Children were asked to think quietly about the room in their home where they kept their toothbrushes. Shortly after this direction, many children denied they had been thinking at all and failed to mention either a toothbrush or a bathroom. In another study, when 5-year-olds were asked to try to have no thoughts at all for about 20 seconds, they reported that they were successful at doing this (Flavell, Green, & Flavell, 2000). By contrast, most of the 8-year-olds said they engaged in mental activity during the 20 seconds and reported specific thoughts.

It is only beyond the preschool years—at approximately 5 to 7 years of age—that children have a deepening appreciation of the mind itself rather than just an understanding of mental states. For example, they begin to recognize that people's behaviors do not necessarily reflect their thoughts and feelings (Flavell, Green, & Flavell, 1993). Not until middle and late childhood do children see the mind as an active constructor of knowledge or processing center (Flavell, Green, & Flavell, 1998) and move from understanding that beliefs can be false to realizing that the same event can be open to multiple interpretations (Carpendale & Chandler, 1996). For example, in one study, children saw an ambiguous line drawing (for example, a drawing that could be seen as either a duck or a rabbit); one puppet told the child she believed the drawing was a duck while another puppet told the child he believed the drawing was a rabbit (see Figure 7.18). Before the age of 7, children said that there was one right answer, and it was not okay for both puppets to have different opinions.

Although most research on children's theory of mind focuses on children around or before their preschool years, at 7 years of age and beyond there are important developments in the ability to understand the beliefs and thoughts of others. While understanding that people may have different interpretations is important, it is also important to recognize that some interpretations and beliefs may still be evaluated on the basis of the merits of arguments and evidence (Kuhn, Cheney, & Weinstock, 2000). In early adolescence, children begin to understand

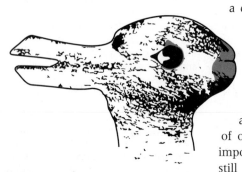

FIGURE 7.18 Ambiguous Line Drawing.

that people can have ambivalent feelings (Harter, 2006). They start to recognize that the same person can feel both happy and sad about the same event. They also engage in more recursive thinking: thinking about what other people are thinking about.

Individual Differences As in other developmental research, there are individual differences in when children reach certain milestones in their theory of mind. For example, preschoolers who have more siblings perform better on theory of mind tasks than preschoolers with fewer siblings, especially if they have older siblings (McAlister & Peterson, 2007). Children who talk with their parents about feelings frequently as 2-year-olds show better performance on theory of mind tasks (Ruffman, Slade, & Crowe, 2002), as do children who frequently engage in pretend play (Harris, 2000).

Executive function, which describes several functions (such as inhibition and planning) that are important for flexible, future-oriented behavior, also may be connected to theory of mind development (Astington & Dack, 2008; Doherty, 2008). For example, in one executive function task, children are asked to say the word *night* when they see a picture of a sun, and the word *day* when they see a picture of a moon and stars. Children who perform better at executive function tasks seem also to have a better understanding of theory of mind (Sabbagh & others, 2006).

Theory of Mind and Autism Another individual difference in understanding the mind involves autism (Doherty, 2008). Approximately 1 in 150 children are estimated to have some type of autism (Centers for Disease Control and Preventation, 2009). Autism can usually be diagnosed by the age of 3 years, and sometimes earlier. Children with autism show a number of behaviors different from children their age, including deficits in social interaction and communication as well as repetitive behaviors or interests. They often show indifference toward others, in many instances preferring to be alone and showing more interest in objects than people.

Children and adults with autism have difficulty in social interactions, often described as huge deficits in theory of mind (Fernyhough, 2008). These deficits are generally greater than deficits in children the same mental age with mental retardation (Baron-Cohen, 1995). Researchers have found that autistic children have difficulty in developing a theory of mind, especially in understanding others' beliefs and emotions (Harris, 2006). Although children with autism tend to do poorly reasoning in false-belief tasks (Peterson, 2005), they can perform much better on reasoning tasks requiring an understanding of physical causality.

Metamemory in Children

Although theory of mind has dominated metacognition research with children in recent years, researchers also have studied children's metamemory. By 5 or 6 years of age, children usually know that familiar items are easier to learn than unfamiliar ones, that short lists are easier than long ones, that recognition is easier than recall, and that forgetting becomes more likely over time (Lyon & Flavell, 1993). However, in other ways young children's metamemory is limited. They don't understand that related items are easier to remember than unrelated ones or that remembering the gist of a

This boy sitting on the sofa is autistic. *What are some characteristics of autistic children? What are some deficits in autistic children's theory of mind?*

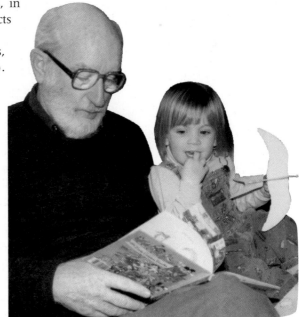

Cognitive developmentalist John Flavell (*left*) is a pioneer in providing insights about children's thinking. Among his many contributions are establishing the field of metacognition and conducting numerous studies in this area, including metamemory and theory of mind studies.

story is easier than remembering information verbatim (Kreutzer, Leonard, & Flavell, 1975). By fifth grade, students understand that gist recall is easier than verbatim recall.

Preschool children also have an inflated opinion of their memory abilities. For example, in one study, a majority of preschool children predicted that they would be able to recall all ten items of a list of ten items. When tested, none of the young children managed this feat (Flavell, Friedrichs, & Hoyt, 1970). As they move through the elementary school years, children give more realistic evaluations of their memory skills (Schneider & Pressley, 1997).

Preschool children also have little appreciation for the importance of cues for memory, such as "It helps when you can think of an example of it." By 7 or 8 years of age, children better appreciate the importance of cueing for memory.

In general, children's understanding of their memory abilities and their skill in evaluating their performance on memory tasks is relatively poor at the beginning of the elementary school years but improves considerably by 11 to 12 years of age (Bjorklund & Rosenbaum, 2000).

Metacognition in Adolescence and Adulthood

In addition to the metacognition changes in memory and theory of mind that occur in childhood, important changes in metacognition take place during adolescence (Kuhn, 2008, 2009). Compared with when they were children, adolescents have an increased capacity to monitor and manage cognitive resources to effectively meet the demands of a learning task. This increased metacognitive ability results in cognitive functioning and learning becoming more effective.

An important aspect of cognitive functioning and learning is determining how much attention will be allocated to an available resource. Evidence is accumulating that adolescents have a better understanding of how to effectively deploy their attention to different aspects of a task than children do (Kuhn, 2008, 2009). In one investigation, 12-year-olds were markedly better than 8-year-olds, and slightly worse than 20-year-olds, at allocating their attention between two tasks (Manis, Keating, & Morrison, 1980). Adolescents may have more resources available to them than children (through increased processing speed, capacity, and automaticity), or they may be more skilled at directing the resources. Further, adolescents have a better meta-level understanding of strategies—that is, knowing the best strategy to use and when to use it in performing a learning task.

Keep in mind, though, that there is considerable individual variation in adolescents' metacognition. Indeed, some experts argue that individual variation in metacognition becomes much more pronounced in adolescence than in childhood (Kuhn & Franklin, 2006). Thus, some adolescents are quite good at using metacognition to improve their learning; others are far less effective.

By middle age, adults have accumulated a great deal of metacognitive knowledge. They can draw on this metacognitive knowledge to help them combat a decline in memory skills. For example, they are likely to understand that they need to have good organizational skills and reminders to help combat the decline in memory skills they face.

Older adults tend to overestimate the memory problems they experience on a daily basis. They seem to be more aware of their memory failures than younger adults and become more anxious about minor forgetfulness than younger adults (Hoyer & Roodin, 2009). Researchers have found that in general older adults are as accurate as younger adults in monitoring the encoding and retrieval of information (Hertzog & Dixon, 2005). However, some aspects of monitoring information, such as source memory (discussed earlier in the chapter), decline in older adults (Herzog & Dixon, 2005; Isingrini, Perrotin, & Souchay, 2008).

Review and Reflect: Learning Goal 5

 Define metacognition, and summarize its developmental changes

REVIEW

- What is metacognition?
- How does the child's theory of mind change during the preschool years?
- How does metamemory typically change during childhood?
- How does metacognition change in adolescence and adulthood?

REFLECT

- How might metacognition be involved in the ability of college students to have better study skills than children?

Reach Your Learning Goals

Information Processing

1 THE INFORMATION-PROCESSING APPROACH: EXPLAIN THE INFORMATION-PROCESSING APPROACH AND ITS APPLICATION TO DEVELOPMENT

The Information-Processing Approach and Its Application to Development

- The information-processing approach analyzes how individuals manipulate information, monitor it, and create strategies for handling it. Attention, memory, and thinking are involved in effective information processing. In the information-processing approach, children's cognitive development results from their ability to overcome processing limitations by increasingly executing basic operations, expanding information-processing capacity, and acquiring new knowledge and strategies. According to Siegler, three important mechanisms of change are encoding (how information gets into memory), automaticity (ability to process information with little or no effort), and strategy construction (creation of new procedures for processing information). Children's information processing is characterized by self-modification, and an important aspect of this self-modification involves metacognition—that is, knowing about knowing.

Speed of Processing Information

- Processing speed increases across the childhood and adolescent years. Processing speed slows in the middle and late adulthood years. However, strategies that people learn through experience can compensate for age-related decline in speed to some degree.

2 ATTENTION: DEFINE ATTENTION, AND OUTLINE ITS DEVELOPMENTAL CHANGES

What Is Attention?

- Attention is the focusing of mental resources. Four ways that people can allocate their attention are selective attention (focusing on a specific aspect of experience that is relevant while ignoring others that are irrelevant); divided attention (concentrating on more than one activity at the same time); sustained attention (maintaining attention to a selected stimulus for a prolonged period of time; also referred to as vigilance); and executive attention (involving action planning, allocating attention to goals, error detection and compensation, monitoring progress on tasks, and dealing with novel or difficult circumstances).

Infancy

- Even newborns can fixate on a contour, but as they get older they scan a pattern more thoroughly. Attention in the first year of life is dominated by the orienting/investigative process. Attention in infancy often occurs through habituation and dishabituation. Joint attention plays an important role in infant development, especially in the infant's acquisition of language.

Childhood and Adolescence

- Salient stimuli tend to capture the attention of the preschooler. After 6 or 7 years of age, there is a shift to more cognitive control of attention. Selective attention improves through childhood and adolescence. Multitasking is an example of divided attention, and it can distract adolescents' attention when they are engaging in a challenging task.

Adulthood

- Attentional skills often are excellent in early adulthood. Older adults are generally less adept than younger adults at selective and divided attention.

3   MEMORY: DESCRIBE WHAT MEMORY IS AND HOW IT CHANGES THROUGH THE LIFE SPAN

What Is Memory?

- Memory is the retention of information over time. Psychologists study the processes of memory: how information is initially placed or encoded into memory, how it is retained or stored, and how it is found or retrieved for a certain purpose later. People construct and reconstruct their memories—the mind does not take an exact photograph of an event and may distort it as it encodes and stores the impression. Schema theory states that people mold memories to fit the information that already exists in their minds.

Infancy

- Infants as young as 2 to 6 months of age display implicit memory, which is memory without conscious recollection as in memory of perceptual-motor skills. However, many experts argue that explicit memory, which is the conscious memory of facts and experiences, does not emerge until the second half of the first year of life. The hippocampus and frontal lobes of the brain are involved in development of memory in infancy. Older children and adults remember little if anything from the first three years of their lives.

Childhood

- One method of assessing short-term memory (the retention of information for up to 15 to 30 seconds, assuming there is no rehearsal of the information) is with a memory-span task, on which there are substantial developmental changes through the childhood years. Working memory (a kind of "mental workbench," where individuals manipulate and assemble information when they make decisions, solve problems, and comprehend language) is linked to children's reading comprehension and problem solving. Young children can remember a great deal of information if they are given appropriate cues and prompts. Strategies can improve children's memory, and older children are more likely to use these than younger children. Imagery and elaboration are two important strategies. Knowledge is an important influence on memory.

Adulthood

- Younger adults have better episodic memory than older adults. Older adults have more difficulty retrieving semantic information. Working memory and processing speed decrease in older adults. Explicit memory is more likely to decline in older adults than is implicit memory. Source memory—remembering where one learned something—declines with age in adulthood. Controversy characterizes whether prospective memory, which is remembering to do something in the future, declines as adults age.

4   THINKING: CHARACTERIZE THINKING AND ITS DEVELOPMENTAL CHANGES

What Is Thinking?

- Thinking involves manipulating and transforming information in memory.

Childhood

- Mandler argues that it is not until about 7 to 9 months of age that infants form conceptual categories, although we do not know precisely when concept formation begins. Infants' first concepts are broad. Over the first two years of life, these broad concepts gradually become more differentiated. Many infants and young children develop an intense interest in a particular category(ies). Critical thinking involves grasping the deeper meaning of ideas, an open mind, and deciding for oneself what to think and do. Children and scientists think alike in some ways, but not alike in others. Children are less influenced by an overall pattern than by happenstance events—they often cling to old theories despite the evidence. Two important aspects of solving problems involve using strategies and using analogies.

Adolescence

- Adolescence is an important transitional period in critical thinking. Decision making increases in adolescence.

Adulthood

- Everyday problem-solving and decision-making effectiveness remain stable in early and middle adulthood; then some aspects decline in late adulthood while others may increase. One aspect of cognition that may improve with aging is expertise. Many older adults preserve decision-making skills reasonably well, although in some cases, memory decline will impair decision making. In the twentieth and twenty-first centuries, successive generations of older adults have been better educated, had work experiences that include a stronger emphasis on cognitively oriented labor, and been healthier. These cohort effects are linked to higher cognitive functioning. There has been considerable increased interest in the cognitive neuroscience of aging that focuses on links between aging, the brain, and cognitive functioning. This field especially relies on fMRI and PET scans to assess brain functioning while individuals are engaging in cognitive tasks. One of the most consistent findings in this field is a decline in the functioning of specific regions in the prefrontal cortex in older adults and links between this decline and poorer performance on complex reasoning, working memory, and episodic memory tasks. Using cognitive skills helps older adults retain a higher level of cognitive functioning. Cognitive training and physical fitness training can help remediate cognitive decline.

5 METACOGNITION: DEFINE METACOGNITION, AND SUMMARIZE ITS DEVELOPMENTAL CHANGES

What Is Metacognition?

- Metacognition is "knowing about knowing."

Theory of Mind

- Theory of mind is the awareness of one's own mental processes and the mental processes of others. Children begin to understand mental states involving perceptions, desires, and emotions from 18 months to 3 years of age and between 3 and 5 years of age come to realize that people can have false beliefs. It is only beyond the early childhood years that children have a deepening appreciation of the mind itself rather than just understanding mental states. Autistic children have difficulty in developing a theory of mind.

Metamemory in Children

- By 5 to 6 years of age, children usually know that familiar items are easier to learn than unfamiliar ones and that short lists are easier than long ones. By 7 to 8 years of age, children better appreciate the importance of cues for memory.

Metacognition in Adolescence and Adulthood

- Adolescents have an increased capacity to monitor and manage resources to effectively meet the demands of a learning task, although there is considerable individual variation in metacognition during adolescence. Metacognition continues to improve in early adulthood, and many middle-aged individuals have accumulated considerable metacognitive knowledge. Older adults tend to overestimate their everyday memory problems.

KEY TERMS

encoding 241
automaticity 241
strategy construction 241
metacognition 241
attention 243
selective attention 243
divided attention 243
sustained attention 243

executive attention 243
joint attention 244
memory 247
schema theory 248
schemas 248
implicit memory 249
explicit memory 250
long-term memory 250

short-term memory 250
working memory 251
elaboration 252
fuzzy trace theory 253
episodic memory 254
semantic memory 254
source memory 255
prospective memory 256

thinking 256
critical thinking 258
mindfulness 258
dual-process model 263
expertise 263
metamemory 268
theory of mind 269

KEY PEOPLE

E-LEARNING TOOLS

Connect to **www.mhhe.com/santrockldt5e** to research the answers and complete these exercises. In addition, you'll find a number of other resources and valuable study tools for Chapter 7, "Information Processing," on this Web site.

Taking It to the Net

1. Six-year-old Matthew is in the habit of asking his parents to repeat every comment or question. They know he does not have a hearing problem—they think he just doesn't pay attention. How can they teach Matthew to pay attention and listen?

2. Twelve-year-old Luke has some learning difficulties. His teacher is interested in finding strategies that will enhance his learning. She wonders whether the use of mnemonics may help Luke both in the classroom and at home. Does Luke benefit from mnemonics?

3. In the past year, 58-year-old Alan has experienced some lapses in memory. He sometimes forgets where he has put his car keys, it may take him a few minutes to recall the name of someone he met on the golf course last week, and it takes him longer to balance his checkbook than it used to. Is Alan showing signs of dementia or merely of normal age-related forgetfulness?

Self-Assessment

In our discussion of memory in adulthood, we discussed a number of study and memory strategies. To evaluate your study skills, complete this self-assessment:

- *My Study Skills*

Health and Well-Being, Parenting, and Education

Build your decision-making skills by trying your hand at the health and well-being, parenting, and education exercises.

Video Clips

The Online Learning Center includes the following videos for this chapter:

- *Children's Eyewitness Testimony*
- *Limits to Memory at Age 3*
- *Memory Ability at Age 4*
- *Memory Ability at Age 7*

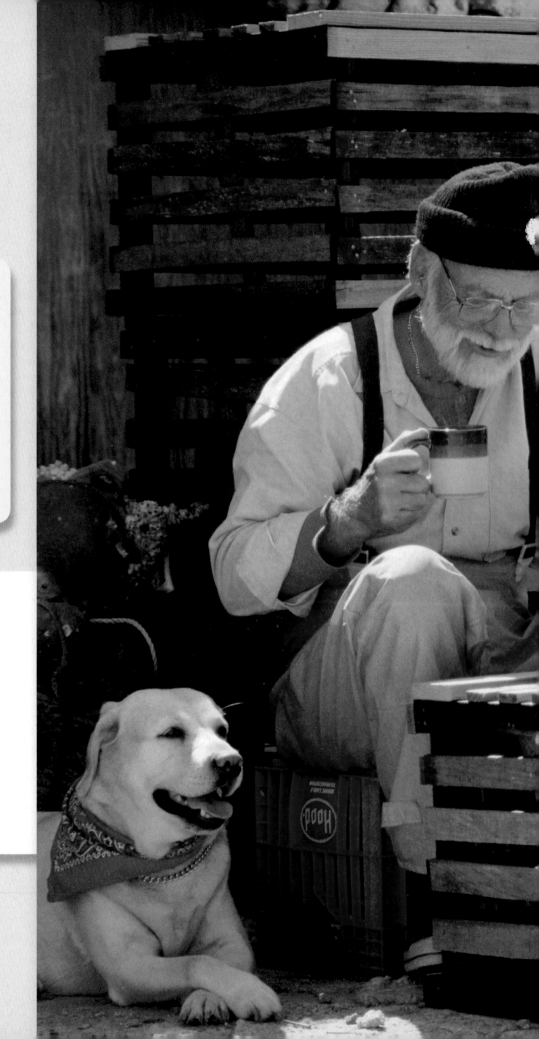

8

> *What a piece of work is a man! How noble in reason! how infinite in faculty! in form, in moving, how express and admirable! in action how like an angel! in apprehension how like a god!*
>
> —WILLIAM SHAKESPEARE
> *English Playwright, 17th Century*

LEARNING GOALS

- ◆ Explain the nature of intelligence.

- ◆ Outline key controversies about differences in IQ scores.

- ◆ Discuss the development of intelligence across the human life span.

- ◆ Describe the characteristics of mental retardation, giftedness, and creativity.

INTELLIGENCE

CHAPTER OUTLINE

PREVIEW

The concept of intelligence has generated many controversies, including whether intelligence is more strongly influenced by heredity or by environment, whether there is cultural bias in intelligence testing, and whether intelligence tests are misused. We explore these controversies, as well as these topics: the extent to which we have a single intelligence or multiple intelligences, the development of intelligence across the life span, and the extremes of intelligence and creativity.

1   THE CONCEPT OF INTELLIGENCE

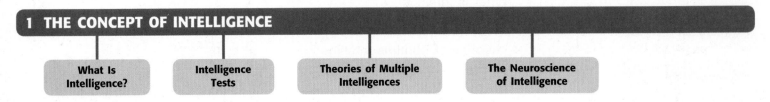

| What Is Intelligence? | Intelligence Tests | Theories of Multiple Intelligences | The Neuroscience of Intelligence |

Intelligence is one of our most prized possessions. However, even the most intelligent people have not been able to agree on how to define and measure the concept of intelligence.

What Is Intelligence?

What does the term *intelligence* mean to psychologists? Some experts describe intelligence as the ability to solve problems. Others describe it as the capacity to adapt and learn from experience. Still others argue that intelligence includes characteristics such as creativity and interpersonal skills.

The problem with intelligence is that, unlike height, weight, and age, intelligence cannot be directly measured. We can't peel back a person's scalp and see how much intelligence he or she has. We can evaluate intelligence only *indirectly* by studying and comparing the intelligent acts that people perform.

The primary components of intelligence are similar to the cognitive processes of thinking and memory that we discussed in Chapter 7, "Information Processing." The differences in how we described these cognitive processes in Chapter 7, and how we discuss intelligence, lie in the concepts of individual differences and assessment. *Individual differences* are the stable, consistent ways in which people are different from one another. Individual differences in intelligence generally have been measured by intelligence tests designed to tell us whether a person can reason better than others who have taken the test (Neukrug & Fawcett, 2010).

How can intelligence be defined? **Intelligence** is the ability to solve problems and to adapt and learn from experiences. But even this broad definition doesn't satisfy everyone. As you will see shortly, Robert J. Sternberg (2008; 2009a, b) proposes that practical know-how should be considered part of intelligence. In his view, intelligence involves weighing options carefully and acting judiciously, as well as developing strategies to improve shortcomings. Also, a definition of intelligence based on a theory such as Vygotsky's, which we discussed in Chapter 6, "Cognitive Developmental Approaches," would have to include the ability to use the tools of the culture with help from more-skilled individuals. Because intelligence is such an abstract, broad concept, it is not surprising that there are so many different ways to define it.

Intelligence Tests

Robert Sternberg (1997) had considerable childhood anxieties about intelligence tests. Because he got so stressed out about taking the tests, he did very poorly on

intelligence The ability to solve problems and to adapt to and learn from experiences.

them. Fortunately, a fourth-grade teacher worked with Robert and helped instill the confidence in him to overcome his anxieties. Not only did he begin performing better on them, but when he was 13, he devised his own intelligence test and began using it to assess classmates—until the chief school-system psychologist found out and scolded him. Sternberg became so fascinated by intelligence that he made its study a lifelong pursuit. Later in this chapter, we discuss his theory of intelligence.

The Binet Tests In 1904, the French Ministry of Education asked psychologist Alfred Binet to devise a method to determine which students would not profit from typical school instruction. Binet and his student Théophile Simon developed an intelligence test to meet this request. The test consisted of 30 items ranging from the ability to touch one's nose or ear when asked to the ability to draw designs from memory and to define abstract concepts.

Binet stressed that the core of intelligence consists of complex cognitive processes, such as memory, imagery, comprehension, and judgment. In addition, he noted that a developmental approach was crucial for understanding intelligence. He proposed that a child's intellectual ability increases with age. Therefore, he tested potential items and determined that age at which a typical child could answer them correctly. Thus, Binet developed the concept of **mental age (MA),** which is an individual's level of mental development relative to others. For an average child, MA scores correspond to *chronological age (CA)*, which is age from birth. A bright child has an MA considerably above CA; a dull child has an MA considerably below CA.

The Binet test has been revised many times to incorporate advances in the understanding of intelligence and intelligence testing. Many revisions were carried out by Lewis Terman, who developed extensive norms and provided detailed, clear instructions for each problem on the test. Terman also applied a concept introduced by William Stern (1912), who coined the term **intelligence quotient (IQ)** to refer to an individual's mental age divided by chronological age multiplied by 100: IQ = MA/CA × 100.

If a child's mental age, as measured by the Binet test, was the same as the child's chronological age, then the child's IQ score was 100. If the measured mental age was above chronological age, then the IQ score was more than 100. If mental age was below chronological age, the IQ score was less than 100. Although this scoring system is no longer used, the term *IQ* is often still used to refer to a score on a standardized intelligence test.

In 2004, the test, now called the Stanford-Binet 5 (Stanford University is where the revisions have been done), was revised to analyze an individual's responses in five content areas: fluid reasoning, knowledge, quantitative reasoning, visual-spatial reasoning, and working memory. A general composite score also is obtained. Today the test is scored by comparing how the test-taker performs compared with other people of the same age. The average score is set at 100.

The current Stanford-Binet is given to individuals from the age of 2 through adulthood. It includes a wide variety of items, some requiring verbal responses; others, nonverbal responses. For example, a 6-year-old is expected to complete the verbal task of defining at least six words, such as *orange* and *envelope,* and the nonverbal task of tracing a path through a maze. An adult with average intelligence is expected to define such words as *disproportionate* and *regard,* explain a proverb, and compare the concepts of idleness and laziness.

Over the years, the Stanford-Binet has been given to thousands of children and adults of different ages. By administering the test to large numbers of individuals selected at random from different parts of the United States, it has been found that the scores approximate a normal distribution (see Figure 8.1). A **normal distribution** is a symmetrical, bell-shaped curve with a majority of the cases falling in the

Alfred Binet constructed the first intelligence test after being asked to create a measure to determine which children could benefit from instruction in France's schools and which could not.

mental age (MA) An individual's level of mental development relative to others.

intelligence quotient (IQ) An individual's mental age divided by chronological age multiplied by 100; devised in 1912 by William Stern.

normal distribution A symmetrical, bell-shaped curve with a majority of the cases falling in the middle of the possible range of scores and few scores appearing toward the extremes of the range.

FIGURE 8.1 The Normal Curve and Stanford-Binet IQ Scores. The distribution of IQ scores approximates a normal curve. Most of the population falls in the middle range of scores. Notice that extremely high and extremely low scores are very rare. Slightly more than two-thirds of the scores fall between 85 and 115. Only about 1 in 50 individuals has an IQ of more than 130, and only about 1 in 50 individuals has an IQ of less than 70.

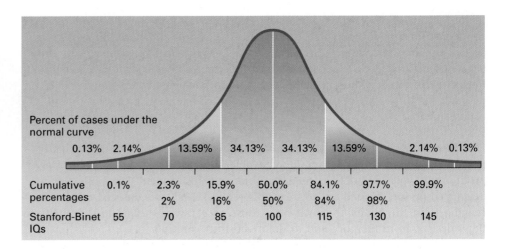

Percent of cases under the normal curve

| 0.13% | 2.14% | 13.59% | 34.13% | 34.13% | 13.59% | 2.14% | 0.13% |

Cumulative percentages	0.1%	2.3%	15.9%	50.0%	84.1%	97.7%	99.9%	
		2%	16%	50%	84%	98%		
Stanford-Binet IQs	55	70	85	100	115	130	145

middle of the range of possible scores and few scores appearing toward the extremes of the range. The Stanford-Binet continues to be one of the most widely used individual tests of intelligence.

Verbal Subscales

Similarities

A child must think logically and abstractly to answer a number of questions about how things might be similar.

Example: "In what way are a lion and a tiger alike?"

Comprehension

This subscale is designed to measure an individual's judgment and common sense.

Example: "What is the advantage of keeping money in a bank?"

Nonverbal Subscales

Block Design

A child must assemble a set of multicolored blocks to match designs that the examiner shows. Visual-motor coordination, perceptual organization, and the ability to visualize spatially are assessed.

Example: "Use the four blocks on the left to make the pattern on the right."

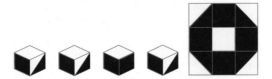

FIGURE 8.2 Sample Subscales of the Wechsler Intelligence Scale for Children–Fourth Edition (WISC-IV). Simulated items similar to those in the Wechsler Intelligence Scale for Children. Copyright © 2003 NCS Pearson, Inc. Reproduced with permission. All rights reserved. "Wechsler Intelligence Scale for Children," "WISC," and "Wechsler" are trademarks, in the U.S. and/or other countries, of Pearson Education, Inc. or its affiliates.

The Wechsler Scales Besides the Stanford-Binet, the other most widely used intelligence tests are the Wechsler scales, developed by David Wechsler. In 1939, Wechsler introduced the first of his scales, designed for use with adults (Wechsler, 1939); the current edition is the Wechsler Adult Intelligence Scale—Third Edition (WAIS-III). The Wechsler Intelligence Scale for Children—Fourth Edition (WISC-IV) is designed for children and adolescents between the ages of 6 and 16, and the Wechsler Preschool and Primary Scale of Intelligence—Third Edition (WPPSI-III) is appropriate for children from the ages of 2 years 6 months to 7 years 3 months of age.

The Wechsler scales not only provide an overall IQ score but also yield several composite scores (for example, the Verbal Comprehension Index, the Working Memory Index, and the Processing Speed Index). These allow the examiner to quickly see the areas in which the individual is strong or weak in different areas of intelligence. Three of the Wechsler subscales are shown in Figure 8.2.

The Use and Misuse of Intelligence Tests Psychological tests are tools. Like all tools, their effectiveness depends on the knowledge, skill, and integrity of the user. A hammer can be used to build a beautiful kitchen cabinet or it can be used as a weapon of assault. Like a hammer, psychological tests can be used for positive purposes or they can be abused.

Intelligence tests have real-world applications as predictors of school and job success (Deary & others, 2007). For example, scores on tests of general intelligence are substantially correlated with school grades and achievement test performance, both at the time of the test and years later (Brody, 2007; Strenze, 2007). IQ in the sixth grade correlates about .60 with the number of years of education the individual will eventually obtain (Jencks, 1979).

Intelligence tests are moderately correlated with work performance (Lubinski, 2000). Individuals with higher scores on tests designed to measure general intelligence tend to get higher-paying, more prestigious jobs (Wagner, 1997; Zagorsky, 2007). However, general IQ tests predict only about one-fourth of the variation in job success, with the majority of job success due to motivation, education, and other factors (Wagner & Sternberg, 1986). Further, the correlations between IQ and achievement decrease the longer people work at a job, presumably because as they gain more job experience they perform better (Hunt, 1995).

Thus, although there are correlations between IQ scores and academic achievement and occupational success, many other factors contribute to success in school and work. These include the motivation to succeed, physical and mental health, and social skills (Sternberg, 2003).

The single number provided by many IQ tests can easily lead to false expectations about an individual (Rosnow & Rosenthal, 1996). Sweeping generalizations are too often made on the basis of an IQ score. For example, imagine that you are a teacher in the teacher's lounge the day after school has started in the fall. You mention a student—Johnny Jones—and a fellow teacher remarks that she had Johnny in class last year; she comments that he was a real dunce and points out that his IQ is 78. You cannot help but remember this information, and it might lead to thoughts that Johnny Jones is not very bright so it is useless to spend much time teaching him. In this way, IQ scores are misused and can become self-fulfilling prophecies (Weinstein, 2004).

Even though they have limitations, tests of intelligence are among psychology's most widely used tools. To be effective, they should be used in conjunction with other information about an individual. For example, an intelligence test alone should not determine whether a child is placed in a special education or gifted class. The child's developmental history, medical background, performance in school, social competencies, and family experiences should be taken into account too.

Theories of Multiple Intelligences

The use of a single score to describe how people perform on intelligence tests suggests intelligence is a general ability, a single trait. Wechsler scales provide scores for a number of intellectual skills, as well as an overall score. Do people have some general mental ability that determines how they perform on all of these tests? Or is intelligence a label for a combination of several distinct abilities? And do conventional intelligence tests measure everything that should be considered part of intelligence? Psychologists disagree about the answers to these questions.

Sternberg's Triarchic Theory   Robert J. Sternberg (1986, 2004, 2007, 2008, 2009a, b; 2010a, b) notes that traditional IQ tests fail to measure some important dimensions of intelligence. Sternberg proposes a **triarchic theory of intelligence** with three main types of intelligence: analytical, creative, and practical.

Analytical, Creative, and Practical Intelligence   To understand what analytical, creative, and practical intelligence mean, let's look at examples of people who reflect these three types of intelligence:

Robert J. Sternberg, who developed the triarchic theory of intelligence.

triarchic theory of intelligence Sternberg's theory that intelligence consists of analytical intelligence, creative intelligence, and practical intelligence.

- Consider Latisha, who scores high on traditional intelligence tests such as the Stanford-Binet and is a star analytical thinker. Sternberg calls Latisha's analytical thinking and abstract reasoning *analytical intelligence*. It is the closest to what has traditionally been called intelligence and what is commonly assessed by intelligence tests. In Sternberg's view of analytical intelligence, the basic unit of analytical intelligence is a *component*, which is a basic unit of information processing. Sternberg's components include the ability to acquire or store information; to retain or retrieve information; to transfer information; to plan, make decisions, and solve problems; and to translate thoughts into performance.

- Todd does not have the best test scores but has an insightful and creative mind. The type of thinking at which Todd excels is called *creative intelligence* by Sternberg. According to Sternberg, creative people like Todd have the ability to solve new problems quickly, but they also learn how to solve familiar problems in an automatic way so their minds are free to handle other problems that require insight and creativity.

- Finally, consider Emanuel, a person whose scores on traditional IQ tests are low but who quickly grasps real-life problems. He easily picks up knowledge about how the world works. Emanuel's "street smarts" and practical know-how indicate that he has what Sternberg calls *practical intelligence*. Practical intelligence includes the ability to keep out of trouble and a knack for getting along with people. Sternberg describes practical intelligence as all of the important information about getting along in the world that you are not taught in school.

Triarchic Theory in the Classroom   Sternberg (2009a; 2010a, b) says that students with different triarchic patterns look different in school. Students with high analytic ability tend to be favored in conventional schools. They often do well in classes in which the teacher lectures and gives objective tests. They often are considered smart students, typically get good grades, do well on traditional IQ tests and the SAT, and later gain admission to competitive colleges.

Students who are high in creative intelligence may not be in the top rung of their class. Creatively intelligent students might not conform to the expectations that teachers have about how assignments should be done. They give unique answers, for which they might get reprimanded or marked down.

Like students high in creative intelligence, students who are practically intelligent often do not relate well to the demands of school. However, these students frequently do well outside the classroom's walls. Their social skills and common sense may allow them to become successful managers, entrepreneurs, or politicians, despite undistinguished school records.

Sternberg (1999) notes that few tasks are purely analytic, creative, or practical. Most tasks require some combination of these skills. For example, when students write a book report, they might (1) analyze the book's main themes, (2) generate new ideas about how the book could have been written better, and (3) think about how the book's themes can be applied to people's lives. Sternberg (2008; Sternberg, Kaufman, & Grigorenko, 2008) argues that it is important for classroom instruction to give students opportunities to learn through all three types of intelligence.

Gardner's Theory of Multiple Intelligences   According to Howard Gardner (1983, 1993, 2002) people have multiple intelligences, and IQ tests measure only a few of these. He argues that IQ tests measure verbal, math, and spatial aspects of intelligence but emphasizes that intelligence involves a number of other abilities. For evidence of the existence of multiple intelligences, Gardner uses information about the ways in which certain cognitive abilities survive particular types of brain damage. He also points to child prodigies and to some individuals who are retarded or autistic but have an extraordinary skill in a particular domain. An example was portrayed by Dustin Hoffman in the movie *Rain Man*. Hoffman's character was autistic but had a remarkable computing ability. In one scene, he helped his brother successfully gamble in Las Vegas by keeping track of all the cards that had been played.

From Verbal Intelligence to Naturalist Intelligence   Gardner has proposed eight types of intelligence. They are described here along with examples of the occupations in which they are reflected as strengths (Campbell, Campbell, & Dickinson, 2004):

- *Verbal.* The ability to think in words and use language to express meaning (occupations: authors, journalists, speakers)

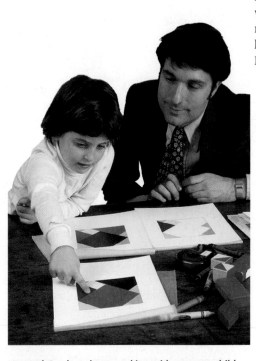

Howard Gardner, here working with a young child, developed the view that intelligence comes in the forms of these eight kinds of skills: verbal, mathematical, spatial, bodily-kinesthetic, musical, intrapersonal, interpersonal, and naturalist.

- *Mathematical.* The ability to carry out mathematical operations (occupations: scientists, engineers, accountants)
- *Spatial.* The ability to think three-dimensionally (occupations: architects, artists, sailors)
- *Bodily-kinesthetic.* The ability to manipulate objects and be physically adept (occupations: surgeons, craftspeople, dancers, athletes)
- *Musical.* A sensitivity to pitch, melody, rhythm, and tone (occupations: composers, musicians, and sensitive listeners)
- *Interpersonal.* The ability to understand and effectively interact with others (occupations: successful teachers, mental health professionals)
- *Intrapersonal.* The ability to understand oneself (occupations: theologians, psychologists)
- *Naturalist.* The ability to observe patterns in nature and understand natural and human-made systems (occupations: farmers, botanists, ecologists, landscapers)

Recently, Gardner has considered adding a ninth type of intelligence to his list of multiple intelligences—*existentialist*, which involves exploring and finding meaning in life, especially regarding questions about life, death, and existence.

Gardner notes that each of the eight intelligences can be destroyed by brain damage, that each involves unique cognitive skills, and that each shows up in exaggerated fashion in the gifted and in individuals with mental retardation or autism. According to Gardner, everyone has all of these intelligences but to varying degrees. As a result, we prefer to learn and process information in different ways. People learn best when they can apply their strong intelligences to the task.

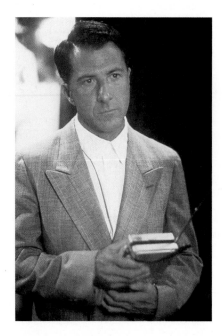

In *Rain Man*, Dustin Hoffman portrayed a man with autism and cognitive deficits who accomplished remarkable feats of counting and mathematics. Such skills are described as *savant skills.* They support the idea that intelligence can be expressed in multiple abilities.

Multiple Intelligences in the Classroom   Currently there is considerable interest in applying Gardner's theory of multiple intelligences to children's education (Campbell, Campbell, & Dickinson, 2004; Hirsch, 2004; Weber, 2005). The goal is to allow students to discover and then explore the domains in which they have natural curiosity and talent. According to Gardner (1983), if teachers give students opportunities to use their bodies, imaginations, and different senses, almost every student finds that she or he is good at something. Even students who are not outstanding in any single area will find that they have relative strengths. Thus, at the Key School in Indianapolis, each day every student is exposed to materials that are designed to stimulate a range of human abilities, including art, music, language skills, math skills, and physical games. In addition, attention is given to understanding oneself and others.

Children in the Key School form "pods," in which they pursue activities of special interest to them. Every day, each child can choose from activities that draw on Gardner's eight frames of mind. The school has pods that range from gardening to architecture to gliding to dancing. *What are some of the main ideas of Gardner's theory and its application to education?*

Emotional Intelligence   Both Sternberg's and Gardner's theories include one or more categories related to social intelligence. In Sternberg's theory, the category is practical intelligence; in Gardner's theory, they are interpersonal intelligence and intrapersonal intelligence. Another theory that emphasizes interpersonal, intrapersonal, and practical aspects of intelligence is called **emotional intelligence,** which has been popularized by Daniel Goleman (1995) in his book *Emotional Intelligence.* The concept of emotional intelligence was initially developed by Peter Salovey and John Mayer (1990), who define it as the ability to perceive and express emotion accurately and adaptively (such as taking the perspective of others), to understand emotion and emotional knowledge (such as understanding the roles that emotions play in friendship and marriage), to use feelings to facilitate thought (such as being in a positive mood, which is linked to creative thinking), and to manage emotions in oneself and others (such as being able to control one's anger).

emotional intelligence The ability to perceive and express emotions accurately and adaptively, to understand emotion and emotional knowledge, to use feelings to facilitate thought, and to manage emotions in oneself and others.

Gardner	Sternberg	Salovey/Mayer
Verbal Mathematical	Analytical	
Spatial Movement Musical	Creative	
Interpersonal Intrapersonal	Practical	Emotional
Naturalistic		

FIGURE 8.3 Comparing Sternberg's, Gardner's, and Salovey/Mayer's Intelligences.

There continues to be considerable interest in the concept of emotional intelligence (Fiori, 2009; Hansenne & Biarchi, 2009). Critics argue that emotional intelligence broadens the concept of intelligence too far and has not been adequately assessed and researched (Matthews, Zeidner, & Roberts, 2006). Figure 8.3 compares Sternberg's, Gardner's, and Salovey/Mayer's intelligences.

Do People Have One or Many Intelligences? Figure 8.3 provides a comparison of Sternberg's, Gardner's and Salovey/Mayer's views. Notice that Sternberg's view is unique in emphasizing creative intelligence and that Gardner's includes a number of types of intelligence that are not addressed by the other views. These theories of multiple intelligence have much to offer. They have stimulated us to think more broadly about what makes up people's intelligence and competence (Sternberg, 2009a, b, c). And they have motivated educators to develop programs that instruct students in different domains.

Theories of multiple intelligences have their critics (Jensen, 2008). Some critics arguing that the research base to support these theories has not yet developed. In particular, some critics say that Gardner's classification seems arbitrary. For example, if musical skills represent a type of intelligence, why don't we also refer to chess intelligence, prize-fighter intelligence, and so on?

A number of psychologists still support Spearman's concept of *g* (general intelligence) (Jensen, 2008; Johnson, te Nijenhuis, & Bouchard, 2008; Reeve & Charles, 2008). For example, one expert on intelligence, Nathan Brody (2007) argues that people who excel at one type of intellectual task are likely to excel in other intellectual tasks. Thus, individuals who do well at memorizing lists of digits are also likely to be good at solving verbal problems and spatial layout problems. This general intelligence includes abstract reasoning or thinking, the capacity to acquire knowledge, and problem-solving ability (Brody, 2000; Carroll, 1993).

Some experts who argue for the existence of general intelligence conclude that individuals also have specific intellectual abilities (Brody, 2007; Chiappe & MacDonald, 2005). In one study, John Carroll (1993) conducted an extensive examination of intellectual abilities and concluded that all intellectual abilities are related to each other, a view that supports the concept of general intelligence but also maintains that there are many specialized abilities as well. Some of these specialized abilities, such as spatial abilities and mechanical abilities, are not adequately reflected in the curriculum of most schools. In sum, controversy still characterizes whether it is more accurate to conceptualize intelligence as a general ability, as specific abilities, or as both (Brody, 2007; Lubinskym 2009; Sternberg, 2009a, 2010a, b). Sternberg (2008, 2009a, b) actually accepts that there is a *g* in the kinds of analytical tasks that traditional IQ tests assess but thinks that the range of intellectual tasks those tests measure is too narrow.

The Neuroscience of Intelligence

In the current era of extensive research on the brain, interest in the neuroscience underpinnings of intelligence has increased (Glascher & others, 2009; Haier, 2009; Neubauer & Fink, 2009; Shenkin & others, 2009). Among the questions about the brain's role in intelligence being explored are these: Is having a big brain linked to higher intelligence? Is intelligence located in certain brain regions? Is how fast the brain processes information linked to intelligence?

Are individuals with a big brain more intelligent than those with a smaller brain? Recent studies using MRI scans to assess total brain volume indicate a moderate correlation (about +.3 to +.4) between brain size and intelligence (Carey, 2007; Luders & others, 2009; Witelson, Beresh, & Kigar, 2006).

Might intelligence be linked to specific regions of the brain? Early consensus was that the frontal lobes are the likely location of intelligence. However, researchers recently have found that intelligence is distributed more widely across brain regions (Haier, 2009; Haier & others, 2009; Karama & others, 2009; Luders & others, 2009). The most prominent finding from brain-imaging studies is that a distributed neural network involving the frontal and parietal lobes is related to higher intelligence (Colom, Jung, & Haier, 2007; Colom & others, 2009; Jung & Haier, 2007) (see Figure 8.4). Albert Einstein's total brain size was average, but a region of his brain's parietal lobe that is very active in processing math and spatial information was 15 percent larger than average (Witelson, Kigar, & Harvey, 1999). Other brain regions that have been linked to higher intelligence (although at a lower level of significance than the frontal/parietal lobe network) include the temporal and occipital lobes, as well as the cerebellum (Luders & others, 2009).

Neuroscientists also are intrigued by the roles that the brain's gray matter (the neuron's cell body) and white matter (axons and dendrites) might play in intelligence (Luders & others, 2009). The most consistent findings indicate that higher intelligence is linked to a higher volume of gray matter (Colom, Jung, & Haier, 2007; Luders & others, 2009). To a lesser degree, some studies also have found a connection between higher intelligence and a higher volume of white matter (Narr & others, 2007).

Examining the neuroscience of intelligence has also led to study of the role that neurological speed might play in intelligence (Waiter & others, 2009). Research results have not been consistent for this possible link, although one recent study did find that speed of neurological functioning was faster for intellectually gifted children than children with average intelligence (Liu & others, 2007).

As advances in the technology to study the brain's functioning continue in coming decades, we are likely to see more specific conclusions about the brain's role in intelligence. As this research proceeds, keep in mind that both heredity and environment likely contribute to links between the brain and intelligence, including the connections we discussed between brain size and intelligence.

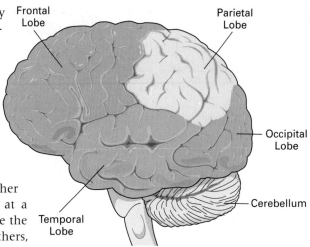

FIGURE 8.4 Intelligence and the Brain. Researchers recently have found that a higher level of intelligence is linked to a distributed neural network in the frontal and parietal lobes. To a lesser extent than the frontal/parietal network, the temporal and occipital lobes, as well as the cerebellum, also have been found to have links to intelligence. The current consensus is that intelligence is likely to be distributed across brain regions rather than being localized in a specific region, such as the frontal lobes.

Review and Reflect: Learning Goal 1

 Explain the nature of intelligence

REVIEW
- What is intelligence?
- What are the main individual tests of intelligence? What are some issues in the use and misuse of intelligence tests?
- What theories of multiple intelligence have been developed? Do people have one intelligence or many intelligences? What are some criticisms of the multiple intelligences concept?
- What are some links between the brain and intelligence?

REFLECT
- A CD-ROM is being sold to parents for testing their child's IQ. What are some potential problems with parents' giving their child an IQ test and interpreting the results?

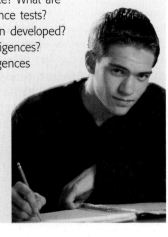

2 CONTROVERSIES AND GROUP COMPARISONS

| The Influence of Heredity and Environment | Group Comparisons and Issues |

We have seen that intelligence is a slippery concept with competing definitions, tests, and theories. It is not surprising, therefore, that attempts to understand the concept of intelligence are filled with controversy. In some cases, the controversies involve comparisons of the intelligence of different groups, such as people from different cultures or ethnic groups.

The Influence of Heredity and Environment

One of the hottest areas in the study of intelligence centers on the extent to which intelligence is influenced by genetics (nature) and the extent to which it is influenced by environment (nurture) (Martinez, 2010). In Chapter 2, "Biological Beginnings," we indicated how difficult it is to tease apart these influences, but that difficulty has not kept psychologists from trying to unravel them.

Genetic Influences To what degree do our genes make us smart? The issue with respect to genetics and intelligence is the degree to which our genes make us smart (Davis, Arden, & Plomin, 2008). A research review found that the difference in the average correlations for identical and fraternal twins was not very high, only .15, (Grigorenko, 2000) (see Figure 8.5).

The concept of heritability attempts to tease apart the effects of heredity and environment in a population. **Heritability** is the portion of the variance in a population that is attributed to genes. The heritability index is computed using correlational techniques. Thus, the highest degree of heritability is 1.00, and correlations of .70 and above suggest a strong genetic influence. A committee of respected researchers convened by the American Psychological Association concluded that by late adolescence, the heritability of intelligence is about .75, which reflects a strong genetic influence (Neisser & others, 1996).

An important point to keep in mind about heritability is that it refers to a specific group (population), *not* to individuals. Researchers use the concept of heritability to try to describe why people differ. Heritability says nothing about why a single individual, like yourself, has a certain intelligence—nor does it say anything about differences *between* groups.

Most research on heredity and environment does not include environments that differ radically. Thus, it is not surprising that many genetic studies show environment to be a fairly weak influence on intelligence (Fraser, 1995).

Researchers have found that the heritability of intelligence increases from as low as .45 in infancy to as high as .80 in late adulthood (McGue & others, 1993; Petrill, 2003). Why might hereditary influences on intelligence increase with age? Possibly as we grow older, our interactions with the environment are shaped less by the influence of others and the environment on us and more by our ability to choose our environments to allow the expression of genetic tendencies (Plomin, 2004). Sometimes children's parents push them into environments that are not compatible with their genetic inheritance (wanting them to be a doctor or an engineer, for example), but as adults these individuals may select their own career environments.

The heritability index has several limitations (Sternberg, Kaufman, & Grigorenko, 2008). It is only as good as the data that are entered into its analysis and the interpretations made from it. The data are virtually all from traditional IQ tests, which some experts believe are not always the best indicator of intelligence (Gardner, 2002; Sternberg, 2009a, b). Also, the heritability index assumes that researchers

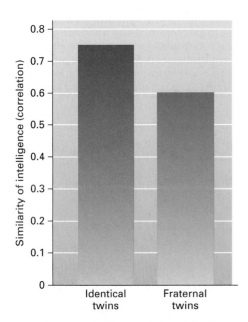

FIGURE 8.5 Correlation Between Intelligence Test Scores and Twin Status. The graph represents a summary of research findings that have compared the intelligence test scores of identical and fraternal twins. An approximate .15 difference has been found with a higher correlation for identical twins (.75) and a lower correlation for fraternal twins (.60).

heritability The portion of the variance in a population that is attributed to genes.

can treat genetic and environmental influences as factors that can be separated, with each part contributing a distinct amount of influence. As we discussed in Chapter 2, "Biological Beginnings," genes and the environment always work together. Genes always exist in an environment, and the environment shapes their activity.

Environmental Influences   Although genetic endowment influences a person's intellectual ability, the environmental experiences of children and adults do make a difference (Grigorenko & Takonishi, 2010; Martinez, 2010). In one study, researchers went into homes and observed how extensively parents from welfare and middle-income professional families talked and communicated with their young children (Hart & Risley, 1995). They found that the middle-income professional parents were much more likely to communicate with their young children than the welfare parents were. And how much the parents communicated with their children in the first three years of their lives was correlated with the children's Stanford-Binet IQ scores at age 3. The more parents communicated with their children, the higher the children's IQs were. Other studies also have found substantial socioeconomic status differences in intelligence (Seifer, 2001).

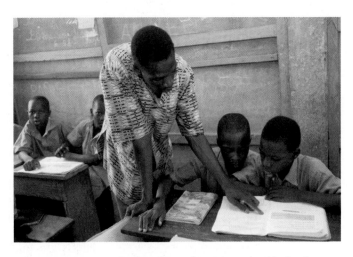

Students in an elementary school in South Africa. *How might schooling influence the development of children's intelligence?*

Schooling also influences intelligence (Ceci & Gilstrap, 2000; Cliffordson & Gustafsson, 2008). The biggest effects have been found when large groups of children received no formal education for an extended period, resulting in lower intelligence.

Another possible effect of education can be seen in rapidly increasing IQ test scores around the world (Flynn, 1999, 2007). IQ scores have been rising so fast that a high percentage of people regarded as having average intelligence in the early 1900s would be considered below average in intelligence today (see Figure 8.6). If a representative sample of people today took the Stanford-Binet test used in 1932, about one-fourth would be defined as having very superior intelligence, a label usually accorded to fewer than 3 percent of the population. Because the increase has taken place in a relatively short time, it cannot be due to heredity, but rather may be due to increasing levels of education attained by a much greater percentage of the world's population or to other environmental factors such as the explosion of information to which people are exposed (Blair & others, 2005). The worldwide increase in intelligence test scores that has occurred over a short time frame has been called the *Flynn effect,* after the researcher who discovered it—James Flynn (1999, 2007).

Keep in mind that environmental influences are complex (Preiss & Sternberg, 2010). Growing up with all the "advantages," for example, does not guarantee success. Children from wealthy families may have easy access to excellent schools, books, travel, and tutoring, but they may take such opportunities for granted and

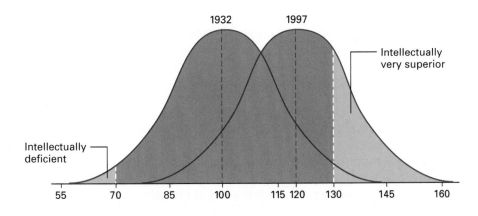

FIGURE 8.6 The Increase in IQ Scores from 1932 to 1997. As measured by the Stanford-Binet test, American children seem to be getting smarter. Scores of a group tested in 1932 fell along a bell-shaped curve with half below 100 and half above. Studies show that if children took that same test today, half would score above 120 on the 1932 scale. Very few of them would score in the "intellectually deficient" end, on the left side, and about one-fourth would rank in the "very superior" range.

fail to develop the motivation to learn and to achieve. In the same way, "poor" or "disadvantaged" does not automatically equal "doomed."

Researchers increasingly are interested in manipulating the early environment of children who are at risk for impoverished intelligence (Gross & others, 2009; Prinz & others, 2009). The emphasis is on prevention rather than remediation. Many low-income parents have difficulty providing an intellectually stimulating environment for their children. Programs that educate parents to be more sensitive caregivers and better teachers, as well as support services such as quality child-care programs, can make a difference in a child's intellectual development (Coltrane & others, 2008).

A review of the research on early interventions concluded that (1) high-quality center-based interventions improve children's intelligence and school achievement; (2) the effects are strongest for poor children and for children whose parents have little education; (3) the positive benefits continue into adolescence, although the effects are smaller than in early childhood or the beginning of elementary school; and (4) the programs that are continued into elementary school have the most sustained long-term effects (Brooks-Gunn, 2003). To read further about environmental influences on intelligence, see the *Research in Life-Span Development* interlude.

Research in Life-Span Development

THE ABECEDARIAN PROJECT

Each morning a young mother waited with her child for the bus that would take the child to school. The child was only 2 months old, and "school" was an experimental program at the University of North Carolina at Chapel Hill. There the child experienced a number of interventions designed to improve her intellectual development—everything from bright objects dangled in front of her eyes while she was a baby to language instruction and counting activities when she was a toddler (Wickelgren, 1999). The child's mother had an IQ of 40 and could not read signs or determine how much change she should receive from a cashier. Her grandmother had a similarly low IQ.

Today, at age 20, the child's IQ measures 80 points higher than her mother's did when the child was 2 months old. Not everyone agrees that IQ can be affected this extensively, but environment can make a substantial difference in a child's intelligence. As behavior geneticist Robert Plomin (1999) has said, even something that is highly heritable (like intelligence) may be malleable through interventions.

The child we just described was part of the Abecedarian Intervention program at the University of North Carolina at Chapel Hill conducted by Craig Ramey and his associates (Campbell, 2007; Ramey & Campbell, 1984; Ramey & Ramey, 1998). They randomly assigned 111 young children from low-income, poorly educated families to either an intervention group, which received full-time, year-round child care along with medical and social work services, or a control group, which received medical and social benefits but no child care. The child-care program included gamelike learning activities aimed at improving language, motor, social, and cognitive skills.

The success of the program in improving IQ was evident by the time the children were 3 years of age. At that age, the experimental group showed normal IQs averaging 101, a 17-point advantage over the control group. Recent follow-up results suggest that the effects are long-lasting. More than a decade later, at 15, children from the intervention group still maintained an IQ advantage of 5 points over the control-group children (97.7 to 92.6) (Campbell, 2007; Campbell & others, 2001; Ramey, Ramey, & Lanzi, 2001). They also did better on standardized tests of reading and math, and were less

The highest-risk children often benefit the most cognitively when they experience early interventions.

—CRAIG RAMEY
Contemporary Psychologist, University of Alabama-Birmingham

likely to be held back a year in school. Also, the greatest IQ gains were made by the children whose mothers had especially low IQs—below 70. At age 15, these children showed a 10-point IQ advantage over a group of children whose mothers' IQs were below 70 but who did not experience the child-care intervention.

In sum, there is a consensus among psychologists that both heredity and environment influence intelligence. This consensus reflects the nature-nurture issue, which was highlighted in Chapter 1, "Introduction." Recall that the nature-nurture issue focuses on the extent to which development is influenced by nature (heredity) and nurture (environment). Although psychologists agree that intelligence is the product of both nature and nurture, there is still disagreement about how strongly each influences intelligence.

Group Comparisons and Issues

Group comparisons in intelligence can involve cultures, ethnic groups, and gender. We begin by examining cross-cultural comparisons and cultural bias in testing.

Cross-Cultural Comparisons Cultures vary in the way they describe what it means to be intelligent (Greenfield, Suzuki, & Rothstein-Fisch, 2006; Matsumoto & Juang, 2008). People in Western cultures tend to view intelligence in terms of reasoning and thinking skills, whereas people in Eastern cultures see intelligence as a way for members of a community to successfully engage in social roles (Nisbett, 2003). One study found that Taiwanese-Chinese conceptions of intelligence emphasize understanding and relating to others, including when to show and when not to show one's intelligence (Yang & Sternberg, 1997).

Elena Grigorenko and her colleagues (2001) have studied the concept of intelligence among rural Africans. They found that people in the Luo culture of rural Kenya view intelligence as consisting of four domains: (1) academic intelligence; (2) social qualities such as respect, responsibility, and consideration; (3) practical thinking; and (4) comprehension. In another study in the same culture, children who scored highly on a test of knowledge about medicinal herbs—a measure of practical intelligence—tended to score poorly on tests of academic intelligence (Sternberg & others, 2001). These results indicated that practical and academic intelligence can develop independently and may even conflict with each other. They also suggest that the values of a culture may influence the direction in which a child develops. In a cross-cultural context, then, intelligence depends a great deal on environment (Sternberg & Grigorenko, 2008).

Cultural Bias in Testing Many of the early intelligence tests were culturally biased, favoring people who were from urban rather than rural environments, middle socioeconomic status rather than low socioeconomic status, and non-Latino White rather than African American (Provenzo, 2002). For example, one question on an early test asked what you should do if you find a 3-year-old child in the street. The correct answer was "call the police." But children from inner-city families who perceive the police as adversaries are unlikely to choose this answer. Similarly, children from rural areas might not choose this answer if there is no police force nearby. Such questions clearly do not measure the knowledge necessary to adapt to one's environment or to be "intelligent" in an inner-city neighborhood or in rural America (Scarr, 1984). Also, members of minority groups who do not speak English or who speak nonstandard English are at a disadvantage in trying to understand questions framed in standard English (Gibbs & Huang, 1989). The *Contexts of Life-Span Development* interlude examines some of the ways intelligence testing can be culturally biased.

"You can't build a hut, you don't know how to find edible roots and you know nothing about predicting the weather. In other words, you do terribly on our I.Q. test."
Cartoon by Sidney Harris. © ScienceCartoonsPlus.com. Used by permission.

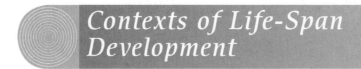

Contexts of Life-Span Development

LARRY P.: INTELLIGENT, BUT NOT ON INTELLIGENCE TESTS

Larry P. is African American and grew up in poverty conditions. When he was 6 years old, he was placed in a class for the "educable mentally retarded" (EMR), which to school psychologists means that Larry learned much more slowly than average children. The primary reason Larry was placed in the EMR class was his very low score of 64 on an intelligence test.

Is there a possibility that the intelligence test Larry was given was culturally biased? Psychologists still debate this issue. A major class-action suit challenged the use of standardized IQ tests to place African American elementary school students in EMR classes. The initial lawsuit, filed on behalf of Larry P., claimed that the IQ test he took underestimated his true learning ability. The lawyers for Larry P. argued that IQ tests place too much emphasis on verbal skills and fail to account for the backgrounds of African American children. Therefore, it was argued, Larry was incorrectly labeled mentally retarded and might forever be saddled with that stigma.

As part of the lengthy court battle involving Larry P., six African American EMR students were independently retested by members of the Bay Association of Black Psychologists in California. The psychologists made sure they established good rapport with the students and made special efforts to overcome the students' defeatism and distraction. For example, items were reworded in terms more consistent with the children's social background, and recognition was given to nonstandard answers that showed a logical, intelligent approach to problems. This testing approach produced scores of 79 to 104—17 to 38 points higher than the scores the students received when initially tested by school psychologists. In every case, the retest scores were above the ceiling for placement in an EMR class.

What was the state's argument for using intelligence tests as one criterion for placing children in EMR classes? Testimony by intelligence testing experts supported the *predictive validity* (using a measure, such as an intelligence test, to predict performance on another measure, such as grades in school) of IQ for different ethnic groups. In Larry's case, the judge ruled that IQ tests are biased and that their use discriminates against ethnic minorities. IQ tests cannot be used now in California to place children in EMR classes. The decision in favor of Larry P. was upheld by an appeals panel. However, in another court case, *Pace v. Hannon* in Illinois, a judge ruled that IQ tests are not culturally biased.

Researchers have developed **culture-fair tests,** which are intelligence tests that are intended not to be culturally biased. Two types of culture-fair tests have been developed. The first includes questions that are familiar to people from all socioeconomic and ethnic backgrounds. For example, a child might be asked how a bird and a dog are different, on the assumption that virtually all children are familiar with birds and dogs. The second type of culture-fair test contains no verbal questions.

Why is it so hard to create culture-fair tests? Most tests tend to reflect what the dominant culture thinks is important (Greenfield & others, 2006). If tests have time limits, these will bias the test against groups not concerned with time. If languages differ, the same words might have different meanings for different language groups. Even pictures can produce bias because some cultures have less experience than others with drawings and photographs (Anastasi & Urbina, 1996).

culture-fair tests Intelligence tests that are intended to not be culturally biased.

Within the same culture, different groups could have different attitudes, values, and motivation, and this could affect their performance on intelligence tests. Items that ask why buildings should be made of brick are biased against children who have little or no experience with brick houses. Questions about railroads, furnaces, seasons of the year, distances between cities, and so on can be biased against groups who have less experience than others with these contexts. Because of such difficulties, Robert Sternberg and his colleagues (Sternberg & Grigorenko, 2008; Zhang & Sternberg, 2010) conclude that there are no culture-fair tests, only *culture-reduced tests.*

Ethnic Comparisons   In the United States, children from African American and Latino families score below children from non-Latino White families on standardized intelligence tests. On the average, African American schoolchildren score 10 to 15 points lower on standardized intelligence tests than non-Latino White schoolchildren do (Brody, 2000; Lynn, 1996). These are *average scores,* however. About 15 to 25 percent of African American schoolchildren score higher than half of non-Latino White schoolchildren do. The reason is that the distribution of scores for African Americans and non-Latino Whites overlap.

As African Americans have gained social, economic, and educational opportunities, the gap between African Americans and non-Latino Whites on standardized intelligence tests has begun to narrow (Ogbu & Stern, 2001). This gap especially narrows in college, where African American and non-Latino White students often experience more similar environments than in the elementary and high school years (Myerson & others, 1998). Also, when children from disadvantaged African American families are adopted into more advantaged middle-socioeconomic-status families, their scores on intelligence tests more closely resemble national averages for middle-socioeconomic-status children than for lower-socioeconomic-status children (Scarr & Weinberg, 1983).

Furthermore, as we have discussed, many experts raise serious questions about the ability of IQ tests to accurately measure a person's intelligence (Sternberg, 2009a; 2010a, b). One potential influence on intelligence test performance is **stereotype threat,** the anxiety that one's behavior might confirm a negative stereotype about one's group (Hollis-Sawyer, & Sawyer, 2008; Kellow & Jones, 2008; Spencer, Logel, & Davies, 2010; Steele & Aronson, 2004). For example, when African Americans take an intelligence test, they may experience anxiety about confirming the old stereotype that Blacks are "intellectually inferior." African American students do more poorly on standardized tests if they believe they are being evaluated. If they believe the test doesn't count, they perform as well as non-Latino White students (Aronson, 2002). However, some critics argue that the extent to which stereotype threat explains the testing gap has been exaggerated (Sackett, Hardison, & Cullen, 2005).

How might stereotype threat affect African American children's scores on tests?

Gender Comparisons   The average scores of males and females do not differ on intelligence tests, but variability in their scores does differ (Brody, 2000). For example, males are more likely than females to have extremely high or extremely low scores. A recent study also revealed that females had faster processing speeds across a number of timed subtests of intelligence such as verbal ability, visual-spatial thinking, reasoning, and memory (Camarata & Woodcock, 2006).

There also are gender differences in specific intellectual abilities (van der Sluis & others, 2008). Males score better than females in some nonverbal areas, such as visual-spatial ability, and females score better than males in some verbal areas, such as the ability to find synonyms for words (Lynn & others, 2004; Reynolds & others, 2008). However, there often is extensive overlap in the scores of females and males in these areas, and there is debate about just how strong the differences are (Hyde, 2007).

stereotype threat The anxiety that one's behavior might confirm a negative stereotype about one's group.

Review and Reflect: Learning Goal 2

2 **Outline key controversies about differences in IQ scores**

REVIEW

- What evidence suggests that genetics influences IQ scores? What evidence suggests that the environment influences IQ scores?
- What do IQ tests tell us about intelligence among people in different cultures and ethnic groups? What do IQ tests tell us about the intelligence of males and females?

REFLECT

- Do you think your performance on standardized tests has provided an accurate reflection of your intelligence?

3 THE DEVELOPMENT OF INTELLIGENCE

| Tests of Infant Intelligence | Stability and Change in Intelligence Through Adolescence | Intelligence in Adulthood |

How can the intelligence of infants be assessed? Is intelligence stable through childhood? Does intelligence decline in older adults and, if so, how much and when? These are some of the questions we explore as we examine the development of intelligence.

Tests of Infant Intelligence

The infant-testing movement grew out of the tradition of IQ testing. However, tests that assess infants are necessarily less verbal than IQ tests for older children. Tests for infants contain far more items related to perceptual-motor development. They also include measures of social interaction.

The most important early contributor to the testing of infants was Arnold Gesell (1934). He developed a measure that helped sort out potentially normal babies from abnormal ones. This was especially useful to adoption agencies, which had large numbers of babies awaiting placement. Gesell's examination was used widely for many years and still is frequently employed by pediatricians to distinguish normal and abnormal infants. The current version of the Gesell test has four categories of behavior: motor, language, adaptive, and personal-social. The **developmental quotient (DQ)** combines subscores in these categories to provide an overall score.

The widely used **Bayley Scales of Infant Development** were developed by Nancy Bayley (1969) in order to assess infant behavior and predict later development. The current version, Bayley-III, has five scales: cognitive, language, motor, socio-emotional, and adaptive (Bayley, 2006). The first three scales are administered directly to the infant, while the latter two are questionnaires given to the caregiver. The Bayley-III also is more appropriate for use in clinical settings than the two previous editions (Lennon & others, 2008).

How should a 6-month-old perform on the Bayley cognitive scale? The 6-month-old infant should be able to vocalize pleasure and displeasure, persistently

developmental quotient (DQ) An overall developmental score that combines subscores on motor, language, adaptive, and personal-social domains in the Gesell assessment of infants.

Bayley Scales of Infant Development Widely used scales, developed by Nancy Bayley, for assessing infant development. The current version, the Bayley-III, has five scales: cognitive, language, motor, socio-emotional, and adaptive; the first three are administered to the infant, the latter two to the caregiver.

search for objects that are just out of immediate reach, and approach a mirror that is placed in front of the infant by the examiner. By 12 months of age, the infant should be able to inhibit behavior when commanded to do so, imitate words the examiner says (such as *Mama*), and respond to simple requests (such as "Take a drink").

The explosion of interest in infant development has produced many new measures, especially tasks that evaluate the ways infants process information (Rose, Feldman, & Wallace, 1992). The Fagan Test of Infant Intelligence is increasingly being used (Fagan, 1992; Fagan, Holland, & Wheeler, 2007). This test focuses on the infant's ability to process information in such ways as encoding the attributes of objects, detecting similarities and differences between objects, forming mental representations, and retrieving these representations. For example, it uses the amount of time babies look at a new object compared with the amount of time they spend looking at a familiar object to estimate their intelligence.

Toosje Thyssen Van Beveren is an infant assessment specialist who administers tests like the Bayley scales and the Fagan Test of Infant Intelligence. To read about her work with infants, see the *Careers in Life-Span Development* profile.

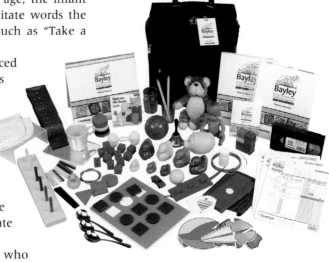

Items used in the Bayley Scales of Infant Development.

Careers in Life-Span Development

Toosje Thyssen Van Beveren, Infant Assessment Specialist

Toosje Thyssen Van Beveren is a developmental psychologist at the University of Texas Medical Center in Dallas. She has a master's degree in child clinical psychology and a Ph.D. in human development.

Her main current work is in a program called New Connections. This 12-week program is a comprehensive intervention for young children (0 to 6 years of age) who were affected by substance abuse prenatally and for their caregivers.

In the New Connections program, Van Beveren conducts assessments of infants' developmental status and progress, identifying delays and deficits. She might refer the infants to a speech, physical, or occupational therapist and monitor the infants' therapeutic services and developmental progress. Van Beveren trains the program staff and encourages them to use the exercises she recommends. She also discusses the child's problems with the primary caregivers, suggests activities they can carry out with their children, and assists them in enrolling their infants in appropriate programs.

During her graduate work at the University of Texas at Dallas, Van Beveren was author John Santrock's teaching assistant for four years in his undergraduate course on development. As a teaching assistant, she attended classes, graded exams, counseled students, and occasionally gave lectures. Each semester, Van Beveren returns to give a lecture on prenatal development and infancy. Van Beveren also teaches part-time in the psychology department at UT-Dallas. She teaches an undergraduate course, "The Child in Society," and a graduate course, "Infant Development."

In Van Beveren's words, "My days are busy and full. The work is often challenging. There are some disappointments but mostly the work is enormously gratifying."

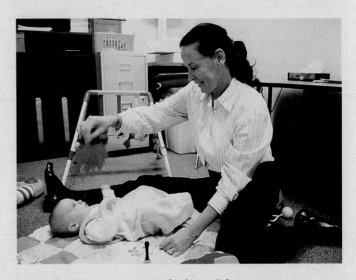

Toosje Thyssen Van Beveren conducting an infant assessment.

Stability and Change in Intelligence Through Adolescence

A recent longitudinal study examined the intelligence of 200 children from 12 months (using the Bayley scales) to 4 years (using the Standford-Binet test) of age (Blaga & others, 2009). The results indicated considerable stability from late infancy through the preschool years.

An early study examined correlations between the IQs of children at a number of different ages (Honzik, MacFarlane, & Allen, 1948). There was a strong relation between IQ scores obtained at the ages of 6, 8, and 9 and IQ scores obtained at the age of 10. For example, the correlation between IQ at the age of 8 and IQ at the age of 10 was .88. The correlation between IQ at the age of 9 and IQ at the age of 10 was .90. These figures show a very high relation between IQ scores obtained in these years. The correlation between IQ in the preadolescent years and IQ at the age of 18 was slightly less but still statistically significant. For example, the correlation between IQ at the age of 10 and IQ at the age of 18 was .70.

What has been said so far about the stability of intelligence has been based on measures of *groups* of individuals. The stability of intelligence also can be evaluated through studies of individuals. Robert McCall and his associates (McCall, Applebaum, & Hogarty, 1973) studied 140 children between the ages of 2½ and 17. They found that the average range of IQ scores was more than 28 points. The scores of one of three children changed by as much as 40 points.

What can we conclude about the stability and change of intelligence in childhood? Intelligence test scores can fluctuate dramatically across the childhood years. Intelligence is not as stable as the original intelligence theorists envisioned. Children are adaptive beings. They have the capacity for intellectual change, but they do not become entirely new intelligent beings. In a sense, children's intelligence changes but has connections to early points in development.

Intelligence in Adulthood

Does intelligence increase or decrease in adulthood? Might older adults have greater wisdom than younger adults? These are among the questions that we explore in this section.

Fluid and Crystallized Intelligence John Horn emphasizes that some abilities increase throughout the life span, whereas others steadily decline from middle adulthood on (Horn, 2007; Horn & Donaldson, 1980). Horn argues that **crystallized intelligence,** an individual's accumulated information and verbal skills, continues to increase throughout the life span. However, he notes that **fluid intelligence,** the ability to reason abstractly, begins to decline in middle adulthood (see Figure 8.7).

Horn's data were collected in a cross-sectional manner. Remember from Chapter 1, "Introduction," that a *cross-sectional study* assesses individuals of different ages at the same point in time. For example, a cross-sectional study might assess the intelligence of groups of 40-, 50-, and 60-year-olds in one evaluation, such as in 1990. The average 40-year-old and the average 60-year-old were born in different eras, which offered different economic and educational opportunities. For example, as the 60-year-olds grew up they likely had fewer educational opportunities, which probably influenced their scores on intelligence tests. Thus, if we find differences between 40- and 60-year-olds on intelligence tests when they are assessed cross-sectionally, these differences might be due to *cohort effects* (due to an individual's time of birth or generation but not to age) related to educational differences rather than to age.

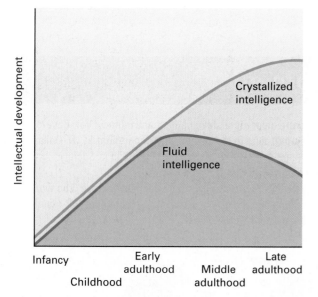

FIGURE 8.7 Fluid and Crystallized Intellectual Development Across the Life Span. According to Horn, crystallized intelligence (based on cumulative learning experiences) increases throughout the life span, but fluid intelligence (the ability to perceive and manipulate information) steadily declines from middle adulthood.

crystallized intelligence An individual's accumulated information and verbal skills, which continues to increase with age, according to Horn.

fluid intelligence The ability to reason abstractly, which begins to decline in middle adulthood, according to Horn.

In contrast, in a *longitudinal study*, the same individuals are studied over a period of time. Thus, a longitudinal study of intelligence in middle adulthood might consist of giving the same intelligence test to the same individuals when they are 40, when they are 50, and when they are 60 years of age. Whether data are collected cross-sectionally or longitudinally makes a difference in what is found about intellectual decline.

The Seattle Longitudinal Study   K. Warner Schaie (1983, 1996, 2000, 2005) has conducted an extensive study of intellectual abilities in the adulthood years. Five hundred individuals initially were tested in 1956. New waves of participants are added periodically. The main mental abilities tested in the Seattle Longitudinal Study are as follows:

- *Verbal ability* (ability to understand ideas expressed in words)
- *Verbal memory* (ability to encode and recall meaningful language units, such as a list of words)
- *Numeric ability* (ability to perform simple mathematical computations such as addition, subtraction, and multiplication)
- *Spatial orientation* (ability to visualize and mentally rotate stimuli in two- and three-dimensional space)
- *Inductive reasoning* (ability to recognize and understand patterns and relationships in a problem and use this understanding to solve other instances of the problem)
- *Perceptual speed* (ability to quickly and accurately make simple discriminations in visual stimuli)

As shown in Figure 8.8, the highest level of functioning for four of the six intellectual abilities occurred in the middle adulthood years (Schaie, 2005). For both women and men, performance on verbal ability, verbal memory, inductive reasoning, and spatial orientation peaked in middle age. Only two of the six abilities—numeric ability and perceptual speed—declined in middle age. Perceptual speed showed the earliest decline, with this beginning in early adulthood.

Notice in Figure 8.8 that decline in functioning for most cognitive abilities began to steepen in the sixties, although the decline in verbal ability did not steepen until

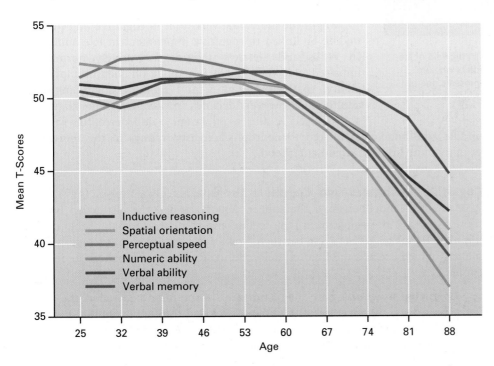

FIGURE 8.8 Longitudinal Changes in Six Intellectual Abilities from Age 25 to Age 88.

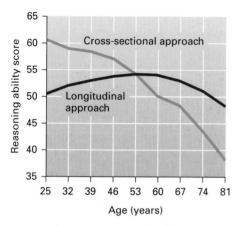

FIGURE 8.9 Cross-Sectional and Longitudinal Comparisons of Inductive Reasoning Ability Across the Adulthood Years. In Schaie's research, the cross-sectional approach revealed declining scores with age; the longitudinal approach showed a slight rise of scores in middle adulthood and only a slight decline beginning in the early part of late adulthood.

K. Warner Schaie (*right*) is one of the leading pioneers in the field of life-span development. He is shown here with two older adults who are actively using their cognitive skills. Schaie's research represents one of the most thorough examinations of how individuals develop and change as they go through the adult years.

cognitive mechanics The "hardware" of the mind, reflecting the neurophysiological architecture of the brain as developed through evolution. Cognitive mechanics involve the speed and accuracy of the processes involving sensory input, attention, visual and motor memory, discrimination, comparison, and categorization.

the mid-seventies. From the mid-seventies through the late eighties, all cognitive abilities showed considerable decline.

When Schaie (1994) assessed intellectual abilities both cross-sectionally and longitudinally, he found decline more likely to occur in the cross-sectional than in the longitudinal assessments. For example, as shown in Figure 8.9, when assessed longitudinally, inductive reasoning increased until toward the end of middle adulthood, when it began to show a slight decline. In contrast, when assessed cross-sectionally, inductive reasoning showed a consistent decline in the middle adulthood years. For the participants in the Seattle Longitudinal Study, middle age was a time of peak performance for both some aspects of crystallized intelligence (verbal ability) and fluid intelligence (spatial orientation and inductive reasoning).

In further analysis, Schaie (2007) recently examined generational differences in parents and their children over a seven-year time frame from 60 to 67 years of age. That is, parents were assessed when they were 60 to 67 years of age; then, when their children reached 60 to 67 years of age, they also were assessed. Higher levels of cognitive functioning occurred for the second generation in inductive reasoning, verbal memory, and spatial orientation, whereas the first generation scored higher on numeric ability. Noteworthy was the finding that the parent generation showed cognitive decline from 60 to 67 years of age, but their offspring showed stability or modest increase in cognitive functioning across the same age range.

The results from Schaie's study that have been described so far focus on *average* cognitive stability or change for all participants across the middle adulthood years. Schaie and Sherry Willis (Schaie, 2005; Willis & Schaie, 2005) recently examined individual differences for the participants in the Seattle study and found substantial individual variations. They classified participants as "decliners," "stable," and "gainers" for three categories—numeric ability, delayed recall (a verbal memory task), and word fluency—from 46 to 60 years of age. The largest percentage of decline (31 percent) or gain (16 percent) occurred for delayed recall; the largest percentage with stable scores (79 percent) occurred for numeric ability. Word fluency declined for 20 percent of the individuals from 46 to 60 years of age.

Might the individual variations in cognitive trajectories in midlife be linked to cognitive impairment in late adulthood? In Willis and Schaie's analysis, cognitively normal and impaired older adults did not differ on measures of verbal ability, spatial orientation, and numeric ability in middle adulthood. However, declines in memory (immediate recall and delayed recall), word fluency, and perceptual speed in middle adulthood were linked to neurophysiologists' ratings of the individuals' cognitive impairment in late adulthood.

Cognitive Mechanics and Cognitive Pragmatics Paul Baltes (1993, 2000, 2003; Baltes, Lindenberger, & Staudinger, 2006) clarified the distinction between those aspects of the aging mind that decline and those that remain stable or even improve. He makes a distinction between "cognitive mechanics" and "cognitive pragmatics," which extends the fluid/crystallized intelligence conceptualization described earlier:

• **Cognitive mechanics** are the "hardware" of the mind and reflect the neurophysiological architecture of the brain developed through evolution. Cognitive mechanics consist of the speed and accuracy of the processes involved in sensory input, attention, visual and motor memory, discrimination, comparison, and categorization. Because of the strong influence of biology, heredity, and health on cognitive mechanics, their decline with aging is likely.

- **Cognitive pragmatics** are the culture-based "software programs" of the mind. Cognitive pragmatics include reading and writing skills, language comprehension, educational qualifications, professional skills, and also the type of knowledge about the self and life skills that help us to master or cope with life. Because of the strong influence of culture on cognitive pragmatics, their improvement into old age is possible. Thus, although cognitive mechanics may decline in old age, cognitive pragmatics may actually improve (see Figure 8.10).

In the Berlin Aging Study, the cognitive mechanic ability of perceptual speed showed the greatest decline with age, whereas the cognitive pragmatic ability of verbal knowledge remained at virtually the same level even when the older adults were in their nineties (Singer & others, 2003). Also, in this study, perceptual speed was more strongly correlated with biological markers such as visual acuity, auditory acuity, and balance/gait—and verbal knowledge was more strongly correlated with sociocultural markers such as years of education, occupational prestige, socioeconomic status, and household income (Baltes, Lindenberger, & Staudinger, 2006).

The distinction between cognitive mechanics and cognitive pragmatics is similar to the one between fluid (mechanics) and crystallized (pragmatics) intelligence that was described earlier. Indeed, the similarity is so strong that some experts now use these terms to describe cognitive aging patterns: *fluid mechanics* and *crystallized pragmatics* (Lovden & Lindenberg, 2007).

Wisdom   As you just saw, Baltes stresses that wisdom is an important aspect of cognitive pragmatics. Baltes and his colleagues (Baltes & Kunzmann, 2004; Baltes, Lindenberger, & Staudinger, 2006; Baltes & Smith, 2008) define **wisdom** as expert knowledge about the practical aspects of life that permits excellent judgment about important matters. This practical knowledge involves exceptional insight about human development and life matters, good judgment, and understanding how to cope with difficult life problems. Thus, wisdom, more than standard conceptions of intelligence, focuses on life's pragmatic concerns and human conditions (Karelitz, Jarvin, & Sternberg, 2010).

In regard to wisdom, research by Baltes and his colleagues (Baltes & Kunzmann, 2004; Baltes, Lindenberger, & Staudinger, 2006; Baltes & Smith, 2008) has found that:

- High levels of wisdom are rare. Few people, including older adults, attain a high level of wisdom. That only a small percentage of adults show wisdom supports the contention that it requires experience, practice, or complex skills.
- The time frame of late adolescence and early adulthood is the main age window for wisdom to emerge. No further advances in wisdom have been found for middle-aged and older adults beyond the level they attained as young adults, but this may have been because the problems Baltes and his colleagues used were not relevant to older adults' lives.
- Factors other than age are critical for wisdom to develop to a high level. For example, certain life experiences, such as being trained and working in a field concerned with difficult life problems and having wisdom-enhancing mentors,

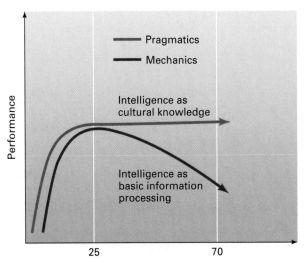

FIGURE 8.10 Theorized Age Changes in Cognitive Mechanics and Cognitive Pragmatics. Baltes argues that cognitive mechanics decline during aging, whereas cognitive pragmatics do not. Cognitive mechanics have a biological/genetic foundation; cognitive pragmatics have an experimental/cultural foundation.

Older adults might not be as quick with their thoughts or behavior as younger people, but wisdom may be an entirely different matter. This older woman shares the wisdom of her experience with a classroom of children. *How is wisdom described by life-span developmentalists?*

cognitive pragmatics The culture-based "software" of the mind. Cognitive pragmatics include reading and writing skills, language comprehension, educational qualifications, professional skills, and also the type of knowledge about the self and life skills that help us to master or cope with life.

wisdom Expert knowledge about the practical aspects of life that permits excellent judgment about important matters.

contribute to higher levels of wisdom. Also, people higher in wisdom have values that are more likely to consider the welfare of others rather than their own happiness.

- Personality-related factors, such as openness to experience, generativity, and creativity, are better predictors of wisdom than cognitive factors such as intelligence.

Robert J. Sternberg (1998, 2009d, e, 2010c), whose triarchic theory of intelligence we discussed earlier in the chapter, argues that wisdom is linked to both practical and academic intelligence. In his view, academic intelligence is a necessary but in many cases insufficient requirement for wisdom. Practical knowledge about the realities of life also is needed for wisdom. For Sternberg, balance between self-interest, the interests of others, and contexts produces a common good. Thus, wise individuals don't just look out for themselves—they also need to consider others' needs and perspectives, as well as the particular context involved. Sternberg assesses wisdom by presenting problems to individuals that require solutions which highlight various intrapersonal, interpersonal, and contextual interests. He also emphasizes that such aspects of wisdom should be taught in schools (Sternberg, 2009d, e; Sternberg, Jarvin, & Reznitskaya, 2010). Sternberg's emphasis on using knowledge for the common good in a manner that addresses competing interests is what mainly differentiates it from Baltes and his colleagues' view of wisdom.

Review and Reflect: Learning Goal 3

3 **Discuss the development of intelligence across the human life span**

REVIEW

- How is intelligence assessed during infancy?
- How much does intelligence change through childhood and adolescence?
- To what extent does intelligence change as adults age? What is wisdom, and how can it be characterized?

REFLECT

- What do you think are the most important cohort effects that can influence the development of intelligence in middle and late adulthood? How are these likely to change in the future?

---

4 THE EXTREMES OF INTELLIGENCE AND CREATIVITY

| Mental Retardation | Giftedness | Creativity |

Mental retardation and intellectual giftedness are the extremes of intelligence. Often intelligence tests are used to identify exceptional individuals. Let's explore the nature of mental retardation and giftedness. Then we explore how creativity differs from intelligence.

Mental Retardation

The most distinctive feature of mental retardation is inadequate intellectual functioning. Long before formal tests were developed to assess intelligence, individuals with mental retardation were identified by a lack of age-appropriate skills in learning and caring for themselves. Once intelligence tests were developed, they were used to identify degrees of mental retardation. But of two individuals with mental retardation who have the same low IQ, one might be married, employed, and involved in the community and the other might require constant supervision in an institution. Such differences in social competence led psychologists to include deficits in adaptive behavior in their definition of mental retardation.

Mental retardation is a condition of limited mental ability in which the individual (1) has a low IQ, usually below 70 on a traditional intelligence test; (2) has difficulty adapting to everyday life; and (3) first exhibits these characteristics by age 18. The age limit is included in the definition of mental retardation because, for example, we don't usually think of a college student who suffers massive brain damage in a car accident, resulting in an IQ of 60, as being "mentally retarded." The low IQ and low adaptiveness should be evident in childhood, not after normal functioning is interrupted by damage of some form. About 5 million Americans fit this definition of mental retardation.

There are several ways of classifying degrees of mental retardation (Hallahan, Kaufmann, Pullen, 2009). Most school systems use the classifications shown in Figure 8.11. It uses IQ scores to categorize retardation as mild, moderate, severe, or profound.

Note that a large majority of individuals diagnosed with mental retardation fit into the mild category. However, these categories are not perfect predictors of functioning. The American Association of Mental Retardation (1992) developed a different classification based on the degree of support required for a person with mental retardation to function at the highest level. As shown in Figure 8.12, these categories of support are intermittent, limited, extensive, and pervasive.

Some cases of mental retardation have an organic cause. *Organic retardation* is mental retardation caused by a genetic disorder or by brain damage. Down syndrome is one form of organic mental retardation, and it occurs when an extra

Type of Mental Retardation	IQ Range	Percentage of Mentally Retarded Individuals
Mild	55 to 70	89
Moderate	40 to 54	6
Severe	25 to 39	4
Profound	Below 25	1

FIGURE 8.11 Classification of Mental Retardation Based on IQ.

A child with Down syndrome. *What causes Down syndrome?*

Intermittent	Supports are provided "as needed." The individual may need episodic or short-term support during life-span transitions (such as job loss or acute medical crisis). Intermittent supports may be low or high intensity when provided.
Limited	Supports are intense and relatively consistent over time. They are time-limited but not intermittent, require fewer staff members, and cost less than more intense supports. These supports likely will be needed for adaptation to the changes involved in the school-to-adult period.
Extensive	Supports are characterized by regular involvement (for example, daily) in at least some setting (such as home or work) and are not time-limited (for example, extended home-living support).
Pervasive	Supports are constant, very intense, and are provided across settings. They may be of a life-sustaining nature. These supports typically involve more staff members and intrusiveness than the other support categories.

FIGURE 8.12 Classification of Mental Retardation Based on Levels of Support Needed.

mental retardation A condition of limited mental ability in which the individual (1) has a low IQ, usually below 70 on a traditional intelligence test; (2) has difficulty adapting to everyday life; and (3) has an onset of these characteristics by age 18.

chromosome is present. Other causes of organic retardation include fragile X syndrome, an abnormality in the X chromosome that was discussed in Chapter 2, "Biological Beginnings"; prenatal malformation; metabolic disorders; and diseases that affect the brain. Most people who suffer from organic retardation have IQs between 0 and 50.

When no evidence of organic brain damage can be found, cases of mental retardation are labeled *cultural-familial retardation.* Individuals with this type of retardation have IQs between 55 and 70. Psychologists suspect that these mental deficits often result from growing up in a below-average intellectual environment. Children who are familially retarded can be identified in schools, where they often fail, need tangible rewards (candy rather than praise), and are highly sensitive to what others expect of them. However, as adults, the familially retarded are usually invisible, perhaps because adult settings don't tax their cognitive skills as sorely. It may also be that the familially retarded increase their intelligence as they move toward adulthood.

Giftedness

There have always been people whose abilities and accomplishments outshine others'—the whiz kid in class, the star athlete, the natural musician. People who are **gifted** have high intelligence or superior talent for something. An IQ of 130 is often used as the low threshold for giftedness, although this figure is arbitrary. Programs for the gifted in most school systems select children who have intellectual superiority and academic aptitude. They tend to overlook children who are talented in the arts or athletics or who have other special aptitudes (Clark, 2008; Karnes & Stephens, 2008, Sternberg, 2010a, b; Winner, 2009).

Until recently, giftedness and emotional distress were thought to go hand-in-hand. English novelist Virginia Woolf, Sir Isaac Newton, Vincent van Gogh, Anne Sexton, Socrates, and Sylvia Plath all had emotional problems. However, these individuals are the exception rather than the rule. In general, no relation between giftedness and mental disorder has been found. Research supports the conclusion that gifted people tend to be more mature and have fewer emotional problems than others, and to grow up in a positive family climate (Feldhusen, 1999).

Characteristics of Children Who Are Gifted   Aside from their abilities, do children who are gifted have distinctive characteristics? Lewis Terman (1925) conducted an extensive study of 1,500 children whose Stanford-Binet IQs averaged 150. Contrary to the popular myth that children who are gifted are maladjusted, Terman found that they were socially well adjusted.

Ellen Winner (1996) described three criteria that characterize gifted children, whether in art, music, or academic domains:

1. *Precocity.* Gifted children are precocious. They begin to master an area earlier than their peers. Learning in their domain is more effortless for them than for ordinary children. In most instances, these gifted children are precocious because they have an inborn high ability.
2. *Marching to their own drummer.* Gifted children learn in a qualitatively different way than ordinary children. For one thing, they need minimal help from adults to learn. In many cases, they resist explicit instruction. They also often make discoveries on their own and solve problems in unique ways.
3. *A passion to master.* Gifted children are driven to understand the domain in which they have high ability. They display an intense, obsessive interest and an ability to focus. They do not need to be pushed by their parents. They motivate themselves, says Winner.

Art prodigy Alexandra Nechita. *What are some characteristics of gifted children?*

gifted Having high intelligence (an IQ of 130 or higher) or superior talent for something.

Life Course of the Gifted   As a 10-year-old, Alexandra Nechita was described as a child prodigy. She paints quickly and impulsively on large canvases, some as large as 5 feet by 9 feet. It is not unusual for her to complete several of these large paintings in a week's time. Her paintings sell for up to $100,000 apiece. When she was only 2 years of age, Alexandra colored in coloring books for hours. She had no interest in dolls or friends. Once she started school, she would start painting as soon as she got home. And she continues to paint—relentlessly and passionately. It is, she says, what she loves to do.

Is giftedness, like Alexandra Nechita's artistic talent, a product of heredity or of environment? Likely both (Sternberg, 2010a, b). Individuals who are gifted recall that they had signs of high ability in a specific area at a very young age, prior to or at the beginning of formal training (Howe & others, 1995). This suggests the importance of innate ability in giftedness. However, researchers also have found that individuals with world-class status in the arts, mathematics, science, and sports all report strong family support and years of training and practice (Bloom, 1985). Deliberate practice is an important characteristic of individuals who become experts in a specific domain. For example, in one study, the best musicians engaged in twice as much deliberate practice over their lives as the least successful ones did (Ericsson, Krampe, & Tesch-Römer, 1993).

Can we predict from infancy who will be gifted as children and adolescents? John Colombo and his colleagues (2004, 2009) have found that measures of infant attention and habituation are not good predictors of high cognitive ability later in development. However, they have discovered a link between assessment with the Home Observation for Measure of the Environment at 18 months of age and high cognitive ability in the preschool years. The best predictor at 18 months of high cognitive ability in the preschool years was the provision of materials and a variety of experiences in the home. These findings illustrate the importance of the cognitive environment provided by parents in the development of children's giftedness.

Do gifted children become gifted and highly creative adults? In Terman's research on children with superior IQs, the children typically became experts in a well-established domain, such as medicine, law, or business. However, they did not become major creators (Winner, 2000). That is, they did not create a new domain or revolutionize an old domain.

One reason that some gifted children do not become gifted adults is that they often have been pushed too hard by overzealous parents and teachers. As a result, they lose their intrinsic (internal) motivation (Winner, 1996, 2006). As adolescents, they may ask themselves, "Who am I doing this for?" If the answer is not for one's self, they may not want to do it anymore. Another reason that gifted children do not become gifted adults is because the criteria for giftedness changes—as an adult, an individual has to actually do something special to be labeled gifted.

Margaret (Peg) Cagle with some of the gifted seventh- and eighth-grade math students she teaches at Lawrence Middle School in Chatsworth, California. Cagle especially advocates challenging students who are gifted to take intellectual risks. To encourage collaboration, she often has students work together in groups of four, and frequently tutors students during lunch hour. As 13-year-old Madeline Lewis commented, "If I don't get it one way, she'll explain it another and talk to you about it and show you until you do get it." Cagle says it is important to be passionate about teaching math and open up a world for students that shows them how beautiful learning math can be (Wong Briggs, 2007, p. 6D).

Domain-Specific Giftedness   Individuals who are highly gifted are typically not gifted in many domains, and research on giftedness is increasingly focused on domain-specific developmental trajectories (Horowitz, 2009; Liben, 2009; Matthews, 2009; Matthews, Subotnik, & Horowitz, 2009; Winner, 2009). During the childhood years, the domain(s) in which individuals are gifted usually emerges. Thus, at some point in the childhood years, the child who is to become a gifted artist or the child who is to become a gifted mathematician begins to show expertise in that domain. Regarding domain-specific giftedness, software genius Bill

Gates (1998), the founder of Microsoft and one of the world's richest persons, commented that sometimes you have to be careful when you are good at something and resist the urge to think that you will be good at everything. Gates says that because he has been so successful at software development, people expect him to be brilliant about other domains about which he is far from being a genius.

Identification of an individual's domain-specific talent and providing the individual individually appropriate and optional educational opportunities needs to be accomplished at the very latest by adolescence (Keating, 2009). During adolescence, individuals who are talented become less reliant on parental support and increasingly pursue their own interests.

A young Bill Gates, founder of Microsoft and now one of the world's richest persons. Like many highly gifted students, Gates was not especially fond of school. He hacked a computer security system when he was 13 and as a high school student, he was allowed to take some college math classes. He dropped out of Harvard University and began developing a plan for what was to become Microsoft Corporation. *What are some ways that schools can enrich the education of such highly talented students as Gates to make it a more challenging, interesting, and meaningful experience?*

Education of Children Who Are Gifted   An increasing number of experts argue that the education of gifted children in the United States requires a significant overhaul, as reflected in these books and reports: *Genius Denied: How to Stop Wasting Our Brightest Young Minds* (Davidson & Davidson, 2004) and *A Nation Deceived: How Schools Hold Back America's Brightest Students* (Colangelo, Assouline, & Gross, 2004).

Underchallenged gifted children can become disruptive, skip classes, and lose interest in achieving. Sometimes these children just disappear into the woodwork, becoming passive and apathetic toward school. It is extremely important for teachers to challenge children who are gifted to reach high expectations (Sternberg, 2010a, b; Webb & others, 2007; Winner, 2006).

Some educators conclude that the inadequate education of children who are gifted has been compounded by the federal government's No Child Left Behind policy, which seeks to raise the achievement level of students who are not doing well in school at the expense of enriching the education of children who are gifted (Clark, 2008; Cloud, 2007). A number of experts argue that too often children who are gifted are socially isolated and underchallenged in the classroom (Karnes & Stephens, 2008; Sternberg, 2010). It is not unusual for them to be ostracized and labeled "nerds" or "geeks." Ellen Winner (1996, 2006) concludes that a child who is truly gifted often is the only such child in the room who does not have the opportunity to learn with students of like ability.

Many eminent adults report that school was a negative experience for them, that they were bored and sometimes knew more than their teachers (Bloom, 1985). Winner stresses that American education will benefit when standards are raised for all children. When some children are still underchallenged, she recommends that they be allowed to attend advanced classes in their domain of exceptional ability, such as allowing some especially precocious middle school students to take college classes in their area of expertise. For example, Bill Gates, founder of Microsoft, took college math classes and hacked a computer security system at 13; Yo-Yo Ma, a famous cellist, graduated from high school at 15 and attended Juilliard School of Music in New York City.

Creativity

We have encountered the term "creative" on several occasions in our discussion of giftedness. What does it mean to be creative? **Creativity** is the ability to think about something in novel and unusual ways and come up with unique, good solutions to problems.

Intelligence and creativity are not the same thing (Sternberg, 2009a, b; Sternberg & Kaufman, 2010). Most creative people are quite intelligent, but the reverse is not necessarily true. Many highly intelligent people (as measured by high scores on conventional tests of intelligence) are not very creative. Many highly intelligent people produce large numbers of products, but they are not necessarily novel.

creativity Ability to think in novel and unusual ways and devise unique, good solutions to problems.

Why don't IQ scores predict creativity? Creativity requires divergent thinking (Guilford, 1967). **Divergent thinking** produces many answers to the same question. In contrast, conventional intelligence tests require **convergent thinking.** For example, a typical item on a conventional intelligence test is, "How many quarters will you get in return for 60 dimes?" There is only one correct answer to this question. In contrast, a question such as "What image comes to mind when you hear the phrase 'sitting alone in a dark room?' " has many possible answers; it calls for divergent thinking.

Steps in the Creative Process   The creative process has often been described as a five-step sequence:

1. *Preparation.* You become immersed in a problem or an issue that interests you and arouses your curiosity.
2. *Incubation.* You churn ideas around in your head. This is the point at which you are likely to make some unusual connections in your thinking.
3. *Insight.* You experience the "Aha!" moment when all pieces of the puzzle seem to fit together.
4. *Evaluation.* Now you must decide whether the idea is valuable and worth pursuing. Is the idea really novel or is it obvious?
5. *Elaboration.* This final step often covers the longest span of time and the hardest work. This is what the famous twentieth-century American inventor Thomas Edison was talking about when he said that creativity is 1 percent inspiration and 99 percent perspiration. Elaboration may require a great deal of perspiration.

Mihaly Csikszentmihalyi (pronounced ME-high CHICK-sent-me-high-ee) (1996) notes that this five-step sequence provides a helpful framework for thinking about how creative ideas are developed. However, he argues that creative people don't always go through the steps in a linear sequence. For example, elaboration is often interrupted by periods of incubation. Fresh insights may appear during incubation, evaluation, and elaboration. And insight might take years or only a few hours. Sometimes the creative idea consists of one deep insight. Other times it's a series of small ones.

Characteristics of Creative Thinkers   Creative thinkers tend to have the following characteristics (Perkins, 1994):

- *Flexibility and playful thinking.* Creative thinkers are flexible and play with problems, which gives rise to a paradox. Although creativity takes hard work, the work goes more smoothly if you take it lightly. In a way, humor greases the wheels of creativity (Goleman, Kaufman, & Ray, 1993). When you are joking around, you are more likely to consider any possibility. Having fun helps to disarm your inner censor, which can condemn your ideas as off-base.

- *Inner motivation.* Creative people often are motivated by the joy of creating. They tend to be less inspired by grades, money, or favorable feedback from others. Thus, creative people are motivated more internally than externally (Runco, 2010).

- *Willingness to risk.* Creative people make more mistakes than their less imaginative counterparts. It's not that they are less proficient, but that they come up with more ideas, more possibilities (Lubart, 2003). They win some, they lose some. For example, the twentieth-century Spanish artist Pablo Picasso created more than 20,000 paintings. Not all of them were masterpieces. Creative thinkers learn to cope with unsuccessful projects and see failure as an opportunity to learn.

What do you mean, "What is it"? It's the spontaneous, unfettered expression of a young mind not yet bound by the restraints of narrative or pictorial representation.
Cartoon by Sidney Harris. © ScienceCartoonsPlus.com. Used by permission.

divergent thinking Thinking that produces many answers to the same question; characteristic of creativity.

convergent thinking Thinking that produces one correct answer; characteristic of the kind of thinking required on conventional intelligence tests.

- *Objective evaluation of work.* Contrary to the stereotype that creative people are eccentric and highly subjective, most creative thinkers strive to evaluate their work objectively. They may use established criteria to make this judgment or rely on the judgments of people they respect. In this manner, they can determine whether further creative thinking will improve their work.

Creativity in Schools   An important teaching goal is to help students become more creative (Beghetto & Kaufman, 2009; Rickards, Moger, & Runco, 2009; Sternberg, 2009a, b, 2010a, b). Teachers need to recognize that students will show more creativity in some domains than in others (Rickards, Moger, & Runco, 2009). A student who shows creative thinking skills in mathematics may not exhibit these skills in art, for example.

School environments that encourage independent work, are stimulating but not distracting, and make resources readily available are likely to encourage students' creativity. There is mounting concern that the U.S. government's No Child Left Behind legislation has harmed the development of students' creative thinking by focusing attention on memorization of materials to do well on standardized tests (Burke-Adams, 2007; Kaufman & Sternberg, 2007).

Some strategies for increasing children's creative thinking include the following:

- *Encourage brainstorming.* **Brainstorming** is a technique in which people are encouraged to come up with creative ideas in a group, play off each other's ideas, and say practically whatever comes to mind that seems relevant to a particular issue. Participants are usually told to hold off from criticizing others' ideas at least until the end of the brainstorming session.

- *Provide environments that stimulate creativity.* Some environments nourish creativity, others inhibit it. Parents and teachers who encourage creativity often rely on children's natural curiosity. They provide exercises and activities that stimulate children to find insightful solutions to problems, rather than ask a lot of questions that require rote answers. Teachers also encourage creativity by taking students on field trips to locations where creativity is valued. Science, discovery, and children's museums offer rich opportunities to stimulate creativity.

What are some good strategies for guiding children in thinking more creatively?

brainstorming Technique in which individuals are encouraged to come up with creative ideas in a group, play off each other's ideas, and say practically whatever comes to mind relevant to a particular issue.

- *Don't overcontrol students.* Teresa Amabile (1993) says that telling children exactly how to do things leaves them feeling that originality is a mistake and exploration is a waste of time. If, instead of dictating which activities they should engage in, you let children select their interests and you support their inclinations, you will be less likely to destroy their natural curiosity (Hennessey & Amabile, 2010).

- *Encourage internal motivation.* Excessive use of prizes, such as gold stars, money, or toys, can stifle creativity by undermining the intrinsic pleasure students derive from creative activities. Creative children's motivation is the satisfaction generated by the work itself. Competition for prizes and formal evaluations often undermine intrinsic motivation and creativity (Amabile & Hennesey, 1992). However, this is not to rule out material rewards altogether.

- *Build children's confidence.* To expand children's creativity, encourage children to believe in their own ability to create something innovative and worthwhile.

Building children's confidence in their creative skills aligns with Bandura's (2008, 2009) concept of *self-efficacy*, the belief that one can master a situation and produce positive outcomes.

- *Guide children to be persistent and delay gratification.* Most highly successful creative products take years to develop. Most creative individuals work on ideas and projects for months and years without being rewarded for their efforts (Sternberg & Williams, 1996). Children don't become experts at sports, music, or art overnight. It usually takes many years of working at something to become an expert at it; so it is with being a creative thinker who produces a unique, worthwhile product.

- *Encourage children to take intellectual risks.* Creative individuals take intellectual risks and seek to discover or invent something never before discovered or invented (Sternberg & Williams, 1996). They risk spending extensive time on an idea or project that may not work. Creative people are not afraid of failing or getting something wrong (Sternberg, 2009a).

- *Introduce children to creative people.* Teachers can invite creative people to their classrooms and ask them to describe what helps them become creative or to demonstrate their creative skills. A writer, poet, musician, scientist, and many others can bring their props and productions to the class, turning it into a theater for stimulating students' creativity.

You can find out about steps you can take to live a more creative life in the following *Applications in Life-Span Development* interlude.

Applications in Life-Span Development

LIVING A MORE CREATIVE LIFE

Leading expert on creativity, Mihaly Csikszentmihalyi (1996), interviewed 90 leading figures in art, business, government, education, and science to learn how creativity works. He discovered that creative people regularly engage in challenges that absorb them. Based on his interviews with some of the most creative people in the world, he concluded that the first step toward a more creative life is to cultivate your curiosity and interest. Here are his recommendations for doing this:

1. *Try to be surprised by something every day.* Maybe it is something you see, hear, or read about. Become absorbed in a lecture or a book. Be open to what the world is telling you. Life is a stream of experiences. Swim widely and deeply in it, and your life will be richer.

2. *Try to surprise at least one person every day.* In a lot of things you do, you have to be predictable and patterned. Do something different for a change. Ask a question you normally would not ask. Invite someone to go to a show or a museum you never have visited.

3. *Write down each day what surprised you and how you surprised others.* Most creative people keep a diary, notes, or lab records to ensure that their experience is not forgotten. Start with a specific task. Each evening, record the most surprising event that occurred that day and your most surprising action. After a few days, reread your notes and reflect on your experiences. After a few weeks,

Leading creativity theorist Mihaly Csikszentmihalyi, in the setting where he gets his most creative ideas.

(continued on next page)

you might see a pattern emerging, one that suggests an area you can explore in greater depth.

4. *When something sparks your interest, follow it.* Usually when something captures your attention, it is short-lived—an idea, a song, a flower. Too often we are too busy to explore the idea, song, or flower further. Or we think these areas are none of our business because we are not experts about them. Yet the world is our business. We can't know which part of it is best suited to our interests until we make a serious effort to learn as much about as many aspects of it as possible.

5. *Wake up in the morning with a specific goal to look forward to.* Creative people wake up eager to start the day. Why? Not necessarily because they are cheerful, enthusiastic types but because they know that there is something meaningful to accomplish each day, and they can't wait to get started.

6. *Take charge of your schedule.* Figure out which time of the day is your most creative time. Some of us are more creative late at night, others early in the morning. Carve out some time for yourself when your creative energy is at its best.

7. *Spend time in settings that stimulate your creativity.* In Csikszentmihalyi's (1996) research, he gave people an electronic pager and beeped them randomly at different times of the day. When he asked them how they felt, they reported the highest levels of creativity when walking, driving, or swimming. "I do my most creative thinking when I'm jogging." These activities are semiautomatic in that they take a certain amount of attention while leaving some time free to make connections among ideas. Another setting in which highly creative people report coming up with novel ideas is the half-asleep, half-awake state we are in when we are deeply relaxed or barely awake.

Changes in Adulthood   At the age of 30, Thomas Edison invented the phonograph, Hans Christian Andersen wrote his first volume of fairy tales, and Mozart composed *The Marriage of Figaro*. One early study of creativity found that individuals' most creative products were generated in their thirties and that 80 percent of the most important creative contributions were completed by age 50 (Lehman, 1960). More recently, researchers have found that creativity often peaks in the forties before declining (Simonton, 1996). However, any generalization about a relationship between age and creative accomplishments must be qualified by consideration of (1) the size of the decline and (2) differences across domains (Simonton, 1996).

Even though a decline in creative contributions is often found in the fifties and later, the decline is often not great. And a recent study of artists from 53 to 75 years of age found no age differences in the artists' perceptions of their creativity (Reed, 2005). An impressive array of creative accomplishments have occurred in late adulthood (Tahir & Gruber, 2003). Benjamin Franklin invented the bifocal lens when he was 78 years old; Wolfgang von Goethe completed *Faust* when he was in his eighties. After a distinguished career as a physicist, Henri Chevreul switched fields in his nineties to become a pioneer in gerontological research. He published his last research paper just a year prior to his death at the age of 103!

Furthermore, the age at which creativity typically declines varies with the domain involved. In philosophy and history, for example, older adults often show as much creativity as when they were in their thirties and forties. In contrast, in lyric poetry, abstract mathematics, and theoretical physics, the peak of creativity is often reached in the twenties or thirties.

Review and Reflect: Learning Goal 4

 Describe the characteristics of mental retardation, giftedness, and creativity

REVIEW

- What is mental retardation, and what are its causes?
- What makes people gifted?
- What makes people creative?

REFLECT

- How many of the tips in the *Applications in Life-Span Development* interlude, on Living a More Creative Life, do you practice? How might you benefit from these suggestions, in addition to becoming more creative?

Reach Your Learning Goals

Intelligence

---

1 THE CONCEPT OF INTELLIGENCE: EXPLAIN THE NATURE OF INTELLIGENCE

What Is Intelligence?

- Intelligence consists of the ability to solve problems and to adapt and learn from experiences. A key aspect of intelligence focuses on its individual variations. Traditionally, intelligence has been measured by tests designed to compare people's performance on cognitive tasks.

Intelligence Tests

- Alfred Binet and his student Théophile Simon developed the first intelligence test; Binet developed the concept of mental age. William Stern developed the concept of IQ for use with the Binet test. Revisions of the Binet test are called the Stanford-Binet, and the current version is the Stanford-Binet 5. The test scores on the Stanford-Binet approximate a normal distribution. The Wechsler scales, created by David Wechsler, are the other main intelligence assessment tool. These tests provide an overall IQ and yield several composite scores, allowing the examiner to see the areas in which the individual is strong or weak in different areas of intelligence. Test scores should be only one type of information used to evaluate an individual. IQ scores can produce unfortunate stereotypes and expectations.

Theories of Multiple Intelligences

- Sternberg's triarchic theory states that there are three main types of intelligence: analytical, creative, and practical. Gardner notes there are eight types of intelligence: verbal, mathematical, spatial, bodily-kinesthetic, musical, interpersonal, intrapersonal, and naturalist. Emotional intelligence is the ability to perceive and express emotion accurately and adaptively, to understand emotion and emotional knowledge, to use feelings to facilitate thought, and to manage emotions in oneself and others. The multiple intelligences approaches have broadened the definition of intelligence and motivated educators to develop programs that instruct students in different domains. Critics maintain that the multiple intelligences theories include classifications that really aren't part of intelligence, such as chess intelligence and prize-fighter intelligence. Critics also say that there isn't enough research to support the concept of multiple intelligences.

The Neuroscience of Intelligence

- There has been a substantial increase in interest in discovering links between the brain and intelligence that has been stimulated by advances in brain imaging. A moderate correlation has been found between overall brain size and intelligence. Recent research has revealed a link between a distributed neural network in the frontal and parietal lobes and intelligence. Research on a connection between neural processing speed and intelligence has produced inconsistent findings.

---

2 CONTROVERSIES AND GROUP COMPARISONS: OUTLINE KEY CONTROVERSIES ABOUT DIFFERENCES IN IQ SCORES

The Influence of Heredity and Environment

- Genetic similarity might explain why identical twins show stronger correlations on intelligence tests than fraternal twins do. Many studies show that intelligence has a reasonably strong heritability component. Criticisms of the heritability concept have been made. In recent decades, there has been a considerable rise in intelligence test scores around the world—called the Flynn effect—and this supports the role of environment in intelligence. Researchers have found that how much parents talk with their children in the first three years of life is correlated with the children's IQs and that being deprived of formal education lowers IQ scores. Ramey's research revealed the positive effects of educational child care on intelligence.

Group Comparisons and Issues

- Cultures vary in the way they define intelligence. Early intelligence tests favored non-Latino White, middle-socioeconomic-status urban individuals. Tests may be biased against certain groups because they are not familiar with a standard form of English, with the content tested, or with the testing situation. Tests are likely to reflect the values and experience of the dominant culture. In the United States, the average score of African American and Latino children is below the average score of non-Latino White children on standardized intelligence tests, but as African Americans have gained economic, social, and educational opportunities, the gap between scores has begun to narrow. Males are more likely than females to have extremely high or extremely low IQ scores. There also are gender differences in specific intellectual abilities.

3 THE DEVELOPMENT OF INTELLIGENCE: DISCUSS THE DEVELOPMENT OF INTELLIGENCE ACROSS THE HUMAN LIFE SPAN

Tests of Infant Intelligence

- Tests designed to assess infant intelligence include the widely used Bayley scales, and a test developed by Gesell was an important early contributor to the developmental testing of infants. The Fagan Test of Infant Intelligence, which assesses how effectively infants process information, is increasingly being used.

Stability and Change in Intelligence Through Adolescence

- Although intelligence is more stable across the childhood and adolescent years than are many other attributes, many children's and adolescents' scores on intelligence tests fluctuate considerably.

Intelligence in Adulthood

- Horn argued that crystallized intelligence continues to increase in middle adulthood, whereas fluid intelligence begins to decline. Schaie found that when assessed longitudinally, inductive reasoning is less likely to decline and more likely to improve than when assessed cross-sectionally in middle adulthood. The highest level of four intellectual abilities (verbal ability, verbal memory, inductive reasoning, and spatial orientation) occurs in middle adulthood. Baltes emphasizes a distinction between cognitive mechanics (the "hardware" of the mind, reflecting the neurophysiological architecture of the brain) and cognitive pragmatics (the culture-based "software" of the mind). Cognitive mechanics are more likely to decline in older adults than are cognitive pragmatics. Wisdom is expert knowledge about the practical aspects of life that permits excellent judgment about important matters. Baltes and his colleagues have found that high levels of wisdom are rare, the time frame of late adolescence and early adulthood is the main age window for the wisdom to emerge, factors other than age are critical for a high level of wisdom to develop, and personality-related factors are better predictors of wisdom than cognitive factors such as intelligence. Sternberg argues that wisdom involves both academic and practical aspects of intelligence—balance between self-interest, the interests of others, and contexts—to produce a common good.

4 THE EXTREMES OF INTELLIGENCE AND CREATIVITY: DESCRIBE THE CHARACTERISTICS OF MENTAL RETARDATION, GIFTEDNESS, AND CREATIVITY

Mental Retardation

- Mental retardation is a condition of limited mental ability in which the individual (1) has a low IQ, usually below 70; (2) has difficulty adapting to everyday life; and (3) has an onset of these characteristics by age 18. Most affected individuals have an IQ in the 55 to 70 range (mild retardation). Mental retardation can have an organic cause (called organic retardation) or be social and cultural in origin if there is no evidence of organic brain damage (called cultural-familial retardation).

- People who are gifted have high intelligence (an IQ of 130 or higher) or superior talent for something. Three characteristics of gifted children are precocity, marching to their own drummer, and a passion to master in their domain. Giftedness is likely a consequence of both heredity and environment. Developmental changes characterize giftedness, and increasingly the domain-specific aspect of giftedness is emphasized. A current concern is the education of children who are gifted.

- Creativity is the ability to think about something in novel and unusual ways and come up with unique solutions to problems. Although most creative people are intelligent, individuals with high IQs are not necessarily creative. Creative people tend to be divergent thinkers; traditional intelligence tests measure convergent thinking. Creativity has often been described as occurring in a five-step process: preparation, incubation, insight, evaluation, and elaboration. Characteristics of creative thinkers include flexibility and playful thinking, inner motivation, a willingness to take risks, and interest in objective evaluation. Creativity often peaks in the forties and then declines, but the decline may be slight and the peak age varies across domains. Csikszentmihalyi notes that cultivating curiosity and interest is the first step toward a more creative life.

KEY TERMS

intelligence 280
mental age (MA) 281
intelligence quotient
    (IQ) 281
normal distribution 281
triarchic theory of
    intelligence 283

emotional
    intelligence 285
heritability 288
culture-fair tests 292
stereotype threat 293
developmental
    quotient (DQ) 294

Bayley Scales of Infant
    Development 294
crystallized
    intelligence 296
fluid intelligence 296
cognitive mechanics 298
cognitive pragmatics 299

wisdom 299
mental retardation 301
gifted 302
creativity 304
divergent thinking 305
convergent thinking 305
brainstorming 306

KEY PEOPLE

Robert J. Sternberg 280
Alfred Binet 281
Théophile Simon 281
Lewis Terman 281
David Wechsler 282
Howard Gardner 284

Daniel Goleman 285
Peter Salovey and John
    Mayer 285
James Flynn 289
Robert Plomin 290
Craig Ramey 290

Elena Grigorenko 291
Arnold Gesell 294
Nancy Bayley 294
Robert McCall 296
John Horn 296
K. Warner Schaie 297

Paul Baltes 298
Ellen Winner 302
John Colombo 303
Mihaly Csikszentmihalyi 305

E-LEARNING TOOLS

Connect to **www.mhhe.com/santrockldt5e** to research the answers and complete these exercises. In addition, you'll find a number of other resources and valuable study tools for Chapter 8, "Intelligence," on this Web site.

Taking It to the Net

1. Penny teaches fifth-grade in a school that has received a grant to pilot a Creative Classrooms Project. The principal has asked Penny to create one month of lesson plans utilizing a creative teaching model. What are some main differences in teaching with this method?

2. Ted and Eva's 10-year-old daughter, Juanita, is experiencing difficulties in school. School personnel have said that Juanita is lazy and unmotivated. They have suggested that Ted and Eva aren't doing enough at home to encourage their daughter. Ted and Eva are very angry and frustrated as they do not agree with this assessment of the situation. What can they do to help Juanita? How should they approach the school?

3. Juan and Carmen's 7-year-old gifted son, Nicholas, attends a school that does not have a gifted program, but the teachers do try to create challenging learning situations within the normal classroom. Nicholas' teacher wants to meet with Juan and Carmen to discuss Nicholas' classroom behavior problems. What types of behavioral challenges do gifted children present in the classroom?

Self-Assessment

To evaluate yourself on various aspects of intelligence and creativity, complete these self-assessments:

- *Evaluating Myself on Gardner's Eight Types of Intelligence*
- *How Emotionally Intelligent Am I?*
- *Examining My Creative Thinking*

Health and Well-Being, Parenting, and Education

Build your decision-making skills by trying your hand at the health and well-being, parenting, and education exercises.

Video Clips

The Online Learning Center includes the following video for this chapter:

- *Intelligence Testing*

9

LEARNING GOALS

◆ Define language, and describe its rule systems.

◆ Describe how language develops through the life span.

◆ Discuss the biological and environmental contributions to language skills.

LANGUAGE DEVELOPMENT

CHAPTER OUTLINE

PREVIEW

In this chapter, we tell the remarkable story of language and how it develops. The questions we explore include these: What is language? What is the course of language development across the life span? What does biology contribute to language? How do different experiences influence language?

1 WHAT IS LANGUAGE?

Defining Language	Language's Rule Systems

In 1799, a nude boy was observed running through the woods in France. The boy was captured when he was 11 years old. He was called the Wild Boy of Aveyron and was believed to have lived in the woods alone for six years (Lane, 1976). When found, he made no effort to communicate. He never learned to communicate effectively. A modern-day wild child named Genie was discovered in Los Angeles in 1970. Genie was locked away in almost complete social isolation during her childhood. At age 13, Genie could not speak or stand erect. Sadly, despite intensive intervention, Genie never acquired more than a primitive form of language. Both cases—the Wild Boy of Aveyron and Genie—raise questions about the biological and environmental determinants of language, topics that we also examine later in the chapter. First, though, we need to define language.

Defining Language

Language is a form of communication—whether spoken, written, or signed—that is based on a system of symbols. Language consists of the words used by a community and the rules for varying and combining them.

Think how important language is in our everyday lives. We need language to speak with others, listen to others, read, and write. Our language enables us to describe past events in detail and to plan for the future. Language lets us pass down information from one generation to the next and create a rich cultural heritage.

All human languages have some common characteristics. These include infinite generativity and organizational rules. **Infinite generativity** is the ability to produce an endless number of meaningful sentences using a finite set of words and rules. Rules describe the way language works. Let's explore what these rules involve.

Language's Rule Systems

When nineteenth-century American writer Ralph Waldo Emerson said, "The world was built in order and the atoms march in tune," he must have had language in mind. Language is highly ordered and organized (Berko Gleason, 2009; Colombo, McCardle, & Freund, 2009). The organization involves five systems of rules: phonology, morphology, syntax, semantics, and pragmatics.

Phonology   Every language is made up of basic sounds. **Phonology** is the sound system of the language, including the sounds that are used and how they may be combined (Menn & Stoel-Gammon, 2009; Stoel-Gammon & Sosa, 2010). For example, English has the initial consonant cluster *spr* as in spring, but no words begin with the cluster *rsp*.

Phonology provides a basis for constructing a large and expandable set of words out of two or three dozen phonemes. A *phoneme* is the basic unit of sound in a language; it is the smallest unit of sound that affects meaning. For example, in English

language A form of communication, whether spoken, written, or signed, that is based on a system of symbols.

infinite generativity The ability to produce an endless number of meaningful sentences using a finite set of words and rules.

phonology The sound system of a language—includes the sounds used and how they may be combined.

the sound represented by the letter *p*, as in the words *pot* and *spot*, is a phoneme. The /p/ sound is slightly different in the two words, but this variation is not distinguished in English, and therefore the /p/ sound is a single phoneme. In some languages, such as Hindi, the variations of the /p/ sound represent separate phonemes.

Morphology **Morphology** refers to the units of meaning involved in word formation. A morpheme is a minimal unit of meaning; it is a word or a part of a word that cannot be broken into smaller meaningful parts. Every word in the English language is made up of one or more morphemes. Some words consist of a single morpheme (for example, *help*), whereas others are made up of more than one morpheme (for example, *helper* has two morphemes, *help* + *er*, with the morpheme *-er* meaning "one who," in this case "one who helps"). Thus, not all morphemes are words by themselves—for example, *pre-*, *-tion*, and *-ing* are morphemes.

Just as the rules that govern phonology describe the sound sequences that can occur in a language, the rules of morphology describe the way meaningful units (morphemes) can be combined in words (Tager-Flusberg & Zukowski, 2009). Morphemes have many jobs in grammar, such as marking tense (for example, she walks versus she walked) and number (she walks versus they walk).

Syntax **Syntax** involves the way words are combined to form acceptable phrases and sentences. If someone says to you, "Bob slugged Tom" or "Bob was slugged by Tom," you know who did the slugging and who was slugged in each case because you have a syntactic understanding of these sentence structures. You also understand that the sentence "You didn't stay, did you?" is a grammatical sentence but that "You didn't stay, didn't you?" is unacceptable and ambiguous.

If you learn another language, English syntax will not get you very far. For example, in English an adjective usually precedes a noun (as in *blue sky*), whereas in Spanish the adjective usually follows the noun (*cielo azul*). Despite the differences in their syntactic structures, however, syntactic systems in all the world's languages have some common ground (Naigles & Swensen, 2010; Tager-Flusberg & Zukowski, 2009). For example, no language we know of permits sentences like the following one:

The mouse the cat the farmer chased killed ate the cheese.

It appears that language users cannot process subjects and objects arranged in too complex a fashion in a sentence.

Semantics **Semantics** refers to the meaning of words and sentences. Every word has a set of semantic features, which are required attributes related to meaning. *Girl* and *women*, for example, share many semantic features, but they differ semantically in regard to age. Words have semantic restrictions on how they can be used in sentences (Li, 2009; Pan & Uccelli, 2009). The sentence *The bicycle talked the boy into buying a candy bar* is syntactically correct but semantically incorrect. The sentence violates our semantic knowledge that bicycles don't talk.

Pragmatics A final set of language rules involves **pragmatics,** the appropriate use of language in different contexts. Pragmatics covers a lot of territory. When you take turns speaking in a discussion or use a question to convey a command ("Why is it so noisy in here?" "What is this, Grand Central Station?"), you are demonstrating knowledge of pragmatics. You also apply the pragmatics of English when you use polite language in appropriate situations (for example, when talking to one's teacher) or tell stories that are interesting, jokes that are funny, and lies that are convincing. In each of these cases, you are demonstrating that you understand the rules of your culture for adjusting language to suit the context.

Pragmatic rules can be complex and differ from one culture to another (Bryant, 2009). Consider the pragmatics of saying "thank you." Even preschoolers' use of the phrase *thank you* varies with sex, socioeconomic status, and the age of the individual they are addressing. If you were to study the Japanese language, you would come

morphology Units of meaning involved in word formation.

syntax The ways words are combined to form acceptable phrases and sentences.

semantics The meanings of words and sentences.

pragmatics The appropriate use of language in different contexts.

Rule System	Description	Examples
Phonology	The sound system of a language. A phoneme is the smallest sound unit in a language.	The word *chat* has three phonemes: /ch/ /a/ /t/. An example of a phonological rule in the English language is that while the phoneme /r/ can follow the phonemes /t/ or /d/ in an English consonant cluster (such as *track* or *drab*), the phoneme /l/ cannot follow these letters.
Morphology	The system of meaningful units involved in word formation.	The smallest sound units that have a meaning are called morphemes or meaning units. The word *girl* is one morpheme or meaning unit; it cannot be broken down any further and still have meaning. When the suffix *s* is added, the word becomes *girls* and has two morphemes because the *s* changed the meaning of the word, indicating that there is more than one girl.
Syntax	The system that involves the way words are combined to form acceptable phrases and sentences.	Word order is very important in determining meaning in the English language. For example, the sentence, "Sebastian pushed the bike" has a different meaning than "The bike pushed Sebastian."
Semantics	The system that involves the meaning of words and sentences.	Knowing the meaning of individual words—that is, vocabulary. For example, semantics includes knowing the meaning of such words as *orange*, *transportation*, and *intelligent*.
Pragmatics	The system of using appropriate conversation and knowledge of how to effectively use language in context.	An example is using polite language in appropriate situations, such as being mannerly when talking with one's teacher. Taking turns in a conversation involves pragmatics.

FIGURE 9.1 The Rule Systems of Language.

face-to-face with countless pragmatic rules about how to say thank you to individuals of various social levels and with various relationships to you.

At this point, we have discussed five important rule systems involved in language. An overview of these rule systems is presented in Figure 9.1.

Review and Reflect: Learning Goal 1

1 **Define language, and describe its rule systems**

REVIEW

- What is language?
- What are language's five main rule systems?

REFLECT

- How good are your family members and friends at the pragmatics of language? Describe an example in which one of the individuals showed pragmatic skills and another in which the person did not.

2 HOW LANGUAGE DEVELOPS

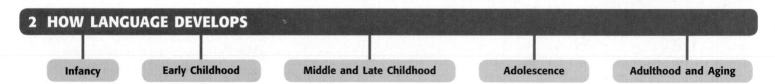

| Infancy | Early Childhood | Middle and Late Childhood | Adolescence | Adulthood and Aging |

In the thirteenth century, Emperor Frederick II of Germany had a cruel idea. He wanted to know what language children would speak if no one talked to them. He selected several newborns and threatened their caregivers with death if they ever talked to the infants. Frederick never found out what language the children spoke because they all died. As we move forward in the twenty-first century, we are still curious about infants' development of language, although our experiments and observations are, to say the least, far more humane than the evil Frederick's.

Infancy

Whatever language they learn, infants all over the world follow a similar path in language development. What are some key milestones in this development?

Babbling and Other Vocalizations   Long before infants speak recognizable words, they produce a number of vocalizations (Jaswal & Fernald, 2007; Sachs, 2009). The functions of these early vocalization are to practice making sounds, to communicate, and to attract attention (Lock, 2004). Babies' sounds go through this sequence during the first year:

Long before infants speak recognizable words, they communicate by producing a number of vocalizations and gestures. *At approximately what ages do infants begin to produce different types of vocalizations and gestures?*

- *Crying.* Babies cry even at birth. Crying can signal distress, but—as we discuss in Chapter 10, "Emotional Development"—different types of cries signal different things.

- *Cooing.* Babies first coo at about 2 to 4 months (Menn & Stoel-Gammon, 2009). These gurgling sounds that are made in the back of the throat usually express pleasure during interaction with the caregiver.

- *Babbling.* In the middle of the first year, babies babble—that is, they produce strings of consonant-vowel combinations, such as *ba, ba, ba, ba.*

Gestures   Infants start using gestures, such as showing and pointing, at about 8 to 12 months of age. They may wave bye-bye, nod to mean "yes," show an empty cup to want more milk, and point to a dog to draw attention to it. Some early gestures are symbolic, as when an infant smacks her lips to indicate food/drink. Pointing is considered by language experts as an important index of the social aspects of language, and it follows this developmental sequence: from pointing without checking on adult gaze to pointing while looking back and forth between an object and the adult. Lack of pointing is a significant indicator of problems in the infant's communication system. For example, failure to engage in pointing characterizes many autistic children.

Recognizing Language Sounds   Long before they begin to learn words, infants can make fine distinctions among the sounds of the language (Menn & Stoel-Gammon, 2009; Sachs, 2009). In Patricia Kuhl's (1993, 2000, 2007, 2009; Kuhl & Damasio, 2009; Kuhl & others, 2006) research, phonemes from languages all over the world are piped through a speaker for infants to hear (see Figure 9.2). A box with a toy bear in it is placed where the infant can see it. A string of identical syllables is played, then the syllables are changed (for example, *ba ba ba ba,* and then *pa pa pa pa*). If the infant turns its head when the syllables change, the box lights up and the bear dances and drums, rewarding the infant for noticing the change.

Kuhl's research (2007, 2009) has demonstrated that from birth up to about 6 months of age, infants are "citizens of the world": They recognize when sounds change most of the time no matter what language the syllables come from. But over the next six months, infants get even better at perceiving the changes in sounds from their "own"

FIGURE 9.2 From Universal Linguist to Language-Specific Listener. In Patricia Kuhl's research laboratory, babies listen to tape-recorded voices that repeat syllables. When the sounds of the syllables change, the babies quickly learn to look at the bear. Using this technique, Kuhl has demonstrated that babies are universal linguists until about 6 months of age, but in the next six months become language-specific listeners. *Does Kuhl's research give support to the view that either "nature" or "nurture" is the source of language acquisition?*

What characterizes the infant's early word learning?

language, the one their parents speak, and they gradually lose the ability to recognize differences that are not important in their own language.

Infants must fish out individual words from the nonstop stream of sound that makes up ordinary speech (Menn & Stoel-Gammon, 2009; Singleton & Ryan, 2009). To do so, they must find the boundaries between words, a task that is very difficult for infants because adults don't pause between words when they speak. Still, infants begin to detect word boundaries by 8 months of age. For example, in one study, 8-month-old infants listened to recorded stories that contained unusual words, such as *hornbill* and *python* (Jusczyk & Hohne, 1997). Two weeks later, the researchers tested the infants with two lists of words, one made up of words in the stories, the other of new, unusual words that did not appear in the stories. The infants listened to the familiar words for a second longer, on average, than to new words.

First Words   Between about 5 to 12 months of age, infants often indicate their first understanding of words. The infant's first spoken word is a milestone eagerly anticipated by every parent. This event usually occurs between 10 to 15 months of age and at an average of about 13 months. However, long before babies say their first words, they have been communicating with their parents, often by gesturing and using their own special sounds. The appearance of first words is a continuation of this communication process (Berko Gleason, 2009).

A child's first words include those that name important people (*dada*), familiar animals (*kitty*), vehicles (*car*), toys (*ball*), food (*milk*), body parts (*eye*), clothes (*hat*), household items (*clock*), and greeting terms (*bye*). These were the first words of babies 50 years ago. They are the first words of babies today. Children often express various intentions with their single words, so that *cookie* might mean, "That's a cookie" or "I want a cookie."

The first words of infants can vary across languages. The first words of English-speaking and Romance-language-speaking infants usually are nouns. However, because of the structure of the Korean language, the first words of Korean infants are most often verbs (Choi & Gopnik, 1995).

On the average, infants understand about 50 words at about 13 months, but they can't say this many words until about 18 months (Menyuk, Liebergott, & Schultz, 1995). Thus, in infancy *receptive vocabulary* (words the child understands) considerably exceeds *spoken vocabulary* (words the child uses).

The infant's spoken vocabulary rapidly increases once the first word is spoken (Pan & Uccelli, 2009; Waxman, 2009). The average 18-month-old can speak about 50 words, but by the age of 2 years can speak about 200 words. This rapid increase in vocabulary that begins at approximately 18 months is called the *vocabulary spurt* (Bloom, Lifter, & Broughton, 1985).

Like the timing of a child's first word, the timing of the vocabulary spurt varies. Figure 9.3 shows the range for these two language milestones in 14 children (Bloom, 1998). On average, these children said their first word at 13 months and had a vocabulary spurt at 19 months. However, the ages for the first word of individual children varied from 10 to 17 months and for their vocabulary spurt from 13 to 25 months.

There are some interesting cross-linguistic differences in word learning. Children learning Mandarin Chinese, Korean, and Japanese acquire more verbs earlier in their development than do children learning English. This cross-linguistic difference reflects the greater use of verbs in the language input to children in these Asian languages.

Some children use a referential style, others an expressive style, in learning words (Melzi & Ely, 2009). A *referential style* refers to more frequently using words that refer to objects, whereas an *expressive style* indicates a greater use of pronouns and socially linked words. Examples of the referential style include words that describe events, people, animals, and food—examples of the expressive style are "hello," "bye-bye,"

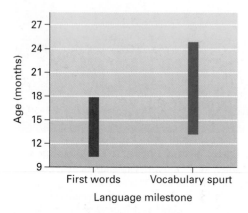

FIGURE 9.3 Variation in Language Milestones. *What are some possible explanations for variations in the timing of these milestones?*

and "thank you." Another example of individual variations is that some children use whole phrases, such as "gimme," "lemme see," and "help me," early in their word learning, whereas other children don't use these whole phrases early on.

Children sometimes overextend or underextend the meanings of the words they use (Woodward & Markman, 1998). *Overextension* is the tendency to apply a word to objects that are inappropriate for the word's meaning. For example, children at first may say *"dada"* not only for "father" but also for other men, strangers, or boys. With time, overextensions decrease and eventually disappear. *Underextension* is the tendency to apply a word too narrowly; it occurs when children fail to use a word to name a relevant event or object. For example, a child might use the word *boy* to describe a 5-year-old neighbor but not apply the word to a male infant or to a 9-year-old male.

Two-Word Utterances   By the time children are 18 to 24 months of age, they usually utter two-word utterances. To convey meaning with just two words, the child relies heavily on gesture, tone, and context. The wealth of meaning children can communicate with a two-word utterance includes the following (Slobin, 1972):

- Identification: "See doggie."
- Location: "Book there."
- Repetition: "More milk."
- Nonexistence: "All gone."
- Possession: "My candy."
- Attribution: "Big car."
- Agent-action: "Mama walk."
- Question: "Where ball?"

These examples are from children whose first language is English, German, Russian, Finnish, Turkish, or Samoan.

Notice that the two-word utterances omit many parts of speech and are remarkably succinct. In fact, in every language, a child's first combinations of words have this economical quality; they are telegraphic. **Telegraphic speech** is the use of short and precise words without grammatical markers such as articles, auxiliary verbs, and other connectives. Telegraphic speech is not limited to two words. "Mommy give ice cream" and "Mommy give Tommy ice cream" also are examples of telegraphic speech.

We have discussed a number of language milestones in infancy. Figure 9.4 summarizes the time at which infants typically reach these milestones.

Early Childhood

Toddlers move rather quickly from producing two-word utterances to creating three-, four-, and five-word combinations. Between 2 and 3 years of age, they begin the transition from saying simple sentences that express a single proposition to saying complex sentences.

As young children learn the special features of their own language, there are extensive regularities in how they acquire that specific language (Berko Gleason, 2009). For example, all children learn the prepositions *on* and *in* before other prepositions. Children learning other languages, such as Russian or Chinese, also acquire the specific features of those languages in a consistent order.

However, some children develop language problems, including speech and hearing problems. To read about the work of one individual who works with children who have speech/language problems, see the *Careers in Life-Span Development* profile.

Around the world, most young children learn to speak in two-word utterances, in most cases at about 18 to 24 months of age. *What implications does this have for the biological basis of language?*

Typical Age	Language Milestones
Birth	Crying
2 to 4 months	Cooing begins
5 months	Understands first word
6 months	Babbling begins
7 to 11 months	Changes from universal linguist to language-specific listener
8 to 12 months	Uses gestures, such as showing and pointing Comprehension of words appears
13 months	First word spoken
18 months	Vocabulary spurt starts
18 to 24 months	Uses two-word utterances Rapid expansion of understanding of words

FIGURE 9.4 Some Language Milestones in Infancy. Despite great variations in the language input received by infants, around the world they follow a similar path in learning to speak.

telegraphic speech The use of short, precise words without grammatical markers such as articles, auxiliary verbs, and other connectives.

Careers in Life-Span Development

Sharla Peltier, Speech Pathologist

A speech pathologist is a health professional who works with individuals who have a communication disorder. Peltier is a speech pathologist in Manitoulin, Ontario, Canada, and works with Native American children in the First Nations schools. She conducts screening for speech/language and hearing problems and assesses infants as young as 6 months of age as well as school-aged children. She works closely with community health nurses to identify hearing problems.

Diagnosing problems is only about half of what Peltier does in her work. She especially enjoys treating speech/language and hearing problems. She conducts parent training sessions to help parents understand and help with their children's language problem. As part of this training, she guides parents in improving their communication skills with their children.

Speech therapist Sharla Peltier, helping a young child improve her language and communication skills.

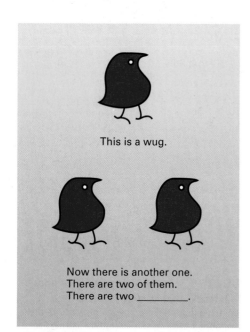

This is a wug.

Now there is another one. There are two of them. There are two _____.

FIGURE 9.5 Stimuli in Berko's Classic Study of Children's Understanding of Morphological Rules. In Jean Berko's study, young children were presented cards such as this one with a "wug" on it. Then the children were asked to supply the missing word and say it correctly.

Understanding Phonology and Morphology During the preschool years, most children gradually become more sensitive to the sounds of spoken words and become increasingly capable of producing all the sounds of their language (National Research Council, 1999). By the time children are 3 years of age, they can produce all the vowel sounds and most of the consonant sounds (Menn & Stoel-Gammon, 2009).

Young children can even produce complex consonant clusters such as *str-* and *-mpt-*. They notice rhymes, enjoy poems, make up silly names for things by substituting one sound for another (such as *bubblegum, bubblebum, bubbleyum*), and clap along with each syllable in a phrase.

By the time children move beyond two-word utterances, they demonstrate a knowledge of morphology rules (Berko Gleason, 2009; Tager-Flusberg & Zukowski, 2009). Children begin using the plural and possessive forms of nouns (such as *dogs* and *dog's*). They put appropriate endings on verbs (such as *-s* when the subject is third-person singular and *-ed* for the past tense). They use prepositions (such as *in* and *on*), articles (such as *a* and *the*), and various forms of the verb *to be* (such as "I *was* going to the store"). Some of the best evidence for changes in children's use of morphological rules occurs in their overgeneralization of the rules, as when a preschool child say "foots" instead of "feet," or "goed" instead of "went."

In a classic experiment that was designed to study children's knowledge of morphological rules, such as how to make a plural, Jean Berko (1958) presented preschool children and first-grade children with cards such as the one shown in Figure 9.5. Children were asked to look at the card while the experimenter read aloud the words on the card. Then the children were asked to supply the missing word. This might sound easy, but Berko was interested in the children's ability to apply the appropriate morphological rule, in this case to say "wugs" with the *z* sound that indicates the plural.

Although the children's answers were not perfect, they were much better than chance. What makes Berko's study impressive is that most of the words were made up for the experiment. Thus, the children could not base their responses on remembering past instances of hearing the words. That they could make the plurals or past tenses of words they had never heard before was proof that they knew the morphological rules.

Changes in Syntax and Semantics Preschool children also learn and apply rules of syntax (Lieven, 2008; Tager-Flusberg & Zukowski, 2009). They show a growing mastery of complex rules for how words should be ordered.

Consider *wh-* questions, such as "Where is Daddy going?" or "What is that boy doing?" To ask these questions properly, the child must know two important differences between *wh-* questions and affirmative statements (for instance, "Mommy is going to work" and "That boy is waiting on the school bus"). First, a *wh-* word must be added at the beginning of the sentence. Second, the auxiliary verb must be inverted—that is, exchanged with the subject of the sentence. Young children learn quite early where to put the *wh-* word, but they take much longer to learn the auxiliary-inversion rule. Thus, preschool children might ask, "Where Daddy is going?" and "What that girl is doing?"

Gains in semantics also characterize early childhood. Vocabulary development is dramatic (Lieven, 2008; Pan & Uccelli, 2009). Some experts have concluded that between 18 months and 6 years of age, young children learn about one new word every waking hour (Gelman & Kalish, 2006)! By the time they enter first grade, it is estimated that children know about 14,000 words (Clark, 1993). However, there are individual variations in children's vocabulary, and children who enter elementary school with a small vocabulary are at risk for developing reading problems (Berninger, 2006).

Why can children learn so many new words so quickly? One possibility is **fast mapping,** which involves children's ability to make an initial connection between a word and its referent after only limited exposure to the word (Woodward, Markman, & Fitzsimmons, 1994). Researchers have found that exposure to words on multiple occasions over several days results in more successful word learning than the same number of exposures in a single day (Childers & Tomasello, 2002).

Language researchers have proposed that young children may use a number of working hypotheses to accomplish their fast mapping (Pan & Uccelli, 2009). One working hypothesis children use is to give a novel label to a novel object. Parents can be especially helpful in aiding children's learning of novel labels for novel objects. As a mother looks at a picture book with her young child, she knows that the child understands the referent for car but not bus, so she says, "That's a *bus,* not a *car.* A bus is bigger than a car." Another working hypothesis children use is that a word refers to a whole object rather than parts of an object such as labeling a tiger a tiger instead of tail or paw. Yet another working hypothesis children invoke is *mutual exclusivity,* in which they give only one name to one object. For example, in the case of a child's dog named Rufus, the child is likely to discard Rufus as a potential referent for *bone* because Rufus already possesses a name. Sometimes children's initial mappings are incorrect. In such cases, they benefit from hearing the words mature speakers use to test and revise their word-referent connections.

Researchers have found that the nature of the talk parents direct to their children is linked with the children's vocabulary growth and the socioeconomic status of families. To read about this link, see the *Research in Life-Span Development* interlude.

> *Children pick up words as pigeons peas.*
> —JOHN RAY
> *English Naturalist, 17th Century*

Research in Life-Span Development

FAMILY ENVIRONMENT AND YOUNG CHILDREN'S LANGUAGE DEVELOPMENT

What characteristics of a family make a difference to a child's language development? Socioeconomic status has been linked with how much parents talk to their children and with young children's vocabulary. Betty Hart and Todd Risley (1995) observed

(continued on next page)

fast mapping A process that helps to explain how young children learn the connection between a word and its referent so quickly.

the language environments of children whose parents were professionals and children whose parents were on welfare. Compared with the professional parents, the parents on welfare talked much less to their young children, talked less about past events, and provided less elaboration. As indicated in Figure 9.6, the children of the professional parents had a much larger vocabulary at 36 months of age than the children of the welfare parents.

Other research has linked how much mothers speak to their infants and the infants' vocabularies. For example, in one study by Janellen Huttenlocher and her colleagues (1991), infants whose mothers spoke more often to them had markedly higher vocabularies. By the second birthday, vocabulary differences were substantial.

However, a recent study of 1- to 3-year-old children living in low-income families found that the sheer amount of maternal talk was not the best predictor of a child's vocabulary growth (Pan & others, 2005). Rather, it was maternal language and literacy skills that were positively related to the children's vocabulary development. For example, when mothers used a more diverse vocabulary when talking with their children, their children's vocabulary benefited, but their children's vocabulary was not related to the total amount of their talkativeness with their children. Also, mothers who frequently used pointing gestures had children with a greater vocabulary. Pointing usually occurs in concert with speech, and it may enhance the meaning of mothers' verbal input to their children.

A recent study revealed that maternal sensitivity (responds warmly to the child's bids and anticipates her child's emotional needs, for example), regardless of socioeconomic status and ethnicity, was positively linked with growth in young children's receptive and expressive language development from 18 to 36 months of age (Pungello & others, 2009). In this study, negative intrusive parenting (physically restraining the child or dominating interaction with the child with unnecessary verbal direction, for example) was related to a slower rate of growth of receptive language.

These research studies and others (NICHD Early Child Care Research Network, 2005) demonstrate the important effect that early speech input and poverty can have on the development of a child's language skills.

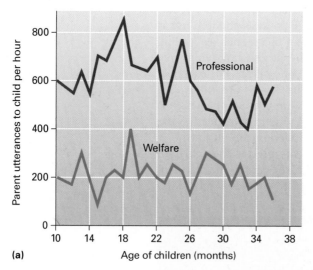

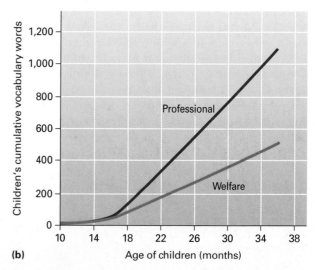

(a)   Age of children (months)   **(b)**   Age of children (months)

FIGURE 9.6 Language Input in Professional and Welfare Families and Young Children's Vocabulary Development. (*a*) In this study (Hart & Risley, 1995), parents from professional families talked with their young children more than parents from welfare families. (*b*) All of the children learned to talk, but children from professional families developed vocabularies that were twice as large as those from welfare families. Thus, by the time children go to preschool, they already have experienced considerable differences in language input in their families and developed different levels of vocabulary that are linked to their socioeconomic context. *Does this study indicate that poverty caused deficiencies in vocabulary development?*

Advances in Pragmatics   Changes in pragmatics also characterize young children's language development (Bryant, 2009; Siegal & Surian, 2010). A 6-year-old is simply a much better conversationalist than a 2-year-old is (Lieven, 2008). What are some of the improvements in pragmatics during the preschool years?

Young children begin to engage in extended discourse (Aktar & Herold, 2008, p. 581). For example, they learn culturally specific rules of conversation and politeness and become sensitive to the need to adapt their speech in different settings. Their developing linguistic skills and increasing ability to take the perspective of others contribute to their generation of more competent narratives.

As children get older, they become increasingly able to talk about things that are not here (grandma's house, for example) and not now (what happened to them yesterday or might happen tomorrow, for example). A preschool child can tell you what she wants for lunch tomorrow, something that would not have been possible at the two-word stage of language development.

Around 4 to 5 years of age, children learn to change their speech style to suit the situation. For example, even 4-year-old children speak to a 2-year-old differently from the way they speak to a same-aged peer; they use shorter sentences with the 2-year-old. They also speak to an adult differently from the way they speak to a same-aged peer, using more polite and formal language with the adult (Shatz & Gelman, 1973).

Early Literacy   The concern about the ability of U.S. children to read and write has led to a careful examination of preschool and kindergarten children's experiences, with the hope that a positive orientation toward reading and writing can be developed early in life (Kim, 2009; Otto, 2010). What should a literacy program for preschool children be like? Instruction should be built on what children already know about oral language, reading, and writing. Further, early precursors of literacy and academic success include language skills, phonological and syntactic knowledge, letter identification, and conceptual knowledge about print and its conventions and functions (Morrow, 2009). Parents and teachers need to provide a supportive environment to help children develop literacy skills (Wagner, 2010). A recent study revealed that children whose mothers had more education had more advanced emergent literacy skills than children whose mothers had less education (Korat, 2009). Another recent study found that literacy experiences (such as how often the child was read to), the quality of the mother's engagement with her child (such as attempts to cognitively stimulate the child), and provision of learning materials (such as age-appropriate learning materials and books) were important home literacy experiences in low-income families that were linked to the children's language development in positive ways (Rodriguez & others, 2009).

Middle and Late Childhood

Children gain new skills as they enter school that include increasingly using language to talk about things that are not physically present, learning what a word is, and learning how to recognize and talk about sounds (Berko Gleason, 2003). They have to learn the *alphabetic principle*, that the letters of the alphabet represent sounds of the language. As children develop during middle and late childhood, changes in their vocabulary and grammar also take place.

Vocabulary, Grammar, and Metalinguistic Awareness   During middle and late childhood, changes occur in the way children organize their mental vocabulary. When asked to say the first word that comes to mind when they hear a word, young children typically provide a word that often follows the word in a sentence. For example, when asked to respond to "dog" the young child may say "barks," or to the word "eat" say "lunch." At about 7 years of age, children begin to respond with a word that is the same part of speech as the stimulus word. For example, a child

What characterizes advances in pragmatics during early childhood?

may now respond to the word "dog" with "cat" or "horse." To "eat," they now might say "drink." This reply is evidence that children now have begun to categorize their vocabulary by parts of speech (Berko Gleason, 2003).

The process of categorizing becomes easier as children increase their vocabulary. Children's vocabulary increases from an average of about 14,000 words at 6 years of age to an average of about 40,000 words by 11 years of age.

Children make similar advances in grammar (Lidz, 2010; Lust, 2007). During the elementary school years, children's improvement in logical reasoning and analytical skills helps them understand such constructions as the appropriate use of comparatives (*shorter, deeper*) and subjunctives ("If you were president . . ."). During the elementary school years, children become increasingly able to understand and use complex grammar, such as the following sentence: *The boy who kissed his mother wore a hat.* They also learn to use language in a more connected way, producing connected discourse. They become able to relate sentences to one another to produce descriptions, definitions, and narratives that make sense. Children must be able to do these things orally before they can be expected to deal with them in written assignments.

These advances in vocabulary and grammar during the elementary school years are accompanied by the development of **metalinguistic awareness,** which is knowledge about language, such as knowing what a preposition is or the ability to discuss the sounds of a language. Metalinguistic awareness allows children "to think about their language, understand what words are, and even define them" (Berko Gleason, 2009, p. 4). It improves considerably during the elementary school years (Pan & Uccelli, 2009). Defining words becomes a regular part of classroom discourse, and children increase their knowledge of syntax as they study and talk about the components of sentences such as subjects and verbs (Melzi & Ely, 2009).

Children also make progress in understanding how to use language in culturally appropriate ways—pragmatics (Bryant, 2009). By the time they enter adolescence, most children know the rules for the use of language in everyday contexts—that is, what is appropriate to say and what is inappropriate to say.

Reading   Before learning to read, children learn to use language to talk about things that are not present; they learn what a word is; and they learn how to recognize sounds and talk about them (Berko Gleason, 2003). If they develop a large vocabulary, their path to reading is eased. Children who begin elementary school with a small vocabulary are at risk when it comes to learning to read (Berko Gleason, 2003).

Vocabulary development plays an important role in reading comprehension (Cunningham, 2009; O'Hara & Pritchard, 2009). For example, one study revealed that a good vocabulary was linked with reading comprehension in second-grade students (Berninger & Abbott, 2005). Having a good vocabulary helps readers access word meaning effortlessly.

How should children be taught to read? Currently, debate focuses on the whole-language approach versus the phonics approach (Otto, 2010; Vacca & others, 2009).

The **whole-language approach** stresses that reading instruction should parallel children's natural language learning. In some whole-language classes, beginning readers are taught to recognize whole words or even entire sentences, and to use the context of what they are reading to guess at the meaning of words. Reading materials that support the whole-language approach are whole and meaningful— that is, children are given material in its complete form, such as stories and poems, so that they learn to understand language's communicative function. Reading is connected with listening and writing skills. Although there are variations in whole-language programs, most share the premise that reading should be integrated with other skills and subjects, such as science and social studies, and that it should focus on real-world material. Thus, a class might read newspapers, magazines, or books, and then write about and discuss them.

In contrast, the **phonics approach** emphasizes that reading instruction should teach basic rules for translating written symbols into sounds. Early phonics-centered

metalinguistic awareness Knowledge about language.

whole-language approach An approach that stresses that reading instruction should parallel children's natural language learning. Reading materials should be whole and meaningful.

phonics approach An approach that emphasizes that reading instruction should teach basic rules for translating written symbols into sounds.

reading instruction should involve simplified materials. Only after children have learned correspondence rules that relate spoken phonemes to the alphabet letters that are used to represent them should they be given complex reading materials, such as books and poems (Cunningham, 2009; Fox, 2010).

Which approach is better? Research suggests that children can benefit from both approaches, but instruction in phonics needs to be emphasized (Fox, 2010; Melzi & Ely, 2009). An increasing number of experts in the field of reading now conclude that direct instruction in phonics is a key aspect of learning to read (Mayer, 2008; Mraz, Padak, & Rasinski, 2008).

Writing Children's writing emerges out of their early scribbles, which appear at around 2 to 3 years of age. In early childhood, children's motor skills usually develop to the point that they can begin printing letters. Most 4-year-olds can print their first names. Five-year-olds can reproduce letters and copy several short words. They gradually learn to distinguish the distinctive characteristics of letters, such as whether the lines are curved or straight, open or closed. Through the early elementary grades, many children continue to reverse letters such as *b* and *d* and *p* and *q* (Temple & others, 1993). At this age, if other aspects of the child's development are normal, letter reversals do not predict literacy problems.

As they begin to write, children often invent spellings. Usually they base these spellings on the sounds of words they hear (Spandel, 2009).

Parents and teachers should encourage children's early writing but not be overly concerned about the formation of letters or spelling. I once had a conference with my youngest daughter's first-grade teacher when she brought home papers with her printing all marked up and sad faces drawn on the paper. Fortunately, the teacher agreed to reduce her criticism of Jennifer's print skills. Printing errors are a natural part of the child's growth. Corrections of spelling and printing should be selective and made in positive ways that do not discourage the child's writing and spontaneity.

Like becoming a good reader, becoming a good writer takes many years and lots of practice. Children should be given many writing opportunities (Graham, 2009). As their language and cognitive skills improve with good instruction, so will their writing skills. For example, developing a more sophisticated understanding of syntax and grammar serves as an underpinning for better writing. So do such cognitive skills as organization and logical reasoning. Through the course of the school years, students develop increasingly sophisticated methods of organizing their ideas. In early elementary school, they narrate and describe or write short poems. In late elementary and middle school, they can combine narration with reflection and analysis in projects such as book reports.

Major concerns about students' writing competence are increasingly being voiced (Graham, 2009; Harris & others, 2008). One study revealed that 70 to 75 percent of U.S. students in grades 4 through 12 are low-achieving writers (Persky, Dane, & Jin, 2003). College instructors report that 50 percent of high school graduates are not prepared for college-level writing (Achieve, Inc., 2005).

As with reading, teachers play a critical role in students' development of writing skills (Graham, 2009; Tompkins, 2010a, b). Effective writing instruction provides guidance about planning, drafting, and revising, not only in elementary school but through college (Mayer, 2008). A recent meta-analysis (use of statistical techniques to combine the results of studies) revealed that the following interventions were the most effective in improving fourth- through twelfth-grade students' writing quality: (1) strategy instruction, (2) summarization, (3) peer assistance, and (4) setting goals (Graham & Perin, 2007).

The observations of classrooms made by Michael Pressley and his colleagues (2007) revealed that students became good writers when

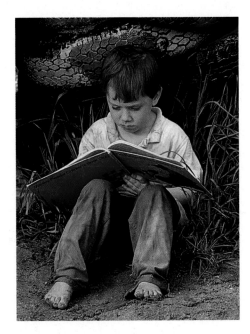

What are the main approaches to teaching children how to read?

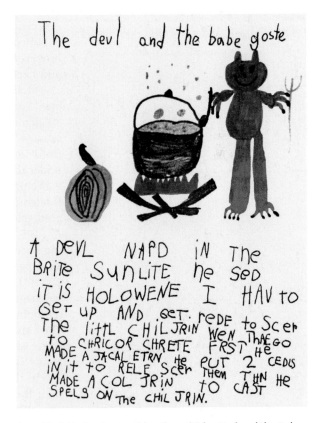

Anna Mudd is the 6-year-old author of "The Devil and the Babe Goste." Anna has been writing stories for at least two years. Her story includes poetic images, sophisticated syntax, and vocabulary that reflect advances in language development. From Jean Berko Gleason, *The Development of Language,* 3rd ed. Published by Allyn & Bacon, Boston, MA. Copyright © 1993 by Pearson Education. Reprinted by permission of the publisher.

teachers spent considerable time on writing instruction and were passionate about teaching students to write. Their observations also indicated that classrooms with students who scored high on writing assessments had walls that overflowed with examples of effective writing, whereas it was much harder to find such examples on the walls of classrooms that had many students who scored low on writing assessments.

Bilingualism and Second-Language Learning   Are there sensitive periods in learning a second language? That is, if individuals want to learn a second language, how important is the age at which they begin to learn it? For many years, it was claimed that if individuals did not learn a second language prior to puberty they would never reach native-language learners' proficiency in the second language (Johnson & Newport, 1991). However, recent research indicates a more complex conclusion: Sensitive periods likely vary across different language systems (Thomas & Johnson, 2008). Thus, for late language learners, such as adolescents and adults, new vocabulary is easier to learn than new sounds or new grammar (Neville, 2006; Werker & Tees, 2005). For example, children's ability to pronounce words with a nativelike accent in a second language typically decreases with age, with an especially sharp drop occurring after the age of about 10 to 12. Also, adults tend to learn a second language faster than children, but their final level of second-language attainment is not as high as children's. And the way children and adults learn a second language differs somewhat. Compared with adults, children are less sensitive to feedback, less likely to use explicit strategies, and more likely to learn a second language from large amounts of input (Thomas & Johnson, 2008).

Some aspects of children's ability to learn a second language are transferred more easily to the second language than others (Paradis, 2010; Pena & Bedore, 2009). A recent research review indicated that in learning to read, phonological awareness is rooted in general cognitive processes and thus transfers easily across languages; however, decoding (converting print words into sounds) is more language-specific and needs to be relearned with each language (Bialystok, 2007).

Students in the United States are far behind their counterparts in many developed countries in learning a second language. For example, in Russia, schools have 10 grades, called *forms,* which roughly correspond to the 12 grades in American schools. Russian children begin school at age 7 and begin learning English in the third form. Because of this emphasis on teaching English, most Russian citizens under the age of 40 today are able to speak at least some English. The United States is the only technologically advanced Western nation that does not have a national foreign-language requirement at the high school level, even for students in rigorous academic programs.

U.S. students who do not learn a second language may be missing more than the chance to acquire a skill (Garcia, 2008). *Bilingualism*—the ability to speak two languages—has a positive effect on children's cognitive development (Gibbons & Ng, 2004). Children who are fluent in two languages perform better than their single-language counterparts on tests of control of attention, concept formation, analytical reasoning, cognitive flexibility, and cognitive complexity (Bialystok, 1999, 2001). They also are more conscious of the structure of spoken and written language and better at noticing errors of grammar and meaning, skills that benefit their reading ability (Bialystok, 1993, 1997).

In the United States, many immigrant children go from being monolingual in their home language to bilingual in that language and in English, only to end up monolingual speakers of English. This is called *subtractive bilingualism,* and it can have negative effects on children, who often become ashamed of their home language.

A current controversy related to bilingualism involves the most effective way of teaching children whose primary language is not English (Diaz-Rico, & Weed, 2010). To read about the work of one bilingual education teacher, see the *Careers in Life-Span Development* profile, and for a discussion of the debate about bilingual education, read the *Contexts of Life-Span Development* interlude that follows.

Careers in Life-Span Development

Salvador Tamayo, Bilingual Education Teacher

Salvador Tamayo teaches bilingual education in the fifth grade at Turner Elementary School in West Chicago. He recently was given a National Educator Award by the Milken Family Foundation for his work in bilingual education. Tamayo especially is adept at integrating technology into his bilingual education classes. He and his students have created several award-winning Web sites about the West Chicago City Museum, the local Latino community, and the history of West Chicago. His students also developed an "I Want to Be an American Citizen" Web site to assist family and community members in preparing for the U.S. Citizenship Test. Tamayo also teaches a bilingual education class at Wheaton College.

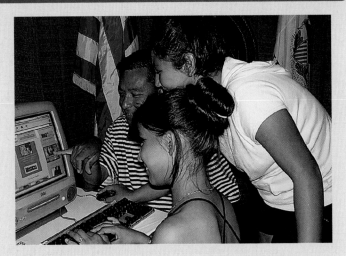

Salvador Tamayo, instructing students in his bilingual education class.

Contexts of Life-Span Development

BILINGUAL EDUCATION

A current controversy related to bilingualism involves the millions of U.S. children who come from homes in which English is not the primary language (Oller & Jarmulowicz, 2010). What is the best way to teach these children?

For the last two decades, the preferred strategy has been *bilingual education,* which teaches academic subjects to immigrant children in their native language while slowly teaching English (Callahan & Colomer, 2009; Haley, 2010). Advocates of bilingual education programs argue that if children who do not know English are taught only in English, they will fall behind in academic subjects. How, they ask, can 7-year-olds learn arithmetic or history taught only in English when they do not speak the language?

Some critics of bilingual programs argue that too often it is thought that immigrant children need only one year of bilingual education. However, in general it takes immigrant children approximately three to five years to develop speaking proficiency and seven years to develop reading proficiency in English (Hakuta, Butler, & Witt, 2001). Also, immigrant children of course vary in their ability to learn English (Lessow-Hurley, 2009; Levine & McCloskey, 2009). Children who come from lower socioeconomic backgrounds have more difficulty than those from higher socioeconomic backgrounds (Hakuta, 2001). Thus, especially for immigrant children from low socioeconomic backgrounds, more years of bilingual education may be needed than they currently are receiving.

Critics who oppose bilingual education argue that as a result of these programs, the children of immigrants are not learning English, which puts them at a permanent disadvantage in U.S. society. California, Arizona, and Massachusetts have significantly reduced the number of bilingual education programs. Some states continue to endorse bilingual education, but the emphasis that test scores be reported separately for English-language learners (students whose main language is not English) in the No Child Left Behind state assessments has shifted attention to literacy in English (Rivera & Collum, 2006; Snow & Kang, 2006).

(continued on next page)

A first- and second-grade bilingual English-Cantonese teacher instructing students in Chinese in Oakland, California. *What have researchers found about the effectiveness of bilingual education?*

What have researchers found regarding outcomes of bilingual education programs? Drawing conclusions about the effectiveness of bilingual education programs is difficult because of variations across programs in the number of years they are in effect, type of instruction, qualities of schooling other than bilingual education, teachers, children, and other factors. Further, no effectively conducted experiments that compare bilingual education with English-only education in the United States have been conducted (Snow & Kang, 2006). Some experts have concluded that the quality of instruction is more important in determining outcomes than the language in which it is delivered (Lesaux & Siegel, 2003).

Research supports bilingual education in that (1) children have difficulty learning a subject when it is taught in a language they do not understand; and (2) when both languages are integrated in the classroom, children learn the second language more readily and participate more actively (Gonzales, Yawkey, & Minaya-Rowe, 2006; Hakuta, 2001, 2005). However, many of the research results report only modest rather than strong support for bilingual education, and some supporters of bilingual education now acknowledge that English-only instruction can produce positive outcomes for English-language learners (Lesaux & Siegel, 2003).

Adolescence

Language development during adolescence includes increased sophistication in the use of words. With an increase in abstract thinking, adolescents are much better than children at analyzing the function a word plays in a sentence.

Adolescents also develop more subtle abilities with words. They make strides in understanding **metaphor,** which is an implied comparison between unlike things. For example, individuals "draw a line in the sand" to indicate a nonnegotiable position; a political campaign is said to be a marathon, not a sprint; a person's faith is shattered. And adolescents become better able to understand and to use **satire,** which is the use of irony, derision, or wit to expose folly or wickedness. Caricatures are an example of satire. More advanced logical thinking also allows adolescents, from about 15 to 20 years of age, to understand complex literary works.

Most adolescents are also much better writers than children are. They are better at organizing ideas before they write, at distinguishing between general and specific points as they write, at stringing together sentences that make sense, and at organizing their writing into an introduction, body, and concluding remarks.

Everyday speech changes during adolescence "and part of being a successful teenager is being able to talk like one" (Berko Gleason, 2005, p. 9). Young adolescents often speak a **dialect** with their peers that is characterized by jargon and slang (Cave, 2002). A dialect is a variety of language that is distinguished by its vocabulary, grammar, or pronunciation. For example, when meeting a friend, instead of saying hello, a young adolescent might say, "Give me five." Nicknames that are satirical and derisive ("Stilt," "Refrigerator," "Spaz") also characterize the dialect of young adolescents. Such labels might be used to show that one belongs to the group and to reduce the seriousness of a situation (Cave, 2002).

What are some changes in language development in adolescence?

Adulthood and Aging

Most research on language development has focused on infancy and childhood. It is generally thought that for most of adulthood individuals maintain their language skills.

In the adolescent and adult years, the development of an identity, a sense of who one is, is an important life task. A distinct personal linguistic style is part of one's special identity (Berko Gleason, 2009; Kotze, 2004). Further psychological goals of early adulthood that call for expanded linguistic skills include both entering the world of work and establishing intimate relations with others. Language development during the adult years varies greatly among individuals, depending on such things as level of education and social and occupational roles. Actors, for instance, must learn not only to be heard by large audiences but to speak the words of others using varying voices and regional dialects. Working people learn the special tones of voice and terminology associated with their own occupational register or code (Berko Gleason, 2005, p. 9).

The vocabulary of individuals often continues to increase throughout most of the adult years, at least until late adulthood (Burko Gleason, 2009). Many older adults "maintain or improve their knowledge of words and word meanings" (Burke & Shafto, 2004, p. 24).

In late adulthood, however, some decrements in language may appear. Among the most common language-related complaints reported by older adults is difficulty in retrieving words to use in conversation and in understanding spoken language in certain contexts (Clark-Cotton & others, 2007). These often involve the *tip-of-the-tongue phenomenon,* in which individuals are confident that they can remember something but just can't quite seem to retrieve it from memory, which we discussed in Chapter 7, "Information Processing" (Thornton & Light, 2006). Older adults also report that in less than ideal listening conditions they can have difficulty in understanding speech. This difficulty is most likely to occur when speech is rapid, when competing stimuli are present (a noisy room, for example), and when they can't see their conversation partner (in a telephone conversation, for example). The difficulty in understanding speech may be due to hearing loss (Gordon-Salant & others, 2006). In general, though, most language skills decline little among older adults if they are healthy (Clark-Cotton & others, 2007; Thornton & Light, 2006).

Some aspects of the phonological skills of older adults are different than those of younger adults (Clark-Cotton & others, 2007). Older adults' speech is typically lower in volume, slower, less precisely articulated, and less fluent (more pauses, fillers, repetition, and corrections). Despite these age differences, the speech skills of most older adults are adequate for everyday communication.

Researchers have found conflicting information about changes in *discourse* (extended verbal expression in speech or writing) with aging. "Some [researchers] have reported increased elaborateness, while others have reported less varied and less complex syntax" (Obler, 2009, p. 459). One aspect of discourse where age differences have been found involves retelling a story or giving instructions for completing a task. When engaging in this type of discourse, older adults are more likely than younger adults to omit key elements, creating discourse that is less fluent and more difficult to follow (Clark-Cotton & others, 2007).

Nonlanguage factors may be responsible for some of the decline in language skills that occur in older adults (Obler, 2009). Slower information-processing speed and a decline in working memory, especially in being able to keep information in mind while processing, likely contribute to lowered language efficiency in older adults (Stine-Morrow, Soderberg Miller, & Hertzog, 2006).

Language does change among individuals with Alzheimer disease (Goral, Clark-Cotton, & Albert, 2007; Obler, 2009). (Recall our discussion of Alzheimer disease in Chapter 4, "Health.") Word-finding difficulties are one of the earliest symptoms of Alzheimer disease, but most individuals with Alzheimer disease retain much of their

What are some differences in the language of younger and older adults?

metaphor An implied comparison between two unlike things.

satire The use of irony, derision, or wit to expose folly or wickedness.

dialect A variety of language that is distinguished by its vocabulary, grammar, or pronunciation.

ability to produce well-formed sentences until the late stages of the disease. Nonetheless, they do make more grammatical errors than older adults without Alzheimer disease.

Review and Reflect: Learning Goal 2

2 **Describe how language develops through the life span**

REVIEW

- What are some key milestones of language development during infancy?
- How do language skills change during early childhood?
- How does language develop in middle and late childhood?
- How does language develop in adolescence?
- How do language skills change during adulthood and aging?

REFLECT

- Should children in the United States be required to learn more than one language? Explain.

---

3 BIOLOGICAL AND ENVIRONMENTAL INFLUENCES

| Biological Influences | Environmental Influences | An Interactionist View of Language |

In the wild, chimps communicate through calls, gestures, and expressions, which evolutionary psychologists believe might be the roots of true language. *How strong is biology's role in language?*

Broca's area An area of the brain's left frontal lobe that is involved in producing words.

Wernicke's area An area of the brain's left hemisphere that is involved in language comprehension.

aphasia A loss or impairment of language processing resulting from damage to Broca's area or Wernicke's area.

We have described how language develops, but we have not explained what makes this amazing development possible. Everyone who uses language in some way "knows" its rules and has the ability to create an infinite number of words and sentences. Where does this knowledge come from? Is it the product of biology? Or is language learned and influenced by experiences?

Biological Influences

Some language scholars view the remarkable similarities in how children acquire language all over the world, despite the vast variation in language input they receive, as strong evidence that language has a biological basis. What role did evolution play in the biological foundations of language?

Evolution and the Brain's Role in Language The ability to speak and understand language requires a certain vocal apparatus as well as a nervous system with certain capabilities. The nervous system and vocal apparatus of humanity's predecessors changed over hundreds of thousands or millions of years. With advances in the nervous system and vocal structures, *Homo sapiens* went beyond the grunting and shrieking of other animals to develop speech. Although estimates vary, many experts hold that humans acquired language about 100,000 years ago, which in evolutionary time represents a very recent acquisition. It gave humans an enormous edge over other animals and increased the chances of human survival (Pinker, 1994).

Some language scholars view the remarkable similarities in how children acquire language all over the world as strong evidence that language has a biological basis. There is evidence that specific regions of the brain are predisposed to be used for language (Bortfeld, Fava, & Boas, 2009; Schwartz & Tropper, 2009). Two regions involved in language were first discovered in studies of brain-damaged individuals: **Broca's area,** an area in the left frontal lobe of the brain involved in producing words, and **Wernicke's area,** a region of the brain's left hemisphere involved in language comprehension (see Figure 9.7). Damage to either of these areas produces types of **aphasia,** which is a loss or impairment of language processing. Individuals with damage to Broca's area have difficulty producing words correctly; individuals with damage to Wernicke's area have poor comprehension and often produce fluent but incomprehensible speech.

Chomsky's Language Acquisition Device (LAD) Linguist Noam Chomsky (1957) proposed that humans are biologically prewired to learn language at a certain time and in a certain way. He said that children are born into the world with a **language acquisition device (LAD),** a biological endowment that enables the child to detect certain features and rules of language, including phonology, syntax, and semantics. Children are prepared by nature with the ability to detect the sounds of language, for example, and follow rules such as how to form plurals and ask questions.

Chomsky's LAD is a theoretical construct, not a physical part of the brain. Is there evidence for the existence of a LAD? Supporters of the LAD concept cite the uniformity of language milestones across languages and cultures, evidence that children create language even in the absence of well-formed input, and biological substrates of language. But, as we see, critics argue that even if infants have something like a LAD, it cannot explain the whole story of language acquisition.

Environmental Influences

Decades ago, behaviorists opposed Chomsky's hypothesis and argued that language represents nothing more than chains of responses acquired through reinforcement (Skinner, 1957). A baby happens to babble "Ma-ma"; Mama rewards the baby with hugs and smiles; the baby says "Mama" more and more. Bit by bit, said the behaviorists, the baby's language is built up. According to behaviorists, language is a complex learned skill, much like playing the piano or dancing.

There are several problems with the behavorial view of language learning. First, it does not explain how people create novel sentences—sentences that people have never heard or spoken before. Second, children learn the syntax of their native language even if they are not reinforced for doing so. Social psychologist Roger Brown (1973) spent long hours observing parents and their young children. He found that parents did not directly or explicitly reward or correct the syntax of most children's utterances. That is, parents did not say "good," "correct," "right," "wrong," and so on. Also, parents did not offer direct corrections such as "You should say two shoes, not two shoe." However, as we see shortly, many parents do expand on their young children's grammatically incorrect utterances and recast many of those that have grammatical errors (Bonvillian, 2005).

The behavioral view is no longer considered a viable explanation of how children acquire language. But a great deal of research describes ways in which children's environmental experiences influence their language skills (Berko Gleason & Ratner, 2009). Many language experts argue that a child's experiences, the specific language to be learned, and the context in which learning takes place can strongly influence language acquisition (Goldfield & Snow, 2009).

Language is not learned in a social vacuum. Most children are bathed in language from a very early age (Meltzoff & Brooks, 2009; Tomasello, 2009). The Wild Boy of Aveyron, who never learned to communicate effectively, had lived in social isolation for years. The support and involvement of caregivers and teachers greatly facilitate a child's language learning (Pan & Uccelli, 2009). One study found that when mothers immediately smiled and touched their 8-month-old infants after they babbled, the infants subsequently made more complex speechlike sounds than when mothers responded to their infants in a random manner (Goldstein, King, & West, 2003) (see Figure 9.8).

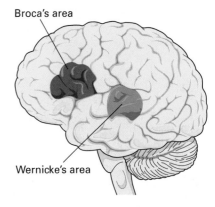

FIGURE 9.7 Broca's Area and Wernicke's Area. Broca's area is located in the frontal lobe of the brain's left hemisphere, and it is involved in the control of speech. Wernicke's area is a portion of the left hemisphere's temporal lobe that is involved in understanding language. *How does the role of these areas of the brain relate to lateralization, which was discussed in Chapter 3?*

FIGURE 9.8 Social Interaction and Babbling. One study focused on two groups of mothers and their 8-month-old infants (Goldstein, King, & West, 2003). One group of mothers was instructed to smile and touch their infants immediately after the babies cooed and babbled; the other group was also told to smile and touch their infants but in a random manner, unconnected to sounds the infants made. The infants whose mothers immediately responded in positive ways to their babbling subsequently made more complex, speechlike sounds, such as *da* and *gu*. The research setting for this study, which underscores how important caregivers are in the early development of language, is shown above.

language acquisition device (LAD) Chomsky's term that describes a biological endowment that enables the child to detect certain features and rules of language, including phonology, syntax, and semantics.

Michael Tomasello (2003, 2006, 2008, 2009; Tomasello & Carpenter, 2007) stresses that young children are intensely interested in their social world and that early in their development they can understand the intentions of other people. His *interaction view* of language emphasizes that children learn language in specific contexts. For example, when a toddler and a father are jointly focused on a book, the father might say, "See the birdie." In this case, even a toddler understands that the father intends to name something and knows to look in the direction of the pointing. Through this joint attention and shared intentions, early in their development children are able to use their social skills to acquire language (Meltzoff & Brooks, 2009; Tomasello, 2008, 2009). One recent study revealed that joint attention at 12 and 18 months predicted language skills at 24 months of age (Mundy & others, 2007).

One intriguing component of the young child's linguistic environment is **child-directed speech,** language spoken in a higher pitch than normal with simple words and sentences (Clark, 2009; Zangl & Mills, 2007). It is hard to use child-directed speech when not in the presence of a baby. As soon as you start talking to a baby, though, you shift into child-directed speech. Much of this is automatic and something most parents are not aware they are doing. Even 4-year-olds speak in simpler ways to 2-year-olds than to their 4-year-old friends. Child-directed speech has the important function of capturing the infant's attention and maintaining communication.

Adults often use strategies other than child-directed speech to enhance the child's acquisition of language, including recasting, expanding, and labeling:

- **Recasting** is rephrasing something the child has said, perhaps turning it into a question or restating the child's immature utterance in the form of a fully grammatical sentence. For example, if the child says, "The dog was barking," the adult can respond by asking, "When was the dog barking?" Effective recasting lets the child indicate an interest and then elaborates on that interest.
- **Expanding** is restating, in a linguistically sophisticated form, what a child has said. For example, a child says, "Doggie eat," and the parent replies, "Yes, the doggie is eating."
- **Labeling** is identifying the names of objects. Young children are forever being asked to identify the names of objects. Roger Brown (1958) called this "the original word game" and claimed that much of a child's early vocabulary is motivated by this adult pressure to identify the words associated with objects.

Parents use these strategies naturally and in meaningful conversations. Parents do not (and should not) use any deliberate method to teach their children to talk, even for children who are slow in learning language. Children usually benefit when parents guide their children's discovery of language rather than overloading them with language; "following in order to lead" helps a child learn language. If children are not ready to take in some information, they are likely to tell you (perhaps by turning away). Thus, giving the child more information is not always better.

Infants, toddlers, and young children benefit when adults read books to and with them (shared reading) (DeLoache & Ganea, 2009; Rodriguez, Hines, & Montiel, 2008; Westerlund & Lagerberg, 2008). In one study, a majority of U.S. mothers in low-income families reported that they were reading to their infants and toddlers with some regularity (Raikes & others, 2006). In this study, non-Latino White, more highly educated mothers who were parenting a firstborn child were more likely to read books to their infants and toddlers than were African American and Latino mothers who were parenting later-born children. Reading daily to children at 14 to 24 months of age was positively related to the children's language and cognitive development at 36 months of age.

Remember, the encouragement of language development, not drill and practice, is the key. Language development is not a simple matter of imitation and reinforcement. To read further about ways that parents can facilitate children's language development, see the *Applications in Life-Span Development* interlude.

*T*he linguistics problems children have to solve are always embedded in personal and interpersonal contexts.

—LOIS BLOOM
Contemporary Psychologist, Columbia University

child-directed speech Language spoken in a higher pitch than normal with simple words and sentences.

recasting Rephrasing a statement that a child has said, perhaps turning it into a question, or restating a child's immature utterance in the form of a fully grammatical sentence.

expanding Restating, in a linguistically sophisticated form, what a child has said.

labeling Identifying the names of objects.

Applications in Life-Span Development

HOW PARENTS CAN FACILITATE INFANTS' AND TODDLERS' LANGUAGE DEVELOPMENT

In *Growing Up with Language,* linguist Naomi Baron (1992) provided ideas to help parents facilitate their child's language development. A summary of her ideas follows:

Infants

- *Be an active conversational partner.* Initiate conversation with the infant. If the infant is in a day-long child-care program, ensure that the baby receives adequate language stimulation from adults.

- *Talk as if the infant understands what you are saying.* Parents can generate self-fulfilling prophecies by addressing their young children as if they understand what is being said. The process may take four to five years, but children gradually rise to match the language model presented to them.

- *Use a language style with which you feel comfortable.* Don't worry about how you sound to other adults when you talk with your child. Your affect, not your content, is more important when talking with an infant. Use whatever type of baby talk with which you feel comfortable.

Toddlers

- *Continue to be an active conversational partner.* Engaging toddlers in conversation, even one-sided conversation, is the most important thing a parent can do to nourish a child linguistically.

- *Remember to listen.* Since toddlers' speech is often slow and laborious, parents are often tempted to supply words and thoughts for them. Be patient and let toddlers express themselves, no matter how painstaking the process is or how great a hurry you are in.

- *Use a language style with which you are comfortable, but consider ways of expanding your child's language abilities and horizons.* For example, using long sentences need not be problematic. Use rhymes. Ask questions that encourage answers other than yes and no. Actively repeat, expand, and recast the child's utterances. Introduce new topics. And use humor in your conversation.

- *Adjust to your child's idiosyncrasies instead of working against them.* Many toddlers have difficulty pronouncing words and making themselves understood. Whenever possible, make toddlers feel that they are being understood.

- *Avoid sexual stereotypes.* Don't let the toddler's sex determine your amount or style of conversation. Many American mothers are more linguistically supportive of girls than of boys, and many fathers talk less with their children than mothers do. Cognitively enriching initiatives from both mothers and fathers benefit both boys and girls.

- *Resist making normative comparisons.* Be aware of the ages at which your child reaches specific milestones (such as the first word, first 50 words), but do not measure this development rigidly against that of other children. Such social comparisons can bring about unnecessary anxiety.

It is a good idea for parents to begin talking to their babies at the start. The best language teaching occurs when the talking is begun before the infant becomes capable of intelligible speech. *What are some other guidelines for parents to follow in helping their infants and toddlers develop their language?*

Our discussion of environmental influences on language development has focused mainly on parents. However, children interact with many other people who can influence their language development, including teachers and peers. A recent study of more than 1,800 4-year-olds focused on ways in which peers might influence children's language development (Masburn & others, 2009). In this study, peers' expressive language abilities were positive linked with young children's receptive and expressive language development.

An Interactionist View of Language

If language acquisition depended only on biology, then Genie and the Wild Boy of Aveyron (discussed at the beginning of the chapter) should have talked without difficulty. A child's experiences influence language acquisition. But we have seen that language does have strong biological foundations. No matter how much you converse with a dog, it won't learn to talk. In contrast, children are biologically prepared to learn language. Children all over the world acquire language milestones at about the same time and in about the same order. However, there are cultural variations in the type of support given to children's language development. For example, caregivers in the Kaluli culture prompt young children to use a loud voice and particular morphemes that direct the speech act performed (calling out) and to refer to names, kinship relations, and places where there has been a shared past experience that indicates a closeness to the person being addressed (Ochs & Schieffelin, 2008; Schieffelin, 2005).

An interactionist view emphasizes that both biology and experience contribute to language development (Bohannon & Bonvillian, 2009). This interaction of biology and experience can be seen in the variations in the acquisition of language. Children vary in their ability to acquire language, and this variation cannot be readily explained by differences in environmental input alone. For children who are slow in developing language skills, however, opportunities to talk and be talked with are important. Children whose parents provide them with a rich verbal environment show many positive benefits. Parents who pay attention to what their children are trying to say, expand their children's utterances, read to them, and label things in the environment, are providing valuable, if unintentional, benefits (Berko Gleason, 2009).

American psychologist Jerome Bruner (1983, 1996) proposed that the sociocultural context is extremely important in understanding children's language development. His view has some similarities with the ideas of Lev Vygotsky, which were briefly described in Chapter 1, "Introduction," and were presented in detail in Chapter 6, "Cognitive Developmental Approaches." Bruner stresses the role of parents and teachers in constructing what he called a *language acquisition support system (LASS)*.

Today, most language acquisition researchers note that children from a wide variety of cultural contexts acquire their native language without explicit teaching. In some cases, they do so even without encouragement. Thus, very few aids are necessary for learning language (Shafer & Garrido-Nag, 2010). However, caregivers greatly facilitate a child's language learning (Berko Gleason, 2009; Goldfield & Snow, 2009).

Review and Reflect: Learning Goal 3

3 Discuss the biological and environmental contributions to language skills

REVIEW

- What are the biological foundations of language?
- What are the environmental aspects of language?
- How does an interactionist view describe language?

REFLECT

- How should parents respond to children's grammatical mistakes in conversation? Should parents allow the mistakes to continue and assume their young children will grow out of them, or should they closely monitor their children's grammar and correct mistakes whenever they hear them?

Reach Your Learning Goals

Language Development

1   WHAT IS LANGUAGE? DEFINE LANGUAGE, AND DESCRIBE ITS RULE SYSTEMS

Defining Language

Language's Rule Systems

- Language is a form of communication, whether, spoken, written, or signed, that is based on a system of symbols. Language consists of all the words used by a community and the rules for varying and combining them. Infinite generativity is the ability to produce an endless number of meaningful sentences using a finite set of words and rules.

- The main rule systems of language are phonology, morphology, syntax, semantics, and pragmatics. Phonology is the sound system of a language, including the sounds used and the sound sequences that may occur in the language. Morphology refers to units of meaning in word formation. Syntax is the way words are combined to form acceptable phrases and sentences. Semantics involves the meaning of words and sentences. Pragmatics is the appropriate use of language in different contexts.

2   HOW LANGUAGE DEVELOPS: DESCRIBE HOW LANGUAGE DEVELOPS THROUGH THE LIFE SPAN

Infancy

Early Childhood

Middle and Late Childhood

Adolescence

Adulthood and Aging

- Among the milestones in infant language development are crying (birth), cooing (2 to 4 months), understanding first word (5 months), babbling (6 months), making the transition from universal linguist to language-specific listener (6 to 12 months), using gestures (8 to 12 months), detecting word boundaries (8 months), first word spoken (13 months), vocabulary spurt (18 months), rapid expansion of understanding words (18 to 24 months), and two-word utterances (18 to 24 months).

- Advances in phonology, morphology, syntax, semantics, and pragmatics continue in early childhood. The transition to complex sentences begins between 2 and 3 years and continues through the elementary school years. Fast mapping provides one explanation for how rapidly young children's vocabulary develops.

- In middle and late childhood, children become more analytical and logical in their approach to words and grammar. Current debate involving how to teach children to read focuses on the whole-language approach versus the phonics approach. Researchers have found strong evidence that the phonics approach should be used in teaching children to read but that children also benefit from the whole-language approach. Children's writing emerges out of scribbling. Advances in children's language and cognitive development provide the underpinnings for improved writing. Recent research indicates a complex conclusion about whether there are sensitive periods in learning a second language. Bilingual education aims to teach academic subjects to immigrant children in their native languages while gradually adding English instruction. Researchers have found that bilingualism does not interfere with performance in either language.

- In adolescence, language changes include more effective use of words; improvements in the ability to understand metaphor, satire, and complex literary works; and improvements in writing.

- For many individuals, knowledge of words and word meanings continues unchanged or may even improve through late adulthood. However, some decline in language skills may occur in retrieving words for use in conversation, in understanding speech, in phonological skills, and in some aspects of discourse. These changes in language skills in older adults likely occur as a consequence of declines in working memory or in speed of processing information, or as a result of disease.

3 BIOLOGICAL AND ENVIRONMENTAL INFLUENCES: DISCUSS THE BIOLOGICAL AND ENVIRONMENTAL CONTRIBUTIONS TO LANGUAGE SKILLS

Biological Influences

- In evolution, language clearly gave humans an enormous edge over other animals and increased their chance of survival. A substantial portion of language processing occurs in the brain's left hemisphere, with Broca's area and Wernicke's area being important left-hemisphere locations. Chomsky argues that children are born with the ability to detect basic features and rules of language. In other words, they are biologically prepared to learn language with a prewired language acquisition device (LAD).

Environmental Influences

- The behavioral view—that children acquire language as a result of reinforcement—has not been supported. Adults help children acquire language through child-directed speech, recasting, expanding, and labeling. Environmental influences are demonstrated by differences in the language development of children as a consequence of being exposed to different language environments in the home. Parents should talk extensively with an infant, especially about what the baby is attending to.

An Interactionist View of Language

- An interactionist view emphasizes the contributions of both biology and experience in language. Bruner proposed that sociocultural context is important in understanding language development in children; he stresses parents' and teachers' roles in constructing a language acquisition support system (LASS).

KEY TERMS

language 316
infinite generativity 316
phonology 316
morphology 317
syntax 317
semantics 317
pragmatics 317

telegraphic speech 321
fast mapping 323
metalinguistic
  awareness 326
whole-language
  approach 326
phonics approach 326

metaphor 330
satire 330
dialect 330
Broca's area 333
Wernicke's area 333
aphasia 333

language acquisition device
  (LAD) 333
child-directed speech 334
recasting 334
expanding 334
labeling 334

KEY PEOPLE

Patricia Kuhl 319
Jean Berko 322

Betty Hart and Todd Risley 323
Janellen Huttenlocher 324

Noam Chomsky 333
Roger Brown 333

Naomi Baron 335
Jerome Bruner 336

E-LEARNING TOOLS

Connect to **www.mhhe.com/santrockldt5e** to research the answers and complete these exercises. In addition, you'll find a number of other resources and valuable study tools for Chapter 9, "Language Development," on this Web site.

Taking It to the Net

1. Todd is working in a child-care center after school. He notices that there is a wide range in the children's use of language, even within age groups. He wonders if there are guidelines that can indicate whether a child is delayed in language development.

2. Lily is about to enter school. Her parents would like her to speak a second language, so they are considering French immersion. They have concerns about her English-language development since immersion will require her to do all of her schoolwork in a second language. They are also wondering if Lily's school success will be affected by the fact that no one in their home can speak French.

3. Jared is concerned because his 7-year-old son, Damion, does not like to read. Damion's second-grade teacher says he is about average for his age, but she has to prod him to do his reading assignments at school. What can Jared do to help Damion become a better reader?

Self-Assessment

Reading and writing skills are two important aspects of language, not only in childhood but also in adulthood. To evaluate your reading and writing skills, complete this self-assignment:

* *Evaluating My Writing Skills*

Health and Well-Being, Parenting, and Education

Build your decision-making skills by trying your hand at the health and well-being, parenting, and education exercises.

Video Clips

The Online Learning Center includes the following videos for this chapter:

* *Babbling at 7.5 Months*
* *First Words at 18 Months*
* *Language Ability at Age 2*
* *Motherese with a 4-Month-Old*
* *Receptive Language*

FOUR

SOCIOEMOTIONAL PROCESSES AND DEVELOPMENT

*Generations will depend
on the ability of all
procreating individuals
to face their children.*

—ERIK ERIKSON
*Danish-Born American
Psychoanalyst, 20th Century*

As children develop, they need "the meeting eyes of love."

They split the universe into two halves: "me and not me." They

juggle the need to curb their will with becoming what they can

freely. Children and youth want to fly but discover that first they

have to learn to stand and walk and climb and dance.

Adolescents try on one face after another, searching for a face

of their own. As adults age, they seek satisfaction in their

emotional lives and search for the meaning of life. Section 4

contains four chapters: "Emotional Development" (Chapter 10),

"The Self, Identity, and Personality" (Chapter 11), "Gender and

Sexuality" (Chapter 12), and "Moral Development, Values, and

Religion" (Chapter 13).

10

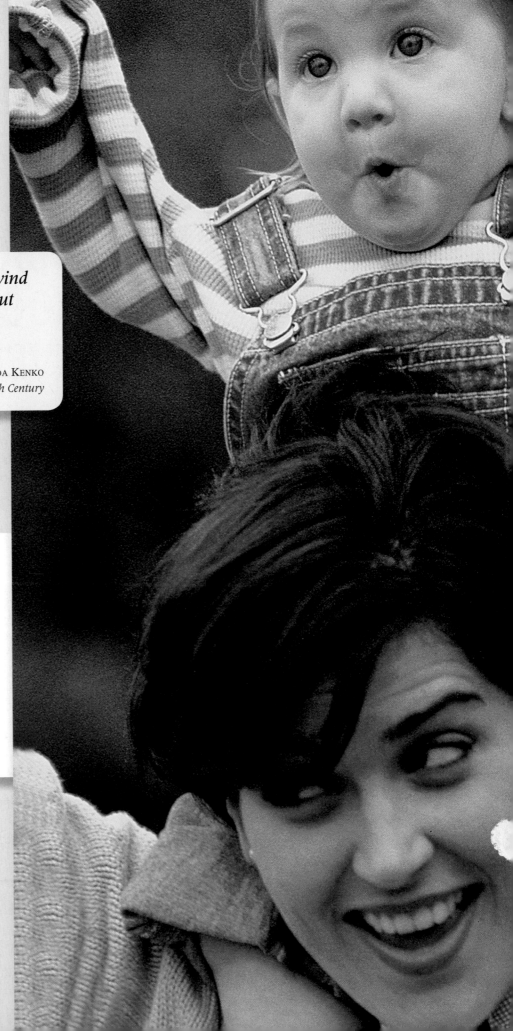

*Blossoms are scattered by the wind
And the wind cares nothing, but
The Blossoms of the heart,
No wind can touch.*

—YOUSHIDA KENKO
Buddhist Monk, 14th Century

LEARNING GOALS

- ◆ Discuss basic aspects of emotion.

- ◆ Describe the development of emotion through the life span.

- ◆ Characterize variations in temperament and their significance.

- ◆ Explain attachment and its development.

EMOTIONAL DEVELOPMENT

CHAPTER OUTLINE

PREVIEW

For many years, emotion was neglected in the study of life-span development. Today, emotion is increasingly important in conceptualizations of development. For example, even as infants, individuals show different emotional styles, display varying temperaments, and begin to form emotional bonds with their caregivers. In this chapter, we study how temperament and attachment change across the human life span. But first, we examine emotion itself, exploring the functions of emotions in people's lives and the development of emotion from infancy through late adulthood.

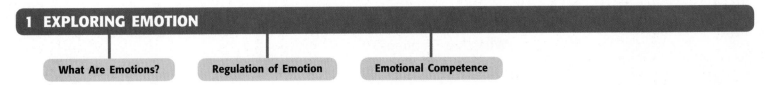

1 EXPLORING EMOTION

What Are Emotions?	Regulation of Emotion	Emotional Competence

Imagine your life without emotion. Emotion is the color and music of life, as well as the tie that binds people together. How do psychologists define and classify emotions, and why are they important to development?

What Are Emotions?

Defining *emotion* is difficult because it is not easy to tell when a child or an adult is in an emotional state. Facial expressions can be misleading, individuals' self-reports of their emotions can be unreliable, and physiological markers (such as increased respiration rate) aren't necessarily linked to specific emotional states. For our purposes, we will adopt Joseph Campos' (2005) definition of **emotion** as feeling, or affect, that occurs when a person is engaged in an interaction that is important to him or her, especially to his or her well-being. Emotion is characterized by behavior that reflects (expresses) the pleasantness or unpleasantness of the state that individuals are in, or the transactions they are experiencing. Emotions also can be more specific and take the form of joy, fear, anger, and so on, depending on how a transaction affects the person—for example, is the transaction a threat, a frustration, a relief, something to be rejected, something unexpected, and so on? And emotions can vary in how intense they are—for example, an infant may show intense fear or only mild fear in a specific situation.

When we think about emotions, a few dramatic feelings such as rage or glorious joy spring to mind. But emotions can be subtle as well, such as uneasiness in a new situation or the feeling of joy a mother has when she holds her baby. Psychologists classify the broad range of emotions in many ways, but almost all classifications designate an emotion as either positive or negative. Positive emotions include enthusiasm, joy, and love. Negative emotions include anxiety, anger, guilt, and sadness.

Emotions are influenced both by biological foundations and by a person's experience. Biology's importance to emotion also is apparent in the changes in a baby's emotional capacities (Bell & Wolfe, 2007). Certain regions of the brain that develop early in life (such as the brain stem, hippocampus, and amygdala) play a role in distress, excitement, and rage, and even infants display these emotions (Goldsmith, 2010; Kagan, 2010). But, as we discuss later in the chapter, infants only gradually develop the ability to regulate their emotions, and this ability seems tied to the gradual maturation of frontal regions of the cerebral cortex (see Chapter 5, "Motor, Sensory, and Perceptual Development") that can exert control over other areas of the brain (Thompson, Meyer, & Jochem, 2008).

emotion Feeling, or affect, that occurs when a person is engaged in an interaction that is important to him or her, especially to his or her well-being.

These biological factors, however, are only part of the story of emotion. Emotions serve important functions in our relationships (Thompson, 2009a, b). As we discuss later in this section, emotions are the first language with which parents and infants communicate. Emotion-linked interchanges, as when a baby cries and a parent sensitively responds, provide the foundation for the infant's developing attachment to the parent.

Social relationships, in turn, provide the setting for the development of a rich variety of emotions (Bridgett & others, 2009; Warren & Stifter, 2008). When toddlers hear their parents quarreling, they often react with distress and inhibit their play. Well-functioning families make each other laugh and may develop a light mood to defuse conflicts. Biological evolution has endowed human beings to be *emotional*, but embeddedness in relationships and culture with others provides diversity in emotional experiences (Novin & others, 2009; Thompson & Virmani, 2010). For example, researchers have found that East Asian infants display less frequent and less positive and negative emotions than non-Latino White infants (Cole & Tan, 2007). Throughout childhood, East Asian parents encourage their children to show emotional reserve rather than to be emotionally expressive (Cole & Tan, 2007). Further, Japanese parents try to prevent children from experiencing negative emotions, whereas non-Latino White mothers more frequently respond after their children become distressed and then help them cope (Rothbaum & Trommsdorff, 2007). In sum, biological evolution has endowed human beings to be emotional, but culture and relationships with others provide diversity in emotional experiences (Eisenberg, 2010; Thompson & Goodman, 2009).

How do Japanese mothers handle their infants' and children's emotional development differently than non-Latino White mothers?

Regulation of Emotion

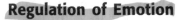

The ability to control one's emotions is a key dimension of development (Eisenberg, 2010; Kopp, 2008; Thompson, 2009a, b). Emotional regulation consists of effectively managing arousal to adapt and reach a goal. Arousal involves a state of alertness or activation, which can reach levels that are too high for effective functioning. Anger, for example, often requires regulation.

In infancy and early childhood, regulation of emotion gradually shifts from external sources to self-initiated, internal sources. Also, with increasing age, children are more likely to improve their use of cognitive strategies for regulating emotion, modulate their emotional arousal, become more adept at managing situations to minimize negative emotion, and choose effective ways to cope with stress.

Of course, there are wide variations in children's ability to modulate their emotions (Calkins, 2007). Indeed, a prominent feature of adolescents with problems is that they often have difficulty managing their emotions.

Parents can play an important role in helping young children regulate their emotions (Eisenberg, 2010; Thompson, Lewis, & Calkins, 2009). Depending on how they talk with their children about emotion, parents can be described as taking an *emotion-coaching* or an *emotion-dismissing* approach (Gottman, 2009). The distinction between these approaches is most evident in the way the parent deals with the child's negative emotions (anger, frustration, sadness, and so on). *Emotion-coaching parents* monitor their children's emotions, view their children's negative emotions as opportunities for teaching, assist them in labeling emotions, and coach them in how to deal effectively with emotions. In contrast, *emotion-dismissing parents* view their role as to deny, ignore, or change negative emotions. Researchers have observed that emotion-coaching parents interact with their children in a less rejecting manner, use more scaffolding and praise, and are more nurturant than are emotion-dismissing parents (Gottman & DeClaire, 1997). Moreover, the children of emotion-coaching parents were better at

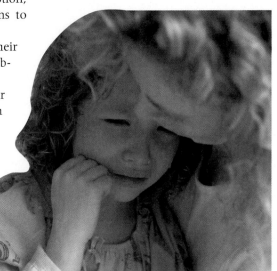

An emotion-coaching parent. *What are some differences in emotion-coaching and emotion-dismissing parents?*

soothing themselves when they got upset, were more effective in regulating their negative affect, focused their attention better, and had fewer behavior problems than the children of emotion-dismissing parents. A recent study revealed that having emotion-dismissing parents is linked with children's poor emotion regulation (Lunkenheimer, Shields, & Cortina, 2007).

A problem that parents face is that young children typically don't want to talk about difficult emotional topics, such as being distressed or engaging in negative behaviors. Among the strategies young children use to avoid these conversations is to not talk at all, change the topic, push away, or run away. In a recent study, Ross Thompson and his colleagues (2009) found that young children were more likely to openly discuss difficult emotional circumstances when they were securely attached to their mother and when their mother conversed with them in a way that validated and accepted the child's views. Thompson and his colleagues (Laible & Thompson, 2000; Ontai & Thompson, 2002) also have found that mothers talk about emotion in a more elaborative manner and are more advanced in their social understanding in a secure attachment relationship.

Emotional Competence

In Chapter 8, "Intelligence," we briefly considered the concept of emotional intelligence. Here we examine a closely related concept, *emotional competence*, which focuses on the adaptive nature of emotional experience. Carolyn Saarni (1999; Saarni & others, 2006) notes that becoming emotionally competent involves developing a number of skills in social contexts that include the following:

Skill	Example
• *Having awareness of one's emotional states*	Being able to differentiate whether one feels sad or anxious
• *Detecting others' emotions*	Understanding when another person is sad rather than afraid
• *Using the vocabulary of emotion terms in socially and culturally appropriate terms*	Appropriately describing a social situation in one culture's when a person is feeling distressed
• *Having empathic and sympathetic sensitivity to others' emotional experiences*	Being sensitive to other people when they are feeling distressed
• *Recognizing that inner emotional states do not have to correspond to outer expressions*	Recognizing that one can feel very angry yet manage one's emotional expression so that it appears more neutral
• *Adaptively coping with negative emotions by using self-regulatory strategies that reduce the intensity or duration of such emotional states*	Reducing anger by walking away from an aversive situation and engaging in an activity that takes one's mind off of the aversive situation
• *Having awareness that the expression of emotions plays a major role in relationships*	Knowing that expressing anger toward a friend on a regular basis is likely to harm the friendship
• *Viewing oneself overall as feeling the way one wants to feel*	Wanting to feel like one can cope effectively with the stress in one's life and feeling that one is successfully doing this

As children acquire these emotional competence skills in a variety of contexts, they are more likely to effectively manage their emotions, become resilient in the face of stressful circumstances, and develop more positive relationships (Denham, Bassett, & Wyatt, 2007).

Review and Reflect: Learning Goal 1

 Discuss basic aspects of emotion

REVIEW

- How is emotion defined?
- What are some developmental changes in the regulation of emotion?
- What constitutes emotional competence, according to Saarni?

REFLECT

- Think back to your childhood and adolescent years. How effective were you in regulating your emotion? Give some examples. Has your ability to regulate your emotions changed as you have grown older? Explain.

---

2 DEVELOPMENT OF EMOTION

| Infancy | Early Childhood | Middle and Late Childhood | Adolescence | Adult Development and Aging |

Does an adult's emotional life differ from an adolescent's? Does a young child's emotional life differ from an infant's? Does an infant even have an emotional life? In this section, we consider an overview of the changes in emotion over the life span, looking not only at changes in emotional experience but also at the development of emotional competence.

Infancy

What are some early developmental changes in emotions? What functions do infants' cries serve? When do infants begin to smile?

Early Emotions Leading expert on infant emotional development, Michael Lewis (2007, 2008) distinguishes between primary emotions and self-conscious emotions. **Primary emotions** are emotions that are present in humans and other animals; these emotions appear in the first six months of the human infant's development. Primary emotions include surprise, interest, joy, anger, sadness, fear, and disgust (see Figure 10.1 for infants' facial expressions of some of these early emotions). In Lewis' classification, **self-conscious emotions** require self-awareness that involves consciousness and a sense of "me." Self-conscious emotions include jealousy, empathy, embarrassment, pride, shame, and guilt—most of these occurring for the first time at some point in the second half of the first year through the second year.

Leading researchers such as Joseph Campos (2005) and Michael Lewis (2007, 2008) debate about how early in the infant and toddler years these emotions first appear and what their sequence is (Campos, 2005; Lewis, 2007). As an indication of the controversy regarding when certain emotions first are displayed by infants, consider jealousy. Some researchers argue that jealousy does not emerge until approximately 18 months of age (Lewis, 2007), whereas others emphasize that it is displayed much earlier (Draghi-Lorenz, 2007). Some research studies suggest that the appearance of jealousy might occur as early as 6 months of age (Hart & others, 2004). In one study, 6-month-old infants observed their mothers giving attention either to a lifelike baby doll (hugging or gently rocking it, for example) or to a book.

Joy   Sadness

Fear   Surprise

FIGURE 10.1 Expression of Different Emotions in Infants.

primary emotions Emotions that are present in humans and other animals, emerge early in life, and are culturally universal; examples are joy, anger, sadness, fear, and disgust.

self-conscious emotions Emotions that require consciousness and a sense of "me"; they include empathy, jealousy, embarrassment, pride, shame, and guilt, most of which first appear at some point in the second half of the first year through the second year.

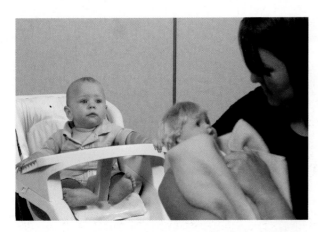

FIGURE 10.2 Research Setting for Sybil Hart's Attempt to Assess the Early Development of Jealousy. An infant becomes distressed when his mother gives attention to a life-like baby doll. *What are some possible interpretations of the infant's distress?*

When mothers directed their attention to the doll, the infants were more likely to display negative emotions, such as anger and sadness, which may have indicated their jealousy (Hart & Carrington, 2002) (see Figure 10.2). On the other hand, their expressions of anger and sadness may have reflected frustration in not being able to have the novel doll to play with.

Emotional Expression and Social Relationships Emotional expressions are involved in infants' first relationships. The ability of infants to communicate emotions permits coordinated interactions with their caregivers and the beginning of an emotional bond between them (Thomann & Carter, 2008; Thompson, 2009a, b). Not only do parents change their emotional expressions in response to infants' emotional expressions, but infants also modify their emotional expressions in response to their parents' emotional expressions. In other words, these interactions are mutually regulated (Bridgett & others, 2009). Because of this coordination, the interactions are described as *reciprocal,* or *synchronous,* when all is going well. Sensitive, responsive parents help their infants grow emotionally, whether the infants respond in distressed or in happy ways (Thompson & Newton, 2009).

Cries and smiles are two emotional expressions that infants display when interacting with parents. These are babies' first forms of emotional communication.

Crying Crying is the most important mechanism newborns have for communicating with their world. The first cry verifies that the baby's lungs have filled with air. Cries also may provide information about the health of the newborn's central nervous system. Newborns even tend to respond with cries and negative facial expressions when they hear other newborns cry (Dondi, Simion, & Caltran, 1999).

Babies have at least three types of cries:

What are some different types of cries?

- **Basic cry.** A rhythmic pattern that usually consists of a cry, followed by a briefer silence, then a shorter inspiratory whistle that is somewhat higher in pitch than the main cry, then another brief rest before the next cry. Some infancy experts stress that hunger is one of the conditions that incite the basic cry.
- **Anger cry.** A variation of the basic cry in which more excess air is forced through the vocal cords.
- **Pain cry.** A sudden long, initial loud cry followed by breath holding; no preliminary moaning is present. The pain cry is stimulated by a high-intensity stimulus.

Most adults can determine whether an infant's cries signify anger or pain (Zeskind, 2007). Parents can distinguish the cries of their own baby better than those of another baby.

Smiling Two types of smiling can be distinguished in infants:

- **Reflexive smile.** A smile that does not occur in response to external stimuli and appears during the first month after birth, usually during sleep.
- **Social smile.** A smile that occurs in response to an external stimulus, typically a face in the case of the young infant. Social smiling occurs as early as 4 to 6 weeks of age in response to a caregiver's voice (Messinger, 2008).

basic cry A rhythmic pattern usually consisting of a cry, a briefer silence, a shorter inspiratory whistle that is higher pitched than the main cry, and then a brief rest before the next cry.

anger cry A cry similar to the basic cry but with more excess air forced through the vocal cords.

pain cry A sudden, initial loud cry followed by breath holding, without preliminary moaning.

The infant's social smile can have a powerful impact on caregivers (Bates, 2008). Following weeks of endless demands, fatigue, and little reinforcement, an infant starts smiling at them and all of the caregivers' efforts are rewarded.

Daniel Messinger (2008) recently described the developmental course of infant smiling. From 2 to 6 months after birth, infants' social smiling increases considerably, both in self-initiated smiles and in smiles in response to others' smiles. At 6 to 12 months, smiles that couple what is called the Duchenne marker (eye constriction) and mouth opening occur in the midst of highly enjoyable interactions and play with parents (see Figure 10.3). In the second year, smiling continues to occur in such positive circumstances with parents, and in many cases an increase in smiling occurs when interacting with peers. Also in the second year, toddlers become increasingly aware of the social meaning of smiles, especially in their relationship with parents.

Infants also engage in *anticipatory smiling,* in which they communicate preexisting positive emotion by smiling at an object and then turning their smile toward an adult. A recent study revealed that anticipatory smiling at 9 months of age was linked to parents' rating of the child's social competence at 2½ years of age (Parlade & others, 2009).

Fear   One of a baby's earliest emotions is fear, which typically first appears at about 6 months of age and peaks at about 18 months. However, abused and neglected infants can show fear as early as 3 months (Campos, 2005). Researchers have found that infant fear is linked to guilt, empathy, and low aggression at 6 to 7 years of age (Rothbart, 2007).

The most frequent expression of an infant's fear involves **stranger anxiety,** in which an infant shows a fear and wariness of strangers. Stranger anxiety usually emerges gradually. It first appears at about 6 months of age in the form of wary reactions. By age 9 months, the fear of strangers is often more intense, reaching a peak toward the end of the first year of life (Scher & Harel, 2008).

Not all infants show distress when they encounter a stranger. Besides individual variations, whether an infant shows stranger anxiety also depends on the social context and the characteristics of the stranger (Kagan, 2008).

Infants show less stranger anxiety when they are in familiar settings. For example, in one study, 10-month-olds showed little stranger anxiety when they met a stranger in their own home but much greater fear when they encountered a stranger in a research laboratory (Sroufe, Waters, & Matas, 1974). Also, infants show less stranger anxiety when they are sitting on their mothers' laps than when placed in an infant seat several feet away from their mothers (Bohlin & Hagekull, 1993). Thus, it appears that, when infants feel secure, they are less likely to show stranger anxiety.

Who the stranger is and how the stranger behaves also influence stranger anxiety in infants. Infants are less fearful of child strangers than adult strangers. They also are less fearful of friendly, outgoing, smiling strangers than of passive, unsmiling strangers (Bretherton, Stolberg, & Kreye, 1981).

In addition to stranger anxiety, infants experience fear of being separated from their caregivers. The result is **separation protest**—crying when the caregiver leaves. Separation protest is initially displayed by infants at approximately 7 to 8 months and peaks at about 15 months (Kagan, 2008). One study revealed that separation protest peaked at about 13 to 15 months in four different cultures (Kagan, Kearsley, & Zelazo, 1978). As indicated in Figure 10.4, the percentage of infants who engaged in separation protest varied across cultures, but the infants reached a peak of protest at about the same age—just before the middle of the second year of life.

Emotional Regulation and Coping

Earlier, we discussed some general developmental changes in emotional regulation across the childhood years. Here we examine in detail how infants develop emotional regulation and coping skills.

*H*e who binds himself to joy.
Does the winged life destroy;
But he who kisses the joy as it flies;
Lives in eternity's sun rise.

—**WILLIAM BLAKE**
English Poet, 19th Century

FIGURE 10.3 A 6-Month-Old's Strong Smile. This strong smile reflects the Duchenne maker (eye constriction) and mouth opening.

reflexive smile A smile that does not occur in response to external stimuli. It happens during the month after birth, usually during sleep.

social smile A smile in response to an external stimulus, which, early in development, typically is a face.

stranger anxiety An infant's fear of and wariness toward strangers; it tends to appear in the second half of the first year of life.

separation protest Reaction that occurs when infants experience a fear of being separated from a caregiver, which results in crying when the caregiver leaves.

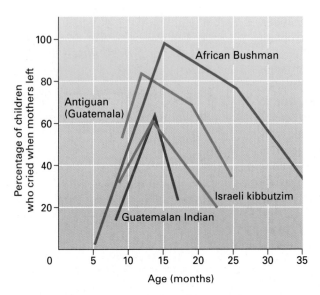

FIGURE 10.4 Separation Protest in Four Cultures.
Note that separation protest peaked at about the same time in all four cultures in this study (13 to 15 months of age) (Kagan, Kearsley, & Zelazo, 1978). However, a higher percentage (100 percent) of infants in an African Bushman culture engaged in separation protest compared with only about 60 percent of infants in Guatemalan Indian and Israeli kibbutzim cultures. *What might explain the fact that separation protest peaks at about the same time in these cultures?*

During the first year of life, the infant gradually develops an ability to inhibit, or minimize, the intensity and duration of emotional reactions (Kopp, 2008). From early in infancy, babies put their thumbs in their mouths to soothe themselves. But, at first, infants mainly depend on caregivers to help them soothe their emotions, as when a caregiver rocks an infant to sleep, sings lullabyes to the infant, gently strokes the infant, and so on.

Later in infancy, when they become aroused, infants sometimes redirect their attention or distract themselves in order to reduce their arousal. By 2 years of age, toddlers can use language to define their feeling states and the context that is upsetting them (Kopp, 2008). A toddler might say, "Feel bad. Dog scare." This type of communication may allow caregivers to help the child in regulating emotion.

Contexts can influence emotional regulation (Thompson, Meyer, & Jochem, 2008). Infants are often affected by fatigue, hunger, time of day, which people are around them, and where they are. Infants must learn to adapt to different contexts that require emotional regulation. Further, new demands appear as the infant becomes older and parents modify their expectations. For example, a parent may take it in stride if a 6-month-old infant screams in a grocery store but may react very differently if a 2-year-old starts screaming.

To soothe or not to soothe—should a crying baby be given attention and soothed, or does this attention spoil the infant? Many years ago, the behaviorist John Watson (1928) argued that parents spend too much time responding to infant crying. As a consequence, he said, parents reward crying and increase its incidence. Some researchers have found that a caregiver's quick, soothing response to crying increased crying (Gewirtz, 1977). However, infancy experts Mary Ainsworth (1979) and John Bowlby (1989) stress that you can't respond too much to infant crying in the first year of life. They argue that a quick, comforting response to the infant's cries is an important ingredient in the development of a strong bond between the infant and caregiver. In one of Ainsworth's studies, infants whose mothers responded quickly when they cried at 3 months of age cried less later in the first year of life (Bell & Ainsworth, 1972).

Controversy still characterizes the question of whether or how parents should respond to an infant's cries. Some developmentalists argue that an infant cannot be spoiled in the first year of life, a view suggesting that parents should soothe a crying infant. This reaction should help infants develop a sense of trust and secure attachment to the caregiver.

Early Childhood

The young child's growing awareness of self is linked to the ability to feel an expanding range of emotions. Young children, like adults, experience many emotions during the course of a day. At times, they also try to make sense of other people's emotional reactions and to control their own emotions.

Expressing Emotions Recall from our earlier discussion that even young infants experience emotions such as joy and fear, but to experience self-conscious emotions, children must be able to refer to themselves and be aware of themselves as distinct from others (Lewis, 2007, 2008). Pride, shame, embarrassment, and guilt are examples of self-conscious emotions. Self-conscious emotions do not appear to develop until self-awareness appears in the last half of the second year of life.

Should a baby be given attention and soothed, or does this spoil the infant? Should the infant's age, type of cry, and circumstances be considered?

During the early childhood years, emotions such as pride and guilt become more common. They are especially influenced by parents' responses to children's behavior. For example, a young child may experience shame when a parent says, "You should feel bad about biting your sister."

Understanding Emotions   Among the most important changes in emotional development in early childhood are an increased understanding of emotion. During early childhood, young children increasingly understand that certain situations are likely to evoke particular emotions, facial expressions indicate specific emotions, emotions affect behavior, and emotions can be used to influence others' emotions (Cole & others, 2009). Between 2 and 4 years of age, children considerably increase the number of terms they use to describe emotions (Ridgeway, Waters, & Kuczaj, 1985). They also are learning about the causes and consequences of feelings (Denham, Bassett, & Wyatt, 2007).

When they are 4 to 5 years of age, children show an increased ability to reflect on emotions. They also begin to understand that the same event can elicit different feelings in different people. Moreover, they show a growing awareness that they need to manage their emotions to meet social standards (Bruce, Olen, & Jensen, 1999). And by 5 years of age, most children can accurately determine emotions that are produced by challenging circumstances and describe strategies they might call on to cope with everyday stress (Cole & others, 2009).

A young child expressing the emotion of shame. *Why is shame called a "self-conscious emotion"?*

Middle and Late Childhood

During middle and late childhood, many children show marked improvement in understanding and managing their emotions. However, in some instances, as when they experience stressful circumstances, their coping abilities can be challenged.

Developmental Changes in Emotion   Here are some important developmental changes in emotions during these years (Kuebli, 1994; Thompson & Goodvin, 2007; Wintre & Vallance, 1994):

- *Improved emotional understanding.* Children in elementary school develop an increased ability to understand such complex emotions as pride and shame. These emotions become less tied to the reactions of other people; they become more self-generated and integrated with a sense of personal responsibility. A child may feel a sense of pride about developing new reading skills or shame after hurting a friend's feelings.

- *Marked improvements in the ability to suppress or conceal negative emotional reactions.* Children now sometimes intentionally hide their emotions. Although a boy may feel sad that a friend does not want to play with him, he may decide not to share those feelings with his parents.

- *The use of self-initiated strategies for redirecting feelings.* In the elementary school years, children reflect more about emotional experiences and develop strategies to cope with their emotional lives. Children can more effectively manage their emotions by cognitive means, such as using distracting thoughts. A boy may be excited about his birthday party later in the afternoon, but still be able to concentrate on his schoolwork during the day.

- *An increased tendency to take into fuller account the events leading to emotional reactions.* A fourth-grader may become aware that her sadness today is influenced by her friend's moving to another town last week.

- *Development of a capacity for genuine empathy.* Two girls see another child in distress on the playground and run to the child and ask if they can help.

Coping with Stress   An important aspect of children's lives is learning how to cope with stress (Coplan & Arbeau, 2008). As children get older, they are able to

What are some effective strategies to help children cope with traumatic events, such as Hurricane Katrina in August 2005?

more accurately appraise a stressful situation and determine how much control they have over it. Older children generate more coping alternatives to stressful conditions and use more cognitive coping strategies (Saarni & others, 2006). For example, older children are better than younger children at intentionally shifting their thoughts to something that is less stressful. Older children are also better at reframing, or changing one's perception of a stressful situation. For example, younger children may be very disappointed that their teacher did not say hello to them when they arrived at school. Older children may reframe this type of situation and think, "She may have been busy with other things and just forgot to say hello."

By 10 years of age, most children are able to use these cognitive strategies to cope with stress (Saarni & others, 2006). However, in families that have not been supportive and are characterized by turmoil or trauma, children may be so overwhelmed by stress that they do not use such strategies (Thabet & others, 2009).

Disasters can especially harm children's development and produce adjustment problems. Among the outcomes for children who experience disasters are acute stress reactions, depression, panic disorder, and post-traumatic stress disorder (Kar, 2009). Proportions of children developing these problems following a disaster depend on such factors as the nature and severity of the disaster, as well as the support available to the children.

The terrorist attacks on the World Trade Center in New York City and the Pentagon in Washington, D.C., on September 11, 2001, and Hurricanes Katrina and Rita in August and September 2005, raised special concerns about how to help children cope with such stressful events. Children who have a number of coping techniques have the best chance of adapting and functioning competently in the face of traumatic events. Here are some recommendations for helping children cope with the stress of especially devastating events (Gurwitch & others, 2001, pp. 4–11):

- *Reassure children of their safety and security.* This step may need to be taken numerous times.
- *Allow children to retell events and be patient in listening to them.*
- *Encourage children to talk about any disturbing or confusing feelings.* Tell them that these are normal feelings after a stressful event.
- *Help children make sense of what happened.* Children may misunderstand what took place. For example, young children "may blame themselves, believe things happened that did not happen, believe that terrorists are in the school, etc. Gently help children develop a realistic understanding of the event" (p. 10).
- *Protect children from reexposure to frightening situations and reminders of the trauma.* This strategy includes limiting conversations about the event in front of the children.

Adolescence

Adolescence has long been described as a time of emotional turmoil (Hall, 1904). Adolescents are not constantly in a state of "storm and stress," but emotional highs and lows do increase during early adolescence (Rosenblum & Lewis, 2003). Young adolescents can be on top of the world one moment and down in the dumps the next. In some instances, the intensity of their emotions seems out of proportion to the events that elicit them (Steinberg, 2009). Young adolescents might sulk a lot, not knowing how to adequately express their feelings. With little or no provocation, they can blow up at their parents or siblings, a response that might reflect the defense mechanism of displacing their feelings onto another person. For some adolescents, such emotional swings can reflect serious problems. Girls are especially vulnerable to depression in adolescence (Nolen-Hoeksema, 2007). But it is important for adults to recognize that moodiness is a normal aspect of early adolescence, and most adolescents make it through these moody times to become competent adults.

Reed Larson and Maryse Richards (1994) found that adolescents reported more extreme emotions and more fleeting emotions than their parents did. For example, adolescents were five times more likely to report being "very happy" and three times more likely to report being "very unhappy" than their parents (see Figure 10.5). These findings lend support to the perception of adolescents as moody and changeable (Rosenblum & Lewis, 2003).

Researchers have also found that from the fifth through the ninth grades, both boys and girls experience a 50 percent decrease in being "very happy" (Larson & Lampman-Petraitis, 1989). In this same study, adolescents were more likely than preadolescents to report mildly negative mood states.

Researchers have discovered that pubertal change is associated with an increase in negative emotions (Archibald, Graber, & Brooks-Gunn, 2003). However, most researchers conclude that hormonal influences are small and that when they occur they usually are associated with other factors, such as stress, eating patterns, sexual activity, and social relationships (Rosenbaum & Lewis, 2003; Susman & Dorn, 2009).

Adolescents' emotional regulation and mood may play a pivotal role in their academic success. One study revealed that sixth- to eighth-grade students who reported more negative affect during regular academic routines had lower grade-point averages than their counterparts who experienced more positive affect during these routines, even when cognitive ability was controlled (Gumora & Arsenio, 2002).

Adult Development and Aging

Like children, adults adapt more effectively when they are emotionally intelligent—when they are skilled at perceiving and expressing emotion, understanding emotion, using feelings to facilitate thought, and managing emotions effectively. (In Chapter 14, "Families, Lifestyles, and Parenting," we examine a number of aspects of relationships that involve emotions.)

Developmental changes in emotion continue through the adult years (Carstensen & Charles, 2010; Kensinger, 2009). The changes often are characterized by an effort to create lifestyles that are emotionally satisfying, predictable, and manageable by making decisions about an occupation, a life partner, and other circumstances. Of course, not all individuals are successful in these efforts. A key theme of "emotional development in adulthood is the adaptive integration of emotional experience into satisfying daily life and successful relationships with others" (Thompson & Goodvin, 2007, p. 402).

As adults become older, is their emotional life different from when they were younger? Researchers have found that across diverse samples—Norwegians, Catholic nuns, African Americans, Chinese Americans, and European Americans—older adults report better control of their emotions and fewer negative emotions than do younger adults (Carstensen, Mikels, & Mather, 2006).

Stereotypes suggest that older adults' emotional landscape is bleak and that most live sad, lonely lives. Researchers have found a different picture (Carstensen & Charles, 2010; Charles & Carstensen, 2009). One study of a very large U.S. sample examined emotions at different ages (Mroczek & Kolarz, 1998). Older adults reported experiencing more positive emotion and less negative emotion than younger adults, and positive emotion increased with age in adults at an accelerating rate (see Figure 10.6).

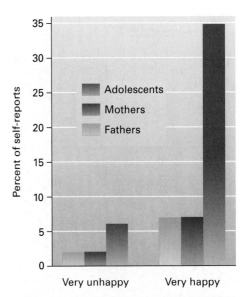

FIGURE 10.5 Self-Reported Extremes of Emotion by Adolescents, Mothers, and Fathers Using the Experience Sampling Method. In the study by Reed Larson and Maryse Richards (1994), adolescents and their mothers and fathers were beeped at random times by researchers using the experience sampling method. The researchers found that adolescents reported more emotional extremes than their parents.

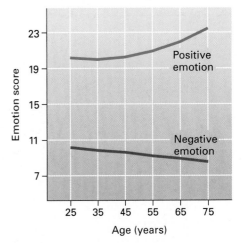

FIGURE 10.6 Changes in Positive and Negative Emotion Across the Adult Years. Positive and negative scores had a possible range of 6 to 30 with higher scores reflecting positive emotion and lower scores negative emotion. Positive emotion increased in the middle adulthood and late adulthood years, while negative emotion declined.

Laura Carstensen (*right*), in a caring relationship with an older woman. Her theory of socioemotional selectivity is gaining recognition as an important theory.

*R*ecent research paints a distinctly positive picture of aging in the emotion domain.

—LAURA CARSTENSEN

Contemporary Psychologist, Stanford University

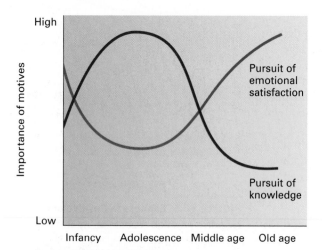

FIGURE 10.7 Idealized Model of Socioemotional Selectivity Through the Life Span. In Carstensen's theory of socioemotional selectivity, the motivation to reach knowledge-related and emotion-related goals changes across the life span.

A recent study also revealed that older adults described their own emotions and the emotions of others more positively than younger adults did (Lockenhoff, Costa, & Lane, 2008). And other recent studies have found that older adults are more inclined to engage in passive emotion self-regulation strategies (distracting oneself from the problem and suppressing feelings, for example) and less inclined to express anger in dealing with interpersonal problems than younger adults are (Blanchard-Fields & Coats, 2007; Coats & Blanchard-Fields, 2008).

Overall, compared with younger adults, the feelings of older adults mellow. Emotional life is on a more even keel, with fewer highs and lows. It may be that although older adults have less extreme joy, they have more contentment, especially when they are connected in positive ways with friends and family. In sum, researchers have found that the emotional life of older adults is more positive than stereotypes suggest (Charles & Carstensen, 2010; Ram & others, 2009).

One theory developed by Laura Carstensen (1991, 1998, 2006, 2008) stands out as important in thinking about developmental changes in adulthood, especially in older adults. **Socioemotional selectivity theory** states that older adults become more selective about their social networks. Because they place a high value on emotional satisfaction, older adults often spend more time with familiar individuals with whom they have had rewarding relationships. This theory argues that older adults deliberately withdraw from social contact with individuals peripheral to their lives while they maintain or increase contact with close friends and family members with whom they have had enjoyable relationships. This selective narrowing of social interaction maximizes positive emotional experiences and minimizes emotional risks as individuals become older. According to this theory, older adults systematically hone their social networks so that available social partners satisfy their emotional needs.

Is there research to support life-span differences in the composition of social networks? Researchers have found that older adults have smaller social networks than for younger adults (Charles & Carstensen, 2010). In one study of individuals 69 to 104 years of age, the oldest participants had fewer peripheral social contacts than the relatively younger participants but about the same number of close emotional relationships (Lang & Carstensen, 1994). And a recent study revealed that compared with younger adults, older adults reported more intense positive emotions with family members, less intense positive emotions with new friends, and equally intense positive emotions with established friends (Charles & Piazza, 2007). Another recent study found that older adults socialize more frequently with their neighbors than middle-aged adults do (Cornwell, Laumann, & Schumm, 2008).

Socioemotional selectivity theory also focuses on the types of goals that individuals are motivated to achieve (Carstensen, 2008; Charles & Carstensen, 2010). According to the theory, motivation for knowledge-related goals starts relatively high in the early years of life, peaks in adolescence and early adulthood, then declines in middle and late adulthood (see Figure 10.7). The trajectory for emotion-related goals is high during infancy and early childhood, declines from middle childhood through early adulthood, and increases in middle and late adulthood.

One of the main reasons given for these changing trajectories in knowledge-related and emotion-related goals involves the perception of time (Charles & Carstensen, 2010). When time is perceived as open-ended, as it is when individuals are younger, people are strongly motivated to pursue information, even at the cost of emotional satisfaction. But as older adults perceive that they have less time left in their lives, they are motivated to spend more time pursuing emotional satisfaction.

Review and Reflect: Learning Goal 2

2 Describe the development of emotion through the life span

REVIEW

- How does emotion develop in infancy?
- What characterizes emotional development in early childhood?
- What changes take place in emotion during middle and late childhood?
- How does emotion change in adolescence?
- What are some key aspects of emotional development in adulthood?

REFLECT

- A mother and father of an 8-month-old baby are having difficulty getting any sleep because the baby wakes up crying in the middle of the night. How would you recommend that they deal with this situation?

3 TEMPERAMENT

| Describing and Classifying Temperament | Biological Foundations and Experience | Goodness of Fit and Parenting |

Do you get upset a lot? Does it take much to get you angry, or to make you laugh? Even at birth, babies seem to have different emotional styles. One infant is cheerful and happy much of the time; another baby seems to cry constantly. These tendencies reflect **temperament,** which is an individual's behavioral style and characteristic way of responding.

Describing and Classifying Temperament

How would you describe your temperament or the temperament of a friend? Researchers have described and classified the temperament of individuals in different ways. Here we examine three of those ways.

Chess and Thomas' Classification Psychiatrists Alexander Chess and Stella Thomas (Chess & Thomas, 1977; Thomas & Chess, 1991) identified three basic types, or clusters, of temperament:

- An **easy child** is generally in a positive mood, quickly establishes regular routines in infancy, and adapts easily to new experiences.
- A **difficult child** reacts negatively and cries frequently, engages in irregular daily routines, and is slow to accept change.
- A **slow-to-warm-up child** has a low activity level, is somewhat negative, and displays a low intensity of mood.

In their longitudinal investigation, Chess and Thomas found that 40 percent of the children they studied could be classified as easy, 10 percent as difficult, and 15 percent as slow to warm up. Notice that 35 percent did not fit any of the three patterns. Researchers have found that these three basic clusters of temperament are moderately stable across the childhood years. A recent study revealed that young

socioemotional selectivity theory The theory that older adults become more selective about their social networks. Because they place high value on emotional satisfaction, older adults often spend more time with familiar individuals with whom they have had rewarding relationships.

temperament An individual's behavioral style and characteristic way of responding.

easy child A temperament style in which the child is generally in a positive mood, quickly establishes regular routines, and adapts easily to new experiences.

difficult child A temperament style in which the child tends to react negatively and cry frequently, engages in irregular daily routines, and is slow to accept change.

slow-to-warm-up child A temperament style in which the child has a low activity level, is somewhat negative, and displays a low intensity of mood.

"Oh, he's cute, all right, but he's got the temperament of a car alarm."

children with a difficult temperament showed more problems when they experienced low-quality child care and fewer problems when they experienced high-quality child care than young children with an easy temperament (Pluess & Belsky, 2009).

Kagan's Behavioral Inhibition Another way of classifying temperament focuses on the differences between a shy, subdued, timid child and a sociable, extraverted, bold child (Asendorph, 2008). Jerome Kagan (2002, 2008, 2010) regards shyness with strangers (peers or adults) as one feature of a broad temperament category called *inhibition to the unfamiliar*. Beginning about 7 to 9 months, inhibited children react to many aspects of unfamiliarity with initial avoidance, distress, or subdued affect.

Kagan has found that inhibition shows considerable stability from infancy through early childhood. One study classified toddlers into extremely inhibited, extremely uninhibited, and intermediate groups (Pfeifer & others, 2002). Follow-up assessments occurred at 4 and 7 years of age. Continuity was demonstrated for both inhibition and lack of inhibition, although a substantial number of the inhibited children moved into the intermediate groups at 7 years of age.

Rothbart and Bates' Classification New classifications of temperament continue to be forged. Mary Rothbart and John Bates (2006) argue that three broad dimensions best represent what researchers have found to characterize the structure of temperament: extraversion/surgency, negative affectivity, and effortful control (self-regulation):

- *Extraversion/surgency* includes "positive anticipation, impulsivity, activity level, and sensation seeking" (Rothbart, 2004, p. 495). Kagan's uninhibited children fit into this category.

- *Negative affectivity* includes "fear, frustration, sadness, and discomfort" (Rothbart, 2004, p. 495). These children are easily distressed; they may fret and cry often. Kagan's inhibited children fit this category.

- *Effortful control (self-regulation)* includes "attentional focusing and shifting, inhibitory control, perceptual sensitivity, and low-intensity pleasure" (Rothbart, 2004, p. 495). Infants who are high on effortful control show an ability to keep their arousal from getting too high and have strategies for soothing themselves. By contrast, children low on effortful control are often unable to control their arousal; they become easily agitated and intensely emotional.

A recent study of school-age children in the United States and China revealed that in both cultures low effortful control was linked to externalizing problems, such as lying, cheating, being disobedient, and being overly aggressive (Zhou, Lengua, & Wang, 2009).

In Rothbart's (2004, p. 497) view, "early theoretical models of temperament stressed the way we are moved by our positive and negative emotions or level of arousal, with our actions driven by these tendencies." The more recent emphasis on effortful control, however, advocates that individuals can engage in a more cognitive, flexible approach to stressful circumstances.

Rothbart and Maria Gartstein (2008, p. 323) recently described the following developmental changes in temperament during infancy. During early infancy, smiling and laughter are emerging as part of the positive affectivity dimension of temperament. Also, by 2 months of age, infants show anger and frustration when their actions don't produce an interesting outcome. During this time, infants often are susceptible to distress and overstimulation. From 4 to 12 months of age, fear and irritability become more differentiated with inhibition (fear) increasingly linked to new and unpredictable experiences. Not all temperament characteristics are in place by the first birthday. Positive emotionality becomes more stable later in infancy and the characteristics of extraversion/surgency can be determined in the toddler period. Improved attention skills in the toddler and preschool years are related to an increase in effortful control, which serves as a foundation for improved self-regulation.

The developmental changes just described reflect normative capabilities of children, not individual differences in children. The development of these capabilities, such as effortful control, allow individual differences to emerge (Bates, 2008). For example, although maturation of the brain's prefrontal lobes must occur for any child's attention to improve and the child to achieve effortful control, some children develop effortful control, others do not. And it is these individual differences in children that are at the heart of what temperament is (Bates, 2008).

Biological Foundations and Experience

How does a child acquire a certain temperament? Kagan (2002, 2008, 2010) argues that children inherit a physiology that biases them to have a particular type of temperament. However, through experience they may learn to modify their temperament to some degree. For example, children may inherit a physiology that biases them to be fearful and inhibited, but they learn to reduce their fear and inhibition to some degree.

Biological Influences   Physiological characteristics have been linked with different temperaments (Rothbart & Bates, 2006). In particular, an inhibited temperament is associated with a unique physiological pattern that includes high and stable heart rate, high level of the hormone cortisol, and high activity in the right frontal lobe of the brain (Kagan, 2008). This pattern may be tied to the excitability of the amygdala, a structure of the brain that plays an important role in fear and inhibition. And the development of effortful control is linked to advances in the brain's frontal lobes (Bates, 2008).

What is heredity's role in the biological foundations of temperament? Twin and adoption studies suggest that heredity has a moderate influence on differences in temperament within a group of people (Buss & Goldsmith, 2007).

Developmental Connections   Do young adults show the same behavioral style and characteristic emotional responses as they did when they were infants or young children? Activity level is an important dimension of temperament. Are children's activity levels linked to their personality in early adulthood? In one longitudinal study, children who were highly active at age 4 were likely to be very outgoing at age 23, which reflects continuity (Franz, 1996). From adolescence into early adulthood, most individuals show fewer emotional mood swings, become more responsible, and engage in less risk-taking behavior, which reflects discontinuity (Caspi, 1998).

What are some ways that developmentalists have classified infants' temperaments? Which classification makes the most sense to you based on your observations of infants?

What are some physiological characteristics of an inhibited temperament?

How is temperament in childhood linked to socioemotional development in adulthood?

goodness of fit The match between a child's temperament and the environmental demands the child must cope with.

Is temperament in childhood linked with adjustment in adulthood? Few longitudinal studies have been conducted on this topic (Caspi, 1998). In one of these studies, children who had an easy temperament at 3 to 5 years of age were likely to be well adjusted as young adults (Chess & Thomas, 1977). In contrast, many children who had a difficult temperament at 3 to 5 years of age were not well adjusted as young adults. Also, other researchers have found that boys with a difficult temperament in childhood are less likely as adults to continue their formal education, whereas girls with a difficult temperament in childhood are more likely to experience marital conflict as adults (Wachs, 2000).

Inhibition is another temperament characteristic that has been studied extensively (Kagan, 2008, 2010). Researchers have found that individuals with an inhibited temperament in childhood are less likely as adults to be assertive or to experience social support, and more likely to delay entering a stable job track (Asendorph, 2008; Wachs, 2000).

Yet another aspect of temperament involves emotionality and the ability to control one's emotions. In one longitudinal study, when 3-year-old children showed good control of their emotions and were resilient in the face of stress, they were likely to continue to handle emotions effectively as adults (Block, 1993). By contrast, when 3-year-olds had low emotional control and were not very resilient, they were likely to show problems in these areas as young adults.

In sum, these studies reveal some continuity between certain aspects of temperament in childhood and adjustment in early adulthood. However, keep in mind that these connections between childhood temperament and adult adjustment are based on only a small number of studies; more research is needed to verify these linkages.

Developmental Contexts   What accounts for the continuities and discontinuities between a child's temperament and an adult's personality? Physiological and heredity factors likely are involved in continuity. Links between temperament in childhood and personality in adulthood also might vary, depending on the contexts in individuals' experience.

Gender can be an important factor shaping the context that influences the fate of temperament (Blakemore, Berenbaum, & Liben, 2009). Parents might react differently to a child's temperament, depending on whether the child is a boy or a girl and on the culture in which they live (Kerr, 2001). For example, in one study, mothers were more responsive to the crying of irritable girls than to the crying of irritable boys (Crockenberg, 1986).

Similarly, the reaction to an infant's temperament may depend, in part, on culture (Cole & Tan, 2007). For example, an active temperament might be valued in some cultures (such as the United States) but not in other cultures (such as China). Indeed, children's temperament can vary across cultures (Cole & Tan, 2007). Behavioral inhibition is more highly valued in China than in North America, and researchers have found that Chinese infants are more inhibited than Canadian infants (Chen & others, 1998). The cultural differences in temperament were linked to parental attitudes and behaviors. Canadian mothers of inhibited 2-year-olds were less accepting of their infants' inhibited temperament, whereas Chinese mothers were more accepting.

In short, many aspects of a child's environment can encourage or discourage the persistence of temperament characteristics (Rothbart & Bates, 2006). One useful way of thinking about these relationships applies the concept of goodness of fit, which we examine next.

Goodness of Fit and Parenting

Goodness of fit refers to the match between a child's temperament and the environmental demands the child must cope with. Some temperament characteristics pose more parenting challenges than others, at least in modern Western societies (Bates & Pettit, 2007). When children are prone to distress, as exhibited by frequent crying and irritability, their parents may eventually respond by ignoring the child's distress or trying to force the child to "behave." In one research study, though, extra support and training for mothers of distress-prone infants improved the quality of mother-infant interaction (van den Boom, 1989).

To read further about some positive strategies for parenting that take into account the child's temperament, see the *Applications in Life-Span Development* interlude.

Applications in Life-Span Development

PARENTING AND THE CHILD'S TEMPERAMENT

What are the implications of temperamental variations for parenting? Although answers to this question necessarily are speculative, these conclusions regarding the best parenting strategies to use in relation to children's temperament were reached by temperament experts Ann Sanson and Mary Rothbart (1995):

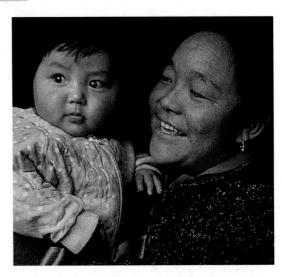

An infant's temperament can vary across cultures. *What do parents need to know about a child's temperament?*

- *Attention to and respect for individuality.* One implication is that it is difficult to generate general prescriptions for "good" parenting. A goal might be accomplished in one way with one child and in another way with another child, depending on the child's temperament. Parents need to be sensitive and flexible to the infant's signals and needs.

- *Structuring the child's environment.* Crowded, noisy environments can pose greater problems for some children (such as a "difficult child") than others (such as an "easygoing" child). We might also expect that a fearful, withdrawing child would benefit from slower entry into new contexts.

- *The "difficult child" and packaged parenting programs.* Programs for parents often focus on dealing with children who have "difficult" temperaments. In some cases, "difficult child" refers to Thomas and Chess' description of a child who reacts negatively, cries frequently, engages in irregular daily routines, and is slow to accept change. In others, the concept might be used to describe a child who is irritable, displays anger frequently, does not follow directions well, or shows some other negative characteristic. Acknowledging that some children are harder than others to parent is often helpful, and advice on how to handle specific difficult characteristics can be useful. However, whether a specific characteristic is difficult depends on its fit with the environment. To label a child "difficult" has the danger of becoming a self-fulfilling prophecy. If a child is identified as "difficult," people may treat the child in a way that actually elicits "difficult" behavior. One recent study did find that having access to experiences that encourage coping and build self-regulatory skills was beneficial to children with a difficult temperament (Bradley & Corwyn, 2008).

Too often, we pigeonhole children into categories without examining the context (Rothbart & Bates, 2006). Nonetheless, caregivers need to take children's temperament into account. Research does not yet allow for many highly specific recommendations, but, in general, caregivers should (1) be sensitive to the individual characteristics of the child, (2) be flexible in responding to these characteristics, and (3) avoid applying negative labels to the child.

Review and Reflect: Learning Goal 3

3 **Characterize variations in temperament and their significance**

REVIEW

- How can temperament be described and classified?
- How is temperament influenced by biological foundations and experience?
- What is goodness of fit? What are some positive parenting strategies for dealing with a child's temperament?

REFLECT

- Consider your own temperament. We described a number of temperament categories. Which one best describes your temperament? Has your temperament changed as you have gotten older? If your temperament has changed, what factors contributed to the changes?

4 ATTACHMENT AND LOVE

Infancy and Childhood   **Adolescence**   **Adulthood**

So far, we have discussed how emotions and emotional competence change over the life span. We have also examined the role of emotional style—in effect, we have seen how emotions set the tone of our experiences in life. But emotions also write the lyrics because they are at the core of our relationships with others. Foremost among these relationships is **attachment,** a close emotional bond between two people. In this section, we focus on two types of attachments: the attachment between children and their parents and romantic attachments.

Infancy and Childhood

Before we describe the attachment in detail, we set the stage for its development by exploring how strong the social orientation of infants is. We also examine their early development of social understanding.

Social Orientation/Understanding   As socioemotional beings, infants show a strong interest in the social world and are motivated to orient to it and understand it. In earlier chapters, we described many of the biological and cognitive foundations that contribute to the infant's development of social orientation and understanding. We call attention to relevant biological and cognitive factors as we explore social orientation; locomotion; intention, goal-directed behavior, and cooperation; and social referencing. Discussing biological, cognitive, and social processes together reminds us of an important aspect of development that we considered in Chapter 1, "Introduction": These processes are intricately intertwined (Diamond, 2007).

Social Orientation   From early in their development, infants are captivated by the social world. As we discussed in our coverage of infant perception in Chapter 5,

attachment A close emotional bond between two people.

"Motor, Sensory, and Perceptual Development," young infants stare intently at faces and are attuned to the sounds of human voices, especially their caregivers' (Ramsey-Rennels & Langlois, 2007). Later, they become adept at interpreting the meaning of facial expressions.

Face-to-face play often begins to characterize caregiver-infant interactions when the infant is about 2 to 3 months of age. The focused social interaction of face-to-face play may include vocalizations, touch, and gestures (Leppanen & others, 2007). Such play is part of many mothers' motivation to create a positive emotional state in their infants (Thompson, 2009a).

In part because of such positive social interchanges between caregivers and infants, by 2 to 3 months of age infants respond differently to people than they do to objects, showing more positive emotion to people than inanimate objects, such as puppets (Legerstee, 1997). At this age, most infants expect people to react positively when the infants initiate a behavior, such as a smile or a vocalization. This finding has been discovered by use of a method called the *still-face paradigm*, in which the caregiver alternates between engaging in face-to-face interaction with the infant and remaining still and unresponsive. As early as 2 to 3 months of age, infants show more withdrawal, negative emotions, and self-directed behavior when their caregivers are still and unresponsive (Adamson & Frick, 2003). The frequency of face-to-face play decreases after 7 months of age as infants become more mobile (Thompson, 2006). A recent meta-analysis revealed that infants' higher positive affect and lower negative affect as displayed during the still-face paradigm were linked to secure attachment at 1 year of age (Mesman, van IJzendoorn, & Bakersman-Kranenburg, 2009).

Infants also learn about the social world through contexts other than face-to-face play with a caregiver (Thompson, 2009a, b). Even though infants as young as 6 months of age show an interest in each other, their interaction with peers increases considerably in the last half of the second year. Between 18 to 24 months of age, children markedly increase their imitative and reciprocal play, such as imitating nonverbal actions like jumping and running (Eckerman & Whitehead, 1999). One recent study involved presenting 1- and 2-year-olds with a simple cooperative task that consisted of pulling a lever to get an attractive toy (Brownell, Ramani, & Zerwas, 2006) (see Figure 10.8). Any coordinated actions of the 1-year-olds appeared to be more coincidental rather than cooperative, whereas the 2-year-olds' behavior was characterized as more active cooperation to reach a goal. As increasing numbers of U.S. infants experience child care outside the home, they are spending more time in social play with other peers. Later in the chapter, we further discuss child care.

Locomotion Recall from earlier in the chapter how important independence is for infants, especially in the second year of life. As infants develop the ability to crawl, walk, and run, they are able to explore and expand their social world. These newly developed self-produced locomotor skills allow the infant to independently initiate social interchanges on a more frequent basis (Laible & Thompson, 2007). Remember from Chapter 5, "Motor, Sensory, and Perceptual Development," that the development of these gross motor skills is the result of a number of factors, including the development of the nervous system, the goal the infant is motivated to reach, and environmental support for the skill (Adolph & Joh, 2009).

Locomotion is also important for its motivational implications (Thompson, 2008). Once infants have the ability to move in goal-directed pursuits, the reward from these pursuits leads to further efforts to explore and develop skills.

Intention, Goal-Directed Behavior, and Cooperation Perceiving people as engaging in intentional and goal-directed behavior is an

A mother and her baby engaging in face-to-face play. *At what age does face-to-face play usually begin, and when does it typically start decreasing in frequency?*

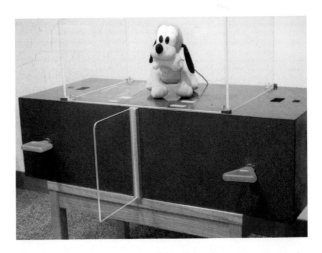

FIGURE 10.8 The Cooperation Task. The cooperation task consisted of two handles on a box, atop which was an animated musical toy, surreptitiously activated by remote control when both handles were pulled. The handles were placed far enough apart that one child could not pull both handles. The experimenter demonstrated the task, saying, "Watch! If you pull the handles, the doggies will sing" (Brownell, Ramani, & Zerwas, 2006).

What is social referencing? What are some developmental changes in social referencing?

important social cognitive accomplishment, and this initially occurs toward the end of the first year (Thompson, 2009a, b). Joint attention and gaze following help the infant to understand that other people have intentions (Meltzoff & Brooks, 2009). Recall from Chapter 7, "Information Processing," that *joint attention* occurs when the caregiver and infant focus on the same object or event. We know that emerging aspects of joint attention occur at about 7 to 8 months, but at about 10 to 11 months of age joint attention intensifies and infants begin to follow the caregiver's gaze. By their first birthday, infants have begun to direct the caregiver's attention to objects that capture their interest (Heimann & others, 2006).

In the study on cooperating to reach a goal that was discussed earlier, 1- and 2-year-olds also were assessed with two social understanding tasks, observation of children's behavior in a joint attention task, and the parents' perceptions of the language the children use about the self and others (Brownell, Ramani, & Zerwas, 2006). Those with more advanced social understanding were more likely to cooperate. To cooperate, the children had to connect their own intentions with the peer's intentions and put this understanding to use in interacting with the peer to reach a goal.

Social Referencing   Another important social cognitive accomplishment in infancy is developing the ability to "read" the emotions of other people. **Social referencing** is the term used to describe "reading" emotional cues in others to help determine how to act in a specific situation. The development of social referencing helps infants to interpret ambiguous situations more accurately, as when they encounter a stranger and need to know whether or not to fear the person (de Rosnay & others, 2006). By the end of the first year, a mother's facial expression—either smiling or fearful—influences whether an infant will explore an unfamiliar environment.

Infants become better at social referencing in the second year of life. At this age, they tend to "check" with their mother before they act; they look at her to see if she is happy, angry, or fearful.

Infants' Social Sophistication and Insight   In sum, researchers are discovering that infants are more socially sophisticated and insightful at younger ages than previously envisioned (Hamlin, Hallinan, & Woodward, 2008; Thompson, 2009a, b). Such sophistication and insight are reflected in infants' perceptions of others' actions as intentionally motivated and goal-directed (Brune & Woodward, 2007) and their motivation to share and participate in that intentionality by their first birthday (Tomasello & Carpenter, 2007). The more advanced social cognitive skills of infants could be expected to influence their understanding and awareness of attachment to a caregiver.

What Is Attachment?   There is no shortage of theories about why infants become attached to a caregiver. Three theorists discussed in Chapter 1, "Introduction"—Freud, Erikson, and Bowlby—proposed influential views.

Freud noted that infants become attached to the person or object that provides oral satisfaction. For most infants, this is the mother, since she is most likely to feed the infant. Is feeding as important as Freud thought? A classic study by Harry Harlow (1958) reveals that the answer is no (see Figure 10.9).

Harlow removed infant monkeys from their mothers at birth; for six months they were reared by surrogate (substitute) "mothers." One surrogate mother was made of wire, the other of cloth. Half of the infant monkeys were fed by the wire mother, half by the cloth mother. Periodically, the amount of time the infant

social referencing "Reading" emotional cues in others to help determine how to act in a specific situation.

monkeys spent with either the wire or the cloth mother was computed. Regardless of which mother fed them, the infant monkeys spent far more time with the cloth mother. Even if the wire mother but not the cloth mother provided nourishment, the infant monkeys spent more time with the cloth mother. And when Harlow frightened the monkeys, those "raised" by the cloth mother ran to the mother and clung to it; those raised by the wire mother did not. Whether the mother provided comfort seemed to determine whether the monkeys associated the mother with security. This study clearly demonstrated that feeding is not the crucial element in the attachment process and that contact comfort is important.

Physical comfort also plays a role in Erik Erikson's (1968) view of the infant's development. Recall Erikson's proposal that the first year of life represents the stage of trust versus mistrust. Physical comfort and sensitive care, according to Erikson (1968), are key to establishing a basic trust in infants. The infant's sense of trust, in turn, is the foundation for attachment and sets the stage for a lifelong expectation that the world will be a good and pleasant place to be.

The ethological perspective of British psychiatrist John Bowlby (1969, 1989) also stresses the importance of attachment in the first year of life and the responsiveness of the caregiver. Bowlby stresses both infants and their primary caregivers are biologically predisposed to form attachments. He argues that the newborn is biologically equipped to elicit attachment behavior. The baby cries, clings, coos, and smiles. Later, the infant crawls, walks, and follows the mother. The immediate result is to keep the primary caregiver nearby; the long-term effect is to increase the infant's chances of survival.

Attachment does not emerge suddenly but rather develops in a series of phases, moving from a baby's general preference for human beings to a partnership with primary caregivers. Following are four such phases based on Bowlby's conceptualization of attachment (Schaffer, 1996):

- *Phase 1: From birth to 2 months.* Infants instinctively direct their attachment to human figures. Strangers, siblings, and parents are equally likely to elicit smiling or crying from the infant.

- *Phase 2: From 2 to 7 months.* Attachment becomes focused on one figure, usually the primary caregiver, as the baby gradually learns to distinguish familiar from unfamiliar people.

- *Phase 3: From 7 to 24 months.* Specific attachments develop. With increased locomotor skills, babies actively seek contact with regular caregivers, such as the mother or father.

- *Phase 4: From 24 months on.* Children become aware of others' feelings, goals, and plans and begin to take these into account in forming their own actions.

Researchers' recent findings that infants are more socially sophisticated and insightful than previously envisioned suggests that some of the characteristics of Bowlby's phase 4, such as understanding the goals and intentions of the attachment figure, appear to be developing in phase 3 as attachment security is taking shape (Thompson, 2008).

Bowlby argued that infants develop an *internal working model* of attachment, a simple mental model of the caregiver, their relationship, and the self as deserving of nurturant care. The infant's internal working model of attachment with the caregiver influences the infant's and later, the child's, subsequent responses to other people (Posada, 2008). The internal model of attachment also has played a pivotal role in the discovery of links between attachment and subsequent emotion understanding, conscious development, and self-concept (Bretherton & Munholland, 2008).

In sum, attachment emerges from the social cognitive advances that allow infants to develop expectations for the caregiver's behavior and to determine the affective quality of their relationship (Thompson, 2009a, b). These social cognitive

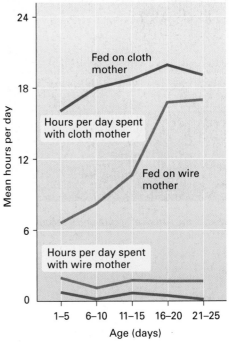

FIGURE 10.9 Contact Time with Wire and Cloth Surrogate Mothers. Regardless of whether the infant monkeys were fed by a wire or a cloth mother, they overwhelmingly preferred to spend contact time with the cloth mother. *How do these results compare with what Freud's theory and Erikson's theory would predict about human infants?*

advances include recognizing the caregiver's face, voice, and other features, as well as developing an internal working model of expecting the caregiver to provide pleasure in social interaction and relief from distress.

In Bowlby's model, what are four phases of attachment?

Individual Differences in Attachment Although attachment to a caregiver intensifies midway through the first year, isn't it likely that the quality of babies' attachment experiences varies? Mary Ainsworth (1979) thought so. Ainsworth created the **Strange Situation,** an observational measure of infant attachment in which the infant experiences a series of introductions, separations, and reunions with the caregiver and an adult stranger in a prescribed order. In using the Strange Situation, researchers hope that their observations will provide information about the infant's motivation to be near the caregiver and the degree to which the caregiver's presence provides the infant with security and confidence.

Based on how babies respond in the Strange Situation, they are described as being securely attached or insecurely attached (in one of three ways) to the caregiver:

What is the nature of secure and insecure attachment?

- **Securely attached babies** use the caregiver as a secure base from which to explore the environment. When in the presence of their caregiver, securely attached infants explore the room and examine toys that have been placed in it. When the caregiver departs, securely attached infants might mildly protest, and when the caregiver returns these infants reestablish positive interaction with her, perhaps by smiling or climbing on her lap. Subsequently, they often resume playing with the toys in the room.
- **Insecure avoidant babies** show insecurity by avoiding the mother. In the Strange Situation, these babies engage in little interaction with the caregiver, are not distressed when she leaves the room, usually do not reestablish contact with her on her return, and may even turn their back on her. If contact is established, the infant usually leans away or looks away.
- **Insecure resistant babies** often cling to the caregiver and then resist her by fighting against the closeness, perhaps by kicking or pushing away. In the Strange Situation, these babies often cling anxiously to the caregiver and don't explore the playroom. When the caregiver leaves, they often cry loudly and push away if she tries to comfort them on her return.
- **Insecure disorganized babies** are disorganized and disoriented. In the Strange Situation, these babies might appear dazed, confused, and fearful. To be classified as disorganized, babies must show strong patterns of avoidance and resistance or display certain specified behaviors, such as extreme fearfulness around the caregiver.

Evaluating the Strange Situation Does the Strange Situation capture important differences among infants? As a measure of attachment, it may be culturally biased. For example, German and Japanese babies often show different patterns of attachment from those of American infants. As illustrated in Figure 10.10, German infants are more likely to show an avoidant attachment pattern and Japanese infants are less likely to display this pattern than U.S. infants (van IJzendoorn & Kroonenberg, 1988). The avoidant pattern in German babies likely occurs because their caregivers encourage them to be independent (Grossmann & others, 1985). Also as shown in Figure 10.10, Japanese babies are more likely than American babies to be categorized as resistant. This may have more to do with the Strange Situation as a measure of attachment than with attachment insecurity itself. Japanese mothers rarely let anyone unfamiliar with their babies care for them. Thus, the Strange Situation might create considerably more stress for Japanese infants than for American infants, who are more accustomed to separation from their

Strange Situation Ainsworth's observational measure of infant attachment to a caregiver that requires the infant to move through a series of introductions, separations, and reunions with the caregiver and an adult stranger in a prescribed order.

securely attached babies Babies who use the caregiver as a secure base from which to explore the environment.

insecure avoidant babies Babies who show insecurity by avoiding the mother.

mothers (Miyake, Chen, & Campos, 1985). Even though there are cultural variations in attachment classification, the most frequent classification in every culture studied so far is secure attachment (van IJzendoorn & Kroonenberg, 1988).

Some critics stress that behavior in the Strange Situation—like other laboratory assessments—might not indicate what infants do in a natural environment. But researchers have found that infants' behaviors in the Strange Situation are closely related to how they behave at home in response to separation and reunion with their mothers (Pederson & Moran, 1996). Thus, many infant researchers stress that the Strange Situation continues to show merit as a measure of infant attachment.

Interpreting Differences in Attachment Do individual differences in attachment matter? Ainsworth notes that secure attachment in the first year of life provides an important foundation for psychological development later in life. The securely attached infant moves freely away from the mother but keeps track of where she is through periodic glances. The securely attached infant responds positively to being picked up by others and, when put back down, freely moves away to play. An insecurely attached infant, by contrast, avoids the mother or is ambivalent toward her, fears strangers, and is upset by minor, everyday separations.

If early attachment to a caregiver is important, it should relate to a child's social behavior later in development. For some children, early attachments seem to foreshadow later functioning (Berlin, Zeanah, & Lieberman, 2008; Cassidy, 2008). In the extensive longitudinal study conducted by Alan Sroufe and his colleagues (2005a, b), early secure attachment (assessed by the Strange Situation at 12 and 18 months) was linked with positive emotional health, high self-esteem, self-confidence, and socially competent interaction with peers, teachers, camp counselors, and romantic partners through adolescence.

For some children, though, there is little continuity (Thompson, 2009a, b). Not all research reveals the power of infant attachment to predict subsequent development. The most consistent link between early attachment and subsequent development occurs for insecure disorganized babies, which likely reflects the abusive rearing conditions experienced by these infants (Bates, 2008). In one longitudinal study, attachment classification in infancy did not predict attachment classification at 18 years of age (Lewis, 1997). In this study, the best predictor of an insecure attachment classification at 18 was the occurrence of parental divorce in the intervening years. Consistently positive caregiving over a number of years is likely an important factor in connecting early attachment and the child's functioning later in development. Indeed, researchers have found that early secure attachment *and* subsequent experiences, especially maternal care and life stresses, are linked with children's later behavior and adjustment (Thompson, 2009a, b).

Some developmentalists note that too much emphasis has been placed on the attachment bond in infancy. Jerome Kagan (2000), for example, emphasizes that infants are highly resilient and adaptive; he argues that they are evolutionarily equipped to stay on a positive developmental course, even in the face of wide variations in parenting. Kagan and others stress that genetic characteristics and temperament play more important roles in a child's social competence than the attachment theorists, such as Bowlby and Ainsworth, are willing to acknowledge (Bakermans-Kranenburg & others, 2007). For example, if some infants inherit a low tolerance for stress, this, rather than an insecure attachment bond, may be responsible for an inability to get along with peers. A recent study found links

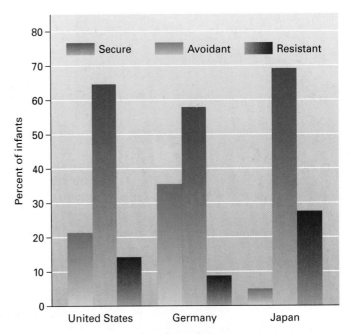

FIGURE 10.10 Cross-Cultural Comparison of Attachment. In one study, infant attachment in three countries—the United States, Germany, and Japan—was measured in the Ainsworth Strange Situation (van IJzendoorn & Kroonenberg, 1988). The dominant attachment pattern in all three countries was secure attachment. However, German infants were more avoidant and Japanese infants were less avoidant and more resistant than U.S. infants. *What are some explanations for differences in how German, Japanese, and U.S. infants respond to the Strange Situation?*

insecure resistant babies Babies who might cling to the caregiver, then resist her by fighting against the closeness, perhaps by kicking or pushing away.

insecure disorganized babies Babies who show insecurity by being disorganized and disoriented.

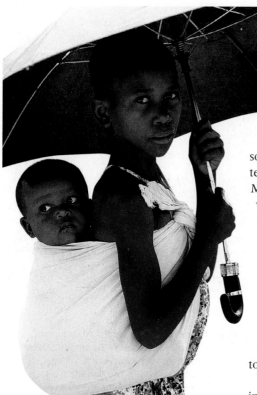

In the Hausa culture, siblings and grandmothers provide a significant amount of care for infants. *How might these variations in care affect attachment?*

between disorganized attachment in infancy, a specific gene, and level of maternal responsiveness. In this study, a disorganized attachment style developed in infancy only when infants had the short version of the serotonin transporter gene—5-*HTTLPR* (Spangler & others, 2009). Infants were not characterized by this attachment style when they had the long version of the gene (Spangler & others 2009). Further, this gene-environment interaction occurred only when mothers showed a low level of responsiveness toward their infants.

Another criticism of attachment theory is that it ignores the diversity of socializing agents and contexts that exists in an infant's world. A culture's value system can influence the nature of attachment (van IJzendoorn & Sagi-Schwartz, 2008). Mothers' expectations for infants to be independent are high in northern Germany, whereas Japanese mothers are more strongly motivated to keep their infants close to them (Grossman & others, 1985; Rothbaum & others, 2000). Not surprisingly, northern German infants tend to show less distress than Japanese infants when separated from their mother. Also, in some cultures, infants show attachments to many people. Among the Hausa (who live in Nigeria), both grandmothers and siblings provide a significant amount of care for infants (Harkness & Super, 1995). Infants in agricultural societies tend to form attachments to older siblings, who are assigned a major responsibility for younger siblings' care. Researchers recognize the importance of competent, nurturant caregivers in an infant's development (Parke & others, 2008). At issue, though, is whether or not secure attachment, especially to a single caregiver, is critical (Lamb, 2005; Thompson, 2009a, b).

Despite such criticisms, there is ample evidence that security of attachment is important to development (Cassidy, 2008; Thompson, 2009c). Secure attachment in infancy is important because it reflects a positive parent-infant relationship and provides the foundation that supports healthy socioemotional development in the years that follow.

Caregiving Styles and Attachment Is the style of caregiving linked with the quality of the infant's attachment? Securely attached babies have caregivers who are sensitive to their signals and are consistently available to respond to their infants' needs (Cassidy, 2009). These caregivers often let their babies have an active part in determining the onset and pacing of interaction in the first year of life. A recent study revealed that maternal sensitivity in responding was linked to infant attachment security (Finger & others, 2009). Another study found that maternal sensitivity in parenting was linked with secure attachment in infants in two different cultures: the United States and Colombia (Posada & others, 2002).

How do the caregivers of insecurely attached babies interact with them? Caregivers of avoidant babies tend to be unavailable or rejecting (Cassidy, 2000). They often don't respond to their babies' signals and have little physical contact with them. When they do interact with their babies, they may behave in an angry and irritable way. Caregivers of resistant babies tend to be inconsistent; sometimes they respond to their babies' needs, and sometimes they don't. In general, they tend not to be very affectionate with their babies and show little synchrony when interacting with them. Caregivers of disorganized babies often neglect or physically abuse them (Benoit, Coolbear, & Crawford, 2008). In some cases, these caregivers are depressed. In sum, caregivers' interactions with infants influence whether infants are securely or insecurely attached to the caregivers (Berlin, Zeenah, & Lieberman, 2008; George & Solomon, 2009).

Developmental Social Neuroscience and Attachment In Chapter 1, "Introduction," we described the emerging field of *developmental social neuroscience* that examines connections between socioemotional processes, development, and the brain. Attachment is one of the main areas in which theory and research on developmental social neuroscience has focused. These connections of attachment and the brain involve the neuroanatomy of the brain, neurotransmitters, and hormones.

Theory and research on the role of the brain's regions in mother-infant attachment is just emerging (de Haan & Gunnar, 2009). A recent theoretical view proposed that the prefrontal cortex likely has an important role in maternal attachment behavior, as do the subcortical (areas of the brain lower than the cortex) regions of the amygdala (which is strongly involved in emotion) and the hypothalamus (Gonzalez, Atkinson, & Fleming, 2009). An ongoing fMRI longitudinal study is exploring the possibility that different attachment patterns can be distinguished by different patterns of brain activity (Strathearn, 2007).

Research on the role of hormones and neurotransmitters in attachment has emphasized the importance of two neuropeptide hormones—oxytocin and vasopressin—in the formation of the maternal-infant bond (Bales & Carter, 2009). Oxytocin, a mammalian hormone that also acts as a neurotransmitter in the brain, is released during breast feeding and by contact and warmth. Oxytocin is especially thought to be a likely candidate in the formation of infant-mother attachment (Bales & Carter, 2009).

The influence of these neuropeptides on the neurotransmitter dopamine in the nucleus accumbens (a collection of neurons in the forebrain that are involved in pleasure) likely is important in motivating approach to the attachment object (de Haan & Gunnar, 2009). Figure 10.11 shows the regions of the brain we have described that are likely important in infant-mother attachment.

In sum, it is likely that a number of brain regions, neurotransmitters, and hormones are involved in the development of infant-mother attachment. Key candidates for influencing this attachment are connections between the prefrontal cortex, amygdala, and hypothalamus; the neuropeptides oxytocin and vasopressin; and the activity of the neurotransmitter dopamine in the nucleus accumbens.

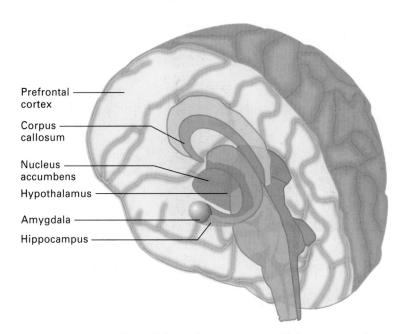

FIGURE 10.11 Regions of the Brain Proposed as Likely Important in Infant-Mother Attachment. *Note:* This illustration shows the brain's left hemisphere. The corpus callosum is the large bundle of axons that connects the brain's two hemispheres.

Mothers and Fathers as Caregivers An increasing number of U.S. fathers stay home full-time with their children (Cohen, 2009; Wong & Rochlen, 2008). As indicated in Figure 10.12, there was a 300-plus percent increase in stay-at-home fathers in the United States from 1996 to 2006. A large portion of the full-time fathers have career-focused wives who provide the main family income. One study revealed that the stay-at-home fathers were as satisfied with their marriage as traditional parents, although they indicated that they missed their daily life in the workplace (Rochlen & others, 2005). In this study, the stay-at-home fathers reported that they tended to be ostracized when they took their children to playgrounds and often were excluded from parent groups.

Can fathers take care of infants as competently as mothers can? Observations of fathers and their infants suggest that fathers have the ability to act as sensitively and responsively as mothers with their infants (Parke & others, 2008). However, although fathers can be active, nurturant, involved caregivers with their infants, many do not choose to follow this pattern (Lamb, 2000).

Do fathers behave differently toward infants than mothers do? Maternal interactions usually center on child-care activities—feeding, changing diapers, bathing. Paternal interactions are more likely to include play (Parke & Buriel,

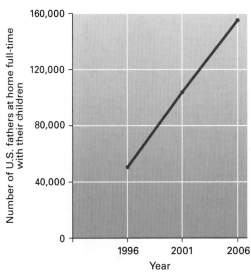

FIGURE 10.12 The Increase in the Number of U.S. Fathers Staying at Home Full-Time with Their Children.

How do most fathers and mothers interact differently with infants?

> W*e have all the knowledge necessary to provide absolutely first-rate child care in the United States. What is missing is the commitment and the will.*
>
> —EDWARD ZIGLER
> *Contemporary Developmental Psychologist, Yale University*

How are child-care policies in many European countries, such as Sweden, different from those in the United States?

2006). Fathers engage in more rough-and-tumble play. They bounce infants, throw them up in the air, tickle them, and so on (Lamb, 2000). Mothers do play with infants, but their play is less physical and arousing than that of fathers.

Child Care   Many U.S. children today experience multiple caregivers. Most do not have a parent staying home to care for them; instead, the children have some type of care provided by others—"child care." Many parents worry that child care will reduce their infants' emotional attachment to them, retard the infants' cognitive development, fail to teach them how to control anger, and allow them to be unduly influenced by their peers. How extensive is child care? Are the worries of these parents justified (Thompson, 2009d)?

Parental Leave   Today far more young children are in child care than at any other time in history. About 2 million children in the United States currently receive formal, licensed child care, and uncounted millions of children are cared for by unlicensed baby-sitters. As described in the *Contexts of Life-Span Development* interlude, many countries provide far more extensive parental leave policies than does the United States.

Contexts of Life-Span Development

CHILD-CARE POLICIES AROUND THE WORLD

Child-care policies around the world vary in eligibility criteria, leave duration, benefit level, and the extent to which parents take advantage of the policies (Tolani & Brooks-Gunn, 2008). Sheila Kammerman (1989, 2000a, b) described five types of parental leave from employment:

- *Maternity leave.* In some countries, the prebirth leave is compulsory as is a 6- to 10-week leave following birth.
  - *Paternity leave.* This is usually much briefer than maternity leave. It may be especially important when a second child is born and the first child requires care.
  - *Parental leave.* This gender-neutral leave usually follows a maternity leave and allows either women or men to share the leave policy or choose which of them will use it. In 1998, the European Union mandated a three-month parental leave.
- *Child-rearing leave.* In some countries, this is a supplement to a maternity leave or a variation on a parental leave. A child-rearing leave is usually longer than a maternity leave and is typically paid at a much lower level.
- *Family leave.* This covers reasons other than the birth of a new baby and can allow time off from employment to care for an ill child or other family members, time to accompany a child to school for the first time, or time to visit a child's school.

Europe led the way in creating new standards of parental leave: The European Union (EU) mandated a paid 14-week maternity leave in 1992. In most European countries today, working parents on leave receive from 70 percent of the worker's prior wage to the full wage and paid leave averages about 16 weeks (Tolani & Brooks-Gunn, 2008). The United States currently allows up to 12 weeks of unpaid leave for caring for a newborn.

Most countries restrict eligible benefits to women employed for a minimum time prior to childbirth (Tolani & Brooks-Gunn, 2008). In Denmark, even unemployed mothers are eligible for extended parental leave related to childbirth. In Germany, child-rearing leave is available to almost all parents. The Nordic countries (Denmark, Norway, and Sweden) have extensive gender-equity family leave policies for childbirth that emphasize the contributions of both women and men (Tolani & Brooks-Gunn, 2008). For example, in Sweden, parents can take an 18-month job-protected parental leave with benefits allowed to be shared by parents and applied to full-time or part-time work.

Variations in Child Care Because the United States does not have a policy of paid leave for child care, child care in the United States has become a major national concern (Belsky, 2009; Howes & Wishard Guerra, 2009). Many factors influence the effects of child care, including the age of the child, the type of child care, and the quality of the program.

The type of child care varies extensively. Child care is provided in large centers with elaborate facilities and in private homes. Some child-care centers are commercial operations; others are nonprofit centers run by churches, civic groups, and employers. Some child-care providers are professionals; others are mothers who want to earn extra money. Figure 10.13 presents the primary care arrangement for children under 5 years of age with employed mothers (Clarke-Stewart & Miner, 2008).

Child-care quality makes a difference. What constitutes a high-quality childcare program for infants? In high-quality child care (Clarke-Stewart & Miner, 2008, p. 273):

> . . . caregivers encourage the children to be actively engaged in a variety of activities, have frequent, positive interactions that include smiling, touching, holding, and speaking at the child's eye level, respond properly to the child's questions or requests, and encourage children to talk about their experiences, feelings, and ideas.

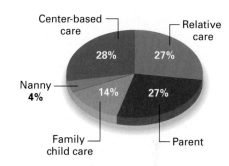

FIGURE 10.13 Primary Care Arrangements in the United States for Children Under 5 Years of Age with Employed Mothers.

High-quality child care also involves providing children with a safe environment, access to age-appropriate toys and participation in age-appropriate activities, and a low caregiver–child ratio that allows caregivers to spend considerable time with children on an individual basis.

In the United States, approximately 15 percent of children 5 years of age and younger experience more than one child-care arrangement. A recent study of 2- and 3-year-old children revealed that an increase in the number of child-care arrangements the children experienced was linked to an increase in behavioral problems and a decrease in prosocial behavior (Morrissey, 2009).

Children are more likely to experience poor-quality child care if they come from families with few resources (psychological, social, and economic) (Cabrera, Hutchens, & Peters, 2006). Many researchers have examined the role of poverty in quality of child care (Giannarelli, Sonenstein, & Stagner, 2006). One study found that extensive child care was harmful to low-income children only when the care was of low quality (Votruba-Drzal & others, 2004). Even if the child was in child care more than 45 hours a week, high-quality care was linked with fewer internalizing problems (anxiety, for example) and externalizing problems (aggressive and destructive behaviors, for example). A recent study revealed that children from low-income families benefited in terms of school readiness and language development when their parents selected higher-quality child care (McCartney & others, 2007).

To read about one individual who provides quality child care to individuals from impoverished backgrounds, see the *Careers in Life-Span Development* profile.

A major, ongoing longitudinal study of U.S. child care was initiated by the National Institute of Child Health and Human Development (NICHD) in 1991. Data were collected on a diverse sample of almost 1,400 children and their families at

Careers in Life-Span Development

Rashmi Nakhre, Child-Care Director

Rashmi Nakhre has two master's degrees—one in psychology the other in child development—and is director of the Hattie Daniels Day Care Center in Wilson, North Carolina. At a "Celebrating a Century of Women" ceremony, Nakhre received the Distinguished Women of North Carolina Award for 1999–2000.

Nakhre first worked at the child-care center soon after she arrived in the United States over 25 years ago. She says that she took the job initially because she needed the money but "ended up falling in love with my job." Nakhre has turned the Wilson, North Carolina, child-care center into a model for other centers. The Hattie Daniels center almost closed several years after she began working there because of financial difficulties. Dr. Nakhre played a major role in raising funds not only to keep it open but to improve it. The center provides quality child care for the children of many Latino migrant workers.

Rashmi Nakhre, child-care director, working with some of the children at her center.

ten locations across the United States over a period of seven years. Researchers used multiple methods (trained observers, interviews, questionnaires, and testing), and they measured many facets of children's development, including physical health, cognitive development, and socioemotional development. Following are some of the results of what is now referred to as the NICHD Study of Early Child Care and Youth Development, or NICHD SECCYD (NICHD Early Child Care Network, 2001, 2002, 2003, 2004, 2005, 2006).

- *Patterns of use.* Many families placed their infants in child care very soon after the child's birth, and there was considerable instability in the child-care arrangements. By 4 months of age, nearly three-fourths of the infants had entered some form of nonmaternal child-care. Almost half of the infants were cared for by a relative when they first entered care; only 12 percent were enrolled in child-care centers. Socioeconomic factors were linked to the amount and type of care. For example, mothers with higher incomes and families that were more dependent on the mother's income placed their infants in child care at an earlier age. Mothers who believed that maternal employment has positive effects on children were more likely than other mothers to place their infant in nonmaternal care for more hours. Low-income families were more likely than more affluent families to use child care, but infants from low-income families who were in child care averaged as many hours as other income groups. In the preschool years, mothers who were single, those with more education, and families with higher incomes used more hours of center-based care than other families. Minority families and mothers with less education used more hours of care by relatives.

- *Quality of care.* Evaluations of quality of care were based on such characteristics as group size, child–adult ratio, physical environment, caregiver characteristics (such as formal education, specialized training, and child-care experience), and caregiver behavior (such as sensitivity to children). An alarming conclusion is that a majority of the child care in the first three years of life was of unacceptable low quality. Positive caregiving by nonparents in child-care settings was infrequent—only 12 percent of the children studied experienced positive nonparental child care (such as positive talk and language stimulation)! Further, infants from low-income families experienced lower quality of child care than infants from higher-income families. When quality of caregivers' care was high, children performed better on cognitive and language tasks, were more cooperative with their mothers during play, showed more positive and skilled interaction with peers, and had fewer behavior problems. Caregiver training and good child–staff ratios were linked with higher cognitive and social competence when children were 54 months of age. Using data collected as part of the NICHD early child care longitudinal study, a recent analysis indicated that higher-quality early child care, especially at 27 months of age, was linked to children's higher vocabulary scores in the fifth grade (Belsky & others, 2007). Higher-quality child care was also related to higher-quality mother-child interaction among the families that used nonmaternal care. Further, poor-quality care was related to an increase of insecure attachment to the mother among infants who were 15 months of age, but only when the mother was low in sensitivity and responsiveness. However, child-care quality was not linked to attachment security at 36 months of age.

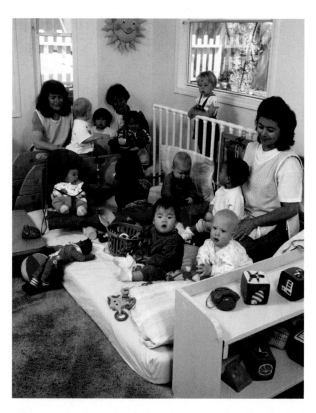

What are some important findings from the national longitudinal study of child care conducted by the National Institute of Child Health and Human Development?

- *Amount of child care.* The quantity of child care predicted some child outcomes. When children spent extensive amounts of time in child care beginning in infancy, they experienced less sensitive interactions with their mother, showed more behavior problems, and had higher rates of illness (Vandell, 2004). Many of these comparisons involved children in child care for less than 30 hours a week versus those in child care for more than 45 hours a week. In general, though, when children spent 30 hours or more per week in child care, their development was less than optimal (Ramey, 2005).

- *Family and parenting influences.* The influence of families and parenting was not weakened by extensive child care. Parents played a significant role in helping children to regulate their emotions. Especially important parenting influences were being sensitive to children's needs, being involved with children, and cognitively stimulating them. Indeed, parental sensitivity has been the most consistent predictor of a secure attachment with child-care experiences being relevant in many cases only when mothers engage in insensitive parenting (Friedman, Melhuish, & Hill, 2009; Thompson, 2009c).

What are some strategies parents can follow in regard to child care? Child-care expert Kathleen McCartney (2003, p. 4) offered this advice:

- *Recognize that the quality of your parenting is a key factor in your child's development.*

- *Make decisions that will improve the likelihood you will be good parents.* "For some this will mean working full-time"—for personal fulfillment, income, or both. "For others, this will mean working part-time or not working outside the home."

- *Monitor your child's development.* "Parents should observe for themselves whether their children seem to be having behavior problems." They need to talk with their child-care providers and their pediatrician about their child's behavior

- *Take some time to find the best child care.* Observe different child-care facilities and be certain that you like what you see. "Quality child care costs money, and not all parents can afford the child care they want. However, state subsidies, and other programs like Head Start, are available for families in need."

Adolescence

Relationships between parents and children continue to be important into the adolescent years. But the adolescent's emotions may become more involved with people outside the family, especially with romantic partners. What do psychologists know about these relationships?

Attachment to Parents   The initial interest in attachment focused on infants and their caregivers. Developmentalists have recently begun to explore the role of secure attachment and related concepts, such as connectedness to parents, during adolescence. Secure attachment to parents in adolescence may facilitate the adolescent's social competence and well-being, as reflected in such characteristics as self-esteem, emotional adjustment, and physical health. In the research of Joseph Allen and his colleagues (Allen, 2007, 2008; Allen & others, 2004, 2007), securely attached adolescents are less likely to engage in problem behaviors. A recent study by Allen and his colleagues (2007) revealed that secure attachment in early adolescence was linked to successful autonomy, good peer relations, and lower incidences of depression and delinquency.

Many studies that assess secure and insecure attachment in adolescence and adulthood use the Adult Attachment Interview (AAI) (George, Main, & Kaplan, 1984). This measure examines an individual's memories of significant attachment relationships. Based on the responses to questions on the AAI, individuals are classified as secure-autonomous (which corresponds to secure attachment in infancy) or as one of three insecure categories:

Dismissing-avoidant attachment is an insecure category in which adolescents deemphasize the importance of attachment. This category is associated with consistent rejection of attachment needs by caregivers. One possible outcome of dismissing-avoidant attachment is that parents and adolescents may mutually distance themselves from each other, which lessens parents' influence. Dismissing-avoidant attachment is linked with violent and aggressive behavior in some adolescents.

Preoccupied-ambivalent attachment is an insecure category in which adolescents are hyper-tuned to attachment experiences. This is thought to occur mainly because parents are inconsistently available to the adolescent, a circumstance that may lead to considerable attachment-seeking behavior, mixed with anger. Conflict with parents may be too high for healthy development.

Unresolved-disorganized attachment is an insecure category in which the adolescent has an unusually high level of fear and is often disoriented. This may result from such traumatic experiences as a parent's death or abuse by parents.

A recent study examined links between adolescent attachment styles and peer relations (Dykas, Ziv, & Cassidy, 2008). Secure-autonomous adolescents were perceived by peers to behave in more prosocial ways, be less shy and withdrawn, and be more socially accepted by peers than insecure-dismissing adolescents.

Dating and Romantic Relationships   Adolescents not only have attachments to their parents. Dating and romantic relationships also can lead to attachment. Adolescents spend considerable time either dating or thinking about dating, which has gone far beyond its original courtship function to become a form of recreation, a source of status and achievement, and a setting for learning about close relationships. One function of dating, though, continues to be mate selection.

Types of Dating and Developmental Changes   Three stages characterize the development of romantic relationships in adolescence (Connolly & McIsaac, 2009):

* *Entry into romantic attractions and affiliations at about 11 to 13 years of age.* This initial stage is triggered by puberty. From 11 to 13, adolescents become

dismissing-avoidant attachment   An insecure attachment style in which adolescents deemphasize the importance of attachment; is associated with consistent experiences of rejection of attachment needs by caregivers.

preoccupied-ambivalent attachment   An insecure attachment style in which adolescents are hyper-tuned to attachment experiences. This is thought to occur mainly because parents are inconsistently available to the adolescent.

unresolved-disorganized attachment   An insecure attachment style in which the adolescent has an unusually high level of fear and is often disoriented. These may result from such traumatic experiences as a parent's death or abuse by parents.

intensely interested in romance, and it dominates many conversations with same-sex friends. Developing a crush on someone is common, and the crush often is shared with a same-sex friend. Young adolescents may or may not interact with the individual who is the object of their infatuation. When dating occurs, it usually occurs in a group setting.

- *Exploring romantic relationships at approximately 14 to 16 years of age.* At this point in adolescence, two types of romantic involvement occur: casual dating and group dating. *Casual dating* emerges between individuals who are mutually attracted. These dating experiences are often short-lived, last a few months at best, and usually endure for only a few weeks. *Dating in groups* is common and reflects embeddedness in the peer context. Friends often act as a third-party facilitator of a potential dating relationship by communicating their friend's romantic interest and confirming whether this attraction is reciprocated.

- *Consolidating dyadic romantic bonds at about 17 to 19 years of age.* At the end of the high school years, more serious romantic relationships develop. This is characterized by strong emotional bonds more closely resembling those in adult romantic relationships. These bonds often are more stable and enduring than earlier bonds, typically lasting one year or more.

Two variations on these stages in the development of romantic relationships in adolescence involve early and late bloomers (Connolly & McIsaac, 2009). *Early bloomers* include 15 to 20 percent of 11- to 13-year-olds who say that they currently are in a romantic relationship and 35 percent who indicate that they have had some prior experience in romantic relationships. *Late bloomers* comprise approximately 10 percent of 17- to 19-year-olds who say that they have had no experience with romantic relationships and another 15 percent who report that they have not engaged in any romantic relationships that lasted more than four months.

In their early exploration of romantic relationships, today's adolescents often find comfort in numbers and begin hanging out together in heterosexual groups. Sometimes they just hang out at someone's house or get organized enough to get someone to drive them to a mall or a movie. Indeed, peers play an important role in adolescent romantic relationships. One study also found that young adolescents increase their participation in mixed-gender peer groups (Connolly & others, 2004). This participation was "not explicitly focused on dating but rather brought boys and girls together in settings in which heterosocial interaction might occur but is not obligatory. We speculate that mixed-gender groups are important because they are easily available to young adolescents who can take part at their own comfort level" (p. 201).

What are dating relationships like in adolescence?

Dating and Adjustment   Researchers have linked dating and romantic relationships with various measures of how well adjusted adolescents are (Collins, Welsh, & Furman, 2009; Connolly & McIsaac, 2009). For example, a recent study of 200 tenth-graders revealed that the more romantic experiences they had, the more they reported higher levels of social acceptance, friendship competence, and romantic competence—however, having more romantic experience also was linked to a higher level of substance use, delinquency, and sexual behavior (Furman, Low, & Ho, 2009). Another recent study of adolescent girls revealed that a higher frequency of dating was linked to having depressive symptoms and emotionally unavailable parents (Steinberg & Davila, 2008). Yet another recent study of adolescent girls found that those who engaged in co-rumination (excessive discussion of problems with friends) were more likely to be involved in a romantic relationship, and together co-rumination and romantic involvement predicted an increase in depressive symptoms (Starr & Davila, 2009).

Dating and romantic relationships at an early age can be especially problematic (Connolly & McIsaac, 2009). Researchers have found that early dating and "going with" someone are linked with adolescent pregnancy and problems at home and school (Florsheim, Moore, & Edgington, 2003).

A recent study examined the influence of a dating partner on the adolescent's adjustment over time (Simon, Aikins, & Prinstein, 2008). Especially important was the positive influence of a high-functioning dating partner on a low-functioning dating partner as the relationship endured. For example, an adolescent who initially reported having a high level of depression but dated an adolescent who reported having a low level of depression indicated that she or he had a lower level of depression 11 months later.

Sociocultural Contexts and Dating   The sociocultural context exerts a powerful influence on adolescents' dating patterns. Values and religious beliefs of various cultures often dictate the age at which dating begins, how much freedom in dating is allowed, whether dates must be chaperoned by adults or parents, and the roles of males and females in dating. For example, Latino and Asian American cultures have more conservative standards regarding adolescent dating than does the Anglo-American culture.

What are some ethnic variations in dating during adolescence?

Dating may be a source of cultural conflict for many adolescents whose families come from cultures in which dating begins at a late age with little freedom, especially for adolescent girls. One study found that Asian American adolescents were less likely to be involved in a romantic relationship in the past 18 months than African American or Latino adolescents (Carver, Joyner, & Udry, 2003). In another study, Latina young adults in the midwestern United States reflected on their dating experiences during adolescence (Raffaelli & Ontai, 2001). They said that their parents placed strict boundaries on their romantic involvement. As a result, the young women recalled that their adolescent dating experiences were filled with tension and conflict. Over half of the Latinas engaged in "sneak dating" without their parents' knowledge.

Adulthood

Attachment and romantic relationships continue to be very important aspects of close relationships in adulthood. Let's explore attachment first, then different types of love.

Attachment   Earlier in this chapter, we discussed the importance of attachment in childhood and adolescence. How do these earlier patterns of attachment and adults' attachment styles influence the lives of adults?

Although relationships with romantic partners differ from those with parents, romantic partners fulfill some of the same needs for adults as parents do for their children (Mikulincer & Shaver, 2008; Shaver & Mikulincer, 2010). Recall that *securely attached* infants are defined as those who use the caregiver as a secure base from which to explore the environment (Cassidy, 2008). Similarly, adults may count on their romantic partners to be a secure base to which they can return and obtain comfort and security in stressful times (Zeifman & Hazan, 2009).

Do adult attachment patterns with partners reflect childhood attachment patterns with parents? In a retrospective study, Cindy Hazen and Phillip Shaver (1987) revealed that young adults who were securely attached in their romantic relationships were more likely to describe their early relationship with their parents as securely attached. In a longitudinal study, infants who were securely attached at 1 year of age were securely attached 20 years later in their adult romantic relationships (Steele & others, 1998). However, in another longitudinal study, links between early attachment styles and later attachment styles were lessened by stressful and disruptive experiences, such as the death of a parent or instability of caregiving (Lewis, Feiring, & Rosenthal, 2000).

Hazen and Shaver (1987) measured attachment styles using the following brief assessment:

> Read each paragraph and then place a check mark next to the description that best describes you:
>
> _____ 1. I find it relatively easy to get close to others and I am comfortable depending on them and having them depend on me. I don't worry about being abandoned or about someone getting too close to me.
>
> _____ 2. I am somewhat uncomfortable being close to others. I find it difficult to trust them completely and to allow myself to depend on them. I get nervous when anyone gets too close to me and it bothers me when someone tries to be more intimate with me than I feel comfortable with.
>
> _____ 3. I find that others are reluctant to get as close as I would like. I often worry that my partner doesn't really love me or won't want to stay with me. I want to get very close to my partner, and this sometimes scares people away.

What are some key dimensions of attachment in adulthood, and how are they related to relationship patterns and well-being?

These items correspond to three attachment styles—secure attachment (option 1 in list) and two insecure attachment styles (avoidant—option 2 in list, and anxious—option 3 in list):

- **Secure attachment style.** Securely attached adults have positive views of relationships, find it easy to get close to others, and are not overly concerned with, or stressed out about, their romantic relationships. These adults tend to enjoy sexuality in the context of a committed relationship and are less likely than others to have one-night stands.

- **Avoidant attachment style.** Avoidant individuals are hesitant about getting involved in romantic relationships and once in a relationship tend to distance themselves from their partner.

- **Anxious attachment style.** These individuals demand closeness, are less trusting, and are more emotional, jealous, and possessive.

The majority of adults (about 60 to 80 percent) describe themselves as securely attached, and not surprisingly adults prefer having a securely attached partner (Shaver & Mikulincer, 2010; Zeifman & Hazan, 2009).

Researchers are studying links between adults' current attachment styles and many aspects of their lives (Campa, Hazan, & Wolfe, 2009; Cowan & Cowan, 2009; Shaver & Mikulincer, 2010). For example, securely attached adults are more satisfied with their close relationships than insecurely attached adults, and the relationships of securely attached adults are more likely to be characterized by trust, commitment, and longevity (Feeney & Collins, 2007). Securely attached adults also are more likely than insecurely attached adults to provide support when they are distressed and more likely to give support when their partner is distressed (Rholes & Simpson, 2007). Also, one study found that adults with avoidant and anxious attachment styles were more likely to be depressed than securely attached adults (Hankin, Kassel, & Abela, 2005). Another study revealed that women with an anxious or avoidant attachment style and men with an avoidant attachment style were more likely to have unwanted but consensual sexual experiences than securely attached adults (Gentzler & Kerns, 2004). And a recent study of young women revealed a link between having an avoidant attachment pattern and a lower incidence of female orgasm (Cohen & Belsky, 2008).

Recent interest in adult attachment also focuses on ways that genes can affect how adults experience the environment (Diamond, 2009). A recent study examined the link between the serotonin transporter gene (*5-HTTLPR*) and adult unresolved

secure attachment style An attachment style that describes adults who have positive views of relationships, find it easy to get close to others, and are not overly concerned or stressed out about their romantic relationships.

avoidant attachment style An attachment style that describes adults who are hesitant about getting involved in romantic relationships and once in a relationship tend to distance themselves.

anxious attachment style An attachment style that describes adults who demand closeness, are less trusting, and are more emotional, jealous, and possessive.

attachment (Caspers & others, 2009). Unresolved attachment was assessed in an attachment interview and involved such speech patterns as indicating that the deceased parent was still playing a major role in the adult's life and giving excessive detail about the death. In this study, parental loss in early childhood was more likely to result in unresolved attachment in adulthood only for individuals who had the short version of the gene; the long version of the gene apparently provided some protection from the negative psychological effects of parental loss. Recall from Chapter 2, "Biological Beginnings," that this type of research is called gene × environment (G × E) interaction.

A recent research review and conceptualization of attachment by leading experts Mario Mikulincer & Phillip Shaver (2008) concluded the following about the benefits of secure attachment. Individuals who are securely attached have a well-integrated sense of self-acceptance, self-esteem, and self-efficacy. They have the ability to control their emotions, are optimistic, and are resilient. Facing stress and adversity, they activate cognitive representations of security, are mindful of what is happening around them, and mobilize effective coping strategies.

Mikulincer and Shaver's (2008) review also concluded that attachment insecurity places couples at risk for relationship problems. For example, when an anxious individual is paired with an avoidant individual, the anxious partner's needs and demands frustrate the avoidant partner's preference for distance in the relationship; the avoidant partner's need for distance causes stress for the anxious partner's need for closeness. The result: Both partners are unhappy in the relationship, and the anxious-avoidant pairing can produce abuse or violence when a partner criticizes or tries to change the other's behavior. Researchers also have found that when both partners have an anxious attachment pattern, the pairing usually produces dissatisfaction with the marriage and can lead to a mutual attack and retreat in the relationship (Feeney & Monin, 2008). When both partners have an anxious attachment style, they feel misunderstood and rejected, excessively dwell on their own insecurities, and seek to control the other's behavior (Mikulincer & Shaver, 2008; Shaver & Mikulincer, 2010).

If you have an insecure attachment style, are you stuck with it and does it doom you to have problematic relationships? Attachment categories are somewhat stable in adulthood, but adults do have the capacity to change their attachment thinking and behavior. It also is important to note that although attachment insecurities are linked to relationship problems, attachment style makes only a moderate-size contribution to relationship functioning and that other factors such as communication skills, effectively dealing with conflict, friendship, and personality traits such as conscientiousness and emotional instability contribute to relationship satisfaction and success (Mikulincer & Shaver, 2008; Shaver & Mikulincer, 2010).

Romantic Love Think for a moment about songs and books that hit the top of the charts. Chances are, they're about love. Poets, playwrights, and musicians through the ages have lauded the fiery passion of romantic love—and lamented the searing pain when it fails. **Romantic love** is also called *passionate love,* or *eros;* it has strong components of sexuality and infatuation, and it often predominates in the early part of a love relationship.

Well-known love researcher Ellen Berscheid (1988) says that it is romantic love we mean when we say that we are "in love" with someone. It is romantic love, she stresses, that we need to understand if we are to learn what love is all about. According to Berscheid, sexual desire is the most important ingredient of romantic love. We discuss sexuality in more detail in Chapter 12, "Gender and Sexuality."

Romantic love includes a complex intermingling of emotions—fear, anger, sexual desire, joy, and jealousy, for example. Obviously, some of these emotions are a source of anguish. One study found that romantic lovers were more likely than friends to be the cause of depression (Berscheid & Fei, 1977).

romantic love Also called passionate love, or eros, this type of love has strong components of sexuality and infatuation, and it often predominates in the early part of a love relationship.

Recently, romantic attraction has not only taken place in person but also over the Internet. More than 16 million individuals in the United States and 14 million in China have tried online matchmaking (Masters, 2008). Some critics argue that online romantic relationships lose the interpersonal connection, whereas others emphasize that the Internet may benefit shy or anxious individuals who find it difficult to meet potential partners in person (Holmes, Little, & Welsh, 2009). One problem with online matchmaking is that many individuals misconstrue their characteristics, such as how old they are, how attractive they are, and their occupation. Despite such dishonesty, researchers have found that romantic relationships initiated on the Internet are more likely than relationships established in person to last for more than two years (Bargh & McKenna, 2004).

Affectionate Love Love is more than just passion. **Affectionate love,** also called companionate love, is the type of love that occurs when individuals desire to have the other person near and have a deep, caring affection for the person.

There is a growing belief that as love matures, passion tends to give way to affection (Berscheid, 2000; Sternberg & Sternberg, 2010; Weis & Sternberg, 2008). One investigation interviewed 102 happily married couples in early (average age 28), middle (average age 45), and late (average age 65) adulthood to explore the nature of age and sex differences in satisfying love relationships (Reedy, Birren, & Schaie, 1981). As indicated in Figure 10.14, passion and sexual intimacy were more important in early adulthood, and feelings of affection and loyalty were more important in later-life love relationships. Young adult lovers also rated communication as more characteristic of their love than their older counterparts. Aside from the age differences, however, there were some striking similarities in the nature of satisfying love relationships. At all ages, emotional security was ranked as the most important factor in love, followed by respect, communication, help and play behaviors, sexual intimacy, and loyalty. The findings in this research also suggested that women believe emotional security is more important in love than men do.

Sternberg's Triangular Theory of Love Clearly, there is more to satisfying love relationships than sex (Berscheid, 2010). One theory of love that captures this idea was proposed by Robert J. Sternberg (1988). His **triangular theory of love** states that love has three main components or dimensions—passion, intimacy, and commitment (see Figure 10.15):

- *Passion*, as described earlier, is physical and sexual attraction to another.
- *Intimacy* is the emotional feelings of warmth, closeness, and sharing in a relationship.
- *Commitment* is our cognitive appraisal of the relationship and our intent to maintain the relationship even in the face of problems.

According to Sternberg, if passion is the only ingredient (with intimacy and commitment low or absent), we are merely experiencing infatuation. This might happen in an affair or a one-night stand. But varying combinations of the dimensions of love create three qualitatively different types of love:

- A relationship marked by intimacy and commitment but low or lacking in passion is called *affectionate love*, a pattern often found among couples who have been married for many years.

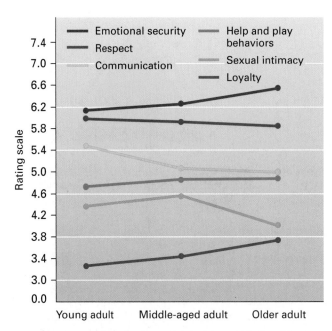

FIGURE 10.14 Changes in Satisfying Love Relationships Across the Adult Years. In the investigation by Reedy, Birren, and Schaie (1981), emotional security was the most important factor in love at all ages. Sexual intimacy was more important in early adulthood, whereas affection and loyalty were more important in the love relationships of older adults. Young adult lovers also rated communication as more important in love than their older counterparts.

affectionate love Also called companionate love, this type of love occurs when individuals desire to have another person near and have a deep, caring affection for the person.

triangular theory of love Sternberg's theory that love includes three types—passion, intimacy, and commitment.

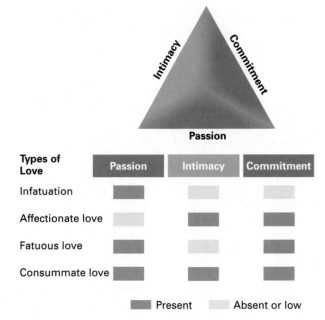

Types of Love	Passion	Intimacy	Commitment
Infatuation	■	□	□
Affectionate love	□	■	■
Fatuous love	■	□	■
Consummate love	■	■	■

■ Present   □ Absent or low

FIGURE 10.15 Sternberg's Triangle of Love. Sternberg identified three dimensions that shape the experience we call love: passion, intimacy, and commitment. Various combinations of the three dimensions produce particular types of love.

• If passion and commitment are present but intimacy is not, Sternberg calls the relationship *fatuous love,* as when one person worships another from a distance.

• If passion, intimacy, and commitment are all strong, the result is *consummate love,* the fullest type of love.

Falling Out of Love The collapse of a close relationship may feel tragic. In the long run, however, our happiness and personal development may benefit from getting over being in love and ending a close relationship.

In particular, falling out of love may be wise if you are obsessed with a person who repeatedly betrays your trust; if you are involved with someone who is draining you emotionally or financially; or if you are desperately in love with someone who does not return your feelings.

Being in love when love is not returned can lead to depression, obsessive thoughts, sexual dysfunction, inability to work effectively, difficulty in making new friends, and self-condemnation. Thinking clearly in such relationships is often difficult, because they are so colored by arousing emotions.

Some people get taken advantage of in relationships (Metts & Cupach, 2007; Tafoya & Spitzberg, 2007). For example, without either person realizing it, a relationship can evolve in a way that creates dominant and submissive roles. Detecting this pattern is an important step toward learning either to reconstruct the relationship or to end it if the problems cannot be worked out. To read further about romantic relationship breakups, see the *Research in Life-Span Development* interlude.

Research in Life-Span Development

PERSONAL GROWTH FOLLOWING A ROMANTIC RELATIONSHIP BREAKUP

Studies of romantic breakups have mainly focused on their negative aspects (Frazier & Cook, 1993; Kato, 2005). Few studies have examined the possibility that a romantic breakup might lead to positive changes.

One study assessed the personal growth that can follow the breakup of a romantic relationship (Tashiro & Frazier, 2003). The participants were 92 undergraduate students who had experienced a relationship breakup in the past nine months. They were asked to describe "what positive changes, if any, have happened as a result of your breakup that might serve to improve your future romantic relationships" (p. 118).

Self-reported positive growth was common following a romantic breakup. Changes were categorized in terms of personal, relational, and environmental changes. The most commonly reported types of growth were personal changes, which included feeling stronger and more self-confident, more independent, and better off emotionally. Relational positive changes included gaining relational wisdom, and environmental positive changes included having better friendships because of the breakup. Figure 10.16 provides examples of these positive changes. Women reported more positive growth than did men.

Change category	Examples of frequently mentioned responses
Personal positives	1. "I am more self-confident." 2. "Through breaking up I found I could handle more on my own." 3. "I didn't always have to be the strong one, it's okay to cry or be upset without having to take care of him."
Relational positives	1. "Better communication." 2. "I learned many relationship skills that I can apply in the future (for example, the importance of saying you're sorry)." 3. "I know not to jump into a relationship too quickly."
Environmental positives	1. "I rely on my friends more. I forgot how important friends are when I was with him." 2. "Concentrate on school more: I can put so much more time and effort toward school." 3. "I believe friends' and family's opinions count—will seek them out in future relationships."

FIGURE 10.16 Examples of Positive Changes in the Aftermath of a Romantic Breakup.

Review and Reflect: Learning Goal 4

  Explain attachment and its development

REVIEW

- What is attachment? How does attachment develop in infancy and childhood? How are caregiving styles related to attachment? How is child care related to children's development?
- How does attachment develop in adolescence? What is the nature of dating and romantic relationships in adolescence?
- What are attachment and love like across the adulthood years?

REFLECT

- How would you describe your attachment style? Why do you think you developed this attachment style?

Reach Your Learning Goals

Emotional Development

1   EXPLORING EMOTION: DISCUSS BASIC ASPECTS OF EMOTION

What Are Emotions?

- Emotion is feeling, or affect, that expresses the pleasantness or unpleasantness of a person's state; it occurs when a person is engaged in an interaction that is important to him or her, especially to his or her well-being. Emotions can be classified as positive or negative and vary in intensity. Today, psychologists note that emotions have both a biological foundation and are influenced by an individual's experiences. Biological evolution endowed humans to be emotional, but culture and relationships with others provide diversity in emotional experiences.

Regulation of Emotion

- The ability to control one's emotions is a key dimension of development. Emotional regulation consists of effectively managing arousal to adapt and reach a goal. In infancy and early childhood, regulation of emotion gradually shifts from external sources to self-initiated, internal sources. Also with increasing age, children are more likely to increase their use of cognitive strategies for regulating emotion, modulate their emotional arousal, become more adept at managing situations to minimize negative emotion, and choose effective ways to cope with stress. Emotion-coaching parents have children who engage in more effective self-regulation of their emotions than do emotion-dismissing parents.

Emotional Competence

- Saarni argues that becoming emotionally competent involves developing a number of skills such as being aware of one's emotional states, discerning others' emotions, adaptively coping with negative emotions, and understanding the role of emotions in relationships.

2   DEVELOPMENT OF EMOTION: DESCRIBE THE DEVELOPMENT OF EMOTION THROUGH THE LIFE SPAN

Infancy

- Infants display a number of emotions early in the first six months, including sadness, surprise, interest, joy, fear, and anger—although researchers debate the onset and sequence of these emotions. Lewis distinguishes between primary emotions and self-conscious emotions. Crying is the most important mechanism newborns have for communicating with their world. Babies have at least three types of cries—basic, anger, and pain cries. Controversy swirls about whether babies should be soothed when they cry, although increasingly experts recommend immediately responding in a caring way in the first year. Social smiling in response to a caregiver's voice occurs as early as 4 to 6 weeks of age. Two fears that infants develop are stranger anxiety and separation from a caregiver (which is reflected in separation protest).

Early Childhood

- Advances in young children's emotions involve expressing emotions, understanding emotions, and regulating emotions. Young children's range of emotions expands during early childhood as they increasingly experience self-conscious emotions such as pride, shame, and guilt. Between 2 and 4 years of age, children use an increasing number of terms to describe emotion and learn more about the causes and consequences of feelings. At 4 to 5 years of age, children show an increased ability to reflect on emotions and understand that a single event can elicit different emotions in different people.

Middle and Late Childhood

- In middle and late childhood, children show a growing awareness about controlling and managing emotions to meet social standards. Also in this age period, they show improved emotional understanding, markedly improve their ability to suppress or conceal negative emotions, use self-initiated strategies for redirecting feelings, have an increased tendency to take into fuller account the events that lead to emotional reactions, and develop a genuine capacity for empathy.

Adolescence

- As individuals go through early adolescence, they are less likely to report being very happy. Moodiness is a normal aspect of early adolescence. Although pubertal change is associated with an increase in negative emotions, hormonal influences are often small, and environmental experiences may contribute more to the emotions of adolescence than hormonal changes.

Adult Development and Aging

- Older adults are better at controlling their emotions than younger adults are, and older adults experience more positive and less negative emotions than younger adults do. An important theory regarding developmental changes in emotion during adulthood, especially late adulthood, is Carstensen's socioemotional selectivity theory. Knowledge-related and emotion-related goals change across the life span; emotion-related goals become more important when individuals get older.

3 TEMPERAMENT: CHARACTERIZE VARIATIONS IN TEMPERAMENT AND THEIR SIGNIFICANCE

Describing and Classifying Temperament

- Temperament is an individual's behavioral style and characteristic way of responding. Developmentalists are especially interested in the temperament of infants. Chess and Thomas classified infants as (1) easy, (2) difficult, or (3) slow to warm up. Kagan argues that inhibition to the unfamiliar is an important temperament category. Rothbart and Bates' view of temperament emphasizes this classification: (1) extraversion/surgency, (2) negative affectivity, and (3) effortful control (self-regulation).

Biological Foundations and Experience

- Physiological characteristics are associated with different temperaments, and a moderate influence of heredity has been found in studies of the heritability of temperament. Children inherit a physiology that biases them to have a particular type of temperament, but through experience they learn to modify their temperament style to some degree. Very active young children are likely to become outgoing adults. In some cases, a difficult temperament at 3 to 5 years of age is linked with adjustment problems in early adulthood. The link between childhood temperament and adult personality depends in part on context, which helps shape the reaction to a child and thus the child's experiences. For example, the reaction to a child's temperament depends in part on the child's gender and on the culture.

Goodness of Fit and Parenting

- Goodness of fit refers to the match between a child's temperament and the environmental demands the child must cope with. Goodness of fit can be an important aspect of a child's adjustment. Although research evidence is sketchy at this point in time, some general recommendations are that caregivers should (1) be sensitive to the individual characteristics of the child, (2) be flexible in responding to these characteristics, and (3) avoid negative labeling of the child.

4 ATTACHMENT AND LOVE: EXPLAIN ATTACHMENT AND ITS DEVELOPMENT

Infancy and Childhood

- Attachment is a close emotional bond between two people. Infants show a strong interest in the social world and are motivated to understand it. Infants orient to the social world early in their development. Face-to-face play with a caregiver begins to occur at about 2 to 3 months of age. Newly developed self-produced locomotion skills significantly expand the infant's ability to initiate social interchanges and explore its social world more independently. Perceiving people as engaging in intentional and goal-directed behavior is an important social cognitive accomplishment, and this occurs toward the end of the first year. Social referencing increases in the second year of life. In infancy, contact comfort and trust are important in the development of attachment. Bowlby's ethological theory stresses that the caregiver and the infant are biologically predisposed to form an attachment. Attachment develops in four phases during infancy. Securely attached babies use the caregiver, usually the mother, as a secure base from which to explore the environment. Three types of insecure attachment are avoidant, resistant, and disorganized. Ainsworth created the Strange Situation, an observational measure of attachment. Ainsworth notes that secure attachment in the first year of life provides an important foundation for psychological development later in life. The strength of the link between early attachment and later development has varied somewhat across studies. Some critics argue that attachment theorists have not given adequate attention to genetics and temperament. Other critics stress that they have not adequately taken into account the diversity of socializing agents and contexts. Cultural variations in attachment have been found, but in all cultures studied to date secure attachment is the most common classification. Caregivers of secure babies are sensitive to the babies' signals and are consistently available to meet their needs. Caregivers of avoidant babies tend to be unavailable or rejecting. Caregivers of resistant babies tend to be inconsistently available to their babies and usually are not very affectionate. Caregivers of disorganized babies often neglect or physically abuse their babies. Increased interest is occurring in the role of the brain in the development of attachment. The hormone oxytocin is a key candidate for influencing the development of maternal-infant attachment. The mother's primary role when interacting with the infant is caregiving; the father's is playful interaction. More U.S. children are in child care now than at any earlier point in history. The quality of child care is uneven, and child care remains a controversial topic. Quality child care can be achieved and seems to have few adverse effects on children. In the NICHD child-care study, infants from low-income families were more likely to receive the lowest quality of care. Also, higher quality of child care was linked with fewer child problems.

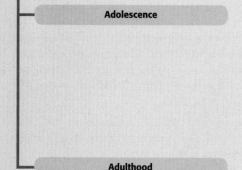

Adolescence

- Securely attached adolescents are referred to as secure-autonomous, whereas insecurely attached adolescents are referred to as dismissing-avoidant, preoccupied-ambivalent, or unresolved-disorganized. Dating, or thinking about dating, becomes an important aspect of many adolescents' lives. Three stages characterize the development of romantic relationships in adolescence: (1) entry into romantic attractions and affiliations at about 11 to 13 years of age, (2) exploring romantic relationships at approximately 14 to 16 years of age, and (3) consolidating dyadic romantic bonds at about 17 to 19 years of age. Early dating is associated with developmental problems. Culture can exert a powerful influence on dating.

Adulthood

- Three adult attachment styles are secure attachment, avoidant attachment, and anxious attachment. Attachment styles in early adulthood are linked with a number of relationship patterns and developmental outcomes. For example, securely attached adults often show more positive relationship patterns than insecurely attached adults. Also, adults with avoidant and anxious attachment styles tend to be more depressed and have more relationship problems than securely attached adults. Romantic love and affectionate love are two important types of love. Romantic love tends to be more important in early adulthood; affectionate love is more likely to be important in later-life love relationships. Sternberg proposed a triangular theory of love that focuses on different combinations of (1) passion, (2) intimacy, and (3) commitment. The collapse of a close relationship can be traumatic, but for some individuals it results in increased self-confidence, relational wisdom, and being better off emotionally. For most individuals, falling out of love is painful and emotionally intense.

KEY TERMS

emotion 344	socioemotional selectivity theory 354	securely attached babies 364	unresolved-disorganized attachment 372
primary emotions 347	temperament 355	insecure avoidant babies 364	secure attachment style 375
self-conscious emotions 347	easy child 355	insecure resistant babies 364	avoidant attachment style 375
basic cry 348	difficult child 355	insecure disorganized babies 364	anxious attachment style 375
anger cry 348	slow-to-warm-up child 355	dismissing-avoidant attachment 372	romantic love 376
pain cry 348	goodness of fit 358	preoccupied-ambivalent attachment 372	affectionate love 377
reflexive smile 348	attachment 360		triangular theory of love 377
social smile 348	social referencing 362		
stranger anxiety 349	Strange Situation 364		
separation protest 349			

KEY PEOPLE

Joseph Campos 344	John Bowlby 350	Mary Rothbart and John Bates 356	Kathleen McCartney 371
Ross Thompson 346	Reed Larson and Maryse Richards 353	Harry Harlow 362	Cindy Hazen and Phillip Shaver 374
Carolyn Saarni 346	Laura Carstensen 354	Erik Erikson 363	Mario Mikulincer 376
Michael Lewis 347	Alexander Chess and Stella Thomas 355	Mary Ainsworth 364	Ellen Berscheid 376
Daniel Messinger 349	Jerome Kagan 356	Alan Sroufe 365	Robert J. Sternberg 377
John Watson 350		Sheila Kammerman 368	
Mary Ainsworth 350			

E-LEARNING TOOLS

Connect to **www.mhhe.com/santrockldt5e** to research the answers and complete these exercises. In addition, you'll find a number of other resources and valuable study tools for Chapter 10, "Emotional Development," on this Web site.

Taking It to the Net

1. Rebecca, a 20-year-old single mother, has had her 6-week-old daughter, who was born prematurely, home for a week. She tells her mother that the infant is the fussiest child she has ever seen. "I can see she is going to be a difficult child," Rebecca says. Is there some connection between premature birth and a fussy temperament?

2. Sam is a 4-year-old who has been having temper tantrums since the age of 2. His parents are concerned about Sam's continuing behavior problems. They would like to try some new strategies to help Sam behave appropriately.

3. Alan and Tina adopted Ben when he was a toddler. As he approaches adolescence, Alan and Tina wonder if he will face any special challenges during this period of his development. They have heard about adopted children who have had great difficulty during the adolescent years. Is there anything they can do to help Ben through this time in his life?

Self-Assessment

To explore attachment and romantic relationships in your life, complete these self-assessments:

- *My Attachment Style*
- *Am I Ready for a Committed Relationship?*
- *Am I a Giver or a Taker in a Romantic Relationship?*
- *What Is My Love Like?*
- *The Characteristics I Desire in a Potential Mate*

Health and Well-Being, Parenting, and Education

Build your decision-making skills by trying your hand at the health and well-being, parenting, and education exercises.

Video Clips

The Online Learning Center includes the following videos for this chapter:

- *Attachment Theory*
- *Adolescent and Parent Emotions*
- *Attachment in Early Childhood*

11

When I say "I," I mean something absolutely unique not to be confused with any other.

—UGO BETTI
Italian Playwright, 20th Century

LEARNING GOALS

- ◆ Discuss the main ways the self is conceptualized.

- ◆ Explain the key facets of identity development.

- ◆ Describe personality and its development in adulthood.

THE SELF, IDENTITY, AND PERSONALITY

CHAPTER OUTLINE

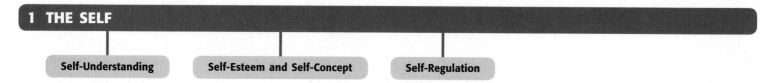

1 THE SELF

Self-Understanding | **Self-Esteem and Self-Concept** | **Self-Regulation**

What do we mean by the concepts of self, identity, and personality? Here are the definitions, and as you will see, there is considerable overlap in them:

- The **self** is all of the characteristics of a person.
- **Identity** is who a person is, representing a synthesis and integration of self-understanding.
- **Personality** refers to the enduring personal characteristics of individuals. Personality is usually viewed as the broadest of the three domains and as encompassing the other two (self and identity).

Theorists and researchers who focus on the self usually argue that the self is the central aspect of the individual's personality and that the self lends an integrative dimension to our understanding of different personality characteristics (Thompson & Goodman, 2009; Thompson & Goodvin, 2005). Several aspects of the self have been studied more than others. These include self-understanding, self-esteem, and self-concept. Let's now turn our attention to how these aspects of the self develop across the human life span.

Self-Understanding

What is self-understanding? **Self-understanding** is the cognitive representation of the self, the substance of self-conceptions. For example, an 11-year-old boy understands that he is a student, a boy, a football player, a family member, a video game lover, and a rock music fan. A 13-year-old girl understands that she is a middle school student, in the midst of puberty, a girl, a soccer player, a student council member, and a movie fan. Self-understanding is based, in part, on roles and membership categories (Harter, 2006). It provides the underpinnings for the development of identity. How does self-understanding develop across the life span?

Infancy   According to leading expert Ross Thompson (2007), studying the self in infancy is difficult mainly because infants cannot tell us how they experience themselves. Infants cannot verbally express their views of the self. They also cannot understand complex instructions from researchers.

A rudimentary form of self-recognition—being attentive and positive toward one's image in a mirror—appears as early as 3 months of age (Mascolo & Fischer, 2007). However, a central, more complete index of self-recognition—the ability to recognize one's physical features—does not emerge until the second year (Thompson, 2006).

One ingenious strategy to test infants' visual self-recognition is the use of a mirror technique, in which first an infant's mother puts a dot of rouge on the

> *The living self has one purpose only: to come into its own fullness of being, as a tree comes into full blossom, or a bird into spring beauty, or a tiger into lustre.*
>
> **—D. H. Lawrence**
> *English Author, 20th Century*

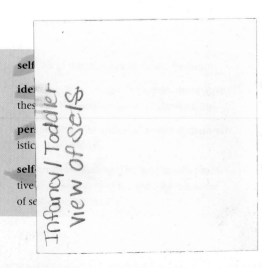

infant's nose. Then an observer watches to see how often the infant touches its nose. Next, the infant is placed in front of a mirror, and observers detect whether nose touching increases. Why does this matter? The idea is that increased nose touching indicates that the infant recognizes the self in the mirror and is trying to touch or rub off the rouge because the rouge violates the infant's view of the self. Increased touching indicates that the infant realizes that it is the self in the mirror but that something is not right since the real self does not have a dot of rouge on it.

Figure 11.1 displays the results of two investigations that used the mirror technique. The researchers found that before they were 1 year old, infants did not recognize themselves in the mirror (Amsterdam, 1968; Lewis & Brooks-Gunn, 1979). Signs of self-recognition began to appear among some infants when they were 15 to 18 months old. By the time they were 2 years old, most children recognized themselves in the mirror. In sum, infants begin to develop a self-understanding called self-recognition at approximately 18 months of age (Hart & Karmel, 1996).

In one study, biweekly assessments from 15 to 23 months of age were conducted (Courage, Edison, & Howe, 2004). Self-recognition gradually emerged over this time, first appearing in the form of mirror recognition, followed by use of the personal pronoun and then by recognizing a photo of themselves. These aspects of self-recognition are often referred to as the first indications of toddlers' understanding of the mental state of "me"—"that they are objects in their own mental representation of the world" (Lewis, 2005, p. 363).

Late in the second year and early in the third year, toddlers show other emerging forms of self-awareness that reflect a sense of me (Thompson, 2006). For example, they refer to themselves such as by saying "Me big"; they label their internal experiences such as emotions; they monitor themselves as when a toddler says, "Me do it"; and say that things are theirs (Bullock & Lutkenhaus, 1990; Fasig, 2000).

Early Childhood   Recent research studies have revealed that young children are more psychologically aware—of themselves and others—than used to be thought (Laible & Thompson, 2007; Thompson & Goodman, 2009). This increased psychological awareness reflects young children's expanding psychological sophistication.

Self-Understanding   Because children can verbally communicate, research on self-understanding in childhood is not limited to visual self-recognition, as it is during infancy. Mainly through interviews, researchers have probed many aspects of children's self-understanding. Here are five main characteristics of self-understanding in young children:

- *Confusion of self, mind, and body.* Young children generally confuse self, mind, and body. Most young children conceive of the self as part of the body, which usually means the head. For them, the self can be described along many material dimensions, such as size, shape, and color.

- *Concrete descriptions.* Preschool children mainly think of themselves and define themselves in concrete terms. A young child might say, "I know my ABC's," "I can count," and "I live in a big house" (Harter, 2006). Although young children mainly describe themselves in terms of concrete, observable features and action tendencies, at about 4 to 5 years of age, as they hear others use psychological trait and emotion terms, they begin to include these in their own self-descriptions (Thompson, 2006). Thus, in a self-description, a 4-year-old might say, "I'm not scared. I'm always happy."

- *Physical descriptions.* Young children also distinguish themselves from others through many physical and material attributes. Says 4-year-old Sandra, "I'm different from Jennifer because I have brown hair and she has blond hair." Says 4-year-old Ralph, "I am different from Hank because I am taller, and I am different from my sister because I have a bicycle."

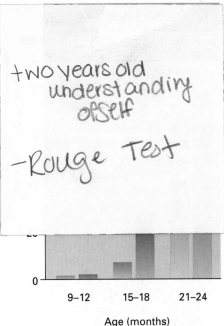

FIGURE 11.1 **The Development of Self-Recognition in Infancy.** The graph shows the findings of two studies in which infants less than 1 year of age did not recognize themselves in the mirror. A slight increase in the percentage of infant self-recognition occurred around 15 to 18 months of age. By 2 years of age, a majority of children recognized themselves. *Why do researchers study whether infants recognize themselves in a mirror?*

- *Active descriptions.* The *active dimension* is a central component of the self in early childhood. For example, preschool children often describe themselves in terms of activities such as play.

- *Unrealistic positive overestimations.* Self-evaluations during early childhood are often unrealistically positive and represent an overestimation of personal attributes (Harter, 2006). A young child might say, "I know all of my ABC's" but does not; or might comment, "I'm never scared," which is not the case. These unrealistic positive overestimations of the self occur because young children (1) have difficulty in differentiating their desired and actual competence, (2) cannot yet generate an ideal self that is distinguished from a real self, and (3) rarely engage in *social comparison*—how they compare with others. Young children's self-evaluations also reflect an inability to recognize that they can possess opposite attributes, such as "good" and "bad" or "nice" and "mean" (Harter, 2006).

Always unrealistically positive.

Young children's self-descriptions are typically unrealistically positive, as reflected in the comment of the 4-year-old above who says he is always happy, which he is not (Harter, 2006). These occur because the children don't yet distinguish between their desired competence and their actual competence, tend to confuse ability and effort (thinking that differences in ability can be changed as easily as can differences in effort), don't engage in spontaneous social comparison of their abilities with those of others, and tend to compare their present abilities with what they could do at an earlier age (by which they usually look quite good). Perhaps as adults we should all be so optimistic about our abilities (Thompson, 2008)!

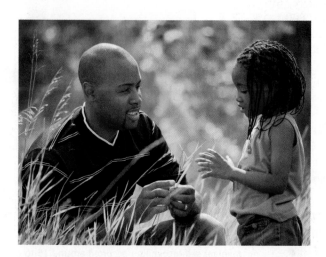

Young children are more psychologically aware of themselves and others than used to be thought. Some children are better than others at understanding people's feelings and desires, and to some degree, these individual differences are influenced by conversations caregivers have with young children about feelings and desires.

Understanding Others   Children also make advances in their understanding of others in early childhood (Heyman, 2008). As we saw in Chapter 7, "Information Processing," young children's theory of mind includes understanding that other people have emotions and desires. And, at about 4 to 5 years, children not only start describing themselves in terms of psychological traits, but they also begin to perceive others in terms of psychological traits. Thus, a 4-year-old might say, "My teacher is nice."

Something important for children to develop is an understanding that people don't always give accurate reports of their beliefs (Heyman, 2008). Researchers have found that even 4-year-olds realize that people may make statements that aren't true to obtain what they want or to avoid trouble (Lee & others, 2002). For example, one recent study revealed that 4- and 5-year-olds were increasingly skeptical of another child's claim to be sick when the children were informed that the child was motivated to avoid having to go to camp (Gee & Heyman, 2007).

Individual differences characterize young children's social understanding (Thompson, 2006). Some young children are better than others at understanding what people are feeling and what they desire, for example. To some degree, these individual differences are linked to conversations caregivers have with young children about other people's feelings and desires, and children's opportunities to observe others talking about people's feelings and desires. For example, a mother might say to her 3-year-old, "You should think about Raphael's feelings next time before you hit him."

Middle and Late Childhood   Children's self-understanding becomes more complex during middle and late childhood. And their social understanding, especially in taking the perspective of others, also increases.

Self-Understanding   Five key changes characterize the increased complexity in children's self-understanding in middle and late childhood:

- *Psychological characteristics and traits.* In middle and late childhood, especially from 8 to 11 years of age, children increasingly describe themselves with psychological characteristics and traits in contrast to the more concrete self-descriptions of younger children. Older children are more likely to describe themselves as *"popular, nice, helpful, mean, smart,* and *dumb"* (Harter, 2006, p. 526).

- *Social descriptions.* In middle and late childhood, children begin to include *social aspects* such as references to social groups in their self-descriptions (Harter, 2006). For example, children might describe themselves as Girl Scouts, as Catholics, or as someone who has two close friends.

- *Social comparison.* Children's self-understanding in middle and late childhood includes increasing reference to social comparison (Harter, 2006). That is, elementary-school-age children increasingly think about what they can do *in comparison with others.*

- *Real self and ideal self.* In middle and late childhood, children begin to distinguish between their real and ideal selves (Harter, 2006). This change involves differentiating their actual competencies from those they aspire to have and think are the most important.

- *Realistic.* In middle and late childhood, children's self-evaluations become more realistic (Harter, 2006). This change may occur because of increased social comparison and perspective taking.

Understanding Others   Earlier we described the advances and limitations of young children's understanding of others. In middle and late childhood, children show an increase in **perspective taking,** the ability to assume other people's perspectives and understand their thoughts and feelings. In Robert Selman's (1980) view, at about 6 to 8 years of age, children begin to understand that others may have a perspective because some people have more access to information. Then, he says, in the next several years, children become aware that each individual is aware of the other's perspective and that putting one's self in the other's place is a way of judging the other person's intentions, purposes, and actions.

Perspective taking is especially thought to be important in whether children develop prosocial or antisocial attitudes and behavior. In terms of prosocial behavior, taking another's perspective improves children's likelihood of understanding and sympathizing with others when they are distressed or in need (Eisenberg, Fabes, & Spinrad, 2006). In terms of antisocial behavior, some researchers have found that children who have a low level of perspective-taking skills engage in more antisocial behavior than children at higher levels (Chandler, 1973).

In middle and late childhood, children also become more skeptical of others' claims. Earlier, we indicated that even 4-year-old children show some skepticism of others' claims. In middle and late childhood, children become increasingly wary of some sources of information about psychological traits. For example, in one study, 10- to 11-year-olds were more likely to reject other children's self-reports that they were *smart* and *honest* than were 6- to 7-year-olds (Heyman & Legare, 2005). The more psychologically sophisticated 10- to 11-year-olds also showed a better understanding than the 6- to 7-year-olds that others' self-reports may involve socially desirable tendencies.

What are some changes in children's understanding of others in middle and late childhood?

perspective taking The ability to assume another person's perspective and understand his or her thoughts and feelings.

Adolescence   The development of self-understanding in adolescence is complex and involves a number of aspects of the self (Harter, 1998, 2006). The tendency to

How does self-understanding change in adolescence?

compare themselves with others continues to increase in the adolescent years. However, when asked whether they engage in social comparison, most adolescents deny it because they are aware that it is somewhat socially undesirable to do so. Let's examine other ways in which the adolescent's self-understanding differs from the child's:

• *Abstract and idealistic thinking.* Remember from our discussion of Piaget's theory of cognitive development in Chapter 6, "Cognitive Developmental Approaches," that many adolescents begin to think in more *abstract* and *idealistic* ways. When asked to describe themselves, adolescents are more likely than children to use abstract and idealistic labels. Consider 14-year-old Laurie's abstract description of herself: "I am a human being. I am indecisive. I don't know who I am." Also consider her idealistic description of herself: "I am a naturally sensitive person who really cares about people's feelings. I think I'm pretty good looking."

• *Self-consciousness.* Adolescents are more likely than children to be *self-conscious* about and *preoccupied* with their self-understanding. This self-consciousness and self-preoccupation reflect adolescent egocentrism, which we discussed in Chapter 6.

• *Contradictions within the self.* As adolescents begin to differentiate their concept of the self into multiple roles in different relationship contexts, they sense potential contradictions between their differentiated selves (Harter, 2006). An adolescent might use this self-description: "I'm moody *and* understanding, ugly *and* attractive, bored *and* inquisitive, caring *and* uncaring, and introverted *and* fun-loving" (Harter, 1986). Young adolescents tend to view these opposing characteristics as contradictory, which can cause internal conflict. However, older adolescents and emerging adults begin to understand why an individual can possess opposing characteristics and integrate these opposing self-labels into their emerging identity (Harter, 2006).

• *The fluctuating self.* The adolescent's self-understanding fluctuates across situations and across time (Harter, 2006). The adolescent's self continues to be characterized by instability until the adolescent constructs a more unified theory of self, usually not until late adolescence or even early adulthood.

What characterizes adolescents' possible selves?

• *Real and ideal selves.* The adolescent's emerging ability to construct ideal selves in addition to actual ones can be perplexing and agonizing to the adolescent. In one view, an important aspect of the ideal or imagined self is the possible self—what individuals might become, what they would like to become, and what they are afraid of (Markus & Nurius, 1986). Thus, adolescents' **possible selves** include both what adolescents hope to be as well as what they dread they will become. The attributes of future positive selves (getting into a good college, being admired, having a successful career) can direct future positive states. The attributes of future negative selves (being unemployed, being lonely, not getting into a good college) can identify what is to be avoided.

• *Self-integration.* In late adolescence and emerging adulthood, self-understanding becomes more *integrative,* with the disparate parts of the self more systematically pieced together (Harter, 2006). Older adolescents are more likely to detect inconsistencies in their earlier self-descriptions as they attempt to construct a general theory of self, an integrated sense of identity.

To read further about the important concept of multiple selves and culture in adolescence, see the *Contexts of Life-Span Development* interlude.

possible selves What adolescents hope to become as well as what they dread they will become.

Contexts of Life-Span Development

MULTIPLE SELVES AND SOCIOCULTURAL CONTEXTS

Differentiation of the self increases across the childhood, adolescent, and adult periods of development (Harter, 2006). Adolescents' portraits of themselves can change, depending on their ethnic and cultural background and experiences.

The multiple selves of ethnically diverse youth reflect their experiences in navigating their multiple worlds of family, peers, school, and community (Rossiter, 2009). Research with American youth of African, Chinese, Filipino, Latino, European, Japanese, and Vietnamese descent, as well as Japanese youth, shows that as youth move across cultural worlds, they can encounter barriers related to language, racism, gender, immigration, and poverty. In each of their different worlds, they might also find resources in other people, in institutions, and in themselves. Youth who find it too difficult to move between worlds can become alienated from their school, family, and peers. However, youth who effectively navigate their various worlds can develop bicultural or multicultural selves and become "culture brokers" for others.

Hazel Markus and her colleagues (1999) stress that it is important to understand how multiple selves emerge through participation in cultural practices. They argue that all selves are culture-specific selves that emerge as individuals adapt to their cultural environments. Markus and her colleagues recognize that cultural groups are characterized by diversity; nonetheless, they conclude that it is helpful to understand the dominant aspects of multiple selves within a culture. Mainstream North American culture promotes and maintains individuality. North Americans, when given the opportunity to describe themselves, often provide not only portraits of their current selves but also notions of their future selves. They also frequently show a need to have multiple selves that are stable and consistent. In Japan, multiple selves are often described in terms of relatedness to others. Self-improvement also is an important aspect of the multiple selves of many Japanese.

How might sociocultural contexts be involved in adolescents' multiple selves?

Adulthood   As individuals move into the traditional college-age years and make the transition from adolescence to adulthood, they begin to engage in more self-reflection about what they want to do with their lives. The extended schooling that takes place in developed countries like the United States and Japan provides time for further self-reflection and understanding of one's self.

Self-Awareness   An aspect of self-understanding that becomes especially important in early adulthood is *self-awareness*—that is, how much a young adult is aware of his or her psychological makeup, including strengths and weaknesses. Many individuals do not have very good awareness of their psychological makeup and skills. For example, how aware is the person that she or he is a good or bad listener, uses the best strategies to solve personal problems, and is assertive rather than aggressive or passive in resolving conflicts? Awareness of strengths and weaknesses in these and many other aspects of life is an important dimension of self-understanding throughout the adult years, and early adulthood is a time when individuals can benefit considerably from improving some of their weaknesses.

Possible Selves   Another aspect of self-understanding that is important in the adult years involves possible selves. Recall that *possible selves* are what individuals might become, what they would like to become, and what they are afraid of becoming (Hoppmann & others, 2007). Adults in their twenties

What characterizes self-awareness and possible selves in young adults?

mention many possible selves that they would like to become and might become. Some of these are unrealistic, such as being happy all of the time and being very rich. As individuals get older, they often describe fewer possible selves and portray them in more concrete and realistic ways. By middle age, individuals frequently describe their possible selves in terms of areas of their life in which they already have performed, such as "being good at my work" or "having a good marriage" (Cross & Markus, 1991). Also, for some individuals, as middle-aged adults, their possible selves center on attaining hoped-for selves, such as acquiring material possessions, but as older adults, they become more concerned with maintaining what they have and preventing or avoiding health problems and dependency (Smith, 2009).

Many individuals continue to revise their possible selves as they go through the adult years. This ability to revise possible selves and adapt them to find a better match between desired and achieved goals may be an important aspect of maintaining positive self-esteem and psychological well-being as individuals get older (Bengtson, Reedy, & Gordon, 1985).

One recent study of older adults (mean age, 81) revealed that hope-related activities had more positive affect and a higher probability of survival over a ten-year period (Hoppmann & others, 2007). Also in this study, hoped-for selves were linked to more likely participation in these domains.

Life Review Another important aspect of self-understanding in adulthood is the *life review*. Life review is prominent in Erikson's final stage of integrity versus despair. Life review involves looking back at one's life experiences, evaluating them, interpreting them, and often reinterpreting them. A leading expert on aging, Robert Butler, recently provided this perspective on life review: ". . . there are chances for pain, anger, guilt, and grief, but there are also opportunities for resolution and celebration, for affirmation and hope, for reconciliation and personal growth" (Butler, 2007, p. 72).

Butler (2007) states that the life review is set in motion by looking forward to death. Sometimes the life review proceeds quietly, at other times it is intense, requiring considerable work to achieve some sense of personality integration. The life review may be observed initially in stray and insignificant thoughts about oneself and one's life history. These thoughts may continue to emerge in brief intermittent spurts or become essentially continuous.

Life reviews can include sociocultural dimensions, such as culture, ethnicity, and gender (Lai, 2007). Life reviews also can include interpersonal, relationship dimensions, including sharing and intimacy with family members or a friend. And life reviews can include personal dimensions, which might involve the creation and discovery of meaning and coherence. These personal dimensions might unfold in such a way that the pieces do or don't make sense to the older adult. In the final analysis, each person's life review is to some degree unique.

As the past marches in review, the older adult surveys it, observes it, and reflects on it (Haber, 2007). Reconsideration of previous experiences and their meaning occurs, often with revision or expanded understanding taking place. This reorganization of the past may provide a more valid picture for the individual, providing new and significant meaning to one's life. It may also help prepare the individual for death, in the process reducing fear.

One aspect of life review involves identifying and reflecting on not only the positive aspects of one's life but also on regrets as part of developing a mature wisdom and self-understanding (Choi & Jun, 2009). The hope is that by examining not only the positive aspects of one's life, but also what an individual has regretted doing, a more accurate vision of the complexity of one's life and possibly increased life satisfaction will be attained (King & Hicks, 2007).

Following is a sampling of recent studies on regrets in older adults:

- For low-income older adults, regrets about education, careers, and marriage were common, but the intensity of regrets was greater for finance/money,

What characterizes a life review in late adulthood?

family conflict and children's problems, loss and grief, and health (Choi & Jun, 2009). Common indications of pride involved children and parenting, careers, volunteering/informal caregiving, having a long/strong marriage, and personal growth.

- Making downward social comparisons, such as "I'm better off than most people," was linked to a reduction in the intensity of regrets in older adults (Bauer, Wrosch, & Jobin, 2008).

- Following the death of a loved one, resolving regrets was related to lower depression and improved well-being (Torges, Stewart, & Nolen-Hoeksema, 2008). In this study, older adults were more likely to resolve their regrets than were younger adults.

Some clinicians use *reminiscence therapy* with their older clients. Reminiscence therapy involves discussing past activities and experiences with another individual or group (Wang, 2007). The therapy may include the use of photographs, familiar items, and video/audio recordings. Some research indicates that reminiscence therapy improves the mood of older adults (Fiske, Wetherell, & Gatz, 2009).

Successful aging, though, doesn't mean thinking about the past all of the time. In one study, older adults who were obsessed about the past were less well adjusted than older adults who integrated their past and present (Wong & Watt, 1991).

Self-Esteem and Self-Concept

High self-esteem and a positive self-concept are important characteristics of children's and adults' well-being (Kaplan, 2009; Orth & others, 2008). **Self-esteem** refers to global evaluations of the self. Self-esteem is also referred to as *self-worth*, or *self-image*. For example, a person may perceive that she or he is not merely a person but a *good* person. Of course, not all people have an overall positive image of themselves. **Self-concept** refers to domain-specific evaluations of the self. Individuals can make self-evaluations in many domains of their lives—academic, athletic, appearance, and so on. In sum, *self-esteem* refers to global self-evaluations, *self-concept* to domain-specific evaluations (Harter, 2006).

Investigators sometimes use the terms *self-esteem* and *self-concept* interchangeably and don't always precisely define them (Donnellan & Robins, 2009). However, the distinction between self-esteem as global self-evaluation and self-concept as domain-specific self-evaluation should help you keep the terms straight.

Issues in Self-Esteem Is self-esteem related to school and adult job performance? There are "only modest correlations between school performance and self-esteem, and these correlations do not indicate that high self-esteem causes good performance" (Baumeister & others, 2003, p. 1). Attempts to increase students' self-esteem have not produced improved academic performance (Davies & Brember, 1999).

In some studies, adult job performance is linked to self-esteem, but the correlations vary greatly and the direction of the causation is not clear (Baumeister & others, 2003). Occupational success might lead to higher self-esteem, but the opposite might occur.

Is self-esteem linked to initiative? Individuals with high self-esteem have greater initiative, and this can produce positive or negative outcomes (Baumeister & others, 2003). High-self-esteem individuals are prone to both prosocial and antisocial actions.

Is self-esteem related to happiness? Self-esteem is strongly related to happiness, and it seems likely that high self-esteem increases happiness, whereas depression lowers it (Baumeister & others, 2003; Van Voorhees & others, 2008).

How is self-esteem related to school performance?

self-esteem The global evaluative dimension of the self. Self-esteem is also referred to as self-worth, or self-image.

self-concept Domain-specific evaluations of the self.

Domain	Harter's U.S. Samples	Other Countries
Physical Appearance	.65	.62
Scholastic Competence	.48	.41
Social Acceptance	.46	.40
Behavioral Conduct	.45	.45
Athletic Competence	.33	.30

FIGURE 11.2 Correlations Between Global Self-Esteem and Domains of Competence. *Note:* The correlations shown are the average correlations computed across a number of studies. The other countries in this evaluation were England, Ireland, Australia, Canada, Germany, Italy, Greece, the Netherlands, and Japan. Recall from Chapter 1 that correlation coefficients can range from −1.00 to +1.00. The correlations between physical appearance and global self-esteem (.65 and .62) are moderately high.

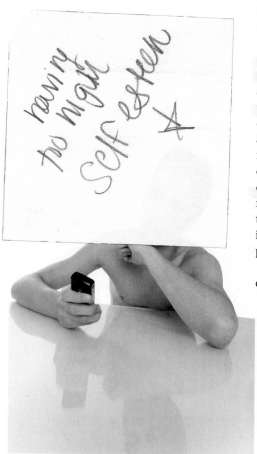

What characterizes narcissistic individuals?

narcissism A self-centered and self-concerned approach toward others.

Is self-esteem related to physical appearance? Self-esteem is related to perceived physical appearance. For example, researchers have found that in adolescence, global self-esteem is correlated more strongly with physical appearance than scholastic competence, social acceptance, behavioral conduct, and athletic competence (Harter, 1999) (see Figure 11.2). This association between perceived physical appearance is not confined to adolescence but holds across the life span from early childhood through middle age (Harter, 1999, 2006).

Is self-esteem linked to depression? A large number of studies have found that individuals with low self-esteem report that they feel more depressed than individuals with high self-esteem (Baumeister & others, 2003). A recent study found that low self-esteem in childhood was linked with depression in adolescence and early adulthood (Orth, Robins, & Roberts, 2008). Low self-esteem has also been implicated in suicide attempts and anorexia nervosa (Fenzel, 1994).

Does self-esteem in adolescence foreshadow adjustment and competence in adulthood? A New Zealand longitudinal study assessed self-esteem at 11, 13, and 15 years of age and adjustment and competence of the same individuals when they were 26 years old (Trzesniewski & others, 2006). The results revealed that adults characterized by poorer mental and physical health, worse economic prospects, and higher levels of criminal behavior were more likely to have had low self-esteem in adolescence than their better-adjusted, more competent adult counterparts.

Can a person have too much self-esteem? Yes, sometimes high self-esteem is undeserved; in fact, some people with high self-esteem are narcissistic and conceited (Krueger, Vohs, & Baumeister, 2008). **Narcissism** refers to a self-centered and self-concerned approach toward others. Typically, narcissistic individuals are unaware of their actual self and how others perceive them. This lack of awareness contributes to their adjustment problems. Narcissists are excessively self-centered and self-congratulatory, viewing their own needs and desires as paramount. As a result, narcissistic individuals rarely show any empathy toward others. In fact, narcissistic individuals often devalue people around them to protect their own precarious self-esteem, yet they often respond with rage and shame when others do not admire them and treat them in accordance with their grandiose fantasies about themselves. Narcissistic persons are at their most grandiose when their self-esteem is threatened. Narcissists may fly into a frenzy if they have given an unsatisfactory performance.

A recent study revealed that narcissistic adolescents were more aggressive than other adolescents, but only when they were shamed (Thomaes & others, 2008). Low self-esteem was not linked to aggression, but narcissism combined with high self-esteem was related to exceptionally high aggression.

Are today's adolescents and emerging adults more self-centered and narcissistic than their counterparts in earlier generations? Research by Jean Twenge and her colleagues (2008a, b) indicated that compared with baby boomers who were surveyed in 1975, twelfth-graders surveyed in 2006 were more self-satisfied overall and far more confident they would be very good employees, mates, and parents. However, another recent large-scale analysis revealed no increase in high school and college students' narcissism from the 1980s through 2007 (Trzesniewski, Donnellan, & Robins, 2008a, b). In sum, the extent to which recent generations of adolescents have higher self-esteem and are more narcissistic than earlier generations is controversial.

An important point needs to be made about much of the research on self-esteem: it is correlational rather than experimental. Remember from Chapter 1, "Introduction," that correlation does not equal causation. Thus, if a correlational study finds an association between self-esteem and depression, it could be equally likely that depression causes low self-esteem or low self-esteem causes depression.

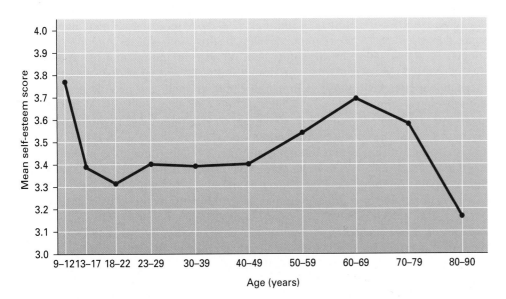

FIGURE 11.3 Self-Esteem Across the Life Span. One cross-sectional study found that self-esteem was high in childhood, dropped in adolescence, increased through early and middle adulthood, then dropped in the seventies and eighties (Robins & others, 2002). More than 300,000 individuals were asked the extent to which they have high self-esteem on a 5-point scale with 5 being "strongly agree" and 1 being "strongly disagree."

Developmental Changes   One cross-sectional study assessed the self-esteem of a very large, diverse sample of 326,641 individuals from 9 to 90 (Robins & others, 2002). About two-thirds of the participants were from the United States. The individuals were asked to respond to the item "I have high self-esteem" on a scale from 1 to 5 with 1 meaning "strongly agree" and 5 meaning "strongly disagree." Self-esteem decreased in adolescence, increased in the twenties, leveled off in the thirties, rose in the fifties and sixties, and then dropped in the seventies and eighties (see Figure 11.3). In most age periods, the self-esteem of males was higher than the self-esteem of females. Let's now explore developmental changes in self-esteem in more detail.

Childhood and Adolescence   Researchers have found that the accuracy of self-evaluations increases across the elementary school years (Harter, 2006). Young children tend to provide inflated views of themselves, but by about 8 years of age most children give more realistic appraisals of their skills (Harter, 2006). For example, older elementary school children who report a positive self-image of themselves in sports indeed are the ones who are reported by peers to be good at athletics.

Adolescents in general have long been described as having low self-esteem (Robins & others, 2002). However, the majority of adolescents actually have a positive self-image. In an extensive cross-cultural study, Daniel Offer and his colleagues (1988) sampled the self-images of adolescents around the world—in the United States, Australia, Bangladesh, Hungary, Israel, Italy, Japan, Taiwan, Turkey, and West Germany. Almost three-fourths of the adolescents had a healthy self-image.

Some researchers note that gender differences in self-esteem emerge by early adolescence, and these were found in the study just described (Robins & others, 2002). Girls and boys enter first grade with roughly equivalent levels of self-esteem. Yet some research studies have shown that by the middle school years girls' self-esteem is significantly lower than boys' (American Association of University Women, 1992). For example, a recent study confirmed that male adolescents have higher self-esteem than do female adolescents (McLean & Breen, 2009). However, other researchers caution that the self-esteem of girls is only slightly lower than boys' and still in the positive range (Harter, 2006; Kling & others, 1999). Researchers also have found that after age 13, girls' self-esteem increases through the remainder of adolescence and in

Researchers have found that after 13 years of age, girls' self-esteem increases.

emerging adulthood (Baldwin & Hoffman, 2002). A recent study examined why some adolescent girls recover and develop healthy self-esteem but others don't (Impett & others, 2008). In this study, both self-esteem and relationship authenticity (a consistency between what one thinks and feels, and what one says and does in relational contexts) increased from the eighth through the twelfth grade. Also, the self-esteem of girls who scored high on relationship authenticity in the eighth grade increased over the course of adolescence more than that of girls who scored low on this measure in the eighth grade.

A current concern is that too many of today's college students grew up receiving empty praise and as a consequence have inflated self-esteem (Graham, 2005; Stipek, 2005). Too often they were given praise for performance that was mediocre or even poor. Now in college, they may have difficulty handling competition and criticism. The title of a book, *Dumbing Down Our Kids: Why American Children Feel Good About Themselves But Can't Read, Write, or Add* (Sykes, 1995), vividly captured the theme that many U.S. children's academic problems stem from unmerited praise as part of an effort to prop up their self-esteem.

Adulthood   Are there differences in the self-esteem of young, middle-aged, and older adults? In the self-esteem study described earlier, self-esteem dropped in late adulthood (Robins & others, 2002). However, some researchers have not found any differences in self-esteem across the age periods of adulthood (McGue, Hirsch, & Lykken, 1993).

Given that older adults have more physical problems, why wouldn't they have lower self-esteem than young or middle-aged adults? One possible reason is that many older adults don't interpret their "losses" as negatively, and don't become as emotionally upset, as younger adults (Carstensen & Freund, 1994). For example, being asked to retire at age 63 may not be nearly as devastating as being fired from a job at 40. Furthermore, as we saw in Chapter 10, "Emotional Development," Laura Carstensen (1998, 2008) argues that knowledge-related goals decrease in older adults, whereas emotion-related goals increase. And many older adults have the ability to reach their emotion-related goals of honing their social network to spend most of their time with the people with whom they have enjoyed satisfying close relationships in the past. Finally, many older adults choose to compare themselves with other older adults rather than younger adults, which can help them maintain their positive self-image (Brandstädter, 1999).

Why might self-esteem decline for some older adults? Explanations include deteriorating physical health and negative societal attitudes toward older adults, although these factors were not examined in the large-scale study just described. Researchers have found that in late adulthood, being widowed, institutionalized, or physically impaired, having a low religious commitment, and experiencing a decline in health are linked to low self-esteem (Giarrusso & Bengtson, 2007).

Even when older adults have physical problems, other aspects of their lives, such as spending time with people whose company they enjoy, can help to buffer any decline in their self-esteem.

[handwritten: five ways to improve self esteem ↙]

Strategies for Increasing Self-Esteem   What are some good strategies for increasing self-esteem? Five ways self-esteem can be improved are (1) to identify the causes of low self-esteem and the domains of competence important to the self, (2) to provide emotional support and opportunities for social approval, (3) to take responsibility for one's own self-esteem, (4) to achieve goals, and (5) to develop effective coping strategies.

Identifying sources of self-esteem—that is, competence in domains important to the self—is critical to improving self-esteem. Susan Harter (1990) points out that the self-esteem enhancement programs of the 1970s and 1980s, in which self-esteem itself was the target and individuals were encouraged to simply feel good about themselves, were ineffective. Rather, Harter notes that intervention must occur at the level of the *causes* of self-esteem if the individual's self-esteem is to improve significantly. Individuals have the highest self-esteem when they perform competently in domains that are important to them. Therefore, people should be encouraged to identify and value areas of competence.

Emotional support and social approval also powerfully influence self-esteem. Some children with low self-esteem come from conflicted families or conditions in which they experienced abuse or neglect—situations in which support was unavailable. In some cases, alternative sources of support can be implemented either informally through the encouragement of a teacher, a coach, or another significant adult or, more formally, through programs such as Big Brothers and Big Sisters. As peer approval becomes increasingly important during adolescence, peer support is an important influence on the adolescent's self-esteem.

Developing self-confidence and believing that one has the ability to do what it takes to improve self-esteem are other good strategies. Although it is helpful to have the social support and emotional approval of others, it is also very important for you to take the initiative to increase your self-esteem.

Achievement can also improve an individual's self-esteem (Baumeister & others, 2003). For example, self-esteem can be enhanced by the straightforward teaching of skills to individuals. People develop higher self-esteem because they know the important tasks to accomplish goals and by carrying out these tasks they are more likely to reach their goals.

Self-esteem often increases when individuals face a problem and try to cope with it rather than avoid it (Frydenberg, 2008). When coping prevails, the individual often faces problems realistically, honestly, and nondefensively. This process leads to favorable self-evaluative thoughts, which then lead to self-generated approval and higher self-esteem. The converse is true of low self-esteem. Unfavorable self-evaluations trigger denial, deception, and avoidance in an attempt to disavow that which has already been glimpsed as true. This process leads to self-generated disapproval as a form of feedback to the self about personal adequacy.

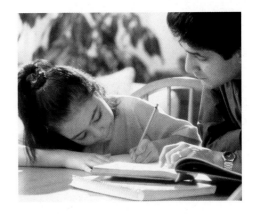

How can parents help children develop higher self-esteem?

Self-Regulation

Self-regulation involves the ability to control one's behavior without having to rely on others' help. Self-regulation includes the self-generation and cognitive monitoring of thoughts, feelings, and behaviors in order to reach a goal. An individual might develop better self-control in the physical, cognitive, or socioemotional domain than in other domains.

Throughout most of the life span, individuals who engage in self-regulation are better achievers and are more satisfied with their lives than their counterparts who let external factors dominate their lives (Schunk, 2008). For example, researchers have found that, compared with low-achieving students, high-achieving students engage in greater self-regulation. They do this by setting more specific learning goals, using more strategies to learn and adapt, self-monitoring more, and more systematically evaluating their progress toward a goal (Schunk, Pintrich, & Meece, 2008).

Infancy and Early Childhood In Chapter 10, "Emotional Development," we discussed the importance of children learning to regulate their emotions as they develop. Emotional regulation is an important aspect of the overall development of self-regulation (Thompson, 2009a, b). How do other aspects of self-regulation develop? Claire Kopp (1982, 1987, 2008) described a sequence for its development early in life. Initially, beginning at about 12 to 18 months of age, infants depend completely on caregivers for reminder signals about acceptable behaviors. At this age, infants begin to show compliance to caregivers' demands. For example, a parent might say, "No. Don't touch!" And the infant doesn't touch.

The next phase of developing self-regulation takes place at approximately 2 to 3 years of age. At this point, children begin to comply with the caregiver's expectations in the absence of external monitoring by the caregiver. Thus, most 2- to 3-year-old children are aware of where they may and may not play and which

self-regulation The ability to control one's behavior without having to rely on others for help.

objects they may and may not touch if they are at home, on a playground, or in the homes of friends and relatives.

Nonetheless, at these young ages, there are clear limitations on self-regulation. Given a strong stimulus, such as a ball rolling down the street or the motivation to explore an interesting place, toddlers often ignore safety or exhortations. Also, only rudimentary aspects of delaying gratification are present at these early ages. For example, when 2-year-olds are confronted with an unexpected delay (such as not being able go outside and play), they often whine and beg to engage in the activity. But there are clear signs of advances in self-initiated regulation, as when young children announce a toy cleanup without prompting from caregivers.

Preschoolers become better at self-control, learning how to resist temptation and giving themselves instructions that keep them focused (Thompson, 2006). Thus, toward the end of the preschool years, children might say to themselves, "No. I can't do that. I'm working," in response to a temptation to stop working and do something else, like play with an attractive toy.

Middle/Late Childhood and Adolescence   One of the most important aspects of the self in middle and late childhood is the increased capacity for self-regulation. This increased capacity is characterized by deliberate efforts to manage one's behavior, emotions, and thoughts, which lead to increased social competence and achievement (Laible & Thompson, 2007).

The increased capacity in self-regulation is linked to developmental advances in the brain's prefrontal cortex, which we discussed in Chapter 3, "Physical Development and Biological Aging." Recall our discussion there of the increased focal activation in the prefrontal cortex that is linked to improvement in cognitive control, which includes self-regulation (Durston & others, 2006).

Few studies of self-regulation have focused on adolescents. On the one hand, advances in cognitive skills (logical thinking, for example), increased introspection, and the greater independence of adolescence might lead to increased self-control. Also, advances in cognitive abilities provide adolescents with a better understanding of the importance of delaying gratification for something desirable (such as a good grade in a class) rather than seeking immediate gratification (listening to rock music rather than studying). On the other hand, an increased sense of invincibility (which can lead to risk taking) and social comparison might produce less self-control.

How does self-regulation change during childhood and adolescence?

Adulthood   Self-control increases in early adulthood and on into the middle adult years (Gatz & Karel, 1993). Researchers have found a decline in perceived self-control in cognitive functioning in older adults (Bertrand & Lachman, 2003).

Although older adults are aware of age-related losses, most still effectively maintain a sense of self-control. The negative effects of age-typical problems, such as a decline in physical and cognitive skills and an increase in illness, may be buffered by a flexible, accommodating control style (Brandstädter & Renner, 1990).

Selective Optimization with Compensation   **Selective optimization with compensation theory** states that successful aging is linked with three main factors: selection, optimization, and compensation (SOC). The theory states that individuals can produce new resources and allocate them effectively to tasks they want to master (Baltes & Smith, 2008). *Selection* is based on the concept that older adults have a reduced capacity and a loss of functioning, which require a reduction in performance in most life domains such as memory and physical skills. *Optimization* suggests that it is possible to maintain performance in some areas through continued practice and the use of new technologies. Examples might include doing crossword puzzles to maintain memory skills and exercising to optimize strength. *Compensation* becomes

selective optimization with compensation theory The theory that successful aging is related to three main factors: selection, optimization, and compensation.

relevant when life tasks require a level of capacity beyond the current level of the older adult's performance potential. Older adults especially need to compensate in circumstances with high mental or physical demands, such as when thinking about and memorizing new material very fast, reacting quickly when driving a car, or running fast. When older adults develop an illness, the need for compensation increases.

Selective optimization with compensation theory was proposed by Paul Baltes and his colleagues (Baltes, 2003; Baltes & Smith, 2008; Baltes, Lindenberger, & Staudinger, 2006). They describe the life of the pianist Arthur Rubinstein (1887–1982) to illustrate their theory. When he was interviewed at 80 years of age, Rubinstein said that three factors were responsible for his ability to maintain his status as an admired concert pianist into old age. First, he mastered the weakness of old age by reducing the scope of his performances and playing fewer pieces (which reflects selection). Second, he spent more time at practice than earlier in his life (which reflects optimization). Third, he used special strategies, such as slowing down before fast segments, thus creating the image of faster playing (which reflects compensation).

The process of selective optimization with compensation is likely to be effective whenever people pursue successful outcomes. What makes SOC attractive to aging researchers is that it makes explicit how individuals can manage and adapt to losses. By using SOC, they can continue to live satisfying lives, although in a more restrictive manner. Loss is a common dimension of old age, although there are wide variations in the nature of the losses involved. Because of this individual variation, the specific form of selection, optimization, and compensation will likely vary depending on the person's life history, pattern of interests, values, health, skills, and resources. To read about some strategies for effectively engaging in selective optimization with compensation, see the *Applications in Life-Span Development* interlude.

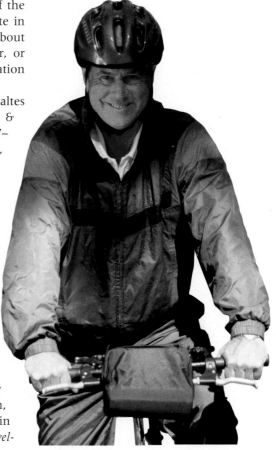

According to selective optimization with compensation theory, what characterizes successful aging?

Applications in Life-Span Development

STRATEGIES FOR EFFECTIVELY ENGAGING IN SELECTIVE OPTIMIZATION WITH COMPENSATION

What are some good strategies that aging adults can engage in to attain selective optimization with compensation? According to Paul Baltes and his colleagues (Baltes, Lindenberger, & Staudinger, 2006; Freund & Baltes, 2002), these strategies are likely to be effective:

Selection Strategies

- Focus on the most important goal at a particular time.
- Think about what you want in life, and commit yourself to one or two major goals.
- To reach a particular goal, you may need to abandon other goals.

Optimization Strategies

- Keep working on what you have planned until you are successful.
- Persevere and keep trying until you reach your goal.
- When you want to achieve something, you may need to be patient until the right moment arrives.

(continued on next page)

Compensation

- When things don't go the way they used to, search for other ways to achieve what you want.
- If things don't go well for you, be willing to let others help you.
- When things don't go as well as in the past, keep trying other ways until you can achieve results that are similar to what you accomplished earlier in your life.

In Baltes' view (2003; Baltes & Smith, 2008), the selection of domains and life priorities is an important aspect of development. Life goals and priorities likely vary across the life course for most people. For many individuals, it is not just the sheer attainment of goals, but rather the attainment of *meaningful* goals, that makes life satisfying. In one study, younger adults were more likely to assess their well-being in terms of accomplishments and careers, whereas older adults were more likely to link well-being with good health and the ability to accept change. And, as you read in Chapter 10, "Emotional Development," in our discussion of socioemotional selectivity theory, emotion-related goals become increasingly important for older adults (Carstensen, 2008; Charles & Carstensen, 2010).

In one cross-sectional study, the personal life investments of 25- to 105-year-olds were assessed (Staudinger, 1996) (see Figure 11.4). From 25 to 34 years of age, participants said that they personally invested more time in work, friends, family, and independence, in that order. From 35 to 54 and 55 to 65 years of age, family became more important than friends to them in terms of their personal investment. Little changed in the rank ordering of persons 70 to 84 years old, but for participants 85 to 105 years old, health became the most important personal investment. Thinking about life showed up for the first time on the most important list for those who were 85 to 105 years old.

25 to 34 Years	35 to 54 Years	55 to 65 Years	70 to 84 Years	85 to 105 Years
Work	Family	Family	Family	Health
Friends	Work	Health	Health	Family
Family	Friends	Friends	Cognitive fitness	Thinking about life
Independence	Cognitive fitness	Cognitive fitness	Friends	Cognitive fitness

FIGURE 11.4 Degree of Personal Life Investment at Different Points in Life. Shown here are the top four domains of personal life investment at different points in life. The highest degree of investment is listed at the top (for example, work was the highest personal investment from 25 to 34 years of age, family from 35 to 54, and health from 85 to 105).

Personal Control Jutta Heckhausen and her colleagues (Haynes & others, 2009; Heckhausen, 2002, 2007; Heckhausen & Heckhausen, 2008; Wrosch, Heckhausen, & Lachman, 2006) argue that it is important to examine control-related strategies and the ability of people to control important outcomes in their lives. They distinguish between primary control striving and secondary control striving:

- *Primary control striving* refers to individuals' efforts to change the external world so that it meets their needs and desires. Primary control strategies are directed at attaining personal goals and overcoming obstacles. Persistence in striving for a goal ("When things don't go according to my plans, my motto is: 'Where there is a will, there's a way'") is an example of a primary control strategy.

- *Secondary control striving* targets individuals' inner worlds and their own motivation, emotion, and mental representation. Examples of secondary control striving are positive reappraisal ("I find I usually learn something from a difficult situation") and lowering aspirations ("When my expectations are not being met, I lower them"). In most instances, primary control is more adaptive than secondary control because in primary control individuals change their environment to meet their own needs and seek gains in their life. In secondary control, they often are trying to minimize losses or maintain their standing.

Primary and secondary control are believed to change through the life span. The ability to control outcomes is expected to increase substantially during the child, adolescent, and early adult years, level off in middle adulthood, and then decline in late adulthood (see Figure 11.5). Secondary control increases in a similar manner through the early adult years, but—unlike primary control—it continues to increase through adulthood (see Figure 11.5). Increasing physical and social challenges to primary control lead older adults to increase the use of secondary control strategies (Heckhausen & Schulz, 1995).

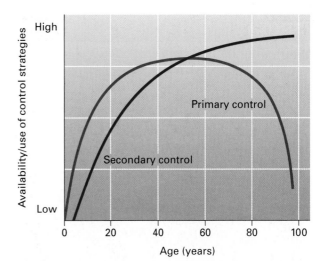

FIGURE 11.5 Theorized Changes in Primary and Secondary Control Strategies Across the Human Life Span. According to Heckhausen, primary control strategies increase in the child, adolescent, and early adult years, then level off in middle age, and finally decline in older adults. However, secondary control strategies continue to increase throughout the adult years.

Review and Reflect: Learning Goal 1

1 Discuss the main ways the self is conceptualized

REVIEW

- How can the terms self, identity, and personality be defined? What is self-understanding, and how does it develop?
- What are self-esteem and self-concept, and how do they develop? How is self-esteem related to performance, initiative, and happiness? Is there a dark side to high self-esteem? What are some ways to increase self-esteem?
- What is self-regulation, and how does it develop?

REFLECT

- If a psychologist had interviewed you when you were 8 years old, 14 years old, and again today, would your self-understanding and self-esteem be different at each of these ages?

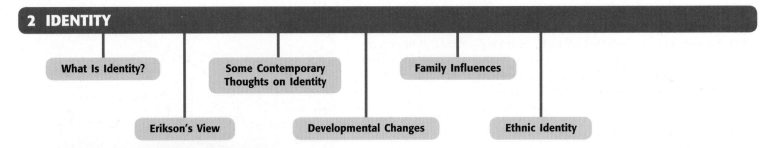

2 IDENTITY

What Is Identity?

Erikson's View

Some Contemporary Thoughts on Identity

Developmental Changes

Family Influences

Ethnic Identity

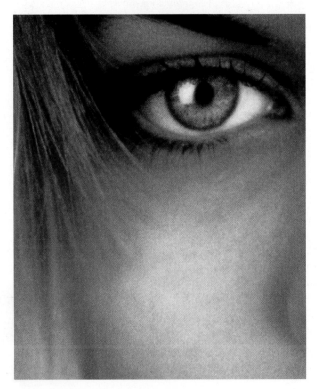

What are some important dimensions of identity?

Erik Erikson.

Who am I? What am I all about? What am I going to do with my life? What is different about me? How can I make it on my own? These questions reflect the search for an identity. By far the most comprehensive and provocative theory of identity development is Erik Erikson's. In this section, we examine his views on identity and some contemporary thoughts on identity. We also discuss research on how identity develops and how social contexts influence that development.

What Is Identity?

Identity is a self-portrait composed of many pieces, including these:

- The career and work path the person wants to follow (vocational/ career identity)
- Whether the person is conservative, liberal, or middle-of-the-road (political identity)
- The person's spiritual beliefs (religious identity)
- Whether the person is single, married, divorced, and so on (relationship identity)
- The extent to which the person is motivated to achieve and is intellectual (achievement, intellectual identity)
- Whether the person is heterosexual, homosexual, or bisexual (sexual identity)
- Which part of the world or country a person is from and how intensely the person identifies with his or her cultural heritage (cultural/ethnic identity)
- The kind of things a person likes to do, which can include sports, music, hobbies, and so on (interests)
- The individual's personality characteristics, such as being introverted or extraverted, anxious or calm, friendly or hostile, and so on (personality)
- The individual's body image (physical identity)

Erikson's View

Questions about identity surface as common, virtually universal, concerns during adolescence. Some decisions made during adolescence might seem trivial: whom to date, whether or not to break up, which major to study, whether to study or play, whether or not to be politically active, and so on. Over the years of adolescence, however, such decisions begin to form the core of what the individual is all about as a human being—what is called his or her identity.

It was Erik Erikson (1950, 1968) who first understood how central questions about identity are to understanding adolescent development. That identity is now believed to be a key aspect of adolescent development is a result of Erikson's masterful thinking and analysis. His ideas reveal rich insights into adolescents' thoughts and feelings, and reading one or more of his books is worthwhile. A good starting point is *Identity: Youth and Crisis* (1968). Other works that portray identity development are *Young Man Luther* (1962) and *Gandhi's Truth* (1969).

Erikson's theory was introduced in Chapter 1, "Introduction." Recall that his fifth developmental stage, which individuals experience during adolescence, is **identity versus identity confusion.** During this time, said Erikson, adolescents are faced with deciding who they are, what they are all about, and where they are going in life.

These questions about identity occur throughout life, but they become especially important for adolescents. Erikson maintains that adolescents face an overwhelming number of choices. As they gradually come to realize that they will be responsible for themselves and their own lives, adolescents search for what those lives are going to be.

The search for an identity during adolescence is aided by a **psychosocial moratorium,** which is Erikson's term for the gap between childhood security and adult autonomy. During this period, society leaves adolescents relatively free of responsibilities and free to try out different identities. Adolescents in effect search their culture's identity files, experimenting with different roles and personalities. They may want to pursue one career one month (lawyer, for example) and another career the next month (doctor, actor, teacher, social worker, or astronaut, for example). They may dress neatly one day, sloppily the next. This experimentation is a deliberate effort on the part of adolescents to find out where they fit in the world. Most adolescents eventually discard undesirable roles.

Youth who successfully cope with conflicting identities emerge with a new sense of self that is both refreshing and acceptable. Adolescents who do not successfully resolve this identity crisis suffer what Erikson calls identity confusion. The confusion takes one of two courses: Individuals withdraw, isolating themselves from peers and family, or they immerse themselves in the world of peers and lose their identity in the crowd.

Erickson's View of Identity

"...must have changed several times since then."

—**Lewis Carroll**
English Writer, 19th Century

Some Contemporary Thoughts on Identity

Contemporary views of identity development suggest that it is a lengthy process, in many instances more gradual and less cataclysmic than Erikson's term *crisis* implies (Phinney, 2008). Today's theorists note that this extraordinarily complex process neither begins nor ends with adolescence (Azmitia, Syed, & Radmacher, 2008; Orbe, 2008). It begins in infancy with the appearance of attachment, the development of a sense of self, and the emergence of independence. It ends with a life review and integration in old age. What is important about identity development in adolescence and emerging adulthood is that for the first time, physical, cognitive, and socioemotional development advance to the point at which the individual can sort through and synthesize childhood identities and identifications to construct a viable path toward adult maturity (Marcia & Carpendale, 2004). Resolution of the identity issue during adolescence and emerging adulthood does not mean that identity will be stable through the remainder of one's life. An individual who develops a healthy identity is flexible and adaptive, open to changes in society, in relationships, and in careers. This openness assures numerous reorganizations of identity throughout the individual's life.

Just as researchers increasingly describe adolescents' and emerging adults' self-understanding in terms of multiple selves, there also is a trend in characterizing adolescents' and emerging adults' identity in terms of multiple identities (Azmitia, Syed, & Radmacher, 2008; Phinney, 2008). Although adolescent and emerging adult identities are preceded by childhood identities, central questions such as "Who am I?" come up more frequently in the adolescent and emerging adult years. During adolescence and emerging adulthood, identities are characterized more strongly by the search for balance between the needs for autonomy and for connectedness.

identity versus identity confusion Erikson's fifth stage of development, which occurs during the adolescent years; adolescents are faced with finding out who they are, what they are all about, and where they are going in life.

psychosocial moratorium Erikson's term for the gap between childhood security and adult autonomy that adolescents experience as part of their identity exploration.

What are some contemporary thoughts about identity formation and development?

Identity formation neither happens neatly, nor is it usually cataclysmic. At the bare minimum, it involves commitment to a vocational direction, an ideological stance, and a sexual orientation. Synthesizing the components of identity can be a long, drawn-out process, with many negations and affirmations of various roles. Identity development gets done in bits and pieces. Decisions are not made once and for all, but must be made again and again. While the decisions might seem trivial at the time—whom to date, whether or not to have intercourse, to break up, to take drugs; whether to go to college or get a job, to study or play, to be politically active or not—over the years, they begin to form the core of what an individual is all about.

A current concern about the development of identity in adolescence and emerging adulthood was voiced in William Damon's (2008) book, *The Path to Purpose*. Damon acknowledges that successful identity development is a long-term process of extended exploration and reflection, and in some instances can involve postponing decisions for a number of years. However, what concerns Damon is that too many of today's youth aren't moving toward any identity resolution. In Damon's (2008, pp. 5, 7) words,

> Their delay is characterized more by indecision than by motivated reflection, more by confusion than by pursuit of clear goals, more by ambivalence than by determination. Directionless shift is not a constructive moratorium in either a developmental or a societal sense. Without a sense of direction, opportunities are lost, and doubt and self-absorption can set in. Maladaptive habits are established and adaptive ones not built. . . . What is too often missing is . . . the kind of wholehearted dedication to an activity or interest that stems from serious purpose, a purpose that can give meaning and direction to life.

In Damon's (2008, p. 47) view, too many youth are left to their own devices in dealing with some of life's biggest questions: "What is my calling? What do I have to contribute to the world? What am I here for?" Damon acknowledges that adults can't make youths' decisions for them, but emphasizes that it is very important for parents, teachers, mentors, and other adults to provide guidance, feedback, and contexts that will improve the likelihood youth will develop a positive identity. Youth need a cultural climate that inspires rather than demoralizes them and supports their chances of reaching their aspirations.

Developmental Changes

Although questions about identity may be especially important during adolescence and emerging adulthood, identity formation neither begins nor ends during these years. It begins with the appearance of attachment, the development of the sense of self, and the emergence of independence in infancy; the process reaches its final phase with a life review and integration in old age. What is important about identity development in adolescence, especially late adolescence, is that for the first time, physical development, cognitive development, and socioemotional development advance to the point at which the individual can sort through and synthesize childhood identities and identifications to construct a viable path toward adult maturity.

Identity Statuses   How do individual adolescents go about the process of forming an identity? Eriksonian researcher James Marcia (1980, 1994) notes that Erikson's theory of identity development contains four *statuses* of identity, or ways of resolving the identity crisis: identity diffusion, identity foreclosure, identity moratorium, and identity achievement. What determines an individual's identity status? Marcia classifies individuals based on the existence or extent of their crisis or commitment (see Figure 11.6). **Crisis** is defined as a period of identity development during which the individual is exploring alternatives. Most researchers use the term *exploration* rather than crisis. **Commitment** is personal investment in identity.

The four statuses of identity are as follows:

- **Identity diffusion** is the status of individuals who have not yet experienced a crisis or made any commitments. Not only are they undecided about occupational and ideological choices, they are also likely to show little interest in such matters.

- **Identity foreclosure** is the status of individuals who have made a commitment but have not experienced a crisis. This occurs most often when parents hand down commitments to their adolescents, usually in an authoritarian way, before adolescents have had a chance to explore different approaches, ideologies, and vocations on their own.

- **Identity moratorium** is the status of individuals who are in the midst of a crisis but whose commitments are either absent or only vaguely defined.

- **Identity achievement** is the status of individuals who have undergone a crisis and have made a commitment.

Let's explore some examples of Marcia's identity statuses. Thirteen-year-old Sarah has neither begun to explore her identity in any meaningful way nor made an identity commitment; she is *identity diffused*. Eighteen-year-old Tim's parents want him to be a medical doctor, so he is planning on majoring in premedicine in college and has not explored other options; he is *identity foreclosed*. Nineteen-year-old Sasha is not quite sure what life paths she wants to follow, but she recently went to the counseling center at her college to find out about different careers; she is in *identity moratorium* status. Twenty-one-year-old Marcelo extensively explored several career options in college, eventually getting his degree in science education, and is looking forward to his first year of teaching high school students; he is *identity achieved*. These examples focused on the career dimension of identity, but remember that identity has a number of dimensions.

Marcia's approach has been sharply criticized by some researchers who conclude that it oversimplifies Erikson's concepts of crisis and commitment and doesn't examine them deeply enough (Coté, 2009; Kroger, 2007).

One way that researchers are examining identity changes in depth is to use a *narrative approach*. This involves asking individuals to tell their life stories and evaluate the extent to which their stories are meaningful and integrated (McAdams & Olson, 2010). The term *narrative identity* "refers to the stories people construct and tell about themselves to define who they are for themselves and others. Beginning in adolescence and young adulthood, our narrative identities are the stories we live by" (McAdams, Josselson, & Lieblich, 2006, p. 4).

Early Adolescence to Adulthood   During early adolescence, most youth are primarily in the identity statuses of *diffusion, foreclosure,* or *moratorium*. According to Marcia (1987, 1996), at least three aspects of the young adolescent's development are important to identity formation. Young adolescents must be confident that they have parental support, must have an established sense of industry, and must be able to take a self-reflective stance toward the future.

A consensus is developing that the key changes in identity are more likely to take place in emerging adulthood or later than in adolescence (Coté, 2009; Phinney, 2008; Syed & Azmitia, 2008). For example, Alan Waterman (1985, 1989, 1992) has found that from the years preceding high school through the last few years of

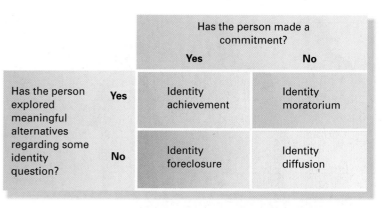

FIGURE 11.6 Marcia's Four Statuses of Identity.

crisis A period of identity development during which the individual is exploring alternatives.

commitment A personal investment in identity.

identity diffusion Marcia's term for the status of individuals who have not yet experienced a crisis (explored meaningful alternatives) or made any commitments.

identity foreclosure Marcia's term for the status of individuals who have made a commitment but have not experienced a crisis.

identity moratorium Marcia's term for the status of individuals in the midst of a crisis, but whose commitments are either absent or vaguely defined.

identity achievement Marcia's term for the status of individuals who have undergone a crisis and have made a commitment.

How does identity change in emerging adulthood?

*A*s long as one keeps
searching, the answers come.

—JOAN BAEZ
American Folk Singer, 20th Century

individuality Characteristic consisting of two dimensions: self-assertion, the ability to have and communicate a point of view; and separateness, the use of communication patterns to express how one is different from others.

connectedness Characteristic consisting of two dimensions: mutuality, sensitivity to and respect for others' views; and permeability, openness to others' views.

college, the number of individuals who are identity achieved increases, whereas the number who are identity diffused decreases. College upperclassmen are more likely to be identity achieved than college freshmen or high school students. Many young adolescents, on the other hand, are identity diffused. These developmental changes are especially true for vocational choice. In terms of religious beliefs and political ideology, fewer college students reach the identity-achieved status; a substantial number are characterized by foreclosure and diffusion. Thus, the timing of identity development may depend on the specific dimension involved (Arehart & Smith, 1990).

Why might college produce some key changes in identity? Increased complexity in the reasoning skills of college students combined with a wide range of new experiences that highlight contrasts between home and college and between themselves and others stimulates them to reach a higher level of integrating various dimensions of their identity (Phinney, 2008).

One of emerging adulthood's themes is not having many social commitments, which gives individuals considerable independence in developing a life path (Arnett, 2006). James Coté (2006, 2009) argues that because of this freedom, developing a positive identity in emerging adulthood requires considerable self-discipline and planning. Without this self-discipline and planning, emerging adults are likely to drift and not follow any particular direction. Coté also stresses that emerging adults who obtain a higher education are more likely to be on a positive identity path. Those who don't obtain a higher education, he says, tend to experience frequent job changes, not because they are searching for an identity but rather because they are just trying to eek out a living in a society that rewards higher education.

Researchers have shown that identity consolidation—the process of refining and enhancing the identity choices that are made in emerging adulthood—continues well into early adulthood and possibly into the early part of middle adulthood (Kroger, 2007). Further, as individuals move from early to middle adulthood they become more certain about their identity. For example, a longitudinal study of college women found that identity certainty increased from the thirties through the fifties (Stewart, Ostrove, & Helson, 2001).

A common pattern of individuals who develop positive identities is called the "MAMA" cycle: *moratorium–achievement–moratorium–achievement.* Individuals may repeat this cycle throughout their lives as personal, family, and societal changes require them to explore new alternatives and develop new commitments (Francis, Fraser, & Marcia, 1989).

Family Influences

Parents are important figures in the adolescent's development of identity (Cooper, Behrens, & Trinh, 2009; Schachter & Ventura, 2008). For example, one study found that poor communication between mothers and adolescents, as well as persistent conflicts with friends, was linked to less positive identity development (Reis & Youniss, 2004). Catherine Cooper and her colleagues (Cooper, Behrens, & Trinh, 2009; Cooper & Grotevant, 1989; Grotevant & Cooper, 1998) have found that a family atmosphere that promotes *both* individuality and connectedness is important in the adolescent's identity development:

- **Individuality** consists of two dimensions: self-assertion, which is the ability to have and communicate a point of view; and separateness, which is the use of communication patterns to express how one is different from others.

- **Connectedness** also consists of two dimensions: mutuality, which involves sensitivity to and respect for others' views; and permeability, which involves openness to others' views.

Ethnic Identity

Throughout the world, ethnic minority groups have struggled to maintain their ethnic identities while blending in with the dominant culture (Erikson, 1968; Liu & others, 2009). **Ethnic identity** is an enduring aspect of the self that includes a sense of membership in an ethnic group, along with the attitudes and feelings related to that membership (Phinney, 2006). Thus, for adolescents from ethnic minority groups, the process of identity formation has an added dimension: the choice between two or more sources of identification—their own ethnic group and the mainstream, or dominant, culture. Many adolescents resolve this choice by developing a *bicultural identity*. That is, they identify in some ways with their ethnic group and in other ways with the majority culture (Phinney, 2008; Phinney & Ong, 2007). A study of Mexican American and Asian American college students found that they identified both with the American mainstream culture and with their culture of origin (Devos, 2006).

Many aspects of sociocultural contexts may influence ethnic identity (Phinney, 2008). Ethnic identity tends to be stronger among members of minority groups than among members of mainstream groups. For example, in one study, the exploration of ethnic identity was higher among ethnic minority college students than among non-Latino White college students (Phinney & Alipra, 1990).

Time is another aspect of the context that influences ethnic identity. The indicators of identity often differ for each succeeding generation of immigrants (Phinney, 2006). First-generation immigrants are likely to be secure in their identities and unlikely to change much; they may or may not develop a new identity. The degree to which they begin to feel "American" appears to be related to whether or not they learn English, develop social networks beyond their ethnic group, and become culturally competent in their new country. Second-generation immigrants are more likely to think of themselves as "American"—possibly because citizenship is granted at birth. For second-generation immigrants, ethnic identity is likely to be linked to retention of their ethnic language and social networks. In the third and later generations, the issues become more complex. Broad social factors may affect the extent to which members of this generation retain their ethnic identities. For example, media images may either discourage or encourage members of an ethnic group from identifying with their group or retaining parts of its culture. Discrimination may force people to see themselves as cut off from the majority group and encourage them to seek the support of their own ethnic culture.

The immediate contexts in which ethnic minority youth live also influence their identity development (Bosma & Kunnen, 2008; Syed & Azmitia, 2008). In the United States, many ethnic minority youth live in pockets of poverty, are exposed to drugs, gangs, and crime, and interact with youth and adults who have dropped out of school or are unemployed. Support for developing a positive identity is scarce. In such settings, programs for youth can make an important contribution to identity development.

Researchers are increasingly finding that a positive ethnic identity is linked to positive outcomes for ethnic minority adolescents. One study found that a positive ethnic identity was related to higher school engagement and lower aggression (Van Buren & Graham, 2003). Also, a recent study revealed that Navajo adolescents' positive ethnic heritage was linked to higher self-esteem, school connectedness, and social functioning (Jones & Galliher, 2007). And a longitudinal study of Latino adolescents found that ethnic identity resolution

Michelle Chin, age 16: "Parents do not understand that teenagers need to find out who they are, which means a lot of experimenting, a lot of mood swings, a lot of emotions and awkwardness. Like any teenager, I am facing an identity crisis. I am still trying to figure out whether I am a Chinese American or an American with Asian eyes."

How do social contexts influence adolescents' ethnic identity?

ethnic identity An enduring aspect of the self that includes a sense of membership in an ethnic group, along with the attitudes and feelings related to that membership.

Careers in Life-Span Development

Armando Ronquillo, High School Counselor

Armando Ronquillo is a high school counselor and admissions advisor at Pueblo High School in a low-income area of Tucson, Arizona. More than 85 percent of the students have a Latino background. Ronquillo was named the top high school counselor in the state of Arizona for the year 2000.

Ronquillo especially works with Latino students to guide them in developing a positive identity. He talks with them about their Latino background and what it's like to have a bicultural identity—preserving important aspects of their Latino heritage but also pursuing what is important to be successful in the contemporary culture of the United States.

Ronquillo believes that helping them stay in school and getting them to think about the lifelong opportunities provided by a college education will benefit their identity development. He also works with parents to help them understand that their child going to college is doable and affordable.

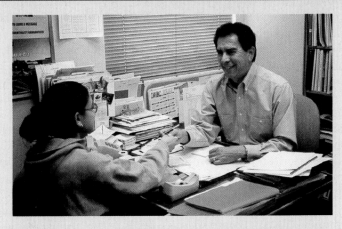

Armando Ronquillo, counseling a Latina high school student about college.

predicted proactive coping with discrimination over time (Umana-Taylor & others, 2008). Further, a recent study found that exploration was an important aspect of establishing a secure sense of one's ethnic identity, which in turn was linked to a positive attitude toward one's own group and other groups (Whitehead & others, 2009). Yet another recent study of Latino youth indicated that growth in identity exploration was linked with a positive increase in self-esteem (Umana-Taylor, Gonzales-Backen, & Guimond, 2009). To read about one individual who guides Latino adolescents in developing a positive identity, see the *Careers in Life-Span Development* profile.

trait theories Theories emphasizing that personality consists of broad dispositions, called traits, which tend to produce characteristic responses.

Big Five factors of personality The view that personality is made up of openness to experience, conscientiousness, extraversion, agreeableness, and neuroticism.

Review and Reflect: Learning Goal 2

 Explain the key facets of identity development

REVIEW

- What does an identity involve?
- What is Erikson's view of identity?
- What are some contemporary thoughts on identity?
- What are the four identity statuses, and how do they change developmentally?
- How does the family influence identity?
- What characterizes ethnic identity?

REFLECT

- Do you think your parents influenced your identity development? If so, how?

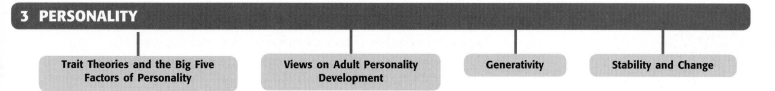

3 PERSONALITY

| Trait Theories and the Big Five Factors of Personality | Views on Adult Personality Development | Generativity | Stability and Change |

Earlier in the chapter, *personality* was defined as the enduring personal characteristics of individuals. Personality psychologists use many strategies in trying to understand the enduring characteristics of individuals. Some of them study the entire personality of individuals; some come up with a list of traits that best describe individuals; others zero in on specific traits or characteristics, such as being introverted or extraverted.

In Chapter 1, "Introduction," we considered several major personality theories—psychoanalytic theories and the social cognitive theory of Albert Bandura. You might wish to review those theories at this time. Here our exploration of personality focuses on trait theory, several views of personality development in adulthood, and studies of stability and change in personality during adulthood.

Trait Theories and the Big Five Factors of Personality

Trait theories state that personality consists of broad dispositions, called traits, that tend to produce characteristic responses. In other words, people can be described in terms of the basic ways they behave, such as whether they are outgoing or friendly or whether they are dominant and assertive. Although trait theorists disagree about which traits make up personality, they agree that traits are the fundamental units and building blocks of personality.

One trait theory that has received considerable attention is the **Big Five factors of personality,** the view that personality is made up of openness to experience, conscientiousness, extraversion, agreeableness, and neuroticism (see Figure 11.7). (Notice that if you create an acronym from these trait names, you will get the word *OCEAN*.) A number of research studies point toward these five factors as important dimensions of personality (Costa & McCrae, 1995; McCrae & Costa, 2006).

Consider recent research on the Big Five factors and adolescent development. The Big Five factor of conscientiousness has emerged as a key predictor of adjustment and competence (Roberts & others, 2009). Following is a sampling of recent research documenting this link:

- Of the Big Five factors, conscientiousness was the best predictor of both high school and college grade-point average (Noftle & Robins, 2007).

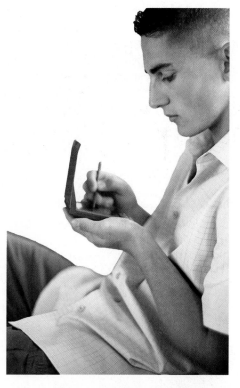

An adolescent with a high level of conscientiousness organizes his daily schedule and plans how to use his time effectively. *What are some characteristics of conscientiousness? How is it linked to adolescents' competence?*

Openness	**C**onscientiousness	**E**xtraversion	**A**greeableness	**N**euroticism
• Imaginative or practical	• Organized or disorganized	• Sociable or retiring	• Softhearted or ruthless	• Calm or anxious
• Interested in variety or routine	• Careful or careless	• Fun-loving or somber	• Trusting or suspicious	• Secure or insecure
• Independent or conforming	• Disciplined or impulsive	• Affectionate or reserved	• Helpful or uncooperative	• Self-satisfied or self-pitying

FIGURE 11.7 The Big Five Factors of Personality. Each of the broad supertraits encompasses more narrow traits and characteristics. Use the acronym OCEAN to remember the Big Five personality factors (openness, conscientiousness, and so on).

- In fifth- to eighth-graders, conscientiousness was linked to better interpersonal relationships: higher-quality friendships, better acceptance by peers, and less victimization by peers (Jensen-Campbell & Malcolm, 2007).

- Adolescents who did not have substance abuse problems or conduct problems were higher in conscientiousness than their counterparts who had these problems (Anderson & others, 2007)

The trait theories have identified a number of characteristics that are important to consider when attempting to understand an individual's personality (Berecz, 2009; Schultz & Schultz, 2009). The trait approach also has led to advances in the assessment of personality through the development of numerous personality tests. However, some psychologists note that the trait approach gives too little attention to environmental factors and puts too much emphasis on stability. These criticisms initially were leveled by social cognitive theorist Walter Mischel (1968). Mischel argued that personality often changes according to the situation. Thus, an individual may behave very differently at a party from the way he would in the library.

Today, most personality psychologists believe that personality is a product of *trait-situation interaction.* In other words, both traits and situational (context) factors must be considered to understand personality. Also, some people are more consistent on some traits and other people are consistent on other traits.

Views on Adult Personality Development

Two important views on adult development are the stage-crisis view and the life-events approach. In examining these approaches, we discuss the extent to which adults experience a midlife crisis and consider how life events influence the individual's development.

The Stage-Crisis View   Erikson's theory, which we discussed earlier, is a stage-crisis view. Here we describe the view of Daniel Levinson and examine the concept of a midlife crisis.

Levinson's Seasons of a Man's Life   In *The Seasons of a Man's Life,* clinical psychologist Daniel Levinson (1978) reported the results of extensive interviews with 40 middle-aged men. The interviews were conducted with hourly workers, business executives, academic biologists, and novelists. Levinson bolstered his conclusions with information from the biographies of famous men and the development of memorable characters in literature. Although Levinson's major interest focused on midlife change, he described a number of stages and transitions in the life span, which are shown in Figure 11.8.

Levinson emphasizes that developmental tasks must be mastered at each of these stages. In early adulthood, the two major tasks to be mastered are exploring the possibilities for adult living and developing a stable life structure. Levinson sees the twenties as a *novice phase* of adult development. At the end of one's teens, a transition from dependence to independence should occur. This transition is marked by the formation of a dream—an image of the kind of life the youth wants to have, especially in terms of a career and marriage.

Era of late adulthood: 60 to ?

Late adult transition: Age 60 to 65

Culminating life structure for middle adulthood: 55 to 60

Age 50 transition: 50 to 55

Entry life structure for middle adulthood: 45 to 50

Middle adult transition: Age 40 to 45

Culminating life structure for early adulthood: 33 to 40

Age 30 transition: 28 to 33

Entry life structure for early adulthood: 22 to 28

Early adult transition: Age 17 to 22

FIGURE 11.8 Levinson's Periods of Adult Development.

The novice phase is a time of reasonably free experimentation and of testing the dream in the real world.

From about the ages of 28 to 33, the man goes through a transition period in which he must face the more serious question of determining his goals. During the thirties, he usually focuses on family and career development. In the later years of this period, he enters a phase of Becoming One's Own Man (or BOOM, as Levinson calls it). By age 40, he has reached a stable location in his career, has outgrown his earlier, more tenuous attempts at learning to become an adult, and now must look forward to the kind of life he will lead as a middle-aged adult.

According to Levinson, the change to middle adulthood lasts about five years (ages 40 to 45) and requires the adult male to come to grips with four major conflicts that have existed in his life since adolescence: (1) being young versus being old, (2) being destructive versus being constructive, (3) being masculine versus being feminine, and (4) being attached to others versus being separated from them. Seventy to eighty percent of the men Levinson interviewed found the midlife transition tumultuous and psychologically painful, as many aspects of their lives came into question. According to Levinson, the success of the midlife transition rests on how effectively the individual reduces the polarities and accepts each of them as an integral part of his being.

The original Levinson data included no females. However, Levinson (1987, 1996) subsequently reported that his stages, transitions, and the crisis of middle age hold for females as well as males.

Midlife Crises Levinson (1978) views midlife as a crisis, believing that the middle-aged adult is suspended between the past and the future, trying to cope with this gap that threatens life's continuity. George Vaillant (1977) concludes that just as adolescence is a time for detecting parental flaws and discovering the truth about childhood, the forties are a decade of reassessing and recording the truth about the adolescent and adulthood years. However, whereas Levinson sees midlife as a crisis, Vaillant notes that only a minority of adults experience a midlife crisis:

> Just as pop psychologists have reveled in the not-so-common high drama of adolescent turmoil, also the popular press, sensing good copy, had made all too much of the mid-life crisis. The term mid-life crisis brings to mind some variation of the renegade minister who leaves behind four children and the congregation that loved him in order to drive off in a magenta Porsche with a 25-year-old striptease artiste. As with adolescent turmoil, mid-life crises are much rarer in community samples. (pp. 222–223)

Vaillant's study—called the Grant Study—involved a follow-up of Harvard University men in their early thirties and in their late forties who initially had been interviewed as undergraduates. Other research has also found that midlife is not characterized by pervasive crises. For example, a longitudinal study of 2,247 individuals found few midlife crises (McCrae & Costa, 1990). The emotional instability of these individuals did not significantly increase during their middle-aged years (see Figure 11.9). In fact, some studies have documented psychological gains among middle-aged adults. For example, one study revealed that individuals from 40 to 60 years of age were less nervous and worried than those under 40. The middle-aged adults reported a growing sense of control in their work as well as more financial security, greater environmental mastery (the ability to handle daily responsibilities), and more autonomy than their younger counterparts. Another study found that adults experienced a peak of personal control and power in middle age (Clark-Plaskie & Lachman, 1999).

Adult development experts have become virtually unanimous in their belief that midlife crises have been exaggerated (Brim, Ryff, & Kessler, 2004; Lachman,

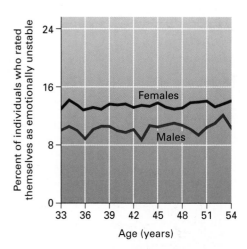

FIGURE 11.9 Emotional Instability and Age. In one longitudinal study, the emotional instability of individuals was assessed from age 33 to age 54 (McCrae & Costa, 1990). No significant increase in emotional instability occurred during the middle-aged years.

*M*id-life crises are greatly exaggerated in America.

—GEORGE VAILLANT
*Contemporary Psychologist,
Harvard University*

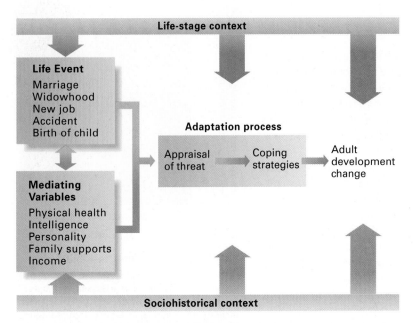

FIGURE 11.10 A Contemporary Life-Events Framework for Interpreting Adult Developmental Change.

2004; Pudrovska, 2009). In sum, (1) the stage theories place too much emphasis on crises in development, especially midlife crises; and (2) there often is considerable individual variation in the way people experience the stages, a topic that we turn to next.

Individual Variations Stage theories especially focus on the universals of adult personality development. They try to pin down stages that all individuals go through in their adult lives. These theories do not adequately address individual variations in adult development. In one extensive study of a random sample of 500 men at midlife, it was concluded that there is extensive individual variation among men (Farrell & Rosenberg, 1981). In the individual variations view, middle-aged adults interpret, shape, alter, and give meaning to their lives (Arpanantikul, 2004).

The ability to set aside unproductive worries and preoccupations is believed to be an important factor in functioning under stress. In Vaillant's (1977, 2002) longitudinal study, pervasive personal preoccupations were maladaptive in both the work and the marriages of college students over a 30-year period after leaving college. Some individuals in this study had personal preoccupations, whereas others did not.

It also is important to recognize how some individuals may experience a midlife crisis in some contexts of their lives but not others (Lachman, 2004). Thus, turmoil and stress may characterize one area of a person's life (such as work) while things are going smoothly in another context (such as family).

Researchers have found that in one-third of the cases in which individuals have reported having a midlife crisis, the crisis is triggered by life events such as a job loss, financial problems, or illness (Wethington, Kessler, & Pixley, 2004). Let's now further explore the role of life events in midlife development.

The Life-Events Approach An alternative to the stage approach to adult development is the life-events approach (Serido, 2009). In the early version of the life-events approach, life events were viewed as taxing circumstances for individuals, forcing them to change their personality (Holmes & Rahe, 1967). Such events as the death of a spouse, divorce, marriage, and so on were believed to involve varying degrees of stress, and therefore likely to influence the individual's development.

Today's life-events approach is more sophisticated (Cui & Vaillant, 1996; Hultsch & Plemons, 1979). The **contemporary life-events approach** emphasizes that how life events influence the individual's development depends not only on the event but also on mediating factors (physical health and family supports, for example), the individual's adaptation to the life event (appraisal of the threat and coping strategies, for example), the life-stage context, and the sociohistorical context (see Figure 11.10).

Consider how the life event of divorce might affect personality. A divorce is likely to be more stressful for individuals who are in poor health and have little family support. One individual may perceive it as highly stressful (less adaptive) rather than a challenge but develop coping strategies to effectively deal with it (more adaptive). And a divorce may be more stressful after many years of marriage when adults are in their fifties than when they have been married only several years and are in their twenties (an example of life-stage context). Finally, adults may be able

contemporary life-events approach
Approach emphasizing that how a life event influences the individual's development depends not only on the event but also on mediating factors, the individual's adaptation to the life event, the life-stage context, and the sociohistorical context.

to cope more effectively with divorce today than several decades ago because divorce has become more commonplace and accepted in today's society (an example of sociohistorical context).

Though the life-events approach is a valuable addition to understanding adult development, it has its drawbacks. One of the most significant drawbacks is that the life-events approach places too much emphasis on change. It does not adequately recognize the stability that, at least to some degree, characterizes adult development. Another drawback is that it may not be life's major events that are the primary sources of stress, but our daily experiences. Enduring a boring but tense job or living in poverty does not show up on scales of major life events. Yet the everyday pounding from these conditions can add up to a highly stressful life and eventually illness. Greater insight into the source of life's stresses might come from focusing more on daily hassles and daily uplifts (O'Connor & others, 2009). Researchers have found that young and middle-aged adults experience a greater daily frequency of stressors than older individuals (Almeida & Horn, 2004).

Generativity

Erikson (1968) argues that middle-aged adults face the issue of **generativity versus stagnation,** which is the name Erikson gave to the seventh stage in his life-span theory. Generativity encompasses adults' desire to leave a legacy of themselves to the next generation. By contrast, stagnation (sometimes called "self-absorption") develops when individuals sense that they have done nothing for the next generation.

Does research support Erikson's theory that generativity is an important dimension of middle age? Yes, it does (Gramling, 2007). One study revealed that parents' generativity was linked to young adult offsprings' successful development (Peterson, 2006). In this study, parents who were generative had young adult children who were conscientious and agreeable. In a longitudinal study of Smith College women, generativity increased from the thirties through the fifties (Cole & Stewart, 1996; Stewart, Ostrove, & Helson, 2001; Zucker, Ostrove, & Stewart, 2002) (see Figure 11.11). In George Vaillant's (2002) longitudinal studies of aging, in middle age, generativity (defined in this study as "taking care of the next generation") was more strongly related than intimacy to whether individuals would have an enduring and happy marriage at 75 to 80 years of age. One participant in Vaillant's studies said, "From twenty to thirty I learned how to get along with my wife. From thirty to forty I learned how to be a success at my job, and at forty to fifty I worried less about myself and more about the children" (p. 114).

Middle-aged adults can develop generativity in a number of ways (Kotre, 1984). Through biological generativity, adults conceive and give birth to an infant. Through parental generativity, adults provide nurturance and guidance to children. Through work generativity, adults develop skills that are passed down to others. And through cultural generativity, adults create, renovate, or conserve some aspect of culture that ultimately survives.

Stability and Change

Recall from Chapter 1, "Introduction," that an important issue in life-span development is the extent to which individuals show stability in their development versus the extent to which they change. A number of longitudinal studies have assessed stability and change in the personality of individuals at different points in their lives (McAdams & Olson, 2010; Roberts & Mroczek, 2008). A common finding is that, in most cases, the less time between measurements of personality characteristics, the more stability they show. Thus, if we measure a person's introversion/extraversion at the age of 20 and then again at age 30, we are likely to find more stability than if we assess the person at the age of 20 and then again at the age of 40.

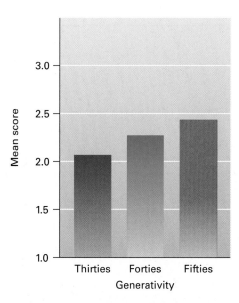

FIGURE 11.11 Changes in Generativity from the Thirties Through the Fifties. Generativity increased in Smith College women as they aged from their thirties through their fifties (Stewart, Ostrove, & Helson, 2001). The women rated themselves on a 3-point scale indicating the extent to which they thought the statements about generativity were descriptive of their lives. Higher scores reflect greater generativity.

generativity versus stagnation The seventh stage in Erikson's life-span theory that encompasses adults' desire to leave a legacy of themselves to the next generation.

Costa and McCrae's Baltimore Study   Earlier we discussed the Big Five factors in personality as an important trait theory. Paul Costa and Robert McCrae (1998; McCrae & Costa, 2006) have studied the Big Five factors in approximately a thousand college-educated women and men from 20 to 96 years of age. Longitudinal data collection initially began in the 1950s to the mid-1960s on people of varying ages and is ongoing. Costa and McCrae found a great deal of stability across the adult years in the Big Five personality factors—emotional stability, extraversion, openness, agreeableness, and conscientiousness. However, recent studies have found age differences in the Big Five factors across the life span. Research on individuals from 16 years of age to the mid-eighties revealed that extraversion and openness decreased with age, whereas agreeableness increased with age (Donnellan & Lucas, 2008). In this study, conscientiousness peaked in middle age. Another study found that conscientiousness continued to develop in late adulthood (Roberts, Walton, & Bogg, 2005), and another study revealed that older adults were more conscientious and agreeable than middle-aged and younger adults (Allemand, Zimprich, & Hendriks, 2008). Yet another study examined developmental changes in the components of conscientiousness (Jackson & others, 2009). In this study, the transition into late adulthood was characterized by increases in these aspects of conscientiousness: impulse control, reliability, and conventionality.

A recent meta-analysis of personality stability and change organized according to the Big Five framework included 92 longitudinal studies spanning 10 to 101 years of age (Roberts, Walton, & Viechtbauer, 2006):

- Results for extraversion were complex until it was subdivided into social dominance (assertiveness, dominance) and social vitality (talkativeness, sociability). Social dominance increased from adolescence through middle adulthood, whereas social vitality increased in adolescence and then decreased in early and late adulthood.

- Agreeableness and conscientiousness increased in early and middle adulthood.

- Neuroticism decreased in early adulthood.

- Openness to experience increased in adolescence and early adulthood and then decreased in late adulthood.

Might some Big Five factors be related to how long older adults live? To find out, read the *Research in Life-Span Development* interlude.

Research in Life-Span Development

THE BIG FIVE FACTORS AND MORTALITY

Researchers have found that some personality traits are associated with the mortality of older adults (Mroczek, Spiro, & Griffin, 2006). In one study, 883 older Catholic clergy were given the NEO Five-Factor Inventory that assesses the Big Five factors in personality (Wilson & others, 2004). The clergy were followed for five years, during which 182 of the 883 clergy died. At the beginning of the study, the average age of the clergy was 75, and 69 percent of them were women. Risk of death nearly doubled in clergy with a high score on neuroticism (90th percentile) compared with a low score (10th percentile) and was halved in clergy who were very high in conscientiousness compared with those who very low. Results for extraversion were mixed, whereas agreeableness and openness were not related to mortality.

Why might a high score on neuroticism and a low score on conscientiousness lead to an earlier death? Researchers have found that high-neuroticism older adults react more emotionally to stressful circumstances than their low-neuroticism counterparts (Mroczek, Spiro, & Griffin, 2006). Over many years, high neuroticism may elevate harmful stress hormones and produce physical damages to the cardiovascular system, thus contributing to mortality. By contrast, individuals who score high on conscientiousness engage in more healthy behaviors than those who score low. For example, low-conscientiousness individuals engage in more risky behaviors, such as excessive drinking and impulsive behaviors that lead to fatal accidents. It also has been proposed that they likely have less healthy diets and are less likely to exercise regularly than high-conscientiousness individuals (Mroczek, Spiro, & Griffin, 2006).

A longitudinal study of more than 1,200 individuals across seven decades revealed that the Big Five personality factor of conscientiousness predicted lower mortality risk from childhood through late adulthood (Martin, Friedman, & Schwartz, 2007). Another longitudinal study recently underscored the importance of the link between neuroticism and mortality in a sample of more than 1,600 aging men (Mroczek & Spiro, 2007). A high level of neuroticism and an increasing level of neuroticism were related to lower survival across an 18-year period (see Figure 11.12).

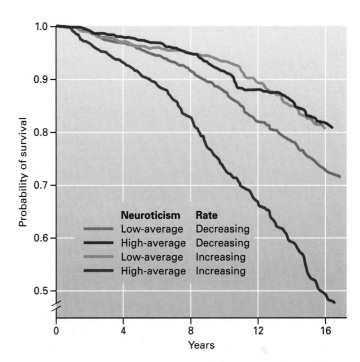

FIGURE 11.12 Link Between Neuroticism and Survival in Aging Men. *Note:* At the beginning of the study, the men were 43 to 91 years old. During the 18-year period of the study, 30 percent of the participants died, with more than 70 percent of the deaths due to cardiovascular disease and cancer.

Berkeley Longitudinal Studies   Most longitudinal studies indicate that neither extreme stability nor extreme change characterizes most people's personality as they go through the adult years. One of the longest-running inquiries is the series of analyses called the Berkeley Longitudinal Studies. Initially, more than 500 children and their parents were studied in the late 1920s and early 1930s. The book *Present and Past in Middle Life* (Eichorn & others, 1981) profiles these individuals as they became middle-aged.

The results from early adolescence through a portion of midlife did not support either extreme in the debate over whether personality is characterized by stability or change. Some characteristics were more stable than others, however. The most stable characteristics were the degree to which individuals were intellectually oriented, self-confident, or open to new experiences. The characteristics that changed the most included the extent the individuals were nurturant or hostile and whether they had good self-control or not.

John Clausen (1993), one of the researchers in the Berkeley Longitudinal Studies, holds that too much attention has been given to discontinuities for all members of the human species, as exemplified in the adult stage theories. Rather, he stresses that some people experience recurrent crises and change a great deal over the life course, whereas others have more stable, continuous lives and change far less.

Helson's Mills College Studies   Another longitudinal investigation of adult personality development was conducted by Ravenna Helson and her colleagues (Helson, 1997; Helson & Wink, 1992; Roberts, Helson, & Klohnen, 2002). They initially studied 132 women who were seniors at Mills College in California in the late 1950s. In 1981, when the women were 42 to 45 years old, they were studied again.

Helson and her colleagues distinguished three main groups among the Mills women: family-oriented (participants who had children), career-oriented (whether or not they also wanted families), and those who followed neither path (women without children who pursued only low-level work). Despite their different college profiles and their diverging life paths, the women in all three groups

What characterized the development of women in Ravenna Helson's Mills College Study?

experienced some similar psychological changes over their adult years. However, the women in the third group changed less than those committed to career or family.

During their early forties, many of the women shared the concerns that stage theorists such as Levinson found in men: concern for young and old, introspectiveness, interest in roots, and awareness of limitations and death. However, the researchers in the Mills College Study concluded that rather than being in a midlife crisis, what was being experienced was *midlife consciousness*. They also indicated that commitment to the tasks of early adulthood—whether to a career or family (or both)—helped women learn to control their impulses, develop interpersonal skills, become independent, and work hard to achieve goals. Women who did not commit themselves to one of these lifestyle patterns faced fewer challenges and did not develop as fully as the other women (Rosenfeld & Stark, 1987). In the Mills study, some women moved toward becoming "pillars of society" in their early forties to early fifties (Helson & Wink, 1992).

George Vaillant's Studies George Vaillant (2002) has conducted three longitudinal studies of adult development and aging: (1) a sample of 268 socially advantaged Harvard graduates born about 1920 (called the "Grant Study"); (2) a sample of 456 socially disadvantaged inner-city men born about 1930; and (3) a sample of 90 middle-SES, intellectually gifted women born about 1910. These individuals have been assessed numerous times (in most cases every two years), beginning in the 1920s to 1940s and continuing today for those still living. The main assessments involve extensive interviews with the participants, their parents, and teachers.

Vaillant categorized 75- to 80-year-olds as "happy-well," "sad-sick," and "dead." He used data collected from these individuals when they were 50 years of age to predict which categories they were likely to end up in at 75 to 80 years of age. Alcohol abuse and smoking at age 50 were the best predictors of which individuals would be dead at 75 to 80 years of age. Other factors at age 50 were linked with being in the "happy-well" category at 75 to 80 years of age: getting regular exercise; avoiding being overweight; being well educated; having a stable marriage; being future-oriented; being thankful and forgiving; empathizing with others; being active with other people; and having good coping skills. Wealth and income at age 50 were not linked with being in the "happy-well" category at 75 to 80 years of age. The results for one of Vaillant's studies, the Grant Study of Harvard men, are shown in Figure 11.13.

Conclusions What can we conclude about stability and change in personality development during the adult years? According to a recent research review by leading researchers Brent Roberts and Daniel Mroczek (2008), there is increasing evidence that personality traits continue to change during the adult years, even into late adulthood. However, in the recent meta-analysis of 92 longitudinal studies described earlier, the greatest change in personality traits occurred in early adulthood—from about 20 to 40 years of age (Roberts, Walton, & Viechbauer, 2006).

Thus, people show more stability in their personality when they reach midlife than when they were younger adults (McAdams & Olson, 2010). These findings support what is called a *cumulative personality model* of personality development, which states that with time and age people become more adept at interacting with their environment in ways that promote increased stability in personality (Caspi & Roberts, 2001).

This does not mean that change is absent throughout middle and late adulthood. Ample evidence shows that social contexts,

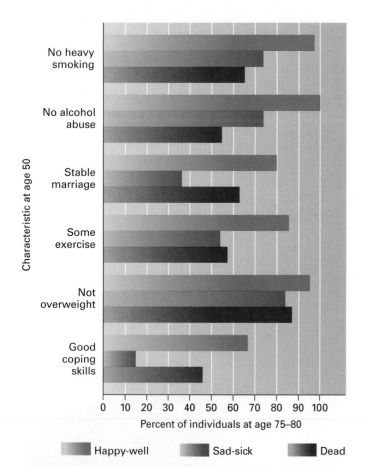

FIGURE 11.13 Links Between Characteristics at Age 50 and Health and Happiness at Age 75 to 80. In a longitudinal study, the characteristics shown above at age 50 were related to whether individuals were happy-well, sad-sick, or dead at age 75 to 80 (Vaillant, 2002).

new experiences, and sociohistorical changes can affect personality development, but the changes in middle and late adulthood are usually not as great as in early adulthood (Mroczek, Spiro, & Griffin, 2006).

In general, changes in personality traits across adulthood also occur in a positive direction. Over time, "people become more confident, warm, responsible, and calm" (Roberts & Mroczek, 2008, p. 33). Such positive changes equate with becoming more socially mature.

In sum, recent research contradicts the old view that stability in personality begins to set in at about 30 years of age (McAdams & Olson, 2009; Roberts & Mroczek, 2008; Roberts, Wood, & Caspi, 2008; Roberts & others, 2009). While there are some consistent developmental changes in the personality traits of large numbers of people, at the individual level people can show unique patterns of personality traits, and these patterns often reflect life experiences related to themes of their specific developmental period (Roberts & Mroczek, 2008). For example, researchers have found that individuals who are in a stable marriage and a solid career track become more socially dominant, conscientious, and emotionally stable as they go through early adulthood (Roberts & Wood, 2006). And, for some of these individuals, there is greater change in their personality traits than for other individuals (Roberts & Mroczek, 2008).

At age 55, actor Jack Nicholson said, "I feel exactly the same as I've always felt: a slightly reined-in voracious beast." Nicholson felt his personality had not changed much. Some others might think they have changed more. *How much does personality change and how does it stay the same through adulthood?*

Review and Reflect: Learning Goal 3

 Describe personality and its development in adulthood

REVIEW

- What are trait theories? What are the Big Five factors of personality?
- What are some views of adult development of personality?
- What is Erikson's view of middle-aged adults?
- What are some major longitudinal studies of adult personality development, and what implications do they have for the stability/change issue?

REFLECT

- Why is it important to examine longitudinal studies when investigating stability and change in development?

Reach Your Learning Goals

The Self, Identity, and Personality

1 THE SELF: DISCUSS THE MAIN WAYS THE SELF IS CONCEPTUALIZED

Self-Understanding

- There is considerable overlap in the concepts of self, identity, and personality. Self is all characteristics of a person, identity is who a person is, and personality consists of the enduring personal characteristics of individuals. Self-understanding is the cognitive representation of the self, the substance of self-conceptions. Developmental changes in self-understanding include the construction of the self in infancy in terms of self-recognition and transformations in self-understanding in childhood (including perspective taking). Self-understanding in early childhood is characterized by confusion of self, mind, and body; concrete, physical, and active descriptions; and unrealistic positive overestimations. Young children display more sophisticated self-understanding and understanding of others than previously thought. Self-understanding in middle and late childhood involves an increase in the use of psychological characteristics and traits, social descriptions, and social comparison; distinction between the real and ideal self; and an increase in realistic self-evaluations. Social understanding also increases in middle and late childhood, especially in taking the perspective of others. Self-definition in adolescence is more abstract and idealistic, involves more contradictions within the self, is more fluctuating, includes concern about the real self versus the ideal self, is characterized by increased self-consciousness, and is more integrative. Developments in adulthood include expanded self-awareness and possible selves and the life reviews of older adults.

Self-Esteem and Self-Concept

- Self-esteem refers to global evaluations of the self; it is also called self-worth, or self-image. Self-concept consists of domain-specific evaluations of the self. Self-esteem can change over time, and low self-esteem is linked with depression. The accuracy of self-evaluations increases across the elementary school years. Some studies have found that self-esteem decreases in adolescence, but overall, most adolescents still have positive self-esteem. Some important aspects of self-esteem include the degree to which it is linked to performance. This varies, as there are only moderate correlations with school performance and varying correlations with job performance; individuals with high self-esteem have greater initiative and this can produce positive or negative outcomes; self-esteem is strongly correlated with happiness; there is a dark side to high self-esteem in that some individuals who have high self-esteem are conceited and narcissistic. Five ways to increase self-esteem are through (1) identifying the causes of low self-esteem and the domains of competence important to the self, (2) providing emotional support and social approval, (3) taking responsibility for one's own self-esteem, (4) achieving goals, and (5) coping.

Self-Regulation

- Self-regulation involves the ability to control one's behavior without having to rely on others' help. Two- to three-year-olds may show rudimentary forms of self-regulation, but many preschoolers show increased self-regulation. Elementary-school-aged children increase their self-regulation. In adolescence, some changes may increase self-regulation; others decrease it. Self-control increases in early and middle adulthood. Self-regulation may vary by domain. For example, older adults often show less self-regulation in the physical domain than younger adults. Baltes proposed the selective optimization with compensation theory of self-regulation. Many older adults show a remarkable ability to engage in self-regulation despite encountering losses. Heckhausen distinguishes between primary and secondary control strategies and has found that secondary control strategies increase through the adult years.

2   IDENTITY: EXPLAIN THE KEY FACETS OF IDENTITY DEVELOPMENT

What Is Identity?

- Identity is a self-portrait with many pieces, including vocational/career identity, political identity, religious identity, relationship identity, sexual identity, and cultural/ethnic identity.

Erikson's View

- Identity versus identity confusion is Erikson's fifth developmental stage, which individuals experience in the adolescent years. At this time, adolescents examine who they are, what they are all about, and where they are going in life. Erikson describes the psychosocial moratorium between childhood security and adult autonomy that adolescents experience, which promotes identity exploration.

Some Contemporary Thoughts on Identity

- In the contemporary view, identity is more gradual than Erikson's term crisis implies, is extraordinarily complex, neither begins nor ends with adolescence, and emphasizes multiple identities. In Damon's view, too many of today's youth are not moving toward any identity resolution.

Developmental Changes

- According to Marcia, various combinations of crisis and commitment produce four identity statuses: identity diffusion, identity foreclosure, identity moratorium, and identity achievement. A number of experts stress that the key developmental changes in identity occur in the late teens and early twenties. "MAMA" cycles—*moratiorum–achievement–moratorium–achievement*—may continue throughout adulthood.

Family Influences

- Adolescents' identity development advances when their relationship with their parents includes both individuality and connectedness.

Ethnic Identity

- Ethnic identity includes a sense of membership in an ethnic group, and the individual's feelings related to belonging to that group. The struggle to maintain an ethnic identity and blend with the dominant culture may present special issues for members of ethnic minority groups, and they may confront these issues for the first time in adolescence. A positive ethnic identity is increasingly linked to positive outcomes for ethnic minority adolescents.

3   PERSONALITY: DESCRIBE PERSONALITY AND ITS DEVELOPMENT IN ADULTHOOD

Trait Theories and the Big Five Factors of Personality

- Trait theories state that personality consists of broad dispositions, called traits, that tend to produce characteristic responses. One trait theory that has received considerable attention is the Big Five factors of personality, the view that personality consists of openness to experience, conscientiousness, extraversion, agreeableness, and neuroticism. Today most psychologists stress that personality is a product of trait-situation interaction.

Views on Adult Personality Development

- Two of the important adult developmental views are the stage-crisis view and the life-events approach. Levinson's and Erikson's theories are stage-crisis views. Midlife crises do not occur nearly as much as the stereotype suggests. What does arise is a midlife consciousness that focuses on such matters as how to adapt to aging. The life-events approach argues that life events and how people adapt to them are important in understanding adult development. There is considerable variation in how people go through the adult stages of development and in how they experience and adapt to life events.

Generativity

- Erikson argues that middle-aged adults face a significant issue in life—generativity versus stagnation—which is the name he gave to the seventh stage in his life-span theory. Generativity encompasses adults' desire to leave a legacy of themselves to the next generation.

Stability and Change

- Four longitudinal studies that have addressed stability and change in adult development are Costa and McCrae's Baltimore Study, the Berkeley Longitudinal Studies, Helson's

Mills College Study, and Vaillant's studies. The longitudinal studies have shown that there are both stability and change in adult personality development. The cumulative personality model states that with time and age personality becomes more stable. Change in personality traits occurs more in early adulthood than middle and late adulthood, but a number of aspects of personality do continue to change after early adulthood. Change in personality traits across adulthood occurs in a positive direction, reflecting social maturity. At the individual level, changes in personality are often linked to life experiences related to a specific developmental period. Some people change more than others.

KEY TERMS

self 386
identity 386
personality 386
self-understanding 386
perspective taking 389
possible selves 390
self-esteem 393
self-concept 393

narcissim 394
self-regulation 397
selective optimization with
    compensation theory 398
identity versus identity
    confusion 403
psychosocial moratorium 403
crisis 405

commitment 405
identity diffusion 405
identity foreclosure 405
identity moratorium 405
identity achievement 405
individuality 406
connectedness 406
ethnic identity 407

trait theories 409
Big Five factors of
    personality 409
contemporary life-events
    approach 412
generativity versus
    stagnation 413

KEY PEOPLE

Robert Selman 389
Hazel Markus 391
Susan Harter 396
Claire Kopp 397
Paul Baltes 399

Jutta Heckhausen 401
Erik Erikson 402
William Damon 404
James Marcia 404
Alan Waterman 406

Walter Mischel 410
Daniel Levinson 410
George Vaillant 411
Paul Costa and Robert
    McCrae 414

John Clausen 415
Ravenna Helson 415
Brent Roberts and Daniel
    Mroczek 416

E-LEARNING TOOLS

Connect to **www.mhhe.com/santrockldt5e** to research the answers and complete these exercises. In addition, you'll find a number of other resources and valuable study tools for Chapter 11, "The Self, Identity, and Personality," on this Web site.

Taking It to the Net

1. Janice has recently been appointed principal of a high school that has a large population of Middle Eastern, Asian, and Hispanic students. She wants to conduct an in-service training for the staff to help them understand the challenges that ethnic students face as they strive to achieve their self-identity and ethnic identity. What challenges do the ethnic students face in resolving their identity crises, and how can the school assist them?

2. Eduardo is the vice president for human resources at a 200-employee manufacturing plant. He wants to use a personality assessment tool to assist him in job selection and in planning interventions for employees who have job-related problems, such as poor motivation, personality problems with co-workers, and conflicts with supervisors. Would an assessment based on the Big Five factor model of personality be a good choice?

Self Assessment

To evaluate your self-esteem, identity, and personality, complete these self-assessments:

• *My Self-Esteem*

• *Exploring My Identity*

• *Am I Introverted or Extraverted?*

Health and Well-Being, Parenting, and Education

Build your decision-making skills by trying your hand at the health and well-being, parenting, and education exercises.

Video Clips

The Online Learning Center includes the following videos for this chapter:

- *Delayed Gratification at Age 4*
- *Self-Perception at 10 Years and 8 Years of Age*
- *Self-Perception at 14 Years of Age*
- *Adolescent Self-Esteem*
- *Life Review at Age 72*
- *Rouge Test at 18 Months*
- *Rouge Test at Age 2*

12

We are born twice over; the first time for existence, the second time for life; once as human beings and later as men or as women.

—JEAN-JACQUES ROUSSEAU
*French-Born Swiss Philosopher,
18th Century*

LEARNING GOALS

◆ Explain biological, social, and cognitive influences on gender.

◆ Discuss gender stereotypes, similarities, and differences.

◆ Describe the development of gender through the life span.

◆ Characterize influences on sexuality, the nature of sexual orientation, and some sexual problems.

◆ Summarize how sexuality develops through the life span.

GENDER AND SEXUALITY

CHAPTER OUTLINE

PREVIEW

As females and males, human beings are involved in the existence and continuation of life. Gender and sexuality—our lives as females and males—are important aspects of human development and are the topics of this chapter.

1 BIOLOGICAL, SOCIAL, AND COGNITIVE INFLUENCES ON GENDER

| What Is Gender? | Biological Influences | Social Influences | Cognitive Influences |

What Is Gender?

Gender refers to the characteristics of people as males and females. **Gender identity** involves a sense of one's own gender, including knowledge, understanding, and acceptance of being male or female (Blakemore, Berenbaum, & Liben, 2009; Egan & Perry, 2001). **Gender roles** are sets of expectations that prescribe how females or males should think, act, and feel. During the preschool years, most children increasingly act in ways that match their culture's gender roles. **Gender-typing** refers to acquisition of a traditional masculine or feminine role. For example, fighting is more characteristic of a traditional masculine role and crying is more characteristic of a traditional feminine role.

One aspect of gender identity involves knowing whether you are a boy or a girl (Martin & Ruble, 2010). Until recently, it was thought that this aspect of gender identity emerged at about 2½ years. However, a recent longitudinal study that explored the acquisition of gender labels in infancy and their implications for gender-typed play revealed that gender identity likely emerges before 2 years of age (Zosuls & others, 2009). In this study, infants began using gender labels on average at 19 months of age, with girls beginning to use gender labels earlier than boys. This gender difference became present at 17 months of age and increased at 21 months of age. Use of gender labels was linked to gender-typed play, indicating that knowledge of gender categories may affect gender-typing earlier than 2 years of age.

A recent study revealed that sex-typed behavior (boys playing with cars and girls with jewelry, for example) increased during the preschool years and children engaging in the most sex-typed behavior during the preschool years still doing so at 8 years of age (Golombok & others, 2008).

Biological Influences

It was not until the 1920s that researchers confirmed the existence of human sex chromosomes, the genetic material that determines our sex. Humans normally have 46 chromosomes, arranged in pairs. A 23rd pair with two X-shaped chromosomes produces a female. A 23rd pair with an X chromosome and a Y chromosome produces a male.

Hormones In Chapter 3, "Physical Development and Biological Aging," we discussed the two classes of hormones that have the most influence on gender: estrogens and androgens. Both estrogens and androgens occur in both females and males, but in very different concentrations.

Estrogens primarily influence the development of female physical sex characteristics and help regulate the menstrual cycle. Estrogens are a general class of

gender The characteristics of people as females or males.

gender identity Involves a sense of one's own gender, including knowledge, understanding, and acceptance of being male or female.

gender role A set of expectations that prescribe how females or males should think, act, or feel.

gender typing Acquisition of a traditional masculine or feminine role.

estrogens A class of sex hormones—an important one of which is estradiol—that primarily influences the development of female sex characteristics and helps regulate the menstrual cycle.

hormones. An example of an important estrogen is estradiol. In females, estrogens are produced mainly by the ovaries.

Androgens primarily promote the development of male genitals and secondary sex characteristics. One important androgen is testosterone. Androgens are produced by the adrenal glands in males and females, and by the testes in males.

In the first few weeks of gestation, female and male embryos look alike. Male sex organs start to differ from female sex organs when a gene on the Y chromosome directs a small piece of tissue in the embryo to turn into testes. Once the tissue has turned into testes, they begin to secrete testosterone. Because in females there is no Y chromosome, the tissue turns into ovaries. To explore biological influences on gender, researchers have studied individuals who are exposed to unusual levels of sex hormones early in development (Blakemore, Berenbaum, & Liben, 2009). Here are four examples of the problems that may occur as a result (Lippa, 2005, pp. 122–124, 136–137):

- *Congenital adrenal hyperplasia (CAH).* Some girls have this condition, which is caused by a genetic defect. Their adrenal glands enlarge, resulting in abnormally high levels of androgens. Although CAH girls are XX females, they vary in how much their genitals look like male or female genitals. Their genitals may be surgically altered to look more like those of a typical female. Although CAH girls usually grow up to think of themselves as girls and women, they are less content with being a female and show a stronger interest in being a male than non-CAH girls (Berenbaum & Bailey, 2003; Ehrhardt & Baker, 1974; Hall & others, 2004). They like sports and enjoy playing with boys and boys' toys. CAH girls usually don't like typical girl activities such as playing with dolls and wearing makeup.

- *Androgen-insensitive males.* Because of a genetic error, a small number of XY males don't have androgen cells in their bodies. Their bodies look female, they develop a female gender identity, and they usually are sexually attracted to males.

- *Pelvic field defect.* A small number of newborns have a disorder called pelvic field defect, which in boys involves a missing penis. These XY boys have normal amounts of testosterone prenatally but usually have been castrated just after being born and raised as females. One study revealed that despite the efforts by parents to rear them as girls, most of the XY children insisted that they were boys (Reiner & Gearhart, 2004). Apparently, normal exposure to androgens prenatally had a stronger influence on their gender identity than being castrated and raised as girls.

- In another intriguing case, one of two identical twin boys lost his penis due to an errant circumcision. The twin who lost his penis was surgically reassigned to be a girl and reared as a girl. Bruce (the real name of the boy) became "Brenda." Early indications were that the sex reassignment had positive outcomes (Money, 1975), but later it was concluded that "Brenda" wasn't adjusted well as a girl (Diamond & Sigmundson, 1997). As a young adult, Brenda became Bruce once again and lived as a man with a wife and adopted children (Colapinto, 2000). Tragically in 2004, when Bruce was 38 years old, he committed suicide.

Although sex hormones alone, of course, do not determine behavior, researchers have found links between sex hormone levels and certain behaviors. The most established effects of testosterone on humans involve aggressive behavior and sexual behavior (Hyde, 2007). Levels of testosterone are correlated with sexual behavior in boys during puberty (Udry & others, 1985). And a recent study revealed that a higher fetal testosterone level measured from amniotic fluid was linked to increased male-typical play, such as increased aggression, in 6- to 10-year-old boys and girls (Auyeung & others, 2009).

androgens A class of sex hormones—an important one of which is testosterone—that primarily promotes the development of male genitals and secondary sex characteristics.

The Evolutionary Psychology View   In Chapter 2, "Biological Beginnings," we described the approach of evolutionary psychology, which emphasizes that adaptation

"How is it gendered?"

Sex differences are adaptations to the differing restrictions and opportunities that a society provides for its men and women.

—ALICE EAGLY
Contemporary Psychologist, Northwestern University

social role theory Eagly's theory that psychological gender differences are caused by the contrasting social roles of women and men.

psychoanalytic theory of gender Stems from Freud's view that preschool children develop a sexual attraction to the opposite-sex parent, then, at 5 or 6 years of age, renounce the attraction because of anxious feelings, subsequently identifying with the same-sex parent and unconsciously adopting the same-sex parent's characteristics.

social cognitive theory of gender The idea that children's gender development occurs through observation and imitation of gender behavior, as well as through the rewards and punishment children experience for behaviors believed to be appropriate or inappropriate for their gender.

during the evolution of humans produced psychological differences between males and females (Buss, 2008). Evolutionary psychologists argue that primarily because of their differing roles in reproduction, males and females faced different pressures in primeval environments when the human species was evolving. In particular, because having multiple sexual liaisons improves the likelihood that males will pass on their genes, natural selection favored males who adopted short-term mating strategies. These males competed with other males to acquire more resources in order to access females. Therefore, say evolutionary psychologists, males evolved dispositions that favor violence, competition, and risk taking.

In contrast, according to evolutionary psychologists, females' contributions to the gene pool were improved by securing resources for their offspring, which was promoted by obtaining long-term mates who could support a family. As a consequence, natural selection favored females who devoted effort to parenting and chose mates who could provide their offspring with resources and protection. Females developed preferences for successful, ambitious men who could provide these resources (Geher & Miller, 2007).

Critics of evolutionary psychology argue that its hypotheses are backed by speculations about prehistory, not evidence, and that in any event people are not locked into behavior that was adaptive in the evolutionary past. Critics also claim that the evolutionary view pays little attention to cultural and individual variations in gender differences (Smith, 2007).

Social Influences

Many social scientists do not locate the cause of psychological gender differences in biological dispositions. Rather, they argue that these differences are due to social experiences. Three theories that reflect this view have been influential.

Alice Eagly (2000; Eagly & Wood, 2010; Wood & Eagly, 2009, 2010) proposed **social role theory,** which states that psychological gender differences result from the contrasting roles of women and men. In most cultures around the world, women have less power and status than men have, and they control fewer resources (UNICEF, 2009). Compared with men, women perform more domestic work, spend fewer hours in paid employment, receive lower pay, and are more thinly represented in the highest levels of organizations. In Eagly's view, as women adapted to roles with less power and less status in society, they showed more cooperative, less dominant profiles than men. Thus, the social hierarchy and division of labor are important causes of gender differences in power, assertiveness, and nurture.

The **psychoanalytic theory of gender** stems from Freud's view that the preschool child develops a sexual attraction to the opposite-sex parent. At 5 or 6 years of age, the child renounces this attraction because of anxious feelings. Subsequently, the child identifies with the same-sex parent, unconsciously adopting the same-sex parent's characteristics. However, developmentalists do not hold that gender development proceeds as Freud proposed. Children become gender-typed much earlier than 5 or 6 years of age, and they become masculine or feminine even when the same-sex parent is not present in the family.

The social cognitive approach discussed in Chapter 1, "Introduction," provides an alternative explanation of how children develop gender-typed behavior (see Figure 12.1). According to the **social cognitive theory of gender,** children's gender development occurs through observation and imitation, and through the rewards and punishments children experience for gender-appropriate and gender-inappropriate behavior (Bussey & Bandura, 1999).

Parents, by action and example, influence their children's and adolescents' gender development (Blakemore, Berenbaum, & Liben, 2009). Parents often use rewards

Theory	Processes	Outcome
Psychoanalytic theory	Sexual attraction to opposite-sex parent at 3 to 5 years of age; anxiety about sexual attraction and subsequent identification with same-sex parent at 5 to 6 years of age	Gender behavior similar to that of same-sex parent
Social cognitive theory	Rewards and punishments of gender-appropriate and -inappropriate behavior by adults and peers; observation and initiation of models' masculine and feminine behavior	Gender behavior

FIGURE 12.1 A Comparison of the Psychoanalytic and Social Cognitive Views of Gender Development. Parents influence their children's development by action and example.

and punishments to teach their daughters to be feminine ("Karen, you are being a good girl when you play gently with your doll") and their sons to be masculine ("Keith, a boy as big as you is not supposed to cry").

Mothers and fathers often interact differently with their children and adolescents. Mothers are more involved with their children and adolescents than are fathers, although fathers increase the time they spend in parenting when they have sons, and they are less likely to become divorced when they have sons (Diekmann & Schmidheiny, 2004; Galambos, Berenbaum, & McHale, 2009; Harris & Morgan, 1991). Mothers' interactions with their children and adolescents often center on caregiving and teaching activities, whereas fathers' interactions often involve leisure activities (Galambos, Berenbaum, & McHale, 2009).

Parents frequently interact differently with sons and daughters, and these gendered interactions that begin in infancy usually continue through childhood and adolescence. In reviewing research on this topic, Phyllis Bronstein (2006) provided these conclusions:

- *Mothers' socialization strategies.* In many cultures mothers socialize their daughters to be more obedient and responsible than their sons. They also place more restrictions on daughters' autonomy.

- *Fathers' socialization strategies.* Fathers show more attention to sons than daughters, engage in more activities with sons, and put forth more effort to promote sons' intellectual development.

Thus, according to Bronstein (2006, pp. 269–270), "Despite an increased awareness in the United States and other Western cultures of the detrimental effects of gender stereotyping, many parents continue to foster behaviors and perceptions that are consonant with traditional gender role norms."

Children also learn about gender from observing other adults in the neighborhood and in the media (Fagot, Rodgers, & Leinbach, 2000). As children get older, peers become increasingly important. Peers extensively reward and punish gender behavior (Leaper & Friedman, 2007). For example, when children play in ways that the culture says are sex-appropriate, they tend to be rewarded by their peers. Those who engage in activities that are considered sex-inappropriate tend to be criticized or abandoned by their peers.

From 4 to about 12 years of age, children spend a large majority of their free play time exclusively with others of their own sex (Maccoby, 2002). What kind of socialization takes place in these same-sex play groups? In one study, researchers observed preschoolers over six months (Martin & Fabes, 2001). The more time boys spent interacting with other boys, the more their activity level, rough-and-tumble play, and sex-typed choice of toys and games increased, and the less time boys spent near adults. By contrast, the more time the preschool girls spent interacting with other girls, the more their activity level and aggression decreased, and the more their girl-type play activities and time spent near adults increased. After watching elementary school children repeatedly

What role does gender play in children's peer relations?

play in same-sex groups, two researchers characterized the playground as "gender school" (Luria & Herzog, 1985).

Cognitive Influences

Observation, imitation, rewards, and punishment—these are the mechanisms by which gender develops according to social cognitive theory. Interactions between the child and the social environment are the main keys to gender development in this view. Some critics who adopt a cognitive approach argue that this explanation pays too little attention to the child's own mind and understanding, and portrays the child as passively acquiring gender roles (Martin, Ruble, & Szkrybalo, 2002).

One influential cognitive theory is **gender schema theory,** which states that gender-typing emerges as children gradually develop gender schemas of what is gender-appropriate and gender-inappropriate in their culture (Blakemore, Berenbaum, & Liben, 2009; Martin & Ruble, 2010). A *schema* is a cognitive structure, a network of associations that guide an individual's perceptions. A *gender schema* organizes the world in terms of female and male. Children are internally motivated to perceive the world and to act in accordance with their developing schemas. Bit by bit, children pick up what is gender-appropriate and gender-inappropriate in their culture, and develop gender schemas that shape how they perceive the world and what they remember. Children are motivated to act in ways that conform with these gender schemas. Thus, gender schemas fuel gender-typing. To read about how gender schemas extend to young children's judgments about occupations, see the *Research in Life-Span Development* interlude.

Research in Life-Span Development

YOUNG CHILDREN'S GENDER SCHEMAS OF OCCUPATIONS

In one study, researchers interviewed children 3 to 7 years old about ten traditionally masculine occupations (airplane pilot, car mechanic) and feminine occupations (clothes designer, secretary), using questions such as these (Levy, Sadovsky, & Troseth, 2000):

- *Example of a traditionally masculine occupation item.* An airplane pilot is a person who "flies airplanes for people." Who do you think would do the best job as an airplane pilot, a man or a woman?

- *Example of a traditionally feminine occupation item.* A clothing designer is a person "who draws up and makes clothes for people." Who do you think would do the best job as a clothes designer, a man or a woman?

As indicated in Figure 12.2, the children had well-developed gender schemas, in this case reflected in stereotypes, of occupations. They "viewed men as more competent than women in masculine occupations, and rated women as more competent than men in feminine occupations" (p. 993). Also, "girls' ratings of women's competence at feminine

gender schema theory The theory that gender-typing emerges as children gradually develop gender schemas of what is gender-appropriate and gender-inappropriate in their culture.

FIGURE 12.2 Children's Judgments About the Competence of Men and Women in Gender-Stereotyped Occupations.

	Boys	Girls
"Masculine Occupations"		
Percentage who judged men more competent	87	70
Percentage who judged women more competent	13	30
"Feminine Occupations"		
Percentage who judged men more competent	35	8
Percentage who judged women more competent	65	92

occupations were substantially higher than their ratings of men's competence at masculine occupations. Conversely, boys' ratings of men's competence at masculine occupations were considerably greater than their ratings of women's competence at feminine occupations" (p. 1002). These findings demonstrate that children as young as 3 to 4 years of age have strong gender schemas regarding the perceived competencies of men and women in gender-typed occupations.

The researchers also asked the children to select from a list of emotions how they would feel if they grew up to have each of the ten occupations. Girls said they would be happy with the feminine occupations and angry or disgusted with the masculine occupations. As expected, boys reversed their choices, saying they would be happy if they grew up to have the masculine occupations but angry and disgusted with the feminine occupations. However, the boys' emotions were more intense (more angry and disgusted) in desiring to avoid the feminine occupations than girls wanting to avoid the masculine occupations. This finding supports other research that indicates gender roles often constrict boys more than girls (Hyde, 2007; Matlin, 2008).

It is important to note that the children in this study were at the height of gender stereotyping. Most older children, adolescents, and adults become more flexible about occupational roles (Hyde, 2007; Leaper & Friedman, 2007).

In sum, cognitive factors contribute to the way children think and act as males and females (Ruble & Martin, 2009). Through biological, social, and cognitive processes, children develop their gender attitudes and behaviors (Blakemore, Berenbaum, & Liben, 2009).

Review and Reflect: Learning Goal 1

Explain biological, social, and cognitive influences on gender

REVIEW
- What is gender? What are some components of gender?
- How does biology influence gender?
- What are three social theories of gender?
- How do cognitive factors influence gender development?

REFLECT
- Does any theory of gender development explain everything you know about differences between men and women? What might an eclectic view of gender development be like? (You might want to review the discussion of an eclectic theoretical orientation in Chapter 1, "Introduction.")

2 GENDER STEREOTYPES, SIMILARITIES, AND DIFFERENCES

| Gender Stereotyping | Gender Similarities and Differences |

To what extent are there real behavioral differences between males and females? Are many of the reported differences just stereotypes?

First imagine that this is a photograph of a baby girl. *What expectations would you have for her?* Then imagine that this is a photograph of a baby boy. *What expectations would you have for him?*

Gender Stereotyping

Gender stereotypes are general impressions and beliefs about females and males. For example, men are powerful; women are weak. Men make good physicians; women make good nurses. Men are good with numbers; women are good with words. Women are emotional; men are not. All of these are stereotypes. They are generalizations about a group that reflect widely held beliefs. Recent research has found that gender stereotypes are, to a great extent, still present in today's world, in the lives of both children and adults (Hyde, 2007). Researchers also have found that boys' gender stereotypes are more rigid than girls' (Blakemore, Berenbaum, & Liben, 2009).

Traditional Masculinity and Femininity A classic study in the early 1970s assessed which traits and behaviors college students believed were characteristic of females and which they believed were characteristic of males (Broverman & others, 1972). The traits associated with males were labeled *instrumental:* they included characteristics such as being independent, aggressive, and power-oriented. The traits associated with females were labeled *expressive:* they included characteristics such as being warm and sensitive.

Thus, the instrumental traits associated with males suited them for the traditional masculine role of going out into the world as the breadwinner. The expressive traits associated with females paralleled the traditional feminine role of being the sensitive, nurturing caregiver in the home. These roles and traits, however, are not just different; they also are unequal in terms of social status and power. The traditional feminine characteristics are childlike, suitable for someone who is dependent and subordinate to others. The traditional masculine characteristics suit one to deal competently with the wider world and to wield authority.

Research continues to find that gender stereotyping is pervasive (Blakemore, Berenbaum, & Liben, 2009; Hyde, 2007). For example, one study found extensive differences in the stereotyping of females' and males' emotions (Durik & others, 2006). Females were stereotyped as expressing more fear, guilt, love, sadness, shame, surprise, and sympathy than their male counterparts. Males were stereotyped as expressing more anger and pride than their female counterparts.

Developmental Changes in Gender Stereotyping Earlier we described how young children stereotype occupations as being "masculine" or "feminine." When do children begin to engage in gender stereotyping? One study examined the extent to which children and their mothers engage in gender stereotyping (Gelman, Taylor, & Nguyen, 2004). The researchers videotaped mothers and their 2-, 4-, and 6-year-old sons and daughters as they discussed a picture book with stereotyped (a male playing football, for example) and nonstereotyped (a female race car driver, for example) gender activities. Children engaged in more gender stereotyping than did their mothers. However, mothers expressed gender concepts to their children by referencing categories of gender ("Why do you think only *men* can be firefighters?" for example), labeling gender ("That looks like a daddy," for example), and contrasting males and females ("Is that a girl job or a boy job?" for example). Gender stereotyping by children was present even in the 2-year-olds, but increased considerably by 4 years of age. This study demonstrated that even when adults don't explicitly engage in gender stereotyping when talking with children, they provide children with information about gender by categorizing gender, labeling gender, and contrasting males and females. Children use these cues to construct an understanding of gender and to guide their behavior (Leaper & Bigler, 2004).

gender stereotypes General impressions and beliefs about females and males.

Gender stereotyping continues to change during middle and late childhood and adolescence (Martin & Ruble, 2010). A recent study of 3- to 10-year-old U.S. children revealed that girls and older children used a higher percentage of gender stereotypes (Miller & others, 2009). In this study, appearance stereotypes were more prevalent on the part of girls, whereas activity (sports, for example) and trait (aggressive, for example) stereotyping was more commonly engaged in by boys. During middle and late childhood, children expanded the range and extent of their gender stereotyping in such areas as occupations, sports, and school tasks. In early adolescence, gender stereotyping might increase again, a topic we address shortly. By late adolescence, gender attitudes become more flexible.

Gender Similarities and Differences

What is the reality behind gender stereotypes? Let's examine some of the differences between the sexes, keeping in mind the following:

- The differences are averages and do not apply to all females or all males.
- Even when gender differences occur, there often is considerable overlap between males and females.
- The differences may be due primarily to biological factors, sociocultural factors, or both.

First, we examine physical similarities and differences, and then we turn to cognitive and socioemotional similarities and differences.

Physical Similarities and Differences We could devote pages to describing physical differences between the average man and the average woman. For example, women have about twice the body fat of men, most concentrated around breasts and hips. In males, fat is more likely to go to the abdomen. On the average, males grow to be 10 percent taller than females. Androgens (the "male" hormones) promote the growth of long bones; estrogens (the "female" hormones) stop such growth at puberty.

Many physical differences between men and women are tied to health. From conception on, females have a longer life expectancy than males, and females are less likely than males to develop physical or mental disorders. Females are more resistant to infection and their blood vessels are more elastic than males'. Males have higher levels of stress hormones, which cause faster clotting and higher blood pressure.

Just how much does gender matter when it comes to brain structure and activity? Among the differences that have been discovered are the following:

- One part of the hypothalamus involved in sexual behavior tends to be larger in men than in women (Swaab & others, 2001).
- An area of the parietal lobe that functions in visuospatial skills tends to be larger in males than in females (Frederikse & others, 2000).
- The areas of the brain involved in emotional expression tend to show more metabolic activity in females than in males (Gur & others, 1995).
- Female brains are smaller than male brains but female brains have more folds; the larger folds (called convolutions) allow more surface brain tissue within the skulls of females than males (Luders & others, 2004).

What are some developmental changes in children's gender stereotyping?

Although some gender differences in brain structure and function have been found, many of these differences are either small or research is inconsistent regarding the differences. Also, when gender differences in the brain have been revealed, in many cases they have not been directly linked to psychological differences (Blakemore, Berenbaum, & Liben, 2009). Although research on gender differences

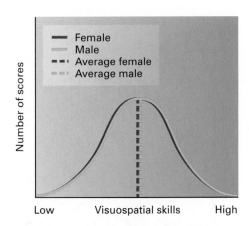

FIGURE 12.3 Visuospatial Skills of Males and Females. Notice that, although an average male's visuospatial skills are higher than an average female's, scores for the two sexes almost entirely overlap. Not all males have better visuospatial skills than all females—the overlap indicates that, although the average male score is higher, many females outperform most males on such tasks.

"So according to the stereotype, you can put two and two together, but I can read the handwriting on the wall."
Copyright © 1994 Joel Pett. All rights reserved.

in the brain is still in its infancy, it is likely that there are far more similarities than differences in the brains of females and males (Hyde, 2007). Similarities and differences in the brains of males and females could be due to evolution and heredity, as well as social experiences.

Cognitive Similarities and Differences No gender differences occur in overall intellectual ability, but in some cognitive areas gender differences do appear (Blakemore, Berenbaum, & Liben, 2009; Galambos, Berenbaum, & McHale, 2009). Some gender experts, such as Janet Shibley Hyde (2007), stress that the cognitive differences between females and males have been exaggerated. For example, Hyde points out that there is considerable overlap in the distributions of female and male scores on visuospatial tasks (see Figure 12.3). However, some researchers have found that males have better visuospatial skills than females (Blakemore, Berenbaum, & Liben, 2009). Despite equal participation in the National Geography Bee, in most years all ten finalists have been boys (Liben, 1995). Also, a recent research review concluded that boys have better visuospatial skills than girls (Halpern & others, 2007).

In the National Assessment of Educational Progress in the United States, fourth- and eighth-grade males continued to slightly outperform females in math through 2007 (National Assessment of Educational Progress, 2005, 2007). However, not all recent studies have shown differences. A recent very large-scale study of more than 7 million U.S. students in grades 2 through 11 revealed no differences in math scores for boys and girls (Hyde & others, 2008).

In the most recent National Assessment of Educational Progress (2005, 2007) reports, girls scored significantly higher than boys in literacy skills, although boys scored slightly higher than girls in math. For example, in reading skills, 41 percent of girls reached the proficient level (compared with 29 percent of boys) and in writing skills, 32 percent of girls were proficient (compared with 16 percent of boys). In math, 25 percent of boys were proficient (compared with 21 percent of girls) and in science, 21 percent of boys were proficient (compared with 16 percent of girls. Clearly, both U.S. boys and girls have room to make considerable improvement in their academic skills.

With regard to school achievement, girls earn better grades and complete high school at a higher rate than boys (Halpern, 2006). Males are more likely than females to be assigned to special/remedial education classes. Girls are more likely to be engaged with academic material, be attentive in class, put forth more academic effort, and participate more in class than boys are (DeZolt & Hull, 2001).

Despite these positive characteristics of girls, the increasing evidence that there is similarity in the math and science skills of girls and boys, and the legislative efforts to attain gender equality in recent years, gender differences in science, technology, and math careers continue to favor boys (Watt, 2008; Watt & Eccles, 2008). Toward the end of high school, girls are less likely to be taking high-level math courses and less likely to plan to enter the so-called "STEM" fields of science—technology, engineering, and math. Thus, the middle school and high school years are especially important in shaping girls' career plans in these areas.

Socioemotional Similarities and Differences Are "men from Mars" and "women from Venus"? Perhaps the gender differences that most fascinate people are those regarding how males and females relate to each other as people. For just about every imaginable socioemotional characteristic, researchers have examined whether there are differences between males and females. Here we examine just two that have been closely studied: (1) aggression and (2) emotion and its regulation.

One of the most consistent gender differences is that boys are more physically aggressive than girls. The difference occurs in all cultures and appears very early in children's development (Baillargeon & others, 2007). The difference in physical aggression is especially pronounced when children are provoked.

Although boys are consistently more physically aggressive than girls, might girls show as much or more verbal aggression, such as yelling, than boys? When verbal aggression is examined, gender differences typically either disappear or are sometimes even more pronounced in girls (Eagly & Steffen, 1986).

Recently, increased interest has been shown in *relational aggression,* which involves harming someone by manipulating a relationship (Coyne & others, 2008). Relational aggression includes such behaviors as trying to make others dislike a certain individual by spreading malicious rumors about the person (Ostrov & others, 2008). Relational aggression comprises a higher percentage of girls' than of boys' overall aggression (Young, Boye, & Nelson, 2006). Relational aggression increases in middle and late childhood (Dishion & Piehler, 2009). A recent study found links between parenting and children's relational aggression (Kuppens & others, 2009). In this study, parents' psychological control was linked to a higher incidence of relational aggression in their children.

What gender differences characterize aggression?

Are there gender differences in emotion? Girls are more likely to express their emotions openly and intensely than are boys, especially in displaying sadness and fear (Blakemore, Berenbaum, & Liben, 2009). Girls also are better at reading others' emotions and more likely to show empathy than are boys (Blakemore, Berenbaum, & Liben, 2009).

An important skill is to be able to regulate and control one's emotions and behavior (Eisenberg, 2010; Thompson, 2009a, b). Boys usually show less self-regulation than girls (Blakemore, Berenbaum, & Liben, 2009). This low self-control can translate into behavior problems.

Gender Controversy   Controversy continues about the extent of gender differences and what might cause them (Blakemore, Berenbaum, & Liben, 2009). As we saw earlier, evolutionary psychologists such as David Buss (2008) argue that gender differences are extensive and caused by the adaptive problems they have faced across their evolutionary history. Alice Eagly (2008) also concludes that gender differences are substantial but reaches a very different conclusion about their cause. She emphasizes that gender differences are due to social conditions that have resulted in women having less power and controlling fewer resources than men.

By contrast, Janet Shibley Hyde (2007; Hyde & others, 2008) concludes that gender differences have been greatly exaggerated, especially fueled by popular books such as John Gray's (1992) *Men Are from Mars, Women Are from Venus* and Deborah Tannen's (1990) *You Just Don't Understand.* She argues that the research indicates females and males are similar on most psychological factors. In a research review, Hyde (2005) summarized the results of 44 meta-analyses of gender differences and similarities. A *meta-analysis* is a statistical analysis that combines the results of many different studies. In most areas, gender differences—including math ability and communication—were either nonexistent or small. Gender differences in physical aggression were moderate. The largest difference occurred on motor skills (favoring males), followed by sexuality (males masturbate more and are more likely to endorse sex in a casual, uncommitted relationship) and physical aggression (males are more physically aggressive than are females).

Hyde's recent summary of meta-analyses is still not likely to quiet the controversy about gender differences and similarities, but further research should continue to provide a basis for more accurate judgments about this controversy.

Gender in Context   In thinking about gender, it is important to consider the context of behavior (Blakemore, Berenbaum, & Liben, 2009; Watt & Eccles, 2008).

In China, females and males are usually socialized to behave, feel, and think differently. The old patriarchal traditions of male supremacy have not been completely uprooted. Chinese women still make considerably less money than Chinese men do, and, in rural China (such as here in the Lixian Village of Sichuan), male supremacy still governs many women's lives.

Gender behavior often varies across contexts. Consider helping behavior. Males are more likely to help in contexts in which a perceived danger is present and they feel competent to help (Eagly & Crowley, 1986). For example, males are more likely than females to help a person who is stranded by the roadside with a flat tire; automobile problems are an area about which many males feel competent. In contrast, when the context involves volunteering time to help a child with a personal problem, females are more likely to help than males are, because there is little danger present and females feel more competent at nurturing. In many cultures, girls show more caregiving behavior than boys do. However, in the few cultures where they both care for younger siblings on a regular basis, girls and boys are similar in their tendencies to nurture (Whiting & Edwards, 1998).

Context is also relevant to gender differences in the display of emotions (Shields,1998). Consider anger. Males are more likely to show anger toward strangers, especially other males, when they think they have been challenged. Males also are more likely than females to turn their anger into aggressive action, especially when the culture endorses such action (Tavris & Wade, 1984).

We find contextual variations regarding gender in specific situations, not only within a particular culture, but also across cultures (Matsumoto & Juang, 2008; Shiraev & Levy, 2010). Sociocultural contexts determine what is considered to be gender-appropriate and gender-inappropriate socioemotional behavior. Not too long ago, it was accepted that boys are made of "snips and snails and puppy dogs' tails" and that girls are made of "sugar and spice and all that's nice." The well-adjusted female was expected to display expressive traits, such as being dependent, nurturant, and uninterested in power. The well-adjusted male was expected to show instrumental traits, such as being independent, aggressive, and power-oriented.

In many cultures around the world, traditional gender roles continue to guide the behavior of males and females (UNICEF, 2009). In China and Iran, for instance, it is still widely accepted for males to engage in dominant behavior and females to behave in subordinate ways. Many Western cultures, such as the United States, have become more flexible about gender behavior and allow for more diversity. For example, although a girl's father might promote traditional femininity, her friends might engage in many traditionally masculine activities, and her teachers might encourage her to be assertive.

In the United States, the cultural backgrounds of adolescents influence how boys and girls will be socialized. In one study, Latino and Latina adolescents were socialized differently as they were growing up (Raffaelli & Ontai, 2004). Latinas experienced far greater restrictions than Latinos in having curfews, interacting with members of the other sex, getting a driver's license, getting a job, and being involved in after-school activities.

Review and Reflect: Learning Goal 2

2 **Discuss gender stereotypes, similarities, and differences**

REVIEW
- What is gender stereotyping, and how extensive is it?
- What are some physical, cognitive, and socioemotional differences between men and women?

REFLECT
- How do your gender behavior and thoughts stack up against the similarities and differences in gender we discussed?

3 GENDER DEVELOPMENT THROUGH THE LIFE SPAN

Childhood   Adolescence   Adulthood and Aging

Here we focus further on gender-related developmental changes in the childhood years. In addition, we discuss some changes that take place in adolescence and adulthood, including adolescents' coming to terms with gender roles and how gender might be linked with aging.

Childhood

Do gender lessons have to be hammered into children's heads year after year? Apparently not, according to gender expert Carole Beal (1994). Instead, what girls and boys learn about gender seems to be learned quickly at certain points in development, especially when new abilities first emerge. For example, toddlers learn a lot about gender when they make their first bids for autonomy and begin to talk. Children form many ideas about what the sexes are like from about 1½ to 3 years of age. Many parents don't really start to think about gender issues involving their child until preschool or kindergarten, but at that point most children have already altered their behavior and learned to think of themselves as a girl or a boy. Few parents have to tell their little boys not to wear pink pants to the first grade! Children show a clear preference for same-sex peers (Vaughn & others, 2001).

The amount, timing, and intensity of gender socialization is different for girls and boys (Beal, 1994). Boys receive earlier and more intense gender socialization than girls do. The social cost of deviating from the expected male role is higher for boys than is the cost for girls of deviating from the expected female role, in terms of peer rejection and parental disapproval. Imagine a girl who is wearing a toy holster, bandanna, and cowboy hat, running around in the backyard pretending to herd cattle. Now imagine a boy who is wearing a flowered hat, ropes of pearls, and lipstick, pretending to cook dinner on a toy stove. Which of these do you have a stronger reaction to—the girl's behavior or the boy's? Probably the boy's. Researchers have found that "effeminate" behavior in boys elicits more negative reactions than does "masculine" behavior in girls (Martin, 1990).

Boys might have a more difficult time learning the masculine gender role because male models are less accessible to young children and messages from adults about the male role are not always consistent. For example, most mothers and teachers would like boys to behave in masculine ways, but also to be neat, well mannered, and considerate. However, fathers and peers usually want boys to behave in another way—independent and engaging in rough-and-tumble play. The mixed messages make it difficult for boys to figure out how to act.

Although gender roles have become more flexible in recent years, the flexibility applies more for girls than for boys (Beal, 1994). Girls can now safely be ambitious, competitive, and interested in sports, but relatively few adults are equally supportive of boys' being gentle, interested in fashion, and motivated to sign up for ballet classes. Instrumental traits and masculine gender roles may be evolving into a new norm for everyone.

Concern about the ways boys are being brought up has been called a "national crisis of boyhood" by William Pollack (1999) in his book *Real Boys*. Pollack says that little has been done to change what he calls the "boy code." Boy code tells boys they should not show their feelings and should act tough, says Pollack. Boys learn the boy code in many contexts—sandboxes, playgrounds, schoolrooms, camps, hangouts—and are taught the code by parents, peers, coaches, teachers, and other adults. Pollack, as well as many others, argues that boys would benefit

Are gender roles more flexible for boys or for girls?

from being socialized to express their anxieties and concerns and to better regulate their aggression.

Adolescence

Early adolescence is another transitional point that seems to be especially important in gender development. Young adolescents have to cope with the enormous changes of puberty. These changes are intensified by their expanding cognitive abilities, which make them acutely aware of how they appear to others. Relations with others change extensively as dating relationships begin and sexuality is experienced.

As females and males experience the physical and social changes of early adolescence, they must come to terms with new definitions of their gender roles (Belansky & Clements, 1992). During early adolescence, individuals develop the adult, physical aspects of their sex. Some theorists and researchers have proposed that, with the onset of puberty, girls and boys experience an intensification of gender-related expectations. Puberty might signal to socializing others—parents, peers, and teachers, for example—that the adolescent is beginning to approach adulthood and therefore should begin to act more in ways that resemble the stereotypical female or male adult. The **gender-intensification hypothesis** states that psychological and behavioral differences between boys and girls become greater during early adolescence because of increased pressures to conform to traditional masculine and feminine gender roles (Galambos, 2004; Hill & Lynch, 1983).

Some researchers have reported evidence of gender intensification in early adolescence (Hill & Lynch, 1983). For example, in one study, sex differences in gender-role attitudes increased across the early adolescent years. Gender-role attitudes were measured by the Attitudes Toward Women Scale (Galambos & others, 1985), which assesses the extent to which adolescents approve of gender-based division of roles. For example, the adolescent is asked such questions as whether girls should have the same freedom as boys. However, not every female and male shows gender intensification during puberty, and the family context influences how strongly gender intensification occurs (Crouter, Manke, & McHale, 1995). A recent longitudinal study of individuals from 7 to 19 years of age revealed stable gender differences in activity interests by the decline in both male- and female-typed activity interests across the 7- to 19-year age range (McHale & others, 2009). The jury is still out on the validity of the gender-intensification hypothesis (Galambos, Berenbaum, & McHale, 2009).

Gender intensification may create special problems for boys. Adopting a strong masculine role in adolescence is increasingly being found to be associated with problem behaviors. Joseph Pleck (1995) argues that what has defined traditional masculinity includes behaviors that do not have social approval but nonetheless validate the adolescent boy's masculinity. That is, in the male adolescent culture, male adolescents perceive that they will be thought of as more masculine if they engage in premarital sex, drink alcohol, take drugs, and participate in delinquent activities.

What is the gender-intensification hypothesis?

gender-intensification hypothesis The view that psychological and behavioral differences between boys and girls become greater during early adolescence because of increased socialization pressures to conform to traditional gender roles.

Adulthood and Aging

How might women's and men's development vary as they go through their adult years? How might gender be linked with aging?

Gender and Communication   Stereotypes about differences in men's and women's attitudes toward communication and about differences in how they communicate with each other have spawned countless cartoons and jokes. Are the supposed differences real?

When Deborah Tannen (1990) analyzed the talk of women and men, she found that many wives complain about their husbands that "He doesn't listen to me anymore" and "He doesn't talk to me anymore." Lack of communication, though high on women's lists of reasons for divorce, is mentioned much less often by men.

Communication problems between men and women may come in part from differences in their preferred ways of communicating. Tannen distinguishes rapport talk from report talk. **Rapport talk** is the language of conversation; it is a way of establishing connections and negotiating relationships. **Report talk** is talk that is designed to give information, which includes public speaking. According to Tannen, women enjoy rapport talk more than report talk, and men's lack of interest in rapport talk bothers many women. In contrast, men prefer to engage in report talk. Men hold center stage through such verbal performances as telling stories and jokes. They learn to use talk as a way of getting and keeping attention.

How extensive are the gender differences in communication? Research has yielded somewhat mixed results. Recent studies do reveal some gender differences (Anderson, 2006). One study of a sampling of students' e-mails found that people could guess the writer's gender two-thirds of the time (Thompson & Murachver, 2001). Another study revealed that women make 63 percent of phone calls and when talking to another woman stay on the phone longer (7.2 minutes) than men do when talking with other men (4.6 minutes) (Smoreda & Licoppe, 2000). However, meta-analyses suggest that overall gender differences in communication are small in both children and adults (Hyde, 2005; Leaper & Smith, 2004).

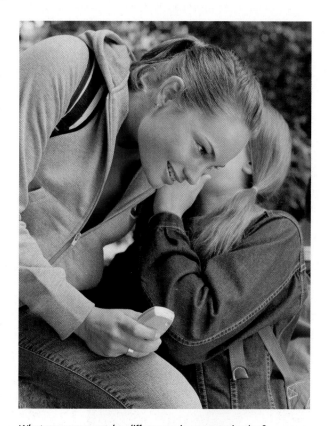

What are some gender differences in communication?

Women's Development   Tannen's analysis of women's preference for rapport talk suggests that women place a high value on relationships and focus on nurturing their connections with others. This view echoes some ideas of Jean Baker Miller (1986), who has been an important voice in stimulating the examination of psychological issues from a female perspective. Miller argues that when researchers examine what women have been doing in life, a large part of it is active participation in the development of others. In Miller's view, women often try to interact with others in ways that will foster the other person's development along many dimensions—emotionally, intellectually, and socially.

Most experts stress that it is important for women not only to maintain their competency in relationships but to be self-motivated, too (Brabeck & Brabeck, 2006). As Harriet Lerner (1989) concludes in her book *The Dance of Intimacy,* it is important for women to bring to their relationships nothing less than a strong, assertive, independent, and authentic self. She emphasizes that competent relationships are those in which the separate "I-ness" of both persons can be appreciated and enhanced while still staying emotionally connected to each other.

In sum, Miller, Tannen, and other gender experts such as Carol Gilligan, note that women are more relationship-oriented than men—and that this relationship orientation should be prized as a skill in our culture more than it currently is. Critics of this view of gender differences in relationships contend that it is too stereotypical (Hyde, 2007; Matlin, 2008). They argue that there is greater individual variation in the relationship styles of men and women than this view acknowledges (Brabeck & Brabeck, 2006).

In the field of the psychology of women, there is increased interest in women of color. To read about the work and views of one individual in this field, see the *Careers in Life-Span Development* profile.

Men's Development   The male of the species—what is he really like? What are his concerns? According to Joseph Pleck's (1995) *role-strain view,* male roles are contradictory and inconsistent. Men not only experience stress when they

rapport talk The language of conversation; a way to establish connections and negotiate relationships; preferred by women.

report talk Language designed to give information, including public speaking; preferred by men.

Careers in Life-Span Development

Cynthia de las Fuentes, College Professor and Counseling Psychologist

Cynthia de las Fuentes is a professor at Our Lady of the Lake University in San Antonio. She obtained her undergraduate degree in psychology and her doctoral degree in counseling psychology at the University of Texas in Austin. Among the courses she teaches are the psychology of women, Latino psychology, and counseling theories.

Dr. de las Fuentes is president of the Division of the Psychology of Women in the American Psychological Association. "Many young women," she says, "take for granted that the women's movement has accomplished its goals—like equal pay for women, or reproductive rights—and don't realize that there is still work to be done. . . . She's interested in learning about people's intersecting identities, like female and Latina, and how the two work together"

Cynthia de las Fuentes.

(Winerman, 2005, pp. 66–67)

violate men's roles, they also are harmed when they do act in accord with men's roles. Here are some of the areas where men's roles can cause considerable strain (Levant, 2001):

- *Health.* Men live 8 to 10 years less than women do. They have higher rates of stress-related disorders, alcoholism, car accidents, and suicide. Men are more likely than women to be the victims of homicide. In sum, the male role is hazardous to men's health.

- *Male-female relationships.* Too often, the male role involves expectations that men should be dominant, powerful, and aggressive and should control women. "Real men," according to many traditional definitions of masculinity, look at women in terms of their bodies, not their minds and feelings, have little interest in rapport talk and relationships, and do not consider women equal to men in work or many other aspects of life. Thus the traditional view of the male role encourages men to disparage women, be violent toward women, and refuse to have equal relationships with women.

- *Male-male relationships.* Too many men have had too little interaction with their fathers, especially fathers who are positive role models. Nurturing and being sensitive to others have been considered aspects of the female role, not the male role. And the male role emphasizes competition rather than cooperation. All of these aspects of the male role have left men with inadequate positive, emotional connections with other males.

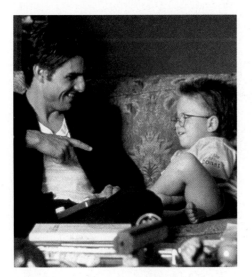

Tom Cruise (*left*) played Jerry Maguire in the movie *Jerry Maguire* with 6-year-old Ray, son of Jerry's love interest. The image of nurturing and nurtured males was woven throughout the movie. Jerry's relationship with Ray was a significant theme in the movie. It is through the caring relationship with Ray that Jerry makes his first genuine movement toward emotional maturity. The boy is guide to the man (Shields, 1998). Many experts on gender stress that men and boys would benefit from engaging in more nurturant behaviors.

To reconstruct their masculinity in more positive ways, Ron Levant (2001) suggests that every man should (1) reexamine his beliefs about manhood, (2) separate out the valuable aspects of the male role, and (3) get rid of those parts of the masculine role that are destructive. All of these involve becoming more "emotionally intelligent"—that is, becoming more emotionally self-aware, managing emotions more effectively, reading emotions better (one's own emotions and others'), and being motivated to improve close relationships.

Gender and Aging Do our gender roles change when we become older adults? Some developmentalists maintain there is decreasing femininity in women and decreasing masculinity in men when they reach the late adulthood years (Gutmann, 1975). The evidence suggests that older men do become more feminine—nurturant, sensitive, and so on—but it appears that older women do not necessarily become more masculine—assertive, dominant, and so on (Turner, 1982). Keep in mind that cohort effects are especially important to consider in areas such as gender roles. As sociohistorical changes take place and are assessed more frequently in life-span investigations, what were once perceived to be age effects may turn out to be cohort effects (Schaie, 2007).

A possible double jeopardy also faces many women—the burden of *both* ageism and sexism (UNICEF, 2006, 2009). The poverty rate for older adult females is almost double that of older adult males.

Not only is it important to be concerned about older women's double jeopardy of ageism and sexism, but special attention also needs to be devoted to female ethnic minority older adults (Leifheit-Limson & Levy, 2009). They face what could be described as triple jeopardy—ageism, sexism, and racism. More information about being female, ethnic, and old appears in the *Contexts of Life-Span Development* interlude.

Contexts of Life-Span Development

BEING FEMALE, ETHNIC, AND OLD

Part of the unfortunate history of ethnic minority groups in the United States has been the negative stereotypes against members of these groups (Albert, 2007). Many have been hampered by their immigrant origins because they are not fluent or literate in English. They may not be aware of the values and norms involved in American social interaction, and they may have lifestyles that differ from those of mainstream America (Angel & Angel, 2006). Often included in these cultural differences is the role of women in the family and in society. Many, but not all, immigrant ethnic groups traditionally have relegated the woman's role to family maintenance. Many important decisions may be made by a woman's husband or parents, and she is often not expected to seek an independent career or enter the workforce except in the case of dire financial need.

Some ethnic minority groups may define an older woman's role as unimportant, especially if she is unable to contribute financially. However, in some ethnic minority groups, an older woman's social status improves. For example, older African American women can express their own needs and can be given status and power in the community. Despite their positive status in the African American family and the African American culture, African American women over the age of 70 are the poorest population group in the United States. Three of five older African American women live alone; most of them are widowed. The low incomes of older African American women translate into less than adequate access to health care. Substantially lower incomes for African American older women are related to the kinds of jobs they hold. Frequently these jobs are not covered by Social Security or, in the case of domestic service, the income of these women is not reported, even when reporting is legally required.

A portrayal of older African American women in cities reveals some of their survival strategies. They highly value the family as a system of mutual support and aid, adhere to the American work ethic, and view religion as a source of strength. The use of religion as a way of coping with stress has a long history in the African American culture, with roots in the slave experience. The African American church came to fulfill needs and functions once met by religion-based tribal and community organizations that African Americans brought from Africa. In one study, the older African American women

(continued on next page)

A special concern is the stress faced by African American elderly women. *What are some ways they cope with stress?*

valued church organizations more than their male counterparts did, especially valuing the church's group activities (Taylor, 1982).

In sum, older African American women have faced considerable stress in their lives (Locher & others, 2005). In the face of this stress, they have shown remarkable adaptiveness, resilience, responsibility, and coping skills. However, many older African American women would indeed benefit from improved support.

Review and Reflect: Learning Goal 3

 3 **Describe the development of gender through the life span**

REVIEW

- What are some developmental changes in gender in childhood?
- How does gender development change during adolescence?
- How does gender development change during adulthood?

REFLECT

- How have your gender attitudes and behavior changed since childhood? Are the changes mainly age changes or do they reflect cohort effects?

4 EXPLORING SEXUALITY

| Biological and Cultural Factors | Sexual Orientation | Sexually Transmitted Infections | Forcible Sexual Behavior and Sexual Harassment |

Now that we have studied the gender aspects of being female and male, let's turn our attention to the sexual aspects. To explore sexuality, we examine biological and cultural factors, sexual orientation, sexually transmitted infections, and forcible sexual behavior and sexual harassment.

Biological and Cultural Factors

We don't need sex for everyday survival, the way we need food and water, but we do need it for the survival of the species. With this important role of sex in mind, let's examine some biological and cultural factors involved in sexuality.

Biological Factors   In our discussion of gender, we discussed the two main classes of sex hormones: estrogens (which primarily promote the development of female physical sex characteristics) and androgens (which mainly promote the development of male physical sex characteristics). The pituitary gland in the brain monitors hormone levels, but it itself is regulated by the hypothalamus. The pituitary gland sends out a signal to the testes or ovaries to manufacture a hormone; then the pituitary gland, through interaction with the hypothalamus, detects when the optimal level of the hormone is reached and maintains this level.

As we move from lower to higher animals, the role of hormones becomes less clear, especially in females. For human males, higher androgen levels are associated with sexual motivation and orgasm frequency (Knussman, Christiansen, &

sexual scripts Stereotyped patterns of expectancies for how people should behave sexually.

traditional religious script Sex is accepted only within marriage; extramarital sex is taboo, especially for women, and sex means reproduction and sometimes affection.

romantic script Sex is synonymous with love; if we develop a relationship with someone and fall in love, it is acceptable to have sex with the person whether we are married or not.

Couwenbergs, 1986). Nonetheless, sexual behavior is so individualized in humans that it is difficult to specify the effects of hormones.

Cultural Factors   Sexual motivation also is influenced by cultural factors (Hock, 2010). The range of sexual values across cultures is substantial. Some cultures consider sexual pleasures "weird" or "abnormal." Consider the people who live on the small island of Ines Beag off the coast of Ireland. They are some of the most sexually repressed people in the world. They know nothing about tongue kissing or hand stimulation of the penis, and they detest nudity. For both females and males, premarital sex is out of the question. Men avoid most sexual experiences because they believe that sexual intercourse reduces their energy level and is bad for their health. Under these repressive conditions, sexual intercourse occurs only at night and takes place as quickly as possible as the husband opens his nightclothes under the covers and the wife raises her nightgown. As you might suspect, female orgasm is rare in this culture (Messinger, 1971).

In contrast, consider the Mangaian culture in the South Pacific. In Mangaia, young boys are taught about masturbation and are encouraged to engage in it as much as they like. At age 13, the boys undergo a ritual that initiates them into sexual manhood. First, their elders instruct them about sexual strategies, including how to help their female partner have orgasms. Then, two weeks later, the boy has intercourse with an experienced woman who helps him hold back ejaculation until she can achieve orgasm with him. By the end of adolescence, Mangaians have sex virtually every day. Mangaian women report a high frequency of orgasms.

As reflected in the behavior of the people in these two different cultures, our sexual motivation is influenced by **sexual scripts.** These are stereotyped patterns of expectancies for how people should behave sexually (Jones, 2006). Two well-known sexual scripts are the traditional religious script and the romantic script. In the **traditional religious script,** sex is accepted only within marriage. Extramarital sex is taboo, especially for women. Sex means reproduction and sometimes affection. In the **romantic script,** sex is synonymous with love. If we develop a relationship with someone and fall in love, it is acceptable to have sex with the person whether or not we are married.

You probably are familiar with some sex differences in sexual scripts. Females tend to link sexual intercourse with love more than males do, and males are more likely to emphasize sexual conquest. Some sexual scripts involve a double standard, such that it is okay for male adolescents to have sex but not females, and that if the female gets pregnant it's her fault for not using contraception.

Sexual Orientation

Our exploration of sexual orientation focuses on heterosexual and same-sex attitudes and behaviors. For example, are there gender differences in sexuality? How often do heterosexual men and women think about sex during a typical day? What is bisexuality? Is there a biological basis for same-sex relations?

Heterosexual Attitudes and Behavior   In a well-designed study, Robert Michael and his colleagues (1994) interviewed nearly 3,500 people from 18 to 50 years of age who were randomly selected (a sharp contrast from earlier samples such as the famous study by Alfred Kinsey and his colleagues in the 1940s). Among the key findings from the 1994 Sex in America survey:

- Americans tend to fall into three categories: One-third have sex twice a week or more, one-third a few times a month, and one-third a few times a year or not at all.

- Married couples have sex the most often and also are the most likely to have orgasms when they do. Figure 12.4 portrays the frequency of sex for married and noncohabiting individuals in the past year.

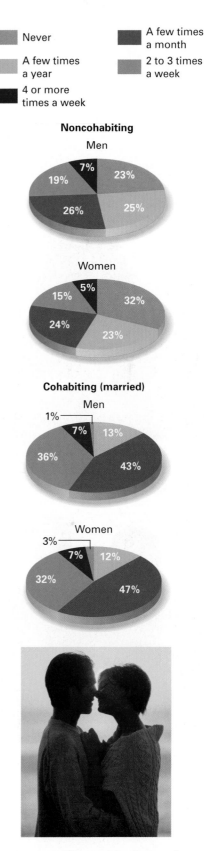

FIGURE 12.4 The 1994 Sex in America Survey. Percentages show noncohabiting and cohabiting (married) males' and females' responses to the question "How often have you had sex in the past year?"

• Most Americans do not engage in kinky sexual acts. When asked what their favorite sexual acts were, the vast majority (96 percent) said that vaginal sex was "very" or "somewhat" appealing. Oral sex was in third place, after an activity that many have not labeled a sexual act—watching a partner undress.

• Adultery is clearly the exception rather than the rule. Nearly 75 percent of the married men and 85 percent of the married women indicated that they have never been unfaithful.

• Men think about sex far more than women do—54 percent of the men said they think about it every day or several times a day, whereas 67 percent of the women said they think about it only a few times a week or a few times a month.

In sum, one of the most powerful messages in the 1994 survey was that Americans' sexual lives are more conservative than previously believed. Although 17 percent of the men and 3 percent of the women said they have had sex with at least 21 partners, the overall impression from the survey was that sexual behavior is ruled by marriage and monogamy for most Americans.

So far, we have mentioned several gender differences in sexuality, such as that men think about sex more often than women do and that women link sexual intercourse with love more than men do. A research review also concluded that men report more frequent feelings of sexual arousal, have more frequent sexual fantasies, and rate the strength of their own sex drive higher than women do (Baumeister, Cantanese, & Vohs, 2001). Men also are more likely to masturbate and have more permissive attitudes about casual premarital sex (Peplau & Fingerhut, 2007).

Attitudes and Behavior of Lesbians and Gay Males Sexual minority individuals include gay males, lesbians, and bisexuals. Being **bisexual** means being sexually attracted to people of both sexes. In the Sex in America survey, 2.7 percent of the men and 1.3 percent of the women indicated that they had had homosexual sex in the past year (Michael & others, 1994).

Why are some individuals lesbian, gay, or bisexual (LGB) and others heterosexual? Speculation about this question has been extensive, but no firm answers are available (Crooks & Baur, 2008; Hock & Williams, 2007). LGBs and heterosexuals have similar physiological responses during sexual arousal and seem to be aroused by the same types of tactile stimulation. Investigators find no differences between LGBs and heterosexuals in a wide range of attitudes, behaviors, and adjustments (Hyde & De Lamater, 2008). Homosexuality once was classified as a mental disorder, but both the American Psychiatric Association and the American Psychological Association discontinued this classification in the 1970s.

Researchers have explored the possible biological basis of same-sex relations. The results of hormone studies have been inconsistent. If gay males are given male sexual hormones (androgens), their sexual orientation does not change. Their sexual desire merely increases. A very early prenatal critical period might influence sexual orientation. In the second to fifth months after conception, exposure of the fetus to hormone levels characteristic of females might cause the individual (male or female) to become attracted to males (Ellis & Ames, 1987). If this critical-period hypothesis turns out to be correct, it would explain why clinicians have found that sexual orientation is difficult, if not impossible, to modify.

With regard to anatomical structures, neuroscientist Simon LeVay (1991) found that an area of the hypothalamus that governs sexual behavior is twice as large (about the size of a grain of sand) in heterosexual males as in gay males. Gay males and heterosexual females had about equal-sized areas in this part of the hypothalamus. Critics of this research point out that many of the gay males in the study had AIDS, and their brains could have been altered by the disease.

An individual's sexual orientation—same-sex, heterosexual, or bisexual—most likely is determined by a combination of genetic, hormonal, cognitive, and

What are some similarities and differences in lesbian and gay male relationships?

bisexual Being sexually attracted to people of both sexes.

environmental factors (Carroll, 2007; Strong & others, 2008). Most experts on same-sex relations stress that no one factor alone causes sexual orientation and that the relative weight of each factor can vary from one individual to the next. No one knows precisely why some individuals are lesbian, gay, or bisexual (Herek, 2000).

Scientists have a clearer picture of what does not cause an individual to be LGB. For example, children raised by gay or lesbian parents or couples are no more likely to be LGB than children raised by heterosexual parents (Patterson & Hastings, 2007). There also is no evidence that being a gay male is caused by a dominant mother or a weak father, or that being a lesbian is caused by girls' choosing male role models.

Many relationship characteristics and gender differences that appear in hetero-sexual relationships also occur in same-sex relationships, although there are some variations (Cohler, 2009; Diamond & Savin-Williams, 2009). In a recent study that compared same-sex couples with opposite-sex dating, engaged, and married dyads, no differences were found in attachment security (Roisman & others, 2008). In this study, one difference between couples was that lesbians were the most effective at working together in positive ways during laboratory observations. Here are the con-clusions about research on gay male and lesbian relationships reached by leading expert Letitia Peplau and her colleagues (Peplau & Fingerhut, 2007):

- Regardless of sexual orientation, most males and females emphasize the importance of affection, trust, and shared interests in a relationship.

- Regardless of sexual orientation, a partner's sexual attraction is more important to men, whereas a partner's personality characteristics are more important to women.

- Lesbians have fewer sex partners than gay men, and lesbians have sex less often than gay males or heterosexual couples.

- Traditional heterosexual marriages involve a gender-based division of labor and greater power by the man, whereas in same-sex couples, regardless of the sex, a more equal distribution of labor and power is emphasized.

- Lesbians have less permissive attitudes about casual sex and sex outside a pri-mary relationship than gay men.

Thus, whether they have a heterosexual or lesbian orientation, for many women, sexuality is strongly linked to a close relationship, with the best context for enjoy-able sex being a committed relationship. This is less so for men (Peplau, Fingerhut, & Beals, 2004).

How can gays and lesbians adapt to a world in which they are a minority? According to psychologist Laura Brown (1989), gays and lesbians experience life as a minority in a dominant majority culture. Brown concludes that lesbians and gay males adapt best when they don't define themselves in polarities, such as trying to live in a separate gay or lesbian world or completely accepting the majority culture. Instead, developing a *bicultural identity* and balancing the demands of the two cul-tures can often lead to more effective coping, says Brown.

A special concern involving sexual minority individuals are the hate-crimes and stigma-related experiences they encounter. In a recent study, approximately 20 per-cent of sexual minority adults reported that they had experienced a person or prop-erty crime related to their sexual orientation, about 50 percent said they had experienced verbal harassment, and more than 10 percent said they had encoun-tered employment or housing discrimination (Herek, 2009).

Sexually Transmitted Infections

Sexually transmitted infections (STIs) are diseases that are contracted primarily through sexual contact. This contact includes oral-genital and anal-genital contact as well as vaginal intercourse (Carroll, 2010). STIs are an increasing health problem,

sexually transmitted infections (STIs) Diseases that are contracted primarily through sexual contact, including oral-genital contact, anal-genital contact, and vaginal intercourse.

affecting about one of every six U.S. adults (National Center for Health Statistics, 2007). The main STIs are those caused by bacteria—gonorrhea, syphilis, and chlamydia—and those caused by viruses—genital herpes, HPV (human papillomavirus), and AIDS (acquired immune deficiency syndrome).

Gonorrhea   Gonorrhea is a sexually transmitted infection that is commonly called the "drip" or the "clap." One of the most common STIs in the United States, it is caused by the bacterium *Neisseria gonorrhoeae,* which thrives in the mucous membranes lining the mouth, throat, vagina, cervix, urethra, and anal tract. The bacterium is spread by contact between the infected moist membranes of one individual and the membranes of another.

Gonorrhea can be successfully treated in its early stages with penicillin or other antibiotics. Untreated, gonorrhea can lead to infections that can move to various organs and can cause infertility. More than 650,000 cases are reported in the United States annually (Centers for Disease Control and Prevention, 2008).

Syphilis   *Syphilis* is a sexually transmitted infection caused by the bacterium *Treponema pallidum,* a spirochete. The spirochete needs a warm, moist environment to survive, and it is transmitted by penile-vaginal, oral-genital, or anal contact. It can also be transmitted from a pregnant woman to her fetus after the fourth month of pregnancy. If the mother is treated before this time with penicillin, syphilis will not be transmitted to the fetus.

In its early stages, syphilis can be effectively treated with penicillin. In its advanced stages, syphilis can cause paralysis or even death. Approximately 40,000 cases of syphilis are reported in the United States each year.

Chlamydia   *Chlamydia* is named for *Chlamydia trachomatis,* a bacterium that spreads by sexual contact and infects the genital organs of both sexes. About 2.8 million Americans are infected with chlamydia each year (National Center for Health Statistics, 2007). About 10 percent of all college students have chlamydia. This STI is highly infectious, and women run a 70 percent risk of contracting it in a single sexual encounter. The male risk is estimated at between 25 and 50 percent.

Males with chlamydia often get treatment because of noticeable symptoms in the genital region; however, most females are asymptomatic. Therefore, many females go untreated and chlamydia spreads to the upper reproductive tract, where it can cause pelvic inflammatory disease (PID). PID, in turn, can result in ectopic pregnancies (a pregnancy in which the fertilized egg is implanted outside the uterus) or infertility. One-quarter of females who have PID become infertile; multiple cases of PID increase the rate of infertility to half. Some researchers suggest that chlamydia is the number one preventable cause of female infertility.

Genital Herpes   *Genital herpes* is a sexually transmitted infection caused by a large family of viruses with many different strains. These strains produce other, nonsexually transmitted infections such as chicken pox and mononucleosis. Three to five days after contact, itching and tingling can occur, followed by an eruption of sores and blisters. The attacks can last up to three weeks and may recur in a few weeks or a few years. In the United States, approximately 20 percent of individuals 12 years of age and older have had a genital herpes infection (National Center for Health Statistics, 2007).

Although drugs such as acyclovir alleviate symptoms, there is no known cure for herpes (Barton, 2005). The virus can be transmitted through nonlatex condoms and foams, making infected individuals reluctant to have sex, angry about the unpredictability of their lives, and fearful that they won't be able to cope with the pain and stress of the next attack. For these reasons, support groups for individuals with herpes have been established.

HPV *HPV* is a virus (human papillomavirus) that causes genital warts on people. The warts can be as large as nickels or so small that they cannot be seen. There are more than a million new cases of HPV each year in the United States. The most common way to contract HPV is by having sex with, or touching the genitals of, someone who already has the virus.

Women with HPV face an increased risk for cervical cancer. Genital warts can be removed by physicians. Sometimes the warts are frozen off; at other times a laser is used to remove them. Although the warts can be removed, it generally is believed that once the virus is acquired, HPV does not go away. In 2007, the Centers for Disease Control and Prevention recommended that all 10- and 12-year-old girls be given Gardasil, a vaccine that helps to fight off HPV and cervical cancer.

HIV and AIDS No single STI has caused more deaths, had a greater impact on sexual behavior, or created more public fear in the last two decades, than AIDS (Hock & Williams, 2007). Here we explore its nature and incidence, how it is transmitted, and prevention.

AIDS is a sexually transmitted syndrome that is caused by a virus, the human immunodeficiency virus (HIV), which destroys the body's immune system. Following exposure to HIV, an individual is vulnerable to germs that a normal immune system could destroy.

Through 2006, 564,427 cases of AIDS in 20- to 39-year-olds had been reported in the United States (National Center for Health Statistics, 2009). In 2006, male-male sexual contact continued to be the most frequent AIDS transmission category (National Center for Health Statistics, 2009). Because of education and the development of more effective drug treatments, deaths due to HIV/AIDS have begun to decline in the United States (National Center for Health Statistics, 2009).

Globally, the total number of individuals living with HIV was 33 million in 2007, with 22 million of these individuals with HIV living in sub-Saharan Africa (UNAIDS, 2008). To put this in perspective, slightly more than 500,000 individuals were living

AIDS Acquired immune deficiency syndrome; caused by the human immunodeficiency virus (HIV), which destroys the body's immune system.

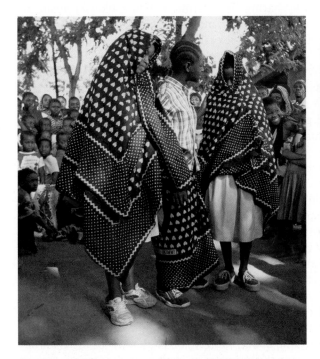

A youth group presents a play in the local marketplace in Morogoro, Tanzania. The play is designed to educate the community about HIV and AIDS.

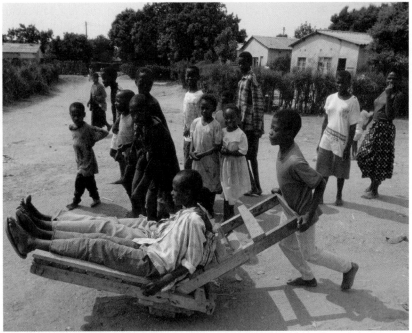

A 13-year-old boy pushes his friends around in his barrow during his break from his work as a barrow boy in a sub-Saharan Africa community. He became the breadwinner in the family because both of his parents died of AIDS.

with AIDS in the United States in 2006 (National Center for Health Statistics, 2009). Approximately half of all new HIV infections around the world occur in the 15- to 24-years-old age category (Campbell, 2009).

Worldwide, the greatest concern about AIDS is in sub-Saharan Africa, where it has reached epidemic proportions (UNICEF, 2009). Adolescent girls in many African countries are especially vulnerable to infection with HIV by adult men. Approximately six times as many adolescent girls as boys have AIDS in these countries. In Kenya, 25 percent of the 15- to 19-year-old girls are HIV-positive, compared with only 4 percent of this age group of boys. In some sub-Saharan countries, less than 20 percent of women and 40 percent of 15- to 19-year-olds reported that they had used a condom the last time they had sexual intercourse (Bankole & others, 2004).

AIDS also has resulted in a dramatic increase in the number of African children and adolescents who are orphaned and left to care for themselves because their parents acquired the disease. In 2006, there were 12 million children and adolescents who had become orphans because of the deaths of their parents due to AIDS (UNICEF, 2006). This figure is expected to increase to 16 million by 2010, which means that AIDS orphans could make up as many as 15 to 20 percent of the population of some sub-Saharan countries. As a result of the dramatic increase in AIDS orphans, more of these children and adolescents are being cared for by their grandmothers or no one, in which case all too often they turn to a lifestyle of crime or prostitution.

There continues to be great concern about AIDS in many parts of the world, not just sub-Saharan Africa (UNICEF, 2009). In the United States, prevention is especially targeted at groups that show the highest incidence of AIDS. These include drug users, individuals with other STIs, young gay males, individuals living in low-income circumstances, Latinos, and African Americans (Centers for Disease Control and Prevention, 2006). Also, in recent years, there has been increased heterosexual transmission of the human immunodeficiency virus in the United States.

Experts say that the human immunodeficiency virus can be transmitted only by the following: sexual contact; sharing hypodermic needles; blood transfusion (which in the last few years has been tightly monitored); other direct contact of cuts or mucous membranes with blood and sexual fluids; or mother-baby transmission (Kalichman, 1996).

Remember that it is not who you are, but what you do, that puts you at risk for getting HIV (Crooks & Baur, 2008). Anyone who is sexually active or uses intravenous drugs is at risk. *No one* is immune. Once an individual is infected, the prognosis is likely illness and possibly death. The only safe behavior is abstinence from sex, which most individuals do not perceive as an option. Beyond abstinence, there is only "safer" behavior, such as sexual behavior without exchange of semen, vaginal fluids, or blood, and sexual intercourse with a condom (Strong & others, 2008).

Just asking a date about his or her sexual behavior does not guarantee protection from the human immunodeficiency virus and other sexually transmitted infections (Caron, 2007; Noam, Zimmerman, & Atwood, 2004). For example, in one investigation, 655 college students were asked to answer questions about lying and sexual behavior (Cochran & Mays, 1990). Of the 422 respondents who said they were sexually active, 34 percent of the men and 10 percent of the women said they had lied so that their partner would be more inclined to have sex with them. Much higher percentages—47 percent of the men and 60 percent of the women—said they had been lied to by a potential sexual partner. When asked what aspects of their past they would be most likely to lie about, more than 40 percent of the men and women said they would understate the number of their sexual partners. Twenty percent of the men, but only 4 percent of the women, said they would lie about results from an HIV blood test.

Protecting Against STIs   What are some good strategies for protecting against HIV and other sexually transmitted infections? They include the following:

- *Know your and your partner's risk status.* Anyone who has had previous sexual activity with another person might have contracted an STI without being aware of it. Get to know a prospective partner before you have sex. Use this time to inform the other person of your STI status and inquire about your partner's. Remember that many people lie about their STI status.

- *Obtain screening tests for STIs.* Many experts recommend that couples who want to begin a sexual relationship should have a medical checkup to rule out STIs before they engage in sex. If cost is an issue, contact your campus health service or a public health clinic.

- *Have protected, not unprotected, sex.* When correctly used, latex condoms help to prevent many STIs from being transmitted. Condoms are more effective in preventing gonorrhea, syphilis, chlamydia, and HIV than herpes.

- *Don't have sex with multiple partners.* One of the best predictors of getting an STI is having sex with multiple partners. Having more than one sex partner elevates the likelihood that you will encounter an infected partner.

What are some strategies for protecting against STIs?

Forcible Sexual Behavior and Sexual Harassment

Too often, sex involves the exercise of power. Here we briefly look at two of the problems that may result: rape and sexual harassment.

Rape   **Rape** is forcible sexual intercourse, oral sex, or anal sex with a person who does not give consent. Legal definitions of rape differ from state to state. For example, in some states, husbands are not prohibited from forcing their wives to have intercourse, although this has been challenged in several states. Because victims may be reluctant to suffer the consequences of reporting rape, the actual incidence is not easily determined (Littleton & Henderson, 2009). It appears that rape occurs most often in large cities, where it has been reported that 8 of every 10,000 women 12 years and older are raped each year. Nearly 200,000 rapes are reported each year in the United States. A recent national study found that 7.8 percent of U.S. ninth- to twelfth-grade students reported that they had been physically forced to have intercourse against their will (Eaton & others, 2008). In this study, 11.3 percent of the female students and 3.8 percent of the male students reported they had been forced to have sexual intercourse.

An increasing concern is **date or acquaintance rape,** which is coercive sexual activity directed at someone with whom the victim is at least casually acquainted (Clark & Carroll, 2008; Wolitzky-Taylor & others, 2008). By some estimates, two-thirds of college freshman women report having been date raped or having experienced an attempted date rape at least once (Watts & Zimmerman, 2002). About two-thirds of college men admit that they fondle women against their will, and half admit to forcing sexual activity.

A number of college and universities describe the *red zone* as a period of time early in the first year of college when women are at especially high risk for unwanted sexual experiences. A recent study revealed that first-year women were more at risk for unwanted sexual experiences, especially early in the fall term, than second-year women (Kimble & others, 2008).

What are some characteristics of date or acquaintance rape?

rape Forcible sexual intercourse, oral sex, or anal sex with a person who does not give consent. Legal definitions of rape differ from state to state.

date or acquaintance rape Coercive sexual activity directed at someone with whom the victim is at least casually acquainted.

FIGURE 12.5 Relationship Between Victim and Offender in Completed and Attempted Rapes of College Women. In a recent phone survey of college women, slightly less than 3 percent of the women said they had experienced a rape or attempted rape during the academic year (Fisher, Cullen, & Turner, 2000). The percentages shown here indicate the relationship between the victim and the offender. *What were some possible advantages and disadvantages of using a phone survey rather than face-to-face interviews to conduct this study?*

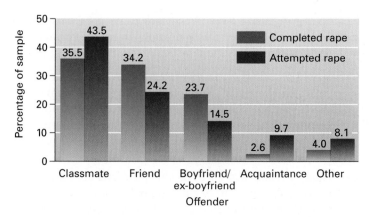

A major study that focused on campus sexual assault involved a phone survey of 4,446 women attending two- or four-year colleges (Fisher, Cullen, & Turner, 2000). In this study, slightly less than 3 percent said that they had experienced either a rape or an attempted rape during the academic year. About one of ten college women said that they had experienced rape in their lifetime. Unwanted or uninvited sexual contacts were widespread, with more than one-third of the college women reporting these incidents. As shown in Figure 12.5, in this study most women (about nine of ten) knew the person who sexually victimized them. Most of the women attempted to take protective actions against their assailants but were then reluctant to report the victimization to the police. Several factors were associated with sexual victimization: living on campus, being unmarried, getting drunk frequently, and experiencing prior sexual victimization.

Although most victims of rape are women, male rape does occur (Ellis, 2002). Men in prisons are especially vulnerable to rape, usually by heterosexual males who use rape as a means of establishing their dominance and power. Though it might seem impossible for a man to be raped by a woman, a man's erection is not completely under his voluntary control, and some cases of male rape by women have been reported (Sarrel & Masters, 1982). Male victims account for fewer than 5 percent of all rapes.

Why does rape occur so often in the United States? Among the causes given are that males are socialized to be sexually aggressive, to regard women as inferior beings, and to view their own pleasure as the most important objective (Adams-Curtis & Forbes, 2004). Researchers have found that male rapists share the following characteristics: Aggression enhances their sense of power or masculinity; they are angry at women in general; and they want to hurt and humiliate the victim (Chiroro & others, 2004). Recent studies also indicate that rape is more likely to occur when alcohol and marijuana are being used (Messman-Moore & others, 2008; Young & others, 2008). Another recent study revealed that a higher level of men's sexual narcissism (assessed by these factors: sexual exploitation, sexual entitlement, low sexual empathy, and sexual skill) was linked to a greater likelihood that they would engage in sexual aggression (Widman & McNulty, 2009).

Rape is a traumatic experience for the victims and those close to them (Herrera & others, 2006; Hock & Williams, 2007). Victims initially feel shock and numbness and are often acutely disorganized. Some show their distress through words and tears; others internalize their suffering. As victims strive to get their lives back to normal, they may experience depression, fear, and anxiety for months or years (Thompson & others, 2003). Sexual dysfunctions, such as reduced sexual desire and an inability to reach orgasm, occur in 50 percent of female rape victims (Sprei & Courtois, 1988). Many victims make changes in their lives—such as moving to a new apartment or refusing to go out at night. Recovery depends on coping abilities, psychological adjustments prior to the assault, and social support. Parents, boyfriend or husband, and others close to the victim are important factors in recovery, as is the availability of professional counseling (Frazier & others, 2004).

Sexual Harassment   **Sexual harassment** takes many forms—from sexist remarks and physical contact (patting, brushing against their bodies) to blatant propositions and sexual assaults (Mitchell, Koen, & Crow, 2008). Millions of women experience sexual harassment each year in work and educational settings (Hynes & Davis, 2009). Sexual harassment of men by women also occurs but to a far lesser extent than sexual harassment of women by men.

A recent survey of 2,000 college women by the American Association of University Women (2006) revealed that 62 percent of them reported that they had experienced sexual harassment while attending college. Most of the college women said that the sexual harassment involved noncontact forms such as crude jokes, remarks, and gestures. However, almost one-third said that the sexual harassment was physical in nature. A recent study of almost 1,500 college women revealed that when they had been sexually harassed they reported an increase in psychological distress, greater physical illness, and an increase in disordered eating (Huerta & others, 2006).

In a recent study of 12- to 18-year-old adolescent girls, 90 percent reported experiencing sexual harassment, 52 percent academic sexism, and 76 percent athletic sexism at least once (Leaper & Brown, 2008). In this study, learning about feminism and gender-conformity pressures was related to increased perceptions of sexism.

Sexual harassment can result in serious psychological consequences for the victim. Sexual harassment is a manifestation of power of one person over another. The elimination of such exploitation requires the development of work and academic environments that provide equal opportunities to obtain education and to develop a career in a climate free of sexual harassment (Das, 2008; Rospenda, Richmond, & Shannon, 2009).

Review and Reflect: Learning Goal 4

 Characterize influences on sexuality, the nature of sexual orientation, and some sexual problems

REVIEW

- How do biology and culture influence sexuality?
- What is the nature of heterosexual and homosexual attitudes and behavior?
- What are some common sexually transmitted infections? What are some good strategies for protecting against STIs?
- What is the nature of forcible sexual behavior and sexual harassment?

REFLECT

- Do you think sex is a matter of doing what comes naturally—that is, sexual behavior is essentially determined by a person's biological drive? Explain your answer.

sexual harassment Sexual persecution that can take many forms—from sexist remarks and physical contact (patting, brushing against their bodies) to blatant propositions and sexual assaults.

---

5 SEXUALITY THROUGH THE LIFE SPAN

| Child Sexuality | Sexuality in Adolescence and Emerging Adulthood | Sexuality and Aging |

So far we have discussed a number of aspects of human sexuality. Now, let's explore sexuality at different points in development, beginning with childhood.

Child Sexuality

Most psychologists doubt Freud's claim that preschool children have a strong sexual attraction to the parent of the other sex. But what are some aspects of child sexuality?

A majority of children engage in some sex play, usually with friends or siblings (Crooks & Baur, 2008; DeLamater & Friedrich, 2002). Child sex play includes exhibiting or inspecting the genitals. Much of this child sex play is likely motivated by curiosity. There does not appear to be any link between such sexual play and sexual adjustment in adolescence or adulthood.

As the elementary school years progress, sex play with others usually declines, although romantic interest in peers may be present. Curiosity about sex remains high in the elementary school years, and children may ask many questions about reproduction and sexuality (Gordon & Gordon, 1989). However, the main surge in sexual interest takes place not in childhood but in early adolescence.

Sexuality in Adolescence and Emerging Adulthood

Adolescence is a critical juncture in the development of sexuality as pubertal changes unfold and individuals develop a sexual identity. And emerging adulthood provides further opportunities for individuals to explore the sexual aspects of their lives.

Sexual arousal emerges as a new phenomenon in adolescence, and it is important to view sexuality as a normal aspect of adolescent development.

—SHIRLEY FELDMAN
Contemporary Psychologist, Stanford University

Adolescence Adolescence is a time of sexual exploration and experimentation, of sexual fantasies and realities, of incorporating sexuality into one's identity. Adolescents have an almost insatiable curiosity about sexuality. They think about whether they are sexually attractive, how to do sex, and what the future holds for their sexual lives. The majority of adolescents eventually manage to develop a mature sexual identity, but most experience times of vulnerability and confusion.

Adolescence is a bridge between the asexual child and the sexual adult. Every society gives some attention to adolescent sexuality. In some societies, adults clamp down and protect adolescent females from males by chaperoning them. Other societies promote very early marriage. Yet others allow some sexual experimentation.

In the United States, children and adolescents learn a great deal about sex from television (Roberts & Foehr, 2008). The messages come from TV commercials, which use sex to sell just about everything, as well as from the content of TV shows. A recent research review concluded that adolescents who view more sexual content on TV are more likely to initiate sexual intercourse earlier than their peers who view less sexual content on TV (Brown & Strasburger, 2007).

Developing a Sexual Identity Mastering emerging sexual feelings and forming a sense of sexual identity is a multifaceted and lengthy process. It involves learning to manage sexual feelings (such as sexual arousal and attraction), developing new forms of intimacy, and learning the skills to regulate sexual behavior to avoid undesirable consequences. An adolescent's sexual identity is influenced by *social norms* related to sex—the extent to which adolescents perceive that their peers are having sex, using protection, and so on. These social norms have important influences on adolescents' sexual behavior. For example, a recent study revealed that when adolescents perceived that their peers were sexually permissive, the adolescents had a higher rate of initiating sexual intercourse and engaging in risky sexual practices (Potard, Courtois, & Rusch, 2008). An individual's sexual identity also can be linked to other developing identities, which were discussed in Chapter 11, "The Self, Identity, and Personality."

An adolescent's sexual identity involves activities, interests, styles of behavior, and an indication of sexual orientation (whether an individual has same-sex or other-sex attractions) (Buzwell & Rosenthal, 1996; Diamond & Savin-Williams, 2009). For example, some adolescents have a high anxiety level about sex, others a low level. Some adolescents are strongly aroused sexually, others less so. Some adolescents are very active sexually, others not at all. Some adolescents are sexually inactive in response to their strong religious upbringing; others go to church regularly, yet their religious training does not inhibit their sexual activity (Thorton & Camburn, 1989).

It is commonly believed that most gay and lesbian individuals quietly struggle with same-sex attractions in childhood, do not engage in heterosexual dating, and gradually recognize that they are gay or lesbian in mid to late adolescence (Diamond & Savin-Williams, 2009). Many youth do follow this developmental pathway, but others do not. For example, many youth have no recollection of same-sex attractions and experience a more abrupt sense of their same-sex attraction in late adolescence (Savin-Williams, 2006). Researchers also have found that the majority of adolescents with same-sex attractions also experience some degree of other-sex attractions (Garofalo & others, 1999). Even though some adolescents who are attracted to same-sex individuals fall in love with these individuals, others claim that their same-sex attractions are purely physical (Diamond & Savin-Williams, 2009).

In sum, gay and lesbian youth have diverse patterns of initial attraction, often have bisexual attractions, and may have physical or emotional attraction to same-sex individuals but do not always fall in love with them (Diamond & Savin-Williams, 2009).

What are some developmental pathways of same-sex attraction in adolescence?

The Timing and Frequency of Adolescent Sexual Behaviors   The timing of sexual initiation varies by country as well as by gender and other socioeconomic characteristics. In one cross-cultural study, among females, the proportion having first intercourse by age 17 ranged from 72 percent in Mali to 47 percent in the United States and 45 percent in Tanzania (Singh & others, 2000). The percentage of males who had their first intercourse by age 17 ranged from 76 percent in Jamaica to 64 percent in the United States and 63 percent in Brazil. Within the United States, male, African American, and inner-city adolescents report being the most sexually active, whereas Asian American adolescents have the most restrictive sexual timetable (Feldman, Turner, & Araujo, 1999).

A recent study examined the role that acculturation might play in Latino adolescents' sexual behavior (McDonald, Manlove, & Ikamullah, 2009). Fewer first-generation Latino adolescents engaged in sexual intercourse before 18 years of age, and fewer first- and second-generation Latino adolescents used contraceptives consistently at 17 years of age than third-generation Latino adolescents. Thus, as acculturation proceeded, the sexual behavior of the Latino adolescents began to more closely resemble that of non-Latino White adolescents—earlier sexual initiation and increased condom use.

In a recent U.S. national survey, 63 percent of twelfth-graders (64 percent of males, 62 percent of females) reported that they had experienced sexual intercourse compared with 34 percent of ninth-graders (39 percent of males, 29 percent of females (MMWR, 2006) (see Figure 12.6). By age 20, 77 percent of U.S. youth have engaged in sexual intercourse (Dworkin & Santelli, 2007). A recent national study indicated that 35 percent of U.S. high school students were currently sexually active (Eaton & others, 2008).

Most studies find that adolescent males are more likely than adolescent females to say that they have had sexual intercourse

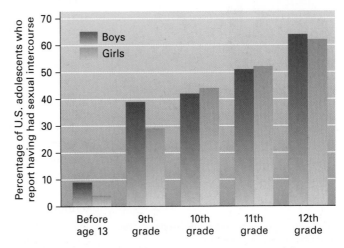

FIGURE 12.6 Timing of Sexual Intercourse in U.S. Adolescents.

and are sexually active (MMWR, 2006). Adolescent males are also more likely than their female counterparts to describe sexual intercourse as an enjoyable experience. And African Americans are more likely to engage in sexual behaviors earlier than other ethnic groups, whereas Asian Americans are more likely to engage in them later (Feldman, Turner, & Araujo, 1999). In the recent national U.S. survey of ninth- to twelfth-graders, 67 percent of African Americans, 51 percent of Latinos, and 43 percent of non-Latino Whites said they had ever experienced sexual intercourse (MMWR, 2006). In this study, 16 percent of African Americans (compared with 7 percent of Latinos and 4 percent of non-Latino Whites) said they had their first sexual experience before 13 years of age. It is important to keep in mind that in studies of adolescent sexuality, ethnic variations in sexual activity often disappear or are diminished when socioeconomic status is controlled for.

Recent research indicates that oral sex is now a common occurrence in U.S. adolescents (Brewster & Harker Tillman, 2008). In a national survey, 55 percent of U.S. 15- to 19-year-old boys and 54 percent of girls said they had engaged in oral sex (National Center for Health Statistics, 2002). What is especially worrisome about the increase in oral sex during adolescence is how casually many engage in the practice. It appears that for many adolescents oral sex is a recreational activity practiced outside an intimate, caring relationship (Walsh & Bennett, 2004). One reason for the increase in oral sex during adolescence is the belief that oral sex is not really sex. Thus, according to this belief, those who engage in oral sex but not sexual intercourse consider themselves virgins. Another reason for the increase is the perception that oral sex is likely to be safer, and less likely to result in sexually transmitted infections than sexual intercourse. Thus, many adolescents appear to be unaware of the health risks linked to oral sex, and the possibility of contracting such infections.

Sexual Risk Factors in Adolescence Many adolescents are not emotionally prepared to handle sexual experiences, especially in early adolescence. Early sexual activity is linked with risky behaviors such as drug use, delinquency, and school-related problems (Dryfoos & Barkin, 2006). In a longitudinal study from 10 to 12 years of age to 25 years of age, early sexual intercourse and affiliation with deviant peers were linked to substance use disorders in emerging adulthood (Cornelius & others, 2007).

In addition to having sex in early adolescence, other risk factors for sexual problems in adolescence include contextual factors such as socioeconomic status (SES), as well as family/parenting and peer factors (Aronowitz, Rennells, & Todd, 2006). The percentage of sexually active young adolescents is higher in low-income areas of inner cities (Silver & Bauman, 2006). Further, having older sexually active siblings or pregnant/parenting teenage sisters places adolescents at an elevated risk of adolescent pregnancy (Miller, Benson, & Galbraith, 2001). A recent study also revealed that not feeling close to their parents, having low self-esteem, and watching television extensively were linked to adolescents being sexually active at 15 years of age (Hyde & Price, 2007). And a recent research review found that an earlier onset of sexual intercourse was linked to living with other than two biological parents and a lower level of parental monitoring (Zimmer-Gembeck & Helfand, 2008). In another study, maternal communication about sex (the extent mothers talked with their adolescents about having sexual intercourse and the negative things that could happen if he got someone pregnant/she got pregnant, for example) was linked with less risky sexual behavior by Latino adolescents (Trejos-Castillo & Vazonyi, 2009). Also, a study of middle school students revealed that better academic achievement was a protective factor in keeping boys and girls from engaging in early initiation of sexual intercourse (Laflin, Wang, & Barry, 2008).

What are some risk factors for developing sexual problems in adolescence?

Cognitive factors are increasingly implicated in sexual risk taking in adolescence (Fantasia, 2008). Two such factors are attention problems and self-regulation (the ability to control one's emotions and behavior). One longitudinal study revealed that attention problems and high rates of aggressive disruptive behavior at school entry increased the risk of multiple problem behaviors (school maladjustment, antisocial behavior, and substance use) in middle school, which in turn was linked to early initiation of sexual activity (Schofield & others, 2008). Another longitudinal study found that weak self-regulation at 8 to 9 years of age and risk proneness (tendency to seek sensation and make poor decisions) at 12 to 13 years of age set the stage for sexual risk taking at 16 to 17 years of age (Crockett, Raffaelli, & Shen, 2006).

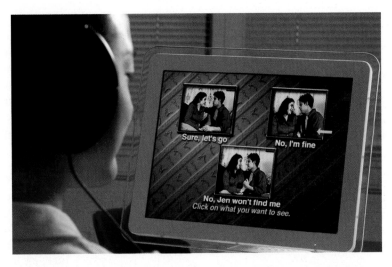

An adolescent participates in an interactive video session developed by Julie Downs and her colleagues at the Department of Social and Decision Making Sciences at Carnegie Mellon University. The videos help adolescents evaluate their responses and decisions in high-risk sexual contexts.

Contraceptive Use   Sexual activity is a normal activity necessary for procreation, but if appropriate safeguards are not taken it brings the risk of unintended, unwanted pregnancy and sexually transmitted infections (Kelly, 2008; Manlove & Terry-Humen, 2007). Both of these risks can be reduced significantly by using certain forms of contraception and barriers (such as condoms) (Breheny & Stephens, 2004).

The good news is that adolescents are increasing their use of contraceptives (Santelli & others, 2007). For example, a recent large-scale study revealed a substantial increase in the use of a contraceptive (61.5 percent in 2007 compared with 46.2 percent in 1991) by U.S. high school students during the last time they had sexual intercourse (Centers for Disease Control and Prevention, 2008).

Although adolescent contraceptive use is increasing, many sexually active adolescents still do not use contraceptives, or they use them inconsistently (Hock & Williams, 2007; Holcombe & others, 2008). Sexually active younger adolescents are less likely than older adolescents to take contraceptive precautions. Younger adolescents are more likely to use a condom or withdrawal, whereas older adolescents are more likely to use the pill or a diaphragm. A recent study also revealed that adolescents with friends who did not use condoms were more likely to not use condoms themselves later during intercourse (Henry & others, 2007).

Researchers also have found that U.S. adolescents use condoms less than their counterparts in Europe. Recent studies of 15-year-olds revealed that in Europe 72 percent of the girls and 81 percent of boys used condoms at last intercourse (Currie & others, 2008); by comparison, in the United States, 62 percent of the girls and 75 percent of the boys used condoms at last intercourse (Santelli, Sandfort, & Orr, 2009). Pill use also continues to be higher in European countries (Santelli, Sandfort, & Orr, 2009). Such comparisons provide insight into why adolescent pregnancy rates are much higher in the United States than in European countries.

Sexually Transmitted Infections   Earlier, we described sexually transmitted infections. Here we focus on their appearance in adolescents. Every year more than 3 million American adolescents (about one-fourth of those who are sexually experienced) acquire an STI (Centers for Disease Control and Prevention, 2008). In a single act of unprotected sex with an infected partner, a teenage girl has a 1 percent risk of getting HIV, a 30 percent risk of acquiring genital herpes, and a 50 percent chance of contracting gonorrhea. In some areas of the United States, as many as 25 percent of sexually active adolescents have contracted chlamydia. Adolescents have a higher incidence of gonorrhea and of chlamydia than young adults.

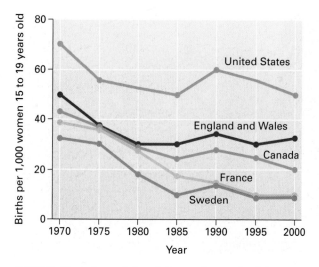

FIGURE 12.7 *Cross-Cultural Comparisons of Adolescent Pregnancy Rates.*

As we discussed earlier, a special concern is the high incidence of AIDS in sub-Saharan Africa (UNICEF, 2009). Adolescent girls in many African countries are vulnerable to being infected with HIV by adult men. Approximately six times as many adolescent girls as boys have AIDS in these countries, whereas in the United States adolescent males are more likely to have AIDS than their female counterparts (Centers for Disease Control and Prevention, 2008). In Kenya, 25 percent of 15- to 19-year-old girls are HIV-positive compared with 4 percent of the boys.

Adolescent Pregnancy   In cross-cultural comparisons, the United States continues to have one of the highest adolescent pregnancy and childbearing rates in the industrialized world, despite a considerable decline in the 1990s (Centers for Disease Control and Prevention, 2003) (see Figure 12.7). The U.S. adolescent pregnancy rate is eight times as high as in the Netherlands. Although U.S. adolescents are no more sexually active than their counterparts in the Netherlands, their adolescent pregnancy rate is dramatically higher.

Despite the negative comparisons of the United States with many other developed countries, in the 1990s and through 2004, there were encouraging trends in U.S. adolescent pregnancy rates. In 2004, births to adolescent girls fell to a record low (Child Trends, 2006). The rate of births to adolescent girls has dropped 30 percent since 1991. Reasons for these declines include increased contraceptive use and fear of sexually transmitted infections such as AIDS. However, as shown in Figure 12.8, the U.S. adolescent birth rate increased in 2006 (Child Trends, 2008).

Latina adolescents are more likely than African American and non-Latina White adolescents to become pregnant (Child Trends, 2008; Santelli, Abraido-Lanza, & Melnikas, 2009) (see Figure 12.8). Latinas also have had the smallest recent declines in adolescent pregnancy and birth rates among ethnic groups in the United States (Ventura & others, 2008). Latina and African American adolescent girls who have a child are also more likely to have a second child than are non-Latino White adolescent girls (Rosengard, 2009). And daughters of teenage mothers are at risk for teenage childbearing, thus perpetuating an intergenerational cycle. A recent study using data from the National Longitudinal Survey of Youth revealed that daughters of teenage mothers were 66 percent more likely to become teenage mothers themselves (Meade, Kershaw, & Ickovics, 2008). In this study, risks that increased the likelihood the

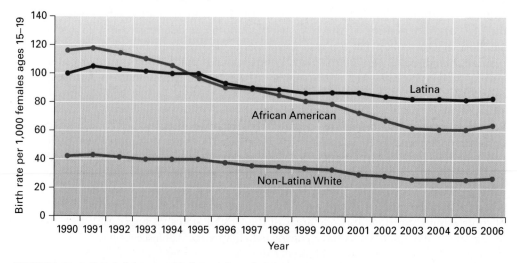

FIGURE 12.8 **U.S. Adolescent Birth Rate by Ethnicity, 1990 to 2006.**

daughters of the teenage mothers would become pregnant included low parental monitoring and poverty.

The consequences of America's high adolescent pregnancy rate are cause for great concern (Key & others, 2008). Adolescent pregnancy creates health risks for both the baby and the mother. Infants born to adolescent mothers are more likely to have low birth weights—a prominent factor in infant mortality—as well as neurological problems and childhood illness (Malamitsi-Puchner & Boutsikou, 2006). Adolescent mothers often drop out of school. Although many adolescent mothers resume their education later in life, they generally do not catch up economically with women who bear children in their twenties. A longitudinal study revealed that these characteristics of adolescent mothers were related to their likelihood of having problems as emerging adults: a history of school problems, delinquency, hard substance use, and mental health problems (Oxford & others, 2006).

Though the consequences of America's high adolescent pregnancy rate are cause for great concern, it often is not pregnancy alone that leads to negative consequences for an adolescent mother and her offspring (Oxford & others, 2006). Adolescent mothers are more likely to come from low-SES backgrounds (Crosby & Holtgrave, 2006). Many adolescent mothers also were not good students before they became pregnant (Malamitsi-Puchner & Boutsikou, 2006). However, not every adolescent female who bears a child lives a life of poverty and low achievement. Thus, although adolescent pregnancy is a high-risk circumstance, and adolescents who do not become pregnant generally fare better than those who do, some adolescent mothers do well in school and have positive outcomes (Ahn, 1994; Leadbeater & Way, 2000).

All adolescents can benefit from comprehensive sexuality education, beginning prior to adolescence and continuing through adolescence (Hyde & DeLamater, 2008). Family and consumer science educators teach life skills, such as effective decision making, to adolescents. To read about the work of one family and consumer science educator, see the *Careers in Life-Span Development* profile. And to learn more about ways to reduce adolescent pregnancy, see the *Applications in Life-Span Development* interlude.

Careers in Life-Span Development

Lynn Blankenship, Family and Consumer Science Educator

Lynn Blankenship is a family and consumer science educator. She has an undergraduate degree in this area from University of Arizona. She has taught for more than 20 years, the last 14 at Tucson High Magnet School.

Blankenship was awarded the Tucson Federation of Teachers Educator of the Year Award for 1999–2000 and the Arizona Association of Family and Consumer Science Teacher of the Year in 1999.

Blankenship especially enjoys teaching life skills to adolescents. One of her favorite activities is having students care for an automated baby that imitates the needs of real babies. She says that this program has a profound impact on students because the baby must be cared for around the clock for the duration of the assignment. Blankenship also coordinates real-world work experiences and training for students in several child-care facilities in the Tucson area.

Lynn Blankenship (*center*) with students carrying their automated babies.

Applications in Life-Span Development

REDUCING ADOLESCENT PREGNANCY

One strategy for reducing adolescent pregnancy, called the Teen Outreach Program (TOP), focuses on engaging adolescents in volunteer community service and stimulates discussions that help adolescents appreciate the lessons they learn through volunteerism (Dryfoos & Barkin, 2006). In one study, 695 adolescents in grades 9 to 12 were randomly assigned to either a Teen Outreach group or a control group (Allen & others, 1997). They were assessed at both program entry and program exit nine months later. The rate of pregnancy was substantially lower for the Teen Outreach adolescents. These adolescents also had a lower rate of school failure and academic suspension.

These are not adolescent mothers, but rather adolescents who are participating in the Teen Outreach Program (TOP), which engages adolescents in volunteer community service. These adolescents are serving as volunteers in a child-care center for crack babies. Researchers have found that such volunteer experiences can reduce the rate of adolescent pregnancy.

Girls, Inc., includes four programs that are intended to increase adolescent girls' motivation to avoid pregnancy until they are mature enough to make responsible decisions about motherhood (Roth & others, 1998). Growing Together, a series of five two-hour workshops for mothers and adolescents, and Will Power/Won't Power, a series of six two-hour sessions that focus on assertiveness training, are for 12- to 14-year-old girls. For older adolescent girls, Taking Care of Business provides nine sessions that emphasize career planning as well as information about sexuality, reproduction, and contraception. Health Bridge coordinates health and education services—girls can participate in this program as one of their club activities. Girls who participated in these programs were less likely to get pregnant than girls who did not participate (Girls, Inc., 1991).

Currently, a major controversy in sex education is whether schools should have an abstinence-only program or a program that emphasizes contraceptive knowledge. Two recent research reviews found that abstinence-only programs do not delay the initiation of sexual intercourse and do not reduce HIV-risk behaviors (Kirby, Laris, & Rolleri, 2007; Underhill, Montgomery, & Operario, 2007). Further, a recent study revealed that adolescents who experienced comprehensive sex education were less likely to report adolescent pregnancies than those who were given abstinence-only sex education or no education (Kohler, Manhart, & Lafferty, 2008).

A number of leading experts on adolescent sexuality now conclude that sex education programs that emphasize contraceptive knowledge do not increase the incidence of sexual intercourse and are more likely to reduce the risk of adolescent pregnancy and sexually transmitted infections than abstinence-only programs (Constantine, 2008; Eisenberg & others, 2008; Hyde & DeLamater, 2008).

Emerging Adulthood   At the beginning of emerging adulthood (age 18), surveys indicate that slightly more than 60 percent of individuals have experienced sexual intercourse, but by the end of emerging adulthood (age 25), most individuals have had sexual intercourse (Lefkowitz & Gillen, 2006). Also, the average age of marriage in the United States is currently 27 for males and 26 for females (Popenoe & Whitehead, 2006). Thus, emerging adulthood is a time frame during which most individuals are "both sexually active and unmarried" (Lefkowitz & Gillen, 2006, p. 235).

Patterns of heterosexual behavior for males and females in emerging adulthood include the following (Lefkowitz & Gillen, 2006):

- Males have more casual sexual partners, and females report being more selective about their choice of a sexual partner.

- Approximately 60 percent of emerging adults have had sexual intercourse with only one individual in the past year, but compared with young adults in their late twenties and thirties, emerging adults are more likely to have had sexual intercourse with two or more individuals.

- Although emerging adults have sexual intercourse with more individuals than young adults, they have sex less frequently. Approximately 25 percent of emerging adults report having sexual intercourse only a couple of times a year or not at all (Michael & others, 1994).

- Casual sex is more common in emerging adulthood than in young adulthood. One study indicated that 30 percent of emerging adults said they had "hooked up" with someone and had sexual intercourse during college (Paul, McManus, & Hayes, 2000).

What are some predictors of risky heterosexual behavior in emerging adults, such as engaging in casual and unprotected sexual intercourse? Some research findings indicate that (Lefkowitz & Gillen, 2006):

- Individuals who became sexually active in adolescence engage in more risky sexual behaviors in emerging adulthood than do their counterparts who delayed their sexual debuts until emerging adulthood (Capaldi & others, 2002).

- More religious emerging adults have had fewer sexual partners and engaged in less risky sexual behaviors than have their less religious counterparts (Lefkowitz, Boone, & Shearer, 2004).

- When emerging adults drink alcohol, they are more likely to have casual sex and less likely to discuss possible risks (Cooper, 2002). A recent study also found that emerging adult women who engaged in casual sex were more likely to report having depressive symptoms than did emerging adult men (Grello, Welsh, & Harper, 2006).

What are some characteristics of sexual patterns in emerging adulthood?

Sexuality and Aging

Earlier in our coverage of sexual orientation, we examined a number of basic ideas about heterosexual and gay male/lesbian attitudes and behavior. Much of what we said there applied to young adults. Here we focus on changes in middle adulthood and late adulthood.

Middle Adulthood What kind of changes characterize the sexuality of women and men as they go through middle age? **Climacteric** is a term that is used to describe the midlife transition in which fertility declines.

Menopause **Menopause** is the time in middle age, usually in the late forties or early fifties, when a woman's menstrual periods cease. The average age at which U.S. women have their last period is 51 (Wise, 2006). However, there is a large variation in the age at which menopause occurs—from 39 to 59 years of age. **Perimenopause** is the transitional period from normal menstrual periods to no menstrual periods at all, which often takes up to 10 years (Maitland & others, 2006). Perimenopause is most common in the forties but can occur in the thirties (O'Connell, 2005). One study of 30- to 50-year-old women found that depressed feelings, headaches, moodiness, and palpitations were the perimenopausal symptoms

climacteric The midlife transition in which fertility declines.

menopause The complete cessation of a woman's menstruation, which usually occurs in the late forties or early fifties.

perimenopause The transitional period from normal menstrual periods to no menstrual periods at all, which often takes up to 10 years.

that these women most frequently discussed with health-care providers (Lyndaker & Hulton, 2004).

With the onset of menopause, there is a dramatic decline in the production of estrogen by the ovaries, which in some women produces "hot flashes," nausea, fatigue, rapid heartbeat, or other symptoms (Cooper & others, 2008). However, menopause overall is not the negative experience for most women it was once thought to be (Bauld & Brown, 2009; Weismuller, 2009). In a large-scale study of Americans in midlife, almost two-thirds of postmenopausal women said they felt relief that their periods had stopped (Brim, 1999). Just over 50 percent of middle-aged women said they did not have hot flashes. A recent study revealed that menopausal symptoms increased in women who smoked cigarettes, drank alcohol, were currently using oral contraceptives, were depressed, and ate high-sugar content foods (Sabia & others, 2008).

Hormone replacement therapy (HRT) augments the declining levels of reproductive hormone production by the ovaries (Nappi, 2009). HRT can consist of various forms of estrogen, and usually a progestin. Concerns about an increased risk of stroke have led the National Institutes of Health (2004) to end part of a major hormone replacement therapy study a year early, telling the women to stop taking the estrogen supplements. Estrogen alone increased the risk of stroke by about the same amount as estrogen combined with progestin. Preliminary data also indicated a trend toward increased risk of dementia (a brain disorder involving deterioration of mental functioning). On the positive side, the study found that estrogen lowered the risk of hip fractures and did not increase the risk of heart attacks or breast cancer. However, recent research studies in a number of countries have found that coinciding with the decreased use of HRT in recent years has been a related decline in the incidence of breast cancer (Dobson, 2009; Parkin, 2009; Vankrunkelsven & others, 2009).

The National Institutes of Health recommend that women who have had their uterus removed, and who are currently taking hormones, should consult with their doctor to determine whether they should continue the hormone therapy. If they are taking the hormone treatment for short-term relief of symptoms, the benefits may outweigh the risks (Schindler, 2006). However, the recent negative hormone therapy results suggest that long-term hormone therapy should be seriously reevaluated (Wathen, 2006). Because of the potential negative effects of HRT, many middle-aged women are seeking alternatives such as regular exercise, dietary supplements, herbal remedies, relaxation therapy, acupuncture, and nonsteroidal medications (Gosden, 2007; Writing Group for the British Menopause Council & others, 2008). For example, one recent study revealed that acupuncture and relaxation therapy reduced the number of hot flashes middle-aged women experienced (Zaborowska & others 2007).

One potential benefit of HRT that has been proposed is that it may help to protect against cognitive aging in women. However, recent research reviews concluded that HRT is not effective in maintaining or improving cognitive functioning in postmenopausal women (Hogervorst & others, 2009; Lethaby & others, 2009).

Hormonal Changes in Middle-Aged Men   Although testosterone production begins to decline about 1 percent a year during middle adulthood, and sperm count usually shows a slow decline, men do not lose their fertility in middle age (Harman, 2007). The drop in testosterone levels, however, can reduce men's sexual drive (Goel & others, 2009). Their erections are less full and less frequent, and require more stimulation to achieve them. In a recent national study of U.S. men 40 years and older, 22 percent said they "sometimes" or "never" get or keep an erection adequate for sexual intercourse (Laumann & others, 2007). The percentage of men with erectile dysfunction increased the older they were and decreased if they engaged in regular exercise and had a college education. As much as 75 percent of the erectile dysfunctions in middle-aged men stem from physiological problems. Researchers have found that two-thirds of men report that erectile dysfunction has impaired their self-esteem, and one-third claim that it has harmed their relationship with their partner (Mirone & others, 2009).

Lifestyle plays a role in erectile dysfunction. Smoking, diabetes, hypertension, and elevated cholesterol levels are implicated in many middle-aged men's erectile problems (Crooks & Bauer, 2008). A recent study revealed that low testosterone levels were related to the presence of metabolic syndrome and a high level of triglycerides (Corona & others, 2009). In another recent study, middle-aged men were randomly assigned to one of two treatment groups: (1) an experimental group that was given detailed, individualized information about the importance of reducing body weight, improved quality of diet, and increased physical activity in reducing erectile dysfunction; and (2) a control group that was provided general information about healthy food choices and increasing physical activity (Esposito & others, 2009). After two years of intervention, the men in the experimental group were more successful in improving their lifestyles and had greater reduction in erectile dysfunction.

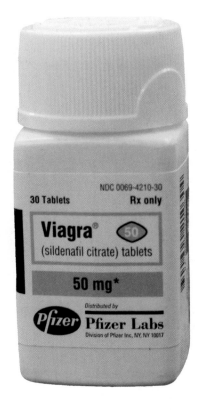

Treatment for men with erectile dysfunction has focused recently on the drug sildenafil (Viagra) and on similar drugs that appeared after Viagra became popular, such as vardenafil (Levitra) and tadalafil (Cialis) (Brock & others, 2009; De Beradis & others, 2009). Viagra works by allowing increased blood flow into the penis, which produces an erection. Its success rate is in the range of 60 to 85 percent (Pavone & others, 2008). Studies continue to show that a high percentage of men who take Viagra for erectile dysfunction are highly satisfied with the effectiveness of the drug (Abdo & others, 2008; McCullough & others, 2008). A recent study revealed that Viagra also improved the self-esteem, confidence, and relationships of men with erectile dysfunction (Glina & others, 2009). Researchers also have found that Levitra and Cialis are as successful as Viagra in treating erectile dysfunction (Rubio-Aurioles & others, 2008; Sharlip & others, 2008).

Although the ability of men and women to function sexually shows little biological decline in middle adulthood, sexual activity usually occurs less frequently than in early adulthood (Waite, Das, & Laumann, 2009). Career interests, family matters, relationship factors, energy level, and routine may contribute to this decline (Avis & others, 2005). In the Sex in America survey, frequency of having sex was greatest for individuals aged 25 to 29 years old (47 percent had sex twice a week or more) and dropped off for individuals in their fifties (23 percent of 50- to 59-year-old males said they had sex twice a week or more, whereas only 14 percent of the females in this age group reported this frequency) (Michael & others, 1994).

Figure 12.9 shows the age trends in frequency of sex from the Sex in America survey. Note, though, that the Sex in America survey may underestimate the

FIGURE 12.9 The Sex in America Survey: Frequency of Sex at Different Points in Adult Development.

	Frequency of Sex				
Age groups	Not at all	A few times a year	A few times a month	2 to 3 times a week	4 or more times a week
Men					
18 to 24	15	21	24	28	12
25 to 29	7	15	31	36	11
30 to 39	8	15	37	23	6
40 to 49	9	18	40	27	6
50 to 59	11	22	43	20	3
Women					
18 to 24	11	16	32	29	12
25 to 29	5	10	38	37	10
30 to 39	9	16	36	33	6
40 to 49	15	16	44	20	5
50 to 59	30	22	35	12	2

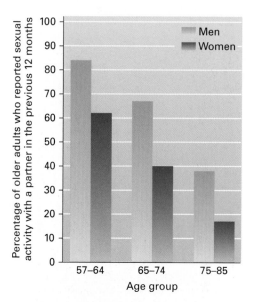

FIGURE 12.10 Sexual Activity in Older Adults with a Partner.

What are some characteristics of sexuality in older adults? How does sexual activity change as older adults go through the late adulthood period?

frequency of sexual activity of middle-aged adults because the data were collected prior to the widespread use of erectile dysfunction drugs such as Viagra. Other research indicates that middle-aged men want sex, think about it more, and masturbate more often than middle-aged women (Stones & Stones, 2007). For many other forms of sexual behavior, such as kissing and hugging, sexual touching, and oral sex, male and female middle-aged adults report similar frequency of engagement (Stones & Stones, 2007). A recent large-scale longitudinal study of women revealed that masturbation increased in early perimenopause but declined during postmenopause (Avis & others, 2009). Also in this study, women's sexual desire decreased by late perimenopause. However, the menopausal transition was not linked to the importance of sex, sexual arousal, frequency of sexual intercourse, emotional satisfaction with a partner, or physical pleasure.

A spouse or live-in partner makes all the difference in whether sexual activity occurs, especially for women over 40 years of age. In one study, 95 percent of women in their forties with partners said that they have been sexually active in the last six months, compared with only 53 percent of those without partners (Brim, 1999). By their fifties, 88 percent of women living with a partner have been sexually active in the last six months, but only 37 percent of those who are neither married nor living with someone say they have had sex in the last six months.

A recent large-scale study of U.S. adults 40 to 80 years of age found that early ejaculation (26 percent) and erectile difficulties (22 percent) were the most common sexual problems of older men, whereas lack of sexual interest (33 percent) and lubrication difficulties (21 percent) were the most common sexual problems of older women (Laumann & others, 2009).

Late Adulthood Aging does induce some changes in human sexual performance, more so in men than in women (Bouman, 2008). Orgasm becomes less frequent in males, occurring in every second to third act of intercourse rather than every time. More direct stimulation usually is needed to produce an erection. From 65 to 80 years of age, approximately one out of four men has serious problems getting or keeping erections; for those over 80 years of age, the percentage rises to one out of two men (Butler & Lewis, 2002). Even when intercourse is impaired by infirmity, other relationship needs persist, among them closeness, sensuality, and being valued as a man or a woman (Bouman, 2008; Hurd Clarke, 2006).

A recent interview study of more than 3,000 adults 57 to 85 years of age revealed that many older adults are sexually active as long as they are healthy (Lindau & others, 2007) (see Figure 12.10). Sexual activity did decline through the later years of life: 73 percent of 57- to 64-year-olds, 53 percent of 65- to 74-year-olds, and 26 percent 75- to 85-year-olds reported that they were sexually active. Even in the sexually active oldest group (75 to 85), more than 50 percent said they still have sex at least two to three times a month. Fifty-eight percent of sexually active 65- to 74-year-olds and 31 percent of 75- to 85-year-olds said they engage in oral sex. As with middle-aged and younger adults, older adults who did not have a partner were far less likely to be sexually active than those who had a partner. For older adults with a partner who reported not having sex, the main reason was poor health, especially the male partner's physical health.

As indicated in Figure 12.10, older women had a lower rate of sexual activity than did men. Indeed, a challenge for a sexually interested older woman is not having a partner. At 70 years of age, only about 35 percent of women have a partner compared with approximately 70 percent of men. Many older women's husbands have died, and many older men are with younger women.

At this point, we have discussed many aspects of sexuality, but we have not examined three influential factors: an individual's morality, values, and religion. In Chapter 13, "Moral Development, Values, and Religion," we explore these topics.

Review and Reflect: Learning Goal 5

 5 **Summarize how sexuality develops through the life span**

REVIEW

- What is the nature of child sexuality?
- How do adolescents develop a sexual identity? How does sexual behavior develop? What are some risk factors for sexual problems during adolescence? What are some patterns of behavior for emerging adults?
- How does sexuality change in middle adulthood? How does sexuality change in late adulthood?

REFLECT

- How would you describe your sexual identity? What contributed to this identity?

Reach Your Learning Goals

CHAPTER 12

Gender and Sexuality

1 BIOLOGICAL, SOCIAL, AND COGNITIVE INFLUENCES ON GENDER: EXPLAIN BIOLOGICAL, SOCIAL, AND COGNITIVE INFLUENCES ON GENDER

What Is Gender?

- Gender refers to the characteristics of people as males and females. Among the components of gender are gender identity, gender roles, and gender-typing.

Biological Influences

- Biological influences on gender include heredity, hormones, and evolution. The 23rd pair of chromosomes with two X-shaped chromosomes produces a female; a 23rd pair with an X and a Y chromosome produces a male. Estrogens primarily influence the development of female physical sex characteristics and help regulate the menstrual cycle. Androgens primarily promote the development of male genitals and secondary sex characteristics. To explore biological influences on gender, researchers have studied individuals who are exposed to unusual levels of sex hormones early in development. Evolutionary psychology argues that adaptation during the evolution of humans produced psychological differences between males and females.

Social Influences

- Three theories have been influential in arguing that psychological differences between the genders are due to social factors. Social role theory states that psychological gender differences result from the contrasting roles of women and men. The psychoanalytic theory of gender stems from Freud's view that the preschool child develops a sexual attraction to the opposite-sex parent, then at 5 or 6 years of age renounces the attraction because of anxious feelings, subsequently identifies with the same-sex parent and unconsciously adopts the characteristics of the same-sex parent. The social cognitive theory of gender states that children learn about gender through observation and imitation and through reward and punishment for gender-appropriate and gender-inappropriate behavior.

Cognitive Influences

- Gender schema theory states that gender-typing emerges as children gradually develop gender schemas of what is gender-appropriate and gender-inappropriate in their culture.

2 GENDER STEREOTYPES, SIMILARITIES, AND DIFFERENCES: DISCUSS GENDER STEREOTYPES, SIMILARITIES, AND DIFFERENCES

Gender Stereotyping

- Gender stereotypes are general impressions and beliefs about males and females. Gender stereotypes are widespread. Gender stereotyping changes developmentally; it is present even at 2 years of age but increases considerably in early childhood. In middle and late childhood, children become more flexible in their gender attitudes, but gender stereotyping may increase again in early adolescence. By late adolescence, gender attitudes are often more flexible.

Gender Similarities and Differences

- There are a number of physical differences in males and females, small or nonexistent cognitive differences—although boys have better visuospatial skills and score slightly higher in math, girls earn better grades and score higher than boys in literacy skills. In addition, there are some socioemotional differences: Males are more physically aggressive and active, but engage in less emotional self-regulation; females show a stronger interest in relationships. Controversy continues to occur regarding how extensive gender differences are and what causes the differences. Gender in context is an important concept—gender behavior often varies across contexts, not only within a particular culture but also across cultures.

3   GENDER DEVELOPMENT THROUGH THE LIFE SPAN: DESCRIBE THE DEVELOPMENT OF GENDER THROUGH THE LIFE SPAN

Childhood

- Children form many ideas about what the sexes are like from about 1½ to 3 years of age. The amount, timing, and intensity of gender socialization are different for girls and for boys. Boys receive earlier and more intense gender socialization than girls do.

Adolescence

- During early adolescence, females and males must come to terms with new definitions of their gender roles as they experience the extensive changes of puberty. There is continued controversy about whether all young adolescents experience gender intensification.

Adulthood and Aging

- Many experts argue that it is important for women to retain their relationship strengths but also to put more energy into self-development. Tannen stresses that many women prefer rapport talk and many men prefer report talk. Men have been successful at achieving, but the male role involves considerable strain. There is diversity in men's experiences, just as there is in women's. Men seem to become more nurturant and sensitive when they get older, but the evidence about whether women tend to become more assertive and dominant when they are older is mixed.

4   EXPLORING SEXUALITY: CHARACTERIZE INFLUENCES ON SEXUALITY, THE NATURE OF SEXUAL ORIENTATION, AND SOME SEXUAL PROBLEMS

Biological and Cultural Factors

- The role of hormones in human sexual behavior is difficult to specify. Sexual motivation is also influenced by cultural factors. Sexual scripts in cultures influence sexual behavior. In some sexual scripts, females link sexual intercourse with love more than do males, the female is to blame if she becomes pregnant, and males tend to emphasize sexual conquest.

Sexual Orientation

- An individual's sexual preference—heterosexual, homosexual, or bisexual—likely is the result of a combination of genetic, hormonal, cognitive, and environmental factors. In the 1994 Sex in America survey, Americans' sexual lives were reported to be more conservative than in earlier surveys. It is generally accepted to view sexual orientation along a continuum. Regardless of sexual orientation, most people emphasize the importance of trust, affection, and shared interests in a relationship.

Sexually Transmitted Infections

- Sexually transmitted infections (STIs) are contracted primarily through sexual contact. The STI that has received the most attention in recent years is AIDS. Gonorrhea, syphilis, chlamydia, genital herpes, and HPV are among the most common STIs. Some good strategies for protecting against STIs include knowing your and your partner's risk status; obtaining screening for STIs; having protected, not unprotected, sex; and not having sex with multiple partners.

Forcible Sexual Behavior and Sexual Harassment

- Rape is forcible sexual intercourse, oral sex, or anal sex with a person who does not give consent. Rape usually produces traumatic reactions in its victims. Sexual harassment occurs when one person uses his or her power over another individual in a sexual manner.

5   SEXUALITY THROUGH THE LIFE SPAN: SUMMARIZE HOW SEXUALITY DEVELOPS THROUGH THE LIFE SPAN

Child Sexuality

- A majority of children engage in some sex play, usually with siblings or friends. Their motivation is probably mainly curiosity, and there does not appear to be a link between sex play and adolescent or adulthood sexual adjustment.

Sexuality in Adolescence and Emerging Adulthood

- Adolescence is a time of sexual exploration and sexual experimentation. Mastering emerging sexual feelings and forming a sense of sexual identity are two challenges of the period. Gay and lesbian youth have diverse patterns of initial attraction, often have bisexual attractions, and may experience same-sex emotional or physical attractions. National U.S. data indicate that by age 20, 77 percent of U.S. high school students have had sexual intercourse. A dramatic increase in oral sex has occurred in adolescence, although many adolescents are unaware of the health risks associated with oral sex. Risk factors for sexual problems include early sexual activity, engaging in delinquency and excessive drinking, living in a low-SES neighborhood, ineffective parenting, and having an older sibling who engages in sex. Contraceptive use by adolescents is increasing. About one in four sexually experienced adolescents acquire a sexually transmitted infection (STI). America's adolescent pregnancy rate is high. Emerging adults have sexual intercourse less frequently than young adults; males have more casual sexual partners and are less selective than females in their partner choice; and by the end of emerging adulthood, most have had sexual intercourse.

Sexuality and Aging

- Menopause usually occurs in the late forties or early fifties. Perimenopause, the transition from normal menstrual periods to no menstrual periods at all, often takes up to 10 years. Hormone replacement therapy (HRT) augments the declining levels of reproductive hormone production by the ovaries. HRT consists of various forms of estrogen, and usually progestin. Although HRT reduces many short-term symptoms of menopause, its long-term use is no longer recommended by the National Institutes of Health because of its association with increased risk of coronary heart disease and stroke. Men do not experience an inability to father children in middle age, although their testosterone level drops. In late adulthood, sexual changes do occur, more so for men than for women.

KEY TERMS

gender 424
gender identity 424
gender role 424
gender-typing 424
estrogens 425
androgens 425
social role theory 426
psychoanalytic theory of gender 426

social cognitive theory of gender 426
gender schema theory 428
gender stereotypes 430
gender-intensification hypothesis 436
rapport talk 437
report talk 437

sexual scripts 441
traditional religious script 441
romantic script 441
bisexual 442
sexually transmitted infections (STIs) 443
AIDS 445

rape 447
date or acquaintance rape 447
sexual harassment 449
climacteric 457
menopause 457
perimenopause 457

KEY PEOPLE

Alice Eagly 426
Sigmund Freud 426
Phyllis Bronstein 427
Janet Shibley Hyde 432

Deborah Tannen 433
Joseph Pleck 436
Jean Baker Miller 437
Harriet Lerner 437

Ron Levant 438
Robert Michael 441
Alfred Kinsey 441
Simon LeVay 442

Letitia Peplau 443
Laura Brown 443

E-LEARNING TOOLS

Connect to **www.mhhe.com/santrockldt5e** to research the answers and complete these exercises. In addition, you'll find a number of other resources and valuable study tools for Chapter 12, "Gender and Sexuality," on this Web site.

Taking It to the Net

1. Travis is gay. One of his classmates, who admits that he thinks that homosexuality is a sin, asked, "Why don't you go to therapy

and get over your problem?" Travis says he doesn't have a problem. Does Travis need therapy to "get over" being gay?

2. Denise, the only female employee in the parts department of a large automobile dealer, tells her mother that she is disgusted by the pornographic calendars hanging on the office wall and tired of the men addressing her as "honey" and "baby doll." Her mother tells her that she may have a sexual harassment claim against her employer. Does she? And, if so, what can Denise do about it?

3. Juan, a California high school student, is taking part in a debate on contraceptive use by adolescents. Where would he find statistics on U.S. teenage pregnancies? What are the rates for his state?

Self-Assessment

To evaluate yourself on various aspects of gender and sexuality, complete these self-assessments:

- *Am I Androgynous?*
- *My Attitudes Toward Women*
- *How Much Do I Know About STIs?*
- *My Knowledge of Sexual Myths and Realities*

Health and Well-Being, Parenting, and Education

Build your decision-making skills by trying your hand at the health and well-being, parenting, and education exercises.

Video Clips

The Online Learning Center includes the following videos for this chapter:

- *Toys for Boys Store Aisle*
- *Toys for Girls Store Aisle*
- *Sex-Typed Play at Age 1*
- *Gender Identity Development*
- *Gender Stereotype Beliefs at Age 6*
- *Sex Differences*
- *Talking About Teen Sex at Age 14*
- *Coming Out*
- *Coping as Teen Parents*
- *Sex in Later Adulthood*
- *Gender Constancy at Age 4*

13

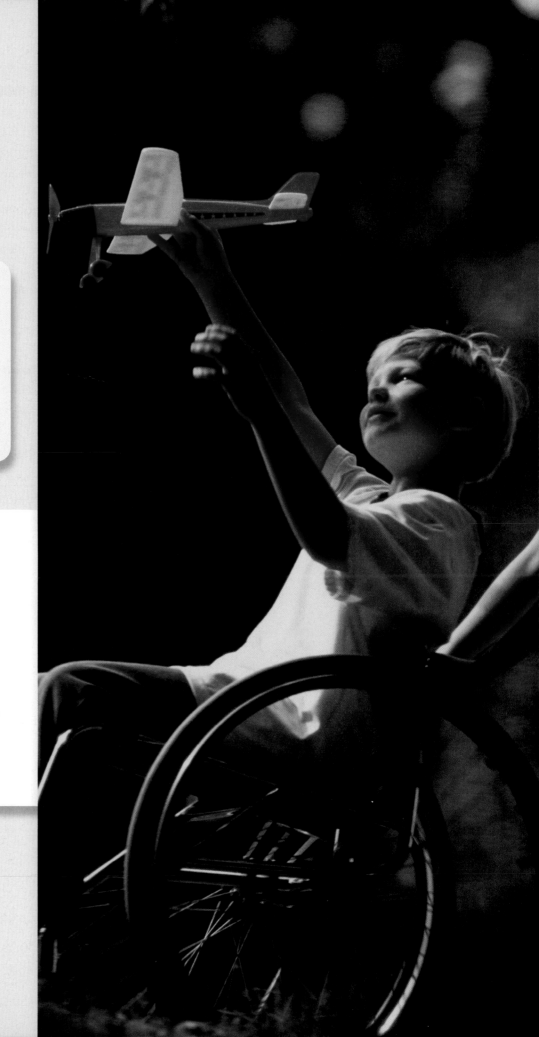

> *It is one of the beautiful compensations of this life that no one can sincerely try to help another without helping himself.*
>
> —CHARLES DUDLEY WARNER
> *American Essayist, 19th Century*

LEARNING GOALS

◆ Discuss theory and research on moral thought, behavior, feeling, and personality.

◆ Explain how parents and schools influence moral development.

◆ Describe the development of prosocial and antisocial behavior.

◆ Characterize the development of values, religion, spirituality, and meaning in life.

MORAL DEVELOPMENT, VALUES, AND RELIGION

CHAPTER OUTLINE

467

PREVIEW

Just as a person's emotional life and sexual life change with age, a person's moral life and spiritual life also develop through the life span. In this chapter, we examine how moral development proceeds. We will also explore how people go beyond questions of right and wrong to search for values, religion, spirituality, and meaning at different points in their lives.

1 DOMAINS OF MORAL DEVELOPMENT

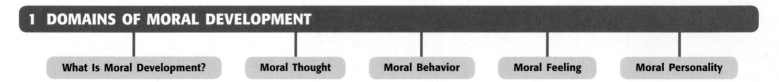

| What Is Moral Development? | Moral Thought | Moral Behavior | Moral Feeling | Moral Personality |

Moral development has been a topic of greatest concern to societies, communities, and families. It is also one of the oldest topics of interest to those who are curious about human nature. Philosophers and theologians have talked about it and written about it for many centuries. In the twentieth century, psychologists began theorizing about and studying moral development.

What Is Moral Development?

Moral development involves changes in thoughts, feelings, and behaviors regarding standards of right and wrong. Moral development has an *intrapersonal* dimension, which regulates a person's activities when she or he is not engaged in social interaction, and an *interpersonal* dimension, which regulates social interactions and arbitrates conflict (Walker, 2004, 2006). To understand moral development, we need to consider four basic questions:

First, how do individuals *reason* or *think* about moral decisions?

Second, how do individuals actually *behave* in moral circumstances?

Third, how do individuals *feel* about moral matters?

Fourth, what characterizes an individual's moral *personality?*

As we consider these four domains in the following sections, keep in mind that thoughts, behaviors, feelings, and personality often are interrelated. For example, if the focus is on an individual's behavior, it is still important to evaluate the person's reasoning. Also, emotions can distort moral reasoning. And moral personality encompasses thoughts, behavior, and feeling.

Moral Thought

How do individuals think about what is right and wrong? Are children able to evaluate moral questions in the same way that adults can? Jean Piaget had some thoughts about these questions. So did Lawrence Kohlberg.

Piaget's Theory   Interest in how children think about moral issues was stimulated by Piaget (1932), who extensively observed and interviewed children from the ages of 4 through 12. Piaget watched children play marbles to learn how they used and thought about the game's rules. He also asked children about ethical issues—theft, lies, punishment, and justice, for example. Piaget concluded that children go through two distinct stages in how they think about morality.

---

moral development Changes in thoughts, feelings, and behaviors regarding standards of right and wrong.

heteronomous morality (Piaget) The first stage of moral development in Piaget's theory, occurring at 4 to 7 years of age. Justice and rules are conceived of as unchangeable properties of the world, removed from the control of people.

autonomous morality The second stage of moral development in Piaget's theory, displayed by older children (about 10 years of age and older). The children become aware that rules and laws are created by people and that, in judging an action, they should consider the actor's intentions as well as the consequences.

immanent justice Piaget's concept that if a rule is broken, punishment will be meted out immediately.

- From 4 to 7 years of age, children display **heteronomous morality,** the first stage of moral development in Piaget's theory. Children think of justice and rules as unchangeable properties of the world, removed from the control of people.

- From 7 to 10 years of age, children are in a transition showing some features of the first stage of moral reasoning and some features of the second stage, autonomous morality.

- From about 10 years of age and older, children show **autonomous morality.** They become aware that rules and laws are created by people, and in judging an action, they consider the actor's intentions as well as the consequences.

Because young children are heteronomous moralists, they judge the rightness or goodness of behavior by considering its consequences, not the intentions of the actor. For example, to the heteronomous moralist, breaking twelve cups accidentally is worse than breaking one cup intentionally. As children develop into moral autonomists, intentions assume paramount importance.

The heteronomous thinker also believes that rules are unchangeable and are handed down by all-powerful authorities. When Piaget suggested to young children that they use new rules in a game of marbles, they resisted. By contrast, older children—moral autonomists—accept change and recognize that rules are merely convenient conventions, subject to change.

The heteronomous thinker also believes in **immanent justice,** the concept that if a rule is broken, punishment will be meted out immediately. The young child believes that a violation is connected automatically to its punishment. Thus, young children often look around worriedly after doing something wrong, expecting inevitable punishment. Immanent justice also implies that if something unfortunate happens to someone, the person must have transgressed earlier. Older children, who are moral autonomists, recognize that punishment occurs only if someone witnesses the wrongdoing and that, even then, punishment is not inevitable.

How do these changes in moral reasoning occur? Piaget argued that, as children develop, they become more sophisticated in thinking about social matters, especially about the possibilities and conditions of cooperation. Piaget stressed that this social understanding comes about through the mutual give-and-take of peer relations. In the peer group, where others have power and status similar to the child's, plans are negotiated and coordinated, and disagreements are reasoned about and eventually settled. Parent-child relations, in which parents have the power and children do not, are less likely to advance moral reasoning, because rules are often handed down in an authoritarian way.

Kohlberg's Theory A second major perspective on moral development was proposed by Lawrence Kohlberg (1958, 1986). Piaget's cognitive stages of development serve as the underpinnings for Kohlberg's theory, but Kohlberg suggested that there are six stages of moral development. These stages, he argued, are universal. Development from one stage to another, said Kohlberg, is fostered by opportunities to take the perspective of others and to experience conflict between one's current stage of moral thinking and the reasoning of someone at a higher stage.

Kohlberg arrived at his view after 20 years of using a unique interview with children. In the interview, children are presented with a series of stories in which characters face moral dilemmas. The following is the most popular Kohlberg dilemma:

> In Europe a woman was near death from a special kind of cancer. There was one drug that the doctors thought might save her. It was a form of radium that a druggist in the same town had recently discovered. The drug was expensive to make, but the druggist was charging ten times what the drug cost him to make.

Piaget extensively observed and interviewed 4- to 12-year-old children as they played games to learn how they used and thought about the games' rules.

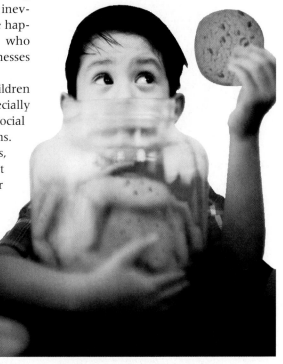

How is this child's moral thinking likely to be different about stealing a cookie depending on whether he is in Piaget's heteronomous or autonomous stage?

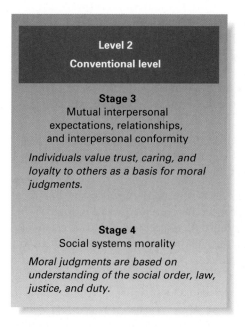

Level 1
Preconventional level

Stage 1
Heteronomous morality

Children obey because adults tell them to obey. People base their moral decisions on fear of punishment.

Stage 2
Individualism, purpose, and exchange

Individuals pursue their own interests but let others do the same. What is right involves equal exchange.

Level 2
Conventional level

Stage 3
Mutual interpersonal expectations, relationships, and interpersonal conformity

Individuals value trust, caring, and loyalty to others as a basis for moral judgments.

Stage 4
Social systems morality

Moral judgments are based on understanding of the social order, law, justice, and duty.

Level 3
Postconventional level

Stage 5
Social contract or utility and individual rights

Individuals reason that values, rights, and principles undergird or transcend the law.

Stage 6
Universal ethical principles

Individuals have developed moral judgments that are based on universal human rights. When faced with a dilemma between law and conscience, they follow a personal, individualized conscience.

FIGURE 13.1 Kohlberg's Three Levels and Six Stages of Moral Development.

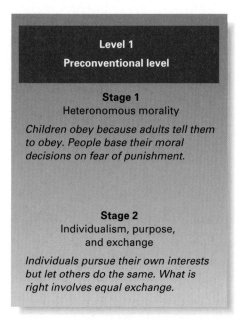

Lawrence Kohlberg, the architect of a provocative cognitive developmental theory of moral development. *What is the nature of his theory?*

preconventional reasoning The lowest level in Kohlberg's theory of moral development. The individual's moral reasoning is controlled primarily by external rewards and punishment.

heteronomous morality (Kohlberg) The first stage of preconventional reasoning in Kohlberg's theory, in which moral thinking is tied to punishment.

He paid $200 for the radium and charged $2,000 for a small dose of the drug. The sick woman's husband, Heinz, went to everyone he knew to borrow the money, but he could only get together $1,000 which is half of what it cost. He told the druggist that his wife was dying and asked him to sell it cheaper or let him pay later. But the druggist said, "No, I discovered the drug, and I am going to make money from it." So Heinz got desperate and broke into the man's store to steal the drug for his wife. (Kohlberg, 1969, p. 379)

This story is one of 11 that Kohlberg devised to investigate the nature of moral thought. After reading the story, the interviewee answers a series of questions about the moral dilemma. Should Heinz have stolen the drug? Was stealing it right or wrong? Why? Is it a husband's duty to steal the drug for his wife if he can get it no other way? Would a good husband steal? Did the druggist have the right to charge that much when there was no law setting a limit on the price? Why or why not?

The Kohlberg Stages   Based on the answers interviewees gave for this and other moral dilemmas, Kohlberg described three levels of moral thinking, each of which is characterized by two stages (see Figure 13.1). A key concept in understanding progression through the levels and stages is that their morality becomes more internal or mature. That is, their reasons for their moral decisions or values begin to go beyond the external or superficial reasons they gave when they were younger. Let's further examine Kohlberg's stages.

Preconventional reasoning is the lowest level of moral reasoning, said Kohlberg. At this level, good and bad are interpreted in terms of external rewards and punishments.

- *Stage 1.* **Heteronomous morality** is the first stage in preconventional reasoning. At this stage, moral thinking is tied to punishment. For example, children think that they must obey because they fear punishment for disobedience.

- *Stage 2.* **Individualism, instrumental purpose, and exchange** is the second stage of preconventional reasoning. At this stage, individuals reason that pursuing their own interests is the right thing to do, but they let others do the same. Thus, they think that what is right involves an equal exchange. They reason that if they are nice to others, others will be nice to them in return.

Conventional reasoning is the second, or intermediate, level in Kohlberg's theory of moral development. At this level, individuals apply certain standards, but they are the standards set by others, such as parents or the government.

- *Stage 3.* **Mutual interpersonal expectations, relationships, and interpersonal conformity** is Kohlberg's third stage of moral development. At this stage, individuals value trust, caring, and loyalty to others as a basis of moral judgments. Children and adolescents often adopt their parents' moral standards at this stage, seeking to be thought of by their parents as a "good girl" or a "good boy."
- *Stage 4.* **Social systems morality** is the fourth stage in Kohlberg's theory of moral development. At this stage, moral judgments are based on understanding the social order, law, justice, and duty. For example, adolescents may reason that in order for a community to work effectively, it needs to be protected by laws that are adhered to by its members.

Postconventional reasoning is the highest level in Kohlberg's theory of moral development. At this level, the individual recognizes alternative moral courses, explores the options, and then decides on a personal moral code.

- *Stage 5.* **Social contract or utility and individual rights** is the fifth Kohlberg stage. At this stage, individuals reason that values, rights, and principles undergird or transcend the law. A person evaluates the validity of actual laws, and social systems in terms of the degree to which they preserve and protect fundamental human rights and values.
- *Stage 6.* **Universal ethical principles** is the sixth and highest stage in Kohlberg's theory of moral development. At this stage, the person has developed a moral standard based on universal human rights. When faced with a conflict between law and conscience, the person reasons that conscience should be followed, even though the decision might bring risk.

Kohlberg noted that these levels and stages occur in a sequence and are age related: before age 9, most children use level 1, preconventional reasoning based on external rewards and punishments, when they consider moral choices. By early adolescence, their moral reasoning is increasingly based on the application of standards set by others. Most adolescents reason at stage 3, with some signs of stages 2 and 4. By early adulthood, a small number of individuals reason in postconventional ways.

What evidence supports this description of development? A 20-year longitudinal investigation found that use of stages 1 and 2 decreased with age (Colby & others, 1983). Stage 4, which did not appear at all in the moral reasoning of 10-year-olds, was reflected in the moral thinking of 62 percent of the 36-year-olds. Stage 5 did not appear until age 20 to 22 and never characterized more than 10 percent of the individuals.

Thus, the moral stages appeared somewhat later than Kohlberg initially envisioned, and reasoning at the higher stages, especially stage 6, was rare. Although stage 6 has been removed from the Kohlberg moral judgment scoring manual, it still is considered to be theoretically important in the Kohlberg scheme of moral development.

Shortly before his death, Kohlberg was contemplating the addition of a seventh stage to his theory, the *cosmic perspective*. He maintained that at this level individuals move beyond considerations of justice and see themselves not just as part of humanity but as part of the universe (Kohlberg & Ryncarz, 1990). In this stage, individuals reflect on such questions as "Why be moral? Why be a just person in a world that appears to be unjust?" Stage 7 has much in common with the emphasis on self-transcendence in Eastern philosophy and religion. Stage 7 thinkers recognize that in experiencing oneness with the universe everything is connected—that is, one person's actions affect everyone else and the consequences revert back to the doer.

individualism, instrumental purpose, and exchange The second Kohlberg stage of preconventional reasoning. At this stage, individuals pursue their own interests but also let others do the same.

conventional reasoning The second, or intermediate, level in Kohlberg's theory of moral development. At this level, individuals abide by certain standards but they are the standards of others such as parents or the laws of society.

mutual interpersonal expectations, relationships, and interpersonal conformity Kohlberg's third stage of moral development. At this stage, individuals value trust, caring, and loyalty to others as a basis of moral judgments.

social systems morality The fourth stage in Kohlberg's theory of moral development. Moral judgments are based on understanding the social order, law, justice, and duty.

postconventional reasoning The highest level in Kohlberg's theory of moral development. At this level, the individual recognizes alternative moral courses, explores the options, and then decides on a personal moral code.

social contract or utility and individual rights The fifth Kohlberg stage of moral development. At this stage, individuals reason that values, rights, and principles undergird or transcend the law.

universal ethical principles The sixth and highest stage in Kohlberg's theory of moral development. Individuals develop a moral standard based on universal human rights.

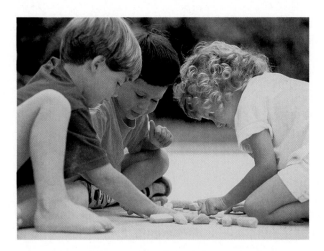

Both Piaget and Kohlberg argued that peer relations are a critical part of the social stimulation that challenges children to advance their moral reasoning. The mutual give-and-take of peer relations provides children with role-taking opportunities that give them a sense that rules are generated democratically.

This 14-year-old boy in Nepal is thought to be the sixth holiest Buddhist in the world. In one study of 20 adolescent male Buddhist monks in Nepal, the issue of justice, a basic theme in Kohlberg's theory, was not a central focus in the monks' moral views (Huebner & Garrod, 1993). Also, the monks' concerns about prevention of suffering and the importance of compassion are not captured in Kohlberg's theory.

Influences on the Kohlberg Stages What factors influence movement through Kohlberg' stages? Although moral reasoning at each stage presupposes a certain level of cognitive development, Kohlberg argued that advances in children's cognitive development did not ensure development of moral reasoning. Instead, moral reasoning also reflects children's experiences in dealing with moral questions and moral conflict.

Several investigators have tried to advance individuals' levels of moral development by having a model present arguments that reflect moral thinking one stage above the individuals' established levels. This approach applies the concepts of equilibrium and conflict that Piaget used to explain cognitive development. By presenting arguments slightly beyond the children's level of moral reasoning, the researchers created a disequilibrium that motivated the children to restructure their moral thought. The upshot of studies using this approach is that virtually any plus-stage discussion, for any length of time, seems to promote more advanced moral reasoning (Walker, 1982).

Kohlberg noted that peer interaction is a critical part of the social stimulation that challenges children to change their moral reasoning. Whereas adults characteristically impose rules and regulations on children, the give-and-take among peers gives children an opportunity to take the perspective of another person and to generate rules democratically. Kohlberg stressed that in principle, encounters with any peers can produce perspective-taking opportunities that may advance a child's moral reasoning.

Kohlberg's Critics Kohlberg's theory provoked debate, research, and criticism (Gibbs, 2009; Narváez & Lapsley, 2009; Power & Higgins-D'Allesandro, 2008). Key criticisms involve the link between moral thought and moral behavior, the roles of culture and the family in moral development, and the significance of concern for others.

Moral Thought and Moral Behavior Kohlberg's theory has been criticized for placing too much emphasis on moral thought and not enough emphasis on moral behavior (Walker, 2004). Moral reasons can sometimes be a shelter for immoral behavior. Corrupt CEOs and politicians endorse the loftiest of moral virtues in public before their own behavior is exposed. Whatever the latest public scandal, you will probably find that the culprits displayed virtuous thoughts but engaged in immoral behavior. No one wants a nation of cheaters and thieves who can reason at the postconventional level. The cheaters and thieves may know what is right yet still do what is wrong. Heinous actions can be cloaked in a mantle of moral virtue.

The mantle of virtue is not necessarily a ruse; it is often taken on sincerely. Social cognitive theorist Albert Bandura (1999, 2002) argues that people usually do not engage in harmful conduct until they have justified the morality of their actions to themselves. Immoral conduct is made personally and socially acceptable by portraying it as serving socially worthy or moral purposes or even as doing God's will. Bandura provides the examples of antiabortion activists who bomb abortion clinics or murder doctors in order to discourage abortions.

Culture and Moral Reasoning Kohlberg emphasized that his stages of moral reasoning are universal, but some critics claim his theory is culturally biased (Miller, 2007). Both Kohlberg and his critics may be partially correct. One review of 45 studies in 27 cultures around the world, mostly non-European, provided support for the universality of Kohlberg's first four stages (Snarey, 1987). As Kohlberg predicted, individuals in diverse cultures developed through these four stages in sequence. A more recent research review revealed support for the qualitative shift from stage 2 to stage 3 across cultures (Gibbs & others, 2007). Stages 5 and 6, however, have not been found in all cultures (Gibbs & others, 2007; Snarey, 1987). Furthermore, Kohlberg's scoring system does not recognize the higher-level moral reasoning of certain cultures, and thus that moral reasoning is more culture-specific that Kohlberg envisioned (Snarey, 1987).

In the view of John Gibbs (2009), most young adolescents around the world use the moral judgment of mutuality (stage 3) that makes intimate friendships possible. And by late adolescence, many individuals also are beginning to grasp the importance of agreed-upon standards and institutions for the common good (stage 4). A main exception, though, is the delayed moral judgment of adolescents who regularly engage in delinquency.

In sum, although Kohlberg's approach does capture much of the moral reasoning voiced in various cultures around the world, his approach misses or misconstrues some important moral concepts in specific cultures (Miller, 2007). To read further about cultural variations in moral reasoning, see the *Contexts of Life-Span Development* interlude.

Contexts of Life-Span Development

MORAL REASONING IN THE UNITED STATES AND INDIA

Cultural meaning systems vary around the world, and these systems shape children's morality (Shiraev & Levy, 2007; Shweder & others, 2006). Consider a comparison of American and Indian Hindu Brahman children (Shweder, Mahapatra, & Miller, 1987). Like people in many other non-Western societies, Indians view moral rules as part of the natural world order. Thus, Indians do not distinguish between physical, moral, and social regulation, as Americans do. For example, in India, violations of food taboos and marital restrictions can be just as serious as acts intended to cause harm to others. In India, social rules are seen as inevitable, much like the law of gravity.

According to William Damon (1988), in those places where culturally specific practices take on profound moral and religious significance, as in India, the moral development of children focuses extensively on their adherence to custom and convention. In contrast, Western moral doctrine tends to elevate abstract principles, such as justice and welfare, to a higher moral status than customs or conventions. As in India, socialization practices in many developing countries actively instill in children a great respect for their culture's traditional codes and practices.

How might Asian Indian children and American children reason differently about moral issues?

Families and Moral Development Kohlberg argued that family processes are essentially unimportant in children's moral development. As noted earlier, he argued that parent-child relationships usually provide children with little opportunity for give-and-take or perspective taking. Rather, Kohlberg said that such opportunities are more likely to be provided by children's peer relations (Brabeck, 2000).

Did Kohlberg underestimate the contribution of family relationships to moral development? Most developmentalists emphasize that parents play more important roles in children's moral development than Kohlberg envisioned (Thompson, 2009d). They stress that parents' communication with children, their discipline techniques, and many other aspects of parent-child relationships influence children's moral development—we will have more to discuss about this topic later in the chapter. Nonetheless, most developmentalists agree with Kohlberg, and Piaget, that peers play an important role in moral development.

Carol Gilligan *(center)* is shown with some of the students she has interviewed about the importance of relationships in a female's development. *What is Gilligan's view of moral development?*

Gender and the Care Perspective   Perhaps the most publicized criticism of Kohlberg's theory has come from Carol Gilligan (1982, 1992, 1996), who argues that Kohlberg's theory reflects a gender bias. According to Gilligan, Kohlberg's theory is based on a male norm that puts abstract principles above relationships and concern for others and sees the individual as standing alone and independently making moral decisions. It puts justice at the heart of morality. In contrast to Kohlberg's **justice perspective,** Gilligan argues for a **care perspective,** which is a moral perspective that views people in terms of their connectedness with others and emphasizes interpersonal communication, relationships with others, and concern for others. According to Gilligan, Kohlberg greatly underplayed the care perspective, perhaps because he was a male, because most of his research was with males rather than females, and because he used male responses as a model for his theory.

In extensive interviews with girls from 6 to 18 years of age, Gilligan and her colleagues found that girls consistently interpret moral dilemmas in terms of human relationships and base these interpretations on listening and watching other people (Gilligan, 1992; Gilligan & others, 2003). However, a meta-analysis (a statistical analysis that combines the results of many different studies) casts doubt on Gilligan's claim of substantial gender differences in moral judgment (Jaffee & Hyde, 2000). And a recent analysis concluded that girls' moral orientations are "somewhat more likely to focus on care for other than on abstract principles of justice, but they can use both moral orientations when needed (as can boys . . .)" (Blakemore, Berenbaum, & Liben, 2009, p 132).

Assessment of Moral Reasoning   Some developmentalists fault the quality of Kohlberg's research and stress that more attention should be paid to the way moral development is assessed (Thoma, 2006). For example, James Rest (1986; Rest & others, 1999) argued that alternative methods should be used to collect information about moral thinking instead of relying on a single method that requires individuals to reason about hypothetical moral dilemmas. Rest also said that Kohlberg's stories are extremely difficult to score. To help remedy this problem, Rest developed his own measure of moral development, called the Defining Issues Test (DIT).

Unlike Kohlberg's procedure, the DIT attempts to determine which moral issues individuals feel are crucial in a given situation by presenting a series of dilemmas and a list of potential considerations in making a decision. In the dilemma of Heinz and the druggist, individuals are asked to rate such matters as whether a community's laws should be upheld or whether Heinz should be willing to risk being injured or caught as a burglar. They might also be asked to list the most important values that govern human interaction. They are given six stories and asked to rate the importance of each issue involved in deciding what ought to be done. Then they are asked to list what they believe are the four most important issues. Rest argued that this method provides a more valid and reliable way to assess moral thinking than Kohlberg's method (Rest & others, 1999).

Researchers also have found that the hypothetical moral dilemmas posed in Kohlberg's stories do not match the moral dilemmas many children and adults face in their everyday lives (Walker, deVries, & Trevethan, 1987). Most of Kohlberg's stories focus on the family and authority. However, when one researcher invited adolescents to write stories about their own moral dilemmas, the adolescents generated dilemmas that were broader in scope, focusing on friends, acquaintances, and other issues, as well as family and authority (Yussen, 1977). The adolescents' moral dilemmas also were analyzed in terms of their content. As shown in Figure 13.2, the moral issues that concerned adolescents more than any others involved interpersonal relationships.

Story Subject	Grade		
	7	9	12
	Percentage		
Alcohol	2	0	5
Civil rights	0	6	7
Drugs	7	10	5
Interpersonal relations	38	24	35
Physical safety	22	8	3
Sexual relations	2	20	10
Smoking	7	2	0
Stealing	9	2	0
Working	2	2	15
Other	11	26	20

FIGURE 13.2 Actual Moral Dilemmas Generated by Adolescents.

Social Conventional Reasoning Some theorists and researchers argue that Kohlberg did not adequately distinguish between moral reasoning and social conventional reasoning (Smetana, 2006; Turiel, 2006). **Social conventional reasoning** focuses on conventional rules that have been established by social consensus in order to control behavior and maintain the social system. The rules themselves are arbitrary, such as using a fork at meals and raising your hand in class before speaking.

In contrast, moral reasoning focuses on ethical issues and rules of morality. Unlike conventional rules, moral rules are not arbitrary. They are obligatory, widely accepted, and somewhat impersonal (Turiel, 2006). Rules pertaining to lying, cheating, stealing, and physically harming another person are moral rules because violation of these rules affronts ethical standards that exist apart from social consensus and convention. Moral judgments involve concepts of justice, whereas social conventional judgments are concepts of social organization.

Recently, a distinction also has been made between moral and conventional issues, which are viewed as legitimately subject to adult social regulation, and personal issues, which are more likely subject to the child's or adolescent's independent decision making and personal discretion (Smetana, 2006; Turiel, 2006). Personal issues include control over one's body, privacy, and choice of friends and activities. Thus, some actions belong to a *personal* domain, not governed by moral strictures or social norms.

Moral Behavior

What are the basic processes responsible for moral behavior? What is the nature of self-control and resistance to temptation? How do social cognitive theorists view moral development?

Basic Processes The processes of reinforcement, punishment, and imitation have been invoked to explain how individuals learn certain responses and why their responses differ from one another (Grusec, 2006). When individuals are reinforced for behavior that is consistent with laws and social conventions, they are likely to repeat that behavior. When provided with models who behave morally, individuals are likely to adopt their actions. Finally, when individuals are punished for immoral behaviors, those behaviors can be eliminated, but at the expense of sanctioning punishment by its very use and of causing emotional side effects for the individual.

These general conclusions come with some important qualifiers. The effectiveness of reward and punishment depends on the consistency and timing with which they are administered. The effectiveness of modeling depends on the characteristics of the model and the cognitive skills of the observer.

Behavior is situationally dependent. Thus, individuals do not consistently display moral behavior in different situations. How consistent is moral behavior? In a classic investigation of moral behavior, one of the most extensive ever conducted, Hugh Hartshorne and Mark May (1928–1930) observed the moral responses of 11,000 children who were given the opportunity to lie, cheat, and steal in a variety of circumstances—at home, at school, at social events, and in athletics. A completely honest or a completely dishonest child was difficult to find. Situation-specific behavior was the rule. Children were more likely to cheat when their friends put pressure on them to do so and when the chance of being caught was slim. However, other analyses suggest that although moral behavior is influenced by situational determinants, some children are more likely than others to cheat, lie, and steal (Burton, 1984).

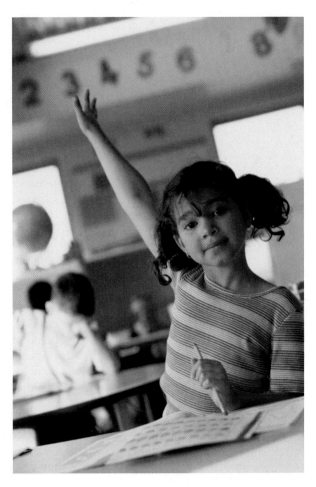

How does social conventional reasoning differ from moral reasoning? What are some examples of social conventional reasoning?

justice perspective A moral perspective that focuses on the rights of the individual; individuals independently make moral decisions.

care perspective The moral perspective of Carol Gilligan; views people in terms of their connectedness with others and emphasizes interpersonal communication, relationships with others, and concern for others.

social conventional reasoning Focuses on conventional rules established by social consensus and convention, as opposed to moral reasoning, which stresses ethical issues.

Resistance to Temptation and Self-Control   When pressures mount for individuals to cheat, lie, or steal, it is important to ask whether they have developed the ability to resist temptation and to exercise self-control (Grusec, 2006). Walter Mischel (1974) argues that self-control is strongly influenced by cognitive factors. Researchers have shown that children can instruct themselves to be more patient and, in the process, show more self-control.

The role of punishment in children's ability to resist temptation has also been studied (Parke, 1972, 1977). For the most part, offering children cognitive rationales (such as reasons why a child should not play with a forbidden toy) enhances most forms of punishment. Cognitive rationales are more effective in getting children to resist temptation over a period of time than punishments that do not use reasoning, such as placing children in their rooms without explaining the consequences for others of the children's deviant behavior.

Social Cognitive Theory   The role of cognitive factors in resistance to temptation and self-control illustrates ways in which cognitions mediate the link between environmental experiences and moral behavior (Grusec, 2006). The relationships between these three elements—environment, cognition, and behavior—are highlighted by social cognitive theorists. The **social cognitive theory of morality** emphasizes a distinction between an individual's moral competence (the ability to perform moral behaviors) and moral performance (performing those behaviors in specific situations) (Mischel & Mischel, 1975). *Moral competencies* include what individuals are capable of doing, what they know, their skills, their awareness of moral rules and regulations, and their cognitive ability to construct behaviors. Moral competence is the outgrowth of cognitive-sensory processes. *Moral performance*, or behavior, however, is determined by motivation and the rewards and incentives to act in a specific moral way.

Albert Bandura (2002) also stresses that moral development is best understood by considering a combination of social and cognitive factors, especially those involving self-control. He proposes that in developing a

> moral self, individuals adopt standards of right and wrong that serve as guides and deterrents for conduct. In this self-regulatory process, people monitor their conduct and the conditions under which it occurs, judge it in relation to moral standards, and regulate their actions by the consequences they apply to themselves. They do things that provide them satisfaction and a sense of self-worth. They refrain from behaving in ways that violate their moral standards because such conduct will bring self-condemnation. Self-sanctions keep conduct in line with internal standards. (Bandura, 2002, p. 102)

Thus, in Bandura's view, self-regulation rather than abstract reasoning is the key to positive moral development.

Moral Feeling

Think about when you do something you sense is wrong. Does it affect you emotionally? Maybe you get a twinge of guilt. And when you give someone a gift, you might feel joy. What role do emotions play in moral development, and how do these emotions develop?

Psychoanalytic Theory   According to Sigmund Freud, guilt and the desire to avoid feeling guilty are the foundation of moral behavior. In Freud's theory, the *superego* is the moral branch of personality. The superego consists of two main components, the ego ideal and conscience. The **ego ideal** rewards the child by conveying a sense of pride and personal value when the child acts according to ideal standards approved by the parents. The **conscience** punishes the child for behaviors disapproved by the parents by making the child feel guilty and worthless.

How do the superego and hence guilt develop? According to Freud, children fear losing their parents' love and being punished for their unacceptable sexual wishes toward the opposite-sex parent. To reduce anxiety, avoid punishment, and

social cognitive theory of morality The theory that distinguishes between moral competence—the ability to produce moral behaviors—and moral performance—performing those behaviors in specific situations.

ego ideal The component of the superego that rewards the child by conveying a sense of pride and personal value when the child acts according to ideal standards approved by the parents.

conscience The component of the superego that punishes the child for behaviors disapproved of by parents by making the child feel guilty and worthless.

maintain parental affection, children identify with the same-sex parent. Through this identification, children *internalize* the parents' standards of right and wrong, which reflect societal prohibitions, and hence develop the superego. Also, the child turns inward the hostility that was previously aimed externally at the same-sex parent. This inwardly directed hostility is then experienced self-punitively (and unconsciously) as guilt. In the psychoanalytic account of moral development, children conform to societal standards to avoid guilt. In this way, self-control replaces parental control.

Freud's claims regarding the formation of the ego ideal and conscience cannot be verified. However, researchers can examine the extent to which children feel guilty when they misbehave. Grazyna Kochanska and her colleagues (Kochanska & Aksan, 2007; Kochanska & others, 2002, 2005, 2008) have conducted a number of studies that explore children's conscience development. In a recent research review of children's conscience, she concluded that young children are aware of right and wrong, have the capacity to show empathy toward others, experience guilt, indicate discomfort following a transgression, and are sensitive to violating rules (Kochanska & Aksan, 2007). In one study, Kochanska and her colleagues (2002) observed 106 preschool children in laboratory situations in which they were led to believe that they had damaged valuable objects. In these mishaps, the behavioral indicators of guilt that were coded by observers included avoiding gaze (looking away or down), body tension (squirming, backing away, hanging head down, covering face with hands), and distress (looking uncomfortable, crying). Girls expressed more guilt than boys did. Children with a more fearful temperament expressed more guilt. Children of mothers who used power-oriented discipline (such as spanking, slapping, and yelling) displayed less guilt.

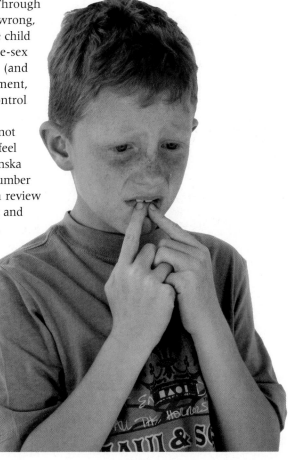

What characterizes a child's conscience?

Empathy   Positive feelings, such as empathy, contribute to the child's moral development (Hastings, Utendale, & Sullivan, 2007; Prinz, 2009). Feeling **empathy** means reacting to another's feelings with an emotional response that is similar to the other's feelings (Damon, 1988). To empathize is not just to sympathize; it is to put oneself in another's place emotionally.

Although empathy is an emotional state, it has a cognitive component—the ability to discern another's inner psychological states, or what we have previously discussed as *perspective taking* (Eisenberg & others, 2002). Infants have the capacity for some purely empathic responses, but for effective moral action, children must learn to identify a wide range of emotional states in others and to anticipate what kinds of action will improve another person's emotional state.

What are the milestones in children's development of empathy? According to an analysis by child developmentalist William Damon (1988), changes in empathy take place in early infancy, at 1 to 2 years of age, in early childhood, and at 10 to 12 years of age.

Global empathy is the young infant's empathic response in which clear boundaries between the feelings and needs of the self and those of another have not yet been established. For example, one 11-month-old infant fought off her own tears, sucked her thumb, and buried her head in her mother's lap after she had seen another child fall and hurt himself. Not all infants cry every time someone else is hurt, though. Many times, an infant will stare at another's pain with curiosity. Although global empathy is observed in some infants, it does not consistently characterize all infants' behavior.

When they are 1 to 2 years of age, infants may feel genuine concern for the distress of other people, but only when they reach early childhood can they respond appropriately to another person's distress. This ability depends on children's new awareness that people have different reactions to situations. By late childhood, they may begin to feel empathy for the unfortunate. To read further about Damon's description of the developmental changes in empathy from infancy through adolescence, see Figure 13.3.

empathy Reacting to another's feelings with an emotional response that is similar to the other's feelings.

Age Period	Nature of Empathy
Early infancy	Characterized by global empathy, the young infant's empathic response does not distinguish between feelings and needs of self and others.
1 to 2 years of age	Undifferentiated feelings of discomfort at another's distress grow into more genuine feelings of concern, but infants cannot translate realization of others' unhappy feelings into effective action.
Early childhood	Children become aware that every person's perspective is unique and that someone else may have a different reaction to a situation. This awareness allows the child to respond more appropriately to another person's distress.
10 to 12 years of age	Children develop an emergent orientation of empathy for people who live in unfortunate circumstances—the poor, the handicapped, and the socially outcast. In adolescence, this newfound sensitivity may give a humanitarian flavor to the individual's ideological and political views.

FIGURE 13.3 Damon's Description of Developmental Changes in Empathy.

moral identity The aspect of personality that is present when individuals have moral notions and commitments that are central to their lives.

The Contemporary Perspective on the Role of Emotion in Moral Development We have seen that classical psychoanalytic theory emphasizes the power of unconscious guilt in moral development but that other theorists, such as Damon, emphasize the role of empathy. Today, many child developmentalists believe that both positive feelings—such as empathy, sympathy, admiration, and self-esteem—and negative feelings—such as anger, outrage, shame, and guilt—contribute to children's moral development (Eisenberg & Fabes, 1998). When strongly experienced, these emotions influence children to act in accord with standards of right and wrong.

Such emotions as empathy, shame, guilt, and anxiety over other people's violations of standards are present early in development and undergo developmental change throughout childhood and beyond (Damon, 1988). These emotions provide a natural base for children's acquisition of moral values, motivating them to pay close attention to moral events (Thompson, 2009d). However, moral emotions do not operate in a vacuum to build a child's moral awareness, and they are not sufficient in themselves to generate moral responses. They do not give the "substance" of moral regulation—the rules, values, and standards of behavior that children need to understand and act on. Moral emotions are inextricably interwoven with the cognitive and social aspects of children's development.

Moral Personality

So far we have examined three key dimensions of moral development: thoughts, behavior, and feelings. Recently, there has been a surge of interest in a fourth dimension: personality (Narváez & Lapsley, 2009; Walker & Frimer, 2009a, b). Thoughts, behavior, and feelings can all be involved in an individual's moral personality. For many years, skepticism characterized the likelihood that a set of moral characteristics or traits could be discovered that would constitute a core of moral personality. Much of this skepticism stemmed from the results of Hartshorne and May's (1928–1930) classic study, and Walter Mischel's (1968) social learning theory and research, which argued that situations trump traits when attempts are made to predict moral behavior. Mischel's (2004) subsequent research and theory and Bandura's (2008, 2009) social cognitive theory have emphasized the importance of "person" factors while still recognizing situational variation. Until recently, though, there has been little interest in studying what might comprise a moral personality. Three aspects of moral personality that have recently been emphasized are (1) moral identity, (2) moral character, and (3) moral exemplars.

Moral Identity A central aspect of the recent interest in the role of personality in moral development focuses on **moral identity.** Individuals have a moral identity when moral notions and commitments are central to their life (Blasi, 2005). In this view, behaving in a manner that violates this moral commitment places the integrity of the self at risk (Narváez & Lapsley, 2009).

Moral Character James Rest (1995) argued that moral character has not been adequately emphasized in moral development. In Rest's view, *moral character* involves having the strength of your convictions, persisting, and overcoming distractions and obstacles. If individuals don't have moral character, they may wilt under pressure or fatigue, fail to follow through, or become distracted and discouraged, and fail to behave morally. Moral character presupposes that the person has set moral goals and that achieving those goals involves the commitment to act in accord with those goals. Rest (1995) also concluded that motivation has not been adequately emphasized in moral development. In Rest's view, *moral motivation* involves prioritizing moral values over other personal values.

Lawrence Walker (2002) has studied moral character by examining people's conceptions of moral excellence. Among the moral virtues people emphasize are "honesty, truthfulness, and trustworthiness, as well as those of care, compassion, thoughtfulness, and considerateness. Other salient traits revolve around virtues of dependability, loyalty, and conscientiousness" (Walker, 2002, p. 74). In Walker's perspective, these aspects of moral character provide a foundation for positive social relationships and functioning.

Moral Exemplars **Moral exemplars** are people who have lived exemplary lives. Moral exemplars have a moral personality, identity, character, and set of virtues that reflect moral excellence and commitment (Walker & Frimer, 2009a, b).

In one study, three different exemplars of morality were examined—brave, caring, and just (Walker & Hennig, 2004). Different personality profiles emerged for the three exemplars. The brave exemplar was characterized by being dominant and extraverted, the caring exemplar by being nurturant and agreeable, and the just exemplar by being conscientious and open to experience. However, a number of traits characterized all three moral exemplars, considered by the researchers to reflect a possible core of moral functioning. This core included being honest and dependable.

Another study examined the personality of exemplary young adults to determine what characterized their moral excellence (Matsuba & Walker, 2004). Forty young adults were nominated by executive directors of a variety of social organizations (such as Big Brothers, AIDS Society, and Ronald McDonald House) as moral exemplars based on their extraordinary moral commitment to these social organizations. They were compared with 40 young adults matched in age, education, and other variables who were attending a university. The moral were exemplars more advanced in moral reasoning, further along in developing an identity, and more likely to be in close relationships.

Rosa Parks (*top photo,* sitting in the front of a bus after the U.S. Supreme Court ruled that segregation was illegal on her city's bus system) and Andrei Sakharov (*bottom photo*) are moral exemplars. Parks (1913–2005), an African American seamstress in Montgomery, Alabama, became famous for her quiet, revolutionary act of not giving up her bus seat to a non-Latino White man in 1955. Her heroic act is cited by many historians as the beginning of the modern civil rights movement in the United States. Across the next four decades, Parks continued to work for progress in civil rights. Sakharov (1921–1989) was a Soviet physicist who spent several decades designing nuclear weapons for the Soviet Union and came to be known as the father of the Soviet hydrogen bomb. However, later in his life he became one of the Soviet Union's most outspoken critics and worked relentlessly to promote human rights and democracy.

Review and Reflect: Learning Goal 1

 Discuss theory and research on moral thought, behavior, feeling, and personality

REVIEW

- What is moral development?
- What are Piaget's and Kohlberg's theories of moral development? What are some criticisms of Kohlberg's theory? What is social conventional reasoning?
- What processes are involved in moral behavior? What is the social cognitive theory of moral development?
- How are moral feelings related to moral development?
- What characterizes moral personality?

REFLECT

- What do you think about these circumstances? (1) A man who had been sentenced to serve ten years for selling a small amount of marijuana walked away from a prison camp after serving only six months of his sentence. Twenty-five years later he was caught. He is now in his fifties and is a model citizen. Should he be sent back to prison? Why or why not? At which Kohlberg stage should your response be placed? (2) A young woman who had been in a tragic accident is "brain dead" and has been kept on life-support systems for four years without ever regaining consciousness. Should the life-support systems be removed? Explain your response. At which Kohlberg stage should your response be placed?

moral exemplars People who have lived exemplary lives—they have a moral personality, identity, character, and set of virtues that reflect moral excellence and commitment.

2 CONTEXTS OF MORAL DEVELOPMENT

Parenting   Schools

So far, we have examined the four main domains of moral development—thoughts, behaviors, feelings, and personality. We saw that both Piaget and Kohlberg noted that peer relations exert an important influence on moral development. What other contexts play a role in moral development? In particular, what are the roles of parents and schools?

Parenting

Both Piaget and Kohlberg held that parents do not provide unique or essential inputs to children's moral development. Parents, in their view, are responsible for providing role-taking opportunities and cognitive conflict, but peers play the primary role in moral development. Research reveals that both parents and peers contribute to children's moral maturity (Walker, Hennig, & Krettenauer, 2000).

In Ross Thompson's (2006, 2009d; Laible & Thompson, 2007; Thompson, McGinley & Meyer, 2006) view, young children are moral apprentices, striving to understand what is moral. They can be assisted in this quest by the "sensitive guidance of adult mentors in the home who provide lessons about morality in everyday experiences" (Thompson, McGinley, & Meyer, 2006). Among the most important aspects of the relationship between parents and children that contribute to children's moral development are relational quality, proactive strategies, and conversational dialogue.

Relational Quality Parent-child relationships introduce children to the mutual obligations of close relationships (Thompson, 2006, 2009d; Laible & Thompson, 2007; Thompson, McGinley, & Meyer, 2006). Parents' obligations include engaging in positive caregiving and guiding children to become competent human beings. Children's obligations include responding appropriately to parents' initiatives and maintaining a positive relationship with parents. A recent study revealed that an early mutually responsive orientation between parents and their infant and a decrease in parents' use of power assertion in disciplining a young child were linked to an increase in the child's internalization and self-regulation (Kochanska & others, 2008). Thus, warmth and responsibility in the mutual obligations of parent-child relationships are important foundations for the positive moral growth in the child.

In terms of relationship quality, secure attachment may play an important role in children's moral development. A secure attachment can place the child on a positive path for internalizing parents' socializing goals and family values (Waters & others, 1990). In one study, secure attachment in infancy was linked to early conscience development (Laible & Thompson, 2000).

Proactive Strategies An important parenting strategy is to proactively avert potential misbehavior by children before it takes place (Thompson, McGinley, & Meyer, 2006). With younger children, being proactive means using diversion, such as distracting their attention or moving them to alternative activities. With older children, being proactive may involve talking with them about values that the parents deem important. Transmitting these values can help older children and adolescents to resist the temptations that inevitably emerge in such contexts as peer relations and the media that can be outside the scope of direct parental monitoring.

What are some aspects of relationships between parents and children that contribute to children's moral development?

Two parenting strategies that work best when older children and adolescents are confronted with situations in which they are exposed to values outside the home that conflict with parents' values are cocooning and pre-arming (Grusec, 2006). *Cocooning* occurs when parents protect children and adolescents from exposure to deviant behavior, and thus the temptation to engage in negative moral behavior. In adolescence, cocooning involves monitoring the contexts in which adolescents spend time and restricting their interaction with deviant peers. In one recent study, reasoned cocooning (providing reasoned explanations for values) was emphasized over controlled cocooning (providing no explanations for restrictions) with adolescents (Padilla-Walker & Thompson, 2005). *Pre-arming* involves anticipating conflicting values and preparing children and adolescents to handle them in their lives outside their home. In using pre-arming, parents discuss strategies with children and adolescents that help them deal with harmful situations.

Conversational Dialogue   Conversations related to moral development can benefit children whether they occur as part of a discipline encounter or outside the encounter in the everyday stream of parent-child interaction (Thompson, 2006, 2009d; Laible & Thompson, 2007; Thompson, McGinley, & Meyer, 2006). The conversations can be planned or spontaneous and can focus on topics such as past events (for example, a child's prior misbehavior or positive moral conduct), shared future events (for example, going somewhere that may involve a temptation and requires positive moral behavior), and immediate events (for example, talking with the child about a sibling's tantrums). Even when they are not intended to teach a moral lesson or explicitly encourage better moral judgment, such conversations can contribute to children's moral development.

Parenting Recommendations   One research review concluded that, in general, children who behave morally tend to have parents who (Eisenberg & Valiente, 2002, p. 134):

- Are warm and supportive rather than punitive.
- Provide opportunities for the children to learn about others' perspectives and feelings.
- Involve children in family decision making and in the process of thinking about moral decisions.
- Model moral behaviors and thinking themselves, and provide opportunities for their children to do so.
- Provide information about what behaviors are expected and why.
- Foster an internal rather than an external sense of morality.

Parents who show this configuration of behaviors likely foster in their children concern and caring about others, and create a positive parent-child relationship.

In addition, parenting recommendations based on Ross Thompson's (2006, 2009d; Laible & Thompson, 2007; Thompson, McGinley, & Meyer, 2006) analysis of parent-child relations suggest that children's moral development is likely to benefit when there are mutual parent-child obligations involving warmth and responsibility, when parents use proactive strategies, and when parents engage children in conversational dialogue.

What are some good strategies parents can adopt to foster their child's moral development?

Schools

However parents treat their children at home, they may feel that they have little control over a great deal of their children's moral education. Children spend extensive time away from their parents at school, and the time spent can influence children's moral development (Narváez & Lapsley, 2009; Lapsley, 2008; Power & others, 2008; Snarey, 2008).

The Hidden Curriculum   More than 60 years ago, educator John Dewey (1933) recognized that even when schools do not have specific programs in moral education, they provide moral education through a "hidden curriculum." The **hidden curriculum** is conveyed by the moral atmosphere that is a part of every school. The moral atmosphere is created by school and classroom rules, the moral orientation of teachers and school administrators, and text materials. Teachers serve as models of ethical or unethical behavior (Mayhew & King, 2008; Sanger, 2008). Classroom rules and peer relations at school transmit attitudes about cheating, lying, stealing, and consideration of others. And through its rules and regulations, the school administration infuses the school with a value system.

Character Education   Currently 40 of 50 states have mandates regarding **character education,** a direct education approach that involves teaching students a basic moral literacy to prevent them from engaging in immoral behavior and doing harm to themselves or others (Carr, 2008). The argument is that such behaviors as lying, stealing, and cheating are wrong, and students should be taught this throughout their education (Berkowitz, Battistich, & Bier, 2008; Davidson, Lickona, & Khmelkov, 2008).

Every school should have an explicit moral code that is clearly communicated to students. Any violations of the code should be met with sanctions. Instruction in specified moral concepts, such as cheating, can take the form of example and definition, class discussions and role playing, or rewards for students exhibiting proper behavior. More recently, an emphasis on the importance of encouraging students to develop a care perspective has been accepted as a relevant aspect of character education (Noddings, 2008; Sherblom, 2008). Rather than just instructing adolescents in refraining from engaging in morally deviant behavior, a care perspective advocates educating students in the importance of engaging in prosocial behaviors, such as considering others feelings, being sensitive to others, and helping others.

Lawrence Walker (2002) argues that it is important for character education to involve more than a listing of moral virtues on a classroom wall. Instead, he emphasizes that children and adolescents need to participate in critical discussions of values; they need to discuss and reflect on how to incorporate virtues into their daily lives. Walker also advocates exposing children to moral exemplars worthy of emulating and getting them to participate in community service. The character education approach reflects the moral personality domain of moral development we discussed earlier in the chapter.

Values Clarification   A second approach to providing moral education is **values clarification**—that is, helping people to clarify what their lives mean and what is worth working for. Unlike character education, which tells students what their values should be, values clarification encourages students to define their own values and understand the values of others (Williams & others, 2003).

Advocates of values clarification say it is value-free. However, critics argue that its content offends community standards and that the values-clarification exercises fail to stress the right behavior.

Cognitive Moral Education   A third approach to moral education, **cognitive moral education,** is based on the belief that students should learn to value such things as democracy and justice as their moral reasoning develops. Kohlberg's theory has served as the foundation for a number of cognitive moral education programs. In a typical program, high school students meet in a semester-long course to discuss a number of moral issues. The instructor acts as a facilitator rather than as a director of the class. The goal is that students will develop more advanced notions of such concepts as cooperation, trust, responsibility, and community (Enright & others, 2008; Power & Higgins-D'Alessandro, 2008).

hidden curriculum The pervasive moral atmosphere that characterizes every school.

character education A direct moral education program in which students are taught moral literacy to prevent them from engaging in immoral behavior.

values clarification A moral education program in which students are helped to clarify what their lives are for and what is worth working for. Students are encouraged to define their own values and understand others' values.

cognitive moral education A moral education program based on the belief that students should learn to value things like democracy and justice as their moral reasoning develops; Kohlberg's theory has been the basis for many of the cognitive moral education programs.

Service Learning   **Service learning** is a form of education that promotes social responsibility and service to the community. In service
learning, adolescents engage in activities such as tutoring, helping older
adults, working in a hospital, assisting at a child-care center, or cleaning up a vacant lot to make a play area. An important goal of service
learning is that adolescents become less self-centered and more strongly
motivated to help others (Catalano, Hawkins, & Toumbourou, 2008;
Hart, Matsuba, & Atkins, 2008). Service learning is often more effective
when two conditions are met (Nucci, 2006): (1) students are given
some degree of choice in the service activities in which they participate, and (2) students are provided opportunities to reflect about their
participation.

Service learning takes education out into the community (Enfield
& Collins, 2008; Nelson & Eckstein, 2008). Adolescent volunteers tend
to be extraverted, committed to others, and have a high level of self-
understanding (Eisenberg & Morris, 2004). Also, a recent study revealed
that adolescent girls participated in service learning more than adolescent boys (Webster & Worrell, 2008).

Researchers have found that service learning benefits adolescents
in a number of ways (Hart, Matsuba, & Atkins, 2008; Reinders &
Youniss, 2006). These improvements in adolescent development related
to service learning include higher grades in school, increased goal setting, higher self-esteem, an improved sense of being able to make a
difference for others, and an increased likelihood that they will serve
as volunteers in the future. A recent study of more than 4,000 high
school students revealed that those who worked directly with individuals in need were better adjusted academically, whereas those who
worked for organizations had better civic outcomes (Schmidt, Shumow, & Kacker,
2007). And, in a recent study, 74 percent of African American and 70 percent of
Latino adolescents said that service-learning programs could have a "fairly or very
big effect" on keeping students from dropping out of school (Bridgeland, Dilulio, &
Wulsin, 2008).

One analysis revealed that 26 percent of U.S. public high schools require students to participate in service learning (Metz & Youniss, 2005). The benefits of
service learning, both for the volunteer and the recipient, suggest that more adolescents should be required to participate in such programs (Enfield & Collins, 2008;
Nelson & Eckstein, 2008).

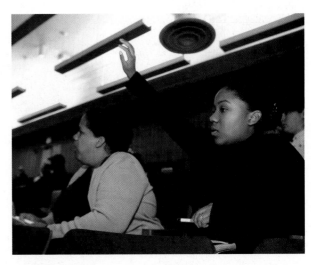

Jewel Cash, seated next to her mother, participating in a
crime-watch meeting at a community center. She is an
exemplar of teenage community involvement. The mayor of
Boston says she is "everywhere." Jewel recently swayed a
neighborhood group to support her proposal for a winter
jobs program. A junior at Boston Latin Academy, she was
raised in one of Boston's housing projects by her mother, a
single parent. Today she is a member of the Boston Student
Advisory Council, mentors children, volunteers at a women's
shelter, and is a member of a neighborhood crime-watch
organization. (*Source:* Silva, 2005)

Cheating   A moral education concern is whether students cheat and how to handle the cheating if they discover it (Anderman & Murdock, 2010; Narváez & others,
2008). Academic cheating can take many forms including plagiarism, using "cheat
sheets" during an exam, copying from a neighbor during a test, purchasing papers,
and falsifying lab results. A 2006 survey revealed that 60 percent of secondary school
students said they had cheated on a test in school during the past year, and one-
third of the students reported that they had plagiarized information from the
Internet in the past year (Josephson Institute of Ethics, 2006).

Why do students cheat? Among the reasons students give for cheating include
the pressure for getting high grades, time pressures, poor teaching, and lack of interest
(Stephens, 2008). In terms of poor teaching, "students are more likely to cheat when
they perceive their teacher to be incompetent, unfair, and uncaring" (Stephens, 2008,
p. 140).

A long history of research also implicates the power of the situation in determining whether students cheat or not (Hartshorne & May, 1928–1930; Murdock,
Miller, & Kohlhardt, 2004; Vandehey, Diekhoff, & LaBeff, 2007). For example, students are more likely to cheat when they are not being closely monitored during a
test; when they know their peers are cheating; when they know whether or not

service learning A form of education that
promotes social responsibility and service to
the community.

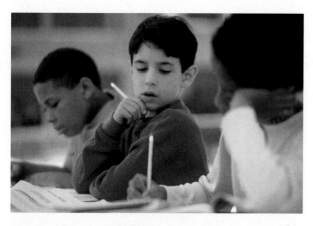

Why do students cheat? What are some strategies teachers can adopt to prevent cheating?

another student has been caught cheating; and when student scores are made public (Anderman & Murdock, 2007; Carrell, Malmstrom, & West, 2008; Harmon, Lambrinos, & Kennedy, 2008).

Among the strategies for decreasing academic cheating are preventive measures such as making sure students are aware of what constitutes cheating, making clear the consequences if they do cheat, closely monitoring students' behavior while they are taking tests, and emphasizing the importance of being a moral, responsible individual who engages in academic integrity. In promoting academic integrity, many colleges have instituted an honor code policy that emphasizes self-responsibility, fairness, trust, and scholarship. However, few secondary schools have developed honor code policies. The Center for Academic Integrity (www.academicintegrity.org/) has extensive materials available to help schools develop academic integrity policies.

An Integrative Approach Darcia Narváez (2006, 2008) emphasizes an *integrative approach* to moral education that encompasses both the reflective moral thinking and commitment to justice advocated in Kohlberg's approach, and developing a particular moral character as advocated in the character education approach. She highlights the Child Development Project as an excellent example of an integrative moral education approach. In the Child Development Project, students are given multiple opportunities to discuss other students' experiences, which inspire empathy and perspective taking, and they participate in exercises that encourage them to reflect on their own behaviors in terms of such values as fairness and social responsibility (Battistich, 2008; Solomon, Watson, & Battistich, 2002). Adults coach students in ethical decision making and guide them in becoming more caring individuals. Students experience a caring community, not only in the classroom, but also in after-school activities and through parental involvement in the program. Research evaluations of the Child Development Project indicate that it is related to an improved sense of community, an increase in prosocial behavior, better interpersonal understanding, and an increase in social problem solving (Battistich, 2008; Solomon & others, 1990).

Another integrative moral education program that is being implemented is called *integrative ethical education* (Holter & Narváez, 2009; Narváez, 2006, 2008; Narváez & others, 2004). This program builds on the concept of expertise that we discussed in Chapter 7, "Information Processing." The goal is to turn moral novices into moral experts by educating students about four ethical skills that moral experts possess: ethical sensitivity, ethical judgment, ethical focus, and ethical action.

Review and Reflect: Learning Goal 2

2 **Explain how parents and schools influence moral development**

REVIEW

- What are some effective parenting strategies for advancing children's moral development?
- What is the hidden curriculum? What are some contemporary approaches to moral education?

REFLECT

- How do you think your parents influenced your moral development?

3 PROSOCIAL AND ANTISOCIAL BEHAVIOR

Prosocial Behavior   **Antisocial Behavior**

Service learning encourages positive moral behavior. This behavior is not just moral behavior but behavior that is intended to benefit other people, and psychologists call it *prosocial behavior* (Eisenberg, & others, 2009). Of course, people have always engaged in antisocial behavior as well. In this section, we take a closer look at prosocial and antisocial behavior, focusing on how they develop.

Prosocial Behavior

Caring about the welfare and rights of others, feeling concern and empathy for them, and acting in a way that benefits others are all components of prosocial behavior. What motivates this behavior, and how does it develop in children?

Altruism and Reciprocity   The purist forms of prosocial behavior are motivated by **altruism,** an unselfish interest in helping another person. Human acts of altruism are plentiful. Think of the hardworking laborer who places $5 in a Salvation Army kettle, the volunteers at homeless shelters, the person who donates a kidney so someone else can live. Altruism is found throughout the human world. It is also taught by every widely practiced religion in the world—Christianity, Judaism, Islam, Hinduism, Buddhism. The circumstances most likely to evoke altruism are empathy for an individual in need or a close relationship between the benefactor and the recipient (Batson, 1989).

The notion of *reciprocity*, which is the obligation to return a favor with a favor pervades human interactions all over the world. Fund-raisers try to exploit the norm of reciprocity when they send free calendars or other knick-knacks in the mail, hoping that you'll feel obligated to reciprocate with a donation to their cause. People feel guilty when they do not reciprocate, and they may feel angry if someone else does not reciprocate. Reciprocity or altruism may motivate many important prosocial behaviors, including sharing.

Sharing and Fairness   William Damon (1988) described a developmental sequence by which sharing develops in children. Most sharing during the first three years of life is done for nonempathetic reasons, such as for the fun of the social play ritual or out of imitation. Then, at about 4 years of age, a combination of empathetic awareness and adult encouragement produces a sense of obligation on the part of the child to share with others. Most 4-year-olds are not selfless saints, however. Children believe they have an obligation to share but do not necessarily think they should be as generous to others as they are to themselves. Neither do their actions always support their beliefs, especially when they covet an object. What is important developmentally is that the child has developed a belief that sharing is an obligatory part of a social relationship and involves a question of right and wrong. These early ideas about sharing set the stage for giant strides that children make in the years that follow.

By the start of the elementary school years, children begin to express more complicated notions of what is fair. Throughout history, varied definitions of fairness have been used as the basis for distributing goods and resolving conflicts. These definitions involve the principles of equality, merit, and benevolence—*equality* means that everyone is treated the same; *merit* means giving extra rewards for hard work, a talented performance, or other laudatory behavior; *benevolence* means giving special consideration to individuals in a disadvantaged condition.

How does children's sharing change from the preschool to the elementary school years?

altruism An unselfish interest in helping another person.

Equality is the first of these principles used regularly by elementary school children. It is common to hear 6-year-old children use the word *fair* as synonymous with *equal* or *same*. By the mid to late elementary school years, children also believe that equity means special treatment for those who deserve it—a belief that applies the principles of merit and benevolence.

Parental advice and prodding certainly foster standards of sharing, but the give-and-take of peer requests and arguments provides the most immediate stimulation of sharing. Parents can set examples that children carry into their interactions and communication with peers, but parents are not present during all of their children's peer exchanges. The day-to-day construction of fairness standards is done by children in collaboration and negotiation with each other. Over the course of many years and thousands of encounters, children's understanding of such notions as equality, merit, benevolence, and compromise deepens. With this understanding comes a greater consistency and generosity in children's sharing (Damon, 1988).

How does prosocial behavior change through childhood and adolescence? Prosocial behavior occurs more often in adolescence than in childhood, although examples of caring for others and comforting someone in distress occur even during the preschool years (Eisenberg, Spinrad, & Sadovsky, 2006).

Two other aspects of prosocial behavior are forgiveness and gratitude. **Forgiveness** is an aspect of prosocial behavior that occurs when the injured person releases the injurer from possible behavioral retaliation (Klatt & Enright, 2009). In one investigation, individuals from the fourth grade through college and adulthood were asked questions about forgiveness (Enright, Santos, & Al-Mabuk, 1989). The individuals were especially swayed by peer pressure in their willingness to forgive others.

Gratitude is a feeling of thankfulness and appreciation, especially in response to someone doing something kind or helpful. A recent study of young adolescents revealed that gratitude was linked to a number of positive aspects of development, including satisfaction with one's family, optimism, and prosocial behavior (Froh, Yurkewicz, & Kashdan, 2009).

Gender and Prosocial Behavior   Are there gender differences in prosocial behavior during childhood and adolescence? Research concludes that there are (Eisenberg & others, 2009). For example, across childhood and adolescence, females engage in more prosocial behavior than males. The largest gender difference occurs for kind and considerate behavior with a smaller difference for sharing.

Altruism and Volunteerism in Older Adults   A recent study of 21,000 individuals 50 to 79 years of age in 21 countries revealed that one-third give back to society, saying that they volunteer now or have volunteered in the past (HSBC Insurance, 2007). In this study, about 50 percent who volunteer reported that they do so for at least one-half day each week. And a recent large-scale U.S. study revealed that volunteering steadily increased from 57 years of age to 85 years of age (Cornwell, Laumann, & Schumm, 2008).

A common perception is that older adults need to be given help rather than give help themselves. However, researchers recently have found that when older adults engage in altruistic behavior and volunteering they benefit from these activities. One study followed 423 older adult couples for five years (Brown & others, 2003). At the beginning of the study, the couples were asked about the extent to which they had given or received emotional or practical help in the past year. Five years later, those who said they had helped others were half as likely to have died. One possible reason for this finding is that helping others may reduce the output of stress hormones, which improves cardiovascular health and strengthens the immune system.

Ninety-eight-year-old volunteer Iva Broadus plays cards with 10-year-old DeAngela Williams in Dallas, Texas. Iva recently was recognized as the oldest volunteer in the Big Sister program in the United States. Iva says that the card-playing helps to keep her memory and thinking skills good and can help DeAngela's as well. *What are some other positive outcomes of volunteering as an older adult?*

forgiveness An aspect of prosocial behavior that occurs when the injured person releases the injurer from possible behavioral retaliation.

gratitude A feeling of thankfulness and appreciation, especially in response to someone's doing something kind or helpful.

Researchers also have found that volunteering as an older adult is associated with a number of positive outcomes (Harootyan, 2007). An early study of individuals 65 years and older found that volunteer workers compared with nonvolunteers were more satisfied with their lives and were less depressed and anxious (Hunter & Linn, 1980). A study of 2,000 older adults in Japan revealed that those who gave more assistance to others had better physical health than their elderly counterparts who gave less assistance (Krause & others, 1999). And, in another study, being a volunteer as an older adult was associated with more positive affect and less negative affect (Greenfield & Marks, 2004). Among the reasons for the positive outcomes of volunteering are its provision of constructive activities and productive roles, social integration, and enhanced meaningfulness.

Antisocial Behavior

Most children and adolescents at one time or another act out or do things that are destructive or troublesome for themselves or others. If these behaviors occur often, psychiatrists diagnose them as conduct disorders. If these behaviors result in illegal acts by juveniles, society labels them *delinquents*. Both problems are much more common in males than in females (Farrington, 2009; Thio, 2010).

Conduct Disorder   **Conduct disorder** refers to age-inappropriate actions and attitudes that violate family expectations, society's norms, and the personal or property rights of others. Children with conduct problems show a wide range of rule-violating behaviors, from swearing and temper tantrums to severe vandalism, theft, and assault (Mannuzza & others, 2004; Sterzer & others, 2005).

As part of growing up, most children and youth break the rules from time to time—they fight, skip school, break curfew, steal, and so on. As many as 50 percent of the parents of 4- to 6-year-old children report that their children steal, lie, disobey, or destroy property at least some of the time (Achenbach, 1997). Most of these children show a decrease in antisocial behavior from 4 to 18 years of age, but adolescents who are referred to psychological clinics for therapy still show high rates of antisocial behavior (Achenbach, 1997).

It has been estimated that about 5 percent of children show serious conduct problems. These children are often described as showing an *externalizing*, or *undercontrolled*, pattern of behavior. Children who show this pattern often are impulsive, overactive, and aggressive and engage in delinquent actions.

Conduct problems in children are best explained by a confluence of causes, or risk factors, operating over time (Dodge & Pettit, 2003). These include possible genetic inheritance of a difficult temperament, ineffective parenting, and living in a neighborhood where violence is the norm.

What are some characteristics of conduct disorder?

Juvenile Delinquency   Closely linked with conduct disorder is **juvenile delinquency,** which refers to actions taken by an adolescent in breaking the law or engaging in behavior that is considered illegal. Like other categories of disorders, juvenile delinquency is a broad concept; legal infractions range from littering to murder. Because the adolescent technically becomes a juvenile delinquent only after being judged guilty of a crime by a court of law, official records do not accurately reflect the number of illegal acts juvenile delinquents commit. Estimates of the number of juvenile delinquents in the United States are sketchy, but FBI statistics indicate that at least 2 percent of all youth are involved in juvenile court cases.

U.S. government statistics reveal that eight of ten cases of juvenile delinquency involve males (Snyder & Sickmund, 1999). In the last two decades, however, there

conduct disorder Age-inappropriate actions and attitudes that violate family expectations, society's norms, and the personal or property rights of others.

juvenile delinquency Actions taken by an adolescent in breaking the law or engaging in illegal behavior.

has been a greater increase in female delinquency than in male delinquency (Snyder & Sickmund, 1999). For both male and female delinquents, rates for property offenses are higher than for other rates of offenses (such as offenses against persons, drug offenses, and public order offenses). Arrests for delinquency still are much higher for adolescent males than for adolescent females.

As adolescents become emerging adults, do their rates of delinquency and crime change? Recent analyses indicate that theft, property damage, and physical aggression decrease from 18 to 26 years of age (Schulenberg & Zarrett, 2006). The peak for property damage is 16 to 18 years of age for males, 15 to 17 years of age for females. However, the peak for violence is 18 to 19 years of age for males and 19 to 21 years of age for females (Farrington, 2004).

A distinction is made between early-onset—before age 11—and late-onset—after 11—antisocial behavior. Early-onset antisocial behavior is associated with more negative developmental outcomes than late-onset antisocial behavior (Schulenberg & Zarrett, 2006). Early-onset antisocial behavior is more likely to persist into emerging adulthood and is associated with more mental health and relationship problems (Roisman, Aguilar, & Egeland, 2004; Stouthamer-Loeber & others, 2004).

Delinquency rates among minority groups and lower-socioeconomic-status youth are especially high in proportion to the overall population of these groups. However, such groups have less influence over the judicial decision-making process in the United States and, therefore, may be judged delinquent more readily than their non-Latino White, middle-socioeconomic-status counterparts.

In the Pittsburgh Youth Study, a longitudinal study focused on more than 1,500 inner-city boys, three developmental pathways to delinquency were as follows (Loeber, Burke, & Pardini, 2009; Loeber & Farrington, 2001; Stouthamer-Loeber & others, 2002):

- *Authority conflict.* Youth on this pathway showed stubbornness prior to age 12, then moved on to defiance and avoidance of authority.
- *Covert.* This pathway included minor covert acts, such as lying, followed by property damage and moderately serious delinquency, then serious delinquency.
- *Overt.* This pathway included minor aggression followed by fighting and violence.

One issue in juvenile justice is whether an adolescent who commits a crime should be tried as an adult (Steinberg, 2009). In one study, trying adolescent offenders as adults increased rather than reduced their crime rate (Myers, 1999). The study evaluated more than 500 violent youth in Pennsylvania, which has adopted a "get tough" policy. Although these 500 offenders had been given harsher punishment than a comparison group retained in juvenile court, they were more likely to be rearrested—and rearrested more quickly—for new offenses once they were returned to the community. These results suggest that the price of short-term public safety attained by prosecuting juveniles as adults might increase the number of criminal offenses over the long run.

One individual whose goal is to reduce juvenile delinquency and help at-risk adolescents cope more effectively with their lives is Rodney Hammond. To read about his work, see the *Careers in Life-Span Development* profile.

Causes of Delinquency What causes delinquency? Many causes have been proposed, including heredity, identity problems, community influences, and family experiences. Erik Erikson (1968), for example, notes that adolescents whose development has restricted them from acceptable social roles or made them feel that they cannot measure up to the demands placed on them may choose a negative identity. Adolescents with a negative identity may find support for their delinquent image among peers, reinforcing the negative identity. For Erikson, delinquency is an attempt to establish an identity, although a negative one.

Careers in Life-Span Development

Rodney Hammond, Health Psychologist

Rodney Hammond described his college experiences: "When I started as an undergraduate at the University of Illinois Champaign-Urbana, I hadn't decided on my major. But to help finance my education, I took a part-time job in a child development research program sponsored by the psychology department. There, I observed inner-city children in settings designed to enhance their learning. I saw first-hand the contribution psychology can make, and I knew I wanted to be a psychologist" (American Psychological Association, 2003, p. 26).

Rodney Hammond went on to obtain a doctorate in school and community psychology with a focus on children's development. For a number of years, he trained clinical psychologists at Wright State University in Ohio and directed a program to reduce violence in ethnic minority youth. There, he and his associates taught at-risk youth how to use social skills to effectively manage conflict and to recognize situations that could lead to violence. Today, Hammond is director of Violence Prevention at the Centers for Disease Control and Prevention in Atlanta. Hammond says that if you are interested in people and problem solving, psychology is a wonderful way to put these together.

(Source: American Psychological Association, 2003, pp. 26–27)

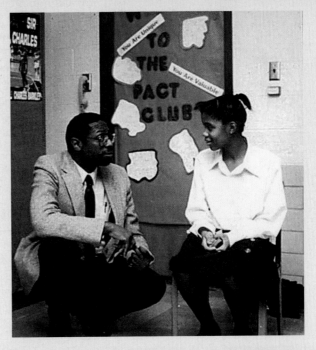

Rodney Hammond, talking with an adolescent about strategies for coping with stress and avoiding risk-taking behaviors.

Although delinquency is less exclusively a phenomenon of lower socioeconomic status than it was in the past, some characteristics of lower-class culture might promote delinquency. The norms of many lower-SES peer groups and gangs are antisocial, or counterproductive, to the goals and norms of society at large. Getting into and staying out of trouble are prominent features of life for some adolescents in low-income neighborhoods (Flannery & others, 2003). Adolescents from low-income backgrounds may sense that they can gain attention and status by performing antisocial actions. Being "tough" and "masculine" are high-status traits for lower-SES boys, and these traits are often measured by the adolescent's success in performing and getting away with delinquent acts. Furthermore, adolescents in communities with high crime rates observe many models who engage in criminal activities. These communities may be characterized by poverty, unemployment, and feelings of alienation toward the middle class. Quality schooling, educational funding, and organized neighborhood activities may be lacking in these communities (Sabol, Coulton, & Korbin, 2004).

Certain characteristics of family support systems are also associated with delinquency (Cavell & others, 2007; Feinberg & others, 2007). Parents of delinquents are less skilled in discouraging antisocial behavior and in encouraging skilled behavior than are parents of nondelinquents. Parental monitoring of adolescents is especially important in determining whether an adolescent becomes a delinquent (Laird & others, 2008). For example, a study of families living in high-risk neighborhoods revealed that parents' lack of knowledge of their young adolescents' whereabouts was linked to whether the adolescents engaged in delinquency later in adolescence (Lahey & others, 2008). And a recent study revealed that maternal monitoring was linked to a lower incidence of delinquency in Latino girls (Loukas, Suizzo, & Prelow, 2007).

What are some factors that influence whether adolescents will become delinquents?

Family discord and inconsistent and inappropriate discipline are also associated with delinquency (Bor, McGee, & Fagan, 2004). A recent study revealed that being physically abused in the first five years of life was linked to a greater risk of delinquency in adolescence (Lansford & others, 2007). And another recent study revealed that harsh discipline at 8 to 10 years of age was linked to which adolescents would persist in criminal activity after age 21 (Farrington, Ttofi, & Coid, 2009).

Rare are the studies that actually demonstrate in an experimental design that changing parenting practices in childhood is related to a lower incidence of juvenile delinquency in adolescence. However, one recent study by Marion Forgatch and her colleagues (2009) randomly assigned divorced mothers with sons to an experimental group (mothers received extensive parenting training) and a control group (mothers received no parenting training) when their sons were in the first to third grades. The parenting training consisted of 14 parent group meetings that especially focused on improving parenting practices with their sons (skill encouragement, limit setting, monitoring, problem solving, and positive involvement). Best practices for emotion regulation, managing interparental conflict, and talking with children about divorce also were included in the sessions. Improved parenting practices and reduced contact with deviant peers were linked with lower rates of delinquency in the experimental group than in the control group at a nine-year follow-up assessment.

An increasing number of studies have found that siblings can have a strong influence on delinquency (Bank, Burraston, & Snyder, 2004). In one study, high levels of hostile sibling relationships and older sibling delinquency were linked with younger sibling delinquency in both brother pairs and sister pairs (Slomkowski & others, 2001).

Having delinquent peers increases the risk of becoming delinquent. For example, a recent study found that peer rejection and having deviant friends at 7 to 13 years of age were linked with increased delinquency at 14 to 15 years of age (Vitaro, Pedersen, & Brendgen, 2007). Also, another recent study revealed that association with deviant peers was linked to a higher incidence of delinquency in male African American adolescents (Bowman, Prelow, & Weaver, 2007).

Cognitive factors, such as low self-control, low intelligence, and lack of sustained attention, are also implicated in delinquency. For example, a recent study revealed that low-IQ serious delinquents were characterized by low self-control (Koolhof & others, 2007). Another recent study found that at age 16 nondelinquents were more likely to have a higher verbal IQ and engage in sustained attention than delinquents (Loeber & others, 2007).

The *Research in Life-Span Development* interlude describes a program that seeks to intervene in the lives of children who show early conduct problems with the goal of reducing their delinquency risk in adolescence.

What roles do peers play in delinquency?

Research in Life-Span Development

FAST TRACK

Fast Track is an intervention that attempts to lower the risk of juvenile delinquency and other problems (Conduct Problems Prevention Research Group, 2007; Dodge & the Conduct Problems Prevention Research Group, 2007; Dodge & others, 2008; Lochman & the Conduct Problems Prevention Research Group, 2007; Nix & the Conduct Problems

Prevention Research Group, 2009; Slough, McMahon, & the Conduct Problems Prevention Research Group, 2008; Thomas & the Conduct Problems Prevention Research Group, 2009). Schools in four areas (Durham, North Carolina; Nashville, Tennessee; Seattle, Washington; and rural central Pennsylvania) were identified as high risk based on neighborhood crime and poverty data. Researchers screened more than 9,000 kindergarten children in the four schools and randomly assigned 891 of the highest-risk and moderate-risk children to intervention or control conditions. The average age of the children when the intervention began was 6.5 years of age.

The 10-year intervention consisted of behavior management training of parents, social cognitive skills training of children, reading tutoring, home visitations, mentoring, and a revised classroom curriculum that was designed to increase socioemotional competence and decrease aggression. Outcomes were assessed in the third, sixth, and ninth grades for the following:

- *Conduct disorder* (multiple instances of behaviors such as truancy, running away, fire setting, cruelty to animals, breaking and entering, and excessive fighting across a 6 month period)
- *Oppositional defiant disorder* (an ongoing pattern of disobedient, hostile, and defiant behavior toward authority figures)
- *Attention deficit hyperactivity disorder* (having one or more of these characteristics over a period of time: inattention, hyperactivity, and impulsivity)
- *Any externalizing disorder* (presence of any of the three disorders previously described)
- *Self-reported antisocial behavior* (a list of 34 behaviors, such as skipping school, stealing, and attacking someone with an intent to hurt the person)

The extensive intervention was successful only for children and adolescents who were identified as the highest risk in kindergarten, lowering their incidence of conduct disorder, attention deficit hyperactivity disorder, any externalized disorder, and antisocial behavior. Positive outcomes for the intervention occurred as early as the third grade and continued through the ninth grade. For example, in the ninth grade the intervention reduced the likelihood that the highest-risk kindergarten children would develop conduct disorder by 75 percent, attention deficit hyperactivity disorder by 53 percent, and any externalized disorder by 43 percent.

Review and Reflect: Learning Goal 3

3 Describe the development of prosocial and antisocial behavior

REVIEW

- How is altruism defined? How does prosocial behavior develop?
- What is conduct disorder? What are key factors in the development of juvenile delinquency

REFLECT

- As the head of a major government agency responsible for reducing delinquency in the United States, what programs would you try to implement?

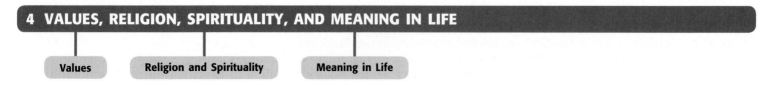

James Garbarino (1999) has interviewed a number of young killers. He concludes that nobody really knows precisely why a tiny minority of youth kill, but that the cause might be a lack of a spiritual center. In many of the youth killers he interviewed, Garbarino found a spiritual or emotional emptiness in which the youth sought meaning in the dark side of life. In contrast, **spirituality** involves a sense of connectedness to a sacred other (God, nature, a higher power). Are spirituality and religion important in your life? How much time have you spent thinking about the meaning of life? What are your values?

Values

Values are beliefs and attitudes about the way things should be. They involve what is important to us. We attach value to all sorts of things: politics, religion, money, sex, education, helping others, family, friends, career, cheating, self-respect, and so on. We carry with us values that influence our thoughts, feelings, and actions (Pratt & others, 2008; Print & others, 2008).

One way of measuring what people value is to ask them what their goals are. Over the past three decades, traditional-aged college students have shown an increased concern for personal well-being and a decreased concern for the well-being of others, especially for the disadvantaged (Pryor & others, 2008). As shown in Figure 13.4, today's college freshmen are more strongly motivated to be well-off financially and less motivated to develop a meaningful philosophy of life than were their counterparts of 20 or even 10 years ago. In 2008, 77 percent of students viewed becoming well-off financially as an "essential" or a "very important" objective compared with only 42 percent in 1971.

There are, however, some signs that U.S. college students are shifting toward a stronger interest in the welfare of society. In the survey just described, interest in developing a meaningful philosophy of life increased from 39 percent to 51 percent of U.S. freshman from 2001 through 2008 (Pryor & others, 2008) (see Figure 13.4). Also in this survey, the percentage of college freshman who said the chances are very good that they will participate in volunteer or community service programs increased from 18 percent in 1990 to 28 percent in 2008 (Pryor & others, 2008).

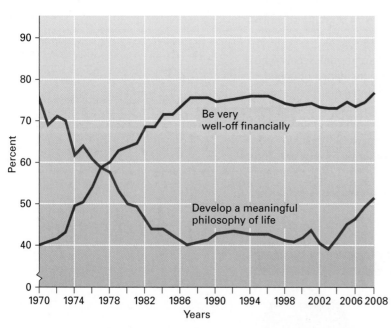

FIGURE 13.4 Changing Freshmen Life Goals, 1968 to 2008. In the last three decades, a significant change has occurred in freshmen students' life goals. A far greater percentage of today's college freshmen state that an "essential" or "very important" life goal is to be well-off financially, and far fewer state that developing a meaningful philosophy of life is an "essential" or a "very important" life goal.

Our discussion of values relates to William Damon's (2008) view that he proposed in *The Path to Purpose: Helping Children Find Their Calling in Life*, which we discussed in Chapter 11, "The Self, Identity, and Personality," Damon concluded that a major difficulty confronting today's youth is their lack of a clear sense of what they want to do with their lives—that too many youths are essentially "rudderless." Damon (2008, p. 8) found that only about 20 percent of 12- to 22-year-olds in the United States expressed "a clear vision of where they want to go, what they want to accomplish in life, and why." He argues that their goals and values too often focus on the short term, such a getting a good grade on a test this week and finding

spirituality A sense of connectedness to a sacred other (God, nature, a higher power).

values Beliefs and attitudes about the way things should be.

a date for a dance, rather than developing a plan for the future based on positive values. As we discussed in Chapter 11, the types of questions that adults can pose to youth to guide them in the direction of developing more purposeful values include: "What's most important in your life? Why do you care about those things? . . . What does it mean to be a good person?" (Damon, 2008, p. 135).

Religion and Spirituality

In Damon's (2008) view, one long-standing source for discovering purpose in life is religion. Religion and spirituality play important roles in the lives of many people around the world (Benson & Roehlkepartain, 2008; Good & Willoughby, 2008; Lerner, Roeser, & Phelps, 2009). What developmental changes characterize religion and spirituality in people's lives?

Childhood, Adolescence, and Emerging Adulthood
Societies use many methods—such as Sunday schools, parochial education, and parental teaching—to ensure that people will carry on a religious tradition. In a recent national study, 63 percent of parents with children at home said they pray or read Scripture with their children and 60 percent reported that they send their children to religious education programs (Pew Research Center, 2008). Does this religious socialization work? In many cases it does (Paloutzian, 2000).

In general, individuals tend to adopt the religious teachings of their upbringing. For instance, individuals who are Catholics by the time they are 25 years of age, and who were raised as Catholics, likely will continue to be Catholics throughout their adult years. If a religious change or reawakening occurs, it is most likely to take place during adolescence. However, it is important to consider the quality of the parent-adolescent relationship (Ream & Savin-Williams, 2003). Adolescents who have a positive relationship with their parents or are securely attached to them are likely to adopt the religious orientation of their parents (Dudley, 1999). Adolescents who have a negative relationship with their parents or are insecurely attached to them may disaffiliate from religion or seek religion-based attachments that are missing in their family system (Streib, 1999).

Religious issues are important to many adolescents and emerging adults, but in the twenty-first century, a downtrend in religious interest among college students has occurred. In the national study of American freshmen described earlier in the chapter in our discussion of values, in 2007, 78 percent said they attended a religious service frequently or occasionally during their senior year in high school, down from a high of 85 percent in 1997 (Pryor & others, 2007). Further, in 2007, more than twice as many first-year students (19 percent) reported that they don't have a religious preference than did first-year students in 1978 (8 percent).

A recent developmental study revealed that religiousness declined from 14 to 20 years of age in the United States (Koenig, McGue, & Iacono, 2008) (see Figure 13.5). In this study, religiousness was assessed with items such as frequency of prayer, frequency of discussing religious teachings, frequency of deciding moral actions for religious reasons, and the overall importance of religion in everyday life. As indicated in Figure 13.5, more change in religiousness occurred from 14 to 18 years of age than from 20 to 25 years of age. Also, attending religious services was highest at 14 years of age, declining from 14 to 18 years of age and increasing at 20 years of age. More change occurred in attending religious services than in religiousness.

Analysis of the World Values Survey of 18- to 24-year-olds revealed that emerging adults in less developed countries were more likely to be religious than their counterparts in more developed countries (Lippman & Keith, 2006). For example, emerging adults' reports of religion being very important in their lives ranged from a low of 0 in Japan to 93 percent in Nigeria, and belief in God ranged from a low of 40 percent in Sweden to a high of 100 percent in Pakistan.

Nina Vasan founded ACS Teens, a nationwide group of adolescent volunteers who support the efforts of the American Cancer Society (ACS). Nina's organization has raised hundreds of thousands of dollars for cancer research, helped change state tobacco laws, and conducted a number of cancer control programs. She created a national letter-writing campaign to obtain volunteers, established a Web site and set up an e-mail network, started a newsletter, and arranged monthly phone calls to communicate ideas and plan projects.

In Nina's words: ". . . I realized that teenagers like myself could make a big difference in the fight against cancer. I knew that the best way to help was to start a teen organization. . . . To be a beneficial part of the human race, it is essential and fundamental to give back to the community and others" (Vasan, 2002, p.1).

Nina Vasan's work on behalf of cancer involved pursuing a purpose. She says that the success of her work involving cancer far outweighs the many honors she has been awarded (Damon, 2008).

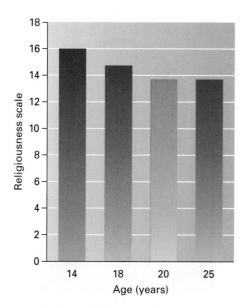

FIGURE 13.5 Developmental Changes in Religiousness from 14 to 25 Years of Age. *Note:* The religiousness scale ranged from 0 to 32 with higher scores indicating stronger religiousness.

Religion and Cognitive Development Adolescence and emerging adulthood can be especially important junctures in religious development (Good & Willoughby, 2008; Lerner, Roeser, & Phelps, 2009). Even if children have been indoctrinated into a religion by their parents, because of advances in their cognitive development adolescents and emerging adults may question what their own religious beliefs truly are.

Many of the cognitive changes thought to influence religious development involve Piaget's cognitive developmental theory, which we discussed in Chapter 6, "Cognitive Developmental Approaches." More so than in childhood, adolescents think more abstractly, idealistically, and logically. The increase in abstract thinking lets adolescents consider various ideas of religious and spiritual concepts. For example, an adolescent might ask how a loving God can possibly exist given the extensive suffering of many people in the world (Good & Willoughby, 2008). Adolescents' increased idealistic thinking provides a foundation for thinking about whether religion provides the best route to a better, more ideal world than the present. And adolescents' increased logical reasoning gives them the ability to develop hypotheses and systematically sort through different answers to spiritual questions (Good & Willoughby, 2008).

Religion and Identity Development During adolescence and emerging adulthood, especially emerging adulthood, identity development becomes a central focus (Coté, 2009; Erikson, 1968). Adolescents and emerging adults want to know answers to questions like these: "Who am I? What am I all about as a person? What kind of life do I want to lead?" As part of their search for identity, adolescents and emerging adults begin to grapple in more sophisticated, logical ways with such questions as "Why am I on this planet? Is there really a God or higher spiritual being, or have I just been believing what my parents and the church imprinted in my mind? What really are my religious views?" A recent analysis of the link between identity and spirituality concluded that adolescence and adulthood can serve as gateways to a spiritual identity that "transcends, but not necessarily excludes, the assigned religious identity in childhood" (Templeton & Eccles, 2006, p. 261).

The Positive Role of Religion in Adolescents' Lives Researchers have found that various aspects of religion are linked with positive outcomes for adolescents (Benson & Roehkepartain 2008; King & Roeser, 2009; Lerner, Roeser, & Phelps, 2009). In a study of 9,700 adolescents, going to church was linked with better grades for students from low-income backgrounds (Regnerus, 2001). Churchgoing may benefit students because religious communities encourage socially acceptable behavior, which includes doing well in school. Churchgoing also may benefit students because churches often offer positive role models for students. A recent study of Indonesian Muslim 13-year-olds revealed that their religious involvement was linked to their social competence, including positive peer relations, academic achievement, emotional regulation, prosocial behavior, and self-esteem (French & others, 2008).

Religion also plays a role in adolescents' health and whether they engage in problem behaviors (King & Roeser, 2009). Researchers have found that religious affiliation is linked to lower rates of delinquent behavior and drug use (Kliewer & Murrelle, 2007). In a recent national random sample of more than 2,000 11- to 18-year-olds, those who were higher in religiosity were less likely to smoke, drink alcohol, use marijuana, be truant from school, engage in delinquent activities, and be depressed than their low-religiosity counterparts (Sinha, Cnaan, & Gelles, 2007).

Many religious adolescents also internalize their religion's message about caring and concern for people (Ream & Savin-Williams, 2003). For example, in one survey, religious youth were almost three times as likely to engage in community service as nonreligious youth (Youniss, McLellan, & Yates, 1999).

Adolescents participating in a youth church group. *What are some positive aspects of religion in adolescents' lives?*

Religion is often an asset to the communities in which adolescents live (Ream & Savin-Williams, 2003). In some instances, religious institutions are the only organizations that initiate efforts to work with adolescents in inner cities. For inner-city youth, as well as other youth, religion offers possible answers to questions about meaning, purpose, and direction in life (Trulear, 2000).

Adulthood and Aging   What role do religion and spirituality play in the lives of adults? Is religion related to adults' health? Is there a point in adult development at which understanding of the meaning of life increases? What is religion like in the lives of older adults?

Religion and Spirituality in Adulthood   How religious are Americans? A recent national poll of more than 35,000 U.S. adults revealed the following: 92 percent said they believe in God, 75 percent reported that they pray at least weekly and 58 percent said they pray every day, 56 percent said that religion is very important, and 39 percent indicated that they attend religious services at least weekly (Pew Research Center, 2008). In the MacArthur Study of Midlife Development, more than 70 percent of U.S. individuals surveyed said they are religious and consider spirituality a major part of their lives (Brim, 1999).

Gender and ethnic differences characterize religious interest and participation. Females have consistently shown a stronger interest in religion than males have (Idler, 2006). Compared with men, they participate more in both organized and personal forms of religion, are more likely to believe in a higher power or presence, and are more likely to feel that religion is an important dimension of their lives. Regarding ethnicity, African Americans and Latinos show higher rates of religious participation than non-Latino White Americans (Idler, 2006).

In thinking about religion and adult development, it is important to consider individual differences. Religion is a powerful influence in some adults' lives, whereas it plays little or no role in others' lives (Myers, 2000). Further, the influence of religion in people's lives may change as they develop. In John Clausen's (1993) longitudinal investigation, some individuals who had been strongly religious in their early adult years became less so in middle age; others became more religious in middle age.

What characterizes religion in adults?

Religion and Health   How might religion and physical health be related? Some cults and religious sects encourage behaviors that are damaging to health such as ignoring sound medical advice (Williams & Sternthal, 2007). For individuals in the religious mainstream, however, there is generally either no link between religion and physical health or a positive effect (Camphell, Yoon, & Johnstone, 2009; McCullough & Willoughby, 2009). A longitudinal study of individuals from 20 to 94 years of age found that women who were highly religious in their twenties had higher self-rated health throughout their lives than did less religious women (McCullough & Laurenceau, 2005). No association between religiousness and health were found for men. Researchers have found that religious commitment helps to moderate blood pressure and hypertension, and that religious attendance is linked to a reduction in hypertension (Gillum & Ingram, 2007). Also, a number of studies have confirmed a positive association between religious participation and longevity (Oman & Thoresen, 2006).

Why might religion promote physical health? There are several possible answers (Hill & Butter, 1995):

- *Lifestyle issues.* For example, religious individuals have lower drug use than their nonreligious counterparts (Gartner, Larson,

Why might religion be linked to physical health?

Careers in Life-Span Development

Gabriel Dy-Liacco, Pastoral Counselor

Gabriel Dy-Liacco is a pastoral counselor at the Pastoral Counseling and Consultation Centers of Greater Washington, D.C. He obtained his Ph.D. in pastoral counseling from Loyola College in Maryland and also has experience as a psychotherapist in such mental health settings as a substance-abuse program, military family center, psychiatric clinic, and community mental health center. As a pastoral counselor, he works with adolescents and adults in the aspects of their life that they show the most concern about—psychological, spiritual, or the interface of both. Having lived in Peru, Japan, and the Philippines, he brings considerable multicultural experience to the counseling setting. Dr. Dy-Liacco also is a professor in the Graduate School of Psychology and Counseling at Regent University in the Washington, D.C., area.

& Allen, 1991). Also, in a recent large-scale study in Mexico, individuals were less likely to smoke cigarettes if religion was important to them and they regularly attended religious services (Benjamins & Buck, 2008).

- *Social networks.* The degree to which individuals are connected to others affects their health. Well-connected individuals have fewer health problems (Benjamins & Finlayson, 2007; Hill & Pargament, 2003). Religious groups, meetings, and activities provide social connectedness for individuals.

- *Coping with stress.* Religion offers a source of comfort and support when individuals are confronted with stressful events (Park, 2007).

Religious counselors often advise people about mental health and coping (Aten & Leach, 2008). To read about the work of one religious counselor, see the *Careers in Life-Span Development* profile. In the *Applications in Life-Span Development* interlude that follows, we further explore links between religion and coping.

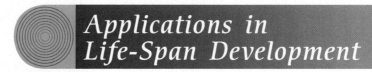

Applications in Life-Span Development

RELIGION AND COPING

What is the relation between religion and the ability to cope with stress? Some psychologists have categorized prayer and religious commitment as defensive coping strategies, arguing that they are less effective in helping individuals cope than are life-skill, problem-solving strategies. However, recently researchers have found that some styles of religious coping are associated with high levels of personal initiative and competence, and that even when defensive religious strategies are initially adopted, they sometimes set the stage for the later appearance of more-active religious coping (Krause, 2006; Paloutzian & Park, 2005). In a study of 850 medically ill patients admitted to an acute-care hospital, religious coping was related to low depression (Koenig & others, 1992).

Religious coping behaviors appear to function quite well during times of high stress. In one study, individuals were divided into those who were experiencing high stress and those with low stress (Manton, 1989). In the high-stress group, spiritual support was significantly related to low depression and high self-esteem. No such links were found in the low-stress group. A recent study revealed that when religion was an important aspect of people's lives, they frequently prayed, and they had positive religious core beliefs, they worried less, were anxious, and had a lower level of depressive symptoms (Rosmarin, Krumrei, & Andersson, 2009). Another recent study

meaning-making coping Drawing on beliefs, values, and goals to change the meaning of a stressful situation, especially in times of chronic stress as when a loved one dies.

found that coping styles that involved collaboration with others and turning to religious groups were more linked to improved psychological adjustment than a self-directing coping style (Ross & others, 2009).

A recent interest in linking religion and coping focuses on **meaning-making coping,** which involves drawing on beliefs, values, and goals to change the meaning of a stressful situation, especially in times of chronic stress as when a loved one dies. In Crystal Park's (2005, 2007, 2009) view, individuals who are religious experience more disruption of their beliefs, values, and goals immediately after the death of a loved one than individuals who are not religious. Eventually, though, individuals who are religious often show better adjustment to the loss. Initially, religion is linked with more depressed feelings about a loved one's death. Over time, however, as religious individuals search for meaning in their loss, the depressed feelings lessen. Thus, religion can serve as a meaning system through which bereaved individuals are able to reframe their loss and even find avenues of personal growth.

In sum, various dimensions of religiousness can help some individuals cope more effectively with their lives (George, 2009; Krause, 2006; Park, 2007, 2009). Religious beliefs can shape a person's psychological perception of pain or disability. Religious cognitions can play an important role in maintaining hope and stimulating motivation toward recovery. Because of its effectiveness in reducing distress, religious coping can help prevent denial of the problem and thus facilitate early recognition and more appropriate health-seeking behavior. Religion also can forestall the development of anxiety and depression disorders by promoting communal or social interaction. Houses of religious worship are a readily available, acceptable, and inexpensive source of support for many individuals, especially the elderly. The socialization provided by religious organizations can help prevent isolation and loneliness (Koenig & Larson, 1998).

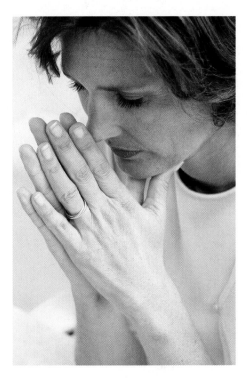

How is religion linked to the ability to cope with stress?

Religion in Older Adults   In many societies around the world, older adults are the spiritual leaders in their churches and communities. For example, in the Catholic Church, more popes have been elected in their eighties than in any other 10-year period of the human life span.

The religious patterns of older adults have increasingly been studied (Benjamins & Finlayson, 2007; McFadden, 2007). A recent study revealed that religious attendance at least weekly compared with never was linked to a lower risk of mortality (Gillum & others, 2008). Another recent study revealed that African American and Caribbean Black older adults reported higher levels of religious participation, religious coping, and spirituality than non-Latino White older adults (Taylor, Chatters, & Jackson, 2007). In yet another recent study, rural older adults' spirituality/religiousness was linked to a lower incidence of depression (Yoon & Lee, 2007).

In one study of individuals from their early thirties through their late sixties/early seventies, a significant increase in spirituality occurred between late middle adulthood (mid-fifties/early sixties) and late adulthood (late sixties/mid-seventies) (Wink & Dillon, 2002) (see Figure 13.6). The spirituality of women increased more than that of men. In this study, spirituality in late adulthood was linked with religiosity in early adulthood (thirties). This finding supports the idea that early religious involvement predisposes individuals to further spiritual development.

Individuals over 65 years of age are more likely than younger people to say that religious faith is the most significant influence in their lives, that they try to put religious faith into practice, and that they attend religious services (Gallup & Bezilla, 1992). In one analysis, most older African Americans and older non-Latino Whites attended religious services several times a month, said religion was important in their lives, read religious materials, listened to religious programming, and prayed frequently (Levin, Taylor, & Chatters, 1994). Also, in this analysis, older women had a stronger interest in religion than did older men.

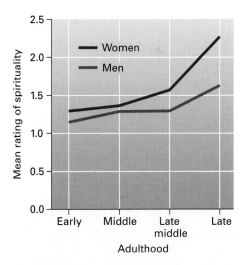

FIGURE 13.6 Level of Spirituality in Four Adult Age Periods. In a longitudinal study, the spirituality of individuals in four different adult age periods—early (thirties), middle (forties), late middle (mid-fifties/early sixties), and late (late sixties/early seventies) adulthood—was assessed (Wink & Dillon, 2002). Based on responses to open-ended questions in interviews, the spirituality of the individuals was coded on a 5-point scale with 5 being the highest level of spirituality and 1 the lowest.

Is religion related to a sense of well-being and life satisfaction in old age? In one study, older adults' self-esteem was highest when they had a strong religious commitment and lowest when they had little religious commitment (Krause, 1995). In another study, older adults who derived a sense of meaning in life from religion had higher levels of life satisfaction, self-esteem, and optimism (Krause, 2003). In this study, African American older adults were more likely to find meaning in religion than non-Latino White older adults. And, in a recent study, older adults who had higher levels of religious attendance had a lower risk of depression (Aranda, 2008).

Religion can meet some important psychological needs in older adults, helping them to face impending death, to find and maintain a sense of meaningfulness in life, and to accept the inevitable losses of old age (Koenig, 2004). In one study, although church attendance decreased among older adults during their last year of life, their feelings of religiousness and the strength or comfort they received from religion were either stable or increased (Idler, Stanislav, & Hays, 2001). Socially, the religious community can serve many functions for older adults, such as social activities, social support, and the opportunity to assume teaching and leadership roles.

Meaning in Life

Austrian psychiatrist Viktor Frankl's mother, father, brother, and wife died in the concentration camps and gas chambers in Auschwitz, Poland. Frankl survived the concentration camp and went on to write about meaning in life. In his book, *Man's Search for Meaning,* Frankl (1984) emphasized each person's uniqueness and the finiteness of life. He believed that examining the finiteness of our existence and the certainty of death adds meaning to life. If life were not finite, said Frankl, we could spend our life doing just about whatever we please because time would continue forever.

Frankl said that the three most distinct human qualities are spirituality, freedom, and responsibility. Spirituality, in his view, does not have a religious underpinning. Rather, it refers to a human being's uniqueness—to spirit, philosophy, and mind. Frankl proposed that people need to ask themselves such questions as why they exist, what they want from life, and what the meaning of their life is.

It is in middle adulthood that individuals begin to be faced with death more often, especially the deaths of parents and other older relatives. Also faced with less time in their life, many individuals in middle age begin to ask and evaluate the questions that Frankl proposed. And, as we indicated in the discussion of religion and coping, meaning-making coping is especially helpful in times of chronic stress and loss.

Roy Baumeister and Kathleen Vohs (2002, pp. 610–611) argue that the quest for a meaningful life can be understood in terms of four main needs for meaning that guide how people try to make sense of their lives:

- *Need for purpose.* "Present events draw meaning from their connection with future events." Purposes can be divided into (1) goals and (2) fulfillments. Life can be oriented toward a future anticipated state, such as living happily ever after or being in love.

- *Need for values.* This "can lend a sense of goodness or positive characterization of life and justify certain courses of action. Values enable people to decide whether certain acts are right or wrong." Frankl's (1984) view of meaning in life emphasized value as the main form of meaning that people need.

- *Need for a sense of efficacy.* This involves the "belief that one can make a difference. A life that had purposes and values but no efficacy would be tragic. The person might know what is desirable but could not do anything with that knowledge." With a sense of efficacy, people believe that they can control

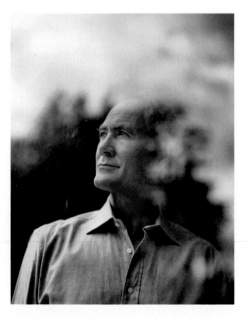

What characterizes the search for meaning in life?

their environment, which has positive physical and mental health benefits (Bandura, 2008, 2009).

- *Need for self-worth.* Most individuals want to be "good, worthy persons. Self-worth can be pursued individually, such as" finding out that one is very good at doing something, or collectively, as when people find self-esteem from belonging to a group or category of people.

Review and Reflect: Learning Goal 4

 Characterize the development of values, religion, spirituality, and meaning in life

REVIEW

- What are values? How are the values of U.S. college students changing?
- How do individuals experience religion and spirituality at different points in the life span?
- How do people seek meaning in life?

REFLECT

- What are the most important aspects of meaning in life? Might the components of meaning in life vary depending on how old someone is? Explain.

Reach Your Learning Goals

CHAPTER 13

Moral Development, Values, and Religion

1 DOMAINS OF MORAL DEVELOPMENT: DISCUSS THEORY AND RESEARCH ON MORAL THOUGHT, BEHAVIOR, FEELING, AND PERSONALITY

What Is Moral Development?

- Moral development involves changes in thoughts, feelings, and behaviors regarding right and wrong. Moral development consists of intrapersonal and interpersonal dimensions.

Moral Thought

- Piaget distinguished between the heteronomous morality of younger children and the autonomous morality of older children. Kohlberg developed a provocative theory of moral reasoning. He argued that development of moral reasoning consists of three levels—preconventional, conventional, and postconventional—and six stages (two at each level). Kohlberg argued that these stages were age-related. Influences on the Kohlberg stages include cognitive development, imitation and cognitive conflict, peer relations, and perspective taking. Criticisms of Kohlberg's theory have been made, especially by Gilligan, who advocates a stronger care perspective. Other criticisms focus on the inadequacy of moral reasoning to predict moral behavior, and culture and family influences, and the assessment of moral reasoning. A distinction can be made between moral reasoning and social conventional reasoning, which concerns social consensus and conventions.

Moral Behavior

- The processes of reinforcement, punishment, and imitation have been used to explain the acquisition of moral behavior, but they provide only a partial explanation. Situational variability is stressed by behaviorists. Cognitions can play a role in resistance to temptation and self-control. Social cognitive theory of morality emphasizes a distinction between moral competence and moral performance.

Moral Feeling

- In Freud's theory, the superego is the moral branch of personality. The superego consists of the ego ideal and the conscience. According to Freud, guilt is the foundation of children's moral behavior. Empathy is an important aspect of moral feelings, and it changes developmentally. In the contemporary perspective, both positive and negative feelings contribute to moral development.

Moral Personality

- Recently, there has been a surge of interest in studying moral personality. This interest has focused on moral identity, moral character, and moral exemplars. Moral character involves having the strength of your convictions, and persisting and overcoming distractions and obstacles. Moral character consists of having certain virtues, such as honesty, truthfulness, loyalty, and compassion. Moral exemplars' identity, character, and virtues reflect moral commitment and excellence.

2 CONTEXTS OF MORAL DEVELOPMENT: EXPLAIN HOW PARENTS AND SCHOOLS INFLUENCE MORAL DEVELOPMENT

Parenting

- Warmth and responsibility in mutual obligations of parent-child relationships provide important foundations for the child's positive moral growth. Moral development can be advanced by these parenting strategies: being warm and supportive rather than punitive; providing opportunities to learn about others' perspectives and feelings; involving children in family decision making; modeling moral behaviors; averting misbehavior before it takes place; and engaging in conversational dialogue related to moral development.

Schools

- The hidden curriculum, initially described by Dewey, is the moral atmosphere of every school. Contemporary approaches to moral education include character education, values clarification, cognitive moral education, service learning, and integrative ethical education. Cheating is a moral education concern and can take many forms. Various aspects of the situation influence whether students will cheat or not.

3   PROSOCIAL AND ANTISOCIAL BEHAVIOR: DESCRIBE THE DEVELOPMENT OF PROSOCIAL AND ANTISOCIAL BEHAVIOR

Prosocial Behavior

- Altruism, which is an unselfish interest in helping another person, and reciprocity often motivate prosocial behaviors (behaviors intended to help others) such as sharing. Damon described a sequence by which children develop their understanding of fairness and come to share more consistently. Peers play a key role in this development. Forgiveness and gratitude are two additional aspects of prosocial behavior. Altruism is linked to having a longer life. Volunteering is associated with higher life satisfaction, less depression and anxiety, better physical health, and more positive affect and less negative affect.

Antisocial Behavior

- Conduct disorder involves age-inappropriate actions and attitudes that violate family expectations, society's norms, and the personal or property rights of others. The disorder is more common in boys than in girls. Juvenile delinquency refers to actions taken by an adolescent in breaking the law or engaging in illegal behavior. In the Pittsburgh Youth Study, pathways to delinquency included conflict with authority, minor covert acts followed by property damage and more serious acts, and overt acts of minor aggression followed by fighting and violence. Associating with peers and friends who are delinquents; low parental monitoring; ineffective discipline; having an older sibling who is a delinquent; living in an urban, high-crime area; having low self-control; and having low intelligence are also linked with delinquency.

4   VALUES, RELIGION, SPIRITUALITY, AND MEANING IN LIFE: CHARACTERIZE THE DEVELOPMENT OF VALUES, RELIGION, SPIRITUALITY, AND MEANING IN LIFE

Values

- Values are beliefs and attitudes about the way things should be. Over the last three decades, traditional-age college students have shown an increased interest in personal well-being and a decreased interest in the welfare of others.

Religion and Spirituality

- Many children, adolescents, and emerging adults show an interest in religion, and religious institutions are designed to introduce them to religious beliefs. Cognitive changes—such as increases in abstract, idealistic, and logical thinking—in adolescence increase the likelihood adolescents will seek a better understanding of religion and spirituality. As part of their search for identity, many adolescents and emerging adults begin to grapple with more complex aspects of religion. A downtrend in religious interest among college students has occurred. When adolescents have a positive relationship with parents or are securely attached to them, they often adopt their parents' religious beliefs. Various aspects of religion are linked with positive outcomes in adolescent development. Religion is an important dimension of many American adults' lives as well as the lives of people around the world. Females have a stronger interest in religion than males do. Although some people in certain religious sects try to avoid using medical treatment, individuals in the religious mainstream generally

Meaning in Life

enjoy a positive or neutral link between religion and physical health. Religious interest often increases in late adulthood.

• Frankl argued that people need to face the finiteness of their life before they understand life's meaning. Faced with the death of older relatives and less time to live themselves, middle-aged adults increasingly examine life's meaning. Baumeister described four main needs that guide how people try to make sense of their lives: (1) need for purpose, (2) need for values, (3) need for a sense of efficacy, and (4) need for self-worth.

KEY TERMS

moral development 468
heteronomous morality (Piaget) 469
autonomous morality 469
immanent justice 469
preconventional reasoning 470
heteronomous morality (Kohlberg) 470
individualism, instrumental purpose, and exchange 470
conventional reasoning 471

mutual interpersonal expectations, relationships, and interpersonal conformity 471
social systems morality 471
postconventional reasoning 471
social contract or utility and individual rights 471
universal ethical principles 471
justice perspective 474

care perspective 474
social conventional reasoning 475
social cognitive theory of morality 476
ego ideal 476
conscience 476
empathy 477
moral identity 478
moral exemplars 479
hidden curriculum 482
character education 482
values clarification 482

cognitive moral education 482
service learning 483
altruism 485
forgiveness 486
gratitude 486
conduct disorder 487
juvenile delinquency 487
spirituality 492
values 492
meaning-making coping 497

KEY PEOPLE

Jean Piaget 468
Lawrence Kohlberg 469
Albert Bandura 472
John Gibbs 473
William Damon 473
Carol Gilligan 474

James Rest 474
Hugh Hartshorne and Mark May 475
Walter Mischel 476
Sigmund Freud 476
Grazyna Kochanska 477

Lawrence Walker 478
Ross Thompson 480
John Dewey 482
Darcia Narváez 484
Marion Forgatch 490
James Garbarino 492

Crystal Park 497
Viktor Frankl 498
Roy Baumeister 498

E-LEARNING TOOLS

Connect to **www.mhhe.com/santrockldt5e** to research the answers and complete these exercises. In addition, you'll find a number of other resources and valuable study tools for Chapter 13, "Moral Development, Values, and Religion," on this Web site.

Taking It to the Net

1. Janet's 15-year-old son, Ryan, has been breaking all of the rules she has set for him. He stays out all night, skips school,

and has been caught stealing on more than one occasion. Janet has been told by a mental health professional that he has conduct disorder. She wonders if this means he will end up in jail as an adult.

2. Liz is worried about her 8-year-old son. Ever since he got a video game with violent action, she can't keep him away from it. He sneaks into the downstairs rec room and plays it when she thinks he is outside. He seems to have gotten

E-Learning Tools **503**

more aggressive, but she wonders if that is just her imagination. Can playing violent video games make children more aggressive?

3. Howard, chairperson of his Methodist church's outreach committee, struggled with problem drinking when he was a young man and credits involvement in the church with his ability to give up alcohol. He wants the church to organize a support group for substance abusers and drug addicts, thinking that if his faith helped him, it can help others. What is the relationship between religious faith and spirituality and recovery from substance abuse?

Self-Assessment

Complete these self-assessments to explore your values, spiritual well-being, and meaning in life:

- *Comparing My Attitudes and Values with Those of Other College Students*
- *My Spiritual Well-Being*
- *What Is My Purpose in Life?*

Health and Well-Being, Parenting, and Education

Build your decision-making skills by trying your hand at the health and well-being, parenting, and education exercises.

FIVE

SOCIAL CONTEXTS OF DEVELOPMENT

Generations will depend on the ability of every procreating individual to face his children.

—ERIK ERIKSON
American Psychotherapist, 20th Century

As children develop, their small world widens as they discover new contexts and people. As they grow through childhood, their parents still cradle their lives, but their lives also are shaped by successive choirs of peers and friends. Parents can give adolescents both roots and wings. When some adults become parents, they recognize for the first time how much effort their parents put in to rearing them. Increasing numbers of adults choose to get married later or not at all. As people age, they come to sense that the generations of living things pass in a short while, and, like runners, they pass on the torch of life. Section 5 contains three chapters: "Families, Lifestyles, and Parenting" (Chapter 14), "Peers and the Sociocultural World" (Chapter 15), and "Schools, Achievement, and Work" (Chapter 16).

14

> *There's no vocabulary for love within a family, love that's lived in but not looked at, love within the light of which all else is seen, the love within which all other love finds speech. That love is silent.*
>
> —T. S. ELIOT
> *American-Born English Poet,*
> *20th Century*

LEARNING GOALS

◆ Describe some important family processes.

◆ Discuss the diversity of adult lifestyles and how they influence people's lives.

◆ Characterize parenting and how it affects children's development.

◆ Explain other aspects of family relationships.

FAMILIES, LIFESTYLES, AND PARENTING

CHAPTER OUTLINE

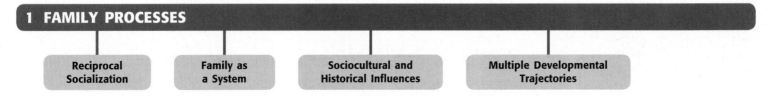

PREVIEW

Love and attachment are two aspects of family life that we discussed in Chapter 10, "Emotional Development." Beyond these emotional ties, what else goes on in families that influences development? And how do the choices that adults make about family life affect their development and the development of their children? These are some of the questions that we will consider in this chapter.

1 FAMILY PROCESSES

Reciprocal Socialization	Family as a System	Sociocultural and Historical Influences	Multiple Developmental Trajectories

As we examine the family and other social contexts of development, keep Urie Bronfenbrenner's (1986, 2004; Bronfenbrenner & Morris, 2006) ecological theory, which we discussed in Chapter 1, "Introduction," in mind. Recall that Bronfenbrenner analyzes the social contexts of development in terms of five environmental systems:

- The *microsystem,* or the setting in which the individual lives, such as a family, the world of peers, schools, work, and so on
- The *mesosystem,* which consists of links between microsystems, such as the connection between family processes and peer relations
- The *exosystem,* which consists of influences from another setting (such as parents' work) that the individual does not experience directly
- The *macrosystem,* or the culture in which the individual lives, such as an ethnic group or a nation
- The *chronosystem,* or sociohistorical circumstances, such as the increase in the numbers of working mothers, divorced parents, stepparent families, gay male and lesbian parents, and multiethnic families in the United States in the last 30 to 40 years

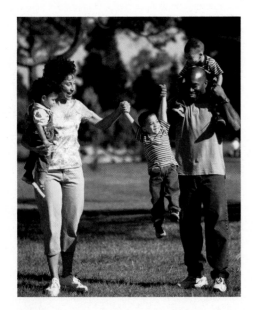

Children socialize parents just as parents socialize children.

reciprocal socialization Socialization that is bidirectional in that children socialize parents just as parents socialize children.

Reciprocal Socialization

Socialization between parents and children is not a one-way process. Parents do socialize children, but socialization in families is reciprocal (Gross & others, 2008). **Reciprocal socialization** is socialization that is bidirectional; children socialize parents just as parents socialize children.

For example, the interaction of mothers and their infants is sometimes symbolized as a dance in which successive actions of the partners are closely coordinated. This coordinated dance can assume the form of synchrony—that is, each person's behavior depends on the partner's previous behavior. Or the interaction can be reciprocal in a precise sense—in which the actions of the partners can be matched, as when one partner imitates the other or when there is mutual smiling.

One important example of early synchronized interaction is mutual gaze or eye contact. In one study, the mother and infant engaged in a variety of behaviors while they looked at each other; by contrast, when they looked away from each other, the rate of such behaviors dropped considerably (Stern & others,

1977). In another study, synchrony in parent-child relationships was positively related to children's social competence (Harrist, 1993).

In short, the behaviors of children and parents involve substantial synchronization (Kuczynski & Parkin, 2007). Another example occurs in *scaffolding*—that is, adjusting the level of guidance to fit the child's performance, as we discussed in Chapter 6, "Cognitive Developmental Approaches." The parent responds to the child's behavior with scaffolding, which in turn affects the child's behavior. For example, in the game peek-a-boo, parents initially cover their babies, then remove the covering, and finally register "surprise" at the babies' reappearance. As infants become more skilled at peek-a-boo, infants gradually do some of the covering and uncovering. Parents try to time their actions in such a way that the infant takes turns with the parent. In addition to peek-a-boo, pat-a-cake and "so-big" are other caregiver games that exemplify scaffolding and turn-taking sequences.

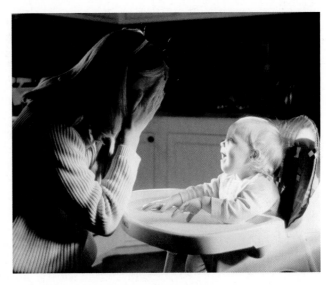

How does the game of peek-a-boo reflect the concept of scaffolding?

Family as a System

As a social system, the family can be thought of as a constellation of subsystems defined in terms of generation, gender, and role. Divisions of labor among family members define particular subunits, and attachments define others. Each family member is a participant in several subsystems—some dyadic (involving two people), some polyadic (involving more than two people). The father and child represent one dyadic subsystem, the mother and father another; the mother-father-child represent one polyadic subsystem, the mother and two siblings another.

These subsystems interact and influence each other (Parke & others, 2008). Thus, as Figure 14.1 illustrates, marital relations, parenting, and infant/child behavior can have both direct and indirect effects on each other (Belsky, 1981). The link between marital relationships and parenting has recently received increased attention. The most consistent findings are that compared with unhappily married parents, happily married parents are more sensitive, responsive, warm, and affectionate toward their children (Grych, 2002).

Researchers have found that promoting marital satisfaction often leads to good parenting. The marital relationship is an important support for parenting (Cox & others, 2008). When parents report more intimacy and better communication in their marriage, they are more affectionate to their children (Grych, 2002). Thus, marriage-enhancement programs may end up improving parenting and helping children. Programs that focus on parenting skills might also benefit from including attention to the participants' marriages.

Sociocultural and Historical Influences

Family development does not occur in a social vacuum. Important sociocultural and historical influences affect family processes, which reflect Bronfenbrenner's concepts of the macrosystem and chronosystem (Bronfenbrenner & Morris, 2006). Both great upheavals such as war, famine, or mass immigration and subtle transitions in ways of life may stimulate changes in families (Elder & Shanahan, 2006). One example is the effect on U.S. families of the Great Depression of the 1930s. During its height, the Depression produced economic deprivation, adult discontent, and depression about living conditions. It also increased marital conflict, inconsistent child rearing, and

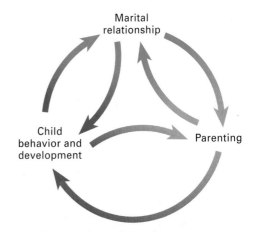

FIGURE 14.1 Interaction Between Children and Their Parents: Direct and Indirect Effects.

Two important changes in families are the increased mobility of families and the increase in television viewing. *What are some other changes?*

unhealthy lifestyles—heavy drinking, demoralized attitudes, and health disabilities—especially in fathers (Elder, 1980).

A major change in families in the last several decades has been the dramatic increase in the immigration of Latino and Asian families into the United States (Liu & others, 2009; Tewari & Alvarez, 2009). Immigrant families often experience stressors uncommon to or less prominent among longtime residents such as language barriers, dislocations and separations from support networks, the dual struggle to preserve identity and to acculturate, and changes in SES status (Clark & King, 2008; Kim & others, 2009; Wong, Kinzie, & Kinzie, 2009). We further discuss some ethnic variations in families later in this chapter and then examine these families more extensively in Chapter 15, "Peers and the Sociocultural World."

Subtle changes in a culture have significant influences on the family (Parke & others, 2008). Such changes include the longevity of older adults, movement to urban and suburban areas, television, computers, and the Internet, and a general dissatisfaction and restlessness.

Early in the twentieth century, middle-aged and older adults were often closely linked to the family (Mead, 1978). Today, older parents may have lost some of their socializing role in the family as many of their children moved considerable distances away. However, as we see later in the chapter, in the twenty-first century, an increasing number of grandparents are raising their grandchildren.

Many of the family moves in the last century have been away from farms and small towns to urban and suburban settings (Mead, 1978). In the small towns and farms, individuals were surrounded by lifelong neighbors, relatives, and friends. Today, neighborhood and extended-family support systems are not nearly as prevalent. Families now move all over the country, often uprooting children from a school and peer group they have known for a considerable length of time. And it is not unusual for this type of move to occur every several years, as one or both parents are transferred from job to job.

The media and technology also play a major role in the changing family (Murray & Murray, 2008). Many children who watch television or work on computers find that parents are too busy working to share this experience with them. Children increasingly experience a world in which their parents are not participants. Instead of interacting in neighborhood peer groups, children come home after school and watch television or log on to a computer. Among the historical changes related to computers, consider the dramatic increase in participation in Internet chat rooms in children's and adolescents' lives.

Another change in families has been an increase in general dissatisfaction and restlessness (Mead, 1978). The result of such restlessness and the tendency to divorce and remarry has been a hodgepodge of family structures, with far greater numbers of divorced and remarried families than ever before in history (Popenoe, 2008). Later in the chapter, we discuss in greater detail such aspects of the changing social world of the child and the family.

Multiple Developmental Trajectories

multiple developmental trajectories Concept that adults follow one trajectory and children another one; how these trajectories mesh is important for understanding the timing of entry into various family tasks.

The concept of **multiple developmental trajectories** refers to the fact that adults follow one trajectory and children another one (Parke & Buriel, 2006; Parke & others, 2008). How adult and child developmental trajectories mesh is important for understanding the timing of entry into various family tasks. Adult developmental trajectories include timing of entry into cohabitation, marriage, or parenthood; child developmental trajectories include timing of child care and entry into middle school. The timing of some family tasks and changes is planned, such as reentry into the workforce or delaying parenthood, whereas the timing of others is not, such as job loss or divorce (Parke & Buriel, 2006).

Review and Reflect: Learning Goal 1

1 **Describe some important family processes**

REVIEW

- What characterizes reciprocal socialization?
- What is the family as a system like?
- How do sociocultural and historical circumstances influence families?
- What is meant by the concept of multiple developmental trajectories?

REFLECT

- What do you predict will be some major changes in families in the remainder of the twenty-first century?

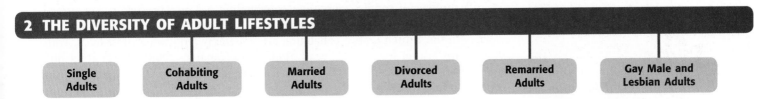

2 THE DIVERSITY OF ADULT LIFESTYLES

| Single Adults | Cohabiting Adults | Married Adults | Divorced Adults | Remarried Adults | Gay Male and Lesbian Adults |

Adults today choose many lifestyles and form many types of families (Benokraitis, 2008). One of the most striking social changes in recent decades is the decreased stigma attached to people who do not maintain what were long considered conventional families. They may choose to live alone, cohabit, marry, divorce, remarry, or live with someone of the same sex. Let's explore each of these lifestyles and how they affect adults.

Single Adults

Over a 30-year period, a dramatic rise in the percentage of single adults has occurred. From 2000 to 2006, there was a significant increase in the United States in single adults from 20 to 29 years of age (U.S. Census Bureau, 2007). In 2000, 64 percent of men in this age range said they were single, but by 2006 the percentage had increased to 73 percent, whereas the comparable percentages for women were 53 percent in 2000 and 62 percent in 2006.

Even when singles enjoy their lifestyles and are highly competent individuals, they often are stereotyped (Koropeckyj-Cox, 2009). Stereotypes associated with being single range from the "swinging single" to the "desperately lonely, suicidal" single. Of course, most single adults are somewhere between these extremes. Common problems of single adults may include forming intimate relationships with other adults, confronting loneliness, and finding a niche in a society that is marriage-oriented.

Advantages of being single include having time to make decisions about one's life course, time to develop personal resources to meet goals, freedom to make autonomous decisions and pursue one's own schedule and interests, opportunities to explore new places and try out new things, and privacy.

Once adults reach the age of 30, there can be increasing pressure to settle down and get married. This is when many single adults make a conscious decision to marry or to remain single. A recent national survey revealed that a higher percentage of singles (58 percent) reported they experienced extreme stress in the past month than married (52 percent) and divorced individuals (48 percent) (American Psychological Association, 2007).

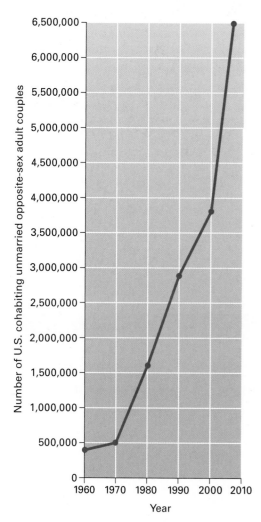

FIGURE 14.2 The Increase in Cohabitation in the United States. Since 1970, there has been a dramatic increase in the number of unmarried adults living together in the United States.

What are some potential advantages and disadvantages of cohabitation?

Approximately 8 percent of all individuals in the United States who reach the age of 65 have never been married. Contrary to the popular stereotype, older adults who have never been married seem to have the least difficulty coping with loneliness in old age. Many of them discovered long ago how to live autonomously and how to become self-reliant.

Cohabiting Adults

Cohabitation refers to living together in a sexual relationship without being married. Cohabitation has undergone considerable changes in recent years (U.S. Census Bureau, 2008) (see Figure 14.2). The percentage of U.S. couples who cohabit before marriage has increased from approximately 11 percent in 1970 to more than 75 percent today (Popenoe, 2009). Cohabiting rates are even higher in some countries—in Sweden, cohabitation before marriage is virtually universal (Stokes & Raley, 2009). A recent study revealed that 59 percent of U.S. women had cohabited at least once by the age of 24 (Schoen, Landale, & Daniels, 2007). Also, emerging adults in low-income circumstances are more likely to cohabit than their higher-earning counterparts (Meier & Allen, 2008).

A number of couples view their cohabitation not as a precursor to marriage but as an ongoing lifestyle. These couples do not want the official aspects of marriage. In the United States, cohabiting arrangements tend to be short-lived, with one-third lasting less than a year (Hyde & DeLamater, 2008). Fewer than one out of ten lasts five years. Of course, it is easier to dissolve a cohabitation relationship than to divorce.

Do cohabiting relationships differ from marriage in other ways? Relationships between cohabiting men and women tend to be more equal than those between husbands and wives (Wineberg, 1994).

Although cohabitation offers some advantages, it also can produce some problems (Popenoe, 2008; Trask & Koivur, 2007). Disapproval by parents and other family members can place emotional strain on the cohabiting couple. Some cohabiting couples have difficulty owning property jointly. Legal rights on the dissolution of the relationship are less certain than in a divorce. A recent study also revealed that cohabiting women experience an elevated risk of partner violence compared with married women (Brownridge, 2008).

Cohabitation and Marital Stability/Happiness If a couple lives together before they marry, does cohabiting help or harm their chances of later having a stable and happy marriage? The majority of studies have found lower rates of marital satisfaction and higher rates of divorce in couples who lived together before getting married (Whitehead & Popenoe, 2003). A recent study revealed that the timing of cohabitation is an important factor in marital satisfaction (Rhoades, Stanley, & Markman, 2009). In this study, couples who cohabited before getting engaged reported lower marital satisfaction, dedication, and confidence, as well as increased likelihood of divorce, than couples who cohabited only after becoming engaged.

In sum, researchers have found either that cohabitation leads to no differences or that cohabitation is not good for a marriage. What might explain the finding that cohabiting is linked with divorce more than not cohabiting? The most frequently given explanation is that the less traditional lifestyle of cohabitation may attract less conventional individuals who are not great believers in marriage in the first place (Whitehead & Popenoe, 2003). An alternative explanation is that the experience of cohabiting changes people's attitudes and habits in ways that increase their likelihood of divorce (Solot & Miller, 2002). And one study revealed that those who cohabit prior to marriage have worse problem-solving skills in marriage than their counterparts who did not cohabit (Cohan & Kleinbaum, 2002).

Cohabiting Older Adults An increasing number of older adults cohabit. In 1960, hardly any older adults cohabited. Today, approximately 4 percent of older adults cohabit (Brown, Lee, & Bulanda, 2006). It is expected that the number of cohabiting older adults will increase even further when baby boomers begin to turn 65 in 2010 and bring their historically more nontraditional values about love, sex, and relationships to late adulthood.

In many cases, the cohabiting is more for companionship than for love. In other cases, for example, when one partner faces the potential for expensive care, a couple may decide to maintain their assets separately and thus not marry. One recent study found that older adults who cohabited had a more positive, stable relationship than younger adults who cohabited, although cohabiting older adults were less likely to have plans to marry their partner (King & Scott, 2005).

Married Adults

Until about 1930, stable marriage was widely accepted as the endpoint of adult development. In the last 70 to 80 years, however, personal fulfillment both inside and outside marriage has emerged as a goal that competes with marital stability. The changing norm of male-female equality in marriage and increasingly high expectations for what a marital relationship should be has produced marital relationships that are more fragile and intense than they were earlier in the twentieth century (Hoelter, 2009).

Marital Trends In recent years, marriage rates in the United States have declined (Waite, 2009). More adults are remaining single longer today, and the average duration of a marriage in the United States is currently just over nine years. In 2007, the U.S. average age for a first marriage climbed to 27.5 years for men and 25.6 years for women, higher than at any point in history (U.S. Census Bureau, 2008). In 1980, the average age for a first marriage in the United States was 24 years for men and 21 years for women. In addition, the increase in cohabitation and a slight decline in the percentage of divorced individuals who remarry contribute to the decline in marriage rates in the United States (Stokes & Raley, 2009).

Despite the decline in marriage rates, the United States is still a marrying society (Popenoe, 2009). More than 90 percent of U.S. women still marry at some point in their lives, although projections indicate that in the future this rate will drop into the 80 to 90 percent range (Popenoe, 2008). For example, one projection is that for U.S. individuals born in 1995, 88 percent of the females and 82 percent of the males will likely marry (Schoen & Standish, 2001). If women and men are going to marry, virtually all do so by the time they are 45 years of age (Popenoe, 2008).

How happy are people who do marry? As indicated in Figure 14.3, the percentage of married individuals in the U.S. who said their marriages were "very happy" declined from the 1970s through the early 1990s, increased around the turn

When two people are under the influence of the most violent, most insane, most delusive, and most transient of passions, they are required to swear that they will remain in that excited, abnormal, and exhausting condition continuously until death do them part.

—GEORGE BERNARD SHAW
Irish Playwright, 20th Century

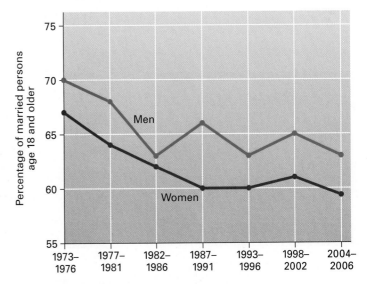

FIGURE 14.3 Percentage of Married Persons Age 18 and Older with "Very Happy" Marriages.

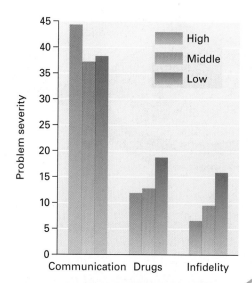

FIGURE 14.4 Severity of Specific Relationship Problems in Low-, Middle-, and High-Income Households. Since 1970, there has been a dramatic increase in the number of unmarried adults living together in the United States.

of the century, but recently has begun to decrease (Popenoe, 2009). Notice in Figure 14.3 that men consistently report being happier in their marriage than women.

Social Contexts   Contexts within a culture and across cultures are powerful influences on marriage. A U.S. study found that although communication was rated as a relatively severe problem regardless of household income, it was rated most severe in high-income households (Karney, Garvan, & Thomas, 2003) (see Figure 14.4). By contrast, drugs and infidelity were rated as more severe problems in low-income households.

Many aspects of marriage vary across cultures. For example, as part of China's efforts to control population growth, a 1981 law sets the minimum age for marriage at 22 years for males, 20 for females. More information about marriage in different cultures appears in the *Contexts of Life-Span Development* interlude.

Contexts of Life-Span Development

MARRIAGE AROUND THE WORLD

The traits that people look for in a marriage partner vary around the world. In one large-scale study of 9,474 adults from 37 cultures on six continents and five islands, people varied most regarding how much they valued chastity—desiring a marital partner with no previous experience in sexual intercourse (Buss & others, 1990). Chastity was the most important characteristic in selecting a marital partner in China, India, Indonesia, Iran, Taiwan, and the Palestinian Arab culture. Adults from Ireland and Japan placed moderate importance on chastity. In contrast, adults in Sweden, Finland, Norway, the Netherlands, and Germany generally said that chastity was not important in selecting a marital partner.

Domesticity is also valued in some cultures and not in others. In this study, adults from the Zulu culture in South Africa, Estonia, and Colombia placed a high value on housekeeping skills in their marital preference. By contrast, adults in the United States, Canada, and all Western European countries except Spain said that housekeeping skill was not an important trait in their partner.

Religion plays an important role in marital preferences in many cultures. For example, Islam stresses the honor of the male and the purity of the female. It also emphasizes

(*a*)   (*b*)   (*c*)

(*a*) In Scandinavian countries, cohabitation is popular; only a small percentage of 20- to 24-year-olds are married. (*b*) Islam stresses male honor and female purity. (*c*) Japanese young adults live at home longer with their parents before marrying than young adults in most other countries.

the woman's role in childbearing, child rearing, educating children, and instilling the Islamic faith in their children.

International comparisons of marriage also reveal that individuals in Scandinavian countries marry later than Americans, whereas their counterparts in many African, Asian, and Latin American countries marry younger (Waite, 2009). In Denmark, for example, almost 80 percent of the women and 90 percent of the men aged 20 to 24 have never been married. In Hungary, less than 40 percent of the women and 70 percent of the men the same age have never been married. In Scandinavian countries, cohabitation is popular among young adults; however, most Scandinavians eventually marry (Popenoe, 2008). In Sweden, on average, women delay marriage until they are 31, men until they are 33. Some countries, such as Hungary, encourage early marriage and childbearing to offset declines in the population. Like Scandinavian countries, Japan has a high proportion of unmarried young people. However, rather than cohabiting as the Scandinavians do, unmarried Japanese young adults live at home longer with their parents before marrying.

What Makes Marriages Work   John Gottman (1994; Gottman & Gottman, 2009; Gottman & Silver, 1999; Gottman & others, 1998) has been studying married couples' lives since the early 1970s. He uses many methods to analyze what makes marriages work. Gottman interviews couples about the history of their marriage, their philosophy about marriage, and how they view their parents' marriages. He videotapes them talking to each other about how their day went and evaluates what they say about the good and bad times of their marriages. Gottman also uses physiological measures to measure their heart rate, blood flow, blood pressure, and immune functioning moment by moment. He also checks back in with the couples every year to see how their marriage is faring. Gottman's research represents the most extensive assessment of marital relationships available. Currently he and his colleagues are following 700 couples in seven studies.

In his research, Gottman has found that seven main principles determine whether a marriage will work or not:

- *Establishing love maps.* Individuals in successful marriages have personal insights and detailed maps of each other's life and world. They aren't psychological strangers. In good marriages, partners are willing to share their feelings with each other. They use these "love maps" to express not only their understanding of each other but also their fondness and admiration.

- *Nurturing fondness and admiration.* In successful marriages, partners sing each other's praises. More than 90 percent of the time, when couples put a positive spin on their marriage's history, the marriage is likely to have a positive future.

- *Turning toward each other instead of away.* In good marriages, spouses are adept at turning toward each other regularly. They see each other as friends. This friendship doesn't keep arguments from occurring, but it can prevent differences from overwhelming the relationship. In these good marriages, spouses respect each other and appreciate each other's point of view despite disagreements.

- *Letting your partner influence you.* Bad marriages often involve one spouse who is unwilling to share power with the other. Although power-mongering is more common in husbands, some wives also show this trait. A willingness to share power and to respect the other person's view is a prerequisite to compromising. A recent study revealed that equality in decision making was one of the main factors that predicted positive marriage quality (Amato & others, 2007).

John Gottman, who has conducted extensive research on what makes marriages work.

> *Unlike most approaches to helping couples, mine is based on knowing what makes marriages succeed rather than fail.*
>
> —JOHN GOTTMAN
> *Contemporary Psychologist, University of Washington*

- *Solving solvable conflicts.* Two types of problems occur in marriage: (1) perpetual and (2) solvable. Perpetual problems include differences about whether to have children and how often to have sex. Solvable problems include not helping each other reduce daily stresses and not being verbally affectionate. Unfortunately, more than two-thirds of marital problems fall into the perpetual category—those that won't go away. Fortunately, marital therapists have found that couples often don't have to solve their perpetual problems for the marriage to work. In his research, Gottman has found that resolving conflicts works best when couples start out solving the problem with a soft rather than a harsh approach, try to make and receive repair attempts, regulate their emotions, compromise, and are tolerant of each other's faults. Conflict resolution is not about one person making changes, it is about negotiating and accommodating each other (Driver & others, 2003).

  Work, stress, in-laws, money, sex, housework, a new baby—these are among the typical areas of marital conflict, even in happy marriages. When there is conflict in these areas, it usually means that a husband and wife have different ideas about the tasks involved, their importance, or how they should be accomplished. If the conflict is perpetual, no amount of problem-solving expertise will fix it. The tension will decrease only when both partners feel comfortable living with the ongoing difference. However, when the issue is solvable, the challenge is to find the right strategy for dealing with it. Strategies include scheduling formal griping sessions about stressful issues, learning to talk about sex in a way that both partners feel comfortable with, and creating lists of who does what to see how household labor is divided.

- *Overcoming gridlock.* One partner wants the other to attend church, the other is an atheist. One partner is a homebody, the other wants to go out and socialize a lot. Such problems often produce gridlock. Gottman stresses that the key to ending gridlock is not to solve the problem, but to move from gridlock to dialogue and to be patient.

- *Creating shared meaning.* The more that partners can speak candidly and respectfully with each other, the more likely it is that they will create shared meaning in their marriage. This also includes sharing goals with one's spouse and working together to achieve each other's goals.

In a provocative book, *Marriage, a History,* Stephanie Coontz (2005) concluded that marriages in America today are fragile not because Americans have become self-centered and career-minded but because expectations for marriage have become unrealistically high compared with previous generations. However, she states that many marriages today are better than in the past, citing the increase in marriages that are equitable, loving, intimate, and protective of children. To make a marriage work, she emphasizes, as does Gottman, that partners need to develop a deep friendship, show respect for each other, and embrace commitment.

In addition to Gottman's view, other experts on marriage argue that such factors as forgiveness and commitment are important aspects of a successful marriage (Fincham, Stanley, & Beach, 2007). These factors function as self-repair processes in healthy relationships. For example, spouses may have a heated argument that has the potential to harm their relationship (Amato, 2007). After calming down, they may forgive each other and repair the damage. Also, spouses who have a strong commitment to each other may in times of conflict sacrifice their personal self-interest for the benefit of the marriage. Commitment especially becomes important when a couple is not happily married and can help them get through hard times with the hope that the future will involve more positive changes in the relationship.

Premarital Education   Premarital education occurs in a group and focuses on relationship advice. Might premarital education improve the quality of a marriage and possibly reduce the chances that the marriage will end in a divorce? Researchers have found that it can (Halford, Markman, & Stanley, 2008). For example, a recent survey of more than 3,000 adults revealed that premarital education was linked to a higher level of marital satisfaction and commitment to a spouse, a lower level of destructive marital conflict, and a 31 percent lower likelihood of divorce (Stanley & others, 2006). The premarital education programs in the study ranged from several hours to 20 hours with a median of 8 hours. It is recommended that premarital education begin approximately six months to a year before the wedding.

What makes marriages work? What are the benefits of having a good marriage?

The Benefits of a Good Marriage Are there any benefits to having a good marriage? There are. Individuals who are happily married live longer, healthier lives than either divorced individuals or those who are unhappily married (Waite, 2009). A recent study assessed 94,000 Japanese 40 to 79 years of age on two occasions: at the beginning of the study and approximately ten years later (Ikeda & others, 2007). Compared with never-married individuals, those who were married had a lower risk of dying in the ten-year period. In another study, women in happy marriages had lower levels of biological and cardiovascular risk factors— such as blood pressure, cholesterol levels, and body mass index—and lower levels of depression, anxiety, and anger than women in unhappy marriages (Gallo & others, 2003). And a recent study indicated that the longer women were married, the less likely they were to develop a chronic health condition and the longer that men were married, the lower their risk was of developing a disease (Dupre & Meadows, 2007).

What are the reasons for these benefits of a happy marriage? People in happy marriages likely feel less physically and emotionally stressed, which puts less wear and tear on a person's body. Such wear and tear can lead to numerous physical ailments, such as high blood pressure and heart disease, as well as psychological problems such as anxiety, depression, and substance abuse.

There is increasing evidence that stressful events of many types reduce the immune system's capabilities, rendering the person vulnerable to disease and infection. Researchers have found that marital stress is linked to immune system dysfunction (Gouin & others, 2009; Kiecolt-Glaser & others, 2005). An unhappy marriage increases an individual's risk of getting sick by approximately one-third and can even shorten a person's life by an average of four years (Gove, Style, & Hughes, 1990).

Marriage in Middle and Late Adulthood What is marriage like for middle-aged adults? How does marriage change in late adulthood?

Middle Adulthood Even some marriages that were difficult and rocky during early adulthood turn out to be better adjusted during middle adulthood (Wickrama & others, 2004). Although the partners may have lived through a great deal of turmoil, they eventually discover a deep and solid foundation on which to anchor their relationship. In middle adulthood, the partners may have fewer financial worries, less housework and chores, and more time with each other. Partners who engage in mutual activities usually view their marriage as more positive at this time.

In midlife, most individuals who are married voice considerable satisfaction with being married. In one large-scale study of individuals in middle adulthood, 72 percent of those who were married said their marriage was either "excellent" or "very good" (Brim, 1999). Possibly by middle age, many of the worst marriages already have dissolved.

What are some adaptations that many married older adults need to make?

*G*row old with me!
The best is yet to be,
The last of life,
For which the first was made.

—ROBERT BROWNING
English Poet, 19th Century

Late Adulthood   In 2005, 65- to 74-year-old U.S. men were more likely to be married than were women in this age range—75 percent of men, 54 percent of women (U.S. Census Bureau, 2005). Twenty-eight percent of women in this age category were widows compared with only 8 percent of men who were widowers.

The time from retirement until death is sometimes referred to as the "final stage in the marriage process." Retirement alters a couple's lifestyle, requiring adaptation. The greatest changes occur in the traditional family, in which the husband works and the wife is a homemaker. The husband may not know what to do with his time, and the wife may feel uneasy having him around the house all of the time. In traditional families, both partners may need to move toward more expressive roles. The husband must adjust from being the provider outside the home to being a helper around the house; the wife must change from being the only homemaker to being a partner who shares and delegates household duties. Marital happiness as an older adult is also affected by each partner's ability to deal with personal conflicts, including aging, illness, and eventual death.

Individuals who are married or partnered in late adulthood are usually happier than those who are single (Lee, 1978). Older adults are more satisfied with their marriages than are young and middle-aged adults (Fingerman & Pitzer, 2007). Indeed, the majority of older adults evaluate their marriages as happy or very happy (Huyck, 1995).

Divorced Adults

Divorce has become epidemic in our culture (Hoelter, 2009). The number of divorced adults rose from 1.8 percent of the adult population in 1960 to 4.8 percent in 1980 to 8.6 percent in 2007 (Popenoe, 2009). The divorce rate was increasing annually by 10 percent, but has been declining since the 1980s (Hernandez, 2007). The divorce rate increased considerably from 1960 to 1980, then gradually declined from the early 1980s to 2005, but recently increased from 2005 to 2007 (Popenoe, 2009).

Although divorce has increased for all socioeconomic groups, those in some groups have a higher incidence of divorce. Youthful marriage, low educational level, low income, not having a religious affiliation, having parents who are divorced, and having a baby before marriage are factors that are associated with increases in divorce (Hoelter, 2009). And these characteristics of one's partner increase the likelihood of divorce: alcoholism, psychological problems, domestic violence, infidelity, and inadequate division of household labor (Hoelter, 2009).

If a divorce is going to occur, it usually takes place early in a marriage; most occur in the fifth to tenth year of marriage (National Center for Health Statistics, 2000) (see Figure 14.5). This timing may reflect an effort by partners in troubled marriages to stay in the marriage and try to work things out. If after several years these efforts don't improve the relationship, they may then seek a divorce.

Even those adults who initiated their divorce experience challenges after a marriage dissolves (Eidar-Avidan, Haj-Yahia, & Greenbaum 2009). Both divorced women and divorced men complain of loneliness, diminished self-esteem, anxiety about the unknowns in their lives, and difficulty in forming satisfactory new intimate relationships.

The stress of separation and divorce places both men and women at risk for psychological and physical difficulties (Rotterman, 2007).

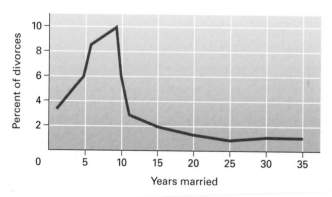

FIGURE 14.5 The Divorce Rate in Relation to Number of Years Married. Shown here is the percentage of divorces as a function of how long couples have been married. Notice that most divorces occur in the early years of marriage, peaking in the fifth to tenth years of marriage.

Separated and divorced women and men have higher rates of psychiatric disorders, admission to psychiatric hospitals, clinical depression, alcoholism, and psychosomatic problems, such as sleep disorders, than do married adults. One analysis of more than 8,000 51- to 61-year-olds revealed that divorce was associated with an increase in chronic health problems (Waite, 2005).

Dealing with Divorce   Psychologically, one of the most common characteristics of divorced adults is difficulty in trusting someone else in a romantic relationship. Following a divorce, though, people's lives can take diverse turns (Tashiro, Frazier, & Berman, 2006). Strategies for divorced adults include the following (Hetherington & Kelly, 2002):

- Think of divorce as a chance to grow personally and to develop more positive relationships.
- Make decisions carefully. The consequences of your decisions regarding work, lovers, and children may last a lifetime.
- Focus more on the future than the past. Think about what is most important for you to go forward in your life, set some challenging goals, and plan how to reach them.
- Use your strengths and resources to cope with difficulties.
- Don't expect to be successful and happy in everything you do. "The road to a more satisfying life is bumpy and will have many detours" (p. 109).
- Remember that "you are never trapped by one pathway. Most of those who were categorized as defeated immediately after divorce gradually moved on to a better life, but moving onward usually requires some effort" (p. 109).

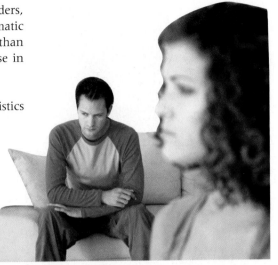

What are some strategies for coping with divorce?

Divorced Middle-Aged and Older Adults   Divorced and separated older adults represented only 8 percent of older adults in 2004 (U.S. Census Bureau, 2006). However, their numbers (2.6 million) have increased considerably since 1990 (1.5 million). Many of these individuals were divorced or separated before they entered late adulthood. The majority of divorced older adults are women, due to their greater longevity and the fact that men are more likely to remarry, thus removing themselves from the pool of divorced older adults (Peek, 2009). Divorce is far less common in older adults than younger adults, likely reflecting cohort effects rather than age effects because divorce was somewhat rare when current cohorts of older adults were young (Peek, 2009).

A survey by AARP (2004) of more than 1 million 40- to 79-year-olds who were divorced at least once in their forties, fifties, or sixties found that staying married because of their children was by far the main reason many people took so long to become divorced. Despite the worry and stress involved in going through the divorce process, three in four of the divorcees said they had made the right decision to dissolve their marriage and reported a positive outlook on life. Sixty-six percent of the divorced women said they initiated the divorce compared with only 41 percent of the divorced men. The divorced women were much more afraid of having financial problems (44 percent) than the divorced men (11 percent). Following are the main reasons the middle-aged and older adults cited for their divorce:

Main Causes for Women

- Verbal, physical, or emotional abuse (23 percent)
- Alcohol or drug abuse (18 percent)
- Cheating (17 percent)

What are some ways that divorce might be more positive or more negative in middle adulthood than in early adulthood?

Main Causes for Men

- No obvious problems, just fell out of love (17 percent)
- Cheating (14 percent)
- Different values, lifestyles (14 percent)

One study found that women who initiated a divorce in midlife were characterized more by self-focused growth and optimism than women whose husbands initiated the divorce (Sakraida, 2005).

Remarried Adults

Adults who remarry usually do so rather quickly, with approximately 50 percent remarrying within three years after their divorce (Sweeney, 2009). Men remarry sooner than women. Men with higher incomes are more likely to remarry than their counterparts with lower incomes. Remarriage occurs sooner for partners who initiate a divorce (especially in the first several years after divorce and for older women) than those who do not (Sweeney, 2009). Only one-third of remarried adults stay married.

Adjustment Evidence on the benefits of remarriage on adults is mixed. Remarried families are more likely to be unstable than first marriages, with divorce more likely to occur—especially in the first several years of the remarried family—than in first marriages (Waite, 2009). Adults who get remarried have a lower level of mental health (higher rates of depression, for example) than adults in first marriages, but remarriage often improves the financial status of remarried adults, especially women (Waite, 2009). Researchers have found that remarried adults' marital relationship is more egalitarian than, and more likely to be characterized by, shared decision making than first marriages (Waite, 2009). Remarried wives also report that they have more influence on financial matters in their new family than do wives in first marriages (Waite, 2009). The complex histories and multiple relationships make adjustment difficult in a stepfamily (Pann & Crosbie-Burnett, 2005). Only one-third of stepfamily couples stay remarried.

Why do remarried adults find it so difficult to stay remarried? For one thing, many remarry not for love but for financial reasons, for help in rearing children, and for a reduction in loneliness. They also might carry into the stepfamily negative patterns that produced failure in an earlier marriage. Remarried couples also experience more stress in rearing children than parents in never-divorced families (Ganong, Coleman, & Hans, 2006).

Among the strategies that help remarried couples cope with the stress of living in a stepfamily are these (Visher & Visher, 1989):

- *Have realistic expectations.* Allow time for loving relationships to develop, and look at the complexity of the stepfamily as a challenge to overcome.
- *Develop new positive relationships within the family.* Create new traditions and ways of dealing with difficult circumstances. Allocation of time is especially important because so many people are involved. The remarried couple needs to allot time alone for each other.

Remarriage and Aging Rising divorce rates, increased longevity, and better health have led to an increase in remarriage by older adults (Coleman, Ganong, & Fine, 2000). What happens when an older adult wants to remarry or does remarry? Researchers have found that some older adults perceive negative social pressure about their decision to remarry (McKain, 1972). These negative sanctions range from raised eyebrows to rejection by adult children. However, the majority of adult children support the decision of their older adult parents to remarry. Researchers have found that remarried parents and stepparents provide less support to adult stepchildren than parents in first marriages (White, 1994).

Gay Male and Lesbian Adults

The legal and social context of marriage creates barriers to breaking up that do not usually exist for most same-sex partners, although an increasing number of states have recognized same-sex marriages. For a number of characteristics, researchers have found that gay male and lesbian relationships are similar—in their satisfactions, loves, joys, and conflicts—to heterosexual relationships (Peplau & Fingerhut, 2007). For example, like heterosexual couples, gay male and lesbian couples need to find the balance of romantic love, affection, autonomy, and equality that is acceptable to both partners (Kurdek, 2003).

Lesbian couples especially place a high priority on equality in their relationships (Peplau & Fingerhut, 2007). Indeed, some researchers have found that gay male and lesbian couples are more flexible in their gender roles than heterosexual individuals are (Marecek, Finn, & Cardell, 1988). And a recent study of couples revealed that over the course of ten years of cohabitation, partners in gay male and lesbian relationships showed a higher average level of relationship quality than heterosexual couples (Kurdek, 2008).

There are a number of misconceptions about gay male and lesbian couples (Hope, 2009; Peplau & Fingerhut, 2007). Contrary to stereotypes, one partner is masculine and the other feminine in only a small percentage of gay male and lesbian couples. Only a small segment of the gay male population has a large number of sexual partners, and this is uncommon among lesbians. Furthermore, researchers have found that gay males and lesbians prefer long-term, committed relationships (Peplau & Fingerhut, 2007). About half of committed gay male couples do have an open relationship that allows the possibility of sex (but not affectionate love) outside the relationship. Lesbian couples usually do not have this open relationship.

What are some characteristics of lesbian and gay male relationships?

Review and Reflect: Learning Goal 2

2 **Discuss the diversity of adult lifestyles and how they influence people's lives**

REVIEW
- What characterizes single adults?
- What are the lives of cohabiting adults like?
- What are some key aspects of the lives of married adults?
- How does divorce affect adults?
- What are the lives of remarried adults like?
- What characterizes the lifestyles of gay male and lesbian adults?

REFLECT
- Which type of lifestyle are you living today? What do you think are its advantages and disadvantages for you? If you could have a different lifestyle, which one would it be? Why?

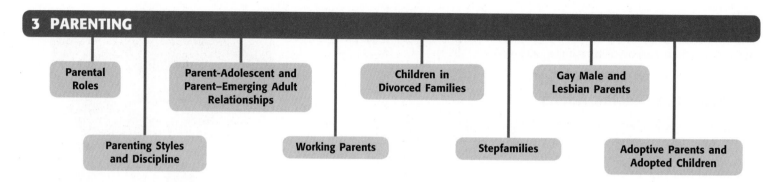

3 PARENTING

Just as there are diverse lifestyles that adults can adopt, so are there diverse styles of parenting and diverse types of parents. Before we examine these diverse styles and types, let's explore the roles of parents.

Parental Roles

Many adults plan when to be parents and consider how parenting will fit with their economic situation. For others, the discovery that they are about to become parents is a startling surprise. In either event, the prospective parents may have mixed emotions and romantic illusions about having a child. The needs and expectations of parents have stimulated many myths about parenting:

Currently, there is a tendency to have fewer children. The number of one-child families is increasing. Is there a best time to have children? What are some of the restrictions individuals face when they become parents? These are some of the questions we now consider.

Timing of Parenthood   As with marriage, the age at which individuals have children has been increasing. In 2005, the average age at which women gave birth for the first time was a record high 25.2 years of age, up from 21 years of age in 2001 (Joint Economic Committee, 2007). As birth control has become common practice, many individuals choose when they will have children and how many children they will raise. They are not only marrying later, but also having children later or not having children at all. The percentage of 40- to 44-year-old U.S. women who remain childless increased from 10 percent in 1976 to 20 percent in 2006 (U.S. Census Bureau, 2008).

What are some of the advantages of having children early or late? Some of the advantages of having children early (in the twenties) are these: (1) the parents are likely to have more physical energy—for example, they can cope better with such matters as getting up in the middle of the night with infants and waiting up until adolescents come home at night; (2) the mother is likely to have fewer medical problems with pregnancy and childbirth; and (3) the parents may be less likely to build up expectations for their children, as do many couples who have waited many years to have children.

There are also advantages to having children later (in the thirties): (1) the parents will have had more time to consider their goals in life, such as what they want from their family and career roles; (2) the parents will be more mature and will be able to benefit from their experiences to engage in more competent parenting; and (3) the parents will be better established in their careers and have more income for child-rearing expenses.

The Transition to Parenting   Whether people become parents through pregnancy, adoption, or stepparenting, they face disequilibrium and must adapt (Claxton & Perry-Jenkins, 2008 Cowan & Cowan, 2000; Lawrence & others, 2009). Parents want to develop a strong attachment with their infant, but they still want to maintain strong attachments to their spouse and friends, and possibly continue their careers. Parents

I looked on child rearing not only as a work of love and duty but as a profession that was fully as interesting and challenging as any honorable profession in the world and one that demanded the best that I could bring to it.

—ROSE KENNEDY
U.S. Public Figure, Philanthropist; 20th Century

ask themselves how this new being will change their lives. A baby places new restrictions on partners; no longer will they be able to rush out to a movie on a moment's notice, and money may not be readily available for vacations and other luxuries. Dual-career parents ask, "Will it harm the baby to place her in child care? Will we be able to find responsible baby-sitters?"

In a longitudinal investigation of couples from late pregnancy until 3½ years after the baby was born, couples enjoyed more positive marital relations before the baby was born than after (Cowan & Cowan, 2000; Cowan & others, 2005). Still, almost one-third showed an increase in marital satisfaction. Some couples said that the baby had both brought them closer together and moved them farther apart; being parents enhanced their sense of themselves and gave them a new, more stable identity as a couple. Babies opened men up to a concern with intimate relationships, and the demands of juggling work and family roles stimulated women to manage family tasks more efficiently and pay attention to their own personal growth.

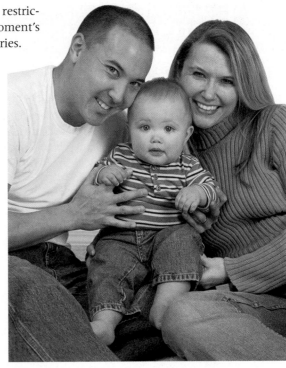

The Bringing Baby Home project is a workshop for new parents that emphasizes strengthening the couples' relationship, understanding and becoming acquainted with the baby, resolving conflict, and developing parenting skills (Gottman, Gottman, & Shapiro, 2009). Evaluations of the project revealed that parents who participated improved in their ability to work together as parents, fathers were more involved with their baby and sensitive to the baby's behavior, mothers had a lower incidence of postpartum depression symptoms, and their baby showed better overall development than participants in a control group (Gottman, 2008; Shapiro & Gottman, 2005).

What characterizes the transition to parenting?

At some point during the early years of the child's life, parents face the difficult task of juggling their roles as parents and as self-actualizing adults. Until recently, nurturing children and having a career were thought to be incompatible, and the nurturing was supposed to be the mother's job. Fortunately, we have come to recognize that a balance between caring and achieving, nurturing and working—although difficult—can be accomplished.

Parents as Managers of Children's Lives Parents can play important roles as managers of children's opportunities, as monitors of their lives, and as social initiators and arrangers (Parke & Buriel, 1998, 2006; Parke & others, 2008). An important developmental task of childhood and adolescence is to develop the ability to make competent decisions in an increasingly independent manner. To help children and adolescents reach their full potential, an important parental role is to be an effective manager, one who finds information, makes contacts, helps structure choices, and provides guidance. Parents who fulfill this important managerial role help children and adolescents to avoid pitfalls and to work their way through a myriad of choices and decisions they face.

Parents can serve as regulators of opportunities for their children's social contact with peers, friends, and adults. From infancy through adolescence, mothers are more likely than fathers to have a managerial role in parenting. In infancy, this might involve taking a child to a doctor and arranging for child care; in early childhood, it might involve a decision about which preschool the child should attend; in middle and late childhood, it might include directing the child to take a bath, to match their clothes and wear clean clothes, and to put away toys; in adolescence, it could involve participating in a parent-teacher conference and subsequently managing the adolescent's homework activity.

A key aspect of the managerial role of parenting is effective monitoring, which is especially important as children move into the adolescent years (Smetana, 2008; Smetana & others, 2009). Monitoring includes supervising an adolescent's choice of social settings, activities, and friends. As we saw in Chapter 13, "Moral Development,

Careers in Life-Span Development

Janis Keyser, Parent Educator

Janis Keyser is a parent educator and teaches in the Department of Early Childhood Education at Cabrillo College in California. In addition to teaching college classes and conducting parenting workshops, she also has coauthored a book with Laura Davis (1997), *Becoming The Parent You Want To Be: A Sourcebook of Strategies for the First Five Years.*

Kayser also writes as an expert on the iVillage Web site (www.parentsplace.com). And she also coauthors a nationally syndicated parenting column, "Growing Up, Growing Together." She is the mother of three, stepmother of five, grandmother of twelve, and great-grandmother of six.

Janis Keyser (*right*), conducting a parenting workshop.

Values, and Religion," a lack of adequate parental monitoring is the parental factor that is related to juvenile delinquency more than any other. A recent interest involving parental monitoring focuses on adolescents' voluntary disclosure, especially about their activities. Researchers have found that adolescents' disclosure to parents about their whereabouts, activities, and friends is linked to positive adolescent adjustment (Smetana & others, 2009).

To read about one individual who helps parents become more effective in managing children's lives, see the *Careers in Life-Span Development* profile.

Parenting Styles and Discipline

A few years ago, there was considerable interest in Mozart CDs that were marketed with the promise that playing them would enrich infants' and young children's brains. Some of the parents who bought them probably thought, "I don't have enough time to spend with my children so I'll just play these intellectual CDs and then they won't need me as much." Similarly, one-minute bedtime stories are being marketed for parents to read to their children (Walsh, 2000). There are one-minute bedtime bear books, puppy books, and so on. Parents who buy them know it is good for them to read with their children, but they don't want to spend a lot of time doing it. Behind the popularity of these products is an unfortunate theme that suggests that parenting can be done quickly, with little or no inconvenience (Sroufe, 2000).

What is wrong with these quick-fix approaches to parenting? Good parenting takes time and effort (Chen, 2009a, b). You can't do it in a minute here and a minute there. You can't do it with CDs.

Of course, it's not just the quantity of time parents spend with children that is important for children's development—the quality of the parenting is clearly important (Bornstein & Zlotnik, 2008). To understand variations in parenting, let's consider the styles parents use when they interact with their children, how they discipline their children, and coparenting.

Calvin and Hobbes

by Bill Watterson

Baumrind's Parenting Styles   Diana Baumrind (1971) argues parents should be neither punitive nor aloof. Rather, they should develop rules for their children and be affectionate with them. She has described four types of parenting styles:

- **Authoritarian parenting** is a restrictive, punitive style in which parents exhort the child to follow their directions and respect their work and effort. The authoritarian parent places firm limits and controls on the child and allows little verbal exchange. For example, an authoritarian parent might say, "You do it my way or else." Authoritarian parents also might spank the child frequently, enforce rules rigidly but not explain them, and show rage toward the child. Children of authoritarian parents are often unhappy, fearful, and anxious about comparing themselves with others, fail to initiate activity, and have weak communication skills. Sons of authoritarian parents may behave aggressively (Hart & others, 2003).

- **Authoritative parenting** encourages children to be independent but still places limits and controls on their actions. Extensive verbal give-and-take is allowed, and parents are warm and nurturant toward the child. An authoritative parent might put his arm around the child in a comforting way and say, "You know you should not have done that. Let's talk about how you can handle the situation better next time." Authoritative parents show pleasure and support in response to children's constructive behavior. They also expect mature, independent, and age-appropriate behavior by children. Children whose parents are authoritative are often cheerful, self-controlled and self-reliant, and achievement-oriented; they tend to maintain friendly relations with peers, cooperate with adults, and cope well with stress.

- **Neglectful parenting** is a style in which the parent is very uninvolved in the child's life. Children whose parents are neglectful develop the sense that other aspects of the parents' lives are more important than they are. These children tend to be socially incompetent. Many have poor self-control and don't handle independence well. They frequently have low self-esteem, are immature, and may be alienated from the family. In adolescence, they may show patterns of truancy and delinquency.

- **Indulgent parenting** is a style in which parents are highly involved with their children but place few demands or controls on them. Such parents let their children do what they want. The result is that the children never learn to control their own behavior and always expect to get their way. Some parents

authoritarian parenting A restrictive, punitive style in which parents exhort the child to follow their directions and to respect their work and effort. Firm limits are placed on the child, and little verbal exchange is allowed.

authoritative parenting A style that encourages children to be independent but still places limits and controls on children's actions; extensive verbal give-and-take is allowed, and parents are warm and nurturant toward the child.

neglectful parenting A style in which the parent is very uninvolved in the child's life.

indulgent parenting A style in which parents are very involved with their children but place few demands or controls on them.

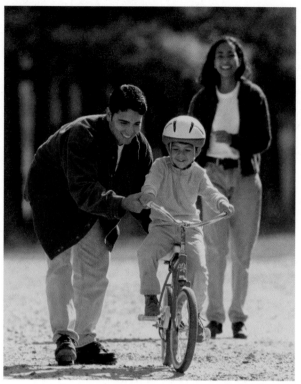

	Accepting, responsive	Rejecting, unresponsive
Demanding, controlling	Authoritative	Authoritarian
Undemanding, uncontrolling	Indulgent	Neglectful

FIGURE 14.6 Classification of Parenting Styles. The four types of parenting styles (authoritative, authoritarian, indulgent, and neglectful) involve the dimensions of acceptance and responsiveness, on the one hand, and demand and control on the other. For example, authoritative parenting involves being both accepting/responsive and demanding/controlling.

We never know the love of our parents until we have become parents.

—HENRY WARD BEECHER
American Clergyman, 19th Century

deliberately rear their children in this way because they believe the combination of warm involvement and few restraints will produce a creative, confident child. However, children whose parents are indulgent rarely learn respect for others and have difficulty controlling their behavior. They might be domineering, egocentric, and noncompliant, and have difficulties in peer relations.

These four classifications of parenting involve combinations of acceptance and responsiveness on the one hand and demand and control on the other (Maccoby & Martin, 1983). How these dimensions combine to produce authoritarian, authoritative, neglectful, and indulgent parenting is shown in Figure 14.6.

Parenting Styles in Context Do the benefits of authoritative parenting transcend the boundaries of ethnicity, socioeconomic status, and household composition? Although some exceptions have been found, evidence linking authoritative parenting with competence on the part of the child occurs in research across a wide range of ethnic groups, social strata, cultures, and family structures (Steinberg, Blatt-Eisengart, & Cauffman, 2006).

Other research with ethnic groups suggests that some aspects of the authoritarian style may be associated with positive child outcomes (Parke & Buriel, 2006). Elements of the authoritarian style may take on different meanings and have different effects depending on the context.

For example, Asian American parents often continue aspects of traditional Asian child-rearing practices that have sometimes been described as authoritarian. The parents exert considerable control over their children's lives. However, Ruth Chao (2005, 2007; Chao & Tseng, 2002) argues that the style of parenting used by many Asian American parents is distinct from the domineering control of the authoritarian style. Instead, Chao argues that the control reflects concern and involvement in their children's lives and is best conceptualized as a type of training. The high academic achievement of Asian American children may be a consequence of their "training" parents (Stevenson & Zusho, 2002).

An emphasis on requiring respect and obedience is also associated with the authoritarian style, but in Latino child rearing this focus may be positive rather than punitive. Rather than suppressing the child's development, it may encourage the development of a different type of self. Latino child-rearing practices encourage the development of a self and identity that is embedded in the family and requires respect and obedience (Dixon, Graber, & Brooks-Gunn, 2008). Furthermore, many Latino families have several generations living together and helping each other (Zinn & Wells, 2000). In these circumstances, emphasizing respect and obedience by children may be part of maintaining a harmonious home and may be important in the formation of the child's identity.

Even physical punishment, another characteristic of the authoritarian style, may have varying effects in different contexts. African American parents are more likely than non-Latino White parents to use physical punishment (Deater-Deckard & Dodge, 1997). However, the use of physical punishment has been linked with increased externalized child problems (such as acting out and high levels of aggression) in non-Latino White families but not in African American families. One explanation of this finding points to the need for African American parents to enforce rules in the dangerous environments in which they are more likely to live (Harrison-Hale, McLoyd, & Smedley, 2004). In this context, requiring obedience to parental authority may be an adaptive strategy to keep children from engaging in antisocial behavior that can have serious consequences for the victim or the perpetrator. As we see soon, though, overall, the use of physical punishment in disciplining children raises many concerns.

Further Thoughts on Parenting Styles   Several caveats about parenting styles are in order. First, the parenting styles do not capture the important themes of reciprocal socialization and synchrony (Laursen & Collins, 2009). Keep in mind that children socialize parents, just as parents socialize children (Kuczyinski & Parkin, 2007). Second, many parents use a combination of techniques rather than a single technique, although one technique may be dominant. Although consistent parenting is usually recommended, the wise parent may sense the importance of being more permissive in certain situations, more authoritarian in others, and yet more authoritative in others. Also, some critics argue that the concept of parenting style is too broad and that more research needs to be conducted to "unpack" parenting styles by studying various components that comprise the styles (Maccoby, 2007). For example, is parental monitoring more important than warmth in predicting child and adolescent outcomes?

Punishment   For centuries, corporal (physical) punishment, such as spanking, has been considered a necessary and even desirable method of disciplining children. Use of corporal punishment is legal in every state in America. A national survey of U.S. parents with 3- and 4-year-old children found that 26 percent of parents reported spanking their children frequently, and 67 percent of the parents reported yelling at their children frequently (Regalado & others, 2004). A cross-cultural comparison found that individuals in the United States were among those with the most favorable attitudes toward corporal punishment and were the most likely to remember it being used by their parents (Curran & others, 2001) (see Figure 14.7).

Despite the widespread use of corporal punishment, there have been surprisingly few research studies on physical punishment, and those that have been conducted are correlational (Kazdin & Benjet, 2003). Clearly, it would be highly unethical to randomly assign parents to either spank or not spank their children in an experimental study. Recall that cause and effect cannot be determined in a correlational study. In one correlational study, spanking by parents was linked with children's antisocial behavior, including cheating, telling lies, being mean to others, bullying, getting into fights, and being disobedient (Strauss, Sugarman, & Giles-Sims, 1997).

A research review concluded that corporal punishment by parents is associated with higher levels of immediate compliance and aggression by the children (Gershoff, 2002). The review also found that corporal punishment is associated with lower levels of moral internalization and mental health (Gershoff, 2002). A longitudinal study found that spanking before age 2 was related to behavioral problems in middle and late childhood (Slade & Wissow, 2004). A recent study discovered that a history of harsh physical discipline was linked to adolescent depression and externalized problems, such as juvenile delinquency (Bender & others, 2007). Another recent study found a link between the use of physical punishment by parents and children's negative behavioral adjustment at 36 months and in the first grade (Mulvaney & Mebert, 2007). And yet another recent study discovered that a history of harsh physical discipline was linked to adolescent depression and externalized problems, such as juvenile delinquency (Bender & others, 2007). Some critics, though, argue that the research evidence is not yet sound enough to warrant a blanket injunction against corporal punishment, especially mild corporal punishment (Baumrind, Larzelere, & Cowan, 2002; Kazdin & Benjet, 2003).

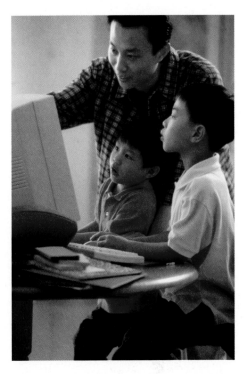

According to Ruth Chao, what type of parenting style do many Asian American parents use?

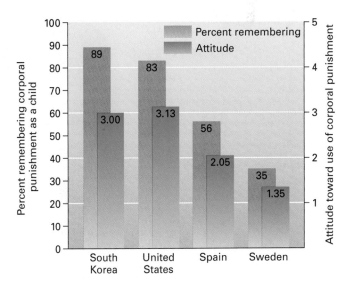

FIGURE 14.7 Corporal Punishment in Different Countries. A 5-point scale was used to assess attitudes toward corporal punishment with scores closer to 1 indicating an attitude against its use and scores closer to 5 suggesting an attitude favoring its use. *Why are studies of corporal punishment correlational studies, and how does that affect their interpretation?*

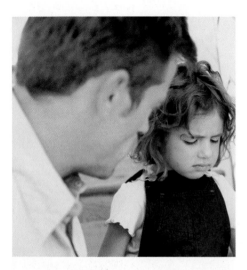

How do most child psychologists recommend handling a child's misbehavior?

What are some reasons for avoiding spanking or similar punishments? The reasons include the following:

- When adults punish a child by yelling, screaming, or spanking, they are presenting children with out-of-control models for handling stressful situations. Children may imitate this aggressive, out-of-control behavior (Sim & Ong, 2005).

- Punishment can instill fear, rage, or avoidance. For example, spanking the child may cause the child to avoid being around the parent and to fear the parent.

- Punishment tells children what not to do rather what to do. Children should be given feedback, such as "Why don't you try this?"

- Punishment can be abusive. Parents might unintentionally become so aroused when they are punishing the child that they become abusive (Ateah, 2005).

Because of reasons such as these, Sweden passed a law in 1979 forbidding parents to physically punish (spank or slap, for example) children. Since the law was enacted, youth rates of delinquency, alcohol abuse, rape, and suicide have dropped in Sweden (Durrant, 2000). These improvements may have occurred for other reasons, such as changing attitudes and opportunities for youth. Nonetheless, the Swedish experience suggests that physical punishment of children may be unnecessary (Durrant, 2008). Many other countries also have passed antispanking laws (Gracia & Herrero, 2008).

Most child psychologists recommend handling misbehavior by reasoning with the child, especially explaining the consequences of the child's actions for others. *Time out,* in which the child is removed from a setting that offers positive reinforcement, can also be effective. For example, when the child has misbehaved, a parent might take away TV viewing for a specified time.

Earlier in this chapter, we described the family as a system and discussed possible links between marital relationships and parenting practices. To read about a family systems study involving marital conflict and the use of physical punishment, see the *Research in Life-Span Development* interlude.

Research in Life-Span Development

MARITAL CONFLICT, INDIVIDUAL HOSTILITY, AND THE USE OF PHYSICAL PUNISHMENT

A longitudinal study assessed couples across the transition to parenting to investigate possible links between marital conflict, individual adult hostility, and the use of physical punishment with young children (Kanoy & others, 2003). Before the birth of the first child, the level of marital conflict was observed in a marital problem-solving discussion; answers to questionnaires regarding individual characteristics were also obtained. Thus, these characteristics of the couples were not influenced by characteristics of the child. When the children were 2 and 5 years old, the couples were interviewed about the frequency and intensity of their physical punishment of the children. At both ages, the parents' level of marital conflict was again observed in a marital problem-solving discussion.

The researchers found that both hostility and marital conflict were linked with the use of physical punishment. Individuals with high rates of hostility on the prenatal measures used more frequent and more severe physical punishment with their children. The same was evident for marital conflict—when marital conflict was high, both mothers and fathers were more likely to use physical punishment in disciplining their young children.

If parents who have a greater likelihood of using physical punishment can be identified in prenatal classes, these families could be encouraged to use other forms of discipline before they get into a pattern of physically punishing their children.

Coparenting   The relationship between marital conflict and the use of punishment highlights the importance of **coparenting,** which is the support that parents provide one another in jointly raising a child. Poor coordination between parents, undermining of the other parent, lack of cooperation and warmth, and disconnection by one parent are conditions that place children at risk for problems (Feinberg & Kan, 2008; McHale, 2009; Talbot, Baker, & McHale, 2009). For example, a recent study revealed that coparenting influenced young children's effortful control above and beyond maternal and paternal parenting by themselves (Karreman & others, 2008).

Parents who do not spend enough time with their children or who have problems in child rearing can benefit from counseling and therapy. To read about the work of marriage and family counselor Darla Botkin, see the *Careers in Life-Span Development* profile.

Child Maltreatment   Unfortunately, punishment sometimes leads to the abuse of infants and children (Cicchetti, & others, 2010; Kennedy, 2009; Miller-Perrin, Perrin, & Kocur, 2009). In 2007, approximately 794,000 U.S. children were found to be victims of child abuse (U.S. Department of Health and Human Services, 2009). Nearly 80 percent of these children were abused by a parent or parents. Laws in many states now require physicians and teachers to report suspected cases of child abuse, yet many cases go unreported, especially those of battered infants.

What characterizes coparenting?

coparenting The support that parents provide one another in jointly raising a child.

Careers in Life-Span Development

Darla Botkin, Marriage and Family Therapist

Darla Botkin is a marriage and family therapist who teaches, conducts research, and engages in marriage and family therapy. She is on the faculty of the University of Kentucky. Botkin obtained a bachelor's degree in elementary education with a concentration in special education and then went on to receive a master's degree in early childhood education. She spent the next six years working with children and their families in a variety of settings, including child care, elementary school, and Head Start. These experiences led Darla to recognize the interdependence of the developmental settings that children and their parents experience (such as home, school, and work). She returned to graduate school and obtained a Ph.D. in family studies from the University of Tennessee. She then became a faculty member in the Family Studies program at the University of Kentucky. Completing further coursework and clinical training in marriage and family therapy, she became certified as a marriage and family therapist.

Botkin's current interests include working with young children in family therapy, gender and ethnic issues in family therapy, and the role of spirituality in family wellness.

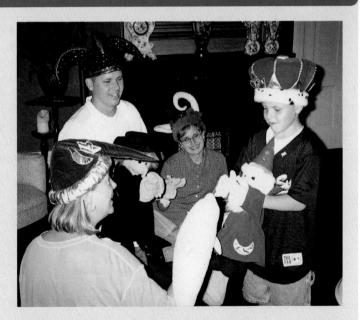

Darla Botkin (*left*), conducting a family therapy session.

Whereas the public and many professionals use the term **child abuse** to refer to both abuse and neglect, developmentalists increasingly use the term **child maltreatment.** This term does not have quite the emotional impact of the term *abuse* and acknowledges that maltreatment includes diverse conditions.

Types of Child Maltreatment   The four main types of child maltreatment are physical abuse, child neglect, sexual abuse, and emotional abuse (National Clearinghouse on Child Abuse and Neglect, 2002, 2004):

- **Physical abuse** is characterized by the infliction of physical injury as a result of punching, beating, kicking, biting, burning, shaking, or otherwise harming a child. The parent or other person may not have intended to hurt the child; the injury may have resulted from excessive physical punishment (Hornor, 2005; Maguire & others, 2005).
- **Child neglect** is characterized by failure to provide for the child's basic needs (Dubowitz, Pitts, & Black, 2004). Neglect can be physical (abandonment, for example), educational (allowing chronic truancy, for example), or emotional (marked inattention to the child's needs, for example). Child neglect is by far the most common form of child maltreatment. In every country where relevant data have been collected, neglect occurs up to three times as often as abuse (Benoit, Coolbear, & Crawford, 2008).
- **Sexual abuse** includes fondling a child's genitals, intercourse, incest, rape, sodomy, exhibitionism, and commercial exploitation through prostitution or the production of pornographic materials (Fitzgerald & others, 2008; Johnson, 2008). In many cases of sexual abuse, there are no outward physical signs of abuse, unlike in incidences of physical abuse.
- **Emotional abuse** (*psychological/verbal abuse/mental injury*)includes acts or omissions by parents or other caregivers that have caused, or could cause, serious behavioral, cognitive, or emotional problems (Gelles & Cavanaugh, 2005).

Although any of these forms of child maltreatment may be found separately, they often occur in combination. Emotional abuse is almost always present when other forms are identified.

The Context of Abuse   No single factor causes child maltreatment (Cicchetti & Rogosch, 2009; Cicchetti & others, 2010). A combination of factors, including the culture, neighborhood, family, and development, likely contribute to child maltreatment (Prinz & others, 2009).

The extensive violence that takes place in American culture is reflected in the occurrence of violence in the family (Azar, 2002). A regular diet of violence appears on television screens, and parents often resort to power assertion as a disciplinary technique. In China, where physical punishment is rarely used to discipline children, the incidence of child abuse is reported to be very low.

The neighborhood in which families live is linked to the incidence of child maltreatment (Kimbrough-Melton & Campbell, 2008; Slep & Heyman, 2008). A number of studies have revealed that child maltreatment is concentrated in areas characterized by low socioeconomic status and lack of resources (Coulton & others, 2007). Other aspects of neighborhoods linked with child maltreatment include child-care burden, residential instability, overcrowding, crime, and per capita density of alcohol outlets (Freisthler, Merritt, & LaScala, 2006). The presence of social networks and social support in neighborhoods can help to buffer the incidence of child maltreatment (Berman, Murphy-Berman, & Melton, 2008; Haski-Leventhal, Ben-Arieh, & Melton, 2008).

The family itself is obviously a key part of the context of abuse. The interactions of all family members need to be considered, regardless of who performs the violent acts against the child (Kim & Cicchetti, 2004). For example, even though the father

---

*C*hild maltreatment involves grossly inadequate and destructive aspects of parenting.

—**D**ante **C**icchetti
Contemporary Developmental Psychologist, University of Minnesota

child abuse The term used most often by the public and many professionals to refer to both abuse and neglect.

child maltreatment The term increasingly used by developmentalists that refers to abuse and neglect, but also includes diverse conditions.

physical abuse Abuse characterized by the infliction of physical injury as a result of punching, beating, kicking, biting, burning, shaking, or otherwise harming a child.

child neglect Failure to provide for the child's basic needs, including physical, educational, or emotional needs.

sexual abuse Fondling the child's genitals, intercourse, incest, rape, sodomy, exhibitionism, and commercial exploitation through prostitution or the production of pornographic materials.

emotional abuse Acts or omissions by parents or other caregivers that have caused, or could cause, serious behavioral, cognitive, or emotional problems.

may be the one who physically abuses the child, contributions by the mother, the child, and siblings also should be evaluated.

Were parents who abuse children abused by their own parents? About one-third of parents who were abused themselves when they were young abuse their own children (Cicchetti & Toth, 2006; Cicchetti & others, 2010). Thus, some, but not a majority, of parents are locked into an intergenerational transmission of abuse (Dixon, Browne, & Hamilton-Giachritsis, 2005). Mothers who break out of the intergenerational transmission of abuse often have at least one warm, caring adult in their background; have a close, positive marital relationship; and have received therapy (Egeland, Jacobvitz, & Sroufe, 1988).

Sexual abuse of women can also have other negative multigenerational outcomes. A recent study revealed that the offspring of mothers who had histories of being sexually abused as children were more likely to be born preterm and be involved in protective services than the children of mothers who had not been sexually abused (Noll & others, 2009). In this study, the mothers who had been sexually abused as children were more likely to drop out of high school, be obese, and have experienced psychiatric problems, substance dependence, and domestic violence than females who had not been sexually abused as children.

Developmental Consequences of Abuse   Among the consequences of child maltreatment in childhood and adolescence are poor emotion regulation, attachment problems, problems in peer relations, difficulty in adapting to school, and other psychological problems such as depression and delinquency (Cichetti & others, 2010; Keil & Price, 2009). As shown in Figure 14.8, maltreated young children in foster care were more likely to show abnormal stress hormone levels than middle-SES young children living with their birth family (Gunnar, Fisher, & the Early Experience, Stress, and Prevention Network, 2006). In this study, the abnormal stress hormone levels were mainly present in the foster children who experienced neglect, best described as "institutional neglect" (Fisher, 2005). Abuse also may have this effect on young children (Gunnar, Fisher, & the Early Experience, Stress, and Prevention Network, 2006). Adolescents who experienced abuse or neglect as children are more likely than adolescents who were not maltreated as children to engage in violent romantic relationships, delinquency, sexual risk taking, and substance abuse (Wekerle & others, 2009).

Later during the adult years, individuals who were maltreated as children often have difficulty in establishing and maintaining healthy intimate relationships (Dozier, Stovall-McClough, & Albus, 2008). As adults, maltreated children are also at higher risk for violent behavior toward other adults—especially dating partners and marital partners—as well as for substance abuse, anxiety, and depression (Miller-Perrin, Perrin, & Kocur, 2009).

An important strategy is to prevent child maltreatment (Cicchetti & others, 2010; McCoy & Keen, 2009). In one study of maltreating mothers and their 1-year-olds, two treatments were effective in reducing child maltreatment: (1) home visitation that emphasized improved parenting, coping with stress, and increasing support for the mother; and (2) psychotherapy that focused on improving maternal-infant attachment (Cicchetti, Toth, and Rogosch, 2005).

Parent-Adolescent and Parent–Emerging Adult Relationships

Even the best parents may find their relationship with their child strained during adolescence, yet attachment to parents is an important aspect of adolescent development. As individuals become emerging adults, their relationship with their parents changes.

Parent-Adolescent Relationships   Important aspects of parent-adolescent relationships include autonomy/attachment and conflict. First, we explore the young adolescent's push for autonomy.

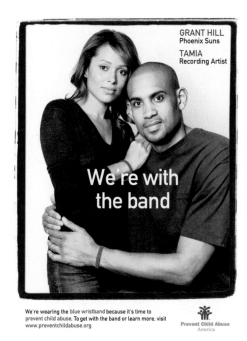

This print ad was created by Prevent Child Abuse America to make people aware of its national blue wristband campaign. The campaign's goal is to educate people about child abuse prevention and encourage them to support the organization.

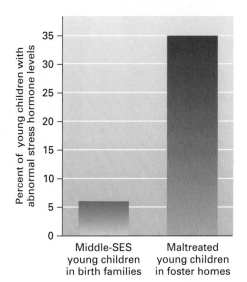

FIGURE 14.8 Abnormal Stress Hormone Levels in Young Children in Different Types of Rearing Conditions.

When I was a boy of 14, my father was so ignorant I could hardly stand to have the man around. But when I got to be 21, I was astonished at how much he had learnt in 7 years.

—MARK TWAIN
American Writer and Humorist, 19th Century

Autonomy and Attachment The young adolescent's push for autonomy and responsibility puzzles and angers many parents. Parents see their teenager slipping from their grasp. They may have an urge to take stronger control as the adolescent seeks autonomy and responsibility. Heated emotional exchanges may ensue, with either side calling names, making threats, and doing whatever seems necessary to gain control. Most parents anticipate that their teenager will have some difficulty adjusting to the changes that adolescence brings, but few parents can imagine and predict just how strong an adolescent's desires will be to spend time with peers or how much adolescents will want to show that it is they—not their parents—who are responsible for their successes and failures.

The ability to attain autonomy and gain control over one's behavior in adolescence is acquired through appropriate adult reactions to the adolescent's desire for control (McElhaney & others, 2009). At the onset of adolescence, the average individual does not have the knowledge to make mature decisions in all areas of life. As the adolescent pushes for autonomy, the wise adult relinquishes control in those areas in which the adolescent can make reasonable decisions but continues to guide the adolescent to make reasonable decisions in areas in which the adolescent's knowledge is more limited. Gradually, adolescents acquire the ability to make mature decisions on their own (Laursen & Collins, 2009).

Gender differences characterize autonomy-granting in adolescence, with boys being given more independence than girls are. In one study, this was especially true in those U.S. families with a traditional gender-role orientation (Bumpus, Crouter, & McHale, 2001). Also, Latino families protect and monitor daughters more closely than sons than is the case in non-Latino White families (Allen & others, 2008).

Cultural differences also characterize adolescent autonomy. In one study, U.S. adolescents sought autonomy earlier than did Japanese adolescents (Rothbaum & others, 2000). In the transition to adulthood, Japanese youth are less likely to live outside the home than Americans are (Hendry, 1999).

Even while adolescents seek autonomy, parent-child attachment remains important (Rothbaum & Trommsdorff, 2007). Mothers maintain more close emotional ties with adolescents, especially daughters, than fathers do (Collins & Steinberg, 2006).

Recall from Chapter 10, "Emotional Development," that one of the most widely discussed aspects of socioemotional development in infancy is secure attachment to caregivers. In the past decade, researchers have explored whether secure attachment also might be an important concept in adolescents' relationships with their parents (Zimmerman, 2007). For example, Joseph Allen and his colleagues (Allen, 2007, 2008; Allen & others, 2003, 2009) have found that securely attached adolescents are less likely than those who were insecurely attached to engage in problem behaviors, such as juvenile delinquency and drug abuse. In a recent longitudinal study, Allen and his colleagues (2009) found that secure attachment at 14 years of age was linked to a number of positive outcomes at 21 years of age, including relationship competence, financial/career competence, and fewer problematic behaviors. In other research, securely attached adolescents had better peer relations than their insecurely attached counterparts (Laible, Carlo, & Raffaeli, 2000). A recent study also revealed that securely attached adolescents in the senior year of high school had a greater capacity for romantic intimacy four years later (Mayseless & Scharf, 2007).

Parent-Adolescent Conflict Although attachment to parents may remain strong during adolescence, the connectedness is not always smooth (Harold, Colarossi, & Mercier, 2007). Early adolescence is a time when conflict with parents escalates (Laursen & Collins, 2009). Much of the conflict involves the everyday events of family life, such as keeping a bedroom clean, dressing neatly, getting home by a

What are strategies that parents can use to guide adolescents in effectively handling their increased motivation for autonomy?

certain time, and not talking incessantly on the phone. The conflicts rarely involve major dilemmas, such as drugs and delinquency.

The increased conflict in early adolescence may be due to a number of factors: the biological changes of puberty, cognitive changes involving increased idealism and logical reasoning, social changes focused on independence and identity, maturational changes in parents, and expectations that are violated by parents and adolescents (Collins & Steinberg, 2006). Adolescents compare their parents with an ideal standard and then criticize their flaws. Many parents see their adolescent changing from a compliant child to someone who is noncompliant, oppositional, and resistant to parental standards. Also, early-maturing adolescents experience more conflict with their parents than do adolescents who mature late or on time (Collins & Steinberg, 2006).

Conflict with parents increases in early adolescence. *What is the nature of this conflict in a majority of American families?*

It is not unusual to hear parents of young adolescents ask, "Is it ever going to get better?" Things usually do get better as adolescents move from early to late adolescence. Conflict with parents often escalates during early adolescence, remains somewhat stable during the high school years, and then lessens as the adolescent reaches 17 to 20 years of age. Parent-adolescent relationships become more positive if adolescents go away to college than if they stay at home and attend college (Sullivan & Sullivan, 1980).

The everyday conflicts that characterize parent-adolescent relationships may serve a positive function. These minor disputes and negotiations facilitate the adolescent's transition from being dependent on parents to becoming an autonomous individual. For example, in one study, adolescents who expressed disagreement with their parents explored identity development more actively than did adolescents who did not express disagreement with their parents (Cooper & others, 1982). One way for parents to cope with the adolescent's push for independence and identity is to recognize that adolescence is a decade-long transitional period in the journey to adulthood, rather than an overnight accomplishment. Recognizing that conflict and negotiation can serve a positive developmental function can tone down parental hostility too. Understanding parent-adolescent conflict, though, is not simple (Riesch & others, 2003).

In sum, the old model of parent-adolescent relationships suggested that parent-adolescent conflict is intense and stressful throughout adolescence. The new model emphasizes that most parent-adolescent conflict is moderate rather than intense and that the moderate conflict can serve a positive function. Figure 14.9 summarizes the

Old Model		New Model
Autonomy, detachment from parents; parent and peer worlds are isolated		Attachment and autonomy; parents are important support systems and attachment figures; adolescent-parent and adolescent-peer worlds have some important connections
Intense, stressful conflict throughout adolescence; parent-adolescent relationships are filled with storm and stress on virtually a daily basis		Moderate parent-adolescent conflict common and can serve a positive developmental function; conflict greater in early adolescence, especially during the apex of puberty

FIGURE 14.9 Old and New Models of Parent-Adolescent Relationships.

old and new models of parent-adolescent relationships, which include changes in thinking about attachment and autonomy.

Still, a high degree of conflict characterizes some parent-adolescent relationships. According to one estimate, parents and adolescents engage in prolonged, intense, repeated, unhealthy conflict in about one in five families (Montemayor, 1982). In other words, 4 to 5 million American families encounter serious, highly stressful parent-adolescent conflict. And this prolonged, intense conflict is associated with a number of adolescent problems—movement out of the home, juvenile delinquency, school dropout, pregnancy and early marriage, membership in religious cults, and drug abuse (Brook & others, 1990). In a recent study of Latino families, higher levels of conflict with either the mother or the father were linked to higher levels of adolescent boys' and girls' internalizing (depression, for example) and externalizing (delinquency, for example) behaviors (Crean, 2008). In this study, conflict with the mother was especially detrimental for Latina girls.

Some cultures are marked by less parent-adolescent conflict than others. American psychologist Reed Larson (1999) studied middle-socioeconomic-status adolescents and their families in India. He observed that in India there seems to be little parent-adolescent conflict and that many families likely would be described as "authoritarian" in Baumrind's categorization. Larson also observed that in India adolescents do not go through a process of breaking away from their parents and that parents choose their youths' marital partners. Researchers have also found considerably less conflict between parents and adolescents in Japan than in the United States (Rothbaum & others, 2000).

Stacey Christensen, age 16: "I am lucky enough to have open communication with my parents. Whenever I am in need or just need to talk, my parents are there for me. My advice to parents is to let your teens grow at their own pace, be open with them so that you can be there for them. We need guidance; our parents need to help but not be too overwhelming."

Conclusions   We have seen that parents play very important roles in adolescent development. Although adolescents are moving toward independence, they still need to stay connected with families (Laursen & Collins, 2009; McElhaney & others, 2009). In the National Longitudinal Study on Adolescent Health (Council of Economic Advisors, 2000) of more than 12,000 adolescents, those who did not eat dinner with a parent five or more days a week had dramatically higher rates of smoking, drinking, using marijuana, getting into fights, and initiating sexual activity. In another study, parents who played an active role in monitoring and guiding their adolescents' development were more likely to have adolescents with positive peer relations and lower drug use than did parents who had a less active role (Mounts, 2002).

Competent adolescent development is most likely when adolescents have parents who show them warmth and mutual respect, demonstrate sustained interest in their lives, recognize and adapt to their cognitive and socioemotional development, communicate expectations for high standards of conduct and achievement, and display constructive ways of dealing with problems and conflict (Small, 1990). These ideas coincide with Diana Baumrind's (1971, 1991) authoritative parenting style.

Emerging Adults' Relationship with Their Parents   For the most part, emerging adults' relationships with their parents improve when they leave home. They often grow closer psychologically to their parents and share more with them than they did before they left home (Arnett, 2007). However, challenges in the parent–emerging adult relationship involve the emerging adult's increasing autonomy by possessing adult status in many areas yet still depending on parents in some manner (Aquilino, 2006). Many emerging adults can make their own decisions about where to live, whether to stay in college, which lifestyle to adopt, whether to get married, and so on. At the

Doonesbury

BY GARRY TRUDEAU

DOONESBURY © 1991 G. B. Trudeau. Reprinted with permission of Universal Press Syndicate. All Rights Reserved.

same time, parents often provide support for their emerging adult children, even after they leave home. This might be accomplished through loans and monetary gifts for education or purchase of a car, and financial contribution to living arrangements, as well as emotional support.

In successful emerging adulthood, individuals separate from their parents without cutting off ties completely or fleeing to some substitute emotional refuge. Complete cutoffs from parents rarely solve emotional problems. Emerging adulthood is a time for young people to sort out emotionally what they will take along from the family of origin, what they will leave behind, and what they will create.

Many emerging adults no longer feel compelled to comply with parental expectations and wishes. They shift to learning to deal with their parents on an adult-to-adult basis, which requires a mutually respectful form of relating in which, by the end of emerging adulthood, individuals can appreciate and accept their parents as they are.

In today's uncertain economic times, many emerging adults continue to live at home or return to live at home after several years of college, after graduation, or as a way to save money after taking a full-time job (Furman, 2005; Paul, 2003). Emerging and young adults also may move back in with their parents after an unsuccessful career or a divorce. And some individuals don't leave home at all until their middle to late twenties because they cannot financially support themselves. Numerous labels have been applied to emerging and young adults who return to their parents' homes to live, including "boomerang kids," and "B2B" (or back-to-bedroom) (Furman, 2005).

As with most family living arrangements, there are both pluses and minuses when emerging adult children live at home or return to live at home. One of the most common complaints voiced by both emerging adults and their parents is a loss of privacy. Emerging adults complain that their parents restrict their independence, cramp their sex lives, reduce their music listening, and treat them as children rather than adults. Parents often complain that their quiet home has become noisy, that they stay up late worrying when their emerging adult children will come home, that meals are difficult to plan because of conflicting schedules, that their relationship as a married couple has been invaded, and that they have to shoulder too much responsibility for their emerging adult children. In sum, when emerging adults return home to live, a disequilibrium in family life is created, which requires considerable adaptation on the part of parents and their emerging adult children.

What are some strategies that emerging adults and their parents can use to get along better? When emerging adults ask to return home to live, parents and their emerging adult children should agree on the conditions and expectations beforehand

What are some strategies that can benefit the relationship between emerging adults and their parents?

(Furman, 2005). For example, they might discuss and agree on whether the emerging adults will pay rent, wash their own clothes, cook their own meals, do any household chores, pay their phone bills, come and go as they please, be sexually active or drink alcohol at home, and so on. If these conditions aren't negotiated at the beginning, conflict often results because the expectations of parents and young adult children will likely be violated. Parents need to treat emerging adult children more like adults than children and let go of much of their parenting role. Parents should not interact with emerging adult children as if they are dependent children who need to be closely monitored and protected but rather should treat them as young adults who are capable of responsible, mature behavior. Emerging adults have the right to choose how much they sleep and eat, how they dress, who they choose as friends and lovers, what career they pursue, and how they spend their money. However, if the emerging adult children act in ways that interfere with their parents' lifestyles, parents need to say so. The discussion should focus not on emerging adults' choices but on how their activities are unacceptable while living with their parents in the same home.

Working Parents

More than one of every two U.S. mothers with a child under the age of 5 is in the labor force; more than two of every three with a child from 6 to 17 years of age is. Maternal employment is a part of modern life, but its effects are still debated.

Work can produce positive and negative effects on parenting (Crouter & McHale, 2005). Recent research indicates that what matters for children's development is the nature of parents' work rather than whether one parent or both parents work outside the home (Clarke-Stewart, 2006; Han, 2009). Ann Crouter (2006) recently described how parents bring their experiences at work into their homes. She concluded that parents who have poor working conditions, such as long hours, overtime work, stressful work, and lack of autonomy at work, are likely to be more irritable at home and engage in less effective parenting than their counterparts who have better work conditions in their jobs. A consistent finding is that children (especially girls) of working mothers engage in less gender stereotyping and have more egalitarian views of gender (Goldberg & Lucas-Thompson, 2008).

Children in Divorced Families

Divorce rates changed dramatically in the United States and many countries around the world in the late twentieth century (Amato & Irving, 2006). The U.S. divorce rate increased enormously in the 1960s and 1970s but has declined since the 1980s. However, the divorce rate in the United States is still much higher than in most other countries.

It is estimated that 40 percent of children born to married parents in the United States will experience their parents' divorce (Hetherington & Stanley-Hagan, 2002). Let's examine some important questions about children in divorced families:

- *Are children better adjusted in intact, never-divorced families than in divorced families?* Most researchers agree that children from divorced families show poorer adjustment than their counterparts in nondivorced families (Hetherington, 2006; Lansford, 2009; Wallerstein, 2008) (see Figure 14.10). Those who have experienced multiple divorces are at greater risk. Children in divorced families are more likely than children in nondivorced families to have academic problems, to show externalized problems (such as acting out and delinquency)

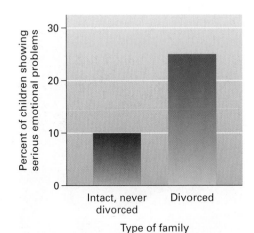

FIGURE 14.10 Divorce and Children's Emotional Problems. In Hetherington's research, 25 percent of children from divorced families showed serious emotional problems compared with only 10 percent of children from intact, never-divorced families. However, keep in mind that a substantial majority (75 percent) of the children from divorced families did not show serious emotional problems.

and internalized problems (such as anxiety and depression), to be less socially responsible, to have less competent intimate relationships, to drop out of school, to become sexually active at an early age, to take drugs, to associate with antisocial peers, to have low self-esteem, and to be less securely attached as young adults (Lansford, 2009). A recent study revealed that adolescent girls with divorced parents were especially vulnerable to developing symptoms of depression (Oldehinkel & others, 2008). Nonetheless, keep in mind that a majority of children in divorced families do not have significant adjustment problems (Ahrons, 2007). One study found that 20 years after their parents had divorced when they were children, approximately 80 percent of adults concluded that their parents' decision to divorce was a wise one (Ahrons, 2004).

Note that marital conflict may have negative consequences for children in the context of marriage or divorce (Cox & others, 2008; Cummings & Merrilees, 2009). A longitudinal study revealed that conflict in nondivorced families was associated with emotional problems in children (Amato, 2006). Indeed, many of the problems that children from divorced homes experience begin during the predivorce period, a time when parents are often in active conflict with each other. Thus, when children from divorced homes show problems, the problems may be due not only to the divorce, but to the marital conflict that led to it (Thompson, 2008).

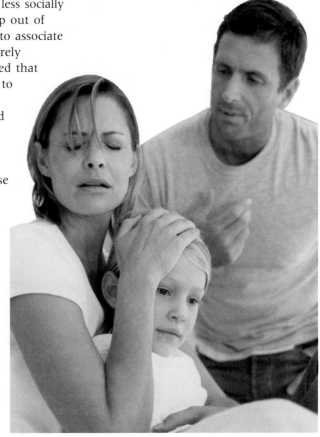

What concerns are involved in whether parents should stay together for the sake of the children or become divorced?

- *Should parents stay together for the sake of the children?* Whether parents should stay in an unhappy or conflicted marriage for the sake of their children is one of the most commonly asked questions about divorce (Deutsch & Pruett, 2009; Hetherington, 2006; Ziol-Guest, 2009). If the stresses and disruptions in family relationships associated with an unhappy, conflictual marriage that erode the well-being of children are reduced by the move to a divorced, single-parent family, divorce can be advantageous. However, if the diminished resources and increased risks associated with divorce also are accompanied by inept parenting and sustained or increased conflict, not only between the divorced couple but also among the parents, children, and siblings, the best choice for the children would be that an unhappy marriage be retained (Hetherington & Stanley-Hagan, 2002). It is difficult to determine how these "ifs" will play out when parents either remain together in an acrimonious marriage or become divorced.

- *How much do family processes matter in divorced families?* Family processes matter a great deal (Lansford, 2009; Pruett & Barker, 2009). When divorced parents' relationship with each other is harmonious, and when they use authoritative parenting, the adjustment of children improves (Hetherington, 2006). A number of researchers have shown that a disequilibrium, which includes diminished parenting skills, occurs in the year following the divorce, but that by two years after the divorce restabilization has occurred and parenting skills have improved (Hetherington, 1989).

- *What factors influence an individual child's vulnerability to suffering negative consequences as a result of living in a divorced family?* Among the factors involved in the child's risk and vulnerability are the child's adjustment prior to the divorce, as well as the child's personality and temperament, gender, and custody situation (Hetherington, 2006). Children whose parents later divorce show poorer adjustment before the breakup (Amato & Booth, 1996). Children who are socially mature and responsible, who show few

As marriage has become a more optional, less permanent institution in contemporary America, children and adolescents are encountering stresses and adaptive challenges associated with their parents' marital transitions.

—E. MAVIS HETHERINGTON
Contemporary Psychologist, University of Virginia

behavioral problems, and who have an easy temperament are better able to cope with their parents' divorce. Children with a difficult temperament often have problems in coping with their parents' divorce (Hetherington, 2006).

• *What role does socioeconomic status play in the lives of children in divorced families?* Custodial mothers experience the loss of about one-fourth to one-half of their predivorce income, in comparison with a loss of only one-tenth by custodial fathers (Emery, 1999). This income loss for divorced mothers is accompanied by increased workloads, high rates of job instability, and residential moves to less desirable neighborhoods with inferior schools (Sayer, 2006).

In sum, many factors are involved in determining how divorce influences a child's development (Hetherington, 2006). To read about some strategies for helping children cope with the divorce of their parents, see the *Applications in Life-Span Development* interlude.

Applications in Life-Span Development

COMMUNICATING WITH CHILDREN ABOUT DIVORCE

Ellen Galinsky and Judy David (1988) developed a number of guidelines for communicating with children about divorce:

• *Explain the separation.* As soon as daily activities in the home make it obvious that one parent is leaving, tell the children. If possible, both parents should be present when children are told about the separation to come. The reasons for the separation are very difficult for young children to understand. No matter what parents tell children, children can find reasons to argue against the separation. It is extremely important for parents to tell the children who will take care of them and to describe the specific arrangements for seeing the other parent.

• *Explain that the separation is not the child's fault.* Young children often believe their parents' separation or divorce is their own fault. Therefore, it is important to tell children that they are not the cause of the separation. Parents need to repeat this point a number of times.

• *Explain that it may take time to feel better.* Tell young children that it's normal not to feel good about what is happening and that many other children feel this way when their parents become separated. It is also okay for divorced parents to share some of their emotions with children, by saying something like "I'm having a hard time since the separation just like you, but I know it's going to get better after a while." Such statements are best kept brief and should not criticize the other parent.

• *Keep the door open for further discussion.* Tell your children to come to you any time they want to talk about the separation. It is healthy for children to express their pent-up emotions in discussions with their parents and to learn that the parents are willing to listen to their feelings and fears.

• *Provide as much continuity as possible.* The less children's worlds are disrupted by the separation, the easier their transition to a single-parent family will be. This guideline means maintaining the rules already in place as much as possible. Children need parents who care enough not only to give them warmth and nurturance but also to set reasonable limits.

- *Provide support for your children and yourself.* After a divorce or separation, parents are as important to children as before the divorce or separation. Divorced parents need to provide children with as much support as possible. Parents function best when other people are available to give them support as adults and as parents. Divorced parents can find people who provide practical help and with whom they can talk about their problems.

Stepfamilies

Not only are parents divorcing more, they are also getting remarried more (Ganong, Coleman, & Hans, 2006). The number of remarriages involving children has grown steadily in recent years. About half of all children whose parents divorce will have a stepparent within four years of parental separation. However, divorces occur at a 10 percent higher rate in remarriages than in first marriages (Cherlin & Furstenberg, 1994).

In some cases, the stepfamily may have been preceded by the death of the spouse. However, by far the largest number of stepfamilies are preceded by divorce rather than death.

Three common types of stepfamily structure are (1) stepfather, (2) stepmother, and (3) blended or complex. In stepfather families, the mother typically had custody of the children and remarried, introducing a stepfather into her children's lives. In stepmother families, the father usually had custody and remarried, introducing a stepmother into his children's lives. In a blended or complex stepfamily, both parents bring children from previous marriages to live in the newly formed stepfamily.

In E. Mavis Hetherington's (2006) most recent longitudinal analyses, children and adolescents who had been in a simple stepfamily (stepfather or stepmother) for a number of years were adjusting better than in the early years of the remarried family and were functioning well in comparison to children and adolescents in conflicted nondivorced families and children and adolescents in complex (blended) stepfamilies. More than 75 percent of the adolescents in long-established simple stepfamilies described their relationships with their stepparents as "close" or "very close." Hetherington (2006) concluded that in long-established simple stepfamilies adolescents seem eventually to benefit from the presence of a stepparent and the resources provided by the stepparent.

Children often have better relationships with their custodial parents (mothers in stepfather families, fathers in stepmother families) than with stepparents (Santrock, Sitterle, & Warshak, 1988). Also, children in simple families (stepmother, stepfather) often show better adjustment than their counterparts in complex (blended) families (Anderson & others, 1999; Hetherington & Kelly, 2002).

As in divorced families, children in stepfamilies show more adjustment problems than children in nondivorced families (Hetherington & Kelly, 2002). The adjustment problems are similar to those found among children of divorced parents—academic problems and lower self-esteem, for example (Anderson & others, 1999). However, it is important to recognize that a majority of children in stepfamilies do not have problems. In one analysis, 25 percent of children from stepfamilies showed adjustment problems compared with 10 percent in intact, never-divorced families (Hetherington & Kelly, 2002). Adolescence is an especially difficult time for the formation of a stepfamily (Anderson & others, 1999). This may occur because becoming part of a stepfamily exacerbates normal adolescent concerns about identity, sexuality, and autonomy.

How does living in a stepfamily influence a child's development?

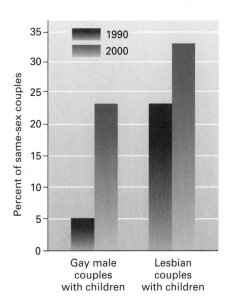

FIGURE 14.11 Amount of Same-Sex Couples with Children.

An increasing number of Hollywood celebrities are adopting children from developing countries. Actress Angelina Jolie recently adopted a baby girl, Zahara (*above*), in Ethiopia.

Gay Male and Lesbian Parents

Increasingly, gay male and lesbian couples are creating families that include children (Patterson, 2009) (see Figure 14.11). Approximately 33 percent of lesbian couples and 23 percent of gay male couples are parents (Patterson, 2004). There may be more than 1 million gay and lesbian parents in the United States today.

Like heterosexual couples, gay male and lesbian parents vary greatly. They may be single or they may have same-gender partners. Many lesbian mothers and gay fathers are noncustodial parents because they lost custody of their children to heterosexual spouses after a divorce.

Most children of gay and lesbian parents were born in a heterosexual relationship that ended in a divorce: in most cases, it was probably a relationship in which one or both parents only later identified themselves as gay male or lesbian. In other cases, lesbians and gay men became parents as a result of donor insemination and surrogates, or through adoption. Parenthood among lesbians and gay men is controversial. Opponents claim that being raised by gay male or lesbian parents harms the child's development. But researchers have found few differences in children growing up with lesbian mothers or gay fathers and children growing up with heterosexual parents (Patterson, 2009). For example, children growing up in gay or lesbian families are just as popular with their peers, and there are no differences in the adjustment and mental health of children living in these families when they are compared with children in heterosexual families (Hyde & DeLamater, 2008). Also, the overwhelming majority of children growing up in a gay male or lesbian family have a heterosexual orientation (Tasker & Golombok, 1997).

Adoptive Parents and Adopted Children

Another variation in the type of family in which children live involves *adoption*, the social and legal process by which a parent-child relationship is established between persons unrelated at birth (Cohen & others, 2008; Rosnati, Montirosso, & Barni, 2008). As we see next, an increase in diversity has characterized the adoption of children in the United States in recent years.

The Increased Diversity of Adopted Children and Adoptive Parents A number of changes have characterized adoptive children and adoptive parents in the last three to four decades (Brodzinsky & Pinderhughes, 2002). In the first half of the 20th century, most U.S. adopted children were healthy, non-Latino White infants who were adopted at birth or soon after; however, in recent decades as abortion became legal and contraception increased, fewer of these infants became available for adoption. Increasingly, U.S. couples adopted a much wider diversity of children—from other countries, from other ethnic groups, children with physical and/or mental problems, and children who had been neglected or abused.

Changes also have characterized adoptive parents in the last three to four decades (Brodzinsky & Pindehughes, 2002). In the first half of the 20th century, most adoptive parents were from non-Latino White middle or upper socioeconomic status backgrounds who were married and did not have any type of disability. However, in recent decades, increased diversity has characterized adoptive parents. Many adoption agencies today have no income requirements for adoptive parents and now allow adults from a wide range of backgrounds to adopt children, including single adults, gay male and lesbian adults, and older adults.

Do these changes matter? They open opportunities for many children and many couples, but possible effects of changes in the characteristics of parents on the outcomes for children are still unknown. For example, in one study, adopted adolescents were more likely to have problems if the adoptive parents had low levels of education (Miller & others, 2000). In another study, international adoptees showed fewer behavior problems and were less likely to be using mental health services than domestic adoptees (Juffer & van IJzendoorn, 2005). More research is needed before definitive conclusions can be reached about the changing demographic characteristics of adoption.

The changes in adoption practice over the last several decades make it difficult to generalize about the average adopted child or average adoptive parent. As we see next, though, some researchers have provided useful comparisons between adopted children and nonadopted children and their families.

Developmental Outcomes for Adopted and Nonadopted Children How do adopted children fare after they are adopted? Children who are adopted very early in their lives are more likely to have positive outcomes than children adopted later in life (Bernard & Dozier, 2008).

In general, adopted children and adolescents are more likely to experience psychological and school-related problems than nonadopted children (Bernard & Dozier, 2008). For example, a meta-analysis (a statistical procedure that combines the results of a number of studies) revealed that adoptees were far more likely to be using mental health services than their nonadopted counterparts (Juffer & van IJzendoorn, 2005). Adopted children also showed more behavior problems than nonadoptees, but this difference was small. A recent large-scale study found that adopted children are more likely to have a learning disability than are nonadopted children (Altarac & Saroha, 2007).

Research that contrasts adopted and nonadopted adolescents has also found positive characteristics among the adopted adolescents. For example, in one study, although adopted adolescents were more likely than nonadopted adolescents to use illicit drugs and to engage in delinquent behavior, the adopted adolescents were also less likely to be withdrawn and more likely to engage in more prosocial behavior, such as being altruistic, caring, and supportive of others (Sharma, McGue, & Benson, 1996).

In short, the vast majority of adopted children (including those adopted at older ages, transracially, and across national borders) adjust effectively, and their parents report considerable satisfaction with their decision to adopt (Brodzinsky & Pinderhughes, 2002). In one recent national study, there were no differences in the antisocial behavior of adopted and nonadopted young adults (Grotevant & others, 2006). A recent research review of 88 studies also revealed no difference in the self-esteem of adopted and nonadopted children, as well as no differences between transracial and same-race adoptees (Juffer & IJzendoorn, (2007). Furthermore, adopted children fare much better than children in long-term foster care or in an institutional environment (Bernard & Dozier, 2008).

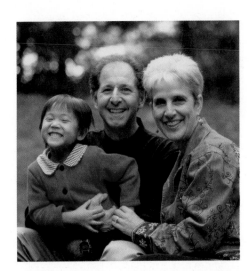

Parenting Adopted Children Many of the keys to effectively parenting adopted children are no different from those for effectively parenting biological children: Be supportive and caring, be involved and monitor the child's behavior and whereabouts, be a good communicator, and help the child to learn to develop self-control. However, parents of adopted children face some unique circumstances (Fontenot, 2007; Wolfgram, 2008). They need to recognize the differences involved in adoptive family life, communicate about these differences, show respect for the birth family, and support the child's search for self and identity.

Because many children begin to ask where they came from when they are about 4 to 6 years old, this is a natural time to begin to talk in simple ways to children about their adoption status (Warshak, 2008). Some parents (although not as many as in the past) decide not to tell their children about the adoption. This secrecy may create psychological risks for the child if he or she later finds out about the adoption.

What are some strategies for parenting adopted children?

Review and Reflect: Learning Goal 3

3 **Characterize parenting and how it affects children's development**

REVIEW

- What are some parental roles?
- What are four main parenting styles? Which parenting style is most often linked with children's social competence? Is physical punishment a wise choice by parents? Does coparenting have positive effects on children? What is the nature of child maltreatment?
- How can parent-adolescent relationships and parent–emerging adult relationships be described?
- What is the link between working parents and children's development?
- How does divorce affect children's development?
- What influence does growing up in a stepfamily have on children's development?
- What characterizes gay male and lesbian parenting?
- How do the lives of adoptive parents and adopted children differ from the lives of nonadoptive parents and nonadopted children?

REFLECT

- What stereotypes exist about children from these types of families: working mother; divorced; stepfamily; gay male and lesbian; and adoptive?

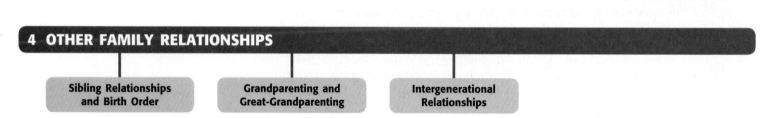

4 OTHER FAMILY RELATIONSHIPS

| Sibling Relationships and Birth Order | Grandparenting and Great-Grandparenting | Intergenerational Relationships |

Important as child-parent relationships are to children's development, other family relationships are also significant. Here we briefly examine sibling relationships, grandparenting and great-grandparenting, and intergenerational relationships.

Sibling Relationships and Birth Order

What are sibling relationships like? How extensively does birth order influence behavior?

Sibling Relationships Approximately 80 percent of American children have one or more siblings—that is, sisters and brothers (Dunn, 2007). Any of you who have grown up with siblings probably have a rich memory of aggressive, hostile interchanges. Siblings in the presence of each other when they are 2 to 4 years of age, on average, have a conflict once every 10 minutes and then the conflicts decrease somewhat from 5 to 7 years of age (Kramer, 2006). What do parents do when they encounter siblings having a verbal or physical confrontation? One study revealed that they do one of three things: (1) intervene and try to help them resolve the conflict, (2) admonish or threaten them, or (3) do nothing at all (Kramer

& Perozynski, 1999). Of interest is that in families with two siblings 2 to 5 years of age, the most frequent parental reaction is to do nothing at all. A recent review concluded that sibling relationships in adolescence are not as close, are not as intense, and are more egalitarian than in childhood (East, 2009).

Negative aspects of sibling relationships, such as high conflict, are linked to negative outcomes for children and adolescents. The negative outcomes can develop not only through conflict but also through direct modeling of a sibling's behavior, as when a younger sibling has an older sibling who has poor study habits and engages in delinquent behavior. By contrast, close and supportive sibling relationships can buffer the negative effects of stressful circumstances in children's and adolescents' lives.

Laurie Kramer (2006), who had conducted a number of research studies on siblings, says that not intervening and letting sibling conflict escalate is not a good strategy. She developed a program titled "More Fun with Sisters and Brothers," which teaches 4- to 8-year-old siblings social skills for developing positive interactions (Kramer & Radey, 1997). Among the social skills taught in the program are how to appropriately initiate play, how to accept and refuse invitations to play, how to take another's perspective, how to deal with angry feelings, and how to manage conflict.

However, conflict is only one of the many dimensions of sibling relations (Steelman & Koch, 2009). Sibling relationships include helping, sharing, teaching, fighting, and playing, and siblings can act as emotional supports, rivals, and communication partners (Howe & Recchia, 2008). One study found that adolescent siblings spent an average of 10 hours a week together with an average of 12 percent of that time spent in constructive time (creative activities such as art, music, and hobbies; sports; religious activities; and games) and 25 percent in nonconstructive time (watching TV and hanging out) (Tucker, McHale, & Crouter, 2003). In Mexican American families, adolescent siblings spend even more time together—more than 17 hours a week (Updegraff & others, 2005).

Judy Dunn (2007), a leading expert on sibling relationships, recently described three important characteristics of sibling relationships:

- *Emotional quality of the relationship.* Both intensive positive and negative emotions are often expressed by siblings toward each other. Many children and adolescents have mixed feelings toward their siblings.

- *Familiarity and intimacy of the relationship.* Siblings typically know each other very well, and this intimacy suggests that they can either provide support or tease and undermine each other, depending on the situation.

Children's sibling relationships are characterized by both sibling rivalry and positive interchanges. *What are some characteristics of these negative and positive interactions?*

• *Variation of the relationship.* Some siblings describe their relationships more positively than others. Thus, there is considerable variation in sibling relationships. We've indicated that many siblings have mixed feelings about each other, but some children and adolescents mainly describe their sibling in warm, affectionate ways, whereas others primarily talk about how irritating and mean a sibling is.

Do parents usually favor one sibling over others—and if so, does it make a difference in an adolescent's development? One recent study of 384 adolescent sibling pairs revealed that 65 percent of their mothers and 70 percent of their fathers showed favoritism toward one sibling (Shebloski, Conger, & Widaman, 2005). When favoritism of one sibling occurred, it was linked to lower self-esteem and sadness in the less-favored sibling.

In some instances, siblings may be stronger socializing influences on the child than parents are (Cicirelli, 1994). Someone close in age to the child—such as a sibling—may be able to understand the child's problems and communicate more effectively than parents can. In dealing with peers, coping with difficult teachers, and discussing such taboo subjects as sex, siblings may have more influence than parents.

Is sibling interaction the same around the world? In industrialized societies, such as the United States, parents tend to delegate responsibility for younger siblings to older siblings primarily to give the parents freedom to pursue other activities. However, in nonindustrialized countries, such as Kenya, the older sibling's role as a caregiver to younger siblings has much more importance. In industrialized countries, the older sibling's caregiving role is often discretionary; in nonindustrialized countries, it is more obligatory (Cicirelli, 1994).

Birth Order Whether a child has older or younger siblings has been linked to development of certain personality characteristics. For example, a recent review concluded that "firstborns are the most intelligent, achieving, and conscientious, while later-borns are the most rebellious, liberal, and agreeable" (Paulhus, 2008, p. 210). Compared with later-born children, firstborn children have also been described as more adult-oriented, helpful, conforming, and self-controlled. However, when such birth-order differences are reported, they often are small.

What might account for even small differences related to birth order? Proposed explanations usually point to variations in interactions with parents and siblings associated with being in a specific position in the family. This is especially true in the case of the firstborn child (Teti, 2001). The oldest child is the only one who does not have to share parental love and affection with other siblings—until another sibling comes along. An infant requires more attention than an older child; thus the firstborn sibling receives less attention after the newborn arrives. Does this result in conflict between parents and the firstborn? In one research study, mothers became more negative, coercive, and restraining and played less with the firstborn following the birth of a second child (Dunn & Kendrick, 1982).

The one-child family is becoming much more common in China because of the strong motivation to limit the population growth in the People's Republic of China. The effects of this policy have not been fully examined. *In general, what have researchers found the only child to be like?*

What is the only child like? The popular conception is that the only child is a "spoiled brat," with such undesirable characteristics as dependency, lack of self-control, and self-centered behavior. But researchers present a more positive portrayal of the only child. Only children often are achievement-oriented and display a desirable personality, especially in comparison with later-borns and children from large families (Falbo & Poston, 1993).

So far, our discussion suggests that birth order might be a strong predictor of behavior. However, an increasing number of family researchers stress that when all of the factors that influence behavior are considered, birth order itself shows limited ability to predict behavior. Think about some of the other important factors in children's lives that influence their behavior beyond birth order.

They include heredity, models of competency or incompetency that parents present to children on a daily basis, peer influences, school influences, socioeconomic factors, sociohistorical factors, and cultural variations. When someone says firstborns are always like this but last-borns are always like that, the person is making overly simplistic statements that do not adequately take into account the complexity of influences on a child's development.

Sibling Relationships in Adulthood   Sibling relationships persist over the entire life span for most adults (Bedford, 2009; Cicirelli, 2009). Eighty-five percent of today's adults have at least one living sibling. Sibling relationships in adulthood may be extremely close, apathetic, or highly rivalrous. The majority of sibling relationships in adulthood have been found to be close (Cicirelli, 2009). Those siblings who are psychologically close to each other in adulthood tended to be that way in childhood. It is rare for sibling closeness to develop for the first time in adulthood (Dunn, 1984). A recent study revealed that adult siblings often provide practical and emotional support to each other (Voorpostel & Blieszner, 2008).

Grandparenting and Great-Grandparenting

The increase in longevity is influencing the nature of grandparenting (Szinovacz, 2009). In 1900 only 4 percent of 10-year-old children had four living grandparents, but in 2000 that figure had risen to more than 40 percent. And in 1990 only about 20 percent of children at 30 years of age had living grandparents, a figure that is projected to increase to 80 percent in 2020 (Hagestad & Uhlenberg, 2007). Further increases in longevity are likely to support this trend in the future, although the current trend in delaying childbearing is likely to undermine it (Szinovacz, 2009).

Grandparents play important roles in the lives of many grandchildren (Thiele & Whelen, 2008). Many adults become grandparents for the first time during middle age. Researchers have consistently found that grandmothers have more contact with grandchildren than grandfathers (Watson, Randolph, & Lyons, 2005). Perhaps women tend to define their role as grandmothers as part of their responsibility for maintaining ties between family members across generations. Men may have fewer expectations about the grandfather role and see it as more voluntary.

Grandparent Roles and Styles   What is the meaning of the grandparent role? Three prominent meanings are attached to being a grandparent (Neugarten & Weinstein, 1964). For some older adults, being a grandparent is a source of biological reward and continuity. For others, being a grandparent is a source of emotional self-fulfillment, generating feelings of companionship and satisfaction that may have been missing in earlier adult-child relationships. And for yet others, being a grandparent is a remote role. A recent study revealed that grandparenting can provide a sense of purpose and a feeling of being valued during middle and late adulthood when generative needs are strong (Thiele & Whelan, 2008).

The grandparent role may have different functions in different families, in different ethnic groups and cultures, and in different situations (Watson, Randolph, & Lyons, 2005). For example, in one study of non-Latino White, African American, and Mexican American grandparents and grandchildren, the Mexican American grandparents saw their grandchildren most frequently, provided the most support for the grandchildren and their parents, and had the most satisfying relationships with their grandchildren (Bengtson, 1985). And in a study of three generations of families in Chicago, grandmothers had closer relationships with their children and grandchildren and gave more personal advice than grandfathers did (Hagestad, 1985).

The diversity of grandparenting also was apparent in an early investigation of how grandparents interacted with their grandchildren (Neugarten & Weinstein,

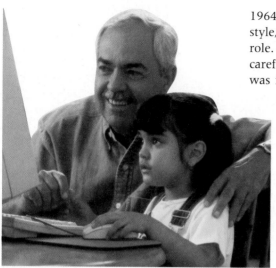

What is the changing profile of grandparents in the United States?

1964). Three styles were dominant—formal, fun-seeking, and distant. In the formal style, the grandparent performed what was considered to be a proper and prescribed role. These grandparents showed a strong interest in their grandchildren, but were careful not to give child-rearing advice. In the fun-seeking style, the grandparent was informal and playful. Grandchildren were a source of leisure activity; mutual satisfaction was emphasized. A substantial portion of grandparents were distant figures. In the distant-figure style, the grandparent was benevolent but interaction was infrequent. Grandparents who were over the age of 65 were more likely to display a formal style of interaction; those under 65 were more likely to display a fun-seeking style.

The Changing Profile of Grandparents An increasing number of U.S. grandchildren live with their grandparents (Hayslip & Kaminski, 2008). In 1980, 2.3 million grandchildren lived with their grandparents, but in 2005 that figure had reached 6.1 million (U.S. Census Bureau, 2006). Divorce, adolescent pregnancies, and drug use by parents are the main reasons that grandparents are thrust back into the "parenting" role they thought they had shed. One study of grandparents raising their grandchildren found that stress was linked with three conditions: younger grandparents, grandchildren with physical and psychological problems, and low family cohesion (Sands & Goldberg-Glen, 2000). A recent study revealed that grandparent involvement was linked with better adjustment for adolescents in single-parent and stepparent families than in two-parent biological families (Attar-Schwartz & others, 2009).

Less than 20 percent of grandparents whose grandchildren move in with them are 65 years old or older. Almost half of the grandchildren who move in with grandparents are raised by a single grandmother. These families are mainly African American (53 percent). When both grandparents are raising grandchildren, the families are overwhelmingly non-Latino White.

Grandparents who take in grandchildren are in better health, are better educated, are more likely to be working outside the home, and are younger than grandparents who move in with their children. According to the 2006 U.S. Census report, a majority of the grandparents living with their children contributed to the family income and provided child care while parents worked. Only about 10 percent of the grandparents who move in with their children and grandchildren are in poverty. Almost half of the grandparents who move in with their children are immigrants. Partly because women live longer than men, more grandmothers than grandfathers live with their children. About 70 percent of the grandparents who move in with their children are grandmothers.

Grandparents who are full-time caregivers for grandchildren are at elevated risk for health problems, depression, and stress (Silverstein, 2009). Caring for grandchildren is linked with these problems in part because full-time grandparent caregivers often are characterized by low-income, minority status, and are not married (Minkler & Fuller-Thompson, 2005). Grandparents who are part-time caregivers are less likely to have the negative health portrait that full-time grandparent caregivers have. In a recent study of part-time grandparent caregivers, few negative effects on grandparents were found (Hughes & others, 2007).

In some cases, divorce may increase grandparents' contact with children, as when grandparents assume a stronger caregiving role; in others, a custodial parent may try to restrict grandparents' time with children. One recent study revealed that when children's relationships with their father deteriorated after a divorce, their relationship with their paternal grandparents was distant, negative, or nonexistent (Ahrons, 2007).

As divorce and remarriage have become more common, a special concern of grandparents is visitation privileges with their grandchildren (Kivnick & Sinclair,

2007). In the last two decades, more states have passed laws giving grandparents the right to petition a court for visitation privileges with their grandchildren, even if a parent objects. Whether such forced visitation rights for grandparents are in the child's best interest is still being debated.

Great-Grandparenting Because of increased longevity, more grandparents today than in the past are also great-grandparents. At the turn of the previous century, the three-generation family was common, but now the four-generation family is common. One contribution of great-grandparents is to transmit family history by telling their children, grandchildren, and great-grandchildren where the family came from, what their members achieved, what they endured, and how their lives changed over the years (Harris, 2002).

There has been little research on great-grandparenting. One study examined the relationship between young adults and their grandparents and great-grandparents (Roberto & Skoglund, 1996). The young adults interacted with and participated in more activities with their grandparents than with their great-grandparents. They also perceived their grandparents to have a more defined role and to be more influential in their lives than great-grandparents.

Intergenerational Relationships

Family is important to most people and connections between generations play important roles in development through the life span (Bengtsson & Psouni, 2008; Swartz, 2008). When 21,000 adults aged 40 to 79 in 21 countries were asked, "When you think of who you are, you think mainly of _____," 63 percent said "family," 9 percent said "religion," and 8 percent said "work" (HSBC Insurance, 2007). In this study, middle-aged and older adults around the world expressed responsibility for the welfare of their families. In all 21 countries, middle-aged and older adults expressed a strong feeling of responsibility between generations in their family with the strongest intergenerational ties indicated in Saudi Arabia, India, and Turkey. More than 80 percent of the middle-aged and older reported that adults have a duty to care for their parents (and parents-in-law) in time of need later in life.

Adults in midlife play important roles in the lives of the young and the old (Ha & Ingersoll-Dayton, 2008). Middle-aged adults share their experience and transmit values to the younger generation. They may be launching children and experiencing the empty nest, adjusting to having grown children return home, or becoming grandparents. They also may be giving or receiving financial assistance, caring for a widowed or sick parent, or adapting to being the oldest generation after both parents have died.

A valuable service that adult children can perform is to coordinate and monitor services for an aging parent who becomes disabled (Huyck, Ayalon, & Yoder, 2006). This might involve locating a nursing home and monitoring its quality, procuring medical services, arranging public service assistance, and handling finances. In some cases, adult children provide direct assistance with daily living, including such activities as eating, bathing, and dressing. Even less severely impaired older adults may need help with shopping, housework, transportation, home maintenance, and bill paying.

A recent study revealed that even when aging parents had health problems, they and their children generally described positive changes in their relationship in recent years (Fingerman & others, 2007). However, in most cases researchers have found that relationships between aging parents and their children are usually characterized by ambivalence. Perceptions include love, reciprocal help, and shared values on

At the beginning of the twentieth century, the three-generation family was common, but now the four-generation family is common as well. Thus, an increasing number of grandparents are also great-grandparents. The four-generation family shown here is the Jordans—author John Santrock's mother-in-law, daughter, granddaughter, and wife.

Middle-aged and older adults around the world show a strong sense of family responsibility. A recent study of middle-aged and older adults in 21 countries revealed the strongest intergenerational ties in Saudi Arabia.

What is the nature of intergenerational relationships?

the positive side and isolation, family conflicts and problems, abuse, neglect, and caregiver stress on the negative side.

With each new generation, personality characteristics, attitudes, and values are replicated or changed (Pratt & others, 2008). As older family members die, their biological, intellectual, emotional, and personal legacies are carried on in the next generation. Their children become the oldest generation and their grandchildren the second generation. As adult children become middle-aged they often develop more positive perceptions of their parents (Field, 1999). In one study, conflicts between mothers and daughters decreased across the life course in both the United States and Japan (Akiyama & Antonucci, 1999).

For the most part, family members maintain considerable contact across generations (Miller-Day, 2004). However, a recent study found that married men and women have a lower incidence of intergenerational contact than never married or divorced individuals (Sarkisian & Gerstel, 2008). In this study, married adults were less likely to live with their parents, keep in touch, and give or receive emotional, financial, or practical help. Nonetheless, another recent study revealed that when young adults have children they are more likely to see their parents than if they don't have children (Bucx, Knijn, & Hagendoorn, 2008).

Both similarity and dissimilarity across generations are found. For example, similarity between parents and an adult child is most noticeable in religion and politics, least in gender roles, lifestyle, and work orientation.

What are the most common conflicts between parents and their adult children? In one study, they included communication and interaction style (such as "He is always yelling" and "She is too critical"), habits and lifestyle choices (such as sexual activity, living arrangements), child-rearing practices and values (such as decisions about having children, being permissive or controlling), politics, religion, and ideology (such as lack of religious involvement) (Clarke & others, 1999). In this study, there were generational differences in perceptions of the main conflicts between parents and adult children. Parents most often listed habits and lifestyle choices; adult children cited communication and interaction style.

Gender differences also characterize intergenerational relationships (Bengtsson & Psouni, 2008; Etaugh & Bridges, 2010). Women have an especially important role in connecting family relationships across generations. Women's relationships across generations are thought to be closer than other family bonds (Merrill, 2009). In one study, mothers and their daughters had much closer relationships during their adult years than mothers and sons, fathers and daughters, and fathers and sons (Rossi, 1989). Also in this study, married men were more involved with their wives' kin than with their own. And maternal grandmothers and maternal aunts were cited twice as often as their counterparts on the paternal side of the family as the most important or loved relative. Also, a recent study revealed that mothers' intergenerational ties were more influential for grandparent-grandchild relationships than fathers' (Monserud, 2008).

The following studies provide further evidence of the importance of intergenerational relationships in children's development:

• Adult children of divorce who were classified as securely attached were less likely to divorce in the early years of their marriage than their insecurely attached counterparts (Crowell, Treboux, & Brockmeyer, 2009).

• Parents who smoked early and often, and persisted in becoming regular smokers, were more likely to have adolescents who became smokers (Chassin & others, 2008).

• Evidence was found for the intergenerational transmission of conduct disorder (multiple delinquent activities) across three generations, with the connection stronger for males than females (D'Onofrio & others, 2007).

Review and Reflect: Learning Goal 4

 Explain other aspects of family relationships

REVIEW

- How do siblings interact with each other? How is birth order linked with developmental outcomes?
- What is the nature of grandparenting and great-grandparenting?
- How do intergenerational relationships influence development?

REFLECT

- Do you have a sibling(s)? If so, what is your relationship like? Has it changed over the years? If you don't have a sibling, how do you think your life would have been different with one or more siblings?

Reach Your Learning Goals

Families, Lifestyles, and Parenting

1 FAMILY PROCESSES: DESCRIBE SOME IMPORTANT FAMILY PROCESSES

Reciprocal Socialization

- Reciprocal socialization is socialization that is bidirectional; children socialize parents just as parents socialize children. Synchrony and scaffolding are two important types of reciprocal socialization.

Family as a System

- The family system consists of subsystems defined by generation, gender, and role. These subsystems interact with each other and can have direct and indirect effects on each other. Each family member participates in dyadic and polyadic subsystems, some defined by division of labor, some by attachments.

Sociocultural and Historical Influences

- Sociocultural and historical contexts influence families, reflecting Bronfenbrenner's concepts of macrosystem and chronosystem. Both great upheavals such as war and subtle transitions in ways of life may influence families. A major change in families in the last several decades has been the extensive immigration of Latino and Asian families into the United States. Media and technology, notably computers, play a major role in the changing family. Increased dissatisfaction and restlessness resulting in divorce and remarriage also are factors.

Multiple Developmental Trajectories

- Adults follow one developmental trajectory and children another one. How these trajectories mesh is important for understanding timing of entry into various family tasks, such as the timing of child care and reentry into the workforce.

2 THE DIVERSITY OF ADULT LIFESTYLES: DISCUSS THE DIVERSITY OF ADULT LIFESTYLES AND HOW THEY INFLUENCE PEOPLE'S LIVES

Single Adults

- Being single has become an increasingly prominent lifestyle. There are advantages and disadvantages to being single, autonomy being one of the advantages. Intimacy, loneliness, and finding a positive identity in a marriage-oriented society are concerns of single adults. Approximately 8 percent of 65-year-old adults have never been married. Many of them cope effectively with loneliness in old age.

Cohabiting Adults

- Cohabitation is an increasing lifestyle for many adults. Cohabitation offers some advantages as well as problems. Cohabitation does not lead to greater marital happiness but rather to no differences or differences suggesting that cohabitation is not good for a marriage. An increasing number of older adults cohabit, in many cases more for companionship than for love.

Married Adults

- Even though adults are remaining single longer and the divorce rate is high, Americans still show a strong predilection for marriage. The age at which individuals marry, expectations about what the marriage will be like, and the developmental course of marriage vary not only over time within a culture, but also across cultures. Gottman has conducted extensive research on what makes marriages work. In his research, these principles characterize good marriages: establishing love maps, nurturing fondness and admiration, turning toward each other instead of away, letting your partner influence you, solving solvable conflicts, overcoming gridlock, and creating shared meaning. Premarital education is associated with positive relationship outcomes. The benefits of marriage include better physical and mental health and a longer life. A majority of middle-aged adults who are married say their marriage is very good or excellent. The time from retirement until death is sometimes called the final stage in the marital process. Married older adults are often happier than single older adults.

Divorced Adults	• The U.S. divorce rate increased dramatically in the twentieth century but began to decline in the 1980s. Marrying young, low educational levels, lack of a religious affiliation, having divorced parents, and having a baby before marriage are factors associated with a higher incidence of divorce. Loneliness, lowered self-esteem, anxiety about the future, and difficulty trusting someone else in a romantic relationship affect divorced men and women. Separated men and women can experience higher rates of chronic health problems, alcoholism, clinical depression, and admissions to psychiatric hospitals. The main causes of divorce for women are verbal, physical, or emotional abuse; alcohol or drug abuse; and cheating—the main causes for men are falling out of love; cheating; and different values, lifestyles.
Remarried Adults	• Divorced adults remarry on average within four years of their divorce. Stepfamilies are complex and adjustment is difficult. Only about one-third of stepfamily couples stay remarried. Rising divorce rates, increased longevity, and better health have led to an increase in remarriage by older adults.
Gay Male and Lesbian Adults	• One of the most striking findings about gay male and lesbian couples is how similar they are to heterosexual couples—for example, gay male and lesbian couples prefer committed, long-term relationships and work to find a balance of romantic love, affection, and autonomy. There are many misconceptions about gay male and lesbian adults.

3 PARENTING: CHARACTERIZE PARENTING AND HOW IT AFFECTS CHILDREN'S DEVELOPMENT

Parental Roles	• Currently, there is a trend toward having children at a later age, having fewer children, and choosing when and if to have children. The transition to parenting involves disequilibrium and adaptation. A key aspect of being a competent parent is effectively managing children's lives.
Parenting Styles and Discipline	• Authoritarian, authoritative, neglectful, and indulgent are four main parenting styles. Authoritative parenting is the style most often associated with children's social competence. Physical punishment is widely used by U.S. parents, but there are a number of reasons why it is not a good choice. Coparenting can have positive effects on children's development if there are parental warmth and cooperation. The four main types of child maltreatment are physical abuse, child neglect, sexual abuse, and emotional abuse. An understanding of child abuse requires information about cultural, familial, and community influences. Child maltreatment places the child at risk for a number of developmental problems.
Parent-Adolescent and Parent–Emerging Adult Relationships	• Adolescents seek to be independent, but secure attachment to parents is positive for development. Conflict with parents often increases in adolescence, but it usually is moderate rather than severe. An increasing number of emerging adults are returning to live at home with their parents, often for economic reasons. Both emerging adults and their parents need to adapt when emerging adults return home to live.
Working Parents	• In general, the nature of parents' work is more important to children's development than whether one or both parents work outside the home. Parenting quality can be affected by long hours, overtime, and lack of autonomy at work. The effects of maternal employment are still debated.
Children in Divorced Families	• Overall, divorce is linked with adjustment problems in children, but not for all children. Whether parents should stay together for the sake of the children is a difficult question to answer. Family processes, such as harmony between parents, quality of parenting, and support systems, matter in divorced children's development. So does socioeconomic status.
Stepfamilies	• Children in stepparent families have more adjustment problems, such as academic problems and lowered self-esteem, than their counterparts in nondivorced families.

Gay Male and Lesbian Parents

Adoptive Parents and Adopted Children

Adolescence is an especially difficult time for remarriage of parents to occur. Restabilization takes longer in stepfamilies than in divorced families.

• Researchers have found few differences between children growing up in gay male or lesbian families and children growing up in heterosexual families.

• Although adopted children and adolescents have more problems than their nonadopted counterparts, the vast majority of adopted children adapt effectively. When adoption occurs very early in development, the outcomes for the child are improved. Because of the dramatic changes that have occurred in adoption in recent decades, it is difficult to generalize about the average adopted child or average adoptive family.

4   OTHER FAMILY RELATIONSHIPS: EXPLAIN OTHER ASPECTS OF FAMILY RELATIONSHIPS

Sibling Relationships and Birth Order

Grandparenting and Great-Grandparenting

Intergenerational Relationships

• Siblings interact with each other in positive and negative ways. Birth order is related in certain ways to child characteristics, but some critics argue that birth order is not a good predictor of behavior. Sibling relationships persist over the entire life span for most adults.

• There are different grandparent roles and styles. Grandmothers spend more time with grandchildren than grandfathers, and the grandmother role involves greater expectations for maintaining ties across generations than the grandfather role. The profile of grandparents is changing, because of such factors as divorce and remarriage. An increasing number of U.S. grandchildren live with their grandparents. Because of increased longevity, more grandparents today are also great-grandparents. One contribution of great-grandparents is family history.

• Family members usually maintain contact across generations. Mothers and daughters have the closest relationships. The middle-aged generation, which may have launched children and be caring for a widowed or sick parent, plays an important role in linking generations by sharing their experiences and transmitting their values to the younger generation.

KEY TERMS

reciprocal socialization 508
multiple developmental
    trajectories 510
authoritarian parenting 525

authoritative
    parenting 525
neglectful parenting 525
indulgent parenting 525

coparenting 529
child abuse 530
child maltreatment 530
physical abuse 530

child neglect 530
sexual abuse 530
emotional abuse 530

KEY PEOPLE

John Gottman 515
Diana Baumrind 525

Joseph Allen 532
Reed Larson 534

Ann Crouter 536
E. Mavis Hetherington 539

Laurie Kramer 543

E-LEARNING TOOLS

Connect to **www.mhhe.com/santrockldt5e** to research the answers and complete these exercises. In addition, you'll find a number of other resources and valuable study tools for Chapter 14, "Families, Lifestyles, and Parenting," on this Web site.

Taking It to the Net

1. Chad is a paralegal in his mother's law firm. His mother just took the case of a woman who announced that she is lesbian, left her husband of ten years, and is fighting for custody of

her two girls, ages 5 and 7. Chad's mother has asked him to find out what the research says about the gender identity and sexual orientation of girls raised by lesbian mothers. What will Chad find?

2. Leslie was raised by very strict parents. She was spanked frequently and was the object of their rage on numerous occasions. Leslie is now the mother of two small children, and she has purposely adopted an indulgent parenting style. She basically lets her children do what they want. How will Leslie's parenting style affect her children?

3. Ellen, expecting her first child in a month, told her mother of her plans to return to work when the baby is 6 months old. "I wish you would reconsider," her mother said. "I was just reading last week about how bad it is for the kids to be in child care, especially so early." "Oh, Mother," Ellen said. "That is old news. The latest research is that child care is good for kids." Who is right?

Self-Assessment

To evaluate your ideas about the best ways to parent children and the extent to which your parents monitored your behavior in adolescence, complete this self-assessment:

• *How Much Did My Parents Monitor My Behavior in Adolescence?*

Health and Well-Being, Parenting, and Education

Build your decision-making skills by trying your hand at the health and well-being, parenting, and education exercises.

Video Clips

The Online Learning Center includes the following videos for this chapter:

• *Relationships with Parents at Age 11*
• *When Second Baby Comes Along*
• *Sibling Differential Treatment*
• *Choosing Not to Cohabitate*
• *Family Reaction to Marriage: Lesbian Couple*
• *Transition to Parenthood: Heterosexual Married Couple*
• *Transition to Parenthood: Lesbian Couple*
• *Interview with Adoptive Parents*
• *Interview with Stay-Home Dad*
• *Cultural Variation in Father Role*

15

> *A man's growth is seen in the successive choirs of his friends.*
>
> —RALPH WALDO EMERSON
> *American Author and Poet,*
> *19th Century*

LEARNING GOALS

- ◆ Discuss peer relations in childhood and adolescence.

- ◆ Explain the role of friendship through the life span.

- ◆ Describe the developmental aspects of play and leisure.

- ◆ Summarize the social aspects of aging.

- ◆ Evaluate sociocultural influences on development.

PEERS AND THE SOCIOCULTURAL WORLD

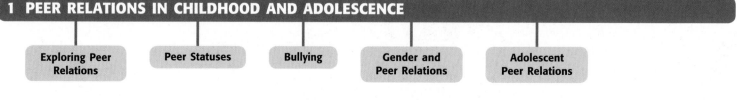

1 PEER RELATIONS IN CHILDHOOD AND ADOLESCENCE

| Exploring Peer Relations | Peer Statuses | Bullying | Gender and Peer Relations | Adolescent Peer Relations |

As children grow older, peer relations consume increasing amounts of their time. In some cases, these relations are positive influences, in others negative.

Exploring Peer Relations

peers Individuals of about the same age or maturity level.

Some important questions in peer relations are: What is the function of a child's peer group? How are peer relations and adult-child relations linked? What are some developmental changes in peer relations during childhood? What role does social cognition play in peer relations? How is emotional regulation involved in peer relations?

Functions of Peer Groups **Peers** are individuals of about the same age or maturity level. Peer groups provide a source of information and comparison about the world outside the family. Children receive feedback about their abilities from their peer group. They evaluate what they do in terms of whether it is better than, as good as, or worse than what other children do. It is hard to do this comparison at home because siblings are usually older or younger.

Both Jean Piaget (1932) and Harry Stack Sullivan (1953) stressed that children learn reciprocity through interaction with their peers. Children explore the meanings of fairness and justice by working through disagreements with peers. They also learn to be keen observers of peers' interests and perspectives in order to smoothly integrate themselves into ongoing peer activities.

Of course, peer influences can be negative as well as positive (Blanton & Burkley, 2008; Snyder & others, 2008). Being rejected or overlooked by peers leads some children to feel lonely or hostile. Further, rejection and neglect by peers are related to an individual's subsequent mental health and criminal problems. Withdrawn children who are rejected by peers or victimized and lonely are at risk for depression. Children who are aggressive with their peers are at risk for developing a number of problems, including delinquency and dropping out of school. Peers can also undermine parental values and control (Masten, 2005).

Keep in mind that the influences of peer experiences vary according to the type of peer experience, developmental status, and outcome (such as achievement, delinquency, depression, and so on) (Brown & others, 2008; Hartup, 2008). "Peers" and "peer group" are global concepts. For example, "peer group" might refer to acquaintances, clique, neighborhood associates, a friendship network, or an activity group (Brown, 1999).

What are some functions of peer group?

Adult-Child and Peer Relations Parents may influence their children's peer relations in many ways, both direct and indirect (Booth-LaForce & Kerns, 2009; Ross & Howe, 2009). Parents affect their children's peer relations through their interactions with their children, how they manage their children's lives, and the opportunities they provide their children. A recent study revealed that warmth, advice giving, and provision of opportunities by mothers and fathers were linked to children's social competence (high prosocial behavior, low aggression), and subsequently to social acceptance (being well liked by peers and teachers) one year later (McDowell & Parke, 2009).

Basic lifestyle decisions by parents—their choices of neighborhoods, churches, schools, and their own friends—largely determine the pool from which their children select possible friends. These choices in turn affect which children their children meet, their purpose in interacting, and eventually which children become their friends.

Researchers also have found that children's peer relations are linked to attachment security and parents' marital quality (Booth-Laforce & Kerns, 2009; Ross & Howe, 2009). Early attachments to caregivers provide a connection to children's peer relations not only by creating a secure base for children to explore social relationships beyond the family but also by conveying a working model of relationships (Hartup, 2009).

Do these results indicate that children's peer relations always are wedded to parent-child relationships? Although parent-child relationships influence children's subsequent peer relations, children also learn other modes of relating through their relationships with peers. For example, rough-and-tumble play occurs mainly with other children, not in parent-child interaction. In times of stress, children often turn to parents, not peers, for support. In parent-child relationships, children learn how to relate to authority figures. With their peers, children are likely to interact on a much more equal basis and to learn a mode of relating based on mutual influence.

Peer Contexts Peer interaction is influenced by contexts, which can include the type of peer the individual interacts with—such as an acquaintance, a crowd, a clique, a friend, a romantic partner—and the situation or location where they are—such as a school, neighborhood, community center, dance, religious setting, sporting event, and so on, as well as the culture in which when the adolescent lives (Brown & others, 2008). As they interact with peers in these various contexts, individuals likely encounter different messages and different opportunities to engage in adaptive and maladaptive behavior that can influence their development (Prinstein & Dodge, 2008).

What are some examples of how social contexts and individual difference factors influence adolescents' peer relations?

Individual Difference Factors   Individual differences among peers also are important to consider in understanding peer relations. Among the wide range of individual differences that can affect peer relations are personality traits, such as how shy or outgoing an individual is. For example, a very shy individual is more likely than a gregarious individual to be neglected by peers and have anxiety about introducing himself or herself to new peers. One individual difference factor that has been found to impair peer relations is the trait of negative emotionality, which involves a relatively low threshold for experiencing anger, fear, anxiety, and irritation. For example, one recent study revealed that adolescents characterized by negative emotionality tended to engage in negative interpersonal behavior when interacting with a friend or a romantic partner (Hatton & others, 2008). Other individual differences include how open the individual is to peer influence and the status/power of the individual and the status/power of the other peer or peer group (Brown & others, 2008). Being in a subordinate social position decreases the likelihood the individual will influence other peers but increases the probability the individual will be open to peer influence.

Developmental Changes in Childhood   Around the age of 3, children already prefer to spend time with same-sex rather than opposite-sex playmates, and this preference increases in early childhood. During these same years, the frequency of peer interaction, both positive and negative, picks up considerably (Hartup, 1983). Although aggressive interaction and rough-and-tumble play increase, the proportion of aggressive exchanges, compared with friendly exchanges, decreases. Many preschool children spend considerable time in peer interaction just playing, conversing with peers, trying out roles, and negotiating rules (Rubin, Bukowski, & Parker, 2006). In early childhood, children distinguish between friends and nonfriends (Howes, 2009). For most young children, a friend is someone to play with. Young preschool children are more likely than older children to have friends who are of different gender and ethnicity (Howes, 2009).

As children enter the elementary school years, reciprocity becomes especially important in peer interchanges. Children play games, function in groups, and cultivate friendships. Until about 12 years of age, their preference for same-sex groups increases. The amount of time children spend in peer interaction also rises during middle and late childhood and adolescence. Researchers estimate that the percentage of time spent in social interaction with peers increases from approximately 10 percent at 2 years of age to more than 30 percent in middle and late childhood (Rubin, Bukowski, & Parker, 2006). Other changes in peer relations as children move through middle and late childhood involve an increase in the size of their peer group and peer interaction that is less closely supervised by adults (Rubin, Bukowski, & Parker, 2006).

Social Cognition   A boy accidentally trips and knocks another boy's soft drink out of his hand. That boy misinterprets the encounter as hostile, which leads him to retaliate aggressively against the boy who tripped. Through repeated encounters of this kind, the aggressive boy's classmates come to perceive him as habitually acting in inappropriate ways.

This example demonstrates the importance of *social cognition*—thoughts about social matters, such as the aggressive boy's interpretation of an encounter as hostile and his classmates' perception of his behavior as inappropriate (Peets, Hodges, & Salmivalli, 2008).

What are some developmental changes in peer relations during childhood?

Children's social cognition about their peers becomes increasingly important for understanding peer relationships in middle and late childhood. Of special interest are the ways in which children process information about peer relations and their social knowledge (Mueller & others, 2008; Rah & Parke, 2008).

Kenneth Dodge (1983) argues that children go through five steps in processing information about their social world. They decode social cues, interpret, search for a response, select an optimal response, and enact. Dodge has found that aggressive boys are more likely to perceive another child's actions as hostile when the child's intention is ambiguous. And, when aggressive boys search for cues to determine a peer's intention, they respond more rapidly, less efficiently, and less reflectively than do nonaggressive children. These are among the social cognitive factors believed to be involved in children's conflicts.

Social knowledge also is involved in children's ability to get along with peers (Bibok, Carpendale, & Lewis, 2008). They need to know what goals to pursue in poorly defined or ambiguous situations, how to initiate and maintain a social bond, and what scripts to follow to get other children to be their friends. For example, as part of the script for getting friends, it helps to know that making positive comments to the peer will make the peer like the child more.

What are some aspects of social cognition that are involved in getting along with peers?

Regulation of Emotion and Peer Relations   Emotions play a strong role in determining whether a child's peer relationships are successful (Saarni & others, 2006). Moody and emotionally negative children are often rejected by their peers, whereas emotionally positive children are often popular (Stocker & Dunn, 1990). The ability to modulate one's emotions is an important skill that benefits children in their relationships with peers (Denham, Bassett, & Wyatt, 2007).

Peer Statuses

Which children are likely to be popular with their peers and which ones are disliked? Developmentalists address these and similar questions by examining *sociometric status*, a term that describes the extent to which children are liked or disliked by their peer group (Cillessen, 2009; LaFontana & Cillessen, 2009). Sociometric status is typically assessed by asking children to rate how much they like or dislike each of their classmates. Or it may be assessed by asking children to nominate the children they like the most and those they like the least.

Developmentalists have distinguished five peer statuses (Wentzel & Asher, 1995):

- **Popular children** are frequently nominated as a best friend and are rarely disliked by their peers.
- **Average children** receive an average number of both positive and negative nominations from their peers.
- **Neglected children** are infrequently nominated as a best friend but are not disliked by their peers.
- **Rejected children** are infrequently nominated as someone's best friend and are actively disliked by their peers.
- **Controversial children** are frequently nominated both as someone's best friend and as being disliked.

Popular children have a number of social skills that contribute to their being well liked (Asher & McDonald, 2009). Researchers have found that popular children give out reinforcements, listen carefully, maintain open lines of communication with

popular children Children who are frequently nominated as a best friend and are rarely disliked by their peers.

average children Children who receive an average number of both positive and negative nominations from their peers.

neglected children Children who are infrequently nominated as a best friend but are not disliked by their peers.

rejected children Children who are infrequently nominated as a best friend and are actively disliked by their peers.

controversial children Children who are frequently nominated both as someone's best friend and as being disliked.

What are some statuses that children have with their peers?

peers, are happy, control their negative emotions, show enthusiasm and concern for others, and are self-confident without being conceited (Hartup, 1983; Rubin, Bukowski, & Parker, 1998). A recent study found that adolescents who had the worst social outcomes at age 14 had been rated as unpopular by their peers at age 13 (McElhaney, Antonishak, & Allen, 2008). Another study revealed that being popular with peers was linked to adaptive and maladaptive behaviors from early to late adolescence (Allen & others, 2005). In this study, popular adolescents decreased their hostile behaviors but increased their use of alcohol and marijuana.

Neglected children engage in low rates of interaction with their peers and are often described as shy by peers. The goal of many training programs for neglected children is to help them attract attention from their peers in positive ways and to hold that attention by asking questions, by listening in a warm and friendly way, and by saying things about themselves that relate to the peers' interests. They also are taught to enter groups more effectively.

Rejected children often have more serious adjustment problems than those who are neglected (Bukowski, Brendgen, & Vitaro, 2007). One study found that in kindergarten, children who were rejected by their peers were less likely to engage in classroom participation, more likely to express a desire to avoid school, and more likely to report being lonely than children who were accepted by their peers (Buhs & Ladd, 2002). The combination of being rejected by peers and being aggressive especially forecasts problems (Dishion & Piehler, 2009; Prinstein & others, 2009). One study evaluated 112 fifth-grade boys over a period of seven years until the end of high school (Kupersmidt & Coie, 1990). The best predictor of whether rejected children would engage in delinquent behavior or drop out of school later during adolescence was aggression toward peers in elementary school.

John Coie (2004, pp. 252–253) gave three reasons why aggressive peer-rejected boys have problems in social relationships:

- "First, the rejected, aggressive boys are more impulsive and have problems sustaining attention. As a result, they are more likely to be disruptive of ongoing activities in the classroom and in focused group play.

- Second, rejected, aggressive boys are more emotionally reactive. They are aroused to anger more easily and probably have more difficulty calming down once aroused. Because of this they are more prone to become angry at peers and attack them verbally and physically. . . .

- Third, rejected children have fewer social skills in making friends and maintaining positive relationships with peers."

Not all rejected children are aggressive (Rubin, Bukowski, & Parker, 2006). Although aggression and its related characteristics of impulsiveness and disruptiveness underlie rejection about half the time, approximately 10 to 20 percent of rejected children are shy.

How can rejected children be trained to interact more effectively with their peers? Rejected children may be taught to more accurately assess whether the intentions of their peers are negative (Bierman, 2004). They may be asked to engage in role playing or to discuss hypothetical situations involving negative encounters with peers, such as when a peer cuts into a line ahead of them. In some programs, children are shown videotapes of appropriate peer interaction and asked to draw lessons from what they have seen (Ladd, Buhs, & Troop, 2004).

Bullying

Significant numbers of students are victimized by bullies (Faris, 2009; Salmivalli & Peets, 2009). In a national survey of more than 15,000 sixth- through tenth-grade students, nearly one of every three students said that they had experienced occasional or frequent involvement as a victim or perpetrator in bullying (Nansel & others, 2001). In this study, bullying was defined as verbal or physical behavior intended to disturb someone less powerful. As shown in Figure 15.1, being belittled about looks or speech was the most frequent type of bullying. A recent study revealed that bullying decreased as students went from the fall of the sixth grade (20 percent were bullied extensively) through the spring of the eighth grade (6 percent were bullied extensively) (Nylund & others, 2007).

Who is likely to be bullied? In the study just described, boys and younger middle school students were most likely to be affected (Nansel & others, 2001). Children who said they were bullied reported more loneliness and difficulty in making friends, whereas those who did the bullying were more likely to have low grades and to smoke and drink alcohol. Researchers have found that anxious, socially withdrawn, and aggressive children are often the victims of bullying (Hannish & Guerra, 2004). Anxious and socially withdrawn children may be victimized because they are nonthreatening and unlikely to retaliate if bullied, whereas aggressive children may be the targets of bullying because their behavior is irritating to bullies (Rubin, Bukowski, & Parker, 2006).

Social contexts also influence bullying (Swearer, Espelage, & Napolitano, 2009). Recent research indicates that 70 to 80 percent of victims and their bullies are in the same school classroom (Salmivalli & Peets, 2009). Classmates are often aware of bullying incidents and in many cases witness bullying. The larger social context of the peer group plays an important role in bullying (Salmivalli & Peets, 2009). In many cases, bullies torment victims to gain higher status in the peer group, and bullies need others to witness their power displays.

What are the outcomes of bullying? A recent study indicated that bullies and their victims in adolescence were more likely to experience depression and engage in suicidal ideation and attempt suicide than their counterparts who were not involved in bullying (Brunstein Klomek & others, 2007). Another recent study revealed that bullies, victims, or those who were both bullies and victims had more health problems (such as headaches, dizziness, sleep problems, and anxiety) than their counterparts who were not involved in bullying (Srabstein & others, 2006). To read further about bullying, see the *Research in Life-Span Development* interlude.

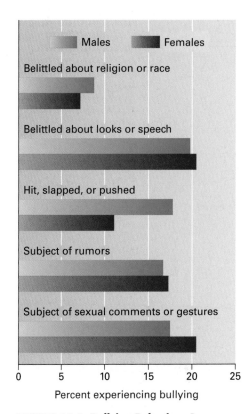

FIGURE 15.1 Bullying Behaviors Among U.S. Youth. This graph shows the type of bullying most often experienced by U.S. youth (Nansel & others, 2001). The percentages reflect the extent to which bullied students said that they had experienced a particular type of bullying. In terms of gender, note that when they were bullied, boys were more likely to be hit, slapped, or pushed than girls were.

Research in Life-Span Development

THE PERSPECTIVE TAKING AND MORAL MOTIVATION OF BULLIES, BULLY-VICTIMS, VICTIMS, AND PROSOCIAL CHILDREN

A recent study explored the roles that perspective taking and moral motivation play in the lives of bullies, bully-victims, victims, and prosocial children (Gasser & Keller, 2009):

- *Bullies* are highly aggressive toward other children but are not victims of bullying.

- *Bully-victims* not only are highly aggressive toward other children but also are the recipients of other children's bullying.

- *Victims* are passive, nonaggressive respondents to bullying.

- *Prosocial children* engage in such positive behaviors as sharing, helping, comforting, and empathizing.

Teacher and peer ratings in 34 classrooms were used to classify 212 7- to 8-year-old boys and girls into the aforementioned four categories. On a 5-point scale (from never to several times a week), teachers rated (1) how often the child bullied others and (2) how

(continued on next page)

often the child was bullied. The ratings focused on three types of bullying and being victimized: physically, verbally, and excluding others. On a 4-point scale (from not applicable to very clearly applicable), teachers also rated children's prosocial behavior on three items: "willingly shares with others," "comforts others if necessary," and "empathizes with others." Peer ratings assessed children's nominations of which children in the classroom acted as bullies, were victimized by bullies, and engaged in prosocial behavior. Combining the teacher and peer ratings after eliminating those that did not agree on which children were bullies, victims, or prosocial children, the final sample consisted of 49 bullies, 80 bully-victims, 33 victims, and 50 prosocial children.

Children's perspective-taking skills were assessed using theory of mind tasks, and moral motivation was examined by interviewing children about aspects of right and wrong in stories about children's transgressions. In one theory of mind task, children were tested to see if they understood that people may have false beliefs about another individual. In another theory of mind task, children were assessed to determine if they understood that people sometimes hide their emotions by showing a different emotion than they really feel. A moral interview also was conducted in which children were told four moral transgression stories (with content about being unwilling to share with a classmate, stealing sweets from a classmate, hiding a victim's shoes, and verbally bullying a victim) and then asked to judge whether the acts were right or wrong and how the participants in the stories likely felt.

The results of the study indicated that only bully-victims—but not bullies—were deficient in perspective taking. Further analysis revealed that both aggressive groups of children—bullies and bully-victims—had a deficiency in moral motivation. The analyses were consistent with a portrait of bullies as socially competent and knowledgeable in terms of perspective-taking skills and being able to effectively interact with peers. However, bullies use this social knowledge for their own manipulative purposes. The analysis also confirmed the picture of the bully as being morally insensitive.

To reduce bullying, teachers and schools can do the following (Cohn & Canter, 2003; Hyman & others, 2006; Limber, 2004; Milsom & Gallo, 2006; Vreeman & Carroll, 2007):

- Get older peers to serve as monitors for bullying and intervene when they see it taking place.

- Develop school-wide rules and sanctions against bullying and post them throughout the school.

- Form friendship groups for children and youth who are regularly bullied by peers.

- Be aware that bullying often occurs outside the classroom, so school personnel may not actually see it taking place. Also, many victims of bullying don't report the bullying to adults. Unsupervised areas such as the playground, bus, and school corridors are common places where students are bullied. If bullying is observed in a classroom or in other locations, a decision needs to be made about whether it is serious enough to report to school authorities or parents.

- Incorporate the message of the antibullying program into places of worship, school, and other community activities where children and youth are involved.

- Encourage parents to reinforce their children's positive behaviors and model appropriate interpersonal interactions.

- Identify bullies and victims early and use social-skills training to improve their behavior. Teaching empathy, especially perspective taking, promoting self-control, and training social skills have been found to reduce the negative behavior of bullies (Macklem, 2003).

What are some strategies to reduce bullying?

Gender and Peer Relations

We know that boys are far more likely to be involved in bullying than girls are. Indeed, there is increasing evidence that gender plays an important role in peer relations, as we saw in Chapter 12, "Gender and Sexuality" (Blakemore, Berenbaum, & Liben, 2009). Gender influences the composition of children's groups, their size, and the interaction within groups (Maccoby, 2002):

- *Gender composition.* Around the age of 3, children already prefer to spend time with same-sex playmates. From 4 to 12 years of age, this preference for playing in same-sex groups increases (see Figure 15.2).

- *Group size.* From about 5 years of age onward, boys tend to associate in larger clusters than girls do. Girls are more likely than boys to play in groups of two or three.

- *Interaction in same-sex groups.* Boys are more likely to participate in organized group games than girls are. They also are more likely to engage in rough-and-tumble play, competition, conflict, ego displays, risk taking, and dominance seeking. And, more than girls' groups, boys' groups seek to attain a group goal (Benenson, Apostolaris, & Parnass, 1997). By contrast, girls are more likely to engage in "collaborative discourse."

Adolescent Peer Relations

Unlike children, whose groups are usually informal collections of friends or neighborhood acquaintances, adolescents are often members of formal and heterogeneous groups, including adolescents who may not be friends and neighborhood acquaintances. Adolescent groups are also more likely than child groups to include boys and girls.

Do these and other peer groups matter? Yes, they do. Researchers have found that the standards of peer groups and the influence of crowds and cliques become increasingly important during adolescence (Brown & others, 2008).

Peer Pressure Young adolescents conform more to peer standards than children do. Around the eighth and ninth grades, conformity to peers—especially to their antisocial standards—peaks (Brown & others, 2008). At this point, adolescents are most likely to go along with a peer to steal hubcaps off a car, draw graffiti on a wall, or steal cosmetics from a store counter. A recent study revealed that 14 to 18 years of age is an especially important time for developing the ability to stand up for what one believes and resist peer pressure to do otherwise (Steinberg & Monahan, 2007). One study also found that U.S. adolescents are more likely than Japanese adolescents to put pressure on their peers to resist parental influence (Rothbaum & others, 2000).

Which adolescents are most likely to conform to peers? Adolescents who are uncertain about their social identity, which can appear in the form of low self-esteem and high social anxiety, are most likely to conform to peers (Prinstein, 2007; Prinstein & Dodge, 2008). This uncertainly often increases during times of transitions, such as school and family transitions. Also peers are more likely to conform when they are in the presence of someone they perceive to have higher status than they do.

Cliques and Crowds Cliques and crowds assume more important roles in the lives of adolescents than in the lives of children (Brown & Larsen, 2009; Brown & others, 2008). **Cliques** are small groups that range from 2 to about 12 individuals and average about 5 to 6 individuals. The clique members are usually of the same sex and about the same age.

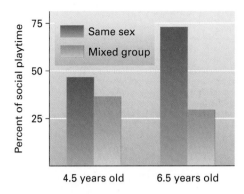

FIGURE 15.2 Developmental Changes in Percentage of Time Spent in Same-Sex and Mixed-Group Settings. Observations of children show that they are more likely to play in same-sex than mixed-group groups. This tendency clearly increases between 4 and 6 years of age.

cliques Small groups that range from 2 to 12 individuals and average about 5 to 6 individuals. Clique members usually are of the same age and same sex and often engage in similar activities, such as belonging to a club or participating in a sport.

What characterizes peer pressure in adolescence?

I didn't belong as a kid, and that always bothered me. If only I'd known that one day my differentness would be an asset, then my early life would have been much easier.

—BETTE MIDLER
Contemporary American Actress

Cliques can form because adolescents engage in similar activities, such as being in a club or on a sports team. Some cliques also form because of friendship. Several adolescents may form a clique because they have spent time with each other and enjoy each other's company. Not necessarily friends, they often develop a friendship if they stay in the clique.

What do adolescents do in cliques? They share ideas and hang out together. Often they develop an in-group identity in which they believe that their clique is better than other cliques.

Crowds are larger than cliques and less personal. Adolescents are usually members of a crowd based on reputation, and they may or may not spend much time together. Many crowds are defined by the activities adolescents engage in (such as "jocks" who are good at sports or "druggies" who take drugs) (Brown & Dietz, 2009; Brown & Larson, 2009). Reputation-based crowds often appear for the first time in early adolescence and usually become less prominent in late adolescence (Collins & Steinberg, 2006).

In one study, crowd membership was associated with adolescent self-esteem (Brown & Lohr, 1987). The crowds included jocks (athletically oriented), populars (well-known students who led social activities), normals (middle-of-the-road students who made up the masses), druggies or toughs (known for illicit drug use or other delinquent activities), and nobodies (low in social skills or intellectual abilities). The self-esteem of the jocks and the populars was highest, whereas that of the nobodies was lowest. One group of adolescents not in a crowd had self-esteem equivalent to that of the jocks and the populars—this group was the independents, who indicated that crowd membership was not important to them. Keep in mind that these data are correlational; self-esteem could increase an adolescent's probability of becoming a crowd member, just as crowd membership could increase the adolescent's self-esteem.

Cultural Variations in Adolescent Peer Relations Peers play an important role in the development of individuals in all cultures. However, cultures vary in how strong the socializing role of peers is (Brown

What characterizes adolescent cliques? How are they different from cliques?

crowds Peer groups that are larger and less personal than cliques; members may or may not spend much time together. Many crowds can be defined by their members' activities—for example, jocks, populars, and druggies.

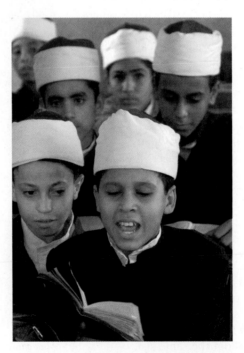

Muslim school in Middle East with boys only.

Street youth in Rio de Janeiro.

& Larson, 2009). In some countries, adults restrict adolescents' access to peers. For example, in many areas of rural India and in Arab countries, opportunities for peer relations in adolescence are severely restricted, especially for girls (Brown & Larson, 2002). If girls attend school in these regions of the world, it is usually in sex-segregated schools. In these countries, interaction with the other sex or opportunities for romantic relationships are restricted (Booth, 2002).

In many countries and regions, though, peers play more prominent roles in adolescents' lives (Brown & Larson, 2002, 2009). For example, in sub-Saharan Africa, the peer group is a pervasive aspect of adolescents' lives (Nsamenang, 2002); similar results have been observed throughout Europe and North America (Arnett, 2002).

In some cultural settings, peers even assume responsibilities usually assumed by parents. For example, street youth in South America rely on networks of peers to help them negotiate survival in urban environments (Welti, 2002).

Review and Reflect: Learning Goal 1

 Discuss peer relations in childhood and adolescence

REVIEW

- What are peers, and what are the functions of peer groups? What are Piaget's and Sullivan's views on peers? How are the worlds of parents and peers distinct but coordinated? What is the developmental course of peer relations in childhood? How is social cognition involved in peer relations? What role does emotional regulation play in peer relations?
- Describe five types of peer statuses.
- What is the nature of bullying?
- How is gender involved in children's peer relations?
- How do adolescent peer groups differ from child peer groups? What are peer pressure and conformity like in adolescence? How are cliques and crowds involved in adolescent development? What are some cultural variations in adolescent peer relations?

REFLECT

- Think back to your childhood and adolescent years.
- Which peer status would you use to describe yourself? How important do you think your peer status was in your development?

2 FRIENDSHIP

| Functions of Friendship | Friendship During Childhood | Friendship During Adolescence and Emerging Adulthood | Adult Friendship |

The world of peers is one of varying acquaintances; we interact with some people we barely know, and with others we know well, every day. It is to the latter type—friends—that we now turn.

Functions of Friendship

Why are friendships important? They serve the following functions (Gottman & Parker, 1987):

- *Companionship.* Friendship provides a familiar partner and play-mate, someone who is willing to spend time with us and join in collaborative activities.

- *Stimulation.* Friendship provides interesting information, excitement, and amusement.

- *Ego support.* Friendship provides the expectation of support, encouragement, and feedback, which helps us maintain an impression of ourselves as competent, attractive, and worthwhile individuals.

- *Social comparison.* Friendship provides information about where we stand vis-à-vis others and how we are doing.

- *Affection and intimacy.* Friendship provides a warm, close, trusting relationship with another individual. **Intimacy in friendships** is characterized by self-disclosure and the sharing of private thoughts. Research reveals that intimate friendships may not appear until early adolescence (Berndt & Perry, 1990).

What characterizes children's friendships?

Friendship During Childhood

Children's friendships are typically characterized by similarity (referred to as *homophily*, the tendency to associate with similar others). Similarity is a central aspect of friendship that may or may not be beneficial (Prinstein & Dodge, 2008). Throughout childhood, friends are more similar than dissimilar in terms of age, sex, ethnicity, and many other factors. Friends often have similar attitudes toward school, similar educational aspirations, and closely aligned achievement orientations.

Although having friends can be a developmental advantage, not all friendships are alike (Laursen & Pursell, 2009; Vitaro, Boivin, & Bukowski, 2009). People differ in the company they keep—that is, who their friends are. Developmental advantages occur when children have friends who are socially skilled, supportive, and oriented toward academic achievement (Crosnoe & others, 2008). However, it is not developmentally advantageous to have coercive, conflict-ridden, and poor-quality friendships (Hartup, 2009; Snyder & others, 2008). To read about strategies for helping children develop friendships, see the *Applications in Life-Span Development* interlude.

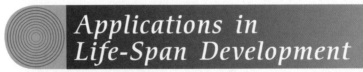

Applications in Life-Span Development

APPROPRIATE AND INAPPROPRIATE STRATEGIES FOR MAKING FRIENDS

Here are some strategies that adults can recommend to children and adolescents for making friends (Wentzel, 1997):

- *Initiate interaction.* Learn about a friend: Ask for his or her name, age, favorite activities. Use these prosocial overtures: Introduce yourself, start a conversation, and invite him or her to do things.

- *Be nice.* Show kindness, be considerate, and compliment the other person.

- *Engage in prosocial behavior.* Be honest and trustworthy: Tell the truth, keep promises. Be generous, share, and be cooperative.

intimacy in friendship Self-disclosure and the sharing of private thoughts.

- *Show respect for yourself and others.* Have good manners, be polite and courteous, and listen to what others have to say. Have a positive attitude and personality.
- *Provide social support.* Show you care.

And here are some inappropriate strategies for making friends that adults can recommend that children and adolescents avoid using (Wentzel, 1997):

- *Be psychologically aggressive.* Show disrespect and have bad manners. Use others, be uncooperative, don't share, ignore others, gossip, and spread rumors.
- *Present yourself negatively.* Be self-centered, snobby, conceited, and jealous; show off, care only about yourself. Be mean, have a bad attitude, be angry, throw temper tantrums, and start trouble.
- *Behave antisocially.* Be physically aggressive, yell at others, pick on them, make fun of them, be dishonest, tell secrets, and break promises.

Friendship During Adolescence and Emerging Adulthood

How are adolescent friendships different from child friendships? What characterizes friendship in emerging adulthood?

Adolescence For most children, being popular with their peers is a strong motivator. The focus of their peer relations is on being liked by classmates and being included in games or lunchroom conversations. Beginning in early adolescence, however, teenagers typically prefer to have a smaller number of friendships that are more intense and intimate than those of young children.

Harry Stack Sullivan (1953) has been the most influential theorist in the study of adolescent friendships. Sullivan argued that friends are also important in shaping the development of children and adolescents. Everyone, said Sullivan, has basic social needs, such as the need for secure attachment, playful companionship, social acceptance, intimacy, and sexual relations. Whether or not these needs are fulfilled largely determines our emotional well-being. For example, if the need for playful companionship goes unmet, then we become bored and depressed; if the need for social acceptance is not met, we suffer a lowered sense of self-worth.

During adolescence, said Sullivan, friends become increasingly important in meeting social needs. In particular, Sullivan argued that the need for intimacy intensifies during early adolescence, motivating teenagers to seek out close friends. If adolescents fail to forge such close friendships, they experience loneliness and a reduced sense of self-worth.

Gossip about peers often dominates the conversation of friends in adolescence (Buhrmester & Chong, 2009). Much of the gossip is characterized by negative comments about others, such as talking about how someone got drunk last weekend, how unattractive someone looked at school yesterday, and how someone could have the nerve to say what they did. In some cases, the negative gossip takes the form of *relational aggression*, which involves spreading disparaging rumors to harm someone (discussed in Chapter 12, "Gender and Sexuality"). However, not all gossip among friends is negative. Some gossip can involve collaborative construction that contributes to developing perspectives on intimacy and close relationships. Friends also can show their trust by disclosing risky opinions. The talk-featured, gossip aspect of friendship is more common in girls than boys.

Many of Sullivan's ideas have withstood the test of time. For example, adolescents report disclosing intimate and personal information to their friends more often than do younger children (Buhrmester, 1998) (see Figure 15.3). Adolescents also say they depend more on friends than on parents to satisfy their needs for companionship, reassurance of worth, and intimacy. The ups and downs of experiences with friends shape adolescents' well-being (Berndt, 2002).

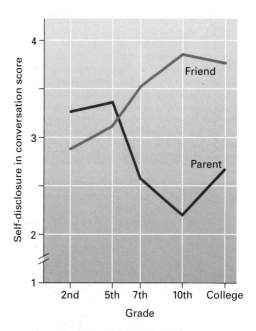

FIGURE 15.3 Developmental Changes in Self-Disclosing Conversations. In this study children and youth completed a 5-point rating scale, with a higher score representing greater self-disclosure (Buhrmester, 1998). The data shown here represent the means for each age group. Self-disclosing conversations with friends increased dramatically in adolescence while declining in an equally dramatic fashion with parents. However, self-disclosing conversations with parents began to pick up somewhat during the college years.

How is adult friendship different among female friends, male friends, and cross-gender friends?

Are the friendships of adolescent girls more intimate than the friendships of adolescent boys? Girls' friendships in adolescence are more likely to focus on intimacy; boys' friendships tend to emphasize power and excitement (Blakemore, Berenbaum, & Liben, 2009; Rose & Smith, 2009). Boys may discourage one another from openly disclosing their problems because self-disclosure is not masculine (Maccoby, 1998).

A recent study of third- through ninth-graders, though, revealed that one aspect of girls' social support in friendship may have costs as well as benefits (Rose, Carlson, & Waller, 2007). In the study, girls' co-rumination (as reflected in excessively discussing problems) predicted not only an increase in positive friendship quality but also an increase in further co-rumination as well as an increase in depressive and anxiety symptoms. One implication of the research is that some girls who are vulnerable to developing internalized problems may go undetected because they have supportive friendships.

The study just described indicates that the characteristics of an adolescent's friends can influence whether the friends have a positive or negative influence on the adolescent. Consider a recent study which revealed that friends' grade-point average was an important positive attribute (Cook, Deng, & Morgano, 2007). Friends' grade-point average was a consistent predictor of positive school achievement and also was linked to a lower level of negative behavior in areas such as drug abuse and acting out. Another recent study found that taking math courses in high school, especially for girls, was strongly linked to the achievement of their best friends (Crosnoe & others, 2008). And as we saw in Chapter 13, "Moral Development, Values, and Religion," having delinquent peers and friends greatly increases the risk of becoming delinquent (Bukowski, Motzoi, & Meyer, 2009).

Although most adolescents develop friendships with individuals who are close to their own age, some adolescents become best friends with younger or older individuals. Do older friends encourage adolescents to engage in delinquent behavior or early sexual behavior? Adolescents who interact with older youth do engage in these behaviors more frequently, but it is not known whether the older youth guide younger adolescents toward deviant behavior or whether the younger adolescents were already prone to deviant behavior before they developed the friendship with the older youth (Billy, Rodgers, & Udry, 1984). A recent study also revealed that over time from the sixth through tenth grades girls were more likely to have older male friends, which places some girls on a developmental trajectory for engaging in problem behavior (Poulin & Pedersen, 2007).

Emerging Adulthood   Many aspects of friendship are the same in emerging adulthood as they were in adolescence. One difference was found, however, in a recent longitudinal study (Collins & van Dulmen, 2006). Close relationships—between friends, family members, and romantic partners—were more integrated and similar in emerging adulthood than they were in adolescence. Also in this study, the number of friendships declined from the end of adolescence through emerging adulthood.

Another research study indicated that best friendships often decline in satisfaction and commitment in the first year of college (Oswald & Clark, 2003). In this study, maintaining communication with high school friends and keeping the same best friends across the transition to college lessened the decline.

Adult Friendship

As in childhood, adult friends tend to be similar in a number of ways. Among the similarities in friendship during the adult years are occupational status, ethnicity, age, marital status, income, education, gender, and religion (Rawlins, 2009).

Gender Differences   As in the childhood and adolescent years, there are gender differences in adult friendships (Clark & Grote, 2003). Women have more close friends than men do, and their friendships are more intimate. When adult female friends get together, they often talk, whereas adult male friends are more likely to engage in activities, especially outdoors. Thus, the adult male pattern of friendship often involves keeping one's distance while sharing useful information. When women talk with their friends, they expect to be able to express their feelings, reveal their weaknesses, and discuss their problems. They anticipate that their friends will listen at length and be sympathetic. In contrast, men are less likely to talk about their weaknesses with their friends, and they want practical solutions to their problems rather than sympathy (Tannen, 1990). Also, adult male friendships are more competitive than those of women (Sharkey, 1993). For example, male friends disagree with each other more. Keep in mind, however, that these differences in same-sex adult friendship tend to be small (Sabini, 1995).

What about female-male friendship? Cross-gender friendships are more common among adults than among elementary school children, but not as common as same-gender friendships (Fehr, 1996). Cross-gender friendships can provide both opportunities and problems. The opportunities involve learning more about common feelings and interests and shared characteristics, as well as acquiring knowledge and understanding of beliefs and activities that historically have been typical of one gender.

Problems can arise in cross-gender friendships because of different expectations. For example, a woman might expect sympathy from a male friend but might receive a directive solution rather than a shoulder to cry on (Tannen, 1990). Another problem that can plague adult cross-gender friendship is unclear sexual boundaries, which can produce tension and confusion (Swain, 1992).

Friendship in Late Adulthood   In early adulthood, friendship networks expand as new social connections are made away from home. In late adulthood, new friendships are less likely to be forged, although some adults do seek out new friendships, especially following the death of a spouse (Zettel-Watson & Rook, 2009).

Aging expert Laura Carstensen and her colleagues (1998, 2008; Carstensen & Charles, 2010; Carstensen, Mikels, & Mather, 2006; Charles & Carstensen, 2007, 2009) concluded that people choose close friends over new friends as they grow older. And as long as they have several close people in their network, they seem content, says Carstensen. Supporting Cartensen's view, recall the recent study we described in Chapter 10, "Emotional Development," that, compared with younger adults, older adults said they tended to experience less intense positive emotions with new friends and equal levels of positive emotions with established friends (Charles & Piazza, 2007) (see Figure 15.4).

The following three studies document the importance of friendship in older adults:

- A study of almost 1,700 U.S. adults 60 years and older revealed that friendships were more important than family relationships in predicting mental health (Fiori, Antonucci, & Cortina, 2006). Even when the researchers controlled for health, age, income, and other factors, older adults whose social contacts were mainly restricted to their family members were more likely to have depressive symptoms. Friends likely provide emotional intimacy and companionship, as well as integration into the community.

- A longitudinal study of adults 75 years of age and older revealed that individuals with close ties with friends were less likely to die across a seven-year age span (Rasulo, Christensen, & Tomassini, 2005). The findings were stronger for women than for men.

- A recent study found that unmarried older adults embedded in a friend-focused network fared better physically and psychologically than unmarried older adults in a restricted network with little friend contact (Fiori, Smith, & Antonucci, 2007).

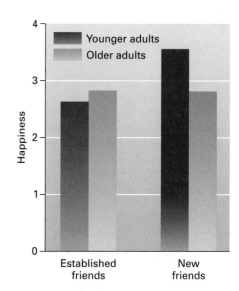

FIGURE 15.4 Happiness of Younger Adults and Older Adults with New and Established Friends. *Note:* The happiness scale ranged from 0 to 6, with participants rating how intensely they experienced happiness (0 = not at all, 6 = extremely intense). Older adults mean age, 71; younger adults mean age, 23.

What are some characteristics of older adults' friendships?

Review and Reflect: Learning Goal 2

 2 **Explain the role of friendship through the life span**

REVIEW

- What are five functions of friendship?
- What is the developmental significance of friendship during childhood?
- How can adolescents' friendships be characterized? What is Sullivan's view on friendship? What are friendships in emerging adulthood like?
- How do friendships vary in adulthood based on gender and age?

REFLECT

- Rank the functions of friendship that were most (1) to least (5) important as you were growing up.

3 PLAY AND LEISURE

Childhood   **Adolescence**   **Adulthood**

Peers and friends often engage in play and enjoy leisure activities together. Let's explore the developmental aspects of play and leisure.

Childhood

An extensive amount of peer interaction during childhood involves play; however, social play is but one type of play. **Play** is a pleasurable activity that is engaged in for its own sake.

Play's Functions   Play is an important aspect of the child's development (Coplan & Arbeau, 2009). Theorists have focused on different aspects of play and highlighted a long list of functions.

According to Freud and Erikson, play helps the child master anxieties and conflicts. Because tensions are relieved in play, the child can cope with life's problems. Play permits the child to work off excess physical energy and to release pent-up tensions. Therapists use **play therapy** both to allow the child to work off frustrations and to analyze the child's conflicts and ways of coping with them. Children may feel less threatened and be more likely to express their true feelings in the context of play.

Piaget (1962) maintained that play advances children's cognitive development. At the same time, he said that children's cognitive development *constrains* the way they play. Play permits children to practice their competencies and acquired skills in a relaxed, pleasurable way. Piaget thought that cognitive structures need to be exercised, and play provides the perfect setting for this exercise. For example, children who have just learned to add or multiply begin to play with numbers in different ways as they perfect these operations, laughing as they do so.

Vygotsky (1962) also considered play to be an excellent setting for cognitive development. He was especially interested in the symbolic and make-believe aspects of play, as when a child substitutes a stick for a horse and rides the stick as if it

*Y*ou are troubled at seeing him spend his early years in doing nothing. What! Is it nothing to be happy? Is it nothing to skip, to play, to run about all day long? Never in his life will he be so busy as now.

—JEAN-JACQUES ROUSSEAU
Swiss-Born French Philosopher, 18th Century

play A pleasurable activity that is engaged in for its own sake.

play therapy Therapy that lets children work off frustrations while therapists analyze their conflicts and coping methods.

were a horse. For young children, the imaginary situation is real. Parents should encourage such imaginary play, because it advances the child's cognitive development, especially creative thought.

Daniel Berlyne (1960) described play as exciting and pleasurable in itself because it satisfies our exploratory drive. This drive involves curiosity and a desire for information about something new or unusual. Play is a means whereby children can safely explore and seek out new information. Play encourages exploratory behavior by offering children the possibilities of novelty, complexity, uncertainty, surprise, and incongruity.

More recently, play has been described as an important context for the development of language and communication skills (Coplan & Arbeau, 2009). Language and communication skills may be enhanced through discussions and negotiations regarding roles and rules in play as young children practice various words and phrases. These types of social interactions during play can benefit young children's literacy skills (Coplan & Arbeau, 2009). And as we discuss in Chapter 16, "Schools, Achievement, and Work," play is a central focus of the child-centered kindergarten and thought to be an essential aspect of early childhood education (Feeney & others, 2010).

An increasing concern is that the large number of hours children spend with electronic media, such as television and computers, takes time away from play (Linn, 2008). An important agenda for parents is to include ample time for play in their children's lives.

Types of Play   The contemporary perspective on types of play emphasizes both cognitive and social aspects of play (Sumaroka & Bornstein, 2008). Among the most widely studied types of children's play today are sensorimotor and practice play, pretense/symbolic play, social play, constructive play, and games.

sensorimotor play Behavior by infants to derive pleasure from exercising their sensorimotor schemes.

practice play Play that involves repetition of behavior when new skills are being learned or when mastery and coordination of skills are required for games or sports.

pretense/symbolic play Play that occurs when a child transforms the physical environment into a symbol.

Sensorimotor and Practice Play   **Sensorimotor play** is behavior by infants to derive pleasure from exercising their sensorimotor schemes. The development of sensorimotor play follows Piaget's description of sensorimotor thought, which we discussed in Chapter 6, "Cognitive Developmental Approaches." Infants initially engage in exploratory and playful visual and motor transactions in the second quarter of the first year of life. For example, at 9 months of age, infants begin to select novel objects for exploration and play, especially responsive objects, such as toys that make noise or bounce. At 12 months of age, infants enjoy making things work and exploring cause and effect.

Practice play involves the repetition of behavior when new skills are being learned or when physical or mental mastery and coordination of skills are required for games or sports. Sensorimotor play, which often involves practice play, is primarily confined to infancy, whereas practice play can be engaged in throughout life. During the preschool years, children frequently engage in practice play. Although practice play declines in the elementary school years, practice play activities such as running, jumping, sliding, twirling, and throwing balls or other objects are frequently observed on the playgrounds at elementary schools.

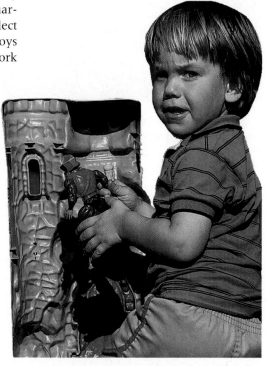

A preschool "superhero" at play.

Pretense/Symbolic Play   **Pretense/symbolic play** occurs when the child transforms the physical environment into a symbol. Between 9 and 30 months of age, children increase their use of objects in symbolic play. They learn to transform objects—substituting them for other objects and acting toward them as if they were these other objects (Smith, 2007). For example, a preschool child treats a table as if it were a car and says, "I'm fixing the car," as he grabs a leg of the table.

Many experts on play consider the preschool years the "golden age" of symbolic/pretense play that is dramatic or sociodramatic in nature. This type of make-believe play often appears at about 18 months of age and reaches a peak at 4 to 5 years of age, then gradually declines.

Some child psychologists conclude that pretend play is an important aspect of young children's development and often reflects advances in their cognitive development, especially as an indication of symbolic understanding. For example, Catherine Garvey (2000) and Angeline Lillard (2006) emphasize that hidden in young children's pretend play narratives are capacities for role-taking, balancing of social roles, metacognition (thinking about thinking), testing of the reality-pretense distinction, and numerous nonegocentric capacities that reveal the remarkable cognitive skills of young children. In one recent analysis, a major accomplishment in early childhood is the development of children's ability to share their pretend play with peers (Coplan & Arbeau, 2009).

Social Play **Social play** is play that involves interaction with peers. Social play increases dramatically during the preschool years (Neuman, 2007). Social play includes varied interchanges such as turn taking, conversations about numerous topics, social games and routines, and physical play (Sumaroka & Bornstein, 2008). Social play often involves a high degree of pleasure on the part of the participants (Sumaroka & Bornstein, 2008).

Constructive Play **Constructive play** combines sensorimotor/practice play with symbolic representation. Constructive play occurs when children engage in the self-regulated creation of a product or a solution (Sawyer & DeZutter, 2007). Constructive play increases in the preschool years as symbolic play increases and sensorimotor play decreases. In the preschool years, some practice play is replaced by constructive play. For example, instead of moving their fingers around and around in finger paint (practice play), children are more likely to draw the outline of a house or a person in the paint (constructive play). Constructive play is also a frequent form of play in the elementary school years, both in and out of the classroom. Constructive play is one of the few playlike activities allowed in work-centered classrooms. For example, if children create a play about a social studies topic, they are engaging in constructive play.

In the elementary school years, children increasingly play games, such as those playing hopscotch here on a school playground.

Games **Games** are activities that are engaged in for pleasure and have rules. Often they involve competition. Preschool children may begin to participate in social games that involve simple rules of reciprocity and turn taking. However, games take on a much stronger role in the lives of elementary school children.

In sum, play ranges from an infant's simple exercise of a new sensorimotor talent to a preschool child's riding a tricycle to an older child's participation in organized games. Note that children's play can involve a combination of the play categories we have discussed. For example, social play can be sensorimotor (rough-and-tumble), symbolic, or constructive.

social play Play that involves interaction with peers.

constructive play Combines sensorimotor/practice play with symbolic representation.

games Activities that are engaged in for pleasure and include rules.

leisure The pleasant times when individuals are free to pursue activities and interests of their own choosing.

Adolescence

Leisure refers to the pleasant times when individuals are free to pursue activities and interests of their own choosing—hobbies, sports, or reading, for example. How much leisure time do U.S. adolescents have compared with adolescents in other countries? How do U.S. adolescents use their leisure time?

Figure 15.5 indicates that U.S. adolescents spend more time in leisure activities than adolescents in other industrialized countries (Larson & Verma, 1999). About 40 to 50 percent of U.S. adolescents' waking hours (not counting summer vacations)

FIGURE 15.5 **Average Daily Leisure Time of Adolescents in Different Regions of the World.**

Activity	Nonindustrial, unschooled populations	Postindustrial, schooled populations		
		United States	Europe	East Asia
TV viewing	Insufficient data	1.5 to 2.5 hours	1.5 to 2.5 hours	1.5 to 2.5 hours
Talking	Insufficient data	2 to 3 hours	Insufficient data	45 to 60 minutes
Sports	Insufficient data	30 to 60 minutes	20 to 80 minutes	0 to 20 minutes
Structured voluntary activities	Insufficient data	10 to 20 minutes	10 to 20 minutes	0 to 10 minutes
Total free time	4 to 7 hours	6.5 to 8.0 hours	5.5 to 7.5 hours	4.0 to 5.5 hours

Note: The estimates in the table are averaged across a 7-day week, including weekdays and weekends. The data for nonindustrial, unschooled populations come primarily from rural peasant populations in developing countries.

is spent in leisure activities compared with 25 to 35 percent in East Asia and 35 to 45 percent in Europe. Whether this additional leisure time is a liability or an asset for U.S. adolescents, of course, depends on how they use it.

The largest amounts of U.S. adolescents' free time are spent using the media and playing, hanging out, and unstructured leisure activities, often with friends. U.S. adolescents spend more time in voluntary structured activities—such as sports, hobbies, and organizations—than East Asian adolescents.

According to Reed Larson (2001), for optimal development U.S. adolescents may have too much unstructured time because when adolescents are allowed to choose what they do with their time, they typically engage in unchallenging leisure activities such as hanging out and watching TV. Although relaxation and social interaction are important aspects of adolescence, it seems unlikely that spending large numbers of hours per week in unchallenging activities fosters development. Structured voluntary activities may provide more promise for adolescent development than unstructured time, especially if adults give responsibility to adolescents, challenge them, and provide competent guidance in these activities (Mahoney, Larson, & Eccles, 2004). A recent study revealed support for Larson's view that structured activities can improve adolescents' initiative (Watts & Caldwell, 2009).

How do U.S. adolescents spend their time differently from European and East Asian adolescents?

Adulthood

As adults, not only must we learn how to work well, but we also need to learn how to relax and enjoy leisure (Iwasaki, 2008). Leisure refers to the pleasant times after work when individuals are free to pursue activities and interests of their own choosing—hobbies, sports, or reading, for example. In an analysis of what U.S. adults regret the most, not engaging in more leisure was one of the top six regrets (Roese & Summerville, 2005).

Leisure can be an especially important aspect of middle adulthood (Mannell, 2000). By middle adulthood, more money is available to many individuals, and there may be more free time and paid vacations. In short, midlife changes may produce expanded opportunities for leisure. For many individuals, middle adulthood is the first time in their lives when they have the opportunity to diversify their interests.

In one study, 12,338 men 35 to 57 years of age were assessed each year for five years regarding whether they took vacations or not (Gump & Matthews, 2000). Then, the researchers examined the medical and death records over nine years for

574

CHAPTER 15 • Peers and the Sociocultural World

men who lived for at least a year after the last vacation survey. Compared with those who never took vacations, men who went on annual vacations were 21 percent less likely to die over the nine years and 32 percent less likely to die of coronary heart disease. The qualities that lead men to avoid taking a vacation tend to promote heart disease, such as not trusting anyone to fill in while you are gone or fearing that you will get behind in your work and someone will replace you. These are behaviors that sometimes have been described as part of the Type A behavioral pattern.

Adults at midlife need to begin preparing psychologically for retirement. Constructive and fulfilling leisure activities in middle adulthood are an important part of this preparation (Kelly, 1996). If adults develop leisure activities that they can continue into retirement, the transition from work to retirement can be less stressful.

How much leisure activity do older adults get? A recent national study revealed that more than half of U.S. adults 60 years and older spend no time in leisure activities (Hughes, McDowell, & Brody, 2008). In this study, 27 percent of the older adults participated in 2½ hours or more of leisure time activities per week. Older adults who were male, younger, non-Latino White, had a higher income status and education, were married, and reported being in better health were more likely to engage in leisure activities.

Sigmund Freud once commented that the two things adults need to do well to adapt to society's demands are to work and to love. To his list we add "to play." In our fast-paced society, it is all too easy to get caught up in the frenzied, hectic pace of our achievement-oriented work world and ignore leisure and play. *Imagine your life as a middle-aged adult. What would be the ideal mix of work and leisure? What leisure activities do you want to enjoy as a middle-aged adult?*

Review and Reflect: Learning Goal 3

3 Describe the developmental aspects of play and leisure

REVIEW

- What are the functions of play? What are the different types of play?
- What is leisure? How do adolescents use their discretionary time?
- What are some key aspects of leisure in adulthood?

REFLECT

- Do you think most young children's and adults' lives today are too structured? Do children and adults have too little time to play? Do U.S. adolescents have too much? Explain.

4 AGING AND THE SOCIAL WORLD

| Social Theories of Aging | Stereotyping of Older Adults | Social Support and Social Integration | Successful Aging |

The death of peers and family members is an expected part of old age. Does it follow that our social world must shrink as we get older? How do social experiences influence the aging process? Let's explore some theories of aging that give social experiences an important role.

Social Theories of Aging

In Chapter 10, "Emotional Development," we discussed *socioemotional selectivity theory,* which states that older adults become more selective about their social networks and may seek greater emotional quality in relationships with friends and family. Researchers have found excellent support for socioemotional selectivity theory (Carstensen & Charles, 2010). Let's consider two other social theories of aging.

Disengagement theory states that to cope effectively, older adults should gradually withdraw from society. This theory was proposed almost half a century ago (Cumming & Henry, 1961). In this view, older adults develop increasing self-preoccupation, lessen emotional ties with others, and show decreasing interest in society's affairs. By following these strategies of disengagement, it was thought that older adults would enjoy enhanced life satisfaction. This theory generated a storm of protest and met with a quick death. We present it because of its historical relevance. Although not formally proposed until 1961, it summarized the prevailing beliefs about older adults in the first half of the twentieth century.

Activity theory states that the more active and involved older adults are, the more likely they will be satisfied with their lives. Thus, activity theory is the exact opposite of disengagement theory. Researchers have found strong support for activity theory, beginning in the 1960s and continuing into the twenty-first century (Neugarten, Havighurst, & Tobin, 1968). One longitudinal study found that a greater overall activity level (which included social activities such as visiting relatives or friends, solitary activities such as hobbies, and productive activities such as volunteer work and gardening) at the beginning of the study was related to greater happiness, better physical and cognitive functioning, and reduced mortality six years later (Menec, 2003). In sum, when older adults are active, energetic, and productive, they age more successfully and are happier than if they disengage from society.

disengagement theory The theory that, to cope effectively, older adults should gradually withdraw from society; this theory is no longer supported.

activity theory The theory that the more active and involved older adults are, the more likely they are to be satisfied with their lives.

ageism Prejudice against other people because of their age, especially prejudice against older adults.

Stereotyping of Older Adults

Social participation by older adults is often discouraged by **ageism,** which is prejudice against others because of their age, especially prejudice against older adults (Leifheit-Limson & Levy, 2009; Roberts, 2008). They are often perceived as incapable of thinking clearly, learning new things, enjoying sex, contributing to the community, or holding responsible jobs. Many older adults face painful discrimination and might be too polite and timid to attack it (Barnes & others, 2008). Because of their age, older adults might not be hired for new jobs or might be eased out of old ones; they might be shunned socially; and they might be edged out of their family life (Tang, 2008).

Ageism is widespread. One study found that men were more likely to negatively stereotype older adults than were women (Rupp, Vodanovich, & Crede, 2005). Research indicates that the most frequent form is disrespect for older adults, followed by assumptions about ailments or frailty caused by age (Palmore, 2004). However, the increased number of adults living to an older age has led to active efforts to improve society's image of older adults, obtain better living conditions for older adults, and gain political clout.

One-hundred-year-old He Jingming , demonstrating his calligraphy skills in China. *How does his behavior contradict stereotyping of older adults?*

Social Support and Social Integration

Social support and social integration play important roles in the physical and mental health of older adults (Birditt, 2009; Kahana, Kahana, & Hammel, 2009). In the *convoy model of social relations,* individuals go through life embedded in a personal network of individuals from whom they give and receive

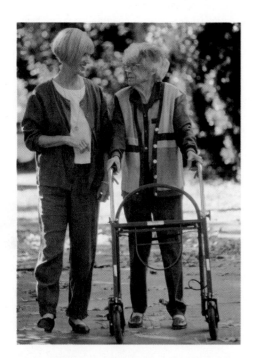

What role does social support play in the health of older adults?

What characterizes social integration in the lives of older adults?

social support (Antonucci, Akiyama, & Sherman, 2007). Social support can help individuals of all ages cope more effectively (Griffiths & others, 2007). For older adults, social support is related to their physical and mental health, including a reduction in symptoms of disease, the ability to meet their own health-care needs, and mortality (Rook & others, 2007). Social support also decreases the probability that an older adult will be institutionalized and is associated with a lower incidence of depression (Cacioppo & others, 2006).

Social support for older adults can be provided by different adults (Antonucci, Akiyama, & Sherman, 2007). Older adults who are married are less likely than nonmarried adults to need formal social supports, such as home nursing care, adult day care, and home-delivered meals. Families play important roles in social support for older adults, but friends also can be invaluable resources for social support. Also, social support for older adults may vary across cultures (Antonucci, Akiyama, & Sherman, 2007). For example, in the United States, the focal support person for an older adult is most likely to be a daughter, whereas in Japan it is most likely to be a daughter-in-law.

Social integration also plays an important role in the lives of many older adults (Rohr & Lang, 2009; von Tilburg, 2009). Remember from our earlier discussion of socioemotional selectivity theory that many older adults choose to have fewer peripheral social contacts and more emotionally positive contacts with friends and family (Carstensen, 2008; Carstensen & Charles, 2009). Thus, a decrease in the overall social activity of many older adults may reflect their greater interest in spending more time in the small circle of friends and families where they are less likely to have negative emotional experiences. A recent large-scale U.S. study revealed that adults in their seventies and eighties had smaller social networks than younger adults (Cornwell, Laumann, & Schumm, 2008). However, in this study, older adults were more likely to socialize with neighbors than were younger adults. Researchers have found that a low level of social integration is linked with coronary heart disease in older adults (Loucks & others, 2006).

Being lonely and socially isolated is a significant health risk factor in older adults (Koropeckyj-Cox, 2009). In one longitudinal study, poor social connections, infrequent participation in social activities, and social disengagement predicted cognitive decline in older adults (Zunzunegui & others, 2003).

Successful Aging

For too long, the positive dimensions of late adulthood were ignored (Carstensen & Charles, 2010; Depp & Jeste, & 2010; McNally, 2009). Throughout this book, we have called attention to the positive aspects of aging. There are many robust, healthy older adults (Terry & others, 2008; Willcox & others, 2008). With a proper diet, an active lifestyle, mental stimulation and flexibility, positive coping skills, good social relationships and support, and the absence of disease, we can maintain many abilities or in some cases even improve them as we get older (Barbieri & others, 2009; Beeri & others, 2009; Rohr & Lang, 2009). Even when individuals develop a disease, improvements in medicine mean that increasing numbers of older adults can still lead active, constructive lives (Depp, Glatt, & Jeste, 2007).

Being active is especially important to successful aging (Hillman, Erickson, & Kramer, 2008). Older adults who get out and go to meetings, participate in church activities, go on trips, and exercise regularly are more satisfied with their lives than their counterparts who disengage from society (Reichstadt & others, 2007). Older adults who are emotionally selective, optimize their choices, and compensate effectively for losses increase their chances of aging successfully (Carstensen, 2008).

Successful aging also involves perceived control over the environment (Heckhausen & Heckhausen, 2008). In Chapter 4, "Health," we discussed how perceived control over the environment had a positive effect on nursing home residents' health and longevity. In recent years, the term *self-efficacy* has often been used to describe perceived control over the environment and the ability to produce positive outcomes (Bandura, 2008, 2009). Researchers have found that many older adults are quite effective in maintaining a sense of control and have a positive view of themselves (Dunbar, Leventhal, & Leventhal, 2007). For example, one study of centenarians found that many were very happy and that self-efficacy and an optimistic attitude were linked to their happiness (Jopp & Rott, 2006). Examining the positive aspects of aging is an important trend in life-span development and is likely to benefit future generations of older adults (Carstensen & Charles, 2010; Depp & Jeste, 2010; McNally, 2009).

John Glenn's space mission is emblematic of our rethinking of older adults in terms of successful aging.

Review and Reflect: Learning Goal 4

 Summarize the social aspects of aging

REVIEW

- What are three social theories of aging?
- How extensively are older adults stereotyped?
- What roles do social support and social integration play in the development of older adults?
- What are some important aspects of successful aging?

REFLECT

- How might aging successfully in late adulthood be related to what people have done earlier in their lives?

5 SOCIOCULTURAL INFLUENCES

| Culture | Socioeconomic Status and Poverty | Ethnicity |

Personal relations with friends and other peers form only part of the social world outside the family that influences development. As we have seen throughout this book, development is also influenced by the sociocultural context. Here we take a closer look at three aspects of that context: culture, socioeconomic status, and ethnicity.

Culture

Recall from Chapter 1, "Introduction," that **culture** refers to the behavior, patterns, beliefs, and all other products of a group of people that are passed on from generation to generation. It results from the interaction between people and their environment over many years. Also remember from Chapter 1 that **cross-cultural studies** compare aspects of two or more cultures. The comparison provides information about

culture The behavior, patterns, beliefs, and all other products of a group of people that are passed on from generation to generation.

cross-cultural studies These studies compare aspects of two or more cultures. The comparison provides information about the degree to which development is similar, or universal, across the cultures, or is instead culture-specific.

the degree to which development is similar, or universal, across cultures, or is instead culture-specific (Schlegal, 2009).

A recent study revealed that from the beginning of the seventh grade through the end of the eighth grade, U.S. adolescents valued academics less and their motivational behavior also decreased (Wang & Pomerantz, 2009). By contrast, the value placed on academics by Chinese adolescents did not change across this time frame and their motivational behavior was sustained. In Chapter 16, "Schools, Achievement, and work" we discuss in greater detail the higher math and science achievement of Asian children when they are compared with U.S. children.

The concept of culture is broad; it includes many components and can be analyzed in many ways (Shiraev & Levey, 2010; Tewari & Alvarez, 2009). Cross-cultural expert Richard Brislin (1993) described a number of characteristics of culture:

- Culture is made up of ideals, values, and assumptions about life that guide people's behavior.
- Culture consists of those aspects of the environment that people make.
- Culture is transmitted from generation to generation, with responsibility for the transmission resting on the shoulders of parents, teachers, and community leaders.
- When their cultural values are violated or their cultural expectations are ignored, people react emotionally.
- It is not unusual for people to accept a cultural value at one point in their lives and reject it at another point. For example, rebellious adolescents and young adults might accept a culture's values and expectations after having children of their own.

Classical research by American psychologist Donald Campbell and his colleagues (Brewer & Campbell, 1976; Campbell & LeVine, 1968) revealed that people in all cultures tend to:

- think that what happens in their culture is "natural" and "correct" and that what happens in other cultures is "unnatural" and "incorrect";
- perceive their cultural customs as universally valid—that is, conclude that "what is good for us is good for everyone";
- behave in ways that favor their cultural group; and
- feel hostile toward other cultural groups.

In other words, people in all cultures tend to display **ethnocentrism,** the tendency to consider one's own group superior to others.

The Relevance of Culture for the Study of Life-Span Development

Global interdependence is an inescapable reality (Shiraev & Levy, 2010). Children, adolescents, and adults are not just citizens of one country; they are citizens of the world—a world that, through advances in transportation and technology, has become increasingly connected. By better understanding cultures around the world, we may be able to interact more effectively with each other and make this planet a more hospitable, peaceful place (Calzada & others, 2009; Greenfield, 2009).

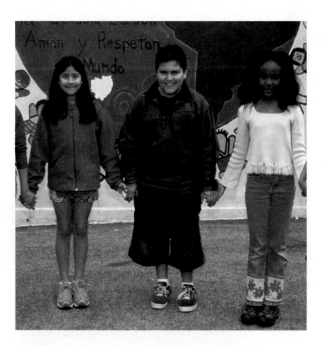

What is culture? How does it influence people's lives?

ethnocentrism The tendency to consider one's own group superior to other groups.

Individualism and Collectivism

What cultural differences are significant in life-span development? One finding in cross-cultural research is that cultures around the world tend to take two very different orientations to life and social relations. That is, cultures tend to emphasize either individualism or collectivism:

- **Individualism** involves giving priority to personal goals rather than to group goals; it emphasizes values that serve the self, such as feeling good, personal distinction and achievement, and independence.
- **Collectivism** emphasizes values that serve the group by subordinating personal goals to preserve group integrity, interdependence of the members, and harmonious relationships.

Figure 15.6 summarizes some of the main characteristics of individualistic and collectivistic cultures. Many Western cultures, such as those of the United States, Canada, Great Britain, and the Netherlands, are described as individualistic; many Eastern cultures, such as those of China, Japan, India, and Thailand, are described as collectivistic.

Many of the assumptions about contemporary ideas in fields like life-span development were developed in individualistic cultures (Triandis, 1994, 2001, 2007). Consider the flurry of *self-terms* in psychology that have an individualistic focus: *self-actualization, self-awareness, self-efficacy, self-reinforcement, self-criticism, self-serving, selfishness,* and *self-doubt* (Lonner, 1988).

Self-conceptions are related to culture. In one study, American and Chinese college students completed 20 sentences beginning with "I am _____" (Trafimow, Triandis, & Goto, 1991). As indicated in Figure 15.7, the American college students were much more likely to describe themselves with personal traits ("I am assertive," for example), whereas the Chinese students were more likely to identify themselves by their group affiliations ("I am a member of the math club," for example).

Some social scientists note that many problems in Western cultures are intensified by the Western cultural emphasis on individualism. The rates of suicide, drug abuse, crime, teenage pregnancy, divorce, child abuse, and mental disorders are higher in individualistic cultures than in collectivistic ones.

A recent analysis proposed four values that reflect parents' beliefs in individualistic cultures about what is required for children's and adolescents' effective development of autonomy: (1) *personal choice*, (2) *intrinsic motivation*, (3) *self-esteem*, and (4) *self-maximization*, which consists of achieving one's full potential (Tamis-LeMonda & others, 2008). The analysis also proposed that three values reflect parents' beliefs in collectivistic cultures: (1) *connectedness to the family and other close relationships*, (2) *orientation to the larger group*, and (3) *respect and obedience*.

Critics of the individualistic and collectivistic cultures concept argue that these terms are too broad and simplistic, especially with globalization increasing (Greenfield, 2009). Regardless of their cultural background, people need both a positive sense of self and connectedness to others to develop fully as human beings. The analysis by Carolyn Tamis-LeMonda and her colleagues (2008) emphasizes that in many families, children are not reared in environments that uniformly endorse individualistic or collectivistic values, thoughts, and actions. Rather, in many families, children are "expected to be quiet, assertive, respectful, curious, humble, self-assured, independent, dependent, affectionate, or reserved depending on the situation, people present, children's age, and social-political and economic circles."

Individualistic	Collectivistic
Focuses on individual	Focuses on groups
Self is determined by personal traits independent of groups; self is stable across contexts	Self is defined by in-group terms; self can change with context
Private self is more important	Public self is most important
Personal achievement, competition, power are important	Achievement is for the benefit of the in-group; cooperation is stressed
Cognitive dissonance is frequent	Cognitive dissonance is infrequent
Emotions (such as anger) are self-focused	Emotions (such as anger) are often relationship based
People who are the most liked are self-assured	People who are the most liked are modest, self-effacing
Values: pleasure, achievement, competition, freedom	Values: security, obedience, in-group harmony, personalized relationships
Many casual relationships	Few, close relationships
Save own face	Save own and other's face
Independent behaviors: swimming, sleeping alone in room, privacy	Interdependent behaviors: co-bathing, co-sleeping
Relatively rare mother-child physical contact	Frequent mother-child physical contact (such as hugging, holding)

FIGURE 15.6 Characteristics of Individualistic and Collectivistic Cultures.

individualism Giving priority to personal goals rather than to group goals; emphasizing values that serve the self, such as feeling good, personal distinction and achievement, and independence.

collectivism Emphasizing values that serve the group by subordinating personal goals to preserve group integrity, interdependence of members, and harmonious relationships.

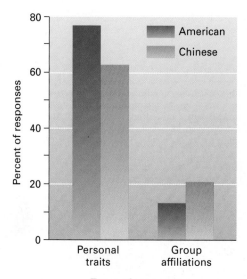

FIGURE 15.7 **American and Chinese Self-Conceptions.** College students from the United States and China completed 20 "I am _____" sentences. Both groups filled in personal traits more than group affiliations. However, the U.S. college students more often filled in the blank with personal traits, the Chinese with group affiliations.

Technology, the Media, and Culture A major change in the lives of children and youth in most cultures around the world is the dramatic increase in their use of technology and media (Strasberger, 2009). According to one analysis, "unlike their parents, they have never known anything but a world dominated by technology. Even their social lives revolve around the Web, iPods, and cellphones" (Jayson, 2006, p. 1D).

There likely are both positive and negative aspects to how the technology revolution is affecting children and youth (Forcier & Descy, 2009). Technology can provide an expansive, rich set of knowledge and used in a constructive way can improve children's and adolescents' education (Egbert, 2009). However, the possible downside of technology was captured in a recent book, *The Dumbest Generation: How the Digital Age Stupefies Young Americans and Jeopardizes Our Future (Or, Don't Trust Anyone Under 30)*, written by Emory University English professor Mark Bauerlein (2008). Among the book's themes are that many of today's youth are more interested in information retrieval than information formation, don't read books and aren't motivated to read them, can't spell without spellcheck, and have become encapsulated in a world of cell phones, iPods, text messaging, YouTube, MySpace, *Grand Theft Auto* (the video's introduction in 2008 had first-week sales of $500 million, dwarfing other movie and video sales), and other technology contexts. In terms of retaining general information and historical facts, Bauerlein may correct. And in terms of some skills, such as adolescents' reading and writing, there is considerable concern as evidenced by U.S. employers spending 1.3 billion dollars a year to teach writing skills to employees (Begley & Interlandi, 2008). However, in terms of cognitive skills, such as thinking and reasoning, Bauerlein likely is wrong given that IQ scores have been rising significantly since the 1930s, as we discussed in Chapter 8, "Inteligence" (Flynn, 2007). Further, there is no research evidence that being immersed in a technological world of iPods and YouTube impairs thinking skills (Begley & Interlandi, 2008).

If the amount of time spent in an activity is any indication of its importance, then there is no doubt that the mass media play important roles in the lives of U.S. children, adolescents, and adults (Roberts, Henriksen, & Foehr, 2009). A national study that surveyed more than 2,000 children and adolescents from 8 through 18 years of age confirmed that they use media heavily (Rideout, Roberts, & Foehr, 2005). The average child and adolescent in the study spent more than 44 hours a week with electronic media. The nearly 6½ hours a day using media compares with approximately 2¼ hours spent with parents, about 1½ hours in physical activity, and 50 minutes in homework. As shown in Figure 15.8, the children and adolescents spent the most time watching TV (nearly 4 hours a day), including videos, DVDs, and live and prerecorded TV. And, as indicated in Figure 15.9, TV viewing and video game playing decline as individuals go through adolescence, whereas time spent listening to music and using a computer increase (Rideout, Roberts, & Foehr, 2005).

A major trend in the use of technology is the dramatic increase in media multitasking (Roberts, Henriksen, & Foehr, 2009). A recent estimate indicates that when media multitasking is taken into account, 8- through 18-year-olds use media an average of eight hours per day (Roberts & Foehr, 2008). For example, it is not unusual for adolescents to simultaneously watch TV while text messaging their friends. In some cases, media multitasking—such as text messaging, listening to an iPod, and updating a YouTube site—is engaged in at the same time as doing homework. It is hard to imagine how that can be a good thing for doing homework efficiently, although there is little research on media multitasking.

Recent research revealed that truckers who text message while they drive have the risk of a crash or near crash that is more than 23 times the rate of nondistracted truckers (Blanco & others, 2009; Hanowski & others, 2009). In this research, cameras continuously observed truck drivers for more than 6 million miles of driving. Texting drew the truckers' eyes away long enough from the road for the truck to travel the length of a football field at 55 miles per hour.

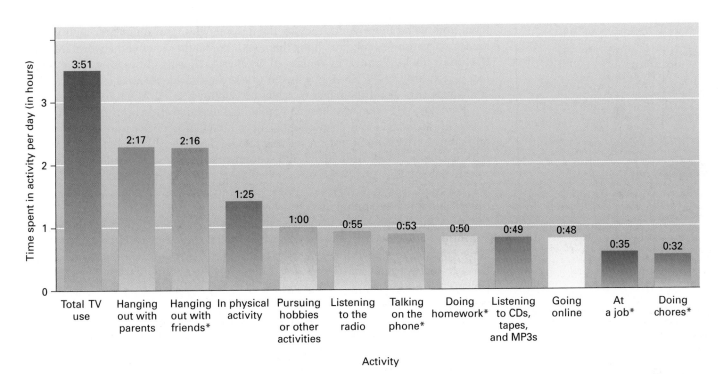

*Data collected among seventh- to twelfth-graders only. All other results are among all 8- to 18-year-olds.

FIGURE 15.8 Amount of Time U.S. 8- to 18-Year-Olds Spend per Day in Different Activities.

Television Few developments during the second half of the twentieth century had a greater impact on children than television (Strasberger, 2009). Many children spend more time in front of the television set than they do with their parents. Although it is only one of the many mass media that affect children's behavior, television may be the most influential. The persuasive capabilities of television are staggering. The 20,000 hours of television watched by the time the average American adolescent graduates from high school are greater than the number of hours spent in the class-room.

Television can have positive or negative effects on children's and adolescents' development. Television can have a positive influence by presenting motivating educational programs, increasing children's and adolescents' information about the world beyond their immediate environment, and providing models of prosocial behavior (Schmidt & Vandewater, 2008; Wilson, 2008). However, television can have a negative influence on children and adolescents by making them passive learners, distracting

FIGURE 15.9 Developmental Changes in the Amount of Time U.S. 8- to 18-Year-Olds Spend with Different Types of Media.

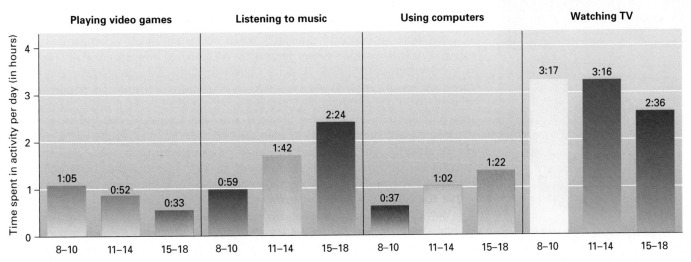

"*Mrs. Horton, could you stop by school today?*"
Copyright © Martha F. Campbell. Reprinted with
permission.

them from doing homework, teaching them stereotypes, providing them with violent models of aggression, and presenting them with unrealistic views of the world (Murray & Murray, 2008). Further, as we saw in Chapter 4, "Health," researchers have found that a high level of TV viewing is linked to a greater incidence of obesity in children and adolescents (Escobar-Chaves & Anderson, 2008).

However, television also has many potential negative effects (Murray & Murray, 2008; Strasberger, 2009). Television has been attacked as one reason for low scores on national achievement tests in reading and mathematics. Television, it is claimed, attracts children away from books and schoolwork. In one study, children who read printed materials, such as books, watched television less than those who did not read (Huston, Seigle, & Bremer, 1983). Furthermore, critics argue that television trains children to become passive learners.

A special concern about television is its exposure of children to violence (Murray & Murray, 2008). What role does televised violence play in children's aggression? Some critics have argued that research results do not warrant the conclusion that TV violence causes aggression (Freedman, 1984). However, many experts insist that TV violence can cause aggressive or antisocial behavior in children (Dubow, Huesmann, & Greenwood, 2007; Murray & Murray, 2008). Of course, television violence is not the only cause of aggression. There is no one cause of any social behavior. Aggression, like all other social behaviors, has multiple determinants. The link between TV violence and aggression in children is influenced by children's aggressive tendencies, their attitudes toward violence, and monitoring of children's exposure to TV violence.

A recent seven-month classroom-based intervention was successful in reducing the amount of time elementary school children watched violent TV and in decreasing their identification with TV superheroes (Rosenkoetter, Rosenkoetter, & Acock, 2009). The classroom-based intervention consisted of 28 lessons of 20 to 30 minutes each that focused on the many ways that television distorts violence.

A recent research review concluded that children and adolescents who experience a heavy media diet of violence are more likely to perceive the world as a dangerous place and to view aggression as more acceptable than their counterparts who see media violence less frequently (Wilson, 2008). Also, another recent research review concluded that there is strong evidence that media violence is a risk factor for aggressive behavior but less evidence linking it to juvenile delinquency and crime (Escobar-Chaves & Anderson, 2008). Much of the media violence described in these two recent research reviews comes from television, but as we see next, it also includes violent video games.

Violent video games, especially those that are highly realistic, also raise concerns about their effects on children and adolescents (Barlett, Anderson, & Swing, 2009). Correlational studies indicate that children and adolescents who extensively play violent electronic games are more aggressive and more likely to engage in delinquent acts than their counterparts who spend less time playing the games or do not play them at all (Anderson, Gentile, & Buckley, 2007; Carnagey, Anderson, & Bushman, 2007).

Are there any positive outcomes when adolescents play video games? Some evidence points to video games improving adolescents' visuospatial skills (Schmidt & Vandewater, 2008). And, Douglas Gentile and his colleagues (2009) conducted three studies of prosocial video games. In one study, Singaporean middle school students who played prosocial video games behaved in more prosocial ways. In a longitudinal study of Japanese children and adolescents, playing prosocial video games predicted later increases in prosocial behavior. In an experimental study, U.S. college students who were randomly assigned to play prosocial video games subsequently behaved more prosocially toward another student. Thus, it is not video games by themselves that have negative outcomes for children and adolescents, but rather the content of the video games (Barlett & Anderson, 2009).

How does television influence children's and adolescents' attention, creativity, and mental ability? Media use has not been found to cause attention deficit hyperactivity disorder but a small link exists between heavy television viewing and nonclinical

How is television violence linked to children's aggression?

attention levels in children and adolescents (Schmidt & Vandewater, 2008). In general, television has not been shown to influence children's and adolescent's creativity but is negatively related to their mental ability (Comstock & Scharrer, 2006).

The more children and adolescents watch TV, the lower their school achievement is (Comstock & Scharrer, 2006). Why might TV watching be negatively linked to children's achievement? Three possibilities involve interference, displacement, and self-defeating tastes/preferences (Comstock & Scharrer, 2006). In terms of interference, having a television on while doing homework can distract children while they are doing cognitive tasks, such as homework. In terms of displacement, television can take away time and attention from engaging in achievement-related tasks, such as homework, reading, writing, and mathematics. Researchers have found that children's reading achievement is negatively linked with the amount of time they watch TV (Comstock & Scharrer, 2006). In terms of self-defeating tastes and preferences, television attracts children to entertainment, sports, commercials, and other activities that capture their interest more than school achievement. Children who are heavy TV watchers tend to view books as dull and boring (Comstock & Scharrer, 2006).

However, some types of television content—such as educational programming for young children—may enhance achievement. In one longitudinal study, viewing educational programs, such as *Sesame Street* and *Mr. Roger's Neighborhood,* as preschoolers was related to a number of positive outcomes through high school, including higher grades, reading more books, and enhanced creativity (Anderson & others, 2001). Newer technologies, especially interactive television, hold promise for motivating children and adolescents to learn and become more exploratory in solving problems.

How might playing violent video games be linked to adolescent aggression?

Computers and the Internet Culture involves change, and nowhere is that change greater than in the technological revolution individuals are experiencing with increased use of computers and the Internet (Brookshear, 2009; Reed, 2009). Society still relies on some basic nontechnological competencies—for example, good communication skills, positive attitudes, and the ability to solve problems and to think deeply and creatively. But how people pursue these competencies is changing in ways and at a speed that few people had to cope with in previous eras. For children to be adequately prepared for tomorrow's jobs, technology needs to become an integral part of their lives (Egbert, 2009; Forcier & Descy, 2008).

With as many as 12 million American adolescents now online, more and more of adolescent life is taking place in a landscape that is inaccessible to many parents (Willoughby, 2008). A recent national survey indicated that 42 percent of U.S. 10- to 17-year-olds had been exposed to online pornography in the past year, with 66 percent of the exposure being unwanted (Wolak, Mitchell, & Finkelhor, 2007).

The Digitally Mediated Social Environment of Adolescents and Emerging Adults
The digitally mediated social environment of adolescents and emerging adults includes e-mail, chat rooms, instant messaging, blogs, social networking sites such as Facebook and MySpace, videosharing and photosharing, multiplayer online computer games, and virtual worlds (Subrahmanyam & Greenfield, 2008; Uhls & Greenfield, 2009). Most of these digitally mediated social interactions began on computers but more recently have also shifted to cell phones, especially smartphones (Roberts, Henriksen, & Foehr, 2009).

The Internet continues to serve as the main focus of digitally mediated social interaction. Chat-room conversations are mainly public and often involve multiple participants and simultaneous conversations; in many cases, the participants are strangers (Subrahmanyam & Greenfield, 2008). Adolescents and emerging adults usually use instant messaging on their computers and cell phones to communicate with friends from school. Gossip is a frequent component of such communication.

One study examined the content of 583 participants in online teen chat rooms (Subrahmanyam, Smahel, & Greenfield, 2006). More than 50 percent of the participants provided identity information, usually their gender. Younger participants

What characterizes the online social environment of adolescents and emerging adults?

(self-described as 10 to 13 years of age) were the most self-disclosing about their identity, older ones the least (self-described as 18 to 24 years of age). Sexual themes comprised 5 percent of the utterances (one sexual comment per minute) and bad/obscene language occurred in 3 percent of the utterances. Females discussed sex in more implicit ways, males in a more explicit manner. Older participants discussed sex more explicitly than did younger participants.

A recent study examined the sequence of using electronic communication technologies that college students in a midwestern university used in managing their social networks (Yang & Brown, 2009). In this study, female college students followed a consistent sequence as their relationships developed, typically beginning by contacting new acquaintenances on Facebook, then moving on to instant messaging, after which they may "exchange cell phone numbers, text each other, talk over their cell phone, and finally schedule a time to meet, if everything went well" (Yang & Brown, 2009, p. 2). Male college students were less likely to follow this sequence as consistently, although they did follow it more when communicating with females than males, suggesting that females may maintain more control over communication patterns.

Recent research has found that approximately one of three adolescents self-disclose better online than in person; in this research, boys report that they feel more comfortable self-disclosing online than do girls (Schouten, Valkenburg, & Peter, 2007; Valkenburg & Peter, 2009). In contrast, girls are more likely to feel comfortable self-disclosing in person than are boys. Thus, boys' self-disclosure may benefit from online communication with friends (Valkenburg & Peters, 2009).

MySpace and Facebook provide opportunities for adolescents and emerging adults to communicate with others who share their interests. Many adolescents and emerging adults who use MySpace and Facebook have apparently thought that the information they placed on the Web sites was private. However, it is easy for anyone to access the information, including parents, college personnel, and employers. For example, all it takes to obtain the information you put on Facebook is an edu e-mail address. Thus, if you are a Facebook or MySpace user, you should never put your Social Security number, address, phone number, or date of birth information on the Web site. Another good strategy is not to put information on Facebook or MySpace that current or future employers might use against you in any way. And a final strategy is to be aware that college administrators and personnel may be able to use the information you place on Facebook or MySpace to evaluate whether you have violated college policies (such as college drug and language harassment policies).

In sum, the Internet holds a great deal of potential for increasing adolescents' educational opportunities. However, the Internet also has limitations and dangers (Uhls & Greenfield, 2009). One recent study revealed the presence of more than 400 self-injury online message boards, with a large majority of the participants describing themselves as 12- to 20-year-old females (Whitlock, Powers, & Eckenrode, 2006). And some youth communicate with strangers in chat rooms and on bulletin boards. An increasing concern is peer bullying and harassment on the Internet (called *cyberbullying*). A recent survey found that peer bullying and harassment both online and offline were the most frequent threats that minors encounter (Palfrey & others, 2009).

The Internet and Aging Adults   The Internet plays an increasingly important role for adults as well as for youth in access to information and communication (Cutler, 2009; Lin, Neafsey, & Strickler, 2009; Rosenberg & others, 2009). A recent study revealed that older adults are clearly capable of learning new technologies (Hickman, Rogers, & Fisk, 2007).

How well are older adults keeping up with changes in technology? Older adults are less likely to have a computer in their home and less likely to use the Internet than younger adults, but older adults are the fastest-growing segment of Internet users (Czaja & others, 2006). Older adults are especially interested in learning to use e-mail and going online for health information (Leung & others, 2007; Westlake & others, 2007). Increasing numbers of older adults use e-mail to communicate with relatives. As with children and younger adults, cautions about the accuracy of information on the Internet—in areas such as health care—need to always be kept in mind (Cutler, 2009).

Aging and Culture   Culture plays an important role in aging (Williams, 2008). What promotes a good old age in most cultures? A recent analysis indicated that these three factors are important in living the "good life" as an older adult: health, security, and kinship/support (Fry, 2007).

What factors are associated with whether older adults are accorded a position of high status in a culture? Seven factors are most likely to predict high status for the elderly in a culture (Sangree, 1989):

- Older persons have valuable knowledge.

- Older persons control key family/community resources.

- Older persons are permitted to engage in useful and valued functions as long as possible.

- There is role continuity throughout the life span.

- Age-related role changes involve greater responsibility, authority, and advisory capacity.

- The extended family is a common family arrangement in the culture, and the older person is integrated into the extended family.

- In general, respect for older adults is greater in collectivistic cultures (such as China and Japan) than in individualistic cultures (such as the United States). However, some researchers are finding that this collectivistic/individualistic difference in respect for older adults is not as strong as it used to be and that in some cases older adults in individualistic cultures receive considerable respect (Antonucci, Vandewater, & Lansford, 2000).

Socioeconomic Status and Poverty

Analyzing cultures represents just one way to understand the social context of lifespan development. Another approach focuses on inequalities present in every society. That is, how do people in a particular society differ in their access to economic, social, and psychological resources, and how do these differences affect their development through life?

What Is Socioeconomic Status?   **Socioeconomic status (SES)** refers to a grouping of people with similar occupational, educational, and economic characteristics. Generally, members of a society have (1) occupations that vary in prestige, and some individuals have more access than others to higher-status occupations; (2) different levels of educational attainment, and some individuals have more access than others to better education; (3) different economic resources; and (4) different degrees of power to influence a community. These differences go together. That is, people with prestigious occupations tend also to have higher levels of educational attainment, more economic resources, and more power. These differences in the ability to control resources and to participate in society's rewards produce unequal opportunities for people (McLoyd & others, 2009). Socioeconomic differences are

Are older adults keeping up with changes in technology?

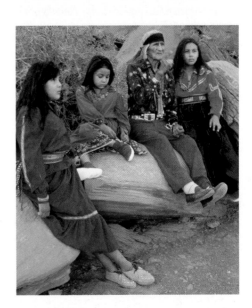

Cultures differ in the amount of prestige they give to older adults. In Navajo culture, older adults are especially treated with respect because of their wisdom and extensive life experiences. *What are some other factors that are linked with respect for older adults in a culture?*

socioeconomic status (SES) A grouping of people with similar occupational, educational, and economic characteristics.

a "proxy for material, human, and social capital within and beyond the family" (Huston & Ripke, 2006, p. 425).

The number of different socioeconomic statuses depends on the community's size and complexity. In most investigators' descriptions of socioeconomic status, two broad categories—low SES and middle SES—are used, although as many as five categories are delineated. Sometimes low SES is described as low-income, working class, or blue collar; sometimes middle SES is described as middle-income, managerial, or white collar. Examples of low-SES occupations are factory worker and maintenance worker. Examples of middle-SES occupations include manager and professional (doctor, lawyer, teacher, accountant, and so on).

What characterizes socioeconomic variations in neighborhoods?

Socioeconomic Variations in Neighborhoods and Families

A parent's SES is likely linked to the neighborhoods in which children live and the schools they attend (Leventhal, Dupéré, & Brooks-Gunn, 2009). Such variations in neighborhood settings can influence children's adjustment (Conger & Conger, 2008). For example, a recent study revealed that neighborhood disadvantage (involving such characteristics as low neighborhood income and unemployment) was linked to less consistent, less stimulating, and more punitive parenting, and ultimately to negative child outcomes (low verbal ability and behavioral problems) (Kohen & others, 2008).

Neighborhood crime and isolation have been linked with low self-esteem and psychological distress in children (Roberts, Jacobson, & Taylor, 1996). Further, schools in low-income neighborhoods have fewer resources than schools in higher-income neighborhoods, and they are more likely to have more students with lower achievement test scores and low rates of graduation with small percentages of students going to college (Garbarino & Asp, 1981).

In America and most Western cultures, differences have been found in child rearing among different SES groups (Hoff, Laursen, & Tardiff, 2002, p. 246):

- "Lower-SES parents (1) are more concerned that their children conform to society's expectations, (2) create a home atmosphere in which it is clear that parents have authority over children," (3) use physical punishment more in disciplining their children, and (4) are more directive and less conversational with their children.

- "Higher-SES parents (1) are more concerned with developing children's initiative" and delay of gratification, (2) "create a home atmosphere in which children are more nearly equal participants and in which rules are discussed as opposed to being laid down" in an authoritarian manner, (3) are less likely to use physical punishment, and (4) "are less directive and more conversational" with their children.

Nevertheless, a sizeable portion of children from low-SES backgrounds are very competent and perform well in school; some perform better than many middle-SES students. When children from low-SES backgrounds achieve well in school, it is not unusual to find a parent or parents making special sacrifices to provide the conditions that contribute to academic success.

So far we have focused on the challenges that many adolescents from low-income families face. However, research by Suniya Luthar and her colleagues (Ansary & Luthar, 2009; Luthar, 2006; Luthar & Goldstein, 2008) found that adolescents from affluent families also face challenges. In her research, adolescents from affluent families are vulnerable to high rates of substance abuse. Also, in the affluent families she has studied, males tend to have more adjustment difficulties than females, with affluent female adolescents especially more likely to attain superior levels of academic success.

Poverty When sixth-graders in a poverty-stricken area of St. Louis were asked to describe a perfect day, one boy said he would erase the world, then he would sit and think. Asked if he wouldn't rather go outside and play, the boy responded, "Are you kidding, out there?" (Children's Defense Fund, 1992). The world is a dangerous and unwelcoming place for too many of America's children, especially those who live in poverty (Children's Defense Fund, 2009). Some children are resilient and cope with the challenges of poverty without any major setbacks, but too many struggle unsuccessfully (Coltrane & others, 2008). Each child of poverty who reaches adulthood unhealthy, unskilled, or alienated keeps our nation from being as competent and productive as it can be (Children's Defense Fund, 2008).

Poverty Rates In 2006, 17 percent of children under 18 years of age were living in families below the poverty line (Federal Interagency Forum on Child and Family Statistics, 2008). This is an increase from 2001 (16.2 percent) but down from a peak of 22.7 percent in 1993. The U.S. figure of 17 percent of children living in poverty is much higher than those from other industrialized nations. For example, Canada has a child poverty rate of 9 percent and Sweden has a rate of 2 percent.

Poverty in the United States is demarcated along family structure and ethnic lines (Federal Interagency Forum on Child and Family Statistics, 2008). In 2006, 42 percent of female-headed families lived in poverty compared with only 8 percent of married-couple families. In 2006, 33 percent of African American families and 27 percent of Latino families lived in poverty, compared with only 10 percent of non-Latino White familes. Compared with non-Latino White children, ethnic minority children are more likely to experience persistent poverty over many years and live in isolated poor neighborhoods where social supports are minimal and threats to positive development abundant (Jarrett, 1995) (see Figure 15.10).

Psychological Ramifications of Poverty Poor children are often exposed to poor health conditions, inadequate housing and homelessness, less effective schools, environmental toxins, and violence (Healey, 2009; Leon-Guerrero, 2009). What are the psychological ramifications of living in poverty? First, the poor are often powerless. At work, they rarely are the decision makers; rules are handed down to them. Second, the poor are often vulnerable to disaster. They are not likely to be given notice before they are laid off from work, and they usually do not have financial resources to fall back on when problems arise. Third, their alternatives are restricted. Only a limited number of jobs are open to them. Even when alternatives are available, the poor might not know about them or be prepared to make a wise decision, because of inadequate education and inability to read well. Fourth, being poor means having less prestige.

One review concluded that compared with their economically more advantaged counterparts, poor children experience widespread environmental inequities (Evans, 2004). For example, as we saw in Chapter 1, "Introduction," one study found that

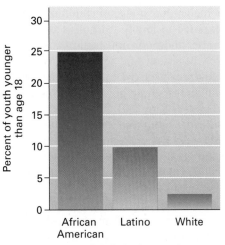

FIGURE 15.10 Percent of Youth Under 18 Who Are Living in Distressed Neighborhoods. *Note:* A distressed neighborhood is defined by high levels (at least one standard deviation above the mean) of (1) poverty, (2) female-headed families, (3) high school dropouts, (4) unemployment, and (5) reliance on welfare.

(*Top*) Children playing in Nueva Era, a low-income area on the outskirts of Nuevo Laredo, Mexico. (*Bottom*) Two boys who live in a poverty section of the South Bronx in New York City. *How does poverty affect the development of children like these?*

a higher percentage of children in poor families than in middle-income families were exposed to family turmoil, separation from a parent, violence, crowding, excessive noise, and poor housing (Evans & English, 2002).

Persistent and long-standing poverty can have especially damaging effects on children (McLoyd & others, 2009). A recent study revealed that the more years children spent in poverty, the more their physiological indices of stress were elevated (Evans & Kim, 2007). Further, one study of more than 30,000 individuals from birth into the adult years found that the greater risk for developmental outcomes took place with persistent and accumulating socioeconomic disadvantage throughout childhood and adolescence (Schoon & others, 2002).

Because of advances in their cognitive growth, adolescents living in poverty conditions likely are more aware of their social disadvantage and the associated stigma than are children (McLoyd & others, 2009). Combined with the increased sensitivity to peers in adolescence, such awareness may cause them to try to hide their poverty status as much as possible from others.

Feminization of Poverty The term **feminization of poverty** refers to the fact that far more women than men live in poverty. A special concern is the high percentage of children and adolescents growing up in mother-headed households in poverty (Leon-Guerrero, 2009). A recent analysis revealed that 42 percent of U.S. children and adolescents birth to 17 years of age were living in poverty in female-headed households compared with only 8 percent in married households (Federal Interagency Forum on Child and Family Statistics, 2008). Vonnie McLoyd (1998) concluded that because poor, single mothers are more distressed than their middle-SES counterparts are, they tend to show low support, nurturance, and involvement with their children. Among the reasons for the high poverty rate of single mothers are women's low pay, infrequent awarding of alimony payments, and poorly enforced child support by fathers (Graham & Beller, 2002).

Families and Poverty One study documented the important links among economic well-being, parenting behavior, and social adjustment (Mistry & others, 2002). Lower levels of economic well-being and elevated perceptions of economic pressure were linked with parenting behavior. Distressed parents reported feeling less effective and capable in disciplining their children and were observed to be less affectionate in parent-child interactions. In turn, less optimal parenting predicted lower teacher ratings of children's social behavior and higher ratings of behavior problems.

Benefits provided to low-income parents may have positive outcomes for children (Burchinal, 2006). For example, the Minnesota Family Investment Program (MFIP) was primarily designed to improve the lives of adults—specifically, to move adults off the welfare rolls and into paid employment. A key element of the program was that it guaranteed that adults who participated in the program would receive more money if they worked than if they did not. When the adults' income rose, how did that affect their children? A study of the effects of MFIP found that increases in the incomes of working poor parents were linked with benefits for their children (Gennetian & Miller, 2002). The children's achievement in school improved, and their behavior problems decreased.

Some studies have shown that poverty interventions are more effective with young children than older children and adolescents (Magnuson, Duncan, & Kalil, 2006; McLoyd & others, 2009). However, a downward trajectory is not inevitable for older children and youth living in poverty, and the success of poverty interventions likely depends on the quality and type of intervention. To read about recent research that explored ways to intervene in family poverty, see the *Contexts of Life-Span Development* interlude.

Vonnie McLoyd (*right*) has conducted a number of important investigations of the roles of poverty, ethnicity, and unemployment in children's and adolescents' development. She has found that economic stressors often diminish children's and adolescents' belief in the utility of education and their achievement strivings.

feminization of poverty The fact that far more women than men live in poverty. Women's low income, divorce, infrequent awarding of alimony, and poorly enforced child support by fathers—which usually leave women with less money than they and their children need to adequately function—are the likely causes.

Contexts of Life-Span Development

IMPROVING RESOURCES FOR FAMILIES IN IMPOVERISHED AREAS: THE NEW HOPE PROGRAM

Might intervention with families of children living in poverty improve children's school performance? In a recent experimental study, Aletha Huston and her colleagues (2006; Duncan, Huston, & Weisner, 2007; Gupta, Thornton, & Huston, 2007) evaluated the effects of New Hope, a program designed to increase parental employment and reduce family poverty, on adolescent development. They randomly assigned families with 6- to 10-year-old children living in poverty to the New Hope program and a control group. New Hope offered adults living in poverty who were employed 30 or more hours a week benefits that were designed to increase family income (a wage supplement that ensured that net income increased as parents earned more) and to provide work supports through subsidized child care (for any child under age 13) and health insurance. Management services were provided to New Hope participants to assist them in job searches and other needs. The New Hope program was available to the experimental-group families for three years (until the children were 9 to 13 years old). Five years after the program began and two years after it had ended, the program's effects on the children were examined when they were 11 to 16 years old. Compared with adolescents in the control group, New Hope adolescents were more competent at reading, had better school performance, were less likely to be in special education classes, had more positive social skills, and were more likely to be in formal after-school arrangements. New Hope parents reported better psychological well-being and a greater sense of self-efficacy in managing their adolescents than control parents did.

SES, Poverty, and Aging Also of special concern are older adults who are poor. Researchers have found that poverty in late adulthood is linked to an increase in physical and mental health problems (Gerst & Mutchler, 2009; Wight & others, 2008). Poverty also is linked to lower levels of physical and cognitive fitness in older adults (Basta & others, 2008). And a recent study revealed that low SES increases the risk of earlier death in older adults (Krueger & Chang, 2008).

Census data suggest that the overall number of older people living in poverty has declined since the 1960s, but in 2006, 9.6 percent of older adults still were living in poverty (U.S. Census Bureau, 2008). In 2006, almost twice as many U.S women 65 years and older (11.5 percent) lived in poverty than did their male counterparts (6.6 percent) (U.S. Census Bureau, 2008). Nineteen percent of single, divorced, or widowed women 65 years and older lived in poverty. Poverty rates among ethnic minorities are two to three times higher than the rate for non-Latino Whites. Combining gender and ethnicity, 60 percent of older African American women and 50 percent of older Latino women who live alone live in poverty. Also, the oldest old are the age subgroup of older adults most likely to be living in poverty.

Many older adults are understandably concerned about their income (Kemper & others, 2008; Svihula & Estes, 2008). The average income of retired Americans is only about half of what they earned when they were fully employed. Although retired individuals need less income for job-related and social activities, adults 65 and over spend a greater proportion of their income for food, utilities, and health care. They spend a smaller proportion for transportation, clothing, pension and life insurance, and entertainment than do adults under the age of 65. Social Security is the

What are some characteristics of older U.S. adults living in poverty conditions?

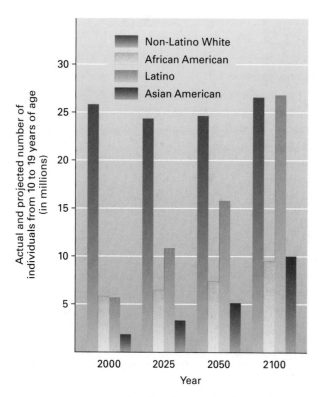

FIGURE 15.11 Actual and Projected Number of U.S. Adolescents Aged 10 to 19, 2000 to 2100. In 2000, there were more than 25 million non-Latino White adolescents aged 10 to 19 years of age in the United States, whereas the numbers for ethnic minority groups were substantially lower. However, projections for 2025 through 2100 reveal dramatic increases in the number of Latino and Asian American adolescents to the point at which in 2100 it is projected that there will be more Latino than non-Latino Whites in the United States and more Asian American than African American adolescents.

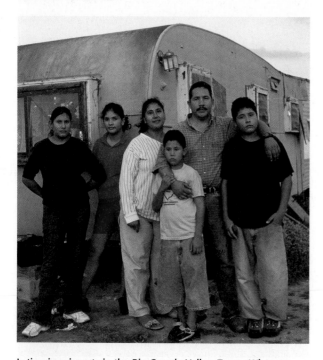

Latino immigrants in the Rio Grande Valley, Texas. *What are some characteristics of the families who have recently immigrated to the United States?*

largest contributor to the income of older Americans (38 percent), followed by assets, earnings, and pensions. There is a special concern about poverty in older women and the role of Social Security in providing a broad economic safety net for them (Slack & Jenson, 2008).

Ethnicity

As our discussion of poverty and aging indicated, differences in SES often overlap with ethnic differences. The United States is a showcase for these differences because it has been a great magnet for people from many ethnic groups. Cultural heritages from every continent have connected and mixed here (Lee & Wong, 2009; Spring, 2008). Native Americans, European Americans, African Americans, Latinos, Chinese Americans, and other groups have retained parts of their culture of origin, lost other parts, and seen some elements transformed as they became part of the mainstream culture.

The United States is more ethnically diverse than ever before (Banks, 2008). Ninety-three languages are spoken in Los Angeles alone. Does it matter which ethnic group a person belongs to? The *Contexts of Life-Span Development* interludes throughout this book have given some examples of how ethnicity can influence development. In Chapter 1, "Introduction," we noted that *ethnicity* is based on cultural heritage and includes characteristics such as nationality, race, religion, and language. Here we explore some additional examples of the role ethnicity plays in development.

Immigration Relatively high rates of minority immigration have contributed to the growth in the proportion of ethnic minorities in the U.S. population (Grigorenko & Takanishi, 2010; Liu & others, 2009; Tewari & Alvarez, 2009). And this growth of ethnic minorities is expected to continue throughout the twenty-first century. Asian Americans are expected to be the fastest-growing ethnic group of adolescents, with a growth rate of almost 600 percent by 2100. Latino adolescents are projected to increase almost 400 percent by 2100. Figure 15.11 shows the actual numbers of adolescents in different ethnic groups in the year 2000, as well as the numbers projected through 2100. Notice that by 2100, Latino adolescents are expected to outnumber non-Latino White adolescents.

Immigrants often experience special stressors (Alvarez, 2009; Clark & King, 2008). These include language barriers, separations from support networks, changes in SES, and the struggle both to preserve ethnic identity and to adapt to the majority culture (Grigorenko & Takanishi, 2010; Liu & others, 2009; Wong, Kinzie, & Kinzie, 2009).

Earlier in the chapter, we discussed the differences in individualist (emphasis on personal goals and the self) and collectivist (emphasis on the group and relationships) cultures. Many of the families that have immigrated in recent decades to the United States, such as Mexican Americans and Asian Americans, come from collectivist cultures in which family obligation and duty to one's family are strong (Fuligni, Hughes, & Way, 2009; Hayashino & Chopra, 2009). Family obligation and duty may take the form of assisting parents in their occupations and contributing to the family's welfare (Fuligni, Hughes, & Way, 2009; Parke & Buriel, 2006). The family work connection often occurs in service and manual labor jobs, such as those in construction, gardening, cleaning, and restaurants.

Parents and children may be at different stages of *acculturation*, the process of adapting to the majority culture. The result may be conflict over cultural values (Greder & Allen, 2007). One study examined values in immigrant (Vietnamese, Armenian, and Mexican) and nonimmigrant families (African American and European American) (Phinney, 1996). In all groups, parents endorsed family obligations more than adolescents did, and the differences between generations generally increased with time in the United States.

Ethnicity and Socioeconomic Status   Research has often failed to tease apart the influences of ethnicity and socioeconomic status (SES). Ethnicity and SES can interact in ways that exaggerate the negative influence of ethnicity because ethnic minority individuals are overrepresented in the lower socioeconomic levels of American society (Healey, 2009; Rowley, Kurtz-Costes, & Cooper, 2008). Consequently, too often researchers have given ethnic explanations for differences that were largely based on socioeconomic status, not ethnicity (Mello, 2009). For example, decades of research on group differences in self-esteem failed to consider the socioeconomic status of African American and non-Latino White American children. When the self-esteem of African American children from low-SES backgrounds is compared with that of non-Latino White American children from middle-SES backgrounds, the differences are often significant but not very informative because of the confounding of ethnicity and SES.

Ethnicity and Families   Families within different ethnic groups in the United States differ in their size, structure, composition, reliance on kinship networks, and levels of income and education (Parke & others, 2008; Umana-Taylor, 2009). Large and extended families are more common among minority groups than among the non-Latino White majority. For example, 19 percent of Latino families have three or more children, compared with 14 percent of African American and 10 percent of non-Latino White families. African American and Latino children interact more with grandparents, aunts, uncles, cousins, and more distant relatives than do non-Latino White children.

Single-parent families are more common among African Americans and Latinos than among non-Latino White Americans (Hattery & Smith, 2007). In comparison with two-parent households, single parents often have more limited resources of time, money, and energy. Ethnic minority parents also are less educated and more likely to live in low-income circumstances than their non-Latino White counterparts. Still, many impoverished ethnic minority families manage to find ways to raise competent children (Gamble & Modry-Mandell, 2008; Harris & Graham, 2007).

Poverty contributes to the stressful life experiences of many ethnic minority children (McLoyd & others, 2009). But even when they are not poor, economic advantage does not enable ethnic minority children to escape entirely the prejudice and discrimination directed at them (Harwood & others, 2002). Although middle-SES ethnic minority children have more resources available to counter the destructive influences of prejudice and discrimination, they still cannot completely avoid the pervasive influence of negative stereotypes about ethnic minority groups.

Vonnie McLoyd (1990) concluded that ethnic minority children experience a disproportionate share of the adverse effects of poverty and unemployment in America today. Thus, many ethnic minority children experience a double disadvantage: (1) prejudice and discrimination because of their ethnic minority status, and (2) the stressful effects of poverty.

Some aspects of home life can help protect ethnic minority children from injustice. The community and the family can filter out destructive racist messages, and parents can present alternative frames of reference to those presented by the majority. The extended family also can serve as an important buffer to stress (Harris & Graham, 2007; Hayashino & Chopra, 2009).

Differences and Diversity   Historical, economic, and social experiences produce differences between various ethnic minority groups, and between ethnic minority groups and the majority non-Latino White group (Cushner, McClelland, & Safford, 2009). Individuals living in a particular ethnic group adapt to the values, attitudes,

Jason Leonard, age 15: "I want America to know that most of us black teens are not troubled people from broken homes and headed to jail. . . . In my relationships with my parents, we show respect for each other and we have values in our house. We have traditions we celebrate together, including Christmas and Kwanzaa."

What characterizes families in different ethnic groups in the United States?

Consider the flowers of a garden: though differing in kind, color, form, and shape, yet, inasmuch as they are refreshed by the waters of one spring, revived by the breath of one wind, invigorated by the rays of one sun, this diversity increases their charm and adds to their beauty. . . .
How unpleasing to the eye if all the flowers and plants, the leaves and blossoms, the fruits, the branches, and the trees of that garden were all of the same shape and color! Diversity of hues, form, and shape enriches and adorns the garden and heightens its effect.

—ABDU'L BAHA
Persian Baha'i Religious Leader, 19th/20th Century

and stresses of that culture. Recognizing and respecting differences is an important aspect of getting along with others in a diverse, multicultural world (Gollnick & Chinn, 2009; Taylor & Whittaker, 2009). Children, like all of us, need to take the perspective of individuals from ethnic groups that are different than their own and think, "If I were in their shoes, what kind of experiences might I have had?" "How would I think and feel if I had grown up in their world?" Such perspective taking often increases empathy and understanding of individuals from ethnic and cultural groups different from one's own.

For too long, differences between any ethnic minority group and non-Latino Whites were conceptualized as *deficits,* or inferior characteristics, on the part of the ethnic minority group. Indeed, research on ethnic minority groups often focused only on a group's negative, stressful aspects. For example, research on African American adolescent females invariably examined such topics as poverty, unwed mothers, and dropping out of school. The current emphasis underscores the strengths of various ethnic groups and is long overdue (Manning & Baruth, 2009). For example, the extended-family support system that characterizes many ethnic groups is now recognized as an important factor in coping.

As we noted in Chapter 1, "Introduction," there also is considerable diversity within each ethnic group. Ethnic minority groups are not homogeneous; they have different social, historical, and economic backgrounds (Hall, 2010; Suyemoto, 2009). For example, Mexican, Cuban, and Puerto Rican immigrants are often lumped together as Latinos, but the typical member of each of these groups had different reasons for migrating, came from varying socioeconomic backgrounds in their native countries, and experience different rates and types of employment in the United States (Coll & others, 1995). The category "Asian Americans" includes people with Chinese, Japanese, Filipino, Korean, and Southeast Asian ancestry. The diversity of Asian Americans is reflected in their educational attainment—for example, 90 percent of Korean American males graduate from high school, but only 71 percent of Vietnamese American males do. Failure to recognize diversity and individual variations results in the stereotyping of an ethnic minority group.

Ethnicity and Aging   Of special concern are ethnic minority older adults, especially African Americans and Latinos, who are overrepresented in poverty statistics (U.S. Census Bureau, 2008). Comparative information about African Americans, Latinos, and non-Latino Whites indicates a possible double jeopardy for elderly ethnic minority individuals. They face problems related to both ageism and racism. One study of more than 4,000 older adults found that African Americans perceived more discrimination than non-Latino Whites (Barnes & others, 2004). Both the wealth and the health of ethnic minority older adults decrease more rapidly than for elderly non-Latino Whites (Angel & Angel, 2006). Older ethnic minority individuals are more likely to become ill but less likely to receive treatment (Hinrichsen, 2006). They also are more likely to have a history of less education, unemployment, worse housing conditions, and shorter life expectancies than their older non-Latino White counterparts (Himes, Hogan, & Eggebeen, 1996). And many ethnic minority workers never enjoy the Social Security and Medicare benefits to which their earnings contribute, because they die before reaching the age of eligibility for benefits (Ciol & others, 2008).

Despite the stress and discrimination older ethnic minority individuals face, many of these older adults have developed coping mechanisms that allow them to survive in the dominant non-Latino White world (Markides & Rudkin, 1996). Extension of family networks helps older minority group individuals cope with the bare essentials of living and gives them a sense of being loved (Antonucci, Vandewater, & Lansford, 2000). Churches in African American and Latino communities provide avenues for meaningful social participation, feelings of power, and a sense of internal satisfaction (Hill & others, 2006). And residential concentrations of ethnic minority groups give their older members a sense of belonging. Thus, it always is important to consider individual variations in the lives of aging minorities. To read about one individual who is providing help for aging minorities, see the *Careers in Life-Span Development* profile.

Careers in Life-Span Development

Norma Thomas, Social Work Professor and Administrator

Dr. Norma Thomas has worked for more than three decades in the field of aging. She obtained her undergraduate degree in social work from Pennsylvania State University and her doctoral degree in social work from the University of Pennsylvania. Thomas' activities are varied. Earlier in her career, as a social work practitioner, she provided services to older adults of color in an effort to improve their lives. she currently is a professor and academic administrator at Widener University in Chester, Pennsylvania, a fellow of the Institute of Aging at the University of Pennsylvania, and the chief executive officer and cofounder of the Center on Ethnic and Minority Aging (CEMA). CEMA was formed to provide research, consultation, training, and services to benefit aging individuals of color, their families, and their communities. Thomas has created numerous community service events that benefit older adults of color, especially African Americans and Latinos. She has also been a consultant to various national, regional, and state agencies in her effort to improve the lives of aging adults of color.

Norma Thomas.

Review and Reflect: Learning Goal 5

 5 **Evaluate sociocultural influences on development**

REVIEW

- How can culture, cross-cultural comparisons, and individualism/collectivism be defined? What are some outcomes of the increase in media use? How is culture related to development?
- What is socioeconomic status? How are socioeconomic status and poverty linked to development?
- What is ethnicity? How is ethnicity involved in development? What are some important aspects of ethnicity to recognize?

REFLECT

- No matter how well intentioned people are, their life circumstances likely have given them some prejudices. If they don't have prejudices toward people with different cultural and ethnic backgrounds, other kinds of people may bring out prejudices in them. For example, prejudices can be developed about people who have certain religious or political conventions, people who are unattractive or too attractive, people with a disability, and people in a nearby town. As a parent or teacher, how would you attempt to reduce children's prejudices?

Reach Your Learning Goals

Peers and the Sociocultural World

1 PEER RELATIONS IN CHILDHOOD AND ADOLESCENCE: DISCUSS PEER RELATIONS IN CHILDHOOD AND ADOLESCENCE

Exploring Peer Relations

- Peers are individuals who are at about the same age or maturity level. Peers provide a means of social comparison and a source of information about the world outside the family. Good peer relations may be necessary for normal social development. Being rejected or neglected by peers is associated with a number of problems. Peer relations can be both positive and negative. Piaget and Sullivan stressed that peer relations provide the context for learning the reciprocal aspects of relationships. Healthy family relations usually promote healthy peer relations. Parents can model or coach their children in ways of relating to peers. Parents' choices of neighborhoods, churches, schools, and their own friends influence the pool from which their children might select possible friends. Rough-and-tumble play occurs mainly in peer relations rather than in parent-child relations. In times of stress, children usually turn to parents rather than peers. Peer relations have a more equal basis than parent-child relations. Contexts and individual difference factors influence peer relations. The frequency of peer interaction, both positive and negative, increases in the preschool years. Children spend even more time with peers in the elementary and secondary school years. Social information-processing skills and social knowledge are important dimensions of social cognition in peer relations. Emotional regulation plays an important role in determining whether a child's peer relationships are successful.

Peer Statuses

- Popular children are frequently nominated as a best friend and are rarely disliked by their peers. Average children receive an average number of both positive and negative nominations from their peers. Neglected children are infrequently nominated as a best friend but are not disliked by their peers. Rejected children are infrequently nominated as a best friend and are actively disliked by their peers. Controversial children are frequently nominated both as one's best friend and as being disliked by peers.

Bullying

- Significant numbers of students are bullied, and bullying in adolescence can result in negative outcomes such as depression and suicidal ideation for both bullies and victims. Anxious, withdrawn children and aggressive children often are victims of bullying, and boys are far more likely to be involved in bullying than girls are.

Gender and Peer Relations

- Gender is linked to peer relations in several ways. From 4 to 12 years of age, preference for playing in same-sex groups increases. Boys' groups are larger than girls' groups, and they participate in more organized games than girls do. Boys are more likely to engage in rough-and-tumble play, competition, ego displays, risk taking, and dominance seeking, whereas girls are more likely to engage in collaborative discourse.

Adolescent Peer Relations

- Child groups are less formal and less heterogeneous than adolescent groups; child groups are also more likely to have same-sex participants. The pressure to conform to peers is strong during adolescence, especially around the eighth and ninth grades. Cliques and crowds assume more importance in the lives of adolescents than children. Membership in certain crowds—especially jocks and populars—is associated with increased self-esteem. Independents also show high self-esteem. Cultures vary in how extensively peers influence adolescents, with some countries restricting adolescents' access to peers more than others, especially for girls. In some cultures, peers assume parental responsibilities.

2   FRIENDSHIP: EXPLAIN THE ROLE OF FRIENDSHIP THROUGH THE LIFE SPAN

Functions of Friendship

- The functions of friendship include companionship, stimulation, ego support, social comparison, and intimacy/affection.

Friendship During Childhood

- Throughout childhood, friends are generally similar—in terms of age, sex, ethnicity, and many other factors. Although having friends is usually a developmental advantage, the quality of friendships varies and having a coercive, conflict-ridden friendship can be harmful.

Friendship During Adolescence and Emerging Adulthood

- Sullivan argued that there is a dramatic increase in the psychological importance of intimacy of close friends in adolescence. Friendships are important sources of support for adolescents. Research findings generally support his view. The friendships of adolescent girls are more intimate than those of adolescent boys. Adolescents who become friends with older individuals engage in more deviant behaviors than their counterparts with same-age friends. Many aspects of friendship are the same in emerging adulthood as in adolescence, although the transition to college can bring changes in friendship.

Adult Friendship

- Friendships play an important role in adult development, especially in providing emotional support. Female, male, and female-male friendships often have different characteristics. Unclear sexual boundaries can produce tension and confusion in cross-gender friendships. Regardless of age, friendship is an important aspect of relationships. In old age, people choose close friends over new friends. Unmarried older adults in a friend-focused network experience better physical and psychological health than those with little friend contact.

3   PLAY AND LEISURE: DESCRIBE THE DEVELOPMENTAL ASPECTS OF PLAY AND LEISURE

Childhood

- The functions of play include affiliation with peers, tension release, advances in cognitive development, and exploration. The contemporary perspective emphasizes both social and cognitive aspects of play. The most widely studied types of play include sensorimotor and practice play, pretense/symbolic play, social play, constructive play, and games.

Adolescence

- Leisure refers to the pleasant times when individuals are free to pursue activities and interests of their own choosing—hobbies, sports, or reading, for example. U.S. adolescents have more discretionary time than adolescents in other industrialized countries, and they often fill this time with unchallenging activities such as hanging out and watching television. U.S. adolescents spend more time in voluntary structured activities—such as hobbies, sports, and organizations—than East Asian adolescents. Some scholars argue that U.S. adolescents have too much unstructured discretionary time that should be replaced with more challenging activities.

Adulthood

- As adults, we not only need to learn to work well, but we also need to learn to enjoy leisure. Midlife may be an especially important time for leisure because of expanded free time, because of the availability of more money to many individuals, and because of psychological preparation for an active retirement.

4   AGING AND THE SOCIAL WORLD: SUMMARIZE THE SOCIAL ASPECTS OF AGING

Social Theories of Aging

- Disengagement theory, in which older adults gradually withdraw from society, has not held up; but socioemotional selectivity theory, in which older adults become more selective about their social networks; and activity theory, in which older adults who are active, energetic, and productive age more successfully and are happier, are viable theories of aging.

Stereotyping of Older Adults

Social Support and Social Integration

Successful Aging

- There is extensive stereotyping of older adults, and ageism—the prejudice against others because of their age—is a common occurrence.

- Social support is an important aspect of helping people cope with stress. Older adults usually have less integrated social networks and engage in less social activity than their younger counterparts, although these findings may be influenced by cohort effects. Families and friends play important social support roles for older adults. Being lonely and socially isolated is a significant health risk factor.

- Increasingly, the positive aspects of aging are being studied. Factors that are linked with successful aging include an active lifestyle, positive coping skills, good social relationships and support, and self-efficacy.

5 SOCIOCULTURAL INFLUENCES: EVALUATE SOCIOCULTURAL INFLUENCES ON DEVELOPMENT

Culture

- Culture refers to the behavior, patterns, beliefs, and all other products of a group of people that are passed on from generation to generation. Cross-cultural comparisons involve the comparison of one culture with one or more cultures, which provides information about the degree to which development is universal or culture-specific. One way that the influence of culture has been studied is to characterize cultures as individualistic (giving priority to personal rather than group goals) or collectivistic (emphasizing values that serve the group). Many experts argue that exposure to television violence can cause increased aggression. Heavy TV watching is linked to lower school achievement. Children and youth also spend substantial amounts of time on the Internet. Adolescents' online time can have positive or negative outcomes. Large numbers of adolescents and emerging adults engage in social networking on MySpace and Facebook. Although older adults are less likely to have a computer and use the Internet than younger adults, they are the fastest-growing segment of Internet users. Respect for the aged may vary across cultures. Factors that predict high status for the older adults across cultures range from the perception that they have valuable knowledge to the belief that they serve useful functions.

Socioeconomic Status and Poverty

- Socioeconomic status (SES) is the grouping of people with similar occupational, educational, and economic characteristics. The neighborhoods, schools, and families of children have SES characteristics that are related to the child's development. Parents from low-SES families are more concerned that their children conform to society's expectations, have an authoritarian parenting style, use physical punishment more in disciplining their children, and are more directive and less conversational with their children than higher-SES parents. Poverty is defined by economic hardship. The subculture of the poor is often characterized not only by economic hardship but also by social and psychological difficulties. Persistent long-lasting poverty especially has adverse effects on children's development. Older adults who live in poverty are a special concern. The majority of older adults face a life of reduced income.

Ethnicity

- Ethnicity is based on cultural heritage, nationality characteristics, race, religion, and language. Immigration brings a number of challenges as children adapt to their new culture. Too often researchers have not teased apart ethnic and socioeconomic status effects. Although not all ethnic minority families are poor, poverty contributes to the stress of many ethnic minority families and between ethnic minority groups and the non-Latino White majority. African American and Latino children are more likely than non-Latino White American children to live in single-parent families and larger families and to have extended family connections. Recognizing differences in ethnicity is an important aspect of getting along with others in a diverse, multicultural world. Too often differences have been described as deficits on the part of ethnic minority individuals. Ethnic groups are not homogeneous. Failure to recognize this diversity results in stereotyping. A special concern involves ethnicity and aging.

KEY TERMS

peers 556
popular children 559
average children 559
neglected children 559
rejected children 559
controversial children 559
cliques 563
crowds 564

intimacy in friendship 566
play 570
play therapy 570
sensorimotor play 571
practice play 571
pretense/symbolic play 571
social play 572
constructive play 572

games 572
leisure 572
disengagement theory 575
activity theory 575
ageism 575
culture 577
cross-cultural studies 577
ethnocentrism 578

individualism 579
collectivism 579
socioeconomic status
  (SES) 585
feminization of
  poverty 588

KEY PEOPLE

Kenneth Dodge 559
John Coie 560
Harry Stack Sullivan 556
Daniel Berlyne 571

Catherine Garvey 572
Angeline Lillard 572
Reed Larson 573
Richard Brislin 578

Donald Campbell 578
Douglas Gentile 582
Suniya Luthar 586
Vonnie McLoyd 588

Aletha Huston 589

E-LEARNING TOOLS

Connect to **www.mhhe.com/santrockldt5e** to research the answers and complete these exercises. In addition, you'll find a number of other resources and valuable study tools for Chapter 15, "Peers and the Sociocultural World," on this Web site.

Taking It to the Net

1. Charise is completing her course work for a Ph.D. in developmental psychology. She does not want to teach and she is not interested in working in a research lab—however, she is very creative and loves young children. Her dissertation advisor suggested that she look into working for a toy company. What role do developmental psychologists play in developing the toys that young children play with?

2. Jeff is the director of the local YMCA's family programs. He would like to conduct a seminar for parents on how to help children cope with peer pressure. What can parents do to help their children resist negative peer pressure?

3. Pauline and Maria are both bright children who attend elementary school. Pauline lives in an upper-class home where education is valued. Maria lives in a low-income home where having enough to eat is more of a concern than educational aspirations. How is Maria likely to be affected by her environment?

Self-Assessment

To examine your ideas about stereotyping related to race and aging, complete these self-assessments:

- *Do I Engage in Racial and Aging Stereotyping?*
- *My Beliefs About Aging*

Health and Well-Being, Parenting, and Education

Build your decision-making skills by trying your hand at the health and well-being, parenting, and education exercises.

Video Clips

The Online Learning Center includes the following videos for this chapter:

- *Children's Social Networks*
- *Parallel Play in the Sandbox*
- *Describing a Best Friend at Age 2*
- *Understanding Friendships at Age 5*
- *Describing a Best Friend at Age 11*
- *Characteristics of Children Who Bully*

16

Life is a gift . . . Accept it.
Life is a puzzle . . . Solve it.
Life is an adventure . . . Dare it.
Life is an opportunity . . . Take it.
Life is a mystery . . . Unfold it.
Life is a mission . . . Fulfill it.
Life is a struggle . . . Face it.
Life is a goal . . . Achieve it.

—AUTHOR UNKNOWN

LEARNING GOALS

◆ Describe the role of schools in development.

◆ Explain the key aspects of achievement.

◆ Discuss career development, work, and retirement.

SCHOOLS, ACHIEVEMENT, AND WORK

CHAPTER OUTLINE

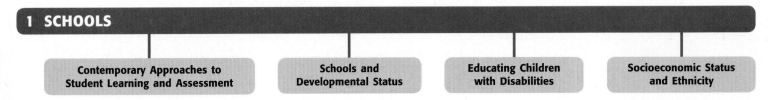

PREVIEW

This chapter is about becoming educated, achieving, and working. We begin the chapter by exploring the importance of schools in development and then examine many aspects of a topic that is closely linked to success in school and life—achievement. The final section of the chapter focuses on key aspects of career development, the role of work across the life span, and retirement as a help or a hindrance to our development.

1 SCHOOLS

Contemporary Approaches to Student Learning and Assessment	Schools and Developmental Status	Educating Children with Disabilities	Socioeconomic Status and Ethnicity

We have discussed many aspects of schools throughout this book but especially in Section 3, "Cognitive Processes and Development." Recall our coverage of applications of Piaget's and Vygotsky's theories to education in Chapter 6, "Cognitive Developmental Approaches," strategies for encouraging children's critical thinking in schools in Chapter 7, "Information Processing," applications of Gardner's and Sternberg's theories of intelligence to education in Chapter 8, "Intelligence," and bilingual education in Chapter 9, "Language Development." Among the topics related to schools that we explore here are contemporary approaches to student learning, education for individuals at different developmental levels, educating children with disabilities, and socioeconomic status and ethnicity in schools.

Contemporary Approaches to Student Learning and Assessment

Controversy swirls about the best way to teach children and how to hold schools and teachers accountable for whether children are learning (Abruscato & DeRosa, 2010; Parkay & Stanford, 2010).

Constructivist and Direct Instruction Approaches   The **constructivist approach** is a learner-centered approach that emphasizes the importance of individuals actively constructing their knowledge and understanding with guidance from the teacher. In the constructivist view, teachers should not attempt to simply pour information into children's minds. Rather, children should be encouraged to explore their world, discover knowledge, reflect, and think critically with careful monitoring and meaningful guidance from the teacher (Eby, Herrell, & Jordan, 2009; Maxim, 2010). The constructivist belief is that for too long in American education children have been required to sit still, be passive learners, and rotely memorize irrelevant as well as relevant information (Armstrong, Henson, & Savage, 2009).

Today, constructivism may include an emphasis on collaboration—children working with each other in their efforts to know and understand (McNeil, 2009). A teacher with a constructivist instructional philosophy would not have children memorize information rotely but would give them opportunities to meaningfully construct the knowledge and understand the material while guiding their learning (Kellough & Carjuzaa, 2009).

By contrast, the **direct instruction approach** is a structured, teacher-centered approach that is characterized by teacher direction and control, high teacher expectations for students' progress, maximum time spent by students on academic tasks,

Is this classroom more likely constructivist or direct instruction? Explain.

constructivist approach A learner-centered approach that emphasizes the individual's active, cognitive construction of knowledge and understanding with guidance from the teacher.

direct instruction approach A teacher-centered approach characterized by teacher direction and control, high expectations for students' progress, and maximum time spent on academic tasks.

and efforts by the teacher to keep negative affect to a minimum. An important goal in the direct instruction approach is maximizing student learning time.

Advocates of the constructivist approach argue that the direct instruction approach turns children into passive learners and does not adequately challenge them to think in critical and creative ways (Abruscato & DeRosa, 2010; Eby, Herrell, & Jordan, 2009). The direct instruction enthusiasts say that the constructivist approaches do not give enough attention to the content of a discipline, such as history or science. They also believe that the constructivist approaches are too relativistic and vague.

Some experts in educational psychology stress that many effective teachers use both a constructivist *and* a direct instruction approach rather than using either one exclusively (Bransford & others, 2006). Further, some circumstances may call more for a constructivist approach, others for a direction instruction approach. For example, experts increasingly recommend an explicit, intellectually engaging direct instruction approach when teaching students with a reading or a writing disability (Berninger, 2006).

Accountability As the public and government have demanded increased accountability of how effectively schools are educating children, state-mandated tests have taken on a more powerful role (Gronlund & Waugh, 2009; Oosterhof, 2009). Most states have or are in the process of identifying objectives that every student in the state is expected to achieve. Teachers are strongly encouraged to incorporate these objectives into their classroom planning and instruction.

Some policy makers argue that state-mandated testing will have a number of positive effects. These include improved student performance; high expectations for all students; identification of poorly performing schools, teachers, and administrators; and improved confidence in schools as test scores increase.

The most visible aspect of state-mandated testing involves the No Child Left Behind (NCLB) Act, the federal legislation that was signed into law in 2002. NCLB is the U.S. government's effort to hold schools and school districts accountable for the success or failure of their students (Yell & Drasgow, 2009). The legislation shifts the responsibility to the states, with states being required to create their own standards for students' achievement in mathematics, English/language arts, and science. In 2006, states were required to give all students annual tests in grades 3 through 8.

A number of criticisms of NCLB have been made (Stiggins, 2008). Critics argue that the NCLB legislation will do more harm than good. One criticism stresses that using a single score from a single test as the sole indicator of students' progress and competence represents a very narrow aspect of students' skills (Lewis, 2007). This criticism is similar to the one leveled at IQ tests, which we considered in Chapter 8, "Intelligence." To more accurately assess student progress and achievement, many psychologists and educators emphasize that a number of measures should be used, including tests, quizzes, projects, portfolios, classroom observations, and so on, rather than a single score on a single test.

Also, the tests schools are using to assess achievement and progress as part of NCLB don't measure such important skills as creativity, motivation, persistence, flexible thinking, and social skills. Critics point out that teachers are spending far too much class time "teaching to the test" by drilling students and having them memorize isolated facts at the expense of more student-centered constructivist teaching that focuses on higher-level thinking skills, which students need for success in life. Many educational psychologists conclude that the challenge is to teach creatively within the structure imposed by NCLB (McMillan, 2007).

Despite such criticisms, the U.S. Department of Education is committed to implementing NCLB, and schools are making accommodations to meet the requirements of this law. Indeed, most educators support the importance of high expectations and high standards of excellence for students. At issue, however, is whether the tests and procedures mandated by NCLB are the best ones for achieving these high standards (Yell & Drasgow, 2009).

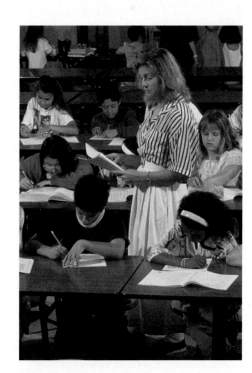

What characterizes the U.S. government's No Child Left Behind legislation? What are some criticisms of No Child Left Behind?

Schools and Developmental Status

Let's now explore how schools work at different developmental levels of students. We begin with early childhood education.

Early Childhood Education   Attending preschool is rapidly becoming the norm for U.S. children. In 2002, 43 states funded pre-kindergarten programs, and 55 percent of U.S. 3- and 4-year-old children attended center-based programs (NAEYC, 2005). Many other 3- and 4-year-old children attend private preschool programs.

There are numerous variations in the way young children are educated (Feeney & others, 2010; Hendrick & Weissman, 2010). The foundation of early childhood education has been the child-centered kindergarten.

The Child-Centered Kindergarten   In the 1840s, Friedrich Froebel's concern for quality education for young children led to the founding of the kindergarten— literally, "a garden for children." The founder of the kindergarten understood that, like growing plants, children require careful nurturing. Unfortunately, too many of today's kindergartens have forgotten the importance of careful nurturing (Krogh & Slentz, 2001).

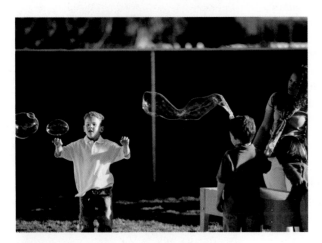

What are some characteristics of the child-centered kindergarten?

Nurturing is still key in the **child-centered kindergarten.** It emphasizes education of the whole child and concern for his or her physical, cognitive, and socioemotional development (Marion, 2010). Instruction is organized around the child's needs, interests, and learning styles. Emphasis is on the process of learning, rather than what is learned (Hendrick & Weissman, 2010). The child-centered kindergarten honors three principles: Each child follows a unique developmental pattern; young children learn best through firsthand experiences with people and materials; and play is extremely important in the child's total development. *Experimenting, exploring, discovering, trying out, restructuring, speaking,* and *listening* are frequent activities in excellent kindergarten programs. Such programs are closely attuned to the developmental status of 4- and 5-year-old children.

The Montessori Approach   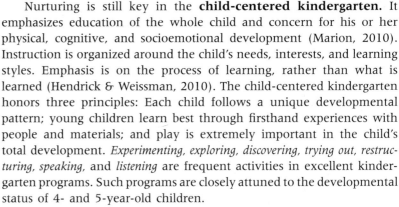 Montessori schools are patterned after the educational philosophy of Maria Montessori (1870–1952), an Italian physician-turned-educator, who crafted a revolutionary approach to young children's education at the beginning of the twentieth century (Wentworth, 1999). Her work began in Rome with a group of children who were mentally retarded. She was successful in teaching them to read, write, and pass examinations designed for normal children. Some time later, she turned her attention to poor children from the slums of Rome and had similar success in teaching them. Her approach has since been adopted extensively in private nursery schools in the United States.

The **Montessori approach** is a philosophy of education in which children are given considerable freedom and spontaneity in choosing activities. They are allowed to move from one activity to another as they desire. The teacher acts as a facilitator rather than a director. The teacher shows the child how to perform intellectual activities, demonstrates interesting ways to explore curriculum materials, and offers help when the child requests it. "By encouraging children to make decisions from an early age, Montessori programs seek to develop self-regulated problem solvers who can make choices and manage their time effectively" (Hyson, Copple, & Jones, 2006, p. 14). The number of Montessori schools in the United States has expanded dramatically in recent years, from one school in 1959 to 355 schools in 1970 to approximately 4,000 in 2005 (Whitescarver, 2006).

Some developmentalists favor the Montessori approach, but others maintain that it neglects children's social development. For example, while Montessori fosters

child-centered kindergarten Education that involves the whole child by considering both the child's physical, cognitive, and socioemotional development and the child's needs, interests, and learning styles.

Montessori approach An educational philosophy in which children are given considerable freedom and spontaneity in choosing activities and are allowed to move from one activity to another as they desire.

independence and the development of cognitive skills, it deemphasizes verbal interaction between the teacher and child and peer interaction. Montessori's critics also argue that it restricts imaginative play and that its heavy reliance on self-corrective materials may not adequately allow for creativity and for a variety of learning styles (Goffin & Wilson, 2001).

Developmentally Appropriate and Inappropriate Education   A growing number of educators and psychologists stress that preschool and young elementary school children learn best through active, hands-on teaching methods such as games and dramatic play. They know that children develop at varying rates and that schools need to allow for these individual differences. They also note that schools should focus on improving children's socioemotional development, as well as their cognitive development (Morrison, 2009). Educators refer to this type of schooling as **developmentally appropriate practice,** which is based on knowledge of the typical development of children within an age span (age appropriateness) as well as the uniqueness of the child (individual appropriateness) (NAEYC, 2009). In contrast, developmentally inappropriate practice for a young child relies on abstract paper-and-pencil activities presented to large groups. Figure 16.1 describes the recently revised recommendations for developmentally appropriate education of the National Association for the Education of Young Children (NAEYC, 2009).

Larry Page and Sergey Brin, founders of the highly successful Internet search engine, Google, recently said that their early years at Montessori schools were a major factor in their success (International Montessori Council, 2006). During an interview with Barbara Walters, they said they learned how to be self-directed and self-starters at Montessori (ABC News, 2005). They commented that Montessori experiences encouraged them to think for themselves and allowed them the freedom to develop their own interests.

One study compared 182 children from five developmentally appropriate kindergarten classrooms (with hands-on activities and integrated curriculum tailored to meet age group, cultural, and individual learning styles) and five developmentally inappropriate kindergarten classrooms (which had an academic, direct instruction emphasis with extensive use of workbooks/worksheets, seatwork, and rote drill/practice activities) in a Louisiana school system (Hart & others, 2003). Children taught in developmentally inappropriate classrooms had slower growth in vocabulary, math application, and math computation. However, not all studies show significant positive benefits for developmentally appropriate education (Hyson, 2007). Among the reasons it is difficult to generalize about research on developmentally appropriate education is that individual programs often vary, and developmentally appropriate education is an evolving concept. Recent changes in the concept have given more attention to sociocultural factors, the teacher's active involvement and implementation of systematic intentions, as well as how strong academic skills should be emphasized and how they should be taught.

Education for Young Children Who Are Disadvantaged   For many years, U.S. children from low-income families did not receive any education before they entered the first grade. Often, they began first grade already several steps behind their classmates in their readiness to learn. In the summer of 1965, the federal government began Project Head Start in an effort to break the cycle of poverty and poor education for young children in the United States. **Project Head Start** is a compensatory program designed to provide children from low-income families the opportunity to acquire the skills and experiences important for success in school. Project Head Start is the largest federally funded program for U.S. children (Hagen & Lamb-Parker, 2008). In 2007, 3 percent of Head Start children were 5 years old, 51 percent were 4 years old, 36 percent were 3 years old, and 10 percent were under 3 years of age (Administration for Children and Families, 2008).

Early Head Start was established in 1995 to serve children from birth to 3 years of age. In 2007, half of all new funds appropriated for Head Start programs were used for the expansion of Early Head Start. Researchers have found positive effects for Early Head Start (Hoffman & Ewen, 2007).

Head Start programs are not all created equal. More attention needs to be given to developing consistently high-quality Head Start programs (Chambers,

developmentally appropriate practice Education that focuses on the typical developmental patterns of children (age appropriateness) and the uniqueness of each child (individual appropriateness). Such practice contrasts with developmentally inappropriate practice, which has an academic, direct instruction emphasis focused largely on abstract paper-and-pencil activities, seatwork, and rote/drill practice activities.

Project Head Start Compensatory education designed to provide children from low-income families the opportunity to acquire the skills and experiences important for school success.

Core Considerations in Developmentally Appropriate Practice

1. **Knowledge to consider in making decisions.**
   In all aspects of working with children, early childhood practitioners need to consider these three areas of knowledge; (a) what is known about child development and learning, especially age-related characteristics; (b) what is known about each child as an individual; and (c) what is known about the social and cultural contexts in which children live.

2. **Challenging and achieveable goals.**
   Keeping in mind desired goals and what is known about the children as a group and individually, teachers plan experiences to promote children's learning and development.

Principles of Child Development and Learning That Inform Practice

1. All the domains of development and learning—physical, cognitive, and social—are important, and they are linked.

2. Many aspects of children's learning and development follow well-documented sequences, with later abilities, skills, and knowledge building on those already acquired.

3. Development and learning proceed at varying rates from child to child, and at uneven rates across different areas of a child's individual functioning.

4. Development and learning result from the interaction of biology and experience.

5. Early experiences have strong effects—both cumulative and delayed—on children's development and learning; optimal periods exist for certain types of development and learning.

6. Development proceeds toward greater complexity, self-regulation, and symbolic or representational capacities.

7. Children develop best when they have secure, consistent relationships with responsive adults and opportunities for positive peer relations.

8. Development and learning occur in and are influenced by multiple social and cultural contexts.

9. Always mentally active in seeking to understand the world around them, children learn in a variety of ways; a wide range of teaching strategies can be effective in guiding children's learning.

10. Play is an important context for developing self-regulation and for promoting language, cognition, and competence.

11. Development and learning advance when children are challenged to achieve at a level just beyond their current mastery and when they are given opportunities to practice newly acquired skills.

12. Children's experiences shape their motivation and approaches to learning, such as persistence, initiative, and flexibility; in turn, these characteristics influence their learning and development.

Guidelines for Developmentally Appropriate Practice

1. **Creating a caring community of learners.**
   Each member of the community should be valued by the others; relationships are an important context through which children learn; practitioners ensure that members of the community feel psychologically safe.

2. **Teaching to enhance development and learning.**
   The teacher takes responsibility for stimulating, directing, and supporting children's learning by providing the experiences that each child needs.

3. **Planning curriculum to achieve important goals.**
   The curriculum is planned to help children achieve goals that are developmentally appropriate and educationally significant.

4. **Assessing children's development and learning.**
   In developmentally appropriate practice, assessments are linked to the program's goals for children.

5. **Establishing reciprocal relationships with families.**
   A positive partnership between teachers and families benefits children's learning and development.

FIGURE 16.1 Recommendations by NAEYC for Developmentally Appropriate Practice in Early Childhood Programs Serving Children from Birth Through Age 8. *Source:* Adapted from: NAEYC (2009). Developmentally appropriate practice in early childhood programs serving children from birth through age 8.

Cheung, & Slavin, 2006). One individual who is strongly motivated to make Head Start a valuable learning experience for young children from disadvantaged backgrounds is Yolanda Garcia. To read about her work, see the *Careers in Life-Span Development* profile.

Evaluations support the positive influence of quality early childhood programs on both the cognitive and social worlds of disadvantaged young children (Schweinhart & others, 2005). One high-quality early childhood education program (although not a Head Start program) is the Perry Preschool program in Ypsilanti, Michigan, a two-year preschool program that includes weekly home visits from program personnel. In analyses of the long-term effects of the program, adults who had been in the Perry Preschool program were compared with a control group of adults from the same background who did not receive the enriched early childhood education (Schweinhart & others, 2005; Weikert, 1993). Those who had been in the Perry

Careers in Life-Span Development

Yolanda Garcia, Director of Children's Services/Head Start

Yolanda Garcia has been the director of the Children's Services Department for the Santa Clara, California, County Office of Education since 1980. As director, she is responsible for managing child development programs for 2,500 3- to 5-year-old children in 127 classrooms. Her training includes two master's degrees, one in public policy and child welfare from the University of Chicago and another in education administration from San Jose State University.

Garcia has served on many national advisory committees that have resulted in improvements in the staffing of Head Start programs. Most notably, she served on the Head Start Quality Committee that recommended the development of Early Head Start and revised performance standards for Head Start programs. Garcia currently is a member of the American Academy of Science Committee on the Integration of Science and Early Childhood Education.

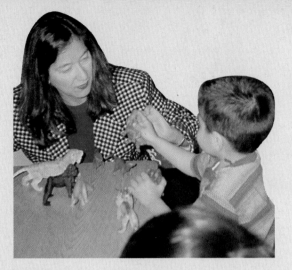

Yolanda Garcia, Director of Children's Services/Head Start, working with some Head Start children in Santa Clara, California.

Preschool program had fewer teen pregnancies and higher high school graduation rates (Weikert, 1993), and at age 40 more were in the workforce, owned their own homes, had a savings account, and had fewer arrests (Schweinhart & others, 2005). In sum, ample evidence indicates that well-designed and well-implemented early childhood education programs are successful with low-income children.

Curriculum Controversy in Early Childhood Education Currently there is controversy about what the curriculum of U.S. early childhood education should be (Hyson, 2007). On one side are those who advocate a child-centered, constructivist approach much like that emphasized by the NAEYC along the lines of developmentally appropriate practice. On the other side are those who advocate an academic, direct instruction approach.

In reality, numerous high-quality early childhood education programs include both academic and constructivist approaches. Many education experts like Lilian Katz (1999), though, worry about academic approaches that place too much pressure on young children to achieve and don't provide any opportunities to actively construct knowledge. Competent early childhood programs also should focus on cognitive development and on socioemotional development, not exclusively on cognitive development (Hyson, 2007).

Elementary School For many children, entering the first grade signals a change from being a "home-child" to being a "school-child"—a situation in which they experience new roles and obligations. Children take up the new role of being a student, interact, develop new relationships, adopt new reference groups, and develop new standards by which to judge themselves. School provides children with a rich source of new ideas to shape their sense of self.

Too often early schooling proceeds mainly on the basis of negative feedback. For example, children's self-esteem in the later part of elementary school is lower than it is in the earlier part, and older children rate themselves as less smart, less good, and less hardworking than do younger ones (Eccles, 2003).

As children make the transition to elementary school, they interact and develop relationships with new and significant others. School provides them with a rich source of new ideas to shape their sense of self.

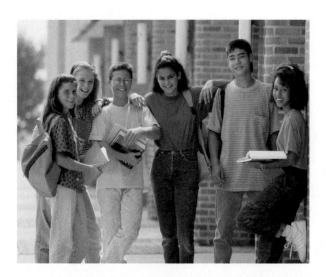

The transition from elementary to middle or junior high school occurs at the same time as a number of other developmental changes. *What are some of these other developmental changes?*

Educating Adolescents What is the transition from elementary to middle or junior high school like? What are the characteristics of effective schools for adolescents?

The Transition to Middle or Junior High School The transition to middle school or junior high school can be stressful (Anderman & Mueller, 2009; Elmore, 2009). Why? The transition takes place at a time when many changes—in the individual, in the family, and in school—are occurring simultaneously. These changes include puberty and related concerns about body image; the emergence of at least some aspects of formal operational thought, including accompanying changes in social cognition; increased responsibility and decreased dependency on parents; change to a larger, more impersonal school structure; change from one teacher to many teachers and from a small, homogeneous set of peers to a larger, more heterogeneous set of peers; and an increased focus on achievement and performance and their assessment. Also, when students make the transition to middle or junior high school, they experience the **top-dog phenomenon,** moving from being the oldest, biggest, and most powerful students in the elementary school to being the youngest, smallest, and least powerful students in the middle or junior high school. A recent study in North Carolina schools revealed that sixth-grade students attending middle schools were far more likely to be cited for discipline problems than their counterparts who were attending elementary schools (Cook & others, 2008).

There can also be positive aspects to the transition to middle or junior high school. Students are more likely to feel grown up, have more subjects from which to select, have more opportunities to spend time with peers and locate compatible friends, and enjoy increased independence from direct parental monitoring. They also may be more challenged intellectually by academic work.

Effective Schools for Young Adolescents Educators and psychologists worry that junior high and middle schools have become watered-down versions of high schools, mimicking their curricular and extracurricular schedules. Critics argue that these schools should offer activities that reflect a wide range of individual differences in biological and psychological development among young adolescents. The Carnegie Foundation (1989) issued an extremely negative evaluation of our nation's middle schools. It concluded that most young adolescents attended massive, impersonal schools, learned from irrelevant curricula, trusted few adults in school, and lacked access to health care and counseling. It recommended that the nation should develop smaller "communities" or "houses" to lessen the impersonal nature of large middle schools; have lower student-to-counselor ratios (10 to 1 instead of several hundred to 1); involve parents and community leaders in schools; develop new curricula; have teachers team teach in more flexibly designed curriculum blocks that integrate several disciplines; boost students' health and fitness with more in-school programs; and help students who need public health care to get it. In sum, many of the Carnegie Foundation's recommendations have not been implemented, and middle schools throughout the nation continue to need a major redesign if they are to be effective in educating adolescents (Eccles & Roeser, 2009; Elmore, 2009).

High School Just as there are concerns about U.S. middle school education, so are there concerns about U.S. high school education (Smith, 2009). Critics stress that many high schools foster passivity and that schools should create a variety of pathways for students to achieve an identity. Many students graduate from high school with inadequate reading, writing, and mathematical skills; of these, many go on to college and have to enroll in remediation classes there. Other students drop out of high school and do not have skills that will allow them to obtain decent jobs, much less to be informed citizens.

top-dog phenomenon The circumstance of moving from the top position in elementary school to the youngest, smallest, and least powerful position in middle or junior high school.

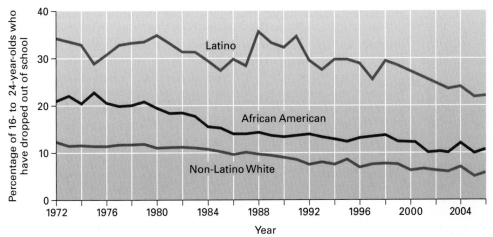

FIGURE 16.2 Trends in High School Dropout Rates. From 1972 through 2006, the school dropout rate for Latinos remained very high (22 percent of 16- to 24-year-olds in 2006). The African American dropout rate was still higher (10 percent) than the non-Latino White rate (6 percent) in 2006. (*Source:* National Center for Education Statistics, 2008a).

In the last half of the twentieth century and the first several years of the twenty-first century, U.S. high school dropout rates declined (National Center for Education Statistics, 2008a) (see Figure 16.2). In the 1940s, more than half of U.S. 16- to 24-year-olds had dropped out of school; by 2006, this figure had decreased to 9.3 percent. The dropout rate of Latino adolescents remains high, although it has been decreasing in the twenty-first century (from 28 percent in 2000 to 22 percent in 2006). The highest dropout rate in the United States, though, likely occurs for Native American youth—less than 50 percent finish their high school education.

Students drop out of schools for many reasons (Jimerson, 2009). In one study, almost 50 percent of the dropouts cited school-related reasons for leaving school, such as not liking school or being expelled or suspended (Rumberger, 1995). Twenty percent of the dropouts (but 40 percent of the Latino students) cited economic reasons for leaving school. One-third of the female students dropped out for personal reasons, such as pregnancy or marriage. A recent study revealed that when children's parents were involved in their school in middle and late childhood and when parents and adolescents had good relationships in early adolescence, a positive trajectory toward academic success was the likely outcome

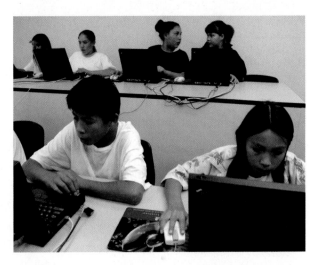

Students in the technology training center at Wellpint Elementary/High School located on the Spokane Indian Reservation in Washington. An important educational goal is to increase the high school graduation rate of Native American adolescents.

(Englund, Egeland, & Collins, 2008). By contrast, those who had poor relationships with their parents were more likely to drop out of high school despite doing well academically and behaviorally.

Early detection of children's school-related difficulties, and getting children engaged with school in positive ways, are important strategies for reducing the dropout rate (Jimerson, 2009). Recently the Bill and Melinda Gates Foundation (2006, 2008) has funded efforts to reduce the dropout rate in schools where dropout rates are high. One strategy that is being emphasized in the Gates' funding is keeping students at risk for dropping out of school with the same teachers through their high school years. The hope is that the teachers will get to know these students much better, their relationship with the students will improve, and they will be able to monitor and guide the students toward graduating from high school.

"I Have a Dream" (IHAD) is an innovative comprehensive, long-term dropout prevention program administered by the National "I Have a Dream" Foundation in New York. Since the National IHAD Foundation was created in 1986, it has grown to number over 180 projects in 64 cities and 27 states serving more than 15,000 children ("I Have a Dream" Foundation, 2009). Local IHAD projects around the country "adopt" entire grades (usually the third or fourth) from public elementary schools, or corresponding age cohorts from public housing developments. These children—"Dreamers"—are then provided with a program of academic, social, cultural,

These adolescents participate in the "I Have a Dream" (IHAD) program, a comprehensive, long-term dropout prevention program that has been very successful. *What are some strategies for reducing high school dropout rates?*

and recreational activities throughout their elementary, middle school, and high school years. When participants complete high school, IHAD provides the tuition assistance necessary for them to attend a state or local college or vocational school.

The IHAD program was created in 1981, when philanthropist Eugene Lang made an impromptu offer of college tuition to a class of graduating sixth-graders at P.S. 121 in East Harlem. Evaluations of IHAD programs have found dramatic improvements in grades, test scores, and school attendance, as well as a reduction of behavioral problems of Dreamers. In a recent analysis of the I Have a Dream program in Houston, 91 percent of the participants received passing grades in reading/English, 83 percent said they liked school, 98 percent said getting good grades is important to them, 100 percent said they plan to graduate from high school, and 94 percent reported they plan to go to college ("I Have a Dream" Foundation, 2009).

Many high school graduates not only are poorly prepared for college, they also are poorly prepared for the demands of the modern workplace. An increasing number of educators note that the nation's high schools need a new mission for the twenty-first century, which addresses the problems listed here (National Commission on the High School Senior Year, 2001):

- More support is needed to enable all students to graduate from high school with the knowledge and skills required to succeed in postsecondary education and careers. Many parents and students, especially those in low-income and minority communities, are unaware of the knowledge and level of skills required to succeed in postsecondary education.

- High schools need to have higher expectations for student achievement. A special concern is the senior year of high school, which has become too much of a party time.

College and Adult Education   Going to college offers many practical benefits, even beyond an education. The more education individuals have, the more income they will earn (*Occupational Outlook Handbook,* 2008–2009). Also, individuals with a college education live two years on the average longer than their counterparts who only graduate from high school. What is the transition to college like? Are adults seeking more education than in the past?

Transition to College   Just as the transition from elementary school to middle or junior high school involves change and possible stress, so does the transition from high school to college. The two transitions have many parallels. Going from being a senior in high school to being a freshman in college replays the top-dog phenomenon of transferring from the oldest and most powerful group of students to the youngest and least powerful group of students that occurred earlier as adolescence began. For many students, the transition from high school to college involves movement to a larger, more impersonal school structure; interaction with peers from more diverse geographical and sometimes more diverse ethnic backgrounds; and increased focus on achievement and its assessment. And like the transition from elementary to middle or junior high school, the transition from high school to college can involve positive features. Students are more likely to feel grown up, have more subjects from which to select, have more time to spend with peers, have more opportunities to explore different lifestyles and values, enjoy greater independence from parental monitoring, and be challenged intellectually by academic work (Santrock & Halonen, 2009).

Today's college students experience more stress and are more depressed than in the past, according to a national study of more than 300,000 freshmen at more than

learning disabilities Disabilities in which children experience difficulty in learning that involves understanding or using spoken or written language; the difficulty can appear in listening, thinking, reading, writing, and spelling. A learning disability also may involve difficulty in doing mathematics. To be classified as a learning disability, the learning problem is not primarily the result of visual, hearing, or motor disabilities; mental retardation; emotional disorders; or environmental, cultural, or economic disadvantage.

500 colleges and universities (Pryor & others, 2008). In 2008, 28 percent (up from 16 percent in 1985) said they frequently "felt overwhelmed with what I have to do." College females were more than twice as likely as their male counterparts (37 to 17 percent, respectively) to say that they felt overwhelmed with all they had to do. And college freshmen in 2008 indicated that they felt more depressed than their counterparts from the 1980s had indicated. The pressure to succeed in college, get a great job, and make lots of money were pervasive concerns of these students.

What makes college students happy? One study of 222 undergraduates compared the upper 10 percent of college students who were very happy with average and very unhappy college students (Diener & Seligman, 2002). The very happy college students were highly social, more extraverted, and had stronger romantic and social relationships than the less happy college students, who spent more time alone (see Figure 16.3).

Adult Education An increasing number of adults older than the traditional college age go to school (Smith & Reio, 2007). *Adult education* refers to all forms of schooling and learning in which adults participate. Adult education includes literacy training, community development, university credit programs, on-the-job training, and continuing professional education (Comings, 2007). Institutions that offer education to adults include colleges, libraries, museums, government agencies, businesses, and churches.

In 1985, individuals over the age of 25 represented 45 percent of the enrollment in credit courses in the United States. At the beginning of the twenty-first century, that figure is now slightly over 50 percent. A large and expanding number of college students are adults who pursue education and advanced degrees on a part-time basis (Smith & Reio, 2007). The increase in adult education is a result of increased leisure time for some individuals and the need to update information and skills for others. Some older adults simply take educational courses because they enjoy learning and want to keep their minds active.

Women represent the majority of adult learners—almost 60 percent. In the 35-and-over age group, women constitute an even greater percentage of the enrollment in adult education—almost 70 percent. Some of these women devoted their early adult lives to parenting and decided to go back to school to enter a new career.

Going back to a classroom after being away from school for a long time can be stressful. However, returning students should realize that they bring a wealth of experience to college and should feel good about the contributions they can make.

Many immigrants to the United States, such as this Spanish-speaking man and woman enrolled in an English class, take adult education classes. *What are some trends in adult education?*

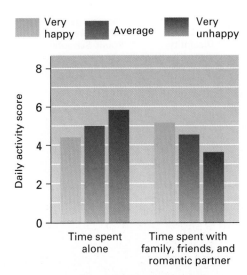

Very happy **Average** **Very unhappy**

Daily activity score

8

6

4

2

0

Time spent alone   Time spent with family, friends, and romantic partner

FIGURE 16.3 Daily Activity Self-Ratings and College Student's Happiness. In this study of undergraduates the daily activity scores reflect mean times with 1 representing no time and 8 reflecting 8 hours per day (Diener & Seligman, 2002). Students were classified as very happy, average, or very unhappy based on their self-ratings.

Educating Children with Disabilities

So far we have discussed schools as they are experienced by the majority of U.S. students. But 13.5 percent of all children from 3 to 21 years of age in the United States receive special education or related services (National Center for Education Statistics, 2008b). Figure 16.4 shows the four largest groups of students with a disability who were served by federal programs in the 2006–2007 school year (National Center for Education Statistics, 2008b). As indicated in Figure 16.4, students with a learning disability were by far the largest group of students with a disability to be given special education, followed by children with speech or language impairments, mental retardation, and emotional disturbance.

Learning Disabilities A child with a **learning disability** has difficulty in learning that involves understanding or using spoken or written language, and the difficulty

Disability	Percentage of All Children in Public Schools
Learning disability	5.4
Speach and language Impairments	3.0
Mental retardation	1.1
Emotional disturbance	.9

FIGURE 16.4 U.S. Children with a Disability Who Receive Special Education Services. Figures are for the 2006–2007 school year and represent the four categories with the highest number and percentage of children. Both learning disability and attention deficit hyperactivity disorder are combined in the learning disabilities category (National Center for Education Statistics, 2008b).

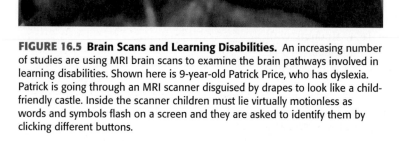

FIGURE 16.5 Brain Scans and Learning Disabilities. An increasing number of studies are using MRI brain scans to examine the brain pathways involved in learning disabilities. Shown here is 9-year-old Patrick Price, who has dyslexia. Patrick is going through an MRI scanner disguised by drapes to look like a child-friendly castle. Inside the scanner children must lie virtually motionless as words and symbols flash on a screen and they are asked to identify them by clicking different buttons.

can appear in listening, thinking, reading, writing, and spelling. A learning disability also may involve difficulty in doing mathematics. To be classified as a learning disability, the learning problem is not primarily the result of visual, hearing, or motor disabilities; mental retardation; emotional disorders; or is not due to environmental, cultural, or economic disadvantage.

From the mid-1970s through the mid-1990s, there was a dramatic increase in the percentage of U.S. students receiving special education services for a learning disability (from 1.8 percent in 1976–1977 to 5.8 percent in 1995–1996), although in the twenty-first century there has been a slight decrease in this percentage (6.1 percent in 2000 to 5.4 percent in 2006–2007) (National Center for Education Statistics, 2008b). Some experts say that the dramatic increase reflected poor diagnostic practices and overidentification. They argue that teachers sometimes are too quick to label children with the slightest learning problem as having a learning disability, instead of recognizing that the problem may rest in their ineffective teaching. Other experts say the increase in the number of children being labeled with a "learning disability" is justified (Hallahan, Kaufmann, & Pullen, 2009).

About three times as many boys as girls are classified as having a learning disability. Among the explanations for this gender difference are a greater biological vulnerability among boys and *referral bias.* That is, boys are more likely to be referred by teachers for treatment because of their behavior.

Diagnosing whether a child has a learning disability is often a difficult task (Fritschmann & Solari, 2008). Because federal guidelines are just that—guidelines—it is up to each state, or in some cases school systems within a state, to determine how to define and implement diagnosis of learning disabilities. The same child might be diagnosed as having a learning disability in one school system and receive services but not be diagnosed and not receive services in another school system. In such cases, parents sometimes will move either to obtain or to avoid the diagnosis.

The most common problem that characterizes children with a learning disability involves reading (Bender, 2008). **Dyslexia** is a category that is reserved for individuals who have a severe impairment in their ability to read and spell (Reid & others, 2009). Children with learning disabilities often have difficulties in handwriting, spelling, or composition. Their writing may be extremely slow, it may be virtually illegible, and they may make numerous spelling errors because of their inability to match up sounds and letters.

Researchers are using brain-imaging techniques in an effort to reveal brain regions that might be involved in learning disabilities (Shaywitz, Gruen, & Shaywitz, 2007) (see Figure 16.5). This research indicates that it is unlikely that learning disabilities reside in a single, specific brain location. More likely, learning disabilities are due to problems in integrating information from multiple brain regions or to subtle difficulties in brain structures and functions.

Many interventions have focused on improving the child's reading ability (Bender, 2008). Intensive instruction over a period of time by a competent teacher can help many children (Simos & others, 2007).

Attention Deficit Hyperactivity Disorder (ADHD) **Attention deficit hyperactivity disorder (ADHD)** is a disability in which children consistently show one or more of these characteristics over a period of time: (1) inattention, (2) hyperactivity, and (3) impulsivity. For an ADHD diagnosis, onset of these characteristics early in childhood is required and the characteristics must be debilitating for the child. Children who are inattentive have difficulty focusing on any one thing and may get bored with a task after only a few minutes. Children who are hyperactive show high levels of physical activity and almost always seem to be in motion. Children who are impulsive have difficulty curbing their reactions and do not do a good job of thinking before they act. Depending on the characteristics that children with ADHD display, they can be diagnosed as (1) ADHD with predominantly inattention, (2) ADHD with predominantly hyperactivity/impulsivity, or (3) ADHD with both inattention and hyperactivity/impulsivity.

The number of children diagnosed and treated for ADHD has increased substantially, by some estimates doubling in the 1990s. The disorder occurs as much as four to nine times more in boys than in girls. There is controversy, however, about the increased diagnosis of ADHD (Gargiulo, 2009). Some experts attribute the increase mainly to heightened awareness of the disorder. Others are concerned that many children are being incorrectly diagnosed (Parens & Johnston, 2009).

Unlike learning disabilities, ADHD is not supposed to be diagnosed by school teams because ADHD is a disorder that appears in the classification of psychiatric disorders called *DSM-IV* with specific diagnostic criteria (Bender, 2008). Although some school teams may diagnose a child as having ADHD, the diagnoses are incorrectly done and can lead to legal problems for schools and teachers. One reason that is given as to why a school team should not do the diagnosis for ADHD is that ADHD is difficult to differentiate from other childhood disorders, and accurate diagnosis requires the evaluation by a specialist in the disorder, such as a child psychiatrist.

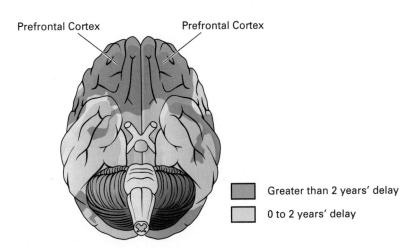

Many children and adolescents show impulsive behavior, such as this boy who is jumping out of his seat and throwing a paper airplane at classmates. *What is the best way for teachers to handle such situations?*

Causes and Course of ADHD   Definitive causes of ADHD have not been found. However, a number of causes have been proposed (Stolzer, 2009). Some children likely inherit a tendency to develop ADHD from their parents (Tripp & Wickens, 2009). Other children likely develop ADHD because of damage to their brain during prenatal or postnatal development (Banerjee, Middleton, & Faraone, 2007). Among early possible contributors to ADHD are cigarette and alcohol exposure during prenatal development and low birth weight (Knopik, 2009).

As with learning disabilities, the development of brain-imaging techniques is leading to a better understanding of the brain's role in ADHD (Shaw & others, 2007). A recent study revealed that peak thickness of the cerebral cortex occurred three years later (10.5 years) in children with ADHD than in children without ADHD (peak at 7.5 years) (Shaw & others, 2007). The delay was more prominent in the prefrontal regions of the brain that are especially important in attention and planning (see Figure 16.6). Researchers also are exploring the roles that various neurotransmitters, such as serotonin, might play in ADHD (Hercigonja Novkovic & others, 2009; Levy, 2009; Rader, McCauley, & Callen, 2009).

The increased academic and social demands of formal schooling, as well as stricter standards for behavioral control, often illuminate the problems of the child with ADHD (Ross & Ross, 2006). Elementary school teachers typically report that the child with ADHD has difficulty working independently, completing seatwork, and organizing work. Restlessness and distractibility also are often noted.

dyslexia A category of learning disabilities involving a severe impairment in the ability to read and spell.

attention deficit hyperactivity disorder (ADHD) A disability in which children consistently show one or more of the following characteristics: (1) inattention, (2) hyperactivity, and (3) impulsivity.

Prefrontal Cortex   Prefrontal Cortex

Greater than 2 years' delay

0 to 2 years' delay

FIGURE 16.6 Regions of the Brain in which children with ADHD Had a Delayed Peak in The Thickness of the Cerebral Cortex. *Note:* The greatest delays occurred in the prefrontal cortex.

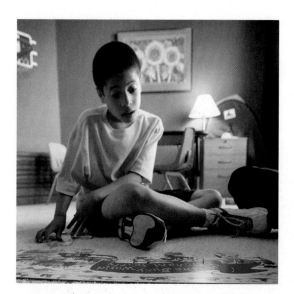

What characterizes autism spectrum disorder?

It used to be thought that ADHD decreased in adolescence, but new estimates suggest that ADHD decreases in only about one-third of adolescents. Increasingly, it is being recognized that these problems may continue into adulthood (Miller, Nigg, & Faraone, 2007).

Treatment of ADHD   Stimulant medication such as methylphenidate. (Ritalin), or amphetamine-dextroamphetamine (Adderall) (which has fewer side effects than Ritalin), is effective in improving the attention of many children with ADHD, but it usually does not improve their attention to the same level as children who do not have ADHD (Brams, Mao, & Doyle, 2009). A recent meta-analysis concluded that behavior management treatments are effective in reducing the effects of ADHD (Fabiano & others, 2009). Researchers have often found that a combination of medication (such as Ritalin) and behavior management improves the behavior of children with ADHD better than medication alone or behavior management alone, although not in all cases (Parens & Johnston, 2009). Other drugs, such as the stimulant called mixed amphetamine salts extended-release (MAS XR) and the nonstimulant atomoxetine (Strattera), are currently being studied in the treatment of children with ADHD, and early findings involving these drugs are promising (Faraone, 2007). A recent experimental study revealed that atomoxetine combined with a psychoeducational treatment was more effective than a placebo drug alone or psychoeducational treatment alone in reducing ADHD symptoms (Svanborg & others, 2009).

Critics argue that many physicians are too quick to prescribe stimulants for children with milder forms of ADHD (Marcovitch, 2004). Also, in 2006, the U.S. government issued a warning about the cardiovascular risks of stimulant medication to treat ADHD.

Autism Spectrum Disorders   **Autism spectrum disorders (ASDs),** also called pervasive developmental disorders, range from the severe disorder labeled autistic disorder to the milder disorder called Asperger syndrome. Autism spectrum disorders are characterized by problems in social interaction, problems in verbal and nonverbal communication, and repetitive behaviors (Goldman & others, 2009; Hall, 2009). Children with these disorders may also show atypical responses to sensory experiences (National Institute of Mental Health, 2008). Autism spectrum disorders can often be detected in children as early as 1 to 3 years of age.

Recent estimates of autism spectrum disorders indicate that they are increasing in occurrence or are increasingly being detected and labeled (Neal 2009). Once thought to affect only 1 in 2,500 individuals, today's estimates suggest that they occur in about 1 in 150 individuals (Centers for Disease Control and Prevention, 2009).

Autistic disorder is a severe developmental autism spectrum disorder that has its onset in the first three years of life and includes deficiencies in social relationships; abnormalities in communication; and restricted, repetitive, and stereotyped patterns of behavior. Estimates indicate that approximately 2 to 5 of every 10,000 young children in the United States have autistic disorder. Boys are about four times more likely to have an autistic disorder than girls.

Asperger syndrome is a relatively mild autism spectrum disorder in which the child has relatively good verbal language, milder nonverbal language problems, and a restricted range of interests and relationships (Bennett & others, 2008). Children with Asperger syndrome often engage in obsessive repetitive routines and preoccupations with a specific subject. For example, a child may be obsessed with baseball scores or railroad timetables.

What causes the autism spectrum disorders? The current consensus is that autism is a brain dysfunction with abnormalities in brain structure and neurotransmitters (Anderson & others, 2009; Gilbert & others, 2009). Genetic factors likely play a role in the development of the autism spectrum disorders (Nishiyama & others, 2009). A recent study revealed that missing or duplicated pieces of DNA on chromosome 16 can raise a child's risk of developing autism 100-fold (Weiss, & others,

autism spectrum disorders (ASDs) Also called pervasive developmental disorders, these range from the severe disorder labeled autistic disorder to the milder disorder called Asperger syndrome. Children with these disorders are characterized by problems in social interaction, verbal and nonverbal communication, and repetitive behaviors.

autistic disorder A severe autism spectrum disorder that has its onset in the first three years of life and includes deficiencies in social relationships; abnormalities in communication; and restricted, repetitive, and stereotyped patterns of behavior.

Asperger syndrome A relatively mild autism spectrum disorder in which the child has relatively good verbal language, milder nonverbal language problems, and a restricted range of interests and relationships.

2008). Estimates are that approximately 1 million U.S. children have an autistic disorder, so about 10,000 of them have this genetic mutation. There is no evidence that family socialization causes autism. Mental retardation is present in some children with autism; others show average or above-average intelligence (McCarthy, 2007).

Boys are four times as likely to have autism spectrum disorders as girls are (Gong & others, 2009). Expanding on autism's male-linkage, Simon Baron-Cohen (2008) recently argued that autism reflects an extreme male brain, especially indicative of males' less effective ability to show empathy and read facial expressions and gestures than girls are. In an attempt to improve these skills in 4- to 8-year-old autistic boys, Baron-Cohen and his colleagues (2007) produced a number of animations on a DVT) that place faces with different emotions on toy trains and tractor characters in a boy's bedroom (see Figure 16.7) (see www.thetransporters.com for a look at a number of the facial expression animations). After watching the animations 15 minutes every weekday for one month, the autistic children's ability to recognize real faces in a different context equaled that of children without autism.

Children with autism benefit from a well-structured classroom, individualized instruction, and small-group instruction. As with children who are mentally retarded, behavior modification techniques are sometimes effective in helping autistic children learn (Hall, 2009). A recent research review concluded that when these behavior modifications are intensely provided and used early in the autistic child's life, they are more effective (Howlin, Magiati, & Charman, 2009).

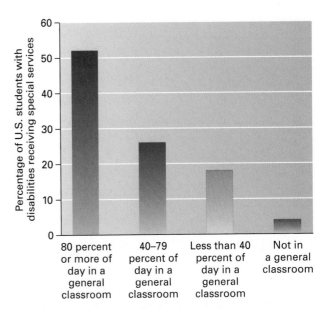

FIGURE 16.7 Percentage of U.S. Students with Disabilities 6 to 21 Years of Age Receiving Special Services in the General Classroom. (*Note:* Data for 2004–2005 School Year; National Center for Education Statistics, 2007).

Educational Issues   Until the 1970s most public schools either refused enrollment to children with disabilities or inadequately served them. In 1975, Public Law 94-142, the Education for All Handicapped Children Act, required that all students with disabilities be given a free, appropriate public education. In 1990, Public Law 94-142 was recast as the Individuals with Disabilities Education Act (IDEA). IDEA was amended in 1997 and then reauthorized in 2004 and renamed the Individuals with Disabilities Education Improvement Act (Turnbull, Huerta, & Stowe, 2009).

IDEA spells out broad mandates for services to all children with disabilities (Carter, Prater, & Dyches, 2009; Smith & others, 2008). These include evaluation and eligibility determination, appropriate education and an individualized education plan (IEP), and education in the least restrictive environment (LRE).

An **individualized education plan (IEP)** is a written statement that spells out a program that is specifically tailored for the student with a disability (Gargiulo, 2009). In general, the IEP should be (1) related to the child's learning capacity, (2) specifically constructed to meet the child's individual needs and not merely a copy of what is offered to other children, and (3) designed to provide educational benefits.

The **least restrictive environment (LRE)** is a setting that is as similar as possible to the one in which children who do not have a disability are educated. This provision of the IDEA has given a legal basis to efforts to educate children with a disability in the regular classroom (Smith & others, 2008). The term **inclusion** describes educating a child with special education needs full-time in the regular classroom (Gargiulo, 2009). Figure 16.7 indicates that in a recent school year slightly more than 50 percent of U.S. students with a disability spent more than 80 percent of their school day in a general classroom.

Many legal changes regarding children with disabilities have been extremely positive (Carter, Prater, & Dyches, 2009). Compared with several decades ago, far more children today are receiving competent, specialized services. For many children, inclusion in the regular classroom, with modifications or supplemental services, is appropriate (Hick & Thomas, 2009). However, some leading experts on special education argue that in some cases the effort to educate children with disabilities in the regular classroom has become too extreme. For example, James Kauffman and his colleagues (Kauffman

Public Law 94-142 mandates free, appropriate education for all children. *What are the aspects of this education?*

individualized education plan (IEP) A written statement that spells out a program tailored to a child with a disability. The plan should be (1) related to the child's learning capacity, (2) specially constructed to meet the child's individual needs and not merely a copy of what is offered to other children, and (3) designed to provide educational benefits.

least restrictive environment (LRE) A setting that is as similar as possible to the one in which children who do not have a disability are educated.

inclusion Education of a child with special education needs full-time in the regular classroom.

& Hallahan, 2005; Kauffman, McGee, and Brigham, 2004) state that inclusion too often has meant making accommodations in the regular classroom that do not always benefit children with disabilities. They advocate a more individualized approach that does not always involve full inclusion but allows options such as special education outside the regular classroom. Kauffman and his colleagues (2004, p. 620) acknowledge that children with disabilities "*do* need the services of specially trained professionals" and "*do* sometimes need altered curricula or adaptations to make their learning possible." However, "we sell students with disabilities short when we pretend that they are not different from typical students. We make the same error when we pretend that they must *not* be expected to put forth extra effort if they are to learn to do some things—or learn to do something in a different way." Like general education, special education should challenge students with disabilities "to become all they can be."

Socioeconomic Status and Ethnicity

Children from low-income, ethnic minority backgrounds have more difficulties in school than do their middle-socioeconomic-status non-Latino White counterparts. Why? Critics argue that schools have not done a good job of educating low-income, ethnic minority students to overcome the barriers to their achievement (Golnick & Chinn, 2009; Taylor & Whittaker, 2009). Let's further explore the roles of socioeconomic status and ethnicity in schools.

The Education of Students from Low-Income Backgrounds

Many children in poverty face problems that present barriers to their learning (McLoyd & others, 2009). They might have parents who don't set high educational standards for them, who are incapable of reading to them, and who don't have enough money to pay for educational materials and experiences, such as books and trips to zoos and museums. They might be malnourished and live in areas where crime and violence are a way of life. A recent study revealed that neighborhood disadvantage (involving such characteristics as low neighborhood income and high unemployment) was linked to less consistent, less stimulating, and more punitive parenting, and ultimately to negative child outcomes such as behavioral problems and low verbal ability (Kohen & others, 2008). Another recent study revealed that the longer children experienced poverty the more detrimental the poverty was to their cognitive development (Najman & others, 2009).

Compared with schools in higher-income areas, schools in low-income areas are more likely to have more students with low achievement test scores, low graduation rates, and small percentages of students going to college; they are more likely to have young teachers with less experience; and they are more likely to encourage rote learning (Leventhal, Dupéré, & Brooks-Gunn, 2009; Nelson & Lee, 2009). Too few schools in low-income neighborhoods provide students with environments that are conducive to learning (Koppelman & Goodheart, 2008). Many of the schools' buildings and classrooms are old and crumbling.

Ethnicity in Schools

More than one-third of all African American and almost one-third of all Latino students attend schools in the 47 largest city school districts in the United States, compared with only 5 percent of all non-Latino White and 22 percent of all Asian American students. Many of these inner-city schools are still segregated, are grossly underfunded, and do not provide adequate opportunities for children to learn effectively. Thus, the effects of SES and the effects of ethnicity are often intertwined (May, 2010; Nieto, 2010).

In *The Shame of the Nation*, Jonathan Kozol (2005) described his visits to 60 U.S. schools in low-income areas of cities in 11

Jill Nakamura, teaching in her first-grade classroom. Jill teaches in a school located in a high-poverty area. She visits students at home early in the school year in an effort to connect with them and develop a partnership with their parents. "She holds a daily afternoon reading club for students reading below grade level . . . In one school year (2004), she raised the percent of students reading at or above grade level from 29 percent to 76 percent" (Wong Briggs 2004, p. 6D).

states. After viewing many schools in which the minority population was 80 to 90 percent, he concluded that school segregation is still present for many poor minority students. Kozol saw many of the inequities just summarized—unkempt classrooms, hallways, and restrooms; inadequate textbooks and supplies; and lack of resources. He also saw teachers mainly instructing students to rotely memorize material, especially as preparation for mandated tests, rather than to engage in higher-level thinking. Kozol also frequently observed teachers using threatening disciplinary tactics to control the classroom.

Even outside inner-city schools, school segregation remains a factor in U.S. education. Almost one-third of all African American and Latino students attend schools in which 90 percent or more of the students are from minority groups (Banks, 2008).

The school experiences of students from different ethnic groups vary considerably (Banks, 2010; Manning & Baruth, 2009; Sleeter & Grant, 2009). African American and Latino students are much less likely than non-Latino White or Asian American students to be enrolled in academic, college preparatory programs and are much more likely to be enrolled in remedial and special education programs. Asian American students are far more likely than other ethnic minority groups to take advanced math and science courses in high school. African American students are twice as likely as Latinos, Native Americans, or non-Latino Whites to be suspended from school.

Following are some strategies for improving relationships among ethnically diverse students:

In *The Shame of the Nation*, Jonathan Kozol (2005) criticized the inadequate quality and lack of resources in many U.S. schools, especially those in the poverty areas of inner cities, that have high concentrations of ethnic minority children. Kozol praises teachers like Angela Lively (*above*), who keeps a box of shoes in her Indianapolis classroom for students in need.

- *Turn the class into a jigsaw classroom.* When Elliot Aronson was a professor at the University of Texas at Austin, the school system contacted him for ideas on how to reduce the increasing racial tension in classrooms. Aronson (1986) developed the concept of "jigsaw classroom," in which students from different cultural backgrounds are placed in a cooperative group in which they have to construct different parts of a project to reach a common goal. Aronson used the term *jigsaw* because he saw the technique as much like a group of students cooperating to put different pieces together to complete a jigsaw puzzle. How might this work? Team sports, drama productions, and music performances are examples of contexts in which students cooperatively participate to reach a common goal.

What are some features of a jigsaw classroom?

- *Encourage students to have positive personal contact with diverse other students.* Contact alone does not do the job of improving relationships with diverse others. For example, busing ethnic minority students to predominantly non-Latino White schools, or vice versa, has not reduced prejudice or improved interethnic relations (Minuchin & Shapiro, 1983). What matters is what happens after children get to school. Especially beneficial in improving interethnic relations is sharing one's worries, successes, failures, coping strategies, interests, and other personal information with people of other ethnicities. When this sharing happens, people tend to look at others as individuals rather than as members of a homogeneous group.

- *Encourage students to engage in perspective taking.* Exercises and activities that help students see others' perspectives can improve interethnic relations. These help students "step into the shoes" of peers who are culturally different and feel what it is like to be treated in fair or unfair ways.

- *Reduce bias.* Teachers can reduce bias by displaying images of children from diverse ethnic and cultural groups, selecting play materials and classroom activities that encourage cultural understanding, helping students resist stereotyping, and working with parents.

Careers in Life-Span Development

James Comer, Child Psychiatrist

James Comer grew up in a low-income neighborhood in East Chicago, Indiana, and credits his parents with leaving no doubt about the importance of education. He obtained a B.A. degree from Indiana University. He went on to obtain a medical degree from Howard University College of Medicine, a Master of Public Health degree from the University of Michigan School of Public Health, and psychiatry training at the Yale University School of Medicine's Child Study Center. He currently is the Maurice Falk Professor of Child Psychiatry at the Yale University Child Study Center and an associate dean at the Yale University Medical School. During his years at Yale, Comer has concentrated his career on promoting a focus on child development as a way of improving schools. His efforts in support of healthy development of young people are known internationally.

Dr. Comer perhaps is best known for the founding of the School Development program in 1968, which promotes the collaboration of parents, educators, and community to improve social, emotional, and academic outcomes for children. His concept of teamwork is currently improving the educational environment in more than 600 schools throughout America.

James Comer (*left*) is shown with some of the inner-city African American children who attend a school that became a better learning environment because of Comer's intervention.

- *View the school and community as a team.* James Comer (2004, 2006) emphasizes that a community, team approach is the best way to educate children. Three important aspects of the Comer Project for Change are (1) a governance and management team that develops a comprehensive school plan, assessment strategy, and staff development plan; (2) a mental health or school support team; and (3) a parents' program. Comer holds that the entire school community should have a cooperative rather than an adversarial attitude. The Comer program is currently operating in more than 600 schools in 26 states. To read further about James Comer's work, see the *Careers in Life-Span Development* profile.

Review and Reflect: Learning Goal 1

 Describe the role of schools in development

REVIEW

- What are some contemporary approaches to student learning?
- How do schools change as children develop?
- What are learning disabilities, ADHD, and autism spectrum disorders? What is involved in educating children with disabilities?
- What roles do socioeconomic status and ethnicity play in schools?

REFLECT

- What was your middle or junior high school like? How did it measure up to the Carnegie Foundation's recommendations?

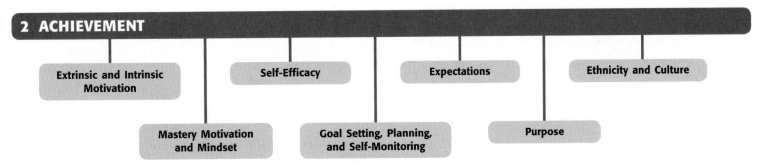

2 ACHIEVEMENT

- Extrinsic and Intrinsic Motivation
- Self-Efficacy
- Expectations
- Ethnicity and Culture
- Mastery Motivation and Mindset
- Goal Setting, Planning, and Self-Monitoring
- Purpose

In any classroom, whoever the teacher is and whatever approach is used, some children achieve more than others. Why? Among the reasons for variations in achievement are characteristics of the child and sociocultural contexts related to motivation.

Extrinsic and Intrinsic Motivation

The behavioral perspective emphasizes the importance of extrinsic motivation. **Extrinsic motivation** involves doing something to obtain something else (the activity is a means to an end). Extrinsic motivation is often influenced by external incentives such as rewards and punishments. For example, a student may study for a test in order to obtain a good grade.

Whereas the behavioral perspective emphasizes extrinsic motivation in achievement, the cognitive perspective stresses the importance of intrinsic motivation. **Intrinsic motivation** involves the internal motivation to do something for its own sake (the activity is an end in itself). For example, a student may study hard for a test because he or she enjoys the content of the course.

Let's first consider the intrinsic motivation of self-determination and personal choice. Next, we identify some developmental changes in intrinsic and extrinsic motivation as students move up the educational ladder. Finally, we draw some conclusions about intrinsic and extrinsic motivation.

Self-Determination and Choice One view of intrinsic motivation emphasizes that students want to believe that they are doing something because of their own will, not because of external success or rewards (Deci, Koestner, & Ryan, 2001). Students' internal motivation and intrinsic interest in school tasks increase when they have opportunities to make choices and take responsibility for their learning

> **extrinsic motivation** Doing something to obtain something else (the activity is a means to an end).
>
> **intrinsic motivation** Doing something for its own sake; involves factors such as self-determination and opportunities to make choices.

Calvin and Hobbes
by Bill Watterson

(Stipek, 2002). In one study, students who were given some choice of activities and when to do them, and were encouraged to take personal responsibility for their behavior, had higher achievement gains and were more likely to graduate from high school than a control group (deCharms, 1984).

Developmental Shifts in Intrinsic and Extrinsic Motivation   Many psychologists and educators stress that it is important for children to develop intrinsic motivation as they grow older. However, as students move from the early elementary school years to the high school years, intrinsic motivation tends to drop (Harter, 1996). In one study, the biggest drop in intrinsic motivation and largest increase in extrinsic motivation occurred between the sixth and seventh grade (Harter, 1981).

Jacquelynne Eccles and her colleagues (Eccles, 2004; Eccles & Roeser, 2009; Wigfield & others, 2006) identified some specific changes in the school context that help to explain the decline in intrinsic motivation. Middle and junior high schools are more impersonal, more formal, more evaluative, and more competitive than elementary schools. Students compare themselves more with other students because they are increasingly graded in terms of their relative performance on assignments and standardized tests.

Conclusions About Intrinsic and Extrinsic Motivation   An overwhelming conclusion of motivation research is that teachers should encourage students to become intrinsically motivated (Eccles & Roeser, 2009). Similarly, teachers should create learning environments that promote students' cognitive engagement and self-responsibility for learning (Anderman & Anderman, 2010; Anderman & Mueller, 2009). That said, the real world includes both intrinsic and extrinsic motivation, and too often intrinsic and extrinsic motivation have been pitted against each other as polar opposites. In many aspects of students' lives, both intrinsic and extrinsic motivation are at work (Cameron & Pierce, 2008). Further, both intrinsic and extrinsic motivation can operate simultaneously. Thus, a student may work hard in a course because she enjoys the content and likes learning about it (intrinsic) and because she wants to earn a good grade (extrinsic) (Schunk, 2008). Keep in mind, though, that many educational psychologists recommend that extrinsic motivation by itself is not a good strategy.

Mastery Motivation and Mindset

The increasingly competitive, impersonal atmosphere of middle schools obviously does not discourage all students. To some, these characteristics represent a challenge. How students typically respond to challenges has a lot to do with how much they achieve (Meece & Eccles, 2009; Reksten, 2009). Becoming cognitively engaged and self-motivated to improve are reflected in individuals with mastery motivation. These individuals also have a growth mindset that they can produce positive outcomes if they put forth the effort.

Mastery Motivation   Carol Dweck and her colleagues (Dweck & Elliott, 1983; Dweck, Mangels, & Good, 2004) have found that individuals respond in two distinct ways to difficult or challenging circumstances. People who display a **mastery orientation** are task-oriented—instead of focusing on their ability, they concentrate on learning strategies and the process of achievement rather than the outcome. Those with a **helpless orientation** seem trapped by the experience of difficulty, and they attribute their difficulty to lack of ability. They frequently say such things as "I'm not very good at this," even though they might earlier have demonstrated their ability through many successes. And, once they view their behavior as failure, they often feel anxious, and their performance worsens even further. Figure 16.8 describes some behaviors that might reflect helplessness (Stipek, 2002).

The student:

- Says "I can't"
- Doesn't pay attention to teacher's instructions
- Doesn't ask for help, even when it is needed
- Does nothing (for example, stares out the window)
- Guesses or answers randomly without really trying
- Doesn't show pride in successes
- Appears bored, uninterested
- Is unresponsive to teacher's exhortations to try
- Is easily discouraged
- Doesn't volunteer answers to teacher's questions
- Maneuvers to get out of or to avoid work (for example, has to go to the nurse's office)

FIGURE 16.8 Behaviors That Suggest a Helpless Orientation.

mastery orientation An orientation in which one is task-oriented—instead of focusing on one's ability, is concerned with learning strategies and the process of achievement rather than the outcome.

helpless orientation An orientation in which one seems trapped by the experience of difficulty and attributes one's difficulty to a lack of ability.

In contrast, mastery-oriented individuals often instruct themselves to pay attention, to think carefully, and to remember strategies that have worked for them in previous situations. They frequently report feeling challenged and excited by difficult tasks, rather than being threatened by them (Anderman & Anderman, 2010). A recent study revealed that seventh- to eleventh-grade students' mastery goals were linked to how much effort they put forth in mathematics (Chouinard, Karsenti, & Roy, 2007).

Another issue in motivation involves whether to adopt a mastery or a performance orientation. Individuals with a **performance orientation** are focused on winning, rather than on achievement outcome, and believe that happiness results from winning. Does this focus mean that mastery-oriented individuals do not like to win and that performance-oriented individuals are not motivated to experience the self-efficacy that comes from being able to take credit for one's accomplishments? No. A matter of emphasis or degree is involved, though. For mastery-oriented individuals, winning isn't everything; for performance-oriented individuals, skill development and self-efficacy take a backseat to winning.

The U.S. government's No Child Left Behind Act (NCLB) emphasizes testing and accountability. Although NCLB may motivate some teachers and students to work harder, motivation experts worry that it encourages a performance rather than a mastery motivation orientation on the part of students (Schunk, Pintrich, & Meece, 2008).

A final point needs to be made about mastery and performance goals: They are not always mutually exclusive. Students can be both mastery- and performance-oriented, and researchers have found that mastery goals combined with performance goals often benefit students' success (Anderman & Anderman, 2010; Schunk, Pintrich, & Meece, 2008).

Mindset   Carol Dweck's (2006, 2007) most recent analysis of motivation for achievement stresses the importance of developing a **mindset,** which she defines as the cognitive view individuals develop for themselves. She concludes that individuals have one of two mindsets: (1) a *fixed mindset*, in which they believe that their qualities are carved in stone and cannot change; or (2) a *growth mindset*, in which they believe their qualities can change and improve through their effort. A fixed mindset is similar to a helpless orientation; a growth mindset is much like having mastery motivation.

In her recent book, *Mindset*, Dweck (2006) argued that individuals' mindsets influence whether they will be optimistic or pessimistic, shape their goals and how hard they will strive to reach those goals, and affect many aspects of their lives, including achievement and success in school and sports. Dweck says that mindsets begin to be shaped as children and adolescents interact with parents, teachers, and coaches, who themselves have either a fixed mindset or a growth mindset. She described the growth mindset of Patricia Miranda:

> [She] was a chubby, unathletic school kid who wanted to wrestle. After a bad beating on the mat, she was told, "You're a joke." First she cried, then she felt: "That really set my resolve. . . . I had to keep going and had to know if effort and focus and belief and training could somehow legitimize me as a wrestler." Where did she get this resolve?
>
> Miranda was raised in a life devoid of challenge. But when her mother died of an aneurysm at age forty, ten-year-old "Miranda . . . [thought] If you only go through life doing stuff that's easy, shame on you." So when wrestling presented a challenge, she was ready to take it on.
>
> Her effort paid off. At twenty-four, Miranda was having the last laugh. She won a spot on the U.S. Olympic team and came home from Athens with a bronze medal. And what was next? Yale Law School, where she earned her law degree in 2007. People urged her to stay where she was already on top, but Miranda felt it was more exciting to start at the bottom again and see what she could grow into this time. (Dweck, 2006, pp. 22–23)

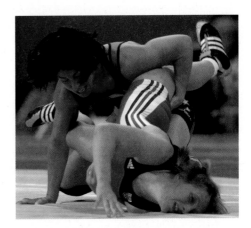

Patricia Miranda (*in blue*) winning the bronze medal in the 2004 Olympics. *What characterizes her growth mindset and how is it different from someone with a fixed mindset?*

performance orientation An orientation in which one focuses on winning, rather than on achievement outcome; happiness is thought to result from winning.

mindset The cognitive view individuals develop for themselves that either is fixed or involves growth.

Dweck (2006) studied first-year premed majors taking their first chemistry class. Students with a growth mindset got higher grades than those with a fixed mindset. Even when they did not do well on a test, the growth mindset students bounced back on the next test. Fixed mindset students typically read and reread the text and class notes or tried to memorize everything verbatim. The fixed mindset students who did poorly on tests concluded that chemistry and maybe premed weren't for them. By contrast, growth mindset students took charge of their motivation and learning, searching for themes and principles in the course and going over mistakes until they understood why they made them. In Dweck's analysis (2006, p. 61), "They were studying to learn, not just ace the test. And, actually, this is why they got higher grades—not because they were smarter or had a better background in science."

Self-Efficacy

Albert Bandura (1997, 2001, 2008, 2009), whose social cognitive theory we described in Chapter 1, "Introduction," stresses that a critical factor in whether or not students achieve is **self-efficacy,** the belief that one can master a situation and produce favorable outcomes. Self-efficacy is the belief that "I can"; helplessness is the belief that "I cannot." Students with high self-efficacy endorse such statements as "I know that I will be able to learn the material in this class" and "I expect to be able to do well at this activity."

Dale Schunk (2008) has applied the concept of self-efficacy to many aspects of students' achievement. In his view, self-efficacy influences a student's choice of activities. Students with low self-efficacy for learning may avoid many learning tasks, especially those that are challenging. By contrast, high-self-efficacy counterparts eagerly work at learning tasks (Schunk, Pintrich, & Meece, 2008; Walsh, 2008). High-self-efficacy students are more likely than low-self-efficacy students to expend effort and persist longer at a learning task.

Goal Setting, Planning, and Self-Monitoring

Self-efficacy and achievement improve when individuals set goals that are specific, proximal, and challenging (Anderman & Mueller, 2009; Schunk, 2008). A nonspecific, fuzzy goal is "I want to be successful." A more concrete, specific goal is "I want to make the honor roll by the end of the semester."

Students can set both long-term (distal) and short-term (proximal) goals. It is okay for individuals to set some long-term goals, such as "I want to graduate from high school" or "I want to go to college," but they also need to create short-term goals, which are steps along the way. "Getting an A on the next math test" is an example of a short-term, proximal goal. So is "Doing all of my homework by 4 p.m. Sunday."

Another good strategy is to set challenging goals (Anderman & Wolters, 2006). A challenging goal is a commitment to self-improvement. Strong interest and involvement in activities are sparked by challenges. Goals that are easy to reach generate little interest or effort. However, goals should be optimally matched to the individual's skill level. If goals are unrealistically high, the result will be repeated failures that lower the individual's self-efficacy.

It is not enough just to set goals. In order to achieve, it also is important to plan how to reach those goals. Being a good planner means managing time effectively, setting priorities, and being organized.

Individuals should not only plan their next week's activities but also monitor how well they are sticking to their plan. Once engaged in a task, they need to monitor their progress, judge how well they are doing on the task, and evaluate the outcomes to regulate what they do in the future (Wigfield & others, 2006). High-achieving children are often self-regulatory learners (Schunk, 2008). For

They can because they think they can.

—Virgil
Roman Poet, 1st Century B.C.E.

self-efficacy The belief that one can master a situation and produce favorable outcomes.

example, high-achieving children monitor their learning and systematically evaluate their progress toward a goal more than low-achieving students do. Encouraging children to monitor their learning conveys the message that they are responsible for their own behavior and that learning requires their active, dedicated participation.

Expectations

An individual's motivation is often influenced by the expectations that parents, teachers, and other adults have for the person's achievement. Children and adolescents benefit when both parents and teachers have high expectations for them and provide the necessary support for them to meet those expectations (Anderman & Anderman, 2010).

Researchers have found that parents' expectations are linked with children's and adolescents' academic achievement (Burchinal & others, 2002). One longitudinal study revealed that children whose mothers had higher academic expectations for them in the first grade were more likely to reach a higher level of educational attainment in emerging adulthood (age 23) than children whose mothers had lower expectations for them in the first grade (Englund, Luckner, & Whaley, 2003).

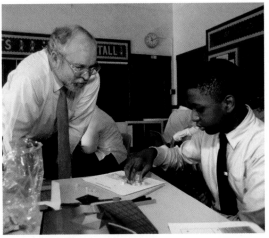

A student and a teacher at Langston Hughes Elementary School in Chicago, a school whose teachers have high expectations for students. *How do teachers' expectations influence students' achievement?*

Too often parents attempt to protect children's and adolescents' self-esteem by setting low standards (Graham, 2005; Stipek, 2005). In reality, it is more beneficial to set standards that challenge them and expect performance at the highest levels they are capable of achieving. Children and adolescents who are not challenged may develop low standards for themselves, and the fragile self-confidence they develop from reaching these low expectations can be shattered the first time they encounter more challenging work and are held to higher standards.

Teachers' expectations also are important influences on children's achievement. In a recent observational study of twelve classrooms, teachers with high expectations spent more time providing a framework for students' learning, asked higher-level questions, and were more effective in managing students' behavior than teachers with average and low expectations (Rubie-Davies, 2007).

In thinking about teachers' expectations, it also is important to examine these expectations in concert with parents' expectations. For example, a recent study revealed that mothers' and teachers' high expectations had a positive effect on urban youths' achievement outcomes, and further that mothers' high achievement expectations for their youth had a buffering effect in the face of low teacher expectations (Benner & Mistry, 2007). In another recent study, teachers' positive expectations for students' achievement tended to protect students from the negative influence of low parental expectations (Wood, Kaplan, & McLoyd, 2007).

How hard students will work can depend on how much they expect to accomplish (Eccles, 2007). If they expect to succeed, they are more likely to work hard to reach a goal than if they expect to fail. As we see later, children's and adolescents' achievement motivation may vary across ethnic groups and cultures.

Purpose

In earlier chapters, we described the view of William Damon (2008) that he proposed in his recent book *The Path to Purpose: Helping Our Children Find Their Calling in Life*. For example, in Chapter 11, "The Self, Identity, and Personality," we discussed the importance of purpose in identity development and in Chapter 13, "Moral Development, Values, and Religion," we indicated that purpose is a key aspect of values. Here we expand on Damon's view and describe how purpose is a missing ingredient in many adolescents' and emerging adults' achievement.

For Damon, *purpose* is an intention to accomplish something meaningful to one's self and contribute something to the world beyond the self. Finding purpose involves answering such questions as "*Why* am I doing this? *Why* does it matter? *Why* is it important for me and the world beyond me? *Why* do I strive to accomplish this end?" (Damon, 2008, pp. 33–34).

In interviews with 12- to 22-year-olds, Damon found that only about 20 percent had a clear vision of where they want to go in life, what they want to achieve, and why. The largest percentage—about 60 percent—had engaged in some potentially purposeful activities, such as service learning or fruitful discussions with a career counselor—but still did not have a real commitment or any reasonable plans for reaching their goals. And slightly more than 20 percent expressed no aspirations and in some instances said they didn't see any reason to have aspirations.

Damon concludes that most teachers and parents communicate the importance of such goals as studying hard and getting good grades, but rarely discuss what the goals might lead to—the purpose for studying hard and getting good grades. Damon emphasizes that too often students focus only on short-term goals and don't explore the big, long-term picture of what they want to do with their life. These interview questions Damon (2008, p. 135) has used in his research are good springboards for getting students to reflect on their purpose:

What's most important to you in your life?

Why do you care about those things?

Do you have any long-term goals?

Why are these goals important to you?

What does it mean to have a good life?

What does it mean to be a good person?

If you were looking back on your life now, how would you like to be remembered?

Ethnicity and Culture

How do ethnicity and culture influence children's achievement? Of course, diversity exists within every group in terms of achievement. But Americans have been especially concerned about two questions related to ethnicity and culture. First, does their ethnicity deter ethnic minority children from high achievement in school? And second, is there something about American culture that accounts for the poor performance of U.S. children in math and science?

Ethnicity   As we discussed in Chapter 15, "Peers and the Sociocultural World," analyzing the effects of ethnicity in the United States is complicated by the fact that a disproportionate number of ethnic minorities have low socioeconomic status. Disentangling the effects of SES and ethnicity can be difficult, and many investigations overlook the socioeconomic status of ethnic minority students. In many instances, when ethnicity *and* socioeconomic status are investigated, socioeconomic status predicts achievement better than ethnicity does. Students from middle- and upper-income families fare better than their counterparts from low-income backgrounds in a host of achievement situations—for example, expectations for success, achievement aspirations, and recognition of the importance of effort (Wigfield & others, 2006).

Sandra Graham (1986, 1990) has conducted a number of studies that reveal stronger socioeconomic status than ethnic differences in achievement. She is struck by how consistently middle-income African American students,

UCLA educational psychologist Sandra Graham is shown talking with adolescent boys about motivation. She has conducted a number of studies which reveal that middle-socioeconomic-status African American students—like their White counterparts—have high achievement expectations and attribute success to internal factors such as effort rather than external factors such as luck.

like their non-Latino White middle-income counterparts, have high achievement expectations and understand that failure is usually due to a lack of effort. An especially important factor in the lower achievement of students from low-income families regardless of their ethnic background is lack of adequate resources, such as an up-to-date computer in the home or even a computer at all, to support students' learning (Schunk, Pintrich, & Meece, 2008).

Cross-Cultural Comparisons In the past decade, the poor performance of American children and youth in math and science compared with other countries has become well publicized. In a large-scale comparison of math and science achievement in fourth-grade students in 2007, the average U.S. fourth-grade math score was higher than 23 of the 35 countries and lower than 8 countries (all in Asia and Europe) (TIMMS, 2008). Fourth-graders from Hong Kong had the highest math score. The average fourth-grade U.S. math score did improve slightly (11 points) from the same assessment in 1995, but some Asian countries improved their scores considerably more—the Hong Kong score was 50 points higher and the Slovenia score 40 points higher in 2007 than in 1995, for example.

In 2007, the fourth-grade U.S. science score was higher than those in 25 countries and lower than those in 4 countries (all in Asia). However, the average U.S. fourth-grade science score decreased 3 points from 1995 to 2007, while the science scores for some countries increased dramatically—63 points in Singapore, 56 points in Latvia, and 55 points in Iran, for example. In the *Research in Life-Span Development* interlude, you can read about Harold Stevenson's efforts to find out why American students fare so poorly in mathematics.

Research in Life-Span Development

CROSS-CULTURAL COMPARISONS IN LEARNING MATH AND MATH INSTRUCTION

Harold Stevenson has been conducting research on children's learning for five decades. His research has explored the reasons for the poor performance of American students. Stevenson and his colleagues (Stevenson, 1995, 2000; Stevenson, Hofer, & Randel, 1999; Stevenson & others, 1990) have completed five cross-cultural comparisons of students in the United States, China, Taiwan, and Japan. In these studies, Asian students consistently outperform American students. And, the longer the students are in school, the wider the gap becomes between Asian and American students—the lowest difference is in the first grade, the highest in the eleventh grade (the highest grade studied).

To learn more about the reasons for these large cross-cultural differences, Stevenson and his colleagues spent thousands of hours observing in classrooms, as well as interviewing and surveying teachers, students, and parents. They found that the Asian teachers spent more of their time teaching math than did the American teachers. For example, more than one-fourth of total classroom time in the first grade was spent on math instruction in Japan, compared with only one-tenth of the time in the U.S. first-grade classrooms. Also, the

Asian grade schools intersperse studying with frequent periods of activities. This approach helps children maintain their attention and likely makes learning more enjoyable. Shown here are Japanese fourth-graders making wearable masks. *What are some differences in the way children in many Asian countries are taught compared with children in the United States?*

(continued on next page)

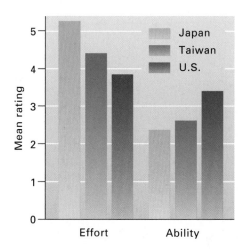

FIGURE 16.9 Mothers' Beliefs About the Factors Responsible for Children's Math Achievement in Three Countries. In one study, mothers in Japan and Taiwan were more likely to believe that their children's math achievement was due to effort rather than innate ability, whereas U.S. mothers were more likely to believe their children's math achievement was due to innate ability (Stevenson, Lee, & Stigler, 1986). If parents believe that their children's math achievement is due to innate ability and their children are not doing well in math, the implication is that they are less likely to think their children will benefit from putting forth more effort.

Asian students were in school an average of 240 days a year, compared with 178 days in the United States.

In addition, differences were found between the Asian and American parents. The American parents had much lower expectations for their children's education and achievement than did the Asian parents. Also, the American parents were more likely to believe that their children's math achievement was due to innate ability; the Asian parents were more likely to say that their children's math achievement was the consequence of effort and training (see Figure 16.9). The Asian students were more likely to do math homework than were the American students, and the Asian parents were far more likely to help their children with their math homework than were the American parents (Chen & Stevenson, 1989).

Review and Reflect: Learning Goal 2

2 Explain the key aspects of achievement

REVIEW

- What are intrinsic motivation and extrinsic motivation? How are they related to achievement?
- How are mastery, helpless, and performance orientations linked with achievement?
- What is self-efficacy, and how is it related to achievement?
- Why are goal setting, planning, and self-monitoring important in achievement?
- How are expectations involved in an individual's achievement motivation?
- What characterizes William Damon's view of the path to purpose in today's youth?
- How do cultural, ethnic, and socioeconomic variations influence achievement?

REFLECT

- Think about several of your own past schoolmates who showed low motivation in school. Why do you think they behaved that way? What teaching strategies may have helped them?

3 CAREERS, WORK, AND RETIREMENT

Career Development — **Work** — **Retirement**

The quality of schooling children experience and the achievement orientation they develop provide the foundation for career success and work when they become adults. Choosing a career, developing in a career, working, and coping with retirement—these are important themes in adulthood.

Career Development

When you were a child, what were your thoughts about a career? How did your thinking about careers change as you became an adolescent? What are they now?

Developmental Changes   Many children have idealistic fantasies about what they want to be when they grow up. For example, many young children want to be superheroes, sports stars, or movie stars. In the high school years, they often have begun to think about careers on a somewhat less idealistic basis. In their late teens and early twenties, their career decision making has usually turned more serious as they explore different career possibilities and zero in on the career they want to enter. In college, this focus often means choosing a major or specialization that is designed to lead to work in a specific field. By their early and mid-twenties, many individuals have completed their education or training and started to enter a full-time occupation. From the mid-twenties through the remainder of early adulthood, individuals often seek to establish their emerging career in a particular field. They may work hard to move up the career ladder and improve their financial standing.

Phyllis Moen (2009a) recently described the *career mystique*, ingrained cultural beliefs that engaging in hard work for long hours through adulthood will produce a path to status, security, and happiness. That is, many individuals have an ideal concept of a career path toward achieving the American dream of upward mobility through occupational ladders. However, the lockstep career mystique has never been a reality for many individuals, especially ethnic minority individuals, women, and poorly educated adults. Further, the career mystique has increasingly become a myth for many individuals in middle-income occupations as global outsourcing of jobs and the 2007–2009 recession have meant reduced job security for millions of Americans.

Personality Types   **Personality type theory** is John Holland's view that it is important to match an individual's personality with a specific career. Holland emphasizes that when individuals find careers that fit their personality, they are more likely to enjoy the work and stay in the job longer than if they'd taken a job not suited to their personality. Holland proposed six basic career-related personality types: realistic, investigative, artistic, social, enterprising, and conventional (see Figure 16.10):

- *Realistic.* These individuals like the outdoors and working in manual activities. They often are less social than other personality types, have difficulty in demanding situations, and prefer to work alone. This personality type matches up best with such jobs as laborer, farmer, truck driver, construction worker, engineer, and pilot.

- *Investigative.* They are interested in ideas more than people, are rather indifferent to social relationships, are troubled by emotional situations, and are often aloof and intelligent. This personality type matches up well with scientific, intellectually oriented professions.

- *Artistic.* They are creative and enjoy working with ideas and materials that allow them to express themselves in innovative ways. They value nonconformity. Sometimes they have difficulties in social relationships. Not many jobs match up with the artistic personality type. Consequently, some artistic individuals work in jobs that are their second or third choices and express their artistic interests through hobbies and leisure.

- *Social.* They like to work with people and tend to have a helping orientation. They like doing social things considerably more than engaging in intellectual tasks. This personality type matches up with jobs in teaching, social work, and counseling.

- *Enterprising.* They also are more oriented toward people than things or ideas. They may try to dominate others to reach their goals. They are often good at persuading others to do things. The enterprising type matches up with careers in sales, management, and politics.

"Your son has made a career choice, Mildred He's going to win the lottery and travel a lot." Copyright © 1985. Reprinted courtesy of Bunny Hoest.

FIGURE 16.10 Holland's Model of Personality Types and Career Choices.

Personality type theory Holland's view that it is important to match an individual's personality with a specific career.

- *Conventional.* They function best in well-structured situations and are skilled at working with details. They often like to work with numbers and perform clerical tasks rather than working with ideas or people. The conventional type matches up with such jobs as accountant, bank teller, secretary, or file clerk.

If all individuals (and careers) fell conveniently into Holland's personality types, career counselors would have an easy job. However, individuals are typically more varied and complex than Holland's theory suggests. Even Holland (1987) states that individuals rarely are pure types, and most persons are a combination of two or three types. Still, the basic idea of matching personality traits to particular careers is an important contribution to the career development field. Holland's personality types are incorporated into the Strong-Campbell Interest Inventory, a widely used measure in career guidance.

Values and Careers   An important aspect of choosing a career is that it also should match up with your values. When people know what they value most— what is important to them in life—they can refine their career choice more effectively. Some values are reflected in Holland's personality types, such as whether a person values working in a career that involves helping others or in a career in which creativity is valued. Among the values that some individuals think are important in choosing a career are working with people they like, working in a career with prestige, making a lot of money, being happy, not having to work long hours, being mentally challenged, having plenty of time for leisure pursuits, working in the right geographical location, and working where physical and mental health are important.

Developing a Sense of Purpose in Career Development   In *The Path to Purpose*, William Damon (2008) described how most youth aren't lacking in ambition when it comes to careers but rather don't have anywhere near an adequate plan for how to reach their career goals. Too many youth drift and aimlessly go through their high school years, Damon says, placing them at risk for not fulfilling their potential and not finding a life pursuit that energizes them.

Damon (2008) also described how too many of today's youth dream about fantasy careers that may have no connection to reality. Too often the youth have no idea about what it takes to become such a career star, and it usually is the case that there is no one in their lives who can help them to reach this career pinnacle. Consider adolescents playing basketball who dream of becoming the next Kobe Bryant and adolescents participating in theater who want to become the next Angelina Jolie, for example.

Monitoring the Occupational Outlook   As you explore the type of work you are likely to enjoy and in which you can succeed, it is important to be knowledgeable about different fields and companies. Occupations may have many job openings one year but few in another year as economic conditions change. Thus, it is critical to keep up with the occupational outlook in various fields. An excellent source for doing this is the U.S. government's *Occupational Outlook Handbook*, which is revised every two years.

According to the 2008–2009 handbook, service industries, especially education and health services, and professional and business services, are projected to account for the most new jobs in the next decade. Education and health services, as well as professional and business services, are projected to have significant growth through 2016.

Projected job growth varies widely by education requirements. Jobs that require a college degree are expected to grow the fastest. Most of the highest-paying occupations require a college degree (*Occupational Outlook Handbook*, 2008–2009). To read about the work of one individual who advises college students about careers, see the *Careers in Life-Span Development* profile.

Careers in Life-Span Development

Grace Leaf, College/Career Counselor

Grace Leaf is a counselor at Spokane Community College in Washington. She has a master's degree in educational leadership and is working toward a doctoral degree in educational leadership at Gonzaga University in Spokane, Washington. Her job involves teaching, orientation for international students, conducting individual and group advising, and doing individual and group career planning. Leaf tries to connect students with goals and values and helps them design an educational program that fits their needs and visions.

Grace Leaf (*standing*) advising college students about potential careers.

Work

Work is one of the most important activities in people's lives. Our developmental coverage of work begins with adolescence and concludes with late adulthood.

Work in Adolescence   One of the greatest changes in adolescents' lives in recent years has been the increased number of adolescents who work part-time and still attend school on a regular basis. Our discussion of adolescents and work focuses on the sociohistorical context of adolescent work and the advantages and disadvantages of part-time work.

Sociohistorical Context of Adolescent Work   Even though education keeps many of today's youth from holding full-time jobs, it has not prevented them from working part-time while going to school (Staff, Messersmith, & Schulenberg, 2009). In 1940, only 1 of 25 tenth-grade males attended school and simultaneously worked part-time. In the 1970s, the number had increased to 1 in 4. Today, it is estimated that 80 to 90 percent of adolescents are employed at some point during high school (Staff, Messersmith, & Schulenberg, 2009). As adolescents go from the eighth to the twelfth grade, their likelihood of working and the average number of hours they work during the school year increases (Staff, Messersmith, & Schulenberg, 2009). In the eighth and tenth grades, the majority of students don't work in paid employment during the school year, but in the twelfth grade only one-fourth don't engage in paid employment during the school year. Almost 10 percent of employed twelfth-graders work more than 30 hours each week during the school year.

Overall, the weight of the evidence suggests that spending large amounts of time in paid labor has limited developmental benefits for youth, and for some it is associated with risky behavior and costs to physical health (Larson, Wilson, & Rickman, 2009; Staff, Messersmith, & Schulenberg, 2009). For example, one research study found that it was not just working that affected adolescents' grades—more important was how long they worked (Greenberger & Steinberg, 1986). Tenth-graders who worked more than 14 hours a week suffered a drop in grades. Eleventh-graders worked up to 20 hours a week before their grades dropped. When adolescents spend more than 20 hours per week working, there is little time to study for tests and to complete homework assignments. In addition, working adolescents felt less involved

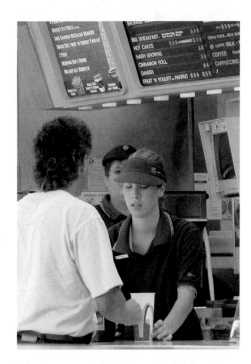

What are some advantages and disadvantages of part-time work during adolescence?

in school, were absent more, and said that they did not enjoy school as much as their nonworking counterparts did. Adolescents who worked long hours also were more frequent users of alcohol and marijuana.

Some youth, though, are engaged in challenging work activities, are provided constructive supervision by adults, and experience favorable work conditions (Staff, Messersmith, & Schulenberg, 2009). For example, work may benefit adolescents in low-income, urban contexts by providing them with economic benefits and adult monitoring. These may increase school engagement and decrease delinquency.

Work in Emerging Adulthood   The work patterns of emerging adults have changed over the course of the last 100 years (Hamilton & Hamilton, 2006, 2009). As an increasing number of emerging adults have participated in higher education, many leave home and begin their career work at later ages. Changing economic conditions have made the job market more competitive for emerging adults and increased the demand for more skilled workers (Gauthier & Furstenberg, 2005).

A diversity of school and work patterns characterizes emerging adults (Borges & others, 2008; Hamilton & Hamilton, 2009). Some emerging adults are going to college full-time; others are working full-time. Some emerging adults work full-time immediately after high school, others after they graduate from college. Many emerging adults who attend college drop out and enter the workforce before they complete their degree; some of these individuals return to college later. Some emerging adults are attending two-year colleges, others four-year colleges; and some are working part-time while going to college, others are not.

The nature of the transition from school to work in emerging adulthood is strongly influenced by the individual's level of education (Hamilton & Hamilton, 2009). In the last two decades, the job market for emerging adults with only a high school education has worsened. The McArthur Foundation Research Network on Emerging Adults recently concluded that for emerging adults who don't go to college, the problem is not jobs but a lack of good jobs (Setterson, Furstenberg, & Rumbaut, 2005). The Research Network also stated that community colleges are an underutilized resource for connecting high schools and employers. A special concern is the large number of students who begin their college education in a community college but don't finish it (Horn & Nevill, 2006).

What about work during college? To read about the pluses and minuses of working during college, see the *Applications in Life-Span Development* interlude.

These emerging adults are college graduates who have started their own business. Emerging adults follow a diversity of work and educational pathways. *What are some of these variations in education and work that characterize emerging adults?*

Applications in Life-Span Development

WORKING DURING COLLEGE

The percentage of full-time U.S. college students who were employed increased from 34 percent in 1970 to 46 percent in 2006 (down from a peak of 52 percent in 2000) (National Center for Education Statistics, 2008c). In this recent survey, 81 percent of part-time U.S. college students were employed.

Working can pay or help offset some costs of schooling, but working also can restrict students' opportunities to learn. For those who identified themselves primarily as students, one national study found that as the number of hours worked per week increased, their grades suffered (National Center for Education Statistics, 2002) (see Figure 16.11). Thus, college students need to carefully examine whether the number of hours they work is having a negative impact on their college success.

Of course, jobs also can contribute to your education. More than 1,000 colleges in the United States offer *cooperative (co-op) programs,* which are paid apprenticeships in a field that you are interested in pursuing. (You may not be permitted to participate in a co-op program until your junior year.) Other useful opportunities for working while going to college include internships and part-time or summer jobs relevant to your field of study. In a national survey of employers, almost 60 percent said their entry-level college hires had co-op or internship experience (Collins, 1996). Participating in these work experiences can be a key factor in whether you land the job you want when you graduate.

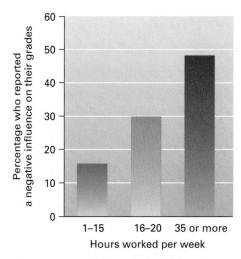

FIGURE 16.11 The Relation of Hours Worked Per Week in College to Grades. Among students working to pay for school expenses, 16 percent of those working 1 to 15 hours per week reported that working negatively influenced their grades. Thirty percent of college students who worked 16 to 20 hours a week said working negatively affected their grades, as did 48 percent who worked 35 hours or more per week.

Work in Adulthood

Both Sigmund Freud and the Russian Count Leo Tolstoy described love and work as the two most important things that adults need to do well. We discussed love in Chapter 10, "Emotional Development," Let's now explore work in the adult years.

The Work Landscape   Do you work to live or live to work? Most individuals spend about one-third of their lives at work. In one survey, 35 percent of Americans worked 40 hours a week, but 18 percent worked 51 hours or more per week (Center for Survey Research at the University of Connecticut, 2000). Only 10 percent worked less than 30 hours a week.

Work defines people in fundamental ways (Schultz & Adams, 2007). It is an important influence on their financial standing, housing, the way they spend their time, where they live, their friendships, and their health (Fouad & Bynner, 2008; Hodson, 2009). Some people define their identity through their work. Work also creates a structure and rhythm to life that is often missed when individuals do not work for an extended period. When unable to work, many individuals experience emotional distress and low self-esteem.

An important consideration regarding work is how stressful it is (Burgard, 2009). A recent national survey of U.S. adults revealed that 55 percent indicated they were less productive because of stress (American Psychological Association, 2007). In this study, 52 percent reported that they considered or made a career decision, such as looking for a new job, declining a promotion, or quitting a job, because of stress in the workplace (American Psychological Association, 2007). In this survey, main sources of stress included low salaries (44 percent), lack of advancement opportunities (42 percent), uncertain job expectations (40 percent), and long hours (39 percent).

Many adults have changing expectations about work, yet employers often aren't meeting their expectations (Grzywacz, 2009; Moen, 2009a, b). For example, current policies and practices often were designed for a single breadwinner (male) workforce and an industrial economy, making these policies and practices out of step with a workforce of women and men, and of single parent and dual earners. Many workers today want flexibility and greater control over the time and timing of their work, and yet most employers offer little flexibility, even though policies like flextime may be "on the books."

What are some characteristics of work settings linked with employees' stress?

The economic recession in 2007–2009 resulted in millions of Americans losing their jobs, such as the individuals in line here waiting to apply for unemployment benefits. *What are some of the potential negative outcomes of the stress caused by job loss?*

Unemployment Unemployment produces stress regardless of whether the job loss is temporary, cyclical, or permanent (Perrucci & Perrucci, 2009). Researchers have found that unemployment is related to physical problems (such as heart attack and stroke), mental problems (such as depression and anxiety), marital difficulties, and homicide (Gallo & others, 2006). A recent study revealed that immune system functioning declined with unemployment and increased with new employment (Cohen & others, 2007).

Stress comes not only from a loss of income and the resulting financial hardships but also from decreased self-esteem (Voydanoff, 1990). Individuals who cope best with unemployment have financial resources to rely on, often savings or the earnings of other family members. The support of understanding, adaptable family members also helps individuals cope with unemployment. Job counseling and self-help groups can provide practical advice on job searching, résumés, and interviewing skills, and also give emotional support.

Dual-Career Couples Dual-career couples may have special problems finding a balance between work and the rest of life (Grzywacz, 2009; Moen, 2009a, b). If both partners are working, who cleans up the house or calls the repairman or takes care of the other endless details involved in maintaining a home? If the couple has children, who is responsible for being sure that the children get to school or to piano practice; who writes the notes to approve field trips or meets the teacher or makes the dental appointments?

Although single-earner married families still make up a sizeable minority of families, the two-earner couple has increased considerably in recent decades. A recent projection indicates that women's share of the U.S. labor force will increase through 2016 (*Occupational Outlook Handbook*, 2008–2009). As more U.S. women work outside the home, the division of responsibility for work and family has changed: (1) U.S. husbands are taking increased responsibility for maintaining the home; (2) U.S. women are taking increased responsibility for breadwinning; and (3) U.S. men are showing greater interest in their families and parenting.

Many jobs have been designed for single earners, usually a male breadwinner, without family responsibilities and the realities of people's actual lives. Consequently, many dual-earner couples engage in a range of adaptive strategies to coordinate their work and manage the family side of the work-family equation (Moen, 2009b). Researchers have found that even though couples may strive for gender equality in dual-earner families, gender inequalities still persist (Cunningham, 2009). For example, women still do not earn as much as men in the same jobs, and this inequity means that gender divisions in how much time each partner spends in paid work, homemaking, and caring for children continue. Thus, dual-earner career decisions often are made in favor of men's greater earning power and women spending more time than men in homemaking and caring for children (Moen, 2009b).

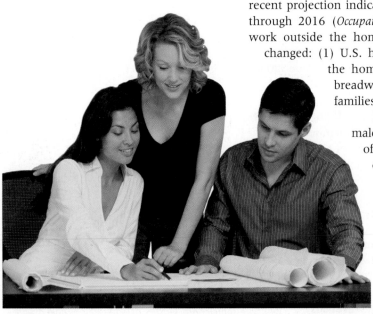

As more women have worked outside the home, how has the division of responsibility for work and family changed?

Careers and Work in Middle Adulthood The role of work—whether a person works in a full-time career, in a part-time job, as a volunteer, or as a homemaker—is central during middle age. Middle-aged adults may reach their peak in position and earnings but also be saddled with financial burdens from rent or mortgage, child care, medical bills, home repairs, college tuition, or bills from nursing homes for care of an elderly parent.

The progression of career trajectories in middle age is diverse, with some individuals having stable careers, whereas others move in and out of the labor force, experiencing layoffs and unemployment (Lachman, 2004). Middle-aged adults also may experience age discrimination in some job situations. Finding a job in midlife may be difficult because technological advances may render the midlife worker's skills outdated.

Some midlife career changes are the consequence of losing one's job; others are self-motivated (Moen, 1998; Moen & Spencer, 2006). Among the work issues that some people face in midlife are recognizing limitations in career progress, deciding whether to change jobs or careers, considering whether to rebalance family and work, and planning for retirement (Sterns & Huyck, 2001).

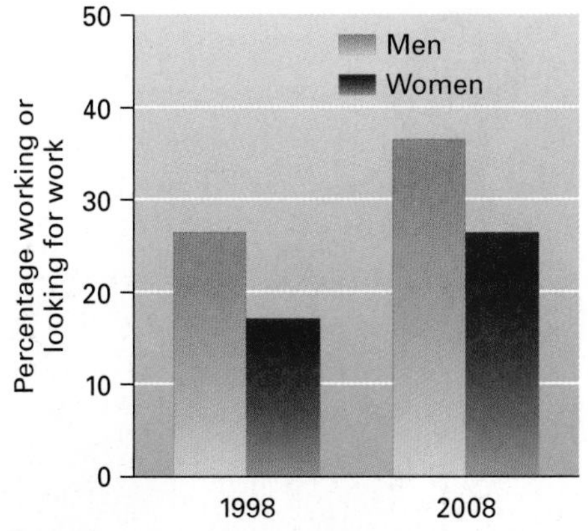

Work in Late Adulthood The percentage of older U.S. adult men still working or returning to work has been increasing since the early 1990s. As more women have entered the workforce, the percentage of older adult women still working also has increased. Figure 16.12 shows the increase in the percentage of men and women 65 years and older still working or looking for work from 1998 to 2008 (U.S. Bureau of Labor Statistics, 2008).

Since the mid-1990s, a significant shift has occurred in the percentage of older adults working part-time or full-time (U.S. Bureau of Labor Statistics, 2008). As shown in Figure 16.13, after 1995, of the adults 65 and older in the workforce, those engaging in full-time work rose substantially and those working part-time decreased considerably. This significant rise in full-time employment likely reflects the increasing number of older adults who realize that they may not have adequate money to fund their retirement.

Cognitive ability is one of the best predictors of job performance in older adults. And older workers have lower rates of absenteeism, fewer accidents, and increased job satisfaction compared with their younger counterparts (Warr, 2004). Thus the older worker can be of considerable value to a company, above and beyond the older worker's cognitive competence. Changes in federal law now allow individuals over the age of 65 to continue working (Shore & Goldberg, 2005). Also, remember from our discussion in Chapter 7, "Information Processing," that substantively complex work is linked with a higher level of intellectual functioning (Schooler, 2007).

In sum, age affects many aspects of work (Cleveland & Shore, 2007). Nonetheless, many studies of work and aging—such as evaluation of hiring and performance—reveal

FIGURE 16.12 Percentage of 65- to 69-Year-Old U.S. Men and Women Working or Looking for Work in 1998 and 2008.

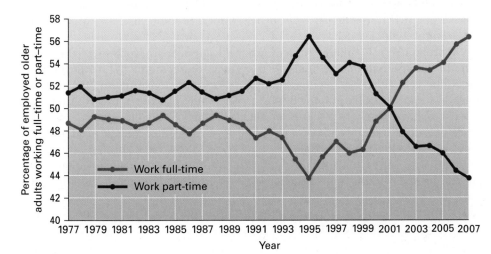

FIGURE 16.13 Percentage of U.S. Adults 65 Years and Older in the Labor Force Who Are Working Full-Time or Part-Time.

inconsistent results. Important contextual factors—such as age composition of departments or applicant pools, occupations, and jobs—all affect decisions about older workers. It also is important to recognize that ageist stereotypes of workers and of tasks can limit older workers' career opportunities and can encourage early retirement or other forms of downsizing that adversely affect older workers (Finkelstein & Farrell, 2007).

Retirement

How is retirement in the United States similar to and different from retirement in other countries? What factors predict whether individuals will effectively adapt to retirement?

Retirement in the United States and Other Countries
What are some life paths that retired individuals follow? Do many people return to the workforce at some point after they have retired? What is retirement like in other countries?

The option to retire is a twentieth-century phenomenon in the United States (Atchley, 2007). It exists largely thanks to the implementation in 1935 of the Social Security system, which gives benefits to older workers when they retire. On the average, today's workers will spend 10 to 15 percent of their lives in retirement. A recent survey revealed that as baby boomers move into their sixties, they expect to delay retirement longer than their parents or grandparents did (Frey, 2007).

In the past, when most people reached an accepted retirement age, such as at some point in their sixties, retirement meant a one-way exit from full-time work to full-time leisure (Atchley, 2007). Leading expert Phyllis Moen (2007) recently described how today, when people reach their sixties, the life path they follow is less clear:

- Some don't retire—they continue in their career jobs.
- Some retire from their career work and then take up a new and different job.
- Some retire from career jobs but do volunteer work.
- Some retire from a postretirement job and go on to yet another job.
- Some move in and out of the workforce, so they never really have a "career" job from which they retire.
- Some who are in poor health move to a disability status and eventually into retirement.
- Some who are laid off define it as "retirement."

Increasingly both spouses are in the workforce and both expect to retire. Historically, retirement has been a male transition but today more and more couples have to plan two retirements, his and hers (Moen & Altobelli, 2007; Moen, Kelly, & Magennis, 2008).

Approximately 7 million retired Americans return to work after they have retired (Putnam Investments, 2006). On average, retired adults return to the labor force four years after retirement (Hardy, 2006). In many instances, the jobs pay much less than their preretirement jobs. In one study of older adults who returned to work, approximately two-thirds said they were happy they had done so, whereas about one-third indicated they were forced to go back to work to meet financial needs (Putnam Investments, 2006).

Just as the life path after individuals reach retirement age may be varied, so are the reasons for working. For example, some older adults who reach retirement age work for financial reasons, others to stay busy, and yet others "to give back" (Moen, 2007). To read about work and retirement in different countries, see the *Contexts of Life-Span Development* interlude.

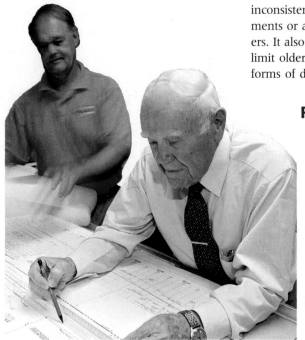

Ninety-two-year-old Russell "Bob" Harrell (*right*) puts in 12-hour days at Sieco Consulting Engineers in Columbus, Indiana. A highway and bridge engineer, he designs and plans roads. James Rice (age 48), a vice president of client services at Sieco, says that Bob wants to learn something new every day and that he has learned many life lessons from being around him. Harrell says he is not planning on retiring. *What are some variations in work and retirement in older adults?*

Contexts of Life-Span Development

WORK AND RETIREMENT AROUND THE WORLD

A recent large-scale study of 21,000 individuals aged 40 to 79 in 21 countries examined patterns of work and retirement (HSBC Insurance, 2007). On average, 33 percent of individuals in their sixties and 11 percent in their seventies were still in some kind of paid employment. In this study, 19 percent of those in their seventies in the United States were still working. As indicated in Figure 16.14, a substantial percentage of individuals expect to continue working as long as possible before retiring (HSBC Insurance, 2007).

In the recent study of work and retirement in 21 countries, Japanese retirees missed the work slightly more than they expected and the money considerably less than they expected (HSBC Insurance, 2007). U.S. retirees missed both the work and the money slightly less than they expected. German retirees were the least likely to miss the work, Turkish and Chinese retirees the most likely to miss it. Regarding the money, Japanese and Chinese retirees were the least likely to miss it, Turkish retirees the most likely to miss it.

Early retirement policies were introduced by many companies in the 1970s and 1980s with an intent to make room for younger workers. However, in the recent survey, there was some indication that an increasing number of adults are beginning to reject the early retirement option as they hear about people who retired and then regretted it. In the 21-country study, on average only 12 percent of individuals in their forties and fifties expected to take early retirement, whereas 16 percent in their sixties and seventies had taken early retirement. Only in Germany, South Korea, and Hong Kong did a higher percentage of individuals expect earlier retirement than in the past.

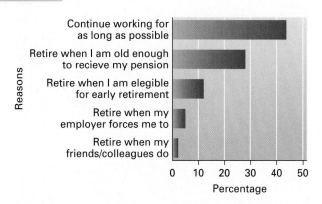

FIGURE 16.14 Reasons Given by People Regarding When They Expect to Retire from Work.

In the recent cross-national study, to what extent did Japanese retirees miss the work and the money in comparison to U.S. retirees?

Adjustment to Retirement Retirement is a process, not an event (Moen, 2007). Much of the research on retirement has been cross-sectional rather than longitudinal and has focused on men rather than women. One recent study found that men had higher morale when they had retired within the last two years compared with men who had been retired for longer periods of time (Kim & Moen, 2002). Another recent study revealed that retired married and remarried women reported being more satisfied with their lives and in better health than retired women who were widowed, separated, divorced, or had never been married (Price & Joo, 2005). And a recent study indicated that women spend less time planning for retirement than men do (Jacobs-Lawson, Hershey, & Neukam, 2005).

Older adults who adjust best to retirement are healthy, have adequate income, are active, are better educated, have an extended social network including both friends and family, and usually were satisfied with their lives before they retired (Raymo & Sweeney, 2006). Older adults with inadequate income and poor health, and who must adjust to other stress that occurs at the same time as retirement, such as the death of a spouse, have the most difficult time adjusting to retirement (Reichstadt & others, 2007). A recent study also found that individuals who had difficulty in adjusting to

What are some keys to adjusting effectively in retirement?

retirement had a strong attachment to work, including full-time jobs and a long work history, lack of control over the transition to retirement, and low self-efficacy (van Solinge & Henkens, 2005).

The U.S. retirement system is in transition. Following are the results of a 2007 survey on retirement (Helman, VanDerhei, & Copeland, 2007):

- Half of the workers were not confident about their pension benefits.
- Many workers count on benefits that won't be there when they retire.
- Workers often don't heed advice about retirement even when they are provided the advice.
- Workers overestimate long-term care coverage.
- Most workers' savings are modest.
- Many workers know little about the Social Security income they will receive when they retire.

Flexibility is also a key factor in whether individuals adjust well to retirement (Shultz & Adams, 2007). When people retire, they no longer have the structured environment they had when they were working, so they need to be flexible and discover and pursue their own interests (Eisdorfer, 1996). Cultivating interests and friends unrelated to work improves adaptation to retirement (Zarit & Knight, 1996).

Planning and then successfully carrying out the plan is an important aspect of adjusting well in retirement. A special concern in retirement planning involves women, who are likely to live longer than men and more likely to live alone (less likely to remarry and more likely to be widowed) (Moen, 2007).

Individuals who view retirement planning only in terms of finances don't adapt as well to retirement as those who have a more balanced retirement plan (Birren, 1996). It is important not only to plan financially for retirement, but to consider other areas of your life as well (Sener, Terzioglu, & Karabulut, 2007). In addition to financial planning, questions individuals need to ask about retirement include: What am I going to do with my leisure time? What am I going to do to stay active? What am I going to do socially? What am I going to do to keep my mind active?

Review and Reflect: Learning Goal 3

 Discuss career development, work, and retirement

REVIEW

- What is involved in the development of a career?
- What are some key aspects of work?
- What characterizes retirement?

REFLECT

- At what age would you like to retire? Or would you prefer to continue working as long as you are healthy? At what age did your father and/or mother retire? How well did they adjust to retirement?

Reach Your Learning Goals

Schools, Achievement, and Work

1 SCHOOLS: DESCRIBE THE ROLE OF SCHOOLS IN DEVELOPMENT

Contemporary Approaches to Student Learning and Assessment

- Contemporary approaches to student learning include the direct instruction approach and the constructivist approach. Today, many effective teachers use both a constructive approach and a direct instruction approach. Increased concern by the public and government in the United States has produced extensive state-mandated testing, which has both strengths and weaknesses, and is controversial. The most visible example of the increased state-mandated testing is the No Child Left Behind federal legislation.

Schools and Developmental Status

- Attending preschool is becoming the norm for children in the United States. The child-centered kindergarten emphasizes the education of the whole child, with special attention to individual variation, the process of learning, and the importance of play in development. The Montessori approach allows children to choose from a range of activities while teachers serve as facilitators. Developmentally appropriate practice focuses on the typical development patterns of children (age appropriateness) and the uniqueness of each child (individual appropriateness). Such practice contrasts with developmentally inappropriate practice, which focuses on abstract pencil-and-paper activities, rote/drill practice activities, and seatwork—with an academic direct instruction approach to learning. The U.S. government has tried to break the poverty cycle with programs such as Head Start. High-quality programs have been shown to have positive social and cognitive effects on disadvantaged children. Controversy characterizes early childhood education curricula. On the one side are the child-centered, constructivist advocates; on the other are those who advocate a direct instruction, academic approach. A special concern is that early elementary school education proceeds too much on the basis of negative feedback to children. The transition from elementary school to middle or junior high school can be stressful—students experience the top-dog phenomenon, going from being the oldest, most powerful, biggest students in elementary school to being the youngest, least powerful, smallest students in middle or junior high school. Successful schools for young adolescents should offer activities that focus on individual differences in their biological and psychological development. Getting students engaged in positive ways and identifying their school-related problems early can help reduce the dropout rate. There are concerns about dropping out of school and improving the high school experience. The transition to college can involve a number of positive and negative experiences. Today's college students experience more stress and are more depressed than in the past, and often feel overwhelmed with all they need to accomplish to be successful.

Educating Children with Disabilities

- An estimated 13.5 percent of U.S. children from 3 to 21 years of age receive special education or related services. Children with learning disabilities have difficulty in learning that involves understanding or using spoken or written language, and the difficulty can appear in listening, thinking, reading, writing, and spelling. A learning disability also may involve difficulty in doing mathematics. To be classified as a learning disability, the learning problem is not primarily the result of visual, hearing, or motor disabilities; mental retardation; emotional disorders; or environmental, cultural, or economic disadvantage. Dyslexia is a category of learning disabilities that involves a severe impairment in the ability to read and spell. Attention deficit hyperactivity disorder (ADHD) is a disability in which individuals consistently show problems in one or more of these areas: (1) inattention, (2) hyperactivity, and (3) impulsivity. ADHD has been increasingly diagnosed. Autism spectrum disorders (ASDs pervasive developmental) refer to a broad range of disorders ranging from the severe autistic disorder to the milder Asperger syndrome. Autism has an onset in the first three years of life, and it involves abnormalities in social relationships and communication. It also is characterized by repetitive behaviors. The current consensus is that autism involves an organic brain dysfunction. In 1975, Public Law 94-142, the Education for All Handicapped Children Act, required that all children with disabilities be given a free, appropriate public education. This law was renamed the Individuals with Disabilities Education Act (IDEA) in 1990 and updated in 2004. IDEA includes requirements that children with disabilities receive an individualized education plan (IEP), which is a written plan that spells out a program tailored to the child, and that they be educated in the least restrictive environment (LRE), which is a setting that is as similar as possible to the one in which children without disabilities are educated. The trend is toward the use of inclusion, which describes educating children with special education needs full-time in the regular classroom, although some aspects of inclusion have recently been criticized.

Socioeconomic Status and Ethnicity

- Children from low-income, ethnic minority backgrounds experience more problems in school than their middle-SES non-Latino white counterparts. They face difficulties at home, such as being malnourished, and at school, such as inadequate textbooks and supplies, that present barriers to learning. The school experiences of children from different ethnic groups vary considerably. A number of strategies, such as turning the class into a jigsaw classroom, can be adopted to improve relationships with diverse others.

2 ACHIEVEMENT: EXPLAIN THE KEY ASPECTS OF ACHIEVEMENT

Extrinsic and Intrinsic Motivation

- Extrinsic motivation involves doing something to obtain something else (a means to an end). Intrinsic motivation involves the internal motivation to do something for its own sake (an end in itself). Overall, most experts recommend that teachers create a classroom climate in which students are intrinsically motivated to learn. One view of intrinsic motivation emphasizes its self-determining characteristics. Giving students some choice and providing opportunities for personal responsibility increase intrinsic motivation. Researchers have found that as students move from the early elementary school years to high school, their intrinsic motivation declines, especially between the sixth and seventh grade. Intrinsic motivation is typically favored by educational psychologists, although in many aspects of achievement, both intrinsic and extrinsic factors are at work.

Mastery Motivation and Mindset

- A mastery orientation is preferred over helpless or performance orientations in achievement situations. Mindset is the cognitive view, either fixed or growth, that individuals develop for themselves. Dweck argues that a key aspect of development is to guide children and adolescents to develop a growth mindset.

Self-Efficacy

- Self-efficacy is the belief that one can master a situation and produce positive outcomes. Bandura stresses that self-efficacy is a critical factor in whether students will achieve. Schunk argues that self-efficacy influences a student's choice of tasks, with low-efficacy students avoiding many learning tasks.

Goal Setting, Planning, and Self-Monitoring

- Setting specific, proximal (short-term), and challenging goals benefits students' self-efficacy and achievement. Being a good planner means managing time effectively, setting priorities, and being organized. Self-monitoring is a key aspect of self-regulation and benefits student learning.

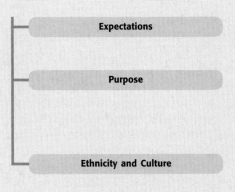

Expectations

- Individuals benefit when their parents, teachers, and other adults have high expectations for their achievement. Students' expectations for success influence their motivation to achieve.

Purpose

- Recently, William Damon has proposed that purpose is an especially important aspect of achievement that has been missing from many adolescents' lives. He argues that too many youth have failed to find a life pursuit that inspires them. Damon argues that youth focus too much on short-term goals and not enough on the big picture of what they want to do with their life.

Ethnicity and Culture

- In most investigations, socioeconomic status predicts achievement better than ethnicity. U.S. children do more poorly on math and science achievement tests than children in Asian countries such as China, Taiwan, and Japan.

3 CAREERS, WORK, AND RETIREMENT: DISCUSS CAREER DEVELOPMENT, WORK, AND RETIREMENT

Career Development

- Many young children have idealistic fantasies about a career. In the late teens and early twenties, their career thinking has usually become more serious. By their early to mid-twenties, many individuals have started in a career. In the remainder of early adulthood, they seek to establish their career and start moving up the career ladder. John Holland proposed that it is important for individuals to choose a career that is compatible with their personality type. It is also important to match up a career to one's values. Damon argues that many of today's youth don't adequately plan for how to reach their career goals. He also states too many youth dream about fantasy careers that have no connection to reality. Service-producing industries will account for the most new jobs in America in the next decade. Jobs that require a college education will be the fastest growing and highest paying.

Work

- Today, the majority of U.S. adolescents work part-time while attending school. Working part-time during adolescence can have advantages or disadvantages, although working too many hours harms students' grades. Forty-six percent of full-time and 81 percent of part-time U.S. college students work while going to college. Working during college can have negative outcomes, especially when students work long hours, or positive outcomes, especially when students participate in co-op programs, internships, or part-time or summer work relevant to their field of study. The work patterns of emerging adults have changed over the last 100 years, and a diversity of school and work patterns now characterize emerging adults. The nature of the transition from school to work is strongly influenced by the individual's education level. Many emerging adults leave home and begin their careers later. Work defines people in fundamental ways and is a key aspect of their identity. Most individuals spend about one-third of their adult lives at work. People often become stressed if they are unable to work, but work also can produce stress, as when there is a heavy workload and time pressure. Unemployment produces stress regardless of whether the job loss is temporary, cyclical, or permanent. Unemployment is related to physical problems, mental problems, and other difficulties. The increasing number of women who work in careers outside the home has led to new work-related issues. There has been a considerable increase in the time men spend in household work and child care. For many people, midlife is a time of reflection, assessment, and evaluation of their current work and what they plan to do in the future. Midlife job or career changes can be self-motivated or forced on individuals. Some individuals continue a life of strong work productivity throughout late adulthood. An increasing number of older U.S. men and women are working, and

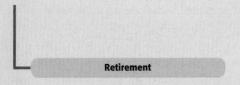

since the mid-1990s there has been a substantial rise in the percentage of older adults who work full-time and a considerable decrease in the percentage of older adults who work part-time.

- A retirement option for older workers is a twentieth-century phenomenon in the United States. The pathways individuals follow when they reach retirement age today are less clear than in the past. Individuals who are healthy, have adequate income, are active, are better educated, have an extended social network of friends and family, and are satisfied with their lives before they retire adjust best to retirement.

KEY TERMS

constructivist approach 600
direct instruction
   approach 600
child-centered
   kindergarten 602
Montessori approach 602
developmentally appropriate
   practice 603
Project Head Start 603

top-dog phenomenon 606
learning disabilities 609
dyslexia 610
attention deficit
   hyperactivity disorder
   (ADHD) 610
autism spectrum disorders
   (ASDs) 612
autistic disorder 612

Asperger syndrome 612
individualized education
   plan (IEP) 613
least restrictive environment
   (LRE) 613
inclusion 613
extrinsic motivation 617
intrinsic motivation 617
mastery orientation 618

helpless orientation 618
performance
   orientation 619
mindset 619
self-efficacy 620
personality type theory 625

KEY PEOPLE

Friedrich Froebel 602
Maria Montessori 602
James Kauffman 613
Jonathan Kozol 614

Elliot Aronson 615
James Comer 615
Carol Dweck 618
Albert Bandura 620

Dale Schunk 620
William Damon 621
Sandra Graham 622
Harold Stevenson 623

John Holland 625
Phyllis Moen 625

E-LEARNING TOOLS

Connect to **www.mhhe.com/santrockldt5e** to research the answers and complete these exercises. In addition, you'll find a number of other resources and valuable study tools for Chapter 16, "Schools, Achievement, and Work," on this Web site.

Taking It to the Net

1. A state's representative to the U.S. Congress wants to decrease funding to the Head Start program. In a debate on the House floor, he maintains that the program is no more expensive than child care. What should the representative know about the latest research into how the Head Start program benefits low-income children and their parents?

2. Charles and Joanne are preparing for their first IEP meeting concerning the education of their 7-year-old daughter, Kara, who has autism. What should they do to prepare for the IEP meeting? What are some things they need to do at the meeting?

3. Juan and Carmen have been married and employed for 30 years. They have enough savings that they do not need to work, so they plan to retire at the end of this year. What should they know about the effects of retirement on their marriage and their individual social and emotional well-being?

Self-Assessment

To evaluate your career interests and assertiveness in job hunting, complete these self-assessments:

- *Evaluating My Career Interests*
- *How Assertive Will I Be in Searching for a Job?*

Health and Well-Being, Parenting, and Education

Build your decision-making skills by trying your hand at the health and well-being, parenting, and education exercises.

Video Clips

The Online Learning Center includes the following videos for this chapter:

- *Overscheduling Our Adolescents*
- *Schools and Public Policy*
- *Retirement*
- *Preschool Teaching*

SECTION SIX

ENDINGS

*Years following years
steal something every
day: At last they steal us
from ourselves away.*

—ALEXANDER POPE
English Poet, 18th Century

Our life ultimately ends–when we approach life's grave

sustained and soothed with unfaltering trust or rave at the close

of day; when at last years steal us from ourselves, and when we

are linked to our children's children's children by an invisible

cable that runs from age to age. This final section contains one

chapter: "Death, Dying, and Grieving" (Chapter 17).

17

Sustained and soothed by an unfaltering trust, approach thy grave, Like one who wraps the drapery of his couch, About him, and lies down to pleasant dreams.

—WILLIAM CULLEN BRYANT
American Poet, 19th Century

LEARNING GOALS

◆ Describe the death system and its cultural and historical contexts.

◆ Evaluate issues in determining death and decisions regarding death.

◆ Discuss death and attitudes about it at different points in development.

◆ Explain the psychological aspects involved in facing one's own death and the contexts in which people die.

◆ Identify ways to cope with the death of another person.

DEATH, DYING, AND GRIEVING

CHAPTER OUTLINE

PREVIEW

In this final chapter of the book, we explore many aspects of death and dying. Among the questions that we ask are: What characterizes the death system and its cultural and historical contexts? How can death be defined? What are some links between development and death? How do people face their own death? How do individuals cope with the death of someone they love?

1 THE DEATH SYSTEM AND CULTURAL CONTEXTS

| The Death System and Its Cultural Variations | Changing Historical Circumstances |

Every culture has a death system, and variations in this death system occur across cultures. Also, when, where, and how people die have changed historically in the United States.

The Death System and Its Cultural Variations

Robert Kastenbaum (2004, 2007, 2009) emphasizes that a number of components comprise the *death system* in any culture. The components include:

These children's parents died when they were swept away by the tsunami in Indonesia in 2004. The death system includes times such as the 2004 tsunami. *What are some other components of the death system?*

- *People.* Because death is inevitable, everyone is involved with death at some point, either their own death or the death of others. Some individuals have a more systematic role with death, such as those who work in the funeral industry and the clergy, as well as people who work in life-threatening contexts such as firemen and policemen.

- *Places or contexts.* These include hospitals, funeral homes, cemeteries, hospices, battlefields, and memorials (such as the Vietnam Veterans Memorial Wall in Washington, D.C.).

- *Times.* Death involves times or occasions—such as Memorial Day in the United States and the Day of the Dead in Mexico—which are times to honor those who have died. Also, anniversaries of disasters such as D-Day in World War II, 9/11/2001, and Hurricane Katrina in 2005, as well as the 2004 tsunami in Southeast Asia that took approximately 100,000 lives, are times when those who died are remembered in special ways such as ceremonies.

- *Objects.* Many objects in a culture are associated with death, including caskets, various black objects such as clothes, arm bands, and hearses.

- *Symbols.* Symbols such as a skull and crossbones, as well as last rites in the Catholic religion and various religious ceremonies, are connected to death.

Kastenbaum (2004, 2007, 2009) also argues that the death system serves certain functions in a culture. These functions include *issuing warnings and predictions* (by such providers as weather-forecasting services and the media, laboratories that analyze test results, and doctors that communicate with patients and their families); *preventing death* (by such people as firefighters, the police, physicians, and researchers who work to improve safety and find cures for diseases); *caring for the dying* (by various health professionals such as physicians and nurses, as well as in places where dying individuals are cared for, such as hospitals or hospices); *disposing of the dead* (removal of the body, whether the body is cremated, and so on); *social consolidation after death* (coping and adapting by family members and friends of the deceased, who often need support and counseling); *making sense of the death* (how people in the society try to understand death); and *killing* (when, how, and for what reasons people in the culture can be killed, such as criminals and whether the death penalty should be given to some individuals). Figure 17.1 describes the functions of the death system in the context of Hurricane Katrina in 2005 (Kastenbaum, 2007, 2009).

What are some cultural variations in the death system? To live a full life and to die with glory were the prevailing goals of the ancient Greeks. Individuals are more conscious of death in times of war, famine, and plague. Whereas Americans are conditioned from early in life to live as though they were immortal, in much of the world this fiction cannot be maintained. Death crowds the streets of Calcutta in daily overdisplay, as it does the scrubby villages of Africa's Sahel. Children live with the ultimate toll of malnutrition and disease, mothers lose as many babies as survive into adulthood, and it is rare that a family remains intact for many years. Even in peasant areas where life is better, and health and maturity may be reasonable expectations, the presence of dying people in the house, the large attendance at funerals, and the daily contact with aging adults prepare the young for death and provide them with guidelines on how to die. By contrast, in the United States it is not uncommon to reach adulthood without having seen someone die.

Most societies throughout history have had philosophical or religious beliefs about death, and most societies have a ritual that deals with death (Bruce, 2007). Death may be seen as a punishment for one's sins, an act of atonement, or a judgment of a just God. For some, death means loneliness; for others, death is a quest for happiness. For still others, death represents redemption, a relief from the trials and tribulations of the earthly world. Some embrace death and welcome it; others abhor and fear it. For those who welcome it, death may be seen as the fitting end to a fulfilled life. From this perspective, how we depart from earth is influenced by how we have lived.

In most societies, death is not viewed as the end of existence—though the biological body has died, the spiritual body is believed to live on. This religious perspective is favored by most Americans as well (Gowan, 2003). Cultural variations in attitudes toward death include belief in reincarnation, which is an important aspect of the Hindu and Buddhist religions (Dillon, 2003). In the Gond culture of India, death is believed to be caused by magic and demons. The members of the Gond culture react angrily to death. In the Tanala culture of Madagascar, death is believed to be caused by natural forces. The members of the Tanala culture show a much more peaceful reaction to death than their counterparts in the Gond culture. Figure 17.2 shows a ritual associated with death in South Korea.

In many ways, we in the United States are death avoiders and death deniers (Norouzieh, 2005). This denial can take many forms:

- The tendency of the funeral industry to gloss over death and fashion lifelike qualities in the dead

A body lies in the flooded streets of New Orleans in the aftermath of Hurricane Katrina.

Death System Function	Hurricane Katrina
Warnings and predictions	Long-standing recognition of vulnerability; clear advance warning of impending disaster.
Preventing death	The hurricane itself could not be prevented; loss of life, social disorganization, and massive property destruction could have been sharply reduced by better advanced planning and emergency response.
Caring for the dying	Medical care was interrupted and undermined by damage to hospitals and communications.
Disposing of the dead	Recovering bodies was delayed, and there were major problems in identifying bodies.
Social consolidation after death	Community cohesiveness and support was negatively impacted by evacuation, scattering of family members, and limited response by overwhelmed human service agencies.
Making sense of death	There was intense criticism of government agencies, whose alleged failures contributed to death and destruction.
Killing	The media reported spikes in lethal violence after the hurricane, but those reports were later found to be inaccurate.

FIGURE 17.1 Hurricane Katrina and Death System Functions.

FIGURE 17.2 A Ritual Associated with Death. Family memorial day at the national cemetery in Seoul, Korea.

- The adoption of euphemistic language for death—for example, *exiting, passing on, never say die,* and *good for life,* which implies forever
- The persistent search for a fountain of youth
- The rejection and isolation of the aged, who may remind us of death
- The adoption of the concept of a pleasant and rewarding afterlife, suggesting that we are immortal
- The medical community's emphasis on prolonging biological life rather than on diminishing human suffering

Changing Historical Circumstances

One historical change involves the age group in which death most often strikes. Two hundred years ago, almost one of every two children died before the age of 10, and one parent died before children grew up. Today, death occurs most often among older adults (Carr, 2009). Life expectancy has increased from 47 years for a person born in 1900 to 78 years for someone born today (U.S. Census Bureau, 2008). In 1900, most people died at home, cared for by their family. As our population has aged and become more mobile, a larger number of older adults die apart from their families (Carr, 2009). In the United States today, more than 80 percent of all deaths occur in institutions or hospitals. The care of a dying older person has shifted away from the family and minimized our exposure to death and its painful surroundings.

Review and Reflect: Learning Goal 1

1 Describe the death system and its cultural and historical contexts

REVIEW

- What characterizes the death system in a culture? What are some cultural variations in the death system?
- What are some changing sociohistorical circumstances regarding death?

REFLECT

- Describe how the United States is a death-denying culture. What could be done to change this?

2 DEFINING DEATH AND LIFE/DEATH ISSUES

Issues in Determining Death	Decisions Regarding Life, Death, and Health Care

Is there one point in the process of dying that is *the* point at which death takes place, or is death a more gradual process? What are some decisions individuals can make about life, death, and health care?

Issues in Determining Death

Twenty-five years ago, determining if someone was dead was simpler than it is today. The end of certain biological functions, such as breathing and blood pressure, and the rigidity of the body (rigor mortis) were considered to be clear signs of death. In the past several decades, defining death has become more complex (Zamperetti & Bellomo, 2009).

Brain death is a neurological definition of death, which states that a person is brain dead when all electrical activity of the brain has ceased for a specified period of time. A flat electroencephalogram (EEG) recording for a specified period of time is one criterion of brain death. The higher portions of the brain often die sooner than the lower portions. Because the brain's lower portions monitor heartbeat and respiration, individuals whose higher brain areas have died may continue breathing and have a heartbeat. The definition of brain death currently followed by most physicians includes the death of both the higher cortical functions and the lower brain stem functions (Truog, 2007).

Some medical experts argue that the criteria for death should include only higher cortical functioning. If the cortical death definition were adopted, then physicians could claim death in a person who has no cortical functioning even though the lower brain stem is functioning. Supporters of the cortical death policy argue that the functions we associate with being human, such as intelligence and personality, are located in the higher cortical part of the brain. They note that when these functions are lost, the "human being" is no longer alive.

Decisions Regarding Life, Death, and Health Care

In cases of catastrophic illness or accidents, patients might not be able to respond adequately to participate in decisions about their medical care. To prepare for this situation, some individuals make earlier choices.

Natural Death Act and Advanced Directive
For many patients in a coma, it has not been clear what their wishes regarding termination of treatment might be if they still were conscious. Recognizing that terminally ill patients might prefer to die rather than linger in a painful or vegetative state, the organization "Choice in Dying" created the living will. This document is designed to be filled in while the individual can still think clearly; it expresses the person's desires regarding extraordinary medical procedures that might be used to sustain life when the medical situation becomes hopeless (Katsetos & Mirarchi, 2009).

Physicians' concerns over malpractice suits and the efforts of people who support the living will concept have produced natural death legislation in many states. For example, California's Natural Death Act permits individuals who have been diagnosed by two physicians as terminally ill to sign an *advance directive*, which states that life-sustaining procedures shall not be used to prolong their lives when death is imminent (Bisson & others, 2009). An advance directive must be signed while the individual still is able to think clearly (Westphal & McKee, 2009). Laws in all 50 states now accept advance directives as reflecting an individual's wishes.

Two recent studies of end-of-life planning revealed the following:

- Only 15 percent of patients 18 years of age and older had a living will (Clements, 2009). Almost 90 percent of the patients reported that it was important to discuss health-care wishes with their family, but only 60 percent of them had done so.
- Characteristics of 64- and 65-year-old adults who were more likely to engage in end-of-life planning (living will, durable power of attorney for health care, and discussion) included (1) being hospitalized in the year prior to the interview, (2) believing that patients rather than physicians should make

brain death A neurological definition of death—an individual is brain dead when all electrical activity of the brain has ceased for a specified period of time.

Terri Schiavo (*right*) shown with her mother in an undated photo. *What issues does the Terri Schiavo case raise?*

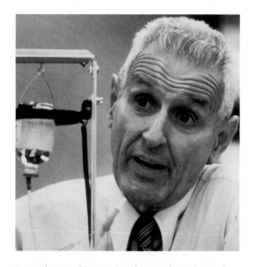

Dr. Jack Kevorkian assisted a number of people in Michigan to end their lives through active euthanasia. *Where do you stand on the use of active euthanasia?*

euthanasia The act of painlessly ending the lives of persons who are suffering from incurable diseases or severe disabilities; sometimes called "mercy killing."

passive euthanasia The withholding of available treatments, such as life-sustaining devices, allowing the person to die.

active euthanasia Death induced deliberately, as by injecting a lethal dose of a drug.

health-care decisions, (3) having less death anxiety, and (4) having survived the painful death of a loved one (Carr & Khodyakov, 2007).

Euthanasia Euthanasia ("easy death") is the act of painlessly ending the lives of individuals who are suffering from an incurable disease or severe disability. Sometimes euthanasia is called "mercy killing." Distinctions are made between two types of euthanasia: passive and active.

- **Passive euthanasia** occurs when a person is allowed to die by withholding available treatment, such as withdrawing a life-sustaining device. For example, this might involve turning off a respirator or a heart-lung machine.
- **Active euthanasia** occurs when death is deliberately induced, as when a lethal dose of a drug is injected.

Technological advances in life-support devices raise the issue of quality of life (Fenigsen, 2008; Givens & Mitchell, 2009). Nowhere was this more apparent than in the highly publicized case of Terri Schiavo, who suffered severe brain damage related to cardiac arrest and a lack of oxygen to the brain. She went into a coma and spent 15 years in a vegetative state. Across the 15 years, whether passive euthanasia should be implemented or whether she should be kept in the vegetative state with the hope that her condition might change for the better was debated between family members and eventually at a number of levels in the judicial system. At one point toward the end of her life in early spring 2005, a court ordered her feeding tube be removed. However, subsequent appeals led to its reinsertion twice. The feeding tube was removed a third and final time on March 18, 2005, and she died 13 days later.

Should individuals like Terri Schiavo be kept alive in a vegetative state? The trend is toward acceptance of passive euthanasia in the case of terminally ill patients. However, a recent study revealed that family members were reluctant to have their relatives disconnected from a ventilator but rather wanted an escalation of treatment for them (Sviri & others, 2009). In this study, most of the individuals said that in similar circumstances they would not want to be chronically ventilated or resuscitated.

The inflammatory argument that once equated this practice with suicide rarely is heard today. However, experts do not yet entirely agree on the precise boundaries or the exact mechanisms by which treatment decisions should be implemented (Gielen, van den Branden, & Broeckaert, 2009; Manthous, 2009; Seale, 2009). Can a comatose patient's life-support systems be disconnected when the patient has left no written instructions to that effect? Does the family of a comatose patient have the right to overrule the attending physician's decision to continue life-support systems? These questions have no simple or universally agreed-upon answers.

The most widely publicized cases of active euthanasia involve "assisted suicide" (Georges & others, 2008; Lofmark & others, 2008). Jack Kevorkian, a Michigan physician, has assisted a number of terminally ill patients to end their lives. After a series of trials, Kevorkian was convicted of second-degree murder and given a 10- to 15-year sentence. After serving 8 years, he was released from prison at age 79 for good behavior in June 2007 and promised not to participate in any further assisted suicides.

Active euthanasia is a crime in most countries and in all states in the United States except three—Oregon, Washington, and Montana. In 1994, the state of Oregon passed the Death with Dignity Act, which allows active euthanasia. In its first decade, 341 individuals were known to have died by active euthanasia in Oregon. In January 2006, the U.S. Supreme Court upheld Oregon's active euthanasia law. In 2008, assisted suicide became legal in Montana, and in 2009, it became legal in Washington state. Active euthanasia is legal in the Netherlands and Uruguay (Pasman & others, 2009; Watson, 2009) in addition to Switzerland, Belgium, and Luxembourg. A recent Canadian study assessed terminally ill cancer patients' views on physician-assisted suicide (Wilson & others, 2007). Slightly more than 60 percent thought that physician-assisted suicide should be legalized, but only 6 percent said they would make a request right away if it were legal. Patients who had a desire for a hastened death were less religious, had been diagnosed as having depression, and had a lower functional living status.

Needed: Better Care for Dying Individuals   Death in America is often lonely, prolonged, and painful. Dying individuals often get too little or too much care. Scientific advances sometimes have made dying harder by delaying the inevitable. And, even though painkillers are available, too many people experience severe pain during the last days and months of life (Mosenthal & others, 2008). Many health-care professionals have not been trained to provide adequate end-of-life care or to understand its importance. A recent study revealed that in many cases doctors don't give dying patients adequate information about how long they are likely to live or how various treatments will affect their lives (Harrington & Smith, 2008). For example, in this study of patients with advanced cancer, only 37 percent of doctors told patients how long they were likely to live.

End-of-life care should include respect for the goals, preferences, and choices of the patient and his or her family (Miyashita & others, 2008). Many patients who are nearing death want companionship.

Care providers are increasingly interested in helping individuals experience a "good death" (Bradley & Brasel, 2009; Carr, 2009). One view is that a good death involves physical comfort, support from loved ones, acceptance, and appropriate medical care. For some individuals, a good death involves accepting one's impending death and not feeling like a burden to others (Carr, 2009).

There are few fail-safe measures for avoiding pain at the end of life. Still, you can follow these suggestions (Cowley & Hager, 1995):

- Make a living will, and be sure there is someone who will draw your doctor's attention to it.

- Give someone the power of attorney, and make sure this person knows your wishes regarding medical care.

- Give your doctors specific instructions—from "Do not resuscitate" to "Do everything possible"—for specific circumstances.

- If you want to die at home, talk it over with your family and doctor.

- Check to see whether your insurance plan covers home care and hospice care.

A hospice nurse in Lansdale, Pennsylvania, visiting a terminally ill patient in the patient's home. *What are some characteristics of hospice care?*

Hospice is a program committed to making the end of life as free from pain, anxiety, and depression as possible (Dunn, 2009). Whereas a hospital's goals are to cure illness and prolong life, hospice care emphasizes **palliative care,** which involves reducing pain and suffering and helping individuals die with dignity (Zaider & Kissane, 2009). Health-care professionals work together to treat the dying person's symptoms, make the individual as comfortable as possible, show interest in the person and the person's family, and help them cope with death (Hupcey, Penrod, & Fenstermacher, 2009; Kelly & others, 2009).

A primary hospice goal is to bring pain under control and to help dying patients face death in a psychologically healthy way. The hospice also makes every effort to include the dying individual's family; it is believed that this strategy benefits not only the dying individual but family members as well, probably diminishing their guilt after the death.

The hospice movement has grown rapidly in the United States. More than 1,500 community groups are involved nationally in establishing hospice programs. Hospices are more likely to serve people with terminal cancer than those with other life-threatening conditions (Kastenbaum, 2007).

hospice A program committed to making the end of life as free from pain, anxiety, and depression as possible. The goals of hospice contrast with those of a hospital, which are to cure disease and prolong life.

palliative care Emphasized in hospice care; involves reducing pain and suffering and helping individuals die with dignity.

Careers in Life-Span Development

Kathy McLaughlin, Home Hospice Nurse

Kathy McLaughlin is a home hospice nurse in Alexandria, Virginia. She provides care for individuals with terminal cancer, Alzheimer disease, and other diseases. There currently is a shortage of home hospice nurses in the United States.

McLaughlin says that she has seen too many people dying in pain, away from home, hooked up to needless machines. In her work as a home hospice nurse, she comments, "I know I'm making a difference. I just feel privileged to get the chance to meet this person who is not going to be around much longer. I want to enjoy the moment with this person. And I want them to enjoy the moment. They have great stories. They are better than novels" (McLaughlin, 2003, p. 1).

Kathy McLaughlin checks the vital signs of Kathryn Francis, 86, who is in an advanced stage of Alzheimer disease.

Currently, approximately 90 percent of hospice care is provided in patients' homes (Hayslip & Hansson, 2007). In some cases, home-based care is provided by community-based health-care professionals or volunteers; in other cases, home-based care is provided by home health-care agencies of Visiting Nurse Associations. Also, some hospice care is provided in free-standing, full-service hospice facilities and in hospice units in hospitals. To read about the work of a home hospice nurse, see the *Careers in Life-Span Development* profile.

Researchers have found that family members provide more positive evaluations of a loved one's quality of life and better psychological adjustment themselves following the loved one's death when in-home hospice services are used than when the loved one is cared for in the final weeks of life in nursing homes, hospitals, or at home with home health nursing services (Teno & others, 2004). One study also revealed that hospice care reduced the increased mortality linked with bereavement by loved ones (Christakis & Iwashyna, 2003).

Review and Reflect: Learning Goal 2

 Evaluate issues in determining death and decisions regarding death

REVIEW
- What are some issues regarding the determination of death?
- What are some decisions to be made regarding life, death, and health care?

REFLECT
- Do you think assisted suicide should be legal? Explain your answer.

3 A DEVELOPMENTAL PERSPECTIVE ON DEATH

Causes of Death | Attitudes Toward Death at Different Points in the Life Span | Suicide

Do the causes of death vary across the human life span? Do we have different expectations about death as we develop through the life span? What are our attitudes toward death at different points in our development? What causes individuals to commit suicide?

Causes of Death

Death can occur at any point in the human life span. Death can occur during prenatal development through miscarriages or stillborn births. Death can also occur during the birth process or in the first few days after birth, which usually happens because of a birth defect or because infants have not developed adequately to sustain life outside the uterus. In Chapter 3, "Physical Development and Biological Aging," we discussed *sudden infant death syndrome (SIDS),* in which infants stop breathing, usually during the night, and die without apparent cause (Dwyer & Ponsonby, 2009). SIDS currently is the leading cause of infant death in the United States, with the risk highest at 2 to 4 months of age (NICHD, 2009).

In childhood, death occurs most often because of accidents or illness. Accidental death in childhood can be the consequence of such things as an automobile accident, drowning, poisoning, fire, or a fall from a high place. Major illnesses that cause death in children are heart disease, cancer, and birth defects.

Compared with childhood, death in adolescence is more likely to occur because of motor vehicle accidents, suicide, and homicide. Many motor vehicle accidents that cause death in adolescence are alcohol-related. We examine suicide in greater depth shortly.

Older adults are more likely to die from chronic diseases, such as heart disease and cancer, whereas younger adults are more likely to die from accidents. Older adults' diseases often incapacitate before they kill, which produces a course of dying that slowly leads to death. Of course, many young and middle-aged adults die of diseases, such as heart disease and cancer.

Attitudes Toward Death at Different Points in the Life Span

The ages of children and adults influence the way they experience and think about death (Silverman & Kelly, 2009). A mature, adultlike conception of death includes an understanding that death is final and irreversible, that death represents the end of life, and that all living things die. Most researchers have found that as children grow, they develop a more mature approach to death (Hayslip & Hansson, 2003).

Childhood Most researchers note that infants do not have even a rudimentary concept of death. However, as infants develop an attachment to a caregiver, they can experience loss or separation and an accompanying anxiety. But young children do not perceive time the way adults do. Even brief separations may be experienced as total losses. For most infants, the reappearance of the caregiver provides a continuity of existence and a reduction of anxiety. We know very little about the infant's actual experiences with bereavement, although the loss of a parent, especially if the caregiver is not replaced, can negatively affect the infant's health.

Even children 3 to 5 years of age have little or no idea of what death means. They may confuse death with sleep or ask in a puzzled way, "Why doesn't it move?" Preschool-aged children rarely get upset by the sight of a dead animal or by being told that a person has died. They believe that the dead can be brought back to life spontaneously by magic or by giving them food or medical treatment. Young children often believe that only people who want to die, or who are bad or careless, actually die. They also may blame themselves for the death of someone they know well, illogically reasoning that the event may have happened because they disobeyed the person who died.

Sometime in the middle and late childhood years more realistic perceptions of death develop. In one early investigation of children's perception of death, children 3 to 5 years of age denied that death exists, children 6 to 9 years of age believed that death exists but happens to only some people, and children 9 years of age and older recognized death's finality and universality (Nagy, 1948). In a review of research on children's conception of death, it was concluded that children probably do not view death as universal and irreversible until about 9 years of age (Cuddy-Casey & Orvaschel, 1997). Most children under 7 do not see death as likely. Those who do perceive it as reversible.

An expert on death and dying, Robert Kastenbaum (2007) takes a different view on developmental dimensions of death and dying. He notes that even very young children are acutely aware of and concerned about *separation* and *loss,* just as attachment theorist John Bowlby (1980) does. Kastenbaum also says that many children work hard at trying to understand death. Thus, instead of viewing young children as having illogical perceptions of death, Kastenbaum thinks a more accurate stance is to view them as having concerns about death and striving to understand it.

The death of a parent is especially difficult for children (Sood & others, 2006). When a child's parent dies, the child's school performance and peer relationships often worsen. For some children, as well as adults, a parent's death can be devastating and result in a hypersensitivity about death, including a fear of losing others close to the individual. In some cases, loss of a sibling can result in similar negative outcomes (Sood & others, 2006). However, a number of factors, such as the quality of the relationship and type of the death (whether due to an accident, long-standing illness, suicide, or murder, for example), can influence the individual's development following the death of a person close to the individual.

Most psychologists stress that honesty is the best strategy in discussing death with children. Treating the concept as unmentionable is thought to be an inappropriate strategy, yet most of us have grown up in a society in which death is rarely discussed.

In addition to honesty, what other strategies can be adopted in discussing death with children? The best response to the child's query about death might depend on the child's maturity level (Aiken, 2000). For example, the preschool child requires a less elaborate explanation than an older child. Death can be explained to preschool children in simple physical and biological terms. Actually, what young children need more than elaborate explanations of death is reassurance that they are loved and will not be abandoned. Regardless of children's age, adults should be sensitive and sympathetic, encouraging them to express their own feelings and ideas.

Adolescence   For many adolescents, the prospect of death, like the prospect of aging, is often regarded as a remote notion that is not very relevant to their lives. However, some adolescents do show a concern for death, both in trying to fathom its meaning and in confronting the prospect of their own demise.

Adolescents develop more abstract conceptions of death than children do. For example, adolescents describe death in terms of darkness, light, transition, or nothingness (Wenestam & Wass, 1987). They also develop religious and philosophical views about the nature of death and whether there is life after death.

Adulthood   There is no evidence that a special orientation toward death develops in early adulthood. An increase in consciousness about death accompanies individuals' awareness that they are aging, which usually intensifies in middle adulthood. In

What are children's and adolescents' attitudes about death? What are some good strategies for helping children and adolescents understand death?

our discussion of middle adulthood, we considered that midlife is a time when adults begin to think more about how much time is left in their lives. Researchers have found that middle-aged adults actually fear death more than do young adults or older adults (Kalish & Reynolds, 1976). Older adults, though, think about death more and talk about it more in conversation with others than do middle-aged and young adults. They also have more direct experience with death as their friends and relatives become ill and die (Hayslip & Hansson, 2003). Older adults are forced to examine the meanings of life and death more frequently than are younger adults.

Younger adults who are dying often feel cheated more than do older adults who are dying (Kalish, 1987). Younger adults are more likely to think they have not had the opportunity to do what they want to with their lives. Younger adults perceive they are losing what they might achieve; older adults perceive they are losing what they have.

In older adults, one's own death may take on an appropriateness it lacked in earlier years. Some of the increased thinking and conversing about death, and an increased sense of integrity developed through a positive life review, may help older adults accept death. Older adults are less likely to have unfinished business than are younger adults. They usually do not have children who need to be guided to maturity, their spouses are more likely to be dead, and they are less likely to have work-related projects that require completion. Lacking such anticipations, death may be less emotionally painful to them. Even among older adults, however, attitudes toward death vary.

Suicide

What are some of the factors that place people at risk for suicide? They include serious physical illnesses, mental disorders, feelings of hopelessness, social isolation, failure in school and work, loss of loved ones, serious financial difficulties, drug use, and a prior suicide attempt (Rhodes & Bethell, 2008).

There are cultural differences in suicide (Oyama & others, 2008; Shah, 2008). The highest rate of suicide for males is in Lithuania (68 per 100,000 population); the lowest is in the Dominican Republic (0 per 100,000 population). The highest rate of suicide for females is in Sri Lanka (17 per 100,000 population) and China; the lowest rate (0 per 100,000 population) occurs in several Caribbean islands, including Aruba and Barbados, and in several middle eastern countries, including Egypt and Jordan (World Health Organization, 2009). The United States' rate of suicide is 18 per 100,000 population for males, 4.5 per 100,000 for females.

Adolescence Suicidal behavior is rare in childhood but escalates in adolescence and then increases further in emerging adulthood (Park & others, 2006). Suicide is the third leading cause of death in 10- to 19-year-olds today in the United States (National Center for Health Statistics, 2008). After increasing to high levels in the 1990s, suicide rates in adolescents have declined in recent years. In 2004, 4,214 U.S. individuals from 15 to 24 years of age committed suicide (Minino, Heron, & Smith, 2006). Emerging adults have triple the rate of suicide as adolescents (Park & others, 2006).

Although a suicide threat should always be taken seriously, far more adolescents contemplate or attempt it unsuccessfully than actually commit it (Miranda & others, 2008). In a national study, in 2005, 17 percent of U.S. high school students said that they had seriously considered or attempted suicide in the last 12 months (Eaton & others, 2006). As shown in Figure 17.3, this percentage has declined since 1991. In the national survey, in 2005, 2.3 percent reported a suicide attempt that

How might older adults' attitudes about death differ from those of younger adults?

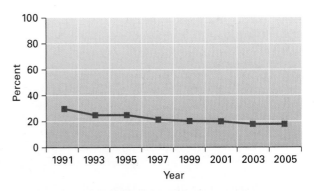

FIGURE 17.3 Percentage of U.S. Ninth- to Twelfth-Grade Students Who Seriously Considered Attempting Suicide in the Previous 12 Months from 1991 to 2005.

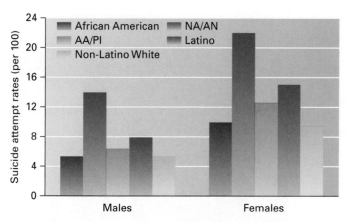

FIGURE 17.4 Suicide Attempts by U.S. Adolescents from Different Ethnic Groups. *Note:* Data shown are for one-year rates of self-reported suicide attempts. NA/AN = Native American/Alaska Native; AA/PI = Asian American/Pacific Islander.

resulted in an injury, poisoning, or drug overdose that had been treated by a doctor. Females were more likely to attempt suicide than males, but males were more likely to succeed in committing suicide. Males use more lethal means, such as guns, in their suicide attempts, whereas adolescent females are more likely to cut their wrists or take an overdose of sleeping pills—methods less likely to result in death.

The suicidal behavior of adolescents varies not only by gender, but also by ethnicity. As shown in Figure 17.4, Native American/ Alaska Native adolescent females are the most likely and African American females the least likely to attempt suicide (Goldston & others, 2008). However, Native American/Alaska Native adolescents are the most likely and non-Latino White females the least likely to actually commit suicide (Goldston & others, 2008). A major risk factor in the high rate of suicide attempts by NA/AN adolescents is their elevated rate of alcohol abuse

Distal, or earlier, experiences often are involved in suicide attempts as well. The adolescent may have a long-standing history of family instability and unhappiness. Just as a lack of affection and emotional support, high control, and pressure for achievement by parents during childhood are related to adolescent depression, such combinations of family experiences also are likely to show up as distal factors in adolescents' suicide attempts.

Adolescents' peer relations also are linked to suicide attempts. A recent research review revealed that prior suicide attempts by members of an adolescent's social groups was linked to the probability the adolescent also would attempt suicide (de Leo & Heller, 2008). Adolescents who attempt suicide may lack supportive friendships. One study found that social isolation was linked with suicide attempts in adolescent girls (Bearman & Moody, 2004).

Just as genetic factors are associated with depression, they also are associated with suicide (Kapornai & Vetro, 2008). The closer a person's genetic relationship to someone who has committed suicide, the more likely that person is to also commit suicide.

What is the psychological profile of the suicidal adolescent? Suicidal adolescents often have depressive symptoms (Ash, 2008). Although not all depressed adolescents are suicidal, depression is the most frequently cited factor associated with adolescent suicide (Bethell & Rhodes, 2008). A sense of hopelessness, low self-esteem, and high self-blame are also associated with adolescent suicide (O'Donnell & others, 2004). One study found that perception of being a burden on others and thwarted belongingness were linked to suicidal thoughts (Van Orden & others, 2008). Another study revealed that overweight middle school students were more likely to think about, plan, and attempt suicide than their counterparts who were not overweight (Whetstone, Morrisey, & Cummings, 2007). And another recent study found that preteen alcohol use was linked to suicide attempts in adolescence (Swahn, Bossarte, & Sullivent, 2008).

Adulthood and Aging U.S. suicide rates remain reasonably stable during early and middle adulthood, then increase in late adulthood (see Figure 17.5) (U.S. Census Bureau, 2006). Older non-Latino White men are more likely to commit suicide than any other group (Garand & others, 2006). One study found that African Americans are less likely to commit suicide than non-Latino Whites, but African Americans commit suicide at a younger age (median age of 34 years compared with 44 years for non-Latino Whites) (Garlow, Purselle, & Heninger, 2005). For all adult age groups (as for adolescents), males are more likely to commit suicide than

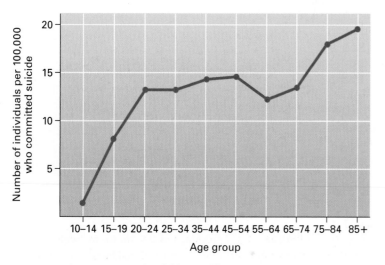

FIGURE 17.5 U.S. Rate of Suicide in Different Age Groups.

are females. The older adult most likely to commit suicide is a male who lives alone, has lost his spouse, and is experiencing failing health (Heisel, 2006).

Are there factors that distinguish between individuals who just think about suicide and those who actually attempt it? One recent study of more than 7,000 adults revealed that suicide attempters were more likely than suicide ideators to be unemployed, have poor health, and have relationship problems (Fairweather & others, 2006).

Older adults are less likely to communicate their suicide intentions than are younger adults and adolescents, and they make fewer attempts (Conwell & Thompson, 2008). However, when older adults attempt suicide, they use more lethal methods and more often succeed (Mitty & Flores, 2008). A surviving spouse is especially at risk for depression or suicide (De Leo, 2002).

Review and Reflect: Learning Goal 3

 3 **Discuss death and attitudes about it at different points in development**

REVIEW

- What are some developmental changes in the cause of death?
- What are some attitudes about death at different points in development?
- Why do people commit suicide? What are some links of suicide to development?

REFLECT

- What is your current attitude about death? Has it changed since you were an adolescent? If so, how?

---

4 FACING ONE'S OWN DEATH

Kübler-Ross' Stages of Dying   Perceived Control and Denial   The Contexts in Which People Die

Knowledge of death's inevitability permits us to establish priorities and structure our time accordingly. As we age, these priorities and structurings change in recognition of diminishing future time. Values concerning the most important uses of time also change. For example, when asked how they would spend six remaining months of life, younger adults described such activities as traveling and accomplishing things they previously had not done; older adults described more inner-focused activities—contemplation and meditation, for example (Kalish & Reynolds, 1976).

Most dying individuals want an opportunity to make some decisions regarding their own life and death (Kastenbaum, 2007). Some individuals want to complete unfinished business; they want time to resolve problems and conflicts and to put their affairs in order.

Kübler-Ross' Stages of Dying

Might there be a sequence of stages we go through as we face death? Elisabeth Kübler-Ross (1969) divided the behavior and thinking of dying persons into five stages: denial and isolation, anger, bargaining, depression, and acceptance.

> *Man is the only animal that finds his own existence a problem he has to solve and from which he cannot escape. In the same sense man is the only animal who knows he must die.*
>
> —ERICH FROMM
> *American Psychotherapist, 20th Century*

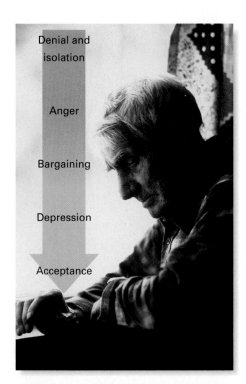

FIGURE 17.6 Kübler-Ross' Stages of Dying. According to Elisabeth Kübler-Ross, we go through five stages of dying: denial and isolation, anger, bargaining, depression, and acceptance. *Does everyone go through these stages, or go through them in the same order? Explain.*

denial and isolation Kübler-Ross' first stage of dying, in which the dying person denies that she or he is really going to die.

anger Kübler-Ross' second stage of dying, in which the dying person's denial gives way to anger, resentment, rage, and envy.

bargaining Kübler-Ross' third stage of dying, in which the dying person develops the hope that death can somehow be postponed.

depression Kübler-Ross' fourth stage of dying, in which the dying person perceives the certainty of her or his death. A period of depression or preparatory grief may appear.

acceptance Kübler-Ross' fifth stage of dying, in which the dying person develops a sense of peace, an acceptance of her or his fate, and, in many cases, a desire to be left alone.

Denial and isolation is Kübler-Ross' first stage of dying, in which the person denies that death is really going to take place. The person may say, "No, it can't be me. It's not possible." This is a common reaction to terminal illness. However, denial is usually only a temporary defense. It is eventually replaced with increased awareness when the person is confronted with such matters as financial considerations, unfinished business, and worry about surviving family members.

Anger is Kübler-Ross' second stage of dying, in which the dying person recognizes that denial can no longer be maintained. Denial often gives way to anger, resentment, rage, and envy. The dying person's question is, "Why me?" At this point, the person becomes increasingly difficult to care for as anger may become displaced and projected onto physicians, nurses, family members, and even God. The realization of loss is great, and those who symbolize life, energy, and competent functioning are especially salient targets of the dying person's resentment and jealousy.

Bargaining is Kübler-Ross' third stage of dying, in which the person develops the hope that death can somehow be postponed or delayed. Some persons enter into bargaining or negotiation—often with God—as they try to delay their death. Psychologically, the person is saying, "Yes, me, but . . ." In exchange for a few more days, weeks, or months of life, the person promises to lead a reformed life dedicated to God or to the service of others.

Depression is Kübler-Ross' fourth stage of dying, in which the dying person perceives the certainty of his or her death. At this point, a period of depression or preparatory grief may appear. The dying person may become silent, refuse visitors, and spend much of the time crying or grieving. This behavior is normal and is an effort to disconnect the self from love objects. Attempts to cheer up the dying person at this stage should be discouraged, says Kübler-Ross, because the dying person has a need to contemplate impending death.

Acceptance is Kübler-Ross' fifth stage of dying, in which the person develops a sense of peace, an acceptance of one's fate, and—in many cases—a desire to be left alone. In this stage, feelings and physical pain may be virtually absent. Kübler-Ross describes this fifth stage as the end of the dying struggle, the final resting stage before death. A summary of Kübler-Ross' dying stages is presented in Figure 17.6.

What is the current evaluation of Kübler-Ross' approach? According to Robert Kastenbaum (2007, 2009), there are some problems with Kübler-Ross' approach:

- The existence of the five-stage sequence has not been demonstrated by either Kübler-Ross or independent research.

- The stage interpretation neglected the patients' situations, including relationship support, specific effects of illness, family obligations, and institutional climate in which they were interviewed.

However, Kübler-Ross' pioneering efforts were important in calling attention to those who are attempting to cope with life-threatening illnesses. She did much to encourage attention to the quality of life for dying persons and their families.

Because of the criticisms of Kübler-Ross' stages, some psychologists prefer to describe them not as stages but as potential reactions to dying. At any one moment, a number of emotions may wax and wane. Hope, disbelief, bewilderment, anger, and acceptance may come and go as individuals try to make sense of what is happening to them.

In facing their own death, some individuals struggle until the end, desperately trying to hang on to their lives. Acceptance of death never comes for them. Some psychologists note that the harder individuals fight to avoid the inevitable death they face and the more they deny it, the more difficulty they will have in dying peacefully and in a dignified way; other psychologists argue that not confronting death until the end may be adaptive for some individuals (Lifton, 1977).

The extent to which people have found meaning and purpose in their lives is linked with how they approach death (Carr, 2009). A recent study revealed that individuals with a chronic, life-threatening illness—congestive heart failure—were trying to understand meaning in life (Park & others, 2008). Another study of 160 individuals with less than three months to live revealed that those who had found purpose and meaning in their lives felt the least despair in the final weeks, whereas dying individuals who saw no reason for living were the most distressed and wanted to hasten death (McClain, Rosenfeld, & Breitbart, 2003). In this and other studies, spirituality helped to buffer dying individuals from severe depression (Smith, McCullough, & Poll, 2003).

Do individuals become more spiritual as they get closer to death? A recent study of more than 100 patients with advanced congestive heart failure who were studied at two times six months apart found that as the patients perceived they were closer to death, they became more spiritual (Park, 2008).

Perceived Control and Denial

Perceived control may work as an adaptive strategy for some older adults who face death. When individuals are led to believe they can influence and control events—such as prolonging their lives—they may become more alert and cheerful. Remember from Chapter 4, "Health," that giving nursing home residents options for control improved their attitudes and increased their longevity (Rodin & Langer, 1977).

Denial also may be a fruitful way for some individuals to approach death. It can be adaptive or maladaptive. Denial can be used to avoid the destructive impact of shock by delaying the necessity of dealing with one's death. Denial can insulate the individual from having to cope with intense feelings of anger and hurt—however, if denial keeps us from having a life-saving operation, it clearly is maladaptive. Denial is neither good nor bad; its adaptive qualities need to be evaluated on an individual basis.

The Contexts in Which People Die

For dying individuals, the context in which they die is important. More than 50 percent of Americans die in hospitals, and nearly 20 percent die in nursing homes. Some people spend their final days in isolation and fear. An increasing number of people choose to die in the humane atmosphere of hospice care.

Hospitals offer several important advantages to the dying individual—for example, professional staff members are readily available, and the medical technology present may prolong life. But a hospital may not be the best place for many people to die. Most individuals say they would rather die at home. Many feel, however, that they will be a burden at home, that there is limited space there, and that dying at home may alter relationships. Individuals who are facing death also worry about the competency and availability of emergency medical treatment if they remain at home.

Review and Reflect: Learning Goal 4

 4 **Explain the psychological aspects involved in facing one's own death and the contexts in which people die**

REVIEW

- What are Kübler-Ross' five stages of dying? What conclusions can be reached about them?
- What roles do perceived control and denial play in facing one's own death?
- What are the contexts in which people die?

REFLECT

- How do you think you will psychologically handle facing your own death?

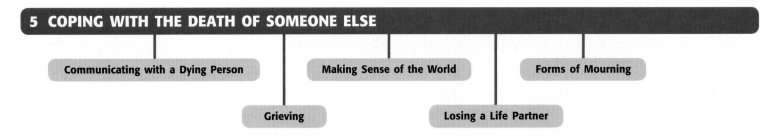

5 COPING WITH THE DEATH OF SOMEONE ELSE

Communicating with a Dying Person   Making Sense of the World   Forms of Mourning

Grieving   Losing a Life Partner

Loss can come in many forms in our lives—divorce, a pet's death, loss of a job—but no loss is greater than that which comes through the death of someone we love and care for: a parent, sibling, spouse, relative, or friend. In the ratings of life's stresses that require the most adjustment, death of a spouse is given the highest number. How should we communicate with a dying individual? How do we cope with the death of someone we love?

Communicating with a Dying Person

Most psychologists stress that it is best for dying individuals to know that they are dying and that significant others know they are dying so they can interact and communicate with each other on the basis of this mutual knowledge. What are some of the advantages of this open awareness for the dying individual? First, dying individuals can close their lives in accord with their own ideas about proper dying. Second, they may be able to complete some plans and projects, can make arrangements for survivors, and can participate in decisions about a funeral and burial. Third, dying individuals have the opportunity to reminisce, to converse with others who have been important in their life, and to end life conscious of what life has been like. And fourth, dying individuals have more understanding of what is happening within their bodies and what the medical staff is doing to them (Kalish, 1981). In the *Applications in Life-Span Development* interlude, you can read further about effective communication strategies with a dying person.

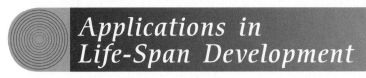

Applications in Life-Span Development

COMMUNICATING WITH A DYING PERSON

Effective strategies for communicating with a dying person include these:

1. Establish your presence, be at the same eye level; don't be afraid to touch the dying person—dying individuals are often starved for human touch.
2. Eliminate distraction—for example, ask if it is okay to turn off the TV. Realize that excessive small talk can be a distraction.
3. Dying individuals who are very frail often have little energy. If the dying person you are visiting is very frail, you may not want to visit for very long.
4. Don't insist that the dying person feel acceptance about death if the dying person wants to deny the reality of the situation; on the other hand, don't insist on denial if the dying individual indicates acceptance.
5. Allow the dying person to express guilt or anger; encourage the expression of feelings.
6. Don't be afraid to ask the person what the expected outcome for the illness is. Discuss alternatives, unfinished business.

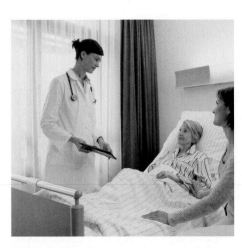

What are some good strategies for communicating with a dying person?

7. Sometimes dying individuals don't have access to other people. Ask the dying person if there is anyone he or she would like to see that you can contact.

8. Encourage the dying individual to reminisce, especially if you have memories in common.

9. Talk with the individual when she or he wishes to talk. If this is impossible, make a later appointment and keep it.

10. Express your regard for the dying individual. Don't be afraid to express love, and don't be afraid to say good-bye.

Grieving

Our exploration of grief focuses on dimensions of grieving, the dual-process model of coping with bereavement, coping and type of death, and cultural diversity in healthy grieving.

Dimensions of Grieving   **Grief** is the emotional numbness, disbelief, separation anxiety, despair, sadness, and loneliness that accompany the loss of someone we love. Grief is not a simple emotional state but rather a complex, evolving process with multiple dimensions (Silverman & Kelly, 2009). In this view, pining for the lost person is one important dimension. Pining or yearning reflects an intermittent, recurrent wish or need to recover the lost person. Another important dimension of grief is separation anxiety, which not only includes pining and preoccupation with thoughts of the deceased person but also focuses on places and things associated with the deceased, as well as on crying or sighing. Grief may also involve despair and sadness, which include a sense of hopelessness and defeat, depressive symptoms, apathy, loss of meaning for activities that used to involve the person who is gone, and growing desolation.

These feelings occur repeatedly shortly after a loss. As time passes, pining and protest over the loss tend to diminish, although episodes of depression and apathy may remain or increase. The sense of separation anxiety and loss may continue to the end of one's life, but most of us emerge from grief's tears, turning our attention once again to productive tasks and regaining a more positive view of life. A recent study of almost 300 recently widowed men and women revealed that in the course of their bereavement, experiencing humor, laughter, and happiness was strongly related to more favorable bereavement adjustment (lower levels of grief and depression) (Lund & others, 2008–2009).

The grieving process is more like a roller-coaster ride than an orderly progression of stages with clear-cut time frames (Lund, 2007). The ups and downs of grief often involve rapidly changing emotions, meeting the challenges of learning new skills, detecting personal weaknesses and limitations, creating new patterns of behavior, and forming new friendships and relationships. For most individuals, grief becomes more manageable over time, with fewer abrupt highs and lows (Bonanno, 2004). But many grieving spouses report that even though time has brought some healing, they have never gotten over their loss. They have just learned to live with it.

An estimated 80 to 90 percent of survivors experience normal or uncompli-cated grief reactions that include sadness and even disbelief or considerable anguish. By six months after their loss, many survivors accept the death as a reality, are more optimistic about the future, and function competently in their everyday lives. However, six months after their loss, approximately 10 to 20 per-cent of survivors have difficulty moving on with their life, feel numb or detached, believe their life is empty without the deceased, and feel that the future has no meaning. This type of grief was initially referred to as complicated grief, but

> *E*veryone can master grief but he who has it.
>
> **—WILLIAM SHAKESPEARE**
> *English Playwright, 17th Century*

grief The emotional numbness, disbelief, sepa-ration anxiety, despair, sadness, and loneliness that accompany the loss of someone we love.

recently leading expert Holly Prigerson and her colleagues (Boelen & Prigerson, 2007; Maciejewski & others, 2007) have advocated use of the term **prolonged grief** to describe grief that involves enduring despair and is still unresolved over an extended period of time. Prolonged grief usually has negative consequences for physical and mental health (Kersting & others, 2009). A person who loses someone he or she was emotionally dependent on is often at greatest risk for developing prolonged grief (Kowalski & Bondmass, 2008). A recent research indicated that African Americans experienced more prolonged grief than non-Latino Whites (Goldsmith & others, 2008).

Another type of grief is **disenfranchised grief,** which describes an individual's grief over a deceased person that is a socially ambiguous loss that can't be openly mourned or supported (Aloi, 2009; Hendry, 2009). Examples of disenfranchised grief include a relationship that isn't socially recognized such as an ex-spouse, a hidden loss such as an abortion, and circumstances of the death that are stigmatized such as death because of AIDS. Disenfranchised grief may intensify an individual's grief because it cannot be publicly acknowledged. This type of grief may be hidden or repressed for many years, only to be reawakened by later deaths.

Dual-Process Model of Coping with Bereavement   The **dual-process model** of coping with bereavement consists of two main dimensions: (1) loss-oriented stressors and (2) restoration-oriented stressors (Stroebe, Schut, & Stroebe, 2005). Loss-oriented stressors focus on the deceased individual and can include grief work and both positive and negative reappraisal of the loss. A positive reappraisal of the loss might include acknowledging that death brought relief at the end of suffering, whereas a negative reappraisal might involve yearning for the loved one and rumination about the death. Restoration-oriented stressors involve the secondary stressors that emerge as indirect outcomes of bereavement. They can include a changing identity (such as from "wife" to "widow") and mastering skills (such as dealing with finances). Restoration rebuilds "shattered assumptions about the world and one's own place in it."

In the dual-process model, effective coping with bereavement often involves an oscillation between coping with loss and coping with restoration. Earlier models often emphasized a sequence of coping with loss through such strategies as grief work as an initial phase, followed by restoration efforts. However, in the dual-process model, coping with loss and engaging in restoration can be carried out concurrently (Richardson, 2007). According to this model, the person coping with death might be involved in grief group therapy while settling the affairs of the loved one. Oscillation might occur in the short term during a specific day as well as across weeks, months, and even years. Although loss and restoration coping can occur concurrently, over time there often is an initial emphasis on coping with loss followed by greater emphasis on restoration.

Coping and Type of Death   The impact of death on surviving individuals is strongly influenced by the circumstances under which the death occurs (Reilly & others, 2008; Silverman & Kelly, 2009). Deaths that are sudden, untimely, violent, or traumatic are likely to have more intense and prolonged effects on surviving individuals and make the coping process more difficult for them (Raphael, Taylor, & McAndrew, 2008; Sveen & Walby, 2008). Such deaths often are accompanied by post-traumatic stress disorder (PTSD) symptoms, such as intrusive thoughts, flashbacks, nightmares, sleep disturbance, problems in concentrating, and others. Death of a child can be especially devastating and extremely difficult for parents to cope with (De Lisle-Porter & Podruchny, 2009; Reder & Serwint, 2009).

Cultural Diversity in Healthy Grieving   Some approaches to grieving emphasize the importance of breaking bonds with the deceased and returning to autonomous lifestyles. People who persist in holding on to the deceased are believed to be in need

How might grieving vary across individuals and cultures?

prolonged grief Grief that involves enduring despair and is still unresolved over an extended period of time.

disenfranchised grief Grief involving a deceased person that is a socially ambiguous loss that can't be openly mourned or supported.

dual-process model A model of coping with bereavement that emphasizes oscillation between two main dimensions: (1) loss-oriented stressors and (2) restoration-oriented stressors.

of therapy. However, some experts on grieving have cast doubt on whether this recommendation is always the best therapeutic advice (Stroebe & others, 1992).

Analyses of non-Western cultures suggest that beliefs about continuing bonds with the deceased vary extensively. Maintenance of ties with the deceased is accepted and sustained in the religious rituals of Japan. In the Hopi of Arizona, the deceased are forgotten as quickly as possible and life is carried on as usual. Their funeral ritual concludes with a break-off between mortals and spirits. The diversity of grieving is nowhere more clear than in two Muslim societies—one in Egypt, the other in Bali. In Egypt, the bereaved are encouraged to dwell at length on their grief, surrounded by others who relate similarly tragic accounts and express their own sorrow. By contrast, in Bali, the bereaved are encouraged to laugh and be joyful.

In sum, people grieve in a variety of ways (Carr, 2009). The diverse grieving patterns are culturally embedded practices. Thus, there is no one right, ideal way to grieve. There are many different ways to feel about a deceased person and no set series of stages that the bereaved must pass through to become well adjusted. What is needed is an understanding that healthy coping with the death of a loved one involves growth, flexibility, and appropriateness within a cultural context.

Making Sense of the World

One beneficial aspect of grieving is that it stimulates many individuals to try to make sense of their world (Carr, 2009; Park, 2009). A common occurrence is to go over again and again all of the events that led up to the death. In the days and weeks after the death, the closest family members share experiences with each other, sometimes reminiscing over family experiences. A recent study revealed that finding meaning in the death of a spouse was linked to a lower level of anger during bereavement (Kim, 2009).

Each individual may offer a piece of death's puzzle. "When I saw him last Saturday, he looked as though he were rallying," says one family member. "Do you think it might have had something to do with his sister's illness?" remarks another. "I doubt it, but I heard from an aide that he fell going to the bathroom that morning," comments yet another. "That explains the bruise on his elbow," says the first individual. "No wonder he told me that he was angry because he could not seem to do anything right," chimes in a fourth family member. So it goes in the attempt to understand why someone who was rallying on Saturday was dead on Wednesday.

When a death is caused by an accident or a disaster, the effort to make sense of it is pursued more vigorously. As added pieces of news come trickling in, they are integrated into the puzzle. The bereaved want to put the death into a perspective that they can understand— divine intervention, a curse from a neighboring tribe, a logical sequence of cause and effect, or whatever it may be.

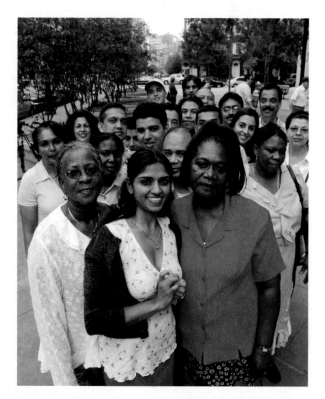

Mary Assanful (*front right*, with other former restaurant workers) worked at Windows on the World restaurant located in the World Trade Center and lost her job when terrorist attacks came She says that she still is not herself and regularly has nightmares. A Ghana native, Mary is still unemployed. She has joined several other workers who are now planning to return by opening a restaurant near Ground Zero. They hope the new restaurant will honor their coworkers who died and provide a focus and meaning for their still-unsettled lives. Mary says that since they have been working on this new project her mind has calmed somewhat.

Losing a Life Partner

In the United States, 18 percent of men and 52 percent of women 75 to 84 years of age were widowed and 32 percent of the men and 75 percent of the women 85 years and older were widowed in 2005 (U.S. Census Bureau, 2006). Those left behind after the death of an intimate partner often suffer profound grief and often endure financial loss, loneliness, increased physical illness, and psychological disorders, including depression (Elwert & Christakis, 2008; Johnson, Zhang, & Prigerson, 2008). How surviving spouses cope varies considerably. A six-year longitudinal study of individuals 80-plus years of age found that the loss of a spouse, especially in men, was related to a lower level of life satisfaction over time (Berg & others, 2009). In another study that included data from 3 years predeath to 18 months postdeath, nearly half of surviving spouses experienced low levels of distress consistently over the 4½ years (Bonanno, Wortman, & Nesse, 2004). In yet another study, widowed individuals were more likely to increase their religious and spiritual beliefs following the death of a spouse, and this increase was linked with a lower level of grief (Brown & others, 2004). And a recent study concluded that chronic grief was more likely to characterize bereaved spouses who were highly dependent on their spouse (Ott & others, 2007).

Widows outnumber widowers by the ratio of 5 to 1, because women live longer than men, because women tend to marry men older than themselves, and because a widowed man is more likely to remarry. Widowed women are probably the poorest group in America. The negative economic consequences for widowed women are greater for African American and Latino women than for non-Latino White women (Angel, Jimenez, & Angel, 2007). A recent study of Mexican Americans 65 years and older revealed that risk of death linked to widowhood was the highest in the first two years following the spouse's death (Stimpson & others, 2007).

Many widows are lonely. The poorer and less educated they are, the lonelier they tend to be. The bereaved are also at increased risk for many health problems, including death (Kowalski & Bondmass, 2008). The following *Research in Life-Span Development* interlude examines the relation of widowhood to health.

Research in Life-Span Development

THE WOMEN'S HEALTH INITIATIVE STUDY OF WIDOWHOOD AND HEALTH

A three-year longitudinal study of more than 130,000 women 50 to 79 years of age in the United States, as part of the Women's Health Initiative, examined the relation of widowhood to physical and mental health, health behaviors, and health outcomes (Wilcox & others, 2003). Women were categorized as (1) remaining married, (2) transitioning from married to widowed, (3) remaining widowed, and (4) transitioning from widowed to married. Widows were further subdivided into the recently widowed (widowed for less than one year) and longer-term widowed (widowed for more than one year).

The measures used to assess the older women's health were:

- *Physical health.* Blood pressure was assessed after five minutes of quiet rest using the average of two readings with 30 seconds between the readings. Hypertension was defined as more than 140/90. Body mass index (BMI) was calculated and used to determine whether a woman was obese. A health survey assessed physical function and health status.

- *Mental health.* Depressive symptoms were assessed by a six-item depression scale, with participants rating the frequency of their depressed thoughts during the past week. The participant's self-report of antidepressant medicine use was also obtained. Information about social functioning and mental health was based on participants' responses on the Social Functioning Scale (Ware, Kosinski, & Dewey, 2000).

- *Health behaviors.* Dietary behaviors were assessed with a modified version of the National Cancer Institute Health Habits and History Questionnaire. Participants also were asked if they smoked tobacco, and if so how much. To assess physical activity, participants were asked how often they walked outside the home each week and the extent to which they engaged in strenuous or moderate exercise. To assess health-care use, they were asked whether they had visited their doctor in the past year.

- *Health outcomes.* Cardiovascular disease and cancer occurrences were assessed annually and any overnight hospitalizations were noted.

At the beginning of the three-year study, married women reported better physical and mental health than, and better health in general, than widowed women. Women who remained married over the three-year period of the study showed stability in mental health, recent widows experienced marked impairments in mental health, and longer-term widows showed stability or slight improvements in mental health. Both groups of widows (recent and longer term) reported more unintentional weight loss across the three years. The findings underscore the resilience of older women and their capacity to reestablish connections but point to the need for services that strengthen social support for those who have difficulty during the transition from marriage to widowhood.

Optimal adjustment after a death depends on various factors (Schultz, Hebert, & Boerner, 2008). Women do better than men largely because, in our society, women are responsible for the emotional life of a couple, whereas men usually manage the finances and material goods (Fry, 2001). Thus, women have better networks of friends, closer relationships with relatives, and experience in taking care of themselves psychologically (Antonucci, Akiyama, & Sherman, 2007). Older widows do better than younger widows, perhaps because the death of a partner is more expected for older women. For their part, widowers usually have more money than widows do, and they are far more likely to remarry.

For either widows or widowers, social support helps them adjust to the death of a spouse (Wortman & Boerner, 2007). The Widow-to-Widow program, begun in the 1960s, provides support for newly widowed women. Volunteer widows reach out to other widows, introducing them to others who may have similar problems, leading group discussions, and organizing social activities. The program has been adopted by the American Association of Retired Persons and disseminated throughout the United States as the Widowed Person's Service. The model has since been adopted by numerous community organizations to provide support for those going through a difficult transition. Other bereavement support groups have been found to improve the well-being of widowed individuals (Maruyama & Atencio, 2008).

One study found that psychological and religious factors—such as personal meaning, optimism, the importance of religion, and access to religious support—were related to the psychological well-being of older adults following the loss of a spouse (Fry, 2001). Other studies have indicated that religiosity and coping skills are related to well-being following the loss of a spouse in late adulthood (Wortmann & Park, 2008).

Two recent studies revealed that volunteering and helping behavior improved the well-being of widowed individuals. In one study, volunteering following spousal loss helped to protect against depressive symptoms and increased self-efficacy (Li, 2007). In another study, following spousal loss, engaging in helping behavior (providing instrumental support to others) was linked to an accelerated decline in the helper's depressive symptoms 6 to 18 months following spousal loss (Brown & others, 2008).

Forms of Mourning

One decision facing the bereaved is what to do with the body. In the United States, in 2006, approximately two-thirds of corpses were disposed of by burial, the remaining one-third by cremation—a significant increase from 15 percent in 1985

A widow leading a funeral procession in the United States.

A crowd gathered at a cremation ceremony in Bali Indonesia, balancing decorative containers on their heads.

(Cremation Association of North America, 2008). Cremation is more popular in the Pacific region of the United States, less popular in the South. Cremation also is more popular in Canada than in the United States and most popular of all in Japan and many other Asian countries.

The funeral is an important aspect of mourning in many cultures. In one study, bereaved individuals who were personally religious derived more psychological benefits from a funeral, participated more actively in the rituals, and adjusted more positively to the loss (Hayslip, Edmondson, & Guarnaccia, 1999). In the United States, the trend is away from public funerals and displaying the dead body in an open casket and toward private funerals followed by a memorial ceremony (Callahan, 2009).

The funeral is an important aspect of mourning in many cultures. The funeral industry has been the source of controversy in recent years. Funeral directors and their supporters argue that the funeral provides a form of closure to the relationship with the deceased, especially when there is an open casket. Their critics claim that funeral directors are just trying to make money and that embalming is grotesque. One way to avoid being exploited during bereavement is to purchase funeral arrangements in advance. However, many adults have not made any funeral arrangements.

In some cultures, a ceremonial meal is held after death; in others, a black armband is worn for one year following a death. Cultures vary in how they practice mourning (Adamolekun, 2001; Shepard, 2002). To learn about two cultures with extensive mourning systems, see the *Contexts of Life-Span Development* interlude.

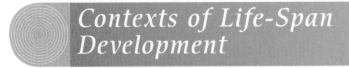

Contexts of Life-Span Development

THE AMISH, TRADITIONAL JUDAISM, AND MOURNING

The family and the community have important roles in mourning in some cultures. Two of those cultures are the Amish and traditional Judaism (Worthington, 1989).

The Amish are a conservative group with approximately 80,000 members in the United States, Ontario, and several small settlements in South and Central America. The Amish live in a family-oriented society in which family and community support is essential for survival. Today, they live at the same unhurried pace as that of their

A funeral procession of horse-drawn buggies on their way to the burial of five young Amish girls who were murdered in October 2006. A remarkable aspect of their mourning involved the outpouring of support and forgiveness they gave to the widow of the murderer.

ancestors, using horses instead of cars and facing death with the same steadfast faith as their forebears. At the time of death, close neighbors assume the responsibility of notifying others of the death. The Amish community handles virtually all aspects of the funeral.

The funeral service is held in a barn in warmer months and in a house during colder months. Calm acceptance of death, influenced by a deep religious faith, is an integral part of the Amish culture. Following the funeral, a high level of support is given to the bereaved family for at least a year. Visits to the family, special scrapbooks and handmade items for the family, new work projects started for the widow, and quilting days that combine fellowship and productivity are among the supports given to the bereaved family. A profound example of the Amish cultures' religious faith and acceptance of death occurred after Charles Roberts shot and killed five Amish school-girls and then apparently took his own life in October 2006 in the small town of Nickel Mines in Bart Township, Pennsylania. Soon after the murders and suicide, members of the Amish community visited his widow and offered their support and forgiveness.

The family and community also have specific and important roles in mourning in traditional Judaism. The program of mourning is divided into graduated time periods, each with its appropriate practices. The observance of these practices is required of the spouse and the immediate blood relatives of the deceased. The first period is *aninut,* the period between death and burial—which must take place within one day. The next two periods make up *avelut,* or mourning proper. The first of these is *shivah,* a period of seven days, which commences with the burial. It is followed by *sheloshim,* the 30-day period following the burial, including shivah. At the end of sheloshim, the mourning process is considered over for all but one's parents. For parents, mourning continues for 11 months, although observances are minimal.

The seven-day period of the shivah is especially important in traditional Judaism. The mourners, sitting together as a group through an extended period, have an opportunity to project their feelings to the group as a whole. Visits from others during shivah may help the mourner deal with feelings of guilt. After shivah, the mourner is encouraged to resume normal social interaction. In fact, it is customary for the mourners to walk together a short distance as a symbol of their return to society. In its entirety, the elaborate mourning system of traditional Judaism is designed to promote personal growth and to reintegrate the individual into the community.

Review and Reflect: Learning Goal 5

5 **Identify ways to cope with the death of another person**

REVIEW

- What are some strategies for communicating with a dying person?
- What is the nature of grieving?
- How is making sense of the world a beneficial outcome of grieving?
- What are some characteristics and outcomes of losing a life partner?
- What are some forms of mourning? What is the nature of the funeral?

REFLECT

- Is there a best or worst way to grieve? Explain.

We have arrived at the end of this book. I hope this book and course have been a window to the life span of the human species and a window to your own personal journey in life.

Our study of the human life span has been long and complex. You have read about many physical, cognitive, and socioemotional changes that take place from conception through death. This is a good time to reflect on what you have learned. Which theories, studies, and ideas were especially interesting to you? What did you learn about your own development?

I wish you all the best in the remaining years of your journey though the human life span.

John W. Santrock

Reach Your Learning Goals

Death, Dying, and Grieving

1   THE DEATH SYSTEM AND CULTURAL CONTEXTS: DESCRIBE THE DEATH SYSTEM AND ITS CULTURAL AND HISTORICAL CONTEXTS

The Death System and Its Cultural Variations

Changing Historical Circumstances

- In Kastenbaum's view, every culture has a death system that involves these components: people, places, times, objects, and symbols. He also argues that the death system serves certain functions in a culture that include issuing warnings and predictions, preventing death, caring for the dying, disposing of the dead, attaining social consolidation after the death, making sense of the death, and killing. Most societies throughout history have had philosophical or religious beliefs about death, and most societies have rituals that deal with death. Most cultures do not view death as the end of existence—spiritual life is thought to continue. Some cultures believe in reincarnation. The United States has been described as more of a death-denying and death-avoiding culture than most cultures.

- When, where, and why people die have changed historically. Today, death occurs most often among older adults. More than 80 percent of all deaths in the United States now occur in a hospital or other institution; our exposure to death in the family has been minimized.

2   DEFINING DEATH AND LIFE/DEATH ISSUES: EVALUATE ISSUES IN DETERMINING DEATH AND DECISIONS REGARDING DEATH

Issues in Determining Death

Decisions Regarding Life, Death, and Health Care

- Twenty-five years ago, determining if someone was dead was simpler than it is today. Brain death is a neurological definition of death, which states that a person is brain dead when all electrical activity of the brain has ceased for a specified period of time. Medical experts debate whether this should mean the higher and lower brain functions or just the higher cortical functions. Most physicians use the cessation of brain function (both higher and lower) as a standard for determining death.

- Decisions regarding life, death, and health care can involve whether to have a living will, euthanasia, and hospice care. Living wills and advance directives are increasingly being used. Euthanasia is the act of painlessly ending the life of a person who is suffering from an incurable disease or severe disability. Distinctions are made between active and passive euthanasia. Hospice care emphasizes reducing pain and suffering rather than prolonging life.

3   A DEVELOPMENTAL PERSPECTIVE ON DEATH: DISCUSS DEATH AND ATTITUDES ABOUT IT AT DIFFERENT POINTS IN DEVELOPMENT

Causes of Death

Attitudes Toward Death at Different Points in the Life Span

- Although death is more likely to occur in late adulthood, death can come at any point in development. In children and younger adults, death is more likely to occur because of accidents; in older adults, death is more likely to occur because of chronic diseases.

- Infants do not have a concept of death. Preschool children also have little or no concept of death. Preschool children sometimes blame themselves for a person's death. In the middle and late childhood years, children develop a more realistic orientation toward death. Most psychologists stress that honesty is the best strategy for helping

667

children cope with death. Death may be glossed over in adolescence. Adolescents have more abstract, philosophical views of death than children do. There is no evidence that a special orientation toward death emerges in early adulthood. Middle adulthood is a time when adults show a heightened consciousness about death and death anxiety. Younger adults who are dying often feel cheated out of the opportunity to achieve what they wanted in life; older adults, who have had an opportunity to live a long life, feel the loss of what they have achieved. Older adults often show less death anxiety than middle-aged adults, but older adults experience and converse about death more. Attitudes about death may vary considerably among adults of any age.

Suicide

- Among the factors that place people at risk for suicide are serious physical illnesses, feelings of hopelessness, social isolation, failure in school and work, loss of loved ones, serious financial difficulties, and depression. Suicidal behavior is rare in childhood but escalates in adolescence. Both earlier and later experiences can influence suicide. U.S. suicide rates remain rather stable in early and middle adulthood, then increase in late adulthood.

4   FACING ONE'S OWN DEATH: EXPLAIN THE PSYCHOLOGICAL ASPECTS INVOLVED IN FACING ONE'S OWN DEATH AND THE CONTEXTS IN WHICH PEOPLE DIE

Kübler-Ross' Stages of Dying

- Kübler-Ross proposed five stages: denial and isolation, anger, bargaining, depression, and acceptance. Not all individuals go through the same sequence. Critics emphasize that many individuals don't go through the stages in the order she proposed.

Perceived Control and Denial

- Perceived control and denial may work together as an adaptive orientation for the dying individual. Denial can be adaptive or maladaptive, depending on the circumstance.

The Contexts in Which People Die

- Most deaths in the United States occur in hospitals; this has advantages, such as availability of medical care and medical technology, and disadvantages, such as the lack of the humane atmosphere of hospice care. Most individuals say they would rather die at home, but they worry that they will be a burden and they worry about the lack of medical care.

5   COPING WITH THE DEATH OF SOMEONE ELSE: IDENTIFY WAYS TO COPE WITH THE DEATH OF ANOTHER PERSON

Communicating with a Dying Person

- Most psychologists recommend an open communication system with the dying. Communication strategies include allowing the dying person to express guilt or anger, examine feelings, and reminisce.

Grieving

- Grief is the emotional numbness, disbelief, separation anxiety, despair, sadness, and loneliness that accompany the loss of someone we love. Grief is multidimensional and in some cases may last for years. Prolonged grief involves enduring despair and is still unresolved after an extended period of time. In the dual-process model of coping with bereavement, oscillation occurs between two dimensions: (1) loss-oriented stressors and (2) restoration-oriented stressors. Grief and coping vary with the type of death. There are cultural variations in grieving.

Making Sense of the World

- The grieving process may stimulate individuals to strive to make sense out of their world; each individual may contribute a piece to death's puzzle.

Losing a Life Partner

- Usually the most difficult loss is the death of a spouse. The bereaved are at risk for many health problems, although there are variations in the distress experienced by a surviving spouse. Social support benefits widows and widowers. Psychological and religious factors and coping skills are related to well-being after the loss of a spouse.

Forms of Mourning

- Forms of mourning vary across cultures. In the United States, approximately two-thirds of corpses are disposed of by burial, one-third by cremation. An important aspect of mourning in many cultures is the funeral. In recent years, the funeral industry has been the focus of controversy. In some cultures, a ceremonial meal is held after death.

KEY TERMS

brain death 647
euthanasia 648
passive euthanasia 648
active euthanasia 648

hospice 649
palliative care 649
denial and isolation 656
anger 656

bargaining 656
depression 656
acceptance 656
grief 659

prolonged grief 660
disenfranchised grief 660
dual-process model 660

KEY PEOPLE

Robert Kastenbaum 644

Holly Prigerson 660

Elisabeth Kübler-Ross 655

E-LEARNING TOOLS

Connect to **www.mhhe.com/santrockldt5e** to research the answers and complete these exercises. In addition, you'll find a number of other resources and valuable study tools for Chapter 17, "Death, Dying, and Grieving," on this Web site.

Taking It to the Net

1. Herman's mother has Parkinson disease. He wants her to make some difficult end-of-life decisions while she still can. He and his mother discuss the options of a health-care power of attorney, a living will, and/or a DNR. What are the different purposes of these documents, and what is the family's involvement in these decisions?

2. Ellen has taken care of her mother throughout her long, lingering illness that has just been diagnosed as terminal. Ellen does not think she alone can provide the type of care necessary to take care of her mother in her final weeks. Her neighbor suggested she contact the local hospice. What does a hospice offer to families in this situation, and how is it different from a nursing home?

3. Since the death of her husband four months ago, 75-year-old Anna has had difficulty sleeping and eating. She spends her days staring out the living room window. Her daughter fears that she is clinically depressed. Her son thinks that she just needs time to go through the grieving process. Is there a typical grieving process? What are the differences between the physical symptoms of grieving and the symptoms of clinical depression?

Self-Assessment

To evaluate your anxiety about death and to complete a living will, complete these self-assessments:

- *How Much Death Anxiety Do I Have?*
- *The Living Will*

Health and Well-Being, Parenting, and Education

Build your decision-making skills by trying your hand at the health and well-being, parenting, and education exercises.

Video Clips

The Online Learning Center includes the following videos for this chapter:

- *Fear of Dying at Age 72*
- *On Dying at Age 71*

GLOSSARY

A

A-not-B error Also called AB̄ error; this occurs when infants make the mistake of selecting the familiar hiding place (A) rather than the new hiding place (B̄) as they progress into substage 4 in Piaget's sensorimotor stage. 213

acceptance Kübler-Ross' fifth stage of dying, in which the dying person develops a sense of peace, an acceptance of her or his fate, and, in many cases, a desire to be left alone. 656

accommodation of the eye The eye's ability to focus and maintain an image on the retina. 190

accommodation Piagetian concept of adjusting schemes to fit new information and experiences. 209

active euthanasia Death induced deliberately, as by injecting a lethal dose of a drug. 648

active (niche-picking) genotype-environment correlations Correlations that exist when children seek out environments they find compatible and stimulating. 66

activity theory The theory that the more active and involved older adults are, the more likely they are to be satisfied with their lives. 575

adolescent egocentrism The heightened self-consciousness of adolescents, which is reflected in adolescents' beliefs that others are as interested in them as they are in themselves, and in adolescents' sense of personal uniqueness and invincibility. 222

adoption study A study in which investigators seek to discover whether, in behavior and psychological characteristics, adopted children are more like their adoptive parents, who provided a home environment, or more like their biological parents, who contributed their heredity. Another form of the adoption study is to compare adoptive and biological siblings. 65

aerobic exercise Sustained activity that stimulates heart and lung functioning. 161

affectionate love Also called companionate love, this type of love occurs when individuals desire to have another person near and have a deep, caring affection for the person. 377

affordances Opportunities for interaction offered by objects that fit within our capabilities to perform activities. 184

ageism Prejudice against other people because of their age, especially prejudice against older adults. 575

AIDS Acquired immune deficiency syndrome; caused by the human immunodeficiency virus (HIV), which destroys the body's immune system. 445

altruism An unselfish interest in helping another person. 485

Alzheimer disease A progressive, irreversible brain disorder characterized by a gradual deterioration of memory, reasoning, language, and, eventually, physical function. 142

amygdala A part of the brain's limbic system that is the seat of emotions such as anger. 116

androgens A class of sex hormones—an important one of which is testosterone—that primarily promotes the development of male genitals and secondary sex characteristics. 425

anger Kübler-Ross' second stage of dying, in which the dying person's denial gives way to anger, resentment, rage, and envy. 656

anger cry A cry similar to the basic cry but with more excess air forced through the vocal cords. 348

animism A facet of preoperational thought—the belief that inanimate objects have life like qualities and are capable of action. 217

anorexia nervosa An eating disorder that involves the relentless pursuit of thinness through starvation. 153

anxious attachment style An attachment style that describes adults who demand closeness, are less trusting, and are more emotional, jealous, and possessive. 375

Apgar Scale A widely used method to assess the health of newborns at one and five minutes after birth; it evaluates infants' heart rate, respiratory effort, muscle tone, body color, and reflex irritability. 87

aphasia A loss or impairment of language processing resulting from damage to Broca's area or Wernicke's area that involves. 333

Asperger syndrome A relatively mild autism spectrum disorder in which the child has relatively good verbal language, milder nonverbal language problems, and a restricted range of interests and relationships. 612

assimilation Piagetian concept in which children use existing schemes to incorporate new information. 208

attachment A close emotional bond between two people. 360

attention deficit hyperactivity disorder (ADHD) A disability in which children consistently show one or more of the following characteristics: (1) inattention, (2) hyperactivity, and (3) impulsivity. 610

attention Focusing of mental resources. 243

authoritarian parenting A restrictive, punitive style in which parents exhort the child to follow their directions and to respect their work and effort. Firm limits are placed on the child, and little verbal exchange is allowed. 525

authoritative parenting A style that encourages children to be independent but still places limits and controls on children's actions; extensive verbal give-and-take is allowed, and parents are warm and nurturant toward the child. 525

autism spectrum disorders (ASDs) Also called pervasive developmental disorders, these range from the severe disorder labeled autistic disorder to the milder disorder called Asperger syndrome. Children with these disorders are characterized by problems in social interaction, verbal and nonverbal communication, and repetitive behaviors. 612

autistic disorder A severe autism spectrum disorder that has its onset in the first three years of life and includes deficiencies in social relationships; abnormalities in communication; and restricted, repetitive, and stereotyped patterns of behavior. 612

automaticity The ability to process information with little or no effort. 241

autonomous morality The second stage of moral development in Piaget's theory, displayed by older children (about 10 years of age and older). The children become aware that rules and laws are created by people and that, in judging an action, they should consider the actor's intentions as well as the consequences. 469

average children Children who receive an average number of both positive and negative nominations from their peers. 559

avoidant attachment style An attachment style that describes adults who are hesitant about getting involved in romantic relationships and once in a relationship tend to distance themselves. 375

B

bargaining Kübler-Ross' third stage of dying, in which the dying person develops the hope that death can somehow be postponed. 656

basic cry A rhythmic pattern usually consisting of a cry, a briefer silence, a shorter inspiratory whistle that is higher pitched than the main cry, and then a brief rest before the next cry. 348

Bayley Scales of Infant Development Widely used scales, developed by Nancy Bayley, for assessing infant development. The current version, the Bayley-III, has five scales: cognitive, language, motor, socio-emotional, and adaptive; the first three are administered to the infant, the latter two to the caregiver. 294

behavior genetics The field that seeks to discover the influence of heredity and environment on individual differences in human traits and development. 65

Big Five factors of personality The view that personality is made up of openness to experience, conscientiousness, extraversion, agreeableness, and neuroticism. 409

biological processes Processes that produce changes in an individual's physical nature. 14

bisexual Being sexually attracted to people of both sexes. 442

bonding The formation of a close connection, especially a physical bond between parents and their newborn in the period shortly after birth. 91

brain death A neurological definition of death—an individual is brain dead when all electrical activity of the brain has ceased for a specified period of time. 647

brainstorming Technique in which individuals are encouraged to come up with creative ideas in a group, play off each other's ideas, and say practically whatever comes to mind relevant to a particular issue. 306

Brazelton Neonatal Behavioral Assessment Scale (NBAS) A test given within 24 to 36 hours after birth to assess newborns' neurological development, reflexes, and reactions to people. 88

Broca's area An area of the brain's left frontal lobe that is involved in producing words. 333

Bronfenbrenner's ecological theory Bronfenbrenner's environmental systems theory that focuses on five environmental systems: microsystem, mesosystem, exosystem, macrosystem, and chronosystem. 27

bulimia nervosa An eating disorder in which the individual consistently follows a binge-and-purge eating pattern. 154

C

care perspective The moral perspective of Carol Gilligan; views people in terms of their connectedness with others and emphasizes interpersonal communication, relationships with others, and concern for others. 474

case study An in-depth look at a single individual. 31

cataracts A thickening of the lens of the eye that causes vision to become cloudy, opaque, and distorted. 192

cellular clock theory Leonard Hayflick's theory that the maximum number of times human cells can divide is about 75 to 80. As we age, our cells have less capability to divide. 130

centration The focusing of attention on one characteristic to the exclusion of all others. 218

cephalocaudal pattern The sequence in which the fastest growth occurs at the top—the head—with physical growth in size, weight, and feature differentiation gradually working from top to bottom. 100

character education A direct moral education program in which students are taught moral literacy to prevent them from engaging in immoral behavior. 482

child abuse The term used most often by the public and many professionals to refer to both abuse and neglect. 530

child-centered kindergarten Education that involves the whole child by considering both the child's physical, cognitive, and socioemotional development and the child's needs, interests, and learning styles. 602

child-directed speech Language spoken in a higher pitch than normal with simple words and sentences. 334

child maltreatment The term increasingly used by developmentalists that refers to abuse and neglect, but also includes diverse conditions. 530

child neglect Failure to provide for the child's basic needs, including physical, educational, or emotional needs. 530

chromosomes Threadlike structures made up of deoxyribonucleic acid, or DNA. 57

chronic disorders Disorders characterized by slow onset and long duration. 140

climacteric The midlife transition in which fertility declines. 107

cliques Small groups that range from 2 to 12 individuals and average about 5 to 6 individuals. Clique members usually are of the same age and same sex and often engage in similar activities, such as belonging to a club or participating in a sport. 563

cognitive mechanics The "hardware" of the mind, reflecting the neurophysiological architecture of the brain as developed through evolution. Cognitive mechanics involve the speed and accuracy of the processes involving sensory input, attention, visual and motor memory, discrimination, comparison, and categorization. 298

cognitive moral education A moral education program based on the belief that students should learn to value things like democracy and justice as their moral reasoning develops; Kohlberg's theory has been the basis for many of the cognitive moral education programs. 482

cognitive pragmatics The culture-based "software" of the mind. Cognitive pragmatics include reading and writing skills, language comprehension, educational qualifications, professional skills, and also the type of knowledge about the self and life skills that help us to master or cope with life. 299

cognitive processes Processes that involve changes in an individual's thought, intelligence, and language. 14

cohort effects Effects due to a person's time of birth, era, or generation but not to actual age. 35

collectivism Emphasizing values that serve the group by subordinating personal goals to preserve group integrity, interdependence of members, and harmonious relationships. 579

commitment A personal investment in identity. 405

concrete operational stage The third Piagetian stage, which lasts from approximately 7 to 11 years of age; children can perform concrete operations, and logical reasoning replaces intuitive reasoning as long as the reasoning can be applied to specific or concrete examples. 219

conduct disorder Age-inappropriate actions and attitudes that violate family expectations, society's norms, and the personal or property rights of others. 487

connectedness Characteristic consisting of two dimensions: mutuality, sensitivity to and respect for others' views; and permeability, openness to others' views. 406

conscience The component of the superego that punishes the child for behaviors disapproved of by parents by making the child feel guilty and worthless. 476

conservation The awareness that altering the appearance of an object or a substance does not change its basic properties. 218

constructive play Combines sensorimotor/practice play with symbolic representation. 572

constructivist approach A learner-centered approach that emphasizes the individual's active, cognitive construction of knowledge and understanding with guidance from the teacher. 600

contemporary life-events approach Approach emphasizing that how a life event influences the individual's development depends not only on the event but also on mediating factors, the individual's adaptation to the life event, the life-stage context, and the sociohistorical context. 412

continuity-discontinuity issue Debate that focuses on the extent to which development involves gradual, cumulative change (continuity) or distinct stages (discontinuity). 20

controversial children Children who are frequently nominated both as someone's best friend and as being disliked. 559

conventional reasoning The second, or intermediate, level in Kohlberg's theory of moral development. At this level, individuals abide by certain standards but they are the standards of others such as parents or the laws of society. 471

convergent thinking Thinking that produces one correct answer; characteristic of the kind of thinking required on conventional intelligence tests. 305

coparenting The support that parents provide one another in jointly raising a child. 529

core knowledge approach States that infants are born with domain-specific innate knowledge systems. Among these domain-specific knowledge systems are those involving space, number sense, object permanence, and language. 214

corpus callosum A large bundle of axon fibers that connects the brain's left and right hemispheres. 116

correlational research A type of research that strives to describe the strength of the relationship between two or more events or characterists. 32

correlation coefficient A number based on a statistical analysis that is used to describe the degree of association between two variables. 32

creativity Ability to think in novel and unusual ways and devise unique, good solutions to problems. 304

crisis A period of identity development during which the individual is exploring alternatives. 405

critical thinking Involves grasping the deeper meaning of ideas, keeping an open mind, and deciding for oneself what to believe or do. 258

cross-cultural studies Comparison of one culture with one or more other cultures. These provide information about the degree to which development is similar, or universal, across cultures, and the degree to which it is culture-specific. 577

cross-sectional approach A research strategy in which individuals of different ages are compared at one time. 34

crowds Peer groups that are larger and less personal than cliques; members may or may not spend much time together. Many crowds can be defined by their members' activities—for example, jocks, populars, and druggies. 564

crystallized intelligence An individual's accumulated information and verbal skills, which continues to increase with age, according to Horn. 296

culture The behavior, patterns, beliefs, and all other products of a group of people that are passed on from generation to generation. 577

culture-fair tests Intelligence tests that are intended to not be culturally biased. 292

D

date or acquaintance rape Coercive sexual activity directed at someone with whom the victim is at least casually acquainted. 447

dementia A global term for any neurological disorder in which the primary symptom is deterioration of mental functioning. 142

denial and isolation Kübler-Ross' first stage of dying, in which the dying person denies that she or he is really going to die. 656

depression Kübler-Ross' fourth stage of dying, in which the dying person perceives the certainty of her or his death. A period of depression or preparatory grief may appear. 656

descriptive research A type of research that aims to observe and record behavior. 32

development The pattern of change that begins at conception and continues through the life span. Most development involves growth, although it also includes decline brought on by aging and dying. 6

developmental quotient (DQ) An overall developmental score that combines subscores on motor, language, adaptive, and personal-social domains in the Gesell assessment of infants. 294

developmentally appropriate practice Education that focuses on the typical developmental patterns of children (age appropriateness) and the uniqueness of each child (individual appropriateness). Such practice contrasts with developmentally inappropriate practice, which has an academic,

direct instruction emphasis focused largely on abstract paper-and-pencil activities, seatwork, and rote/drill practice activities. 603

dialect A variety of language that is distinguished by its vocabulary, grammar, or pronunciation. 330

difficult child A temperament style in which the child tends to react negatively and cry frequently, engages in irregular daily routines, and is slow to accept change. 355

direct instruction approach A teacher-centered approach characterized by teacher direction and control, high expectations for students' progress, and maximum time spent on academic tasks. 600

disenfranchised grief Grief involving a deceased person that is a socially ambiguous loss that can't be openly mourned or supported. 660

disengagement theory The theory that, to cope effectively, older adults should gradually withdraw from society; this theory is no longer supported. 575

dishabituation The recovery of a habituated response after a change in stimulation. 186

dismissing-avoidant attachment An insecure attachment style in which adolescents deemphasize the importance of attachment; is associated with consistent experiences of rejection of attachment needs by caregivers. 372

divergent thinking Thinking that produces many answers to the same question; characteristic of creativity. 305

divided attention Concentration on more than one activity at the same time. 243

DNA A complex molecule that contains genetic information and has a double helix shape. 57

Down syndrome A chromosomally transmitted form of mental retardation, caused by the presence of an extra copy of chromosome 21. 61

dual-process model A model of coping with bereavement that emphasizes oscillation between two main dimensions: (1) loss-oriented stressors and (2) restoration-oriented stressors. 660

dual-process model States that decision making is influenced by two systems—one analytical and one experiential, which compete with each other; in this model, it is the experiential system—monitoring and managing actual experiences—that benefits adolescent decision making. 263

dynamic systems theory A theory proposed by Esther Thelen that seeks to explain how infants assemble motor skills for perceiving and acting. 172

dyslexia A category of learning disabilities involving a severe impairment in the ability to read and spell. 610

E

easy child A temperament style in which the child is generally in a positive mood, quickly establishes regular routines, and adapts easily to new experiences. 355

eclectic theoretical orientation An orientation that does not follow any one theoretical approach, but rather selects from each theory whatever is considered the best in it. 28

ecological view The view proposed by the Gibsons that people directly perceive information in the world around them. Perception brings people in contact with the environment in order to interact with it and adapt to it. 184

egocentrism The inability to distinguish between one's own and someone else's perspective; an important feature of preoperational thought. 216

ego ideal The component of the superego that rewards the child by conveying a sense of pride and personal value when the child acts according to ideal standards approved by the parents. 476

elaboration Engagement in more extensive processing of information, benefiting memory. 252

embryonic period The period of prenatal development that occurs from two to eight weeks after conception. During the embryonic period, the rate of cell differentiation intensifies, support systems for the cells form, and organs appear. 69

emotion Feeling, or affect, that occurs when a person is engaged in an interaction that is important to him or her, especially to his or her well-being. 344

emotional abuse Acts or omissions by parents or other caregivers that have caused, or could cause, serious behavioral, cognitive, or emotional problems. 530

emotional intelligence The ability to perceive and express emotions accurately and adaptively, to understand emotion and emotional knowledge, to use feelings to facilitate thought, and to manage emotions in oneself and others. 285

empathy Reacting to another's feelings with an emotional response that is similar to the other's feelings. 477

encoding The process by which information gets into memory. 241

epigenetic view Perspective that emphasizes that development is the result of an ongoing, bidirectional interchange between heredity and environment. 67

episodic memory Retention of information about the where and when of life's happenings. 254

equilibration A mechanism that Piaget proposed to explain how children shift from one stage of thought to the next. 209

Erikson's theory Theory that proposes eight stages of human development. Each stage consists of a unique developmental task that confronts individuals with a crisis that must be resolved. 22

estradiol A hormone associated in girls with breast, uterine, and skeletal development. 104

estrogens A class of sex hormones—an important one of which is estradiol—that primarily influences the development of female sex characteristics and helps regulate the menstrual cycle. 424

ethnic gloss Use of an ethnic label such as African American or Latino in a superficial way that portrays an ethnic group as being more homogeneous than it really is. 38

ethnic identity An enduring aspect of the self that includes a sense of membership in an ethnic group, along with the attitudes and feelings related to that membership. 407

ethnicity A characteristic based on cultural heritage, nationality characteristics, race, religion, and language. 10

ethnocentrism The tendency to consider one's own group superior to other groups. 578

ethology Theory stressing that behavior is strongly influenced by biology, is tied to evolution, and is characterized by critical or sensitive periods. 26

euthanasia The act of painlessly ending the lives of persons who are suffering from incurable diseases or severe disabilities; sometimes called "mercy killing." 648

evocative genotype-environment correlations Correlations that exist when the child's characteristics elicit certain types of environments. 65

evolutionary psychology Emphasizes the importance of adaptation, reproduction, and "survival of the fittest" in shaping behavior. 55

executive attention Cognitive process involving action planning, allocating attention to goals, error detection and compensation, monitoring progress on tasks, and dealing with novel or difficult circumstances. 243

expanding Restating, in a linguistically sophisticated form, what a child has said. 334

experiment Carefully regulated procedure in which one or more factors believed to influence the behavior being studied are manipulated while all other factors are held constant. 33

expertise Having extensive, highly organized knowledge and understanding of a particular domain. 263

explicit memory Conscious memory of facts and experiences. 250

extrinsic motivation Doing something to obtain something else (the activity is a means to an end). 617

F

fast mapping A process that helps to explain how young children learn the connection between a word and its referent so quickly. 323

feminization of poverty The fact that far more women than men live in poverty. Women's low income, divorce, infrequent awarding of alimony, and poorly enforced child support by fathers—which usually leave women with less money than they and their children need to adequately function—are the likely causes. 588

fertilization A stage in reproduction whereby an egg and a sperm fuse to create a single cell, called a zygote. 58

fetal alcohol spectrum disorders (FASD) A cluster of abnormalities that appears in the offspring of mothers who drink alcohol heavily during pregnancy. 75

fetal period The prenatal period of development that begins two months after conception and lasts for seven months, on average. 70

fine motor skills Motor skills that involve finely tuned movements, such as any activity that requires finger dexterity. 181

fluid intelligence The ability to reason abstractly, which begins to decline in middle adulthood, according to Horn. 296

forgiveness An aspect of prosocial behavior that occurs when the injured person releases the injurer from possible behavioral retaliation. 486

formal operational stage The fourth and final Piagetian stage, which appears between the ages of 11 and 15; individuals move beyond concrete experiences and think in more abstract and logical ways. 221

fragile X syndrome A chromosomal disorder involving an abnormality in the X chromosome, which becomes constricted and often breaks. 61

free-radical theory A microbiological theory of aging that states that people age because when their cells metabolize energy, they generate waste that includes unstable oxygen molecules, known as free radicals, that damage DNA and other cellular structures. 131

fuzzy trace theory Theory stating that memory is best understood by considering two types of memory representations: (1) verbatim memory trace, and (2) gist. In this theory, older children's better memory is attributed to the fuzzy traces created by extracting the gist of information. 253

G

games Activities that are engaged in for pleasure and include rules. 572

gender The characteristics of people as females or males. 10

gender identity Involves a sense of one's own gender, including knowledge, understanding, and acceptance of being male or female. 424

gender-intensification hypothesis The view that psychological and behavioral differences between boys and girls become greater during early adolescence because of increased socialization pressures to conform to traditional gender roles. 436

gender role A set of expectations that prescribe how females or males should think, act, or feel. 424

gender schema theory The theory that gender-typing emerges as children gradually develop gender schemas of what is gender-appropriate and gender-inappropriate in their culture. 428

gender stereotypes General impressions and beliefs about females and males. 430

gender typing Acquisition of a traditional masculine or feminine role. 424

gene × enviroment (G × E) interaction The interaction of a specific measured variation in the DNA and a specific measured aspect of the enviroment. 67

generativity versus stagnation The seventh stage in Erikson's life-span theory that encompasses adults' desire to leave a legacy of themselves to the next generation. 413

genes Units of hereditary information composed of DNA. Genes direct cells to reproduce themselves and assemble proteins that direct body processes. 57

genotype All of a person's actual genetic material. 59

germinal period The period of prenatal development that takes place in the first two weeks after conception; it includes the creation of the zygote, continued cell division, and the attachment of the zygote to the wall of the uterus. 69

gifted Having high intelligence (an IQ of 130 or higher) or superior talent for something. 302

glaucoma Damage to the optic nerve because of the pressure created by a buildup of fluid in the eye. 192

gonadotropins Hormones that stimulate the testes or ovaries. 103

gonads The sex glands—the testes in males, the ovaries in females. 103

goodness of fit The match between a child's temperament and the environmental demands the child must cope with. 358

grasping reflex A reflex that occurs when something touches an infant's palms. The infant responds by grasping tightly. 174

gratitude A feeling of thankfulness and appreciation, especially in response to someone doing something kind or helpful. 486

grief The emotional numbness, disbelief, separation anxiety, despair, sadness, and loneliness that accompany the loss of someone we love. 659

gross motor skills Motor skills that involve large-muscle activities, such as walking. 174

growth hormone deficiency The absence or deficiency of growth hormone produced by the pituitary gland to stimulate body growth. 102

H

habituation Decreased responsiveness to a stimulus after repeated presentations of the stimulus. 186

helpless orientation An orientation in which one seems trapped by the experience of difficulty and attributes one's difficulty to a lack of ability. 618

heritability The portion of the variance in a population that is attributed to genes. 288

heteronomous morality (Kohlberg) The first stage of preconventional reasoning in Kohlberg's theory, in which moral thinking is tied to punishment. 470

heteronomous morality (Piaget) The first stage of moral development in Piaget's theory, occurring at 4 to 7 years of age. Justice and rules are conceived of as unchangeable properties of the world, removed from the control of people. 469

hidden curriculum The pervasive moral atmosphere that characterizes every school. 482

hormonal stress theory The theory that aging in the body's hormonal system can lower resistance to stress and increase the likelihood of disease. 132

hormones Powerful chemical substances secreted by the endocrine glands and carried through the body by the bloodstream. 103

hospice A program committed to making the end of life as free from pain, anxiety, and depression as possible. The goals of hospice contrast with those of a hospital, which are to cure disease and prolong life. 649

hypothalamus A structure in the brain that is involved with eating and sexual behavior. 103

hypotheses Specific assumptions and predictions that can be tested to determine their accuracy. 21

hypothetical-deductive reasoning Piaget's formal operational concept that adolescents have the cognitive ability to develop hypotheses about ways to solve problems and can systematically deduce which is the best path to follow in solving the problem. 222

I

identity Who a person is, representing a synthesis and integration of self-understanding. 386

identity achievement Marcia's term for the status of individuals who have undergone a crisis and have made a commitment. 405

identity diffusion Marcia's term for the status of individuals who have not yet experienced a crisis (explored meaningful alternatives) or made any commitments. 405

identity foreclosure Marcia's term for the status of individuals who have made a commitment but have not experienced a crisis. 405

identity moratorium Marcia's term for the status of individuals in the midst of a crisis, but whose commitments are either absent or vaguely defined. 405

identity versus identity confusion Erikson's fifth stage of development, which occurs during the adolescent years; adolescents are faced with finding out who they are, what they are all about, and where they are going in life. 403

imaginary audience That aspect of adolescent egocentrism that involves feeling one is the center of attention and sensing that one is on stage. 222

immanent justice Piaget's concept that if a rule is broken, punishment will be meted out immediately. 469

implicit memory Memory without conscious recollection—memory of skills and routine procedures that are performed automatically. 249

inclusion Education of a child with special education needs full-time in the regular classroom. 613

individualism Giving priority to personal goals rather than to group goals; emphasizing values that serve the self, such as feeling good, personal distinction and achievement, and independence. 579

individualism, instrumental purpose, and exchange The second Kohlberg stage of preconventional reasoning. At this stage, individuals pursue their own interests but also let others do the same. 470

individuality Characteristic consisting of two dimensions: self-assertion, the ability to have and communicate a point of view; and separateness, the use of communication patterns to express how one is different from others. 406

individualized education plan (IEP) A written statement that spells out a program tailored to a child with a disability. The plan should be (1) related to the child's learning capacity, (2) specially constructed to meet the child's individual needs and not merely a copy of what is offered to other children, and (3) designed to provide educational benefits. 613

indulgent parenting A style in which parents are very involved with their children but place few demands or controls on them. 525

infinite generativity The ability to produce an endless number of meaningful sentences using a finite set of words and rules. 316

information-processing theory Theory emphasizing that individuals manipulate information, monitor it, and strategize about it. Central to this theory are the processes of memory and thinking. 24

insecure avoidant babies Babies who show insecurity by avoiding the mother. 364

insecure disorganized babies Babies who show insecurity by being disorganized and disoriented. 364

insecure resistant babies Babies who might cling to the caregiver, then resist her by fighting against the closeness, perhaps by kicking or pushing away. 364

intelligence The ability to solve problems and to adapt to and learn from experiences. 280

intelligence quotient (IQ) An individual's mental age divided by chronological age multiplied by 100; devised in 1912 by William Stern. 281

intermodal perception The ability to integrate information about two or more sensory modalities, such as vision and hearing. 197

intimacy in friendship Self-disclosure and the sharing of private thoughts. 566

intrinsic motivation Doing something for its own sake; involves factors such as self-determination and opportunities to make choices. 617

intuitive thought substage The second substage of preoperational thought, occurring between approximately 4 and 7 years of age. Children begin to use primitive reasoning and want to know the answers to all sorts of questions. 217

J

joint attention Focus by individuals on the same object or event; requires an ability to track another's behavior, one individual's directing another's attention, and reciprocal interaction. 244

justice perspective A moral perspective that focuses on the rights of the individual; individuals independently make moral decisions. 474

juvenile delinquency Actions taken by an adolescent in breaking the law or engaging in illegal behavior. 487

K

kangaroo care A way of holding a preterm infant so that there is skin-to-skin contact. 90

Klinefelter syndrome A chromosomal disorder in which males have an extra X chromosome, making them XXY instead of XY. 61

kwashiorkor Severe malnutrition caused by a deficiency in protein in which the child's legs and abdomen swell with fluids. 149

L

labeling Identifying the names of objects. 334

laboratory A controlled setting in which many of the complex factors of the "real world" are removed. 30

language A form of communication, whether spoken, written, or signed, that is based on a system of symbols. 316

language acquisition device (LAD) Chomsky's term that describes a biological endowment that enables the child to detect certain features and rules of language, including phonology, syntax, and semantics. 333

lateralization Specialization of function in one hemisphere or the other of the cerebral cortex. 111

learning disabilities Disabilities in which children experience difficulty in learning that involves understanding or using spoken or written language; the difficulty can appear in listening, thinking, reading, writing, and spelling. A learning disability also may involve difficulty in doing mathematics. To be classified as a learning disability, the learning problem is not primarily the result of visual, hearing, or motor disabilities; mental retardation; emotional disorders; or environmental, cultural, or economic disadvantage. 609

least restrictive environment (LRE) A setting that is as similar as possible to the one in which children who do not have a disability are educated. 613

leisure The pleasant times when individuals are free to pursue activities and interests of their own choosing. 572

life-span perspective The perspective that development is lifelong, multidimensional, multidirectional, plastic, multidisciplinary, and contextual; involves growth, maintenance, and regulation of loss; and is constructed through biological, sociocultural, and individual factors working together. 7

life span The upper boundary of life, the maximum number of years an individual can live. The maximum life span of humans is about 120 years of age. 127

longitudinal approach A research strategy in which the same individuals are studied over a period of time, usually several years or more. 34

long-term memory A relatively permanent and unlimited type of memory. 250

low birth weight infants Infants that weigh less than 5½ pounds at birth. 88

M

macular degeneration A vision problem in the elderly that involves deterioration of the macula of the retina. 192

marasmus Severe malnutrition due to insufficient caloric intake. 149

mastery orientation An orientation in which one is task-oriented—instead of focusing on one's ability, is concerned with learning strategies and the process of achievement rather than the outcome. 618

meaning-making coping Drawing on beliefs, values, and goals to change the meaning of a stressful situation, especially in times of chronic stress as when a loved one dies. 497

meiosis A specialized form of cell division that occurs to form eggs and sperm (or gametes). 58

memory Retention of information over time. 247

menarche A girl's first menstrual period. 102

menopause The complete cessation of a woman's menstruation, which usually occurs in the late forties or early fifties. 457

menopause The time in middle age, usually in the late forties or early fifties, when a woman's menstrual periods cease. 107

mental age (MA) An individual's level of mental development relative to others. 281

mental retardation A condition of limited mental ability in which the individual (1) has a low IQ, usually below 70 on a traditional intelligence test; (2) has difficulty adapting to everyday life; and (3) has an onset of these characteristics by age 18. 301

metacognition "Knowing about knowing." 241

metalinguistic awareness Knowledge about language. 326

metamemory Knowledge about memory. 268

metaphor An implied comparison between two unlike things. 330

mindfulness Being alert, mentally present, and cognitively flexible while going through life's everyday activities and tasks. 258

mindset The cognitive view individuals develop for themselves that either is fixed or involves growth. 619

mitochondrial theory The theory that aging is caused by the decay of mitochondria, tiny cellular bodies that supply energy for function, growth, and repair. 131

mitosis Cellular reproduction in which the cell's nucleus duplicates itself; two new cells are formed, each containing the same DNA as the original cell, arranged in the same 23 pairs of chromosomes. 58

Montessori approach An educational philosophy in which children are given considerable freedom and spontaneity in choosing activities and are allowed to move from one activity to another as they desire. 602

moral development Changes in thoughts, feelings, and behaviors regarding standards of right and wrong. 468

moral exemplars People who have lived exemplary lives—they have a moral personality, identity, character, and set of virtues that reflect moral excellence and commitment. 479

moral identity The aspect of personality that is present when individuals have moral notions and commitments that are central to their lives. 478

Moro reflex A startle response that occurs in reaction to a sudden, intense noise or movement. When startled, the newborn arches its back, throws its head back, and flings out its arms and legs. Then the newborn rapidly closes its arms and legs to the center of the body. 173

morphology Units of meaning involved in word formation. 317

multiple developmental trajectories Concept that adults follow one trajectory and children another one; how these trajectories mesh is important for understanding the timing of entry into various family tasks. 510

mutual interpersonal expectations, relationships, and interpersonal conformity Kohlberg's third stage of moral development. At this stage, individuals value trust, caring, and loyalty to others as a basis of moral judgments. 471

myelination The process of encasing axons with a myelin sheath, which helps increase the speed and efficiency of information processing. 111

N

narcissism A self-centered and self-concerned approach toward others. 394

natural childbirth Method attempting to reduce the mother's pain by decreasing her fear through education about childbirth and relaxation techniques during delivery. 85

naturalistic observation Observing behavior in real-world settings. 31

nature-nurture issue Debate about whether development is primarily influenced by nature or nurture. Nature refers to an organism's biological inheritance, nurture to its environmental experiences. The "nature proponents" claim biological inheritance is the more important influence on development; the "nurture proponents" claim that environmental experiences are more important. 19

neglected children Children who are infrequently nominated as a best friend but are not disliked by their peers. 559

neglectful parenting A style in which the parent is very uninvolved in the child's life. 525

Neonatal Intensive Care Unit Network Neurobehavioral Scale (NNNS) An "offspring" of the NBAS, a test that provides a more comprehensive analysis of the newborn's behavior, neurological and stress responses, and regulatory capacities. 88

neo-Piagetians Developmentalists who have elaborated on Piaget's theory, emphasizing attention to children's strategies; information-processing speed; the task involved; and division of the problem into more precise, smaller steps. 225

neurogenesis The generation of new neurons. 118

neurons Nerve cells that handle information processing at the cellular level. 70

nonnormative life events Unusual occurrences that have a major impact on an individual's life. 8

nonshared environmental experiences The child's own unique experiences, both within the family and outside the family, that are not shared by another sibling; thus, experiences occurring within the family can be part of the "nonshared environment." 66

normal distribution A symmetrical, bell-shaped curve with a majority of the cases falling in the middle of the possible range of scores and few scores appearing toward the extremes of the range. 281

normative age-graded influences Influences that are similar for individuals in a particular age group. 8

normative history-graded influences Influences that are common to people of a particular generation because of historical circumstances. 8

O

object permanence The Piagetian term for one of an infant's most important accomplishments: understanding that objects continue to exist even when they cannot directly be seen, heard, or touched. 212

operations Reversible mental actions that allow children to do mentally what before they had done only physically. 216

organization Piagetian concept of grouping isolated behaviors and thoughts into a higher-order, more smoothly functioning cognitive system. 209

organogenesis Process of organ formation that takes place during the first two months of prenatal development. 70

osteoporosis A disorder that involves an extensive loss of bone tissue and is the main reason many older adults walk with a marked stoop. Women are especially vulnerable to osteoporosis. 141

P

pain cry A sudden, initial loud cry followed by breath holding, without preliminary moaning. 348

palliative care Emphasized in hospice care; involves reducing pain and suffering and helping individuals die with dignity. 649

Parkinson disease A chronic, progressive disease characterized by muscle tremors, slowing of movement, and partial facial paralysis. 145

passive euthanasia The withholding of available treatments, such as life-sustaining devices, allowing the person to die. 648

passive genotype-environment correlations Correlations that exist when the biological parents, who are genetically related to the child, provide a rearing environment for the child. 65

peers Individuals of about the same age or maturity level. 556

perception The interpretation of sensation. 184

performance orientation An orientation in which one focuses on winning, rather than on achievement outcome; happiness is thought to result from winning. 619

perimenopause The transitional period from normal menstrual periods to no menstrual periods at all, which often takes up to 10 years. 457

personal fable The part of adolescent egocentrism that involves an adolescent's sense of personal uniqueness and invincibility. 222

personality The enduring personal characteristics of individuals. 386

personality type theory Holland's view that it is important to match an individual's personality with a specific career. 626

perspective taking The ability to assume another person's perspective and understand his or her thoughts and feelings. 389

phenotype Observable and measurable characteristics such as height, hair color, and intelligence. 59

phenylketonuria (PKU) A genetic disorder in which an individual cannot properly metabolize phenylalanine, an amino acid; PKU is now easily detected—but, if left untreated, results in mental retardation and hyperactivity. 62

phonics approach An approach that emphasizes that reading instruction should teach basic rules for translating written symbols into sounds. 326

phonology The sound system of a language—includes the sounds used and how they may be combined. 316

physical abuse Abuse characterized by the infliction of physical injury as a result of punching, beating, kicking, biting, burning, shaking, or otherwise harming a child. 530

Piaget's theory Theory stating that children actively construct their understanding of the world and go through four stages of cognitive development. 23

pituitary gland An important endocrine gland that controls growth and regulates other glands. 103

play A pleasurable activity that is engaged in for its own sake. 570

play therapy Therapy that lets children work off frustrations while therapists analyze their conflicts and coping methods. 570

popular children Children who are frequently nominated as a best friend and are rarely disliked by their peers. 559

possible selves What adolescents hope to become as well as what they dread they will become. 390

postconventional reasoning The highest level in Kohlberg's theory of moral development. At this level, the individual recognizes alternative moral courses, explores the options, and then decides on a personal moral code. 471

postformal thought Thinking that is reflective, relativistic, and contextual; provisional; realistic; and open to emotions and subjective. 233

practice play Play that involves repetition of behavior when new skills are being learned or when mastery and coordination of skills are required for games or sports. 571

pragmatics The appropriate use of language in different contexts. 317

precocious puberty The term used to describe the very early onset and rapid progression of puberty. 105

preconventional reasoning The lowest level in Kohlberg's theory of moral development. The individual's moral reasoning is controlled primarily by external rewards and punishment. 470

prefrontal cortex The highest level of the frontal lobes that is involved in reasoning, decision making, and self-control. 116

preoccupied-ambivalent attachment An insecure attachment style in which adolescents are hypertuned to attachment experiences. This is thought to occur mainly because parents are inconsistently available to the adolescent. 372

preoperational stage The second Piagetian developmental stage, which lasts from about 2 to 7 years of age; children begin to represent the world with words, images, and drawings. 216

prepared childbirth Developed by French obstetrician Ferdinand Lamaze, a childbirth strategy similar to natural childbirth but one that includes a special breathing technique to control pushing in the final stages of labor and details about anatomy and physiology. 85

pretense/symbolic play Play that occurs when a child transforms the physical environment into a symbol. 571

preterm infants Infants born three weeks or more before the pregnancy has reached its full term. 88

primary emotions Emotions that are present in humans and other animals, emerge early in life, and are culturally universal; examples are joy, anger, sadness, fear, and disgust. 347

Project Head Start Compensatory education designed to provide children from low-income families the opportunity to acquire the skills and experiences important for school success. 603

prolonged grief Grief that involves enduring despair and is still unresolved over an extended period of time. 660

prospective memory Remembering to do something in the future. 256

proximodistal pattern The sequence in which growth starts at the center of the body and moves toward the extremities. 101

psychoanalytic theories Theories that describe development as primarily unconscious and heavily colored by emotion. Behavior is merely a surface characteristic, and the symbolic workings of the mind have to be analyzed to understand behavior. Early experiences with parents are emphasized. 21

psychoanalytic theory of gender Stems from Freud's view that preschool children develop a sexual attraction to the opposite-sex parent, then, at 5 or 6 years of age, renounce the attraction because of anxious feelings, subsequently identifying with the same-sex parent and unconsciously adopting the same-sex parent's characteristics. 426

psychosocial moratorium Erikson's term for the gap between childhood security and adult autonomy that adolescents experience as part of their identity exploration. 403

puberty A period of rapid physical maturation involving hormonal and bodily changes during early adolescence. 102

R

rape Forcible sexual intercourse, oral sex, or anal sex with a person who does not give consent. Legal definitions of rape differ from state to state. 447

rapport talk The language of conversation; a way to establish connections and negotiate relationships; preferred by women. 437

recasting Rephrasing a statement that a child has said, perhaps turning it into a question, or restating a child's immature utterance in the form of a fully grammatical sentence. 334

reciprocal socialization Socialization that is bidirectional in that children socialize parents just as parents socialize children. 508

reflexes Built-in reactions to stimuli that govern the newborn's movements, which are automatic and beyond the newborn's control. 173

reflexive smile A smile that does not occur in response to external stimuli. It happens during the month after birth, usually during sleep. 348

rejected children Children who are infrequently nominated as a best friend and are actively disliked by their peers. 559

report talk Language designed to give information, including public speaking; preferred by men. 437

romantic love Also called passionate love, or eros, this type of love has strong components of sexuality and infatuation, and it often predominates in the early part of a love relationship. 376

romantic script Sex is synonymous with love; if we develop a relationship with someone and fall in love, it is acceptable to have sex with the person whether we are married or not. 441

rooting reflex A newborn's built-in reaction that occurs when the infant's cheek is stroked or the side of the mouth is touched. In response, the infant turns its head toward the side that was touched, in an apparent effort to find something to suck. 173

S

satire The use of irony, derision, or wit to expose folly or wickedness. 331

scaffolding In cognitive development, a term Vygotsky used to describe the changing level of support over the course of a teaching session, with the more-skilled person adjusting guidance to fit the child's current performance level. 227

schemas Mental frameworks that organize concepts and information. 248

schema theory Theory stating that people mold memories to fit information that already exists in their minds. 248

schemes In Piaget's theory, actions or mental representations that organize knowledge. 208

secure attachment style An attachment style that describes adults who have positive views of relationships, find it easy to get close to others, and are not overly concerned or stressed out about their romantic relationships. 375

securely attached babies Babies who use the caregiver as a secure base from which to explore the environment. 364

selective attention Focusing on a specific aspect of experience that is relevant while ignoring others that are irrelevant. 243

selective optimization with compensation theory The theory that successful aging is related to three main factors: selection, optimization, and compensation. 398

self All of the characteristics of a person. 386

self-concept Domain-specific evaluations of the self. 393

self-conscious emotions Emotions that require consciousness and a sense of "me"; they include empathy, jealousy, embarrassment, pride, shame, and guilt, most of which first appear at some point in the second half of the first year through the second year. 347

self-efficacy The belief that one can master a situation and produce favorable outcomes. 620

self-esteem The global evaluative dimension of the self. Self-esteem is also referred to as self-worth, or self-image. 393

self-regulation The ability to control one's behavior without having to rely on others for help. 397

self-understanding The individual's cognitive representation of the self, the substance of self-conceptions. 386

semantic memory A person's knowledge about the world, including fields of expertise, general academic knowledge, and "everyday knowledge" about meaning of words, famous individuals, important places, and common things. 254

semantics The meanings of words and sentences. 317

sensation Reaction that occurs when information interacts with sensory receptors—the eyes, ears, tongue, nostrils, and skin. 184

sensorimotor play Behavior by infants to derive pleasure from exercising their sensorimotor schemes. 571

sensorimotor stage The first of Piaget's stages, which lasts from birth to about 2 years of age; infants construct an understanding of the world by coordinating sensory experiences (such as seeing and hearing) with physical, motoric actions. 209

separation protest Reaction that occurs when infants experience a fear of being separated from a caregiver, which results in crying when the caregiver leaves. 349

seriation The concrete operation that involves ordering stimuli along a quantitative dimension (such as length). 220

service learning A form of education that promotes social responsibility and service to the community. 483

sexual abuse Fondling the child's genitals, intercourse, incest, rape, sodomy, exhibitionism, and commercial exploitation through prostitution or the production of pornographic materials. 530

sexual harassment Sexual persecution that can take many forms—from sexist remarks and physical contact (patting, brushing against their bodies) to blatant propositions and sexual assaults. 449

sexually transmitted infections (STIs) Diseases that are contracted primarily through sexual contact, including oral-genital contact, anal-genital contact, and vaginal intercourse. 443

sexual scripts Stereotyped patterns of expectancies for how people should behave sexually. 441

shape constancy Recognition that an object remains the same even though its orientation to us changes. 189

shared environmental experiences Siblings' common experiences, such as their parents' personalities or intellectual orientation, the family's socioeconomic status, and the neighborhood in which they live. 66

short-term memory Retention of information for up to 15 to 30 seconds, without rehearsal of the information. Using rehearsal, individuals can keep the information in short-term memory longer. 251

sickle-cell anemia A genetic disorder that affects the red blood cells and occurs most often in African Americans. 62

size constancy Recognition that an object remains the same even though the retinal image of the object changes as you move toward or away from the object. 188

slow-to-warm-up child A temperament style in which the child has a low activity level, is somewhat negative, and displays a low intensity of mood. 355

small for date infants Infants whose birth weights are below normal when the length of pregnancy is considered; also called small for gestational age infants. Small for date infants may be preterm or full-term. 88

social cognitive theory of gender The idea that children's gender development occurs through observation and imitation of gender behavior, as well as through the rewards and punishment children experience for behaviors believed to be appropriate or inappropriate for their gender. 426

social cognitive theory of morality The theory that distinguishes between moral competence—the ability to produce moral behaviors—and moral performance—performing those behaviors in specific situations. 476

social cognitive theory Theoretical view which holds that behavior, environment, and cognition are the key factors in development. 25

social constructivist approach An emphasis on the social contexts of learning and construction of knowledge through social interaction. Vygotsky's theory reflects this approach. 230

social contract or utility and individual rights The fifth Kohlberg stage of moral development. At this stage, individuals reason that values, rights, and principles undergird or transcend the law. 471

social conventional reasoning Focuses on conventional rules established by social consensus and convention, as opposed to moral reasoning, which stresses ethical issues. 475

social play Play that involves interaction with peers. 572

social policy A government's course of action designed to promote the welfare of its citizens. 11

social referencing "Reading" emotional cues in others to help determine how to act in a specific situation. 362

social role theory Eagly's theory that psychological gender differences are caused by the contrasting social roles of women and men. 426

social smile A smile in response to an external stimulus, which, early in development, typically is a face. 348

social systems morality The fourth stage in Kohlberg's theory of moral development. Moral judgments are based on understanding the social order, law, justice, and duty. 471

socioeconomic status (SES) Refers to a person's position in society based on occupational, educational, and economic characteristics. 585

socioemotional processes Processes that involve changes in an individual's relationships with other people, emotions, and personality. 14

socioemotional selectivity theory The theory that older adults become more selective about their social networks. Because they place high value on emotional satisfaction, older adults often spend more time with familiar individuals with whom they have had rewarding relationships. 354

source memory The ability to remember where something is learned. 255

spirituality A sense of connectedness to a sacred other (God, nature, a higher power). 492

stability-change issue Debate as to whether and to what degree we become older renditions of our early experience (stability) or whether we develop into someone different from who we were at an earlier point in development (change). 19

standardized test A test with uniform procedures for administration and scoring. Many standardized tests allow a person's performance to be compared with the performance of other individuals. 31

stereotype threat The anxiety that one's behavior might confirm a negative stereotype about one's group. 293

stranger anxiety An infant's fear of and wariness toward strangers; it tends to appear in the second half of the first year of life. 349

Strange Situation Ainsworth's observational measure of infant attachment to a caregiver that requires the infant to move through a series of introductions, separations, and reunions with the caregiver and an adult stranger in a prescribed order. 364

strategy construction Creation of new procedures for processing information. 241

sucking reflex A newborn's built-in reaction of automatically sucking an object placed in its mouth. The sucking reflex enables the infant to get nourishment before it has associated a nipple with food. 173

sudden infant death syndrome (SIDS) Condition that occurs when an infant stops breathing, usually during the night, and suddenly dies without an apparent cause. 123

sustained attention The ability to maintain attention to a selected stimulus for a prolonged period of time. 243

symbolic function substage The first substage of preoperational thought, occurring roughly between the ages of 2 and 4. In this substage, the young child gains the ability to represent mentally an object that is not present. 216

syntax The ways words are combined to form acceptable phrases and sentences. 317

T

telegraphic speech The use of short, precise words without grammatical markers such as articles, auxiliary verbs, and other connectives. 321

temperament An individual's behavioral style and characteristic way of responding. 355

teratogen Any agent that can potentially cause a birth defect or negatively alter cognitive and behavioral outcomes. 73

testosterone A hormone associated in boys with the development of genitals, an increase in height, and a change in voice. 104

theory An interrelated, coherent set of ideas that helps to explain phenomena and make predictions. 21

theory of mind Awarness of one's own mental processes and the mental processes of others. 269

thinking Manipulating and transforming information in memory, in order to reason, reflect, evaluate ideas and solve problems, and make decisions. 256

top-dog phenomenon The circumstance of moving from the top position in elementary school to the youngest, smallest, and least powerful position in middle or junior high school. 606

traditional religious script Sex is accepted only within marriage; extramarital sex is taboo, especially for women, and sex means reproduction and sometimes affection. 441

trait theories Theories emphasizing that personality consists of broad dispositions, called traits, which tend to produce characteristic responses. 409

transitivity The ability to logically combine relations to understand certain conclusions. Piaget argued that an understanding of transitivity is characteristic of concrete operational thought. 221

triangular theory of love Sternberg's theory that love includes three types—passion, intimacy, and commitment. 377

triarchic theory of intelligence Sternberg's theory that intelligence consists of analytical intelligence, creative intelligence, and practical intelligence. 283

Turner syndrome A chromosomal disorder in females in which either an X chromosome is missing, making the person XO instead of XX, or part of one X chromosome is deleted. 62

twin study A study in which the behavioral similarity of identical twins is compared with the behavioral similarity of fraternal twins. 65

U

universal ethical principles The sixth and highest stage in Kohlberg's theory of moral development. Individuals develop a moral standard based on universal human rights. 471

unresolved-disorganized attachment An insecure attachment style in which the adolescent has an unusually high level of fear and is often disoriented. These may result from such traumatic experiences as a parent's death or abuse by parents. 372

V

values Beliefs and attitudes about the way things should be. 492

values clarification A moral education program in which students are helped to clarify what their lives are for and what is worth working for. Students are encouraged to define their own values and understand others' values. 482

visual preference method A method developed by Fantz to determine whether infants can distinguish one stimulus from another by measuring the length of time they attend to different stimuli. 185

Vygotsky's theory Sociocultural cognitive theory that emphasizes how culture and social interaction guide cognitive development. 24

W

Wernicke's area An area of the brain's left hemisphere that is involved in language comprehension. 333

whole-language approach An approach that stresses that reading instruction should parallel children's natural language learning. Reading materials should be whole and meaningful. 326

wisdom Expert knowledge about the practical aspects of life that permits excellent judgment about important matters. 299

working memory A mental "workbench" where individuals manipulate and assemble information when making decisions, solving problems, and comprehending written and spoken language. 251

X

XYY syndrome A chromosomal disorder in which males have an extra Y chromosome. 62

Z

zone of proximal development (ZPD) Vygotsky's term for tasks too difficult for children to master alone but that can be mastered with guidance and assistance from adults or more-skilled children. 226

zygote A single cell formed through fertilization. 58

REFERENCES

A

Aalsma, M., Lapsley, D. K., & Flannery, D. (2006). Narcissism, personal fables, and adolescent adjustment. *Psychology in the Schools, 43,* 481–491.

AARP. (2004). *The divorce experience: A study of divorce at midlife and beyond.* Washington, DC: Author.

Abbott, A. (2003). Restless nights, listless days. *Nature, 4235,* 896–898.

Abbott, R. D., White, I. R., Ross, G. W., Masaki, K. H., Curb, J. D., & Petrovitch, H. (2004). Walking and dementia in physically capable elderly men. *Journal of the American Medical Association, 292,* 1447–1453.

ABC News. (2005, December 12). Larry Page and Sergey Brim. Retrieved June 24, 2006, from www.Montessori.org/enews/barbara_Walters.html

Abdo, C. H., Afif-Abdo, J., Otani, F., & Machado, A. C. (2008). Sexual satisfaction among patients with erectile dysfunction treated with counseling, sildenafil, or both. *Journal of Sexual Medicine, 5,* 1720–1726.

Abellan van Kan, G., Rolland, Y., Nourhashemi, F., Coley, N., Andrieu, S., & Vellas, B. (2009). Cardiovascular disease risk factors and progression of Alzheimer's disease. *Dementia and Geriatric Cognitive Disorders, 27,* 240–246.

Abruscato, J. A., & DeRosa, D. A. (2010). *Teaching children science: A discovery approach* (7th ed.). Boston: Allyn & Bacon.

Accornero, V. H., Amado, A. J., Morrow, C. E., Xue, L., Anthony, J. C., & Bandstra, E. S. (2007). Impact of prenatal cocaine exposure on attention and response inhibition as assessed by continuous performance tests. *Journal of Developmental and Behavioral Pediatrics, 28,* 195–205.

Achenbach, T. M. (1997). What is normal? What is abnormal? Developmental perspectives on behavioral and emotional problems. In S. S. Luthar, J. A. Burack, D. Cicchetti, & J. R. Weisz (Eds.), *Developmental psychopathology: Perspectives on adjustment, risk, and disorder.* New York: Cambridge University Press.

Achieve, Inc. (2005). *An action agenda for improving America's high schools.* Washington, DC: Author.

Adamolekun, K. (2001). Survivors' motives for extravagant funerals among the Yorubas of Western Nigeria. *Death Studies, 25,* 609–619.

Adams, J. C. (2009). lmmunocytochemical traits of type IV fibrocytes and their possible relation to cochlear function and pathology. *Journal of the Association for Research in Otolaryngology, 10,* 369–382.

Adams-Curtis, L. E., & Forbes, G. B. (2004). College women's experiences of sexual coercion: A review of cultural, perpetrator, victim, and situational variables. *Drama, Violence, and Abuse, 5,* 91–122.

Adamson, L., & Frick, J. (2003). The still face: A history of a shared experimental paradigm. *Infancy, 4,* 451–473.

Administration for Children and Families. (2008). *Statistical fact sheet fiscal year 2008.* Washington, DC: Author.

Adolph, K. E. (1997). Learning in the development of infant locomotion. *Monographs of the Society for Research in Child Development, 62* (3, Serial No. 251).

Adolph, K. E., & Berger, S. E. (2005). Physical and motor development. In M. H. Bornstein & M. E. Lamb (Eds.), *Developmental psychology* (5th ed.). Mahwah, NJ: Erlbaum.

Adolph, K. E., & Joh, A. S. (2009). Multiple learning mechanisms in the development of action. In A. Needham & A. Woodward (Eds.), *Learning and the infant mind.* New York: Oxford University Press.

Adolph, K. E., Joh, A. S., Franchak, J. M., Ishak, S., & Gill, S. V. (2008). Flexibility in the development of action. In J. Bargh, P. Gollwitzer, & E. Morsella (Eds.), *Oxford handbook of human action.* Oxford, UK: Oxford University Press.

Adolph, K. E., Karasik, L. B., & Tamis-LeMonda, C. S. (2010, in press). Moving between cultures: Cross-cultural research on motor development. In M. Bornstein & L. R. Cote (Ed.), *Handbook of cross-cultural developmental science. Vol. 1: Domains of development across cultures.* Clifton, NJ: Psychology Press.

Afanas'ev, I. (2009). Superoxide and nitric oxide in senescence and aging. *Frontiers in Bioscience, 14,* 3899–3912.

Agency for Healthcare Research and Quality. (2007). *Evidence report/technology assessment 153: Breastfeeding and maternal and health outcomes in developed countries.* Rockville, MD: U.S. Department of Health and Human Services.

Aggarwal, N. T., Wilson, R. S., Beck, T. L., Bienias, J. L., Berry-Kravis, E., & Bennett, D. A. (2005). The apolipoprotein E epsilon4 allele and incident Alzheimer's disease in persons with mild cognitive impairment. *Neurocase, 11,* 3–7.

Agras, W. S., Hammer, L. D., McNicholas, P., & Kraemer, H. C. (2004). Risk factors for childhood overweight: A prospective study from birth to 9.5 years. *Journal of Pediatrics, 145,* 20–25.

Ahn, N. (1994). Teenage childbearing and high school completion: Accounting for individual heterogeneity. *Family Planning Perspectives, 26,* 17–21.

Ahrons, C. (2004). *We're still family.* New York: HarperCollins.

Ahrons, C. (2007). Family ties after divorce: Long-term implications for children. *Family Process, 46,* 53–65.

Ahrons, C. R. (2007). Family ties after divorce: Long-term implications for children. *Family Process, 46,* 53–65.

Aiken, L. (2000). *Dying, death, and bereavement* (4th ed.). Mahwah, NJ: Erlbaum.

Aimone, J. B., Wiles, J., & Gage, F. H. (2009). Computational influence of adult neurogenesis on memory encoding. *Neuron, 61,* 187–202.

Ainsworth, M. D. S. (1979). Infant-mother attachment. *American Psychologist, 34,* 932–937.

Akey, J. (2009). Inherited variation in gene expression. *Annual Review of Genomics and Human Genetics* (Vol. 10). Palo Alto, CA: Annual Reviews.

Akiyama, H., & Antonucci, T. C. (1999, November). *Mother-daughter dynamics over the life course.* Paper presented at the meeting of the Gerontological Association of America, San Francisco.

Aktar, N., & Herold, K. (2008). Pragmatic development. In M. M. Haith & J. B. Benson (Eds.), *Encyclopedia of infant and early childhood development.* Oxford, UK: Elsevier.

Albert, S. M. (2007). Cultural and ethnic influences on aging. In J. E. Birren (Ed.), *Encyclopedia of gerontology* (2nd ed.). San Diego: Academic Press.

Alberts, A., Elking, D., & Ginsberg, S. (2007). The personal fable and risk-taking in early adolescence. *Journal of Youth and Adolescence, 36,* 71–76.

Aldwin, C. M., Spiro, A., & Park, C. L. (2006). Health, behavior, and optimal aging. In J. E. Birren & K. W. Schaie (Eds.), *Handbook of*

the psychology of aging (6th ed.). San Diego: Academic Press.

Alessi, C. A. (2007). Sleep. In J. E. Birren (Ed.), *Encyclopedia of gerontology* (2nd ed.). San Diego: Academic Press.

Allan, M. F., Eisen, E. J., & Pomp, D. (2005). The M16 mouse: An outbred animal model of early onset polygenic obesity and diabesity. *Obesity Research, 12*, 1397–1407.

Allemand, M., Zimprich, D., & Hendriks, A. A. J. (2008). Age differences in five personality domains across the life span. *Developmental Psychology, 44*, 758–770.

Allen, E. G., Freeman, S. B., Druschel, C., Hobbs, C. A., O'Leary, L. A., Romitti, P. A., Royle, M. H., Torfs, C. P., & Sherman, S. L. (2009, in press). Maternal age and risk for trisomy 21 assessed by the origin of chromosome nondisjunction: A report from the Atlanta and National Down Syndrome Projects. *Human Genetics, 125*, 41–52.

Allen, J. P. (2007, March). *A transformational perspective on the attachment system in adolescence.* Paper presented at the meeting of the Society for Research in Child Development, Boston.

Allen, J. P. (2008). The attachment system in adolescence. In J. Cassidy & P. R. Shaver (Eds.), *Handbook of attachment* (2nd ed.). New York: Guilford.

Allen, J. P., McElhaney, K. B., Kuperminc, G. P., & Jodl, K. M. (2004). Stability and change in attachment security across adolescence. *Child Development, 75*, 1792–1805.

Allen, J. P., Mc Elhaney, K. B., Land, D. J., Kuperminc, G. P., Moore, C. W., O'Beirne-Kelly, H., & Kilmer, S. L. (2003). A secure base in adolescence: Markers of attachment security in the mother-adolescent relationship. *Child Development, 74*, 294–307.

Allen, J. P., & others. (2009, April). *Portrait of the secure teen as an adult: Predictions from attachment to family, peer, and romantic relationship functioning.* Paper presented at the meeting of the Society for Research in Child Development, Denver.

Allen, J. P., Philliber, S., Herring, S., & Kuperminc, G. P. (1997). Preventing teen pregnancy and academic failure: Experimental evaluation of a developmentally-based approach. *Child Development, 68*, 729–742.

Allen, J. P., Porter, M., McFarland, C., McElhaney, K. B., & March, P. (2007). The relationship of attachment security to adolescents' paternal and peer relationships, depression, and externalizing behavior. *Child Development, 78*, 1222–1239.

Allen, J. P., Porter, M. R., McFarland, C. F., Marsh, P. A., & McElhaney, K. B. (2005). The two faces of adolescents' success with peers: Adolescent popularity, social adaptation, and deviant behavior. *Child Development, 76* (3), 747–760.

Allen, M. C. (2008). Neurodevelopmental outcomes of preterm infants. *Current Opinion in Neurology, 21*, 123–128.

Allen, M., Svetaz, M. V., Hardeman, R., & Resnick, M. D. (2008, February). *What research tells us about Latino parenting practices and their relationship to youth sexual behavior.* The National Campaign to Prevent Teen and Unplanned Pregnancy. Retrieved December 2, 2008, from www.TheNationalCampaign.org

Allstate Foundation. (2005). *Teen driving—Chronic: A report on the state of teen driving.* Northbrook, IL: Author.

Alm, B., Lagercrantz, H., & Wennergren, G. (2006). Stop SIDS-sleeping solitary supine, sucking smoother, stopping smoking substitutes. *Acta Paediatrica, 95*, 260–262.

Almeida D. M., & Horn, M. C. (2004). Is daily life more stressful during middle adulthood? In C. D. Ryff & R. C. Kessler (Eds.), *A portrait of midlife in the United States.* Chicago: University of Chicago Press.

Almeida, O. P., Garrido, G. J., Lautenschlager, N. T., Hulse, G. K., Jamrozik, K., & Flicker, L. (2008). Smoking is associated with reduced cortical gray matter density in brain regions associated with incipient Alzheimer disease. *American Journal of Geriatric Psychiatry, 16*, 92–98.

Aloi, J. A. (2009). Nursing the disenfranchised: Women who have relinquished an infant for adoption. *Journal of Psychiatric and Mental Health Nursing, 16*, 27–81.

Als, H., & Butler, S. C. (2008). Screening, newborn, and maternal well-being. In M. M. Haith & J. B. Benson (Eds.), *Encyclopedia of infant and early childhood development.* Oxford, UK: Elsevier.

Altarac, M., & Saroha, E. (2007). Lifetime prevalence of learning disability among U.S. children. *Pediatrics, 119* (Suppl. 1), S77–S83.

Altimer, L. (2008). Shaken baby syndrome. *Journal of Perinatal and Neonatal Nursing, 22*, 68–76.

Alvarez, A. (2009). Racism: "It isn't fair." In N. Tewari & A. Alvarez (Eds.), *Asian American psychology.* Clifton, NJ: Psychology Press.

Alvarez, A., & del Rio, P. (2007). Inside and outside the zone of proximal development: An eco-functional reading of Vygotsky. In H. Daniels, J. Wertsch, & M. Cole (Eds.), *The Cambridge companion to Vygotsky.* New York: Cambridge University Press.

Alzheimer's Association. (2009). 2009 Alzheimer's disease facts and figures. *Alzheimer's Disease and Dementia, 5*, 234–270.

Amabile, T. (1993). (Commentary). In D. Goleman, P. Kafman, & M. Ray, (Eds.), *The creative spirit.* New York: Plume.

Amabile, T. M., & Hennesey, B. A. (1992). The motivation for creativity in children. In A. K. Boggiano & T. S. Pittman (Eds.), *Achievement and motivation.* New York: Cambridge University Press.

Amato, P., & Irving, S. (2006). Historical trends in divorce and dissolution. In M. A. Fine & J. H. Harvey (Eds.), *Handbook of divorce and relationship dissolution.* Mahwah, NJ: Erlbaum.

Amato, P. R. (2006). Marital discord, divorce, and children's well-being: Results from a 20-year longitudinal study of two generations. In A. Clarke-Stewart & J. Dunn (Eds.), *Families count.* New York: Cambridge University Press.

Amato, P. R. (2007). Transformative processes in marriage: Some thoughts from a sociologist. *Journal of Marriage and the Family, 69*, 305–309.

Amato, P. R., & Booth, A. (1996). A prospective study of divorce and parent-child relationships. *Journal of Marriage and the Family, 58*, 356–365.

Amato, P. R., Booth, A., Johnson, D. R., & Rogers, S. J. (2007). *Alone together: How marriage in America is changing.* Cambridge, MA: Harvard University Press.

American Academy of Pediatrics (AAP) Work Group on Breastfeeding. (1997). Breastfeeding and the use of human milk. *Pediatrics, 100*, 1035–1039.

American Academy of Pediatrics Task Force on Infant Positioning and SIDS (AAPTFIPS). (2000). Changing concepts of sudden infant death syndrome. *Pediatrics, 105*, 650–656.

American Association of University Women. (1992). *How schools shortchange girls: A study of major findings on girls and education.* Washington, DC: Author.

American Association of University Women. (2006). *Drawing the line: Sexual harassment on campus.* Washington, DC: Author.

American Association on Mental Retardation, Ad Hoc Committee on Terminology and Classification. (1992). *Mental retardation* (9th ed.). Washington, DC: Author.

American Psychological Association. (2003). *Psychology: Scientific problem solvers.* Washington, DC: Author.

American Psychological Association. (2007). *Stress in America.* Washington, DC: Author.

American Public Health Association. (2006). *Understanding the health culture of recent immigrants to the United States.* Retrieved December 5, 2006, from www.apha.org/ppp/red/Intro.htm

Amsterdam, B. K. (1968). *Mirror behavior in children under two years of age.* Unpublished doctoral dissertation, University of North Carolina, Chapel Hill.

Anastasi, A., & Urbina, S. (1996). *Psychological testing* (7th ed.). Upper Saddle River, NJ: Prentice Hall.

Anderman, E. M., & Anderman, L. H. (2010). *Classroom motivation.* Upper Saddle River, NJ: Merrill.

Anderman, E. M., & Mueller, C. E. (2009, in press). Middle school transitions and adolescent development: Disentangling psychological, social, and biological effects. In J. Meece & J. Eccles (Eds.), *Handbook of research on schools, schooling, and human development.* Clifton, NJ: Psychology Press.

Anderman, E. M., & Murdock, T. B. (Eds.). (2007). *Psychology of academic cheating.* San Diego: Academic Press.

Anderman, E. M., & Wolters, C. A. (2006). Goals, values, and affect: Influences on student motivation. In P. A. Alexander & P. H. Winne (Eds.), *Handbook of educational psychology* (2nd ed.). Mahwah, NJ: Erlbaum.

Anderson, B. M., & others. (2009). Examination of associations of genes in the serontonin system to autism. *Neurogenetics, 10,* 209–216.

Anderson, C. A., Gentile, D. A., & Buckley, K. E. (2007). *Violent video game effects on children and adolescents.* New York: Oxford University Press.

Anderson, D. R., Huston, A. C., Schmitt, K., Linebarger, D. L., & Wright, J. C. (2001). Early childhood viewing and adolescent behavior: The recontact study. *Monographs of the Society for Research in Child Development, 66* (1, Serial No. 264).

Anderson, E., Greene, S. M., Hetherington, E. M., & Clingempeel, W. G. (1999). The dynamics of parental remarriage. In E. M. Hetherington (Ed.), *Coping with divorce, single parenting, and remarriage.* Mahwah, NJ: Erlbaum.

Anderson, J. L., Waller, D. K., Canfield, M. A., Shaw, G. M., Watkins, M. L., & Werler, M. M. (2005). Maternal obesity, gestational diabetes, and central nervous system birth defects. *Epidemiology, 16,* 87–92.

Anderson, K. G., Tapert, S. F., Moadab, I., Crowley, T. J., & Brown, S. A. (2007). Personality risk profile for conduct disorder and substance use disorders in youth. *Addictive Behaviors, 32,* 2377–2382.

Anderson, P. A. (2006). The evolution of biological sex differences in communication. In K. Dindia & D. J. Canary (Eds.), *Sex differences and similarities in communication.* Mahwah: NJ: Erlbaum.

Anderson, R. M., & Weindruch, R. (2007). Metabolic reprogramming in dietary restriction. *Interdisciplinary Topics in Gerontology, 35,* 18–38.

Angel, J. L., Jimenez, M. A., & Angel, R. J. (2007). The economic consequences of widowhood for older minority women. *Gerontologist, 47,* 224–234.

Angel, L., Fay, S., Bourazzaoui, B., Granjon, L., & Isingrini, M. (2009). Neural correlates of cued recall in young and older adults: An event-related potential study. *Neuroreport, 20,* 75–79.

Angel, R. J., & Angel, J. L. (2006). Diversity and aging in the United States. In R. H. Binstock & L. K. George (Eds.), *Handbook of aging and the social sciences* (6th ed.). San Diego: Academic Press.

Ansary, N. S., & Luthar, S. S. (2009). Distress and academic achievement among adolescents of affluence: A study of externalizing and internalizing problem behaviors and school performance. *Development and Psychopathology, 21,* 319–341.

Anspaugh, D. J., Hamrick, M. H., & Rosato, F. D. (2009). *Wellness* (7th ed.). New York: McGraw-Hill.

Antonarakis, S. E. (2009). Whole genome association studies: What have we learned and where do we go from here? *Annual Review of Genomics and Human Genetics* (Vol. 10). Palo Alto, CA: Annual Reviews.

Antonucci, T. C., Akiyama, H., & Sherman, A. M. (2007). Social networks, support, and integration. In J. E. Birren (Ed.), *Encyclopedia of gerontology* (2nd ed.). San Diego: Academic Press.

Antonucci, T. C., Vandewater, E. A., & Lansford, J. E. (2000). Adulthood and aging: Social processes and development. In A. Kazdin (Ed.), *Encyclopedia of psychology.* Washington, DC, & New York: American Psychological Association and Oxford University Press.

Aquilino, W. S. (2006). Family relationships and support systems in emerging adulthood. In J. J. Arnett & J. L. Tanner (Eds.), *Emerging adults in America.* Washington, DC: American Psychological Association.

Ara, I., Vicente-Rodriguez, G., Jimenez-Ramirez, J., Dorado, C., Serrano-Sanchez, J. A., & Calber, J. A. (2004). Regular participation in sports is associated with enhanced physical fitness and lower fat mass in prepubertal boys. *International Journal of Obesity and Related Metabolic Disorders, 28,* 1585–1593.

Araceli, G., Castro, J., Cesena, J., & Toro, J. (2005). Anorexia nervosa in male adolescents: Body image, eating attitudes, and psychological traits. *Journal of Adolescent Health, 36,* 221–226.

Aranda, M. P. (2008). Relationship between religious involvement and psychological well-being: A social justice *perspective. Health and Social Work, 33,* 9–21.

Archibald, A. B., Graber, J. A., & Brooks-Gunn, J. (2003). Pubertal processes and physical growth in adolescence. In G. R. Adams & M. Berzonsky (Eds.), *Handbook on adolescence.* Malden, MA: Blackwell.

Arehart, D. M., & Smith, P. H. (1990). Identity in adolescence: Influences on dysfunction and psychosocial task issues. *Journal of Youth and Adolescence, 19,* 63–72.

Armstrong, D. G., Henson, K. T., & Savage, T. V. (2009). *Teaching today* (8th ed.). Boston: Allyn & Bacon.

Arnett, J. J. (1990). Contraceptive use, sensation seeking, and adolescent egocentrism. *Journal of Youth and Adolescence, 19,* 171–180.

Arnett, J. J. (2002). Adolescents in Western countries in the 21st century: Vast opportunities—for all? In B. B. Brown, R. W. Larson, & T. S. Saraswathi (Eds.), *The world's youth.* New York: Cambridge University Press.

Arnett, J. J. (2006). Emerging adulthood: Understanding the new way of coming of age. In J. J. Arnett & J. L. Tanner (Eds.), *Emerging adults in America.* Washington, DC: American Psychological Association.

Arnett, J. J. (2007). Socialization in emerging adulthood. In J. E. Grusec & P. D. Hastings (Eds.), *Handbook of socialization.* New York: Guilford.

Aronowitz, T., Rennells, R. E., & Todd, E. (2006). Ecological influences of sexuality on early adolescent African American females. *Journal of Community Mental Health, 23,* 113–122.

Aronow, W. S. (2007). Cardiovascular system. In J. E. Birren (Ed.), *Encylcopedia of gerontology* (2nd ed.). San Diego: Academic Press.

Aronson, E. (1986, August). *Teaching students things they think they already know about: The case of prejudice and desegregation.* Paper presented at the meeting of the American Psychological Association, Washington, DC.

Aronson, J. (2002). Stereotype threat: Contending and coping with unnerving expectations. In J. Aronson (Ed.), *Improving academic achievement.* San Diego: Academic Press.

Arpanantikul, M. (2004). Midlife experiences of Thai women. *Journal of Advanced Nursing, 47,* 49–56.

Arterberry, M. E. (2008). Perceptual development. In M. M. Haith & J. B. Benson (Eds.), *Encyclopedia of infant and early childhood development.* Oxford, UK: Elsevier.

Asendorph, J. B. (2008). Shyness. In M. M. Haith & J. B. Benson (Eds.), *Encyclopedia of infant and early childhood development.* Oxford, UK: Elsevier.

Ash, P. (2008). Suicidal behavior in children and adolescents. *Journal of Psychosocial Nursing and Mental Health Services, 46,* 26–30.

Asher, S. R., & McDonald, K. L. (2009). The behavioral basis of acceptance, rejection, and perceived popularity. In K. H. Rubin, W. M. Bukowski, & B. Laursen (Eds.), *Handbook of peer interactions, relationships, and groups.* New York: Guilford.

Aslin, R. N. (2009). The role of learning in cognitive development. In A. Woodward & A. Needham (Eds.), *Learning and the infant mind.* New York: Oxford University Press.

Aslin, R. N., Jusczyk, P. W., & Pisoni, D. B. (1998). Speech and auditory processing during infancy: Constraints on and precursors to language. In W. Damon (Ed.), *Handbook of child psychology* (5th ed. Vol. 2). New York: Wiley.

Aslin, R. N., & Lathrop, A. L. (2008). Visual perception. In M. M. Haith & J. B. Benson (Eds.), *Encyclopedia of infant and early childhood development.* Oxford, UK: Elsevier.

Assanand, S., Dias, M., Richardson, E., & Waxier-Morrison, N. (1990). The South Asians. In N. Waxier-Morrison, J. M. Anderson, & E. Richardson (Eds.), *Cross-cultural caring.* Vancouver, BC: UBC Press.

Astington, J. W., & Dack, L. A. (2008). Theory of mind. In M. M. Haith & J. B. Benson (Eds.), *Encyclopedia of infant and early childhood development.* Oxford, UK: Elsevier.

Atchley, R. C. (2007). Retirement. In J. E. Birren (Ed.), *Encyclopedia of gerontology* (2nd ed.). San Diego: Academic Press.

Ateah, C. A. (2005). Maternal use of physical punishment in response to child misbehavior: Implications for child abuse prevention. *Child Abuse and Neglect, 29,* 169–185.

Aten, J., & Leach, M. (2008). (Eds.). *Spirituality and the therapeutic process: A comprehensive resource from intake to termination.* Washington, DC: American Psychological Association.

Atkinson, R. M., Ryan, S. C., & Turner, J. A. (2001). Variation among aging alcoholic patients in treatment. *American Journal of Geriatric Psychiatry, 9,* 275–282.

Attar-Schwartz, S., Tan, J. P., Buchanan, A., Flouri, E., & Griggs, J. (2009). Grandparenting and adolescent development in two-parent biological, lone-parent, and step-families. *Journal of Family Psychology, 23,* 67–75.

Aubert, G., & Lansdorp, P. M. (2008). Telomeres and aging. *Physiological Review, 88,* 557–579.

Auyeung, B., Baron-Cohen, S., Ashwin, E., Knickmeyer, R., Taylor, K., Hackett, G., & Hines, M. (2009). Fetal testosterone predicts sexually differentiated childhood behavior in girls and boys. *Psychological Science, 20,* 144–148.

Avent, N. D., Plummer, Z. E., Madgett, T. E., Maddocks, D. G., & Soothill, P. W. (2008). Post-genomic studies and their application to non-invasive prenatal diagnosis. *Seminars in Fetal and Neonatal Medicine, 13,* 91–98.

Avis, N. E., Brockwell, S., Randolph, J. F., Shen, S., Cain, V. S., Orly, M., & Greendale, G. A. (2009). Longitudinal changes in sexual functioning as women transition through menopause: Results from the Study of Women's Health Across the Nation. *Menopause, 16,* 442–452.

Avis, N. E., Zhao, X., Johannes, C. B., Ory, M., Brockwell, S., & Greendale, G. A. (2005). Correlates of sexual function among multi-ethnic middle-aged women: Results from the Study of Women's Health Across the Nation (SWAN). *Menopause, 12,* 385–398.

Avramopoulos, D. (2009). Genetics of Alzheimer's disease: Recent advances. *Genome Medicine, 27,* 34.

Azar, S. T. (2002). Parenting and child maltreatment. In M. H. Bornstein (Ed.), *Handbook of parenting* (2nd ed., Vol. 4). Mahwah, NJ: Erlbaum.

Azmitia, M., Syed, M., & Radmacher, K. (Eds.). (2008). On the intersection of personal and social identities: Introduction and evidence from a longitudinal study of emerging adults. *New Directions for Child and Adolescent Development, 120,* 1–16.

B

Babizhayev, M. A., Minasyan, H., & Richer, S. P. (2009). Cataract halos: A driving hazard in aging populations: Implications of the Halometer DG test for assessment of intraocular light scatter. *Applied Ergonomics, 40,* 545–553.

Bachman, J. G., O'Malley, P. M., Schulenberg, J., Johnston, L. D., Bryant, A. L., & Merline, A. C. (2002). *The decline of substance abuse in young adulthood.* Mahwah, NJ: Erlbaum.

Bachman, J. G., O'Malley, P. M., Schulenberg, J. E., Johnson, L. D., Freedman-Doan, P., & Messersmith, E. E. (2008). *The education-drug use connection.* Clifton, NJ: Psychology Press.

Badaly, D., & Adolph, K. E. (2008). Beyond the average: Infants take steps longer than their leg length. *Infant Behavior and Development 31,* 554–558.

Baddeley, A. (1990). *Human memory: Theory and practice.* Boston: Allyn & Bacon.

Baddeley, A. (2001). *Is working memory still working?* Paper presented at the meeting of the American Psychological Association, San Francisco.

Baddeley, A. D. (2007) Working memory: Multiple models, multiple mechanisms. In H. L. Roediger, Y. Dudai, & S. M. Fitzpatrick (Eds.), *Science of memory: Concepts.* Oxford: Oxford University Press.

Baddeley, A. D. (2007). *Working memory, thought and action.* New York: Oxford University Press.

Baddeley, A., Eysenck, M., & Anderson, M. (2009). *Memory.* New York: Psychology Press.

Baezner, H., & others. (2008). Association of gait and balance disorders with age-related white matter changes: The LADIS study. *Neurology, 70,* 935–942.

Bahrick. H. P. (1984). Semantic memory content in permastore: Fifty years of memory for Spanish learned in school. *Journal of Experimental Psychology: General, 113,* 1–35.

Bahrick, H. P., Bahrick, P. O., & Wittlinger, R. P. (1975). Fifty years of memory for names and faces: A cross-sectional approach. *Journal of Experimental Psychology: General, 104,* 54–75.

Bahrick, L. E., & Hollich, G. (2008). Intermodal perception. In M. M. Haith & J. B. Benson (Eds.), *Encyclopedia of infant and early childhood development.* Oxford, UK: Elsevier.

Baillargeon, R. (1995). The object concept revisited: New directions in the investigation of infants' physical knowledge. In C. E. Granrud (Ed.), *Visual perception and cognition in infancy.* Hillsdale, NJ: Erlbaum.

Baillargeon, R. (2004). The acquisition of physical knowledge in infancy: A summary in eight lessons. In U. Goswami (Ed.), *Blackwell handbook of childhood cognitive development.* Malden, MA: Blackwell.

Baillargeon, R. (2008). Innate ideas revisited: For a principle of persistence in infants' physical reasoning. *Perspectives on Psychological Science, 3,* 2–13.

Baillargeon, R., & DeVos, J. (1991). Object permanence in young children: Further evidence. *Child Development, 62,* 1227–1246.

Baillargeon, R., Li, J., Ng, W., & Yuan, S. (2009). A new account of infants' physical rea-

soning. In A. Woodward & A. Needham (Eds.), *Learning and the infant mind* (pp. 66–116). New York: Oxford University Press.

Baillargeon, R. H., Zoccolillo, M., Keenna, K., Cote, S., Perusse, D., Wu, H.-X., Boivin, M., & Tremblay, R. E. (2007). Gender differences in physical aggression: A prospective population-based survey of children before and after two years of age. *Developmental Psychology, 43,* 13–26.

Bajanowski, T., Brinkmann, B, Mitchell, E. A., Vennemann, M. M., Leukel, H. W., Larsch, K. P., Beike, J., & the GeSID Group. (2008). Nicotine and cotinine in infants dying from sudden infant death syndrome. *International Journal of Legal Medicine, 122,* 23–28.

Bakeman, R., & Brown, J. V. (1980). Early interaction: Consequences for social and mental development at three years. *Child Development, 51,* 437–447.

Bakermans-Kranenburg, M. J., Breddels-Van Bardewijk, F., Juffer, F., Velderman, M. H., & van IJzenddorn, M. H. (2007). Insecure mothers with temperamentally reactive infants. In F. Juffer, M. J. Bakermans-Kranenburg, & M. H. van IJzendoorn (Eds.), *Promoting positive parenting.* Mahwah, NJ: Erlbaum.

Baldwin, S. A., & Hoffman, J. P. (2002). The dynamics of self-esteem: A growth-curve analysis. *Journal of Youth and Adolescence, 31,* 101–113.

Bales, K. L., & Carter, C. S. (2009). Neuroendocrine mechanisms of social bonds and child-parent attachment, from the child's perspective. In M. de Haan & M. R. Gunnar (Eds.), *Handbook of development social neuroscience.* New York: Guilford.

Balkau, B., & others. (2007). International Day for the Evaluation of Abdominal Obesity (IDEA): A study of waist circumference, cardiovascular disease, and diabetes mellitus in 168,000 primary care patients in 63 countries. *Circulation, 116,* 1942–I951.

Ball, K., Burton, N. W., & Brown, W. J. (2009). A prospective study of overweight, physical activity, and depressive symptoms in young women. *Obesity, 17,* 66–71.

Ball, K., Edwards, J. D., & Ross, L. A. (2007). The impact of speed of process training on cognitive and everyday functions. *Journals of Gerontology B: Psychological Sciences and Social Sciences, 62,* P19–P31.

Ballantine, J. H., & Hammock, J. H. (2009). *The sociology of education* (6th ed.). Upper Saddle River, NJ: Prentice Hall.

Balsano, A. B., Theokas, C., & Bobek, D. L. (2009). A shared commitment to youth: The integration of theory, research practice, and social policy. In R. M. Lerner & L. Steinberg (Eds.), *Handbook of adolescent psychology* (3rd ed.). New York: Wiley.

Baltes, P. B. (1987). Theoretical propositions of life-span developmental psychology: On the dynamics between growth and decline. *Developmental Psychology, 23,* 611–626.

Baltes, P. B. (1993). The aging mind: Potentials and limits. *Gerontologist, 33,* 580–594.

Baltes, P. B. (2000). Life-span developmental theory. In A. Kazdin (Ed.), *Encyclopedia of psychology.* Washington, DC, & New York: American Psychological Association and Oxford University Press.

Baltes, P. B. (2003). On the incomplete architecture of human ontogeny: Selection, optimization, and compensation as foundation for developmental theory. In U. M. Staudinger & U. Lindenberger (Eds.), *Understanding human development.* Boston: Kluwer.

Baltes, P. B. (2006). *Facing our limits: The very old and the future of aging.* Unpublished manuscript, Max Planck Institute, Berlin.

Baltes, P. B., & Kunzmann, U. (2004). The two faces of wisdom: Wisdom as a general theory of knowledge and judgment about excellence in mind and virtue vs. wisdom as everyday realization in people and products. *Human Development, 47,* 290–299.

Baltes, P. B., & Kunzmann, U. (2007). Wisdom and aging: The road toward excellence in mind and character. In D. C. Park & N. Schwarz (Eds.), *Cognitive aging: A primer* (2nd ed.). New York: Psychology Press.

Baltes, P. B., & Lindenberger, U. (1997). Emergence of a powerful connection between sensory and cognitive functions across the adult life span: A new window to the study of cognitive aging? *Psychology and Aging, 12,* 12–21.

Baltes, P. B., Lindenberger, U., & Staudinger, U. M. (2006). Lifespan theory in developmental psychology. In W. Damon & R. Lerner (Eds.), *Handbook of child psychology* (6th ed.). New York: Wiley.

Baltes, P. B., Reuter-Lorenz, P., & Rösler, F. (Eds.). (2006). *Lifespan development and the brain.* New York: Cambridge University Press.

Baltes, P. B., & Smith, J. (2003). New frontiers in the future of aging: From successful aging of the young old to the dilemmas of the fourth age. *Gerontology, 49,* 123–135.

Baltes, P. B., & Smith, J. (2008). The fascination of wisdom: Its nature, ontogeny, and function. *Perspectives on Psychological Science, 3,* 56–64.

Bandura, A. (1997). *Self-efficacy.* New York: W. H. Freeman.

Bandura, A. (1998, August). *Swimming against the mainstream: Accentuating the positive aspects of humanity.* Paper presented at the meeting of the American Psychological Association, San Francisco.

Bandura, A. (1999). Moral disengagement in the perpetuation of inhumanities. *Personality and Social Psychology Review, 3,* 193–209.

Bandura, A. (2001). Social cognitive theory. *Annual Review of Psychology* (Vol. 52). Palo Alto, CA: Annual Reviews.

Bandura, A. (2002). Selective moral disengagement in the exercise of moral agency. *Journal of Moral Education, 31,* 101–119.

Bandura, A. (2007). Self-efficacy in health functioning. In S. Ayers & others (Eds.), *Cambridge handbook of psychology, health and medicine* (2nd ed.). New York: Cambridge University Press.

Bandura, A. (2008). Reconstrual of "Free Will" from the Agentic Perspective of Social Cognitive Theory. In J. Baer, J. C. Kaufman & R. F. Baumeister (Eds.), *Are we free?: Psychology and free will.* Oxford, UK: Oxford University Press.

Bandura, A. (2009). Self-efficacy. In S. Clegg & J. Bailey (Eds.), *International encyclopedia of organizational studies.* Thousand Oaks, CA: Sage.

Bandura, A. (2009, in press). Social and policy impact of social cognitive theory. In M. Mark, S. Donaldson, & B. Campbell (Eds.), *Social psychology and program/policy evaluation.* New York: Guilford.

Bandura, A. (2010a, in press). Self-efficacy. In D. Matsumoto (Ed.), *Cambridge dictionary of psychology.* New York: Cambridge University Press.

Bandura, A. (2010b, in press). Self-reinforcement. In D. Matsumoto (Ed.), *Cambridge dictionary of psychology.* New York: Cambridge University Press.

Banerjee, T. D., Middleton, F., & Faraone, S. V. (2007). Environmental risk factors for attention-deficit hyperactivity disorder. *Acta Pediatrica, 96,* 1269–1274.

Bank, L., Burraston, B., & Snyder, J. (2004). Sibling conflict and ineffective parenting as predictors of adolescent boys' antisocial behavior and peer difficulties: Additive and interactive effects. *Journal of Research on Adolescence, 14,* 99–125.

Bankole, A., Singh, S., Woog, V., & Wulf, D. (2004). *Risk and protection: Youth and HIV/AIDS in sub-Saharan Africa.* New York: Alan Guttmacher Institute.

Banks, J. A. (2008). *Introduction to multicultural education* (4th ed.). Boston: Allyn & Bacon.

Banks, J. A. (Ed.) (2010). *Multicultural education.* New York: Routledge.

Banks, M. S. (2005). The benefits and costs of combining information between and within the senses. In J. J. Reiser, J. J. Lockman, & C. A. Nelson (Eds.), *The role of action in learning and development.* Mahwah, NJ: Erlbaum.

Banks, S., & Dinges, D. F. (2008). Behavioral and physiological consequences of sleep restriction. *Journal of Clinical Sleep Medicine, 15,* 519–528.

Barabasz, A., & Perez, N. (2007). Salient findings: Hypnotizability as core construct and the clinical utility of hypnosis. *International Journal of Clinical Hypnosis, 55,* 372–379.

Barbieri, M., Boccardi, V., Papa, M., & Paolisso, G. (2009). Metabolic journey to healthy longevity. *Hormone Research, 71* (Suppl. 1), S24–S27.

Barbu-Roth, M., Anderson, D. I., Despres, A., Provasi, J., Cabrol, D., & Campos, J. J. (2009). Neonatal stepping in relation to terrestrial optical flow. *Child Development, 80,* 8–14.

Bargh, J. A., & McKenna, K. Y. A. (2004). The Internet and social life. *Annual Review of Psychology* (Vol. 55). Palo Alto, CA: Annual Reviews.

Barlett, C. P., & Anderson, C. A. (2009). Violent video games and public policy. In T. Bevc & H. Zapf (Eds.), *Wie wir spielen, was wir werden: Computerspiele in unserer Gesellschaft.* Konstanz: UVK Verlagsgesellschaft. (German version)

Barlett, C. P., & Anderson, C. A., & Swing, E. L. (2009). Video game effects confirmed, suspected and speculative: A review of the evidence. *Simulation and Gaming, 40,* 377–403.

Barnes, L. L., de Leon, C. F., Lewis, T. T., Bienias, J. L., Wilson, R. S., & Evans, D. A. (2008). Perceived discrimination and mortality in a population-based study of older adults. *American Journal of Public Health, 98,* 1241–1247.

Barnes, L. L., Mendes de Leon, C. F., Wilson, R. S., Bienias, J. L., Bennett, D. A., & Evans, D. A. (2004). Racial differences in perceived discrimination in a community population of older Blacks and Whites. *Journal of Aging and Health, 16,* 315–317.

Baron, N. S. (1992). *Growing up with language.* Reading, MA: Addison-Wesley.

Baron-Cohen, S. (1995). *Mindblindness: An essay on autism and theory of mind.* Cambridge, MA: MIT Press.

Baron-Cohen, S. (2008). Autism, hypersystemizing, and truth. *Quarterly Journal of Experimental Psychology, 61,* 64–75.

Baron-Cohen, S., Golan, O., Chapman, E., & Granader, Y. (2007). Transported to a world of emotion. *The Psychologist, 20,* 76–77.

Barrett, T. M., Davis, E. F., & Needham, A. (2007). Learning about tools in infancy. *Developmental Psychology, 43,* 352–368.

Barrett, T. M., & Needham, A. (2008). Developmental differences in infants' use of an object's shape to grasp it securely. *Developmental Psychobiology, 50,* 97–106.

Barron, J., Petrilli, F., Strath, L., & McCaffrey, R. (2007). Successful interventions for smoking cessation in pregnancy. *MCN American Journal of Maternal and Child Nursing, 32,* 42–47.

Barry, R. A., Kochanska, G., & Philibert, R. A. (2008). G × E interaction in the organization of attachment: Mothers' responsiveness as a moderator of children's genotypes. *Journal of Child Psychology and Psychiatry, 49,* 1313–1320.

Bart, W. M., & Peterson, D. P. (2008). Stanford-Binet test. In N. J. Salkind (Ed.), *Encyclopedia of educational psychology.* Thousand Oaks, CA: Sage.

Barton, S. E. (2005). Reducing the transmission of genital herpes. *British Medical Journal, 330,* 157–158.

Bartsch, K., & Wellman, H. M. (1995) *Child talk about the mind.* Oxford University Press.

Basaran, A. (2007). Progesterone to prevent preterm delivery: Enigma or ready? *American Journal of Obstetrics and Gynecology, 197,* 686.

Bass, J. E., Contant, T. L., & Carin, A. A. (2009). *Teaching science as inquiry* (11th ed.). Boston: Allyn & Bacon.

Basta, N. E., Matthews, F. E., Chatfield, M. D., Brayne, C., & MRC-CFAS. (2008). Community-level socio-economic status and cognitive and functional impairment in the older population. *European Journal of Public Health, 18,* 48–54.

Bates, J. E. (2008). Unpublished review of J. W. Santrock's *Children,* 11th ed. (New York: McGraw-Hill).

Bates, J. E., & Pettit, G. S. (2007). Temperament, parenting, and socialization. In J. E. Grusec & P. D. Hastings (Eds.), *Handbook of socialization.* New York: Guilford.

Bates, J. E., Viken, R. J., Alexander, D. B., Beyers, J., & Stockton, L. (2002). Sleep and adjustment in preschool children: Sleep diary reports by mothers relate to behavior reports by teachers. *Child Development, 73,* 62–74.

Batson, C. D. (1989). Personal values, moral principles, and the three path model of prosocial motivation. In N. Eisenberg & J. Reykowski (Eds.), *Social and moral values.* Hillsdale, NJ: Erlbaum.

Battistich, V. A. (2008). The Child Development Project: Creating caring school communities. In L. Nucci & D. Narváez (Eds.), *Handbook of moral and character education.* Clifton, NJ: Psychology Press.

Bauer, I., Wrosch, C., & Jobin, J. (2008). I'm better off than most people: The role of social comparisons for coping with regret in young adulthood and old age. *Psychology and Aging, 23,* 800–811.

Bauer, M. E., Jeckel, C. M., & Luz, C. (2009). The role of stress factors during aging of the immune system. *Annals of the New York Academy of Sciences, 1153,* 139–152.

Bauer, P. J. (2006). Event memory. In W. Damon & R. Lerner (Eds.), *Handbook of child psychology* (6th ed.). New York: Wiley.

Bauer, P. J. (2009). Learning and memory: Like a horse and carriage. In A. Needham & A. Woodward (Eds.), *Learning and the infant mind.* New York: Oxford University Press.

Bauer, P. J., Wenner, J. A., Dropik, P. I., & Wewerka, S. S. (2000). Parameters of remembering and forgetting in the transition from infancy to early childhood. *Monographs of the Society for Research in Child Development, 65* (4, Serial No. 263).

Bauerlein, M. (2008). *The dumbest generation: How the digital age stupefies young Americans and jeopardizes our future (Or, don't trust anyone under 30).* New York: Tarcher.

Bauld, R., & Brown, R. F. (2009). Stress, psychological stress, psychological factors, menopause symptoms, and physical health in women. *Maturitas, 62,* 160–165.

Baum, N. H., & Crespi, C. A. (2007). Testosterone replacement in elderly men. *Geriatrics, 62,* 15–18.

Baumeister, R. F., Campbell, J. D., Krueger, J. I., & Vohs, K. D. (2003). Does high self-esteem cause better performance, interpersonal success, happiness, or healthier lifestyles? *Psychological Science in the Public Interest, 4* (1), 1–44.

Baumeister, R. F., Catanese, K. R., & Vohs, K. D. (2001). Is there a gender difference in strength of sex drive? *Personality and Social Psychology Review, 5,* 242–273.

Baumeister, R. F., & Vohs, K. D. (2002). The pursuit of meaningfulness in life. In C. R. Snyder & S. J. Lopez (Eds.), *Handbook of positive psychology.* New York: Oxford University Press.

Baumrind, D. (1971). Current patterns of parental authority. *Developmental Psychology Monographs, 4* (1, Pt. 2).

Baumrind, D. (1991). Effective parenting during the early adolescent transition. In P. A. Cowan & E. M. Hetherington (Eds.), *Advances in family research* (Vol. 2). Hillsdale, NJ: Erlbaum.

Baumrind, D., Larzelere, R. B., & Cowan, P. A. (2002). Ordinary physical punishment: Is it harmful? Comment on Gershoff. *Psychological Bulletin, 128,* 590–595.

Bayley, N. (1969). *Manual for the Bayley Scales of Infant Development.* New York: Psychological Corporation.

Bayley, N. (2006). *Bayley Scales of Infant and Toddler Development* (3rd ed.). San Antonio: Harcourt Assessment.

Beal, C. R. (1994). *Boys and girls: The development of gender roles.* New York: McGraw-Hill.

Bearman, P. S., & Moody, J. (2004). Suicide and friendships among American adolescents. *American Journal of Public Health, 94,* 89–95.

Bearman, S. K., Presnall, K., Martinez, E., & Stice, E. (2006). The skinny on body dissatisfaction: A longitudinal study of adolescent girls and boys. *Journal of Youth and Adolescence, 35,* 217–229.

Bechtold, A. G., Busnell, E. W., & Salapatek, P. (1979, April.) *Infants' visual localization of visual and auditory targets.* Paper presented at the meeting of the Society for Research in Child Development, San Francisco.

Bedford, V. H. (2009). Sibling relationships: Adulthood. In D. Carr (Ed.), *Encyclopedia of the life course and human development.* Boston: Gale Cengage.

Beeri, M. S., Lee, H., Cheng, H., Wollman, D., Silverman, J. M., & Prohovnik, I. (2009, in press). Memory activation in healthy nonagenarians. *Neurobiology of Aging.*

Beets, M. W., & Foley, J. T. (2008). Association of father involvement and neighborhood quality with kindergartners' physical activity: A multilevel structural equation model. *American Journal of Health Promotion, 22,* 195–203.

Beghetto, R. A., & Kaufman, J. C. (2009, in press). *Nurturing creativity in the classroom.* New York: Cambridge University Press.

Begley, S., & Interlandi, J. (2008, July 2). The dumbest generation? Don't be dumb. Retrieved July 15, 2008, from www.newsweek.com/id/138536

Belansky, E. S., & Clements, P. (1992, March). *Adolescence: A crossroads for gender-role transcendence or gender-role intensification.* Paper presented at the meeting of the Society for Research on Adolescence, Washington, DC.

Bell, K. N., & Oakley, G. P. (2009). Update on prevention of folic acid–preventable spina bifida and anencephaly. *Birth Defects Research Part A: Clinical and Molecular Teratology, 85,* 102–107.

Bell, M. A., & Fox, N. A. (1992). The relations between frontal brain electrical activity and cognitive development during infancy. *Child Development, 63,* 1142–1163.

Bell, M. A., & Wolfe, C. D. (2007). The cognitive neuroscience of early socioemotional development. In C. A. Brownell & C. B. Kopp (Eds.), *Socioemotional development in the toddler years.* New York: Guilford.

Beeghly, M., Martin, B., Rose-Jacobs, R., Cahral, H., Heeren, T., Augustyn, M., Bellinger, D., & Frank, D. A. (2006). Prenatal cocaine exposure and children's language functioning at 6 and 9.5 years: Moderating effects of child age, birthweight, and gender. *Journal of Pediatric Psychology, 31,* 98–115.

Bell, S. M., & Ainsworth, M. D. S. (1972). Infant crying and maternal responsiveness. *Child Development, 43,* 1171–1190.

Belsky, J. (1981). Early human experience: A family perspective. *Developmental Psychology, 77,* 3–23.

Belsky, J. (2009). Classroom composition, childcare history, and social development: Are children effects disappearing or spreading? *Social Development, 18,* 230–238.

Belsky, J., Vandell, D. L., Burchinal, M., Clarke-Stewart, A., McCartney, K., Owen, M. T., & the NICHD Early Child Care Research Network. (2007). Are there long-term effects of early child care. *Child Development, 78,* 681–701.

Bender, W. N. (2008). *Learning disabilities* (6th ed.). Boston: Allyn & Bacon.

Bender, H. L., Allen, J. P., McElhaney, K. B., Antonishak, J., Moore, C. M., Kello, H. O., & Davis, S. M. (2007). Use of harsh discipline and developmental outcomes in adolescence. *Development and Psychopathology, 19,* 227–242.

Bendersky, M., & Sullivan, M. W. (2007). Basic methods in infant research. In A. Slater & M. Lewis (Eds.), *Introduction to infant development* (2nd ed.). New York: Oxford University Press.

Benenson, J. E., Apostolaris, N. H., & Parnass, J. (1997). Age and sex differences in dyadic and group interaction. *Developmental Psychology, 33,* 538–543.

Bengtson, V. L. (1985). Diversity and symbolism in grandparental roles. In V. L. Bengtson & J. Robertson (Eds.), *Grandparenthood.* Newbury Park, CA: Sage.

Bengtson, V. L., Reedy, M. N., & Gordon, C. (1985). Aging and self-conceptions: Personality processes and social contexts. In J. E. Birren & K. W. Schaie (Eds.), *Handbook of the psychology of aging.* New York: Van Nostrand Reinhold.

Bengtson, H., & Psouni, E. (2008). Mothers' representations of caregiving and their adult children's representations of attachment: Intergenerational concordance and relations to beliefs about mothering. *Scandinavian Journal of Psychology, 49,* 247–257.

Benjamins, M. R., & Buck, A. C. (2008). Religion: A sociocultural predictor of health behavior in Mexico. *Journal of Aging and Health, 20,* 290–305.

Benjamins, M. R., & Finlayson, M. (2007). Using religious services to improve health: Findings from a sample of middle-aged and older adults with multiple sclerosis. *Journal of Aging and Health, 19,* 537–553.

Benner, A. D., & Mistry R. S. (2007). Congruence of mother and teacher educational expectations and low-income youth's academic competence. *Journal of Educational Psychology, 99,* 140–153.

Bennett, T., Szatmari, P., Bryson, S., Volden, J., Zwaigenbaum, L., Vaccarella, L., Duku, E., & Boyle, M. (2008). Differentiating autism and Asperger syndrome on the basis of language delay or impairment. *Journal of Autism and Developmental Disorders, 38,* 616–625.

Benninghoven, D., Tetsch, N., Kunzendorf, S., & Jantschek, G. (2007). Body image in patients with eating disorders and their mothers, and the role of family functioning. *Comprehensive Psychiatry, 48,* 118–123.

Benoit, D., Coolbear, J., & Crawford, A. (2008). Abuse, neglect, and maltreatment of infants. In M. M. Haith & J. B. Benson (Eds.), *Encyclopedia of infant and early childhood development.* Oxford, UK: Elsevier.

Benokraitis, N. (2008). *Marriages and families* (6th ed.). Upper Saddle River, NJ: Prentice Hall.

Benson, A. C., Torode, M. E., & Fiatarone Singh, M. A. (2008). The effects of high-intensity progressive resistance training on adiposity in children: A randomized controlled trial. *International Journal of Obesity, 32,* 1016–1027.

Benson, L., Baer, H. J., & Kaelber, D. C. (2009). Trends in the diagnosis of overweight and obesity in children and adolescents: 1999–2007. *Pediatrics, 123,* el53–el58.

Benson, P. L., & Roehlkepartain, E. C. (2008). Spiritual development: A missing priority in youth development. *New Directions for Youth Development, 118,* 13–28.

Berecz, J. M. (2009). *Theories of personality.* Boston: Allyn & Bacon.

Berenbaum, S. A., & Bailey, J. M. (2003). Effects on gender identity of prenatal androgens and genital appearance: Evidence from girls with congenital adrenal hyperplasia. *Journal of Clinical Endocrinology and Metabolism, 88,* 1102–1106.

Berg, A. I., Hoffman, L., Hassing, L. B., McClean, G. E., & Johansson, B. (2009). What matters, and what matters most, for change in life satisfaction in the oldest-old? A study over 6 years among individuals 80+. *Aging and Mental Health, 13,* 191–201.

Berk, L. E. (1994). Why children talk to themselves. *Scientific American, 271* (5), 78–83.

Berk, L. E., & Spuhi, S. T. (1995). Maternal interaction, private speech, and task performance in preschool children. *Early Childhood Research Quarterly, 10,* 145–169.

Berko, J. (1958). The child's learning of English morphology. *Word, 14,* 150–177.

Berko Gleason, J. (2003). Unpublished review of J. W. Santrock's *Life-span development,* 9th ed. (New York: McGraw-Hill).

Berko Gleason, J. (2009). The development of language: An overview. In J. Berko Gleason & N. Ratner (Eds.), *The development of language* (7th ed.). Boston: Allyn & Bacon.

Berko Gleason, J., & Ratner, N. B. (Eds.). (2009). *The development of language* (7th ed.), Boston: Allyn & Bacon.

Berkowitz, M. W., Battistich, V. A., & Bier, M. (2008). What works in character education: What is known and what needs to be known. In L. Nucci & D. Narváez (Eds.), *Handbook of moral and character education.* Clifton, NJ: Psychology Press.

Berlin, C. M., Paul, I. M., & Vesell, E. S. (2009). Safety issues of maternal drug therapy during breastfeeding. *Clinical Pharmacology and Therapeutics, 85,* 20–22.

Berlin, L. J., Cassidy, J., & Appleyard, K. (2008). The influence of early attachment on other relationships. In J. Cassidy & P. R. Shaver (Eds.), *Handbook of attachment* (2nd ed.). New York: Guilford.

Berlin, L. J., Zeanah, C. H., & Lieberman, A. F. (2008). Prevention and intervention programs for supporting early attachment. In J. Cassidy & P. R. Shaver (Eds.), *Handbook of attachment* (2nd ed.). New York: Guilford.

Berlyne, D. E. (1960). *Conflict, arousal, and curiosity.* New York: McGraw-Hill.

Berman, J. J., Murphy-Berman, V., & Melton, G. B. (2008). Strong communities: What did participants actually do? *Family and Community Health, 31,* 126–135.

Bernard, K., & Dozier, M. (2008). Adoption and foster placement. In M. M. Haith &

J. B. Benson (Eds.), *Encyclopedia of infant and early childhood development.* Oxford, UK: Elsevier.

Berndt, T. J. (2002). Friendship quality and social development. *Current Directions in Psychological Science 11,* 7–10.

Berndt, T. J., & Perry, T. B. (1990). Distinctive features and effects of early adolescent friendships. In R. Montemayor (Ed.), *Advances in adolescent research.* Greenwich, CT: JAI Press.

Berninger, V. W. (2006). Learning disabilities. In W. Damon & R. Lerner (Eds.), *Handbook of child psychology* (6th ed.). New York: Wiley.

Berninger, V. W., & Abbott, R. (2005, April). *Paths leading to reading comprehension in at-risk and normally developing second-grade readers.* Paper presented at the meeting of the Society for Research in Child Development, Atlanta.

Berntsen, D. & Rubin, D. C. (2002). Emotionally charged autobiographical memories across the life span: The recall of happy, sad, traumatic, and involuntary memories. *Psychology and Aging, 17,* 636–652.

Berry, P., Kelley-Bock, M., & Rei, C. (2008). Confident living program for senior adults experiencing vision and hearing loss. *Care Management Journal, 9,* 31–35.

Berscheid, E. (1988). Some comments on love's anatomy: Or, whatever happened to old-fashioned lust? In R. J. Sternberg (Ed.), *Anatomy of love.* New Haven, CT: Yale University Press.

Berscheid, E. (2000). Attraction. In A. Kazdin (Ed.), *Encyclopedia of psychology.* Washington, DC, & New York: American Psychology Association and Oxford University Press.

Berscheid, E. (2010). Love in the fourth dimension. *Annual Review of Psychology* (Vol. 61). Palo Alto, CA: Annual Reviews.

Berscheid, E., & Fei, J. (1977). Sexual jealousy and romantic love. In G. Clinton & G. Smith (Eds.), *Sexual jealousy.* Englewood Cliffs, NJ: Prentice Hall.

Bertenthal, B. I. (2008). Perception and action. In M. M. Haith & J. B. Benson (Eds.), *Infant and early childhood development.* Oxford, UK: Elsevier.

Bertenthal, B. I., Longo, M. R., & Kenny, S. (2007). Phenomenal permanence and the development of predictive tracking in infancy. *Child Development, 78,* 350–363.

Bertrand, R. M., & Lachman, M. E. (2003). Personality development in adulthood and old age. In I. B. Weiner (Ed.), *Handbook of psychology* (Vol. VI). New York: Wiley.

Beskin, M., & Gulgoz, S. (2009). Reliance on schemas in source memory: Age differences and similarities of schemas. *Neuropsychology, Development, and Cognition. Section B: Aging, Neuropsychology, and Cognition, 16,* 1–2.

Bessette, L., Jean, S., Davison, K. S., Roy, S., Ste-Marie, L. G., & Brown, J. P. (2009, in press). Factors influencing the treatment of osteoporosis following fragility fracture. *Osteoporosis International.*

Best, D. L. (2010). Gender. In M. H. Bornstein (Ed.), *Handbook of cultural developmental science.* New York: Psychology Press.

Betensky, J. D., Contrada, R. J., & Leventhal, E. (2009). Cardiovascular disease. In D. Carr (Ed.), *Encyclopedia of the life course and human development.* Boston: Gale Cengage.

Bethell, J., & Roades, A. E. (2008). Adolescent depression and emergency department use: The roles of suicidality and deliberate self-harm. *Current Psychiatry Reports, 10,* 53–59.

Betz, C., & Sowden, L. (2008). *Mosby's pediatric nursing reference* (6th ed.). Oxford, UK: Elsevier.

Beydoun, M. A., & Wang, Y. (2009). Gender-ethnic disparity in BMI and waist circumference distribution shifts in U.S. adults. *Obesity, 17,* 169–176.

Beyene, Y. (1986). Cultural significance and physiological manifestations of menopause: A biocultural analysis. *Culture, Medicine, and Psychiatry, 10,* 47–71.

Bialystok, E. (1993). Metalinguistic awareness: The development of children's representations in language. In C. Pratt & A. Carton (Eds.), *Systems of representation in children.* London: Wiley.

Bialystok, E. (1997). Effects of bilingualism and biliteracy on children's emerging concepts of print. *Developmental Psychology, 33,* 429–440.

Bialystok, E. (1999). Cognitive complexity and attentional control in the bilingual mind. *Child Development, 70,* 537–604.

Bialystok, E. (2001). *Bilingualism in development: Language, literacy, and cognition.* New York: Cambridge University Press.

Bialystock, E. (2007). Acquisition of literacy in preschool children: A framework for research. *Language Learning, 57,* 45–77.

Bian, Z., & Andersen, G. J. (2008) Aging and the perceptual organization of 3-D scenes. *Psychology and Aging, 23,* 342–352.

Bibok, M. B., Carpendale, J. I. M., & Lewis, C. (2008). Social knowledge and social skill: An action-based view of social understanding. In U. Mueller, J. I. M. Carpendale, N. Budwig, & B. W. Sokol (Eds.), *Social life and social knowledge.* Philadelphia: Psychology Press.

Bielak, A. A. M., Hughes, T. F., Small, B. J., & Dixon, R. A. (2007). It's never too late to engage in lifestyle activities: Significant concurrent but not change relationships between lifestyle activities and cognitive speed. *Journals of Gerontology B: Psychological Sciences and Social Sciences, 62,* P331–P339.

Bierman, K. L. (2004). *Peer rejection.* New York: Guilford.

Bill and Melinda Gates Foundation. (2006). *The silent epidemic: Perspectives on high school dropouts.* Seattle: Author.

Bill and Melinda Gates Foundation. (2008). *Report gives voice to dropouts.* Retrieved July 5, 2008, from www.gatesfoundation.org/UnitedStates/Education/TransformingHighSchools/Related…

Billy, J. O. G., Rodgers, J. L., & Udry, J. R. (1984). Adolescent sexual behavior and friendship choice. *Social Forces, 62,* 653–678.

Binder, T., & Vavrinkova, B. (2008). Prospective randomized comparative study of the effect of buprenorphine, methadone, and heroin on the course of pregnancy, birth weight of newborns, early postpartum adaptation, and the course of neonatal abstinence syndrome (NAS). *Neuroendocrinology Letters, 29,* 80–86.

Birch, S., & Bloom, P. (2003). Children are cursed: An asymmetric bias in mental state attribution. *Psychological Science, 14,* 283–286.

Birditt, K. S. (2009). Spousal caregiving. In D. Carr (Ed.), *Encyclopedia of the life course and human development.* Boston: Gale Cengage.

Birren, J. E. (Ed.). (1996). *Encyclopedia of gerontology.* San Diego: Academic Press.

Birren, J. E. (2002). Unpublished review of J. W. Santrock's *Life-span development,* 9th ed. (New York: McGraw-Hill).

Bisiacchi, P. S., Tarantino, V., & Ciccola, A. (2008). Aging and prospective memory: The role of working memory and monitoring processes. *Aging: Clinical and Experimental Research, 20,* 569–577.

Bisson, J. I., Hampton, V., Rosser, A., & Holm, S. (2009). Developing a care pathway for advance decisions and power of attorney: A qualitative study. *British Journal of Psychiatry, 194,* 55–61.

Bjorklund, D. F. (2005). *Children's thinking differences* (4th ed.). Belmont, CA: Wadsworth.

Bjorklund, D. F. (2007). *Why youth is not wasted on the young.* Maiden, MA: Blackwell.

Bjorklund, D. F., Dukes, C., & Brown, R. D. (2009). *The development of memory strategies in infancy and childhood.* In M. Courage & N. Cowan (Eds.). New York: Psychology Press.

Bjorklund, D. F., & Pellegrini, A. D. (2002). *The origins of human nature.* New York: Oxford University Press.

Bjorklund, D. R., & Rosenbaum, K. (2000). Middle childhood: Cognitive development. In A. Kazdin (Ed.), *Encyclopedia of psychology.* Washington, DC, & New York: American Psychological Association and Oxford University Press.

Black, M. M., & Hurley, K. M. (2007). Helping children develop healthy eating habits. In Tremblay, R. E., Barr, R. G., Peters, R. D., & Boivin, M. (Eds.), *Encyclopedia on early childhood development.* Retrieved March 19, 2008, from *www.child-encyclopedia.com/documents/BlackHurleyANGxp_rev-Eating.pdf*

Black, M. M., Hurley, K. M., Oberlander, S. E., Hager, E. R., McGill, A. E., White, N. T., & Quigg, A. M. (2009). Participants' comments on changes in the revised special supplemental nutrition program for women, infants, and children food packages: The Maryland food preference study. *Journal of the American Dietetic Association, 109,* 116–123.

Black, M. M., & Lozoff, B. (2008). Nutrition and diet. In M. M. Haith & J. B. Benson (Eds.), *Encyclopedia of infant and early childhood development.* Oxford, UK: Elsevier.

Blaga, O. M., Shaddy, D. J., Anderson, C. J., Kannass, K. N., Little, T. D., & Colombo, J. (2009). Structure and continuity of intellectual development in early childhood. *Intelligence, 37,* 106–113.

Blaine, S. M., & others. (2008). Interactive genetic counseling role-play: A novel educational strategy for family physicians. *Journal of Genetic Counseling, 17,* 189–195.

Blair, C., Gamson, D., Thorne, S., & Baker, D. (2005). Rising mean IQ: Cognitive demand of mathematics education for young children, population exposure to formal schooling, and the neurobiology of the prefrontal cortex. *Intelligence, 33,* 93–106.

Blair, S. N. (1990, January). Personal communication. Aerobics Institute, Dallas.

Blair, S. N., Kohl, H. W., Paffenbarger, R. S., Clark, D. G., Cooper, K. H., & Gibbons, L. W. (1989). Physical fitness and all-cause mortality: A prospective study of healthy men and women. *Journal of the American Medical Association, 262,* 2395–2401.

Blakemore, J. E. O., Berenbaum, S. A. & Liben, L. S. (2009). *Gender development.* Clifton, NJ: Psychology Press.

Blanchard-Fields, F. (2007). Everyday problem solving and emotion. *Current Directions in Psychological Science, 16,* 26–31.

Blanchard-Fields, F., & Coats, A. (2007). *Emotions in everyday problems: Age differences in elicitation and regulation.* Unpublished manuscript, Department of Psychology, Georgia Tech University, Atlanta.

Blanco, M., Hickman, J. S., Olson, R. L., Bocanegra, J. L., Hanowski, R. J., Nakata, A., Greening, M., Madison, P., Holbrook, G. T., & Bowman, D. (2009, in press). *Investigating critical incidents, driver restart period, sleep quantity, and crash countermeasures in commercial operations using naturalistic data collection: Final report* (Contract No. DTFH61-01-C-00049, Task Order # 23). Washington, DC: Federal Motor Carrier Safety Administration.

Blanton, H., & Burkley, M. (2008). Deviance regulation theory: Applications to adolescent social influence. In M. J. Prinstein & K. A. Dodge (Eds.), *Understanding peer influence in children and adolescents.* New York: Guilford.

Blasi, A. (2005). Moral character: A psychological approach. In D. K. Lapsley & F. C. Power

(Eds.), *Character psychology and character education.* Notre Dame, IN: University of Notre Dame Press.

Blass, E. (2008). Suckling. In M. M. Haith & J. B. Benson (Eds.), *Encyclopedia of infant and early childhood development.* Oxford, UK: Elsevier.

Blazer, D. G., & Steffens, D. (Eds.). (2009). Textbook of geriatric psychiatry (4th ed.). Arlington, VA: American Psychiatric Publishing.

Block, J. (1993). Studying personality the long way. In D. Funder, R. D. Parke, C. Tomlinson-Keasey, & K. Widaman (Ed.), *Studying lives through time.* Washington, DC: American Psychological Association.

Bloom, B. (1985). *Developing talent in young people.* New York: Ballentine.

Bloom, L. (1998). Language acquisition in its developmental context. In W. Damon (Ed.), *Handbook of child psychology* (5th ed., Vol. 2). New York: Wiley.

Bloom, L., Lifter, K., & Broughton, J. (1985). The convergence of early cognition and language in the second year of life: Problems in conceptualization and measurement. In M. Barrett (Ed.), *Single word speech.* London: Wiley.

Bloom, P., & German, T. P. (2000). Two reasons to abandon the false belief task as a test of theory of mind. *Cognition, 77,* B25–B31.

Bloor, C., & White, F. (1983). Unpublished manuscript. University of California at San Diego, LaJolla, CA.

Bodrova, E., & Leong, D. J. (2007). *Tools of the mind* (2nd ed.). Geneva: International Bureau of Education, UNESCO.

Boelen, P. A., & Prigerson, H. G. (2007). The influence of symptoms of prolonged grief disorder, depression, and anxiety on quality of life among bereaved adults: A prospective study. *European Archives of Psychiatry and Clinical Neuroscience, 257,* 444–452.

Bohannon, J. N., & Bonvillian, J. D. (2009). Theoretical approaches to language acquisition. In J. Berko Gleason & N. B. Ratner (Eds.), *The development of language.* Boston: Allyn & Bacon.

Bohlin, G., & Hagekull B. (1993). Stranger wariness and sociability in the early years. *Infant Behavior and Development, 16,* 53–67.

Bojesen, A., & Gravholt, C. H. (2007). Klinefelter syndrome in clinical practice. *Nature Clinical Practice: Urology, 4,* 192–204.

Bolling, C. F., & Daniel, S. R. (2008). Obesity. In M. M. Haith & J. B. Benson (Eds.), *Encyclopedia of infant and early childhood development.* Oxford, UK: Elsevier.

Bolte, G., Fromme, H., & the GME Study Group. (2009). Socioeconomic determinants of children's environmental tobacco smoke exposure and family's home smoking policy. *European Journal of Public Health, 19,* 52–58.

Bonanno, G. A. (2004). Loss, trauma, and human resilience: Have we underestimated the human capacity to thrive after extremely aversive events? *American Psychologist, 59,* 20–28.

Bonanno, G. A., Wortman, C. B., & Nesse, R. M. (2004). Prospective patterns of resilience and maladjustment during widowhood. *Psychology and Aging, 19,* 260–271.

Bondare, W. (2007). Brain and central nervous system. In J. E. Birren (Ed.), *Encyclopedia of gerontology* (2nd ed.). San Diego: Academic Press.

Bonjour, J. P., Gueguen, L., Palacios, C., Shearer, M. J., & Weaver, C. M. (2009). Minerals and vitamins in bone health: The potential value of dietary enhancement. *British Journal of Nutrition, 101,* 1581–1596.

Bonvillian, J. (2005). Unpublished review of J. W. Santrock's *Topical life-span development,* 3rd ed. (New York: McGraw-Hill).

Booth, A. (2006). Object function and categorization in infancy: Two mechanisms of facilitation. *Infancy, 10,* 145–169.

Booth, M. (2002). Arab adolescents facing the future: Enduring ideals and pressures to change. In B. B. Brown, R. W. Larson, & T. S. Saraswathi (Eds.), *The world's youth.* New York: Cambridge University Press.

Booth-LaForce, C., & Kerns, K. A. (2009). Child-parent attachment relationships, peer relationships, and peer-group functioning. In K. H. Rubin, W. M. Bukowksi, & B. Laursen (Eds.), *Handbook of peer interactions, relationships, and groups.* New York: Guilford.

Bor, W., McGee, T. R., & Pagan, A. A. (2004). Early risk factors for adolescent antisocial behavior: An Australian longitudinal study. *Australian and New Zealand Journal of Psychiatry, 35,* 365–372.

Borges, N. J., McNally, C. J., Maguire, C. P., Werth, J. L., & Britton, P. J. (2008). Work, health, diversity, and social justice: Expanding and extending the discussion. *The Counseling Psychologist, 36,* 127–131.

Bornstein, M. H. (1975). Qualities of color vision in infancy. *Journal of Experimental Child Psychology, 19,* 401–409.

Bornstein, M. H., & Zlotnik, D. (2008). Parenting styles and their effects. In M. M. Haith & J. B. Benson (Ed.), *Encyclopedia of infant and early childhood development.* Oxford, UK: Elsevier.

Boron, J. B., Willis, S. L., & Schaie, K. W. (2007). Cognitive training gain as a predictor of mental status. *Journals of Gerontology B: Psychological Sciences and Social Sciences, 62,* P45–P52.

Borowski, K., & Niebyl, J. R. (2008). Drugs in pregnancy. In J. Studd, S. L. Tan, & F. A. Cherenak (Eds.), *Progress in obstetrics and gynecology.* London: Elsevier.

Bortfeld, H., Fava, E., & Boas, D. A. (2009). Identifying cortical lateralization of speech processing in infants using near-infrared spectroscopy. *Developmental Neuropsychology, 34,* 52–65.

Bosma, H. A., & Kunnen, E. S. (2008). Identity-in-context is not yet identity development-in-context. *Journal of Adolescence, 31,* 281–289.

Bostock, C. V., Soiza, R. L., & Whalley, L. J. (2009). Genetic determinants of aging processes and diseases in later life. *Maturitas, 62,* 225–229.

Botwinick, J. (1978). *Aging and behavior* (2nd ed.). New York: Springer.

Boukydis, C. F., & Lester, B. M. (2008). Mother-infant consultation during drug treatment: Research and innovative clinical practice. *Harm Reduction Journal, 5,* 6.

Bouman, W. P. (2008). Sexuality in later life. In R. Jacoby, C. Oppenheimer, T. Dening, & A. Thomas (Eds.), *Oxford textbook of old age psychiatry.* Oxford University Press.

Boveris, A., & Navarro, A. (2008). Brain mitochondrial dysfunction in aging. *IUBMB Life, 60,* 308–314.

Bower, T. G. R. (1966). Slant perception and shape constancy in infants. *Science, 151,* 832–834.

Bowlby, J. (1969). *Attachment and loss* (Vol. 1). London: Hogarth Press.

Bowlby, J. (1980). *Attachment and loss:* Vol. 3. *Loss, sadness, and depression.* New York: Basic Books.

Bowlby, J. (1989). *Secure and insecure attachment.* New York: Basic Books.

Bowman, M. A., Prelow, H. M., & Weaver, S. R. (2007). Parenting behaviors, association with deviant peers, and delinquency in African American adolescents: A mediated-moderation model. *Journal of Youth and Adolescence, 36,* 517–527.

Boyer, K., & Diamond, A. (1992). Development of memory for temporal order in infants and young children. In A. Diamond (Ed.), *Development and neural bases of higher cognitive function.* New York: New York Academy of Sciences.

Boyle, J., & Cropley, M. (2004). Children's sleep: Problems and solutions. *Journal of Family Health Care, 14,* 61–63.

Brabeck, M. M. (2000). Kohlberg, Lawrence. In A. Kazdin (Ed.), *Encyclopedia of psychology.* Washington, DC, and New York: American Psychological Association and Oxford University Press.

Brabek, M. M., & Brabek, K. M. (2006). Women and relationships. In J. Worell & C. D. Goodheart (Eds.), *Handbook of girls' and women's psychological health.* New York: Oxford University Press.

Brabyn, J. A., Schneck, M. E., Haegerstrom-Portnoy, G., & Lott, L. (2001). The Smith-Kettlewell Institute (SKI). Longitudinal study of vision function and its impact among the elderly: An overview. *Ophthalmology and Vision Science, 78,* 2464–2469.

Bracken, M. B., Eskenazi, B., Sachse, K., McSharry, J., Hellenbrand, K., & Leo-Summers, L. (1990). Association of cocaine use with sperm concentration, motility, and morphology. *Fertility and Sterility, 53*, 315–322.

Bradley, C. T., & Brasel, K. J. (2009). Developing guidelines for patients who would benefit from palliative care services in the surgical intensive care unit. *Critical Care Medicine, 37*, 946–950.

Bradley, R. H., & Corwyn, R. F. (2008). Infant temperament, parenting, and externalizing behavior in first grade: A test of the differential susceptibility hypothesis. *Journal of Child Psychology and Psychiatry, 49*, 124–131.

Brainerd, C. J., & Reyna, V. F. (1993). Domains of fuzzy-trace theory. In M. L. Howe & R. Pasnak (Eds.), *Emerging themes in cognitive development*. New York: Springer.

Brainerd, C. J., & Reyna, V. F. (2004). Fuzzy-trace theory and memory development. *Developmental Review, 24*, 396–439.

Brams, H., Mao, A. R., & Doyle, R. L. (2009). Onset of efficacy of long-lasting psychostimulants in pediatric attention-deficit/hyperactivity disorder. *Postgraduate Medicine, 120*, 69–88.

Brandstädter, J. (1999). Sources of resilience in the aging self: Toward integrated perspectives. In T. M. Hess & R. Blanchard-Fields (Eds.), *Social cognition and aging*. San Diego: Academic Press.

Brandstädter, J., & Renner, G. (1990). Tenacious goal pursuit and flexible goal adjustment: Explication and age-related analysis of assimilative and accommodative strategies of coping. *Psychology and Aging, 5*, 58–67.

Bransford, J., & others. (2006). Learning theories in education. In P. A. Alexander & P. H. Winne (Eds.), *Handbook of educational psychology* (2nd ed.). Mahwah, NJ: Erlbaum.

Brazelton, T. B. (1956). Sucking in infancy. *Pediatrics, 17*, 400–404.

Breheny, M., & Stephens C. (2004). Barriers to effective contraception and strategies for overcoming them among adolescent mothers. *Public Health Nursing, 21*, 220–227.

Brendgen, R. M. (2009). Aggression, childhood and adolescence. In D. Carr (Ed.), *Encyclopedia of the life course and human development*. Boston: Gale Cengage.

Brenes, G. A., Williamson, J. D., Messier, S. P., Rejeski, W. J., Pahor, M., Ip, E., & Penninx, B. W. (2007). Treatment of minor depression in older adults: A pilot study comparing sertraline and exercise. *Aging and Mental Health, 11*, 61–68.

Brennan, M., Horowitz, A., & Su, Y. P. (2005). Dual sensory loss and its impact on everyay competence. *Gerontologist, 45*, 337–346.

Brent, R. L. (2009). Saving lives and changing family histories: Appropriate counseling of pregnant women and men and women of reproductive age concerning the risk of diagnostic radiation exposure during and before pregnancy. *American Journal of Obstetrics and Gynecology, 200*, 4–24.

Bretherton, I., & Munholland, K. A. (2008). Internal working models in attachment relationships: Elaborating a central construct in attachment theory. In J. Cassidy & P. R. Shaver (Eds.), *Handbook of attachment* (2nd ed.). New York: Guilford.

Bretherton, I., Stolberg, U., & Kreye, M. (1981). Engaging strangers in proximal interaction: Infants' social initiative. *Developmental Psychology, 17*, 746–755.

Brewer, M. B., & Campbell, D. T. (1976). *Ethnocentrism and intergroup attitudes.* New York: Wiley.

Brewster, K. L., & Harker Tillman, K. (2008). Who's doing it? Patterns and predictors of youths' oral sexual experiences. *Journal of Adolescent Health, 42*, 73–80.

Bridgeland, J. M., Dilulio, J. J., & Wulsin, S. C. (2008). *Engaged for success.* Washington, DC: Civic Enterprises.

Bridgett, D. J., Gartstein, M. A., Putnam, S. P., McKay, T., Iddins, E., Robertson, C., Ramsay, K., & Rittmueller, A. (2009). Maternal and contextual influences and the effect of temperament development during infancy on parenting in toddlerhood. *Infant Behavior and Development, 32*, 103–116.

Bril, B. (1999). Dires sur l'enfant selon les cultures. Etat des lieux et perspectives. In B. Brill, P. R. Dasen, C. Sabatier, & B. Krewer (Eds.), *Propos sur l'enfant et l'adolescent. Quels enfants pour quelles cultures?* Paris: L'Harmattan.

Brim, G., Ryff, C. D., & Kessler, R. (Eds.). (2004). *How healthy we are: A national study of well-being in midlife.* Chicago: University of Chicago Press.

Brim, O. (1999). *The MacArthur Foundation study of midlife development.* Vero Beach, FL: MacArthur Foundation.

Brislin, R. (1993). *Understanding culture's influence on behavior.* Fort Worth, TX: Harcourt Brace.

Brock, G., Glina, S., Moncada, I., Watts, S., Xu, L., Wolka, A., & Kopernicky, V. (2009). Likelihood of tadalafil-associated adverse events in integrated multiclinical trial datadase: Classification tree analysis in men with erectile dysfunction. *Urology, 73*, 756–761.

Brodsky, J. L., Viner-Brown, S., & Handler, A. S. (2009, in press). Changes in maternal cigarette smoking among pregnant WIC participants in Rhode Island. *Maternal and Child Health Journal.*

Brody, N. (2000). Intelligence. In A. Kazdin (Ed.), *Encyclopedia of psychology.* Washington, DC, & New York: American Psychological Association and Oxford University Press.

Brody, N. (2007). Does education influence intelligence? In P. C. Kyllonen, R. D. Roberts, & L. Stankov (Eds.), *Extending intelligence.* Mahwah, NJ: Erlbaum.

Brodzinsky, D. M., & Pinderhughes, E. (2002). Parenting and child development in adoptive families. In M. H. Bornstein (Ed.), *Handbook of parenting* (Vol. 1). Mahwah, NJ: Erlbaum.

Bronfenbrenner, U. (1986). Ecology of the family as a context for human development: Research perspectives. *Developmental Psychology, 22*, 723–742.

Bronfenbrenner, U. (2004). *Making human beings human.* Thousand Oaks, CA: Sage.

Bronfenbrenner, U., & Morris, P. (1998). The ecology of developmental processes. In W. Damon (Ed.), *Handbook of child psychology* (5th ed., Vol. 1). New York: Wiley.

Bronfenbrenner, U., & Morris, P. A. (2006). The ecology of developmental processes. In W. Damon & R. Lerner (Eds.), *Handbook of child psychology* (6th ed.). New York: Wiley.

Bronstein, P. (2006). The family environment: Where gender role socialization begins. In J. Worell & C. D. Goodheart (Eds.), *Handbook of girls' and women's psychological health.* New York: Oxford University Press.

Brook, J. S., Brook, D. W., Gordon, A. S., Whiteman, M., & Cohen, P. (1990). The psychological etiology of adolescent drug use: A family interactional approach. *Genetic, Social, and General Psychology Monographs, 116*, 110–267.

Brooker, R. J. (2009). *Genetics* (3rd ed.). New York: McGraw-Hill.

Brooks, J. G., & Brooks, M. G. (1993). *The case for constructivist classrooms.* Alexandra VA: Association for Supervision and Curriculum.

Brooks, J. G., & Brooks, M. G. (2001). *The case for constructivist classrooms* (2nd ed.). Upper Saddle River, NJ: Erlbaum.

Brooks, R., & Meltzoff, A. N. (2005). The development of gaze in relation to language. *Developmental Science, 8*, 535–543.

Brooks-Gunn, J. (2003). Do you believe in magic?: What we can expect from early childhood programs. *Social Policy Report of the Society for Research in Child Development, XVII* (No. 1), 1–13.

Brooks-Gunn, J., & Warren, M. P. (1989). The psychological significance of secondary sexual characteristics in 9- to 11-year-girls. *Child Development 59*, 161–169.

Brookshear, J. G. (2009). *Computer science* (10th ed.). Upper Saddle River, NJ: Addison-Wesley.

Broverman, I., Vogel, S., Broverman, D., Clarkson, F., & Rosenkranz, P. (1972). Sex-role stereotypes: A current appraisal. *Journal of Social Issues, 28*, 59–78.

Brown, A. L. (1990). Domain-specific principles affect learning and transfer in children. *Cognitive Science, 14*, 107–133.

Brown, A. L., Kane, M. J., & Echols, K. (1986). Young children's mental models determine analogical transfer across problems with a common goal structure. *Cognitive Development 1*, 103–122.

Brown, B. B. (1999). Measuring the peer environment of American adolescents. In S. L. Friedman & T. D. Wachs (Eds.), *Measuring environment across the life span*. Washington, DC: American Psychological Association.

Brown, B. B., Bakken, J. P., Ameringer, S. W., & Mahon, S. D. (2008). A comprehensive conceptualization of the peer influence process in adolescence. In M. J. Prinstein & K. A. Dodge (Eds.), *Understanding peer influence in children and adolescents*. New York: Guilford.

Brown, B. B., & Dietz, E. L. (2009). Informal peer groups in middle childhood and adolescence. In K. H. Rubin, W. M. Bukowski, & B. Laursen (Eds.), *Handbook of peer interactions, relationships, and groups*. New York: Guilford.

Brown, B. B., & Larson, J. (2009). Peer relationships in adolescence. In R. M. Lerner & L. Steinberg (Eds.), *Handbook of adolescent psychology*, (3rd ed.). New York: Wiley.

Brown, B. B., & Larson, R. W. (2002). The kaleidoscope of adolescence: Experiences of the world's youth at the beginning of the 21st century. In B. B. Brown, R. W. Larson, & T. S. Saraswathi (Eds.), *The world's youth*. New York: Cambridge University Press.

Brown, B. B., & Lohr, M. J. (1987). Peergroup affiliation and adolescent self-esteem: An integration of ego-identity and symbolic-interaction theories. *Journal of Personality and Social Psychology, 52*, 47–55.

Brown, J. D., & Strasburger, V. C. (2007). From Calvin Klein to Paris Hilton and MySpace: adolescents, sex, and the media. *Adolescent Medicine: State of the Art Reviews, 18*, 484–507.

Brown, L. S. (1989). New voices, new visions: Toward a lesbian/gay paradigm for psychology. *Psychology of Women Quarterly, 13*, 445–458.

Brown, M., Keynes, R., & Lumsden, A. (2001). *The developing brain*. New York: Oxford University Press.

Brown, R. (1958). *Words and things*. Glencoe, IL: Free Press.

Brown, R. (1973). *A first language: The early stages*. Cambridge, MA: Harvard University Press.

Brown, S. L., Brown, R. M., House, J. S., & Smith, D. M. (2008). Coping with spousal loss: Potential buffering effects of self-reported helping behavior. *Personality and Social Psychology Bulletin, 34*, 849–861.

Brown, S. L., Lee, G. R., & Bulanda, J. R. (2006). Cohabitation among older adults: A national portrait. *Journals of Gerontology B: Psychological Sciences and Social Sciences, 61*, S71–S79.

Brown, S. L., Nesse, R. M., House, J. S., & Utz, R. L. (2004). Religion and emotional compensation: Results from a prospective study of widowhood. *Personality and Social Psychology Bulletin, 30*, 1165–1174.

Brown, S. L., Nesse, R. M., Vinokur, A. D., & Smith, D. M. (2003). Providing social support may be more beneficial than receiving it: Results from a prospective study of mortality. *Psychologial Science, 14*, 320–327.

Brown, W. H., Pfeiffer, K. A., McIver, K. L., Dowda, M., Addy, C. L., & Pate, R. R. (2009). Social and environmental factors associated with preschoolers' nonsedentary physical activity. *Child Development, 80*, 45–58.

Brown-Borg, H. M. (2007). Hormonal regulation of longevity in mammals. *Aging Research Reviews, 6*, 28–45.

Brownell, C. A., Ramani, G. B., & Zerwas, S. (2006). Becoming a social partner with peers: Cooperation and social understanding in one- and two-year-olds. *Child Development, 77*, 803–821.

Brownridge, D. A. (2008). The elevated risk for violence against cohabiting women: A comparison of three nationally representative surveys of Canada. *Violence Against Women, 14*, 809–832.

Bruce, A. (2007). Time(lessness): Buddhist perspectives and end-of-life. *Nursing Philosophy, 8*, 151–157.

Bruce, J. M., Olen, K., & Jensen, S. J. (1999, April). *The role of emotion and regulation in social competence*. Paper presented at the meeting of the Society for Research in Child Development, Albuquerque.

Bruck, M., & Ceci, S. J. (1999). The suggestibility of children's memory. *Annual Review of Psychology, 50*, 419–439.

Bruck, M., Ceci, S. J., & Hembrooke, H. (1998). Reliability and credibility of young children's reports: From research to policy and practice. *American Psychologist, 53* (2), 136–151.

Bruck, M., Ceci, S. J., & Principe, G. F. (2006). The child and the law. In W. Damon & R. Lerner (Eds.), *Handbook of child psychology* (6th ed.). New York: Wiley.

Bruck, M., & Melnyk, L. (2004). Individual differences in children's suggestibility: A review and a synthesis. *Applied Cognitive Psychology. 18*, 947–996.

Bruine de Bruin, W., Parker, A., & Fischhoff, B. (2007). Can teens predict significant life events? *Journal of Adolescent Health, 41*, 208–210.

Brune, C. W., & Woodward, A. L. (2007). Social cognition and social responsiveness in 10-month-old infants. *Journal of Cognition and Development, 2*, 3–27.

Bruner, J. S. (1983). *Child talk*. New York: W. W. Norton.

Bruner, J. S. (1996). *The culture of education*. Cambridge, MA: Harvard University Press.

Bruni, O., Ferri, R., Novelli, L., Finotti, E., Miano, S., & Guilleminault, C. (2008). NREM sleep instability in children with sleep terrors: The role of slow wave activity interruptions. *Clinical Neuropsychology, 119*, 985–992.

Brunstein Klomek, A., Marrocco, F., Kleinman, M., Schofield, I. S., & Gould, M. S. (2007). Bullying, depression, and suicidality in adolescents. *Journal of the American Academy of Child and Adolescent Psychiatry, 46*, 40–49.

Bryant, J. B. (2009). Language in social contexts: Communication competence in the preschool years. In J. Berko Gleason & N. Ratner (Eds.), *The development of language* (7th ed.). Boston: Allyn & Bacon.

Brynes, J. P. (2008). Piaget's cognitive-developmental theory. In M. M. Haith & J. B. Benson (Eds.), *Encyclopedia of infant and early childhood development*. Oxford, UK: Elsevier.

Bucur, B., & Madden, D. J. (2007). Information processing/cognition. In I. E. Birren (Ed.)., *Encyclopedia of gerontology* (2nd ed.). San Diego: Academic Press.

Bucx, F., van Wel, F., Knijn, T., & Hagendoorn, L. (2008). Intergenerational contact and the life course status of young adult children. *Journal of Marriage and the Family, 70*, 144–156.

Buhimschi, C. S., & Weiner, C. P. (2009). Medications in pregnancy and lactation: Part 1. Teratology. *Obstetrics and Gynecology, 113*, 166–188.

Buhrmester, D. (1998). Need fulfillment, interpersonal competence, and the developmental contexts of early adolescent friendship. In W. M. Bukowski & A. F. Newcomb (Eds.), *The company they keep: Friendship in childhood and adolescence*. New York: Cambridge University Press.

Buhrmester, D., & Chong, C. M. (2009). Friendship in adolescence. In H. Reis & S. Sprecher (Eds.), *Encyclopedia of human relationships*. Thousand Oaks, CA: Sage.

Buhs, E. S., & Ladd, G. W. (2002). Peer rejection as antecedent of young children's school adjustment: An examination of mediating processes. *Developmental Psychology, 37*, 550–560.

Bukowski, R., & others. (2008, January). *Folic acid and preterm birth*. Paper presented at the meeting of the Society for Maternal-Fetal Medicine, Dallas.

Bukowski, W. M., Brendgen, M., & Vitaro, F. (2007). Peers and socialization: Effects on externalizing and internalizing problems. In J. E. Grusec & P. D. Hastings (Eds.), *Handbook of socialization*. New York: Guilford.

Bukowski, W. M., Motzoi, C., & Meyer, F. (2009). Friendship as process, function, and outcome. In K. H. Rubin, W. M. Bukowski, & B. Laursen (Eds.), *Handbook of peer interactions, relationships, and groups*. New York: Guilford.

Bulik, C. M., Berkman, N. D., Brownley, K. A., Sedway, J. A., & Lohr, K. N. (2007). Anorexia nervosa treatment: A systematic review of randomized controlled trials. *International Journal of Eating Disorders, 40*, 310–320.

Bullock, M., & Lutkenhaus, P. (1990). Who am I? Self-understanding in toddlers. *Merrill-Palmer Quarterly, 36*, 217–238.

Bumpus, M. F., Crouter, A. C., & McHale, S. M. (2001). Parental autonomy granting during adolescence: Exploring gender differences in context. *Developmental Psychology, 37,* 161–173.

Burchinal, M. (2006). Childcare subsidies, quality, and preferences among low-income families. In N. Cabrera, R. Hutchens, H. E. Peters, & L. Peters (Eds.), *From welfare to child-care.* Mahwah, NJ; Erlbaum.

Burchinal, M. R., Peisner-Feinberg, E., Pianta, R., & Howes, C. (2002). Development of academic skills from preschool through second grade: Family and classroom predictors of developmental trajectories. *Journal of School Psychology, 40* (5), 415–436.

Burgard, S. (2009). Job characteristics and job stress. In D. Carr (Ed.), *Encyclopedia of the life course and human development.* Boston: Gale Cengage.

Burke, D. M., & Shafto, M. A. (2004). Aging and language production. *Current Directions in Psychological Science, 13,* 21–24.

Burke, H. M., Zautra, A. J., Davis, M. C., Schultz, A. S., & Reich, J. W. (2003). Arthritis and musculoskeletal conditions. In I. B. Weiner (Ed.), *Handbook of psychology* (Vol. IX). New York: Wiley.

Burke-Adams, A. (2007). The benefits of equalizing standards and creativity: Discovering a balance in instruction. *Gifted Child Quarterly, 30,* 58–63.

Burns, C., Dunn, A., Brady, M., Starr, N. B., & Blosser, C. (2009). *Pediatric primary care.* Oxford, UK: Elsevier.

Burton, R. V. (1984). A paradox in theories and research in moral development In W. M. Kurtines & J. L. Gewirtz (Eds.), *Morality, moral behavior, and moral development.* New York: Wiley.

Bushnell, I. W. R. (2003). Newborn face recognition. In O. Pascalis & A. Slater (Eds.), *The development of face processing in infancy and early childhood.* New York: NOVA Science.

Buss, D. M. (1995). Psychological sex differences: Origins through sexual selection. *American Psychologist, 50,* 164–168.

Buss, D. M. (2004). *Evolutionary psychology* (2nd ed.). Boston: Allyn & Bacon.

Buss, D. M. (2008). *Evolutionary psychology* (3rd ed.). Boston: Allyn & Bacon.

Buss, D. M., & others. (1990). International preferences in selecting mates: A study of 37 cultures. *Journal of Cross-Cultural Psychology, 21,* 5–47.

Buss, K. A., & Goldsmith, H. H. (2007). Biobehavioral approaches to early socioemotional development. In C. A. Brownell & C. B. Kopp (Eds.), *Socioemotional development in the toddler years.* New York: Guilford.

Bussey, K., & Bandura A. (1999). Social cognitive theory of gender development and differentiation. *Psychological Review, 106,* 676–713.

Butcher, K., Sallis, J. F., Mayer, J. A., & Woodruff, S. (2008). Correlates of physical activity guideline compliance for adolescents in 100 cities. *Journal of Adolescent Health, 42,* 360–368.

Butler, R. N. (2007). Life review. In J. E. Birren (Ed.), *Encyclopedia of gerontology* (2nd ed.). San Diego: Academic Press.

Butler, R. N., & Lewis, M. (2002). *The new love and sex after 60.* New York: Ballentine.

Buzwell, S., & Rosenthal, D. (1996). Constructing a sexual self: Adolescents' sexual self-perceptions and sexual risk-taking. *Journal of Research on Adolescence, 6,* 489–513.

Bybee, R. W., Powell, J. C., & Trowbridge, L. W. (2008). *Teaching secondary science* (9th ed.). Upper Saddle River, NJ: Prentice Hall.

Byrd-Williams, C. E., Shaibi, G. Q., Sun, P., Lane, C. J., Ventura, E. E., Davis, J. N., Kelly, L. A., & Goran, M. I. (2008). Cardiorespiratory fitness predicts change in adiposity in overwight Hispanic boys. *Obesity, 16,* 1072–1077.

Byrnes, J. P. (2008). Piaget's cognitive developmental theory. In M. M. Haith & J. B. Benson (Eds.), *Encyclopedia of infant and early childhood development.* Oxford, UK: Elsevier.

C

Cabeza, R. (2002). Hemispheric asymmetry reduction in older adults: The HAROLD model. *Psychology and Aging, 17,* 85–100.

Cabeza, R., Nyberg, L., & Park, D. (Eds.). (2009). *Cognitive neuroscience of aging.* New York: Oxford University Press.

Cabrera, N., Hutchens, R., & Peters, H. E. (Eds.). (2006). *From welfare to childcare.* Mahwah, NJ: Erlbaum.

Cacioppo, J. T., Hughes, M. E., Waite, L. J., Hawkley, L. C., & Thisted, R. A. (2006). Loneliness as a specific risk factor for depressive symptoms: Cross-sectional and longitudinal analyses. *Psychology and Aging, 21,* 140–151.

Cahill, L., Haier, R. J., White, N. S., Fallen, J., Kilparaick, L., Lawrence, C., Potkin, S. G., & Alkire, M. T. (2001). Sex-related differences in amygdala activity during emotionally influenced memory storage. *Neurobiology of Learning and Memory, 75,* 1–9.

Caley, L., Syms, C., Robinson, L., Cederbaum, J., Henry, M., & Shipkey, N. (2008). What human service professionals know and want to know about fetal alcohol syndrome. *Canadian Journal of Clinical Pharmacology, 15,* e117–e123.

Calkins, S. D. (2007). The emergence of self-regulation: Biological and behavioral control mechanisms supporting toddler competencies. In C. A. Brownell & C. B. Kopp (Eds.), *Socioemotional development in the toddler years.* New York: Guilford.

Callahan, D. (2009). Death, mourning, and medical progress. *Perspectives in Biology and Medicine, 52,* 103–115.

Callahan, R., & Colomer, S. (2009). Bilingual education. In D. Carr (Ed.), *Encyclopedia of the life course and human development.* Boston: Gale Cengage.

Callaway, L. K., Lust, K., & McIntyre, H. D. (2005). Pregnancy outcomes in women of very advanced maternal age. *Obstetric and Gynecology Survey, 60,* 562–563.

Callisaya, M. L., Blizzard, L., Schmidt, M. D., McGinley, J. L., & Srikanth, V. K. (2008). Sex modifies the relationship between age and gait: A population-based study of older adults. *Journals of Gerontology A: Biological Sciences and Medical Sciences, 63,* 165–170.

Calzada, E. J., Brotman, L. M., Huang, K. Y., Bat-Chava, Y., & Kingston, S. (2009). Parent cultural adaptation and child functioning in culturally diverse, urban families of preschoolers. *Journal of Applied Developmental Psychology, 30,* 515–524.

Camarata, S., & Woodock, R. W. (2006). Sex differences in processing speed: Developmental effects in males and females. *Intelligence, 34,* 231–252.

Cameron, J., & Pierce, D. (2008). Intrinsic versus extrinsic motivation. In N. J. Salkind (Ed.), *Encyclopedia of educational psychology.* Thousand Oaks, CA: Sage.

Campa, M. I., Hazan, C., & Wolfe, J. E. (2009). The form and function of attachment behavior in the daily lives of young adults. *Social Development, 18,* 288–304.

Campbell, C. A. (2009). AIDS. In D. Carr (Ed.), *Encyclopedia of the life course and human development.* Boston: Gale Cengage.

Campbell, D. A., Lake, M. F., Falk, M., & Backstrand, J. R. (2006). A randomized controlled trial of continuous support by a lay doula. *Journal of Obstetrics and Gynecology: Neonatal Nursing, 35,* 456–464.

Campbell, D. T., & LeVine, K. A. (1968). Ethnocentrism and intergroup relations. In R. Abelson & others (Eds.), *Theories and cognitive consistency: A sourcebook.* Chicago: Rand-McNally.

Campbell, F. A. (2007). The malleability of the cognitive development of children of low-income African-American families: Intellectual test performance over twenty-one years. In P. C. Kyllonen, R. D. Roberts, & L. Stankov (Eds.), *Extending intelligence.* Mahwah, NJ: Erlbaum.

Campbell, F. A., Pungello, E. P., Miller-Johnson, S., Burchinal, M., & Ramey, C. T. (2001). The development of cognitive and academic abilities: Growth curves from an early childhood educational experiment. *Developmental Psychology, 37,* 231–243.

Campbell, J. D., Yoon, D. P., & Johnstone, B. (2009, in press). Determining relationship between physical health and spiritual experience, religious practices, and congregational support in a heterogeneous sample. *Journal of Religion and Health.*

Campbell, L., Campbell, B., & Dickinson, D. (2004). *Teaching and learning through multiple intelligence* (3rd ed.). Boston: Allyn & Bacon.

Campos, J. (2005). Unpublished review of J. W. Santrock's *Life-span development,* 11th ed. (New York: McGraw-Hill).

Campos, J. J., Langer, A., & Krowitz, A. (1970). Cardiac responses on the visual cliff in prelocomotor human infants. *Science, 170,* 196–197.

Candow, D. G., & Chilibeck, P. O. (2005). Differences in size, strength, and power of upper and lower body muscle groups in young and older men. *Journals of Gerontology A: Biological Sciences and Medical Sciences, 60,* 148A–156A.

Canfield, R. L., & Haith, M. M. (1991). Young infants' visual expectations for symmetric and asymmetric stimulus sequences. *Developmental Psychology, 27,* 198–208.

Cansino, S. (2009). Episodic memory decay along the adult lifespan: A review of behavioral and neurophysiological evidence. *International Journal of Psychophysiology, 71,* 64–69.

Capaldi, D. M., Stoolmiller, M., Clark, S., & Owen, L. D. (2002). Heterosexual risk behaviors in at-risk young men from early adolescence to young adulthood: Prevalence, prediction, and association with STD contraction. *Developmental Psychology, 38,* 394–406.

Cardelle-Elawar, M. (1992). Effects of teaching metacognitive skills to students with low mathematics ability. *Teaching and Teacher Education, 8* (2), 109–121.

Carey, D. P. (2007). Is bigger really better? The search for brain size and intelligence in the twenty-first century. In S. Della Sala (Ed.), *Tall tales about the mind and brain: Separating fact from fiction.* Oxford, UK: Oxford University Press.

Carlsen, K. H., & Carlsen, K. C. (2008). Respiratory effects of tobacco smoking on infants and young children. *Pediatric Respiratory Reviews, 9,* 11–20.

Carlson, S. M., & Zelazo, P. D. (2008). Symbolic thought. In M. M. Haith & J. B. Benson (Eds.), *Encyclopedia of infant and early childhood development.* Oxford, UK: Elsevier.

Carnagey, N. L., Anderson, C. A., & Bushman, B. J. (2007). The effect of video game violence on physiological desensitization to real-life violence. *Journal of Experimental Social Psychology, 43,* 489–496.

Carnegie Foundation. (1989). *Turning points: Preparing youth for the 21st century.* New York: Author.

Caron, S. (2007). *Sex matters for college students* (2nd ed.). Upper Saddle River, NJ: Prentice Hall.

Carpendale, J. I., & Chandler, M. J. (1996). On the distinction between false belief understanding and subscribing to an interpretive theory of mind. *Child Development, 67,* 1686–1706.

Carpendale, J. I. M., Muller, U., & Bibok, M. B. (2008). Piaget's theory of cognitive development. In N. J. Salkind (Ed.), *Encyclopedia of educational psychology.* Thousand Oaks, CA: Sage.

Carr, D. (2008) Character education as the cultivation of virtue. In L. Nucci & D. Narváez (Eds.), *Handbook of moral and character education.* Clifton, NJ: Psychology Press.

Carr, D. (2009). Death and dying. In D. Carr (Ed.). *Encyclopedia of the life and course and human development.* Boston: Gale Cengage.

Carr, D., & Khodyakov, D. (2007). End-of-life health care planning among young-old adults: An assessment of psychosocial influences. *Journals of Gerontology B: Psychological Sciences and Social Sciences, 62,* S135–S141.

Carrell, S. E, Malmstrom, F. V., & West, J. E. (2008). Peer effects in academic cheating. *Journal of Human Resources, 43,* 173–207.

Carroll, J. (1993). *Human cognitive abilities.* New York: Cambridge University Press.

Carroll, J. L. (2007). *Sexuality now* (2nd ed.). Belmont, CA: Wadsworth.

Carroll, J. L. (2010). *Sexuality now* (3rd ed.). Boston: Cengage.

Carskadon, M. A. (Ed.). (2002). *Adolescent sleep patterns.* New York: Cambridge University Press.

Carskadson, M. A. (2004). Sleep difficulties in young people. *Archives of Pediatric and Adolescent Health, 158,* 597–598.

Carskadon, M. A. (2005). Sleep and circadian rhythms in children and adolescents: Relevance for athletic performance of young people. *Clinical Sports Medicine, 24,* 319–328.

Carskadon, M. A. (2006, April). *Adolescent sleep: The perfect storm.* Paper presented at the meeting of the Society for Research on Adolescence, San Francisco.

Carstensen, L. L. (1991). Selectivity theory: Social activity in life-span context. *Annual Review of Gerontology and Geriatrics, 11,* 195–217.

Carstensen, L. L. (1998). A life-span approach to social motivation. In J. Heckhausen & C. Dweck (Eds.), *Motivation and self-regulation across the life span.* New York: Cambridge University Press.

Carstensen, L. L. (2006). The influence of a sense of time on human development. *Science, 312,* 1913–1915.

Carstensen, L. L. (2008, May). *Long life in the 21st century.* Paper presented at the meeting of the Association for Psychological Science, Chicago.

Carstensen, L. L., & Freund, A. M. (1994). Commentary: The resilience of the aging self. *Developmental Review, 14,* 81–92.

Carstensen, L. L., Mikels, J. A., & Mather, M. (2006). Aging and the intersection of cognition, motivation and emotion. In J. Birren & K. W. Schaie (Eds.), *Handbook of the psychology of aging* (6th ed.). San Diego: Academic Press.

Carter, N., Prater, M. A., & Dyches, T. T. (2009). *What every teacher should know about: Adaptations and accommodations for students with mild to moderate disabilities.* Upper Saddle River, NJ: Prentice Hall.

Cartwright, R., Agargun, M. Y., Kirkby, J., & Friedman, J. K. (2006). Relation of dreams to waking concerns. *Psychiatry Research, 141,* 261–270.

Carvalho Bos, S., & others. (2009). Sleep and behavioral/emotional problems in children: A population-based study. *Sleep Medicine, 10,* 66–74.

Carver, K., Joyner, K., & Udry, J. R. (2003). National estimates of adolescent romantic relationships. In P. Florsheim (Ed.), *Adolescent romantic relationships and sexual behavior.* Mahwah, NJ: Erlbaum.

CASA. (2007). *The importance of family dinners IV.* New York: National Center for Addiction and Substance Abuse, Columbia University.

Case, R. (1987). Neo-Piagetian theory. Retrospect and prospect. *International Journal of Psychology, 22,* 773–791.

Case, R. (1999). Conceptual development in the child and the field: A personal view of the Piagetian legacy. In E. K. Skolnick, K. Nelson, S. A. Gelman, & P. H. Miller (Eds.), *Conceptual development.* Mahwah, NJ: Erlbaum.

Case, R., Kurland, D. M., & Goldberg, J. (1982). Operational efficiency and the growth of short-term memory span. *Journal of Experimental Child Psychology, 33,* 386–404.

Casey, B. J., Getz, S., & Galvan, A. (2008). The adolescent brain. *Developmental Review, 28,* 42–77.

Casey, B. J., Jones, R. M., & Hare, T. A. (2008). The adolescent brain. *Annals of the New York Academy of Sciences, 1124,* 111–126.

Casey, P. H. (2008). Growth of low birth weight preterm children. *Seminars in Perinatology, 32,* 20–27.

Caspers, K. M., Paraiso, S., Yucuis, R., Troutman, B., Arndt, S., & Philibert, R. (2009). Association between the serotonin transporter polymorphism (5-HTTLPR) and adult unresolved attachment. *Developmental Psychology, 45,* 64–76.

Caspi, A. (1998). Personality development across the life course. In W. Damon (Ed.), *Handbook of child psychology* (Vol. 3). New York: Wiley.

Caspi, A., & Roberts, B. W. (2001). Personality development across the life course: The argument for change and continuity. *Psychological Inquiry, 12,* 49–66.

Caspi, A., Sugden, K., Moffitt, T. E., Taylor, A., Craig, I., Harrington, H., McClay, J., Mill, J., Martin, J., Braithwaite, A., & Poulton, R. (2003). Influence of life stress on depression: Moderation by a polymorphism in the 5-HTT gene. *Science, 301,* 386–389.

Cassidy, J. (2008). The nature of the child's ties. In J. Cassidy & P. R. Shaver (Eds.), *Handbook of attachment* (2nd ed.). New York: Guilford.

Catalano, R. F., Hawkins, J. D., & Toumbourou, J. W. (2008). Positive youth development in the United States: History, efficacy, and links to moral and character education. In L. Nucci & D. Narváez (Eds.), *Handbook of moral and character education.* Clifton, NJ: Psychology Press.

Cavanagh, S. E. (2009). Puberty. In D. Carr (Ed.), *Encyclopedia of the life course and human development.* Boston: Gale Cengage.

Cave, R. K. (2002, August). *Early adolescent language: A content analysis of child development and educational psychology textbooks.* Unpublished doctoral dissertation, University of Nevada–Reno, Reno, NV.

Cavell, T. A., Hymel, S., Malcolm, K. T., & Seay, A. (2007). Socialization and interventions for antisocial youth. In J. E. Grusec & P. D. Hastings (Eds.), *Handbook of socialization.* New York: Gulford.

Ceci, S. J. (2000). Bronfenbrenner, Urie. In A. Kazdin (ed.), *Encyclopedia of psychology.* Washington, DC, & New York: American Psychological Association and Oxford University Press.

Ceci, S. J., & Gilstrap, L. L. (2000). Determinants of intelligence: Schooling and intelligence. In A. Kazdin (Ed.), *Encyclopedia of psychology.* Washington, DC, & New York: American Psychological Association and Oxford University Press.

Ceci, S. J., Paierno, P. B., & Kulkovsky, S. (2007). Representational constraints on children's suggestibility. *Psychological Science, 18,* 503–509.

Center for Survey Research at the University of Connecticut. (2000). *Hours on the job.* Storrs: Author.

Centers for Disease Control and Prevention. (2008). *Aging.* Atlanta: Author.

Centers for Disease Control and Prevention. (2003). Births: Final data for 2002. *National Vital Statistics Reports, 52* (10), 1–5.

Centers for Disease Control and Prevention. (2008). *National Health Interview Study,* Atlanta: Author.

Centers for Disease Control and Prevention. (2008). *Sexually transmitted diseases.* Atlanta: Author.

Centers for Disease Control and Prevention. (2009). *Autism and developmental disabilities monitoring (ADDM) network.* Atlanta: Author.

Centers for Disease Control and Prevention. (2009). *Autism.* Atlanta: Author.

Centers for Disease Control and Prevention. (2009). *Body mass index for children and teens.* Atlanta: Author.

Centers for Disease Controls and Prevention. (2008). *SIDS.* Retrieved April 26, 2008, from www.cdc.gov/SIDS/index.htm

Cepeda, M. S., Carr, D. B., Lau, J., & Alvarez, H. (2006). Music for pain relief. *Cochrane Database of Systematic Reviews, 2,* CD004843.

Cetin, I., & Alvino, G. (2009). Intrauterine growth restriction: Implications for placental metabolism and transport: A review. *Placenta, 30,* 577–582.

Chaillet, N., & Dumont, A. (2007). Evidence-based strategies for reducing cesarean section rates: A meta-analysis. *Birth, 34,* 53–64.

Chambers, B., Cheung, A. C. K., & Slavin, R. F. (2006). Effective preschool programs for children at risk of school failure: A best-evidence synthesis. In B. Spodek & O. N. Saracho (Eds.), *Handbook of research on the education of young children.* Mahwah, NJ: Erlbaum.

Chan, C. (2008). Childhood obesity and adverse health effects in Hong Kong. *Obesity Reveiws, 9* (Suppl. 1), S87–S90.

Chandler, M. (1973). Egocentrism and antisocial behavior: The assessment and training of social perspective-taking skills. *Developmental Psychology, 9,* 326–332.

Chang, J. S. (2009). Parental smoking and childhood leukemia. *Methods in Molecular Biology, 472,* 103–137.

Chang, M. Y., Chen, C. H., & Huang, K. F. (2006). A comparison of massage effects on labor pain using the McGill Pain Questionnaire. *Journal of Nursing Research, 14,* 190–197.

Chao, R. K. (2005, April). *The importance of Guan in describing control of immigrant Chinese.* Paper presented at the meeting of the Society for Research in Child Development, Atlanta.

Chao, R. K. (2007, March). *Research with Asian Americans: Looking back and moving forward.* Paper presented at the meeting of the Society for Research in Child Development, Boston.

Chao, R., & Tseng, V. (2002). Parenting of Asians. In M. H. Bornstein, (Ed.), *Handbook of parenting* (Vol. 4, 2nd ed.). Mahwah, NJ: Erlbaum.

Charles, S. C., & Piazza, J. R. (2007). Memories of social interactions: Age differences in emotional intensity. *Psychology and Aging, 22,* 300–309.

Charles, S. T., & Carstensen, L. L. (2007). Emotion and aging. In J. J. Gross (Ed.), *Handbook of emotion regulation.* New York: Gulford.

Charles, S. T., & Carstensen, L. L. (2009). Socioemotional selectivity theory. In H. Reis & S. Sprecher (Eds.), *Encyclopedia of human relationships.* Thousand Oaks, CA: Sage.

Charles, S. T., & Carstensen, L. L. (2010). Social and emotional aging. *Annual Review of Psychology,* Vol. 61. Palo Alto, CA: Annual Reviews.

Charles, S. T., Reynolds, C. A., & Gatz, M. (2001). Age-related differences and change in positive and negative affect over 23 years. *Journal of Personality and Social Psychology, 80,* 136–151.

Charness, N., & Bosman, E. A. (1992). Human factors and aging. In F. I. M. Craik & T. A. Salthouse (Eds.), *The handbook of aging and cognition.* Hillsdale, NJ: Erlbaum.

Chassin, L., Hussong, A., & Beltran, I. (2009). Adolescent substance use. In R. M. Lerner & L. Steinberg (Eds.), *Handbook of adolescent psychology* (3rd ed.). New York: Wiley.

Chassin, L., Presson, C., Seo, D. C., Sherman, S. J., Macy, J., Wirth, R. J., & Curran, P.

(2008). Multiple trajectories of cigarette smoking and the intergenerational transmission of smoking: A multigenerational, longitudinal study of a midwestern community sample. *Health Psychology, 27,* 819–828.

Chaytor, N., & Schmitter-Edgecombe, M. (2004). Working memory and aging: A cross-sectional and longitudinal analysis using a self-ordered pointing task. *Journal of the International Neuropsychological Society, 10,* 489–503.

Chehab, O., Quertani, M., Souiden, Y., Chaieb, K., & Mahdouani, K. (2008). Plasma antioxidants and human aging: A study on a health elderly Tunisian population. *Molecular Biotechnology, 40,* 27–37.

Chen, C., & Stevenson, H. W. (1989). Homework: A cross-cultural examination. *Child Development, 60,* 551–561.

Chen D., & Guarente, L. (2007). SIR2: A potential target for calorie restriction mimetics. *Trends in Molecular Medicine, 13,* 64–71.

Chen, M. Y., Liou, Y. M., & Wu, J. Y. (2008). The relationship between TV/computer time and adolescents' health-promoting behavior: A secondary data analysis. *Journal of Nursing Research, 16,* 75–85.

Chen, M. Y., Wang, E. K., & Jeng, Y. J. (2006). Adequate sleep among adolescents is positively associated with health status and health-related behaviors. *BMC Public Health, 6,* 59.

Chen, X., Hastings, P. D., Rubin, K. H., Chen, H., Cen, G., & Stewart, S. L. (1998). Childrearing attitudes and behavioral inhibition in Chinese and Canadian toddlers: A cross-cultural study. *Developmental Psychology, 34,* 677–686.

Chen, X., & others. (2009). Interactions of IL-12A and IL-12B polymorphisms on the risk of cervical cancer in Chinese women. *Clinical Cancer Research, 15,* 400–405.

Chen, Z. Y. (2009a). Parenting style. In D. Carr (Ed.), *Encyclopedia of the life course and human development.* Boston: Gale Cengage.

Chen, Z. Y. (2009b). Parent-child relationships, childhood, and adolescence. In D. Carr (Ed.), *Encyclopedia of the life course and human development.* Boston: Gale Cengage.

Cheng, M. H., Lee, S. J., Wang, P. M., & Fuh, J. L. (2007). Does menopausal transition affect the quality of life? A longitudinal study of middle-aged women in Kinmen. *Menopause, 14,* 885–90.

Cheok, M. H., Pottier, N., Kager, L., & Evans, W. E. (2009). Pharmacogenetics in acute lymphoblastic leukemia. *Seminars in Hematology, 46,* 39–51.

Cherkas, L. F., & others. (2008). The association between physical activity in leisure time and leukocyte telomere length. *Archives of Internal Medicine, 168,* 154–158.

Cherlin, A. J., & Furstenberg, F. F. (1994). Stepfamilies in the United States: A reconsideration. In J. Blake & J. Hagen (Eds.), *Annual*

Review of Sociology (Vol. 20) Palo Alto, CA: Annual Reviews.

Chess, S., & Thomas, A. (1977). Temperamental individuality from childhood to adolescence. *Journal of Child Psychiatry, 16,* 218–226.

Chi, M. T. (1978). Knowledge structures and memory development In R. S. Siegler (Ed.), *Children's thinking. What develops?* Hillsdale, NJ: Erlbaum.

Chiappe, D., & MacDonald, K. (2005). The evolution of domain-general mechanisms in intelligence and learning. *Journal of General Psychology, 132,* 5–40.

Chia, P., Sellick, K., & Gan, S. (2006). The attitudes and practices of neonatal nurses in the use of kangaroo care. *Australian Journal of Advanced Nursing, 23,* 20–27.

Chiappetta, E. L., & Koballa, T. R. (2010). *Science instruction in the middle and secondary schools* (7th ed.). Boston: Allyn & Bacon.

Chiba, T. & others. (2009). Amyloid-beta causes of memory impairment by disturbing the JAK2/STAT3 axis in hippocampal neurons. *Molecular Psychiatry, 14,* 206–222.

Childers, J. B., & Tomasello, M. (2002). Two-year-olds learn novel nouns, verbs, and conventional actions from massed or distributed exposures. *Developmental Psychology, 38,* 967–978.

Children's Defense Fund. (1992). *The state of America's children, 1992.* Washington, DC: Author.

Children's Defense Fund. (2008). *Children's welfare and mental health.* Retrieved November 8, 2008, from www.childrensdefense.org

Children's Defense Fund. (2009). *Policy initiatives.* Retrieved January 26, 2009, from www.childrensdefense.org

Children's Defense Fund. (2009). *The state of America's children, 2009.* Washington, DC: Author.

Child Trends. (2006). *Facts at a glance.* Washington, DC: Author.

Child Trends. (2008, July). *Facts at a glance.* Washington, DC: Author.

Chiroro, P., Bohner, G., Viki, G. T., & Jarvis, C. I. (2004). Rape myth acceptance and rape proclivity: Expected dominance versus expected arousal as mediators in acquaintance rape situations. *Journal of Interpersonal Violence, 19,* 427–442.

Chiu, M. M. (2007). Families, economies, cultures, and science achievements in 41 countries: Country-, school-, and student-level analyses. *Journal of Family Psychology, 21,* 510–519.

Chodosh, J., Kado, D. M., Seeman, T. E., & Karlamangla, A. S. (2007). Depressive symptoms as a predictor of cognitive decline: MacArthur Studies of Successful Aging. *American Journal of Geriatric Psychiatry, 15,* 406–415.

Choi, N. G., & Jun, J. (2009). Life regrets and pride among low-income older adults: Relationships with depressive symptoms, current life stressors, and coping resources. *Aging and Mental Health, 13,* 213–225.

Choi, S. & Gopnik, A. (1995). Early acquisition of verbs in Korean: A cross-linguistic study. *Journal of Child Language, 22,* 497–529.

Chomsky, N. (1957). *Syntactic structures.* The Hague: Mouton.

Chouinard, R., Karsenti, T., & Roy, N. (2007). Relations among competence beliefs, utility value, achievement goals, and effort in mathematics. *British Journal of Educational Psychology, 77,* 501–517.

Christakis, N. A., & Iwashyna, T. J. (2003). The health impact of health care on families: A matched cohort study of hospice use by decedents and mortality outcomes in surviving, widowed spouses. *Social Science and Medicine, 57,* 465–475.

Chu, S. Y., Callaghan, W. M., Bish, C. L., & D'Angelo, D. (2009). Gestational weight gain by body mass index among U.S. women delivering live births, 2004–2005: Fueling future obesity. *American Journal of Obstetrics and Gynecology, 200,* e1–e7.

Chung, J. K., Park, S. H., Lee, W. J., & Lee, S. J. (2009). Bilateral cataract surgery: A controlled clinical trial. *Japan Journal of Ophthalmology, 53,* 107–113.

Cicchetti, D., & Rogosch, F. A. (2009, in press). Adaptive coping under conditions of extreme stress: Multi-level influences on the determinants of resilience in maltreated children. In E. Skinner & M. J. Zimmer-Gembeck (Eds.), *Coping and the development of regulation. New Directions in Child and Adolescent Development,* San Francisco: Jossey-Bass.

Cicchetti, D., & Toth, S. L. (2006). Developmental psychopathology and preventive intervention. In W. Damon & R. Lerner (Eds.), *Handbook of child psychology* (6th ed.). New York: Wiley.

Cicchetti, D., Toth, S. L., Nilsen, W. J., & Manly, J. T. (2010, in press). What do we know and why does it matter? The dissemination of evidence-based interventions for child maltreatment. In H. R. Schaffer & K. Durkin (Eds.), *Blackwell handbook of developmental psychology in action.* Oxford, UK: Blackwell.

Cicchetti, D., Toth, S. L., & Rogusch, F. A. (2005). *A prevention program for child maltreatment.* Unpublished manuscript, University of Rochester, Rochester, NY.

Cicirelli, V. G. (1991). Sibling relationships in adulthood. *Marriage and Family Review, 16,* 291–310.

Cicirelli, V. G. (1994). Sibling relationships in cross-cultural perspective. *Journal of Marriage and Family, 56,* 7–20.

Cicirelli, V. G. (2009). Sibling relationships, later life. In D. Carr (Ed.), *Encyclopedia of the life course and human development.* Boston: Gale Cengage.

Cillessen, A. H. N. (2009). Sociometric methods. In K. H. Rubin, W. M. Bukowski, & B. Laursen (Eds.), *Handbook of peer interactions, relationships, and groups.* New York: Guilford.

Cimarolli, V. R. (2009). Sensory impairments. In D. Carr (Ed.), *Encyclopedia of the life course and human development.* Gale Cengage.

Ciol, M. A., Shumway-Cook, A., Hoffman, J. M., Yorkston, K. M., Dudgeon, B. J., & Chan, L. (2008). Minority disparities in disability between Medicare beneficiaries. *Journal of the American Geriatrics Society, 56,* 444–453.

Clancy, S. M., & Hoyer, W. J. (1994). Age and skill in visual search. *Developmental Psychology, 30,* 545–552.

Clark, B. (2008). *Growing up gifted* (7th ed.). Upper Saddle River, NJ: Prentice Hall.

Clark, E. V. (1993). *The lexicon in acquisition.* New York: Cambridge University Press.

Clark, E. V. (2009). What shapes children's language? Child-directed speech and the process of acquisition. In V. C. M. Gathercole (Ed.), *Routes to language: Essays in honor of Melissa Bowerman.* New York: Psychology Press.

Clark, M. D., & Carroll, M. H. (2008). Acquaintance rape scripts of women and men: Similarities and differences. *Sex Roles, 58,* 616–625.

Clark, M. S. & Grote, N. K. (2003). Close relationships. In I. B. Weiner (Ed.), *Handbook of psychology* (Vol. 5). New York: Wiley.

Clark, R. L., & King, R. B. (2008). Social and economic aspects of immigration. *Annals of the New York Academy of Sciences, 1136,* 289–297.

Clark-Cotton, M. R., Williams, R. K., & Goral, M. (2007). Language and communication in aging. In J. E. Birren (Ed.), *Encyclopedia of gerontology* (2nd ed.). San Diego: Academic Press.

Clark-Plaskie, M., & Lachman, M. E. (1999). The sense of control in midlife. In S. L. Willis & J. D. Reid (Eds.), *Life in the middle.* San Diego: Academic Press.

Clarke, E. J., Preston, M., Raksin, J., & Bengtson, V. L. (1999). Types of conflicts and tensions between older adults and adult children. *Gerontologist, 39,* 261–270.

Clarke-Stewart, A. (2006). What have we learned: Proof that families matter, policies for families and children, prospects for future research. In A. Clarke-Stewart & J. Dunn (Eds.), *Families count.* New York: Cambridge University Press.

Clarke-Stewart, A. K., & Miner, J. L. (2008). Child and day care, effects of. In M. M. Haith & J. B. Benson (Eds.), *Encyclopedia of infant and early childhood development.* Oxford, UK: Elsevier.

Clausen, J. A. (1993). *American lives.* New York: Free Press.

Claxton, A., & Perry-Jenkins, M. (2008). No fun anymore: Leisure and marital quality across the transition to parenthood. *Journal of Marriage and the Family, 70,* 28–43.

Clearfield, M. W., Diedrich, F. J., Smith, L. B., & Thelen, E. (2006). Young infants reach correctly in A-not-B tasks: On the development of stability and perseveration. *Infant Behavior and Development, 29,* 435–444.

Clearfield, M. W., Dineva, E. Smith, L. B., Diedrich, F. J., & Thelen, E. (2009). Cue salience and infant perserverative reaching: Tests of the dynamic field theory. *Developmental Science, 12,* 26–40.

Clements, J. M., (2009, in press). Patient perceptions on the use of advanced directives and life prolonging technology. *American Journal of Hospice and Palliative Care.*

Cleveland, J. N., & Shore, L. M. (2007). Work and employment: Individual. In J. E. Birren (Ed.), *Encyclopedia of gerontology* (2nd ed.). San Diego: Academic Press.

Cliffordson, C., & Gustafsson, J. E. (2008). Effects of age and schooling on intellectual performance: Estimates obtained from analysis of continuous variation in age and length of schooling. *Intelligence, 36,* 143–152.

Clifton, R. K., Morrongiello, B. A., Kulig, J. W., & Dowd, J. M. (1981) Developmental changes in auditory localization in infancy. In R. N. Aslin, J. R. Alberts, & M. R. Petersen (Eds.), *Development of perception* (Vol. 1). Orlando, FL: Academic Press.

Clifton, R. K., Muir, D. W., Ashmead, D. H., & Clarkson, M. G. (1993). Is visually guided reaching in early infancy a myth? *Child Development, 64,* 1099–1110.

Cloud, J. (2007, August 27). Failing our geniuses. *Time,* 40–47.

Coats, A. H., & Blanchard-Fields, F. (2008). Emotion regulation in interpersonal problems: The role of cognitive-emotional complexity, emotion regulation goals, and expressivity. *Psychology and Aging, 23,* 39–51.

Coatsworth, J. D., & Conway, D. E. (2009). The effects of autonomy-supportive coaching, need satisfaction, and self-perceptions on initiative and identity youth swimmers. *Developmental Psychology, 45,* 320–328.

Cochran, S. D., & Mays, V. M. (1990). Sex, lies, and HIV. *New England Journal of Medicine, 322,* 774–775.

Cohan, C. L., & Kleinbaum, S. (2002). Toward a greater understanding of the cohabitation effect: Premarital cohabitation and marital communication. *Journal of Marriage and Family, 64,* 180–192.

Cohen, D. (2009). *What every man should know about being a dad.* New York: Psychology Press.

Cohen, D., & Belsky, J. (2008). Avoidant romantic attachment and female orgasm: Testing an emotion-regulation hypothesis. *Attachment and Human Development, 10,* 1–10.

Cohen, F., Kemeny, M. E., Zegans, L. S., Johnson, P., Kearney, K. A., & Stites, D. P. (2007). Immune function declines with unemployment and recovers after stressor termination. *Psychosomatic Medicine, 69,* 225–234.

Cohen, L. B. (2002, April). *Can infants really add and subtract?* Paper presented at the meeting of the International Conference on Infant Studies, Toronto.

Cohen, L. B. (2009). Commentary on Part I: Unresolved issues in infant categorization. In D. H. Rakison & L. M. Oakes (Eds.), *Early category and concept development.* New York: Oxford University Press.

Cohen, N. J., Lojkasek, M., Zadeh, Z. Y., Pugliese, M., & Kiefer, H. (2008). Children adopted from China: A prospective study of their growth and development. *Journal of Child Psychology and Psychiatry, 49,* 458–468.

Cohler, B. J. (2009). Gays and lesbians, adulthood. In D. Carr (Ed.), *Encyclopedia of the life course and human development.* Boston: Gale Cengage.

Cohn, A., & Canter, A. (2003). *Bullying: Facts for schools and parents.* Washington, DC: National Association of School Psychologists Center.

Coie, J. D. (2004). The impact of negative social experiences on the development of antisocial behavior. In J. B. Kupersmidt & K. A. Dodge (Eds.), *Children's peer relations: From development to intervention.* Washington, DC: American Psychological Association.

Coker, R. H., Williams, R. H., Kortebein, P. M., Sullivan, D. H., & Evans, W. J. (2009, in press). Influence of exercise intensity on abdominal fat and adiponectin in elderly adults. *Metabolic Syndrome and Related Disorders.*

Colangelo, N. C., Assouline, S. G., & Gross, M. U. M. (2004). *A nation deceived: How schools hold back America's brightest students.* Retrieved March 6, 2005, from http://nationdeceived.org/

Colapinto, J. (2000). As *nature made him.* New York: Simon & Schuster.

Colby, A., Kohlberg, L., Gibbs, J., & Lieberman, M. (1983). A longitudinal study of moral judgment. *Monographs of the Society for Research in Child Development, 48* (21, Serial No. 201).

Colcombe, S. J., Erickson, K. I., Scalf, P. E., Kim, J. S., Prakash, R., McAuely, E., Elavsky, S., Marquex, D. X., Hu, L., & Kramer, A. F. (2006). Aerobic exercise training increases brain volume in aging humans. *Journals of Gerontology: A Biological Sciences and Medical Sciences, 61,* 1166–1170.

Colcombe, S. J., & Karmer, A. F. (2003). Fitness effects on the cognitive function of older adults: A meta-analytic study. *Psychological Science, 14,* 125–130.

Cole, E. R., & Stewart, A. J. (1996). Black and white women's political activism: Personality development, political identity and social responsibility. *Journal of Personality and Social Psychology, 71,* 130–140.

Cole, M. (2006). Culture and cognitive development in phylogenetic, historical, and ontogenetic perspective. In W. Damon & R. Lerner (Eds.), *Handbook of child psychology* (6th ed.). New York: Wiley.

Cole, P. M., Dennis, T. A., Smith-Simon, K. E., & Cohen, L. H. (2009, in press). Preschoolers' emotion regulation strategy understanding: Relations with emotion socialization and child self-regulation. *Social Development.*

Cole, P. M., & Tan, P. Z. (2007). Emotion socialization from a cultural perspective. In J. E. Grusec & P. D. Hastings (Eds.), *Handbook of socialization.* New York: Guilford.

Coleman, M., Ganong, L., & Fine, M. (2000). Reinvestigating remarriage: Another decade of progress. *Journal of Marriage and the Family, 62,* 1288–1307.

Coleman, P. D. (1986, August). *Regulation of dendritic extent: Human aging brain and Alzheimer's disease.* Paper presented at the meeting of the American Psychological Association, Washington, DC.

Coleman-Phox, K., Odouli, R., & Li, D.-K. (2008). Use of a fan during sleep and the risk of sudden infant death syndrome. *Archives of Pediatric and Adolescent Medicine, 162,* 963–968.

Coll, C. T. G., Erkut, S., Alarcon, O., Garcia, H. A. V., & Tropp, L. (1995, March). *Puerto Rican adolescents and families: Lessons in construct and instrument development.* Paper presented at the meeting of the Society for Research in Child Development, Indianapolis.

Collins, M. (1996, Winter). The job outlook for '96 grads. *Journal of Career Planning,* 51–54.

Collins, W. A., & Steinberg, L. (2006). Adolescent development in interpersonal context. In W. Damon & R. Lerner (Eds.), *Handbook of child psychology* (6th ed.). New York: Wiley.

Collins, W. A., & van Dulmen, M. (2006). The significance of middle childhood peer competence for work and relationships in early adulthood. In A. C. Huston & M. N. Ripke (Eds.), *Developmental contexts in middle childhood.* New York: Cambridge University Press.

Collins, W. A., Welsh, D. P., & Furman, W. (2009). Adolescent romantic relationships. *Annual Review of Clinical Psychology* (Vol. 5). Palo Alto, CA: Annual Reviews.

Colom, R., Jung, R. E., & Haier, R. J. (2007). General intelligence and memory span: Evidence for a common neuro-anatomic framework. *Cognitive Neuropsychology, 24* (8), 867–878.

Colombo, J., McCardle, P., & Freund, L. (Eds.). (2009). *Infant pathways to language.* Clifton, NJ: Psychology Press.

Colombo, J., Shaddy, D. J., Blaga, O. M., Anderson, C. J., & Kannass, K. N. (2009). High cognitive ability in infancy and early childhood. In F. D. Horowitz, R. F. Subotnik, & D. J. Matthews (Eds.), *The development of giftedness and talent across the life span.* Washington, DC: American Psychological Association.

Colombo, J., Shaddy, D. J., Richman, W. A., Maikranz, J. M., & Blaga, O. M. (2004). The developmental course of attention in infancy and preschool cognitive outcome. *Infancy, 4,* 1–38.

Colom, R., & others. (2009). Gray matter correlates of fluid, crystallized, and spatial intelligence. *Intelligence, 37,* 124–135.

Coltrane, S. L., Parke, R. D., Schofield, T. J., Tsuha, S. J., Chavez, M., & Lio, S. (2008). Mexican American families and poverty. In D. R. Crane & T. B. Heaton (Eds.), *Handbook of families and poverty.* Thousand Oaks. CA: Sage.

Comer, J. (2004). *Leave no child behind.* New Haven, CT: Yale University Press.

Comer, J. (2006). Child development: The under-weighted aspect of intelligence. In P. C. Kyllonen, R. D. Roberts, & L. Stankov (Eds.), *Extending intelligence.* Mahwah, NJ: Erlbaum.

Comings, J. (2007). Persistence: Helping adult students reach their goals. In J. Comings, B. Garner, & C. Smith (Eds.), *Review of adult learning and literacy* (Vol. 7). Mahwah, NJ: Erlbaum.

Commodari, E., & Guarnera, M. (2008). Attention and aging. *Aging: Clinical and Experimental Research, 20,* 578–584.

Commoner, B. (2002). Unraveling the DNA myth: The spurious foundation of genetic engineering. *Harper's Magazine, 304,* 39–47.

Commons, M. L., & Richards, F. A. (2003). Four postformal stages. In J. Demick & C. Andreoletti (Eds.), *Handbook of adult development.* New York: Kluwer.

Commons, M. L., Sinnott, J. D., Richards, F. A., & Armon, C. (1989). *Adult development. Vol. 1: Comparisons and applications of developmental models.* New York: Praeger.

Comstock, G., & Scharrer, E. (2006). Media and popular culture. In W. Damon & R. Lerner (Eds.), *Handbook of child psychology* (6th ed.). New York: Wiley.

Concannon, P., & others. (2009). Genome-wide scan for linkage to type 1 diabetes in 2,496 multiplex families from the Type 1 Diabetes Genetics Consortium. *Diabetes, 58,* 1018–1022.

Conduct Problems Prevention Research Group. (2007). The Fast Track randomized controlled trial to prevent externalizing psychiatric disorders: Findings from grades 3 to 9. *Journal of the American Academy of Child and Adolescent Psychiatry 46,* 1250–1262.

Conger, R., & Conger, K. J. (2008). Understanding the processes through which economic hardship influences rural families and children. In D. R. Crane & T. B. Heaton (Eds.), *Handbook of families and poverty.* Thousand Oaks, CA: Sage.

Connides, I. A. (2009). *Family ties and aging (2nd ed.).* Thousand Oaks, CA: Sage.

Connolly, J. A., & McIsaac, C. (2009). Romantic relationships in adolescence. In R. M. Lerner & L. Steinberg (Eds.), *Handbook of adolescent psychology* (3rd ed.). New York: Wiley.

Connolly, J., Craig, W., Goldberg, A., & Pepler, D. (2004). Mixed-gender groups, dating, and romantic relationships in early adolescence. *Journal of Research on Adolescence, 14,* 185–207.

Constantine, N. A. (2008). Editorial: Converging evidence leaves policy behind: Sex education in the United States. *Journal of Adolescent Health, 42,* 324–326.

Contestabile, A. (2009). Benefits of caloric restriction on brain aging and related pathological states: Understanding mechanisms to devise novel therapies. *Current Medicinal Chemistry, 16,* 350–361.

Conwell, Y., & Thompson, C. (2008). Suicidal behavior in elders. *Psychiatric Clinics of North America, 31,* 333–356.

Cook, H. L., Patel, P. J., & Tufail, A. (2008). Age-related macular degeneration: Diagnosis *and management. British Medical Bulletin, 85,* 127–149.

Cook, J. A., & others. (2005). Integration of psychiatric and vocational services: A multisite. randomized, controlled trial of supported employment. *American Journal of Psychiatry, 162,* 1948–1956.

Cook, M., & Birch, R. (1984). Infant perception of the shapes of tilted plane forms. *Infant Behavior and Development, 7,* 389–402.

Cook, P. J., MacCoun, R., Muschkin, C., & Vigdor, J. (2008). The negative impacts of starting middle school in the sixth grade. *Journal of Policy Analysis and Management, 27,* 104–121.

Cook, T. D., Deng, Y., & Morgano, E. (2007). Friendship influences during early adolescence: The special role of friends' grade point average. *Journal of Research on Adolescence, 17,* 325–356.

Coontz, S. (2005). *Marriage: A history.* New York: Penguin.

Cooper, A. R., & Moley, K. H. (2008). Maternal tobacco use and its preimplantation effects on fertility: More reasons to stop smoking. *Seminars in Reproductive Medicine, 26,* 204–212.

Cooper, C., Harvey, N., Javaid, K., Hanson, M., & Dennison, E. (2008). Growth and bone development. *Nestle Nutrition Workshop Series, 61,* 53–68.

Cooper, C., Katona, C., Orrell, M., & Livingston, G. (2008). Coping strategies, anxiety, and depression in caregivers of people with Alzheimer's disease. *International Journal of Geriatric Psychiatry, 23,* 929–936.

Cooper, C. R., Behrens, R., & Trinh, N. (2009, in press). Identity development. In R. A. Shweder, T. R. Bidell, A. C. Daily, S. D. Dixon, P. J. Miller, & J. Model (Eds.), *The Chicago companion to the child.* Chicago: University of Chicago Press.

Cooper, C. R., & Grotevant, H. D. (1989, April). *Individuality and connectedness in the family and adolescent's self and relational competence.* Paper presented at the meeting of the Society for Research in Child Development, Kansas City.

Cooper, C. R., Grotevant, H. D., Moore, M. S., & Condon, S. M. (1982, August). *Family support and conflict: Both foster adolescent identity and role taking.* Paper presented at the meeting

of American Psychological Association, Washington, DC.

Cooper, M. L. (2002). Alcohol use and risky sexual behavior among college students and youth: Evaluating the evidence. *Journal of Studies on Alcohol, 14,* 101–107.

Cooper, R., Mishra, G., Clennell, S., Guralnik, J., & Kuh, D. (2008). Menopausal status and physical performance in midlife: Findings from a British birth cohort study. *Menopause, 15,* 1043–1044.

Coplan, R. J., & Arbeau, K. A. (2008, in press). The stresses of a brave new world: Shyness and adjustment in kindergarten. *Journal of Research in Childhood Education.*

Coplan, R. J., & Arbeau, K. A. (2009). Peer interactions and play in early childhood. In K. H. Rubin, W. M. Bukowski, & B. Laursen (Eds.), *Handbook of peer interactions, relationships, and groups.* New York: Guilford.

Corbetta, D., & Snapp-Childs, W. (2009). Seeing and touching: The role of sensory-motor experience on the development of reaching. *Infant Behavior and Development, 32,* 44–58.

Cordier, S. (2008). Evidence for a role of paternal exposure in developmental toxicity. *Basic and Clinical Pharmacology and Toxicology, 102,* 176–181.

Cornelius, J. R., Clark, D. B., Reynolds, M., Kirisci, L., & Tarter, R. (2007). Early age of first sexual intercourse and affiliation with deviant peers predict development of SUD: A prospective longitudinal study. *Addictive Behavior, 32,* 850–854.

Cornwell, B., Laumann, E. O., & Schumm, P. L. (2008). The social connectedness of adults: A national profile. *American Sociological Review, 73,* 185–203.

Corona, G., & others. (2009, in press). The age-related decline of testosterone is associated with different specific symptoms and signs in patients with sexual dysfunction. *International Journal of Andrology.*

Corso, J. F. (1977). Auditory perception and communication. In J. E. Birren & K. W. Schaie (Eds.), *Handbook of the psychology of aging* (2nd ed.). New York: Van Nostrand Reinhold.

Costa, P. T., & McCrae, R. R. (1995). Solid ground on the wetlands of personality: A reply to Black. *Psychological Bulletin, 117,* 216–220.

Costa, P. T., & McCrae, R. R. (1998). Personality assessment. In H. S. Friedman (Ed.), *Encyclopedia of mental health* (Vol. 3). San Diego: Academic Press.

Cote, J. E. (2006). Emerging adulthood as an institutionalized moratorium: Risks and benefits to identity formation. In J. J. Arnett & J. L. Tanner (Eds.), *Emerging adults in America.* Washington, DC: American Psychological Association.

Coté, J. E. (2009). Identity formation and self-development in adolescence. In R. M. Lerner & L. Steinberg (Eds.), *Handbook of adolescent psychology* (3rd ed.), New York: Wiley.

Coulton, C. J., Crampton, D. S., Spilsbury, J. C., & Korbin, J. E. (2007). How neighborhoods influence child maltreatment: A review of the literature and alternative pathways. *Child Abuse and Neglect, 31,* 1117–1142.

Council of Economic Advisors. (2000). *Teens and their parents in the 21st century: An examination of trends in teen behavior and the role of parent involvement.* Washington, DC: Author.

Courage, M. L., Edison, S. C., & Howe, M. L. (2004). Variability in the early development of visual self-recognition. *Infant Behavior and Development, 27,* 509–532.

Courage, M. L., Howe, M. L., & Squires, S. E. (2004). Individual differences in 3.5 month olds' visual attention: What do they predict at 1 year? *Infant Behavior and Development, 127,* 19–30.

Courage, M. L., & Richards, J. E. (2008). Attention. In M. M. Haith & J. B. Benson (Eds.), *Encyclopedia of infant and early childhood development.* Oxford, UK: Elsevier.

Cousineau, T. M., Goldstein, M., & Franco, D. L. (2005). A collaborative approach to nutrition education for college students. *Journal of American College Health, 53,* 79–84.

Cowan, P. A., & Cowan, C. P. (2009). Couple relationships: A missing link between adult attachment and child outcomes. *Attachment and Human Development, 11,* 1–4.

Cowan, P. A., & Cowan, C. P. (2009, in press). How working with couples fosters children's development: From prevention science to public policy. In M. S. Schultz, M. K. Pruett, P. K. Kerig, & R. D. Parke (Eds.), *Feathering the nest: Couple relationships, couples interventions, and children's development.* Washington, DC: American Psychological Association.

Cowan, P., & Cowan, C. (2000). *When partners become parents: The big life change for couples.* Mahwah, NJ: Erlbaum.

Cowan, P., Cowan, C., Ablow, J., Johnson, V. K., & Measelle, J. (2005) *The family context of parenting in children's adaptation to elementary school.* Mahwah, NJ: Erlbaum.

Cowley, G., & Hager, M. (1995, December 4). Terminal care: Too painful, too prolonged. *Newsweek,* pp. 74–75.

Cox, J. E., & Nelson, D. (2008). The relationship between thinking patterns and emotional skills. *Journal of Humanistic Counseling, Education, and Development, 47* (1), 1–9.

Cox, M. J., Neilbron, N., Mills-Koonce, W. R., Pressel, A., Oppenheimer, C. W., & Szwedo, D. E. (2008). Marital relationship. In M. M. Haith & J. B. Benson (Eds.), *Encyclopedia of infant and early childhood development.* Oxford, UK: Elsevier.

Coyne, S. M., Archer, J., Eslea, M., & Liechty, T. (2008). Adolescent perceptions of indirect forms of relational aggression: Sex of perpetrator effects. *Aggressive Behavior, 34,* 577–583.

Crane, D. R., & Heaton, T. B. (Eds.) (2008). *Handbook of families and poverty.* Thousand Oaks, CA: Sage.

Crean, H. F. (2008). Conflict in the Latino parent-youth dyad: The role of emotional support from the opposite parent. *Journal of Family Psychology, 22,* 484–493.

Cremation Association of North America. (2008). *Statistics.* Retrieved December 9, 2008, from www.cremationassociation.org/.

Creswell, J. W. (2008). *Educational research* (3rd ed.). Upper Saddle River, NJ: Prentice Hall.

Crews, J. E., & Campbell, V. A. (2004). Vision impairment and hearing loss among community-dwelling older Americans: Implications for health and functioning. *American Journal of Public Health, 94,* 823–829.

Crockenberg, S. B. (1986). Are temperamental differences in babies associated with predictable differences in caregiving? In J. V. Lerner & R. M. Lerner (Eds.), *Temperament and social interaction during infancy and childhood.* San Francisco: Jossey-Bass.

Crockett, L. J., Raffaeli, M., & Shen, Y.-L. (2006). Linking self-regulation and risk proneness to risky sexual behavior: Pathways through peer pressure and early substance use. *Journal of Research on Adolescence, 16,* 503–525.

Crooks, R. L., & Baur, K. (2008). *Our sexuality* (10th ed.). Belmont, CA: Wadsworth.

Crosby, R. A., & Holtgrave, D. R. (2006). The protective value of social capital against teen pregnancy: A state-level analysis. *Journal of Adolescent Health, 38,* 556–559.

Crosnoe, R., Riegle-Crumb, C., Field, S., Frank, K., & Muller, C. (2008). Peer group contexts of girls' and boys' academic experiences. *Child Development, 79,* 139–155.

Cross, S., & Markus, H. (1991). Possible selves across the lifespan. *Human Development, 34,* 230–255.

Crossman, A. M., Scullin, M. H., & Melnyk, L. (2004). Individual and developmental differences in suggestibility. *Applied Cognitive Psychology, 18,* 941–945.

Crouter, A. C. (2006). Mothers and fathers at work. In A. Clarke-Stewart & J. Dunn (Eds.), *Families count.* New York: Cambridge University Press.

Crouter, A. C., Manke, B. A., & McHale, S. M. (1995). The family context of gender intensification in early adolescence. *Child Development, 66,* 317–329.

Crouter, A. C., & McHale, S. (2005). The long arm of the job revisited: Parenting in dual-earner families. In T. Luster & L. Okagaki (Eds.), *Parenting.* Mahwah, NJ: Erlbaum.

Crowell, J. A., Treboux, D., & Brockmeyer, S. (2009). Parental divorce and adult children's attachment representations and marital status. *Attachment and human development, 11,* 87–101.

Crowley, K., Callahan, M. A., Tenenbaum, H. R., & Allen, E. (2001). Parents explain more to boys than to girls during shared scientific thinking. *Psychological Science, 12,* 258–261.

Csaba, A., Bush, M. C., & Saphier, C. (2006). How painful are amniocentesis and chorionic villus sampling? *Prenatal Diagnosis, 26,* 35–38.

Csikszentmihalyi, M. (1996). *Creativity.* New York: HarperCollins.

Csikszentmihalyi, M. (1997). *Finding flow: The psychology of engagement with everyday life.* New York: Basic Books.

Cuddy-Casey, M., & Orvaschel, H. (1997). Children's understanding of death in relation to child suicidality and homicidality. *Death Studies, 17,* 33–45.

Cui, X., & Vaillant, G. E. (1996). Antecedents and consequences of negative life events in adulthood: A longitudinal study. *American Journal of Psychiatry, 153,* 21–26.

Cumming, E., & Henry, W. (1961). *Growing old.* New York: Basic Books.

Cummings, E. M., & Merrilees, C. E. (2009, in press). Identifying the dynamic processes underlying links between marital conflict and child adjustment. In M. S. Schultz, M. K. Pruett, P. K. Kerig, & R. D. Parke (Eds.), *Feathering the nest: Couple relationships, couples interventions, and children's development.* Washington, DC: American Psychological Association.

Cummings, M. (2009). *Human heredity* (8th ed.). Boston: Cengage.

Cunningham, M. (2009). Housework. In D. Carr (Ed.), *Encyclopedia of the life course and human development.* Boston: Gale Cengage.

Cunningham, P. M. (2009). *What really matters in vocabulary.* Boston: Allyn & Bacon.

Cunningham, W., & Hyson, D. (2006). The skinny on high-protein, low-carbohydrate diets. *Preventive Cardiology, 9,* 166–171.

Curran, K., DuCette, J., Eisenstein, J., & Hyman, I. A. (2001, August). *Statistical analysis of the cross-cultural data: The third year.* Paper presented at the meeting of the American Psychological Association, San Francisco.

Currie, C., & others. (2008). *Inequalities in young people's health: HBSC international report from the 2005/2006 survey.* Geneva: World Health Organization.

Cushner, K. H., McClelland, A., & Safford, P. (2009). *Human diversity in education* (6th ed.). New York: McGraw-Hill.

Cutler, S. J. (2009). Media and technology use, later life. In D. Carr (Ed.), *Encyclopedia of the life course and human development.* Boston: Gale Cengage.

Cuzon, V. C., Yeh, P. W., Yanagawa, Y., Obata, K., & Yeh, H. H. (2008). Ethanol consumption during early pregnancy alters the disposition of tangentially migrating GABAnergic interneurons in the fetal cortex. *Journal of Neuroscience, 28,* 1854–1864.

Czaja, S. J., Charness, N., Fisk, A. D., Hertzog, C., Nair, S. N., Rogers, W. A., & Sharit, J. (2006). Factors predicting the use of technology: Findings from the Center for Research and Education on Aging and Technology (CREATE). *Psychology and Aging, 21,* 333–352.

D

Dahl, R. E. (2004). Adolescent brain development: A period of vulnerabilities and opportunities. *Annals of the New York Academy of Sciences, 1021,* 1–22.

Dahl, R. E. (2007, August). *Adolescent brain development.* Paper presented at the meeting of the American Psychological Association, San Francisco.

Dahle, C. L., Jacobs, B. S., & Raz, N. (2009). Aging, vascular risk, and cognition: Blood glucose, pulse pressure, and cognitive performance in healthy adults. *Psychology and Aging, 24,* 154–162.

Damon, W. (1988). *The moral child.* Free Press.

Damon, W. (2008). *The path to purpose: Helping our children find their calling in life.* New York: Free Press.

Daniels, H. (2007). Pedagogy. In H. Daniels, J. Wertsch, & M. Cole (Eds.), *The Cambridge companion to Vygotsky.* New York: Cambridge University Press.

Danner, D., Snowdon, D., & Friesen, W. (2001). Positive emotions in early life and longevity: Findings from the Nun Study. *Journal of Personality and Social Psychology, 80* (5), 814–813.

Darwin, C. (1859). *On the origin of species.* London: John Murray.

Das, A. (2008, in press). Sexual harassment at work in the United States. *Archives of Sexual Behavior.*

Dasen, P. R. (1977). Are cognitive processes universal? A contribution to cross-cultural Piagetian psychology. In N. Warran (Ed.), *Studies in cross-cultural psychology* (Vol. 1). London: Academic Press.

Dasen, P. R., Ngini, L., & Lavalée, M. (1979). Cross-cultural training studies of concrete operations. In L. H. Eckenberger, W. J. Lonner, & Y. H. Poortinga (Eds.), *Cross-cultural contributions to psychology.* Boston: Allyn & Bacon.

Datar, A., & Sturm, R. (2004). Physical education in elementary school and body mass index: Evidence from the early childhood longitudinal study. *American Journal of Public Health, 94,* 1501–1506.

Davidson, D. (1996). The effects of decision characteristics on children's selective search of predecisional information. *Acta Psychologica, 92,* 263–281.

Davidson, J., & Davidson, B. (2004). *Genius denied: How to stop wasting our brightest young minds.* New York: Simon & Schuster.

Davidson, M., Lickona, T., & Khmelkov, V. (2008). A new paradigm for high school character education. In L. Nucci & D. Narváez (Eds.), *Handbook of moral and character education.* Clifton, NJ: Psychology Press.

Davidson, M. R., London, M. L., & Ladewig, P. A. (2008). *Olds' maternal-newborn nursing and women's health across the lifespan* (8th ed.). Upper Saddle River, NJ: Prentice Hall.

Davies, J., & Brember, I. (1999). Reading and mathematics attainments and self-esteem in years 2 and 6—an eight-year cross-sectional study. *Educational Studies, 25,* 145–157.

Davis, B. E., Moon, R. Y., Sachs, M. C., & Ottolini, M. C. (1998). Effects of sleep position on infant motor development. *Pediatrics, 102,* 1135–1140.

Davis, C. L., Tomporowski, P. O., Boyle, C. A., Waller, J. L., Miller, P. H., Nagieri, J. A., & Gregoski, M. (2007). Effects of aerobic exercise on overweight children's cognitive functioning: A randomized controlled trial. *Research Quarterly for Exercise and Sport, 78,* 510–519.

Davis, D. K. (2005). Leading the midwifery renaissance. *RCM Midwives, 8,* 264–268.

Davis, K. F., Parker, K. P., & Montgomery, G. L. (2004). Sleep in infants and young children: Part one: Normal sleep. *Journal of Pediatric Health Care, 18,* 65–71.

Davis, L., & Keyser, J. (1997). *Becoming the parent you want to be: A sourcebook of strategies for the first five years.* New York: Broadway Books.

Davis, O. S. P., Arden, R., & Plomin, R. (2008). g in middle childhood: Moderate genetic and shared environmental influence diverse measures of general cognitive ability at 7, 9, and 10 years in large population sample of twins. *Intelligence, 36,* 68–80.

Davison, G. C., & Neale, J. M. (2010). *Abnormal psychology* (11th ed.). New York: Wiley.

Day, N. L., Goldschmidt, L., & Thomas, C. A. (2006). Prenatal marijuana exposure contributes to the prediction of marijuana use at age 14. *Addiction, 101,* 1313–1322.

Day, R. H., & McKenzie, B. E. (1973). Perceptual shape constancy in early infancy. *Perception, 2,* 315–320.

Deary, I. J., Strand, S., Smith, P., & Fernandes, C. (2007). Intelligence and educational achievement. *Intelligence, 35,* 13–21.

Deater-Deckard, K., & Dodge K. (1997). Externalizing behavior problems and discipline revisited: Non-linear effects and variation by culture, context and gender. *Psychological Inquiry, 8,* 161–75.

De Berardis, G., Pellegrini, F., Franciosi, M., Pamparana, F., Morelli, P., Togoni, G., Nicolueei, A., & the EDEN study group. (2009). Management of erectile dysfunction in general practice. *Journal of Sexual Medicine, 6,* 1127–1134.

DeCasper, A. J., & Spence, M. J. (1986). Prenatal maternal speech influences newborn's perception of speech sounds. *Infant Behavior and Development, 9,* 133–150.

deCharms, R. (1984). Motivation enhancement in educational settings. In R. Arnes & C. Arnes (Eds.), *Research on motivation in education* (Vol. 1). Orlando: Academic Press.

Deci, E. L., Koestner, R., & Ryan, R. M. (2001). Extrinsic rewards and intrinsic motivation in education: Reconsidered once again. *Review of Educational Research, 71,* 1–28.

Declercq, E., Cunningham, D. K., Johnson, C., & Sakala, C. (2008). Mothers' reports of postpartum pain associated with vaginal and cesarean deliveries: Results of a national survey. *Birth, 35,* 16–24.

Deeny, S. P., & others. (2008). Exercise, APOE, and working memory: MEG and behavioral evidence for benefit of exercise in epsilon4 carriers. *Biological Psychology, 78,* 179–187.

de Haan, M., & Gunnar, M. R. (Eds.). (2009). *Handbook of developmental social neuroscience.* New York: Guilford.

de Haan, M., & Martinos, M. (2008). Brain function. In M. M. Haith & J. B. Benson (Eds.), *Encyclopedia of infant and early childhood development.* Oxford, UK: Elsevier.

Delaloye, C., & others. (2009). The contribution of aging to the understanding of the dimensionality of executive functions. *Archives of Gerontology and Geriatrics, 49,* e51–e59.

DeLamater, J., & Friedrich, W. (2002) Human sexual development. *Journal of Sex Research, 39,* 10–14.

de la Torre, J. C. (2008). Pathophysiology of neuronal energy crisis in Alzheimer's disease. *Neurodegenerative Diseases, 5,* 126–132.

De Leo, D. (2002). Struggling against suicide: The need for an integrative approach. *Crisis, 23,* 23–31.

de Leo, D., & Heller, T. (2008). Social modeling in the transmission of suicidality. *Crisis, 29,* 11–19.

De Lisle-Porter, M., & Podruchny, A. M. (2009). The dying neonate: Family-centered end-of-life care. *Neonatal Network, 28,* 75–83.

DeLoache, J. S. (1989). The development of representation in young children. In H. W. Reese (Ed.), *Advances in child development and behavior.* New York: Academic Press.

DeLoache, J. S. (2004). Early development of the understanding and use of symbolic artifacts. In U. Goswami (Ed.), *Blackwell handbook of childhood cognitive development.* Malden, MA: Blackwell.

DeLoache, J. S., & Ganea, P. A. (2009). Symbol-based learning in infancy. In A. Woodward & A. Needham (Eds.), *Learning and the infant mind.* New York: Oxford University Press.

DeLoache. J. S., Miller, K. F., & Pierroutsakos, S. L. (1998). Reasoning and problem solving. In D. Kuhn & R. S. Siegler (Eds.), *Handbook of child psychology* (5th ed., Vol. 2). New York: Wiley.

DeLoache, J. S., Simcock, G., & Macari, S. (2007). Planes, trains, automobiles—and tea-sets: Extremely intense interests in very young children. *Developmental Psychology, 43*, 1579–1586.

Demetriou, A., Christou, C., Spanoudis, G., & Platsidou, M. (2002). The development of mental processing: Efficiency, working memory, and thinking. *Monographs of the Society for Research in Child Development, 67* (1, Serial No. 268).

Dempster, F. N. (1981). Memory span: Sources of individual and developmental differences. *Psychological Bulletin, 80*, 63–100.

Denham, S. A., Bassett, H. H., & Wyatt, T. (2007). The socialization of emotional competence. In J. E. Grusec & P. D. Hastings (Eds.), *Handbook of socialization.* New York: Guilford.

Denmark, F. L., Russo, N. F., Frieze, I. H., & Eschuzur, J. (1988). Guidelines for avoiding sexism in psychological research: A report of the ad hoc committee on nonsexist research. *American Psychologist, 43*, 582–585.

Denney, N. (1986, August). *Practical problem solving.* Paper presented at the meeting of the American Psychological Association, Washington, DC.

Denney, N. W. (1990). Adult age differences in traditional and practical problem solving. *Advances in Psychology, 72*, 329–349.

Dennis, N. A., & Cabeza, R. (2008). Neuroimaging of healthy cognitive aging. In F. I. M. Craik & T. A. Salthouse (Eds.), *Handbook of aging and cognition* (3rd ed.). Mahwah, NJ: Erlbaum.

Depp, C. A., Glatt, S. J., & Jeste, D. V. (2007). Recent advances in research on successful or healthy aging. *Current Psychiatry Reports, 9*, 7–13.

Depp, C. A., & Jeste, D. V. (2010). Successful aging. *Annual Review of Clinical Psychology* (Vol. 6). Palo Alto, CA: Annual Reviews.

Der Ananian, C., & Prohaska, T. R. (2007). Exercise and physical activity. In J. E. Birren (Ed.), *Encyclopedia of gerontology* (2nd ed.). San Diego: Academic Press.

de Rosnay, M., Cooper, P. J., Tsigaras, N., & Murray, L. (2006). Transmission of social anxiety from mother to infant: An experimental study using a social referencing paradigm. *Behavior Research and Therapy, 44*, 1165–1175.

DeSantis, L. (1998). Building healthy communities with immigrants and refugees. *Journal of Transcultural Nursing, 9*, 20–31.

Deutsch, R., & Pruett, M. K. (2009). Child adjustment and high conflict divorce. In R. M. Galatzer-Levy and L. Kraus (Eds.), *The scientific basis of custody decisions* (2nd ed.). New York: Wiley.

Devos, T. (2006). Implicit bicultural identity among Mexican American and Asian American college students. *Cultural Diversity and Ethnic Psychology, 12*, 381–402.

Dewey, J. (1933). *How we think.* Lexington, MA: D. C. Heath.

DeZolt, D. M., & Hull, S. H. (2001). Classroom and school climate. In J. Worell (Ed.), *Encyclopedia of women and gender.* San Diego: Academic Press.

Diamond, A. D. (1985). Development of the ability to use recall to guide action, as indicated by infants' performance on AB. *Child Development, 56*, 868–883.

Diamond, A. D. (2007). Interrelated and interdependent. *Developmental Science, 10*, 152–158.

Diamond, A. D. (2009). The interplay of biology and environment broadly defined. *Developmental Psychology, 45*, 1–8.

Diamond, A. D., Casey, B. J., & Munakata, Y. (2010). *Developmental cognitive neuroscience.* New York: Oxford University Press.

Diamond, L. M., & Savin-Williams, R. (2009). Adolescent sexuality. In R. M. Lerner & L. Steinberg (Eds.), *Handbook of adolescent psychology* (3rd ed.). New York: Wiley.

Diamond, M., & Sigmundson, H. K. (1997). Sex reassignment at birth: Long-term review and clinical implications. *Archives of Pediatric and Adolescent Medicine, 151*, 295–304.

Diaz-Rico, L. T. (2008). *A course for teaching English learners.* Boston: Allyn & Bacon.

Diaz-Rico, L. T. & Weed, K. Z. (2010). *Crosscultural, language, and academic achievement* (4th ed.). Boston: Allyn & Bacon.

Diego, M. A., Field, T., & Hernandez-Reif, M. (2008). Temperature increases in preterm infants during massage therapy. *Infant Behavior and Development, 31*, 149–152.

Diego, M. A., Field, T., Hernandez-Reif, M., Schanberg, S., Kuh, C., & Gonzales-Quinterto, V. H. (2009). Prenatal depression restricts fetal growth. *Early Human Development, 85*, 65–70.

Diekmann, A., & Schmidheiny, K. (2004). Do parents of girls have a higher risk of divorce? An eighteen-country study. *Journal of Marriage and the Family, 66*, 651–660.

Diener, E., & Seligman, M. E. P. (2002). Very happy people. *Psychological Science, 13*, 81–84.

Dillaway, H. E. (2005). Menopause is the "good old": Women's thoughts about reproductive aging. *Gender and Society, 19*, 398–417.

Dillon, J. (2003). Reincarnation: The technology of death. In C. D. Bryant (Ed.), *Handbook of death and dying.* Thousand Oaks, CA: Sage.

DiPietro, J. (2008). Unpublished review of J. W. Santrock's, *Children,* 11th ed. (New York: McGraw-Hill).

Dishion, T. J., & Piehler T. F. (2009). Deviant by design: Peer contagion in development, interventions and school. In K. H. Rubin, W. M. Bukowski, & B. Laursen (Eds.), *Handbook of peer interactions, relationship, and groups.* New York: Guilford.

Dixon, L., Browne, K., & Hamilton-Giachritsis, C. (2005). Risk factors of parents abused as children: A mediational analysis of the intergenerational continuity of child maltreatment (Part I). *Journal of Child Psychology and Psychiatry and Allied Disciplines. 46*, 47–57.

Dixon, R. A., Kurzman, D., & Friesen, I. C. (1993). Handwriting performance in younger and older adults: Age, familiarity, and practice effects. *Psychology and Aging, 8* (3), 360–370.

Dixon, S. V., Graber, J. A., & Brooks-Gunn, J. (2008). The roles of respect for parental authority and parenting practices in parent-child conflict among African American, Latino, and European American families. *Journal of Family Psychology, 22*, 1–10.

Dobson, R. (2009). Breast cancer incidence falls as women give up HRT. *British Medical Journal, 338*, 791.

Dodge, K. A. (1983). Behavioral antecedents of peer social status. *Child Development, 54*, 1386–1399.

Dodge, K. A., Greenberg, M. T., Malone, P. S., & the Conduct Problems Prevention Research Group. (2008). Testing an idealized dynamic cascade model of the development of serious violence in adolescence. *Child Development, 79*, 1907–1927.

Dodge, K. A., & Pettit, G. S. (2003), A biopsychosocial model of the development of chronic conduct problems in adolescence. *Developmental Psychology, 39*, 349–371.

Dodge, K. A., & the Conduct Problems Prevention Research Group. (2007, March). *The impact of Fast Track on adolescent conduct disorder.* Paper presented at the meeting of the Society for Research in Child Development, Boston.

Doherty, M. (2008). *Theory of mind.* Philadelphia: Psychology Press.

Dondi, M., Simion, F., & Caltran, G. (1999). Can newborns discriminate between their own cry and the cry of another newborn infant? *Developmental Psychology, 35* (2), 418–426.

Dong, G. H., Ma, Y. N., Ding, H. L., Cao, Y., Zhao, Y. D., & He, Q. C. (2008). Effects of housing characteristics and home environmental factors on respiratory symptoms in 10,784 elementary school children from northeast China. *Respiration, 76*, 82–91.

Donnellan, M. B., & Lucas, R. E. (2008). Age differences in the Big Five across the life span: Evidence from two national samples. *Psychology and Aging, 23*, 558–566.

Donnellan, M. B., & Robins, R. W. (2009). The development of personality across the lifespan. In G. Matthews and P. Corr (Eds), *Cambridge handbook of personality psychology.* Cambridge, UK: Cambridge University Press.

D'Onofrio, B. M. (2008). Nature vs. nurture. In M. M. Haith & J. B. Benson (Eds.), *Encyclopedia of infant and early childhood development.* Oxford, UK: Elsevier.

D'Onofrio, B. M., & others. (2007). Intergenerational transmission of childhood conduct problems: A children of twins study. *Archives of General Psychiatry, 64,* 820–829.

Dontigny, L., & others. (2008). Rubella in pregnancy. *Journal of Obstetrics and Gynecology Canada, 30,* 152–168.

Dorn, L. D., Dahl, R. E., Woodward, H. R., & Biro, F. (2006). Defining the boundaries of early adolescence: A user's guide to assessing pubertal status and pubertal timing in research with adolescents. *Applied Developmental Science, 10,* 30–56.

Dorrian, J., Tolley, C., Lamond, N., van den Heuvel, C., Pincombe, J., Rogers, A. E., & Drew, D. (2008). Sleep and errors in a group of Australian hospital nurses at work and during the commute. *Applied Ergonomics, 39,* 605–613.

Doty, R. L., & Shah, M. (2008). Taste and smell. In M. M. Haith & J. B. Benson (Eds.), *Encyclopedia of infant and early childhood development.* Oxford, UK: Elsevier.

Dowda, M., Brown, W. H., McIver, K. L., Pfeiffer, K. A., O'Neill, J. R., Addy, C. L., & Pate, R. R. (2009). Policies and characteristics of the preschool environment and physical activity of young children. *Pediatrics, 123,* e261–e266.

Dozier, M., Stovall-McClough, K. C., & Albus, K. E. (2008). Attachment and psychopathology in adulthood. In J. Cassidy & P. R. Shaver (Eds.), *Handbook of attachment* (2nd ed.), New York: Guilford.

Draghi-Lorenz, R. (2007, July). *Self-conscious emotions in young infants and the direct perception of self and others in interaction.* Paper presented at the meeting of the International Society for Research on Emotions, Sunshine Coast, Australia.

Driver, J., Tabares, A., Shapiro, A., Nahm, E. Y., & Gottman, J. M. (2003). Interactional patterns in marital success and failure: Gottman laboratory studies. In F. Walsh (Ed.), *Normal family processes* (3rd ed.). New York: Guilford.

Druzhyna, N. M., Wilson, G. L., & LeDoux, S. P. (2008). Mitochondrial DNA repair in aging and disease. *Mechanisms of Aging and Development, 129,* 383–390.

Dryfoos, J. G., & Barkin, C. (2006). *Adolescence: Growing up in America today.* New York: Oxford University Press.

Duan, W., & others. (2008). Sertraline slows disease progression and increases neurogenesis in N171–82Q mouse model of Huntington's disease. *Neurobiology of Disease, 30,* 312–322.

Dubow, E. F., Huesmann, L. R., & Greenwood, D. (2007). Media and youth socialization. In J. E. Grusec & P. D. Hastings (Eds.), *Handbook of socialization.* New York: Guilford.

Dubowitz, H., Pitts, S. C., & Black, M. M. (2004). Measurement of three subtypes of child neglect. *Child Maltreatment, 9,* 344–356.

Dudley, R. L. (1999). Youth religious commitment over time: Longitudinal study of retention. *Review of Religious Research, 41,* 110–121.

Dunbar, L., Leventhal, H., & Leventhal, E. A. (2007). Self-regulation, health, and behavior. In J. E. Birren (Ed.), *Encyclopedia of gerontology* (2nd ed.). San Diego: Academic Press.

Duncan, G. J., Huston, A. C., & Weisner, T. (2007). *Higher ground: New hope for working poor families and their children.* New York: Russell Sage.

Dunn, G. P. (2009). Principles and core competencies of surgical palliative care: An overview. *Otolaryngologic Clinics of North American, 42,* 1–13.

Dunn, J. (1984). Sibling studies and the developmental impact of critical incidents. In P. B. Baltes & O. G. Brim (Eds.), *Life-span development and behavior* (Vol. 6). Orlando, FL: Academic Press.

Dunn, J. (2007). Siblings and socialization. In J. E. Grusec & P. D. Hastings (Eds.), *Handbook of socialization.* New York: Guilford.

Dunn, J., & Kendrick, C. (1982). *Siblings.* Cambridge, MA: Harvard University Press.

Dunn, N. F., Miller, R., Griffioen, A., & Lee, C. A. (2008). Carrier testing in haemophilia A and B: Adult carriers' and their partners' experiences and their views on the testing of young females. *Haemophilia, 14,* 584–592.

Dupre, M. E., & Meadows, S. O. (2007). Disaggregating the effects of marital trajectories on health. *Journal of Family Issues, 28,* 623–652.

Dupuy, A. M., Jaussent, I., Lacroux, A., Durant, R., Cristol, J. P., & Delcourt, C. (2007). Waist circumference adds to the variance in plasma C-reactive protein levels in elderly patients with metabolic syndrome. *Gerontology, 53,* 91–101.

Duque, G., Demontiero, O., & Troen, B. R. (2009). Prevention and treatment of senile osteoporosis and hip fractures. *Minerva Medica, 100,* 79–94.

Durieux-Smith, A., Fitzpatrick, E., & Whittingham, J. (2008). Universal newborn hearing screening: A question of evidence. *International Journal of Audiology, 47,* 1–10.

Durik, A. M., Hyde, J. S., Marks, A. C., Roy, A. L., Anaya, D., & Schultz, G. (2006). Ethnicity and gender stereotypes of emotions. *Sex Roles, 54,* 429–445.

Durrant, J. E. (2000). Trends in youth crime and well-being since the abolition of corporal punishment in Sweden. *Youth and Society, 3,* 437–455.

Durrant, J. E. (2008). Physical punishment, culture, and rights: Current issues for professionals. *Journal of Developmental and Behavioral Pediatrics, 29,* 55–66.

Durston, S., Davidson, M. C., Tottenham, N. T., Galvan, A., Spicer, J., Fossella, J. A., & Casey, B. J. (2006). A shift from diffuse to focal cortical activity with development. *Developmental Science, 9,* 1–8.

Dweck, C. S. (2006). *Mindset.* New York: Random House.

Dweck, C. S. (2007). Boosting achievement with messages that motivate. *Education Canada, 47,* 6–10.

Dweck, C. S., & Elliott, E. (1983). Achievement motivation. In P. Mussen (Ed.), *Handbook of child psychology* (4th ed., Vol. 4). New York: Wiley.

Dweck, C. S., Mangels, J. A., & Good, C. (2004). Motivational effects on attention, cognition, and performance. In D. Y. Dai & R. J. Sternberg (Eds.), *Motivation, emotion, and cognition.* Mahwah, NJ: Erlbaum.

Dworkin, S. L., & Santelli, J. (2007). Do abstinence-plus interventions reduce sexual risk behavior among youth? *PLoS Medicine, 4,* 1437–1439.

Dwyer, T., & Ponsonby, A. L. (2009). Sudden infant death syndrome and prone sleeping position. *Annals of Epidemiology, 19,* 245–249.

Dykas, M. J., Ziv, Y., & Cassidy, J. (2008). Attachment and peer relations in adolescence. *Social Development, 10,* 123–141.

E

Eagly, A. H. (2000). Gender roles. In A. Kazdin (Ed.), *Encyclopedia of psychology.* Washington, DC, & New York: American Psychological Association and Oxford University Press.

Eagly, A. H., & Crowley, M. (1986). Gender and helping behavior: A meta-analytic review of the social psychological literature. *Psychological Bulletin, 100,* 283–308.

Eagly, A. H., & Steffen, V. J. (1986). Gender and aggressive behavior: A meta-analytic review of the social psychological literature. *Psychological Bulletin, 100,* 309–330.

Eagly, A. H., & Wood, W. (2010, in press). Gender roles in a biosocial world. In P. van Lange, A. Kruglanski, & E. T. Higgins (Eds.), *Handbook of theories in social psychology.* Thousand Oaks, CA: Sage.

East, P. (2009). Adolescent relationships with siblings. In R. M. Lerner & L. Steinberg (Eds.), *Handbook of adolescent psychology* (3rd ed.). New York: Wiley.

Eaton, D. K., & others. (2006). Youth risk behavior surveillance—United States, 2005. *MMWR Surveillance Summary, 55,* 1–108.

Eaton, D. K., & others. (2008). Youth risk behavior surveillance—United States, 2007. *MMWR Surveillance Summaries, 57,* 1–131.

Eaton, W. O. (2008). Milestones: Physical. In M. M. Haith & J. B. Benson (Eds.), *Encyclopedia of infant and early childhood development.* Oxford, UK: Elsevier.

Eby, J. W., Herrell, A. L., & Jordan, M. L. (2009). *Teaching in elementary school: A reflective approach* (5th ed.). Boston: Allyn & Bacon.

Eccles, J. (2003). Education: Junior and high school. In G. Adams & M. Berzonsky (Eds.), *Blackwell handbook of adolescence.* Malden, MA: Blackwell.

Eccles, J. S. (2004). Schools, academic motivation, and stage-environment fit. In R. Lerner & L. Steinberg (Eds.), *Handbook of adolescent psychology*. New York: Wiley.

Eccles, J. S. (2007). Families, schools, and developing achievement-related motivations and engagement. In J. E. Grusec & P. D. Hastings (Eds.), *Handbook of socialization.* New York: Guilford.

Eccles, J. S., & Roeser, R. W. (2009). Schools, academic motivation, and stage-environment fit. In R. M. Lerner & L. Steinberg (Eds.), *Handbook of adolescent psychology* (3rd ed.). New York: Wiley.

Eckerman, C., & Whitehead, H. (1999). How toddler peers generate coordinated action: A cross-cultural exploration. *Early Education and Development, 10,* 241–266.

Eckstein, K. C., Mikhail, L. M., Ariza, A. J., Thomson, J. S., Millard, S. C, Binns, H. J., & the Pediatric Practice Research Group. (2006). Parents' perception of their child's weight and health. *Pediatrics, 117,* 681–690.

Effros, R. B. (2009). Kleemeier Award Lecture 2008—The canary in the coal mine: Telomeres and human healthspan. *Journals of Gerontology A: Biological Sciences and Medical Sciences, 64,* 511–515.

Egan, S. K., & Perry, D. G. (2001). Gender identity: A multidimensional analysis with implications for psychosocial adjustment. *Developmental Psychology, 37,* 451–463.

Egbert, J. L. (2009). *Supporting learning with technology.* Boston: Allyn & Bacon.

Egeland, B., Jacobvitz, D., & Sroufe, L. A. (1988). Breaking the cycle of abuse. *New Directions for Child Development, 11,* 77–92.

Ehrhardt, A. A., & Baker, S. W. (1974). Fetal androgens, human central nervous system differentiation, and behavior sex differences. In R. C. Friedman, R. M. Richart, & R. L. Vande Wiele (Eds.), *Sex differences in behavior.* New York: Wiley.

Eichorn, D. H., Clausen, J. A., Haan, N., Honzik, M. P., & Mussen, P. H. (Eds.), (1981). *Present and past in middle life.* New York: Academic Press.

Eider-Avidan, D., Haj-Yahia, M. M., & Greenbaum, C. W. (2009). Divorce is part of my life . . . resilience, survival, and vulnerability: Young adults' perceptions of the implications of parental divorce. *Journal of Marital and Family Therapy, 35,* 30–46.

Einstein, G. O., & McDaniel, M. A. (2005). Prospective memory, *Current Directions in Psychological Science, 14,* 286–290.

Eisdorfer, C. (1996, December). Interview. *APA Monitor,* p. 35.

Eisenberg, M. E., Bernat, D. H., Bearinger, L. H., & Resnick, M. D. (2008). Support for comprehensive sexuality education: Perspectives from parents of school-aged youth. *Journal of Adolescent Research, 42,* 352–359.

Eisenberg, N. (2010, in press). Emotional regulation in children. *Annual Review of Clinical Psychology* (Vol. 6). Palo Alto, CA: Annual Reviews.

Eisenberg, N., & Fabes, R. A. (1998). Prosocial development. In N. Eisenberg (Ed.), *Handbook of child psychology* (5th ed., Vol. 3). New York: Wiley.

Eisenberg, N., Fabes, R. A., Guthrie, I. K., & Reiser, M. (2002). The role of emotionality and regulation in children's social competence and adjustment. In L. Pulkkinen & A. Caspi (Eds.), *Paths to successful development.* New York: Cambridge University Press.

Eisenberg, N., Fabes, R. A., & Spinrad, T. L. (2006). Prosocial development. In W. Damon & R. Lerner (Eds.), *Handbook of child psychology* (6th ed.). New York: Wiley.

Eisenberg, N., & Morris, A. S. (2004). Moral cognitions and prosocial responding in adolescence. In R. Lerner & L. Steinberg (Eds.), *Handbook of adolescent psychology* (2nd ed.). New York: Wiley.

Eisenberg, N., Morris, A. S., McDaniel, B., & Spinrad, T. L. (2009). Moral cognitions and prosocial responding in adolescence. In R. M. Lerner & L. Steinberg (Eds.), *Handbook of adolescent psychology* (3rd ed.). New York: Wiley.

Eisenberg, N., & Valiente, C. (2002). Parenting and children's prosocial and moral development. In M. H. Bornstein (Ed.), *Handbook of parenting* (2nd ed.). Mahwah, NJ: Erlbaum.

Elder, G. H. (1980). Adolescence in historical perspective. In J. Adelson (Ed.), *Handbook of adolescent psychology.* New York: Wiley.

Elder, G. H., & Shanahan, M. J. (2006). The life course and human development. In W. Damon & R. Lerner (Eds.), *Handbook of child psychology* (6th ed.). New York: Wiley.

Elias, J. W., & Wagster, M. V. (2007). Developing context and background underlying cognitive intervention/training studies in older populations. *Journals of Gerontology B: Psychological Sciences and Social Sciences, 62,* 5–10.

Eliasieh, K., Liets, L. C., & Chalupa, L. M. (2007). Cellular reorganization in the human retina during normal aging. *Investigative Ophthalmology and Visual Science, 48,* 2824–2830.

Elkind, D. (1976). *Child development and education. A Piagetian perspective.* New York: Oxford University Press.

Elkind, D. (1978). Understanding the young adolescent. *Adolescence, 13,* 127–134.

Ellis, C. D. (2002). Male rape. *Collegian, 9,* 34–39.

Ellis, L., & Ames, M. A. (1987). Neurohormonal functioning and sexual orientation. *Psychological Bulletin, 101,* 233–258.

Elmore, R. F. (2009). Schooling adolescents. In R. M. Lerner & L. Steinberg (Eds.), *Handbook of adolescent psychology* (3rd ed.). New York: Wiley.

El-Sheikh, M., Buckhalt, J. A., Mize, J., & Acebo, C. (2006). Marital conflict and disruption of children's sleep. *Child Development, 77,* 31–43.

Elwert, F., & Christakis, N. A. (2008). The effect of widowhood on mortality by the causes of death of both spouses. *American Journal of Public Health, 98,* 2092–2098.

Emery, R. E. (1999). *Renegotiating family relationships* (2nd ed.). New York: Guilford.

Enfield, A., & Collins, D. (2008). The relationship of service-learning, social justice, multicultural competence, and civic engagement. *Journal of College Student Development, 49,* 95–109.

Enger, E., Ross, F. C., & Bailey, D. (2009). *Concepts in biology* (13th ed.). New York: McGraw-Hill.

Engle, P. L., & Black, M. M. (2008). The effect of poverty on child development and educational outcomes. *Annals of the New York Academy of Sciences, 1136,* 243–256.

Engler, A. J., Ludington-Hoe, S. M., Cusson, R. M., Adams, R., Bahnsen, M., Brumbaugh, E., Coates, P., Grief, J., McHargue, L., Ryan, D. L., Settle, M., & Williams, D. (2002). Kangaroo care: National survey of practice, knowledge, barriers, and perceptions. *American Journal of Maternal/Child Nursing, 27,* 146–153.

Englund, M. M., Egeland, B., & Collins, W. A. (2008). Exceptions to high school dropout predictions in a low-income sample: Do adults make a difference? *Journal of Social Issues. 64,* 77–93.

Englund, M. M., Luckner, A. E., & Whaley, G. (2003, April). *The importance of early parenting for children's long-term educational attainment.* Paper presented at the meeting of the Society for Research in Child Development, Tampa.

Ennett, S. T., Bauman, K. E., Hussong, A., Paris, R., Foshee, V. A., & Cai, L. (2006). The peer context of adolescent substance use: Findings from social network analysis. *Journal of Research on Adolescence, 16,* 159–186.

Enright, M. S., Schaefer, L. V., Schaefer, P., & Schaefer, K. A. (2008). Building a just adolescent community. *Montessori Life, 20,* 36–42.

Enright, R. D., Santos, M. J. D., & Al-Mabuk, R. (l989). The adolescent as forgiver. *Journal of Adolescence, 12,* 95–110.

Ensembl Human. (2008). *Explore the Homo sapiens genome.* Retrieved April 14, 2008, from www.ensembl.org/Homo_sapiens/index.html

Entringer, S., Kumsta. R., Hellhammer, D. H., Wadhwa, P. D., & Wust, S. (2009). Prenatal exposure to maternal psychosocial stress and HPA axis regulation in young adults. *Hormones and Behavior, 55,* 292–298.

Epel, E. S. (2009). Psychological and metabolic stress: A recipe for accelerated cellular aging. *Hormones, 8,* 7–22.

Erickson, K. I., & others. (2009, in press). Aerobic fitness is associated with hippocampal volume in elderly humans. *Hippocampus.*

Erickson, K. I., Colcombe, S. J., Wadhwa, R. Bherer, L., Peterson, M. S., Scalf, P. E., Kim, J. S., Alvarado, M., & Kramer, A. F.

(2007). Training-induced plasticity in older adults: Effects of training on hemispheric asymmetry. *Neurobiology of Aging, 28,* 272–283.

Erickson, K. I., Prakash, R. S., Voss, M. W., Chaddock, L., Hu, L., Morris, K. S., White, S. M., Wojcicki, T. R., McAuley, E., & Kramer, A. F. (2009, in press). Aerobic fitness is associated with hippocampal volume in elderly humans. *Hippocampus.*

Ericsson, K. A., Krampe, R., & Tesch-Römer, C. (1993). The role of deliberate practice in the acquisition of expert performance. *Psychological Review, 100,* 363–406.

Erikson, E. H. (1950), *Childhood and society.* New York: W. W. Norton.

Erikson, E. H. (1962). *Young man Luther.* New York: W. W. Norton.

Erikson, E. H. (1968). *Identity: Youth and crisis.* New York: W. W. Norton.

Erikson, E. H. (1969). *Gandhi's truth.* New York: W. W. Norton.

Eriksson, U. J. (2009). Congenital malformations in diabetic pregnancy. *Seminar's in Fetal and Neonatal Medicine, 14,* 85–93.

Erixon-Lindroth, N., Farde, L., Wahlin, T. B., Sovago, J., Hallidin, C., & Backman, L. (2005). The role of the striatal dopamine transporter in cognitive aging. *Psychiatry Research, 138,* 1–12.

Erlich, B. S., & Isaacowitz, D. M. (2002). Does subjective well-being increase with age? *Perspectives in Psychology, 5,* 20–26.

Ernst, M., & Mueller, S. C. (2008). The adolescent brain: Insights from functional neuroimaging research. *Developmental Neuroscience, 68,* 729–743.

Escobar-Chaves, S. L., & Anderson, C. A. (2008). Media and risky behavior. *The Future of Children, 18* (1), 147–180.

Eskildsen, M., & Price, T. (2009). Nursing home care in the USA. *Geriatrics and Gerontology International, 9,* 1–6.

Esposito, K., & others. (2009). Effects of intensive lifestyle changes on erectile dysfunction in men. *Journal of Sexual Medicine, 6,* 243–250.

Etaugh, C., & Bridges, J. S. (2010). *Women's lives* (2nd ed.). Boston: Allyn & Bacon.

Evans, G. W. (2004). The environment of childhood poverty. *American Psychologist, 59,* 77–92.

Evans, G. W., & English, G. W. (2002). The environment of poverty. *Child Development, 73,* 1238–1248.

Evans, G. W., & Kim, P. (2007). Childhood poverty and health: Cumulative risk exposure and stress dysregulation. *Psychological Science, 18,* 953–957.

F

Fabiano, G. A., Pelham, W. E., Coles, E. K., Gnagy, E. M., Chronis-Tuscano, A., & O'Connor, B. C. (2009). A meta-analysis of behavioral treatments for attention deficit/ hyperactivity disorder. *Clinical Psychology Review, 29,* 129–140.

Fadnes, L. T., Engebretsen, I. M., Wamani, H., Wangisi, J., Tumwine, J. K., & Tylleskar, T. (2009). Need to optimize infant feeding counseling: A cross-sectional survey among HIV-positive mothers in Eastern Uganda. *BMC Pediatricsk, 9* (1), 2.

Fagan, J. F. (1992). Intelligence: A theoretical viewpoint. *Current Directions in Psychological Science, 1,* 82–86.

Fagan, J. F., Holland, C. R., & Wheeler, K. (2007). The prediction, from infancy, of adult IQ and achievement. *Intelligence, 35,* 225–231.

Fagot, B. J., Rodgers, C. S., & Leinbach, M. D. (2000). Theories of gender socialization. In T. Eckes & H. M. Trautner (Eds.), *The developmental social psychology of gender.* Mahwah, NJ: Erlbaum.

Fahey, T. D., Insel, P. M., & Roth, W. T. (2009). *Fit and well* (8th ed.). New York: McGraw-Hill.

Fair, D., & Schlaggar, B. L. (2008). Brain development. In M. M. Haith & J. B. Benson (Eds.), *Encyclopedia of infant and early childhood development.* Oxford, UK: Elsevier.

Fairweather, A. K., Anstey, K. J., Rodgers, B., & Butterworth, P. (2006). Factors distinguishing suicide attempters from suicide ideators in a community sample: Social issues and physical health problems. *Psychological Medicine, 31,* 1–11.

Fakhoury, J., Nimmo, G. A., & Autexier, C. (2007). Harnessing telomerase in cancer Therapeutics. *Anticancer Agents and Medicinal Chemistry, 7,* 475–484.

Falbo, T., & Poston, D. L. (1993). The academic, personality, and physical outcomes of only children in China. *Child Development, 64,* 18–35.

Fanklin, S. S. (2006). Hypertension in older people: Part I. *Journal of Clinical Hypertension, 8,* 444–449.

Fantasia, H. C. (2008). Concept analysis: Sexual decision-making in adolescence. *Nursing Forum, 43,* 80–90.

Fantz, R. L. (1963). Pattern vision in newborn infants. *Science, 140,* 286–297.

Farage, M. A., Miller, K. W., Berardesca, E., & Malbach, H. I. (2009). Clinical implications of aging skin: Cutaneous disorders in the elderly. *American Journal of Clinical Dermatology, 10,* 73–86.

Faraone, S. V. (2007). Stimulant therapy in the management of ADHD: Mixed amphetamine salts (extended release). *Expert Opinion on Pharmacotherapy, 8,* 2127–2134.

Farin, A., Liu, C. Y., Langmoen, I. A., & Apuzzo, M. L. (2009). The biological restoration of central nervous system architecture and function: Part 2—emergence of the realization of adult neurogenesis. *Neurosurgery, 64,* 581–600.

Faris, R. (2009). Bullying and peer victimization. In D. Carr (Ed.), *Encyclopedia of the life course and human development.* Boston: Gale Cengage.

Farooqui, T., & Farooqui, A. A. (2009). Aging: An important factor for the pathogenesis of neurogenerative diseases. *Mechanisms of Aging and Development, 130,* 203–215.

Farrell, M. P., & Rosenberg, S. D. (1981). *Men at mid-life.* Boston: Auburn House.

Farrington, D. (2004). Conduct disorder, aggression and delinquency. In R. Lerner & L. Steinberg (Eds.), *Handbook of adolescent psychology.* New York: Wiley.

Farrington, D. P. (2009). Conduct disorder, aggression, and delinquency. In R. M. Lerner & L. Steinberg (Eds.), *Handbook of adolescent psychology* (3rd ed.). New York: Wiley.

Farrington, D. P., Ttofi, M. M., & Coid, J. W. (2009). Development of adolescence-limited, late-onset, and persistent offenders from 8 to 48. *Aggressive Behavior, 35,* 150–163.

Fasig, L. (2000). Toddlers' understanding of ownership: Implications for self-concept development. *Social Development, 9,* 370–382.

Fear, N. T., Hey, K., Vincent, T., & Murphy, M. (2007). Paternal occupation and neural tube defects: A case-control study based on the Oxford Record Linkage Study register. *Pediatric and Perinatal Epidemiology, 21,* 163–168.

Federal Interagency Forum on Child and Family Statistics. (2002). *Key national indicators of well-being.* Washington, DC: U.S. Government Printing Office.

Federal Interagency Forum on Child and Family Statistics. (2008). *America's children: Key indicators of well-being.* Washington, DC: U.S. Government Printing Office.

Feeney, B. C., & Collins, N. L. (2007). Interpersonal safe haven and secure base caregiving processes in adulthood. In W. S. Rholes & J. A. Simpson (Eds.), *Adult attachment.* New York: Guilford.

Feeney, B. C., & Monin, J. K. (2008). An attachment-theoretical perspective on divorce. In J. Cassidy & P. R. Shaver (Eds.), *Handbook of attachment* (2nd ed.). New York: Guilford.

Feeney, M. P., & Sanford, C. A. (2004). Age effects in the middle ear: Wideband acoustical measures. *Journal of the Acoustical Society of America, 116,* 3546–3558.

Feeney, S., Moravcik, E., Nolte, S., & Christensen, D. (2010). *California version of who am I in the lives of children* (8th ed.). Upper Saddle River, NJ: Prentice Hall.

Fehr, B. (1996). *Friendship processes.* Thousand Oaks, CA: Sage.

Feinberg, M. E., Button, T. M., Neiderhiser, J. M., Reiss, D., & Hetherington, E. M. (2007). Parenting and antisocial behavior and depression: Evidence of genotype × parenting environment interaction. *Archives of General Psychiatry, 64,* 457–465.

Feinberg, M. E., & Kan, M. L. (2008). Establishing family foundations: Intervention effects on coparenting, parent/infant well-being, and parent-child relations. *Journal of Family Psychology, 22,* 253–263.

Feldhusen, J. (1999). Giftedness and creativity. In M. A. Runco & S. Pritzker (Eds.), *Encyclopedia of creativity.* San Diego: Academic Press.

Feldman, S. S., Turner, R., & Araujo, K. (1999). Interpersonal context as an influence on sexual timetables of youths: Gender and ethnic effects. *Journal of Research on Adolescence, 9,* 25–52.

Feng, L., Ng, T. P., Chuah, L., Niti, M., & Kua, E. H. (2006). Homocysteine, folate, and vitamin B-12 and cognitive performance in older Chinese adults: Findings from the Singapore Longitudinal Aging Study. *American Journal of Clinical Nutrition 84,* 1506–1512.

Fenigsen, R. (2008). Other people's lives: Reflections on medicine, ethics, and euthanasia. *Issues in Law and Medicine, 23,* 281–297.

Fenzel, L. M. (1994, February). *A prospective study of the effects of chronic strains on early adolescent self-worth and school adjustment.* Paper presented at the meeting of the Society for Research on Adolescence, San Diego.

Ferber, S. G., & Makhoul, I. R. (2008). Neurobehavioral assessment of skin-to-skin effects on reaction to pain in preterm infants: A randomized, controlled within-subject trial. *Acta Pediatrica, 97,* 171–176.

Ferguson, D. M., Harwood, L. J., & Shannon, F. T. (1987). Breastfeeding and subsequent social adjustment in 6- to 8-year-old children. *Journal of Child Psychology and Psychiatry, 28,* 378–386.

Fernyhough, C. (2008). Getting Vygotskian about theory of mind: Mediation, dialogue, and the development of social understanding. *Developmental Review, 28,* 225–262.

Ferrini, A. F., & Ferrini, R. (2008). *Health in the later years* (4th ed.). New York: McGraw-Hill.

Fidler, D. J. (2008). Down syndrome. In M. M. Haith & J. B. Benson (Eds.), *Encyclopedia of infant and early childhood development.* Oxford, UK: Elsevier.

Field, D. (1999). A cross-cultural perspective on continuity and change in social relations in old age: Introduction to a special issue. *International Journal of Aging and Human Development, 48,* 257–262.

Field, T. M. (2001). Massage therapy facilitates weight gain in preterm infants. *Current Directions in Psychological Science, 10,* 51–55.

Field, T. M. (2003). Stimulation of preterm infants. *Pediatrics Review, 24,* 4–11.

Field, T. M. (2007). *The amazing infant.* Malden, MA: Blackwell.

Field, T. M., & Diego, M. (2008). Vagal activity, early growth, and emotional development. *Infant Behavior and Development, 31,* 361–373.

Field, T. M., Diego, M., & Hernandez-Reif, M. (2007). Massage therapy research. *Developmental Review, 27,* 75–89.

Field, T. M., Diego, M., & Hernandez-Reif, M. (2008). Prematurity and potential predictors. *International Journal of Neuroscience, 118,* 277–289.

Field, T. M., Diego, M., Hernandez-Reif, M., Deeds, O., Holder, V., Schanberg, S., & Kuhn, C. (2009). Depressed pregnant black women have a greater incidence of prematurity and low birthweight outcomes. *Infant Behavior and Development, 32,* 10–16.

Field, T. M., & Hernandez-Reif, M. (2008). Touch and pain. In M. M. Haith & J. B. Benson (Eds.), *Encyclopedia of infant and early childhood development.* Oxford, UK: Elsevier.

Field, T. M., Grizzle, N., Scafidi, P., & Schanberg, S. (1996). Massage and relaxation therapies' effects on depressed adolescent mothers. *Adolescence, 31,* 903–911.

Field, T. M., Hernandez-Reif, M., Feijo, L., & Freedman, J. (2006). Prenatal, perinatal, and neonatal stimulation. *Infant Behavior and Development, 29,* 24–31.

Field, T. M., Hernandez-Reif, M., Freedman, J. (2004, Fall). Stimulation programs for preterm infants. *SRCD Social Policy Reports, XVIII* (No. 1), 1–20.

Figueiredo, P. A., Powers, S. K., Ferreira, R. M., Appell, H. J., & Duarta, J. A. (2009). Aging impairs skeletal muscle mitochondrial bioenergetic function. *Journals of Gerontology A: Biological Sciences and Medical Sciences, 64,* 21–33.

Finch, C. E. (2009). The neurobiology of middle-age has arrived. *Neurobiology of Aging, 30,* 515–520.

Fincham, F. D., Stanley, S. M., & Beach, S. R. H. (2007). Transformative processes in marriage: An analysis of emerging trends. *Journal of Marriage and the Family, 69,* 275–292.

Finger, B., Hans, S. L., Bernstein, V. J., & Cox, S. M. (2009). Parent relationship quality and infant-mother attachment. *Attachment and Human Development, 11,* 285–306.

Fingerman, K. L., Hay, E. L., Kamp Dush, C. M., Cichy, K. E., & Hosterman, S. (2007). Parents' and offspring's perceptions of change and continuity when parents experience the transition to old age. *Advances in Life Course Research, 12,* 275–306.

Fingerman, K. L., & Pitzer, L. (2007). Socialization in old age. In J. E. Grusec & P. D. Hastings (Eds.), *Handbook of socialization.* New York: Guilford.

Finkelstein, L. M., & Farrell, S. K. (2007). An expanded view of age bias in the workplace. In K. S. Shultz & G. A. Adams (Eds.), *Aging and work in the 21st century.* Mahwah, NJ: Erlbaum.

Finning, K. M., & Chitty, L. S. (2008). Noninvasive fetal sex determination: Impact on clinical practice. *Seminars in Fetal and Neonatal Medicine, 13,* 69–75.

Fiori, K. L., Antonucci, T. C., & Akiyama, H. (2009, in press). Profiles of social relations among older adults: A cross-cultural approach. *Ageing and Society.*

Fiori, K. L., Antonucci, T. C., & Cortina, K. S. (2006). Social network typologies and mental health among older adults. *Journals of Gerontology B: Psychological Sciences and Social Sciences, 61,* P25–P32.

Fiori, K. L., Smith, J., & Antonucci, T. C. (2007). Social network types among older adults: A multidimensional approach. *Journals of Gerontology B: Psychological Sciences and Social Sciences, 62,* P322–P330.

Fiori, M. (2009). A new look at emotional intelligence: A dual-process framework. *Peronality and Social Psychology Bulletin, 13,* 21–44.

Fischer, K. W. (2008). Dynamic cycles of cognitive and brain development: Measuring growth in mind, brain, and education. In A. M. Battro, K. W. Fischer & P. Léna (Eds.), *The educated brain.* Cambridge, UK: Cambridge University Press.

Fischer, K. W., & Bidell, T. L. (2006). Dynamic development of action and thought. In W. Damon & R. Lerner (Eds.), *Handbook of child psychology* (6th ed.). New York: Wiley.

Fischer, K. W., & Pruyne, E. (2003). Reflective thinking in adulthood. In J. Demick & C. Andreoletti (Eds.), *Handbook of adult development.* New York: Kluwer.

Fisher, B. S., Cullen, F. T., & Turner, M. G. (2000). *The sexual victimization of college women.* Washington, DC: National Institute of Justice.

Fisher, P. A. (2005, April). *Translational research on underlying mechanisms of risk among foster children: Implications for prevention science.* Paper presented at the meeting of the Society for Research in Child Development, Washington, DC.

Fiske, A., Wetherell, J. L., & Gatz, M. (2009). Depression in older adults. *Annual Review of Clinical Psychology* (Vol. 5). Palo Alto, CA: Annual Reviews.

Fitzgerald, M. M. J., Schneider, R. A., Salstrom, S., Zinzow, H. M., Jackson, J., & Fossel, R. V. (2008). Child sexual abuse, early family risk, and childhood parentification: Pathways to current psychosocial adjustment. *Journal of Family Psychology, 22,* 320–324.

Fivush, R. (2009). Sociocultural perspectives in autobiographical memory. In M. Courage & N. Cowan (Eds.), *The development of memory in infancy and childhood.* New York: Psychology Press.

Flannery, D. J., Hussey, D., Biebelhausen, L., & Wester, K. (2003). Crime, delinquency, and youth gangs. In G. Adams & M. Berzonsky (Eds.), *Blackwell handbook of adolescence.* Malden, MA: Blackwell.

Flavell, J. H. (2004). Theory-of-mind development. *Merrill-Palmer Quarterly, 50,* 274–290.

Flavell, J. H., Friedrichs, A., & Hoyt, J. (1970). Developmental changes in memorization processes. *Cognitive Psychology, 1,* 324–340.

Flavell, J. H., Green, F. L., & Flavell, E. R., (1993). Children's understanding of the stream of consciousness. *Child Development, 64*, 95–120.

Flavell, J. H., Green, F. L., & Flavell, E. R. (1995). The development of children's knowledge about attentional focus. *Developmental Psychology, 31*, 706–712.

Flavell, J. H., Green, F. L., & Flavell, E. R. (1998). The mind has a mind of its own: Developing knowledge about mental uncontrollability. *Cognitive Development, 13*, 127–138.

Flavell, J. H., Green, F. L., & Flavell, E. R. (2000). Development of children's awareness of their own thoughts. *Journal of Cognition and Development, 1*, 97–113.

Flavell, J. H., Miller, P. H., & Miller, S. (2002). *Cognitive development* (4th ed.). Upper Saddle River, NJ: Prentice Hall.

Flavell, J., Mumme, D., Green, F., and Flavell E. (1992). Young children's understanding of different types of beliefs. *Child Development, 63*, 960–977.

Fletcher, A. C., Steinberg, L., & Williams-Wheeler, M. (2004). Parental influences on adolescent problem behavior: Revisiting Stattin and Kerr. *Child Development, 75*, 781–796.

Fletcher, A. E., Breeze, E., & Shetty, P. S. (2003), Antioxidant vitamins and mortality in older persons. *American Journal of Nutrition, 78*, 999–1010.

Flint, M. S., Baum, A., Chambers, W. H., & Jenkins, F. J. (2007). Induction of DNA damage, alteration of DNA repair, and transcriptional activation by stress hormones. *Psychoneuroendocrinology, 32*, 470–479.

Flom, R., & Pick, A. D. (2003). Verbal encouragement and joint attention in 18-month-old infants. *Infant Behavior and Development, 26*, 121–134.

Flora, S. J. (2007). Role of free radicals and antioxidants in health and disese. *Cellular and Molecular Biology, 53*, 1–2.

Florence, N. (2010). *Multiculturalism 101*. New York: McGraw-Hill.

Floriani, V., & Kennedy, C. (2008). Promotion of physical activity in children. *Current Opinion in Pediatrics, 20*, 90–95.

Florsheim, P., Moore, D., & Edgington, C. (2003). Romantic relationships among pregnant and parenting adolescents. In P. Florsheim (Ed.), *Adolescent romantic relations and sexual behavior*. Mahwah, NJ: Erlbaum.

Flynn, J. R. (1999). Searching for justice: The discovery of IQ gains over time. *American Psychologist, 54*, 5–20.

Flynn, J. R. (2007). The history of the American mind in the 20th century: A scenario to explain gains over time and a case for the irrelevance of *g*. In P. C. Kyllonen, R. D. Roberts, & L. Stankov (Eds.), *Extending intelligence*. Mahwah, NJ: Erlbaum.

Flynn, L., Budd, M., & Modelski, J. (2008). Enhancing resource utilization among pregnant adolescents. *Public Health Nursing, 25*, 140–148.

Fonseca, E. B., Celik, E., Parra, M., Singh, M., Nicolaides, K. H., & the Fetal Medicine Foundation Second Trimester Screening Group. (2007). Progesterone and the risk of preterm birth among women with a short cervix. *New England Journal of Medicine, 357*, 462–469.

Fontana, L. (2008). Calorie restriction and cardiometabolic health. *European Journal of Cardiovascular Prevention and Rehabilitation, 15*, 3–9.

Fontana, L. (2009). The scientific basis of caloric restriction leading to longer life. *Current Opinion in Gastroenterology, 25*, 144–150.

Fontenot, M. B. (2007). Transition and adaptation to adoptive motherhood. *Journal of Obstetrics, Gynecologic, and Neonatal Nursing, 36*, 175–182.

Food & Nutrition Service. (2009). *The new look of the women, infants, and children (WIC) program*. Retrieved January 21, 2009, from www.health.state.ny.us/prevention/nutrition/wic/the_new_look_of_wic.htm

Forcier, R. C., & Descy, D. E. (2008). *Computer as an educational tool* (5th ed.). Boston: Allyn & Bacon.

Forgatch, M. S., Patterson, G. R., Degarmo, D. S., & Beldavs, Z. G. (2009). Testing the Oregon delinquency model with 9-year follow-up of the Oregon Divorce Study. *Development and Psychopathology, 21*, 637–660.

Forrester, M. B. (2007). Oxycodone abuse in Texas, 1998–2004. *Journal of Toxicology and Environment Health A, 70*, 534–538.

Forrester, M. B., & Merz, R. D. (2007). Genetic counseling utilization by families with offspring affected by birth defects, Hawaii, 1986–2003. *American Journal of Medical Genetics A, 143*, 1045–1052.

Fouad, N. A., & Bynner, J. (2008) Work transitions. *American Psychologist, 63*, 241–251

Fowler, C. G., & Leigh-Paffenroth, E. D. (2007). Hearing. In J. E. Birren (Ed.), *Encyclopedia of gerontology* (2nd ed). San Diego: Academic Press.

Fowler-Brown, A., & Kahwati, L. C. (2004). Prevention and treatment of overweight in children and adolescents. *American Family Physician, 69*, 2591–2598.

Fox, B. J. (2010). *Phonics and structural analysis for the teacher of reading* (10th ed.). Boston: Allyn & Bacon.

Fozard, J. L. (2000). Sensory and cognitive changes with age. In K. W. Schaie & M. Pietrucha (Eds.), *Mobility and transportation in the elderly*. New York: Springer.

Fozard, J. L., & Gordon-Salant, S. (2001). Changes in vision and hearing with aging. In J. E. Birren & K. W. Schaie (Eds.), *Handbook of the psychology of aging* (5th ed.). San Diego: Academic Press.

Francis, J., Fraser, G., & Marcia, J. E. (1989). *Cognitive and experimental factors in moratorium-achievement (MAMA) cycles*. Unpublished manuscript, Department of Psychology, Simon Fraser University, Burnaby, British Columbia.

Frankl, V. (1984). *Man's search for meaning*. New York: Basic Books.

Franz, C. E. (1996). The implications of preschool tempo and motoric activity level for personality decades later. Reported in Caspi, A. (1998). Personality development across the life course. In W. Damon (Ed.), *Handbook of child psychology* (Vol. 3). New York: Wiley, p. 337.

Fraser, S. (Ed.). (1995). *The bell curve wars: Race, intelligence, and the future of America*. New York: Basic Books.

Fratelli, N., Papageorghiou, A. T., Prefumo, F., Bakalis, S., Homfray, T., & Thilaganathan, B. (2007). Outcome of prenatally diagnosed agenesis of the corpus callosum. *Prenatal Diagnosis, 27*, 512–517.

Frazier, P. A., & Cook, S. W. (1993). Correlates of distress following heterosexual relationship dissolution. *Journal of Social and Personal Relationships, 10*, 55–67.

Frazier, P., Tashiro, T., Herman, M., Steger, M., & Long, J. (2004). Correlates of levels and patterns of positive life changes following sexual assault. *Journal of Consulting and Clinical Psychology, 72*, 19–30.

Frederikse, M., Lu, A., Aylward, E., Barta, P., Shanha, T., & Pearlson, G. (2000). Sex differences in inferior lobule volume in schizophrenia. *American Journal of Psychiatry, 157*, 422–427.

Fredrikson, K., Rhodes, J., Reddy, R., & Way, N. (2004). Sleepless in Chicago: Tracking the effects of sleep loss during middle school years. *Child Development, 75*, 84–95.

Freedman, J. L. (1984). Effects of television violence on aggressiveness. *Psychological Bulletin, 96*, 227–246.

Freeman, K. E., & Gehl, K. S. (1995, March). *Beginnings, middles, and ends: 24-month-olds' understanding of analogy*. Paper presented at the meeting of the Society for Research in Child Development, Indianapolis.

Freisthler, B., Merritt, D. H., & LaScala, E. A. (2006). Understanding the ecology of child maltreatment: A review of the literature and directions for future research. *Child Maltreatment, 11* (3), 263–280.

French, D. C., Eisenberg, N., Vaughan, J., Purwono, U., & Suryanti, T. A. (2008). Religious involvement and the social competence and adjustment of Indonesian Muslim adolescents. *Developmental Psychology, 44*, 597–611.

Fretts, R. C., Zera, C., & Heffner, C. Z. (2008). Maternal age and pregnancy. In M. M. Haith & J. B. Benson (Eds.), *Encyclopedia of infant and early childhood development*. London, UK: Elsevier.

Freud, S. (1917). *A general introduction to psycho-analysis*. New York: Washington Square Press.

Freund, A. M., & Baltes, P. B. (2002). Life-management strategies of selection, optimization, and compensation: Measurement by self-report and construct validity. *Journal of Personality and Social Psychology, 82*, 642–662.

Frey, W. H. (2007). *Mapping the growth of older America: Seniors and boomers in the early 21st century*. Washington, DC: The Brookings Institution.

Friedman, S. L., Melhuish, E. & Hill, C. (2009, in press). Childcare research at the dawn of a new millennium: An update. In G. Bremner & T. Wachs, (Eds.) *Wiley-Blackwell handbook of infant development* (2nd ed.). Oxford, UK: Wiley-Blackwell.

Frisco, M. L. (2009). Obesity, childhood and adolescence. In D. Carr (Ed.), *Encyclopedia of the life course and human development*. Boston: Gale Cengage.

Fritschmann, N. S., & Solari, E. J. (2008). Learning disabilities. In N. J. Salkind (Ed.), *Encyclopedia of educational psychology*. Thousand Oaks, CA: Sage.

Froh, J. J., Yurkewicz, C., & Kashdan, T. B. (2009). Gratitude and subjective well-being in early adolescence: Examining gender differences. *Journal of Adolescence, 32*, 633–650.

Fry, C. L. (2007). Comparative and cross-cultural studies. In J. E. Birren (Ed.), *Encyclopedia of gerontology* (2nd ed.). San Diego: Academic Press.

Fry, P. S. (2001). The unique contribution of key existential factors to the prediction of psychological well-being of older adults following spousal loss. *The Gerontologist, 41*, 69–81.

Frydenberg, E. (2008). *Adolescent coping*. Clifton, NJ: Psychology Press.

Fukunaga, A., Uematsu, H., & Sugimoto, K. (2005). Influences of age on taste perception and oral somatic sensation. *Journals of Gerontology A: Biological Sciences and Medical Sciences, 60*, 109A–113A.

Fuligni, A. J., & Hardway, C. (2006). Daily variations in adolescents' sleep, activities, and psychological well-being. *Journal of Research on Adolescence, 16*, 353–378.

Fuligni, A. J., Hughes, D. L., & Way, N. (2009). Ethnicity and immigration. In R. M. Lerner & L. Steinberg (Eds.), *Handbook of adolescent psychology* (3rd ed.). New York: Wiley.

Furman, E. (2005). *Boomerang nation*. New York: Fireside.

Furman, W., Low, S., & Ho, M. (2009). Romantic experience and psychosocial adjustment in middle adolescence. *Journal of Clinical Child and Adolescent Psychology, 38*, 1–16.

Furth, H. G., & Wachs, H. (1975). *Thinking goes to school*. New York: Oxford University Press.

G

Gable, S., Chang, Y., & Krull, J. L. (2007). Television watching and frequency of family meals are predictive of overweight onset and persistence in a national sample of preschool children. *Journal of the American Dietetic Association, 107*, 53–61.

Gaff, C. L., Williams, J. K., & McInerney, J. D. (2008). Genetics in health practice and education special issue. *Journal of Genetic Counseling, 17*, 143–144.

Gagliese, L. (2009). Pain and aging: The emergence of a new subfield of pain research. *Journal of Pain, 10*, 343–353.

Galambos, N. L. (2004). Gender and gender role development in adolescence. In R. Lerner & L. Steinberg (Eds.), *Handbook of adolescence*. New York: Wiley.

Galambos, N. L., Berenbaum, S. A., & McHale, S. M. (2009). Gender development in adolescence. In R. M. Lerner & L. Steinberg (Eds.), *Handbook of adolescent psychology* (3rd ed.). New York: Wiley.

Galambos, N. L., Petersen, A. C., Richards, M., & Gitleson, I. B. (1985). The Attitudes toward Women Scale for Adolescents (AWSA): A study of reliability and validity. *Sex Roles, 13*, 343–356.

Galinsky, E., & David, J. (1988). *The preschool years: Family strategies that work—from experts and parents*. New York: Times Books.

Gallagher, J. J. (2007). *Teaching science for understanding*. Upper Saddle River, NJ: Prentice Hall.

Gallo, L. C., Troxel, W. M., Matthews, K. A., & Kuller, L. W. (2003). Marital status and quality in middle-aged women: Associations with levels and trajectories of cardiovascular risk factors. *Health Psychology, 22*, 453–463.

Gallo, W. T., Bradley, E. H., Dubin, J. A., Jones, R. N., Falba, T. A., Teng, H.-M., & Kasl, S. V. (2006). The persistence of depressive symptoms in older workers who experience involuntary job loss: Results from the health and retirement survey. *Journals of Gerontology B: Psychological Sciences, and Social Sciences, 61*, S221–S228.

Galloway, J. C., & Thelen, E. (2004). Feet first: Object exploration in young infants. *Infant Behavior and Development, 27*, 107–112.

Gallup, G. W., & Bezilla, R. (1992). *The religious life of young Americans*. Princeton, NJ: Gallup Institute.

Gamble, W. C., & Modry-Mandell, K. (2008). Family relations and the adjustment of young children of Mexican descent: Do family cultural values moderate these associations. *Social Development, 17*, 358–379.

Ganong, L., Coleman, M., & Hans, J. (2006). Divorce as prelude to stepfamily living and the consequences of re-divorce. In M. A. Fine & J. H. Harvey (Eds.), *Handbook of divorce and relationship dissolution*. Mahwah, NJ: Erlbaum.

Gao, X., Yuan, S., Jayaraman, S., & Gursky, O. (2009). Differential stability of high-density lipoprotein subclasses: Effects of particle size and protein composition. *Journal of Molecular Biology, 387*, 628–638.

Garand, L., Mitchell, A. M., Dietrick, A., Hijjawi, S. P., & Pan, D. (2006). Suicide in older adults: Nursing assessment of suicide risk. *Issues in Mental Health Nursing, 27*, 355–370.

Garbarino, J. (1999). *Lost boys: Why our sons turn violent and how we can save them*. New York: Free Press.

Garbarino, J., & Asp, C. F. (1981). *Successful schools and competent students*. Lexington, MA: Lexington Books.

Garcia, E. E. (2008). Bilingual education in the United States. In J. Altarriba & R. R. Heredia (Eds.), *An introduction to bilingualism*. Philadelphia: Psychology Press.

Garcia-Bournissen, F., & others. (2008). Fetal exposure to isotretinoin—an international problem. *Reproductive Toxicology, 25*, 124–128.

Gardner, D. S., Hosking, J., Metcalf, B. S., An, J., Voss, L. D., & Wilkin, T. J. (2009). Contribution of early weight gain to childhood overweight and metabolic health: A longitudinal study (EarlyBird 36). *Pediatrics, 123*, e67–e73.

Gardner, H. (1983). *Frames of mind*. New York: Basic Books.

Gardner, H. (2002). The pursuit of excellence through education. In M. Ferrari (Ed.), *Learning from extraordinary minds*. Mahwah, NJ: Erlbaum.

Gardner, M., & Steinberg, L. (2005). Peer influence on risk taking, risk preference, and risky decision making in adolescence and adulthood. *Developmental Psychology, 41*, 625–635.

Garel, C. (2008). Fetal MRI: What is the future? *Ultrasound in Obstetrics and Gynecology, 31*, 123–128.

Gargiulo, R. M. (2009). *Special education in contemporary society*. Thousand Oaks, CA: Sage.

Garlow, S. J., Purselle, D., & Heninger, M. (2005). Ethnic differences in patterns of suicide across the life cycle. *American Journal of Psychiatry, 162*, 319–323.

Garofalo, R., Wolf, R. C., Wissow, L. S., Woods, E. R., & Goodman, E. (1999). Sexual orientation and risk of suicide attempts among a representative sample of youth. *Archives of Pediatrics and Adolescent Medicine, 153*, 487–493.

Garshasbi, A., & Faghih Zadeh, S. (2005). The effect of exercise on the intensity of low back pain in pregnant women. *International Journal of Gynecology and Obstetrics, 88*, 271–275.

Gartner, J., Larson, D. B., & Allen, G. D. (1991). Religious commitment and mental health: A review of the empirical literature. *Journal of Psychology and Theology, 19*, 6–25.

Garvey, C. (2000). *Play* (enlarged ed.). Cambridge, MA: Harvard University Press.

Gasser, L., & Keller, M. (2009, in press). Are the competent the morally good? Perspective taking and moral motivation of children involved in bullying. *Social Development.*

Gates, W. (1998, July 20). Charity begins when I'm ready (interview). *Fortune Magazine.*

Gathwala, G., Singh, B., & Balhara, B. (2008). KMG facilitates mother baby attachment in low birth weight infants. *Indian Journal of Pediatrics, 75,* 43–47.

Gatz, M., & Karel, M. J. (1993). Individual change in perceived control over 20 years. Special Issue: Planning and control processes across the life span. *International Journal of Behavioral Development, 16* (2), 305–322.

Gatz, M., Reynolds, C. A., Fratiglioni, L., Johansson, B., Mortimer, J. A., Berg, S., Fiske, A., & Pedersen, N. L. (2006). Role of genes and environments for explaining Alzheimer's disease. *Archives of General Psychiatry, 63,* 168–174.

Gaudreau, P., Amiot, C. E., & Vallerand, R. J. (2009). Trajectories of affective states in adolescent hockey players: Turning point and motivational antecedents. *Developmental Psychology, 45,* 307–319.

Gauthier, A. M., & Furstenberg, F. F. (2005). Historical trends in the patterns of time use among young adults in developed countries. In R. A. Setterson, F. F. Furstenberg, & R. G. Rumbaut (Eds.), *On the frontier of adulthood: Theories, research, and social policy.* Chicago: University of Chicago Press.

Gauvain, M. (2008). Vygotsky's sociocultural theory. In M. M. Haith & J. B. Benson (Eds.), *Encyclopedia of infant and early childhood development.* Oxford, UK: Elsevier.

Gauvain, M., & Parke, R. D. (2010). Socialization. In M. H. Bornstein (Ed.), *Handbook of cultural developmental science.* New York: Psychology Press.

Gay, L. R., Millis, G., & Airasian, P. W. (2009). *Educational research* (9th ed.). Upper Saddle River, NJ: Prentice Hall.

Gaziano, J. M., & others. (2009). Vitamins E and C in prevention of prostate and total cancer in men: The Physicians Health Study II randomized controlled trial. *Journal of the American Medical Association, 301,* 52–62.

Geda, Y. E., & others. (2008, June 7). *Exercise and mild cognitive impairment.* Paper presented at the meeting of the American Academy of Neurology, Chicago.

Gee, C. L., & Hayman, G. D. (2007). Children's evaluations of other people's self-descriptions. *Social Development, 16,* 800–810.

Geher, G., & Miller, G. (Eds.). (2007). *Mating intelligence.* Mahwah, NJ: Erlbaum.

Gelles, R. J., & Cavanaugh, M. M. (2005). Violence, abuse, and neglect in families and intimate relationships. In P. C. McKenry & S. J. Price (Eds.), *Families and change* (3rd ed.). Thousand Oaks, CA: Sage.

Gelman, R. (1969). Conservation acquisition: A problem of learning to attend to relevant attributes. *Journal of Experimental Child, 7,* 67–87.

Gelman, R., & Williams, E. M. (1998). Enabling constraints for cognitive development and learning. In W. Damon (Ed.), *Handbook of child psychology* (5th ed., Vol. 4). New York: Wiley.

Gelman, S. A. (2009). Learning from others: Children's construction of concepts. *Annual Review of Psychology* (Vol. 60). Palo Alto, CA: Annual Reviews.

Gelman, S. A., & Kalish, C. W. (2006). Conceptual development. In W. Damon & R. Lerner (Eds.), *Handbook of child psychology* (6th ed.). New York: Wiley.

Gelman, S. A., & Opfer, I. E. (2004). Development of the animate-inanimate distinction. In U. Goswami (Ed.), *Blackwell handbook of childhood cognitive development.* Malden, MA: Blackwell.

Gelman, S. A., Taylor, M. G., & Nguyen, S. P. (2004). Mother-child conversations about gender. *Monographs of the Society for Research in Child Development 69* (1, Serial No. 275).

Gennetian, L. A., & Miller, C. (2002). Children and welfare reform: A view from an experimental welfare reform program in Minnesota. *Child Development, 73,* 601–620.

Gentile, D. A., Anderson, C. A., Yukawa, S., Ihori, N., Saleem, M., Ming, L. K., Shibuya, A., Liau, A. K., Khoo, A., & Sakamoto, A. (2009). The effects of prosocial video games on prosocial behaviors: International evidence from correlational, experimental, and longitudinal studies. *Personality and Social Psychology Bulletin, 35,* 752–763.

Gentzler, A. L., & Kerns, K. A. (2004). Associations between insecure attachment and sexual experiences. *Personal Relationships, 11,* 249–266.

George, C., Main, M., & Kaplan, N. (1984). *Attachment interview with adults.* Unpublished manuscript, University of California, Berkeley.

George, C., & Solomon, J. (2009). The caregiving system: A behavioral systems approach to parenting. In J. Cassidy & P. R. Shaver (Eds.), *Handbook of attachment* (2nd ed.). New York: Guilford.

George, L. K. (2009). Religious and spirituality, later life. In D. Carr (Ed.), *Encyclopedia of the life course and human development.* Boston: Gale Cengage.

Georges, J. J., The, A. M., Onwuteaka-Philipsen, B. D., & van der Wal, G. (2008). Dealing with requests for euthanasia: A qualitative study investigating the experience of general practitioners. *Journal of Medical Ethics, 34,* 150–155.

Gerards, F. A., Twisk, J. W., Fetter, W. P., Wijnaendts, L. C., & van Vugt, J. M. (2008). Predicting pulmonary hypoplasia with 2- or 3-dimensional ultrasonography in complicated pregnancies. *American Journal of Gynecology and Obstetrics, 198,* e1–e6.

Gerrard, M., Gibbons, F. X., Houihan, A. E., Stock, M. L., & Pomery, E. A. (2008). A dual-process approach to health risk decision-making. *Developmental Review, 28,* 29–61.

Gershoff, B. T. (2002). Corporal punishment by parents and associated child behaviors and experiences: A meta-analysis and theoretical review. *Psychological Bulletin, 128,* 539–579.

Gerst, K., & Mutchler, J. E. (2009). Poverty, later life. In D. Carr (Ed.), *Encyclopedia of the life course and human development.* Boston: Gale Cengage.

Gerstof, D., Herlitz, A., & Smith, J. (2006). Stability of sex differences in cognition in advanced old age: The role of education and attrition. *Journals of Gerontology B: Psychological Sciences and Social Sciences, 61,* P245–P249.

Gesell, A. (1934). *An atlas of infant behavior.* New Haven, CT: Yale University Press.

Gesell, A. L. (1934). *Infancy and human growth.* New York: Macmillan.

Gewirtz, J. (1977). Maternal responding and the conditioning of infant crying: Directions of influence within the attachment-acquisition process. In B. C. Etzel, J. M. LeBlanc, & D. M. Baer (Eds.), *New developments in behavioral research.* Hillsdale, NJ: Erlbaum.

Ghetti, S., & Alexander, K. W. (2004). "If it happened, I would remember it": Strategic use of event memorability in the rejection of false autobiographical events. *Child Development, 75,* 542–561.

Giannarelli, F., Sonenstein, E., & Stagner, M. (2006). Child care arrangements and help for low-income families with young children: Evidence from the National Survey of America's Families. In N. Cabrera, R. Hutchens, & H. E. Peters (Eds.), *From welfare to childcare.* Mahwah, NJ: Erlbaum.

Giarrusso, R., & Bengtson, V. L. (2007). Self-esteem. In J. E. Birren (Ed.), *Encyclopedia of gerontology* (2nd ed.). San Diego: Academic Press.

Gibbons, J., & Ng, S. H. (2004). Acting bilingual and thinking bilingual. *Journal of Language and Social Psychology, 23,* 4–6.

Gibbons, R. D., Hedeker, D., & DuToit, S. (2009). Advances in analysis of longitudinal data. *Annual Review of Clinical Psychology* (Vol. 5). Palo Alto, CA: Annual Reviews.

Gibbs, J. C. (2009). Moral development. In S. J. Lopez & A. Beauchamp (Eds.), *Encyclopedia of positive psychology.* Washington, DC: American Psychological Association.

Gibbs, J. C., Basinger, K. S., Grime, R. L., & Snarey, J. R. (2007). Moral judgment across cultures: Revisiting Kohlberg's universality claims. *Developmental Review, 27,* 443–500.

Gibbs, J. T., & Huang, L. N. (1989). A conceptual framework for assessing and treating minority youth. In J. T. Gibbs & L. N. Huang (Eds.). *Children of color.* San Francisco: Jossey-Bass.

Gibson, E. J. (1969). *Principles of perceptual learning and development.* New York: Appleton-Century-Crofts.

Gibson, E. J. (1989). Exploratory behavior in the development of perceiving, acting, and the acquiring of knowledge. *Annual Review of Psychology* (Vol. 39). Palo Alto, CA: Annual Reviews.

Gibson, E. J. (2001). *Perceiving the affordances.* Mahwah, NJ: Erlbaum.

Gibson, E. J., Riccio, G., Schmuckler, M. A., Stoffregen, T. A., Rosenberg, D., & Taormina, J. (1987). Detection of the traversability of surfaces by crawling and walking infants. *Journal of Experimental Psychology: Human Perception and Performance. 13,* 533–544.

Gibson, E. J., & Walk, R. D. (1960). The "visual cliff." *Scientific American, 202,* 64–71.

Gibson, J. J. (1966). *The senses considered as perceptual systems.* Boston: Houghton Mifflin.

Gibson, J. J. (1979). *The ecological approach to visual perception.* Boston: Houghton Mifflin.

Gibson, L. Y., Bryne, S. M., Blair, E., Davis, E. A., Jacoby, P., & Zubrick, S. R. (2008). Clustering of psychological symptoms in overweight children. *Australian and New Zealand Journal of Psychiatry, 42,* 118–125.

Giedd, J. N. (2007, September 27). Commentary in S. Jayson "Teens driven to distraction." *USA Today,* pp. D1–2.

Giedd, J. N. (2008). The teen brain: Insights from neuroimaging. *Journal of Adolescent Health, 42,* 335–343.

Giedd, J. N., Lalonde, F. M., Celano, M. J., White, S. L., Wallace, G. L., Lee, N. R., & Lenroot, R. K. (2009). Anatomical brain magnetic imaging of typically developing children and adolescents. *Journal of the American Academy of Child and Adolescent Psychiatry, 48,* 465–470.

Gielen, J., Van den Branden, S., & Broeckaert, B. (2009). Religion and nurses' attitudes to euthanasia and physician assisted suicide. *Nursing Ethics, 16,* 303–318.

Gilbert, S. J., Meuwese, J. D., Towgood, K. J., Frith, C. D., & Burgess, P. W. (2009). Abnormal functional specialization within medial prefrontal cortex in high-functioning autism: A multi-voxel similarity analysis. *Brain, 132,* 869–878.

Gilligan, C. (1982). *In a different voice.* Cambridge, MA: Harvard University Press.

Gilligan, C. (1992, May). *Joining the resistance: Girls' development in adolescence.* Paper presented at the symposium on development and vulnerability in close relationships, Montreal, Quebec.

Gilligan, C. (1996). The centrality of relationships in psychological development: A puzzle, some evidence, and a theory. In G. G. Noam & K. W. Fischer (Eds.), *Development and vulnerability in close relationships.* Hillsdale, NJ: Erlbaum.

Gilligan, C., Spencer, R., Weinberg, M. K., & Bertsch, T. (2003). On the listening guide: A voice-centered relational model. In P. M. Carnic & J. E. Rhodes (Eds.), *Qualitative research in psychology.* Washington, DC: American Psychological Association.

Gill, S. V., Adolph, K. E., & Vereijken, B. (2009, in press). Change in action: How infants learn to walk down slopes. *Developmental Science.*

Gillum, R. F., & Ingram, D. D. (2007). Frequency of attendance at religious services, hypertension, and blood pressure: The third National Health and Nutrition Examination Survey. *Psychosomatic Medicine, 68,* 382–385.

Gillum, R. F., King, D. E., Obisesan, T. O., & Koenig, H. G. (2008). Frequency of attendance at religious services and mortality in a U.S. national cohort. *Annals of Epidemiology, 18,* 124–129.

Girls, Inc. (1991). *Truth, trusting, and technology: New research on preventing adolescent pregnancy.* Indianapolis: Author.

Givens, J. L., & Mitchell, J. L. (2009). Concerns about end-of-life care and support for euthanasia. *Journal of Pain and Symptom Management, 38,* 167–173.

Glascher, J., & others. (2009). Lesion mapping of cognitive abilities linked to intelligence. *Neuron, 61,* 681–691.

Glaser, R., & Kiecolt-Glaser, J. K. (2005). Stress-induced immune dysfunction: Implications for health. *Nature Review: Immunology, 5,* 243–251.

Glasser, A. (2008). Restoration of accommodation: Surgical options for correction of presbyopia. *Clinical and Experimental Optometry, 91,* 279–295.

Glina, S., Damiao, R., Abdo, C., AfifAbdo, J., Tseng, L.-J., & Stecher, V. (2009). Self-esteem, confidence, and relationships in Brazilian men with erectile dysfunction receiving sildenafil citrate: A randomized, parallel-group, double-blind, placebo-controlled study in Brazil. *Journal of Sexual Medicine, 6,* 268–275.

Gliori, G., Imm, P., Anderson, H. A., & Knobeloch, L. (2006). Fish consumption and advisory awareness among expectant women. *Wisconsin Medicine Journal, 105,* 41–44.

Glisky, E. L., & Kong, L. L. (2008). Do young and older adults rely on different processes in source memory tasks? A neuropsychological study. *Journal of Experimental Psychology: Learning, Memory, and Cognition, 34,* 809–822.

Gluck, J., & Bluck, S. (2007). Looking back across the life span: A life story account of the reminiscence bump. *Memory and Cognition, 35,* 1928–1939.

Gluck, M. E., Venti, C. A., Lindsay, R. S., Knowler, W. C., Salbe, A. D., & Krakoff, J. (2009, in press). Maternal influence, not diabetic intrauterine environment, predicts children's energy intake. *Obesity.*

Glynn, L. M., Schetter, C. D., Hobel, C. J., & Sandman, C. A. (2008). Pattern of perceived stress and anxiety in pregnancy predicts preterm birth. *Health Psychology, 27,* 43–51.

Goel, A., Sinha R. J., Dalela, D., Sankhwar, S., & Singh, V. (2009). Andropause in Indian men: A preliminary cross-sectional study. *Urology Journal, 6,* 40–46.

Goel, M. S., McCarthy, E. P., Phillips, R. S., & Wee, C. C. (2004). Obesity among U.S. immigrant subgroups by duration of residence. *Journal of the American Medical Association, 292,* 2860–2867.

Goffin, S. G., & Wilson, C. S. (2001). *Curriculum models and early childhood education. Appraising the relationship* (2nd ed.). Upper Saddle River, NJ: Prentice Hall.

Goh, V. I., & Koren, G. (2008). Folic acid in pregnancy and fetal outcomes. *Journal of Obstetrics and Gynecology, 28,* 3–13.

Golanska, E., & others. (2009, in press). Earlier onset of Alzheimer's disease: Risk polymorphisms within PRNP, PRND, CYP46, and APOE genes. *Journal of Alzheimer's Disease.*

Goldberg, W. A., & Lucas-Thompson, R. (2008). Maternal and paternal employment, effects of. In M. M. Haith & J. B. Benson (Eds.), *Encyclopedia of infant and early childhood development.* Oxford, UK: Elsevier.

Goldenberg, R. L., & Culhane, J. F. (2007). Low birth weight in the United States. *American Journal of Clinical Nutrition, 85* (Suppl.), S584–S590.

Goldfield, B. A., & Snow, C. E. (2009). Individual differences: Implications for the study of language acquisition. In J. Berko Gleason & N. B. Ratner (Eds.), *The development of language.* Boston: Allyn & Bacon.

Goldman, S., Wang, C., Salgado, M. W., Greene, P. E., Kim, M., & Rapin, I. (2009). Motor stereotypies in children with autism and other developmental disorders. *Developmental Medicine and Child Neurology, 51,* 30–38.

Goldschmidt, L., Richardson, G. A., Willford, J., & Day, N. L. (2008). Prenatal marijuana exposure and intelligence test performance at age 6. *Journal of the American Academy of Child and Adolescent Psychiatry, 47,* 254–263.

Goldsmith, B., Borrison, R. S., Vanderwerker, L. C., & Prigerson, H. G. (2008). Elevated rates of prolonged grief disorder in African Americans. *Death Studies, 32,* 352–365.

Goldsmith, H. (2010, in press). Human development: Biological and genetic processes in development. *Annual Review of Psychology* (Vol. 61). Palo Alto, CA: Annual Reviews.

Goldsmith, H. H. (2008). Behavior genetics. In M. M. Haith & J. B. Benson (Eds.), *Encyclopedia of infant and early childhood development.* Oxford, UK: Elsevier.

Goldstein, M. H., King, A. P., & West, M. J. (2003). Social interaction shapes babbling: Testing parallels between birdsong and speech. *Proceedings of the National Academy of Sciences USA, 100,* 8030–8035.

Goldston, D. B., Molock, S. D., Whitbeck, L. B., Murakami, J. L., Zayas, L. H., & Hall, G. C. (2008). Cultural considerations in adolescent suicide prevention and psychosocial treatment. *American Psychologist, 63,* 14–31.

Goleman, D. (1995). *Emotional intelligence.* New York: Basic Books.

Goleman, D., Kaufman, P., & Ray, M. (1993). *The creative spirit.* New York: Plume.

Gollnick, D. M., & Chinn, P. C. (2009). *Multicultural education in a pluralistic society* (8th ed.). Boston: Allyn & Bacon.

Golombok, S., Rust, J., Zervoulis, K., & Croudace, T., Golding, J., & Hines, M. (2008). Developmental trajectories of sex-typed behavior in boys and girls: A longitudinal general population study of children aged 2.5–8 years. *Child Development, 79,* 1583–1593.

Gong, X., & others. (2009). An investigation of ribosomal protein L10 gene in autism spectrum disorders. *BMC Medical Genetics, 10,* 7.

Gonzalez, A., Atkinson, L., & Fleming, A. S. (2009). Attachment and the comparative psychobiology of mothering. In M. de Haan & M. R. Gunnar (Eds.), *Handbook of developmental social neuroscience.* New York: Guilford.

Gonzalez, V., Yawkey, T. D., & Minaya-Rowe, L. (2006). *English-as-a-second-language (ESL) teaching and learning.* Boston: Allyn & Bacon.

Good, M., & Willoughby, T. (2008). Adolescence as a sensitive period for spiritual development. *Child Development Perspectives, 2,* 32–37.

Goodman, G. S., Batterman-Faunce, J. M., & Kenney, R. (1992). Optimizing children's testimony: Research and social policy issues concerning allegations of child sexual abuse. In D. Cicchetti & S. Toth (Eds.), *Child abuse, child development and social policy.* Norwood, NJ: Ablex.

Gopnik, A., & Schulz, L. (Eds.). (2007). *Causal learning.* New York: Oxford University Press.

Goral, M., Clark-Cotton, M. R., & Albert, M. L. (2007). Language disorders: General. In J. E. Birren (Ed.), *Encyclopedia of gerontology* (2nd ed.). San Diego: Academic Press.

Gordon, S., & Gordon, J. (1989). *Raising a child conservatively in a sexually permissive world.* New York: Simon & Schuster.

Gordon-Salant, S., Veni-Komshian, G. H., Fitzgibbons, P. J., & Barrett, S. (2006). Age related differences in identification of temporal cues in speech segments. *Journal of the Acoustical Society of America, 129,* 2455–2466.

Gortmaker, S. L., Peterson, K., Wiecha, J., Sobol, A. M., Dixit, S., Fox, M. K., & Laird, N. (1999). Reducing obesity via a school-based interdisciplinary intervention among youth. *Archives of Pediatric and Adolescent Medicine, 153,* 409–418.

Gosden, R. G. (2007). Menopause. In J. E. Birren (Ed.), *Encyclopedia of gerontology* (2nd ed.). San Diego: Academic Press.

Goswami, S. K., & Das, D. K. (2009, in press). Resveratrol and chemoprevention. *Cancer Letters.*

Gottlieb, G. (2007). Probabalistic epigenesis. *Developmental Science, 10,* 1–11.

Gottlieb, G., Wahlsten, D., & Lickliter, R. (2006). The significance of biology for human development: A developmental psychobiological systems view. In W. Damon & R. Lerner (Eds.), *Handbook of child psychology* (6th ed.). New York: Wiley.

Gottman, J. M. (1994). *Why marriages succeed or fail.* New York: Simon & Schuster.

Gottman, J. M. (2008). *Research on parenting.* Retrieved March 25, 2008, from www.gottman.com/parenting/research

Gottman, J. M. (2009). *Research on parenting.* Retrieved January 29, 2009, from www.gottman.com/parenting/research

Gottman, J. M., Coan, J., Carrere, S., & Swanson, C. (1998). Predicting marital happiness and stability from newlywed interactions. *Journal of Marriage and the Family, 60,* 5–22.

Gottman, J. M., & DeClaire, J. (1997). *The heart of parenting. Raising an emotionally intelligent child.* New York: Simon & Schuster.

Gottman, J. M., & Gottman, J. S. (2009). Gottman method of couple therapy. In A. S. Gurman (Ed.), *Clinical handbook of couple therapy* (4th ed.). New York: Guilford.

Gottman, J. M., Gottman, J. S., & Shapiro, A. (2009, in press). A new couples approach to interventions for the transition to parenthood. In M. S. Schultz, M. K. Pruett, P. K. Kerig, & R. D. Parke (Eds.), *Feathering the nest: Couple relationships, couples interventions, and children's development.* Washington, DC: American Psychological Association.

Gottman, J. M., & Parker, J. G. (Eds.). (1987). *Conversations of friends.* New York: Cambridge University Press.

Gottman, J. M., & Silver, N. (1999). *The seven principles for making marriages work.* New York: Crown.

Gouin, J. P., Glaser, R., Loving, T. J., Malarkey, W. B., Stowell, J., Houts, C., & Kiecolt-Glaser, J. K. (2009, in press). Attachment avoidance predicts inflammatory responses to marital conflict. *Brain, Behavior, and Immunity.*

Gould, E. (2007). How widespread is neurogenesis in mammals? *Nature Review: Neuroscience, 8,* 481–488.

Gove, W. R., Style, C. B., & Hughes, M. (1990). The effect of marriage on the well-being of adults: A theoretical analysis. *Journal of Health and Social Behavior, 24,* 122–131.

Gow, A. J., Johnson, W., Pattie, A., Whiteman, M. C., Starr, J., & Deary, I. J. (2008). Mental ability in childhood and cognitive aging. *Gerontology, 54,* 177–186.

Gowan, D. E. (2003). Christian beliefs concerning death and life after death. In C. D. Bryant (Ed.), *Handbook of death and dying.* Thousand Oaks, CA: Sage.

Graber, J. A. (2008). Pubertal and neuroendocrine development and risk for depressive disorders. In N. B. Allen & L. Sheeber (Eds.), *Adolescent emotional development and the emergence of depressive disorders.* New York: Cambridge University Press.

Gracia, E., & Herrero, J. (2008). Is it considered violence? The acceptability of physical punishment of children in Europe. *Journal of Marriage and the Family, 70,* 210–217.

Grady, C. L. (2008). Cognitive neuroscience of aging. *Annals of the New York Academy of Sciences, 1124,* 127–144.

Graham, J. E., Christian, L. M., & Kiecolt-Glaser, J. K. (2006). Stress, age, and immune function: Toward a lifespan approach. *Journal of Behavioral Medicine, 29,* 389–400.

Graham, J. H., & Beller, A. H. (2002). Nonresident fathers and their children: Child support and visitation from an economic perspective. In C. S. Tamis-LeMonda & N. Cabrera (Eds.), *The handbook of father involvement.* Mahwah, NJ: Erlbaum.

Graham, S. (1986, August). *Can attribution theory tell us something about motivation in blacks?* Paper presented at the meeting of the American Psychological Association, Washington, DC.

Graham, S. (1990). Motivation in Afro-Americans. In G. L. Berry & J. K. Asamen (Eds.), *Black students: Psychosocial issues and academic achievement.* Newbury Park, CA: Sage.

Graham, S. (2005, February 16). Commentary in *USA Today,* p. 2D.

Graham, S. (Ed.). (2006). Our children too: A history of the first 25 years of the Society for Research in Child Development. *Monographs of the Society for Research in Child Development* (Vol. 71, No. 1), 1–227.

Graham, S. (2009). Teaching writing. In P. Hogan (Ed.), *Cambridge encyclopedia of language sciences.* Cambridge, UK: Cambridge University Press.

Graham, S., & Olinghouse, N. (2009). Learning and teaching writing. In E. Anderman & L. Anderman (Eds.), *Psychology of classroom learning.* Farmington Hills, MI: Thomas Gale.

Graham, S., & Perin, D. (2007). A meta-analysis of writing instruction for adolescent students. *Journal of Educational Psychology, 99,* 445–476.

Gramling, L. F. (2007). Women in young and mid-adulthood: Theory advancement and retroduction. *ANS Advances in Nursing Science, 30,* 95–107.

Graven, S. (2006). Sleep and brain development. *Clinical Perinatology, 33,* 693–706.

Gray, J. (1992). *Men are from Mars, women are from Venus.* New York: HarperCollins.

Gray, K. A., Day, N. L., Leech, S., Richardson, G. A. (2005). Prenatal marijuana exposure: Effect on child depressive symptoms at ten years of age. *Neurotoxicology and Teratology, 27,* 439–448.

Graziano, A. M., & Raulin, M. L. (2010). *Research methods* (7th ed.). Boston: Allyn & Bacon.

Greder, K. A., & Allen, W. D. (2007). Parenting in color: Culturally diverse perspectives on parenting. In B. S. Trask & R. R. Hamon (Eds.), *Cultural diversity and families.* Thousand Oaks, CA: Sage.

Gredler, M. E. (2008). Vygotsky's cultural historical theory of development. In N. J. Salkind (Ed.), *Encyclopedia of educational psychology.* Thousand Oaks, CA: Sage.

Gredler, M. E. (2009). Hiding in plain sight: The stages of mastery/self-regulation in Vygotsky's cultural-history theory. *Educational Psychologist, 44,* 1–19.

Greenberger, E., & Steinberg, L. (1986). *When teenagers work: The psychological social costs of adolescent employment.* New York: Basic Books.

Greene, M. F. (2009). Making small risks even smaller. *New England Journal of Medicine, 360,* 183–184.

Greenfield, L. A., & Marks, N. F. (2004). Formal volunteering as a protective factor for older adults' psychological well-being. *Journals of Gerontology B: Psychological Sciences and Social Sciences, 59,* S258–S264.

Greenfield, P. M. (1966). On culture and conservation. In J. S. Bruner, R. P. Oliver, & P. M. Greenfield (Eds.), *Studies in cognitive growth.* New York: Wiley.

Greenfield, P. M. (2009). Linking social change and developmental change: Shifting pathways of human development. *Developmental Psychology, 43,* 401–418.

Greenfield, P. M., & Suzuki, L. K. (1998). Culture and human development. In I. E. Siegel & K. A. Renninger (Eds.), *Handbook of child psychology* (5th ed., Vol. 4). New York: Wiley.

Greenfield, P. M., Suzuki, L. K., & Rothstein-Fisch, C. (2006). Cultural pathways through human development. In W. Damon & R. Lerner (Eds.), *Handbook of child psychology* (6th ed.). New York: Wiley.

Greenfield, P. M., Trumbull, E., Keller, H., Rothstein-Fisch, C., Suzuki, L., & Quiroz, B. (2006). Cultural conceptions of learning and development. In P. A. Alexander & P. H. Winne (Eds.), *Handbook of educational psychology* (2nd ed.). Mahwah, NJ: Erlbaum.

Greer, F. R., Sicherer, S. H., Burks, A. W., & the Committee on Nutrition and Section on Allergy and Immunology. (2008). Effects of early nutritional interventions on the development of atopic disease in infants and children: The role of maternal dietary restriction, breast feeding, timing of introduction of complementary foods, and hydrolyzed formulas. *Pediatrics, 121,* 183–191.

Grello, C. M., Welsh, D. P., & Harper, M. S. (2006). No strings attached: The nature of casual sex in college students. *The Journal of Sex Research, 43,* 255–267.

Griffiths, R., Horsfall, J., Moore, M., Lane, D., Kroon, V., & Langdon, R. (2007). Assessment of health, well-being, and social connections: A survey of women living in Western Sydney. *International Journal of Nursing Practice, 13,* 3–13.

Grigorenko, E. (2000). Heritability and intelligence. In R. J. Sternberg (Ed.), *Handbook of intelligence.* New York: Cambridge University Press.

Grigorenko, E. L., Geissler, P., Prince, R., Okatcha, F., Nokes, C., Kenney, D. A., Bundy, D. A., & Sternberg, R. J. (2001). The organization of Luo conceptions of intelligence: A study of implicit theories in a Kenyan village. *International Journal of Behavioral Development, 25,* 367–378.

Grigorenko, E. L., & Takanishi, R. (2010, in press). *Handbook of U.S. immigration and education.* New York: Springer.

Gronlund, N. E., & Waugh, C. K. (2009). *Assessment of student achievement* (9th ed.). Upper Saddle River, NJ: Prentice Hall.

Gropman, A. L., & Adams, D. R. (2007). Atypical patterns of inheritance. *Seminars in Pediatric Neurology, 14,* 34–45.

Gross, D., Garvey, C., Julion, W., Fogg, L., Tucker, S., & Mokros, H. (2009). Efficacy of the Chicago Parent Program with low-income African American and Latino parents of young children. *Prevention Science, 10,* 54–65.

Gross, H. E., Shaw, D. S., Moilanen, K. L., Dishion, T. J., & Wilson, M. N. (2008). Reciprocal models of child behavior and depressive symptoms in mothers and fathers in a sample of children at risk for early conduct problems. *Journal of Family Psychology, 22,* 742–751.

Grossmann, K., Grossmann, K. E., Spangler, G., Suess, G., & Unzner, L. (1985). Maternal sensitivity and newborns' orientation responses as related to quality of attachment in northern Germany. In I. Bretherton & E. Waters (Eds.), Growing points of attachment theory and research. *Monographs of the Society for Research in Child Development, 50* (1–2, Serial No. 209).

Grotevant, H. D., & Cooper, C. R. (1998). Individuality and connectedness in adolescent development: Review and prospects for research on identity, relationships, and context. In E. Skoe & A. von der Lippe (Eds.), *Personality development in adolescence: A cross-national and life-span perspective.* London: Routledge.

Grotevant, H. D., van Dulmen, M. H. M., Dunbar, N., Nelson-Christinedaughter, J., Christensen, M., Fan, X., & Miller, B. C. (2006). Antisocial behavior of adoptees and nonadoptees: Prediction from early history and adolescent relationships. *Journal of Research on Adolescence, 16,* 105–131.

Grusec, J. (2006). Development of moral behavior and a conscience from a socialization perpective. In M. Killen & J. G. Smetana (Eds.), *Handbook of moral development.* Mahwah, NJ: Erlbaum.

Grych, J. M. (2002). Marital relationships and parenting. In M. H. Bornstein (Ed.), *Handbook of parenting.* Mahwah, NJ: Erlbaum.

Grzywacz, J. G. (2009). Work-family conflict. In D. Carr (Ed.), *Encyclopedia of the life course and human development.* Boston: Gale Cengage.

Gu, D., Dupre, M. E., Sautter, J., Zhu, H., Liu, Y., & Yi, Z. (2009). Frailty and mortality among Chinese at advanced ages. *Journals of Gerontology A: Biological Sciences and Medical Sciences, 64,* 279–289.

Gualtieri, C. T., & Johnson, L. G. (2008). Age-related cognitive decline in patients with mood disorders. *Progress in Neuropsychopharmacology and Biological Psychiatry, 32,* 962–967.

Guelinckx, I., Devlieger, R., Beckers, K., & Vansant, G. (2008). Maternal obesity: Pregnancy complications, gestational gain, and nutrition. *Obesity Review, 9,* 140–150.

Guilford, J. P. (1967). *The structure of intellect.* New York: McGraw-Hill.

Guillem, F, & Mograss, M. (2005). Gender differences in memory processing: Evidence from event-related potentials to faces. *Brain and Cognition, 57,* 84–92.

Guillot M. (2009). Life expectancy. In D. Carr (Ed.), *Encyclopedia of the life course and human development.* Gale Cengage.

Gumora, G., & Arsenio, W. (2002). Emotionality, emotion regulation, and school performance in middle school children. *Journal of School Psychology, 40,* 395–413.

Gump, B., & Matthews, K. (2000 March). *Annual vacations, health, and death.* Paper presented at the meeting of American Psychosomatic Society, Savannah, GA.

Gunnar, M., & Quevado, K. (2007). The neurobiology of stress and development. *Annual Review of Psychology* (Vol. 58). Palo Alto, CA: Annual Reviews.

Gunnar, M. R., Fisher, P. A., & the Early Experience, Stress, and Prevention Network. (2006). Bringing basic research on early experience and stress neurobiology to bear on preventive interventions for neglected and maltreated children. *Development and Psychopathology, 18,* 651–677.

Gunnar, M. R., Malone, S., & Fisch, R. O. (1987). The psychobiology of stress and coping in the human neonate: Studies of the adrenocortical activity in response to stress in the first week of life. In T. Field, P. McCabe, & N. Scheiderman (Eds.). *Stress and coping.* Hillsdale, NJ: Erlbaum.

Guo, G., & Tillman, K. H. (2009). Trajectories of depressive symptoms, dopamine D2 and D4 receptors, family socioeconomic status, and social support in adolescence and young adulthood. *Psychiatric Genetics, 19,* 14–26.

Guo, S. S., Wu, W., Chumlea, W. C., & Roche, A. F. (2002). Predicting overweight and obesity in adulthood from body mass index values in childhood and adolescence. *American Journal of Clinical Nutrition, 76,* 653–658.

Gupta, A., Thornton, J. W., & Huston, A. C. (2008). Working families should not be poor—the New Hope program. In D. R. Crane & T. B. Heaton (Eds.), *Handbook of families and poverty.* Thousand Oaks, CA: Sage.

Gur, R. C., Mozley, L. H., Mozley, P. D., Resnick, S. M., Karp, J. S., Alavi, A., Arnold, S. E., & Gur, R. E. (1995). Sex differences in regional cerebral glucose metabolism during a resting state. *Science, 267,* 528–531.

Gurevich-Panigrahi, T., Panigrahi, S., Wiechec, E., & Los, M. (2009). Obesity: Pathophysiology and clinical management. *Current Medicinal Chemistry, 16,* 506–521.

Gurwitch, R. H., Silovksy, J. F., Schultz, S., Kees, M., & Burlingame, S. (2001). *Reactions and guidelines for children following trauma/disaster.* Norman, OK: Department of Pediatrics, University of Oklahoma Health Sciences Center.

Gutchess, A. H., Welsch, R. C., Hedden, T., Bangert, A., Minear, M., Liu, L. L., & Park, D. C. (2005). Aging and the neural correlates of successful picture encoding: Frontal activations compensate for decreased medial-temporal activity. *Journal of Cognitive Neuroscience, 17,* 84–96.

Gutmann, D. L. (1975). Parenthood: A key to the comparative study of the life cycle. In N. Datan & L. Ginsberg (Eds.), *Life-span developmental psychology: Normative life crises.* New York: Academic Press.

Guzzetta, A., Pecini, C., Biagi, L., Tosetti, M., Brizzolara, D., Chilosi, A., Cipriani, P., Petacchi, E., & Cioni, G. (2008). Language organization in left perinatal stroke. *Neuropediatrics, 39,* 157–163.

H

Ha, J. H., & Ingersoll-Dayton, B. (2008). The effect of widowhood on intergenerational ambivalence. *Journals of Gerontology B: Psychological Sciences and Social Sciences, 63,* S49–S58.

Haber, D. (2007). Life review: Implementation, theory, research, and therapy. *International Journal of Aging and Human Development, 63,* 153–171.

Hackney, M. E., & Earhart, G. M. (2009, in press). Health-related quality of life and alternative forms of exercise in Parkinson disease. *Parkinsonism and Related Disorders.*

Haga, M. (2008). The relationship between physical fitness and motor competence in children. *Child: Child Care and Health Development, 34,* 329–334.

Hagen, J. W., & Lamb-Parker, F. G. (2008). Head Start. In M. M. Haith & J. B. Benson (Eds.), *Encyclopedia of infant and early childhood development.* Oxford, UK: Elsevier.

Hagestad, G. O. (1985). Continuity and connectedness. In V. L. Bengtson (Ed.), *Grandparent-hood.* Beverly Hills, CA: Sage.

Hagestad, G. O., & Uhlenberg, P. (2007). The impact of demographic changes on relations between age groups and generations: A comparative perspective. In K. W. Schaie & P. Uhlenberg (Eds.), *Demographic changes and the well-being of older persons.* New York: Springer.

Hagg, T. (2009). From neurotransmitters to neurotrophic factors to neurogenesis. *Neuroscientist, 15,* 20–27.

Hahn, D. B., Payne, W. A., & Lucas, E. B. (2009). *Focus on health* (9th ed.). New York: McGraw-Hill.

Hahn, S., Zhong, X. Y., & Holzgreve, W. (2008). Recent progress in non-invasive prenatal diagnosis. *Seminars in Fetal and Neonatal Medicine, 13,* 57–62.

Hahn, W. K. (1987). Cerebral lateralization of function: From infancy through childhood. *Psychological Bulletin, 101,* 376–392.

Haier, R. J. (2009). Neuro-intelligence, neurometrics, and the next phase of brain imaging studies. *Intelligence, 37,* 121–123.

Haier, R. J., & others. (2009). Gray matter and intelligence factors: Is there a neuro-*g*? *Intelligence, 37,* 136–144.

Haith, M. M., & Benson, J. B. (1998). Infant cognition. In W. Damon (Ed.). *Handbook of child psychology* (5th ed., Vol. 2). New York: Wiley.

Haith, M. M., Hazen, C., & Goodman, G. S. (1988). Expectation and anticipation of dynamic visual events by 3.5 month old babies. *Child Development, 59,* 467–479.

Hakuta, K. (2001, April 5). *Key policy milestones and directions in the education of English language learners.* Paper prepared for the Rockefeller Foundation Symposium, Leveraging change: An emerging framework for educational equity, Washington, DC.

Hakuta, K. (2005, April). *Bilingualism at the intersection of research and public policy.* Paper presented at the meeting of the Society for Research in Child Development, Atlanta.

Hakuta, K., Butler, Y. G., & Witt, D. (2001). *How long does it take English learners to attain proficiency?* Berkeley, CA: The University of California Linguistic Minority Research Institute Policy Report 2000–1.

Hale, S. (1990). A global developmental trend in cognitive processing speed. *Child Development, 61,* 653–663.

Haley, M. H. (2010). *Brain-compatible differentiated instruction for English language learners.* Boston: Allyn & Bacon.

Halford, G. S. (2008). Cognitive developmental theories. In M. M. Haith & J. B. Benson (Eds.), *Encyclopedia of infant and early childhood development.* Oxford, UK: Elsevier.

Halford, W. K., Markman, H. J., & Stanley, S. (2008). Strengthening couples' relationships with education: Social policy and public health perspectives. *Journal of Family Psychology, 22,* 497–505.

Hall, C. M., Jones, J. A., Meyer-Bahlburg, H. F., Dolezal, C., Coleman, M., Foster, P., Price, D. A., & Clayton, P. E. (2004). Behavioral and physical masculinization are related to genotype in girls with congenital adrenal hyperplasia. *Journal of Clinical Endocrinology Metabolism, 89,* 419–424.

Hall, G. N. (2010). *Multicultural psychology* (2nd ed.). Upper Saddle River, NJ: Prentice Hall.

Hall, G. S. (1904). *Adolescence* (Vols. 1 & 2). Englewood Cliffs, NJ: Prentice Hall.

Hall, L. (2009). *Autism spectrum disorders: From therapy to practice.* Boston: Allyn & Bacon.

Hall, W. J. (2008). Centenarians: Metaphor becomes reality. *Archives of Internal Medicine, 168,* 262–263.

Hallahan, D. P., Kauffman, J. M., & Pullen, P. C. (2009). *Exceptional learners* (11th ed.). Boston: Allyn & Bacon.

Halpern, D. (2001). Sex difference research: Cognitive abilities. In J. Worell (Ed.), *Encyclopedia of women.* San Diego: Academic Press.

Halpern, D. F. (2006). Girls and academic success: Changing patterns of academic achievement. In J. Worell & C. D. Goodheart (Eds.), *Handbook of girls' and women's psychological health.* New York: Oxford University Press.

Halpern, D. F. (2007). The nature and nurture of critical thinking. In R. J. Sternberg, H. Roediger, & D. Halpern (Eds.), *Critical thinking in psychology.* New York: Cambridge University Press.

Halpern, D. F., Benbow, C. P., Geary, D. C., Gur, R. C., Hyde, J. S., & Gernsbacher, M. A. (2007). The science of sex differences in science and mathematics. *Psychological Science in the Public Interest, 8,* 1–51.

Hamilton, S. F., & Hamilton, M. A. (2006). School, work, and emerging adulthood. In J. J. Arnett & J. L. Tanner (Eds.), *Emerging adults in America.* Washington, DC: American Psychological Association.

Hamilton, S. F., & Hamilton, M. A. (2009). The transition to adulthood: Challenges of poverty and structural lag. In R. M. Lerner & L. Steinberg (Eds.). *Handbook of adolescent psychology* (3rd ed.). New York: Wiley.

Hamlin, J. K., Hallinan, E. V., & Woodward, A. L. (2008). Do as I do: 7-month-old infants selectively reproduce others' goals. *Developmental Science, 11,* 487–494.

Hampton, T. (2008). Scientists build map of imprinted genes. *Journal of the American Medical Association, 299,* 161.

Han, W. J. (2009). Maternal employment. In D. Carr (Ed.), *Encyclopedia of the life course and human development.* Boston: Gale Cengage.

Hancox, R. J., Milne, B. J., & Poulton, R. (2004). Association between child and adolescent television viewing and adult health: A longitudinal birth cohort study. *Lancet, 364,* 257–262.

Hankin, B. L., Kassel, J. D., & Abela, J. R. (2005). Adult attachment dimensions and specificity of emotional distress symptoms: Prospective investigations of cognitive risk and interpersonal stress generation as mediating mechanisms. *Personality and Social Psychology Bulletin, 31,* 131–151.

Hannan, M. A., Faraji, B., Tanguma, J., Longoria, N., & Rodriguez, R. C. (2009). Maternal milk concentration of zinc, iron, selenium, and iodine and its relationship to dietary intake. *Biological Trace Element Research, 127,* 6–15.

Hannish, L. D., & Guerra, N. G. (2004). Aggressive victims, passive victims, and bullies: Developmental continuity or developmental change? *Merrill-Palmer Quarterly, 50,* 17–38.

Hanowski, R. J., Olson, R. L., Hickman, J. S., & Bocanegra, J. (2009, September). *Driver distraction in commercial vehicle operations.* Paper presented at the First International Conference on Driver Distraction and Inattention, Gothenburg, Sweden.

Hansenne, M., & Bianchi, J. (2009). Emotional intelligence and personality in major depression: Trait versus state effects. *Psychiatry Research, 166,* 63–68.

Hardy, M. (2006). Older Workers. In R. H. Binstock & L. K. George (Eds.), *Handbook of aging and the social sciences* (6th ed.). San Diego: Academic Press.

Harkins, S. W., & Scott, R. B. (2007). Pain and presbyalgos. In J. E. Birren (Ed.), *Encyclopedia of aging* (2nd ed.). San Diego: Academic Press.

Harkness, S., & Super, E. M. (1995). Culture and parenting. In M. H. Bornstein (Ed.), *Handbook of parenting* (Vol. 3). Hillsdale, NJ: Erlbaum.

Harlow, H. F. (1958). The nature of love. *American Psychologist, 13,* 673–685.

Harman, S. M. (2007). Andropause. In J. E. Birren (Ed.), *Encyclopedia of gerontology* (2nd ed.). San Diego: Academic Press.

Harmon, O. R., Lambrinos, J., & Kennedy, P. (2008). Are online exams an invitation to cheat? *Journal of Economic Education, 39,* 116–125.

Harold, R. D., Colarossi, L. G., & Mercier, L. R. (2007). *Smooth sailing or stormy waters: Family transitions through adolescence and their implications for practice and policy.* Mahwah, NJ: Erlbaum.

Harootyan, R. A. (2007). Volunteer activity in older adults. In J. E. Birren (Ed.), *Encyclopedia of gerontology* (2nd ed.). San Diego: Academic Press.

Harridge, S. D. R., & Saltin, B. (2007). Neuromuscular system. In J. E. Birren (Ed.), *Encyclopedia of gerontology* (2nd ed.). San Diego: Academic Press.

Harrington, S. E., & Smith, T. J. (2008), The role of chemotherapy at the end of life: "When is enough, enough?" *Journal of the American Medical Association, 299,* 2667–2678.

Harris, G. (2002). *Grandparenting: How to meet its responsibilities.* Los Angeles: The Americas Group.

Harris, K. M., & Morgan, S. P. (1991). Fathers, sons, and daughters: Differential parental involvement in parenting. *Journal of Marriage and the Family, 53,* 531–544.

Harris, K. R., Graham, S., Mason, L., & Friedlander, B. (2008). *Powerful-writing strategies for all students.* Baltimore, MD: Brookes.

Harris, L. (1975). *The myth and reality of aging in America.* Washington, DC: National Council on Aging.

Harris, P. L. (2000). *The work of the imagination.* Oxford University Press.

Harris, P. L. (2006). Social cognition. In W. Damon & R. Lerner (Eds.), *Handbook of child psychology* (6th ed.). New York: Wiley.

Harris, Y. R., & Graham, J. A. (2007). *The African American child.* New York: Springer.

Harrison-Hale, A. O., McLoyd, V. C., & Smedley, B. (2004). Racial and ethnic status: Risk and protective processes among African-American families. In K. L. Maton, C. J. Schellenbach, B. J. Leadbetter, & A. L. Solarz (Eds.), *Investing in children, families, and communities.* Washington, DC: American Psychological Association.

Harrist, A. W. (1993, March). *Family interaction styles as predictors of children's competence: The role of synchrony and nonsynchrony.* Paper presented at the biennial meeting of the Society for Research in Child Development, New Orleans.

Hart, B., & Risley, T. R. (1995). *Meaningful differences in the everyday experience of young Americans.* Baltimore: Paul H. Brookes.

Hart, C. H., Yang, C., Charlesworth, R., & Hurts, D. C. (2003, April). *Early childhood teachers' curriculum beliefs, classroom practices, and children's outcomes: What are the connections?* Paper presented at the biennial meeting of the Society for Research in Child Development, Tampa.

Hart, D., Burock, D., London, B., & Atkins, R. (2003). Prosocial development, antisocial development, and moral development. In A. M. Slater & G. Bremner (Eds.), *An introduction to developmental psychology.* Malden, MA: Blackwell.

Hart, D., & Karmel, M. P. (1996). Self-awareness and self-knowledge in humans, great apes, and monkeys. In A. Russori, K. Bard, & S. Parker (Eds.), *Reaching into thought.* New York: Cambridge University Press.

Hart, D., Matsuba, M. K., & Atkins, R. (2008). The moral and civic effects of learning to serve. In L. Nucci & D. Narváez (Eds.), *Handbook of moral and character education.* Clifton, NJ: Psychology Press.

Hart, S., & Carrington, H. (2002). Jealousy in 6-month-old infants. *Infancy, 3,* 395–402.

Hart, S., Carrington, H., Tronick, E. Z., & Carroll, S. R. (2004). When infants lose exclusive maternal attention: Is it jealousy? *Infancy, 6,* 57–78.

Harter, S. (1981). A new self-report scale of intrinsic versus extrinsic orientation in the classroom: Motivational and informational components. *Developmental Psychology, 17,* 300–312.

Harter, S. (1986). Processes underlying the construction, maintenance, and enhancement of the self-concept of children. In J. Suls & A. Greenwald (Eds.), *Psychological perspective on the self* (Vol. 3). Hillsdale, NJ: Erlbaum.

Harter, S. (1990). Processes underlying adolescent self-concept formation. In R. Montemayor, G. R. Adams, & T. P. Gullotta (Eds.), *From childhood to adolescence: A transitional period?* Newbury Park, CA: Sage.

Harter, S. (1996). Teacher and classmate influences on scholastic motivation, self-esteem, and level of voice in adolescents. In J. Juvonen & K. R. Wentzel (Eds.), *Social motivation.* New York: Cambridge University Press.

Harter, S. (1998). The development of self-representations. In W. Damon (Ed.), *Handbook of child psychology* (5th ed., Vol. 3). New York: Wiley.

Harter, S. (1999). *The construction of the self.* New York: Guilford.

Harter, S. (2006). The self. In W. Damon & R. Lerner (Eds.), *Handbook of child psychology* (6th ed.). New York: Wiley.

Hartshorne, H., & May, M. S. (1928–1930). *Moral studies in the nature of character: Studies in deceit* (Vol. 1); *Studies in self-control* (Vol. 2); *Studies in the organization of character* (Vol. 3). New York: Macmillan.

Hartup, W. W. (1983). The peer system. In P. H. Mussen (Ed.), *Handbook of child psychology* (4th ed., Vol. 4). New York: Wiley.

Hartup, W. W. (2008). Peer interaction: What causes what? *Journal of Abnormal Child Psychology, 33,* 387–394.

Hartup, W. W. (2009). Critical issues and theoretical viewpoints. In K. H. Rubin, W. M. Bukowski, & B. Laursen (Eds.), *Handbook of peer interactions, relationships, and groups.* New York: Guilford.

Hartwell, L. (2008). *Genetics* (3rd ed.). New York: McGraw-Hill.

Harwood, R., Leyendecker, B., Carlson, V., Asencio, M., & Miller, A. (2002). Parenting among Latino families in the U.S. In M. H. Bornstein (Ed.), *Handbook of parenting* (2nd ed.). Mahwah, NJ: Erlbaum.

Hasher, L. (2003. February 28). Commentary in "The wisdom of the wizened." *Science, 299,* 1300–1302.

Hasher, L., Chung, C., May, C. P., & Foong, N. (2001). Age, time of testing, and proactive interference. *Canadian Journal of Experimental Psychology, 56,* 200–207.

Haski-Leventhal, D., Ben-Arieh, A., & Melton, G. B. (2008). Between neighborliness and volunteerism: Participants in the strong communities initiative. *Family and Community Health, 31,* 150–161.

Hastings, P. D., Utendale, W. T., & Sullivan, C. (2007). The socialization of prosocial development. In J. E. Grusec & P. D. Hastings (Eds.), *Handbook of socialization*. New York: Guilford.

Hattery, A. J., & Smith, E. (2007). *African American families*. Thousand Oaks, CA: Sage.

Hatton, H., Donnellan, M. B., Maysn, K., Feldman, B. J., Larsen-Riffe, D., & Conger, R. D. (2008). Family and individual difference predictors of trait aspects of negative interpersonal behaviors during emerging adulthood. *Journal of Family Psychology, 22*, 448–455.

Hauser, R. A., & Zesiewicz, T. A. (2007). Advances in the pharmacologic management of early Parkinson disease. *Neurologist, 13*, 126–132.

Hausman, B. L. (2005). Risky business: Framing childbirth in hospital settings. *Journal of Medical Ethics, 26*, 23–38.

Hawkes, C. (2006). Olfaction in neurogenerative disorder. *Advances in Oto-rhino-laryngology, 63*, 133–151.

Hayashino, D., & Chopra, S. B. (2009). Parenting and raising families. In N. Tewari & A. Alvarez (Eds.), *Asian American psychology*. Clifton, NJ: Psychology Press.

Hayflick, L. (1977). The cellular basis for biological aging. In C. E. Finch & L. Hayflick (Eds.), *Handbook of the biology of aging*. New York: Van Nostrand.

Haynes, T. J., Heckhausen, J., Chipperfield, J. G., Newall, N. E., & Perry, R. P. (2009). Primary and secondary control strategies: Implications for health and well-being among older adults. *Journal of Social and Clinical Psychology 28*, 165–195.

Hayslip, B., Edmondson, R., & Guarnaccia, C. (1999, November). *Religiousness, perceptions of funerals, and bereavement adjustment in adulthood*. Paper presented at the meeting of the Gerontological Society of America, San Francisco.

Hayslip, B., & Hansson, R. (2003). Death awareness and adjustment across the life span. In C. D. Bryant (Ed.), *Handbook of death and dying*. Thousand Oaks, CA: Sage.

Hayslip, B., & Hansson, R. O. (2007). Hospice. In J. E. Birren (Ed.), *Encyclopedia of gerontology* (2nd ed.). San Diego: Academic Press.

Hayslip, B., & Kaminski, P. L. (Eds.). (2008). *Parenting the custodial grandchild*. New York: Springer.

Hazan, C., & Shaver, P. R. (1987). Romantic love conceptualized as an attachment process. *Journal of Personality and Social Psychology, 52*, 522–524.

Healey, J. F. (2009). *Race, ethnicity and class* (5th ed.). Thousand Oaks, CA: Sage.

Healey, M. K., & Hasher, L. (2009). Limitations to the deficit attenuation hypothesis: Aging and decision making. *Journal of Consumer Psychology, 19*, 17–22.

Heckhausen, J. (2002). Developmental regulation transitions of life-course transitions: A control theory approach. In L. Pulkkinen & A. Caspi

(Eds.), *Paths to successful development: Personality in the life course*. New York: Cambridge University Press.

Heckhausen, J. (2007). The motivation-volition divide and its resolution in action-phase models of behavioral and developmental regulation. *Research in Human Development, 4*, 163–180.

Heckhausen, J., & Heckhausen, H. (2008). *Motivation and action*. New York: Cambridge University Press.

Heckhausen, J., & Schultz, R. (1995). A life-span theory of control. *Psychological Review, 102*, 284–304.

Hedberg, P., Ohrvik, J., Lonnberg, I., & Nilsson, G. (2009). Augmented blood pressure response to exercise is associated with improved long-term survival in older people. *Heart, 95*, 1072–1078.

Hedden, T., & Gabrielli, J. D. E. (2004). Insights into the aging mind: A view from cognitive neuroscience. *Nature Reviews: Neuroscience, 5*, 87–97.

Hegaard, H. K., Hedegaard, M., Damm, P., Ottesen, B., Petersson, K., & Henriksen, T. B. (2008). Leisure time physical activity is associated with a reduced risk of preterm delivery. *American Journal of Obstetrics and Gynecology, 198*, e1–e5.

Heimann, M., Strid, K., Smith, L., Tjus, T., Ulvund, S. E., & Meltzoff, A. N. (2006). Exploring the relation between memory, gestural communication, and the emergence of language in infancy: A longitudinal study. *Infant and Child Development, 75*, 233–249.

Heinig, M. J., Ishii, K. D., Banuelos, J. L., Campbell, E., O'Laughlin, C., & Becerra, L. E. (2009). Sources and acceptance of infant-feeding advice among low-income women. *Journal of Human Lactation, 25*, 163–172.

Heisel, M. J. (2006). Suicide and its prevention in older adults. *Canadian Journal of Psychiatry, 51*, 143–154.

Helman, C. (2008). Inside T. Boone Pickens' brain. *Forbes*. Retrieved June 15, 2008, from http://www.forbes.com/billionaires/forbes/2008/0630/076.html

Helman, R., VanDerhei, J., & Copeland, C. (2007). The retirement system in transition: The 2007 Retirement Confidence Survey. *Employment Benefit Research Institute Issue Brief, 304* (1), 4–24.

Helmuth, L. (2003). The wisdom of the wizened. *Science, 299*, 1300–1302.

Helson, R. (1997, August). *Personality change: When is it adult development?* Paper presented at the meeting of the American Psychological Association, Chicago.

Helson, R., & Wink, P. (1992). Personality change in women from the early 40s to early 50s. *Psychology and Aging, 7*, 46–55.

Helzner, E. P., & others. (2009). Contribution of vascular risk factors to the progression of Alzheimer disease. *Archives of Neurology, 66*, 343–348.

Henderson, A. J. (2008). The effects of tobacco smoke exposure on respiratory health in school-aged children. *Pediatric Respiratory Reviews, 9*, 21–28.

Hendrick, J., & Weissman, P. (2010). *Whole child, the: Developmental education for the early years* (9th ed.). Upper Saddle River, NJ: Prentice Hall.

Hendry, C. (2009). Incarceration and the tasks of grief: A narrative review. *Journal of Advanced Nursing, 65*, 270–278.

Hendry, J. (1999). *Social anthropology*. New York: Macmillan.

Hennessey, B. A., & Amabile, T. M. (2010). Creativity. *Annual Review of Psychology* (Vol. 61). Palo Alto, CA: Annual Reviews.

Henriksen, T. B., Hjollund, N. H., Jensen, T. K., Bonde, J. P., Andersson, A. M., Kolstad, H., Ernst, E., Giwereman, A., Skakkebaek, N. E., & Olsen, J. (2004). Alcohol consumption at the time of conception and spontaneous abortion. *American Journal of Epidemiology, 160*, 661–667.

Henry, D. B., Schoeny, M. E., Deptula, D. P., & Slavick, J. T. (2007). Peer selection and socialization effects on adolescent intercourse without a condom and attitudes about the costs of sex. *Child Development, 78*, 825–838.

Hercigonja Novkovic, V., Rudan, V., Pivac, N., Nedic, G., & Muck-Seler, D. (2009). Platelet serotonin concentration in children with attention-deficit/hyperactivity disorder. *Neuropsychobiology, 59*, 17–22.

Herek, G. (2000). Homosexuality. In A. Kazdin (Ed.), *Encyclopedia of psychology*. Washington, DC, & New York: American Psychological Association and Oxford University Press.

Herek, G. M. (2009). Hate crimes and stigma-related experiences among sexual minority adults in the United States: Prevalence estimates from a national probability sample. *Journal of Interpersonal Violence, 24*, 54–74.

Hermann-Giddens, M. E. (2007). The decline in the age of menarche in the United States: Should we be concerned? *Journal of Adolescent Health, 40*, 201–203.

Hernandez, D. J. (2007). Changes in the demographics of families over the course of American history. In A. S. Skolnick & J. H. Skolnick (Eds.), *Family in transition* (14th ed.). Boston: Allyn & Bacon.

Hernandez, D. J., Denton, N. A., & Macartney, S. E. (2010). Children of immigrants and the future of America. In Grigorenko, E. L., Takanishi, R. (Eds.) (2010). *Immigration, diversity, and education*. New York: Routledge.

Hernandez, R. J., Bayer, Z. C., Brushfield, A. M., Pirogrovsky, E., Murphy, C., & Gilbert, P. E. (2008). Effect of encoding condition on source memory for odors in healthy young and older adults. *Gerontology, 54*, 187–192.

Hernandez-Reif, M., Diego, M., & Field, T. (2007). Preterm infants show reduced stress behaviors and activity after 5 days of massage therapy. *Infant Behavior and Development, 30,* 557–561.

Heron, M. P., Hoyert, D. L., Xu, J., Scott, C. & Tejada-Vera, B. (2008, June 11). *Deaths: Preliminary data for 2006. National Vital Statistics Reports,* 56 (16), 1–52.

Herrera, V. M., Koss, M. P., Bailey, J., Yuan, N. P., & Lichter, E. L. (2006). An overview of policies that impact the psychological well-being of girls and women. In J. Worell & C. D. Goodheart (Eds.), *Handbook of girls' and women's psychological health.* New York: Oxford University Press.

Herrmann, M., King, K., & Weitzman, M. (2008). Prenatal tobacco smoke and postnatal secondhand smoke exposure and child neurodevelopment. *Current Opinion in Pediatrics, 20,* 184–190.

Hertzog, C., & Dixon, R. A. (2005). Metacognition in midlife. In S. L. Willis & M. Martin (Eds.), *Middle adulthood: A lifespan perspective.* Thousand Oaks, CA: Sage.

Hertz-Picciotto, I., Park, H. Y., Dostal, M., Kocan, A., Trnovec, T., & Sram, R. (2008). Prenatal exposure to persistent and non-persistent organic compounds, and effects on immune system development. *Basic and Clinical Pharmacology and Toxicology, 102,* 146–154.

Hess, T. M., Auman, C., Colcombe, S. J., & Rahhal, T. A. (2003). The impact of stereotype threat on age differences in memory performance. *Journals of Gerontology B: Psychological Sciences and Social Sciences, 58,* P3–P11.

Hetherington, E. M. (1989). Coping with family transitions: Winners, losers, and survivors. *Child Development, 60,* 1–14.

Hetherington, E. M. (1993). An overview of the Virginia Longitudinal Study of Divorce and Remarriage with a focus on early adolescence. *Journal of Family Psychology, 7,* 39–56.

Hetherington, E. M. (2006). The influence of conflict, marital problem solving, and parenting on children's adjustment in nondivorced, divorced, and remarried families. In A. Clarke-Stewart & J. Dunn (Eds.), *Families count.* New York: Cambridge University Press.

Hetherington, E. M., & Kelly, J. (2002). *For better or for worse: Divorce reconsidered.* New York: Norton.

Hetherington, E. M., & Stanley-Hagan, M. (2002). Parenting in divorced and remarried families. In M. Bornstein (Ed.), *Handbook of parenting* (2nd ed.). Mahwah, NJ: Erlbaum.

Heuwinkel, M. K. (1996). New ways of learning: 5 new ways of teaching. *Childhood Education, 72,* 27–31.

Heyman, G. D. (2008). Children's critical thinking when learning from others. *Current Directions in Psychological Science, 17,* 344–347.

Heyman, G. D., & Legare, C. H. (2005). Children's evaluation of sources of information about traits. *Developmental Psychology, 41,* 636–647.

Hibell, B., Andersson, B., Bjarnasson, T., & others. (2004). *The ESPAD report 2003: Alcohol and other drug use among students in 35 European countries. Stockholm:* The Swedish Council for Information on Alcohol and Other Drugs (CAN) and Council of Europe Pompidou Group.

Hick, P., & Thomas, G. (Eds.). (2009). *Inclusion and diversity in education.* Thousand Oaks, CA: Sage.

Hickman, J. M., Rogers, W. A., & Fisk, A. D. (2007). Training older adults to use new technology. *Journals of Gerontology B: Psychological Sciences and Social Sciences, 62 (Special Issue),* P77–P84.

Hietanen, A., Era, P., Sorri, M., & Heikkinen, E. (2004). Changes in hearing in 80-year-old people: A 10-year follow-up study. *International Journal of Audiology, 43,* 126–135.

Highfield, R. (2008, April 30). *Harvard's baby brain research lab.* Retrieved January 24, 2009, from www.telegraph.co.uk/scienceandtechnology/science/sciencenews/3341166/Harvards...

Hill, J. P., & Lynch, M. E. (1983). The intensification of gender-related role expectations during early adolescence. In J. Brooks-Gunn & A. C. Petersen (Eds.), *Girls at puberty: Biological and psychosocial perspectives.* New York: Plenum Press.

Hill, P. C., & Butter, E. M. (1995). The role of religion in promoting physical health. *Journal of Psychology and Christianity, 14,* 141–155.

Hill, P. C., & Pargament, K. I. (2003). Advances in conceptualization and measurement of religion and spirituality: Implications for physical and mental health research. *American Psychologist, 58,* 64–74.

Hill, T. D., Burdette, A. M., Angel, J. L., & Angel, R. J. (2006). Religious attendance and cognitive functioning among older Mexican Americans. *Journals of Gerontology B: Psychological Sciences and Social Sciences, 61,* P31–P39.

Hillman, C. H., Buck, S. M., Themanson, J. R., Pontifex, M. B., & Castelli, D. M. (2009). Aerobic fitness and cognitive development: Event-related brain potential and task performance indices of executive control in preadolescent children. *Developmental Psychology, 45,* 114–129.

Hillman, C. H., Erickson, K. I., & Kramer, A. F. (2008). Be smart, exercise your heart: Exercise affects on the brain and cognition. *Nature Reviews: Neuroscience, 9,* 58–65.

Hills, A. P., King, N. A., & Armstrong, T. P. (2007). The contribution of physical activity and sedentary behaviors to the growth and development of children and adolescents: Implications for overweight and obesity. *Sports Medicine, 37,* 533–545.

Himes, C. L., Hogan, D. P., & Eggebeen, D. J. (1996). Living arrangements of minority elders. *Journals of Gerontology B, Psychological Sciences and Social Sciences, 51,* S42–S48.

Hingson, R. W., Heeren, T., & Winter, M. R. (2006). Age at drinking onset and alcohol dependence: Age at onset, duration, and severity. *Archives of Pediatric and Adolescent Medicine, 160,* 739–746.

Hinks, A., & others. (2009). Identification of a novel susceptibility locus for juvenile idiopathic arthritis by genome-wide association analysis. *Arthritis and Rheumatism, 60,* 258–263.

Hinrichsen, G. A. (2006). Why multicultural issues matter for practitioners working with older adults. *Psychology and Aging, 37,* 29–35.

Hirsh, R. (2004). *Early childhood curriculum: Incorporating multiple intelligences, developmentally appropriate practices, and play.* Boston: Allyn & Bacon.

Hock, R. R. (2010). *Human sexuality* (2nd ed.). Upper Saddle River, NJ: Prentice Hall.

Hock, R. R., & Williams, S. (2007). *Human sexuality.* Upper Saddle River, NJ: Prentice Hall.

Hockenberry, M., & Wilson, D. (2009). *Wong's essentials of pediatric nursing.* Oxford, UK: Elsevier.

Hodapp, R. M., & Dykens, E. M. (2006). Mental retardation. In W. Damon & R. Lerner (Eds.), *Handbook of child psychology.* Mahwah, NJ: Erlbaum.

Hodson, R. (2009). Employment. In D. Carr (Ed.), *Encyclopedia of the life course and human development.* Boston: Gale Cengage.

Hoefnagels, M. (2009). *Biology.* New York: McGraw-Hill.

Hoelter, L. (2009). Divorce and separation. In D. Carr (Ed.), *Encyclopedia of the life course and human development.* Boston: Gale Cengage.

Hoff, E., Laursen, B., & Tardiff, T. (2002). Socioeconomic status and parenting. In M. H. Bornstein (Ed.), *Handbook of parenting* (2nd ed.) Mahwah, NJ: Erlbaum.

Hoffman, E., & Ewen, D. (2007). Supporting families, nurturing young children. *CLASP Policy Brief No. 9,* 1–11.

Hoffman, J. P. (2009). Drug use, adolescent. In D. Carr (Ed.), *Encyclopedia of the life course and human development.* Boston: Gage Cengage.

Hofheimer, J. A., & Lester, B. M. (2008). Neuropsychological assessment. In M. M. Haith & J. B. Benson (Eds.), *Encyclopedia of infant and early childhood development.* Oxford, UK: Elsevier.

Hofman, M. A., & Swaab, D. F. (2006). Living by the clock: The circadian pacemaker older people. *Aging Research and Review, 5,* 33–51.

Hogervorst, E., Yaffe, K., Richards, M., & Huppert, F. A. (2009). Hormone replacement therapy to maintain cognitive function in women with dementia. *Cochrane Database of Systematic Reviews, 1,* No. CD003799.

Holcombe, E., Carrier, D., Manlove, J., & Ryan, S. (2008, February). Contraceptive use patterns across teens' sexual relationships. *Child fact sheet.* Washington, DC: Child Trends.

Holland, J. L. (1987). Current status of Holland's theory of careers: Another perspective. *Career Development Quarterly, 36,* 24–30.

Hollich, G., Newman, R. S., & Jusczyk, P. W. (2005). Infants' use of synchronized visual information to separate streams of speech. *Child Development, 76,* 598–613.

Hollier, L., & Wendel, G. (2008). Third trimester antiviral prophylaxis for preventing maternal genital herpes simplex virus (HSV) recurrences and neonatal infection. *Cochrane Database of Systematic Reviews, 1,* CD004946.

Hollis, J. F., & others. (2008). Weight loss during the intensive intervention phase of the weight-loss maintenance trial. *American Journal of Preventive Medicine, 35,* 118–126.

Hollis-Sawyer, L. A., & Sawyer, T. P. (2008). Potential stereotype threat and face validity effects on cognitive-based test performance in the classroom. *Educational Psychology, 28,* 291–304.

Holmes, R. M., Little, K. C., & Welsh, D. (2009). Dating and romantic relationships, adulthood. In D. Carr (Ed.), *Encyclopedia of the life course and human development.* Boston: Gale Cengage.

Holmes, T. H., & Rahe, R. H. (1967). The social readjustment rating scale. *Journal of Psychosomatic Research, 11,* 213–218.

Holstein, B. E., Due, P. Almind, G., & Avlund, K. (2007). Eight-year change in functional ability among 70- to 95-year-olds. *Scandinavian Journal of Public Health, 35,* 243–249.

Holter, A., & Narváez, D. (2009). Moral Education. In E. Anderman & L. Anderman (Eds.), *Psychology of classroom learning: An encyclopedia.* Boston: Gale Cengage.

Holzgrabe, U., Kapkova, P., Alptuzun, V., Scheiber, J., & Kugelmann, E. (2007). Targeting acetylcholinesterase to treat neurodegeneration. *Expert Opinion on Therapeutic Targets, 11,* 161–179.

Holzman, L. (2009). *Vygotsky at work and play.* Clifton, NJ: Psychology Press.

Honzik, M. P., MacFarlane, I. W., & Allen, L. (1948). The stability of mental test performance between two and eighteen years. *Journal of Experimental Education, 17,* 309–324.

Hood, B. M. (1995). Gravity rules for 2- to 4 year-olds? *Cognitive Development, 10,* 577–598.

Hooper, S. R., & others. (2008). Executive functions in young males with fragile X syndrome in comparison to mental age-matched controls: Baseline findings from a longitudinal study. *Neuropsychology, 22,* 36–47.

Hope, D. A. (2009). Contemporary perspectives on lesbian, gay, and bisexual identities: Introduction. *Nebraska Symposium on Motivation, 54,* 1–4.

Hopkins, B. (1991). Facilitating early motor development: An intracultural study of West Indian mothers and their infants living in Britain. In J. K. Nugent, B. M. Lester, & T. B. Brazelton (Eds.), *The cultural context of infancy.*

Vol. 2: Multicultural and interdisciplinary approaches to parent-infant relations. New York: Ablex.

Hopkins, B., & Westra, T. (1988). Maternal handling and motor development: An intracultural study. *Genetic Psychology Monographs, 14,* 377–420.

Hopkins, B., & Westra, T. (1990). Motor development, maternal expectations, and the role of handling. *Infant Behavior and Development, 13,* 117–122.

Hoppmann, C. A., Gerstorf, D., Smith, J., & Klumb, P. L. (2007). Linking possible selves and behavior: Do domain-specific hopes and fears translate into daily activities in very old age? *Journals of Gerontology B: Psychological Sciences and Social Sciences, 62,* P104–P111.

Horn, J. (2007). Spearman, *g*, expertise, and the nature of human cognitive capacity. In P. C. Kyllonen, R. D. Roberts, & L. Stankov (Eds.), *Extending intelligence.* Mahwah, NJ: Erlbaum.

Horn, J. L., & Donaldson, G. (1980). Cognitive development II: Adulthood development of human abilities. In O. G. Brim & J. Kagan (Eds.), *Constancy and change in human development.* Cambridge, MA: Harvard University Press.

Horn, L., & Nevill, S. (2006). *Profile of undergraduates in U.S. postsecondary education institutions: 2003–2004: With a special analysis of community college students* (NCES 2006-184). Washington, DC: National Center for Education Statistics.

Horne, R. S., Franco, P., Adamson, T. M., Groswasser, J., & Kahn, A. (2002). Effects of body position on sleep and arousal characteristics in infants. *Early Human Development, 69,* 25–33.

Hornor, G. (2005). Physical abuse: Recognition and reporting. *Journal of Pediatric Health Care, 19,* 4–11.

Horowitz, F. D. (2009). Introduction: A developmental understanding of giftedness and talent. In F. D. Horowitz, R. F. Subotnik, & D. J. Matthews (Eds.), *The development of giftedness and talent across the life span.* Washington, DC: American Psychological Association.

Horsthemke, B., & Buiting, K. (2008). Genomic imprinting and imprinting defects in humans. *Advances in Genetics, 61,* 225–246.

Horwitz, E. K. (2008). *Becoming a language teacher.* Boston: Allyn & Bacon.

Hourigan, S. R., Nitz, J. C., Brauer, S. G., O'Neill, S., Wong, J., & Richardson, C. A. (2008). Positive effects of exercise on falls and fracture risk in osteopenic women. *Osteoporosis International, 19,* 1077–1086.

Houston, D. K., & others. (2009). Overweight and obesity over the adult life course and incident mobility limitation in older adults: The Health, Aging, and Body Composition Study. *American Journal of Epidemiology, 169,* 927–936.

Howard, R. A., & others. (2008). Physical activity, sedentary behavior, and the risk of colon and rectal cancer in the NIH-AARP Diet and Health Study. *Cancer Causes and Control, 19,* 939–953.

Howe, M. J. A., Davidson, J. W., Moore, D. G., & Sloboda, J. A. (1995). Are there early childhood signs of musical ability? *Psychology of Music, 23,* 162–176.

Howe, N., & Recchia, H. E. (2008). Siblings and sibling rivalry. In M. M. Haith & J. B. Benson (Eds.), *Encyclopedia of infant and early childhood development.* Oxford, UK: Elsevier.

Howell, D. C. (2010). *Statistical methods for psychology* (7th ed.). Boston: Cengage.

Howell, K. K., Lynch, M. E., Platzman, K. A., Smith, G. H., & Coles, C. D. (2006). Prenatal alcohol exposure and ability, academic achievement, and school functioning in adolescence: A longitudinal follow-up. *Journal of Pediatric Psychology, 31,* 116–126.

Howes, C. (2009). Friendship in early childhood. In K. H. Rubin, W. M. Bukowski, & B. Laursen (Eds.), *Handbook of peer interactions, relationships, and groups.* New York: Guilford.

Howes, C., & Wishard Guerra, A. G. (2009, in press). Networks of attachment relationships in low-income children of Mexican heritage: Infancy through preschool. *Social Development.*

Howlin, P., Magiati, I., & Charman, T. (2009). Systematic review of early intensive behavioral interventions with autism. *American Journal on Intellectual and Developmental Disabilities, 114,* 23–41.

Hoyer, W. J., & Roodin, P. A. (2009). *Adult development and aging* (6th ed.), New York: McGraw-Hill.

Hoyert, D. L., Mathews, T. J., Menacker, F., Strobino, D. M., & Guyer, B. (2006). Annual summary of vital statistics: 2004. *Pediatrics, 117,* 168–183.

Hrabosky, J. I., Masheb, R. M., White, M. A., & Grilo, C. M. (2007). Overvaluation of shape and weight in binge eating disorder. *Journal of Consulting and Clinical Psychology, 75,* 175–180.

HSBC Insurance. (2007). *The future of retirement: The new old age-global report.* London: Author.

Hu, H., & others. (2007). Fetal lead exposure at each stage of pregnancy as a predictor of infant mental development. *Environmental Health Perspectives, 114,* 1730–1735.

Huang, J. H., DeJong, W., Towvim, L. G., & Schneider, S. K. (2009). Sociodemographic and psychobehavioral characteristics of U.S. college students who abstain from alcohol. *Journal of American College Health, 57,* 395–410.

Huebner, A. M., & Garrod, A. C. (1993). Moral reasoning among Tibetan monks: A study of Buddhist adolescents and young adults in Nepal. *Journal of Cross-Cultural Psychology, 24,* 167–185.

Huerta, M., Cortina, L. M. Pang, J. S., Torges, C. M., & Magley, V. J. (2006). Sex and power in the academy: Modeling sexual harassment in the lives of college women. *Personality and Social Psychology Bulletin, 32,* 616–628.

Hueston, W. J., Geesey, M. E., & Diaz, V. (2008). Prenatal care initiation among pregnant teens in the United States: An analysis over 25 years. *Journal of Adolescent Health, 42,* 243–248.

Hughes, J. P., McDowell, M. A., & Brody, D. J. (2008). Leisure-time physical activity among U.S. adults 60 or more years of age: Results from NHANES 1999–2004. *Journal of Physical Activity and Health, 5,* 347–358.

Hughes, M. E., Waite, L. J., LaPierre, T. A., & Luo, Y. (2007). All in the family: The impact of caring for children on grandparents' health. *Journals of Gerontology B: Psychological Sciences and Social Sciences, 62,* S108–S119.

Hughes, P. C. Reported in Fozard, J. L., & Popkin, S. J. (1978). Optimizing adult development. *American Psychologist, 33,* 975–989.

Hultsch, D. F., Hertzog, C., Small, B. J., & Dixon, R. A. (1999). Use it or lose it: Engaged lifestyle as a buffer of cognitive decline in aging? *Psychology and Aging, 14,* 245–263.

Hultsch, D. F., & Plemons, J. K. (1979). Life events and life-span development. In P. B. Baltes & O. G. Brim (Eds.), *Life-span development and behavior.* New York: Academic Press.

Humphreys, C. (2007). A health inequalities perspective on violence against women. *Health and Social Care in the Community, 15,* 120–127.

Hunt, E. (1995). *Will we be smart enough? A cognitive analysis of the coming work force.* New York: Russell Sage.

Hunt, N. D., Hyun, D. H., Allard, J. S., Minor, R. K., Mattson, M. P., Ingram, D. K., & de Cabo, R. (2006). Bioenergetics of aging and calorie restriction. *Aging Research Review, 5,* 125–143.

Hunter, K. I., & Linn, M. W. (1980). Psychosocial differences between elderly volunteers and non-volunteers. *International Journal of Aging and Human Development, 12,* 205–213.

Hupcey, J. E., Penrod, J., & Fenstermacher, K. (2009, in press). A model of palliative care for heart failure. *American Journal of Hospice and Palliative Care.*

Hurd Clarke, L. (2006). Older women and sexuality: Experiences in marital relationships across the life course. *Canadian Journal of Aging, 25,* 129–140.

Hurt, H., Brodsky, N. L., Roth, H., Malmud, F., & Glannetta, J. M. (2005). School performance of children with gestational cocaine exposure. *Neurotoxicology and Teratology, 27,* 203–211.

Huston, A. C., & Bentley, A. D. (2010). Human development in societal context. *Annual Review of psychology,* Vol. 61. Palo Alto, CA: Annual Reviews.

Huston, A. C., Epps, S. R., Shim, M. S., Duncan, G. J., Crobsy, D. A., & Ripke, M. N. (2006). Effects of a poverty intervention program last from middle childhood to adolescence. In A. C. Huston & M. N. Ripke (Eds.), *Developmental contexts of middle childhood: Bridges to adolescence and adulthood.* New York: Cambridge University Press.

Huston, A. C., & Ripke, M. N. (2006). Experiences in middle childhood and children's development: A summary and integration of research. In A. C. Huston & M. N. Ripke (Eds.), *Developmental contexts in middle childhood.* New York: Cambridge University Press.

Huston, A. C., Seigle, J., & Bremer, M. (1983, April). *Family environment and television use by preschool children.* Paper presented at the Society for Research in Child Development meeting, Detroit.

Hutchinson, D. M., & Rapee, R. M. (2007). Do friends share similar body image and eating problems? The role of social networks and peer influences in early adolescence. *Behavior Research and Therapy, 45,* 1557–1577.

Huttenlocher, J., Haight, W., Bruk, A., Seltzer, M., & Lyons, T. (1991). Early vocabulary growth: Relation to language input and gender. *Developmental Psychology, 27,* 236–248.

Huttenlocher, P. R., & Dabholkar, A. S. (1997). Regional differences in synaptogenesis in human cerebral cortex. *Journal of Comparative Neurology, 37 (2),* 167–178.

Huyck, M. H. (1995). Marriage and close relationships of the marital kind In R. Blieszner & V. H. Bedford (Eds.), *Handbook of aging and the family.* Westport, CT: Greenwood.

Huyck, M. H., Ayalon, L., & Yoder, J. (2007). Using mixed methods to evaluate the use of a caregiver strain measure to assess outcomes of a caregiver support program for caregivers of older adults. *International Journal of Geriatric Psychiatry, 22,* 160–165.

Hyde, D. C., & Spelke, E. S. (2009). All numbers are not equal: An electrophysiological investigation of small and large number representations. *Journal of Cognitive Neuroscience, 21,* 1039–1053.

Hyde, D. R. (2009). *Introduction to genetic principles.* New York: McGraw-Hill.

Hyde, J. S. (2005). The gender similarities hypothesis. *American Psychologist, 60,* 581–592.

Hyde, J. S. (2007). *Half the human experience* (7th ed.). Boston: Houghton Mifflin.

Hyde, J. S., & DeLamater, J. D. (2008). *Human sexuality* (10th Ed.). New York: McGraw-Hill.

Hyde, J. S., Lindberg, S. M., Linn, M. C., Ellis, A. B., & Williams, C. C. (2008). Gender similarities characterize math performance. *Science, 321,* 494–495.

Hyde, J. S., & Price, M. (2007, November). *When two isn't better than one: Predictors of early sexual activity in adolescence using a cumulative risk model.* Paper presented at the meeting of the Society for the Scientific Study of Sexuality, Indianapolis.

Hyman, L., Kay, B., Tabori, A., Weber, M., Mahon, M., & Cohen, I. (2006). Bullying: Theory, research, and interventions. In C. M. Evertson & C. S. Weinstein (Eds.), *Handbook of classroom management.* Mahwah, NJ: Erlbaum.

Hynes, K., & Davis, K. D. (2009). Gender in the workplace. In D. Carr (Ed.), *Encyclopedia of the life course and human development.* Boston: Gale Cengage.

Hyson, M. (2007). Curriculum. In R. New & M. Cochran (Eds.), *Early childhood education: An international encyclopedia of early childhood education.* New York: Greenwood.

Hyson, M. C., Copple, C., & Jones, J. (2006). Early childhood development and education. In W. Damon & R. Lerner (Eds.), *Handbook of child psychology* (6th ed.). New York: Wiley.

I

Idler, E. (2006). Religion and aging. In R. H. Binstock & L. K. George (Eds.), *Handbook of aging and the social sciences* (6th ed.). San Diego: Academic Press.

Idler, E. L., Stanislav, V. K., & Hays, J. C. (2001). Patterns of religious practice and belief in the last year of life. *Journals of Gerontology B: Psychological Sciences and Social Sciences, 56,* S326–S334.

Ige, F., & Shelton, D. (2004). Reducing the risk of sudden infant death syndrome (SIDS) in African-American communities. *Journal of Pediatric Nursing, 19,* 290–292.

"I Have a Dream" Foundation. (2009). *About us.* Retrieved July 9, 2009, from http://www.ihad.org.

IJzerman, M. J., Renzenbrink, G. J., & Geurts, A. C. (2009). Neuromuscular stimulation after stroke: From technology to clinical development. *Expert Reviews of Neurotherapeutics, 9,* 541–552.

Ikeda, A., & others. (2007). Marital status and mortality among Japanese men and women: The Japanese Collaborative Cohort Study. *BMC Public Health, 7,* 73.

Imada, T., Zhang, Y., Cheour, M., Taulu, S., Ahonen, A., & Kuhl, P. K. (2007). Infant speech perception activates Broca's area: A developmental magnetoencephalography study. *Neuroreport, 17,* 957–962.

Impett, E. A., Schoolder, D., Tolman, L., Sorsoli, L., & Henson, J. M. (2008). Girls' relationship authenticity and self-esteem across adolescence. *Developmental Psychology, 44,* 722–733.

Inglehart, R. (1990). *Culture shift in advanced industrial society.* Princeton, NJ: Princeton University Press.

Insel, P. M., & Roth, W. T. (2010). *Core concepts in Health* (11th ed.). New York: McGraw-Hill.

International Montessori Council. (2006). Much of their success on prime-time television. Retrieved June 24, 2006, from www.Montessori.org/enews/Barbara_walters.html

Ip, S., Chung, M., Raman, G., Chew, P., Magula, N., Devine, D., Trikalinos, T., & Lau, J. (2007). Breastfeeding and maternal and infant health outcomes in developed countries. *Evidence Report/Technology Assessment, 153,* 1–86.

Isacson, O., & Kordower, J. H. (2008). Future of cell and gene therapies for Parkinson's disease. *Annals of Neurology, 64* (Suppl. 2), S122–S138.

Isella, V., Mapelli, C., Morielli, N., Pelati, O., Franceschi, M., & Appollonio, I. M. (2008). Age-related quantitative and qualitative changes in decision-making ability. *Behavioral Neurology, 19*, 59–63.

Isen, J., & Baker, L. A. (2008). Genetic disorders: Sex-linked. In M. M. Haith & J. B. Benson (Eds.), *Encyclopedia of infant and early childhood development*. Oxford, UK: Elsevier.

Isen, J. D., Baker, L. A., Raine, A., & Bezdjian, S. (2009). Genetic and environmental influences on the Junior Temperament and Character Inventory in a preadolescent twin sample. *Behavior Genetics, 39*, 36–47.

Ishikawa, Y., & others. (2009, in press). Spinal curvature and postural balance in patients with osteoporosis. *Osteoporosis International.*

Isingrini, M., Perrotin, A., & Souchay, C. (2008). Aging, metamemory regulation, and executive functioning. *Progress in Brain Research, 169*, 377–392.

Issuree, P. D., Pushpraraj, P. N., Pervaiz, S., & Melendez, A. J. (2009, in press). Resveratrol attenuates C5a-induced inflammatory responses in vitro and in vivo by inhibiting phospholipase D and sphingosine kinase activities. *FACEB Journal.*

Iwamoto, J., Sato, Y., Takeda, T., & Matsumoto, H. (2009, in press). Role of sport and exercise in the maintenance of female bone health. *Journal of Bone and Mineral Metabolism.*

Iwasaki, Y. (2008). Pathways to meaning-making through leisure-like pursuits in global contexts. *Journal of Leisure Research, 40*, 231–249.

Izard, V., Dehaene-Lambertz, G., & Dehaene, S. (2008). Distinct cerebral pathways for object identity and number in human infants. *PLoS Biology, 6*, e11.

J

Jackson, J. J., & others. (2009). Not all conscientiousness scales change alike: A multimethod, multisample study of age differences in the facets of conscientiousness. *Journal of Personality and Social Psychology, 96*, 446–459.

Jackson, S. L. (2008). *Research methods.* Belmont, CA: Wadsworth.

Jacobs, J. M., Hammerman-Rozenberg, R., Cohen, A., & Stressman, J. (2008). Reading daily predicts reduced mortality among men from a cohort of community-dwelling 70-year-olds. *Journals of Gerontology B: Psychological Sciences and Social Sciences, 63*, S73–S80.

Jacobs-Lawson, J. M., Hershey, D. A., & Neukam, K. A. (2005). Gender differences in factors that influence time spent planning for retirement. *Journal of Women and Aging, 16*, 55–69.

Jaddoe, V. W., Troe, E. J., Hofman, A., Mackenbach, J. P., Moll, H. A., Steegers, E. A., & Witteman, J. C. (2008). Active and passive smoking during pregnancy and the risks of low birthweight and preterm birth: The Generation R Study. *Pediatric and Perinatal Epidemiology, 22*, 162–171.

Jafar, T. H. (2009). Children, obesity, and high blood pressure: Asian population at high risk. *American Journal of Hypertension, 22*, 6–7.

Jaffee, S., & Hyde, J. S. (2000). Gender differences in moral orientation: A meta-analysis. *Psychological Bulletin, 126*, 703–726.

Jagust, W., & D'Esposito, M. (Eds.). (2009, in press). *Imaging the human brain.* Oxford, UK: Oxford University Press.

Jagust, W. J., & others. (2008). Neuropathological basis of magnetic resonance images in aging and dementia. *Annals of Neurology, 63*, 72–80.

James, A. H., Brancazio, L. R., & Price, T. (2008). Aspirin and reproductive outcomes. *Obstetrical and Gynecological Survey, 63*, 49–57.

James, D. C., & Dobson, B. (2005). Position of the American Dietetic Association: Promoting and supporting breastfeeding. *Journal of the American Dietetic Association, 105*, 810–818.

James, W. (1890/1950). *The principles of psychology.* New York: Dover.

Jamieson, P. E., & Romer, D. (2008). Unrealistic fatalism in U.S. youth ages 14–22: Prevalence and characteristics. *Journal of Adolescent Health, 42*, 154–160.

Janacek, R. J., Anderson, N., Liu, M., Zheng, S., Yang, Q., & Tso, P. (2005). Effects of yo-yo diet, caloric restriction, and olestra on tissue distribution of hexachlorobenzene. *American Journal of Physiology and Gastrointestinal Liver Physiology, 288*, G292–C299.

Jarrett, R. L. (1995). Growing up poor: The family experiences of socially mobile youth in low-income African-American neighborhoods. *Journal of Adolescent Research, 10*, 111–135.

Jaswal, V. K., & Fernald, A. (2007). Learning to communicate. In A. Slater & M. Lewis (Eds.), *Introduction to infant development* (2nd ed.). New York: Oxford University Press.

Jayson, S. (2006, June 29). The "millenials" come of age. *USA Today,* pp. 1–2D.

Jencks, C. (1979). *Who gets ahead? The determinants of economic success in America.* New York: Basic Books.

Jenkins, J. M., & Astington, J. W. (1996). Cognitive factors and family structure associated with theory of mind development in young children. *Developmental Psychology, 32*, 70–78.

Jensen, A. R. (2008). Book review. *Intelligence, 36*, 96–97.

Jenson-Campbell, L. A., & Malcolm, K. T. (2007). The importance of conscientiousness in adolescent interpersonal relationships. *Personality and Social Psychology Bulletin, 33*, 368–383.

Jessberger, S., & Gage, F. H. (2008). Stem-cell-associated structural and functional plasticity in the aging hippocampus. *Psychology and Aging, 23*, 684–691.

Ji, B. T., Shu, X. O., Linet, M. S., Zheng, W., Wacholde, S., Gao, Y. T., Ying, D. M., & Jin, E. (1997). Paternal cigarette smoking and the risk of childhood cancer among offspring of nonsmoking mothers. *Journal of the National Cancer Institute, 89*, 238–244.

Ji, C. Y., & Chen, T. J. (2008). Secular changes in stature and body mass index for Chinese youth in sixteen major cities, 1950s–2005. *American Journal of Human Biology, 20*, 530–537.

Jimerson, S. R. (2009). High school dropout. In D. Carr (Ed.), *Encyclopedia of the life course and human development.* Boston: Gale Cengage.

Johnson, A. D., Tarrant, K., & Brooks-Gunn, J. (2008). Early childhood education and care: An opportunity to enhance the lives of poor children. In D. R. Crane & T. B. Heaton (Eds.), *Handbook of families and poverty.* Thousand Oaks, CA: Sage.

Johnson, A. N. (2007). Factors influencing implementation of kangaroo holding in a special care nursery. *MCN American Journal of Maternal Child Nursing, 32*, 25–29.

Johnson, G. B., & Losos, J. (2010). *The living world* (6th ed.). New York: McGraw-Hill.

Johnson, H. L., Erbelding, E. J., & Ghanem, K. G. (2007). Sexually transmitted infections during pregnancy. *Current Infectious Disease Reports, 9*, 125–133.

Johnson, J. G., Zhang, B., & Prigerson, H. G. (2008). Investigation of a developmental model of risk for depression and suicidality following spousal bereavement. *Suicide and Life-Threatening Behavior, 38*, 1–12.

Johnson, J. S., & Newport, E. L. (1991). Critical period effects on universal properties of language: The status of subjacency in the acquisition of a second language. *Cognition, 39*, 215–258.

Johnson, M. (2008, April 30). Commentary in R. Highfield *Harvard's baby brain research lab.* Retrieved January 24, 2008, from www.telegraph.co.uk/scienceandtechnology/science/sciencenews/3341166/Harvards-baby-brain-research-lab.html

Johnson, M. H., Grossmann, T. and Cohen-Kadosh, K. (2009) Mapping functional brain development: Building a social brain through interactive specialization. *Developmental Psychology, 45*, 151–159.

Johnson, M. H., Grossman, T., & Farroni, T. (2009). The social cognitive neuroscience of infancy: Illuminating the early development of social brain functions. *Advances in Child Development and Behavior, 36*, 331–372.

Johnson, R. J. (2008). Advances in understanding and treating childhood sexual abuse:

Implications for research and policy. *Family and Community Health, 31,* (Suppl. 1), S24–S31.

Johnson, S. (2007). Cognitive and behavioral outcomes following very preterm birth. *Seminars in Fetal and Neonatal Medicine, 12,* 363–373.

Johnson, S. P. (2004). Development of perceptual completion in infancy. *Psychological Science, 15,* 769–775.

Johnson, S. P. (2009a, in press). Perceptual completion in infancy. In S. P. Johnson (Ed.), *Neoconstructivism: The new science of cognitive development.* New York: Oxford University Press.

Johnson, S. P. (2009b, in press). A constructivist view of object perception in infancy. In L. M. Oakes, C. H. Cashon, M. Casasola, & D. H. Rakison (Eds.), *Early perceptual and cognitive development.* New York: Oxford University Press.

Johnson, S. P. (2009c). Developmental origins of object perception. In A. Woodward & A. Needham (Eds.), *Learning and the infant mind.* New York: Oxford University Press.

Johnson, S. P., Bremner, J. G., Slater, A., & Mason, U. (2000). The role of good form in young infants, perception of partly occluded objects. *Journal of Experimantal Child Psychology, 76,* 1–25.

Johnson, W., te Nijenhuis, J., & Bouchard, T. J. (2008). Still just 1 *g*: Consistent results from five test batteries. *Intelligence, 36,* 81–95.

John-Steiner, V. (2007). Vygotsky on thinking and speaking. In H. Daniels, J. Wertsch, & M. Cole (Eds.), *The Cambridge companion to Vygotsky.* New York: Cambridge University Press.

Johnston, A. P., De Lisio, M., & Parise, G. (2008). Resistance training, sarcopenia, and the mitochondrial theory of aging. *Applied Physiology, Nutrition, and Metabolism, 31,* 191–199.

Johnston, B. B. (2008). Will increasing folic acid in fortified grain products further reduce neural tube defects without causing harm?: Consideration of the evidence. *Pediatric Research, 63,* 2–8.

Johnston, C. C., Filion, F., Campbell-Yeo, M., Goulet, C., Bell, L., McNaughton, K., & Bryon, J. (2009). Enhanced kangaroo care for heel lance in preterm neonates: A crossover trial. *Journal of Perinatology, 29,* 51–56.

Johnston, L. D., O'Malley, P. M., Bachman, J. G., & Schulenberg, J. E. (2006). *Monitoring the Future national survey results on drug use, 1975–2005. Volume II: College students and adults ages 19–45* (NIH Publication No. 06-5884). Bethesda, MD: National Institute on Drug Abuse

Johnston, L. D., O'Malley, P. M., Bachman, J. G., & Schulenberg, J. E. (2009). *Monitoring the Future national results on adolescent drug use: Overview of key findings, 2008.* Bethesda, MD: National Institute of Drug Abuse.

Joint Economic Committee. (2007, February). *Investing in raising children.* Washington, DC: U.S. Senate.

Jolly, C. A. (2005). Diet manipulation and prevention of aging, cancer, and autoimmune disease. *Current Opinions in Clinical Nutrition and Metabolic Care, 8,* 382–387.

Jones, D. C., Bain, N., & King, S. (2008). Weight and muscularity concerns as longitudinal predictors of body image among early adolescent boys: A test of the dual path model. *Body Image, 5,* 195–204.

Jones, M. C. (1965). Psychological correlates of somatic development. *Child Development, 36,* 899–911.

Jones, M. D. & Galliher, R. V. (2007). Navajo ethnic identity: Predictors of psychosocial outcomes in Navajo adolescents. *Journal of Research on Adolescence, 17,* 683–696.

Jones, R. (2006). Sex scripts and power: A framework to explain urban women's HIV sexual risk with male partners. *Nursing Clinics of North America, 41,* 425–436.

Jopp, D., & Rott, C. (2006). Adaptation in very old age: Exploring the role of resources and attitudes. *Psychology and Aging, 21,* 266–280.

Jordan, S. J., & others. (2008). Serous ovarian, fallopian tube, and primary peritoneal cancers: A comprehensive epidemiological analysis. *International Journal of Cancer, 122,* 1598–1603.

Jorgensen, M. E., Borch-Johnsen, K., & Bjerregaard, P. (2006). Lifestyle modifies obesity-associated risk of cardiovascular disease in a genetically homogeneous population. *American Journal of Clinical Nutrition, 84,* 29–36.

Josephson Institute of Ethics. (2006). *2006 Josephson Institute report card on the ethics of American youth. Part one—integrity.* Los Angeles: Josephson Institute.

Juffer, F., & van IJzendoorn, M. H. (2005). Behavior problems and mental health referrals of international adoptees: A meta-analysis. *Journal of the American Medical Association, 293,* 2501–2513.

Juffer, F., & van IJzendoorn, M. H. (2007). Adoptees do not lack self-esteem: A meta-analysis of studies on self-esteem of transracial, international, and domestic adoptees. *Psychological Bulletin, 133,* 1067–1083.

Jung, R. E., & Haier, R. J. (2007). The Parieto-Frontal Integration Theory (P-FIT) of intelligence: Converging neuroimaging evidence. *Behavioral and Brain Sciences, 30,* 135–187.

Jusczyk, P. W., & Hohne, E. A. (1997). Infants' memory for spoken words. *Science, 277,* 1984–1986.

Jylhava, J., & others. (2009). Genetics of C-reactive protein and complement factor H have an epistatic effect on carotid artery compliance: The Cardiovascular Risk in Young Finns Study. *Clinical and Experimental lmmunology, 155,* 53–58.

K

Kadenbach, B., Ramzan, R., & Vogt, S. (2009). Degenerative diseases, oxidative stress, and cytochrome c oxidase function. *Trends in Molecular Medicine, 15,* 139–147.

Kagan, J. (2002). Behavioral inhibition as a temperamental category. In R. J. Davidson, K. R. Scherer, & H. H. Goldsmith (Eds.), *Handbook of affective sciences.* New York: Oxford University Press.

Kagan, J. (2008). Fear and wariness. In M. M. Haith & J. B. Benson (Eds.), *Encyclopedia of infant and early childhood development.* Oxford, UK: Elsevier.

Kagan, J. (2008). Temperament. In A. Kazdin (Ed.), *Encyclopedia of psychology.* Washington, DC, & New York: American Psychological Association and Oxford University Press.

Kagan, J. (2010). Emotions and temperament. In M. H. Bornstein (Ed.), *Handbook of cultural developmental science.* New York: Psychology Press.

Kagan, J. J., Kearsley, R. B., & Zelazo, P. R. (1978). *Infancy: Its place in human development.* Cambridge, MA: Harvard University Press.

Kagan, S. H. (2008). Faculty profile, University of Pennsylvania School of Nursing. Retrieved April 25, 2008, from www.nursing.upenn.edu/faculty/profile.asp?pid=33

Kahana, E., Kahana, B., & Hammel, R. (2009). Stress in later life. In D. Carr (Ed.), *Encyclopedia of the life course and human development.* Boston: Gale Cengage.

Kahn, J. A., Huang, B., Gillman, M. W., Field, A. E., Austin, S. B., Colditz, G. A., & Frazier, A. L. (2008). Patterns and determinants of physical activity in U.S. adolescents. *Journal of Adolescent Health, 42,* 369–377.

Kail, R. (2000). Speed of information processing: Developmental change and links to intelligence. *Journal of School Psychology, 38,* 51–62.

Kail, R. V. (2007). Longitudinal evidence that increases in processing speed and working memory enhance children's reasoning. *Psychological Science, 18,* 312–313.

Kajantie, E., & others. (2008). Young adults with very low birth weight: Leaving the parental home and sexual relationships—Helsinki Study of Very Low Birth Weight Adults. *Pediatrics, 122,* e62–e72.

Kalichman, S. (1996). *Answering your questions about AIDS.* Washington, DC: American Psychological Association.

Kalish, R. A. (1981). *Death, grief, and caring relationships.* Monterey, CA: Brooks/Cole.

Kalish, R. A. (1987). Death. In G. L. Maddox (Ed.), *Encyclopedia of aging.* New York: Springer.

Kalish, R. A., & Reynolds, D. K. (1976). *An overview of death and ethnicity.* Farmingdale, NY: Baywood.

Kamii, C. (1985). *Young children reinvent arithmetic: Implications of Piaget's theory.* New York: Teachers College Press.

Kamii, C. (1989). *Young children continue to reinvent arithmetic.* New York: Teachers College Press.

Kammerman, S. B. (1989). Child care, women, work, and the family: An international overview of child-care services and related policies.

In J. S. Lande, S. Scarr, & N. Gunzenhauser (Eds.), *Caring for children: Challenge to America*. Hillsdale, NJ: Erlbaum.

Kammerman, S. B. (2000a). Parental leave policies. *Social Policy Report of the Society for Research in Child Development, XIV* (No. 2), 1–15.

Kammerman, S. B. (2000b). From maternity to paternity child leave policies. *Journal of the Medical Women's Association, 55,* 98–99.

Kandler, C., Riemann, R., & Kampfe, N. (2009). Genetic and personality mediation between measures of personality and family environment in twins reared together. *Behavior Genetics, 39,* 24–35.

Kane, R. L. (2007). Health care and services. In J. E. Birren (Ed.), *Encyclopedia of gerontology* (2nd ed.). San Diego: Academic Press.

Kanoy, K., Ulku-Steiner, B., Cox, M., & Burchinal, M. (2003). Marital relationship and individual psychological characteristics that predict physical punishment of children. *Journal of Family Psychology, 17,* 20–28.

Kaplan, H. B. (2009). Self-esteem. In D. Carr (Ed.), *Encyclopedia of the life course and human development*. Boston: Gale Cengage.

Kapornai, K., & Vetro, A. (2008). Depression in children. *Current Opinion in Psychiatry, 21,* 1–7.

Kar, N. (2009). Psychological impact of disasters on children: Review of assessment and interventions. *World Journal of Pediatrics, 5,* 5–11.

Karama, S., & others. (2009). Positive association between cognitive ability and cortical thickness in a representative sample of healthy 6 to 18 year olds. *Intelligence, 37,* 145–155.

Karelitz, T. M., Jarvin, L., & Sternberg, R. J. (2010, in press). The meaning of wisdom and its development throughout life. In W. Overton (Ed.), *Handbook of lifespan human development*. New York: Wiley.

Karnes, F. A., & Stephens, K. R. (2008). *Achieving excellence: Educating the gifted and talented*. Upper Saddle River, NJ: Prentice Hall.

Karney, B. R., Garvan, C. W., & Thomas, M. S. (2003). *Family formation in Florida—2003 baseline survey of attitudes, beliefs, and demographics relating to marriage and family formation*. Gainesville, FL: University of Florida. Retrieved September, 10, 2006, from *http://www.phhp.ufl.edu/~uspringe/FMP/Publications/REPORT.pdf*

Karpov, Y. V. (2006). *The neo-Vygotskian approach to child development*. New York: Cambridge University Press.

Karreman, A., van Tuijl, C., van Aken, M. A. G., & Dekovic, M. (2008). Parenting, coparenting, and effortful control in preschoolers. *Journal of Family Psychology, 22,* 30–40.

Kastenbaum, R. J. (2004). *Death, society, and human experience* (8th ed.). Boston: Allyn & Bacon.

Kastenbaum, R. J. (2007). *Death, society, and human experience* (9th ed.). Boston: Allyn & Bacon.

Kastenbaum, R. J. (2009). *Death society, and human experience* (10th ed.). Boston: Allyn & Bacon.

Kato, T. (2005). The relationship between coping with stress due to romantic break-ups and mental health. *Japanese Journal of Social Psychology, 20,* 171–180.

Katsetos, A. D., & Mirarchi, F. L. (2009, in press). A living will misinterpreted as a NDR order: Confusion compromises patient care. *Journal of Emergency Medicine.*

Katz, L. (1999). Curriculum disputes in early childhood education. *ERIC Clearinghouse on Elementary and Early Childhood Education,* Document EDO-PS-99-13.

Katz, P. R., Karuza, J., Intrator, O., & Mor, V. (2009). Nursing home physician specialists: A response to the workforce crisis in long-term care. *Annals of Internal Medicine, 150,* 411–413.

Kauffman, J. M., & Hallahan, D. P. (2005). *Special education: What it is and why we need it.* Boston: Allyn & Bacon.

Kauffman, J. M., McGee, K., & Brigham, M. (2004). Enabling or disabling? Observations on changes in special education. *Phi Delta Kappan, 85,* 613–620.

Kaufman, J. C., & Sternberg, R. J. (2007). Resource review: Creativity. *Change, 39,* 55–58.

Kaur G., Roberti, M., Raul, F., & Pendurthi, U. R. (2007). Suppression of human monocyte tissue factor induction by red wine phenolics and synthetic derivatives of resveratrol. *Thrombosis Research, 119,* 247–256.

Kavsek, M. (2009). The perception of subjective contours and neon color spreading figures in young infants. *Attention, Perception, and Psychophysics, 71,* 412–420.

Kazdin, A. E., & Benjet, C. (2003). Spanking children: Evidence and isues. *Current Directions in Psychological Science, 12,* 99–103.

Keating, D. P. (1990). Adolescent thinking. In S. S. Feldman & G. R. Elliott (Eds.), *At the threshold: The developing adolescent.* Cambridge, MA: Harvard University Press.

Keating, D. P. (2004). Cognitive and brain development. In R. Lerner & L. Steinberg (Ed.), *Handbook of adolescent psychology.* New York: Wiley.

Keating, D. P. (2007). Understanding adolescent development: Implications for driving safety. *Journal of Safety Research, 38,* 147–157.

Keating, D. P. (2009). Developmental science and giftedness: An integrated life-span framework. In F. D. Horowitz, R. F. Subotnik, & D. J. Matthews (Eds.), *The development of giftedness and talent across the life span.* Washington, DC: American Psychological Association.

Keen, R. (2005). Unpublished review of J. W. Santrock's *Topical life-span development,* 3rd ed. (New York: McGraw-Hill).

Keijer, J., & van Schothorst, E. M. (2008). Adipose tissue failure and mitochondria as a possible target for improvement by bioactive food components. *Current Opinion in Lipidology, 19,* 4–10.

Keil, V., & Price, J. M. (2009). Social information-processing patterns of maltreated children in two social domains. *Journal of Applied Developmental Psychology, 30,* 43–52.

Kellman, P. J., & Arterberry, M. E. (2006). Infant visual perception. In W. Damon & R. Lerner (Eds.), *Handbook of child psychology* (6th ed). New York: Wiley.

Kellman, P. J., & Banks, M. S. (1998). Infant visual perception. In W. Damon (Eds.), *Handbook of child psychology* (5th ed., Vol. 2). New York:

Kellogg, R. T. (2007). *Fundamentals of cognitive psychology.* Thousand Oaks, CA: Sage.

Kellough, R. D., & Carjuzaa, J. D. (2009). *Teaching in the middle and secondary schools* (9th ed.). Boston: Allyn & Bacon.

Kellow, J. T., & Jones, B. D. (2008). The effects of stereotypes on the achievement gap: Reexamining the academic performance of African American high school students. *Journal of Black Psychology, 34,* 94–120.

Kelly, D. J., Liu, S., Lee, K., Quinn, P. C., Pascalls, Slater, A. M., & Ge, L. (2009). Development of the other-race effect in infancy: Evidence towards universality? *Journal of Experimantal Child Psychology, 104,* 105–114.

Kelly, D. J., & others. (2007). Cross-race preferences for same-race faces extend beyond the African versus Caucasian contrast in 3-month-old infants. *Infancy, 11,* 87–95.

Kelly, G. F. (2008). *Sexuality today* (9th ed.). New York: McGraw-Hill.

Kelly, J. P., Borchert, J., & Teller, D. Y. (1997). The development of chromatic and achromatic sensitivity in infancy as tested with the sweep VEP. *Vision Research, 37,* 2057–2072.

Kelly, J. R. (1996). Leisure. In J. E. Birren (Ed.), *Encyclopedia of gerontology* (Vol. 2). San Diego: Academic Press.

Kelly, L., & others. (2009). Palliative care of First Nations people: A qualitative study of bereaved family members. *Canadian family Physician, 55,* 394–395.

Kemper, P., Weaver, P., Short, P. F., Shea, D., & Rang, H. (2008). Meeting the need for personal care among the elderly: Does Medicaid home care spending matter. *Health Services Research, 43,* 344–362.

Kempermann, G., Gast, D., & Gage, F. H. (2002). Neuroplasticity in old age: Sustained five-fold induction of hippocampal neurogenesis by long-term environmental enrichment. *Annals of Neurology, 52,* 135–152.

Kempermann, G., van Praag, H., & Gage, F. H. (2000). Activity-dependent regulation of neuronal plasticity and self repair. *Progress in Brain Research, 127,* 35–48.

Kennedy, K. M., & Raz, N. (2009). Aging white matter and cognition: Differential effects of regional variations in diffusion properties of memory, executive functioning, and speed. *Neuropsychologia, 47,* 916–927.

Kennedy, M. A. (2009). Child abuse. In D. Carr (Ed.), *Encyclopedia of the life course and human development.* Boston: Gale Cengage.

Kennell, J. H. (2006). Randomized controlled trial of skin-to-skin contact from birth versus conventional incubator for physiological stabilization in 1200 g to 2199 g newborns. *Acta Paediatica (Sweden), 95,* 15–16.

Kennell, J. H., & McGrath, S. K. (1999). Commentary: Practical and humanistic lessons from the third world for perinatal caregivers everywhere. *Birth, 26,* 9–10.

Kenner, C., Sugrue, N. M., & Finkelman, A. (2007). How nurses around the world can make a difference. *Nursing for Women's Health, 11,* 468–473.

Kensinger, E. A. (2009). *Emotional memory across the adult lifespan.* New York: Psychology Press.

Kerr, M. (2001). Culture as a context for temperament. In T. D. Wachs & G. A. Kohnstamm (Eds.), *Temperament in context.* Mahwah, NJ: Erlbaum.

Kersting, A., Kroker, K., Horstmann, J., Ohrmann, P., Baune, B. T., Arolt, V., & Suslow, T. (2009, in press). Complicated grief in patients with unipolar depression. *Journal of Affective Disorders.*

Kessen, W., Haith, M. M., & Salapatek, P. (1970). Human infancy. In P. H. Mussen (Ed.), *Manual of child psychology* (3rd ed., Vol. 1). New York: Wiley

Ketcham, C. J., & Stelmack, G. E. (2001). Age-related declines in motor control. In J. E. Birren & K. W. Schaie (Eds.), *Handbook of the psychology of aging.* (5th ed.). San Diego: Academic Press.

Key, J. D., Gebregziabher, M. G., Marsh, L. D., & O'Rourke, K. M. (2008). Effectiveness of an intensive, school-based intervention for teen mothers. *Journal of Adolescent Health, 42,* 394–400.

Kiecolt-Glaser, J. K., Loving, T. J., Stowell, J. R., Malarkey, W. B., Lemeshow, S., Dickinson, S. L., & Glaser, R. (2005). Hostile marital interactions, proinflammatory cytokine production, and wound healing. *Archives of General Psychiatry, 62,* 1377–1384.

Kiecolt-Glaser, J. K., Preacher, K. J., MacCallum, R. C., Atkinson, C., Malarkey, W. B., & Glaser, R. (2003). Chronic stress and age-related increases in the proinflammatory cytokine IL-6. *Proceedings of the National Academy of Sciences USA, 100,* 9090–9095.

Kim, J., & Cicchetti, D. (2004). A longitudinal study of child maltreatment, mother-child relationship quality and maladjustment: The role of self-esteem and social competence. *Journal of Abnormal Child Psychology, 32,* 341–354.

Kim, J. A., Wei, Y., & Sowers, J. R. (2008). Role of mitochondrial dysfunction in insulin resistance. *Circulation Research, 102,* 401–414.

Kim, J. E., & Moen, P. (2002). Retirement transitions, gender, and psychological well-being: A life-course, ecological model. *Journals of Gerontology B: Psychological Sciences and Social Sciences, 57,* P212–P222.

Kim, S., & Hasher, L. (2005). The attraction effect in decision making: Superior performance by older adults. *Quarterly Journal of Experimental Psychology, 58A,* 120–133.

Kim, S. H. (2009). The influence of finding meaning and worldview of accepting death on anger among bereaved older spouses. *Aging and Mental Health, 13,* 38–45.

Kim, S. Y., Su, J., Yancura, L., Yee, B. (2009). Asian American and Pacific Islander families. In N. Tewari & A. Alvarez (Eds.), *Asian American psychology.* Clifton, NJ: Psychology Press.

Kim, Y. K. (2009). The relationship between home literacy practices and developmental trajectories of emergent literacy and conventional literacy skills for Korean children. *Reading and Writing, 22,* 57–84.

Kimber, L., McNabb, M., McCourt, C., Haines, A., & Brocklehurst, P. (2008). Massage or music for pain relief in labour: A pilot randomised placebo controlled trial. *European Journal of Pain, 12,* 961–969.

Kimble, M., Neacsiu, A. D., Flack, W. F., & Horner, J. (2008). Risk of unwanted sex for college women: Evidence for a red zone. *Journal of American College Health, 57,* 331–338.

Kimbrough-Melton, R. J., & Campbell, D. (2008). Strong communities for children: A community-wide approach to prevention of child abuse and neglect. *Family and Community Health, 31,* 100–112.

Kimmel, A. J. (2007). *Ethical issues in behavioral research.* Malden, MA: Blackwell.

King, A. A., DeBraun, M. R., & White, D. A. (2008). Need for cognitive rehabilitation for children with sickle-cell disease and strokes. *Expert Review of Neurotherapeutics, 8,* 291–296.

King, L. A., & Hicks, J. A. (2007). Whatever happened to "What might have been?" Regrets, happiness, and maturity. *American Psychologist, 62,* 625–636.

King, P. E., & Roeser, R. W. (2009). Religion and spirituality in adolescent development. In R. M. Lerner & L. Steinberg (Eds.), *Handbook of adolescent psychology* (3rd ed.). New York: Wiley.

King, V., & Scott, M. E. (2005). A comparison of cohabiting relationships among older and younger adults. *Journal of Marriage and the Family, 67,* 271–285.

Kingston, N. (2008). Standardized tests. In N. J. Salkind (Ed.), *Encyclopedia of educational psychology.* Thousand Oaks, CA: Sage.

Kinney, H. C., Richerson, G. B., Dymecki, S. M., Darnall, R. A., & Nattie, E. E. (2009). The brainstem and serotonin in sudden infant death syndrome. *Annual Review of Pathology, 4,* 517–550.

Kinney, J. (2009). *Loosening the grip* (9th ed.). New York: McGraw-Hill.

Kirby, D. B., Laris, B. A., & Rolleri, L. A. (2007). Sex and HIV education programs: Their impact on sexual behavior of young people throughout the world. *Journal of Adolescent Health 40,* 206–217.

Kirkpatrick, R. M., McGue, M., & Iacono, W. G. (2009). Shared-environment contributions to high cognitive ability. *Behavioral Genetics, 39,* 406–416.

Kisilevsky, B. S., Hains, S. M., Lee, K., Xic, X., Huang, H., Ye, H. H., Zhang, K., & Wang, Z. (2003). Effects of experience on fetal voice recognition. *Psychological Science, 14,* 220–224.

Kisilevsky, B. S., & others. (2009). Fetal sensitivity to properties of maternal speech and language. *Infant Behavior and Development, 32,* 59–71.

Kitchener, K. S., & King, P. M. (1981). Reflective judgment: Concepts of justification and their relationship to age and education. *Journal of Applied Developmental Psychology, 2,* 89–111.

Kivnik, H. Q., & Sinclair, H. M. (2007). Grandparenthood. In J. E. Birren (Ed.), *Encyclopedia of gerontology* (2nd ed.). San Diego: Academic Press.

Klaczynski, P. (2001). The influence of analytic and heuristic processing on adolescent reasoning and decision making. *Child Development. 72,* 844–861.

Klaczynski, P. A., & Narasimham, G. (1998). Development of scientific reasoning biases: Cognitive versus ego-protective explanations. *Developmental Psychology, 34,* 175–187.

Klatt, J., & Enright, R. (2009). Investigating the place of forgiveness within the positive youth development paradigm. *Journal of moral Education, 38,* 35–52.

Klaus, M., & Kennell, H. H. (1976). *Maternal-infant bonding.* St. Louis: Mosby.

Klein, S. B. (2009). *Learning.* Thousand Oaks, CA: Sage.

Kliewer, W., & Murrelle, L. (2007). Risk and protective factors for adolescent substance use: Findings from a study in selected Central American countries. *Journal of Adolescent Health, 40,* 448–455.

Klima, C., Norr, K., Conderheld, S., & Handler, A. (2009). Introduction of Centering-Pregnancy in a public health clinic. *Journal of Midwifery and Women's Health, 54,* 27–34.

Kling, K. C., Hyde, J. S., Showers, C. J., & Buswell, B. N. (1999). Gender differences in self-esteem: A meta-analysis. *Psychological Bulletin, 125,* 470–500.

Knopik, V. S. (2009). Maternal smoking during pregnancy and child outcomes: Real or spurious? *Developmental Neuropsychology, 34,* 1–36.

Knuiman, M. W., Hung, J., Divitini, M. L., Davis, T. M., & Beilby, J. P. (2009). Utility of the metabolic syndrome and its components in the prediction of incident cardiovascular disease: A prospective cohort study. *European Journal of Cardiovascular Prevention and Rehabilitation, 16,* 235–241.

Knussmann, R., Christiansen, K., & Couwenbergs, C. (1986). Relations between sex hormone levels and sexual behavior in men. *Archives of Sexual Behavior, 15,* 429–45.

Kochanska, G., & Aksan, N. (2007). Conscience in childhood: Past, present, and future. *Merrill-Palmer Quarterly, 50,* 299–310.

Kochanska, G., Aksan, N., Prisco, T. R., & Adams, E. E. (2008). Mother-child and father-child mutually responsive orientation in the first 2 years and children's outcomes at preschool age: Mechanisms of influence. *Child Development, 79,* 30–44.

Kochanska, G., Forman, D. R., Aksan, N., & Dunbar, S. B. (2005). Pathways to conscience: Early mother-child mutually responsive orientation and children's moral emotion, conduct, and cognition. *Journal of Child Psychology and Psychiatry, 46,* 19–34.

Kochanska, G., Gross, J. N., Lin, M., & Nichols, K. E. (2002). Guilt in young children: Development, determinants, and relations with a broader set of standards. *Child Development, 73,* 461–482.

Kochanska, G., Philibert, R. A., & Barry, R. A. (2009, in press). Interplay of genes and early mother-child relationship in the development of self-regulation from toddler to preschool age. *Journal of Child Psychology and Psychiatry.*

Koenig, H. G. (2004). Religion, spirituality, and medicine: Research findings and implications for clinical practice. *Southern Medical Journal, 97,* 1194–2000.

Koenig, H. G., Cohen, H. J., Blazer, D. G., Pieper, C., Meador, K. G., Shelp, F., Goldi, V., & DiPasquale, R. (1992). Religious coping and depression in elderly hospitalized medically ill men. *American Journal of Psychiatry, 149,* 1693–1700.

Koenig, H. G., & Larson, D. B. (1998). Religion and mental health. In H. S. Friedman (Ed.), *Encyclopedia of mental health* (Vol. 3). San Diego: Academic Press.

Koenig, L. B., McGue, M., & Iacono, W. G. (2008). Stability and change in religousness during emerging adulthood. *Developmental Psychology, 44,* 523–543.

Kohen, D. E., Leventhal, T., Dahinten, V. S., & McIntosh, C. N. (2008). Neighborhood disadvantage: Pathways of effects for young children. *Child Development, 79,* 156–169.

Kohlberg, L. (1958). *The development of modes of moral thinking and choice in the years 10 to 16.* Unpublished doctoral dissertation, University of Chicago.

Kohlberg, L. (1969). Stage and sequence: The cognitive-developmental approach to socialization. In D. A. Goslin (Ed.), *Handbook of socialization theory and research.* Chicago: Rand McNally.

Kohlberg, L. (1986). A current statement on some theoretical issues. In S. Modgil & C. Modgil (Eds.), *Lawrence Kohlberg.* Philadelphia: Palmer.

Kohlberg, L., & Ryncarz, R. A. (1990) Beyond justice reasoning: Moral development and consideration of a seventh stage. In C. N. Alexander & E. J. Langer (Eds.), *Higher stages of human development.* New York: Oxford University Press.

Kohler, P. K., Manhart, L. E., & Lafferty, W. E. (2008). Abstinence-only and comprehensive sex education and the initiation of sexual activity and teen pregnancy. *Journal of Adolescent Health, 42,* 344–351.

Kohler, T. S., Kim, J., Feia, K., Bodie, J., Johnson, N., Makhlouf, A., & Monga, M. (2008). Prevalence of androgen deficiency in men with erectile dysfunction. *Urology, 71,* 693–697.

Kohn, D. (2009). Adolescent thinking. In R. M. Lerner & L. Steinberg (Eds.), *Handbook of adolescent psychology* (3rd ed.), New York: Wiley.

Koolhof, R., Loeber, R., Wei, E. H., Pardini, D., & D'escury, A. C. (2007). Inhibition deficits of serious delinquent boys of low intelligence. *Criminal Behavior and Mental Health, 77,* 274–292.

Kopp, C. B. (1982). The antecedents of self-regulation. *Developmental Psychology, 18,* 199–214.

Kopp, C. B. (1987). The growth of self-regulation: Caregivers and children. In N. Eisenberg (Ed.), *Contemporary topics in developmental psychology.* New York: Wiley.

Kopp, C. B. (2008). Self-regulatory processes. In M. M. Haith & J. B. Benson (Eds.), *Encyclopedia of infant and early childhood development.* Oxford, UK: Elsevier.

Koppelman, K., & Goodheart, L. (2000). *Understanding human differences* (2nd ed.). Boston: Allyn & Bacon.

Korantzopoulos, P., Kolettis, T. M., Galaris, D., & Goudevenos, J. A. (2007). The role of oxidative stress in the pathogenesis and perpetuation of atrial fibrillation. *International Journal of Cardiology, 115,* 135–143.

Korat, O. (2009). The effect of maternal teaching talk on children's emergent literacy as a function of type of activity and maternal education level. *Journal of Applied Developmental Psychology, 30,* 34–42.

Koropeckyj-Cox, T. (2009). Singlehood. In D. Carr (Ed.), *Encyclopedia of the life course and human development.* Boston: Gale Cengage.

Korres, S., & others. (2008). Outcomes and efficacy of newborn hearing screening: Strengths and weaknesses (success or failure?). *Laryngoscope, 118,* 1253–1256.

Korrick, S. A., & Sagiv, S. K. (2008). Polychlorinated biphenyls, organopesticides, and neurodevelopment. *Current Opinion in Pediatrics, 20,* 198–204.

Koster, A., & others. (2008). Joint effects of adiposity and physical activity on incident mobility limitation in older adults. *Journal of the American Geriatric Society, 56,* 636–643.

Kotovsky, L., & Baillargeon, R. (1994). Calibration-based reasoning about collision events in 11-month-old infants. *Cognition, 51,* 107–129.

Kotre, J. (1984). *Outliving the self: Generativity and the interpretation of lives.* Baltimore: Johns Hopkins University Press.

Kotze, E. (2004). Language and identity—the Afrikaans community in the U.K. *Collections in Anthropology, 28* (Suppl. 1), 63–72.

Koulougliolti, C., Cole, R., & Kitzman, H. (2008). Inadequate sleep and unintentional injuries in young children. *Public Health Nursing, 25,* 106–114.

Kowalski, S. D., & Bondmass, M. D. (2008). Physiological and psychological symptoms of grief in widows. *Research in Nursing and Health, 31,* 23–30.

Kozol, J. (2005). *The shame of the nation.* New York: Crown.

Krakoff, L. R. (2008). Older patients need better guidelines for optimal treatment of high blood pressure: 1 size fits few. *Hypertension, 51,* 817–818.

Kramer, A. F., Larish, J., Weber, T., & Bardell, L. (1999). Training for executive control: Task coordination strategies and aging. In D. Gopher & A. Koriat (Eds.), *Attention and performance XVII.* Cambridge, MA: MIT Press.

Kramer, A. F., & Madden, D. J. (2008). Attention. In F. I. M. Craik & T. A. Salthouse (Eds.), *Handbook of aging and cognition* (3rd ed.). Mahwah, NJ: Erlbaum.

Kramer, A. F., & Morrow, D. (2009, in press). Cognitive training and expertise. In D. Park & N. Schwartz (Eds.), *Cognitive aging: A primer.* New York: Psychology Press.

Kramer, D., Kahlbaugh, P. E., & Goldston, R. B. (1992). A measure of paradigm beliefs about the social world. *Journal of Gerontology: Psychological Sciences, 47,* P180–P189.

Kramer, L. (2006, July 10). Commentary in J. Kluger, "How your siblings make you who you are." *Time,* pp. 46–55.

Kramer, L., & Perozynski, L. (1999). Parental beliefs about managing sibling conflict. *Developmental Psychology, 35,* 489–499.

Kramer, L., & Radey, C. (1997). Improving sibling relationships among young children: A social skills training model. *Family Relations, 46,* 237–246.

Kranz, S., Lin, P. J., & Wagstaff, D. A. (2007). Children's dairy intake in the United States: Too little, too fat? *Journal of Pediatrics, 151,* 642–646.

Krause, N. (1995). Religiosity and self-esteem among older adults. *Journal of Gerontology B: Psychological Sciences and Social Sciences, 50,* P236–P246.

Krause, N. (2003). Religious meaning and subjective well-being in late life. *Journals of Gerontology B: Psychological Sciences and Social Sciences, 50,* S160–S170.

Krause, N. E. (2006). Religion and aging. In J. E. Birren & K. W. Schaie (Eds.), *Handbook of the psychology of aging.* San Diego: Academic Press.

Krause, N., Ingersoll-Dayton, B., Liang, J., & Sugisawa, H. (1999). Religion, social behavior, and health among the Japanese elderly. *Journal of Health and Social Behavior, 40,* 405–421.

Kreutzer, M. A., Leonard, C., & Flavell, J. H. (1975). An interview study of children's knowledge about memory. *Monographs of the Society for Research in Child Development, 40* (1, Serial No. 159).

Kroger, J. (2007). *Identity development: Adolescence through adulthood* (2nd ed.). Thousand Oaks, CA: Sage.

Krogh, K. L., & Slentz, S. L. (2001). *Teaching young children.* Mahwah, NJ: Erlbaum.

Krueger, J. I., Vohs, K. D., & Baumeister, R. F. (2008). Is the allure of self-esteem a mirage after all? *American Psychologist, 63,* 64–65.

Krueger, P. M., & Chang, V. W. (2008). Being poor and coping with stress: Health behaviors and the risk of death. *American Journal of Public Health, 98,* 889–896.

Kruger, J., Blanck, H. M., & Gillespie, C. (2006). Dietary and physical activity behaviors among adults successful at weight loss management. *International Journal of Behavioral Nutrition and Physical Activity, 3,* 17.

Ksir, C. J., Chart, C. L., & Ray, O. S. (2008). *Drugs, society, and human behavior* (12th ed.). New York: McGraw-Hill.

Kübler-Ross, E. (1969). *On death and dying.* New York: Macmillan.

Kuczynski, L., & Parkin, C. N. (2007). Agency and bidirectionality in socialization: Interactions, transactions, and relational dialectics. In J. E. Grusec & P. D. Hastings (Eds.), *Handbook of socialization.* New York: Guilford.

Kuebli, J. (1994, March). Young children's understanding of everyday emotions. *Young Children,* pp. 36–48.

Kuhl, P. K. (1993). Infant speech perception: A window on psycholinguistic development. *International Journal of Psycholinguistics, 9,* 33–56.

Kuhl, P. K. (2000). A new view of language acquisition. *Proceedings of the National Academy of Sciences USA, 97* (22), 11850–11857.

Kuhl, P. K. (2007). Is speech learning "gated" by the social brain? *Developmental Science, 10,* 110–120.

Kuhl, P. K. (2009). Linking infant speech perception to language acquisition: Phonetic learning predicts language growth. In J. Colombo, P. McCardle, & L. Freund (Eds.), *Infant pathways to language.* New York: Psychology Press.

Kuhl, P. K., & Damasio, A. (2009, in press). Language. In E. R. Kandel, J. H. Schwartz, T. M. Jessell, S. Siegelbaum, & J. Hudspeth (Eds.), *Principles of neural science* (5th ed.). New York: McGraw-Hill.

Kuhl, P. K., Stevens, E., Hayashi, A., Deguchi, T., Kiritani, S., & Iverson, P. (2006). Infants show a facilitation for native language phonetic perception between 6 and 12 months. *Developmental Science, 9,* F13–F21.

Kuhn, D. (1998). Afterword to Volume 2: Cognition, perception, and language. In W. Damon (Ed.), *Handbook of child psychology* (5th ed., Vol. 2). New York: Wiley.

Kuhn, D. (2006). *Education for thinking.* Cambridge: Harvard University Press.

Kuhn, D. (2008). Formal operations from a twenty-first century perspective. *Human Development, 51,* 48–55.

Kuhn, D. (2009). Adolescent thinking. In R. M. Lerner & L. Steinberg (Eds.), *Handbook of adolescent psychology* (3rd ed.). New York: Wiley.

Kuhn, D., Cheney, R., & Weinstock, M. (2000). The development of epistemological understanding. *Cognitive Development, 15,* 309–328.

Kuhn, D., & Franklin, S. (2006). The second decade: What develops (and how)? In W. Damon & R. Lerner (Eds.), *Handbook of child psychology* (6th ed.). New York: Wiley.

Kuhn, D., Schauble, L. & Garcia-Mila, M. (1992). Cross-domain development of scientific reasoning. *Cognition and Instruction, 9,* 285–327.

Kupersmidt, J. B., & Coie, J. D. (1990). Preadolescent peer status, aggression, and school adjustment as predictors of externalizing problems in adolescence. *Child Development, 61,* 1350–1363.

Kuppens, S., Grietens, H., Onghena, P., & Michiels, D. (2009). Relations between parental psychological control and childhood relational aggression: Reciprocal in nature? *Journal of Clinical Child and Adolescent Psychology, 38,* 117–131.

Kurdek, L. A. (2003). Differences between gay and lesbian cohabiting couples. *Journal of Social and Personal Relationships, 20,* 411–436.

Kurdek, L. A. (2008). Change in relationship quality for partners from lesbian, gay male, and heterosexual couples. *Journal of Family Psychology, 22,* 701–711.

Kuriyama, S., & Mayor, R. (2009). A role for Syndecan-4 in neural induction ERK- and PKC-dependent pathways. *Development, 136,* 575–584.

L

Labouvie-Vief, G. (1986, August). *Modes of knowing and life-span cognition.* Paper presented at the meeting of the American Psychological Association, Washington, DC.

Labouvie-Vief, G. (2006). Emerging structures of adult thought. In J. J. Arnett & J. L. Tanner (Eds.), *Emerging adults in America.* Washington, DC: American Psychological Association.

Lacey, J., Cate, H., & Broadway, D. C. (2009). Barriers to adherence with glaucoma medications: A qualitative research study. *Eye, 23,* 924–932.

Lachman, M. E. (2004). Development in midlife. *Annual Review of Psychology* (Vol. 55). Palo Alto, CA: Annual Reviews.

Ladd, G., Buhs, E., & Troop, W. (2004). School adjustment and social skills training. In P. K. Smith & C. H. Hart (Eds.), *Blackwell handbook of childhood social development.* Malden, MA: Blackwell.

Laflin, M. T., Wang, J., & Barry, M. (2008). A longitudinal study of adolescent transition from virgin to nonvirgin status. *Journal of Adolescent Health, 42,* 228–236.

LaFontana, K. M., & Cillessen, A. H. N. (2009, in press). Developmental changes in the priority of perceived status in childhood and adolescence. *Social Development.*

Lafreniere, D., & Mann, N. (2009). Anosmia: Loss of smell in the elderly. *Otolaryngologic Clinics of North America, 42,* 123–131.

Lahey, B. B., Van Hulle, C. A., D'Onofrio, B. M., Rodgers, J. L., & Waldman, I. D. (2008). Is parental knowledge of their adolescent offspring's whereabouts and peer associations spuriously associated with offspring delinquency? *Journal of Abnormal Child Psychology, 36,* 807–823.

Lai, D. W. L. (2007). Cultural aspects of reminiscence and life review. In J. A. Kunz & G. Soltys (Eds.), *Transformational reminiscence: Life story work.* New York: Springer.

Laible, D. J., Carlo, G., & Raffaeli, M. (2000). The differential relations of parent and peer attachment to adolescent adjustment. *Journal of Youth and Adolescence, 29,* 45–53.

Laible, D. J., & Thompson, R. A. (2000). Mother-child discourse, attachment security, shared positive affect, and early conscience development. *Child Development, 71,* 1424–1440.

Laible, D. J., & Thompson, R. A. (2007). Early socialization: A relationship perspective. In J. E. Grusec & P. D. Hastings (Eds.), *Handbook of socialization.* New York: Guilford.

Laird, R. D., Criss, M. M., Pettit, G. S., Dodge, K. A., & Bates, J. E. (2008). Parents' monitoring knowledge attenuates the link between antisocial friends and adolescent delinquent behavior. *Journal of Abnormal Child Psychology, 36,* 299–310.

Lamb, M. E. (1994). Infant care practices and the application of knowledge. In C. B. Fisher & R. M. Lerner (Eds.), *Applied developmental psychology.* New York: McGraw-Hill.

Lamb, M. E. (2000). The history of research on father involvement: An overview. *Marriage and Family Review, 29,* 23–42.

Lamb, M. E. (2005). Attachments, social networks, and developmental contexts. *Human Development, 48,* 108–112.

Lamb, M. E., Bornstein, M. H., & Teti, D. M. (2002). *Development in infancy* (4th ed.). Mahwah, NJ: Erlbaum.

Lamont, R. F., & Jaggat, A. N. (2007). Emerging drug therapies for preventing spontaneous labor and preterm birth. *Expert Opinion on Investigational Drugs, 16,* 337–345.

Lampl, M. (2008). Physical growth. In M. M. Haith & J. B. Benson (Eds.), *Encyclopedia of infant and early childhood development.* Oxford, UK: Elsevier.

Landau, L. I. (2008). Tobacco smoke exposure and tracking of lung function into adult life. *Pediatric Respiratory Reviews, 9,* 39–44.

Lane H. (1976). *The wild boy of Aveyron.* Cambridge, MA: Harvard University Press.

Lane, R. M., & He, Y. (2009). Emerging hypotheses regarding the influences of butyrylcholinesterase-K variant, APOE epsilon 4, and hyperhomocysteinemia in neurogenerative dementias. *Medical Hypotheses, 73,* 230–250.

Langer, E. J. (2005). *On becoming an artist.* New York: Ballentine.

Langer, E. J. (2007, August). *Counterclockwise: Mindfulness and aging.* Paper presented at the meeting of the American Psychological Association, San Francisco.

Lang, F. R., & Carstensen, L. L. (1994). Close emotional relationship in late life: Further support for proactive aging in the social domain. *Psychology and Aging, 9,* 315–324.

Lanham-New, S. A. (2008). Importance of calcium, vitamin D, and vitamin K for osteoporosis prevention and treatment. *Proceedings of the Nutrition Society, 67,* 163–176.

Lansford, J. E. (2009). Parental divorce and children's adjustment. *Perspectives on Psychological Science, 4,* 140–152.

Lansford, J. E., Miller-Johnson, S., Berlin, L. J., Dodge, K. A., Bates, J. E., & Pettit, G. S. (2007). Early physical abuse and later violent delinquency: A prospective longitudinal study. *Child Maltreatment, 12,* 233–245.

Lapsley, D. (2008). Moral self-identity as the aim of education. In L. Nucci & D. Narváez (Eds.), *Handbook of moral and character education.* Clifton, NJ: Psychology Press.

Larson, R. (1999, September). Unpublished review of J. W. Santrock's *Adolescence,* 8th ed. (New York: McGraw-Hill).

Larson, R., & Lampman-Petraitis, C. (1989). Daily emotional states as reported by children and adolescents. *Child Development, 60,* 1250–1260.

Larson, R., & Richards, M. H. (1994). *Divergent realities.* New York: Basic Books.

Larson, R., & Verma, S. (1999). How children and adolescents spend their time around the world: Work, play, and developmental opportunities. *Psychological Bulletin, 125,* 701–736.

Larson, R. W. (2001) How U. S. children spend time: What it does (and doesn't) tell us about their development. *Current Directions in Psychological Science, 10,* 160–164.

Larson, R. W., Wilson, S., & Rickman, A. (2009). Globalization, societal change, and adolescence across the world. In R. M. Lerner & L. Steinberg (Eds.), *Handbook of adolescent psychology* (3rd ed.). New York: Wiley.

Larson-Meyer, D. E., & others. (2008). Effect of 6-month calorie restriction and exercise on serum and liver lipids and markers of liver function. *Obesity, 16,* 1355–1362.

Latendresse, G. (2009). The interaction between chronic stress and pregnancy: Preterm birth from biobehavioral perspective. *Journal of Midwifery and Women's Health, 54,* 8–17.

Laumann, E. G., West, S., Glasser, D., Carson, C., Rosen, R., & Kang, J. H. (2007). Prevalence and correlates of erectile dysfunction by race and ethnicity among men aged 40 or older in the United States: From the male attitudes regarding sexual health survey. *Journal of Sexual Medicine, 4,* 57–65.

Laumann, E. O., Glasser, D. B., Neves, R. C., & Moreira, E. D. (2009). A population-based survey of sexual activity, sexual problems, and associated help-seeking behavior patterns in mature adults in the United States of America. *International Journal of Impotence Research, 21,* 171–178.

Laursen, B. & Collins, W. A. (2009). Parent-child relationships in adolescence. In R. M. Lerner & L. Steinberg (Eds.), *Handbook of adolescent psychology* (3rd ed.). New York: Wiley.

Laursen, B., & Pursell, G. (2009). Conflict in peer relationships. In K. H. Rubin, W. M. Bukowski, & B. Laursen (Eds.), *Handbook of peer interaction, relationships, and groups.* New York: Guilford.

Lavoie, B. A., Mehta, R., & Thornton, A. R. (2008). Linear and nonlinear changes in the auditory brainstem response of aging humans. *Clinical Neuropsychology, 119,* 772–785.

Lawrence, E., Rothman, A. D., Cobb, R. J., & Bradbury, T. N. (2009, in press). Marital satisfaction across the transition to parenthood. In M. S. Schultz, M. K. Pruett, P. K. Kerig, & R. D. Parke (Eds.), *Feathering the nest: Couple relationships, couples interventions, and children's development.* Washington, DC: American Psychological Association.

Lawrence, J. M., Contreras, R., Chen, W., & Sacks, D. A. (2008). Trends in the prevalence of preexisting diabetes and gestational diabetes mellitus among a racially/ethnically diverse population of pregnant women, 1999–2005. *Diabetes Care, 31,* 899–904.

Lawrence, L., Shaha, S., & Lillis, K. (2008). Observational study of helmet use among children skiing and skateboarding. *Pediatric Emergency Care, 24,* 219–221.

Lawrence, R. A. (2008). Breastfeeding. In M. M. Haith & J. B. Benson (Eds.), *Encyclopedia of infant and early childhood development.* Oxford, UK: Elsevier.

Leach, P. (1990). *Your baby and child: From birth to age five.* New York: Knopf.

Leadbeater, B. J., & Way, N. (2000). *Growing up fast.* Mahwah, NJ: Erlbaum.

Leaper, C., & Bigler, R. S. (2004). Commentary: Gender language and sexist thought. *Monographs of the Society for Research in Child Development, 69* (1, Serial No. 275), 128–142.

Leaper, C., & Brown, C. S. (2008). Perceived experience of sexism among adolescent girls. *Child Development, 79,* 685–704.

Leaper, C., & Friedman, C. K. (2007). The socialization of gender. In J. E. Grusec & P. D. Hastings (Eds.), *Handbook of socialization.* New York: Guilford.

Leaper, C., & Smith, T. E. (2004). A meta-analytic review of gender variations in children's language use: Talkativeness, affiliative speech, and assertive speech. *Developmental Psychology, 40,* 993–1027.

Leasure, J. L., & Decker, L. (2009, in press). Social isolation prevents exercise-induced proliferation of hippocampal progenitor cells in female rats. *Hippocampus.*

Lee, B. K., Glass, T. A., McAfee, M. J., Wand, G. S., Bandeen-Roche, K., Bolla, K. I., & Schwartz, B. S. (2007). Associations of salivary cortisol with cognitive function in the Baltimore memory study. *Archives of General Psychiatry, 64,* 810–818.

Lee, E., Mitchell-Herzfeld, S. D., Lowenfels, A. A., Greene, R., Dorabawila, V., & DuMont, K. A. (2009). Reducing low birth weight through home visitation: A randomized controlled trial. *American Journal of Preventive Medicine, 36,* 154–160.

Lee, G. R. (1978). Marriage and morale in late life. *Journal of Marriage and the Family, 40,* 131–139.

Lee, H. Y., Lee, E. L., Pathy, P., & Chan, Y. H. (2005). Anorexia nervosa in Singapore: An eight-year retrospective study. *Singapore Medical Journal, 46,* 275–281.

Lee, I. M., Hsieh, C., & Paffenbarger, O. (1995). Exercise intensity and longevity in men. *Journal of the American Medical Association, 273,* 1179–1184.

Lee, I. M., & Skerrett, P. J. (2001). Physical activity and all-cause mortality: What is the dose-response relation? *Medical Science and Sports Exercise, 33* (6 Suppl.), 5459–5471.

Lee, K., Cameron, C. A., Doucette, J., & Talwar, V. (2002). Phantoms and fabrications: Young children's detection of implausible lies. *Child Development, 73,* 1688–1702.

Lee, S. J., & Wong, A. N. (2009). The model minority and the perceptual foreigner: Stereotypes of Asian Americans. In N. Tewari & A. Alvarez (Eds.), *Asian American psychology.* Clifton, NJ: Psychology Press.

Leedy, P. D., & Ormrod, J. E. (2010). *Practical research* (9th ed.). Upper Saddle River, NJ: Prentice Hall.

Lefkowitz, E. S., Boone, T. L., & Shearer, T. L. (2004). Communication with best friends about sex-related topics during emerging adulthood. *Journal of Youth and Adolescence, 33,* 339–351.

Lefkowitz, E. S., & Gillen, M. M. (2006). "Sex is just a normal part of life": Sexuality in emerging adulthood. In J. J. Arnett & J. L. Tanner (Eds.), *Emerging adults in America.* Washington, DC: American Psychological Association.

Legerstee, M. (1997). Contingency effects of people and objects on subsequent cognitive functioning in 3-month-old infants. *Social Development, 6,* 307–321.

Legge, G. E., Madison, C., Vaughn, B. N., Cheong, A. M., & Miller, J. C. (2008). Retention of high tactile acuity throughout the lifespan in blindness. *Perception and Psychophysics, 70,* 1471–1488.

Lehman, H. C. (1960). The age decrement in outstanding scientific creativity. *American Psychologist, 15,* 128–134.

Lehrer, R., & Schauble, L. (2006). Scientific thinking and scientific literacy. In W. Damon & R. Lerner (Eds.), *Handbook of child psychology* (6th ed.). New York: Wiley.

Leifheit-Limson, E., & Levy, B. (2009). Ageism/age discrimination. In D. Carr (Ed.), *Encyclopedia of the life course and human development.* Boston: Gale Cengage.

Lempers, J. D., Flavell, E. R., & Flavell, J. H. (1977). The development in very young children of tacit knowledge concerning visual perception. *Genetic Psychology Monographs, 95,* 3–53.

Lennon, E. M., Gardner, J. M., Karmel, B. Z., & Flory, M. J. (2008). Bayley Scales of Infant Development. In M. M. Haith & J. B. Benson (Eds.), *Encyclopedia of infant and early childhood development.* Oxford, UK: Elsevier.

Lenoir, C. P., Mallet, E, & Calenda, E. (2000). Siblings of sudden infant death syndrome and near miss in about 30 families: Is there a genetic link? *Medical Hypotheses, 54,* 408–411.

Lenz, B. K. (2004). Tobacco, depression, and lifestyle choices in the pivotal early college years. *Journal of American College Health, 52,* 213–219.

Leonardi-Bee, J. A., Smyth, A. R., Britton, J., & Coleman, T. (2008). Environmental tobacco smoke and fetal health: Systematic review and meta-analysis. *Archives of Disease in Childhood: Fetal and Neonatal Edition, 93,* F351–F361.

Leon-Guerrero, A. (2009). *Social problems* (2nd ed.). Thousand Oaks, CA: Sage.

Leppanen, J. M., Moulson, M., Vogel-Farley, V. K., & Nelson, C. A. (2007). An ERP study of emotional face processing in the adult and infant brain. *Child Development, 78,* 232–245.

Lerner, H. G. (1989). *The dance of intimacy.* New York: Harper & Row.

Lerner, R. M., Boyd, M., & Du, D. (2009, in press). Adolescent development. In I. B. Weiner

& C. B. Craighead (Eds.). *Encyclopedia of psychology* (4th ed). Hoboken, NJ: Wiley.

Lerner, R. M., Roeser, R. W., & Phelps, E. (Eds.). (2009, in press). *Positive youth development and spirituality: From theory to research.* West Conshohocken, PA: Templeton Foundation Press.

Lesaux, N. K., & Siegel, L. S. (2003). The development of reading in children who speak English as a second language. *Developmental Psychology, 39,* 1005–1019.

Lessow-Hurley, J. (2009). *The foundations of dual language instruction* (5th ed.). Boston: Allyn & Bacon.

Lester, B. M., Tronick, E. Z., & Brazelton, T. B. (2004). The Neonatal Intensive Care Unit Network Neurobehavioral Scale procedures. *Pediatrics, 113* (Suppl.), S641–S667.

Lester, B. M., Tronick, E. Z., LaGasse, L., Seifer, R., Bauer, C. R., Shankaran, S., Bada, H. S., Wright, L. L., Smeriglio, V. L., Lu, J., Finnegan, L. P., & Maza, P. L. (2002). The maternal lifestyle study: Effects of substance exposure during pregnancy on neurodevelopmental outcome in 1-month-old infants. *Pediatrics, 110,* 1182–1192.

Lethaby, A., Hogervorst, E., Richards, M., Yesufu, A., & Yaffe, K. (2009). Hormone replacement therapy for cognitive function in postmenopausal women. *Cochrane Database of Systematic Reviews, 1,* No. CD003122.

Leung, A., Ko, P., Chan, K. S., Chi, I., & Chow, N. (2007). Searching health information via the web: Hong Kong Chinese older adults' experience. *Public Health Nursing, 24,* 169–175.

Levant, R. F. (2001). Men and masculinity. In J. Worell (Ed.), *Encyclopedia of women and gender.* San Diego: Academic Press.

LeVay, S. (1991). A difference in the hypothalamic structure between heterosexual and homosexual men. *Science, 253,* 1034–1037.

Levelt, W. J. M. (1989). *Speaking: From intention to articulation.* Cambridge, MA: MIT Press.

Levene, M. I., & Chervenak, F. A. (2009). *Fetal and neonatal neurology and neurosurgery* (4th ed.). London: Elsevier.

Leventhal, T., Dupéré, V., & Brooks-Gunn, J. (2009). Neighborhood influences on adolescent development. In R. M. Lerner & L. Steinberg (Eds.), *Handbook of adolescent psychology* (3rd ed.). New York: Wiley.

Levin, J. S., Taylor, R. J., & Chatters, L. M. (1994). Race and gender differences in religiosity among older adults: Findings from four national surveys. *Journal of Gerontology, 49,* S137–S145.

Levine, L. N., & McCloskey, M. L. (2009). *Teaching learners of English in mainstream classrooms (K-8).* Boston: Allyn & Bacon.

Levine, T. P., & others. (2008). Effects of cocaine exposure on special education in school-aged children. *Pediatrics, 122,* e83–e91.

Levinson, D. J. (1978). *The seasons of a man's life.* New York: Knopf.

Levinson, D. J. (1987, August). *The seasons of a woman's life.* Paper presented at the meeting of the American Psychological Association, New York.

Levinson, D. J. (1996). *Seasons of a woman's life.* New York: Alfred Knopf.

Levy, B. R., Slade, M. D., & Gill, T. M. (2006). Hearing decline predicted by elders' stereotypes. *Journals of Gerontology B: Psychological Sciences and Social Sciences, 61,* P82–P87.

Levy, F. (2009). Dopamine vs noradrenaline: Inverted-U effects and ADHD theories. *Australian and New Zealand Journal of Psychiatry, 43,* 101–108.

Levy, G. D., Sadovsky, A. L., & Troseth, G. L. (2000). Aspects of young children's perceptions of gender-typed occupations. *Sex Roles, 42,* 993–1006.

Levykh, M. G. (2008). The affective establishment and maintenance of Vygotsky's zone of proximal development. *Educational Theory, 58,* 83–101.

Lewis, A. C. (2007). Looking beyond NCLB. *Phi Delta Kappan, 88,* 483–484.

Lewis, B. A., Kirchner, H. L., Short, E. J., Minnes, S., Weishampel, P., Satayathum, S., & Singer, L. T. (2007). Prenatal cocaine and tobacco effects on children's language trajectories. *Pediatrics, 120,* e78–e85.

Lewis, M. (1997). *Altering fate: Why the past does not predict the future.* New York: Guilford.

Lewis, M. (2005). Selfhood. In B. Hopkins (Ed.), *The Cambridge Encyclopedia of child development.* Cambridge, UK: Cambridge University Press.

Lewis, M. (2007). Early emotional development. In A. Slater & M. Lewis (Eds.), *Introduction to infant development.* Malden, MA: Blackwell.

Lewis, M. (2008). The emergence of human emotions. In M. Lewis, J. M. Haviland Jones, & L. Feldman Barrett (Eds.), *Handbook of emotions* (3rd ed.). New York: Guilford

Lewis, M., & Brooks-Gunn, J. (1979). *Social cognition and the acquisition of the self.* New York: Plenum.

Lewis, M., Feiring, C., & Rosenthal, S. (2000). Attachment over time. *Child Development, 71,* 707–720.

LeWitt, P. A. (2009). Levodopa therapeutics for Parkinson's disease: New developments. *Parkinsonism and Related Disorders, 15* (Suppl. 1), S31–S34.

Li, C., Ford, E. S., McGuire, L. C., & Mokdad, A. H. (2007). Increasing trends in weight circumference and abdominal obesity among U.S. adults. *Obesity, 15,* 216–224.

Li, D., Liao, C., Yi, C., & Pan, M. (2006). Amniocentesis for karyotyping prior to induction of abortion at second trimester. *Prenatal Diagnosis, 26,* 192.

Li, D. K., Willinger, M., Petitti, D. B., Odulil, R. K., Liu, L., & Hoffman, H. J. (2006). Use of a dummy (pacifier) during sleep and risk of sudden infant death syndrome (SIDS): Population based case-control study. *British Medical Journal, 332,* 18–22.

Li, L., Law, C., Lo Conte, R., & Power, C. (2009). Intergenerational influences on childhood body mass index: The effect of parental body mass index trajectories. *American Journal of Clinical Nutrition, 89,* 551–557.

Li, M. D., Lou, X. Y., Chen, G., Ma, J. Z., & Elston, R. C. (2008). Gene-gene interactions among CHRNA4, CHRNB2, BDNF, and NTRK2 in nicotine dependence. *Biological Psychiatry, 64,* 951–957.

Li, P. (2009). What's in a lexical system? Discovering meaning through an interactive eye. In V. C. M. Gathercole (Ed.), *Routes to language: Essays in honor of Melissa Bowerman.* New York: Psychology Press.

Li, Y. (2007). Recovering from spousal bereavement in later life: Does volunteer participation play a role? *Journals of Gerontology B: Psychological Sciences and Social Sciences, 62,* S257–S266.

Li, Y., Yang, X., Zhai, F., Piao, J., Zhao, W. Zhang, J., & Ma, G. (2008). Childhood obesity and its health consequence in China. *Obesity Reviews, 9* (Suppl. 1), S82–S86.

Liben, L. S. (1995). Psychology meets geography: Exploring the gender gap on the national geography bee. *Psychological Science Agenda, 8,* 8–9.

Liben, L. S. (2009). Giftedness during childhood: The spatial-graphic domain. In F. D. Horowitz, R. F. Subotnik, & D. J. Matthews (Eds.), *The development of giftedness and talent across the life span.* Washington, DC: American Psychological Association.

Libert, S., Cohen, D., & Guarente, L. (2008). Neurogenesis directed by Sirt1. *Nature: Cell Biology, 10,* 373–374.

Lidz, J. (2010). The abstract nature of syntactic representations: Consequences for a theory of learning. In E. Hoff & M. Shatz (Eds.), *Blackwell handbook of language development* (2nd ed.). Malden, MA: Blackwell.

Lie, E., & Newcombe, N. (1999). Elementary school children's explicit and implicit memory for faces of preschool classmates. *Developmental Psychology, 35,* 102–112.

Lieberman, E., Davidson, K., Lee-Parritz, A., & Shearer, E. (2005). Changes in fetal position during labor and their association with epidural analgesia. *Obstetrics and Gynecology, 105,* 974–982.

Liegeois, F., Connelly, A., Baldeweg, T., & Vargha-Khadem, F. (2008). Speaking with a single cerebral hemisphere: fMRI language organization after hemispherectomy in childhood. *Brain and Language, 106,* 195–203.

Lieven, E. (2008). Language development: Overview. In M. M. Haith & J. B. Benson (Eds.), *Encyclopedia of infant and early childhood development.* Oxford, UK: Elsevier.

Liew, L. P., & Norbury, C. J. (2009). Telomere maintenance: All's well that ends well. *Archives of Toxicology, 83,* 407–416.

Lifton, R. J. (1977). The sense of immortality: On death and the continuity of life. In H. Feifel (Ed.), *New meanings of death.* New York: McGraw-Hill.

Lillard, A. (2006). Pretend play in toddlers. In C. A. Brownell & C. B. Kopp (Eds.), *Socioemotional development in the toddler years.* New York: Oxford University Press.

Lima, J. J., Blake, K. V., Tantisira, K. G., & Weiss, S. T. (2009). Pharmacogenetics of asthma. *Current Opinion in Pulmonary Medicine, 15,* 57–62.

Limber, S. P. (2004), Implementation of the Olweus Bullying Prevention Program in American schools: Lessons learned from the field. In D. L. Espelage, & S. M. Swearer (Eds.), *Bullying in American schools.* Mahwah, NJ: Erlbaum.

Lin, C. A., Neafsey, P. J., & Strickler, Z. (2009). Usability testing by older adults of a computer-mediated health communication program. *Journal of Health Communication, 14,* 102–118.

Lin, J., & others. (2009). Vitamins C and E and beta-carotene supplementation and cancer risk: A randomized controlled trial. *Journal of the National Cancer Institute, 101,* 14–23.

Lindau, S. T., Schumm, L. P., Laumann, E. O., Levinson, W., O'Muircheartaigh, C. A., & Waite, L. J. (2007). A study of sexuality and health among older adults in the United States. *New England Journal of Medicine, 357,* 762–774.

Lindenberger, U., & Ghisletta, P. (2009). Cognitive and sensory declines in old age: Gauging the evidence for a common cause. *Psychology and Aging, 24,* 1–16.

Linn, S. (2008). *The case for make believe: Saving play in a commercialized world.* New York: The New Press.

Lippa, R. A. (2005). *Gender, nature, and nurture* (2nd ed.). Mahwah, NJ: Erlbaum.

Lippman, L. A., & Keith, J. D. (2006). The demographics of spirituality among youth: International perspectives. In E. Roehlkepartain, P. E. King, L. Wagener, & P. L. Benson (Eds.), *The handbook of spirituality in childhood and adolescence.* Thousand Oaks, CA: Sage.

Lipton, J., & Spelke, E. (2004). Discrimination of large and small numerosities by human infants. *Infancy, 5,* 271–290.

Littleton, H., & Henderson, C. E. (2009). If she is not a victim, does that mean she was not traumatized?: Evaluation of predictors of PTSD symptomatology in rape victims. *Violence Against Women, 15,* 148–167.

Liu, A., Hu, X., Ma, G., Cui, Z., Pan, Y., Chang, S. Zhao, W., & Chen, C. (2008). Evaluations of a classroom-based physical activity promoting program. *Obesity Reviews, 9* (Suppl. 1), S130–S134.

Liu, C. H., Murakami, J., Iap, S., & Nagayama Hall, G. C. (2009). Who are Asian Americans? An overview of history, immigration, and communities. In N. Tewari & A. Alvarez (Eds.), *Asian American psychology.* Clifton, NJ: Psychology Press.

Liu, D., Wellman, H. M., Tardif, T., & Sabbagh, M. A. (2008). Theory of mind development in Chinese children: A meta-analysis of false-belief understanding across cultures and languages. *Developmental Psychology, 44,* 523–531.

Liu, T., Shi, J., Zhang, Q., Zhao, D., & Yang, J. (2007). Neural mechanisms of auditory sensory processing in children with high intelligence. *Neuroreport, 18* (15), 1571–1575.

Liu, X., & Liu, L. (2005). Sleep habits and insomnia in a sample of elderly persons in China. *Sleep, 28,* 1579–1587.

Locher, J. L., Ritchie, C. S., Roth, D. L., Baker, P. S., Bodner, E. V., & Allman, R. M. (2005). Social isolation, support, and capital and nutritional risk in an older sample: Ethnic and gender differences. *Social Science Medicine, 60,* 747–761.

Lochman, J., & the Conduct Problems Prevention Research Group. (2007, March). *Fast Track intervention outcomes in the middle school years.* Paper presented at the meeting of the Society for Research in Child Development.

Lock, A. (2004). Preverbal communication. In U. Goswami (Ed.), *Blackwell handbook of childhood cognitive development.* Malden, MA: Blackwell.

Lock, M. (1998). Menopause: Lessons from anthropology. *Psychosomatic Medicine, 60,* 410–419.

Lockenhoff, C. E., Costa, P. T., & Lane, R. D. (2008). Age differences in descriptions of emotional experiences in oneself and others. *Journals of Gerontology B: Psychological Sciences and Social Sciences, 63,* P92–P99.

Lockl, K., & Schneider, W. (2007). Knowledge about the mind: Links between theory of mind and later metamemory. *Child Development, 78,* 147–167.

Loeber, R., Burke, J., & Pardini, D. (2009). The etiology and development of antisocial and delinquent behavior. *Annual Review of Psychology* (Vol. 60). Palo Alto, CA: Annual Reviews.

Loeber, R., & Farrington, D. P. (Eds.). (2001). *Child delinquents: Development, intervention and service needs.* Thousand Oaks CA: Sage.

Loeber, R., Pardini, D. A., Stouthamer-Loeber, M., & Raine, A. (2007). Do cognitive, physiological, and psychosocial risk and promotive factors predict desistance from delinquency in males? *Development and Psychopathology, 19,* 867–887.

Loehlin, J. C., Horn, J. M., & Ernst, J. L. (2007). Genetic and environmental influences on adult life outcomes: Evidence from the Texas Adoption Project. *Behavior Genetics, 37,* 463–476.

Lofmark, R., & others. (2008). Physicians' experiences with end-of-life decision-making:

Survey in 6 European countries and Australia. *BMC Medicine, 12,* 4.

Longo-Mbenza, B., Lukoki, L. E., & M'buyambia-Kabangu, J. R. (2007). Nutritional status, socio-economic status, heart rate, and blood pressure in African school children and adolescents. *International Journal of Cardiology, 121,* 171–177.

Lonner, W. J. (1988, October). *The introductory psychology text and cross-cultural psychology: A survey of cross-cultural psychologists.* Bellingham: Western Washington University, Center for Cross-cultural Research.

Lorenz, K. Z. (1965). *Evolution and the modification of behavior.* Chicago: University of Chicago Press.

Loucks, E. B., & others. (2006). Association of educational level with inflammatory markers in the Framington Offspring Study. *American Journal of Epidemiology, 163,* 622–628.

Loukas, A., Suizzo, M.-A., & Prelow, H. M. (2007). Examining resource and protective factors in the adjustment of Latino youth in low income families: What role does maternal acculturation play? *Journal of Youth and Adolescence, 36,* 489–501.

Lovden, M., & Lindenberger, U. (2007). Intelligence. In J. E. Birren (Ed.), *Encyclopedia of gerontology* (2nd ed.). San Diego: Academic Press.

Lu, M. C., & Lu, J. S. (2008). Prenatal care. In M. M. Haith & J. B. Benson (Eds.), *Encyclopedia of infant and early childhood development.* Oxford, UK: Elsevier.

Lubart, T. I. (2003). In search of creative intelligence. In R. J. Sternberg, J. Lautrey, & T. I. Lubert (Eds.), *Models of intelligence: International perspectives.* Washington, DC: American Psychological Association.

Luber, B., Habeck, C., Trott, C. T., Friedman, D., & Moeller, J. R. (2004). A ghost of retrieval past: A functional network of alpha EEG related to source memory in elderly humans. *Brain Research: Cognitive Brain Research, 20,* 144–155.

Lubinski, D. (2000). Measures of intelligence: Intelligence tests. In A. Kazdin (Ed.), *Encyclopedia of psychology.* Washington, DC, & New York: American Psychological Association and Oxford University Press.

Lubinski, D. (2009). Exceptional cognitive ability: The phenotype. *Behavior Genetics, 39,* 350–358.

Luders, E., Narr, K. L., Thompson, P. M., Rex, D. E., Uancke, L., Steinmetz, H., & Toga, A. W. (2004). Gender differences in cortical complexity. *Nature Neuroscience, 7,* 799–800.

Luders, E., Narr, K. L., Thompson, P. M., & Toga, A. W. (2009). Neuroanatomical correlates of intelligence. *Intelligence, 37,* 156–163.

Ludington-Hoe, S. M., Lewis, T., Morgan, K., Cong, X., Anderson, L., & Reese, S. (2006). Breast and infant temperatures with twins during kangaroo care. *Journal of Obstetric, Gynecologic, and Neonatal Nursing, 35,* 223–231.

Lund, D. A. (2007). Bereavement and loss. In J. E. Birren (Ed.), *Encyclopedia of gerontology* (2nd ed.). San Diego: Academic Press.

Lund, D. A., Utz, R., Caserta, M. S., & De Vries, B. (2008–2009). Humor, laughter, and happiness in the lives of recently bereaved spouses. *Omega, 58,* 87–105.

Lunkenheimer, E. S., Shields, A. M., & Cortina, K. S. (2007). Parental emotion coaching and dismissing in family interaction. *Social Development, 16,* 232–248.

Luo, L., & Craik, F. I. M. (2008). Aging and memory: A cognitive approach. *Canadian Journal of Psychology, 53,* 346–353.

Luo, Y., Kaufman. L., & Baillargeon, R. (2009). Young infants' reasoning about events involving inert and self-propelled objects. *Cognitive Psychology, 58,* 441–486.

Luria, A., & Herzog, E. (1985, April). *Gender segregation across and within settings.* Paper presented at the biennial meeting of the Society for Research in Child Development, Toronto.

Lust, B. C. (2007). *Child language.* New York: Cambridge University Press.

Lustig, C., & Hasher, L. (2009, in press). Interference. In R. Schulz, L. Noelker, K. Rockwood, & R. Sprott (Eds). *Encyclopedia of aging* (4th ed). New York: Springer.

Luthar, S. S. (2006). Resilience in development: A synthesis of research across five decades. In D. Cicchetti & D. J. Cohen (Eds.), *Developmental psychopathology: Vol. 3. Risk, disorder, and adaptation* (2nd ed.). Hoboken, NJ: Wiley.

Luthar, S. S., & Goldstein, A. S. (2008). Substance use and related behaviors among suburban late adolescents: The importance of perceived parent containment. *Development, and Psychopathology, 20,* 591–614.

Lyndaker, C., & Hulton, L. (2004). The influence of age on symptoms of perimenopause. *Journal of Obstetric, Gynecological, and Neonatal Nursing, 33,* 340–347.

Lynn, R. (1996). Racial and ethnic differences in intelligence in the U.S. on the Differential Ability Scale. *Personality and Individual Differences, 26,* 271–273.

Lynn, R., Allik, J., Pullman, H., & Laidra, K. (2004). Sex differences on the progressive matrices among adolescents: Some data from Estonia. *Personality and Individual Differences, 36,* 1249–1255.

Lyon, T. D., & Flavell, J. H. (1993). Young children's understanding of forgetting over time. *Child Development, 64,* 789–800.

M

Maccoby, E. E. (1998). The two sexes: Growing up apart, coming together. Cambridge, MA: Harvard University Press.

Maccoby, E. E. (2002). Gender and group presence. *Current Directions in Psychological Science, 11,* 54–58.

Maccoby, E. E. (2007). Historical overview of socialization theory and research. In J. E. Grusec & P. D. Hastings (Eds.), *Handbook of socialization.* New York: Guilford.

Maccoby, E. E., & Martin, J. A. (1983). Socialization in the context of the family: Parent-child interaction. In P. H. Mussen (Ed.), *Handbook of child psychology* (4th ed., Vol. 4). New York: Wiley.

MacDorman, M. F., Declercq, E., Menacker, F., & Malloy, M. H. (2008). Neonatal mortality for primary cesarean and vaginal births to low-risk women: Application of an "intention-to-treat" model. *Birth, 35,* 3–8.

MacFarlane, J. A. (1975). Olfaction in the development of social preferences in the human neonate. In *Parent-infant interaction.* Ciba Foundation Symposium No. 33. Amsterdam: Elsevier.

Machaalani, R., & Waters, K. A. (2008). Neuronal cell death in the sudden infant death-syndrome brainstem and associations with risk factors. *Brain, 131,* 218–228.

Maciejewski, P. K., Zhang, B., Block, S. D., & Prigerson, H. G. (2007). An empirical examination of the stage theory of grief. *Journal of the American Medical Association, 297,* 716–723.

Maciokas, J. B., & Crognale, M. A. (2003). Cognitive and attentional changes with age: Evidence from attentional blink deficits. *Experimental Aging Research, 29,* 137–153.

Macklem, G. L. (2003). *Bullying and teasing: Social power in children's groups.* New York: Kluwer Academic/Plenum.

Madden, D. J. (2007). Aging and visual attention. *Current Directions in Psychological Science, 16,* 70–74.

Madden, D. J., Gottlob, L. R., Denny, L. L., Turkington, T. G., Provenzale, J. M., Hawk, T. C., & others. (1999). Aging and recognition memory: Changes in regional cerebral blood flow associated with components of reaction time distributions. *Journal of Cognitive Neuroscience, 11,* 511–520.

Mader, S. S. (2010). *Biology* (10th ed.). New York: McGraw-Hill.

Magnuson, K., Duncan, G. J., & Kalil, A. (2006). The contribution of middle childhood contexts to adolescent achievement and behavior. In A. C. Huston & M. N. Ripke (Eds.), *Developmental contexts in middle childhood.* New York: Cambridge University Press.

Magnusson, S. J., & Palinscar, A. S. (2005). Teaching to promote the development of scientific knowledge and reasoning about light at the elementary school level. In *How people learn.* Washington, DC: National Academies Press.

Maguire, S., Mann, M. K., Sibert, J., & Kemp, A. (2005). Are there patterns of bruising in childhood which are diagnostic or suggestive of abuse? A systematic review. *Archives of Diseases in Childhood, 90,* 182–186.

Mahoney, J. L., Larson, R. W., & Eccles, J. S. (Eds.). (2004). *Organized activities as contexts of development.* Mahwah, NJ: Erlbaum.

Maitland, T. E., Gomez-Marin, O., Weddle, D. O., & Fleming, L. B. (2006). Associations of nationality and race with nutritional status during perimenopause: Implications for public health practice. *Ethnicity and Disease, 16,* 201–216.

Malamitsi-Puchner, A., & Boutsikou, T. (2006). Adolescent pregnancy and perinatal outcome. *Pediatric Endocrinology Review, 3* (Suppl. 1), 170–171.

Malizia, B. A., Hacker, M. R., & Penzias, A. S. (2009). Cumulative live-birth rates after in vitro fertilization. *New England Journal of Medicine, 360,* 236–243.

Mamtani, M., Patel, A., & Kulkarni, H. (2008). Association of the pattern of transition between arousal states in neonates with the cord blood lead level. *Early Human Development, 84,* 231–235.

Mandler, J. (2000). Unpublished review of J. W. Santrock's *Life-span development,* 8th ed. (New York: McGraw-Hill).

Mandler, J. M. (2004). *The foundations of mind.* New York: Oxford University Press.

Mandler, J. M. (2006). *Jean Mandler.* Retrieved January 15, 2006, from http://cogsci.ucsd.edu/-jean/

Mandler, J. M. (2009). Conceptual categorization. In D. H. Rakison & L. M. Oakes (Eds.), *Early category and concept development.* New York: Oxford University Press.

Mandler, J. M., & McDonough, L. (1993). Concept formation in infancy. *Cognitive Development, 8,* 291–318.

Manheimer, R. J. (2007). Education and aging. In J. E. Birren (Ed.), *Encyclopedia of gerontology* (2nd ed.). San Diego: Academic Press.

Manis, F. R., Keating, D. P., & Morrison, F. J. (1980). Developmental differences in the allocation of processing capacity. *Journal of Experimental Child Psychology, 29,* 156–169.

Manlove, J., & Terry-Humen, E. (2007). Contraceptive use patterns within females' first sexual relationships: The role of relationships, partners and methods. *Journal of Sexual Research, 44,* 3–16.

Mannell, R. C. (2000). Older adults, leisure, and wellness. *Journal of Leisurability, 26,* 3–10.

Manning, M. L., & Baruth, L. G. (2009). *Multicultural education of children and adolescents* (5th ed.). Boston: Allyn & Bacon.

Mannuzza, S., Klein, R. G., Abikoff, H., & Moulton, J. L. (2004). Significance of childhood conduct problems for later development of conduct disorder among children with ADHD: A prospective follow-up study. *Journal of Abnormal Child Psychology, 32,* 565–573.

Manthous, C. A. (2009). Why not physician-assisted death? *Critical Care Medicine, 37,* 1206–1209.

Manton, K. I. (1989). The stress-buffering role of spiritual support: Cross-sectional and prospective investigations. *Journal for the Scientific Study of Religion, 28,* 310–223.

Marcia, J. E. (1987). The identity status approach to the study of ego identity development. In T. Honess & K. Yardley (Eds.), *Self and identity: Perspectives across the lifespan.* London: Routledge & Kegan Paul.

Marcia, J. E. (1990). Ego identity development. In J. Adelson (Ed.), *Handbook of adolescent psychology.* New York: Wiley.

Marcia, J. E. (1994). The empirical study of ego identity. In H. A. Bosma, T. L. G. Graafsma, H. D. Grotevant, & D. J. De Levita (Eds.), *Identity and development.* Newbury Park, CA: Sage.

Marcia, J. E. (1996). Unpublished review of J. W. Santrock's *Adolescence,* 7th ed. (Dubuque, IA: Brown & Benchmark).

Marcia, J. E., & Carpendale, J. (2004). Identity: Does thinking make it so? In C. Lightfoot, C. Lalonde, & M. Chandler (Eds.), *Changing conceptions of psychological life.* Mahwah, NJ: Erlbaum.

Marcovitch, H. (2004). Use of stimulants for attention deficit hyperactivity disorder: AGAINST. *British Medical Journal, 329,* 908–909.

Marcus, D. L., Mulrine, A., & Wong, K. (1999, September 13). How kids learn. *U.S. News & World Report,* pp. 44–50.

Marecek, J., Finn, S. E., & Cardell, M. (1988). Gender roles in the relationships of lesbians and gay men. In J. P. De Cecco (Ed.), *Gay relationships.* New York: Harrington Park Press.

Margran, T. H., & Boulton, M. (2005). Sensory impairment. In M. L. Johnson (Ed.), *The Cambridge handbook of age and aging.* New York: Cambridge University Press.

Margrett, J. A., & Deshpande-Kamat, N. (2009). Cognitive functioning and decline. In D. Carr (Ed.), *Encyclopedia of the life course and human development.* Boston: Gale Cengage.

Marinucci, L., Balloni, S., Bodo, M., Carinci, F., Pezzetti, F., Stabellini, G., Carmela, C., & Lumare, E. (2009). Patterns of some extracellular matrix gene expression are similar in cells from cleft lip-palate patients and in human palatal fibroblasts to diazepam in culture. *Toxicology, 257,* 10–16.

Marion, M. C. (2010). *Introduction to early childhood education.* Upper Saddle River, NJ: Prentice Hall.

Markides, K. S., & Rudkin, L. (1996). Race and ethnic diversity. In J. E. Birren (Ed.), *Encyclopedia of gerontology* (Vol. 2). San Diego: Academic Press.

Marko, M. G., Ahmed, T., Bunnell, S. C., Wu, D., Chung, H, Huber, B. T., & Meydani, S. N. (2007). Age-associated decline in effective immune synapse formation of CD4(+) T cells is reversed by vitamin E supplementation. *Journal of Immunology, 178,* 1443–1449.

Markovic, K., Reulbach, U., Vassiliadu, A., Lunkenheimer, J., Lunkenheimer, B. Spannenberger, R., & Thuerauf, N. (2007). Good news for elderly persons: Olfactory pleasure increases at later stages of the life span. *Journals of Gerontology A: Biological Sciences and Medical Sciences, 62,* 1287–1293.

Markus, H. R., Mullally, P. R., & Kitayama, S. (1999). *Selfways: Diversity in modes of cultural participation.* Unpublished manuscript, Department of Psychology, University of Michigan.

Markus, H. R., & Nurius, P. (1986). Possible selves. *American Psychologist, 41,* 954–969.

Marshall, P. J., & Kenney, J. W. (2009). Biological perspectives on the effects of early psychosocial experience. *Developmental Review, 29,* 96–119.

Martin, C. L. (1990). Attitudes and expectations about children with nontraditional traditional gender roles. *Sex Roles, 22,* 151–165.

Martin, C. L., & Fabes, R. A. (2001). The stability and consequences of young children's same-sex peer interactions. *Developmental Psychology, 37,* 431–446.

Martin, C. L., & Ruble, D. N. (2010). Patterns of gender development. *Annual Review of Psychology* (Vol. 61). Palo Alto, CA: Annual Reviews.

Martin, C. L., Ruble, D. N., & Szkrybalo, J. (2002). Cognitive theories of early gender development. *Psychological Bulletin, 128,* 903–933.

Martin, J. A., Hamilton, B. E., Sutton, P. D., Ventura, S. J., Menacker, F., & Munson, M. L. (2005, September). Births: Final data for 2003. *National Vital Statistics Reports, 54* (No. 2), 1–116.

Martin, L. R., Friedman, H. S., & Schwartz, J. E. (2007). Personality and mortality risk across the lifespan: The importance of conscientiousness as a biopsychosocial attribute. *Health Psychology, 26,* 428–436.

Martinez, M. E. (2010). *Learning and cognition.* Upper Saddle River, NJ: Merrill.

Maruthy, S., & Mannarukrishnaiah, J. (2008). Effect of early onset otitis media on brainstem and cortical auditory processing. *Behavioral and Brain Functions, 4,* 17.

Maruyama, N. C., & Atencio, C. V. (2008). Evaluating a bereavement support group. *Palliative Support and Care, 6,* 43–49.

Mascolo, M. F., & Fischer, K. (2007). The co-development of self and socio-moral emotions during the toddler years. In C. A. Brownell & C. B. Kopp (Eds.), *Transitions in early development.* New York: Guilford.

Mashburn, A. J., Justice, L. M., Downer, J. T., & Pianta, R. C. (2009). Peer effects on children's language achievement during pre-kindergarten. *Child Development, 80,* 686–702.

Masley, S. C., Weaver, W., Peri, G., & Phillips, S. E. (2008). Efficacy of lifestyle changes in modifying practical markers of wellness and aging. *Alternative Therapies in Health and Medicine, 14,* 24–29.

Massey, Z., Rising, S. S., & Ickovics, J. (2006). CenteringPregnancy group prenatal care: Promoting relationship-centered care. *Journal of Obstetric, Gynecologic, and Neonatal Nursing, 35*, 286–294.

Mast, B. T., & Healy, P. J. (2009). Dementias. In D. Carr (Ed.), *Encyclopedia of the life course and human development.* Boston: Gale Cengage.

Masten, A. S. (2001). Ordinary magic: Resilience processes in development. *American Psychologist, 56*, 227–238.

Masten, A. S. (2004). Regulatory processes, risk and resilience in adolescent development. *Annals of the New York Academy of Sciences, 1021*, 310–319.

Masten, A. S. (2005). Peer relationships and psychopathology in developmental perspective: Reflections on progress and promise. *Journal of Clinical Child and Adolescent Psychology, 34*, 87–92.

Masten, A. S. (2007). Resilience in developing systems: Progress and promise as the fourth wave rises. *Development and Psychopathology, 19*, 921–930.

Masten, A. S. (2009a). Ordinary magic: Lessons from research on resilience in human development. *Education Canada, 49*, 28–32.

Masten, A. S. (2009b). Resilience in children and youth: A practical guide. *Schools for all encyclopedia.* Vancouver: Health Canada and the Health and Learning Knowledge Centre of the Canadian Council.

Masters, C. (2008, January 17). We just clicked. *Time*, pp. 84–89.

Matlin, M. W. (2008). *The psychology of women* (6th ed.). Belmont, CA: Wadsworth.

Matsuba, M. K., & Walker, L. J. (2004). Extraordinary moral commitment: Young adults involved in social organizations. *Journal of Personality, 72*, 413–436.

Matsuda, H. (2007). Role of neurogimaging in Alzheimer's disease, with emphasis on brain profusion SPECT. *Journal of Nuclear Medicine, 27*, 570–577.

Matsumoto, D. C., & Juang, L. (2008). *Culture and psychology* (4th ed.). Belmont, CA: Wadsworth.

Matthews, C. E., Jurj, A. L., Shu, X. O., Yang, G., Li, Q., Gao, Y. T., & Zheng, W. (2007). Influence of exercise, walking, cycling, and overall nonexercise physical activity on mortality in Chinese women. *American Journal of Epidemiology, 165*, 1343–1350.

Matthews, D. J. (2009). Developmental transitions in giftedness and talent: Childhood into adolescence. In F. D. Horowitz, R. F. Subotnik, & D. J. Matthews (Eds.), *The development of giftedness and talent across the life span.* Washington, DC: American Psychological Association.

Matthews, D. J., Subotnik, R. F., & Horowitz, F. D. (2009). A developmental perspective on giftedness and talent: Implications for research, policy, and practice. In F. D.

Horowitz, R. F. Subotnik, & D. J. Matthews (Eds.), *The development of giftedness and talent across the life span.* Washington, DC: American Psychological Association.

Matthews, G., Zeidner, M., & Roberts, R. D. (2006). Models of personality and affect for education: A review and synthesis. In P. A. Alexander & P. M. Wynne (Eds.), *Handbook of educational psychology* (2nd ed.). Mahwah, NJ: Erlbaum.

Matthews, J. D., & Cramer, E. P. (2006). Envisioning the adoption process to strengthen gay- and lesbian-headed families: Recommendations for adoption professionals. *Child Welfare, 85*, 317–340.

Maurer, D., & Salapatek, R. (1976). Developmental changes in the scanning of faces by young infants. *Child Development, 47*, 523–527.

Mausbach, B. T., & others. (2007). Stress-related reduction in personal mastery is associated with reduced immune cell beta2-adrenergic receptor sensitivity. *International Psychogeriatics, 4*, 1–13.

Maxim, G. W. (2010). *Dynamic social studies for constructive classrooms* (9th ed.). Boston: Allyn & Bacon.

May, S. (2010). Critical multiculturalism and education. In J. A. Banks (Ed.), *The Routledge international companion to multicultural education.* Oxford, UK: Routledge.

Mayer, K. D., & Zhang, L. (2009). Short- and long-term effects of cocaine abuse during pregnancy on heart development. *Therapeutic Advances in Cardiovascular Disease, 3*, 7–16.

Mayer, R. E. (2008). *Curriculum and instruction* (2nd ed.). Upper Saddle River, NJ: Prentice Hall.

Mayhew, M. J., & King, P. (2008). How curricular content and pedagogical strategies affect moral reasoning development in college students. *Journal of Moral Education, 37*, 17–40.

Maynard, A. E. (2008). What we thought we knew and how we came to know it: Four decades of cross-cultural research from a Piagetian point of view. *Human Development, 51*, 56–65.

Mayseless, O., & Scharf, M. (2007). Adolescents' attachment representations and their capacity for intimacy in close relationships. *Journal of Research on Adolescence, 17*, 23–50.

Mbonye, A. K., Neema, S., & Magnussen, P. (2006). Treatment-seeking practices for malaria in pregnancy among rural women in Mukono district, Uganda. *Journal of Biosocial Science, 38*, 221–237.

Mbugua Gitau, G., Liversedge, H., Goffey, D., Hawton, A., Liversedge, N., & Taylor, M. (2009). The influence of maternal age on the outcomes of pregnancy complicated by bleeding at less than 12 weeks. *Acta Obstetricia et Gynecologica Scandinavica, 88*, 116–118.

McAdams, D. P., Josselson, R., & Lieblich, A. (Eds.). (2006.). *Identity and story: Creating self in narrative.* Washington, DC: American Psychological Association Press.

McAdams, D. P., & Olson, B. D. (2010). Personality development: Continuity and change over the life course. *Annual Review of Psychology* (Vol. 61). Palo Alto, CA: Annual Reviews.

McAlister, A., & Peterson, C. (2007). A longitudinal study of child siblings and theory of mind development. *Cognitive Development, 22*, 258–270.

McAnarney, E. R. (2008). Adolescent brain development: Forging new links? *Journal of Adolescent Health, 42*, 321–323.

McBurney, D. H., & White, T. L. (2010). Research methods (8th ed.). Boston: Cengage.

McCall, R. B., Applebaum, M. I., & Hogarty, P. S. (1973). Developmental changes in mental performance. *Monographs of the Society for Research in Child Development, 38* (Serial No. 150).

McCarter, R. J. M. (2006). Differential aging among skeletal muscles. In E. J. Masoro & S. N. Austad (Eds.). *Handbook of the psychology of aging* (6th ed.). San Diego: Academic Press.

McCarthy, J. (2007). Children with autism spectrum disorders and intellectual disability. *Current Opinion in Psychiatry, 20*, 472–476.

McCartney, K. (2003, July 16). Interview with Kathleen McCartney in A. Bucuvalas, "Child care and behavior." *HGSE News*, pp. 1–4. Cambridge, MA: Harvard Graduate School of Education.

McCartney, K., Dearing, E., Taylor, B. A., & Bub, K. L. (2007). Quality child care supports the achievement of low-income children: Direct and indirect pathways through caregiving and the home environment. *Journal of Applied Developmental Psychology, 28*, 411–426.

McClain, C. S., Rosenfeld, B., & Breitbart, W. S. (2003, March). *The influence of spirituality on end-of-life despair in cancer patients close to death.* Paper presented at the meeting of American Psychosomatic Society, Phoenix.

McCoy, M. L., & Keen, S. M. (2009). *Child abuse and neglect.* New York: Psychology Press.

McCrae, C., & Dubyak, P. (2009). Sleep patterns and behavior. In D. Carr (Ed.), *Encyclopedia of the life course and human development.* Boston: Gale Cengage.

McCrae, R. R., & Costa, P. T. (1990). *Personality in adulthood.* New York: Guilford.

McCrae, R. R., & Costa, P. T. (2006). Cross-cultural perspectives on adult personality trait development. In D. K. Mroczek & T. D. Little (Eds.), *Handbook of personality development.* Mahwah, NJ: Erlbaum.

McCullough, A. R., Steidle, C. P., Klee, B., & Tseng, L. J. (2008). Randomized, double-blind, cross-over trial of sildenafil in men with moderate erectile dysfunction: Efficacy at 8 and 12 hours postdose. *Urology, 71*, 686–692.

McCullough, M. E., & Laurenceau, J. P. (2005). Religiousness and the trajectory of self-rated health across adulthood. *Personality and Social Psychology Bulletin, 31*, 560–573.

McCullough, M. E., & Willoughby, B. L. (2009). Religion, self-regulation, and self-control: Associations, explanations, and implications. *Psychological Bulletin, 135,* 69–93.

McDonald, J. A., Manlove, J., & Ikamullah, E. N. (2009). Immigration measures and reproductive health among Hispanic youth: Findings from the National Longitudinal Survey of Youth, 1997–2003. *Journal of Adolescent Health, 44,* 14–24.

McDowell, D. J., & Parke, R. D. (2009). Parental correlates of children's peer relations: An empirical test of a tripartite model. *Developmental Psychology, 45,* 224–235.

McElhaney, K. B., Allen, J. P., Stephenson, J. C., & Hare, A. L. (2009). Attachment and autonomy during adolescence. In R. M. Lerner & L. Steinberg (Eds.), *Handbook of adolescent psychology* (3rd ed.), New York: Wiley.

McElhaney, K. B., Antonishak, J., & Allen, J. P. (2008). "They like me, they like me not": Popularity and adolescents' perceptions of acceptance predicting social functioning over time. *Child Development, 79,* 720–731.

McEniery, C. M., & others. (2008). Central pressure: Variability and impact of cardiovascular risk factors: The Anglo-Cardiff Collaborative Trial II. *Hypertension, 51,* 1476–1482.

McFadden, S. H. (2007). Religion and spirituality. In J. E. Birren (Ed.), *Encyclopedia of gerontology* (2nd ed.). San Diego: Academic Press.

McFarlin, B. L. (2009). Solving the puzzle of prematurity. *American Journal of Nursing, 109,* 60–63.

McGarvey, C., McDonnell, M., Hamilton, K., O'Regan, M., & Matthews, T. (2006). An 8 year study of risk factors for SIDS: Bed-sharing versus non-bed-sharing. *Archives of Disease in Childhood, 91,* 318–323.

McGue, M., Bouchard, T. J., Iacono, W. G., & Lykken, D. T. (1993). Behavioral genetics of cognitive ability: A life-span perspective. In R. Plomin & G. E. McClearn (Eds.), *Nature, nurture, and psychology*. Washington, DC: American Psychological Association.

McGue, M., Hirsch, B., & Lykken, D. T. (1993). Age and the self-perception of ability: A twin analysis. *Psychology and Aging, 8,* 72–80.

McGuigan, M. R., Tatasciore, M., Newton, R. U., & Pettigrew, S. (2009). Eight weeks of resistance training can significantly alter body composition in children who are overweight or obese. *Journal of Strength and Conditioning Research, 23,* 80–85.

McHale, J. P. (2009, in press). Shared child-rearing in nuclear, fragile, and kinship systems: Evolution, dilemmas, and promise of a coparenting framework. In M. S. Schultz, M. K. Pruett, P. K. Kerig, & R. D. Parke (Eds.), *Feathering the nest: Couple relationships, couples interventions, and children's development.* Washington, DC: American Psychological Association.

McHale, J., & Sullivan, M. (2007). Family systems. In M. Hersen & A. Gross (Eds.), *Handbook of clinical psychology* (Vol. II). New York: Wiley.

McHale, S. M., Kim, J.-Y., Dotterer, A. M., Crouter, A. C, & Booth, A. (2009). The development of gendered interests and personality qualities from middle childhood through adolescence: A biosocial analysis. *Child Development, 80,* 482–495.

McKain, W. C. (1972). A new look at older marriages. *The Family Coordinator, 21,* 61–69.

McLaughlin, K. (2003, December 30). Commentary in K. Painter, "Nurse dispenses dignity for dying." *USA Today,* Section D, pp. 1–2.

McLean, K. C., & Breen, A. V. (2009). Processes and content of narrative identity development in adolescence: Gender and well-being. *Developmental Psychology, 45,* 702–710.

McLoyd, V. C. (1990). The impact of economic hardship on Black families and children: Psychological distress, parenting, and socioemotional development. *Child Development, 61,* 311–346.

McLoyd, V. C. (1998). Children in poverty: Development, public policy, and practice. In W. Damon (Ed.), *Handbook of child psychology* (5th ed., Vol. 4). New York: Wiley.

McLoyd, V. C., Kaplan, R., Purtell, K. M., Bagley, E., Hardaway, C. R., & Smalls, C. (2009). Poverty and socioeconomic disadvantage in adolescence. In R. M. Lerner & L. Steinberg (Eds.), *Handbook of adolescent psychology* (3rd ed.). New York: Wiley.

McLoyd, V. C., Purtell, I. M., Bagley, E., Hardaway, C. R., Smalls, C. (2009). Poverty and socioeconomic disadvantage in adolescence. In R. M. Lerner & L. Steinberg (Eds.), *Handbook of adolescent psychology* (3rd ed.). New York: Wiley.

McMillan, J. H. (2007). *Classroom assessment* (4th ed.). Boston: Allyn & Bacon.

McMillan, J. H. (2008). *Educational research* (5th ed.). Boston: Allyn & Bacon.

McMillan, J. H., & Schmacher, S. (2010). *Research in education: Evidence-based inquiry.* (7th ed.). Upper Saddle River, NJ: Merrill.

McMillen, I. C., MacLaughlin, S. M., Muhlhausler, B. S., Gentili, S., Duffield, J. L., & Morrison, J. L. (2008). Developmental origins of adult health and disease: The role of periconceptional and foetal nutrition. *Basic and Clinical Pharmacology and Toxicology, 102,* 82–89.

McMullen, S. L., Lipke, B., & LeMura, C. (2009). Sudden infant death syndrome prevention: A model program for NICUs. *Neonatal Network, 28,* 7–12.

McNally, J. W. (2009). Quality of life. In D. Carr (Ed.), *Encyclopedia of the life course and human development.* Boston: Gale Cengage.

McNamara, F., & Sullivan, C. E. (2000). Obstructive sleep apnea in infants. *Journal of Pediatrics, 136,* 318–323.

McNeil, J. D. (2009). *Contemporary curriculum* (7th ed.). New York: Wiley.

McNeill, G., & others. (2007). Effect of multivitamin and multiple supplementation on cognitive function in men and women aged 65 years and over: A randomized controlled trial. *Nutrition Journal, 6,* 10.

Mead, M. (1978, Dec. 30–Jan. 5). The American family: An endangered species. *TV Guide,* pp. 21–24.

Meade, C. S., Kershaw, T. S., & Ickovics, J. R. (2008). The intergenerational cycle of teenage motherhood: An ecological approach. *Health Psychology, 27,* 419–429.

Meece, J., & Eccles, J. (Eds.). (2009). *Handbook of research on schools, schooling, and human development.* Clifton, NJ: Psychology Press.

Meeks, T. W., & Jeste, D. V. (2009). Neurobiology of wisdom: A literature review. *Archives of General Psychiatry, 66,* 355–365.

Meier, A., & Allen, G. (2008, Spring). Intimate relationship development during the transition to adulthood. *New Directions for Child and Adolescent Development, 119,* 25–39.

Meis, P. J., & Peaceman, A. M. (2003). Prevention of recurrent preterm delivery by 17-alpha-hydroxyprogesterone caproate. *New England Journal of Medicine, 348,* 2379–2385.

Mello, Z. R. (2009). Racial/ethnic group and socioeconomic status variation in educational and occupational expectations from adolescence to adulthood. *Journal of Applied Developmental Psychology, 30,* 494–504.

Meltzoff, A. N. (2008). Unpublished review of J. W. Santrock's *Life-span development,* 12th ed. (New York: McGraw-Hill).

Meltzoff, A. N., & Brooks, R. (2009). Social cognition: The role of gaze following in early word learning. In J. Colombo, P. McCardle, & L. Freund (Eds.), *Infant pathways in language.* Clifton, NJ: Psychology Press.

Meltzoff, A. N., & Moore, M. K. (1998). Object representation, identity, and the paradox of early permanence: Steps toward a new framework. *Infant Behavior and Development, 21,* 201–235.

Melzi, G., & Ely, R. (2009). Language development in the school years. In J. B. Gleason & N. Ratner (Eds.), *The development of language* (7th ed.). Boston: Allyn & Bacon.

Mendle, J., Turkheimer, E., & Emery, R. E. (2007). Detrimental psychological outcomes associated with early pubertal timing in adolescent girls. *Developmental Review, 27,* 151–171.

Menec, V. H. (2003). The relation between everyday activities and successful aging: A 6-year longitudinal study. *Journals of Gerontology B: Psychological Sciences and Social Sciences, 58,* 574–582.

Menias, C. O., Elsayes, K. M., Peterson, C. M., Huete, A., Gratz, B. I., & Bhalla, S. (2007). CT of pregnancy-related complications. *Emergency Radiology, 13,* 299–306.

Menn, L., & Stoel-Gammon, C. (2009). Phonological development: Learning sounds and sound patterns. In J. Berko Gleason (Ed.), *The development of language* (7th ed.). Boston: Allyn & Bacon.

Mennuti, M. T. (2008). Genetic screening in reproductive health care. *Clinical Obstetrics and Gynecology, 51*, 3–23.

Mensah, G. A., & Brown, D. W. (2007). An overview of cardiovascular disease burden in the United States. *Health Affairs, 26*, 38–48.

Menshikova, E. V., Ritov, B. V., Fairfull, L., Ferrell, R. E., Kelley, D. E., & Goodpaster, B. H. (2006). Effects of exercise on mitochondrial content and function in aging human skeletal muscle. *Journals of Gerontology A: Biological Sciences and Medical Sciences, 61*, 534–540.

Menyuk, P., Liebergott, J., & Schultz, M. (1995). *Early language development in full-term and premature infants.* Hillsdale, NJ: Erlbaum.

Mercer, N. (2008). Talk and the development of reasoning and understanding. *Human Development, 51*, 90–100.

Meredith, N. V. (1978). Research between 1960 and 1970 on the standing height of young children in different parts of the world. In H. W. Reece & I. P. Lipsitt (Eds.), *Advances in child development and behavior* (Vol. 12). New York: Academic Press.

Merrill, D. M. (2009). Parent-child relationships: Later-life. In D. Carr (Ed.), *Encyclopedia of the life course and human development.* Boston: Gale Cengage.

Mesman, J., van IJzendoorn, M. H., & Bakersman-Kranenburg, M. J. (2009). The many faces of the still-face paradigm: A review and meta-analysis. *Dvelopmental Review, 29*, 120–162.

Messinger, D. (2008). Smiling. In M. M. Haith & J. B. Benson (Eds.), *Encyclopedia of infant and early childhood development.* Oxford, UK: Elsevier.

Messinger, J. C. (1971). Sex and repression in an Irish folk community. In D. S. Marshall & R. C. Suggs (Eds.), *Human sexual behavior: Variations in the ethnic spectrum.* New York: Basic Books.

Messman-Moore, T. L., Coates, A. A., Gaffey, K. J., & Johnson, C. F. (2008). Sexuality, substance use, and susceptibility to victimization: Risk for rape and sexual coercion in a prospective sample of college women. *Journal of Interpersonal Violence, 23*, 1730–1746.

Mestre, J. M., Guil, R., Lopes, P. N., Salovey, P., & Gil-Olarte, P. (2007). Emotional intelligence and social and academic adaptation to school. *Psicothema, 18*, S112–S117.

Metts, S., & Cupach, W. R. (2007). Responses to relational transgressions. In M. Tafoya & B. H. Spitzberg (Eds.), *The dark side of interpersonal communication.* Mahwah, NJ: Erlbaum.

Metz, E. C., & Youniss, J. (2005). Longitudinal gains in civic development through school-based required service. *Political Psychology, 26*, 413–437.

Michael R. T., Gagnon, J. H., Laumann, E. O., & Kolata, G. (1994). *Sex in America.* Boston: Little, Brown.

Middleton, L. E., Kirkland, S. A., Maxwell, C. J., Hogan, D. B., & Rockwood, K. (2007). Exercise: A potential contributing factor to the relationship between folate and dementia. *Journal of the American Geriatric Society, 55*, 1095–1098.

Mikulincer, M., & Shaver, P. R. (2008). Adult attachment and affect regulation. In J. Cassidy & P. R. Shaver (Eds.), *Handbook of attachment* (2nd ed.). New York: Guilford.

Miller, B. C., Benson, B., & Galbraith, K. A. (2001). Family relationships and adolescent pregnancy risk: A research synthesis. *Developmental Review, 21*, 1–38.

Miller, B. C., Fan, X., Christensen, M., Grotevant, H. D., & von Dulmen, M. (2000). Comparisons of adopted and nonadopted adolescents in a large, nationally representative sample. *Child Development, 71*, 1458–1473.

Miller, C. F., Lurye, L. E., Zusuls, K. M., & Ruble, D. N. (2009). Accessibility of gender stereotype domains: Developmental and gender differences in children. *Sex Roles, 60*, 870–881.

Miller, J. B. (1986). *Toward a new psychology of women* (2nd ed.). Boston: Beacon Press.

Miller, J. G. (2007). Insights into moral development from cultural psychology. In M. Killen & J. G. Smetana (Eds.), *Handbook of moral development.* Mahwah, NJ: Erlbaum.

Miller, M. A., & Cappuccio, F. P. (2007). Inflammation, sleep, obesity, and cardiovascular disease. *Current Vascular Pharmacology, 5*, 92–102.

Miller R. A. (2009). Cell stress and aging: New emphasis on multiplex resistance mechanisms. *Journals of Gerontology A: Biological Sciences and Medical Sciences, 64*, 179–182.

Miller, T. W., Nigg, J. T., & Faraone, S. V. (2007). Axis I and II comorbidity in adults with ADHD. *Journal of Abnormal Psychology, 116*, 519–528.

Miller-Day, M. A. (2004). *Communication among grandmothers, mothers, and adult daughters.* Mahwah, NJ: Erlbaum.

Miller-Perrin, C. L., Perrin, R. D., & Kocur, J. L. (2009). Parental physical and psychological aggression: Psychological symptoms in young adults. *Child Abuse and Neglect, 33*, 1–11.

Mills, B., Reyna, V., & Estrada, S. (2008). Explaining contradictory relations between risk perception and risk taking. *Psychological Science, 19*, 429–433.

Mills, D., & Mills, C. (2000). *Hungarian kindergarten curriculum translation.* London: Mills Production.

Milsom, A., & Gallo, L. L. (2006). Bullying in middle schools: Prevention and intervention. *Middle School Journal, 37*, 12–19.

Minde, K., & Zelkowitz, P. (2008). Premature babies. In M. M. Haith & J. B. Benson (Eds.), *Encyclopedia of infant and early childhood development.* Oxford, UK: Elsevier.

Minino, A. M., Heron, M. P., & Smith, B. L. (2006, June 28). Deaths: Preliminary data for 2004. *National Vital Statistics Reports, 54*, 1–49.

Minkler, M., & Fuller-Thompson, E. (2005). African American grandparents raising grandchildren: A national study using the Census 2000 American Community Survey. *Journals of Gerontology B: Psychological Sciences and Social Sciences, 60*, S82–S92.

Minnesota Family Investment Program. (2009). *Longitudinal study of early MFIP recipients.* Retrieved January 12, 2009, from www.dhs.state.mn.us/main/idcplg?IdcService=GET_DYNAMIC_CONVERSION&...

Minuchin, P. O., & Shapiro, E. K. (1983). The school as a context for social development. In P. H. Mussen (Ed.), *Handbook of child psychology* (4th ed., Vol. 4). New York: Wiley.

Miranda, R., Scott, M., Hicks, R., Wilcox, H. C., Harris Munfakh, J. L., & Shaffer, D. (2008). Suicide attempt characteristics, diagnoses, and future attempts: Comparing multiple attempters to single attempters and ideators. *Journal of the American Academy of Child and Adolescent Psychiatry, 47*, 32–40.

Mirone, V., Fusco, F., Rossi, A., Sicuteri, R., & Montorsi, F. (2009). Tadalafil and vardenafil vs sildenafil: A review of patient-preferences studies. *BJU International, 103*, 1212–1217.

Mischel, W. (1968). *Personality and assessment.* New York: Wiley.

Mischel, W. (1974). Process in delay of gratification. In L. Berkowitz (Ed.), *Advances in experimental social psychology* (Vol. 7). New York: Academic Press.

Mischel, W. (2004). Toward an integrative science of the person. *Annual Review of Psychology* (Vol. 55). Palo Alto, CA: Annual Reviews.

Mischel, W., & Mischel, H. (1975, April). *A cognitive social-learning analysis of moral development.* Paper presented at the meeting of the Society for Research in Child Development, Denver.

Mistry, R. S., Vandewater, E. A., Huston, A. C., & McLoyd, V. C. (2002). Economic well-being and children's social adjustment: The role of family process in an ethnically diverse low-income sample. *Child Development, 3*, 935–951.

Mitchell, E. A. (2007). Recommendations for sudden infant death syndrome prevention: A discussion document. *Archives of Disease in Childhood, 92*, 155–159.

Mitchell, E. A. (2009). What is the mechanism of SIDS? Clues from epidemiology. *Developmental Psychobiology, 51*, 215–222.

Mitchell, E. A., Stewart, A. W., Crampton, P., & Salmond, C. (2000). Deprivation and sudden infant death syndrome. *Social Science and Medicine, 51*, 147–150.

Mitchell, M. L., & Jolley, J. M. (2010). *Research design explained* (7th ed.). Boston: Cengage.

Mitchell, M. S., Koen, C. M., & Crow, S. M. (2008). Harassment: It's not (all) about sex! Part I: The evolving legal framework. *Health Care Management, 27,* 13–22.

Mitty, E., & Flores, S. (2008). Suicide in late life. *Geriatric Nursing, 29,* 160–165.

Miura, K., & others. (2009). Four blood pressure indexes and the risk of stroke and myocardial infarction in Japanese men and women: A meta-analysis of 16 cohort studies. *Circulation, 119,* 1892–1898.

Miyake, K., Chen, S., & Campos, J. (1985). Infants' temperament, mothers' mode of interaction and attachment in Japan: An interim report. In I. Bremerton & F. Waters (Eds.), Growing points of attachment theory and research. *Monographs of the Society for Research in Child Development, 50* (1–2, Serial No. 109), 276–297.

Miyashita, M., Sato, K., Morita, T., & Suzuki, M. (2008). Effect of a population-based educational intervention focusing on end-of-life home care, life-prolonging treatment, and knowledge about palliative care. *Palliative Medicine, 22,* 376–382.

MMWR. (2006, June 9). *Youth risk behavior surveillance—United States, 2005* (Vol. 255). Atlanta: Centers for Disease Control and Prevention.

Moen, P. (1998). Recasting careers: Changing reference groups, risks, and realities. *Generations, 22,* 40–45.

Moen, P. (2007). Unpublished review of J. W. Santrock's *Life-span development,* 12th ed. (New York: McGraw-Hill).

Moen, P. (2009a). Careers. In D. Carr (Ed.), *Encyclopedia of the life course and human development.* Boston: Gale Cengage.

Moen, P. (2009b). Dual-career couples. In D. Carr (Ed.), *Encyclopedia of the life course and human development.* Boston: Gale Cengage.

Moen, P., & Altobelli, J. (2007). Strategic selection as a retirement project: Will Americans develop hybrid arrangements? In J. James & P. Wink (Eds.), *The crown of life: Dynamics of the early postretirement period.* New York: Springer.

Moen, P., Kelly, E., and Magennis, R. (2008). Gender strategies: Social and institutional convoys, mystiques, and cycles of control. In M. C. Smith & T. G. Reio (Eds.), *Handbook of research on adult development and learning.* Mahwah, NJ: Erlbaum.

Moen, P., & Spencer, D. (2006). Converging divergences in age, gender, health, and well-being. In R. H. Binstock L. K. George (Eds.), *Handbook of aging and the social sciences* (6th ed.). San Diego: Academic Press.

Moffitt, T. E., Caspi. A., & Rutter, M. (2006). Measured gene-environment interactions in psychopathology. *Perspectives on Psychological Science, 1,* 5–27.

Moise, K. J. (2005). Fetal RhD typing with free DNA I maternal plasma. *American Journal of Obstetrics and Gynecology, 192,* 663–665.

Moleti, C. A. (2009). Trends and controversies in labor induction. *MCN American Journal of Maternal and Child Nursing, 34,* 40–47.

Mollenkopf, H. (2007). Mobility and flexibility. In J. E. Birren (Ed.), *Encyclopedia of gerontology* (2nd ed.). San Diego: Academic Press.

Money, J. (1975). Ablato penis: Normal male infant sex-reassigned as a girl. *Archives of Sexual Behavior, 4,* 65–71.

Monserud, M. A. (2008). Intergenerational relationships and affectual solidarity between grandparents and young adults. *Journal of Marriage and the Family, 70,* 182–195.

Montan, S. (2007). Increased risk in the elderly parturient. *Current Opinion in Obstetrics and Gynecology, 19,* 110–112.

Montemayor, R. (1982). The relationship between parent-adolescent conflict and the amount of time adolescents spend with parents, peers, and alone. *Child Development, 53,* 1512–1519.

Moody, H. R. (2009). *Aging* (6th ed.). Thousand Oaks, CA: Sage.

Moore, D. (2001). *The dependent gene.* New York: W. H. Freeman.

Moos, B. (2007). Who'll care for aging boomers? *Dallas Morning News,* pp. A1–A2.

Morokuma, S., & others. (2008). Developmental change in fetal response to repeated low-intensity sound. *Developmental Science, 11,* 47–52.

Morra, S., Gobbo, C., Marini, Z., & Sheese, R. (2007). *Cognitive development: Neo-Piagetian perspectives.* Mahwah, NJ: Erlbaum.

Morris, D. S., Tenkku, L. E., Salas, J., Xaverius, P. K., & Mengel, M. B. (2008). Exploring pregnancy-related changes in alcohol consumption between Black and White women. *Alcoholism: Clinical and Experimental Research, 32,* 505–512.

Morrison, G. S. (2009). *Early childhood education today* (11th ed.). Upper Saddle River, NJ: Prentice Hall.

Morrissey, T. W. (2009). Multiple child-care arrangements and young children's behavioral outcomes. *Child Development, 80,* 59–76.

Morrow, L. (2009). *Literacy development in the early years.* Boston: Allyn & Bacon.

Moschonis, G., Grammatikaki, E., & Manios, Y. (2008). Perinatal predictors of overweight at infancy and preschool childhood: The GENESIS study. *International Journal of Obesity, 32,* 39–47.

Moseley, L., & Gradisar, M. (2009). Evaluation of a school-based intervention for adolescent sleep problems. *Sleep, 32,* 334–341.

Mosenthal, A. C., Murphy, P. A., Barker, L. K., Lavery, R., Retano, A., & Livingston, D. H. (2008). Changing the culture around end-of-life care in the trauma intensive care unit. *Journal of Trauma, 64,* 1587–1593.

Most, O. L., Kim, J. H., Arsian, A. A., & Klauser, C. (2009). Maternal and neonatal outcomes in early glucose tolerance testing in an obstetric population in New York City. *Journal of Perinatal Medicine, 37,* 114–117.

Moster, D., Lie, T. L., & Markestad, T. (2008). Long-term medical and social consequences of preterm birth. *New England Journal of Medicine, 359,* 262–273.

Mottershead, N. (2006). Hypnosis: Removing labor from birth. *Practicing Midwife, 9,* 26–27, 29.

Moulson, M. C., & Nelson, C. A. (2008). Neurological development. In M. M. Haith & J. B Benson (Eds.), *Encyclopedia of infant and early childhood development.* Oxford, UK: Elsevier.

Mounts, N. S. (2002). Parental management of adolescent peer relationships in context: The role of parenting style. *Journal of Family Psychology, 16,* 58–69.

Mraz, M. A. (2009). The physical manifestations of shaken baby syndrome. *Journal of Forensic Nursing, 5,* 26–30.

Mraz, M., Padak, N. D., & Rasinski, T. V. (2008). *Evidence-based instruction in reading.* Boston: Allyn & Bacon.

Mroczek, D. K., & Kolarz, C. M. (1998). The effect of age on positive and negative affect: A developmental perspective on happiness. *Journal of Personality and Social Psychology, 75,* 1333–1349.

Mroczek, D. K., & Spiro, A. (2007). Personality change influences mortality in older men. *Psychological Science, 18,* 371–376.

Mroczek, D. K., Spiro, A., & Griffin, P. W. (2006). Personality and aging. In J. E. Birren & K. W. Schaie (Eds.), *Handbook of the psychology of aging* (6th Ed.). San Diego: Academic Press.

Mueller, A. S. (2009). Body image, childhood and adolescence. In D. Carr (Ed.), *Encyclopedia of the life course and human development.* Boston: Gale Cengage.

Mueller, U., Carpendale, J. I. M., Budwig, N., & Sokol, B. W. (Eds.). (2008). *Social life and social knowledge.* Philadelphia: Psychology Press.

Muhler, M. R., Hartmann, C., Werner, W., Meyer, O., Bollmann, R., & Klingebiel, R. (2007). Fetal MRI demonstrates glioependymal cyst in a case of sonographic unilateral ventriculomegaly. *Pediatric Radiology, 37,* 391–395.

Mukherjee, S., Lekli, I., Gurusamy, N., Bertelli, A. A., & Das, D. K. (2009). Expression of the longevity proteins by both red and white wines and their cardioprotective components, resveratrol, tyrosol, and hyrdoxytyrosol. *Free Radical Biology and Medicine, 46,* 573–578.

Mullis, P. E., & Tonella, P. (2008). Regulation of fetal growth: Consequences and impact of being born small. *Best Practice Research: Clinical Endocrinology and Metabolism, 22,* 173–190.

Mulvaney, M. K., & Mebert, C. J. (2007). Parental corporal punishment predicts behavioral problems in early childhood. *Journal of Family Psychology, 21,* 389–397.

Mundy, P., Block, J., Delgado, C., Pomares, Y., Van Hecke, A. V., & Parlade, M. V. (2007). Individual differences and the development of joint attention in infancy. *Child Development, 78,* 938–954.

Murdock, T. B., Miller, A., & Kohlhardt, J. (2004). Effects of classroom context variables on high school students' judgments of the acceptability and likelihood of *cheating. Journal of Educational Psychology, 96,* 765–777.

Murphy, M. M., & Mazzocco, M. M. (2008). Mathematics learning disabilities in girls with fragile X or Turner syndrome during late elementary school. *Journal of Learning Disabilities, 41,* 29–46.

Murray, J. P., & Murray, A. D. (2008). Television: Uses and effects. In M. M. Haith & J. B. Benson (Eds.), *Encyclopedia of infant and early childhood development.* Oxford, UK: Elsevier.

Musch, D. C., & others. (2009). Visual field progression in the Collaborative Initial Glaucoma Treatment Study: The impact of treatment and other baseline factors. *Ophthalmology, 116,* 200–2007.

Mussen, P. H., Honzik, M., & Eichorn, D. (1982). Early adult antecedents of life satisfaction at age 70. *Journal of Gerontology, 37,* 316–322.

Mustelin, L., Silventoinen, K., Pietilainen, K., Risssanen, A., & Kaprio, J. (2009). Physical activity reduces the influence of genetic effects on BMI and waist circumference: A study of young adult twins. *International Journal of Obesity, 33,* 29–36.

Myers, D. (2008, June 2). Commentary in S. Begley & J. Interlandi, The dumbest generation? Don't be dumb. Retrieved July 22, 2008, from www.newsweek.com/id/138536/

Myers, D. G. (2000). *The American paradox.* New Haven, CT: Yale University Press.

Myers, D. G. (2010). *Psychology* (9th ed.). New York: Worth.

Myers, D. L. (1999). *Excluding violent youths from juvenile court: The effectiveness of legislative waiver.* Doctoral dissertation. University of Maryland, College Park.

Myerson, J., Rank, M. R., Raines, F. Q., & Schnitzler, M. A. (1998). Race and general cognitive ability: The myth of diminishing returns in education. *Psychological Science, 9,* 139–142.

N

Nader P. R., Bradley, R. H., Houts, R. M., McRitchie, S. L., & O'Brian, M. (2008). Moderate-to-vigorous physical activity from 9 to 15 years. *Journal of the American Medical Association, 300,* 295–305.

Nabet, C., Lelong, N., Ancel, P. Y., Saurel-Cubizolles, M. J., & Kaminski, M. (2007). Smoking during pregnancy according to obstetric complications and parity: Results of the EUROPOP study. *European Journal of Epidemiology, 22,* 715–721.

Nader, P., O'Brien, M., Houts, R., Bradley, R., Belsky, J., Corsnoe, R., Friedman, S., Mei, Z., & Susman, E. J. (2006). Identifying risk for obesity in early childhood. *Pediatrics, 118,* e594–e601.

NAEYC. (2005). *Critical facts about young children and early childhood programs in the United States.* Washington, DC: Author.

NAEYC. (2009, in press). Developmentally appropriate practice in early childhood programs serving children from birth through age 8. *Young Children.*

Nagy, M. (1948). The child's theories concerning death. *Journal of Genetic Psychology, 73,* 3–27.

Naigles, L. R., & Swensen, L. D. (2010). Syntactic supports for word learning. In E. Hoff & M. Shatz (Eds.), *Blackwell handbook of language development* (2nd ed.). Malden, MA: Blackwell.

Najman, J. M., Hayatbakhsh, M. R., Heron, M. A., Bor, W., O'Callaghan, M. J., & Williams, G. M. (2009). The impact of episodic and chronic poverty on child cognitive development. *Journal of Pediatrics, 154,* 284–289.

Nansel, T. R., Overpeck, M., Pilla, R., Ruan, W., Simons-Morton, B., & Scheidt, P. (2001). Bullying behaviors among U.S. youth. *Journal of the American Medical Association, 285,* 2094–2100.

Napierski-Prancl, M. (2009). Eating disorders. In D. Carr (Ed.), *Encyclopedia of the life course and human development.* Boston: Gale Cengage.

Nappi, R. E., & Polatti, F. (2009). The use of estrogen therapy in women's sexual functioning. *Archives of Sexual Medicine, 6,* 603–606.

Narberhaus, A., Segarra, D., Caldu, X., Gimenez, M., Pueyo, R., Botet, F., & Junque, C. (2008). Corpus callosum and prefrontal functions in adolescents with history of very preterm birth. *Neuropsychologia, 46,* 111–116.

Narr, K. L., & others. (2007). Relationships between IQ and regional cortical gray matter thickness in healthy adults. *Cerebral Cortex, 17,* 2163–2171.

Narváez, D. (2006). Integrative ethical education. In M. Killen & J. Smetana (Eds.), *Handbook of moral development.* Mahwah, NJ: Erlbaum.

Narváez, D. (2008). Four Component Model. In F. C. Power, R. J. Nuzzi, D. Narváez, D. K. Lapsley, & T. C. Hunt (Eds.). *Moral education: A handbook.* Westport, CT: Greenwood.

Narváez, D., Bock, T., Endicott, L., & Lies, J. (2004). Minnesota's Community Voices and Character Education Project. *Journal of Research in Character Education, 2,* 89–112.

Narváez, D., & Lapsley, D. (Eds.) (2009, in press). *Moral personality, identity, and character: An interdisciplinary future.* New York: Cambridge University Press.

Narváez, D., Lynchard, N., Vaydich, J., & Mattan, B. (2008, March). *Cheating: Explicit recognition, implicit evaluation, moral judgment and honor code training.* Paper presented at the annual meeting of the Society for Research in Adolescence, Chicago.

Nash, C. (2008, June 2). Commentary in S. Begley & J. Interlandi, The dumbest generation? Don't be dumb. Retrieved July 22, 2008, from www.newsweek.com/id/138536/

Nash, J. M. (1997, February 3). Fertile minds. *Time,* pp. 50–54.

Nathalie, P., & Jean-Noel, O. (2008). Processing of amyloid precursor protein and amyloid peptide neurotoxicity. *Current Alzheimer Research, 5,* 92–99.

National Assessment of Educational Progress. (2005). *The nation's report card, 2005.* Washington, DC: U.S. Department of Education.

National Assessment of Educational Progress. (2007). *The nation's report card, 2007.* Washington, DC: U.S. Department of Education.

National Center for Education Statistics. (2002). *Work during college.* Washington, DC: U.S. Office of Education.

National Center for Education Statistics. (2008a). *School dropout rates.* Washington, DC: U.S. Department of Education.

National Center for Education Statistics. (2008b). *The Condition of Education, 2008. Indicator 8. Children and youth with disabilities in public schools.* Washington, DC: U.S. Department of Education.

National Center for Education Statistics. (2008c). *Contexts of post-secondary education.* Washington, DC: U.S. Department of Education.

National Center for Health Statistics. (2000). *Health United States, 1999.* Atlanta: Centers for Disease Control and Prevention.

National Center for Health Statistics. (2002). *Health United States, 2002.* Hyattsville, MD: Centers for Disease Control and Prevention.

National Center for Health Statistics. (2002). *Sexual behavior and selected health measures: Men and women 15–44 years of age. United States, 2002,* PHS 2003–1250. Atlanta: Centers for Disease Control and Prevention.

National Center for Health Statistics. (2006). *Health United States.* Atlanta: Centers for Disease Control and Prevention.

National Center for Health Statistics. (2006). *HIV/AIDS.* Atlanta: Centers for Disease Control and Prevention.

National Center for Health Statistics. (2007). *Health, United States, 2007.* Hyattsville, MD: Author.

National Center for Health Statistics. (2008a). *Table 115: Deaths and death rates, by leading couses of death and age: 2005.* Atlanta: Centers for Disease Control and Prevention.

National Center for Health Statistics. (2008b). *Table 117: Death rates from heart disease,* *by selected characteristics: 1980 to 2005.* Atlanta: Centers for Disease Control and Prevention.

National Center for Health Statistics. (2008c). *Table 119: Death rates from malignant neoplasms, by selected characteristics: 1990 to 2005.* Atlanta: Centers for Disease Control and Prevention.

National Center for Health Statistics. (2008, June 11). *U.S. mortality rate drops sharply in 2006, latest data show.* Atlanta: Centers for Disease Control and Prevention.

National Center for Health Statistics. (2008). *Suicide.* Retrieved August 10, 2009, from www.cdc.gov/injury.

National Center for Health Statistics. (2009). *HIV/AIDS statistics and surveillance.* Atlanta: Centers for Disease Control and Prevention.

National Center for Health Statistics. (2009, January 7). *Public release statement: Preterm births rise 36 percent since early 1980s.* Atlanta: Centers for Disease Control and Prevention.

National Center on Skaken Baby Syndrome. (2008). *Shaken baby syndrome.* Retrieved October 16, 2008, from www.dontshake.org/

National Clearinghouse on Child Abuse and Neglect. (2002). *What is child maltreatment?* Washington, DC: Administration for Children and Families.

National Clearinghouse on Child Abuse and Neglect. (2004). *What is child abuse and neglect?* Washington, DC: U.S. Department of Health and Human Services.

National Commission on the High School Year. (2001). *Youth at the crossroads: Facing high school and beyond.* Washington, DC: The Education Trust.

National Institute of Mental Health. (2004). *Austism spectrum disorders.* Bethesda, MD: Author.

National Institute of Mental Health. (2008). *Autism spectrum disorders (pervasive developmental disorders).* Retrieved January 6, 2008, from http://www.nimh.nih.gov/Publicat/autism.cfm.

National Institute of Neurological Disorders and Stroke. (2009). *Understanding Sleep.* Bethesda, MD: Author.

National Institutes of Health. (2004, March 2). *NIH asks participants in Women's Health Initiative estrogen-alone study to stop study pills, begin follow-up phase* (Press Release). Bethesda, MD: Author.

National Institutes of Health. (2008). *Clinical trial.gov.* Retrieved April 22, 2008, from http://clinicaltrials.gov/ct2/show/NCT00059293?cond=%22Intracranial+Embolism%22&r...

National Research Council. (1999). *Starting out right: A guide to promoting children's reading success.* Washington, DC: National Academy Press.

National Sleep Foundation. (2003). *Sleep in America poll: Sleep and aging.* Washington, DC: Author.

National Sleep Foundation. (2009). *Children and sleep.* Retrieved July 6, 2009, from www.sleepfoundation.org/site/c.huIXKjM0IxF/b.2418873/k.B9AD/Children_and_S1...

Neal, A. R. (2009). Autism. In D. Carr (Ed.), *Encyclopedia of the life course and human development.* Boston: Gale Cengage.

Needham, A. (2009). Learning in infants' object perception, object-directed action, and tool use. In A. Needham & A. Woodward (Eds.), *Learning and the infant mind.* New York: Oxford University Press.

Needham, A., Barrett, T., & Peterman, K. (2002). A pick-me-up for infants' exploratory skills: Early simulated experiences reaching for objects using "sticky mittens" enhances young infants' object exploration skills. *Infant Behavior and Development, 25,* 279–295.

Neisser, U. (2004). Memory development: New questions and old. *Developmental Review, 24,* 154–158.

Neisser, U., Boodoo, G., Bouchard, T. J., Boykin, A. W., Brody, N., Ceci, S. J., Halpern, D. E., Loehlin, J. C., Perioff, R. J., Sternberg, R., & Urbina, S. (1996). Intelligence: Knowns and unknowns. *American Psychologist, 51,* 77–101.

Nelson, C. (2006). Unpublished review of J. W. Santrock's *Topical life-span development,* 4th ed. (New York: McGraw-Hill).

Nelson, C. A. (2003). Neural development and lifelong plasticity. In R. M. Lerner, F. Jacobs, & D. Wertlieb (Eds.), *Handbook of applied developmental science* (Vol. 1). Thousand Oaks, CA: Sage.

Nelson, C. A. (2007). A developmental cognitive neuroscience approach to the study of atypical development: A model system involving infants of diabetic mothers. In D. Coch, G. Dawson, & K. W. Fischer (Eds.), *Human behavior, learning, and the developing brain.* New York: Guilford.

Nelson, C. A. (2008). Unpublished review of J. W. Santrock's *Life-span development: A topical approach,* 5th ed. (New York: McGraw-Hill).

Nelson, C. A. (2009). Brain development and behavior. In A. M. Rudolph, C. Rudolf, L. First, G. Lister, & A. A. Gersohon (Eds.), *Rudolph's pediatrics* (22nd ed.). New York: McGraw-Hill.

Nelson, F. A., Yu, L. M., Williams, S., & the International Child Care Practices Study Group Members. (2005). International Child Care Practices Study: Breastfeeding and pacifier use. *Journal of Human Lactation, 21,* 289–295.

Nelson, J. A., & Eckstein, D. (2008). A service-learning model for at-risk adolescents. *Education and Treatment of Children, 31,* 223–237.

Nelson, K. (1999). Levels and modes of representation: Issues for the theory of conceptual change and development. In E. K. Skolnick, K. Nelson, S. A. Gelman, & P. H. Miller (Eds.), *Conceptual development.* Mahwah, NJ: Erlbaum.

Nelson, S. L., & Lee, J. C. (2009). Socioeconomic inequality in education. In D. Carr (Ed.), *Encyclopedia of the life course and human development.* Boston: Gale Cengage.

Neubauer, A. C., & Fink, A. (2009). Intelligence and neural efficiency: Measures of brain activation versus measures of functional connectivity in the brain. *Intelligence, 37,* 223–229.

Neugarten, B. L. (1988, August). *Policy issues for an aging society.* Paper presented at the meeting of the American Psychological Association, Atlanta.

Neugarten, B. L., Havighurst, R. J., & Tobin, S. S. (1968). Personality and patterns of aging. In B. L. Neugarten (Ed.), *Middle age and aging.* Chicago: University of Chicago Press.

Neugarten, B. L., & Weinstein, K. K. (1964). The changing American grandparent. *Journal of Marriage and the Family, 26,* 199–204.

Neukrug, E. S., & Fawcett, R. C. (2010). *Essentials of testing and assessment* (2nd ed.). Boston: Cengage.

Neuman, S. B. (2007). Social contexts for literacy development. In K. A. Roskos & J. F. Christie (Eds.), *Play and literacy in early childhood.* Mahwah, NJ: Erlbaum.

Neville, H. J. (2006). Different profiles of plasticity within human cognition. In Y. Munakata & M. H. Johnson (Eds.), *Attention and performance XXI: Processes of change in brain and cognitive development.* Oxford, UK: Oxford University Press.

Nevsimalova, S. (2009). Narcolespy in childhood. *Sleep Medicine Reviews, 13,* 169–180.

Newburg, D. S., & Walker, W. A. (2007). Protection of the neonate by the innate immune system of developing gut and of human milk. *Pediatric Research, 61,* 2–8.

Newcomb, M. D., & Bentler, P. M. (1989). Substance use and abuse among children and teenagers. *American Psychologist, 44,* 242–248.

Newcombe, N., & Fox, N. (1994). Infantile amnesia: Through a glass darkly. *Child Development, 65,* 31–40.

Newell, K., Scully, D. M., McDonald, P. V., & Balllargeon, R. (1989). Task constraints and infant grip configurations. *Developmental Psychobiology, 22,* 817–832.

Newman, A. B., & others. (2006). Association of long-distance corridor walk performance with mortality, cardiovascular disease, mobility limitation, and disability. *Journal of the American Medical Association. 295,* 2018–2026.

Newman, A. B., & others. (2009). Long-term function in an older cohort—The Cardiovascular Health Study All-Stars Study. *Journal of the American Geriatrics Society, 57,* 432–440.

Newsom, A. J. (2008). Ethical aspects arising from non-invasive fetal diagnosis. *Seminars in Fetal and Neonatal Medicine, 13,* 103–108.

Newton, I. G., Forbes, M. E., Linville, M. C., Pang, H., Tucker, E. W., Riddle, D. R., & Brunso-Bechtoid, J. K. (2008). Effects of aging and caloric restriction on dentate gyrus synapses and glutamate receptor subunits. *Neurobiology of Aging, 29,* 1308–1318.

Ney, D. M., Hull, A. K., van Calcar, S. C., Liu, X., & Etzel, M. R. (2008). Dietary glycomacropeptide supports growth and reduces the concentrations of phenylalanine in plasma and brain in a murine model of phenylketonuria. *Journal of Nutrition, 138,* 316–322.

Niamtu, J. (2009). Complications of fillers and Botox. *Oral and Maxillofacial Surgery Clinics of North America, 21,* 13–21.

NICHD. (2009). *SIDS.* Retrieved August 10, 2009, from www.nichd.nih.gov/publications/pubs/safe_sleep_gen.cfm

NICHD Early Child Care Research Network. (2001). Nonmaternal care and family factors in early development: An overview of the NICHD Study of Early Child Care. *Journal of Applied Developmental Psychology, 22,* 457–492.

NICHD Early Child Care Research Network. (2002). Structure → Process → Outcome: Direct and indirect effects of child care quality on young children's development. *Psychological Science, 13,* 199–206.

NICHD Early Child Care Research Network. (2003). Does amount of time spent in child care predict socioemotional adjustment during the transition to kindergarten? *Child Development, 74,* 976–1005.

NICHD Early Child Care Research Network. (2004). Type of child care and children's development at 54 months. *Early Childhood Research Quarterly, 19,* 203–230.

NICHD Early Child Care Research Network. (2005). *Child care and development.* New York: Guilford.

NICHD Early Child Care Research Network. (2005). Duration and developmental timing of poverty and children's cognitive and social development from birth through third grade. *Child Development, 76,* 795–810.

NICHD Early Child Care Research Network. (2005). Predicting individual differences in attention, memory, and planning in first graders from experiences at home, child care, and school. *Developmental Psychology, 41,* 99–114.

NICHD Early Child Care Research Network. (2006). Infant-mother attachment classification: Risk and protection in relation to changing maternal quality. *Developmental Psychology, 42,* 38–58.

NICHD Early Child Care Research Network. (2009, in press). Family-peer linkages: The meditational role of attentional processes. *Social Development.*

Nieto, S. (2010). Multicultural education in the United States: Historical realities ongoing challenges, and transformative possibilities. In J. A. Banks (Ed.), *The Routledge international companion to multicultural education.* Oxford, UK: Routledge.

Nilsson, K. W., Oreland, L., Dronstrand, R., & Leppert, J. (2009). Smoking as a product of gene-environment interaction. *Upsala Journal of Medical Sciences, 114,* 100–107.

Nippold, M. A. (2009). School-age children talk about chess: Does knowledge drive syntactic complexity? *Journal of Speech, Language, and Hearing Research,* 856–871.

Nisbett, R. (2003). *The geography of thought.* New York: Free Press.

Nishiyama, T., Tanial, H., Miyachi, T., Ozaki, K., Tomita, M., & Sumi, S. (2009). Genetic correlation between autistic traits and IQ in a population-based sample of twins with autism spectrum disorders (ASDs). *Journal of Human Genetics, 54,* 56–61.

Nix, R. L., Bierman, K. L., McMahon, R. J., & the Conduct Problems Prevention Research Group. (2009). How attendance and quality of therapeutic engagement affect treatment response in parent behavior management training. *Journal of Consulting and Clinical Psychology, 77,* 429–438.

Nixon, G. M., & others. (2008). Short sleep duration in middle childhood: Risk factors and consequences. *Sleep, 31,* 71–78.

Noam, S. M., Zimmerman, R. S., & Atwood, K. A. (2004). Safer sex and sexually transmitted infections from a relationship perspective. In J. H. Harvey & A. Wetzel (Eds.), *The handbook of sexuality in close relationships.* Mahwah, NJ: Erlbaum.

Noddings, S. N. (2008). Caring and moral education. In L. Nucci & D. Narváez (Ed.), *Handbook of moral and character education.* Clifton, NJ: Psychology Press.

Noftle, E. E., & Robins, R. W. (2007). Personality predictors of academic outcomes: Big Five correlates of GPA and SAT scores. *Journal of Personality and Social Psychology, 93,* 116–130.

Noland, H., Price, J. H., Dake, J., & Telijohann, S. K. (2009). Adolescents' sleep behaviors and perceptions of sleep. *Journal of School Health, 79,* 224–230.

Noland, J. S., Singer, L. T., Short, E. J., Minnes, S., Arendt, R. E., Kirchner, H. L., & Bearer, C. (2005). Prenatal drug exposure and selective attention in preschoolers. *Neurotoxicology and Teratology, 27,* 429–438.

Nolen-Hoeksema, S. (1990). *Sex differences in depression.* Stanford, CA: Stanford University Press.

Nolen-Hoeksema, S. (2007). *Abnormal psychology* (4th ed.). New York: McGraw-Hill.

Nolen-Hoeksema, S. (2010). *Abnormal psychology* (5th ed.). New York: McGraw-Hill.

Noll, J. G., Trickett, P. K., Harris, W. W., & Putnam, F. W. (2009). The cumulative burden borne by offspring whose mothers were sexually abused as children: Descriptive results from a multigenerational study. *Journal of Interpersonal Violence, 24,* 424–429.

Nomoto, M., & others. (2009). Inter- and intra-individual variation in L-dopa pharmacokinetics in the treatment of Parkinson's disease. *Parkinsonism and Related Disorders, 15* (Suppl. 1), S21–S24.

Norbury, G., & Norbury, C. J. (2008). Non-invasive prenatal diagnosis of single gene disorders: How close are we? *Seminars in Fetal and Neonatal Medicine, 13,* 76–83.

Nordberg, A. (2008). Amyloid plaque imaging in vivo: Current achievement and future prospects. *European Journal of Nuculear Medicine and Molecular Imaging, 35* (Suppl. 1), S46–S50.

Norgard, B., Puho, E., Czeilel, A. E., Skriver, M. V., & Sorensen, H. T. (2006). Aspirin use during early pregnancy and the risk of congenital abnormalities. *American Journal of Obstetrics and Gynecology, 192,* 922–923.

Norouzieh, K. (2005). Case management of the dying child. *Case Manager, 16,* 54–57.

Nottelmann, E. D., Susman, E. J., Blue, J. H., Inoff-Germain, G., Dorn, L. D., Loriaux, D. L., Cutler, G. B., & Chrousos, G. P. (1987). Gonadal and adrenal hormone correlates of adjustment in early adolescence. In R. M. Lerner & T. T. Foch (Eds.), *Biological-pychosocial interactions in early adolescence.* Hillsdale, NJ: Erlbaum.

Novin, S., Banderjee, R., Dadkhah, A., Rieffe, C. (2009). Self-reported use of emotional display rules in the Netherlands and Iran: Evidence for sociocultural influence. *Social Development, 18,* 397–411.

Nsamenang, A. B. (2002). Adolescence in sub-Saharan Africa: An image constructed from Africa's triple heritage. In B. B. Brown, R. W. Larson, & T. S. Saraswathi (Eds.), *The world's youth.* New York: Cambridge University Press.

Nucci, L. (2006). Education for moral development. In M. Killen & J. Smetana (Eds.), *Handbook of moral development.* Mahwah, NJ: Erlbaum.

Nyaronga, D., & Wickrama, K. A. S. (2009). Health behaviors, childhood and adolescence. In D. Carr (Ed.), *Encyclopedia of the life course and human development.* Boston: Gale Cengage.

Nyiti, R. M. (1982). The validity of "cultural differences explanations" for cross-cultural variation in the rate of Piagetian cognitive development. In D. Wagner & H. Stevenson (Eds.), *Cultural perspectives on child development.* New York: W. H. Freeman.

Nylund, K., Bellmore, A., Nishina, A., & Graham, S. (2007). Subtypes, severity, and structural stability of peer victimization: What does latent class analysis say? *Child Development, 78,* 1706–1722.

O

Oakes, L. M. (2008). Categorization skills and concepts. In M. M. Haith & J. B. Benson (Eds.), *Encyclopedia of infant and early childhood development.* Oxford, UK: Elsevier.

Oakes, L. M., Kannass, K. N., & Shaddv, D. J. (2002). Developmental changes in endogenous control of attention: The role of target familiarity on infants' distraction latency. *Child Development, 73,* 1644–1655.

Obel, C., & others. (2009). Smoking during pregnancy and hyperactivity-inattention in the offspring—comparing results from three Nordic cohorts. *International Journal of Epidemiology, 38,* 698–705.

Obenauer, S., & Maestre, L. A. (2008). Fetal MRI of lung hypoplasia: Imaging findings. *Clinical Imaging, 32,* 48–50.

Oberlander, T. F., Bonaguro, R. J., Misri, S., Papsdorf, M., Ross, C. J., & Simpson, E. M. (2008). Infant serotonin transporter (SLC6A4) promoter genotype is associated with adverse neonatal outcomes after prenatal exposure to serotonin reuptake inhibitor medications. *Molecular Psychiatry, 13,* 65–73.

Obler, L. K. (2009). Developments in the adult years. In J. Berko Gleason & N. B. Ratner (Eds.), *The development of language* (7th ed.). Boston: Allyn & Bacon.

O'Bryant, S. E., & others. (2009, in press). Brain-derived neurotrophic factor levels in Alzheimer's disease. *Journal of Alzheimer's Disease.*

Occupational Outlook Handbook. (2008–2009). Washington, DC: U.S. Department of Labor, Bureau of Labor Statistics.

Ochs, E., & Schieffelin, B. (2008). *Language socialization and language acquisition.* In P. A. Duff & N. H. Hornberger (Eds.), *Encyclopedia of language ond education.* New York: Springer.

O'Connell, E. (2005). Mood, energy, cognition, and physical complaints: A mind/body approach to symptom management during the climacteric. *Journal of Obstetrics, Gynecologic, and Neonatal Nursing, 34,* 274–279.

O'Connor, A. B., & Roy, C. (2008). Electric power plant emissions and public health. *American Journal of Nursing, 108,* 62–70.

O'Connor, D. B., Conner, M., Jones, F., McMillan, B., & Ferguson, E. (2009). Exploring the benefits of conscientiousness: An investigation of the role of daily stressors and health benefits. *Annals of Behavioral Medicine, 37,* 184–196.

O'Donnell, L., O'Donnell, C., Wardlaw, D. M., & Stueve, A. (2004). Risk and resiliency factors influencing suicidality among urban African American and Latino youth. *American Journal of Community Psychology, 33,* 37–49.

Offer, D., Ostrov, E., Howard, K. I., & Atkinson, R. (1988). *The teenage world: Adolescents' self-image in ten countries.* New York: Plenum Press.

Ogbu, J., & Stern, P. (2001). Caste status and intellectual development. In R. J. Sternberg & E. L. Grigorenko (Eds.), *Environmental effects on cognitive abilities.* Mahwah, NJ: Erlbaum.

Ogden, C. L., Carroll, M. D., & Flegal, K. M. (2008). High body mass index for age among U.S. children and adolescents, 2003–2006. *Journal of the American Medical Association, 299,* 2401–2405.

O'Gorman, C. S., Hamid, M. A., & Fox, G. P. (2005). Universal neonatal hearing screening. *Irish Medical Journal, 98,* 86–87.

O'Hara, S., & Pritchard, R. (2009). *Teaching vocabulary with hypermedia, 6–12.* Boston: Allyn & Bacon.

Oken, E., & Bellinger, D. C. (2008). Fish consumption, methylmercury, and child neurodevelopment. *Current Opinion in Pediatrics, 20,* 178–183.

Okonkwo, O. C., Crowe, M., Wadley, V. G., & Ball, K. (2008). Visual attention and self-regulation of driving among older adults. *International Geriatrics, 20,* 162–173.

Oldehinkel, A. J., Ormel, J., Veenstra, R., De Winter, A., & Verhulst, F. C. (2008). Parental divorce and offspring depressive symptoms: Dutch developmental trends during early adolescence. *Journal of Marriage and the Family, 70,* 284–293.

Olds, D. L., & others. (2004). Effects of home visits by paraprofessionals and nurses: Age four follow-up of a randomized trial. *Pediatrics, 114,* 1560–1568.

Olds, D. L., & others. (2007). Effects of nurse home visiting on maternal and child functioning: Age-9 follow-up of a randomized trial. *Pediatrics, 120,* e832–e845.

Oller, D. K., & Jarmulowicz, L. (2010). Language and literacy in bilingual children in the early school years. In E. Hoff & M. Shatz (Eds.), *Blackwell handbook of language development* (2nd ed.) Malden, MA: Blackwell.

Olsho, L. W., Harkins, S. W., & Lenhardt, M. L. (1985). Aging and the auditory system. In J. E. Birren & K. W. Schaie (Eds.), *Handbook of the psychology of aging* (2nd ed.). New York: Van Nostrand Reinhold.

Olson, B. H., Haider, S. J., Vangjel, L., Bolton, T. A., & Gold, J. G. (2009b, in press). A quasi-experimental evaluation of a breastfeeding support program for low income women in Michigan. *Maternal and Child Health Journal.*

Olson, B. H., Horodynski, M. A., Brophy-Herb, H., & Iwanski, K. C. (2009a, in press). Health professionals' perspectives on the infant feeding practices of low income mothers. *Maternal and Child Health Journal.*

Olson, H. C., King, S., & Jirikowic, T. (2008). Fetal alcohol spectrum disorders. In M. M. Haith & J. B. Benson (Eds.), *Encyclopedia of infant and early childhood development.* Thousand Oaks, CA: Sage.

Oman, D., & Thoresen, C. E. (2006). Do religion and spirituality influence health? In R. F. Paloutzian & C. L. Park (Eds.), *Handbook of the psychology of religion and spirituality.* New York: Guilford.

Ono, M. Y., Farzin, F., & Hagerman, R. J. (2008). Fragile X syndrome. In M. M. Haith & J. B. Benson (Eds.), *Encyclopedia of infant and early childhood development.* Oxford, UK: Elsevier.

Ontai, L. L., & Thompson, R. A. (2002). Patterns of attachment and maternal discourse effects on children's emotion understanding from 3 to 5 years of age. *Social Development, 11,* 433–450.

Oostdam, N., van Poppel, M. N., Eekohff, E. M., Wouters, M. G., & van Mechelen, W. (2009). Design of FitFor2 study: The effects of an exercise program on insulin sensitivity and plasma glucose levels in pregnant women at high risk for gestational diabetes. *BMC Pregnancy and Childbirth, 9,* 1.

Oosterhof, A. (2009). *Developing and using classroom assessments* (4th ed.). Upper Saddle River, NJ: Prentice Hall.

Orbe, M. P. (2008). Theorizing multidimensional identity negotiation: Reflections on the lived experiences of first-generation college students. *New Directions for Child and Adolescent Development, 120,* 81–95.

Orecchia, R., Lucignani, G., & Tosi, G. (2008). Prenatal irradiation and pregnancy: The effects of diagnostic imaging and radiation therapy. *Recent Results in Cancer Research, 178,* 3–20.

Orhan, G., Orhan, I., Subutay-Oztekin, N., Ak, F., & Sener, B. (2009). Recent anticholinesterase pharmaceuticals of natural origin and their synthetic analogues for the treatment of Alzheimer's disease. *Recent Patents on CNS Drug Discovery, 4,* 43–51.

Ornstein, P., Gordon, B. N., & Larus, D. (1992). Children's memory for a personally experienced event: Implications for testimony. *Applied Cognition and Psychology, 6,* 49–60.

Orth, U., Robins, R. W., & Roberts, B. W. (2008). Low self-esteem prospectively predicts depression in adolescence and young adulthood. *Journal of Personality and Social Psychology, 95,* 695–708.

Ostrov, J. M., Ries, E. E., Staffacher, K., Godleski, S. A., & Mullins, A. D. (2008). Relational aggression, physical aggression, and deception during early childhood: A multimethod, multi-informant short-term longitudinal study. *Journal of Clinical Child and Adolescent Psychology, 37,* 664–675.

Oswald, D. L., & Clark, E. M. (2003). Best friends forever? High school best friendships and the transition to college. *Personal Relationships, 10,* 187–196.

Oswiecimska, J. M., & others. (2008). Growth hormone therapy in boy with panhypopituitarism may induce pilomatricoma recurrence: Case report. *Neuroendocrine Letters, 29,* 51–54.

Otiniano, M. E., Du, X. L., Maldonado, M. R., Ray, L., & Markides, K. (2005). Effect of metabolic syndrome on heart attack and mortality in Mexican-American elderly persons: Findings of 7-year follow-up from the Hispanic established population for the epidemiological study of the elderly. *Journals of Gerontology: Biological Sciences and Medical Sciences, 60,* 466A–470A.

Ott, C. H., Lueger, R. J., Kelber, S. T., & Prigerson, H. G. (2007). Spousal bereavement in older adults: Common, resilient, and chronic grief with defining characteristics. *Journal of Nervous and Mental Disease, 195,* 332–341.

Otto, B. W. (2010). *Language development in early childhood* (3rd ed.). Upper Saddle River, NJ: Merrill.

Oude, L. H., Baur, L., Jansen, H., Shrewsbury, V. A., O'Malley, C., Stolk, R. P., & Summerbell, C. D. (2009). Interventions for treating obesity in children. *Cochrane Database of Systematic Reviews, 1,* CDOO1872.

Oxford, M. L., Gilchrist, L. D., Gillmore, M. R., & Lohr, M. J. (2006). Predicting variation in the life course of adolescent mothers as they enter adulthood. *Journal of Adolescent Health, 39,* 20–36.

Oyama, H., Sakashita, T., Ono, Y., Fujita, M., & Koida, J. (2008). Effect of community-based intervention using depression screening on elderly suicide risk: A meta-analysis of the evidence from Japan. *Community Mental Health Journal, 44,* 311–320.

Ozaki, K., & Ando, J. (2009). Direction of causation between shared and non-shared environmental factors. *Behavioral Genetics, 39,* 321–336.

Ozer E. M., & Irwin, C. (2009). Adolescent and youth adult health: From basic health status to clinical interventions. In R. M. Lerner & L. Steinberg (Eds.), *Handbook of adolescent psychology* (3rd ed.). New York: Wiley.

P

Padilla-Walker, L. M., & Thompson, R. A. (2005). Combating conflicting messages of values: A closer look at parental strategies. *Social Development, 14,* 305–323.

Paffenbarger, R. S., Hyde, R. T., Wing, A. L., Lee, I., Jung, D. L., & Kampter, J. B. (1993). The association of changes in physical-activity level and other life-style characteristics with mortality among men. *New England Journal of Medicine, 328,* 538–545.

Painter, K. (2008, June 16). Older, wiser, but less active. *USA Today,* p. 4D.

Palfrey, J., Sacco, D., Boyd, D., & DeBonis, L. (2009). *Enhancing child safety and online technologies.* Cambridge, MA: Berkman Center for Internet and Society.

Pallas, M., Verdaguer, E., Tajes, M., Gutierrez-Cuesta, J., & Camins, A. (2008). Modulation of sirtuins: New targets for antiaging. *Recent Patents on CNS Drug Discovery, 3,* 61–69.

Palmore, E. B. (2004). Research note: Ageism in Canada and the United States. *Journal of Cross Cultural Gerontology, 19,* 41–46.

Paloutzian, R. F. (2000). *Invitation to the psychology of religion* (3rd ed.). Needham Heights, MA: Allyn & Bacon.

Paloutzian, R. K., & Park, C. L. (Eds.). (2005). *Handbook of the psychology of religion and sprituality.* New York: Guilford.

Pan, B. A., Rowe, M. L., Singer, J. D., & Snow, C. E. (2005). Maternal correlates of growth in toddler vocabulary production in low-income families. *Child Development, 76,* 763–782.

Pan, B. A., & Uccelli, P. (2009). Semantic development, in J. Berko Gleason & N. Ratner (Eds.), *The development of language* (7th ed.). Boston: Allyn & Bacon.

Pang, V. O. (2005). *Multicultural education.* (3rd ed.). New York: McGraw-Hill.

Paradis, J. (2010). Second language acquisition in children. In E. Hoff & M. Shatz (Eds.), *Blackwell handbook of language development* (2nd ed.). Malden, MA: Blackwell.

Parens, E., & Johnston, J. (2009). Facts, values, and attention-deficit hyperactivity disorder (ADHD): An update on the controversies. *Child and Adolescent Psychiatry and Mental Health, 3,* 1.

Park, C. L. (2005). Religion as a meaning-making system. *Psychology of Religion Newsletter, 30* (2), 1–9.

Park, C. L. (2007). Religiousness/spirituality and health: A meaning systems perspective. *Journal of Behavioral Medicine, 30,* 319–328.

Park, C. L. (2008). Estimated longevity and changes in spirituality in the context of advanced congestive heart failure. *Palliative and Supportive Care, 6,* 1–9.

Park, C. L. (2009, in press). Meaning making in cancer survivorship. In P. T. P. Wong (ed.). *Handbook of Meaning* (2nd ed.). Thousand Oaks, CA: Sage.

Park, C. L., Malone, M. R., Suresh, D. P., Bliss, D., & Rosen, R. I. (2008). Coping, meaning in life, and the quality of life in congestive heart failure patients. *Quality of Life Research, 17,* 21–26.

Park, D. C., & Gutchess, A. H. (2005). Long-term memory and aging: A cognitive neuroscience perspective. In R. Cabeza, L. Nyberg, & D. Park (Eds.), *Cognitive neuroscience of aging: Linking cognitive and cerebral aging.* New York: Oxford University Press.

Parkay, F. W., & Stanford, B. H. (2010). *Becoming a teacher* (8th ed.). Upper Saddle River, NJ: Prentice Hall.

Park, D., & Reuter-Lorenz, P. (2009). The adaptive brain: Aging and neurocognitive scaffolding. *Annual Review of Psychology* (Vol. 60). Palo Alto, CA: Annual Reviews.

Park, D. W., Baek, K., Kim, J. R., Lee, J. J., Ryu, S. H., Chin, B. R., & Baek, S. H. (2009). Resveratrol inhibits foam cell formation via NADPH oxidase 1-mediated reactive oxygen species and monocyte chemotactic protein-1. *Experimental Molecular Medicine, 41,* 171–179.

Park, M. J., Mulye, T. P., Adams, S. H., Brindis, C. D., & Irwin, C. E. (2006) The health status of young adults in the United States. *Journal of Adolescent Health, 39,* 305–317.

Park, T. R., Brooks, J. M., Chrischilles, E. A., & Bergus, G. (2008). Estimating the effect of treatment changes when treatment benefits are heterogeneous: Antibiotics and otitis media. *Value in Health, 11,* 304–314.

Parke, R. D. (1972). Some effects of punishment on childen's behavior. In W. W. Hartup (Ed.), *The young child* (Vol. 2). Washington, DC:

National Association for the Education of Young Children.

Parke, R. D. (1977). Some effects of punishment on children's behavior—revisited. In E. M. Hetherington & R. D. Parke (Eds.), *Readings in contemporary child psychology.* New York: McGraw-Hill.

Parke, R. D., & Buriel, R. (1998). Socialization in the family. In N. Eisenberg (Ed.), *Handbook of child psychology* (5th ed., Vol. 3). New York: Wiley.

Parke, R. D., & Buriel, R. (2006). Socialization in the family: Ethnic and ecological perspectives. In W. Damon & R. Lerner (Eds.), *Handbook of child psychology* (6th ed.). New York: Wiley.

Parke, R. D., Leidy, M. S., Schofield, T. J., Miller, M. A., & Morris, K. L. (2008). Socialization. In M. M. Haith & J. B. Benson (Eds.), *Encyclopedia of infant and early childhood development.* Oxford, UK: Elsevier.

Parkin, D. M. (2009). Is the recent fall in incidence of post-menopausal breast cancer in UK related to changes in use of hormone replacement therapy? *European Journal of Cancer, 45,* 1649–1653.

Parlade, M. V., Messinger, D. S., Delgado, C. D., Kaiser, M. Y., Van Hecke, A. V., & Mundy, P. C. (2009). Anticipatory smiling: Linking early affective communication and social outcome. *Infant Behavior and Development, 32,* 33–43.

Partnership for a Drug-Free America. (2005). *Partnership Attitude Tracking Study.* New York: Author.

Pascalls, O., & Kelly, D. J. (2008). Face processing. In M. M. Haith & J. B. Benson (Eds.), *Encyclopedia of infant and early childhood development.* Oxford, UK: Elsevier.

Pasman, H. R., & others. (2009). Policy statements and practice guidelines for medical end-of-life decisions in Dutch health care institutions: Developments in the past decade. *Health Policy, 92,* 79–88.

Patel, S. R., & Hu, F. B. (2008). Short sleep duration and weight gain: A systematic review. *Obesity, 16,* 643–653.

Patrick, M. E., Abar, C., & Maggs, J. L. (2009). Drinking, adolescent. In D. Carr (Ed.), *Encyclopedia of the life course and human development.* Boston: Gale Cengage.

Patterson, C. J. (2004). What differences does a civil union make? Changing pubic policies and the experiences of same-sex couples: Comment on Solomon, Rothblum, and Balsam (2004). *Journal of Family Psychology, 18,* 287–289.

Patterson, C. J. (2009). Lesbian and gay parents and their children: A social science perspective. *Nebraska Symposium on Motivation, 54,* 147–182.

Patterson, C. J., & Hastings, P. D. (2003). Socialization in the context of family diversity. In J. E. Grusec & P. D. Hastings (Eds.), *Handbook of socialization.* New York: Guilford.

Paul, E. L., McManus, B., & Hayes, A. (2000). "Hookups": Characteristics and correlates of college students' spontaneous and anonymous sexual experiences. *The Journal of Sexual Research, 37,* 76–88.

Paul, P. (2003, Sept/Oct). The PermaParent trap. *Psychology Today, 36* (5), 40–53.

Pauley, S., Kopecky, B., Beisel, K., Soukup, G., & Fritzsch, B. (2008). Stem cells and molecular strategies to restore hearing. *Panminerva Medicine, 50,* 41–53.

Paulhus, D. L. (2008). Birth order. In M. M. Haith & J. B. Benson (Eds.), *Encyclopedia of infant and early childhood development.* Oxford, UK: Elsevier.

Pauli-Pott, U., Friedl, S., Hinney, A., & Hebebrand, J. (2009). Serotonin transporter gene polymorphism (5-HTTLPR), environmental conditions, and developing negative emotionality and fear in early childhood. *Journal of Neural Transmission, 116,* 503–512.

Paus, T. (2009). Brain development. In R. M. Lerner & L. Steinberg (Eds.), *Handbook of adolescent psychology* (3rd ed.). New York: Wiley.

Paus, T., Toro, R., Leonard, G., Lerner, J. V., Lerner, R. M., Perron, M., Pike, G. B., Richer, L., Steinberg, L., Veillete, S., & Pausova, Z. (2008). Morphological properties of the action-observation cortical network in adolescents with low and high resistance to peer influence. *Social Neuroscience, 3,* 303–316.

Pavone, C., Curto, F., Anello, G., Serretta, V., Almasio, P. L., & Pavone-Macaluso, M. (2008). Prospective, randomized crossover comparison of sublingual apopmorphine (3 mg) with oral sildenafil (50 mg) for male erectile dysfunction. *Journal of Urology, 179* (Suppl. 5), S92–S94.

Payer, L. (1991). The menopause in various cultures. In H. Burger & M. Boulet (Eds.), *A portrait of menopause.* Park Ridge, NJ: Parthenon.

Paz-Alonso, P. M., Larson, R. P., Castelli, P., Alley, D., & Goodman, G. S. (2009). Memory development: Emotion, stress, and trauma. In M. Courage & N. Cowan (Eds.), *The development of memory in infancy and childhood.* New York: Psychology Press.

Pearson, N., Biddle, S. J., & Gorely, T. (2009). Family correlates of fruit and vegetable consumption in children and adolescents: A systematic review. *Public Health Nutrition, 12,* 267–283.

Pederson, D. R., & Moran, G. (1996). Expressions of the attachment relationship outside of the Strange Situation. *Child Development, 67,* 915–927.

Pedroso, F. S. (2008). Reflexes. In M. H. Haith & J. B. Benson (Eds.), *Encyclopedia of infant and early childhood development.* Oxford, UK: Elsevier.

Peek, M. K. (2009). Marriage in later life. In D. Carr (Ed.), *Encyclopedia of the life course and human development.* Boston: Gale Cengage.

Peets, K., Hodges, E. V. E., & Salmivalli, C. (2008). Affect-congruent social cognitive evaluations and behaviors. *Child Development, 79,* 170–185.

Pei, J. R., Rinaldi, C. M., Rasmussen, C., Massey, V., & Massey, D. (2008). Memory patterns of acquisition and retention of verbal and nonverbal information in children with fetal alcohol spectrum disorders. *Canadian Journal of Clinical Pharmacology, 15,* e44–e56.

Pena, E., & Bedore, J. A. (2009). Bilingualism. In R. G. Schwartz (Ed.), *Handbook of child language disorders.* Clifton, NJ: Psychology Press.

Pepeu, G., & Giovannini, M. G. (2009). Cholinesterase inhibitors and beyond. *Current Alzheimer Research, 6,* 86–96.

Peplau, L. A., & Fingerhut, A. (2007). The close relationships of lesbians and gay men. *Annual Review of Psychology* (Vol. 58). Palo Alto, CA: Annual Reviews.

Peplau, L. A., Fingerhut, A., & Beals, K. P. (2004). Sexuality in the relationships of lesbians and gay men. In J. H. Harvey & K. Wenzel (Eds.), *The handbook of sexuality in close relationships.* Mahwah, NJ: Erlbaum.

Perkins, D. (1994, September). Creativity by design. *Educational Leadership,* pp. 18–25.

Perls, T. T. (2007). Centenarians. In J. E. Birren (Ed.), *Encyclopedia of gerontology* (2nd ed.). San Diego: Academic Press.

Perrucci, C. C., & Perrucci, R. (2009). Unemployment. In D. Carr (Ed.), *Encyclopedia of the life course and human development.* Boston: Gale Cengage.

Perry, W. G. (1970). *Forms of intellectual and ethical development in the college years.* New York: Holt, Rinehart & Winston.

Persky, H. R., Dane, M. C., & Jin, Y. (2003). *The nation's report card: Writing 2002.* Washington, DC: U.S. Department of Education.

Peskin, H. (1967). Pubertal onset and ego functioning. *Journal of Abnormal Psychology, 72,* 1–15.

Peters, B. R., Litovsky, R., Parkinson, A., & Lake, J. (2007) Importance of age and post-implantation experience on speech perception measures in children with sequential bilateral cochlear implants. *Otology and Neurotology, 28,* 649–657.

Peterson, C. C. (2005). Mind and body: Concepts of human cognition, physiology and false belief in children with autism or typical development. *Journal of Autism and Developmental Disorders, 35,* 487–497.

Peterson, M. B., Wang, Q., & Willems, P. J. (2008). Sex-linked deafness. *Clinical Genetics, 73,* 14–23.

Peterson, M. J., & others. (2009). Physical activity as a preventive factor for frailty: The Health, Aging, and Body Composition Study. *Journals of Gerontology A: Biological Sciences and Medical Sciences, 64,* 61–68.

Peterson, R. C., & Negash, S. (2008). Mild cognitive impairment: An overview. *CNS Spectrum, 13,* 45–53.

Petrill, S. A. (2003). The development of intelligence: Behavioral genetic approaches. In R. J. Sternberg, J. Lautrey, & T. I. Lubert (Eds.), *Models of intelligence: International perspectives.* Washington, DC: American Psychological Association.

Petrill, S. A., Kovas, Y., Hart, S. A., Thompson, L. A., & Plomin, R. (2009). The genetic and environmental etiology of high math performance in 10 year old twins. *Behavioral Genetics, 39,* 371–379.

Pew Research Center. (2008). *Pew forum on religion and public life: U.S. Religious Landscape Survey.* Washington, DC: Author.

Pfeifer, M., Goldsmith, H. H., Davidson, R. J., & Rickman, M. (2002). Continuity and change in inhibited and uninhibited children. *Child Development, 73,* 1474–1485.

Phinney, J. S. (1996). When we talk about American ethnic groups, what do we mean? *American Psychologist, 51,* 918–927.

Phinney, J. S. (2006, April). *Acculturation and adaptation of immigrant adolescents in thirteen countries.* Paper presented at the meeting of the Society for Research on Adolescence, San Francisco.

Phinney, J. S. (2008). Bridging identities and disciplines: Advances and challenges in understanding multiple identities. *New Directions for Child and Adolescent Development, 120,* 97–109.

Phinney, J. S., & Alipura, L. L. (1990). Ethnic identity in college students from four ethnic groups. *Journal of Adolescence, 13,* 171–183.

Phinney, J. S., & Ong, A. D. (2007). Conceptualization and measurement of ethnic identity: Current status and future directions. *Journal of Counseling Psychology, 54,* 271–281.

Piaget, J. (1932). *The moral judgment of the child.* New York: Harcourt Brace Jovanovich.

Piaget, J. (1954). *The construction of reality in the child.* New York: Basic Books.

Piaget, J. (1962). *Play, dreams, and imitation in childhood.* New York: W. W. Norton.

Piaget, J., & Inhelder, B. (1969). *The child's conception of space* (F. J. Langdon & J. L. Lunger, Trans.). New York: Norton.

Pierce, G. F., Lillicrap, D., Pipe, S. W., & Vandenriessche, T. (2007). Gene therapy, bioengineered clotting factors, and novel technologies for hemophilia treatment. *Journal of Thrombosis and Haemostasis, 5,* 901–906.

Pihlajamaki, M., Jauhiainen, A. M., & Soininen, H. (2009). Structural and functional MRI in mild cognitive impairment. *Current Alzheimer Research, 6,* 179–185.

Ping, H., & Hagopian, W. (2006). Environmental factors in the development of type 1 diabetes. *Reviews in Endocrine and Metabolic Disorders, 7,* 149–162.

Pinker, S. (1994). *The language instinct.* New York: HarperCollins.

Pinkhardt, E. H., Kassubek, J., Brummer, D., Koeich, M., Ludolph, A. C., Fegert, J. M., & Ludolph, A. G. (2009). Intensified testing for attention deficit hyperactivity disorder (ADHD) in girls should reduce depression and smoking in adult females and the prevalence of ADHD in the longterm. *Medical Hypotheses, 72,* 409–412.

Pinquart, M., & Sorensen, S. (2006). Gender differences in caregiver stressors, social resources, and health: An updated meta-analysis. *Journals of Gerontology B: Psychological Sciences and Social Sciences, 61,* P33–P45.

Pipe, M. (2008). Children and eyewitnesses: Memory in the forensic context. In M. Courage & N. Cowan (Eds.), *The development of memory in infancy and childhood.* Philadelphia: Psychology Press.

Pipe, M. E., & Salmon, K. (2009). Memory development and the forensic context. In M. Courage & N. Cowan (Eds.), *The development of memory in infancy and childhood.* New York: Psychology Press.

Pitkanen, T., Lyyra, A. L., & Pulkkinen L. (2005). Age of onset of drinking and the use of alcohol in adulthood: A follow-up study from age 8–42 for females and males. *Addiction, 100,* 652–661.

Pleck, J. H. (1995). The gender-role strain paradigm. In R. F. Levant & W. S. Pollack (Eds.), *A new psychology of men.* New York: Basic Books.

Plomin, R. (1999). Genetics and general cognitive ability. *Nature, 402* (Suppl.), C25–C29.

Plomin, R. (2004). Genetics and developmental psychology. *Merrill-Palmer Quarterly, 50,* 341–352.

Plomin, R., DeFries, J. C., & Fulker, D. W. (2007). *Nature and nurture during infancy and early childhood.* New York: Cambridge University Press.

Plomin, R., DeFries, J. C., McClearn, G. E., & McGuffin, P. (2009). *Behavioral genetics* (5th ed.). New York: Worth.

Pluess, M., & Belsky, J. (2009). Differential susceptibility to rearing experience: The case of childcare. *Journal of Child Psychology and Psychiatry, 50,* 396–404.

Polivy, J., Herman, C. P., Mills, J., & Brock, H. (2003). Eating disorders in adolescence. In G. Adams & M. Berzonsky (Eds.), *Blackwell handbook of adolescence.* Malden, MA: Blackwell.

Pollack, W. (1999). *Real boys.* New York: Owl Books.

Pollitt, E. P., Gorman, K. S., Engle, P. L., Martorell, R., & Rivera, J. (1993). Early supplementary feeding and cognition. *Monographs of the Society for Research in Child Development, 58* (7, Serial No. 235).

Poole, D. A., & Lindsay, D. S. (1996). *Effects of parents' suggestions, interviewing techniques, and age on young children's event reports.* Presented at the NATO Advanced Study Institute. Port de Bourgenay, France.

Popenoe, D. (2008). *Cohabitation, marriage, and child wellbeing: A cross-national perspective.* Piscataway, NJ: The National Marriage Project, Rutgers University.

Popenoe, D. (2009). *The state of our unions, 2008. Updates of social indicators: Tables and charts.* Piscataway, NJ: The National Marriage Project.

Popenoe, D., & Whitehead, B. (2006). *The state of our unions, 2006.* New Brunswick, NJ: The National Marriage Project, Rutgers University.

Posada, G. (2008). Attachment. In M. M. Haith & J. B. Benson (Eds.), *Encyclopedia of infant and early childhood development.* Oxford, UK: Elsevier.

Posada, G., Jacobs, A., Richmond, M. K., Carbonell, O. A., Alzate, G., Bustamante, M. R., & Quiceno, J. (2002). Maternal caregiving and infant security in two cultures. *Developmental Psychology, 38,* 67–78.

Posner, M. I., & Rothbart, M. K. (2007). *Educating the human brain.* Washington, DC: American Psychological Association.

Posner, M. I., & Rothbart, M. K. (2007). Research on attention networks as a model for the integration of psychological sciences. *Annual Review of Psychology, 58,* 1–23.

Potard, C., Courtois, R., & Rusch, E. (2008). The influence of peers on risky behavior during adolescence. *European Journal of Contraception and Reproductive Health Care, 13,* 264–270.

Pott, W., Albayrak, O., Hebebrand, J., & Pauli-Pott, U. (2009). Treating childhood obesity: Family background variables and the child's success in a weight-controlled intervention. *International Journal of Eating Disorders, 42,* 284–289.

Poulin, F., & Pedersen, S. (2007). Developmental changes in gender composition of friendship networks in adolescent girls and boys. *Developmental Psychology, 43,* 1484–1496.

Poulin-Dubois, D., & Graham, S. A. (2007). Cognitive processes in early word learning. In E. Hoff & M. Shatz (Eds.), *Blackwell handbook of language development.* Malden, MA: Blackwell.

Powell, J. L. (2009). Global aging. In D. Carr (Ed.), *Encyclopedia of the life course and human development.* Boston: Gale Cengage.

Powell, K. (2006). Neurodevelopment: How does the teenage brain work? *Nature, 442,* 865–867.

Power, F. C., & Higgins-D'Alessandro, A. (2008). The Just Community Approach to moral education and moral atmosphere of the school. In L. Nucci & D. Narváez (Eds.), *Handbook of moral and character education.* Clifton, NJ: Psychology Press.

Power, F. C., Narváez, D., Nuzzi, R., Lapsley, D., & Hunt, T. (Eds.). (2008) *Moral education: A handbook.* Westport, CT: Greenwood.

Pratt, C., & Bryant, P. E. (1990). Young children understand that looking leads to knowing (so long as they are looking in a single barrel). *Child Development, 61,* 973–982.

Pratt, M. W., Norris, J. E., Cressman, K., Lawford, H., & Hebblethwaite, S. (2008). Parents' stories of grandparenting concerns in the three-generational family: Generativity, optimism, and forgiveness. *Journal of Personality, 76,* 581–604.

Pratt, M. W., Norris, J. E., Hebblewaite, S., & Arnold, M. O. (2008). International transmission of values: Family generality and adolescents' narratives of parent and grandparent value teaching. *Journal of Personality, 76,* 171–198.

Preiss, D., & Sternberg, R. J. (Eds.). (2010, in press). *From genes to context: Perspectives on learning, teaching, and human development.* New York: Springer.

Pressley, M. (2003). Psychology of literacy and literacy instruction. In I. B. Weiner (Ed.), *Handbook of psychology* (Vol. 7). New York: Wiley.

Pressley, M. (2007). Achieving best practices. In L. B. Bambrell, L. M. Morrow, & M. Pressley I (Eds.), *Best practices in literacy instruction.* New York: Guilford.

Pressley, M., Allington, R., Wharton-McDonald, R., Block, C. C., & Morrow, L. M. (2001). *Learning to read: Lessons from exemplary first grades.* New York: Guilford.

Pressley, M., Cariligia-Bull, T., Deane, S., & Schneider, W. (1987). Short-term memory, verbal competence, and age as predictors of imagery instructional effectiveness. *Journal of Experimental Child Psychology, 43,* 194–211.

Pressley, M., Dolezal, S. E., Raphael, L. M., Welsh, L. M., Bogner, K., & Roehrig, A. D. (2003). *Motivating primary-grade teachers.* New York: Guilford.

Pressley, M., Mohan, L., Fingeret, L., Reffitt, K., & Raphael-Bogaert, L. R. (2007). Writing instruction in engaging and effective elementary settings. In S. Graham, C. A. MacArthur, & J. Fitzgerald (Eds.), *Best practices in writing instruction.* New York: Guilford.

Pressley, M., Raphael, L. Gallagher, D., & DiBella, J. (2004). Providence–St. Mel School: How a school that works for African-American students works. *Journal of Educational Psychology, 96,* 216–235.

Presson, J. C., & Jenner, J. C. (2008). *Biology.* New York: McGraw-Hill.

Price, C. A., & Joo, E. (2005). Exploring the relationship between marital status and women's retirement satisfaction. *International Journal of Aging and Human Development, 61,* 37–55.

Prinstein, M. J. (2007). Moderators of peer contagion: A longitudinal examination of depression socialization between adolescents and their best friends. *Journal of Clinical Child and Adolescent Psychology, 36,* 159–170.

Prinstein, M. J., & Dodge, K. A. (2008). Current issues in peer influence. In M. J. Prinstein & K. A. Dodge (Eds.), *Understanding peer influence in children and adolescents.* New York: Guilford.

Prinstein M. J., Rancourt, D., Guerry, J. D., & Browne, C. B. (2009). Peer reputations and psychological adjustment. In K. H. Rubin,

W. M. Bukowksi, & B. Laursen (Eds.), *Handbook of peer interactions, relationships, and groups.* New York: Guilford.

Print, M., Ugarte, C., Naval, C., & Mihr, A. (2008). Moral and human rights education: The contribution of the United Nations. *Journal of Moral Education, 37,* 115–132.

Prinz, J. (2009, in press). *The emotional construction of morals.* New York: Oxford University Press.

Prinz, R. J., Sanders, M. R., Shapiro, C. J., Whitaker, D. J., & Lutzker, J. R. (2009). Population-based prevention of child maltreatment: The Trip P System Population Trial. *Prevention Science, 10,* 1–12.

Provenzo, E. F. (2002). *Teaching, learning, and schooling in American culture: A critical perspective.* Boston: Allyn & Bacon.

Pruett, M. K., & Barker, R. K. (2009, in press). Effectively intervening with divorcing parents and their children: What works and how it works. In M. S. Schultz, M. K. Pruett, P. K. Kerig, & R. D. Parke (Eds.), *Feathering the nest: Couple relationships, couples interventions, and children's development.* Washington, DC: American Psychological Association.

Pryor, J. H., Hurtado, S., DeAngelo, L., Sharkness, J., Romero, L. C., Korn, W. S., & Tran, S. (2008). *The American freshman: National norms for fall 2008.* Los Angeles: Higher Education Institute, UCLA.

Pryor, J. H., Hurtado, S., Sharkness, J., & Korn, W. S. (2007). *The American freshman: National norms for fall, 2007.* Los Angeles: Higher Education Research Institute, UCLA.

Pudrovska, T. (2009). Midlife crises and transitions. In D. Carr (Ed.), *Encyclopedia of the life course and human development.* Boston: Gale Cengage.

Pujol, J., Lopez-Sala, A., Sebastian-Galles, N., Deus, J., Cardoner, N., Soriano-Mas, C., Moreno, A., & Sans, A. (2004). Delayed myelination in children with developmental delay detected by volumetric MRI. *Neuroimage, 22,* 897–903.

Pungello, E. P., Iruka, I. U., Dotterer, A. M., Mills-Koonce, R., & Reznick, J. S. (2009). The effects of socioeconomic status, race, and parenting on language development in early childhood. *Developmental Psychology, 45,* 544–557.

Putnam Investments. (2006). *Survey of the working retired.* Franklin, MA: Author.

Q

Quinn, P. C. (2009a). Concepts are not just for objects: Categorization of spatial relation information by infants. In D. H. Rakison & L. M. Oakes (Eds.), *Early category and concept development.* New York: Oxford University Press.

Quinn, P. C. (2009b, in press). Born to categorize. In U. Goswami (Ed.), *Blackwell handbook of childhood cognitive development.* (2nd ed.). Oxford, UK: Blackwell.

Quinn, P. C., & Bhatt, R. S. (2009, in press). Transfer and scaffolding of perceptual grouping occurs across organizing principles in 3- to 7-month-old infants. *Psychological Science.*

Quinn, P. C., Lee, K., Pascalls, O., & Slater, A. M. (2009, in press). Perceptual development: Face perception. In E. B. Goldstein (Ed.), *Encyclopedia of perception.* Thousand Oaks, CA: Sage.

R

Raabe, A., & Müller, W. U. (2008). Radiation exposure during pregnancy. *Neurosurgery Review, 31,* 351–352.

Rader, B., McCauley, L., & Callen, E. C. (2009). Current strategies in the diagnosis and treatment of childhood attention-deficit/hyperactivity disorder. *American Family Physician, 79,* 657–665.

Raffaelli, M., & Ontai, L. (2001). "She's sixteen years old and there's boys calling over to the house": An exploratory study of sexual socialization in Latino families. *Culture, Health, and Sexuality, 3,* 295–310.

Raffaelli, M., & Ontai, L. L. (2004). Gender socialization in Latino/a families: Results from two retrospective studies. *Sex Roles, 50,* 287–299.

Rafii, M. S., & Aisen, P. S. (2009). Recent developments in Alzheimer's disease therapeutics. *BMC Medicine, 7,* 7.

Rafla, N., Nair, M. S., & Kumar, S. (2008). Exercise in pregnancy. In J. Studd, S. L. Tan, & F. A. Cherenak (Eds.), *Progress in obstetrics and gynecology.* Oxford, UK: Elsevier.

Rah, Y., & Parke, R. D. (2008). Pathways between parent-child interactions and peer acceptance: The role of children's social information processing. *Social Development, 17,* 341–357.

Raikes, H., Pan, B. A., Luze, G., Tamis-LeMonda, C. S., Brooks-Gunn, J., Constantine, J., Tarullo, L. B., Raikes, H. A., & Rodriquez, E. T. (2006). Mother-child bookreading in low-income families: Correlates and outcomes during the first three years of life. *Child Development, 77,* 924–953.

Rakison, D. H., & Oakes, L. M. (2009). *Early category and concept development.* New York: Oxford University Press.

Ram, N., Morrelli, S., Lindberg, C., & Carstensen, L. L. (2009). From static to dynamic. The ongoing dialetic about human development. In K. W. Schaie & R. P. Abeles (Eds.), *Social structures and aging individuals: Continuing challenges.* New York: Psychology Press.

Ramey, C. T., & Campbell, F. A. (1984). Preventive education for high-risk children: Cognitive consequences of the Carolina Abecedarian Project. *American Journal of Mental Deficiency, 88,* 515–523.

Ramey, C. T., & Ramey, S. L. (1998). Early prevention and early experience. *American Psychologist, 53,* 109–120.

Ramey, C. T., Ramey, S. L., & Lanzi, R. G. (2001). Intelligence and experience. In R. J. Sternberg & E. I. Grigorenko (Eds.), *Environment effects on cognitive development.* Mahwah, NJ: Erlbaum.

Ramey, S. L. (2005). Human developmental science serving children and families: Contributions of the NICHD Study of Early Child Care. In NICHD Early Child Care Network (Eds.), *Child care and development.* New York: Guilford.

Ram, K. T., Bobby, P., Hailpern, S. M., Lo, J. C., Schocken, M., Skurnick, J., & Santoro, N. (2008). Duration of lactation is associated with lower prevalence of the metabolic syndrome in midlife—SWAN, the study of women's health across the nation. *American Journal of Obstetrics and Gynecology, 198,* e1–e6.

Ram, N., Morelli, S., Lindberg, C., & Carstensen, L. L. (2008). From static to dynamic: The ongoing dialectic about human development. In K. W. Schaie & R. P. Abeles (Eds.), *Social structures and aging individuals: Continuing challenges.* Mahwah, NJ: Erlbaum.

Ramsey-Rennels, J. L., & Langlois, J. H. (2007). How infants perceive and process faces. In A. Slater & M. Lewis (Eds.), *Introduction to infant development* (2nd ed.). Malden, MA: Blackwell.

Rapaport, S. (1994, November 28). Interview. *U.S. News & World Report,* p. 94.

Raphael, B., Taylor, M., & McAndrew, V. (2008). Women, catastrophe, and mental health. *Australia and New Zealand Journal of Psychiatry, 42,* 13–23.

Rasinski, T. V., & Padak, N. (2008). *From phonics to fluency* (2nd ed.). Boston: Allyn & Bacon.

Rasulo, D., Christensen, K., & Tomassini, C. (2005). The influence of social relations on mortality in later life: A study on elderly Danish twins. *The Gerontologist, 45,* 601–608.

Ratcliffe, S. D. (2008). *Family medicine obstetrics* (3rd ed.). Oxford, UK: Elsevier.

Rathunde, K., & Csikszentmihalyi, M. (2006). The developing person: An experiential perspective. In W. Damon & R. Lerner (Eds.), *Handbook of child psychology* (6th ed.). New York: Wiley.

Rawlins, W. K. (2009). *The compass of friendship.* Thosand Oaks, CA: Sage.

Raymo, J. M., & Sweeney, M. M. (2006). Work-family conflict and retirement preferences. *Journals of Gerontology B: Psychological Sciences and Social Sciences, 61,* S161–S169.

Ream, G. L., & Savin-Williams, R. (2003). Religious development in adolescence. In G. Adams & M. Berzonksy (Eds.), *Blackwell handbook of adolescence.* Malden, MA: Blackwell.

Reddy Thavanati, P. K., Kanala, K. R, de Dies, A. E., & Cantu Garza, J. M. (2008). Age-related correlation between antioxidant enzymes and DNA damage with smoking and body mass index. *Journals of Gerontology A: Biological Sciences and Medical Sciences, 63,* 360–364.

Reder, E. A., & Serwint, J. R. (2009). Until the last breath: Exploring the concept of hope for parents and health care professionals during a child's serious illness. *Archives of Pediatric and Adolescent Medicine, 163,* 653–657.

Redinbaugh, E. M., MacCallum, J., & Kiecolt-Glaser, J. K. (1995). Recurrent syndromal depression in caregivers. *Psychology and Aging, 10,* 358–368.

Redmond, N., & White, A. (2008). Age related macular degeneration: Visual impairment with advancing age. *British Journal of Community Nursing, 13,* 68–75.

Reeb, B. C., Fox, N. A., Nelson, C. A., & Zeanah, C. H. (2009). The effects of early institutionalization on social behavior and underlying neural correlates. In M. de Haan & M. Gunnar (Eds.), *Handbook of social developmental neuroscience.* Malden, MA: Blackwell.

Reece, E. A. (2008). Obesity, diabetes, and links to congenital defects: A review of the evidence and recommendations for intervention. *Journal of Maternal-Fetal and Neonatal Medicine, 2l,* 173–180.

Reed, D. (2009). *Balanced introduction to computer science* (2nd ed.). Upper Saddle River, NJ: Prentice Hall.

Reed, I. C. (2005). Creativity: Self-perceptions over time. *International Journal of Aging and Development, 60,* 1–18.

Reedy, M. N., Birren, J. E., & Schaie, K. W. (1981). Age and sex differences in satisfying relationships across the adult life span. *Human Development, 24,* 52–66.

Reeve, C. L., & Charles, J. E. (2008). Survey of opinions on the primacy of *g* and social consequences of ability testing: A comparison of expert and non-expert views. *Intelligence, 36,* 681–688.

Regalado, M., Sareen, H., Inkelas, M., Wissow, L. S., & Halfon, N. (2004). Parents' discipline of young children: Results from the National Survey of Early Childhood Health. *Pediatrics, 113,* 1952–1958.

Regnerus, M. D. (2001). *Making the grade: The influence of religion upon the academic performance of youth in disadvantaged communities.* Report 01-04, Center for Research on Religion and Urban Civil Society, University of Pennsylvania.

Reichstadt, J., Depp, C. A., Palinkas, L. A., Folsom, D. P., & Jeste, D. V. (2007). Building blocks of successful aging. *American Journal of Geriatric Psychiatry, 15,* 194–201.

Reid, G., Fawcett, A., Manis, F., & Siegel, L. (2009). *The SAGE handbook of dyslexia.* Thousand Oaks, CA: Sage.

Reid, P. T., & Zalk, S. R. (2001). Academic environments: Gender and ethnicity in U. S. higher education. In J. Worell (Ed.), *Encyclopedia of women and gender.* San Diego: Academic Press.

Reilly, D. E., Hastings, R. P., Vaughan, F. L., & Huws, J. C. (2008). Parental bereavement and the loss of a child with intellectual disabilities: A review of the literature. *Intellectual and Developmental Disabilities, 46,* 27–43.

Reinders, H., & Youniss, J. (2006). School-based required community service and civic development in adolescence. *Applied Developmental Science, 10,* 2–12.

Reiner, W. G., & Gearhart, J. P. (2004). Discordant sexual identity in some genetic males with cloacal exstrophy assigned to female sex at birth. *New England Journal of Medicine, 350,* 333–341.

Reis, O., & Youniss, J. (2004). Patterns of identity change and development in relationships with mothers and friends. *Journal of Adolescent Research, 19,* 31–44.

Rejeski, W. J., King A. C., Katula, J. A., Kritchevsky, S., Miller, M. E., Walkup, M. P., Glynn, N. W., Pahor, M., & LIFE investigators. (2008). Physical activity in perfrail older adults: Confidence and satisfaction related to physical function. *Journals of Gerontology B: Psychological Sciences and Social Sciences, 63,* P19–P26.

Reksten, L. E. (2009). *Sustaining extraordinary achievement.* Thousand Oaks, CA: Sage.

Rendell, P. G., McDaniel, M. A., Forbes, R. D., & Einstein, G. O. (2007). Age-related effects in prospective memory are modulated by ongoing task complexity and relation to target cue. *Neuropsychology, Development, and Cognition, Section B: Neuropsychology and Cognition, 14,* 236–256.

Repacholi, B. M., & Gopnik, A. (1997). Early reasoning about desires: Evidence from 14- and 18-month olds. *Developmental Psychology, 33,* 12–21.

Rest, J., Narváez, D., Bebeau, M., & Thoma, S. (1999). *Postconventional moral thinking: A neo-Kohlbergian approach.* Hillsdale, NJ: Erlbaum.

Rest, J. R. (1986). *Moral development: Advances in theory and research.* New York: Praeger.

Rest, J. R. (1995). *Concerns for the social-psychological development of youth and educational strategies: Report for the Kaufmann Foundation.* Minneapolis: University of Minnesota, Department of Educational Psychology.

Reuter-Lorenz, P. A., Jonides, J., Smith, E. S., Hartley, A., Miller, A., Marshuetz, C., & others. (2000). Age differences in the frontal lateralization of verbal and spatial working memory revealed by PET. *Journal of Cognitive Neuroscience, 12,* 174–187.

Reutzel, D. R., & Cooter, R. B. (2008). *Teaching children to read* (5th ed.). Upper Saddle River, NJ: Prentice Hall.

Rey-Lopez, J. P., Vicente-Rodriguez, G., Biosca, M., & Moreno, L. A. (2008). Sedentary behavior and obesity development in children and adolescents. *Nutrition, Metabolism, and Cardiovascular Diseases, 18,* 242–251.

Reyna, V., & Farley, F. (2006). Risk and rationality in adolescent decision-making: Impli-

cations for theory, practice, and public policy. *Psychological Science in the Public Interest, 7,* 1–44.

Reyna, V. F., & Rivers, S. E. (2008). Current theories of risk and decision making. *Developmental Review, 28,* 1–11.

Reynolds, M. R., Keith, T. Z., Ridley, K. P., & Patel, P. O. (2008). Sex differences in latent general and broad cognitive abilities for children and youth: Evidence from higher-order MG-MACS and MIMIC models. *Intelligence, 36,* 236–260.

Reznick, J. S. (2009). Working memory in infants and toddlers. In M. Courage & N. Cowan (Eds.), *The development of memory in infancy and childhood.* New York: Psychology Press.

Rhoades, G. K., Stanley, S. M., & Markman, H. J. (2009). The pre-engagement cohabitation effect: A replication and extension of previous findings. *Journal of Family Psychology, 23,* 107–111.

Rhodes, A. E., & Bethell, J. (2008). Suicide ideators without major depression—whom are we not reaching? *Canadian Journal of Psychiatry, 53,* 125–130.

Rholes, W. S., & Simpson, J. A. (2007). Introduction: New directions and emerging issues in adult attachment. In W. S. Rholes & J. A. Simpson (Eds.), *Adult attachment.* New York: Guilford.

Richardson, C. R., Faulkner, G., McDevitt, J., Skrinar, G. S., Hutchinson, D. S., & Piette, J. D. (2005). Integrating physical activity into mental health services for persons with serious mental illness. *Psychiatric Services, 56,* 324–331.

Richardson, E. D., & Marottoli, R. A. (2003). Visual attention and driving behaviors among community-living older persons. *Journals of Gerontology A: Biological Sciences and Medical Sciences, 58,* M832–M836.

Richardson, G. A., Goldschmidt, L., & Larkby, C. (2008). Effects of prenatal cocaine exposure on growth: A longitudinal analysis. *Pediatrics, 120,* e1017–e1027.

Richardson, G. A., Goldschmidt, L., & Willford, J. (2008). The effects of prenatal use on infant development. *Neurotoxicology and Teratology, 30,* 96–106.

Richardson, V. E. (2007). A dual process model of grief counseling: Findings from the Changing Lives of Older Couples (CLOC) Study. *Journal of Gerontological Social Work, 45,* 311–329.

Richmond, E. J., & Rogol, A. D. (2007). Male pubertal development and the role of androgen therapy. *Nature General Practice: Endocrinology and Metabolism, 3,* 338–344.

Rickards, T., Moger, S., & Runco, M. (Eds.). (2009). *The Routledge companion to creativity.* Milton Park, UK: Routledge.

Rideout, V., Roberts, D. P., & Foehr, U. G. (2005). *Generation M.* Menlo Park, CA: Kaiser Family Foundation.

Ridgeway, D., Waters, E., & Kuczaj, S. A. (1985). Acquisition of emotion-descriptive language: Receptive and productive vocabulary norms for ages 18 months to 6 years. *Developmental Psychology, 21,* 901–908.

Riesch, S. K., Gray, J., Hoefs, M., Keenan, T., Ertil, T., & Mathison, K. (2003). Conflict and conflict resolution: Parent and young teen perceptions. *Journal of Pediatric Health Care, 17,* 22–31.

Rigaud, D., Verges, B., Colas-Linhart, N., Petiet, Moukkaddem, M., Van Wymelbeke, V., & Brondel, L. (2007). Hormonal and psychological factors linked to the increased thermic effect of food in malnourished fasting anorexia nervosa. *Journal of Clinical Endocrinology and Metabolism, 92,* 1623–1629.

Riley, K. P., Snowdon, D. A., Derosiers, M. F., & Markesbery, W. R. (2005). Early life linguistic ability, late life cognitive function, and neuropathology: Findings from the Nun Study. *Neurobiology of Aging, 26,* 341–347.

Rimmer, J. H., Rauworth, A. E., Wang, E. C., Nicola, T. L., & Hill, B. (2009). A preliminary study to examine the effects of aerobic and therapeutic (nonaerobic) exercise on cardio-respiratory fitness and coronary risk reduction in stroke survivors. *Archives of Physical Medicine and Rehabilitation, 90,* 407–412.

Rimsza, M. E., & Kirk, G. M. (2005). Common medical problems of the college student. *Pediatric Clinics of North America, 52,* 9–24.

Rink, J. E. (2009). *Designing the physical education curriculum.* New York: McGraw-Hill.

Rivera, C., & Collum, E. (Eds.). (2006). *State assessment policy and practice for English language learners.* Mahwah, NJ: Erlbaum.

Rivers, S. E., Reyna, V. F., & Mills, B. (2008). Risk taking under the influence: A fuzzy-trace theory of emotion in adolescence. *Developmental Review, 28,* 107–144.

Rizvi, A. A. (2007). Management of diabetes in older adults. *American Journal of Medical Science, 333,* 35–47.

Rizzo, M. S. (1999, May 8). Genetic counseling combines science with a human touch. *Kansas City Star,* p. 3.

Robbins, G., Powers, D., & Burgess, S. (2008). *A fit way of life.* New York: McGraw-Hill.

Roberto, K. A., & Skoglund, R. R. (1996). Interactions with grandparents and great-grandparents: A comparison of activities, influences, and relationships. *International Journal of Aging and Human Development, 43,* 107–117.

Roberts, B. W., Helson, R., & Klohnen, E. C. (2002). Personality development and growth in women across 30 years: Three perspectives. *Journal of Personality, 70,* 79–102.

Roberts, B. W., Jackson, J. J., Fayard, J. V., Edmonds, G., & Meints, J. (2009, in press). Conscientiousness. In M. Leary & R. Hoyle (Eds.), *Handbook of individual differences in social behavior.* New York: Guilford.

Roberts, B. W., & Mroczek, D. (2008). Personality trait change in adulthood. *Current Directions in Psychological Science, 17,* 31–35.

Roberts, B. W., Walton, K. E., & Bogg, T. (2005). Conscientiousness and health across the life course. *Review of General Psychology, 9,* 156–168.

Roberts, B. W., Walton, K. E., & Viechtbauer, W. (2006). Pattern of mean-level change in personality traits across the life course: A meta-analysis of longitudinal studies. *Psychological Bulletin, 132,* 1–25.

Roberts, B. W., & Wood, D. (2006). Personality development in the context of the Neo-Socioanalytic Model of personality. In D. Mroczek & T. Little (Eds.), *Handbook of personality development.* Mahwah, NJ: Erlbaum.

Roberts, B. W., Wood, D., & Caspi, A. (2008). Personality development. In O. P. John, R. W. Robins, & L. A. Pervin (Eds.), *Handbook of personality: Theory and research* (3rd ed.). New York: Guilford.

Roberts, D. F., & Foehr, U. G. (2008). Trends in media use. *The Future of Children, 18* (1), 11–37.

Roberts, D. F., Henriksen, L., & Foehr, U. G. (2009). Adolescence, adolescents, and the media. In R. M. Lerner & L. Steinberg (Eds.), *Handbook of adolescent psychology* (3rd ed.). New York: Wiley.

Roberts, D., Jacobson, L., & Taylor, R. D. (1996, March). *Neighborhood characteristics, stressful life events, and African-American adolescents' adjustment.* Paper presented at the meeting of the Society for Research on Adolescence, Boston.

Roberts, J. M. (2008). The parameters of prejudice: Knowledge of ethics and age bias. *Journal of Gerontological Social Work, 50,* 65–79.

Roberts, S. B., & Rosenberg, I. (2006). Nutrition and aging: Changes in the regulation of energy metabolism with aging. *Physiology Review, 86,* 651–667.

Robins, R. W., Trzesniewski, K. H., Tracey, J. L., Potter, J., & Gosling, S. D. (2002). Age differences in self-esteem from age 9 to 90. *Psychology and Aging, 17,* 423–434.

Rochlen, A. B., McKelley, R. A., Suizzo, M.-A., & Scaringi, V. (2008). Predictors of relationship satisfaction, psychological well-being, and life-satisfaction among stay-at-home fathers. *Psychology of Men and Masculinity, 9,* 17–28.

Rode, S. S., Chang, P., Fisch, R. O., & Sroufe, L. A. (1981). Attachment patterns of infants separated at birth. *Developmental Psychology, 17,* 188–191.

Rodgers, W. (1982). Trends in reported happiness within demographically defined subgroups 1957–1978. *Social Forces, 60,* 826–842.

Rodin, J., & Langer, E. J. (1977). Long-term effects of a control-relevant intervention with the institutionalized aged. *Journal of Personality and Social Psychology, 35,* 397–402.

Rodriguez, B. L., Hines, R., & Montiel, M. (2009). Mexican-American mothers of low and middle socioeconomic status: Communication behaviors and interactive strategies during shared book reading. *Language, Speech, and Hearing Services in Schools, 40,* 271–282.

Rodriguez, E. T., Tamis-LeMonda, C. S., Spellman, M. E., Pan, B. A., Riakes, H., Lugo-Gil, J., & Luze, G. (2009, in press). The formative role of home literacy experiences across the first three years of life in children from low-income families. *Journal of Applied Developmental Psychology.*

Roese, N. J., & Summerville, A. (2005). What we regret most ... and why. *Personality and Social Psychology Bulletin, 31,* 1273–1285.

Rogers, W. A., & Fisk, A. D. (2001). Attention in cognitive aging research. In J. E. Birren & K. W. Schaie (Eds.), *Handbook of the psychology of aging* (5th ed.). San Diego: Academic Press.

Rohr, M. K., & Lang, F. R. (2009). Aging well together—a mini-review. *Gerontology, 55,* 333–343.

Rohrer, J. F., Pierce, J. R., & Blackburn, C. (2005). Lifestyle and mental health. *Preventive Medicine, 40,* 438–443.

Roisman, G. I., Aguilar, B., & Egeland, B. (2004). Antisocial behavior in the transition to adulthood: The independent and interactive roles of developmental history and emerging developmental tasks. *Developmental and Psychopathology, 16,* 857–872.

Roisman, G. I., Clausell, E., Holland, A., Fortuna, K., & Elieff, C. (2008). Adult romantic relationships as contexts of human development: A multimethod comparison of same-sex couples with opposite-sex dating, engaged, and married dyads. *Developmental Psychology, 44,* 91–101.

Rönnlund, M., Nyberg, L., Bäckman, L., & Nilsson, L. G. (2005). Stability, growth, and decline in adult life span development of declarative memory: Cross-sectional and longitudinal data from a population-based study. *Psychology and Aging, 20,* 3–18.

Rook, K. S., Mavandadi, S., Sorkin, D. H., & Zettel, L. A. (2007). Optimizing social relationships as a resource for health and wellbeing in later life. In C. M. Aldwin, C. L. Park, & A. Spiro (Eds.), *Handbook of health psychology and aging.* New York: Guilford.

Rose, A. J., Carlson, W., & Waller, E. M. (2007). Prospective associations of co-rumination with friendship and emotional adjustment: Considering the socioemotional trade-offs of co-rumination. *Developmental Psychology, 43,* 1019–1031.

Rose, A. J., & Smith, R. L. (2009). Sex differences is peer relationships. In K. H. Rubin, W. M. Bukowski, & B. Laursen (Eds.), *Handbook of peer interactions, relationships, and groups.* New York: Guilford.

Rosenberg, L., Kottorp, A., Winblad, B., & Nygard, L. (2009). Perceived difficulty in everyday technology use among older adults with or without cognitive deficits. *Scandinavian Journal of Occupational Therapy, 16,* 1–11.

Rosenblith, J. F. (1992). *In the beginning* (2nd ed.). Newbury Park, CA: Sage.

Rosenblum, G. D., & Lewis, M. (2003). Emotional development in adolescence. In G. Adams & M. Berzonsky (Eds.), *Blackwell handbook of adolescence.* Malden, MA: Blackwell.

Rosenfeld, A., & Stark, E. (1987, May). The prime of our lives. *Psychology Today*, pp. 62–72.

Rosenfeld, R. G., & Bakker, B. (2008). Compliance and persistence in pediatric and adult patients receiving growth hormone therapy. *Endocrine Practice, 14,* 143–154.

Rosengard, C. (2009). Confronting the intendedness of adolescent rapid repeat pregnancy. *Journal of Adolescent Health, 44,* 5–6.

Rosenheck, R. (2008). Fast food consumption and increased caloric intake: A systematic review of a trajectory towards weight gain and obesity risk. *Obesity Reviews, 9,* 535–547.

Rosenkoetter, L. I., Rosenkoetter, S. E., & Acock, A. C. (2009). Television violence: An intervention to reduce its impact of children. *Journal of Applied Developmental Psychology, 30,* 381–397.

Rosenstein, D., & Oster, H. (1988). Differential facial responses to four basic tastes in newborns. *Child Development, 59,* 1555–1568.

Rose, S. A., Feldman, J. F., & Wallace, I. F. (1992). Infant information processing in relation to six-year cognitive outcomes. *Child Development, 63,* 1126–1141.

Roskos, K. A., & Christie, J. F. (Eds.). (2007). *Play and literacy in early childhood.* Mahwah, NJ: Erlbaum.

Rosmarin, D. H., Krumrei, E. J., & Andersson, G. (2009). Religion as a predictor of psychological distress in two religious communities. *Cognitive Behavior Therapy, 38,* 54–64.

Rosnati, R., Montirosso, R., & Barni, D. (2008). Behavioral and emotional problems among Italian international adoptees and non-adopted children: Father's and mother's reports. *Journal of Family Psychology, 22,* 541–549.

Rosnow, R. L., & Rosenthal, R. (2008). *Beginning behavioral research* (6th ed.). Upper Saddle River, NJ: Prentice Hall.

Rospenda, K. M., Richman, J. A., & Shannon, C. A. (2009). Prevalence and mental health correlates of harassment and discrimination in the workplace: Results from a national study. *Journal of Interpersonal Violence, 24,* 819–843.

Ross, E., & Ross, B. C. (2006). The identification of ADHD. *Infants and Young Children, 19,* 164–167.

Ross, J. L., & others. (2008). Cognitive and motor development during childhood in boys with Klinefelter syndrome. *American Journal of Medical Genetics A, 146,* 708–719.

Ross, K., Handel, P. J., Clark, E. M., & Vander Wal, J. S. (2009, in press). The relationship between religion and religious coping: Religious coping as a moderator between coping and adjustment. *Journal of Religion and Health.*

Ross, H., & Howe, N. (2009). Family influences on children's peer relationships. In K. H. Rubin, W. M. Bukowksi, & B. Laursen (Eds.), *Handbook of peer interactions, relationships, and groups.* New York: Guilford.

Rossi, A. S. (1989). A life-course approach to gender, aging, and intergenerational relations. In K. W. Schaie & C. Schooler (Eds.), *Social structure and aging.* Hillsdale, NJ: Erlbaum.

Rossi, S., Miniussi, C., Pasqualetti, P., Babiloni, C., Rossini, P. M., & Cappa, S. F. (2005). Age-related functional changes of prefrontal cortex in long-term memory: A repetitive transcranial magnetic stimulation study. *Journal of Neuroscience, 24,* 7939–7944.

Rossiter, M. (2009). Possible selves and career transition: Implications for serving nontraditional students. *Journal of Continuing Higher Education, 57,* 61–71.

Rossit, S., & Harvey, M. (2008). Age-related differences in corrected and inhibited pointing movements. *Experimental Brain Research. 185,* 1–10.

Roth, J. L., Brooks-Gunn, J., Murray, L., & Foster, W. (1998). Promoting healthy adolescents: Synthesis of youth development program evaluations. *Journal of Research on Adolescence, 8,* 423–459.

Rothbart, M. K. (2004). Temperament and the pursuit of an integrated developmental psychology. *Merrill-Palmer Quarterly, 50,* 492–505.

Rothbart, M. K. (2007). Temperament, development, and personality. *Current Directions in Psychological Science, 16,* 207–212.

Rothbart, M. K., & Bates, J. E. (2006). Temperament. In W. Damon & R. Lerner (Eds.), *Handbook of child psychology* (6th ed.). New York-Wiley.

Rothbart, M. K., & Gartstein, M. A. (2008). Temperament. In M. M. Haith & J. B. Benson (Eds.), *Encyclopedia of infant and early childhood development.* Oxford, UK: Elsevier.

Rothbaum, F., Poll, M., Azuma, H., Miyake, K., & Weisz, J. (2000). The development of close relationships in Japan and the United States: Paths of symbiotic harmony and generative tension. *Child Development, 71,* 1121–1142.

Rothbaum, F., & Trommsdorff, G. (2007). Do roots and wings complement or oppose one another?: The socialization of relatedness and autonomy in cultural context. In J. E. Grusec & P. D. Hastings (Eds.), *Handbook of socialization.* New York: Guilford.

Rothbaum, F., Weisz, J., Pott, M., Miyake, K., & Morelli, G. (2000). Attachment and culture: Security in the United States and Japan. *American Psychologist, 55,* 1093–1104.

Rotterman, M. (2007). Marital breakdown and subsequent depression. *Health Reports, 18,* 33–44.

Rovee-Collier, C. (1987). Learning and memory in children. In J. D. Osofsky (Ed.), *Handbook of infant development* (2nd ed.). New York: Wiley.

Rovee-Collier, C. (2004). Infant learning and memory. In U. Goswami (Ed.), *Blackwell handbook of childhood cognitive development.* Malden, MA: Blackwell.

Rovee-Collier, C. (2007). The development of infant memory. In N. Cowan & M. Courage (Eds.), *The development of memory in childhood.* Philadelphia: Psychology Press.

Rovee-Collier, C., & Cuevas, K. (2009). The development of infant memory. In M. Courage & N. Cowan (Eds.), *The development of memory in infancy and childhood.* New York: Psychology Press.

Rovers, M. M., de Kok, I. M., & Schilder, A. G. (2006). Risk factors for otitis media: An international perspective. *International Journal of Otorhinoloaryngology, 70,* 1251–1256.

Rovner, B. W., Casten, R. J., Leiby, B. E., & Tasman, W. S. (2009). Activity loss is associated with cognitive decline in age-related macular degeneration. *Alzheimer's and Dementia, 5,* 12–17.

Rowley, S. R., Kurtz-Costes, B., & Cooper, S. M. (2008). The role of schooling in ethnic minority achievement and attainment. In J. Meece and J. Eccles (Eds.), *Handbook of research on schools, schooling, and human development.* London: Routledge.

Rozzini, R., Ranhoff, A., & Trabucchi, M. (2007). Alcoholic beverage and long-term mortality in elderly people living at home. *Journals of Gerontology A: Biological Sciences and Medical Sciences, 62,* M1313–M1314.

Rubie-Davies, C. M. (2007). Classroom interactions: Exploring the practices of high- and low-expectation teachers. *British Journal of Educational Psychology, 77,* 289–306.

Rubin, K. H., Bukowski, W., & Parker, J. (2006). Peer interactions, relationships, and groups. In W. Damon & R. Lerner (Eds.), *Handbook of child psychology* (6th ed.). New York: Wiley.

Rubio-Aurioles, E., Casabé, A., Torres, L. O., Quinzaños, L., Glina, S., Filimon, I., Kopernicky, V., & Leñero, E. (2008). Efficacy and safety of tadalafil in the treatment of Latin American men with erectile dysfunction: Results of integrated analysis. *Journal of Sexual Medicine, 5,* 1965–1976.

Ruble, D. N., & Martin, C. (2010). Gender-role development. *Annual Review of Psychology* (Vol. 61). Palo Alto, CA: Annual Reviews.

Ruble, D. N., Martin, C. L., & Berenbaum, S. A. (2006). Gender development. In W. Damon & R. Lerner (Eds.), *Handbook of child psychology* (6th ed.). New York: Wiley.

Ruff, H. A., & Capozzoli, M. C. (2003). Development of attention and distractibility in the first 4 years of life. *Developmental Psychology, 39,* 877–890.

Ruffman, T., Slade, L., & Crowe, E. (2002). The relation between children's and mothers' mental state language and theory-of-mind understanding. *Child Development, 73,* 734–751.

Rumberger, R. W. (1995). Dropping out of middle school: A multilevel analysis of students and schools. *American Education Research Journal, 3,* 583–625.

Runco, M. (Ed.). (2010, in press). *Encyclopedia of creativity.* New York: Elsevier.

Rupp, D. E., Vodanovich, S. J., & Crede, M. (2005). The multidimensional nature of ageism: Construct validity and group differences. *Journal of Social Psychology, 145,* 335–362.

Russ, S., Regalado, M., & Halfon, N. (2008). Healthcare. In M. M. Haith & J. B. Benson (Eds.), *Encyclopedia of infant and early childhood development.* Oxford, UK: Elsevier.

Russell, L. B., & Rice, D. P. (2009). Health care use, later life. In D. Carr (Ed.), *Encyclopedia of the life course and human development.* Gale Cengage.

Ryan-Harshman, M., & Aldoori, W. (2008). Folic acid and prevention of neural tube defects. *Canadian Family Physician, 54,* 36–38.

Rypma, B., Eldreth, D. A., & Rebbechi, D. (2007). Age-related differences in activation-performance relations in delayed-response tasks: A multiple component analyses. *Cortex, 43,* 65–76.

S

Saarni, C. (1999). *The development of emotional competence.* New York: Guilford.

Saarni, C., Campos, J., Camras, L. A., & Witherington, D. (2006). Emotional development. In W. Damon & R. Lerner (Eds.), *Handbook of child psychology* (6th ed.). New York: Wiley.

Sabbagh, K. (2009). *Remembering our childhood: How memory betrays us.* New York: Oxford University Press.

Sabbagh, M. A., Xu, F., Carlson, S. M., Moses, L. J., & Lee, K. (2006). The development of executive functioning and theory of mind: A comparison of Chinese and U. S. preschoolers. *Psychological Science, 17,* 74–81.

Sabia, S., Fournier, A., Mesrine, S., Boutron-Rualt, M. C., & Clavel-Chapelon, F. (2008). Risk factors for onset of menopausal symptoms: Results from a large cohort study. *Maturitas, 60,* 108–121.

Sabini, J. (1995). *Social psychology* (2nd ed.). New York: Norton.

Sabol, W. J., Coulton, C. J., & Korbin, J. F. (2004). Building community capacity for violence prevention. *Journal of Interpersonal Violence, 19,* 322–340.

Sachs, J. (2009). Communication development in infancy. In J. Berko Gleason & N. B. Ratner (Eds.), *The development of language* (7th ed.). Boston: Allyn & Bacon.

Sackett, P. R., Hardison, C. M., & Cullen, M. J. (2005). On interpreting research on stereotype threat and test performance. *American Psychologist, 60,* 271–272.

Sadeh, A. (2008). Sleep. In M. M. Haith & J. B. Benson (Eds.), *Encyclopedia of infant and early childhood development.* Oxford, UK: Elsevier.

Saffran, J. R., Werker, J. F., & Werner, L. A. (2006). The infant's auditory world: Hearing, speech, and the beginnings of language. In W. Damon & R. Lerner (Eds.), *Handbook of child psychology* (6th ed.). New York: Wiley.

Sahni, S., Hannan, M. T., Gagnon, D., Blumberg, J., Cupples, L. A., Kiel, D. P., & Tucker, K. L. (2009, in press). Protective effect of total and supplemental vitamin C intake on the risk of hip fracture—a 17-year follow-up from the Framingham Osteoporosis Study. *Osteoporosis International.*

Saint Onge, J. M. (2009). Mortality. In D. Carr (Ed.), *Encyclopedia of the life course and human development.* Gale Cengage.

Sakamaki, R., Toyama, K., Amamoto, R., Liu, C. J., & Shinfuku, N. (2005). Nutritional knowledge, food habits, and health attitude of Chinese university students—a cross-sectional study. *Nutrition Journal, 9,* 4.

Sakamoto, Y., & others. (2009). Effect of exercise, aging, and functional capacity on acute secretory immunoglobulin: A response in elderly people over 75 years of age. *Geriatrics and Gerontology International, 9,* 81–88.

Sakraida, T. J. (2005). Divorce transition differences of midlife women. *Issues in Mental Health Nursing, 26,* 225–249.

Salazar-Martinez, E., Allen, B., Fernandez-Ortega, C, Torres-Mejia, G., Galal, O., & Lazcano-Ponce, E. (2006). Overweight and obesity status among adolescents from Mexico and Egypt. *Archives of Medical Research, 37,* 535–542.

Salmivalli, C., & Peets, K. (2009). Bullies, victims, and bully-victim relationships in middle childhood and adolescence. In K. H. Rubin, W. M. Bukowski, & B. Laursen (Eds.), *Handbook of peer interactions, relationships, and groups.* New York: Guilford.

Salmon, J., Campbell, K. J., & Crawford, D. A. (2006). Television viewing habits associated with obesity risk factors: A survey of Melbourne schoolchildren. *Medical Journal of Australia, 184,* 64–67.

Salovey, P., & Mayer, J. D. (1990). Emotional intelligence. *Imagination, Cognition, and Personality, 9,* 185–211.

Salthouse, T. A. (1988). Cognitive aspects of motor functioning. *Annals of the New York Academy of Sciences, 515,* 33–41.

Salthouse, T. A. (1991). *Theoretical perspectives on cognitive aging.* Hillsdale, NJ: Erlbaum.

Salthouse, T. A. (1994). The nature of the influence of speed on adult age differences in cognition. *Developmental Psychology 30,* 240–259.

Salthouse, T. A. (2007). Reaction time. In J. E. Birren (Ed.), *Encyclopedia of gerontology* (2nd ed.). San Diego: Academic Press.

Salthouse, T. A. (2009). When does age-related cognitive decline begin? *Neurobiology of Aging, 30,* 507–514.

Sanchez-Johnsen, L. A., Fitzgibbon, M. L., Martinovich, Z., Stolley, M. R., Dyer, A. R., **& Van Horn, L.** (2004). Ethnic differences in correlates of obesity between Latin-American and black women. *Obesity Research, 12,* 652–660.

Sando, S. B., & others. (2008). APOE episolon 4 lowers age at onset and is a high risk factor for Alzheimer's disease: A case-control study from central Norway. *BMC Neurology, 8,* 9.

Sands, R. G., & Goldberg-Glen, R. S. (2000). Factors associated with stress among grandparents raising their grandchildren. *Family Relations, 49,* 97–105.

Sanger, M. N. (2008). What we need to prepare teachers for the moral nature of their work. *Journal of Curriculum Studies, 40,* 169–185.

Sangree, W. H. (1989). Age and power: Life-course trajectories and age structuring of power relations in East and West Africa. In D. I. Kertzer & K. W. Schaie (Eds.), *Age structuring in comparative perspective.* Hillsdale, NJ: Erlbaum.

Sanson, A., & Rothbart, M. K. (1995). Child temperament and parenting. In M. H. Bornstein (Ed.), *Handbook of parenting* (Vol. 4). Hillsdale, NJ: Erlbaum.

Santelli, J., Sandfort, T. G., & Orr, M. (2009). U.S./European differences in condom use. *Journal of Adolescent Health, 44,* 306.

Santelli, J. S., Abraido-Lanza, A. F., & Meinikas, A. J. (2009). Migration, acculturation, and sexual and reproductive health of Latino adolescents. *Journal of Adolescent Health, 44,* 3–4.

Santelli, J. S., Lindberg, L. D., Finer, L. B., & Sing, S. (2007). Explaining recent declines in adolescent pregnancy in the United States: The contribution of abstinence and contraceptive use. *American Journal of Public Health, 97,* 150–156.

Santo, J. L., Portuguez, M. W., & Nunes, M. L. (2009). Cognitive and behavioral status of low birth weight preterm children raised in a developing country at preschool age. *Journal of Pediatrics, 85,* 35–41.

Santrock, J. W., & Halonen, J. A. (2009). *Your guide to college success* (6th ed.). Belmont, CA: Wadsworth.

Santrock, J. W., Sitterle, K. A., & Warshak, R. A. (1988). Parent-child relationships in stepfather families. In P. Bronstein & C. P. Cowan (Eds.), *Fatherhood today: Men's changing roles in the family.* New York: Wiley.

Sarkisian, N., & Gerstel, N. (2008). Till marriage do us part: Adult children's relationship with their parents. *Journal of Marriage and the Family, 70,* 360–376.

Sarrel, P., & Masters, W. (1982). Sexual molestation of men by women. *Archives of Human Sexuality, 11,* 117–131.

Sausenthaler, S., Kompauer, I., Mielck, A., Borte, M., Herbarth, O., Schaaf, B., von Berg, A., & Heinrich, J. (2007). Impact of parental education and income equality on children's food intake. *Public Health Nutrition, 10,* 24–33.

Sawyer, R. K., & DeZutter, S. (2007). Improvisation: A lens for play and literacy research. In K. A. Roskos & J. F. Christie (Eds.), *Play and literacy in early childhood.* Mahwah, NJ: Erlbaum.

Sayer, L. C. (2006). Economic aspects of divorce and relationship dissolution. In M. A. Fine & J. H. Harvey (Eds.), *Handbook of divorce and relationship dissolution.* Mahwah, NJ: Erlbaum.

Scarr, S. (1984, May). Interview. *Psychology Today,* pp. 59–63.

Scarr, S. (1993). Biological and cultural diversity: The legacy of Darwin for development. *Child Development, 64,* 1333–1353.

Scarr, S., & Weinberg, R. A. (1983). The Minnesota adoption studies: Genetic differences and malleability. *Child Development, 54,* 182–259.

Schachter, E. P., & Ventura, J. J. (2008). Identity agents: Parents as active and reflective participants in their children's identity formation. *Journal of Research on Adolescence, 18,* 449–476.

Schaffer, H. R. (1996). *Social development.* Cambridge, MA: Blackwell.

Schaie, K. W. (1977). Toward a stage theory of adult cognitive development. *Human Development, 8,* 129–138.

Schaie, K. W. (1983). Consistency and changes in cognitive functioning of the young-old and old-old. In M. Bergner, U. Lehr, E. Lang, & R. Schmidt-Scherzer (Eds.), *Aging in the eighties and beyond.* New York: Springer.

Schaie, K. W. (1994). The life course of adult intellectual abilities. *American Psychologist, 49,* 304–313.

Schaie, K. W. (1996). *Intellectual development in adulthood: The Seattle Longitudinal Study.* New York: Cambridge University Press.

Schaie, K. W. (2000). The impact of longitudinal studies on understanding development from young adulthood to old age. *International Journal of Behavioral Development, 24,* 257–266.

Schaie, K. W. (2000). Unpublished review of J. W. Santrock's *Life-span development,* 8th ed. (New York: McGraw-Hill).

Schaie, K. W. (2005). *Developmental changes in intelligence: The Seattle Longitudinal Study.* New York: Oxford University Press.

Schaie, K. W. (2007). Generational differences: Age-period-cohort. In J. E. Birren (Ed.), *Encyclopedia of gerontology* (2nd ed.). San Diego: Academic Press.

Schaie, K. W. (2008a). Historical processes and patterns of cognitive aging, In S. M. Hofer & D. F. Alwin (Eds.), *Handbook on cognitive aging: Interdisciplinary perspective.* Thousand Oaks, CA: Sage.

Schaie, K. W. (2008b). A lifespan developmental perspective of psychological aging. In K. Laidlaw & B. G. Knight (Eds.), *The handbook of emotional disorders in late life: Assessment and treatment.* Oxford, UK: Oxford University Press.

Schaie, K. W. (2009, in press). "When does age-related cognitive decline begin?" Salthouse again reifies the "cross-sectional fallacy." *Neurobiology of Aging.*

Scheibe, S., Freund, A. M., & Baltes, P. B. (2007). Toward a developmental psychology of Sehnsucht (life-longings): The optimal (utopian) life. *Developmental Psychology, 43,* 778–795.

Scher, A., & Harel, J. (2008). Separation and stranger anxiety. In M. M. Haith & J. B. Benson (Eds.), *Encyclopedia of infant and early childhood development.* Oxford, UK: Elsevier.

Schiavone, F., Charton, R. A., Barrick, T. R., Morris, R. G., & Markus, H. G. (2009). Imaging age-related cognitive decline: A comparison of diffusion tensor and magnetization transfer fMRI. *Journal of Magnetic Resonance Imaging, 29,* 23–30.

Schieber, F. (2006). Vision and aging. In J. E. Birren & K. W. Schaie (Eds.), *Handbook of the psychology of aging* (6th ed.). San Diego: Academic Press.

Schieffelin, B. (2005). *The give and take of everyday life.* Tucson, AZ: Fenestra.

Schiff, W. J. (2009). *Nutrition for healthy living.* New York: McGraw-Hill.

Schiffman, S. S. (2007). Smell and taste. In J. B. Birren (Ed.), *Encyclopedia of gerontology* (2nd ed.). San Diego: Academic Press.

Schindler, A. E. (2006). Climacteric symptoms and hormones. *Gynecological Endocrinology, 22,* 151–154.

Schlegal, A. (2009). Cross-cultural issues in the study of adolescent development. In R. M. Lerner & L. Steinberg (Eds.), *Handbook of adolescent psychology* (3rd ed.). New York: Wiley.

Schlegel, M. (2000). All work and play. *Monitor on Psychology, 31* (11), 50–51.

Schmidt, J., Shumow, L., & Kacker, H. (2007). Adolescents' participation in service activities and its impact on academic, behavioral, and civic outcomes. *Journal of Youth and Adolescence, 36,* 127–140.

Schmidt, L. A., Miskovic, V., Boyle, M. H., & Saigal, S. (2008). Shyness and timidity in young adults who were born at extremely low birth weight. *Pediatrics, 122,* e181–e187.

Schmidt, M. E., & Vandewater, E. A. (2008). Media and attention, cognition, and school achievement. *The Future of Children, 18* (1), 64–85.

Schmidt, S., & others. (2006). Cigarette smoking strongly modifies the association of LOC387715 and age-related macular degeneration. *American Journal of Human Genetics, 78,* 852–864.

Schmidt, U. (2003). Aetiology of eating disorders in the 21st century: New answers to old questions. *European Child and Adolescent Psychiatry, 12* (Suppl. 1), 1130–1137.

Schneider, W. (2004). Memory development in childhood. In P. Smith & C. Hart (Eds.), *Blackwell handbook of childhood cognitive development.* Maiden, MA: Blackwell.

Schneider, W., & Pressley, M. (1997). *Memory development between two and twenty.* Mahwah, NJ: Erlbaum.

Schoen, R., Landale, N. S., & Daniels, K. (2007). Family transitions in young adulthood. *Demography, 44,* 807–820.

Schoen, R., & Standish, N. (2001). "The retrenchment of marriage: Results from marital status life tables for the United States, 1995." *Population and Development Review, 27,* 553–563.

Schofield, H. L., Bierman, K. L., Heinrichs, B., Nix, R. L., & the Conduct Problems Prevention Research Group. (2008). Predicting early sexual activity with behavior problems exhibited at school entry and in early adolescence. *Journal of Abnormal Child Psychology, 36,* 1175–1180.

Scholnick, E. K. (2008). Reasoning in early development. In M. M. Haith & J. B. Benson (Eds.), *Encyclopedia of infant and early childhood development.* Oxford, UK: Elsevier.

Schooler, C. (2007). Use it—and keep it, longer, probably: A reply to Salthouse (2006). *Perspectives on Psychological Science, 2,* 24–29.

Schooler, C., Mulatu, S., & Oates, G. (1999). The continuing effects of substantively complex work on the intellectual functioning of older workers. *Psychology and Aging, 14,* 483–506.

Schoon, I., Bynner, J., Joshi, H., Parsons, S., Wiggins, R. D., & Sacker, A. (2002). The influence of context, timing, and duration of risk experiences for the passage from childhood to midadulthood. *Child Development, 73,* 1486–1504.

Schouten, A. P., Valkenburg, P. M., & Peter, J. (2007). Precursors and underlying processes of adolescents' online self-disclosure: Developing and testing an "Internet-attribute-perception" model. *Media Psychology, 10,* 292–314.

Schreiber, L. R. (1990). *The parents' guide to kids' sports.* Boston: Little, Brown.

Schulenberg, J. E., Maggs, J. L., Steinman, K. J., & Zucker, R. A. (2001). Development matters: Taking the long view on substance abuse etiology and intervention during adolescence. In P. M. Monti, S. M. Colbyk, & T. A. O'Leary (Eds.), *Adolescents, alcohol, and substance abuse.* New York: Guilford.

Schulenberg, J. E., & Zarrett, N. R. (2006). Mental health during emerging adulthood: Continuities and discontinuities in course, content, and meaning. In J. J. Arnett & J. Tanner (Eds.), *Advances in emerging adulthood.* Washington, DC: American Psychological Association.

Schultz, D. P., & Schultz, S. E. (2009). *Theories of personality* (9th ed.). Belmont, CA: Wadsworth.

Schultz, K. A., & Adams, G. A. (Eds.). (2007). *Aging and work in the 21st century.* Mahwah, NJ: Erlbaum.

Schultz, R., & Curnow, C. (1988). Peak performance and age among super athletes: Track and field, swimming, baseball, tennis, and golf. *Journal of Gerontology, 43,* P113–P120.

Schulz, R., Hebert, R., & Boerner, K. (2008). Bereavement after caregiving. *Geriatrics, 63,* 20–22.

Schunk, D. H. (2008). *Learning theories: An educational perspective* (5th ed.). Upper Saddle River, NJ: Prentice Hall.

Schunk, D. H., Pintrich, P. R., & Meece, J. L. (2008). *Motivation in education: Theory, research, and applications* (3rd ed.). Upper Saddle River, NJ: Prentice Hall.

Schwartz, R. G., & Tropper, B. (2009). Neurobiology. In R. G. Schwartz (Ed.), *Handbook of child language disorders*. Clifton, NJ: Psychology Press.

Schweinhart, L. J., Montie, J., Xiang, Z., Barnett, W. S., Belfield, C. R., & Mores, M. (2005). *Lifetime effects: The High/Scope Perry Preschool Study Through Age 40*. Ypsilanti, MI: High/Scope Press.

Scialfa, C. T., & Kline, D. W. (2007). Vision. In J. E. Birren (Ed.), *Encyclopedia of gerontology* (2nd ed.). San Diego: Academic Press.

Scourfield, J., Van den Bree, M., Martin, N., & McGuffin, P. (2004). Conduct problems in children and adolescents: A twin study. *Archives of General Psychiatry, 61*, 489–496.

Seale, C. (2009). Legalization of euthanasia or physician-assisted suicide: Survey of doctors' attitudes. *Palliative Medicine, 23*, 205–212.

Seeman, T. E., Berkman, L. F., Charpentier, P. A., Balzer, D. G., Albert, M. S., & Tinetti, M. E. (1995). Behavioral and psychological predictors of physical performance: MacArthur Studies of Successful Aging. *Journals of Gerontology: A Biological Sciences and Medical Sciences, 50*, M177–M183.

Segal, B. (2007). Addiction: General. In J. E. Birren (Ed.), *Encyclopedia of gerontology* (2nd ed.). San Diego: Academic Press.

Segovia, A., Arco, A. D., & Mora, F. (2009). Environmental enrichment, prefrontal cortex, stress, and aging of the brain. *Journal of Neural Transmission, 116*, 1007–1016.

Seidenfeld, M. E., Sosin, E., & Rickert, V. I. (2004). Nutrition and eating disorders in adolescents. *Mt. Sinai Journal of Medicine, 71*, 155–161.

Seifer, R. (2001). Socioeconomic status, multiple risks, and development of intelligence. In R. J. Sternberg & E. L. Grigorenko (Eds.), *Environmental effects on cognitive abilities*. Mahwah, NJ: Erlbaum.

Sellner, J., Buonomano, R., Nedeltchev, K., Findling, O., Schroth, G., Surbek, D. V., & Leib, S. L. (2009). A case of maternal herpes simplex virus encephalitis during pregnancy. *Nature Clinical Practice: Neurology, 5*, 51–56.

Selman, R. L. (1980). *The growth of interpersonal understanding*. New York: Academic Press.

Semmler, C., Ashcroft, J., van Jaarsveld, C. H., Carnell, S., & Wardle, J. (2009). Development of overweight in children in relation to parental weight and socioeconomic status. *Obesity, 17*, 814–820.

Sener, A., Terzioglu, R. G., & Karabulut, E. (2007). Life satisfaction and leisure activities during men's retirement: A Turkish sample. *Aging and Mental Health, 11*, 30–36.

Serido, J. (2009). Life events. In D. Carr (Ed.), *Encyclopedia of the life course and human development*. Boston: Gale Cengage.

Sesso, H. D., & others. (2008). Vitamins E and C in the prevention of cardiovascular disease in men: The Physicians' Health Study II randomized controlled trial. *Journal of the American Psychological Association, 300*, 2095–2202.

Settersten, R. A., Furstenberg, F. F., & Rumbaut, R. G. (Eds.). (2005). *On the frontier of adulthood: Theory, research, and public policy*. Chicago: University of Chicago Press.

Shafer, V. L., & Garrido-Nag, K. (2010). The neurodevelopmental bases of language. In E. Hoff & M. Shatz (Eds.), *Blackwell handbook of language development* (2nd ed.). Malden, MA: Blackwell.

Shah, A. (2008). The relationship between elderly suicide rates and the human development index: A cross-national study of secondary data from the World Health Organization and the United Nations. *International Psychogeriatrics, 16*, 1–16.

Shan, Z. Y., Liu, J. Z., Sahgal, V., Wang, B., & Yue, G. H. (2005). Selective atrophy of left hemisphere and frontal lobe of the brain in older men. *Journals of Gerontology A: Biological Sciences and Medical Sciences, 60*, A165–A174.

Shanley, D. P., & Kirkwood, T. B. (2006). Caloric restriction does not enhance longevity in all species and is unlikely to do so in humans. *Biogerontology, 7*, 165–168.

Shapiro, A. F., & Gottman, J. M. (2005). Effects on marriage of a psycho-education intervention with couples undergoing the transition to parenthood, evaluation at 1-year post-intervention. *Journal of Family Communication, 5*, 1–24.

Sharkey, W. (1993). Who embarrasses whom? Relational and sex differences in the use of intentional embarrassment. In P. J. Kalbfleisch (Ed.), *Interpersonal communication*. Mahwah, NJ: Erlbaum.

Sharlip, I. D., Shumaker, B. P., Hakim, L. S., Goldfischer, E., Natanegra, F., & Wong, D. G. (2008). Tadalafil is efficacious and well tolerated in the treatment of erectile dysfunction (ED) in men over 65 years of age: Results from multiple observations in men with ED in national tadalafil study in the United States. *Journal of Sexual Medicine, 5*, 716–725.

Sharma, A. R., McGue, M. K., & Benson, P. L. (1996). The emotional and behavioral adjustment of adopted adolescents: Part I: Age at adoption. *Children and Youth Services Review, 18*, 101–114.

Sharts-Hopko, N. (2009). Low vision and blindness among midlife and older adults: A review of the nursing research literature. *Holistic Nursing Practice, 23*, 94–100.

Shatz, M., & Gelman, R. (1973). The development of communication skills: Modifications in the speech of young children as a function of the listener. *Monographs of the Society for Research in Child Development, 38* (Serial No. 152).

Shaver, P., & Mikulincer, M. (2010, in press). Recent advances in the study of close relationships. *Annual Review of Psychology* (Vol. 61). Palo Alto, CA: Annual Reviews.

Shaw, P., Eckstrand, K., Sharp, W., Blumenthal, J., Lerch, J. P., Greenstein, D., Clasen, L., Evans, A., Giedd, J., & Rapoport, J. L. (2007). Attention-deficit/hyperactivity disorder is characterized by a delay in cortical maturation. *Proceedings of the National Academy of Sciences USA, 104* (49), 19649–19654.

Shay, J. W., & Wright, W. E. (2007). Hallmarks of telomeres in aging research. *Journal of Pathology, 211*, 114–123.

Shaya, F. T., Flores, D., Gbarayor, C. M., & Wang, J. (2008). School-based obesity interventions: A literature review. *Journal of School Health, 78*, 189–196.

Shaywitz, S. E., Gruen, J. R., & Shaywitz, B. A. (2007). Management of dyslexia, its rationale, and underlying neurobiology. *Pediatric Clinics of North America, 54*, 609–623.

Shea, A. K., & Steiner, M. (2008). Cigarette smoking during pregnancy. *Nicotine and Tobacco Research, 10*, 267–278.

Shebloski, B., Conger, K. J., & Widaman, K. F. (2005). Reciprocal links among differential parenting, perceived partiality, and self worth: A three-wave longitudinal study. *Journal of Family Psychology, 19*, 633–642.

Shema, L., Ore, L., Ben-Shachar, M., Haj, M., & Linn, S. (2007). The association between breastfeeding and breast cancer occurrence among Israeli Jewish women: A case control study. *Journal of Cancer Research and Clinical Oncology, 133*, 903.

Shen, J. (2009). Evaluation of environmental and personal susceptibility characteristics that modify genetic risks. *Methods in Molecular Biology, 471*, 163–177.

Shenkin, S. D., Rivers, C. S., Deary, I. J., Starr, J. M., & Wardlaw, J. M. (2009). Maximum (prior) brain size, not atrophy, correlates with cognition in community-dwelling older people: A cross-sectional study. *BMC Geriatrics, 9*, 12.

Shepard, G. H. (2002). Three days for weeping: Dreams, emotions, and death in the Peruvian Amazon. *Medical Anthropology Quarterly, 16*, 200–229.

Sherblom, S. (2008). The legacy of the "care challenge": Re-envisioning the outcome of the justice-care debate. *Journal of Moral Education, 37*, 81–98.

Sheridan, M., & Nelson, C. A. (2008, in press). Neurobiology of fetal and infant development: Implications for mental health. In C. H. Zeanah (Ed.), *Handbook of infant mental health* (3rd ed.). New York: Guilford.

Sherwood, A., Light, K. C., & Blumenthal, J. A. (1989). Effects of aerobic exercise training on hemodynamic responses during psychosocial stress in normotensive and borderline hypertensive Type A men: A preliminary report. *Psychosomatic Medicine, 51,* 123–136.

Shields, M. (2006). Overweight and obesity among children and youth. *Health Reports, 17,* 27–42.

Shields, S. A. (1998, August). *What Jerry Maguire can tell us about gender and emotion.* Paper presented at the meeting of the International Society for Research on Emotions, Würzburg, Germany.

Shin, C. Y., Yun, K. E., & Park, H. S. (2009, in press). Blood pressure has a greater impact on cardiovascular mortality than other components of metabolic syndrome in Koreans. *Atherosclerosis.*

Shiraev, E., & Levy, D. (2007). *Cross-cultural psychology: Critical thinking and critical applications* (3rd ed.). Belmont, CA: Wadsworth.

Shiraev, E., & Levy, D. (2010). *Cross-cultural psychology* (4th ed.). Boston: Allyn & Bacon.

Shore, L. M., & Goldberg, C. B. (2005). Age discrimination in the work place. In R. L. Dipobye & A. Colella (Eds.), *Discrimination at work.* Mahwah, NJ: Erlbaum.

Shors, T. J. (2009). Saving new brain cells. *Scientific American, 300,* 46–52.

Shoup, J. A., Gattshall, M., Dandamudi, P., & Estabrooks, P. (2008). Physical activity, quality of life, and weight status in overweight children. *Quality of Life Research, 17,* 407–412.

Shultz, K. S., & Adams, G. A. (Eds.). (2007). *Aging and work in the 21st century.* Mahwah, NJ: Erlbaum.

Shweder, R., Goodnow, J., Hatano, G., Le Vine, R. A., Markus, H., & Miller, P. (2006). The cultural psychology of development. In W. Damon & R. Lerner (Eds.), *Handbook of child psychology* (6th ed.). New York: Wiley.

Shweder, R., Mahapatra, M., & Miller, J. (1987). Culture and moral development. In J. Kagan & S. Lamb (Eds.), *The emergence of morality in young children.* Chicago: University of Chicago Press.

Siedlecki, K. L. (2007). Investigating the structure and age invariance of episodic memory across the adult life span. *Psychology and Aging, 22,* 251–268.

Siegal, M., & Surian, L. (2010). Conversational understanding in young children. In E. Hoff & M. Shatz (Eds.), *Blackwell handbook of language development* (2nd ed.). Malden, MA: Blackwell.

Siegler, I. C., Poon, L. W., Madden, D. J., Dilworth-Anderson, P., Schaie, K. W., Willis, S. L., & Martin, P. (2009). Psychological aspects of normal aging. In D. G. Blazer & D. Steffens (Eds.), *Textbook of geriatric psychiatry* (4th ed.). Arlington, VA: American Psychiatric Publishing.

Siegler, R. S. (2006). Microgenetic analysis of learning. In W. Damon & R. Lerner (Eds.), *Handbook of child psychology* (6th ed.). New York: Wiley.

Siegler, R. S. (2007). Cognitive variability. *Developmental Science 10,* 104–109.

Siegler, R. S. (2009). Improving preschoolers' number sense using information processing theory. In O. A. Barbarin & K. Miller (Ed.), *Handbook of child development and early education.* New York: Guilford.

Silva, C. (2005, October 31). When teen dynamo talks, city listens. *Boston Globe,* pp. 81–84.

Silver, E. J., & Bauman, L. J. (2006). The association of sexual with attitudes, beliefs and risk behaviors of inner-city adolescents. *Journal of Research on Adolescence, 16,* 29–45.

Silverman, P. R., & Kelly, M. (2009). *A parent's guide to raising grieving children.* New York: Oxford University Press.

Silverstein, M. (2009). Caregiving. In D. Carr (Ed.), *Encyclopedia of the life course and human development.* Boston: Gale Cengage.

Sim, T. N., & Ong, L. P. (2005). Parent punishment and child aggression in a Singapore Chinese preschool sample. *Journal of Marriage and the Family, 67,* 85–99.

Simard, V., Nielsen, T. A., Tremblay, R. E., Boivan, M., & Montplaisir, J. Y. (2008). Longitudinal study of bad dreams in preschool-aged children: Prevalence, demographic correlates, risk, and protective factors. *Sleep, 31,* 62–70.

Simkin, P., & Bolding, A. (2004). Update on nonpharmacologic approaches to relieve labor pain and prevent suffering. *Journal of Midwifery and Women's Health, 49,* 489–504.

Simm, A., Nass, N., Bartling, B., Hofmann, B., Silber, R. E., & Navarrete Santos, A. (2008). Potential biomarkers of aging. *Biological Chemistry, 389,* 257–265.

Simon, V. A., Aikins, J. W., & Prinstein, M. J. (2008). Romantic partner selection and socialization during early adolescence. *Child Development, 79,* 1676–1692.

Simons, J. S., Dodson, C. S., Bell, D., & Schacter, D. L. (2004). Specific- and partial-source memory: Effects of aging. *Psychology and Aging, 19,* 689–694.

Simonton, D. K. (1996). Creativity. In J. E. Birren (Ed.), *Encyclopedia of aging.* San Diego: Academic Press.

Simos, P. G., Fletcher, J. M., Sarkari, S., Billingsley, R. L., Denton, C., & Papanicolaou, A. C. (2007). Altering the brain circuits for reading through intervention: A magnetic source imaging study. *Neuropsychology, 21,* 485–496.

Simpson, C. F., Punjabi, N. M., Wolfenden, L., Shardell, M., Shade, D. M., & Fried, L. P. (2005). Relationship between lung function and physical performance in disabled older women. *Journals of Gerontology A: Biological Sciences and Medical Sciences, 60,* A350–A354.

Singer, T., Verhaeghen, P., Ghisletta, P., Lindenberger, U., & Baltes, P. B. (2003). The fate of cognition in very old age: Six-year longitudinal findings in the Berlin Aging Study. *Psychology and Aging, 18,* 318–331.

Singh, S., Wulf, D., Samara, R., & Cuca, Y. P. (2000). Gender differences in the timing of first intercourse: Data from 14 countries. *International Family Planning Perspectives, 26,* 21–28, 43.

Singleton, D., & Ryan, L. (2009). *Understanding child language acquisition.* New York: Oxford University Press.

Sinha, J. W., Cnaan, R. A., & Gelles, R. J. (2007). Adolescent risk behaviors and religion: Findings from a national study. *Journal of Adolescence, 30,* 231–249.

Sinnott, J. D. (2003). Postformal thought and adult development. Living in balance. In J. Demick & C. Andreoletti (Eds.), *Handbook of adult development.* New York: Kluwer.

Siow, H. M., Cameron, D. B., & Ganley, T. J. (2008). Acute knee injuries in skeletally immature athletes. *Physical Medicine and Rehabilitation Clinics of North America, 19,* 319–345.

Sivell, S., & others. (2008). How risk is perceived, constructed, and interpreted by clients in clinical genetics, and the effects on decision making: A review. *Journal of Genetic Counseling, 17,* 30–63.

Skakibaei, M., Harikumar, K. B., & Aggarwal, B. B. (2009). Resveratrol addiction: To die or not to die. *Molecular Nutrition and Food Research, 53,* 115–128.

Skinner, B. F. (1938). *The behavior of organisms: An experimental analysis.* New York: Appelton-Century-Crofts.

Skinner, B. F. (1957). *Verbal behavior.* New York: Appleton-Century-Crofts.

Slack, T., & Jensen, L. (2008). Employment hardship among older workers: Does residential and gender inequality extend into old age? *Journals of Gerontology B: Psychological Sciences and Social Sciences, 63,* S15–S24.

Slade, E. P., & Wissow, L. S. (2004). Spanking in early childhood and later behavior problems: A prospective study. *Pediatrics, 113,* 1321–1330.

Slater, A., Field, T., & Hernandez-Reif, M. (2007). The development of the sense. In A. Slater & M. Lewis (Eds.), *Introduction to infant development* (2nd ed.). New York: Oxford University Press.

Slater, A., Morison, V., & Somers, M. (1988). Orientation discrimination and cortical function in the human newborn. *Perception, 17,* 597–602.

Slawta, J. N., & Deneui, D. (2009, in press). Be a fit kid: Nutrition and physical activity for the fourth grade. *Health Promotion Practice.*

Sleeter, C. E., & Grant, C. A. (2009). *Making choices for multicultural education* (6th ed.). New York: Wiley.

Slep, A. M. S., & Heyman, R. E. (2008). Public health approaches to family maltreatment prevention: Resetting family psychology's sights from the home to the community. *Journal of Family Psychology, 22,* 518–528.

Slobin, D. (1972, July). Children and language. They learn the same way around the world. *Psychology Today,* pp. 71–76.

Slomkowski, C., Rende, R., Conger, K. J., Simons, R. L., & Conger, R. D. (2001). Sisters, brothers, and delinquency: Social influence during early and middle adolescence. *Child Development, 72,* 271–283.

Slough, N. M., McMahon, R. J., & the Conduct Problems Prevention Research Group. (2008). Preventing serious conduct problems in school-age youth: The Fast Track program. *Cognitive and Behavioral Practice, 15,* 3–17.

Smaldone, A., Honig, J. C., & Byrne, M. W. (2007). Sleepless in America: Inadequate sleep and relationships to health and well-being of our nation's children. *Pediatrics, 119* (Suppl. 1), S29–S37.

Small, S. A. (1990). *Preventive programs that support families with adolescents.* Washington, DC: Carnegie Council on Adolescent Development.

Smetana, J. (2006). Social domain theory. In M. Killen & J. G. Smetana (Eds.), *Handbook of moral development.* Mahwah, NJ: Erlbaum.

Smetana, J. G. (2008). "It's 10 o'clock: Do you know where your children are?" Recent advancements in understanding parental monitoring and adolescents' information management. *Child Development Perspectives, 2* (1), 19–25.

Smetana, J. G., Villalobos, M., Tasopoulos-Chan, M., Gettman, D. C., & Campione-Barr, N. (2009). Early and middle adolescents' disclosure about activities in different domains. *Journal of Adolescence, 32,* 693–713.

Smith, B. (2007). *The psychology of sex and gender.* Boston: Allyn & Bacon.

Smith, C. A., & Crowther, C. A. (2004). Acupuncture for the induction of labor. *Cochrane Database of Systematic Review, 1,* CD0029262.

Smith, D. L. (2008). Birth complications and outcomes. In M. M. Haith & J. B. Benson (Eds.), *Encyclopedia of infant and early childhood development.* Oxford, UK: Elsevier.

Smith, J. (2009). Self. In D. Carr (Ed.), *Encyclopedia of the life course and human development.* Boston: Gale Cengage.

Smith, J. B. (2009). High school organization. In D. Carr (Ed.), *Encyclopedia of the life course and human development.* Boston: Gale Cengage.

Smith, L. B. (1999). Do infants possess innate knowledge structures? The con side. *Developmental Science, 2,* 133–144.

Smith, L. M., Chang, L., Yonekura, M. L., Gilbride, K., Kuo, J., Poland, R. E., Walot, I., & Ernst, T. (2001). Brain proton magnetic resonance spectroscopy and imaging in children exposed to cocaine in utero. *Pediatrics, 107,* 227.

Smith, L. M., & others. (2008). Prenatal methamphetamine use and neonatal neurobehavioral outcome. *Neurotoxicology and Teratology, 30,* 20–28.

Smith, M. C., & Reio, T. G. (2007) (Eds.). *The handbook on adult development and learning.* Mahwah, NJ: Erlbaum.

Smith, P. K. (2007). Pretend play and children's cognitive and literacy development: Sources of evidence and some lessons from the past. In K. A. Roskos & J. F. Christie (Eds.), *Play and literacy in early childhood.* Mahwah, NJ: Erlbaum.

Smith, R. P. (2009). *Netter's obstetrics and gynecology* (2nd ed.). London: Elsevier.

Smith, T. B., McCullough, M. E., & Poll, J. (2003). Religiousness and depression: Evidence (for a main effect and the moderating influence of stressful life events. *Psychological Bulletin, 129,* 614–636.

Smith, T. E. C., Polloway, E. A., Patten, J. R., & Dowdy, C. A. (2008). *Teaching students with special needs in inclusive settings* (5th ed.). Boston: Allyn & Bacon.

Smithbattle, L. (2007). Legacies of advantage and disadvantage: The case of teen mothers. *Public Health Nursing, 24,* 409–420.

Smoreda, Z., & Licoppe, C. (2000). Gender-specific use of the domestic telephone. *Social Psychology Quarterly, 63,* 238–252.

Snarey, J. (1987, June). A question of morality. *Psychology Today,* pp. 6–8.

Snarey, J. (2008). Moral education in the cognitive developmental tradition. In L. Nucci & D. Narvàez (Eds.), *Handbook of moral and character education.* Clifton, NJ: Psychology Press.

Snijders, B. E., & others. (2007). Breast-feeding duration and infant atopic manifestations, by maternal allergic status, in the first two years of life (KOALA study). *Journal of Pediatrics, 151,* 347–351.

Snow, C. E., & Kang, J. Y. (2006). Becoming bilingual, biliterate, and bicultural. In W. Damon & R. Lerner (Eds.), *Handbook of child psychology* (6th ed.). New York: Wiley.

Snowdon, D. A. (1997). Aging and Alzheimer's disease: Lessons from the nun study. *Gerontologist, 37,* 150–156.

Snowdon, D. A. (2002). *Aging with grace: What the Nun Study teaches us about leading longer, healthier, and more meaningful lives.* New York: Bantam.

Snowdon, D. A. (2003). Healthy aging and dementia: Findings from the Nun Study. *Annals of Internal Medicine, 139,* 450–454.

Snowdon, D. A., Tully, C. L., Smith, C. D., Riley, K. P., & Markesbery, W. R. (2000). Serum folate and the severity of atrophy of the neocortex in Alzheimer's disease: Findings from the Nun Study. *American Journal of Clinical Nutrition, 71,* 993–998.

Snyder, H. N., & Sickmund, M. (1999, October). *Juvenile offenders and victims: 1999 national report.* Washington, DC: National Center for Juvenile Justice.

Snyder, J., Schreperman, L., McDachern, A., Earner, S., Johnson, K., & Provines, J. (2008). Peer deviancy training and peer coercion: Dual processes associated with early-onset conduct problems. *Child Development, 79,* 252–268.

Snyder, K. A., & Torrence, C. M. (2008). Habituation and novelty. In M. M. Haith & J. B. Benson (Eds.), *Encyclopedia of infant and early childhood development.* Oxford, UK: Elsevier.

Solomon, D., Watson, M. S., & Battistich, V. A. (2002). Teaching and school effects on moral/prosocial development. In V. Richardson (Ed.), *Handbook for research on teaching.* Washington, D. C.: American Educational Research Association.

Solomon, D., Watson, P., Schapes, E., Battistich, V., & Solomon, J. (1990). Cooperative learning as part of a comprehensive program designed to promote prosocial development. In S. Sharan (Ed.), *Cooperative learning.* New York: Praeger.

Solot, D., & Miller, M. (2002). *Unmarried to each other.* New York: Marlowe.

Sonnen, J. A., & others. (2009). Free radical damage to cerebral cortex in Alzheimer's disease, microvascular injury, and smoking. *Annals of Neurology, 65,* 226–229.

Sood, A. B., Razdan, A., Weller, E. B., & Weller, R. A. (2006). Children's reactions to parental and sibling death. *Current Psychiatry Reports, 8,* 115–120.

Sophian, C. (1985). Perseveration and infants' search: A comparison of two- and three-location tasks. *Developmental Psychology, 21,* 187–194.

Sottero, B., Gamba, P., Gargiulo, S., Leonarduzzi, G., & Poli, G. (2009). Cholesterol oxidation products and disease: An emerging topic of interest in medicinal chemistry. *Current Medicinal Chemistry, 16,* 685–705.

Spandel, V. (2009). *Creating young writers* (3rd ed.). Boston: Allyn & Bacon.

Spangler, G., Johann, M., Ronai, Z., & Zimmermann, P. (2009). Genetic and environmental influence on attachment disorganization. *Journal of Child Psychology and Psychiatry, 50,* 952–961.

Sparks, D. L., Hunsaker, J. C., Scheff, S. W., Kryscio, R. J., Henson, H., & Markesbery, W. R. (1990). Cortical senile plaques in coronary artery disease, aging, and Alzheimer's disease. *Neurobiology of Aging, 11,* 601–607.

Spelke, E. S. (1979). Perceiving bimodally specified events in infancy. *Developmental Psychology, 5,* 626–636.

Spelke, E. S. (1991). Physical knowledge in infancy: Reflections on Piaget's theory. In S. Carey & R. Gelman (Eds.), *The epigenesis of mind: Essays on biology and cognition.* Hillsdale, NJ: Erlbaum.

Spelke, E. S. (2000). Core knowledge. *American Psychologist, 55,* 1233–1243.

Spelke, E. S., Breinlinger, K., Macomber, J., & Jacobson, K. (1992). Origins of knowledge. *Psychological Review, 99,* 605–632.

Spelke, E. S., & Hespos, S. J. (2001). Continuity, competence, and the object concept. In E. Dupoux (Ed.), *Language, brain, and behavior.* Cambridge, MA: Bradford/MIT Press.

Spelke, E. S., & Kinzler, K. D. (2007). Core knowledge. *Developmental Science 10,* 89–96.

Spelke, E. S. & Kinzler, K. D. (2009). Innateness, learning and rationality. *Cognitive Development Perspectives, 3,* 96–98.

Spelke, E. S., & Owsley, C. J. (1979). Intermodal exploration and knowledge in infancy. *Infant Behavior and Development, 2,* 13–28.

Spence, A. P. (1989). *Biology of human aging.* Englewood Cliffs, NJ: Prentice Hall.

Spencer, J. (2009). *Dynamic systems and connectionist approaches to development.* New York: Oxford University Press.

Spencer, J. P., Blumberg, M. S., McMurray, B., Robinson, S. R., Samuelson, L. K., & Tomlin, J. B. (2009). Short arms and talking eggs: Why we should no longer abide the nativist-empiricist debate. *Child Development Perspectives, 3,* 79.

Spencer, S., Logel, C., & Davies, P. G. (2010). Stereotype threat. *Annual Review of Psychology* (Vol. 61). Palo Alto, CA: Annual Reviews.

Speranza, M., Corcos, M., Loas, G., Stephan, P., Guilbaud, O., Perez-Diaz, F., Venisse, J. L., Bizouard, P., Halfon, O., Flament, M., & Jeammet, P. (2005). Depressive personality dimensions and alexithymia in eating disorders. *Psychiatry Research, 135,* 153–163.

Spironelli, C., & Angrilli, A. (2009). Developmental aspects of automatic word processing: Language lateralization of early ERP components in children, young adults, and middle-aged adults. *Biological Psychology, 80,* 35–45.

Sprei, J. E., & Courtois, C. A. (1988). The treatment of women's sexual dysfunctions arising from sexual assault. In R. A. Brown & J. R. Fields (Eds.), *Treatment of sexual problems in individual and couples therapy.* Great Neck, NY: PMA.

Spring, J. (2008). *American education* (13th ed.). New York: McGraw-Hill.

Spring, J. (2010). *Deculturalization and the struggle for equality* (6th ed.). New York: McGraw-Hill.

Srabstein, J. C., McCarter, R. J., Shao, C., & Huang, Z. J. (2006). Morbidities associated with bullying behaviors in adolescents: School based study of American adolescents. *International Journal of Adolescent Medicine and Health, 18,* 587–596.

Sroufe, L. A. (2000, Spring). The inside scoop on child development: Interview. *Cutting through the hype.* Minneapolis: College of Education and Human Development, University of Minnesota.

Sroufe, L. A., Egeland, B., Carlson, E., & Collins, W. A. (2005a). The place of early attachment in developmental context. In K. E. Grossmann, K. Grossmann, & E. Waters (Eds.), *The power of longitudinal attachment research: From infancy and childhood to adulthood.* New York: Guilford.

Sroufe, L. A., Egeland, B., Carlson, E., & Collins, W. A. (2005b). The place of early attachment in developmental context. In K. E.

Grossmann, K. Grossmann, & E. Waters (Eds.), *The power of longitudinal attachment research: From infancy and childhood to adulthood.* New York: Guilford.

Sroufe, L. A., Waters, E., & Matas, L. (1974). Contextual determinants of infant affectional response. In M. Lewis & L. Rosenblum (Eds.), *Origins of fear.* New York: Wiley.

Staff, J., Messersmith, E. E., & Schulenberg, J. E. (2009). Adolescents and the world of work. In R. M. Lerner & L. Steinberg (Eds.), *Handbook of adolescent psychology* (3rd ed.). New York: Wiley.

Stanford University Medical Center. (2008). *Growth hormone deficiency.* Sanford, CA: Pituitary Center, Stanford University.

Stanley, S. M., Amato, P. R., Johnson, C. A., & Markman, H. J. (2006). Premarital education, marital quality, and marital stability: Findings from a large, household survey. *Journal of Family Psychology, 20,* 117–126.

Staplin, L., Lococo, K., & Sim, J. (1993). *Traffic maneuver problems of older drivers.* Report No. FHWA-RD-92-092. McLean, VA: Federal Highway Administration.

Starr, C., Evers, C., & Starr, L. (2010). *Biology today and tomorrow with physiology* (3rd ed.). Boston: Cengage.

Starr, L. R., & Davila, J. (2009). Clarifying co-rumination: Associations with internalizing symptoms and romantic involvement among adolescent girls. *Journal of Adolescence, 32,* 19–37.

Stater, A. M., Riddell, P., Quinn, P. C., Pascalls, O., Lee, K., & Kelly, D. J. (2009, in press). Visual perception. In G. Bremner & T. Wachs (Eds.), *Blackwell handbook of infant development.* (2nd ed.). Oxford, UK: Blackwell.

Staudinger, U. M. (1996). Psychologische Produktivität und Selbstenfaltung im Alter. In M. M. Baltes & L. Montada (Eds.), *Produktives Leben im Alter.* Frankfurt: Campus.

Steele, C. M., & Aronson, J. A. (2004). Stereotype threat does not live by Steele and Aronson (1995) alone. *American Psychologist, 59,* 47–48.

Steele, J., Waters, E., Crowell, J., & Treboux, D. (1998, June). *Self-report measures of attachment: Secure bonds to other attachment measures and attachment theory.* Paper presented at the meeting of the International Society for the Study of Personal Relationships, Saratoga Springs, NY.

Steelman, L. C., & Koch, P. R. (2009). Sibling relationships, childhood, and adolescence. In D. Carr (Ed.), *Encyclopedia of the life course and human development.* Boston: Gale Cengage.

Steinberg, L. (2004). Risk taking in adolescence: What changes, and why? *Annals of the New York Academy of Sciences, 1021,* 51–58.

Steinberg, L. (2008). A social neuroscience perspective on adolescent risk-taking *Developmental Review, 28,* 78–106.

Steinberg, L. (2009). Adolescent development and juvenile justice. *Annual Review of Clinical*

Psychology (Vol. 5). Palo Alto, CA: Annual Reviews.

Steinberg, L., Blatt-Eisengart, I., & Cauffman, E. (2006). Patterns of competence and adjustment among adolescents from authoritative, authoritarian, indulgent, and neglectful homes: A replication in a sample of serious juvenile offenders. *Journal of Research on Adolescence, 16,* 47–58.

Steinberg, L., Cauffman, E., Woolard, J., Graham, S., & Banich, M. (2009, in press). Are adolescents less mature than adults? Minors' access to abortion, the juvenile death penalty, and the alleged APA "flip-flop." *American Psychologist.*

Steinberg, L., & Monahan, K. (2007). Age differences in resistance to peer influence. *Developmental Psychology, 43,* 1531–1543.

Steinberg, S. J., & Davila, J. (2008). Romantic functioning and depressive symptoms among early adolescent girls: The moderating role of parental emotional availability. *Journal of Clinical Child and Adolescent Psychology, 37,* 350–362.

Steiner, J. E. (1979). Human facial expressions in response to taste and smell stimulation. In H. Reese & L. Lipsitt (Eds.), *Advances in child development and behavior* (Vol. 13). New York: Academic Press.

Steinhausen, H. C., Blattmann, B., & Pfund, F. (2007). Developmental outcome in children with intrauterine exposure to substances. *European Addiction Research, 13,* 94–100.

Steming, C. (2008). CenteringPregnancy: Group prenatal care. *Creative Nursing, 14,* 182–183.

Stephens, J. M. (2008). Cheating. In N. J. Salkind (Ed.), *Encyclopedia of educational psychology.* Thousand Oaks, CA: Sage.

Stern, D. N., Beebe, B., Jaffe, J., & Bennett, S. L. (1977). The infant's stimulus world during social interaction: A study of caregiver behaviors with particular reference to repetition and tuning. In H. R. Schaffer (Ed.), *Studies in mother-infant interaction.* London: Academic Press.

Sternberg, K., & Sternberg, R. J. (2010, in press). Love. In H. Pashler (Ed.), *Encyclopedia of the mind.* Thousands Oaks, CA: Sage.

Sternberg, R. J. (1986). *Intelligence applied.* San Diego: Harcourt Brace Jovanovich.

Sternberg, R. J. (1988). *The triangle of love.* New York: Basic Books.

Sternberg, R. J. (1997). Educating intelligence: Infusing the triarchic theory into instruction. In R. J. Sternberg & E. Grigorenko (Eds.), *Intelligence, heredity, and environment.* New York: Cambridge University Press.

Sternberg, R. J. (1998) A balance theory of wisdom. *Review of General Psychology, 2,* 347–365.

Sternberg, R. J. (1999). Intelligence. In M. A. Runco & S. Pritzker (Eds.), *Encyclopedia of creativity.* San Diego: Academic Press.

Sternberg, R. J. (2003). Contemporary theories of intelligence. In I. B. Weiner (Ed.), *Handbook of psychology* (Vol. 7). New York: Wiley.

Sternberg, R. J. (2004). Individual differences in cognitive development. In U. Goswami (Ed.), *Blackwell handbook of childhood cognitive development.* Malden, MA: Blackwell.

Sternberg, R. J. (2007). Critical thinking in psychology: It really is critical. In R. J. Sternberg, H. Roediger, & D. Halpern (Eds.), *Critical thinking in psychology.* New York: Cambridge University Press.

Sternberg, R. J. (2007). *g, g's,* or Jeez: Which is the best model for developing abilities, competencies, and expertise? In P. C. Kyllonen, R. D. Roberts, & L. Stankov (Eds.), *Extending intelligence: Enhancement and new constructs.* Mahwah, NJ: Erlbaum.

Sternberg, R. J. (2008). The triarchic theory of successful intelligence. In N. Salkind (Ed.), *Encyclopedia of educational psychology.* Thousand Oaks, CA: Sage.

Sternberg, R. J. (2009a). *Cognitive psychology* (5th ed.). Belmont, CA: Cengage.

Sternberg, R. J. (2009b, in press). Intelligence. In M. E. Laur (Ed.), *Chicago companion to the child.* Chicago: University of Chicago Press.

Sternberg, R. J. (2009c, in press). The triarchic theory of successful intelligence. In B. Kerr (Ed.), *Encyclopedia of giftedness, creativity, and talent.* Thousand Oaks, CA: Sage.

Sternberg, R. J. (2009d, in press). Wisdom. In S. J. Lopez (Ed.), *Encyclopedia of positive psychology.* Blackwell.

Sternberg, R. J. (2009e, in press). Wisdom, intelligence, creativity, synthesized: A model of giftedness. In T. Balchin, B. Hymer, & D. Matthews (Eds.), *International companion to gifted education.* London: RoutledgeFalmer.

Sternberg, R. J. (2010a, in press). Intelligence. In B. McGaw, P. Peterson, & E. Baker (Eds.), *International encyclopedia of education* (3rd ed.). New York: Elsevier.

Sternberg, R. J. (2010b, in press). The triarchic theory of successful intelligence. In B. Kerr (Ed.), *Encyclopedia of giftedness, creativity, and talent.* Thousand Oaks, CA: Sage.

Sternberg, R. J. (2010c, in press). Wisdom, intelligence, and creativity synthesized: A model of successful leadership for an uncertain and challenging future. *The School Administrator.*

Sternberg, R. J. (2010, in press). Assessment of gifted students for identification purposes: New techniques for a new millennium. *Learning and Individual Differences.*

Sternberg, R. J., & Grigorenko, E. L. (2008). Ability testing across cultures. In L. A. Suzuki & J. G. Ponterotto (Eds.), *Handbook of multicultural assessment* (3rd ed.). San Francisco: Jossey-Bass.

Sternberg, R. J., Jarvin, L., & Grigorenko, E. L. (2009, in press). *Teaching for intelligence, creativity, and wisdom.* Thousand Oaks, CA: Corwin.

Sternberg, R. J., Jarvin, L., & Reznitskaya, A. (2010, in press). Teaching for wisdom through history: Infusing wise thinking skills in the school curriculum. In M. Ferrari (Ed.), *Teaching for wisdom.* Amsterdam: Springer.

Sternberg, R. J., & Kaufman, J. C. (2010, in press). Intelligence (as related to creativity). In M. Runco (Ed.), *Encyclopedia of creativity.* New York: Elsevier.

Sternberg, R. J., Kaufman, J. C., & Grigorenko, E. L. (2008). *Applied intelligence.* New York: Cambridge University Press.

Sternberg, R. J., Nokes, K., Geissler, P. W., Prince, R., Okatcha, F., Bundy, D. A., & Grigorenko, E. L. (2001). The relationship between academic and practical intelligence: A case study in Kenya. *Intelligence, 29,* 401–418.

Sternberg, R. J., & Williams, W. M. (1996.) *How to develop student creativity.* Alexandria, VA: ASCD.

Stern, W. (1912). The psychological methods of testing intelligence. *Educational Psychology Monographs* (No. 13).

Sterns, H. L., Barrett, G. V., & Alexander, R. A. (1985). Accidents and the aging individual. In J. E. Birren & K. W. Schaie (Eds.), *Handbook of the psychology of aging.* New York: Van Nostrand Reinhold.

Sterns, H. L., & Huyck, H. (2001). The role of work in midlife. In M. E. Lachman (Ed.), *Handbook of midlife development.* New York: Wiley.

Sterzer, P., Stadler, C., Krebs, A., Klemschmidt, A., & Poustka, F. (2005). Abnormal neural responses to emotional visual stimuli in adolescents with conduct disorder. *Biological Psychiatry, 57,* 7–15.

Stevens, J. C., Alvarez-Reeves, M., Dipietro, L., Mack, G. W., & Green, B. G. (2003). Decline of tactile acuity in aging: A study of body site, blood flow, and lifetime habits of smoking and physical activity. *Somatosensory and Motor Research, 20,* 271–279.

Stevenson, H. G., Lee, S., & Stigler, J. W. (1986). Mathematics achievement of Chinese, Japanese, and American children. *Science, 231,* 693–699.

Stevenson, H. W. (1995). Mathematics achievement of American students: First in the world by the year 2000? In C. A. Nelson (Ed.), *Basic and applied perspectives on learning, cognition, and development.* Minneapolis: University of Minnesota Press.

Stevenson, H. W. (2000). Middle childhood: Education and schooling. In A. Kazdin (Ed.), *Encyclopedia of psychology.* Washington, DC, & New York: American Psychological Association and Oxford University Press.

Stevenson, H. W., Hofer, B. K., & Randel, B. (1999). *Middle childhood: Education and schooling.* Unpublished manuscript, Department of Psychology, University of Michigan, Ann Arbor.

Stevenson, H. W., Lee, S., Chen, C., Stigler, J. W., Hsu, C., & Kitamura, S. (1990). Contexts of achievement. *Monograph of the Society for Research in Child Development, 55* (Serial No. 221).

Stevenson, H. W., & Zusho, A. (2002). Adolescence in China and Japan: Adapting to a changing environment. In B. B. Brown, R. W. Larson, & T. S. Saraswathi (Eds.), *The world's youth.* New York: Cambridge University Press.

Stewart, A. J., Ostrove, J. M., & Helson, R. (2001). Middle aging in women: Patterns of personality change from the 30s to the 50s. *Journal of Adult Development, 8,* 23–37.

Stice, E., Presnell, K., & Spangler, D. (2002). Risk factors for binge eating onset in adolescent girls: A 2-year prospective investigation. *Health Psychology, 21,* 131–138.

Stiggins, R. (2008). *Introduction to student-involved assessment for learning* (5th ed.). Upper Saddle River, NJ: Prentice Hall.

Stimpson, J. P., Kuo, Y. F., Ray, L. A., Raji, M. A., & Peek, M. K. (2007). Risk of mortality related to widowhood in older Mexican Americans. *Annals of Epidemiolog, 17,* 313–319.

Stine-Morrow, E. A. L., Parisi, J. M., Morrow, D. G., Greene, J., & Park, D. C. (2007). An engagement model of cognitive optimization through adulthood. *Journals of Gerontology B: Psychological Sciences and Social Sciences, 62,* P62–P69.

Stine-Morrow, E. A. L., Soederberg Miller, L. M., & Hertzog, C. (2006). Aging and self-regulated language processing. *Psychological Bulletin, 132,* 582–606.

Stipek, D. J. (2002). *Motivation to learn* (4th ed.). Boston: Allyn & Bacon.

Stipek, D. J. (2005, February 16). Commentary in *USA Today,* p. 1D.

Stocker, C., & Dunn, J. (1990). Sibling relationships in childhood: Links with friendships and peer relationships. *British Journal of Developmental Psychology, 8,* 227–244.

Stoel-Gammon, C. & Sosa, A. V. (2010). Phonological development. In E. Hoff & M. Shatz (Eds.), *Blackwell handbook of language development* (2nd ed.). Malden, MA: Blackwell.

Stokes, C. E., & Raley, R. K. (2009). Cohabitation. In D. Carr (Ed.), *Encyclopedia of the life course and human development.* Boston: Gale Cengage.

Stolzer, J. M. (2009). Attention deficit/hyperactivity disorder. In D. Carr (Ed.), *Encyclopedia of the life course and human development* Boston: Gale Cengage.

Stones, M., & Stones, L. (2007). Sexuality, sensitivity, and intimacy. In J. E. Birren (Ed.), *Encyclopedia of gerontology* (2nd ed.). San Diego: Academic Press.

Stouthamer-Loeber, M., Loeber, R., Wei, E., Farrington, D. P., & Wikstrom, P. H. (2002). Risk and promotive effects in the explanation of persistent serious delinquency in boys. *Journal of Consulting and Clinical Psychology, 70,* 111–123.

Stoutheimer-Loeber, M., Wei, E., Loeber, R., & Masten, A. (2004). Desistance from serious delinquency in the transition to adulthood. *Development and Psychopathology, 16,* 897–918.

Strandberg, T. E., Strandberg, A. Y., Slaomaa, V. V., Pitkala, K., Tilvis, R. S., & Miettinen, T. A. (2007). Alcoholic beverage preference, 29-year mortality, and quality of life in men in old age. *Journals of Gerontology A: Biological Sciences and Medical Sciences, 62,* M213–M218.

Strasberger, V. C. (2009). Why do adolescent health researchers ignore the impact of the media? *Journal of Adolescent Health, 44,* 203–205.

Strathearn, L. (2007). Exploring the neurobiology of attachment. In L. C. Mayes, P. Fonagy, & M. Target (Eds.), *Developmental science and psychoanalysis.* London: Karnac Press.

Strauss, M. A., Sugarman, D. B., & Giles-Sims, J. (1997). Spanking by parents and subsequent antisocial behavior in children. *Archives of Pediatrics and Adolescent Medicine, 151,* 761–767.

Streib, H. (1999). Off-road religion? A narrative approach to fundamentalist and occult orientations of adolescents. *Journal of Adolescence, 22,* 255–267.

Strenze, T. (2007). Intelligence and socioeconomic success: A meta-analytic review of longitudinal research. *Intelligence, 35,* 401–426.

Striegel-Moore, R. H., Silberstein, L. R., & Rodin, J. (1993). The social self in bulimia nervosa: Public self-consciousness, social anxiety, and perceived fraudulence. *Journal of Abnormal Psychology, 102,* 297–303.

Stringer, M., Ratcliffe, S. J., Evans, E. C., & Brown, L. P. (2005). The cost of prenatal care attendance and pregnancy outcomes in low-income working women. *Journal of Obstetrical, Gynecologic, and Neonatal Nursing, 34,* 551–560.

Stroebe, M., Gergen, M. H., Gergen, K. J., & Stroebe, W. (1992). Broken hearts or broken bonds: Love and death in historical perspective. *American Psychologist, 47,* 1205–1212.

Stroebe, M., Schut, H., & Stroebe, W. (2005). Attachment in coping with bereavement: A theoretical integration. *Review of General Psychology, 9,* 48–66.

Strong, B., DeVault, C., Sayad, B., & Yarber, W. (2008). *Human sexuality* (5th ed.). New York: McGraw-Hill.

Stroobant, N., Buijs, D., & Vingerhoets, G. (2009). Variation in brain lateralization during various language tasks: A functional transcranial Doppler study. *Behavioral Brain Research, 199,* 190–196.

Studenski, S., Carlson, M. C., Fillet, H., Greenough, W. T., Kramer, A. F., & Rebok, G. W. (2006). From bedside to bench: Does mental and physical activity promote cognitive vitality in late life? *Science of Aging, Knowledge, and Environment, 10,* e21.

Sturm, R. (2005). Childhood obesity—what we can learn from existing data and social trends. *Prevention of Chronic Diseases, 2,* A12.

Subrahmanyam, K., & Greenfield, P. (2008). Online communication and adolescent relationships. *The Future of Children, 18* (1), 119–146.

Subrahmanyam, K., Smahel, D., & Greenfield, P. (2006). Connecting developmental constructions on the internet: Identity presentation and sexual exploration in online chat rooms. *Developmental Psychology, 42,* 395–406.

Substance Abuse and Mental Health Services Administration. (2005). Substance use tables [online database]. Retrieved November 15, 2005, from *http://www.icpsr.umich.edu/*

Suetta, C., Andersen, J. L., Dalgas, U., Berget, J., Koskinen, S. O., Aagaard, P., Magnusson, S. P., & Kjaer, M. (2008). Resistance training induces qualitative changes in muscle morphology, muscle architecture, and muscle function in postoperative patients. *Journal of Applied Physiology, 105,* 180–186.

Sugimoto, M., Kuze, M., & Uji, Y. (2008). Ultrasound biomicroscopy for membranous congenital cataract. *Canadian Journal of Ophthalmology, 43,* 7–8.

Sugita, Y. (2004). Experience in early infancy is indispensable for color perception. *Current Biology, 14,* 1267–1271.

Sui, X., LaMonte, M. J., Laditka, J. N., Hardin, J. W., Chase, N., Hooker, S. P., & Blair, S. N. (2007). Cardiorespiratory fitness and adiposity as mortality predictors in older adults. *Journal of the American Medical Association, 298,* 2507–2516.

Sullivan, H. S. (1953). *The interpersonal theory of psychiatry.* New York: W. W. Norton.

Sullivan, K., & Sullivan, A. (1980). Adolescent-parent separation. *Developmental Psychology, 16,* 93–99.

Suman, R. P., Udani, R., & Nanavati, R. (2008). Kangaroo mother care for low birth weight infants: A randomized controlled trial. *Indian Pediatrics, 45,* 17–23.

Sumaroka, M., & Bornstein, M. H. (2008). Play. In M. M. Haith & J. B. Benson (Eds.), *Encyclopedia of infant and early childhood development.* Oxford, UK: Elsevier.

Sun, S. S., Liang, R., Huang, T. T., Daniels, S. R., Arsianian, S., Liu, K., Grave, G. D., & Siervogel, R. M. (2008). Childhood obesity predicts adult metabolic syndrome: The Fels Longitudinal Study. *Journal of Pediatrics, 152,* 191–200.

Sunstein, C. R. (2008). Adolescent risk-taking and social meaning: A commentary. *Developmental Review, 28,* 145–152.

Super, C., & Harkness, S. (1997). The cultural structuring of child development. In J. W. Berry, Y. H. Poortinga, & J. Pandey (Eds.), *Handbook of cross-cultural psychology: Vol. 2. Theory and method.* Boston: Allyn & Bacon.

Susman, E. J., & Dorn, L. D. (2009). Puberty: Its role in development. In R. M. Lerner & L. Steinberg (Eds.), *Handbook of adolescent psychology* (3rd ed). New York: Wiley.

Susman, E. J., & others. (2009, in press). Trajectories of the characteristics of pubertal development: Timing, rate, and synchrony. *Journal of the American Medical Association.*

Susman, E. J., & Rogol, A. (2004). Puberty and psychological development. In R. Lerner & L. Steinberg (Eds.), *Handbook of adolescent psychology.* New York: Wiley.

Suvas, S. (2008). Advancing age and immune cell dysfunction: Is it reversible or not? *Expert Opinion on Biological Therapy, 8,* 657–658.

Suyemoto, K. L. (2009). Multiracial Asian Americans. In N. Tewari & A. Alvarez (Eds.), *Asian American psychology.* Clifton, NJ: Psychology Press.

Suzuki, A., Sekiguchi, S., Asano, S., & Itoh, M. (2008). Pharmacological topics of bone metabolism: Recent advances in pharmacological management of osteoporosis. *Journal of Pharmacological Science, 106,* 530–535.

Svanborg, P., Thernlund, G., Gustafsson, P. A., Hägglöf, B., Poole, L., & Kadesjö, B. (2009). Efficacy and safety of atomoxetine as add-on psychoeducation in the treatment of attention deficit/hyperactivity disorder: A randomized, double-bind, placebo-controlled study in stimulant-naïve Swedish children and adolescents. *European Child and Adolescent Psychiatry, 18,* 240–249.

Sveen, C. A., & Walby, F. A. (2008). Suicide survivors' mental health and grief reactions: A systematic review of controlled studies. *Suicide and Life-Threatening Behavior, 38,* 13–29.

Sveistrup, H., Schneiberg, S., McKinley, P. A., McGadyen, B. J., & Levin, M. F. (2008). Head, arm and trunk coordination during reaching in children. *Experimental Brain Research, 188,* 237–247.

Svihula, J., & Estes, C. L. (2008). Social security politics: Ideology and reform. *Journals of Gerontology B: Psychological Sciences and Social Sciences, 62,* S79–S89.

Sviri, S., Garbg, Y., Stav, I., Rubinow, A., Linton, D. M., Caine, Y. G., & Marcus, E. L. (2009). Contraindications in end-of-life decisions for self and other, expressed by relatives of chronically ventilated persons. *Journal of Critical Care, 24,* 293–301.

Swaab, D. F., Chung, W. C., Kruijver, P. P., Hofman, M. A., & Ishunina, T. A. (2001). Structural and functional sex differences in the human hypothalamus. *Hormones and Behavior, 40,* 93–98.

Swahn, M., Bossarte, R. M., & Sullivent, E. E. (2008). Age of alcohol use initiation, suicidal behavior, and peer and dating violence victimization and perpetration among high-risk, seventh-grade adolescents. *Pediatrics, 121,* 297–305.

Swain, S. L., & Nikolich-Zugich, J. (2009). Key research opportunities in immune system aging. *Journals of Gerontology A: Biological Sciences and Medical Sciences, 64,* 183–186.

Swain, S. O. (1992). Men's friendship with women. In P. M. Nardi (Ed.), *Gender in intimate relationships.* Belmont, CA: Wadsworth.

Swamy, G. K., Ostbye, T., & Skjaerven, R. (2008). Association of preterm birth with long-term survival, reproduction, and next generation preterm birth. *Journal of the American Medical Association, 299,* 1429–1436.

Swanson, C. R., Sesso, S. L., & Emborg, M. E. (2009). Can we prevent Parkinson's disease. *Frontiers in Bioscience, 14,* 1642–1660.

Swanson, H. L. (1999). What develops in working memory? A life span perspective. *Developmental Psychology, 35,* 986–1000.

Swartz, T. T. (2008, Spring). Family capital and the invisible transfer of privilege: Intergenerational support and social class in early adulthood. *New Directions in Child and Adolescent Development, 119,* 11–24.

Swearer, S. M., Espelage, D. L., & Napolitano, S. A. (2009). *Bullying prevention and intervention.* New York: Guilford.

Sweeney, M. M. (2009). Remarriage. In D. Carr (Ed.), *Encyclopedia of the life course and human development.* Boston: Gale Cengage.

Sweeting, H. N. (2008). Gendered dimensions of obesity in childhood and adolescence. *Nutrition Journal, 7,* 1.

Syed, M., & Azmitia, M. (2008). A narrative approach to ethnic identity in emerging adulthood: Bringing life to the identity status model. *Developmental Psychology, 2008,* 1012–1027.

Sykes, C. J. (1995). *Dumbing down our kids: Why American children feel good about themselves but can't read, write, or add.* New York: St. Martin's Press.

Szinovacz, M. E. (2009). Grandparenthood. In D. Carr (Ed.), *Encyclopedia of the life course and human development.* Boston: Gale Cengage.

T

Tabira, T. (2009). Decorated plaques in Alzheimer's disease. *Annals of Neurology, 65,* 4–6.

Taddio, A. (2008). Circumcision. In M. M. Haith & J. B. Benson (Eds.), *Encyclopedia of infant and early childhood development.* Oxford, UK: Elsevier.

Tafoya, M., & Spitzberg, B. H. (2007). The dark side of infidelity. In B. H. Spitzberg and W. R. Cupach (Eds.), *The dark side of interpersonal communication.* Mahwah, NJ: Erlbaum.

Tager-Flusberg, H. & Zukowski, A. (2009). Putting words together: Morphology and syntax in the preschool years. In J. Berko Gleason & N. Ratner (Eds.), *The development of language* (7th ed.). Boston: Allyn & Bacon.

Tahir, L., & Gruber, H. B. (2003). Developmental trajectories and creative work in late life. In J. Demick & C. Andreoletti (Eds.), *Handbook of adult development,* New York: Kluwer.

Talaro, K. P. (2008). *Foundations of microbiology* (6th ed.). New York: McGraw-Hill.

Talbot, J., Baker, J. K., & McHale, J. P. (2009). Sharing the love: Prebirth adult attachment status and coparenting adjustment during infancy. The transition to parenthood. *Parenting: Science & Practice, 9,* 56–77.

Taler, S. J. (2009). Hypertension in women. *Current Hypertension Reports, 11,* 23–28.

Talge, N. M., Neal, C., Glover, V., and the Early Stress, Translational Research and Prevention Science Network: Fetal and Neonatal Experience on Child and Adolescent Mental Health. (2007). Antenatal maternal stress and long-term effects on neurodevelopment: How and why? *Journal of Child Psychology and Psychiatry, 48,* 245–261.

Tamis-LeMonda, C. S., & McFadden, K. E. (2010). The United States of America. In M. H. Bornstein (Ed.), *Handbook of cultural developmental science.* New York: Psychology Press.

Tamis-LeMonda, C. S., Way, N., Hughes, D., Yoshikawa, H., Kallman, R. K., & Niwa, E. Y. (2008). Parents' goals for children: The dynamic coexistence of individualism and collectivism in cultures and individuals. *Social Development, 17,* 183–209.

Tang, K. L. (2008). Taking older people's rights seriously: The role of international law. *Journal of Aging and Social Policy, 20,* 99–117.

Tanne, D. (1990). *You just don't understand: Women and men in conversatin.* New York: Ballantine.

Tashiro, T., & Frazier, P. (2003). "I'll never be in a relationship like that again": Personal growth following romantic relationship break-ups. *Personal Relationships, 10,* 113–128.

Tashiro, T., Frazier, P., & Berman, M. (2006). Stress-related growth following divorce and relationship dissolution. In M. A. Fine & J. H. Harvey (Eds.), *Handbook of divorce and relationship dissolution.* Mahwah, NJ: Erlbaum.

Tasker, F. L., & Golombok, S. (1997). *Growing up in a lesbian family: Effects on child development.* New York: Guilford.

Tauman, R., & Gozal, D. (2006). Obesity and obstructive sleep apnea in children. *Pediatric Respiratory Reviews, 7,* 247–259.

Taveras, E. M., Rifas-Shiman, S. L., Oken, E., Gunderson, E. P., & Gillman, M. W. (2008). Short sleep duration in infancy and risk of childhood overweight. *Archives of Pediatric and Adolescent Medicine, 162,* 305–311.

Tavris, C., & Wade, C. (1984). *The longest war: Sex differences in perspective* (2nd ed.). San Diego: Harcourt Brace Jovanovich.

Taylor, F. M. A., Ko, R., & Pan, M. (1999). Prenatal and reproductive health care. In E. J. Kramer, S. L. Ivey, & Y.-W. Ying (Eds.), *Immigrant women's health.* San Francisco: Jossey-Bass.

Taylor, L. S., & Whittaker, C. R. (2009). *Bridging multiple worlds* (2nd ed.). Boston: Allyn & Bacon.

Taylor, R. J., Chatters, L. M., & Jackson, J. S. (2007). Religious and spiritual involvement among older African Americans, Caribbean Blacks, and non-Hispanic Whites: Findings from the National Survey of American life. *Journals of Gerontology B: Psychological Sciences and Social Sciences, 62,* S238–S250.

Taylor, S. P. (1982). Mental health and successful coping among Black women. In R. C. Manuel (Ed.), *Minority aging.* Westport, CT: Greenwood.

Temple, B., Janzen, B. L., Chad, K., Bell, G., Reeder, B., & Martin, L. (2008). The health benefits of a physical activity program for older adults living in congregate housing. *Canadian Journal of Public Housing, 99,* 36–40.

Temple, C., Nathan, R., Temple, R., & Burris, N. A. (1993). *The beginnings of writing* (3rd ed.). Boston: Allyn & Bacon.

Templeton, J. L., & Eccles, J. S. (2005). The relation between spiritual development and identity processes. In E. Roehlkepartain, P. E. King, L. Wagener, & P. L. Benson (Eds.), *The handbook of spirituality in childhood and adolescence.* Thousand Oaks, CA: Sage.

Teno, J. M., Clarridge, B. R., Casey, V., Welch, L. C., Welch, T., Shield, R., & Mor, V. (2004). Family perspectives on end-of-life care at the last place of care. *Journal of the American Medical Association, 291,* 88–93.

Terman, L. (1925). *Genetic studies of genius. Vol. 1: Mental and physical traits of a thousand gifted children.* Stanford, CA: Stanford University Press.

Terry, D. F., Nolan, V. G., Andersen, S. L., Perls, T. T., & Cawthon, R. (2008b). Association of longer telomeres with better health in centenarians. *Journals of Gerontology A: Biological Sciences and Medical Sciences, 63,* 809–812.

Terry, D. F., Sebastiani, P., Andersen, S. L., & Perls, T. T. (2008). Disentangling the roles of disability and morbidity in survival to exceptional old age. *Archives of Internal Medicine, 168,* 277–283.

Teti, D. (2001). Retrospect and prospect in the psychological study of sibling relationships. In J. P. McHale & W. S. Grolnick (Eds.), *Retrospect and prospect in the psychological study of families.* Mahwah, NJ: Erlbaum.

Tewari, A., & Shah, G. K. (2008). Presbyopia-correcting intraocular lens: What retinal surgeons should know. *Retina, 28,* 535–537.

Tewari, N., & Alvarez, A. (Eds.). (2009). *Asian American psychology.* New York: Psychology Press.

Thabet, A. A., Ibraheem, A. N., Shivram, R., Winter, E. A., & Vostanis, P. (2009). Parenting support and PTSD in children of a war zone. *International Journal of Social Psychiatry, 55,* 225–227.

Tharp, R. G. (1994). Intergroup differences among Native Americans in socialization and child cognition: An ethnogenetic analysis. In P. M. Greenfield & R. Cocking (Eds.), *Cross-cultural roots of minority child development.* Mahwah, NJ: Erlbaum.

Tharp, R. G., & Gallimore, R. (1988). *Rousing minds to life: Teaching, learning, and schooling in social context.* New York: Cambridge University Press.

Thelen, E. (2000). Perception and motor development. In A. Kazdin (Ed.), *Encyclopedia of psychology,* Washington, DC, & New York: American Psychological Association and Oxford University Press.

Thelen, E., Corbetta, D., Kamm, K., Spencer, J. P., Schneider, K., & Zernicke, R. F. (1993). The transition to reaching: Mapping intention and intrinsic dynamics. *Child Development, 64,* 1058–1098.

Thelen, E., & Smith, L. B. (1998). Dynamic systems theory. In W. Damon (Ed.), *Handbook of child psychology* (5th ed., Vol. 1.). New York Wiley.

Thelen, E., & Smith, L. B. (2006). Dynamic development of action and thought. In W. Damon & R. Lerner (Eds.), *Handbook of child psychology* (6th ed.). New York: Wiley.

Theokas, C. (2009). Youth sports participation—a view of the issues: Introduction to the special section. *Developmental Psychology, 45,* 303–306.

Thiele, D. M., & Whelan, T. A. (2008). The relationship between grandparent satisfaction, meaning, and generativity. *International Journal of Aging and Human Development, 66,* 21–48.

Thio, A. (2010). *Deviant behavior* (10th ed.). Boston: Allyn & Bacon.

Thomaes, S., Bushman, B. J., Stegge, H., & Olthof, T. (2008). Trumping shame by blasts of noise: Narcissism, self-esteem, shame, and aggression in young adolescents. *Child Development, 79,* 1792–1801.

Thomann, C. R., & Carter, A. S. (2008). Social and emotional development theories. In M. M. Haith & J. B. Benson (Eds.), *Encyclopedia of infant and early childhood development.* Oxford, UK: Elsevier.

Thomas, A., & Chess, S. (1991). Temperament in adolescence and its functional significance. In R. M. Lerner, A. C. Petersen, & J. Brooks-Gunn (Eds.), *Encyclopedia of adolescence* (Vol. 2). New York: Garland.

Thomas, D. E., Bierman, K. L., Thompson, C., & the Conduct Problems Prevention Research Group. (2009, in press). Double jeopardy: Child and school characteristics that undermine school readiness and predict disruptive behavior at school entry. *School Psychology Review.*

Thoma, S. J. (2006). Research on the Defining Issues Test. In M. Killen & J. Smetana (Eds.), *Handbook of moral development.* Mahwah, NJ: Erlbaum.

Thomas, M. S. C., & Johnson, M. H. (2008). New advances in understanding sensitive periods in brain development. *Current Directions in Psychological Science, 17,* 1–5.

Thompson, D. R., Obarzanek, E., Franko, D. L., Barton, B. A., Morrison, J., Biro, F. M., **Daniels, S. R., & Striegel-Moore, R. H.** (2007). Childhood overweight and cardiovascular disease risk factors: The National Heart, Lung, and Blood Institute Growth and Health Study. *Journal of Pediatrics, 150,* 18–25.

Thompson, K. M., Crosby, R. D., Wonderlich, S. A., Mitchell, J. E., Redline, J., Demuth, G., Smyth, J., & Haseltine, B. (2003). Psychopathology and sexual trauma in childhood and adulthood. *Journal of Traumatic Stress, 16,* 35–38.

Thompson, P. M., Giedd, J. N., Woods, R. P., MacDonald, D., Evans, A. C., & Toga, A. W. (2000). Growth patterns in the developing brain detected by using continuum mechanical tensor maps. *Nature, 404,* 190–193.

Thompson, R., & Murachver, T. (2001). Predicting gender from electronic discourse. *British Journal of Social Psychology, 40,* 193–208.

Thompson, R. A. (2006). The development of the person. In W. Damon & R. Lerner (Eds.), *Handbook of child psychology* (6th ed.). New York: Wiley.

Thompson, R. A. (2007). Unpublished review of J. W. Santrock's *Children,* 10th ed. (New York: McGraw-Hill).

Thompson, R. A. (2008). Unpublished review of J. W. Santrock's *Life-span development,* 12th ed. (New York: McGraw-Hill).

Thompson, R. A. (2009a, in press). Emotional development. In R. A. Schweder (Ed.), *The Chicago companion to the child.* Chicago: University of Chicago Press.

Thompson, R. A. (2009b, in press). Feeling and understanding through the prism of relationships. In S. D. Calkins & M. A. Bell (Eds.), *Child development at the intersection of emotion and cognition.* Washington, DC: American Psychological Association.

Thompson, R. A. (2009c). Making the most of small effects. *Social Development, 18,* 247–251.

Thompson, R. A. (2009d, in press). Early foundations: Conscience and the development of moral character. In D. Narváez & D. Lapsley (Eds.), *Moral self, identity and character: Prospects for a new field of study.* New York: Cambridge University Press.

Thompson, R. A. (2009e, in press). The child care debate 20 years later. *Social Development.*

Thompson, R. A., & Goodman, M. (2009). Development of self, relationships, and socioemotional competence: Foundations of early school success. In O. A. Barbarin & B. H. Wasak (Eds.), *Handbook of child development and early education.* New York: Guilford.

Thompson, R. A., & Goodvin, R. (2005). The individual child: Temperament, emotion, and personality. In M. H. Bornstein & M. Lamb (Eds.), *Developmental science* (5th ed.). Mahwah, NJ: Erlbaum.

Thompson, R. A., & Goodvin, R. (2007). Taming the tempest in the teapot: Emotion regulation in toddlers. In C. A. Brownell & C. B. Kopp (Eds.), *Socioemotional development in toddlers.* New York: Guilford.

Thompson, R. A., Lewis, M., & Calkins, S. D. (2009, in press). Reassessing emotion regulation. *Child Development Perspectives.*

Thompson, R. A., McGinley, M., & Meyer, S. (2006). Understanding values in relationships. In M. Killen & J. G. Smetana (Eds.), *Handbook of moral development.* Mahwah, NJ: Erlbaum.

Thompson, R. A., Meyer, S. A., & Jochem, R. (2008). Emotion regulation. In M. M. Haith & J. B. Benson (Eds.), *Encyclopedia of infant and early childhood development.* Oxford, UK: Elsevier.

Thompson, R. A., Meyer, S., Virmani, E., Waters, S., Raikes, H. A., & Jochem, R. (2009, April). *Parent-child relationships, conversation, and developing emotion regulation.* Paper presented at the meeting of the Society for Research in Child Development, Denver.

Thompson, R. A., & Nelson C. A. (2001). Developmental science and the media. *American Psychologist, 56,* 5–15.

Thompson, R. A., & Newton, E. (2009). Infant-caregiver communication. In H. T. Reis & S. Sprecher (Eds.), *Encyclopedia of human relationships.* Thousand Oaks, CA: Sage.

Thompson, R. A., & Virmani, E. A. (2009, in press). Creating persons: Culture, self, and personality development. In M. H. Bornstein (Ed.), *Handbook of cross-cultural developmental science.* Clifton, NJ: Psychology Press.

Thoni, A., & Moroder, L. (2004). Waterbirth: A safe and natural delivery method. Experience after 1355 waterbirths in Italy. *Midwifery Today, 70,* 44–48.

Thorley, V. (2009). Guidelines to improve maternity practices and support breast-feeding are readily available. *Southern Medical Journal, 102,* 222–223.

Thornton, J. G. (2007). Progesterone and preterm labor—still no definite answers. *New England Journal of Medicine, 357,* 499–501.

Thornton, R., & Light, L. L. (2006). Language comprehension and production in normal aging. In J. E. Birren & K. W. Schaie (Eds.), *Handbook of the psychology of aging* (6th ed.). San Diego: Academic Press.

Thornton, W. J. L., & Dumke, H. A. (2005). Age differences in everyday problem-solving and decision-making effectiveness: A meta-analytic review. *Psychology and Aging, 20,* 85–99.

Thorton, A., & Camburn, D. (1989). Religious participation and sexual behavior and attitudes. *Journal of Marriage and the Family, 49,* 117–128.

Tierney, M. C., Yao, C., Kiss, A., & McDowell, I. (2005). Neuropsychological tests accurately predict incident Alzheimer disease after 5 and 10 years. *Neurology, 64,* 1853–1859.

TIMMS. (2008). *Trends in International Mathematics and Science Study, 2007.* Washington, DC: National Center for Education Statistics.

Tiran, D. (2008). *Bailliere's midwives' dictionary* (11th ed.). Oxford, UK: Elsevier.

Tita, A. T., & others. (2009). Timing of elective repeat cesarean delivery at term and neonatal outcomes. *New England Journal of Medicine, 360,* 111–1120.

Tolani, N., & Brooks-Gunn, J. (2008). Family support, international trends. In M. M. Haith & J. B. Benson (Eds.), *Encyclopedia of infant and early childhood development.* Oxford, UK: Elsevier.

Tomasello, M. (2006). Acquiring linguistic constructions. In W. Damon & R. Lerner (Eds.), *Handbook of child psychology* (6th ed.). New York: Wiley.

Tomasello, M. (2009, in press). *Why we cooperate.* Cambridge, MA: MIT Press.

Tomasello, M., & Carpenter, M. (2007). Shared intentionality. *Developmental Science 10,* 121–125.

Tomaseno, M. (2003). *Constructing a language: A usage-based theory of language acquisition.* Cambridge, MA: Harvard University Press.

Tompkins, G. E. (2010a). *Literacy for the 21st century* (5th ed.). Boston: Allyn & Bacon.

Tompkins, G. E. (2010b). *Literacy in the middle grades* (2nd Ed.). Boston: Allyn & Bacon.

Tompkins, S. A., & Bell, P. A. (2009). Examination of a psychoeducational intervention and a respite grant in relieving psychosocial stressors associated with being an Alzheimer's caregiver. *Journal of Gerontological Social Work, 52,* 89–104.

Torges, C. M., Stewart, A. J., Nolen-Hoeksema, S. (2008). Regret resolution, aging, and adapting to loss. *Psychology and Aging, 23,* 169–180.

Tough, S. C., Newburn-Cook, C., Johnston, D. W., Svenson, L. W., Rose, S., & Belik, J. (2002). Delayed childbearing and its impact on population rate changes in lower birth weight, multiple birth, and preterm delivery. *Pediatrics, 109,* 399–403.

Trafimow, D., Triandis, H. C., & Goto, S. G. (1991). Some tests of the distinction between the prime and collective self. *Journal of Personality and Social Psychology, 60,* 649–655.

Trask, B. S., & Koivur, M. (2007). Trends in marriage and cohabitation. In B. S. Trask & R. R. Hamon (Eds.), *Cultural diversity and families.* Thousand Oaks, CA: Sage.

Treffers, P. E., Eskes, M., Kleiverda, G., & van Alten, D. (1990). Home births and minimal medical interventions. *Journal of the American Medical Association, 246,* 2207–2208.

Trehub, S. E., Schneider, B. A., Thorpe, L. A., & Judge, P. (1991). Observational measures of auditory sensitivity in early infancy. *Developmental Psychology, 27,* 40–49.

Trejos-Castillo, E., & Vazonyi, A. T. (2009). Risky sexual behavior in first and second generation Hispanic immigrant youth. *Journal of Youth and Adolescence, 38,* 719–731.

Triandis, H. C. (1994). *Culture and social behavior.* New York: McGraw-Hill.

Triandis, H. C. (2001). Individualism and collectivism. In D. Matsumoto (Ed.), *The handbook of culture and psychology.* New York: Oxford University Press.

Triandis, H. C. (2007). Culture and psychology: A history of their relationship. In S. Kitayama & D. Cohen (Eds.), *Handbook of cultural psychology.* New York: Guilford.

Triche, E. W., & Hossain, N. (2007). Environmental factors implicated in the causations of adverse pregnancy outcome. *Seminars in Perinatology, 31,* 240–242.

Trimble, J. E. (1988, August). *The enculturation of contemporary psychology.* Paper presented at the meeting of the American Psychological Association, Orleans.

Trimmer, P. A., & Bennett, J. P. (2009). The cybrid model of sporadic Parkinson's disease. *Experimental Neurology, 218,* 320–325.

Tripp, G., & Wickens, J. R. (2009, in press). Neurobiology of ADHD. *Psychopharmacology.*

Trost, S. G., Fees, B., & Dzewaltowski, D. (2008). Feasibility and efficacy of "move and learn" physical activity curriculum in preschool children. *Journal of Physical Activity and Health, 5,* 88–103.

Troster, A. I. (2009). Neuropsychology of deep brain stimulation in neurology and psychiatry. *Frontiers in Bioscience, 14,* 1857–1879.

Trulear, H. D. (2000). *Faith-based institutions and high-risk youth: First report to the field.* Philadelphia: Public/Private Ventures.

Truog, R. D. (2007). Brain death—too flawed to endure, too ingrained to abandon. *Journal of Law, Medicine, and Ethnics, 35,* 273–281.

Trzesniewski, K. H., Donnellan, M. B., Moffitt, T. E., Robins, R. W., Poulton, R., & Caspi, A. (2006). Low self-esteem during adolescence predicts poor health, criminal behavior, and limited economic prospects during adulthood. *Developmental Psychology, 42,* 381–390.

Trzesniewski, K. H., Donnellan, M. B., & Robins, R. W. (2008a). Do today's young people really think they are so extraordinary? An examination of secular trends in narcissism and self-enhancement. *Psychological Science, 19,* 181–188.

Trzesniewski, M., Donnellan, M. B., & Robins, R. W. (2008b). Is "Generation Me" really more narcissistic than previous generations? *Journal of Personality, 76,* 903–918.

Tucker, C. J., McHale, S. M., & Crouter, A. C. (2003). Conflict resolution: Links with adolescents' family relationships and individual well-being. *Journal of Family Issues, 24,* 715–726.

Tucker, J. S., Ellickson, P. L., & Klein, M. S. (2003). Predictors of the transition to regular smoking during adolescence and young adulthood. *Journal of Adolescent Health, 32,* 314–324.

Tucker-Drob, E. M., Johnson, K. E., & Jones, R. N. (2009). The cognitive reserve hypothesis: A longitudinal examination of age-associated declines in reasoning and processing speed. *Developmental Psychology, 45,* 431–446.

Turiel, E. (2006). The development of morality. In W. Damon & R. Lerner (Eds.), *Handbook of child psychology* (6th ed.). New York: Wiley.

Turnbull, H. R., Huerta, N., & Stowe, M. (2009). *What every teacher should know about: The Individuals with Disabilities Education Act as amended in 2004* (2nd ed.). Upper Saddle River, NJ: Prentice Hall.

Turner, B. F. (1982). Sex-related differences in aging. In B. B. Wolman (Ed.), *Handbook of developmental psychology.* Englewood Cliffs NJ: Prentice Hall.

Twenge, J. M., Konrath, S., Foster, J. D., Campbell, W. K., & Bushman, B. J. (2008a). Egos inflating over time: A cross-temporal meta-analysis of the Narcissistic Personality Inventory. *Journal of Personality, 76,* 875–902.

Twenge, J. M., Konrath, S., Foster, J. D., Campbell, W. K., & Bushman, B. J. (2008b). Further evidence of an increase in narcissism among college students. *Journal of Personality, 76,* 919–928.

Tyas, S. L., Salazar, J. C., Snowdon, D. A., Desrosiers, M. F., Riley, K. P., Mendiondo, M. S., & Kryscio, R. J. (2007). Transitions to mild cognitive impairments, dementia, and death: Findings from the Nun Study. *American Journal of Epidemiology, 165,* 1231–1238.

U

Uba, L. (1992). Cultural barriers to health care for Southeast Asian refugees. *Public Health Reports, 107,* 544–549.

Udry, J. R., & others. (1985). Serum androgenic hormones motivate sexual behavior in adolescent boys. *Fertility and Sterility, 43,* 90–94.

Uhls, Y. T., & Greenfield, P. M. (2009, in press). Adolescents and electronic communication: Risks, benefits, and ideas for parenting. To appear at www.education.com

Umana-Taylor, A. J. (2009). Research with Latino early adolescents. *Journal of Early Adolescence, 29,* 5–15.

Umana-Taylor, A. J., Gonzales-Backen, M. A., & Guimond, A. B. (2009). Latino adolescents' ethnic identity: Is there a developmental progression and does growth in ethnic identity predict growth in self-esteem? *Child Development, 80,* 391–405.

Umana-Taylor, A. J., Vargas-Changes, D., Garcia, C. D., & Gonzales-Backen, M. (2008). A longitudinal examination of Latino adolescents' ethnic identity, coping with discrimination, and self-esteem. *Journal of Early Adolescence, 28,* 16–50.

UNAIDS. (2008). *UNAIDS World AIDS Day Report.* New York: United Nations.

Underhill, K., Montgomery, P., & Operario, D. (2007). Sexual abstinence programs to prevent HIV infection in high-income countries. *British Medical Journal, 335,* 248.

UNICEF. (2003). *The state of the world's children, 2003.* Geneva: Author.

UNICEF. (2004). *The state of the world's children, 2002.* Geneva: Author.

UNICEF. (2005). *The state of the world's children, 2005.* Geneva: Author.

UNICEF. (2006). *The state of the world's children, 2006.* Geneva: Author.

UNICEF. (2007). *The state of the world's children, 2007.* Geneva: Author.

UNICEF. (2009). *The state of the world's children, 2009.* Geneva: Author.

UNICEF. (2010). *The state of the world's children, 2010.* Geneva: Author.

United Nations. (2002). *Improving the quality of life of girls.* New York: Author.

Updegraff, K. A., McHale, S., Whiteman, S. D., Thayer, S. M., & Delgado, M. Y. (2005). Adolescent sibling relationships in Mexican American families: Exploring the role of familism. *Journal of Family Psychology, 19,* 512–522.

U.S. Bureau of Labor Statistics. (2008). *Employment of older workers.* Washington, DC: U.S. Department of Labor.

U.S. Census Bureau. (2005). Marital Status and living arrangements. Washington, DC: Author.

U.S. Census Bureau. (2006). *Death statistics.* Washington, DC: Author.

U.S. Census Bureau. (2006). *Statistical abstracts of the United States.* Washington, DC: U.S. Government Printing Office.

U.S. Census Bureau. (2008). *Death statistics.* Washington, DC: Auther.

U.S. Census Bureau. (2008). *Population statistics.* Washington, DC: U.S. Department of Labor.

U.S. Department of Energy. (2001). *The human genome project.* Washington, DC: Author.

U.S. Department of Health and Human Services. (2009). *Child maltreatment, 2007.* Washington, DC: U.S. Government Printing Office.

U.S. Department of Health and Human Services. (2009). *Folic acid.* Retrieved January 26, 2009, from www.cdc.gov/ncbddd/folicacid/

U.S. Food and Drug Administration. (2004, March 19). *An important message for pregnant women and women of childbearing age who may become pregnant about the risk of mercury in fish.* Washington, DC: Author.

V

Vacca, J. A., Vacca, R. T., Gove, M. K., Burkey, L. C., Lenhart, L. A., & McKeon, C. A. (2009). *Reading and learning to read* (7th ed.). Boston: Allyn & Bacon.

Vaillant, G. E. (1977). *Adaptation to life.* Boston: Little, Brown.

Vaillant, G. E. (2002). *Aging well.* Boston: Little, Brown.

Valkenburg, P. M., & Peter, J. (2009). Social consequences of the Internet for adolescents. *Current Directions in Psychological Science, 18,* 1–5.

Van Beveren, T. T. (2008, January). *Personal conversation.* Richardson, TX: Department of Psychology, University of Texas at Dallas.

Van Buren, E., & Graham, S. (2003). *Redefining ethnic identity: Its relationship to positive and negative school adjustment outcomes for minority youth.* Paper presented at the meeting of the Society for Research in Child Development, Tampa.

Vandehey, M., Diekhoff, G., & LaBeff, E. (2007). College cheating: A 20-year follow-up and the addition of an honor code. *Journal of College Development, 48,* 468–480.

Vandell, D. L. (2004). Early child care: The known and unknown. *Merrill-Palmer Quarterly, 50,* 387–414.

van den Boom, D. C. (1989). Neonatal irritability and the development of attachment. In G. A. Kohnstamm, J. E. Bates, & M. K. Rothbart (Eds.), *Temperament in childhood.* New York: Wiley.

van den Heuvel, A., & Marteau, T. M. (2008). Cultural variation in values attached to informed choice in the context of prenatal diagnosis. *Seminars in Fetal and Neonatal Medicine, 13,* 99–102.

van der Borght, K., & others. (2009, in press). Physical exercise leads to rapid adaptations in hippocampal vasculature: Temporal dynamics and relationship to cell proliferation and neurogenesis. *Hippocampus.*

van der Sluis, S., & others. (2008). Sex differences on the WISC-R in Belgium and the Netherlands. *Intelligence, 36,* 48–67.

van Hof, P., van der Kamp, J., & Savelsbergh, G. J. (2008). The relation between infants' perception of catchableness and the control of catching. *Developmental Psychology, 44,* 182–194.

van IJzendoorn, M. H., & Kroonenberg, P. M. (1988). Cross-cultural patterns of attachment: A meta-analysis of the Strange Situation. *Child Development, 59,* 147–156.

van IJzendoorn, M. H., & Sagi-Schwartz, A. (2008). Cross-cultural patterns of attachment: Universal and contextual dimensions. In J. Cassidy & P. R. Shaver (Eds.), *Handbook of attachment* (2nd ed.). New York: Guilford.

Vankrunkelsven, P., & others. (2009, in press). Reduction in hormone replacement therapy use and declining breast cancer incidence in the Belgian province of Limburg. *Breast Cancer Research and Treatment.*

Van Orden, K. A., Witte, T. K., Gordon, K. H., Bender, T. W., & Joiner, T. E. (2008). Suicidal desire and the capability for suicide: Tests of the interpersonal-psychological theory of suicidal behavior among adults. *Journal of Consulting and Clinical Psychology, 76,* 72–83.

van Praag, H. (2008). Neurogenesis and exercise: Past and future directions. *Neuromolecular Medicine, 10,* 128–140.

van Praag, H. (2009). Exercise and the brain: Something to chew on. *Trends in Neuroscience, 32,* 283–290.

Van Remmen, H., & Jones, D. P. (2009). Current thoughts on the role of mitochondria and free radicals in the biology of aging. *Journals of Gerontology A: Biological Sciences and Medical Sciences, 64,* 171–174.

van Solinge, H., & Henkens, K. (2005). Couples' adjustment to retirement: A multi-factor panel study. *Journals of Gerontology B: Psychological Sciences and Social Sciences, 60,* S11–S20.

Van Voorhees, B. W., & others. (2008). Protective and vulnerability factors predicting new-onset depressive episode is a representative of U.S. adolescents. *Journal of Adolescent Health, 42,* 605–616.

Vasan, N. (2002). Commentary in "18-year-old inductees." Retrieved April 24, 2009, from http://thekidshalloffame.com/CustomPage19.html

Vasdev, G. (2008). *Obstetric anesthesia.* Oxford, UK: Elsevier.

Vaughn, B. E., Colvin, T. N., Azria, M. R., Caya, L., & Krzysik, L. (2001). Dyadic analyses of friendship in a sample of preschool-aged children attending Headstart. *Child Development, 71,* 862–878.

Vellone, E., Piras, G., Talucci, C., & Cohen, M. Z. (2008). Quality of life for caregivers of people with Alzheimer's disease. *Journal of Advanced Nursing, 61,* 222–231.

Venners, S. A., Wang, X., Chen, C., Wang, L., Chen, D., Guang, W., Huang, A., Ryan, L., O'Conner, J., Lasley, B., Overstreet, J., Wilcox, A., & Xu, X. (2005). Paternal smoking and pregnancy loss: A prospective study using a biomarker of pregnancy. *American Journal of Epidemiology, 159,* 993–1001.

Ventura, S. J., Abma, C., Mosher, W. D., & Henshaw, S. K. (2008). Estimated pregnancy rates by outcome for the United States, 1990–2004. *National Vital Statistics Reports, 56,* 1–25, 28.

Vernazza-Martin, S., Tricon, V., Martin, N., Mesure, S., Azulay, J. P., & Le Pellec-Muller, A. (2008, in press). Effect of aging on coordination between equilibrium and movement: What changes? *Experimental Brain Research.*

Vicente-Rodriguez, G., & others. (2008). Television watching, videogames, and excess of body weight in Spanish adolescents: The AVENA Study. *Nutrition, 24,* 654–662.

Viikari, J., Niinikoski, H., Raitakari, O. T., & Simell, O. (2009). The initiatives and outcomes for cardiovascular risks that can be achieved through pediatric counseling. *Current Opinion in Lipidology, 20,* 17–23.

Villegas, R., Gao, Y. T., Yang, G., Li, H. L., Elasy, T., Zheng, W., & Shu, X. O. (2008). Duration of breast-feeding and the incidence of type 2 diabetes mellitus in the Shanghai Women's Health Study. *Diabetologia, 51,* 258–266.

Vina, J., Borras, C., Gambini, J., Sastre, J., & Pallardo, F. V. (2005). Why females live longer than males: Control of longevity by hormones. *Science of Aging Knowledge Environment, 23,* e17.

Visher, E., & Visher, J. (1989). Parenting coalitions after remarriage: Dynamics and therapeutic guidelines. *Family Relations, 38,* 65–70.

Visootsak, J., & Sherman, S. (2007). Neuropsychiatric and behavioral aspects of trisomy 21. *Current Psychiatry Reports, 9,* 135–140.

Visser, M., Simonsick, E. M., Colbert, L. H., Brach, J., Rubin, S. M., Kritchevsky, S. B., Newman, A. B., & Harris, T. B. (2005). Type and intensity of activity and risk of mobility limitation: The mediating role of muscle parameters. *Journal of the American Geriatrics Society, 53,* 762–770.

Vitaro, F., Boivin, M., & Bukowski, W. M. (2009). The role of friendship in child and adolescent psychosocial development. In K. H. Rubin, W. M. Bukowski, & B. Laursen (Eds.), *Handbook of peer interaction, relationships, and groups.* New York: Guilford.

Vitaro, F., Pedersen, S., & Brendgen, M. (2007). Children's disruptiveness, peer rejection, friends' deviancy, and delinquent behaviors: A process-oriented approach. *Development and Psychopathology, 19,* 433–453.

Vogel, I., Brug, J., Hosli, E. J., van der Ploeg, C. P., & Raat, H. (2008b). MP3 players and hearing loss: Adolescents' perceptions of loud music and hearing conservation. *Journal of Pediatrics, 152,* 400–404.

Vogel, I., Brug, J., van de Ploeg, C. P., & Raat, H. (2008a). Young people's exposure to loud music: A summary of the literature. *American Journal of Preventive Medicine, 33,* 124–133.

von Hofsten, C. (2008). Motor and physical development manual. In M. M. Haith & J. B. Benson (Eds.), *Encyclopedia of infant and early childhood development.* Oxford, UK: Elsevier.

von Tilburg, T. (2009). Social integration/isolation, later life. In D. Carr (Ed.), *Encyclopedia of the life course and human development.* Boston: Gale Cengage.

Voorpostel, M., & Blieszner, R. (2008). Intergenerational solidarity and support between adult siblings. *Journal of Marriage and the Family, 70,* 157–167.

Vorster, H. H., & Kruger, A. (2007). Poverty, malnutrition, underdevelopment, and cardiovascular disease: A South African perspective. *Cardiovascular Journal of Africa, 18,* 321–324.

Votruba-Drzal, E., Coley, R. L., & Chase-Lansdale, P. I. (2004). Child care and low-income children's development: Direct and moderated effects. *Child Development, 75,* 296–312.

Voydanoff, P. (1990). Economic distress and family relations: A review of the eighties. *Journal of Marriage and the Family, 52,* 1099–1115.

Vreeman, R. C., & Carroll, A. E. (2007). A systematic review of school-based interventions to prevent bullying. *Archives of Pediatric and Adolescent Medicine, 161,* 78–88.

Vurpillot, E. (1968). The development of scanning strategies and their relation to visual differentiation. *Journal of Experimental Child Psychology, 6,* 632–650.

Vygotsky, L. S. (1962). *Thought and language.* Cambridge, MA: MIT Press.

W

Wachs, T. D. (2000). *Necessary but not sufficient.* Washington, DC: American Psychological Association.

Wagner, D. A. (2010). Literacy. In M. H. Bornstein (Ed.), *Handbook of cultural developmental science.* New York: Psychology Press.

Wagner, R. K. (1997). Intelligence, training, and employment. *American Psychologist, 52,* 1059–1069.

Wagner, R. K., & Sternberg, R. J. (1986). Tacit knowledge and intelligent functioning in the everyday world. In R. J. Sternberg & R. K. Wagner (Eds.), *Practical intelligence.* New York: Cambridge University Press.

Waite, L. (2005, June). *The case for marriage.* Paper presented at the ninth annual Smart Marriages conference, Dallas.

Waite, L. J. (2009). Marriage. In D. Carr (Ed.), *Encyclopedia of the life course and human development.* Boston: Gale Cengage.

Waite, L. J., Das, A., & Laumann, E. O. (2009). Sexual activity, later life. In D. Carr (Ed.), *Encyclopedia of the life course and human development.* Boston: Gale Cengage.

Waiter, G. D., & others. (2009). Exploring possible neural machanisms of intelligence differences using processing speed and working memory tasks. *Intelligence, 37,* 199–206.

Walker, L. (1982). The sequentiality of Kohlberg's stages of moral development. *Child Development, 53,* 1130–1136.

Walker, L. (2006). Gender and morality. In M. Killen & J. G. Smetana (Eds.), *Handbook of moral development.* Mahwah, NJ: Erlbaum.

Walker, L. J. (2002). Moral exemplarity. In W. Damon (Ed.), *Bringing in a new era of character education.* Stanford, CA: Hoover Press.

Walker, L. J. (2004). Progress and prospects in the psychology of moral development. *Merrill-Palmer Quarterly, 50,* 546–557.

Walker, L. J., deVries, B., & Trevethan, S. D. (1987). Moral stages and moral orientation in real-life and hypothetical dilemmas. *Child Development, 58,* 842–858.

Walker, L. J., & Frimer, J. A. (2009a, in press). Moral personality exemplified. In D. Narváez & D. K. Lapsley (Eds.), *Moral personality, identity, and character: Prospects for new field of study.* New York: Cambridge University Press.

Walker, L. J., & Frimer, J. A. (2009b, in press). Being good for goodness' sake: Transcendence in the lives of moral heroes. In P. K. Oser & W. M. M. H. Veugelers (Eds.), *Getting involved: Global citizenship development and sources of moral values.* Rotterdam, the Netherlands: Sense.

Walker, L. J., & Hennig, K. H. (2004). Differing conceptions of moral exemplars: Just, brave, and caring. *Journal of Personality and Social Psychology, 86,* 629–647.

Walker, L. J., Hennig, K. H., & Krettenauer, T. (2000). Parent and peer contexts for children's moral development. *Child Development, 71,* 1033–1048.

Walker, N., Philbin, D. A., & Fisk, A. D. (1997). Age-related differences in movement control: Adjusting submovement structure to optimize performance. *Journals of Gerontology B: Psychological Sciences and Social Sciences, 52,* P42–P50.

Wallenborg, K., & others. (2009). Red wine triggers cell death and thiroredoxin reductase inhibition: Effects beyond resveratrol and SIRT 1. *Experimental Cell Research, 315,* 1360–1371.

Wallerstein, J. S. (2008). Divorce. In M. M. Haith & J. B. Benson (Eds.), *Encyclopedia of infant and early childhood development.* Oxford, UK: Elsevier.

Walsh, D., & Bennett, N. (2004). *WHY do they act that way?: A survival guide to the adolescent brain for your teen.* New York: Free Press.

Walsh, J. (2008). Self-efficacy. In N. J. Salkind (Ed.), *Encyclopedia of educational psychology.* Thousand Oaks, CA: Sage.

Walsh, L. A. (2000, Spring). The inside scoop on child development: Interview. *Cutting through the hype.* Minneapolis: College of Education and Human Development, University of Minnesota.

Walsh, L. V. (2006). Beliefs and rituals in traditional bath attendant practice in Guatemala. *Journal of Transcultural Nursing, 17,* 148–154.

Walston, J. D., & others. (2009, in press). Inflammation and stress-related candidate genes, plasma interleukin-6 levels, and longevity in older adults. *Experimental Gerontology.*

Walters, E., & Readier, K. S. (1994). Anorexia nervosa and anorexia-like symptoms in a population based twin sample. *American Journal of Psychiatry, 152,* 62–71.

Walters, M. W., Boggs, K. M., Ludington-Hoe, S., Price, K. M., & Morrison, B. (2007). Kangaroo care at birth for full term infants: A pilot study. *MCN American Journal of Maternal Child Nursing, 32,* 375–381.

Wandell, P. E., Carlsson, A. C., & Theobold, H. (2009). The association between BMI value and long-term mortality. *International Journal of Obesity, 33,* 577–582.

Wang, A. L., Lukas, T. J., Yan, M., Du, N., Tso, M. O., & Neufeld, A. H. (2009). Autophagy and exosomes in the aged retinal pigment epithelium: Possible relevance to drusen formation and age-related macular degeneration. *PLoS ONE, 4,* e4160.

Wang, J., Eslinger, P. J., Smith, M. B., & Yang, Q. X. (2005). Functional magnetic resonance imaging study of human olfaction and normal aging. *Journals of Gerontology A: Biological Sciences and Medical Sciences, 60,* 510–514.

Wang, J. J. (2007). Group reminiscence therapy for cognitive and affective function of demented elderly in Taiwan. *International Journal of Geriatric Psychiatry, 22,* 1235–1240.

Wang, L., Goldstein, F. C., Veledar, E., Levey, A. I., Lah, J. J., Meltzer, C. C., Holder, C. A., & Mao, H. (2009). Alterations in cortical thickness and white matter integrity in mild cognitive impairment measured by whole-brain cortical thickness mapping and diffusion tensor imaging. *AJNR. American Journal of Neuroradiology, 30,* 893–899.

Wang, L. Y., Chyen, D., Lee, L., & Lowry, R. (2008). The association between body mass index in adolescence and obesity in adulthood. *Journal of Adolescent Health, 42,* 512–518.

Wang, Q., & Pomerantz, E. M. (2009). The motivational landscape of early adolescence in the United States and China: A longitudinal study. *Child Development, 80,* 1272–1287.

Wardlaw, G. M., & Hempl, J. (2007). *Perspectives in nutrition.* (7th ed.). New York: McGraw-Hill.

Wardlaw, G. M., & Smith, A. M. (2009). *Contemporary nutrition* (7th ed.). New York: McGraw-Hill.

Wardle, J., Carnell, S., Haworth, C. M., & Plomin, R. (2008). Evidence for a strong genetic influence on childhood adiposity despite the force of the obesogenic environment. *American Journal of Clinical Nutrition, 87,* 398–404.

Ward, W. F., Qi, W., Van Remmen, H., Zackert, W. E., Roberts, L. J., & Richardson, A. (2005). Effects of age and caloric restriction on lipid peroxidation: Measurement of oxidative stress by F-isoprostane levels. *Journals of Gerontology A: Biological Sciences and Medical Sciences, 60,* 847–851.

Ware, J. E., Kosinski, M., & Dewey, J. E. (2000). *How to score Version 2 of the SF-36 Health Survey.* Boston: Quality Metric.

Warr, P. (1994). Age and employment. In M. Dunnette, L. Hough, & H. Triandis (Eds.), *Handbook of industrial and organizational psychology* (Vol. 4). Palo Alto, CA: Consulting Psychologists Press.

Warren, H., & Stifter, C. A. (2008). Maternal emotion-related socialization and preschoolers' developing self-awareness. *Social Development, 17,* 239–258.

Warshak, R. A. (2008, January), Personal communication. Department of Psychology, University of Texas at Dallas, Richardson.

Waterman, A. S. (1985). Identity in the context of adolescent psychology. In A. S. Waterman (Ed.), *Identity in adolescence: Processes and contents.* San Francisco: Jossey-Bass.

Waterman, A. S. (1989). Curricula interventions for identity change: Substantive and ethical considerations. *Journal of Adolescence, 12,* 389–400.

Waterman, A. S. (1992). Identity as an aspect of optimal psychological functioning. In G. R. Adams, T. P. Gullotta, & R. Montemayor (Eds.), *Adolescent identity formation.* Newbury Park, CA: Sage.

Waters, E., Kondo-Ikemura, K., Posada, G., & Richters, J. E. (1990). Learning to love: Mechanisms and milestones. In M. Gunnar & L. A. Sroufe (Eds.), *Minnesota symposia on child psychology* (Vol. 23). Mahwah, NJ: Erlbaum.

Wathen, C. N. (2006). Health information seeking in context: How women make decisions regarding hormone replacement therapy. *Journal of Health Communication, 11,* 477–493.

Watson, J. A., Randolph, S. M., & Lyons, J. L. (2005). African-American grandmothers as health educators in the family. *International Journal of Aging and Human Development, 60,* 343–356.

Watson, J. B. (1928). *Psychological care of infant and child.* New York: W. W. Norton.

Watson, R. (2009). Luxembourg is to allow euthanasia from 1 April. *British Medical Journal, 338,* 1248.

Watt, H. M. G. (2008). Gender and occupational outcomes: An introduction. In H. M. G. Watt & J. S. Eccles (Eds.), *Gender and occupational outcomes.* American Psychological Association.

Watt, H. M. G., & Eccles, J. S. (Eds.). (2008). *Gender and occupational outcomes.* American Psychological Association.

Watts, C. E., & Caldwell, L. L. (2009, in press). The influence of parenting practices, adolescent self-determination and adolescent initiative on structured and unstructured activity involvement of adolescents. *Journal of Leisure Research.*

Watts, C., & Zimmerman, C. (2002). Violence against women: Global scope and magnitude. *Lancet, 359,* 1232–1237.

Waxman, S. (2009). How infants discover distinct word types and map them to distinctive meanings. In J. Colombo, P. McCardle, & L. Freund (Eds.), *Infant pathways to language.* Clifton, NJ: Psychology Press.

Webb, J. T., Gore, J. L., Mend, E. R., & DeVries, A. R. (2007). *A parent's guide to gifted children.* Scottsdale, AZ: Great Potential Press.

Weber, E. (2005). *MI strategies in the classroom and beyond.* Boston: Allyn & Bacon.

Webster, N. S., & Worrell, F. C. (2008). Academically-talented adolescents' attitudes toward service in the community. *Gifted Child Quarterly, 52,* 170–179.

Wechsler, D. (1939). *The measurement of adult intelligence.* Baltimore: Williams & Wilkins.

Wechsler, H., Davenport, A., Sowdall, G., Moetykens, B., & Castillo, S. (1994). Health and behavioral consequences of binge drinking in college. *Journal of the American Medical Association, 272,* 1672–1677.

Wechsler, H., Lee, J. E., Kuo, M., Seibring, M., Nelson, T. F., & Lee, H. (2002). Trends in college binge drinking during a period of increased prevention efforts: Findings from 4 Harvard School of Public Health college alcohol study surveys: 1993–2001. *Journal of American College Health, 50,* 203–217.

Wehren, L. E., Hawkes, W. G., Hebel, J. R., Orwig, D. L., & Magaziner, J. (2005). Bone mineral density, soft tissue body composition, strength, and functioning after hip fracture. *Journals of Gerontology A: Biological Sciences and Medical Sciences, 60,* A80–A84.

Wei, M., Fabrizio, P., Hu, J., Ge, H., Cheng, C., Li, L., & Longo, V. D. (2008). Life span extension by calorie restriction depends on Riml5 and transcription factors downstream of Ras/PKA, Tor, and Sch9. *PloS Genetics, 4,* el3.

Weikert, D. P. (1993). Long-term, positive effects in the Perry Preschool Head Start Program. Unpublished data, High Scope Foundation, Ypsilanti, MI.

Weiner, C. P., & Buhischi, C. (2009). *Drugs for pregnant and lactating women* (2nd ed.). London: Elsevier.

Weinstein, R. S. (2004). *Reaching higher: The power of expectations in schooling.* Cambridge, MA: Harvard University Press.

Weis, K., & Sternberg, R. J. (2008). The nature of love. In S. F. Davis & W. H. Buskist (Eds.), *21st century psychology: A reference handbook* (Vol. 2). Thousand Oaks, CA: Sage.

Weismiller, D. G. (2009). Menopause. *Primary Care, 36,* 199–226.

Weiss, L. A., & others. (2008). Association between microdeletion and microduplication at 16p11.2 and autism. *New England Journal of Medicine, 358,* 667–675.

Wekerle, C., Leung, E., Wall, A. M., Macmillan, H., Boyle, M., Trocme, N., & Waechter, R. (2009). The contribution of childhood emotional abuse to teen dating violence among child protective services–involved youth. *Child Abuse and Neglect, 33,* 45–58.

Welford, A. T. (1994). Between bodily changes and performance: Some possible reasons for slowing with age. *Experimental Aging Research, 10* (2), 73–88.

Wellman, H. M., Cross, D., & Watson, J. (2001). Meta-analysis of theory-of-mind development: The truth about false belief. *Child Development, 72,* 655–684.

Wellman, H. M., Lopez-Duran, S., Labounty, J., & Hamilton, B. (2008). Infant attention to intentional action predicts preschool theory of mind. *Developmental Psychology, 44,* 618–623.

Wellman, H. M. & Woolley, J. D. (1990). From simple desires to ordinary beliefs: The early development of everyday psychology. *Cognition, 35,* 245–275.

Wells, J. C., Hallal, P. C., Reichert, F. F., Menezes, A. M., Araujo, C. L., & Victora, C. G. (2008). Sleep patterns and television viewing in relation to obesity and blood pressure: Evidence from an adolescent Brazilian birth cohort. *Internal Journal of Obesity, 32,* 1042–1049.

Welti, C. (2002). Adolescents in Latin America: Facing the future with skepticism. In B. B. Brown, R. W. Larson, & T. S. Saraswathi (Eds.), *The world's youth.* New York: Cambridge University Press.

Wenestam, C. G., & Wass, H. (1987). Swedish and U.S. children's thinking about death: A qualitative study and cross-cultural comparison. *Death Studies, 11,* 99–121.

Weng, X., Odouli, R., & Li, D. K. (2008). Maternal caffeine consumption during pregnancy and the risk of miscarriage: A prospective cohort study. *American Journal of Obstetrics and Gynecology, 198,* e1–e8.

Wenger, N. S., & others (2003). The quality of medical care provided to vulnerable community-dwelling older patients. *Annals of Internal Medicine, 139,* 740–747.

Wengreen, H. J., & others. (2007). Antioxidant intake and cognitive function of elderly men and women: The Cache County Study. *Journal of Nutrition, Health, and Aging, 11,* 230–237.

Wentworth, R. A. L. (1999). *Montessori for the millennium.* Mahwah, NJ: Erlbaum.

Wentzel, K. (1997). Student motivation in middle school: The role of perceived pedagogical caring. *Journal of Educational Psychology, 89,* 411–419.

Wentzel, K. R., & Asher, S. R. (1995). The academic lives of neglected, rejected, popular, and controversial children. *Child Development, 66,* 754–763.

Werker, J. F., & Tees, R. C. (2005). Speech perception as a window for understanding plasticity and commitment in language systems of the brain. *Developmental Psychobiology, 46,* 233–251.

Wertsch, J. (2008). From social interaction to higher psychological processes. *Human Development, 51,* 66–79.

Westerlund, M., & Lagerberg, D. (2008). Expressive vocabulary in 18-month-old children in relation to demographic factors, mother and child characteristics, communication style, and shared reading. *Child: Care, Health, and Development, 34,* 257–266.

Westlake, C., Evangelista, L. S., Stromberg, A., Ter-Galstanyan, A., Vazirani, S., & Dracup, K. (2007). Evaluation of a web-based education and counseling pilot for older heart failure patients. *Progress in Cardiovascular Nursing, 22,* 20–26.

Westling, E., Andrews, J. A., Hampson, S. E., & Peterson, M. (2008). Pubertal timing and substance use: The effects of gender, parental monitoring, and deviant peers. *Journal of Adolescent Health, 42,* 555–563.

Westphal, D. M., & Mckee, S. A. (2009). End-of-life decision making in the intensive care unit: Physician and nurse perspective. *American Journal of Medical Quality, 24,* 222–228.

Wethington, E., Kessler, R., & Pixley, J. (2004). Turning points in adulthood. In G. Brim, C. D. Ryff, & R. Kessler (Eds.), *How healthy we are: A national study of well-being in midlife.* Chicago: University of Chicago Press.

Wheeden, A., Scafidi, F. A., Field, T., Ironson, G., Valdeon, C. & Bandstra, E. (1993) Massage effects on cocaine-exposed preterm neonates. *Journal of Developmental and Behavioral Pediatrics, 14,* 318–322.

Wheeler, P. G., Bresnahan, K., Shephard, B. A., Lau, J., & Balk, E. M. (2004). Short stature and functional impairments: A systematic review. *Archives of Pediatric and Adolescent Medicine, 158,* 236–243.

Whetstone, L. M., Morrissey, S. L., & Cummings, D. M. (2007). Children at risk: The association between perceived weight status and suicidal thoughts and attempts in middle school youth. *Journal of School Health, 77,* 59–66.

Whiffen, V. (2001). Depression. In J. Worell (Ed.), *Encyclopedia of women and gender.* San Diego: Academic Press.

Whitehead, B. D., & Popenoe, D. (2003). *The state of our unions.* Piscataway, NJ: The National Marriage Project, Rutgers University.

Whitehead, K. A., Ainsworth, A. T., Wittig, M. A., & Gadino, B. (2009). Implications of ethnic identity exploration and ethnic identity affirmation and belonging for intergroup attitudes among adolescents. *Journal of Research on Adolescence, 19,* 123–135.

White, J. W., & Frabutt, J. M. (2006). Violence against girls and women. In J. Worell & C. D. Goodheart (Eds.), *Handbook of girls' and women's psychological health.* New York: Oxford University Press.

White, L. 1994. Stepfamilies over the life course: Social support. In A. Booth & J. Dunne (Eds.), *Stepfamilies: Who benefits and who does not.* Hillsdale, NJ: Erlbaum.

Whitescarver, K. (2006, April). *Montessori rising: Montessori education in the United States, 1955–present.* Paper presented at the meeting of the American Education Research Association, San Francisco.

Whiting, B. B., & Edwards, C. P. (1998). *Children of different worlds.* Cambridge, MA: Harvard University Press.

Whitlock, J. L., Powers, J. L., & Eckenrode, J. (2006). The virtual cutting edge: The internet and adolescent self-injury. *Developmental Psychology, 42,* 407–417.

Whittle, S., Yap, M. B., Yucel, M., Fornito, A., Simmons, J. G., Sheeber, L., & Allen, N. B. (2008). Prefrontal and amygdala volumes are related to adolescents' affective behaviors during parent-adolescent interactions. *Proceedings of the National Academy of Sciences USA, 105,* 3652–3657.

Wickelgren, I. (1999). Nurture helps to mold able minds. *Science, 283,* 1832–1834.

Wickham, S. (2009). *Midwifery: Best practice.* London: Elsevier.

Wickrama, K. A. S., Brynt, C. M., Conger, R. D., & Meehan, J. M. (2004). Change and continuity in marital relationships during the middle years. In R. D. Conger, F. O. Lorenz, & K. A. S. Wickrama (Eds.), *Continuity and change in family relations.* Mahwah, NJ: Erlbaum.

WIC New York. (2009). *The new look of the women, infants, and children (WIC) program.* Retrieved January 21, 2009, from www.health.state.ny.us/prevention/nutrition/wic/the_new_look of wic.htm

Widman, L., & McNulty, J. K. (2009, in press). Sexual narcissism and the perpetration of sexual aggression. *Archives of Sexual Behavior.*

Wiersman, W., & Jurs, S. G. (2009). *Research methods In education* (9th ed.). Upper Saddle River, NJ: Prentice Hall.

Wiesner, M., & Ittel, A. (2002). Relations of pubertal timing and depressing symptoms to substance use in early adolescence. *Journal of Early Adolescence, 22,* 5–23.

Wigfield, A., Byrnes, J. P., & Eccles, J. S. (2006). Development during early and middle adolescence. In P. A. Alexander & P. H. Winne (Eds.), *Handbook of educational psychology* (2nd ed.). Mahwah, NJ: Erlbaum.

Wigfield, A., Eccles, J. S., Schiefele, U., Roeser, R., & Davis-Kean, P. (2006). Development of achievement motivation. In W. Damon & R. Lerner (Eds.), *Handbook of child psychology* (6th ed.). New York: Wiley.

Wight, R. G., Cummings, J. R., Miller-Martinez, D., Karlamangla, A. S., Seeman, T. E., & Aneshensel, C. S. (2008). A multilevel analysis of urban neighborhood socioeconomic disadvantage and health in late life. *Social Science and Medicine, 66,* 862–872.

Wilcox, S., Evenson, K. R., Aragaki, A., Wassertheil-Smoller, S., Mouton, C. P., & Loevinger, B. L. (2003). The effects of widowhood on physical and mental health, health behaviors, and health outcomes: The Women's Health Initiative. *Health Psychology, 22,* 513–522.

Willcox, B. J., Willcox, M. D., & Suzuki, M. (2002). *The Okinawa Program.* New York: Crown.

Willcox, D. C., Willcox, B. J., He, Q., Wang, N. C., & Suzuki, M. (2008). They really are that old: A validation study of centenarian prevalence in Okinawa. *Journals of Gerontology A: Biological Sciences and Medical Sciences, 63,* 338–349.

Willcox, D. C., Willcox, B. J., Sokolovsky, J., & Sakihara, S. (2007). The cultural context of "successful aging" among older women weavers in a northern Okinawan village: The role of productive activity. *Journal of Cross Gerontology, 22,* 137–165.

Williams, D. D., Yancher, S. C., Jensen, L. C., & Lewis, C. (2003). Character education in a public high school: A multi-year inquiry into unified studies. *Journal of Moral Education, 32,* 3–33.

Williams, D. R., & Sternthal, M. J. (2007). Spirituality, religion, and health: Evidence and research directions. *Medical Journal of Australia, 186* (Suppl.), S47–S50.

Williams, J. H., & Ross, L. (2007). Consequences of prenatal toxin exposure for mental health in children and adolescents: A systematic review. *European Child and Adolescent Psychiatry, 16,* 243–253.

Williams, M. E. (1995). *The American Geriatric Society's complete guide to aging and health.* New York: Harmony Books.

Williams, T. R. (2008). A cultural and global perspective of United States health care perspective. *Seminars in Radiation Onocology, 18,* 175–185.

Williamson, J., Goldman, J., & Marder, K. S. (2009). Genetic aspects of Alzheimer disease. *Neurologist, 15,* 80–86.

Williamson, J. D., & others. (2009). Changes in cognitive function in a randomized trial of physical activity: Results of the Lifestyle Interventions and Independence for Elders Pilot Study. *Journals of Gerontology A: Biological Sciences and Medical Sciences, 64,* 688–694.

Willis, S. L., & Nesselroade, C. S. (1990). Long-term effects of fluid ability training in old age. *Developmental Psychology, 26,* 905–910.

Willis, S. L., & Schaie, K. W. (2005). Cognitive trajectories in midlife and cognitive functioning in old age. In S. L. Willis & M. Martin (Eds.), *Middle adulthood.* Thousand Oaks, CA: Sage.

Willis, S. L., & Schaie, K. W. (2006). A co-constructionist view of the third age: The case of cognition. *Annual Review of Gerontology and Geriatrics, 26,* 131–152.

Willoughby, T. (2008). A short-term longitudinal study of internet and computer game use by adolescent boys and girls: Prevalence, frequency of use, and psychosocial predictors. *Developmental Psychology, 44,* 195–204.

Wilson, B. J. (2008). Media and children's aggression, fear, and altruism. *The Future of Children, 18* (1), 87–118.

Wilson, K. G., & others. (2007). Desire for euthanasia or physician-assisted suicide in palliative cancer care. *Health Psychology, 26,* 314–323.

Wilson, R. S., Mendes de Leon, C. F., Barnes, L. L., Schneider, J. A., Bienias, J., Evans, D. A., & Bennett, D. A. (2002). Participation in cognitively stimulating activities and risk of incident Alzheimer disease. *Journal of the American Medical Association, 287,* 742–748.

Wilson, R. S., Mendes de Leon, C. F., Bienas, J. L., Evans, D. A., & Bennett, D. A. (2004). Personality and mortality in old age. *Journals of Gerontology B: Psychological Sciences and Social Sciences, 59,* 110B–116B.

Wilson, R. S., & others. (2009). Educational attainment and cognitive decline in old age. *Neurology, 72,* 460–465.

Windle, W. F. (1940). *Physiology of the human fetus.* Philadelphia: W. B. Saunders.

Wineberg, H. (1994). Marital reconciliation in the United States: Which couples are successful? *Journal of Marriage and the Family, 56,* 80–88.

Winerman, L. (2005, January). Leading the way. *Monitor on Psychology, 36* (1), 64–67.

Wink, P., & Dillon, M. (2002). Spiritual development across the adult life course: Findings from a longitudinal study. *Journal of Adult Development, 9,* 79–94.

Winner, E. (1986, August). Where pelicans kiss seals. *Psychology Today,* pp. 24–35.

Winner, E. (1996). *Gifted children: Myths and realities.* New York: Basic Books.

Winner, E. (2000). The origins and ends of giftedness. *American Psychologist, 55,* 159–169.

Winner, E. (2006). Development in the arts: Drawing and music. In W. Damon & R. Lerner (Eds.), *Handbook of child psychology* (6th ed.). New York: Wiley.

Winner, E. (2009). Toward broadening our understanding of giftedness: The spatial domain. In F. D. Horowitz, R. F. Subotnik, & D. J. Matthews (Eds.), *The development of giftedness and talent across the life span.* Washington, DC: American Psychological Association.

Wintre, M. G., & Vallance, D. D. (1994). A developmental sequence in the comprehension of emotions: Intensity, multiple emotions, and valence. *Developmental Psychology, 30,* 509–514.

Wise, P. M. (2006). Aging of the female reproductive system. In E. J. Masoro & S. N. Austad (Eds.), *Handbook of the biology of aging* (6th ed.). San Diego: Academic Press.

Witelson, S. F., Beresh, H., & Kigar, D. L. (2006). Intelligence and brain size in 100 post-mortem brains: Sex, lateralization and age factors. *Brain, 129,* 386–398.

Witelson, S. F., Kigar, D. L., & Harvey, T. (1999). The exceptional brain of Albert Einstein. *The Lancet, 353,* 2149–2153.

Witkin, H. A., Mednick, S. A., Schulsinger, R., Bakkestrom, E., Christiansen, K. O., Goodenbough, D. K., Hirchhofn, K., Lunsteen, C., Owen, D. R., Philip, J., Ruben, D. B., & Stocking, M. (1976). Criminality in XYY and XXY men. *Science, 193,* 547–555.

Witte, A. V., Fobker, M., Gellner, R., Knecht, S., & Fioel, A. (2009). Caloric restriction improves memory in elderly humans. *Proceedings of the National Academy of Sciences USA, 106,* 1255–1260.

Wittmeier, K. D., Mollard, R. C., & Kriellaars, D. J. (2008). Phsyical activity intensity and risk of overweight and adiposity in children. *Obesity, 16,* 415–420.

Wolak, J., Mitchell, K., & Finkelhor, D. (2007). Unwanted and wanted exposure to online pornography in a national sample of youth Internet users. *Pediatrics, 119,* 247–257.

Wolfgram, S. M. (2008). Openness in adoption: What we know so far—a critical review of the literature. *Social Work, 53,* 133–142.

Wolitzky-Taylor, K. B., Ruggiero, K. J., Danielson, C. K., Resnick, H. S., Hanson, R. F., Smith, D. W., Saunders, B. E., & Kilpatrick, D. G. (2008). Prevalence and correlates of dating violence in a national sample of adolescents. *Journal of the American Academy of Child and Adolescent Psychiatry, 47,* 755–762.

Wolraich, M., Dworkin, P., Drotar, D., & Perrin, E. (2008). *Developmental-behavioral pediatrics.* Oxford, UK: Elsevier.

Women's Sports Foundation. (2001). *The 10 commandments for parents and coaches in youth sports.* Eisenhower Park, NY: Author.

Wong, E. C., Kinzie, J. D., & Kinzie, M. (2009). Stress, refugees, and trauma. In N. Tewari & A. Algarez (Eds.), *Asian American psychology.* Clifton, NJ: Psychology Press.

Wong, M. M., Brower, K. J., & Zucker, R. A. (2009). Childhood sleep problems, early onset of substance use, and behavioral problems in adolescence. *Sleep Medicine, 10,* 787–796.

Wong, P. T. P., & Watt, L. M. (1991). What types of reminiscence are associated with successful aging? *Psychology and Aging, 6,* 272–279.

Wong, Y. J., & Rochlen, A. B. (2005). Demystifying the inexpressive male: New directions and implications for counseling and research. *Psychology of Men and Masculinity, 6,* 62–72.

Wong Briggs, T. (2007, October 18). An early start for learning. *USA Today,* p. 6D.

Wood, A. C., Rijsdijk, F., Saudino, K. J., Asherson, P., & Kuntei, J. (2008). High heritability for a composite index of children's activity level measures. *Behavior Genetics, 38,* 266–276.

Wood, A. H., & Eagly, A. H. (2010, in press). Gender. In S. Fiske, D. Gilbert, & G. Lindzey (Eds.), *Handbook of social psychology.* New York: Oxford University Press.

Wood, D., Kaplan, R., & McLoyd, V. C. (2007). Gender differences in educational expectations of urban, low-income African American youth: The role of parents and school. *Journal of Youth and Adolescence, 36,* 417–427.

Wood, M. D., Vinson, D. C., & Sher, K. J. (2001). Alcohol use and misuse. In A. Baum, T. A. Revenson, & J. E. Singer (Eds.), *Handbook of health psychology.* Mahwah, NJ: Erlbaum.

Woodward, A., Markman, E., & Fitzsimmons, C. (1994). Rapid word learning in 13- and 18-month-olds. *Developmental Psychology, 30,* 553–556.

Woodward, A., & Needham, A. (Eds.). (2009). *Learning and the infant mind.* New York: Oxford University Press.

Woodward, A. L., & Markman, E. M. (1998). Early word learning. In D. Kuhn & R. S. Siegler (Eds.), *Handbook of child psychology* (5th ed., Vol. 2). New York: Wiley.

Wood, W., & Eagly, A. H. (2009). Gender identity. In M. R. Leary & R. H. Hoyle (Eds.),

Handbook of individual differences in social behavior (pp. 109–125). New York: Guilford.

Woollacott, M. (2007). Balance, posture, and gait. In J. E. Birren (Ed.), *Encyclopedia of gerontology* (2nd ed.). San Diego: Academic Press.

World Health Organization. (2000, February 2). *Adolescent health behavior in 28 countries.* Geneva: Author.

World Health Organization. (2009). *Suicide rates per 100,000 by country, year and sex (Table).* Retrieved July 27, 2009, from www.who.int/mental_health/prevention/suicide_rates/en/print...

Worthington, E. L. (1989). Religious faith across the life span: Implications for counseling and research. *Counseling Psychologist, 17,* 555–612.

Worthman, C. M. (2010). Survival and health. In M. H. Bornstein (Ed.), *Handbook of cultural developmental science.* New York: Psychology Press.

Wortman, C. B., & Boerner, K. (2007). Reactions to death of a loved one: Beyond the myths of coping with loss. In H. S. Friedman & R. C. Silver (Eds.), *Foundations of health psychology.* New York: Oxford University Press.

Wortmann, J. H., & Park, C. L. (2008). Religion and spirituality in adjustment following bereavement: An integrative review. *Death Studies, 32,* 703–736.

Writing Group for the British Menopause Society Counsel & others. (2008). Non-estrogen based treatments for menopausal symptoms. *Menopause International, 14,* 88–90.

Wrosch, C., Heckhausen, J., & Lachman, M. E. (2006). Goal management across adulthood and old age: The adaptive value of primary and secondary control. In D. K. Mroczek & T. D. Little (Eds.), *Handbook of personality development.* Mahwah, NJ: Erlbaum.

Wu, T., Gao, X., Chen, M., & van Dam, R. M. (2009, in press). Long-term effectiveness of diet-plus-exercise interventions vs. diet-only interventions for weight loss: A meta-analysis. *Obesity Review.*

Wu, Y. H., Cheng, M. L., Ho, H. Y., Chiu, D. T., & Wang, T. C. (2009). Telomerase prevents accelerated senescence in glucose-6-phosphate dehydrogenase (G6PD)-deficient human fibroblasts. *Journal of Biomedical Science, 16,* 18.

Wynn, K. (1992). Addition and subtraction by human infants. *Nature, 358,* 749–570.

X

Xu, F., Spelke, E., & Goddard, S. (2005). Number sense in human infants. *Developmental Science, 8,* 88–101.

Xu, Q., Parks, C. G., DeRoo, L. A., Cawthon, R. M., Sandler, D. P., & Chen, H. (2009). Multivitamin use and telomere length in women. *American Journal of Clinical Nutrition, 89,* 1857–1863.

Y

Yamasue, K., Hayashi, T., Ohshige, K., Tochikubo, O., & Souma, T. (2008). Masked hypertension in elderly managerial employees and retirees. *Clinical and Experimental Hypertension, 30,* 203–211.

Yang, C., & Brown, B. (2009, April). *From Facebook to cell calls: Layers of electronic intimacy in college students' peer relations.* Paper presented at the meeting of the Society for Research in Child Development, Denver.

Yang, S., & Sternberg, R. J. (1997). Taiwanese Chinese people's conceptions of intelligence. *Intelligence, 25,* 21–36.

Yang, Y. (2008). Social inequalities in happiness in the United States, 1972–2004: An age-period-cohort analysis. *American Sociological Review, 73,* 204–226.

Yasnitsky, A., & Ferrari, M. (2008). From Vygotsky ot Vygotskian psychology: Introduction to the history of the Kharkov School. *Journal of the History of the Behavioral Sciences, 44,* 119–145.

Yassine, H. N., Marchetti, C. M., Krishna, R. K., Vrobel, T. R., Gonzalez, F., & Kirwin, J. P. (2009). Effects of exercise and caloric restriction on insulin resistance and cardiometabolic risk factors in older obese adults—a randomized trial. *Journals of Gerontology A: Biological Sciences and Medical Sciences, 64,* 90–95.

Yates, L. B., Djuousse, L., Kurth, T., During, J. E., & Gaziano, J. M. (2008). Exceptional longevity in men: Modifiable factors associated with survival and function to age 90 years. *Archives of Internal Medicine, 168,* 284–290.

Yell, M. L., & Drasgow, E. (2009). *What every teacher should know about No Child Left Behind* (2nd ed.). Upper Saddle River, NJ: Prentice Hall.

Yen, S. C. (2008). Short-term memory. In N. J. Salkind (Ed.), *Encyclopedia of educational psychology.* Thousand Oaks, CA: Sage.

Yokoya, T., Demura, S., & Sato, S. (2009). Three-year follow-up of the fall risk and physical function characteristics of the elderly participating in a community exercise class. *Journal of Physiological Anthropology, 28,* 55–62.

Yoon, C. Cole, C. A., & Lee, M. P. (2009). Consumer decision making and aging: Current knowledge and future directions. *Journal of Consumer Psychology, 19,* 2–16.

Yoon, D. P., & Lee, E. K. (2007). The impact of religiousness, spirituality, and social support on psychological well-being among older adults in rural areas. *Journal of Gerontological Social Work, 48,* 281–298.

Yoshida, S., Kozu, T., Gotoda, T., & Saito, D. (2006). Detection and treatment of early cancer in high-risk populations. *Best Practice and Research: Clinical Gastroenterology, 20,* 745–765.

Young, A., Grey, M., Abbey, A., Boyd, C. J., & McCabe, S. E. (2008). Alcohol-related sexual assault victimization among adolescents: Prevalence, characteristics, and correlates. *Journal of Studies on Alcohol and Drugs, 69,* 39–48.

Young, A. M., Morales, M., McCabe, S. E., Boyd, C. J., & Darcy, H. (2005). Drinking like a guy: Frequent binge drinking among undergraduate women. *Substance Use and Misuse, 40,* 241–267.

Young, E. L., Boye, A. E., & Nelson, D. A. (2006). Relational aggression: Understanding, identifying, and responding in schools. *Psychology in the Schools, 43,* 297–312.

Young, K. T. (1990) American conceptions of infant development from 1955 to 1984: What the experts are telling parents. *Child Development, 61,* 17–28.

Youngblade, L. M., Storch, E. A., & Nackashi, J. A. (2007). In W. B. Carey, A. C. Crocker, W. L. Coleman, H. M. Feldman, & E. R. Elias (Eds.), *Developmental-behavioral pediatrics* (4th ed.). London: Elsevier.

Youniss, J., McLellan, J. A., & Yates, M. (1999). Religion, community service, and identity in American youth. *Journal of Adolescence, 22,* 243–253.

Yuan, T. F. (2008). GABA effects on neurogenesis: An arsenal of regulation. *Science Signaling, 1,* jc1.

Yussen, S. R. (1977). Characteristics of moral dilemmas written by adolescents. *Developmental Psychology, 13,* 162–163.

Z

Zaborowska, E., & others. (2007). Effects of acupuncture, applied relaxation, estrogens, and placebo on hot flushes in postmenopausal women: An analysis of two prospective, parallel, randomized studies. *Climacteric, 10,* 38–45.

Zagorsky, J. L. (2007). Do you have to be smart to be rich? The impact of IQ on wealth, income, and financial distress. *Intelligence, 35,* 489–501.

Zahodne, L. B., & others. (2009, in press). Greater improvement in quality of life following deep brain stimulation surgery in the globus pallidus as compared to the subthalamic nucleus. *Journal of Neurology.*

Zaider, T., & Kissane, D. (2009). The assessment and management of family distress during palliative care. *Current Opinion in Supportive and Palliative Care, 3,* 67–71.

Zamperetti, N., & Bellomo, R. (2009). Total brain failure: A new contribution to the President's Council of Bioethics to the definition of death according to the neurological standard. *Intensive Care Medicine, 35,* 1305–1307.

Zangl, R., & Mills, D. L. (2007). Increased brain activity to infant-directed speech in 6- and 13-month-old infants. *Infancy, 11,* 31–62.

Zarit, S. H., & Knight, B. G. (Eds.). (1996). *A guide to psychotherapy and aging.* Washington, DC: American Psychological Association.

Zeifman, D., & Hazan, C. (2009). Pair bonds as attachments: Reevaluating the evidence. In J. Cassidy & P. R. Shaver (Ed.), *Handbook of attachment* (2nd ed.). New York: Guilford.

Zelinski, E. M., & Kennison, R. F. (2007). Not your parents' test scores: Cohort reduces psychometric aging effects. *Psychology and Aging, 22,* 546–557.

Zeller, M. H., Reiter-Purtill, J., & Ramey, C. (2008). Negative peer perceptions of obese children in the classroom environment. *Obesity, 16,* 755–762.

Zeskind, P. S. (2007). Impact of the cry of the infant at risk on psychosocial development. In R. E. Tremblay, R. deV Peters, M. Boivin, & R. G. Barr (Eds.), *Encyclopedia on early childhood development.* Montreal: Centre of Excellence for Early Childhood Development. Retrieved November 24, 2008, from www.child-encyclopedia.com/en-ca/list-of-topics.html

Zettel-Watson, L., & Rook, K. S. (2009). Friendship, later life. In D. Carr (Ed.), *Encyclopedia of the life course and human development.* Boston: Gale Cengage.

Zhang, L. F., & Sternberg, R. J. (2009). Learning in a cross-cultural perspective. In T. Husén & T. N. Postlethwaite (Eds.), *International encyclopedia of education* (3rd ed.), *Learning and cognition.* Oxford UK: Elsevier.

Zhou, F., Shefer, A., Yuan, K., & Nuorti, J. P. (2008). Trends in acute otitis media-related health care utilization by privately insured young children in the United States, 1997–2004. *Pediatrics, 121,* 253–260.

Zhou, Q., Lengua, L. J., & Wang, Y. (2009). The relations of temperament reactivity and effortful control to children's adjustment problems in the United States and China. *Developmental Psychology, 45,* 724–739.

Zhu, D., Kang, Q., Huang, P. Y., He, T. C., & Xie, P. (2009). Neurogenesis-related genes expression profiling of mouse fibroblastic stem cells inducted by Wnt signaling. *Neural Research, 31,* 200–203.

Zimmer-Gembeck, M. J., & Helfand, M. (2008). Ten years of longitudinal research on U.S. adolescent sexual behavior: Developmental correlates of sexual intercourse, and the importance of age, gender, and ethnic background. *Developmental Review, 28,* 153–224.

Zimmerman, P. (2007, March). *Attachment in adolescence.* Paper presented at the meeting of the Society for Research in Child Development, Boston.

Zinn M. B., & Wells, B. (2000). Diversity within Latino families: New lessons for family social science. In D. M. Demo, K. R. Allen, & M. A. Fine (Eds.), *Handbook of family diversity.* New York: Oxford University Press.

Ziol-Guest, K. M. (2009). Child custody and support. In D. Carr (Ed.), *Encyclopedia of the life course and human development.* Boston: Gale Cengage.

Zosuls, K. M., Ruble, D. N., Tamis-LeMonda, C. S., Shrout, P. E., Bornstein, M. H., & Greulich, F. K. (2009). The acquisition of gender labels in infancy: Implications for gender-typed play. *Developmental Psychology, 45,* 688–701.

Zou, Y., Misri, S., Shay, J. W., Pandita, T. K., & Wright, W. E. (2009). Altered states of telomere deprotection and the two-stage mechanism of replicative aging. *Molecular and Cellular Biology, 29,* 2390–2397.

Zucker, A. N., Ostrove, J. M., & Stewart, A. J. (2002). College educated women's personality development in adulthood: Perceptions and age differences. *Psychology and Aging, 17,* 236–244.

Zunzunegui, M., Alvarado, B. E., Del Ser, T., & Vtero, A. (2003). Social networks, social integration, and social engagement determine cognitive decline in community-dwelling Spanish older adults. *Journals of Gerontology B: Psychological Sciences and Social Sciences, 58,* S93–S100.

Photo Credits

Section Openers

1: Left to right: © Getty RF, © PunchStock RF; © Veer RF, © Getty RF; 2: © John P. Kelly Photographer; 3: © Tom & Dee Ann McCarthy/Corbis; 4: © Julian Hirshowitz/The Stock Market/Corbis; 5: © Ariel Skelley/Corbis; 6: © Dennis Stock/Magnum Photos

Chapter 1

Opener: © Chuck Savage/Corbis; p. 8 (top): Courtesy of Paul Baltes, Margaret Baltes Foundation; p. 8 (bottom): © Adam Tanner/Reuters/Corbis; p. 9 (top): © Paul Bartan/Corbis; p. 9 (bottom): © National Associate for the Education of Young Children, Robert Maust/Photo Agora; p. 11: © Naser Siddique/UNICEF Bangladesh; p.12 (top): Courtesy of Marian Wright Edelman, The Children's Defense Fund, photograph by Rick Reinhard; p. 12 (bottom): © Nathan Benn/Corbis; p. 14 (top): © iStock Photos; p. 14 (Prenatal): Courtesy of Landrum Shettles; p. 14 (Infancy): John Santrock; p. 14 (Early childhood): © Dynamic Graphics Group/PunchStock RF; p. 14 (Middle childhood): © Corbis RF; p. 14 (Adolescence): © ComstockPictureQuest RF; p. 14 (Early adulthood): © Vol. 155/Corbis RF; p. 14 (Middle adulthood): © Corbis RF; p. 14 (Late adulthood): © Corbis RF; p. 18 (top): © Jay Syverson/Corbis; p. 18 (bottom): © Owaki-Kulla/Corbis; p. 19: © Joel Gordon 1995; p. 21: © Bettmann/Corbis; p. 22: © Ted Streshinsky/Bettmann/Corbis; p. 24 (top): © Yves de Braine/Stock Photo; p. 24 (bottom): A. R. Lauria/Dr. Michael Cole, Laboratory of Human Cognition, University of California, San Diego; p. 25 (top): © Creatas Images/Jupiter Images RF; p. 25 (bottom): © AP/Wide World Photos; p. 26 (top): Courtesy Albert Bandura; p. 26 (bottom): Photo by Nina Leen/Timepix/Getty Images News Service; p. 27: © Corbis RF; p. 28: Courtesy of Urie Bronfenbrenner; p. 30: © Jeffrey Greenberg/Photo Researchers; p. 31: © Bettmann/Corbis; p. 32: © S. Fraser/Photo Researchers; p. 35 (top): © AP/Wide World Photos; p. 35 (middle): © Lawrence Migdale/Photo Researchers; p. 35 (bottom): © McGraw-Hill Companies, Inc./John Thoeming, photographer; p. 37: Courtesy of Pam Reid; p. 38 (top): © Steve Schaefer/AFP/Getty; p. 38 (bottom): © Stuart McClymont/Stone/Getty; p. 44: Courtesy Valerie Pang; p. 47: Courtesy Katherine Duchen Smith

Chapter 2

Opener: Photo Lennart Nilsson/Albert Bonniers Forlag AB, *A Child is Born*, Dell Publishing Company; p. 54: © Frans Lemmens/Corbis; p. 55: © Alan and Sandy Carey/Getty RF; p. 56: © David Wilkie; p. 57: © Rick Rickman; 2.4: © Don W. Fawcett/Photo Researchers; 2.5 (top & bottom): © Custom Medical Stock Photo; p. 61: © 1989 Joel Gordon Photography; p. 62 (top): From R. Simensen and R. Curtis Rogers, "Fragile X Syndrome," *American Family Physician*, 39 (5): 186, May 1989. © American Academy of Family Physicians.; p. 62 (bottom): © Andrew Eccles/JBGPHOTO. COM; p. 64: Courtesy of Holly Ishmael; p. 65: © Myrleen Ferguson Cate/Photo Edit; p. 67: © Duomo/Corbis; 2.10a-c: Photo Lennart Nilsson/Albert Bonniers Forlag AB., *A Child is Born*, Dell Publishing Company; 2.11: © Lennart Nilsson/Albert Bonniers Forlag AB; p. 72: © 2006 Spina Bifida camp photo; p. 72 (bottom): © Jacques Pavlovsky/Sygma/Corbis; 2.12: © Larry Berman; p. 75: Streissguth A. P., Clarren, S. K., & Jones, K. L. "Natural History of the Fetal Alcohol Syndrome: A 10-year follow-up of eleven

patients" in *The Lancet*, 2, 85–91; p. 76 (top): © Will & Deni McIntyre/Photo Researchers; p. 76 (bottom): © John Chiasson; p. 78 (top): © Betty Press/Woodfin Camp & Associates; p. 78 (bottom): © iStock Photos; p. 79: © Alon Reininger/Contact Press Images; p. 80 (top): © David Butow/Corbis SABA; p. 80 (bottom): © R.I.A. Novosti/Gamma/H.P.P./Eyedea; p. 81 (top): © Stockbyte/Getty RF; p. 81 (bottom): © Charles Gupton/Stock Boston; p. 82: © Sharon Schindler Rising, Centering Pregnancy Program; p. 83: © Viviane Moos/Corbis; p. 84 (top): © SIU/Peter Arnold, Inc.; p. 84 (bottom): © Marjorie Shostak/Anthro-Photo; p. 85: © Corbis/RF; p. 86 (top): Courtesy of Linda Pugh; p. 86 (middle): © Dr. Holly Beckwith; p. 86 (bottom): © Nova Development RF; 2.14: © Stephen Marks, Inc./The Image Bank/Getty; p. 88 (bottom): © Charles Gupton/Stock Boston; p. 90: Courtesy of Dr. Susan M. Ludington; p. 91: Courtesy of Dr. Tiffany Field

Chapter 3

Opener: © Lori Adamski Peek/Stone/Getty; p. 101: © Bob Daemmrich/The Image Works; p. 102: © Janis Christie/Getty RF; p. 105: © Jon Feingersh, 2009; p. 106 (top): © Corbis RF; p. 106 (middle): © Bettmann/Corbis; p. 106 (bottom): © Matthew Mendelsohn/Corbis; p. 107 (top): © George V. Mann, M. D.; p. 107 (bottom): © Ryan McVay/Photodisc/Getty RF; p.108: © 1998 Tom & Dee McCarthy/The Stock Market/Corbis; p. 109: © AP Photo/Jacqueline Larma; 3.5: © A. Glauberman/Photo Researchers; 3.7: Photo Lennart Nilsson/Albert Bonniers Forlag; 3.8a&b: Courtesy of Dr. Harry T. Chugani, Children's Hospital of Michigan; 3.9a: © David Grubin Productions, Inc. Reprinted by permission.; 3.9b: Image courtesy of Dana Boatman, Ph.D., Department of Neurology, John Hopkins University, reprinted with permission from *The Secret Life of the Brain*, Joseph Henry Press; 3.10: © 1990 Kenneth Jarecke/Contact Press Images; 3.11: © Steve Gschmeissner/Photo Researchers; p. 117: © Duomo/Corbis; 3.16 (left & right): Courtesy of Dr. Fred Gage; 3.17: From R. Cabeza, et al., "Age-related differences in neural activity during memory encoding and retrieval: A positron emission tomography study" in *Journal of Neuroscience*, 17, 391–400, 1997.; 3.18a: Courtesy of Denise Park, University of Texas at Dallas Center for Brain Health; 3.18b: © Michael O'Brien; p. 120 (bottom left & right): © James Balog; p. 122: © C Squared Studios/Getty RF; p. 123: © SuperStock; p. 124: © BrandXPictures/PunchStock RF; p. 125: © Richard Hutchings/Photo Edit; p. 126: © Jim LoScalzo; p. 127: © Ingram Publishing/SuperStock RF; p. 128 (top): © AP/Wide World Photos; p. 128 (left): Courtesy New England Centenarian Study at Boston University Medical Center; p. 128 (middle): © Waldo McBurney; p. 128 (right): Courtesy New England Centenarian Study at Boston University Medical Center; p. 130: © 2002 USA Today Library, Paul Wiseman, photographer. Reprinted with permission; 3.23: Courtesy of Dr. Jerry Shay; 3.24: © J. Bavosi/Photo Researchers

Chapter 4

Opener: © Paul Barton/Corbis; p. 139: © Tom Stewart/Corbis; p. 141: © George Gardner/The Image Works; p. 142 (left): © PunchStock RF; p. 142 (middle): © Corbis RF; p. 142 (right): © Taxi/Getty; 4.4a&b: © Alfred Pasieka/Science Photo Library/Photo Researchers; p. 144 (top): © Ira Wyman/Sygma/Corbis; p. 144 (middle): © Bettmann/Corbis; p. 144 (bottom): © Ansgar Photography/zefa/Corbis

RF; p. 145: © AP/Wide World Photos; p. 146: © Rex Curry; p. 148: © Bruce McAllister/Image Works; p. 149: © Bob Daemmrich/The Image Works; p. 150: Courtesy of Barbara Deloin; p. 151: © L. Perez/zefa/Corbis; p. 152: © Jules Frazier/Getty RF; p. 154 (top): © Karen Kasmausk/Corbis; p. 154 (bottom): © Ian Thraves/Alamy; p. 155: © iStock Photos; 4.13 (top & bottom): © Ethan Hill; p. 157 (bottom): © Stockbyte/Getty RF; p. 159: © Aerial Skelley/Corbis; p. 160: © 2007 Dallas Morning News, photographer Vernon Bryant; 4.16: Courtesy of Colin M. Bloor; p. 161 (bottom): © Randy M. Ury/Corbis; p. 162: © Ingram Publishing/Fotosearch RF; p. 163: © Bob Daemmrich/Stock Boston; p. 165 (top): © Josh Reynolds; p. 165 (bottom): © Chuck Savage/Corbis; p. 166: © Joe Raelle/Newsmakers/Getty; p. 167: © Norbert Schaefer/Corbis

Chapter 5

Opener: Photodisc/Getty RF; p. 172: Courtesy of Esther Thelen; p. 173: © Corbis/PictureQuest RF; 5.1a&b: © Petit Format/Photo Researchers; p. 174 (bottom): © Fabio Caardosa/zefa/Corbis; 5.2 (top & bottom): © Dr. Karen Adolph, New York University; p. 177 (top): © Michael Greenlar/The Image Works; p. 177 (bottom): © Frank Baily Studios; p. 178 (top): © Joel Gordon 1993; p. 178 (bottom): © PhotoDisc/Getty RF; p. 179 (top): © SW Productions/Brand X/Corbis RF; p. 179 (bottom): © Corbis RF; p. 180: © Frederick Reglain/Gamma/Gamma/H.P.P./Eyedea Presse; p. 181: © Newstockimages/SuperStock RF; 5.5: Courtesy Amy Needham, Duke University; p. 182 (bottom): © Digital Vision/Getty RF; p. 183: © Doug Menuez/Getty RF; p. 184: © Mika/zefa/Corbis; 5.6: Adapted from "The Origin of Form and Perception" by R. L. Frantz © 1961 by *Scientific American*. Photo by David Linton; 5.8 a-d: Courtesy of Dr. Charles Nelson; 5.10: © Enrico Ferorelli; 5.11: © Dr. Bruce Hood, University of Bristol, England; p. 191: © Steve Prezant/Corbis; 5.13: © Argentum/Photo Researchers; 5.14a: © Michael Siluk; 5.14b: © Dr. Melanie Spence, University of Texas at Dallas; p. 194: © Frank Leonhardt/dpa/Corbis; 5.16: © Jean Guichard/Sygma/Corbis; 5.17 a-c: From D. Rosenstein and H. Oster, "Differential Facial Responses to Four Basic Tastes in Newborns," *Child Development*, Vol. 59, 1988. © Society for Research in Child Development, Inc.; 197: © Jose Luis Pelaez, Inc./Corbis; p. 198: © Digital Vision/PunchStock RF; p. 199 (top): © Tom Stewart/Corbis; p. 199 (bottom): © Corbis RF

Chapter 6

Opener: © Tim Pannell/Corbis RF; p. 208: © Archives Jean Piaget, Universite De Geneve, Switzerland; p. 209: © Laura Dwight/Corbis; p. 211: © PunchStock RF; 6.3 (top & bottom): © Doug Goodman/Photo Researchers; p. 214: © Don Mason/Corbis; p. 215: © Joe McNally; 6.7: © Paul Fusco/Magnum Photos; p. 220: © Sean Sprague, SpraguePhoto.com; p. 221: © David Young-Wolff/Photo Edit; p. 222: © Stewart Cohen/Stone/Getty; p. 224: © Punchstock RF; p. 225: © M & E Bernheim/Woodfin Camp; 6.10: © Elizabeth Crews/The Image Works; p. 227 (bottom): © James Wertsch/Washington University in St. Louis; p. 228: © Gabe Palmer/Corbis; 6.11: Images courtesy of E. Bodrova and D. J. Leong, from *Tools of the Mind*, 2007; 6.12 (left): A. R. Lauria/Dr. Michael Cole, Laboratory of Human Cognition, University of California, San Diego; 6.12 (right): © Bettmann/Corbis; p. 232: © Image100/CORBIS RF; p. 233: © Johnny Le Fortune/zefa/Corbis

Images/Getty RF; p. 632: © Greg Sailor; p. 633: © Chuck Savage/Corbis; p. 634: © Bronwyn Kidd/Getty RF

Chapter 17

Opener: © Stan Honda/AP Wide World Photos; p. 644: © Lynsey Addario/Corbis; p. 645: © Robert Galbrait/Reuters/Corbis; 17.2: © Patrick Ward/Stock Boston; p. 648 (top): © Handout Courtesy of the Schiavo Family/Corbis; p. 648 (bottom): © The Detroit News; p. 649: © Matthew Barrick, Carring Photography; p. 650: © 2003 USA Today, photographer Tim Dillon; p. 652: © Mika/zefa/Corbis; p. 653: © Norbert Schaefer/Corbis; 17.6: © Eastcott Momatinck/Image Works; p. 658: © M. Thomsen/zefa/Corbis; p. 660: © Phyllis Picarci/Image State; p. 661: © Jennifer S. Altman; p. 664 (left): © Paul Almasy/Corbis; p. 664 (right): © Hermine Dreyfuss; p. 665: Courtesy of The Baltimore Sun Media Group. All Rights Reserved

Text/Line Art Credits

Chapter 1

Figure 1.1 From Santrock, *Life-Span Development*, 10th ed., p. 7. Copyright © 2006 The McGraw-Hill Companies. Reproduced with permission of The McGraw-Hill Companies. **Figure 1.3** From *State of the World's Children*, 2004, Geneva, Switzerland, UNICEF. Reprinted with permission from UNICEF. **Figure 1.4** From Santrock, *Life-Span Development*, 12th ed., Fig. 1.4, p. 13. Copyright © 2009 The McGraw-Hill Companies. Reproduced with permission of The McGraw-Hill Companies. **Figure 1.5** From Santrock, *Life-Span Development*, 12th ed., Fig. 1.5, p. 14. Copyright © 2009 The McGraw-Hill Companies. Reproduced with permission of The McGraw-Hill Companies. **Figure 1.8** From Santrock, *Life-Span Development*, 12th ed., Fig. 1.8, p. 18. Copyright © 2009 The McGraw-Hill Companies. Reproduced with permission of The McGraw-Hill Companies. **Figure 1.10** From Santrock, *Life-Span Development*, 8th ed. Copyright © 2002 The McGraw-Hill Companies. Reproduced with permission of The McGraw-Hill Companies. **Figure 1.11** From Santrock, *Child Development*, 9th ed. Copyright © 2001 The McGraw-Hill Companies. Reproduced with permission of The McGraw-Hill Companies. **Figure 1.13** From Santrock, *Children*, 5th ed. Copyright © 1997 The McGraw-Hill Companies. Reproduced with permission of The McGraw-Hill Companies. **Figure 1.14** Claire B. Kopp & Joanne B. Krakow, *The Child: Development in Social Context*. Copyright ©1982, p. 648. Prentice-Hall Publishing. **Figure 1.16** From Santrock, *Life-Span Development*, 12th ed., Fig. 1.15, p. 32. Copyright © 2009 The McGraw-Hill Companies. Reproduced with permission of The McGraw-Hill Companies. **Figure 1.17** From Crowley, et al., 2001, "Parents Explain More Often to Boys Than to Girls During Shared Scientific Thinking," *Psychological Science*, 12(3), pp. 258–261. Reprinted by permission of Wiley-Blackwell Publishers. **Figure 1.18** From Santrock, *Children*, 5th ed. Copyright © 1997 The McGraw-Hill Companies. Reproduced with permission of The McGraw-Hill Companies. **Figure 1.19** From Santrock, *Child Development*, 9th ed. Copyright © 2001 The McGraw-Hill Companies. Reproduced with permission of The McGraw-Hill Companies.

Chapter 2

Figure 2.2 From P.B. Baltes, U.M. Staudinger & U. Lindenberger, 1999, "Lifespan Psychology," *Annual Review of Psychology*, 50, p. 474, Fig. 1. Reprinted with permission from the Annual Review of Psychology. Copyright © 1999 by Annual Reviews. www.annualreviews.org **Figure 2.3** From Santrock, *Child Development*, 9th ed. Copyright © 2001 The McGraw-Hill Companies. Reproduced with permission of The McGraw-Hill Companies. **Figure 2.6** From Santrock, *Life-Span Development*, 8th ed. Copyright © 2002 The McGraw-Hill Companies. Reproduced with permission of The McGraw-Hill Companies. **Figure 2.7** From Santrock, *Life-Span Development*, 8th ed. Copyright © 2002 The McGraw-Hill Companies. Reproduced with permission of The McGraw-Hill Companies. **Figure 2.8** From Santrock, *Children*, 7th ed. Copyright © 2003 The McGraw-Hill Companies. Reproduced with permission of The McGraw-Hill Companies. **Figure 2.10** From Santrock, *Children*, 5th ed. Copyright © 1997 The McGraw-Hill Companies. Reproduced with permission of The McGraw-Hill Companies. **Figure 2.14** From Virginia A. Apgar, 1953, "A Proposal for a New Method of Evaluation of a Newborn Infant," in *Anesthesia and Analgesia*, Vol. 32, pp. 260–267. Reprinted with permission from Lippincott Williams & Wilkins/Wolters Kluwer Health.

Chapter 3

Figure 3.2 From Santrock, *Adolescence*, 8th ed. Copyright © 2001 The McGraw-Hill Companies. Reproduced with permission of The McGraw-Hill Companies. **Figure 3.3** From Santrock, *Children*, 10th ed., Fig. 14.2, p. 472. Copyright © 2008 The McGraw-Hill Companies. Reproduced with permission of The McGraw-Hill Companies. **Figure 3.4** From *Newsweek*, "Health for Life" Special Section, Fall/Winter 2001. Copyright © 2001 Newsweek, Inc. Used by permission and protected by the copyright laws of the U.S. The printing, copying, redistribution, or retransmission of the material without express written permission is prohibited. **Figure 3.7** From Santrock, *Child Development*, 9th ed. Copyright © 2001 The McGraw-Hill Companies. Reproduced with permission of The McGraw-Hill Companies. **Figure 3.13** From Santrock, *Psychology*, 7th ed. Copyright © 2003 The McGraw-Hill Companies. Reproduced with permission of The McGraw-Hill Companies. **Figure 3.14** From *Human Biology and Ecology*, Second Edition, by Albert Damon. W.W. Norton & Company, Inc., 1977. **Figure 3.20** From data in Eaton, D.J., et al., 2008. *Youth Risk Behavior Surveillance—United States*, MMWR, Vol. 57, 131, after data from Table 95. Atlanta: Centers for Disease Control & Prevention. **Figure 3.21** From *The Psychology of Death, Dying and Bereavement*, by Richard Schulz, Copyright © 1978. Reproduced with permission of The McGraw-Hill Companies. **Figure 3.22** From *The Okinawa Program*, by Bradley J. Willcox and D. Craig Willcox, Makoto Suzuki. Copyright © 2001 by Bradley J. Willcox, D. Craig Willcox and Makoto Suzuki. Used by permission of Clarkson/Potter Publishers, an imprint of the Crown Publishing Group, a division of Random House, Inc.

Chapter 4

Figure 4.2 From M.J. Parker, et al., 2006, "The Health Status of Young Adults in the U.S.," *Journal of Adolescent Health*, 39(3), Fig. 1, p. 310. Reprinted with permission from Elsevier, obtained via RightsLink. **Figure 4.5** Adapted from Janice K. Kiecolt-Glaser, et al., 2003, "Chronic Stress and Age-Related Increases in the Proinflammatory Cytokine IL-6," *Proceedings of the National Academy of Science USA*, 100(15), after Figure 1. Copyright © 2003 National Academy of Sciences, U.S.A. Used with permission. **Figure 4.6** From *Nursing Home Use by the "Oldest Old" Sharply Declines*, by Lisa Alecxih, The Lewin Group, November 21, 2006, Reprinted with permission. **Figure 4.10** From data in Eaton, D.J., et al., 2008. *Youth Risk Behavior Surveillance—United States*, MMWR, Vol. 57, 131, after data from Table 70. Atlanta: Centers for Disease Control & Prevention. **Figure 4.12** After data presented by Judy Kruger, Heidi Michels Blanck, and Cathleen Gillespie, 2006, "Dietary and Physical Activity Behaviors Among Adults Successful at Weight Loss Management," *International Journal of Behavioral Nutrition and Physical Activity*, 3, 17. Excerpts used with permission from the original publisher, BioMed Central, Ltd. **Figure 4.14** From Nader, P.R., Bradley, R.H., Houts, R.M., McRitchie, S.L., O'Brian, M., 2008. "Moderate to Vigorous Physical Activity From 9 to 15 Years," *Journal of the American Medical Association*, 300, 295–305, Figure 3. Reprinted by permission of the American Medical Association. **Figure 4.15** After Eaton, D.J., et al., 2008. *Youth Risk Behavior Surveillance—United States*, MMWR, Vol. 57, 131, Table 74. Atlanta: Centers for Disease Control & Prevention. **Figure 4.18** From Santrock, *Life-Span Development*, 12th ed., Figure 17.19, p. 547. Copyright © 2009 The McGraw-Hill Companies. Reproduced with permission of The McGraw-Hill Companies. **Figure 4.19** From National Institute on Drug Abuse, Washington, DC.

Chapter 5

Figure 5.3 From Santrock, *Child Development*, 9th ed. Copyright © 2001 The McGraw-Hill Companies. Reproduced with permission of The McGraw-Hill Companies. P. 179 From *Parents' Guide to Girls' Sports*. Reprinted by permission of the Women's Sports Foundation. **Figure 5.6a** Adapted from Alexander Semenoick, in R.L. Franz, "The Origin of Form Perception," *Scientific American*, 1961. **Figure 5.7** From Slater, A., Morison, V. & Somers, M., 1988, "Orientation Discrimination and Cortical Functions in the Human Newborn," *Perception*, Vol. 17, pp. 597–602, Fig. 1 and Table 1. Reprinted by permission. **Figure 5.12** Adapted from J.A. Brabyn, et al., The Smith-Kettlewell Institute (SKI) "Longitudinal Study of Vision Function and Its Impact on the Elderly: An Overview," *Optometry and Vision Science*, 78(5): 264–269, May 2001. Used with permission by Dr. John Brabyn. **Figure 5.15** From Santrock, *Life-Span Development*, 8th ed. Copyright © 2002 The McGraw-Hill Companies. Reproduced with permission of The McGraw-Hill Companies.

Chapter 6

Figure 6.4 From R. Baillargeon & J. DeVos, 1991, "Object Permanence in Young Infants: Further Evidence," *Child Development*, 62(6), pp. 1227–1246. Reprinted by permission from Wiley-Blackwell Publishers. **Figure 6.5** From Santrock, *Psychology*, 7th ed. Copyright © 2003 The McGraw-Hill Companies. Reproduced with permission of The McGraw-Hill Companies. **Figure 6.6** From *The Symbolic Drawings of Young Children*, by Dennie Palmer Wolf, Annenberg Institute, Brown University. Reprinted by permission. **Figure 6.7** From Santrock, *Life-Span Development*, 8th ed. Copyright © 2002 The McGraw-Hill Companies. Reproduced with permission of The McGraw-Hill Companies. **Figure 6.8** From Santrock, *Life-Span Development*, 8th ed. Copyright © 2002 The McGraw-Hill Companies. Reproduced with permission of The McGraw-Hill Companies. **Figure 6.9** From Santrock, *Life-Span Development*, 8th ed. Copyright © 2002 The McGraw-Hill Companies. Reproduced with permission of The McGraw-Hill Companies. **Figure 6.11** From E. Bodrova & D. Leong, 2001, *Tools of the Mind: A Case Study of Implementing the Vygotskian Approach in American Early Childhood and Primary Classrooms*, pp. 36, 38. Copyright © UNESCO: IBE 2001.

Chapter 7

Figure 7.2 From Salthouse, 1994, "The Nature of the Influence of Speed on Adult Age Differences in Cognition," *Developmental Psychology*, p. 30, 240–259. Copyright © 1994 by the American Psychological Association. Reprinted with permission. **Figure 7.4** From E. Vurpillot, 1968, "The Development of Scanning Strategies," *Journal of Experimental Child Psychology*, 6(4), 632–650, Figure 1. Reprinted with permission from Elsevier, obtained via RightsLink. **TA Figure 7.7** From Santrock, *Psychology*, 7th ed. Copyright © 2003 The McGraw-Hill Companies. Reprinted with permission of the McGraw-Hill Companies. **Figure 7.8** From Dempster, 1981, "Memory Span," *Psychological Bulletin*, Vol. 80, pp. 63–100. Copyright © 1981 American Psychological Association. Adapted with permission. **Figure 7.12** From M. Ronnlund, et al., 2005, "Stability, Growth, and Decline in Adult Life Span Development of Declarative Memory," *Psychology and Aging*, 20, p. 11, Fig. 2. Copyright © 2005 American Psychological Association. Reprinted with permission. **Figure 7.14** From DeLoache, Judy S.; Simcock, Gabrielle; Macari, Suzanne, "Planes, Trains, Automobiles—and Tea Sets: Extremely Intense Interests in Very Young Children," *Developmental Psychology*, 2007(Nov), Vol. 43(6), 1579–1586. Copyright © 2007 American Psychological Association. Reprinted with permission. **Figure 7.16** After Wellman, Cross & Watson, 2001, "Meta-Analysis of Theory-of-Mind Development: The Truth About False Belief," *Child Development*, 72(3), pp. 655–684. Reprinted by permission of Wiley-Blackwell Publishers. **Figure 7.17** From Uta Frith, *Autism: Explaining the Enigma*, p. 83. Blackwell Publishing, 1989. Reprinted by permission of Wiley-Blackwell Publishers.

Chapter 8

Figure 8.1 From Santrock, *Children*, 5th ed. Copyright © 1997 The McGraw-Hill Companies. Reproduced with permission of The McGraw-Hill Companies. **Figure 8.5** From Robert Sternberg (ed.), 2000, *Handbook of Intelligence*. New York: Cambridge University Press. **Figure 8.6** From "The

Increase in IQ Scores from 1932 to 1997," by Dr. Ulric Neisser. Reprinted by permission. **Figure 8.7** From Santrock, *Life-Span Development*, 8th ed. Copyright © 2002 The McGraw-Hill Companies. Reproduced with permission of The McGraw-Hill Companies. **Figure 8.8** Schaie, K.W., *Developmental Influences on Adult Intelligence: The Seattle Longitudinal Study*, 2005, Oxford University Press, p. 127, Figure 5.7a. Reprinted by permission of Oxford University Press, Inc. **Figure 8.9** From Santrock, *Life-Span Development*, 8th ed. Copyright © 2002 The McGraw-Hill Companies. Reproduced with permission of The McGraw-Hill Companies. **Figure 8.10** From Santrock, *Life-Span Development*, 10th ed. Copyright © 2006 The McGraw-Hill Companies. Reproduced with permission of The McGraw-Hill Companies. **Figure 8.11** From Santrock, *Educational Psychology*, 1st ed. Copyright © 2001 The McGraw-Hill Companies. Reproduced with permission of The McGraw-Hill Companies. **Figure 8.12** From Morton Hunt, *The Universe Within: A New Science Explores the Human Mind*, 1982. Copyright © 1982 by Morton Hunt.

Chapter 9

Figure 9.1 Reprinted by permission of Sherrel Haight, Ph.D. **Figure 9.3** From Santrock, *Children*, 7th ed. Copyright © 2003 The McGraw-Hill Companies. Reproduced with permission of The McGraw-Hill Companies. **Figure 9.4** From Santrock, *Children*, 7th ed. Copyright © 2003 The McGraw-Hill Companies. Reproduced with permission of The McGraw-Hill Companies. **Figure 9.5** From Jean Berko, 1958, "The Child's Learning of English Morphology," in *Word*, Vol. 14, p. 154. Reprinted by permission of the author. **Figure 9.6** From Hart & Risley, (1995), *Meaningful Differences in the Everyday Experiences of Young American Children*, Baltimore: Paul H. Brookes Publishing Co, Inc. Reprinted by permission. **Figure 9.7** From Santrock, *Child Development*, 10th ed. Copyright © 2005 The McGraw-Hill Companies. Reproduced with permission of The McGraw-Hill Companies.

Chapter 10

Figure 10.4 Reprinted by permission of the publisher from *Infancy: Its Place in Human Development*, by Jerome Kagan, Richard B. Kearsley and Philip R. Zelazo, p. 107, Cambridge, Mass.: Harvard University Press, Copyright © 1978 by the President and Fellows of Harvard College. **Figure 10.6** From D. Mroczek and C.M. Kolarz, 1998, "The Effect of Age in Positive and Negative Affect," in *Journal of Personality and Social Psychology*, Vol. 75, pp. 1333–1349. Copyright © 1998 by the American Psychological Association. Reproduced with permission. **Figure 10.7** From L. Carstensen, et al., "The Social Context of Emotional Experience," *Annual Review of Geriatrics and Gerontology*, Schaie/Lawton, eds., 1997, Vol. 17, p. 331, Fig. 12.2. Reproduced with the permission of Springer Publishing Company, LLC, New York, NY 10036. **Figure 10.9** From Santrock, *Life-Span Development*, 11th ed. Copyright © 2008 The McGraw-Hill Companies. Reproduced with permission of The McGraw-Hill Companies. **Figure 10.11** From M.H. van Ijzendoorn & P.M. Kroonenberg, 1988, "Cross-Cultural Patterns of Attachment: A Meta-Analysis of the Strange Situation," *Child Development*, 59(1), pp. 147–156. Reprinted by permission of Wiley-Blackwell Publishers. **Figure 10.14** From M.N. Reedy, J.E. Birren & K.W. Schaie, 1981, "Age and Sex Differences in Satisfying Relationships Across the Adult Life Span," *Human Development*, 24, pp. 52–66. Reprinted with permission, S. Karger AG, Basel, Switzerland. **Figure 10.15** From Robert J. Sternberg, 1988, *The Triangle of Love*, New York: Basic Books. With permission from the author. **Figure 10.16** From T. Tashiro & P. Frazier, 2003, "I'll Never Be in a Relationship Like That Again: Personal Growth Following Romantic Relationship Breakups," *Personal Relationships*, 10(1), pp. 113–128, after Table 1, p. 120. Reprinted by permission of Wiley-Blackwell Publishers.

Chapter 11

Figure 11.1 From M. Lewis & J. Brooks-Gunn, *Social Cognition and the Acquisition of the Self*, 1979, p. 64. Reprinted with permission, Springer-SBM B.V. **Figure 11.2** From S. Harter, 1999, *The Construction of the Self*, Table 6.1. New York: Guilford Press. Reprinted by permission of Guilford Press. **Figure 11.3** From R.W. Robins, et al., 2002, "Global Self-Esteem Across the Life-Span," in *Psychology and Aging*, Vol. 17, pp. 423–434. Copyright © 2002 by the American Psychological Association. Reproduced with permission. **Figure 11.5** From R. Schulz and J. Heckhausen, 1996, "A Life Span Model of Successful Aging," *American Psychologist*, Vol. 51, pp. 702–714. Copyright © 1997 by the American Psychological Association. Reproduced with permission. **Figure 11.6** From Santrock, *Life-Span Development*, 8th ed. Copyright © 2002 The McGraw-Hill Companies. Reproduced with permission of The McGraw-Hill Companies. **Figure 11.7** From Santrock, *Psychology*, 6th ed. Copyright © 2000 The McGraw-Hill Companies. Reproduced with permission of The McGraw-Hill Companies. **Figure 11.11** From Stewart, Osgrove & Helson, 2002, "Middle Aging in Women: Patterns of Personality Change from the 30s to the 50s," Fig. 3, *Journal of Adult Development*, Vol. 8, pp. 23–37. Reprinted with kind permission from Springer Science & Business Media. **Figure 11.12** From Mroczek & Spiro, 2007, "Personality Change Influences Mortality in Older Men," *Psychological Science*, 18(5), Figure 1, p. 375. Reprinted by permission of Wiley-Blackwell Publishers.

Chapter 12

Figure 12.2 From G. Levy, A. Sadovsky & G. Troseth, 2000, "Aspects of Young Children's Perceptions of Gender-Typed Occupations," *Sex Roles*, 42, Table 1. p. 1000. Reprinted with kind permission from Springer Science & Business Media. **Figure 12.4** From *Sex in America*, by Robert Michael. Copyright © CSG Enterprises, Inc., Edward O. Laumann, Robert T. Michael, and Gina Kolata. By permission of Hachette Book Group, on behalf of Edward O. Laumann. **Figure 12.5** From Fisher, Cullen & Turner, 2000, *The Sexual Victimization of College Women*, Exhibit 8, p. 19. Reprinted by permission of the National Institute of Justice. **Figure 12.6** From Santrock, *Life-Span Development*, 12th ed., Fig. 11.5, p. 362. Copyright © 2009 The McGraw-Hill Companies. Reproduced with permission of The McGraw-Hill Companies. **Figure 12.7** From Darroch, et al., 2000, "Teenage Sexual and Reproductive Behavior in Developed Countries: Can Progress Be Made?" *Occasional Report*, New York: The Alan Guttmacher Institute, 2001 No. 3, p. 4. Reprinted by permission of the Alan Guttmacher Institute. **Figure 12.8** "U.S. Adolescent Birth Rate by Ethnicity," from *Child Trends*, July 2008, Facts at a Glance. Washington, DC: Child Trends. Reprinted by permission obtained via The Copyright Clearance Center. **Figure 12.10** From Santrock, *Life-Span Development*, 12th ed., Fig. 17.13, p. 542. Copyright © 2009 The McGraw-Hill Companies. Reproduced with permission of The McGraw-Hill Companies.

Chapter 13

Figure 13.4 From Santrock, *Adolescence*, 8th ed. Copyright © 2001 The McGraw-Hill Companies. Reproduced with permission of The McGraw-Hill Companies. **Figure 13.6** From P. Wink & M. Dillon, 2002, "Spiritual Development Over the Adult Life Course: Findings From a Longitudinal Study," *Journal of Adult Development*, 9, pp. 79–84. Kluwer Academic Publishers.

Chapter 14

Figure 14.2 "The Increase in Cohabitation in the United States," from U.S. Bureau of the Census, 2000. **Figure 14.3** "The National Marriage Project," Figure 4, Copyright © 2008 by The National Marriage Project at the University of Virginia. Reprinted by permission of the National Marriage Project. **Figure 14.4** From Karney & Bradbury, 2005, "Contextual Influences on Marriage: Implications for Policy and Intervention," *Current Directions in Psychological Science*, (14)4, pp. 171–174, Fig. 2. Reprinted by permission of Wiley-Blackwell Publishers. **Figure 14.5** "The Divorce Rate in Relation to Number of Years Married," from U.S. Bureau of the Census, 2000. **Figure 14.7** From "Corporal Punishment in Different Countries," K. Curran, J. DuCette, J. Eisenstein, I. Hyman, August 2001, "Statistical Analysis of the Cross-Cultural Data: The Third Year." Paper presented at APA meeting, San Francisco, CA. Reprinted with permission. **Figure 14.8** From Gunnar, M.R., Fisher, P.A., 2008, "The Early Experience Stress and Prevention Network: Bringing Basic Research on Early Experience and Stress Neurobiology to Bear on Preventative Interventions for Neglected and Maltreated Children," *Development and Psychopathology*, 18, 651–677. Fig. 4 on p. 666. Reprinted with the permission of Cambridge University Press. **P. 519** From *For Better or Worse: Divorce Reconsidered*, by E. Mavis Hetherington and John Kelly. Copyright © 2002 by E. Mavis Hetherington and John Kelly. Used by permission of W.W. Norton & Company, Inc.

Chapter 15

Figure 15.1 From Nansel, et al., 2001, "Bullying Behaviors Among U.S. Youth," *Journal of the American MedicalAssociation*, Vol. 285, pp. 2094–2100. **Figure 15.2** From Maccoby & Jacklin, 1987, "Gender Segregation in Childhood," in H.W. Reese (ed.), *Advances in Child Development and Behavior*, Vol. 20, San Diego: Academic Press. Reprinted with permission from Elsevier, obtained via RightsLink. **Figure 15.3** From Santrock, *Child Development*, 11th ed. Copyright © 2007 The McGraw-Hill Companies. Reproduced with permission of The McGraw-Hill Companies. **Figure 15.5** From R.W. Larson, 2001, "How U.S. Children and Adolescents Spend Time: What it Does (and Doesn't) Tell Us About Their Development," *Current Directions in Psychological Science*, 10(5), pp. 160–164, Table 1. Reprinted by permission from Wiley-Blackwell Publishers. **Figure 15.6** From H.C. Triandis, 1995, *Individualism & Collectivism*. Boulder, CO: Westview Press. Copyright © 1995 The Perseus Books Group. Reprinted with permission. **Figure 15.7** From Trafimow, et al., 1997, "The Effects of Language and Priming on the Relative Accessibility of the Private Self and the Collective Self," *Journal of Cross-Cultural Psychology*, 28, pp. 107–123. Reprinted by permission obtained via RightsLink. **Figure 15.10** From Santrock, *Adolescence*, 8th ed. Copyright © 2001 The McGraw-Hill Companies. Reproduced with permission of The McGraw-Hill Companies. **Figure 15.11** "Actual and Projected Number of U.S. Adolescents Aged 10 to 19, 2000–2100," from U.S. Bureau of the Census, 2002, National Population Projects, Summary Files.

Chapter 16

Figure 16.1 "Core Considerations in Developmentally Appropriate Practice in Early Childhood," adapted from the NAEYC position statement: http://www.naeyc.org/positionstatements/dap. Copyright © 2009 National Association for the Education of Young Children. **Figure 16.2** From U.S. Department of Commerce, Census Bureau. *Current Population Survey (CPS), October (1972–2005)*, the National Center for Education Statistics, NCES 2007–059, Figure 2, U.S. Department of Education. **Figure 16.3** From Diener & Seligman, 2002, "Very Happy People," *Psychological Science*, 13(1), pp. 81–84. Reprinted by permission from Wiley-Blackwell Publishers. **Figure 16.4** Figure from the National Center for Education Statistics, 2003. **Figure 16.6** From Santrock, *Educational Psychology*, 4th ed., Fig. 6.3, p. 200. Copyright © 2009 The McGraw-Hill Companies. Reproduced with permission of The McGraw-Hill Companies. **Figure 16.8** From D. Stipek, *Motivation to Learn*, 4th ed., Table 5.3. Boston: Allyn & Bacon. Copyright © 2002. Reproduced with permission of Pearson Education, Inc. **Figure 16.9** From Stevenson, Lee & Stigler, 1986, "Mathematics Achievement of Chinese, Japanese and American Children," *Science*, Vol. 231, pp. 693–699, Figure 6. Reprinted by permission obtained via RightsLink. **Figure 16.10** Reproduced by special permission of the publisher, Psychological Assessment Resources, Inc., 16204 North Florida Avenue, Lutz, FL 33549, from Making Vocational Choices, Third Edition. Copyright © 1973, 1985, 1992, 1997 by Psychological Assessment Resources, Inc. All rights reserved. **Figure 16.11** From Santrock, *Adolescence*, 11th ed. Copyright © 2007 The McGraw-Hill Companies. Reproduced with permission of The McGraw-Hill Companies. **Figure 16.12** U.S. Bureau of Labor Statistics. **Figure 16.13** U.S. Bureau of Labor Statistics. **Figure 16.14** "Reasons Given by People Regarding When They Expect to Retire From Work," HSBC Insurance, 2007. Reprinted by permission.

Chapter 17

Figure 17.3 Center for Disease Control, Atlanta, GA. **Figure 17.4** From D.B. Goldston, et al., 2008, Cultural Consideration in Adolescent Suicide Prevention and Psychosocial Treatment, *American Psychologist*, 63, 14–31, Figure 2, p. 15. Copyright © 2008 by the American Psychological Association. Reproduced with permission.